REDS

John Williams has been studying football as a sociologist for the past 30 years and is the author of several books on Liverpool FC, including *Rafa*, *Into the Red*, *Kennedy's Way* and *The Miracle of Istanbul*.

REDS

LIVERPOOL FOOTBALL CLUB
THE BIOGRAPHY

John Williams

MAINSTREAM
PUBLISHING

EDINBURGH AND LONDON

First published in Great Britain in 2010 by
MAINSTREAM PUBLISHING COMPANY
(EDINBURGH) LTD
7 Albany Street
Edinburgh EH1 3UG

ISBN 9781845966829

A catalogue record for this book is available
from the British Library

Typeset in Caslon and Franklin Gothic

Printed in Great Britain by
Clays Ltd, St Ives plc

1 3 5 7 9 10 8 6 4 2

ACKNOWLEDGEMENTS

This book has taken much longer to produce than I thought it would. I want to thank those who have been waiting patiently for it to be born. But many more thanks are also in order. Much of the research for this text was undertaken by ploughing through the Liverpool press and connected sources, and my dedicated researcher David Gould did as much of this crucial spadework as anyone else. I want to thank him for his excellent job, and I hope that his beloved Stoke City continue to survive – and more – in the heady Premier League. We both want to thank the staff at the Liverpool Central Library for looking after us so well during our many visits there between 2006 and 2008. I must also thank my dear friend Cathy Long for letting me stay over in her flat in Liverpool when I most needed to. I could not have completed this work without my Liverpool base.

My friends and colleagues David Gould, Andrew Ward, Stephen Hopkins, Neil Carter, Viet-Hai Phung and Alec McAuley all read early versions of some of these chapters and offered many useful comments and scholarly support. Andrew Ward, especially, is a terrific writer and researcher as well as being a very good friend. Andrew helped me restructure chapters when I was in danger of losing my way. I also 'entertained' some of my fellow Liverpool supporters in the Flat Iron pub in Liverpool with ad hoc and often obscure stories taken from the text, and even the occasional historical football quiz about Liverpool FC. I thank them, as always, for their tolerance, humour and interest. They are the very best of knowledgeable Liverpool supporters. James Cleary and Adrian Killen gave me great advice on pictures and Liverpool FC's past, and Ken Rogers at Trinity Mirror was kind enough, initially, to ask me to write this book. When the book transferred to Mainstream Publishing, Bill Campbell, Claire Rose and Graeme Blaikie performed heroics in keeping the whole thing on track. Finally, Stephen Done at the Liverpool FC museum read an early version of the text, and he offered many priceless correctives and pieces of sound guidance and advice. He also allowed me to look at the surviving official Liverpool FC minute books (1914–56), for which I am eternally grateful.

At home, as I tried valiantly to pull all this material together, my partner Sylvia offered her usual love, patience and encouragement, and my precious toddler granddaughters, Millie and Sasha, kept me amused and full of energy when things started to flag. They were even joined later on in the piece by little Esmée. Despite her US heritage, Sasha will be well schooled by her mother in the Reds tradition, and at just three years of age Millie can already sing whole sections of the Fernando Torres song and is now busy learning 'You'll Never Walk Alone' – though her sudden and strange obsession with sharks and other matters has proved a distraction to her much more important Liverpool FC schooling. Her uncle Seb will help keep her focused on the main task.

I also want to say here that a number of sources, in particular, were completely invaluable as I tried to make sense of Liverpool FC's extraordinary history. Tony Matthews' *Who's Who of Liverpool* is an excellent and comprehensive starting point for pen pictures of Liverpool players, going right back to the earliest days of the club. All Liverpool fans should own a copy. As he will no doubt notice, I used his research so frequently I could not always attribute it, and I give my heartfelt thanks (and sheepish apologies) to him here. Likewise, Brian Pead's *Liverpool: A Complete Record 1892–1990* is a very useful guide to the club's early formations and playing records, and Eric Doig and Alex Murphy's *The Essential History of Liverpool* is indispensable for its accuracy and detail. Vital too is the club website lfchistory.net for providing lots of crucial historical information about the club and its players.

The *Football League Players' Records 1888–1939* by Michael Joyce got me out of many tight spots in trying to establish the identities of early opponents of Liverpool Football Club and to track their careers, and Jack Rollin's *Rothmans Book of Football Records* did the same for crowd data information and for relevant Football League tables. Simon Inglis's terrific account of the history of the Football League, *League Football and the Men Who Made It*, was exceptionally useful for keeping me up to date with wider developments in the game as we lurched, uncertainly, towards the present. Finally, John Belchem's wonderful edited collection in celebration of the city of Liverpool, *Liverpool 800: Culture, Character and History*, gave me plenty to contemplate – and to rely upon – concerning history, culture and social change in the city. I hope I have done no gross disservice in the text to any of these indispensable works.

When I use a source directly and extensively, I have indicated this fact in the text, though I must reiterate I used the standard Liverpool FC reference books and sites rather more liberally than such formal referencing suggests. Finally, I have tried to report on events covered in this book quite critically, as a researcher, and not simply with a supporter's feverish eye: the reader will have to judge how well (or how badly) I have done in this respect. Needless to say, all the errors in the text – though only some of the insights – are mine and mine alone.

For the lost 135, Heysel and Hillsborough

CONTENTS

INTRODUCTION

For the year 2008, and despite its many doubters, the city of Liverpool was a spectacularly successful European Capital of Culture. This is a fitting reason, in itself, for the production of a book during that halcyon period that celebrates the history and cultural significance of football and of Liverpool Football Club in the city. Without doubt, football is as much a feature of the cultural heritage and artistic landscape of the city of Liverpool as any theatre production, media installation or art exhibition.

As many people have noted, Liverpool is something of a city on the edge, both geographically and culturally. Despite its considerable Welsh and Scottish in-migrations, Liverpool has typically looked westwards, to Ireland and the United States, rather than back to Britain or southwards to Continental Europe, for its inspiration and for much of its cultural history. It has many of the independent and distinctive characteristics of a city on the margins, a place at the end of the line even. Rather like other great peripheral cities of Europe that have football at their cultural heart, such as Marseille and Naples, Liverpool has an uneasy and shifting relationship with its national host, often preferring to look inwards rather than to national forms of identification. In this sense, T-shirts that describe Liverpool football supporters in the city as 'Scouse not English' are making rather more than a joke.

Accordingly, the city of Liverpool has a highly idiosyncratic set of cultural reference points, whether they be the city's Irish, Welsh or Scottish cultural influences; its old traveller stories and sea shanties; its bastardised versions of American jazz and soul music; the beat traditions of the Beatles and their many imitators; the deep creativity of the shoal of Liverpool poets and artists, past and present; or else the incredible native imagination of local football supporters in their endless task of producing new songs and banners in praise of their heroes on and off the football pitch. Indeed, there can be few places in the world where complex football songs are created so prodigiously or sung with such gusto. And there is nowhere – anywhere – in the world where one minute these anthems are likely to be pumping out to the rhythms of rousing Irish Republican choruses and then, the next, being delivered to the strains of deeply Loyalist hymns or other melodies assiduously collected from around the globe. Football in Liverpool is, quite simply, a text constructed as much by the club's avid supporters as it is by its players, managers and even directors. It is much more important today than any religious or political divide, or indeed any other schism shaped by difference, fashion or creed. But it is also interesting to note, as I have frequently done in this text, that *playing* weekend football, in Liverpool's parks and public spaces, has often been opposed fiercely by local religious leaders and for much longer than was the case in many other major English cities.

There can be few places other than in Liverpool, too, where football has quite the specific cultural-political resonances that it has – and has had – in the city. As this book, I hope, shows, football on Merseyside has variously been a focus for civic rivalry and celebration, as in the early 1900s; a local bulwark against the effects of economic depression, as in the 1920s and 1930s, and in many periods that followed; a crucial site for the recovery of local pride and a sense of community, as in the post-war reconstruction period of the 1940s and 1950s; part of a celebration of the youthful energy and the brief creative world dominance of popular culture on Merseyside in the 1960s; a potential escape, abroad, from the privations of central government meddling and cruelty and a focus for mutual community support, as in the successful and tragic 1980s; and a site for global fusion, as it increasingly seems to be in the 2000s.

But football is also important in Liverpool – perhaps most important of all – in its own terms: as an individual and collective physical performance and a local class and masculinity rite. In this last respect, I have tried to chart the near constant struggle of women in the city to play and watch the game, often against the fiercest male opposition. This fight, thankfully, is still being waged, though it is far from won. Football in England offers a very specific, but also a highly complex, range of traditional working-class aesthetic archetypes – the brave and rugged defender; the powerful and constructive midfielder; the creative and elegant winger; the cool and nerveless striker – in addition to a set of collective and individual cultural practices that many men – and increasingly women – in the city of Liverpool continue to identify with very strongly. As the author Arthur Hopcraft points out in his brilliant 1968 book on the game, *The Football Man*, football in cities such as Liverpool is not just a sport people take to, like cricket or tennis – it has both conflict and beauty and is inherent in the people. Football is something that is built into the urban psyche, and in Liverpool it really *matters* to the people who live there. It does so as poetry or fine art matters for some people and alcohol does to others. A *combined* love of alcohol and football as occurs in Liverpool and similar cities, it goes without saying, is an especially potent mix.

There are certainly few more informed, animated, articulate and passionate forums in the city than at the tables and bars in north Liverpool pubs as kick-off approaches at Anfield. The same has been true for more than 100 years and will doubtless continue to be the case for decades to come. And this huge passion remains despite the awful disasters that beset football in the 1980s, in which Liverpool Football Club and its fans played no small role as both perpetrators and victims. It has also survived the recent hyper-commercialisation of the game and its movement – because of price and restricted access to tickets – out of the reach of many of those local people who used regularly to attend football. Instead, Liverpool supporters now travel to the city from far and wide – I was born and raised in the nearby borough of Bootle but now drive in from the East Midlands for home games – and new groups of supporters including British Asians and Continental Liverpool followers now find their places on the Kop, as well as on websites and in Internet chat rooms. This is while bars and pubs in and around Liverpool are packed on Saturday and Sunday afternoons to watch the local football clubs play live on television. This new media consumption of top-level football in cities such as Liverpool often occurs via jerky TV 'feeds' usually illegally procured from mysterious countries from around the globe. It is all part of the contradictory new globalisation and democratisation of football support, in an era when the price of a seat for a top-level game in England is now forbidding for many supporters.

Nor is football an arena today simply for the celebration of *local* talent – as if this was ever the case. In the first Liverpool v. Everton Football League derby match, way back in 1894, the Liverpool side was packed with alien Scots, and the local press in the city was full of complaints about the lack of opportunity for young men from the area to play for the top Merseyside clubs. Very few would make it into the Liverpool team before the First World War. Not much has changed in over a century, except that the clubs' players are now drawn in not just from over the border but from around the world, and that top-level footballers today can earn more in a *week* than many people would take five years, or more, to accumulate. Gone are the pre-celebrity football days when Liverpool players walked to the ground with the crowds that worshipped them. Or – as the great Billy Liddell did in the 1950s – they caught the tram to Anfield to undertake their (part-time) jobs as football professionals for Liverpool. Football today has its transient mercenaries, of course. But, we might also ask, are some of today's football millionaires – Jamie Carragher, for one – or even the recent international Liverpool heroes – Germany's Didi Hamann or Finland's Sami

Hyypiä, for example – *really* any less 'of' the city of Liverpool, or less typical of its football traditions and dedication, than earlier Reds heroes who may have been more local and earned peanuts by comparison? I wonder.

This book deals in some detail with periods when ordinary professional footballers were not especially high earners, nor nationally known. I am especially interested here in the span of almost 90 years from the late 1870s, when football began to emerge on Merseyside from diverse political roots, up to 1965 when Liverpool Football Club under Bill Shankly finally managed to win the FA Cup for the first time. This long period takes up much of the first part of the main text, and here I introduce readers to great names in the club's past, such as its first successful manager Tom Watson, the wonderful all-rounder Alex Raisbeck, and the totemic Reds goalkeeper for three decades Elisha Scott. I also explore great Liverpool sides of the past, such as the 1901 and 1906 championship teams and the Liverpool squad containing Scott that won back-to-back league titles in 1922 and 1923. But the FA Cup had certainly been Liverpool Football Club's central concern almost since the club was formed in 1892, and this was especially the case after the first Liverpool Football League championship was won near the beginning of the twentieth century.

From that point on, the FA Cup was the holy grail, *the* prime target for the Anfield board and probably for most of the club's players and supporters. Liverpool had actually come much closer to succeeding in this grand quest, at various moments, than its two losing FA Cup finals before 1965 (1914 and 1950) might suggest. But finally winning the FA Cup in 1965 seemed like something of the end of a journey, a 'natural' point of closure to the early part of the story of Liverpool FC and the people who made it. The long period before 1965 – lengthy stretches of aspiration and hope, flecked by occasional moments of real success – is much less well known to most of the club's followers, for obvious reasons. After 1965, the footballing landscape of Europe opened up to Liverpool and set quite a different set of challenges.

I also cover, of course, the great years of Shankly and Paisley, and these will be quite well known to most Liverpool supporters. There is a fixation with managers at Liverpool that it is difficult to trace anywhere else in England. I deal with the main reasons for the decline of the club after the end of the boot-room era and with the terrible disasters at both Heysel (1985) and Hillsborough (1989) that played a major part in shaping that decline and the recent supporter traditions around the club. I discuss the successes and problems of the new Continental influences at Liverpool in recent years and try to bring the Anfield story right up to date in the closing chapters, and especially in the epilogue, by looking at aspects of the new ownership arrangements at Liverpool. Throughout the text, I have tried to provide some wider cultural and economic context for football in the city by offering brief descriptions of events and debates that were going on in and around the city at the time. This is in order better to locate developments at Liverpool Football Club in both time and space. This seems to me what a real football club history that dwells on the sport's local cultural significance should try to do.

I also try, wherever possible, to draw on the contemporaneous voices of football supporters and other people in Liverpool, admittedly taken mainly from the letters pages of the local press. This, I think, adds more cogency to the story and tells us something about how people saw relations with the club and football in the city at that time. I do, necessarily, begin my account of the history of Liverpool FC, briefly, with a discussion of the early years of *Everton* Football Club, especially when the Blues played at Anfield. This is done in order to cover the origins of association football itself, and to try to tell the reader something about how and why organised football overtook rugby in the city of Liverpool in the late nineteenth century. I also describe here, of course, how Liverpool Football Club emerged following the famous split from Everton in 1892, and how the emerging character of the two clubs has developed and differed ever since.

At the very end of the book, I say something about the possibilities of choosing a 'best-ever' Liverpool side. In many ways, this is a rather fatuous task, for obvious reasons, but it is also a very entertaining and diverting one. I have spent many happy hours in Liverpool pubs and elsewhere doing just this kind of thing, and I would guess many other readers have done the same. Most of us are constrained in this task to choosing players we have seen live or glimpsed on television. Arguments will continue to rage on this score, and rightly so. Limits of space have meant that I have said very little in support of my own choices, but I think the main text does this for me. What I try to do in this final section is to show just how limiting most discussions currently are about the 'greatest-ever' Liverpool team. This is simply because they tend to ignore the first 70 years, or so, of the club's history.

My selections consciously try to counter that tendency, and they are aimed at getting the reader at least to think about earlier periods in the history of the club. A number of my own selections come from the era before Bill Shankly produced his first great Liverpool side in the early 1960s and before Bob Paisley produced a team to dominate the game from the mid-1970s. This may surprise and even appal some readers, but there are players from earlier periods who also have their claims to be considered among the club's greatest-ever servants. I hope this book convinces on this matter. It should go at least some way to explaining why clearly exceptional Liverpool players of more recent eras, such as Ian St John, Ray Clemence, Phil Neal, Kevin Keegan, John Barnes, Graeme Souness, Ian Rush and also many other past and recent stars, have not made it into my own all-time 'best' Liverpool XI. Readers will have to make up their own minds on this and on many other issues I try to cover. At least we can all agree that the story of Liverpool Football Club – and of football in the city of Liverpool – has been a joyous and remarkable one, if one also characterised by vital moments of real human drama and occasional terrible loss. This is, of course, what makes the modern Liverpool Football Club precisely what it is. Come on, you Red Men!

John Williams
April 2010

1

FOOTBALL IN LIVERPOOL
From the Very Beginning

STIRRINGS DOWN SOUTH

Despite what many Scousers and other Liverpool fans might like to think, association football didn't actually originate in Liverpool at all. In fact, the first of a series of meetings about establishing football as the national game took place in the Freemason's Tavern in Great Queen Street, London, on 26 October 1863. A group of ex-public schoolboys were trying to agree on a common set of laws for football by setting up the Football Association (FA). The meeting barely raised a murmur in the great Victorian city of Liverpool. It was certainly not reported in the local press. Why should it be? Here, after all, was a small group of southern-based toffs mulling over ideas originally coined by Cambridge University graduates. They wanted a common set of laws for a ball game – association football – to be played in Harrow, Eton and a selection of England's elite public schools. Why on earth should this little sporting cabal register even a blip of interest in the resplendent, prosperous great working port of Liverpool of the north?

Folk versions of something called 'football' had existed for centuries in England, of course. Rivers, streams and other local landmarks mapped out the playing areas. Essentially, these were brutal, public-holiday free-for-alls for local young bucks – a sort of legitimised mass brawl over possession of a ball or keg. Occasionally, they ended fatally for some of those involved. Lancashire was a special site for sporting matches organised by pub landlords for gambling purposes. The city of Liverpool was dominated by a slightly milder version of this anarchic ritual that came codified from the English public schools. In fact, the first recorded non-school football match played under Rugby School rules in the north of England took place at the Edge Hill cricket ground, Liverpool, in 1857. It was played between men from Liverpool and Manchester but was described extravagantly as a fixture that pitched 'Rugby School' against 'the World'. Fifty players were involved, most of them ex-Rugby public schoolboys and sons of Liverpool's merchant class. Signs of what would become the association game there were none. Although early versions of 'football' often meant a mixing and matching of handling and kicking, rugby was king in mid-nineteenth-century Liverpool. The Liverpool Rugby Union Club was founded in 1862, and rugby in the city seemed just as its elite supporters wanted it to be: upper or middle class in personnel, and violent and uncompromising in play. Manchester opponents (always keen rivals for Liverpudlians, even then) commented a few years later, after a trip to the city to play rugby football, that, 'Anyone who played in the match at Queen's Park [Liverpool] in or about 1865 would remember it, as we were overmatched and roughly handled. Some of us had to be helped out of the railway carriage on arrival at Manchester Victoria station.'[1] Great stuff.

The association men at the FA did seem to have a rather more democratic view than their rugby opponents about the possibilities of spreading a new common football code *downwards* among working people in cities such as Liverpool, as well as to the new urban middle classes. This would only be possible, of course, as long as football could be stripped of some of the violent excesses of the past. They were determined to get their way, even fiddling the votes at early meetings in order to keep their vision on track.[2] With a little more diplomacy or tact, the FA might have successfully compromised with its opponents by agreeing to establish *two* football codes: one for association football and the other for rugby football. This strategy would have boosted FA membership and increased its early national importance. Instead, the hackers and handlers would eventually set up their own rival body, outside the FA. Nor did the FA men do much even to try to *explain* or spread their modest new football laws. In any case, people in the city of Liverpool seemed largely disinterested in them. Elsewhere, the new laws served to confuse early FA members and other football clubs rather than offer any real clarity. In fact, many existing football clubs chose to adopt *some* aspects of the FA laws and to reject others, thus producing a bewildering series of hybrid football codes.[3] It looked as if this obscure new southern sporting body – and its fancy new association-football code – was actually going nowhere fast.

In 1871, the embryonic world of football was turned on its head. The Rugby Football Union was formed, and, partly as a response, the FA launched the world's first national sporting knockout competition: the FA Cup was born. Two thousand fans, drawn mainly from the London social elites, watched the first FA Cup final at the Kennington Oval in 1872. A team of ex-public schoolboys from Wanderers defeated ex-public schoolboys representing Royal Engineers, 1–0. Predictably, there were no reports of this historic southern encounter in the Liverpool press. But by the late 1870s the first real *northern* working-class football hero, Fergus Suter, a Scottish stonemason, had already emerged – not in Liverpool but in East Lancashire. Football in this part of the north seemed to be a continuation of local traditions rather than something especially encouraged by the public schools or the FA.

As football was being dragged kicking and screaming into the mainstream of English public life, the great seaport of Liverpool remained resolutely a cricket and rugby city. In Yorkshire, and in some parts of Lancashire, cup competitions for largely working-class northern rugby were established in the late 1870s. But the controlling elitist ex-public school rugby clubs in the great cities of Liverpool and Manchester refused, point blank, to play any competitive cup rugby football. Their argument was that 'gentlemen' should play only friendly sporting fixtures, 'for the good of the game'. More importantly, these social elites feared being drawn to play against their social inferiors in a cup competition. They might even come across veiled professionals. This kind of social superiority (or rank snobbery, if you like) provided just the sort of social and cultural sporting vacuum that association football would eventually rush to fill in Liverpool. Over the next decade or so, ordinary working-class people in the north and Midlands increasingly began to link up with social reformers, employers and middle-class patrons to form association football clubs in and around cities such as Sheffield, Birmingham and Nottingham.

LEFT BEHIND LIVERPOOL

But why was association football for working people in the 1870s already well established in places such as East Lancashire, South Yorkshire and the Midlands, but not so at all in Liverpool? By 1880, for example, the local press in Birmingham was reporting on eight hundred and eleven local football contests while the Liverpool press could find only two on Merseyside. For one thing, the Liverpool area lacked the folk forms of football that had been common in East Lancashire and around Sheffield. For another, the incredible economic and cultural span between Liverpool's elite rich, its ranks of clerks in the middle and the squalid, urban poor at the bottom meant that there was much less of the sort of social mixing and paternalism that was now common in other British cities. There were plenty of returning ex-Harrow public schoolboys living in Liverpool who might have been expected to spread association football. But because of the stark divisions between rich and poor in the city, sport could not be so easily passed down from local social elites, as had happened elsewhere. And, in any case, the poor in Liverpool's docklands had neither the space nor the good health to play sport.[4]

In the 1860s and early 1870s, northern and Midlands association football clubs had been made up mainly of players from the upper and middle classes. Then, from the middle of the 1870s, as the sport mushroomed from the bottom up, new football clubs began to develop for working people out of existing institutions, such as cricket clubs and churches. New football clubs were often inspired by the Victorian doctrine of 'Muscular Christianity', a form of community engineering from above aimed at combining the restraint and sobriety of Methodism with the obvious benefits of physical activity and healthy competition for working people. Football was seen by liberal elites as an improving form of 'moral cleansing' for the urban poor. It might even help 'save' the souls of the working class, people who could otherwise be easily tempted by the connected evils of fecklessness, crime, drinking and gambling.

Some of her critics – and even her friends – might well have argued that the Liverpool of the 1870s and 1880s was in urgent need of a good dose of moral cleansing. This heaving and turbulent nineteenth-century English seaport probably seemed a rather odd place compared to the average English provincial town of the time. But it fitted perfectly well with the outlook in transient Continental seaports such as Hamburg and Marseille, or great cities across the Atlantic. An American visitor of the time thought Liverpool to be a modern marvel, 'the Chicago of England', and the *London Illustrated News* on 15 May 1886 described it as 'the New York of Europe, a world city rather than merely British provincial'. Many of Liverpool's Victorian residents were moulded, for good or ill, by this same sense of being cosmopolitans, authentic citizens of the world.[5]

Liverpool's selective affluence, its nod to cosmopolitanism and its flamboyant identity as a thriving global port was also reflected in the conviviality and sheer liveliness of the city centre – and in the fact that by 1874 there was a grand total of 2,585 places in the city from which beer and spirits were sold. But this largesse also meant that public drunkenness – especially among Merseyside street children, criminals and the poor – was a regular local focus for moral concern and regulation among those who were occasionally forced into rubbing shoulders with the lower orders. This included the city's civic leaders and members of the press. Liverpool's wonderful municipal Victorian finery, its extensive programme of public lectures, an impulse for self improvement and its sheer commercial dynamism stood cheek by jowl with incredible levels of desperation and deprivation. One overseas visitor to the city remarked that he had seen such vast wealth and poverty in other cities but 'never before had I seen the two so jammed together'.[6]

Among the worst affected by poverty and poor health was Liverpool's Irish community, especially Catholic families who were originally from the south and west of Ireland and who were part of the group of 580,000 Irish who passed through the port at the height of the great potato famine in 1846 and 1847. Many of the Irish who then settled in Liverpool drew attention to themselves in the northern end of the city mainly through their sheer numbers and levels of unemployment and poverty, and the diseases they suffered, caused by malnutrition and overcrowded and unsanitary housing conditions. With one of the highest mortality rates in Britain, Liverpool in the mid-nineteenth century was publicly labelled as 'the Black Spot on the Mersey'.[7] Amidst the deprivation, squalor and filth, idle hands inevitably turned to gangs, violence and crime. The so-called 'cornermen' who stood outside Liverpool pubs or on street corners demanding money for beer from passers-by became notorious. Public panics about the alleged existence of organised criminal gangs in the city, including the 'High Rip Gang', the 'Bridge Boys' and the 'Canal Bankers', all contributed, periodically, in the wider public's mind to a sense that Victorian Liverpool was a violent, chaotic and potentially lawless place. The city of Liverpool was now already established as a place of extremes: it hosted high culture and global commerce but also crime and destitution in an uneasy and often seemingly unequal balance. It was a stigma that would prove difficult to shift.

As well as divisions of poverty and ill health, the peculiar occupational structure of Liverpool also held back the spread of football on Merseyside. It was shaped by the port and its processing industries, and it meant that it was much more difficult for the vast majority of working people in the city to find free time for playing and supporting *any* sport. The Liverpool workforce had to lobby long and persistently for change in this area, with even most skilled workers in the city being unable to attain a shorter working week until as late as 1872. By contrast, beginning with the Ten Hours Act of 1847, East Lancashire textile workers had been granted a two o'clock end to work on Saturdays by 1850, reduced to one o'clock in 1874. The Ten Hours Act meant that cotton spinners now worked 55 hours rather than 70 hours, and for these workers 'it became a practice, mostly on Saturdays, to play football and cricket, which had never been done before'.[8] Most men in Birmingham did not have to work Saturday afternoons from the 1870s.

By contrast, because of the casual nature of their employment practices and the lack of care shown by dock employers for their workers, the mass of Liverpool's dockworkers had much less power to bargain with their bosses, and they would only gain Saturday afternoons off from work in April 1890 – fully two years *after* the formation of the Football League.[9] Conditions for working people in Liverpool lagged behind as the profits poured into the city coffers.

TURNING RUGBY MEN TO FOOTBALL

Another reason for the late uptake of football in Liverpool was probably the fact that rugby remained such a powerful force in the city and that it continued to be so jealously guarded by its local social elites. But things were changing fast, and not just on Merseyside. With the establishment of the Lancashire FA Cup and other local football competitions from 1879 onwards, and especially after the national FA Cup successes of the working-class clubs of Blackburn in the late 1870s and early 1880s, previously exclusively rugby-playing areas of the north-west of England were now rapidly converting, en masse, to football. Preston and Burnley – later, founder members of the Football League – were originally staunch rugby towns, but by the early 1880s both had become football strongholds. Previously high-profile supporters of the rugby code, including the great Fergus Suter himself, by now had turned from rugby to association football.[10] The spread of football in what were previously rugby havens was like a bush fire. Local football derbies between Liverpool's emerging association clubs, such as Everton FC and Bootle FC, now began to be reported on at some length by the Liverpool press. By 1882, exhibition football matches were being staged on Stanley Park, featuring teams selected by top local footballers – one match attracted one thousand four hundred fans. By 1883, the *Liverpool Daily Post* was routinely carrying results of the national FA Cup ties, and it even ran an account of an FA meeting in London on law changes for the association game. How times had changed. Finally, football was stirring on Merseyside.

As the association game began to challenge rugby's dominance in the parks and in the sporting press on Merseyside, another man to turn away from rugby in order to champion football was to play a crucial role in developing football in the city. Irishman and future Everton FC, Liverpool FC and Football League stalwart 'Honest' John McKenna would help shape the modern game, but his conversion from rugby was also a vital moment in the history of Liverpool Football Club. John McKenna had arrived in the city in 1854 as part of the great Irish diaspora that flooded into the sprawling mix of chaos and opportunity that was mid-nineteenth-century Liverpool. At the age of 17, McKenna had become a grocer's boy and then a vaccination officer before later becoming a sergeant major in the Lancashire Artillery military regiment. A keen rugby man when the sport was still dominant in Liverpool, this 'man of action' McKenna was eventually dismayed by rugby's avowed elitism and violence. But he was immediately impressed by the sheer competitiveness and the spectator potential of the new football cup competitions that were sweeping the north-west of England in the late 1870s. Football, with its simplicity, more civilised laws, its mixed constituents and its wider social appeal, certainly chimed well with McKenna's keen entrepreneurial instincts. He noticed that in 1880 an East Lancashire football derby between Blackburn Rovers and Darwen was already attracting an extraordinary 10,000 spectators, many of them cotton workers. He reasoned that there was money to be made by smart businessmen in association football on Merseyside.

But football was much more than a commercial proposition for McKenna. He had his values – he worked with the poor and destitute for the West Derby Union and he deplored gambling – and he was also openly envious of the way the national football cup successes of the clubs of East Lancashire, Blackburn Olympic and Rovers, drew great publicity and brass-band welcome-home parties in these small towns for winning the southerners' FA Cup. He now desperately wanted to bring this sort of national sporting triumph to his adopted city of Liverpool. He would not have to wait too long. After a late start, by the early 1880s Liverpool had a stock of new association clubs, including Everton, Stanley Park, the ex-public school Liverpool Ramblers, Bootle FC, Druids, Bootle Wanderers, Anfield, Tranmere, Toxteth Wanderers, St Peters and Liverpool Linden. More were forming all the time. McKenna would throw his lot in with the rising Everton club and its charismatic president, 'King' John Houlding. By 1886, the new Liverpool Cup competition could attract 20 clubs from inside the city in its inaugural season. Within one extraordinary decade, between 1878 and the launch of the Football League in 1888, the city of Liverpool would move from having no association football at all to attracting the largest crowds to football matches anywhere in the world.

THE MYSTERIOUS BIRTH OF EVERTON FC AND THE COURT OF KING JOHN

In this place of extreme contrasts, boasting both plenty and abject poverty, local association clubs now rapidly started to form on Merseyside. Everton FC was established in a slightly more affluent area of the north end of Liverpool after a meeting in the Queen's Head Hotel in November 1879. The Anglican Everton United Church Football Club had been set up earlier that year by a group of curates from St John's College in Cambridge University led by the 25-year-old Reverend Alfred Keely. Keely had been spreading the virtues of Muscular Christianity via football in both Bootle and Liverpool. St Saviour's Church had provided the core of the United team, Methodism its values.

The exact origins of Everton FC remain contentious. The club is popularly believed to have grown out of a club at the St Domingo's New Connexion Methodist Chapel, which was supposedly formed in 1878 and which initially played cricket. The Reverend Ben Swift Chambers, a Yorkshire Methodist, is thought to have coaxed young men into playing football for St Domingo's. Leading early Everton committee members George Mahon and Will Cuff were prominent New Connexion Methodists. But one recent historian can find no trace of the St Domingo's Football Club, suggesting that the St Domingo's football team might have been a clever fiction invented later by Everton's directors in order to undermine the early role played at Everton by local brewer and Liverpool FC founder John Houlding.[11] But there is at least one reference in the *Liverpool Courier*, on 20 October 1879, to St Domingo's actually playing an association fixture against the Everton Church Club on Stanley Park. This was just before Everton FC was formed.[12] John Houlding, a prominent local Conservative politician and Orangeman, had been on the lay vestry at St Saviour's, and, through Everton United, he could have been involved in the early days of Everton FC before 1881, by which time he had become the club's first president. Houlding, no doubt, already had plans to exploit his links with the new football club for commercial and political gain, aspirations which were very out of tune with the ideals of both Cambridge curates and Merseyside Methodists.

Clerks dominated these early Merseyside sports clubs – Liverpool was a financial hub so was full of them – and by 1881 Everton FC had regular fixtures against local clubs and teams from nearby Lancashire and Cheshire, as well as matches with clubs from Manchester. In September 1882, the *Liverpool Courier* was already suggesting that football was overtaking rugby in Liverpool in terms of its popularity, and it was now seen as an entertainment by fans and players, even if it was still regarded by some of its patrons as a bulwark against drink and crime. By 1885, twenty-five out of the one hundred and twelve football clubs playing in the city had connections with religious organisations, and the origins of four out of five of the Merseyside clubs that eventually played professional football were in religious groups.

The growing ambitions of Everton were signalled by the appointment of John Houlding to the office of club president. Houlding owned a house and a pub – the Sandon Hotel – virtually overlooking Everton's home patch on Stanley Park. The Everton-born brewer and politician, now approaching 50, had been educated to no great level at Liverpool College and had begun his working life at 11 years of age as a lowly errand boy in a customs house. He followed this with a spell as a cowman's assistant; his father was a cowman, but the plague had damaged the milk business, and the impatient young Houlding soon moved on. He then became a drayman and later a foreman and chief brewer in the Clarkson Brewery – all before he had reached 21 years of age. Houlding eventually set up his own successful brewing business in the city, the Tynemouth Street Brewery in Everton, producing Houlding's Sparkling Ales. There were few people in 1880s Liverpool – certainly few drinkers or politicians, or few of the poor of the Everton district – who had not heard of Councillor John Houlding.

There were some obvious early tensions inside the Everton club. Its original philosophies – about sobriety, Methodism and liberalism – clashed somewhat with those of the self-made and charismatic patrician Tory politician and businessman John Houlding. The latter's political antennae for identifying compassionately with the grassroots, and his honed commercial interests in cashing in on the obvious connections between working people, drink and sport, were already well known in the city. Houlding, according to the *Liverpool Mercury*, was 'one of the most remarkable of men for, while not possessing any great educational advantages . . . he read and studied to such an extent that there was not a topic of conversation that he was unable to hold his own and give an intelligent opinion on'. Houlding was also chairman of the Everton Conservative Association, a leading Freemason and a staunch Unionist at a time when the city of Liverpool, like most other places in England, was effectively subject to one-party rule.

Houlding's reliable local political and cultural contacts, his 'common touch' shown by his poor-law work with young people in the city and with the elderly stuck in poverty, and his work as a great publicist for the asssociation game (and especially for Everton FC) all meant that, despite his many failings, what he had to offer football clubs in Liverpool seemed like an unbeatable combination. Houlding appeared unstoppable. He was such a major public personality and positive force for the club, a man who talked in a language that ordinary people could understand, that the local press soon dubbed him 'Honest' John or 'King John of Everton'.[13] Eventually, however, Houlding's commercial and political instincts, his lingering suspicions of Methodism and his powerful Liberal opponents on the Everton board would end King John's football reign in this half of Liverpool. But it would also help start, from scratch, another football dynasty in the city at a new association club.[14]

Like many local parks' clubs, most of Everton's early games were friendly affairs and fixtures in local cup competitions fought out on Stanley Park. Everton even met a football club called 'Liverpool' at Walton Stiles in the Liverpool Cup in January 1883, defeating their hapless hosts 8–0. But Everton's fiercest rivals by now were certainly north-end neighbours Bootle FC. Their keenly fought-out local contests often spilled over into disputes and crowd disturbances. Even the *Liverpool Echo* was by now picking up on the significance of these local rivalries and on the wider national impact of the 'football fever'. The *Echo* carried a major report on 2 April 1883 on the history-making FA Cup final at the Oval between Old Etonians and Blackburn Olympic. Sensationally, Olympic had won 2–1, and the *Echo* made much of the sharp contrast between the elite followers of the public-school club and those of the Lancastrian tribe, the 'artisan class', who followed their Blackburn heroes to London. 'Co'om Olympics, put on another shovelful!' the visiting spectators reportedly urged on their team, much to the *Echo*'s amusement. But such passion seemed to do the trick: the northern working classes at last began to colonise what would become *their* sport.

HERE COME THE PROFESSIONALS

Because of their FA Cup exploits, Olympic were now offered hard cash to take up new fixtures around the country. Eyeing up this East Lancashire success and its obvious commercial possibilities, John Houlding wanted to develop the Everton club for their own place in the FA Cup (achieved in 1886) by collecting gate money from the few hundred regular fans who followed the club, free of charge, on Stanley Park. In 1883, and for one season only, Everton hired an enclosed field, Coney Green, off Priory Road, near the Anfield Cemetery. The club won the Liverpool Cup and also played some of the top Lancashire clubs, but the noise from home supporters disturbed the club's new landlord William Cruitt and probably those who were paying their last respects next door. Everton FC were turfed out, and the club moved to a field owned by John Orrell on the other side of Stanley Park, much closer to Houlding's Sandon Hotel and wedged between Anfield Road and Walton Breck Road. John Houlding negotiated the deal and acted as representative tenant. Everton players would get changed and drink afterwards in the Sandon Hotel, a pub named by Houlding after a local Tory grandee. The *Daily Post* reported on 29 September 1884 that 'Everton has had to seek a new home during the recess and have been fortunate to secure a capital one near to the Sandon Hotel, the headquarters of the club . . . Today the new ground will be opened with a match against Earlestown, the runners-up for the last cup contest.'

Everton easily disposed of Earlestown, 5–0. Association football had finally arrived at what would later become Liverpool's Anfield Road ground. King John would now build up the club's crowds and the stadium facilities. Until, that is, the great Merseyside football split of 1892 effectively handed all this over to a new Liverpool Football Club – controlled by the same John Houlding.

The city of Liverpool had few skilled footballers at this time. As we have seen, the sport had arrived very late to Merseyside, and it would take time to become embedded among working people. As football crowds grew and matches became more important in the north of England, so recruiting and holding on to the best talent – and keeping it fresh, especially for big FA Cup matches – meant that football clubs had to scout more intensively and also 'invent' jobs for migrant footballers, whilst also paying them to play.

Professionalism in football was opposed, mainly in the south, because it was feared that business values would soon supersede sporting ones if payment for play became the norm. Paying footballers in this way did not especially concern ordinary working people in the north. But many local spectators and commentators *were* strongly opposed to the notion that players should be brought in from *outside* the area to represent their clubs. Why not give local talent a chance? This was certainly the position taken by the *Daily Post* on 25 October 1884 when it pointed out that professionalism and local English players worked perfectly well in cricket. Professionalism was not the problem for the *Post* and the rest of the Liverpool press – it was 'foreign' recruits. Such debates about football 'outsiders' would continue, no less passionately of course, more than 100 years later.

When Everton opened up their 1886–87 roster of 'friendly' fixtures at Anfield against Glasgow Rangers, the money that was now in the sport had begun to show its face. The *Daily Post* on 30 October 1886 reported, 'The Everton committee are doing their level best for the comfort and accommodation of their patrons.' Certainly, the Anfield ground had undergone considerable redevelopment and was already taking shape as a recognisable modern football stadium – even including some seating provision for football writers, as the *Post* reported:

> The ground is now completely enclosed, a stand capable of seating about 400 persons has been erected, and for one hundred yards on the opposite side a substantial wooden terrace has been constructed with standing room for 800, whilst just behind the rails a bench has been run the whole length of the ground . . . The members of the Fourth Estate have not been forgotten either, as a space has been allotted to that body on the front bench of the stand.

More than 5,000 people attended the Rangers match (including, no doubt, some local Irish Catholic Everton followers from the north end), and with Everton recent winners of the Liverpool Senior Cup, and capable of attracting big gates, the club urgently needed new challenges. Entry into the FA Cup signalled some important progress, and in 1887 a crowd in excess of 8,000 fans watched the club's FA Cup third-replay victory against Bolton at Anfield. All human life was here, according to the local press, as 'the immense concourse of spectators swarmed across the ground after the final whistle had sounded' and '800 colleens . . . dainty maids, clad in minks and victorines . . . came rushing through the portals – a sight for gods and mortals'. To their female fans' delight, Everton won the tie, but seven of their Scottish players were later deemed to be 'veiled professionals', and the club forfeited the win and was suspended from all football for one month. Also, because of the length of time it had taken to complete the tie, Everton had been forced to postpone valuable friendly fixtures with other clubs, including with a fuming Bootle FC. Football clubs of the size and ambition of Everton and Bootle needed a new structure, a fixed and reliable list of contests for which they could offer fans season tickets. They needed a football league.

McGREGOR'S 1888 UNION OF CLUBS

It was William McGregor, a Scottish Methodist draper and director of Aston Villa, who, at 41 years of age, first dreamed up the idea of a football league. Some suggested that he borrowed the concept from unofficial press tables for English cricket's County Championship. Others thought the idea might have come from the baseball leagues in the USA, which had been operating since 1876. Whatever the source, McGregor toured football clubs in the north and Midlands in the summer of 1887 to try to gather support for his project. But he received only a mixed reception: not everyone shared his enthusiasm for radical change. Unimpressed by the response from his travels – football clubs were worried by travel costs and losing valued local contests, and were unsure a league would even work – McGregor then sent a letter to the nation's top professional clubs (professionalism had been reluctantly sanctioned in a limited way by the FA in 1885). He had just two replies, although representatives from seven clubs eventually met for further discussions at the Anderton Hotel in London on 22 March 1888. The northern giants, Preston and Bolton Wanderers, were absent but apparently still keen on the league concept. Preston and Bolton, along with all the other clubs at this first meeting – Stoke, West Bromich Albion, Burnley, Wolverhampton Wanderers, Blackburn Rovers, Notts County and Aston Villa – became founder members of the new Football League. Nine clubs were now tied up: just three more to find. Everton, Accrington and Derby County were then invited to a second meeting, at the Royal Street Hotel in Manchester on 17 April at 6.30 p.m. Here the new league was formed, and McGregor's 'Football Union' was renamed the Football League. There was no club from Sheffield or anywhere in Yorkshire involved, and none at all from the south of England.

Why invite modest Accrington to join, and why seek out Everton? Why, indeed? *Athletic News* commented, acidly, that some of the chosen 12 had been 'knocked into smithereens by teams who, so far, have been left out in the cold'. Bootle Football Club was surely one of these.[15] Accrington's league claims were supported by the other Lancashire clubs, and the town was at least easy to reach by rail, an important consideration. *Both* Merseyside clubs could not be invited to join, because McGregor had decided it should be only one club per local area. Bootle FC was a better bet on the playing side than Everton, but Everton had better facilities and was attracting bigger crowds at Anfield. Everton's gates were already worth twice those of Bootle.[16] In 1888, Bootle had already beaten three proposed Football League clubs – Blackburn Rovers, Accrington and Burnley – in the run up to the new league's formation. But it made no odds: Bootle were out and the more commercially attractive Everton were in.

Everton made a raft of signings in the summer of 1888, including the brilliant Scot Nick Ross from Preston North End. Ross had teeth that were 'discoloured almost green to the gums and he hissed through them as he played' yet he was described as 'the champion back of the world'.[17] His defensive kicks were legendary, routinely clearing the Kemlyn Road chimney pots. Ross could also be difficult: he wanted a hand in coaching and selection, but he was 'just another player' to the Everton hierarchy. 'Too many cooks have spoiled the Everton broth,' opined the Lancashire press, 'and Ross has done quite right in showing his independence and his contempt for the childish mismanagement.'

With Ross and other signings newly on board on the first day of Football League fixtures on 8 September 1888, it was the Anfield ground that drew the biggest crowd of the day as an estimated 10,000 watched Everton beat Accrington 2–1. Anfield stadium security was sorely tested, as one 'hulking fellow tore down a portion of hoarding and 50 followed him through the breach'. Later, 'a little urchin trespassed on the grass and got a "free kick" from an elderly steward'. Then, a 'little young fellow went for the official without ceremony, leaving him prostrate with blood streaming from his face'.[18] Welcome, indeed, to league football in Liverpool.

Everton were widely chided in the Lancashire press in these early days for their spendthrift ways and their alleged player poaching, but also for their on-pitch aggression. Their approach was described locally as a kind of 'football forcing . . . the most expensive, the dearest lot of players that has ever been got together'. The club recruited 36 professionals, paying more than £100 per week for them. They certainly showed the necessary ruthlessness. The Scottish full-back Alec Dick was known as a 'savage' defender. His hack on an Aston Villa forward produced a punch missed by the officials, and Dick was routinely involved in fist fights on the field. Dick also allegedly once butted a spectator, and his bad language on the pitch was notorious. He was the first Football League player officially cautioned and then suspended. Everton, it was said, in this first, turbulent season, were 'singularly disliked in official quarters'.

Everton struggled in this first season, and after an Anfield defeat 0–1 to West Bromwich Albion, 'hero' Nick Ross got home later that night to find that Everton supporters had smashed all the windows in his house. The local press described the affair as 'rag-tag and bobtail footballism with a vengeance'. Ross might have escaped lightly in the circumstances, because some British football fans were already showing that they could be frighteningly critical. For example, around this time the Glasgow Rangers captain Donald Gow received a parcel at Ibrox Park from an anonymous fan following a bad run of results. Its message needed little decoding: the package contained the neatly arranged carcasses of 11 dead mice.[19]

Everton's apparent chaos was sometimes matched by that of the Football League itself in its first season. Matches often seemed to be as badly organised as the old friendly fixtures before them, because clubs frequently turned up late for matches and some had even 'lost' players en route. Everton played a total of 61 matches in the first league season, only 22 of them in the Football League. John Houlding ensured that they also played 41 of those games at Anfield, thus raking in the receipts.

The new Football League worked essentially because of the good sense of its members and the commitment of the clubs to make it work – but also because of British engineering and the existence of the Lancashire and Yorkshire railways to take players and spectators to matches: they covered five hundred and ninety miles and three hundred and nine stations, none more than two miles apart. On 19 January 1889, Everton hosted champions-elect Preston North End in a match between the best and the best supported of all the original league clubs. Everton lost 0–2 in front of 15,000 fans, the largest Football League crowd that first season. The local press described the Anfield grandeur as a 'huge circus, with its two immense galleries, rising tier after tier, and its covered stands, stretching the length of the ground'. Liverpool was rapidly becoming unrivalled as the country's premier centre for supporting association football. But as Bootle Football Club began to ail, so Everton FC now needed a credible local rival to really get the competitive sporting juices working in the city. Although no one yet knew it, King John Houlding of Everton was about to provide his colleagues on the Everton board with just what they desired.

CHAPTER 1 REFERENCES

1. Booth, *The Father of Modern Sport*, p. 39
2. Harvey, *Football: The First Hundred Years – The Untold Story*
3. Harvey, *Football: The First Hundred Years – The Untold Story*
4. Preston, 'The Origins and Development of Association Football in the Liverpool District, *c*.1879–*c*.1915'
5. Milne, 'Maritime Liverpool', p. 257
6. Marne, 'Whose Public Space Was It Anyway? Class, Gender and Ethnicity in the Creation of Sefton and Stanley Parks, Liverpool: 1858–1872', p. 425
7. Pooley, 'Living in Liverpool: The Modern City', pp. 173 and 187
8. Williams, *The Code War*, p. 49
9. Physick, *Played in Liverpool*, p. 15; Mason, *Association Football and English Society 1863–1915*
10. Collins, *Rugby's Great Split*, p. 38
11. Preston, 'The Origins and Development of Association Football in the Liverpool District, *c*.1879–*c*.1915', pp. 103–5
12. Lupson, *Across the Park*, p. 17
13. Lupson, *Thank God for Football!*, p. 59
14. Kennedy and Kennedy, 'Ambiguity, Complexity and Convergence: The Evolution of Liverpool's Irish Football Clubs'
15. Inglis, *League Football and the Men Who Made It*, p. 8
16. Preston, 'The Origins and Development of Association Football in the Liverpool District, *c*.1879–*c*.1915', p. 67
17. Sanders, *Beastly Fury*, p. 113
18. Taw, *Football's Twelve Apostles*, pp. 127 and 146
19. Taw, *Football's Twelve Apostles*, p. 179

2

LIVERPOOL OUT OF EVERTON
One Seed, Two Clubs

THE GREAT SPLIT: 1892 AND ALL THAT

Recovering successfully from their various trials in 1889, Everton Football Club actually fulfilled one of King John Houlding's great football ambitions by winning the 1891 Football League championship and with it the newly bought league-championship trophy. But it was not exactly a vintage year for football. High-spending Everton lost seven times and secured just twenty-nine points from twenty-two matches. Like any good modern chairman, Houlding was reportedly 'much disgusted' with his players for losing the final 'dead' league match against Burnley, especially in light of the reported substantial players' wage bill at Everton of some £80 or £90 a week. Couldn't these guys start to *earn* what they were paid? Houlding himself had reportedly loaned Everton more than £2,300 over the previous five years so had cause to demand more.

But 1891 *was* a vintage football year on Merseyside in another important sense. It signalled the official adoption by the sport of an authentic Liverpool invention: the goal-net. Liverpool city engineer J.A. Brodie had first considered the problem of a mechanism for confirming goals scored in August 1889. Matches between Everton and Bootle especially had supporters crammed into grounds and inevitably balanced along the touchlines. They could trip or baulk players, and, standing behind the goals, they sometimes loitered with the intention of keeping opposing shots out. Everton had even had a clear goal ruled out at an early Football League match against Accrington. By November 1890, after a trial on Stanley Park, the new goal-net was approved by the Patent Office. In September 1891, both the Lancashire League and the Football League made goal-nets compulsory, and they were also used at international and FA Cup final matches.[1] But despite Brodie's ingenuity, more than a century later even some professional football clubs have still not worked out how to design nets to avoid the ball rebounding out and embarrassing some half-awake referee.

There were also, in 1891, already the beginnings of administrative and financial rumblings from inside the Everton club. After a defeat by West Bromwich Albion in September 1891, the *Liverpool Review* reported on Houlding's plans to convert the Everton club into a limited company, with shares valued at £12,000: 'The players will have to do better if the shares are to be taken up at all quickly.' Houlding, as the representative tenant at Anfield, had effectively been Everton's landlord, and he was charging the club rent, which had increased from a figure of £100 to a weighty £240 a year by 1888 – and was still rising. Houlding saw this arrangement as a reasonable business deal: the success of the Football League had raised the value of the rent at Anfield. Everton's committee, led by George Mahon, an accountant, now asked for a long-term lease, which Houlding refused. Houlding claimed, instead, the rights for himself to the exclusive sale of refreshments to the club's fans. This was some nerve – and King John was some businessman and local politician. Houlding now proposed that Everton must also use adjacent land he owned for training, which would raise the total club rent to £370 a year. Either that or the club could convert to a limited company and purchase the land owned by Houlding and Orrell, including the stands and offices, for a total of just over £8,737. Otherwise, Orrell insisted that the Anfield land would be used for building and that Everton FC would have to move to a new site.

Understandably, all this left a rather bad taste in the mouth of Everton's Methodist founders, led by Mahon, who had been exploring the possibility of renting nearby land for just £50. After initially seeming to accept Houlding's corporate solution to the Everton 'problem', finally, on 15 September 1891, a general meeting was held in the Royal Street Hotel, at which the president produced a valuation and prospectus for the purchase of the Anfield land. The prospect of being faced with buying Anfield from John Houlding and his associates was too much for the growing band of men inside Everton who disliked King John's brewing businesses and his corporate style. Another solution would have to be sought for this problem. The *Liverpool Echo* reported that an Everton member had told a shareholders' meeting that 'it seemed to him we could expect nothing but the policy of Shylock from Mr Houlding. He was determined to have his pound of flesh, or intimidate the club into accepting his scheme.' George Mahon, leading for Houlding's opponents at Everton, put forward the motion that this proposal 'should not be entertained'. It was comfortably passed, and Houlding threatened to evict the club from Anfield. Time was now fast running out to patch things up. The anti-Houlding men at Everton were effectively looking to establish their own limited liability company so that they could purchase land for a new stadium. They even thought they had seen a suitable site, some wasteland just on the other side of Stanley Park at Mere Green Field. It would later be known, of course, as Goodison Park.[2]

This angry stand-off between Houlding and his rivals inside Everton was definitely heading for a fall, though on 8 January 1892 the Houlding-loyal *Liverpool Review* still felt able to report that 'The malcontents in the Everton club are climbing down nicely to the King of Everton's ideas. Seemingly, they were ill advised to quarrel with him.' This was overly optimistic. John McKenna was by now, with vice chair William Barclay, one of a dwindling number of Houlding allies around Everton. For local-born entrepreneurs and public figures such as John Houlding, involvement in football was part of the wider moral and political appeal that local elites felt they had to make to working people. But, frankly, he just didn't need all these football problems, because he had real difficulties with national and local party politics. The death of a local Conservative MP in the Everton division had made Houlding seem like a local shoo-in for the job. All seemed set, especially as the brewer epitomised popular Toryism in his support for male working-class leisure interests – sport and the pub – against the fanaticism of the Liverpool abstentionists.[3] But then the tide turned; temperance reformers began to gain ground in the city, especially around the issue of 'drunken children'. It was no help when Houlding's dispute inside Everton began to turn publicly sour at the same time. King John was also perhaps too much of a maverick and just *too* popular locally among working people for the national Tory bigwigs. Perhaps because of his obvious personal local popularity, he was strongly opposed by the Tory hierarchy and the constituency party in Liverpool, and Houlding was eventually forced to withdraw his candidacy to avoid splitting the party.

By now John Houlding's prominent position at Everton Football Club was also fading fast for lack of internal support. His opponents attempted to set up a new limited liability company using the Everton name, only to find that Houlding had mischievously registered 'Everton Football Club and Athletics Grounds Company, Limited' just 24 hours before. On 15 March, Houlding was ejected from Everton's ruling committee at a meeting at a Presbyterian school in Royal Street. He refused to chair the meeting as club president, and he learned that the Football League had sided with his opponents in the matter of company name. His arrival was cheered, but out of the five hundred Everton members present 'only eighteen or twenty stood by the King', reported the *Liverpool Review* on 19 March 1892. But the newspaper also rubbished rumours that Houlding had been undone in his sporting business by political radicals inside the club, arguing that, 'If the Everton football club was polled tomorrow, it is safe to say that the majority would be found Tory to the backbone.'

Others suggested otherwise: that it was Liberals and Methodist non-conformists at Everton – Mahon and club director and church choirmaster Will Cuff, especially – who were opposed to Houlding's commercial brewing interests and who most wanted Everton distanced from the drinks trade. It also seems clear that Houlding's opponents at Everton FC probably wanted to establish a much more democratic ownership and membership structure for their club, whereas, for all his good works with the poor in the city, the Tory King John wanted to tap into local working-class community support whilst still maintaining overall corporate control of the club. The *Liverpool Echo*, no great fan, had described Houlding, disparagingly, as a 'one man government' at Everton. The later, rather uneven, spread of share ownership at the two clubs rather confirmed this view of Houlding's dictatorial tendencies, with Liverpool FC's shares being concentrated in the hands of far fewer shareholders than were Everton's.[4] This meant much more autocratic control of the club by its directors than typically existed at Goodison Park, where it was one share, one vote and much more of a members' club than a corporate business. Everton's shares were also well spread among manual workers (36 per cent), whilst Liverpool FC could claim very few obviously working-class shareholders (just 5 per cent) under John Houlding.[5]

The *Review* also carried, on 26 March 1892, a *Private Eye*-like near-spoof account, provided by an 'insider', of the raucous special general meeting (officially closed to the press) that finally ejected Houlding and his followers from the Everton club. It starts with a preamble and a brief account of director Tom Howarth's pro-Houlding speech, and then things really began to hot up:

> 9.30 [John] McKenna rises and is received with terrible howls of execration and cries of 'Lie down McKenna!' 'Traitor!', etc. This is kept up all the time he is on his feet. Is cried down. Cheers, jumps up again. Howled down. Ditto. Howarth resumes, but is again interrupted. Members say he is only spouting to waste time.

> 9.45 Vote taken for Goodison Road. No question as to the majority.

> 9.50 Clayton moved that Mr Houlding, Mr Howarth and Mr Nisbet be removed. [William] Barclay (secretary) says he would like to hear Mr Houlding defend himself.

> 10.10 Houlding's speech (the chairman hopes members will give him a silent hearing because he has been ill). This is given with but few exceptions.

General opinion of speech is that he should have communicated as a gentleman should and have acknowledged them.

10.25 Mr Houlding's speech lasted a quarter of an hour. Wilson deeply regrets having to leave the [Anfield] ground though the majority of the committee have his entire sympathy. Loud cheers and cries of 'Good old Bob!', etc. Motion put to meeting. Honestly think there were not fifty voted against it. Howarth wants to speak, as regards being removed from the committee. But meeting will not hear him . . .

10.35 Members in hurry to close as there are only a few minutes to sup ale. Vote to chairman and loud cheering.

The whole sorry affair took just over an hour. When ale had been supped by the members and the dust had finally settled on what had been a poisonous dispute, Houlding claimed that it was not his business plans for Everton but the 'teetotal fanaticism' of his opponents that had forced his actions and produced the split. In truth, it had probably been both. His very public face in the city, his drinks firm and his 'direct' methods in business and public relations never seemed quite to fit at Everton. The dispute over rental charges also marked Houlding as an obvious 'outsider' in the Everton camp: he sometimes seemed to treat the club, at least in the eyes of his opponents, in a high-handed way as just another business client.

Was it greed or politics or drink or even personality clashes that forced Houlding out of Everton FC? The local politician certainly had many enemies in the Merseyside press. The temperance-supporting *Daily Post* of 19 March, for example, congratulated the board for 'trying to rid the Everton Club of an influence that had apparently grown stronger year after year'. The *Liverpool Echo* argued that Houlding was both autocratic and patronising, a man who liked to lead his colleagues 'by the nose'. Not unreasonably, Houlding felt unjustly treated in these accounts, and he also proved something of a poor loser, obstructing the Everton officials as they tried to remove their property from Anfield. The ever-loyal *Liverpool Review* of 19 March offered its own, much more misty-eyed, assessment of Houlding's recent treatment and decline and his considerable contribution to the Everton club. In a lengthy editorial lament, entitled 'Houlding Kicked Offside', the *Review* also offered its views of the possible future for both Houlding and the now vacant Anfield ground:

Oh, football. There seems to be as much gratitude in you in so far as 'King Houlding' is concerned as there is in politics ... Years ago, 'King Houlding' advanced the then struggling but rising Everton Football Club funds at a small rate of interest. He also assisted the organisation in other ways, for which the members were righteously thankful. As a landlord he lent the club a ground, at a moderate rental, to play on. He advanced money to erect grandstands and provide all the rest of the paraphernalia of a first-class football club. Things went on swimmingly and the Everton players made a name second to none, hardly, in the football world. Then came a change o'er the scene. Things were not what they seemed.

As the club prospered the rental of the ground was increased and the interest asked by the landlord for money advanced increased perceptively. There were mumblings and grumblings and finally the storm burst ... The King has been kicked and the victorious host has elected to migrate to a fresh field and pastures new ... All this is very sad and, a large number of onlookers think, very stupid ... And it really is a pity that a man like 'King Houlding' should be mixed up in such an unseemly tangle as that which has been going on at Everton Football Club. Perhaps 'King Houlding' will run a new football club in the present ground at Oakfield Road? If he does, the migrators to the new ground in Goodison Road will have a rival to beat.

There was much to support in this spirited defence. After all, it was Houlding who had provided Everton with the use of the Anfield Road ground, and he had later followed it with loans at excellent rates for ground improvements. Now, as Everton began to achieve some financial success, he surely had a right to expect some return on his investment. But Houlding's sometimes lofty approach to the club's affairs, coupled with his brewing interests, had brought him into direct conflict with Liberal opponents on the Everton board, and at a time when politics in the city were changing.[6] Houlding was astute enough to know very well the importance of football to local politics in a bubbling working-class Victorian city such as Liverpool – which is one reason why he was determined to form *another* professional football club just as soon as he possibly could.

LIVERPOOL FC IS BORN – BUT REJECTED BY THE FOOTBALL LEAGUE

Though the *Liverpool Review* might have had an inside track on John Houlding's future plans, paradoxically, on 28 May 1892, it also criticised Houlding for spending just too much of his time on football-related business. But almost from the outset of the dispute at Anfield, King John seemed to have designs on forming a new club at Oakfield Road. After all, he had a ready-made football stadium at cost, and Anfield might offer the rump of a new supporter base, too. He could run the new club as he liked, without interference. After failing to hold on to the Everton name, Houlding arguably trumped his erstwhile colleagues by choosing a club name much more in keeping with modern times and the emerging town and *city* rivalries that were now keenly promoted by the Football League. Anticipating the use of the Orrell-owned land for other sports, he adopted the rather grand name of Liverpool Football Club and Athletic Grounds Company Limited. Typically, he charged his new club £100 in rent – this was still business after all – but then donated £500 to its empty coffers.

Unsurprisingly, Liverpool's new board would be largely free from the sorts of Liberal influence that had plagued Houlding at Everton, and it would also be Catholic-free, dominated by prominent local Conservatives, Protestant Unionists and Freemasons and people involved in overlapping local civic, political and business organisations. Initially, it also involved Houlding's son William and his son-in-law Thomas Knowles, who came from a Wigan family with brewing and mining interests. Out of the original forty-six subscribers who established Liverpool FC, seventeen were Freemasons, and of the original six directors of the club, four were of the same persuasion – between 1892 and 1914, fifteen out of twenty-three Liverpool directors were members of the Masonic order.[7] Houlding clearly wanted his own people around him. But, unlike the situation in Glasgow prior to the formation of Celtic FC, the existing major football clubs on Merseyside were never entirely closed to local Irish influence – both Liverpool and Everton had Irish shareholders. Despite the obvious marginalisation, and the discrimination aimed at the Liverpool Irish, the major football clubs in the city were never fated to carry quite the weight of sectarian identification and enmity as they would in Glasgow. There was also, partly as a consequence, no real groundswell of popular support in Liverpool for the specifically *Irish* football clubs that were formed in the city but which soon went under because of financial and organisational problems and lack of local support.[8]

A new football chapter was now beginning at Oakfield Road, Anfield. The embryonic Liverpool Football Club was born into a city with the keenest possible rivals any sporting club could possibly have: a club whose owners positively hated Liverpool FC's hierarchy and its politics, and who were now digging the foundations of a new stadium in a field less than a mile away. Everybody in the city of Liverpool knew this was going to be some sporting rivalry. The irrepressible Houlding immediately applied to the Football League for membership for his new Liverpool club. It seemed like perfect timing. For the 1892–93 season, the league was expanding from 14 to 16 clubs in the First Division, with the creation of a whole new Second Division made up of 12 clubs. On the face of it, then, possibly *fourteen* new league places were up for grabs, and none of the competition looked particularly strong. But the new Liverpool club was turned down flat by the league, on the mysterious grounds that they 'did not comply to regulations'.

What could this mean? The Liverpool stadium could not be at fault: it was first class for the time, with four seasons of First Division football already behind it. And Houlding had quickly sent John McKenna off to Scotland (where else?) to find a team worthy of playing league football for Liverpool. Merseyside certainly seemed well capable of supporting another Football League club, so there could be few complaints about Liverpool lacking a local spectator base. It has been suggested that Liverpool was rejected by the league because it refused to consider joining any competition other than the First Division.[9] But objections orchestrated by Houlding's opponents at Everton FC were probably the crucial factor in blocking Liverpool's application to join the Football League.[10]

The new football war in Liverpool had started – and it was already a dirty business. The men from the Football League also probably wanted to teach the uppity Houlding a lesson on Everton's behalf – Methodists stick together. But there were other factors involved. The Football League had a membership application for the Second Division from Bootle FC to consider. Accepting Bootle and holding up the new Liverpool Football Club probably carried some moral force with William McGregor and his Football League management committee. These must have seemed like the obvious cards to play. Finally, the Football League also wanted to expand *outside* of its original Lancashire/ Liverpool and Midlands bases, so accepting *three* clubs from the Merseyside area might have seemed a little excessive. So, in 1892, while rejecting Houlding's Liverpool, the Football League reached for the first time into Manchester, Cheshire, Lincolnshire and South Yorkshire for new members.

At Anfield, Houlding had kept with him at least a few loyal supporters from the old Everton club: directors Frank Brettle and Sam Crosbie went right back to the old Stanley Park days, and William Barclay and Edwin Berry had also stayed loyal to King John. But pretty much all the decent players had moved across to Goodison Park – they were, after all, contracted to the recent Football League champions. And who knew at what level the new Anfield club might be playing? With John McKenna ostensibly acting as main scout, player recruiter and club manager, there was at least the basis for the administration of a new football club, especially given some much needed time to sort things out while fiddling about in the Lancashire League. The Liverpool press was convinced that when the names of these new Anfield signings were revealed they would prove 'to include some of the best known and cleverest exponents of the game'. Time would tell.

THE TEAM OF THE MACS

The highly capable right-back Andrew Hannah had joined Everton in 1889 and had captained the side, winning a league-championship medal for Everton at Anfield in 1891. Now he signed for John McKenna and Liverpool, and he would be captain for them, too, a unique feat: captain of *both* of the senior Liverpool clubs when each was based at Anfield. Hannah was experienced, reliable and mentally strong and was still only 27 years old when he joined Liverpool in July 1892. He was a leader and just the sort of solid character required to offer continuity, backbone and on-field direction to the new Liverpool side. He played in front of Liverpool-born goalkeeper Sid Ross. On the left side of defence was an ex-Everton and Scotland international full-back, the 'flaming, big burly' Duncan McLean, a no-nonsense, wide-of-girth stopper described later as a 'champion back' in the Football League. Joe McQue, a 22-year-old centre-half from Glasgow, was signed by McKenna from Celtic's reserves. Good in the air, he liked to score the occasional goal (14 in 142 appearances), but his main strength was in his defensive resolve: Liverpool would concede only 18 goals in their first season in the Second Division of the Football League in 1893–94, with McQue invariably a formidable barrier at the back.

From Leith Athletic, McKenna picked up the McQueen brothers, Matt and Hugh. Half-back Matt McQueen eventually played one hundred and three times for Liverpool whilst winning two Second Division titles in the process. He was an extraordinarily versatile player, an intelligent man who could play anywhere – including 20 times in goal for Liverpool in the Football League. He later qualified as a referee. A real Liverpool servant, McQueen later became a Liverpool director and also managed the club to the 1923 league title before ill health forced his retirement. Unlike Matt, younger brother Hugh, a clever winger with an accurate shot, was something of a maverick off the field. He once leapt from a Southport springboard during a Liverpool training camp and had to be hauled out of the water spluttering for breath – he couldn't swim. John McCartney, a tough-tackling, elegant-passing ex-cotton worker from Ayrshire, anchored the Liverpool midfield for five years until he left for New Brighton Tower, and another Scot, right-winger Tom Wyllie, came from Everton and was reputedly Liverpool FC's first professional player. Malcolm

McVean signed as a semi-professional from Third Lanark and played in all five forward positions for the Liverpool club between 1892 and 1897. He scored in Liverpool's first competitive fixture, in 1892, and also claimed the club's first Football League goal, in September 1893, in a 2–0 victory over Middlesbrough Ironopolis. He died, still a young man, in 1907.

The city of Liverpool to which these Scottish signings had migrated echoed aspects of Glasgow and its environs. Although not quite hosting the pernicious sectarian divide that existed north of the border, Catholic v. Protestant riots were still a pretty routine feature of Liverpool life. However, a survey of one hundred and six houses in the Everton area in January 1893 found that only four heads of households claimed any connection with church or chapel. Meanwhile, the Broughton Terrace mosque and its members in Liverpool were routinely attacked by so-called 'respectable' Christians. One unfortunate Muslim worshipper was stabbed in the face.

While poverty and squalor continued to characterise much of the north end of the city, the Scottish-rooted Liverpool Caledonian football club was now established at 'a grand ground' at Woodcroft Park in Wavertree in the south of the city. It was reported in the local press to represent 'Scotia's sons in Liverpool'. Caledonian were obviously well backed, and they were reportedly 'determined to make the winter game in Liverpool their own' as the game expanded. 'Football in Liverpool is rapidly becoming a national kind of business,' reported the *Liverpool Review* in an editorial on 11 June 1892. From £2 a week or up to £300 a year – 'and for eight months' work only' – Liverpool FC's own agents were reported by the local press to be seeking a nucleus of a new team north of the border among the 'Scottish Professors', 'to the extent of £1,000 for the season'.

The *Review* calculated that Scotland might provide up to one-quarter of the new Liverpool FC team – it would be much more, of course – and thus that as much as £4,000 would be needed to pay for the whole of John McKenna's squad. Here was serious money being spent on sport. Cue a new local media panic about football wages and 'foreign' players in the city: 'Football appears to pay professional players better than running a bank,' complained the *Liverpool Review*. All this was before Liverpool FC had even played its first friendly fixture. The *Liverpool Review* editorial continued with questions about 'outsiders' and wages that would still be asked in press columns and public houses in the city and elsewhere almost 120 years later:

How long is this kind of thing to go on? Liverpool is very fond of football, but are local football devotees likely to pay for it at this price? Next season we will have Everton, the Liverpool Caledonians, Liverpool and Bootle in full swing as the leading quartet of local clubs, besides many smaller fry. In nearly every football club of any pretensions, some, if not all, of the players are paid. It is no exaggeration to say that Liverpool's football bill for players during the 1892–93 season will reach to between £12,000 and £15,000. And the men who will take the vast bulk of the coin will be Scotchmen, who are still *the* exponents of the game. That is Liverpool football up to date.

A few days later, the *Review* concluded, glumly, that 'footballers are becoming of more importance than prime ministers'. John Houlding was reported to be prepared to pay his new recruits some £300 a year on average, which the newspaper equated, uncertainly, to the extraordinary payment of three shillings a minute for their football services. Local charities were also argued to be losing money as football crowds grew: 'Do the coppers and the sixpences now go to princely paid footballers?' it asked. The *Review* reminded its readers that Liverpool was an impoverished city full of 'ragged urchins' and neglected 'offal', a place where 'children of the gutter huddle together hungry and unwashed'. Officially, the average proportion of paupers to population in Liverpool was one in twenty-four, compared to one in sixty-one for the county, and one in forty-one for the whole of England and Wales. The city, it was claimed locally, was invaded in 1892 by 'habitual drunks, indigent paupers from foreign lands and . . . stowaway sailors', not to mention prostitutes in the guise of the alleged '10,000 loose women of Liverpool'. Could such wages for mere footballers be justified alongside this kind of want, chaos and depravity?

By 27 August 1892, a 'Liverpool Football War' was predicted in the local press. The four premier local clubs now began to take shape, thus replacing the tired old Everton–Bootle duopoly as the new Goodison Park was officially opened for business. 'War will be waged until the end of April. How many dead and wounded there will be during the eight months of carnage remains to be seen.' Clearly, tabloid newspaper reporting styles pre-date the rise of the rapacious British red tops. 'Everybody is talking about it,' continued the *Liverpool Review*, arguing strongly that football had a unique cross-class appeal in the city: The mechanic is as enthusiastic as the hobbledehoy and the schoolboy. Practice games on the several grounds during the past few nights have been followed with unwonted, almost feverish, excitement. How tenaciously will the actual warfare be followed?' How tenaciously, indeed.

AN EVERTON AND LIVERPOOL FOOTBALL TAKEOVER

On Thursday, 1 September 1892, Liverpool, playing in blue-and-white quarters, hosted Midland League champions Rotherham Town in a friendly match, the club's first-ever fixture at Anfield. Would anyone turn up to see Houlding's new project, especially after all the antagonism at Everton? Despite the new club's claim that 'no better game will be held in any plot in the neighbourhood', Anfield contained no more than a handful of curious fans, who witnessed a 7–1 home drubbing of the visitors.[11] Preston's Higher Walton club was Liverpool's first Lancashire League opponents just two days later. A couple of hundred local supporters turned up to watch an 8–0 Liverpool landslide. There were no *English* players in the Liverpool team, let alone any Scousers. Perhaps this was one of the reasons why the fans were staying away. But with two points gained and fifteen home goals scored in two fixtures, it was not for the lack of entertainment that home support was still reluctant. But things can soon change in football.

Middlesbrough Ironopolis crushed an outclassed Liverpool 0–5 in their next away fixture, another friendly match. It was a result mitigated for the Liverpool press by a 'railway journey of 140 miles and a heavy meal afterwards . . . not exactly the kind of things to prepare eleven men for an hour and a half of football'. It seemed like a fair point.

'The football madness has again bitten us badly – *very* badly this year,' commented an overheated *Liverpool Review* on 10 September 1892, noting that as far as spectators were concerned 'on present form, Everton and the Caledonians appear to have the pull'. This may have been because, according to the press at least, 'spectators on the Everton ground have made some mutual compact not to support the Liverpool club when playing away, but to patronise Bootle'.

Cunning John Houlding had his own plans to overcome these negative sentiments from across Stanley Park. Recalling his very modest origins in the north end of the city where he had once 'bathed in pits' with other local boys, he sent complimentary Anfield season tickets 'to a number of gentlemen who, for the past few years, have done their best towards assisting association football in Liverpool and the neighbourhood'. He was using his 'common touch' again to try to launch his new football club, as well as attempting to revive his ailing political career. This marketing strategy might even have helped do the trick, because later in September a remarkable 6,000 fans (it was probably more like 4,000) were reported by the Liverpool press to have turned up at a match at Anfield. In December 1892, some 4,000 fans were present to watch the visitors Blackpool claim the first away victory against

Liverpool at Anfield, a 0–2 defeat for their hosts. This was hardly a shock. The Seasiders had already crushed the Reds on the northern coast by an even more convincing score of 0–3.

Despite this first deflating home loss, the crowd figures suggested that perhaps the new football club at Oakfield Road really did have a future in the city. Indeed, estimated average crowds at Liverpool in this first Lancashire League championship season reached a very healthy 5,217, compared to 13,230 at First Division Everton. The average gate for Everton had also actually *grown* by 3,000 from the previous season, suggesting that most Evertonians had remained just that: loyal to Everton. A substantial proportion of the crowds now following Liverpool were probably entirely *new* football fans, or perhaps football supporters who had previously followed other local clubs in the city.

'At all events,' the *Liverpool Review* commented on Liverpool FC in its first season, 'the team is growing in public favour. All the unsportsmanlike talk about "boycott" is likely to be falsified. And why should it not?' Moreover, all the Liverpool FC company shares had been taken up, and the Anfield ground was now owned freehold, meaning that the new club's financial position 'need scarcely be discussed'. John Houlding had exactly what he wanted: undisputed control of a financially sound football club, which was also potentially a popular political base. Prestigious southern clubs, such as the public-school Corinthians, were already turning to the barely established Liverpool Football Club for their lucrative friendly fixtures in the area. 'How is it, may I ask,' mused 'Centre' rhetorically in the *Liverpool Review*, 'that the Corinthians approached *Liverpool* before Everton for dates? Are the ex-champions of the league getting into bad repute?'

All of this conjecture and 'puffing up' of Liverpool FC must have really riled Everton and their followers. As must another local story: that the Goodison club was making a 'handsome present' to a local pressman who had 'materially assisted in the club's welfare'. This reporter must surely be 'the best scribe at the game in this district', stated Centre, archly. Were the mighty Everton really trying to *buy* local press favours in the face of the early successes of these Anfield upstarts?

Everton sensitivities were also on show in the anger expressed when the two club committees could not agree on the venue for the annual Christmas theatrical charity match to be played in the city in 1892 to raise funds for local hospitals. The match, involving top local players, had previously been played at Anfield, of course. But then it had always been hosted by Everton – who, not unreasonably as the senior club, now wanted it staged at their new Goodison Park home. A reported 'slanging match' ensued between the rival committees, with Everton resisting any compromise suggestion from Houlding that the fixture should now be staged at a neutral venue, or even at each of the major grounds in alternate years. The affair was dubbed 'childishly absurd' and 'football foolery' by the *Liverpool Review*, which concluded that 'the selfishness seems to be largely on the side of the Everton committee'. The enmity between Mahon's followers and Houlding and his allies was obviously holding fast.

By this early stage, too, King John told the local press that the new Liverpool already had 30 players to call upon, with 16 reported to be of 'first XI' potential. This strong squad was now starting to perform, even beating the mighty Aston Villa in Birmingham in a friendly fixture on a Monday early in November 1892, thus producing a reported 'great rejoicing' on the Anfield side of the city.

As Liverpool FC grew ever more powerful, and especially as its rather spiteful rivalry with Everton began to capture the local public imagination, so the other two clubs among the premier four in the city – Bootle FC and Liverpool Caledonian – began to fall on harder times. Caledonian could not even make it intact to Christmas 1892, with much of its traditional local Scottish support now draining towards the developing 'team of the Macs' over at Anfield. Bootle resigned from the Football League the following year. Liverpool FC had also had the advantage over these two rivals inasmuch as the population around the Anfield stadium showed a sizeable proportion of residents drawn from the relatively affluent middle and lower-middle classes, key constituencies in building up support for early professional football clubs.[12] In short, the residential site for Bootle FC probably lacked some of the crucial demographics for sustainable Victorian football-club growth, which depended initially more on the presence and patronage of clerks and bookkeepers than it did on the keenness of manual workers.

Evidence of the scale of early travelling football support, of rival fan exchanges and also of the growing interest in football among the higher classes in the city was provided by the *Liverpool Review* of 11 February 1893, on the eve of First Division Everton hosting Nottingham Forest:

> At about midday, a tram heavily laden with Notts. Forest supporters, each sporting the colours of the club and each supporter cheering loudly, was proceeding along Dale Street, where a number of gentlemen in tall hats and frock coats raised a counter-shout. Of course, this led to a lot of good-natured banter, which was at once exceedingly diverting and a good advertisement for the match. Gentleman from 'Change are, just at present, taking an hilarious interest in football matters.

These obviously well-heeled local gentlemen from the Liverpool Exchange financial district might even have attended this Everton fixture, where it was reported that 'a well-known local bookmaker' had promised local players a £5 note if they won: they did. Not that working people and the poor were excluded from involvement in the sport in the city – far from it. Some attended matches, and at least they could all *play* a form of football. The Liverpool press was soon complaining, for example, that the previously harmless 'improvised footballs of paper and rags tightly tied with cord' were now being replaced on Liverpool streets by 'stones converted into footballs'. The local urchins of Merseyside must have their sport, too.

A fine Lancashire League unbeaten run meant that Liverpool could still edge ahead of Blackpool as champions if they could just defeat Southport Central away in their last fixture. In a chaotic scene familiar to all Sunday footballers, the match was delayed by 40 minutes because no match official turned up. A local spectator was eventually persuaded to take charge, but the visitors could manage only a 1–1 draw. No matter: Blackpool also failed to win, and, on goal average (sixty-six for, nineteen against), Liverpool FC won its first title in its first season, winning seventeen out of twenty-two matches, losing three (two to Blackpool) and finishing top of the Lancashire League with thirty-six points.

There was only the small matter of the Liverpool Cup final left – which, after sweetly defeating Bootle 1–0 in the semi-final, Liverpool played out against 'a mixed team of the renowned Everton organisation' in an early example of player rotation. Everton, in fact, were also committed to playing a lucrative friendly at Renton in Scotland on the same day, so their resources were inevitably stretched. Despite training at Hoylake on a mixture of 'teetotalism, good living, skipping rope and golf', Everton's first team had already contested, and lost, the 1893 FA Cup final (0–1 to Wolves) at Fallowfield, Manchester, in chaotic circumstances. There were crowd incursions, and the press and FA dignitaries were harried from their seats by some of the estimated 60,000 present. The *Daily Post* of 1 April 1893 was justifiably scathing about the facilities offered by their near neighbours and regional city rivals, and about the hapless FA arrangements for the final: 'They should have taken precautions . . . and had something more than matchwood barricades and a handful of "dummies" in blue to protect the field and the players from invasion.' The Liverpool press was also angry – and not for the last time – about a football-induced rise in rail fares, this time from Liverpool to Manchester, and about the FA putting profit – 'a commercial affair to make a pot of money out of' – before the safety and comfort of fans. The men from Merseyside had made their point: Goodison Park would host the next FA Cup final, in 1894, for the first and last time.

The Liverpool Cup final, the first competitive Everton v. Liverpool derby, was blighted by another issue: accusations by Everton of foul play and refereeing ineptitude. How little really changes in the game. Liverpool won the cup 1–0 in a decidedly rugged affair, the goal scored by Tom Wyllie. Everton were denied a possible penalty and angrily lodged an immediate protest 'against the general incompetence of the referee'.[13] The cup was not presented because of this determined and sour response and the inquiry that followed, thus short-circuiting planned celebrations at the Sandon Hotel, with a beaming John Houlding eager to hold court. Everton lost much public support for their transparently surly attitude. 'It was rather paltry of them,' concluded the *Liverpool Review*, 'to protest against the referee in the match and so spoil the victor's chance of carrying the cup in triumph off the ground. A waggonette and four, I believe, was waiting for the winning team and cup.' The Liverpool horses would have to delay, although Everton's protest was eventually overruled and the trophy finally ended up in the Sandon Hotel after all. But this was not the story's end. Perhaps some light-fingered Evertonians could still not accept this inaugural derby defeat, because both the Lancashire League and Liverpool cups were soon stolen, with Liverpool Football Club forced to cough up £127 to replace them. It was a sad (and expensive) end to a highly promising first season of competitive football for John Houlding's new sporting concern. His ambitions for his new club continued to burn brightly.

THE FOOTBALL FEVER FINISHED IN LIVERPOOL?

Lancashire League football was a start, right enough, but Houlding and McKenna had much bigger plans. The latter 'allowed his Irish impulses to carry him away' in 1893 by applying for membership of the Second Division of the Football League.[14] In fact, the timing was just right: Rotherham Town and Newcastle United had already been elected into the Second Division, and, aiming for two sections of sixteen clubs each, the Football League had advertised for two more clubs to join. Within a few days, Liverpool, Woolwich Arsenal, Middlesbrough Ironopolis, Doncaster Rovers and Loughborough all applied, with Woolwich Arsenal joining Liverpool as the league's choices, thus including two clubs from the same city and expanding the competition into the south for the first time. This was a brave move, considering the travelling costs to London for other clubs, but it was also a vital one if the Football League was ever to be considered a truly national affair.[15] Ironopolis would get their chance of league football after all when Accrington later resigned, and when struggling Bootle FC collapsed because of financial pressures this scotched the league plan for symmetry between the two divisions: it would be a sixteen-club First Division but a fifteen-club second section for 1893–94.

Bootle FC's sad demise could only strengthen Liverpool FC locally, of course. Anfield was now the undisputed second football base in the city. The failure of local clubs even produced alarming 'THE FOOTBALL FEVER FINISHED' headlines in the Liverpool press in May, though the *Liverpool Review* used the local vernacular to reassure its readers: 'Football – it's a gran' game chiel, ye ken an. In Leverpule the people are fair gone crazy o'it.' Which, translated, meant that football had not lost its hold on the Liverpool public. The *Review* also argued that it was actually a good thing that Houlding and Everton had been at such divisive loggerheads in 1892 because the new Goodison Park was 'perfection . . . accommodation unrivalled and supreme'. The city now had two first-class football stadiums instead of just one.

Culturally, at this time, Liverpool and its surrounds were an extraordinary mix. The city's civic fathers were committed to providing a typically Victorian range of cultural exercises and excursions, including museums, galleries, lectures and the theatre, all aimed at the moral and social 'improvement' of its better-off citizens. Working people also had their leisure pursuits, of course – including sport – so it would be wrong to paint a picture of working-class life that was too bleak or dismal.[16] It was often gently philanthropic purveyors of working-class leisure, such as the brewer A.B. Walker, who also donated funds for local elite cultural provision, in this case in the shape of the splendid new Walker Art Gallery.[17]

Liverpool's streets were still routinely depicted as being populated at night by roguish young 'Dicky Sams', vagabonds, thieves and wretched drunks. The inebriated antics of late-night engine drivers and guards on the Liverpool trains caused one local letter writer to have 'trembled for his own life and that of fellow passengers'. 'Brutal Bootle' had a measly 64 police officers to cope with its widespread drunken violence and burglary. The New Year's Eve celebrations in Liverpool in the early 1890s also brought press complaints about inebriated men and women who were colourfully reported to be 'indulging in conduct from which even a Mexican nigger might have shrunk'.

The local police in Liverpool often seemed little better disposed than some of the excitable football supporters, street ruffians or drunkards they were supposedly patrolling. In May 1893, an indignant letter to the *Liverpool Review* recalled a genial Liverpool constable who offered the reader a yuletide drink. 'While struggling to pull a large bottle out of his coat-tail pocket,' the correspondent reported, 'he suddenly slipped on the frozen pavement and sat in the gutter. The bottle smashed with a loud noise, and the only remaining whisky was in the lining of his pocket.' So much, it seems, for the sobriety of the law.

Also in May that year (1893), the drink flowed in the Sandon Hotel when John Houlding, 'the lion at the evening', finally got his hands on the Lancashire League cup (albeit briefly). Liverpool Football Club meanwhile had strengthened for the winter challenges that lay ahead by signing Patrick Gordon, a right-sided forward, from Everton's reserves, Jimmy Stott, a Darlington-born goal-hungry striker from Middlesbrough who scored 14 goals in just 17 Liverpool appearances, and Scottish utility forward Davy Henderson, with whom Stott briefly formed a useful striking partnership. But most important of all turned out to be the signing of Liverpool-born Thomas 'Harry' Bradshaw from Cheshire's Northwich Victoria, a dashing left-sided attacking winger who would play 138 league and FA Cup games for the club, scoring 53 times.

After so many imported journeymen, Harry Bradshaw was the first authentic locally born hero of the Liverpool supporters. No wonder the Merseyside crowds loved him. The historian Thomas Preston has shown that between 1893 and 1914 only 10.7 per cent of Liverpool's players actually came from the Liverpool area – an average of about one local player in each Reds team. This early history puts into perspective complaints today about a Liverpool club with too few Scousers. Forty-six per cent of Reds players came from Scotland, especially from the football hotbed mining areas of Dumbartonshire. Everton recruited fewer Scots (36 per cent) and only slightly more locals (15 per cent).[18]

Signing for Liverpool also meant good prospects of a public-house tenancy for players on retirement – a favourite with veterans – because of the local influence in the brewing business of John Houlding. But there would be no pub to run for Bradshaw. Scandalously, the local man played but once for England – being callously dropped after a 6–0 demolition of Northern Ireland. Harry would score many crucial goals for his club before eventually leaving for Spurs after almost five years of fruitful service. But like many Victorian players his football career was tragically brief, his retirement non-existent: Bradshaw died of consumption in 1899, aged just 26 years.

A 2–0 debut Liverpool win at fellow Football League new boys Ironopolis was followed by the first Liverpool FC Football League match at Anfield, a 4–0 victory over Lincoln City, with the hosts famously fielding eight 'Macs'. There were plenty of Liverpool-based Scots present, boosting the home crowd, reported to be around the 5,000 mark. At the next home league match (v. Small Heath), the crowd continued to grow with late arrivals, and up to 8,000 finally saw Liverpool turn around 3–1 up and add two more second-half goals with no reply. Three matches, three wins: this league football must have looked easy for the 'Houlding satellites' as they were described locally. As the *Liverpool Review* put it on 16 September 1893, referring to match-day transport chaos as the football thrived, 'The old Anfield glories may be revived and the traffic once again goes crashing up London Road.' Liverpool remained serene and unbeaten in the league into the new year. They had lost only one of twenty-six games in total, and this a prestigious 'friendly' fixture against formidable Football League founder members Preston North End.

The city of Liverpool at this time was rapidly becoming a national centre for sport. Over one weekend in January 1894, the Rugby International Board met on Merseyside and then the management committee of the Football League convened there. 'When Liverpool [FC] gets into the First Division,' commented the *Liverpool Review*, 'we shall be even a bigger football centre than Sheffield, which is at present the only town possessing two first league clubs.' In fact, the combined gates of Liverpool and Everton were *already* larger than those combined in Sheffield. Everton's match attendances were bigger than anywhere else in England (which probably meant the world), and Liverpool's were growing fast. The city was already looking like the world capital for football and would soon host the sport's biggest club fixture of them all, the FA Cup final.

Ever alert for a bit of helpful publicity, on 18 January 1894 John Houlding hosted a dinner for his unbeaten Liverpool team and club officials 'when the harmony which exists between players, committees and president was very happily exemplified'. Liverpool FC presented its leader with a silver kettle, lamp and stand, in a near-parody of public self-promotion and congratulation. 'No wonder,' commented a clearly smitten *Liverpool Review*, 'the Liverpool Football Club carry all before them in the league when the members are privately so well in league with each other.' It was more free media blather for the club. In February, Liverpool FC showed its growing stature, if not its class, by paying fellow Second Division club Grimsby Town £100 to relocate their home FA Cup tie against Liverpool to Anfield, where a reported 'seven or eight thousand people lined the enclosure'. Town paid heavily for their greed, with a 3–0 win for Liverpool in a wind-ruined encounter, one notable for an unusual loss of temper for the generally unflappable Reds captain Andy Hannah.

Everton's brave FA Cup defeat at Stoke City came with complaints that the referee – a Mr Kingscott – could not keep pace with the game and so missed vital penalty claims within the 12-yard area, then in place across the full width of the pitch. Why not, asked the Liverpool press, forward looking as always, 'appoint a couple of sub-referees whose sole duty it shall be to watch the play . . . within each of the 12-yard lines?' One hundred and fifteen years later, in

2009, UEFA would finally take notice of Merseyside on this score, at least for Europa League matches.

At home against bottom club Northwich Victoria on 3 February 1894, a puny crowd, barely enough to populate the goal ends, turned out to see Liverpool triumph 4–1. Many more locals were watching Everton's *reserve* games. Liverpool FC, clearly, still had plenty of ground to make up, and their fans might have been bored by its poor opposition. But here at least one could detect the first signs of the legendary wit and playfulness of Anfield crowds. The club's supporters followed the goals and tried, gallantly – as they would have to do over many years to come – to create some energy and interest out of a miserably uneven encounter. According to the *Liverpool Review*, 'So one-sided was the game that it was taken quite humorously by the spectators, and the visitors had to undergo a lot of ironical comments in the way of shouts to "play up".' The report went on to describe the voluntary evacuation of the away-goal end at the interval, leaving the Liverpool goalkeeper abandoned. 'It was amazing to notice how at half-time the sightseers all emigrated, as one man, in the direction of the Northwich goal leaving McOwen, who might have played skittles on the halfway line had he so chosen.'

Things were very different when Liverpool next hosted, because the match was against Preston North End in the second round of the FA Cup, drawing an 18,000 crowd. The Anfield pitch barriers were broken down in half a dozen places, but 'very good humouredly, the crowd did not interfere with play and violate the game as a cup tie'. This general orderliness was to be the Liverpool Way over many years to come. More than £450 was taken at the turnstiles, a club record. 'Here, ladies and gentlemen,' said the *Review* grandly, 'is something significant to con over. Is the Liverpool organisation to, at last, mount the financial rudder, as they have already done in form?' The match was played in 'typical Liverpool Football Club weather', wind and rain, and contained 'some very earnest, not to say rough, play'. The crowd was described as 'quite divided' in its partisanship, leading the local press to speculate that opposing Evertonians might have been present. In fact, Everton had arranged a friendly home fixture at the same time with Sheffield United at Goodison Park to act as a spoiler for Liverpool's great day and to try to hold on to their own support. Liverpool scored early on through David Henderson and then McVean, but North End replied to make it 2–1 at the interval. The visitors 'meant serious business' after the break and soon equalised through Frank Becton, but a centre to Henderson produced the Liverpool winner: 3–2. This was a huge moment. 'Last Saturday,' said Centre in the local press later, 'Liverpool quite extinguished Everton in the public interest. It was indeed a novelty to find an overflow Anfield audience seeking refuge and entertainment at Goodison Park.' People locked out at Liverpool FC? Supporters moping over at Everton? What next?

The major local security concern in the city of Liverpool in 1894 was about the possible presence of anarchists and the danger of 'dynamiters lurking around'. But Everton's chief concern was something almost equally explosive: it was about their neighbours' rapid rise and the Reds' possible promotion and FA Cup double. Everton's play was already described locally as 'clever, scientific and fascinating' compared to the more rough-edged, prosaic approach of Liverpool. These labels would endure. But the Anfield club was certainly challenging the traditional Blue ascendancy. Missing both Henderson and Jim McBride, a 'large and enthusiastic following' from Liverpool paid two shillings from Exchange Station on a football-excursion train to the next FA Cup match. It was to no avail: in a bog at Bolton Wanderers the Reds' FA Cup run hit the buffers, with a sobering 0–3 defeat. Nevertheless, the prospects for Liverpool promotion were exciting local football followers in the city, and even the Everton board might have perked up at the promise of raised gate receipts with Liverpool FC as direct rivals the following season. The 'Linesman' welcomed the Red advance in the local press, but he did so in strangely Alan Partridge-like tones:

> Verily, Liverpool proceeds apace. It is all for the best. We can easily support two first class football organisations in Liverpool and healthy rivalry will begat better fare. Anfield at Everton, and Everton at Anfield – in First League games. Aha! Aha! Commence to save up your three-penny bits my brethren, for there are joyful things in store for us, and the prices may be raised.

Raised prices for football would certainly be an issue in the Merseyside FA Cup final year of 1894.

LIVERPOOL: FA CUP FINAL CITY

Perhaps promotion for Liverpool to the First Division would bring more efficient match-programme sales at Anfield? The local press certainly hoped so: they relied on local urchins to provide a 'Bill of Play' on match days, but complained that these young 'demons' were never on the right side of the ground. In fact, all of the city of Liverpool would need to raise its organisational game soon, because towards the end of March 1894 the city would offer all that was best in popular culture and sport in a single weekend. It was, arguably, the greatest sporting and entertainment weekend so far in the life of any provincial English city. The world-famous Grand National meeting in racing was hosted at nearby Aintree, the FA Cup final in football was played out at Goodison Park, and versions of *HMS Pinafore* and *Cinderella* ran to packed houses at the city's main theatres. Football in the city was positively booming: in six Liverpool and Everton home matches over four days during the Easter period between 23 and 26 March 1894, an unprecedented 59,000 people attended. 'These have been record times,' confirmed the Linesman. 'The city has never shown so well in the football firmament as it has during the last fortnight . . . If this kind of thing goes on Liverpool will be the greatest football centre in the kingdom.'

The city of Liverpool was a veritable kaleidoscope of colours and cultures at this time: from the 'courtly nobles, knights and dames' who mingled with 'the common herd' on Grand National day, in what was as much a social carnival as a mere race meeting;[19] to the sharp Liverpool street pedlars who showed their enterprise by knocking out exotic tortoises from flat-topped barrows; the finery and pomp of the city theatre crowds; and the loud revelry and public display of the football enthusiasts from Nottinghamshire (Notts County) and Lancashire (Bolton Wanderers) who descended on Goodison Park in 1894 for the only Merseyside FA Cup final.

Moving *out* of Liverpool, meanwhile, as if to remind observers of the city's continuing core problems of poverty and destitution in the face of all this sporting carnival and consumption, were 420 boys and 430 girls who had been 'snatched from poverty and crime by various agencies' and were now embarking from the dockside to Canada in search of better lives. The charitable John Houlding had established the Fazackerly College Homes for Children in the city, and he would later visit these young Merseyside exports in Canada, taking a large tin of Everton toffees with him to remind them of home. Charity clearly has its limits. If there were 'fewer broad acres preserved for the rich,' the *Liverpool Review* observed wisely, 'such wholesale migration might be unnecessary'.

Despite apparent local enthusiasm aplenty, Merseyside's only FA Cup final was a cruel disappointment. Two poorly supported and low-quality sides (Notts County were below Liverpool in the Second Division, and Bolton had recently been well beaten by Everton) produced a one-sided contest (4–1 to County), a gate of only 23,000 and paltry receipts of £1,300. The Liverpool press knew the game was up right away and claimed, mischievously, that nearby Manchester's advantage in this respect was that it was 'not so satiated with first-class football and consequently are not so exacting in their demands'. Ticket prices were deemed locally to be 'absurd', but even the one-shilling areas of the ground were not filled for the final. This drew local comment that football fans in the city were lamentably narrow followers of their *clubs* rather than the game at large. But the *Daily Post* probably had it about right when it observed on 7 April 1894 that it was impossible 'to tempt the people to pay an especially high fee to see the "Trotters" get thrashed by a Second Division club, as the public had pretty much made up their minds they would be'. An unbalanced FA Cup contest could not overcome local affiliation. The city of Liverpool, it seemed, had had its chance for FA Cup glory, and, in the direst of circumstances, it was deemed by the elites at the FA to have failed to deliver.

UNBEATEN – BUT ONLY JUST

Intense *local* football affinities were soon to the fore once more on Merseyside, especially at Goodison Park on 7 April 1894. On the same day, thus far unbeaten Second Division Liverpool were 0–2 down at Burslem Port Vale. This latest score was posted by a reporter in front of the press box at Goodison, to predictably loud cheers from gloating Evertonians. At that same moment, 'numerous obstreperous gamins' openly celebrated the fact that all-conquering Liverpool had apparently 'been knocked'. In fact, the Reds later recovered with goals from McVean and Matt McQueen to draw 2–2, thus saving their proud league record. 'What a grim spirit of antagonism there is even now,' concluded the *Liverpool Review*, 'between the supporters of Goodison and Anfield.' The incident had repercussions later when the winning Liverpool result in the post-season Test match (between the top Second Division and bottom First Division club to decide on the promotion/relegation issue) was *not* posted by the press at Goodison Park. Enraged Everton fans now surged to the press box and accused the reporters of cowardice – for being too afraid to put up a *positive* Liverpool scoreline. This was all too much for the Goodison correspondent from the *Liverpool Review*, who commented, 'How contemptible is the attitude which the Everton people are taking up in regard to Liverpool – an attitude so unsportsmanlike that no amount of argument and sophistry can explain it away . . . The Everton officials should remember that the hallmark of a gentleman lies in the fact that he even treats his supposed inferiors with respect.'

Today, this would seem overly alarmist, even priggish: the application of a highly moralistic middle-class tone to (mainly) working men who were clearly beginning to identify strongly with their own football clubs. In so doing, these Blues supporters were developing a predictable antipathy towards the fate of their near neighbours and rivals in a city that undoubtedly had something of a 'democratic swagger' derived from its sea trading, but in which quite extreme forms of localism were also already defining features.[20] Unbeaten Liverpool would soon join Everton in the top tier. But not before a huge scare. Facing Burslem, once more, in their final Second Division league fixture at Anfield, a clearly nervous Liverpool soon went behind to a goal scored from midfield that deceived goalkeeper McOwen – 'a terrible and most surprising shot'. Liverpool then laid siege to the Port Vale goal, but they could not score, until a 'scrimmage' occurred on the visitors' goal-line, providing 'a dangerous and unedifying' spectacle.

The scrimmage was something akin to a ruck in modern rugby but was then a staple part of association football. Eventually, both teams' players 'piled on top of each other in a struggling, kicking and also a fighting mass', the ball lying somewhere beneath them. The referee allowed this quite legal affair to continue for some two minutes, causing spectators to 'gasp in dismay'. He then blew up in despair at ever seeing the leather again, deciding on a drop ball right on the Burslem goal-line. This was simply a recipe, surely, for another ball-obscuring mass brawl, but something else occurred. The referee 'threw up the ball in the middle of the twenty-one men and after a report like a gun, into the net it went and the Liverpool record was saved'. It was the unlikely figure of Reds captain Andrew Hannah who had rescued the day, scoring his only ever goal for the club in the process. Liverpool scored another late goal, through McQue, to win the match 2–1.

It was extraordinary that no player was badly injured here, because the very real dangers of playing football at this time should not be underestimated. A correspondent to the *Liverpool Review* on 21 April 1894, for example, reported on 341 football 'accidents' during the current season, with 24 ending in death. No such list was compiled for football in Liverpool, but football mortalities were still depressingly routine affairs in Britain.

So, for the first and only time in its history, Liverpool FC would finish a season unbeaten in the Football League. Not even Bob Paisley would achieve this feat. The new league club had won every home match and had drawn just six out of twenty-eight fixtures, ending up eight points clear of second-placed Small Heath. But Liverpool still had to beat the First Division's bottom club, Newton Heath, in a one-off Test match to confirm their promotion. The contest, at Ewood Park, Blackburn, in front of 5,000 fans, was comfortable enough, with Matt McQueen 'as cool and safe as a cold-store brick building' and McLean 'practically faultless' hitting a free-kick deflected in by Pat Gordon, later added to by Bradshaw's 'low, lightning shot' for a routine 2–0 Reds win. As the *Liverpool Review* pointed out, the celebrations for this first Liverpool FC title in the Football League were suitably exuberant:

Needless to say, there were great rejoicings among the Liverpool contingent after the victory and on arriving at Tithebarn Street station the team was met by an enormously big and correspondingly enthusiastic crowd. Different players were carried shoulder high to their special conveyance and after lubrication at the Alexandra Hotel the men drove off to the Sandon, where another tremendous reception awaited them . . . The team have done wonders; so, indeed, have the committee and officials of the club.

The truth was that for all their magnificent Football League record, this Liverpool team had been mainly functional and determined in the Second Division, with a well organised defence (only six goals conceded in fourteen home fixtures) and an inconsistent if resolute attack. After the Reds had impressively seen off Preston North End in the FA Cup, First Division Bolton Wanderers had quite casually crushed Liverpool in the next round. Did the club really have the necessary quality to survive higher up the embryonic football food chain? It would, as it turned out, prove to be a very difficult test indeed.

CHAPTER 2 REFERENCES

1. Physick, *Played in Liverpool*, pp. 84–7
2. Corbett, *Everton: The School of Science*
3. Kennedy and Collins, 'Community Politics in Liverpool and the Governance of Professional Football in the Late Nineteenth Century', p. 768
4. Kennedy and Collins, p. 776
5. Kennedy, 'Locality and Professional Football Club Development', p. 383
6. Kennedy and Collins, p. 788
7. Kennedy, 'Class, Ethnicity and Civic Governance', p. 847
8. Kennedy and Kennedy, 'Ambiguity, Complexity and Convergence: The Evolution of Liverpool's Irish Football Clubs'
9. Taylor, *The Leaguers*, p. 7
10. Inglis, *League Football and the Men Who Made It*, p. 25
11. Wilson, *All Change at Anfield*, p. 2
12. Kennedy, 'Locality and Professional Football Club Development', p. 384
13. Young, *Football on Merseyside*, p. 45
14. Young, *Football on Merseyside*, p. 46
15. Inglis, *League Football and the Men Who Made It*, p. 31
16. Pooley, 'Living in Liverpool: The Modern City', p. 236
17. Milne, 'Maritime Liverpool', p. 289

18. Preston, 'The Origins and Development of Association Football in the Liverpool District *c.*1879–*c.*1915', p. 125
19. Pooley, 'Living in Liverpool: The Modern City', p. 254
20. Milne, 'Maritime Liverpool', p. 308

3

TURNING ICE INTO FIRE
Tom Watson, the First Great Liverpool Manager

THE 'FOOTBALL FEVER' RETURNS TO MERSEYSIDE

With the Second Division title in the Reds bag, the much anticipated Senior Liverpool Cup 'derby' final between Liverpool and Everton of 1894 proved to be a huge let-down. According to the local press, it produced 'farcical football', with Everton 'contemptibly' fielding a combination (reserve) side and Liverpool, apparently in an angry response to their neighbours' cynicism, a team of amateurs. Weakened football teams are no modern invention. The message was already clear enough: the Football League and the national FA Cup were now becoming increasingly important trophies for these dominant local clubs. Local football was already on the long slide into relative obscurity – though even sixty years later derby games like this one in local cup competitions could still draw very large crowds on Merseyside.

According to the local press, the joyful Liverpool FC Second Division championship celebrations meant that a sporting disease was back on Merseyside:

> This city has the football fever especially violently and badly; it will have it ever so much worse in the future. And those colossal sums paid by spectators to witness a football fray of ninety minutes' duration. What does this mean?

There was much more of this sort of incendiary stuff in the Liverpool press. 'The city of Liverpool will invariably be the scene of crush, enthusiasm, excitement,' said the *Liverpool Review* in a lengthy editorial of 19 May 1894. 'In other words, of the football fever. When the two XIs of local champions meet – Whish!!! Crash!!! Bash!!! Bang!!! Hurroo!!!' Was this exuberant irony or simply proof of the early existence of tabloid styles of journalism on Merseyside? Liverpool FC, it was said, was looking for yet more new recruits, and, once again, the football kingdom of Scotland would be freely drawn upon. Moreover, football was already more important in the city even than politics. The *Review* continued on its tack:

> The fact remains, be it a sign of moral degeneration or not, that in Liverpool football and footballers are more discussed than are other games or any other class of gamester. Council and Imperial Parliament matters sink into insignificance in most companies when the great winter game is turned on tap. It may sound ironical and an exaggeration, but it is very questionable whether in political circles a change of Prime Minister is more anxiously and vehemently discussed than the transfer of some famous footballer is in football circles . . . In short, it is everywhere. And there is no use denying the fact. Liverpool, and Liverpool men, take a very forefront place where the game is concerned . . . In the future, Liverpool will prove itself to be its biggest and most financially successful centre.

In the years that followed, of course, regional rivals Manchester would have plenty to say on this last point. And the general antipathy between the two cities that would light up the next century was already plain to see during the royal opening of the Manchester Ship Canal in 1894. Liverpool people, it was reported in the city's press, could look towards 'Cottonopolis' only with 'grim humour and unconcern'. There was no use denying the fact, it was conceded on Merseyside, 'that the two cities had been at open and secret warfare for a considerable time'. These north-west rivals also shared in another rather ghoulish competition: only Salford had a higher mortality rate than Liverpool among all large towns and cities in England. There seemed to be some local agreement that 'there are probably more social sores to be seen in Liverpool than in any other city outside London'. You didn't have to look too far from Anfield for evidence. 'I have had occasion to travel along Sheil Road late at night,' a correspondent told the *Review* on 11 August 1894, 'and many are the disgusting sights I have witnessed. It is quite time that something was done to clear the neighbourhood of the drunken and abandoned creatures who infest it.'

Partly because of press reports such as these, the 'curse' of puritanism was now also at large along the Mersey, aimed at 'saving' working people and the Liverpool destitute from an early grave. There were public calls for more prohibitions in the city on the evils of betting, drink, tobacco and even dancing. This was part of a long history of Liverpool's middle classes attempting to regulate and 'purify' free entertainment and the public use of the streets in the city. Certainly, Liverpool had a national reputation for drunkenness, though the chief constable at the time stressed that Liverpool police simply *arrested* more drunks than happened elsewhere.[1]

In the face of this moral onslaught and the burgeoning social ills of the city, perhaps the only sensible answer was a radical one: to emigrate. In the 1890s, to be American was to be modern, a view reflected in Liverpool's showy transatlantic waterfront and its expansive ambitions.[2] A passage to America from Liverpool could be bought for just £2 in 1894, a sum that included the 'agent's commission, the seven days' food on board and the usual kit for steerage passengers'. Some 'Dicky Sams' took the American route to a new life, forsaking both the social and moral reformers in the city *and* the beautiful game. Those who stayed put in Liverpool awaited the city's first authentic derby match in the vertiginously dizzy atmosphere of the First Division of the Football League.

THE NEW ANFIELD – AND FIRST DIVISION BLUES

With the new season now on the horizon, Liverpool FC finally looked to extend the Anfield grandstands into some of the adjacent land owned by Joseph Orrell (brother of John). But John Houlding rejected Orrell's proposed price for the deal, and there was even brief press talk of the club touring and training in the USA and then relocating to *another* arena in the city for their first season in the top flight. It seemed as if the club was back to the sorts of problems that had plagued football at Anfield in 1892. But agreement was eventually reached with the vendor, thus ensuring new facilities and that 'Anfield will, indeed, be a Paradise compared to what it was before'.

Anticipation for the new season was now acute, with the Linesman even offering in the local press a useful glossary of football terms for potential new supporters and helpfully reporting for those who did not know that match officials were paid one guinea plus rail and cab fare per match, with optional overnight accommodation. The Everton match diary for the forthcoming season also included Liverpool's fixtures for the first time, a commercial decision, no doubt, but also a sign that the two major clubs in the city might co-exist on friendlier terms than had previously been possible. In fact, these rivals would share a match-day programme until the 1935–36 season.

An 'enormous crowd' gathered on Tuesday, 22 August 1894 to witness a pre-season practice match in the 'newly equipped and greatly improved Anfield ground'. The rudimentary pitch markings they gazed upon would be pretty unfamiliar to today's sporting eye, consisting of a centre line, two twelve-yard lines (instead of penalty boxes) and two semi-circles at either end of the pitch instead of six-yard boxes. Only in 1902 was a rectangular penalty area and a penalty spot introduced, along with six-yard boxes to replace the old semi-circles. The crowd was reported to be reluctant to leave the empty ground and instead 'stood still gazing at the imposing skeleton of the handsome new grandstand, which is now in course of construction'. Because of its imposing height and unusual length this new Main Stand, in the fawning view of the *Liverpool Review*, 'will be without doubt the greatest grandstand on any football ground in the kingdom'. Anfield could now hold up to 30,000 fans, with 3,500 under cover in the new stand and 3,500 standing in the Paddock below. It already exhibited the dimensions and grandeur of a modern sports stadium.

The best seats at Anfield would now cost 21 shillings for a season ticket, with tickets in other covered stands costing 15 shillings. An uncovered standing season ticket was 7s 6d (which was soon withdrawn). There were price reductions for older members, and 'ladies' could get season tickets for half price in the rather patronising hope that their presence at football might help to gentle the more boisterous male throng. The plan was also to reconstruct the goal-end terracing into a half-moon shape by the opening day of the new season to allow better viewing and to give the stadium an even more handsome appearance. Given a good first season at the top level, the Liverpool board also planned to replace the old (Kemlyn Road) stand with one to mirror that constructed on the Main Stand side. Alas, Liverpool Football Club would not have a good season at their first attempt at the First Division – not by a long chalk.

Why did Liverpool fail so badly in this its first season in the top flight? They ended rock bottom with twenty-two points and relegation, taking ten matches even to register their first victory and a further eight attempts for their next. Well, it was a familiar football tale: the new signings did not impress. The 5 ft 9 in. Willie McCann from Paisley Abercorn, the Scotland reserve team goalkeeper, shipped 39 goals in his 15 League outings. He stayed only eight months. Wales international full-back Abel Hughes played only one match, none in the Football League. At least David Hannah – newly arrived cousin of Andrew – managed to score in the Anfield derby in November, contributing to the point that was saved thanks to a last-minute penalty by Jimmy Ross in a 2–2 draw.

Star signing Ross, £75 from Preston North End, did much better than most, with 12 league goals in his first season and 40 goals in total in 85 Liverpool appearances. He was a tough and fiery character with an abrasive tongue and wit, a man who had scored eight of the record twenty-six goals that Preston had once put past Hyde in the FA Cup. He was also credited with some early coaching at Anfield.[3] But his arrival at Liverpool also came with complications. Jimmy's more famous footballing brother Nick died tragically at just 31 years of age, and on his death bed he begged brother Jimmy to stay loyal to Preston North End. Understandably, this plea made relations with Ross's new club rather 'strained and awkward'. Jimmy eventually settled down at Anfield, but he could not get Liverpool firing despite John Houlding telling his players, inelegantly, during the pre-season that a league title would make him 'die content and live contenteder'.

By the time the first Football League derby game in Liverpool arrived on 13 October 1894, the Reds were already in trouble at the foot of the table. The players retired to Hightown to prepare in the week before the match. The contest at Goodison Park was rough and ready, with Everton unbalanced by an early injury to Bell and Liverpool desperately trying to raise the tempo. But the Blues showed their extra class – they began the season with eight straight wins and eventually finished league runners-up. Everton managed to claim a half-time lead, a header by McInnes. Liverpool strived hard for parity in the second half but were caught on the break by Alex Latta for the crucial second goal in an eventual 0–3 defeat. The return, at Anfield a month later, was a much tighter affair and ended in stalemate. But elsewhere Liverpool's defence was too readily shipping goals – five without reply at West Bromwich, Aston Villa and Sheffield Wednesday, respectively – and the club's players were also falling like ninepins to injury and illness. Despite a mini-revival after New Year, there would be no avoiding the privations and tensions of the promotion and relegation Test match on this form and with this luck. It duly arrived after a last-day thrashing at home to Preston, by 2–5. At Ewood Park, once more, for the nerve-jangling relegation-deciding contest, not even the sending off of the Bury goalkeeper for a wild kick to the stomach of a Liverpool forward could help the Anfield men. Liverpool surrendered the Test match 0–1 – and with it their hard-won place in the First Division.

RISINGS FROM BELOW

Liverpool, still in shock, reinforced for their return to the Second Division by signing striker Fred Geary from Everton, a goalscoring inside-left Frank Becton from Preston North End to link up brilliantly with Harry Bradshaw, and two much-needed new defenders, a stylish Scottish footballing right-back Archie Goldie from Clyde and the reliable Edinburgh-born Tom Wilkie on the left. Bill Dunlop had also signed from Paisley Abercorn in January 1895, and, after a slow start punctuated by injury, he was to be the mainstay of the Liverpool defence for the next 13 years. He was unarguably the most consistent Liverpool full-back until Phil Neal took over the mantle in the 1970s. Tom Cleghorn, a fiery little left-half from Leith who was signed from Blackburn Rovers in 1896, added further energy to the left side.

But it was the £100 that Liverpool paid Leith Athletic for 20-year-old centre-forward George Allan that proved the key investment. Allan had fire in his boots and in his belly, scoring twenty-five goals in just twenty league games and three more in the vital play-off matches. Allan's antics once so upset the legendary Sheffield United goalkeeper Willie 'Fatty' Foulke that the keeper conceded a penalty by up-turning Allan and jamming the forward's head in the mud. Allan managed 56 goals in just 96 Liverpool appearances, but he tragically died from illness at just 24 years of age, his huge potential only partially fulfilled.

The Reds were Second Division champions again in 1896, this time on goal difference, with a league record 106 goals scored – runners-up Manchester City managed just 63. The 18th of February 1896 marked the club's record league win, 10–1 against hapless Rotherham Town, a match in which 'Liverpool might almost as well have won by 20 goals, so persistently did they attack and shoot'. Liverpool scored an astonishing sixty-five goals in just fourteen home matches, but still had to face a post-season mini-league of play-off matches, in which they played the two lowest-placed First Division clubs, home and away, for the right to be promoted once again.

After beating the same opponents 4–0 at Anfield, a poor 0–0 draw at Small Heath was explained locally by a lengthy rail trip for the players (which took from 1.30 p.m. to 5.15 p.m.) to this Monday evening fixture, but a crucial 2–0 home victory against West Brom in front of 20,000 fans was the key result to send the Anfield club back into the top flight. The press suggested this home scoreline had been 'arranged' because Liverpool later casually lost the away match at Albion by the same score, playing 'fancy touches' and using 'gallery tricks'. Both clubs were eventually promoted as a result. This accusation was certainly hard on George Allan, because when he scored in the first match with 'a truly memorable effort, the sphere travelling into the net at thunderbolt rate, there was a loud, long and lusty demonstration' on the Anfield terraces. The negative publicity and press concern about alleged match-fixing was enough to stir the men at the Football League to wonder just how long the controversial Test matches could survive the obvious threat of corruption. It was a routine fear around English football fixtures right up until the First World War.

LIVERPOOL, SPORT CITY – FOR MEN

The year 1896 had been an eventful one for the city of Liverpool and its environs: it marked the opening of the Anfield crematorium and the Palm House in Sefton Park, as well as the extension of the overhead railway line and the opening of the new Wirral railway. Crabs caught off the Isle of Man were reportedly becoming a 'toothsome dish' in the city, and in March 1896 Liverpool was labelled, to some acclaim – if not among local social reformers – the 'greatest beer drinking city in the United Kingdom'. Early in 1897, the electric light was used in nearby New Brighton for the first time and would soon arrive in Bootle. The period also signalled a welcome upturn in commercial and industrial activity in the city after many years of depression.

Meanwhile, brewer, football-club owner and local councillor John Houlding spoke in a conference in Glasgow in 1896 on the rather prosaic topic of 'The History of the Treatment and Disposal of City Refuse in Liverpool During the Past 50 Years'. As a young man, the pragmatic Houlding had seen the effects of the plague on his father's milk business, and he now championed better sanitation for the Merseyside poor – including ending the practice of dumping raw urban refuse into the Mersey estuary. Houlding was also carefully making his football club a local force in his adopted city: the Anfield men acquired the red-and-white municipal colours of the city of Liverpool in 1896. From 1901, the club crest incorporated the Liverpool liver bird.

But football did not hold everyone's imagination in Liverpool. In June 1896, a crowd of some 5,000 at Newsome Park watched the Union club play Everton in a baseball match, a signal of the Liverpool–USA cultural exchanges, though strangely the scorers could not agree on the final result. The year produced, too, the first mention of 'lady footballers' in the city, who were summarily dismissed by local reporters (as they were elsewhere) as 'too funny for words, merely making the game ridiculous'. These women played a match in North Wales in July under the auspices of the newly formed British Ladies Football Association. 'This being the first appearance of the new women in the football field,' commented the *Liverpool Review*, 'the visitors, the majority of whom were attired in knickerbockers and short skirts, attracted considerable attention and although there was a gate of a thousand there was no hooting.'

On 1 August, the *Review* reported, with obvious satisfaction, that the women's team had 'bust up' after its organiser had ended up in hospital with scarlet fever. Football was clearly regarded as no pastime for 'respectable' women – it might even have been organised in Liverpool by 'do-gooding' social reformers. 'Other members of the company, some fifteen in number, were practically destitute,' it was reported. 'Several of the girls receive relief from the parochial authorities and in some instances food was supplied to them by the police. What a fiasco!' Women on Merseyside would face a long struggle throughout much of the next century to be accepted as footballers, or even as active club supporters.

TOM WATSON, THE FIRST LIVERPOOL FC MANAGER

Finally, in 1896, there was the arrival in the city of the 'silver tongued' Tom Watson at Liverpool Football Club, 'football's first prototype of the modern football manager'.[4] On 1 August 1896, the *Liverpool Review* announced this extraordinary news:

> Mr Tom Watson, who has done such a very great deal for the Sunderland Football Club, has undertaken the secretaryship of the Liverpool Football Club. This is undeniably a good stroke on the part of the Liverpool management and it would appear that now, at any rate, the Anfield Roaders will not figure in the Test matches for a very long time.

John Houlding certainly wanted to avoid the risk of an immediate slide out of the First Division, but this was, by any measure, an audacious move. Watson was, arguably, as important in the early development of the Liverpool club as Bill Shankly and Bob Paisley were to prove to be in the post-war era. Tom Watson was born in Newcastle in 1859, the son of a skilled worker who was a supporter of the independent educational tradition. This meant that as a child Tom studied both in Newcastle and in York. Watson had no real playing career to talk of, but he became very active and influential in local football administration in the north-east in the 1880s, founding the Rosehill club in 1881. Watson then acted as honorary secretary at both the Newcastle East End and Newcastle West End clubs, where he was charged with recruiting capable Scottish professionals. By the late 1880s, some directors were beginning to realise that running a professional football club was a full-time project, requiring deep knowledge of both players and administration. It was his work with the so-called 'Team of All the Talents' at Sunderland FC that cemented Watson's reputation for innovative tactics and leadership. He had brought three league titles to the north-east, in 1892, '93 and '95.

Watson was now thinking of retirement, but he was headhunted for Liverpool by John McKenna and William Houlding, who was now Liverpool's chairman. John Houlding had moved upstairs as president and was soon to become the mayor of Liverpool. McKenna accepted that the Liverpool club now needed someone to work full-time with the players and to deal with administration on the playing side – though Everton and many other clubs continued to resist the very notion of anything approaching the modern football manager. McKenna also accepted that Liverpool should pay top money, given Watson's impressive record, so an annual salary of £300 was agreed, generally assumed to be the largest in football. Watson was also a Freemason, so he fitted in very well with the Liverpool FC hierarchy. In fact, much of Watson's own responsibilities at Liverpool were focused on financial matters at Anfield. It was unlikely he had complete autonomy in team selection, which probably only came to the manager after the arrival at Melwood of Bill Shankly late in 1959. But the local press soon described Liverpool as 'Watson's team', and he clearly exerted considerable influence in player selection, thus beginning the cult of the football manager that became such a prominent part of the Anfield tradition.

What Tom Watson provided was positive direction and cohesion in both team and financial affairs, and also a considerable flair for public relations and the constructive use of the press, especially as the game grew in its popularity and status. These approaches were very much the mark of the modern, media-friendly football manager, of course. Bill Shankly again comes to mind. As Jimmy Catton, editor of *Athletic News*, put it when reflecting about the gregarious Watson, 'No secretary contrived to be mentioned in print so often as Tom Watson of Liverpool. He loved to see his name in good type. It was a little weakness of his – and quite pardonable, for most people have their spice of vanity, although they take pains to conceal it.'[5] Despite Watson's much heralded arrival, in which he was soon reported to be 'rapidly getting things in order' whilst 'the eyes of the football world are turned in the direction of the city', the Liverpool team which consolidated its place in the First Division was pretty much the same as that which had blasted its way out of the Second Division.

But Liverpool soon showed obvious signs on the pitch of Watson's more 'scientific' influence on tactics and organisation. The impact was akin to that of the Continentals Gérard Houllier and Rafa Benítez a century later. Watson insisted, for example, that Liverpool adopted a very different approach to that of the club's last First Division campaign, notably a much stronger concentration on defence. This meant that barely an away goal was scored at Anfield in three months. Admittedly, this cautious philosophy did not always go down well with local scribes. After a dull 0–0 home draw against West Bromwich in November 1896, for example, and under the headline 'What Fans Want', the *Liverpool Review* concluded, 'This kind of thing will not raise Liverpool's status. The man who pays his sixpence and is the supporter of football wants to see goals scored. He wants something for his money and a draw, as in this case of 0–0, narks him. The motto should be "Score boys, score".' A 1–2 defeat at Goodison in early October hardly improved Watson's Anfield standing either, though the 'good humours' displayed by the Liverpool football public at the match – presumably through gritted teeth – 'were a pattern to the football world and to followers of any other sport'.

By early November 1896, after humbling Sunderland 3–0 at Anfield in mist and drizzle that the visitors thought unfit for play, a resilient but prosaic Liverpool topped the entire Football League for the first time in the club's short history. Eventually, though, it would be Liverpool's 'well organised, swift-covering and ruthless-tackling defence' that would be the key to their healthy showing, with the Reds finishing fifth to Everton's seventh and conceding only 38 goals, the same number as champions Aston Villa.[6] Despite forward George Allan's best efforts, Liverpool could only score 46 times in 30 matches. A turn-of-the-year 3–3 home draw with Villa, a match described as 'the finest at Anfield for a very long time', was atypical but also symbolic of Liverpool's obvious improvement under Watson and their capability at this level. By mid-January, Liverpool were second in the league to Villa but had played four games more. They were never really serious title contenders. Club discipline at Anfield was also occasionally challenged at this time – and was quickly re-established: three 'class' players – reputedly Wilkie, Allan and Neil – were credited with 'setting out on a bout of so-called enjoyment' a few hours before an important Lancashire Cup tie with Bolton in January. They were summarily dropped by Watson.

This was also the first season (1896–97) to offer the real possibility of an all-Merseyside FA Cup final – it would actually be delayed by almost 90 years. Liverpool reached a semi-final for the first time, meeting with Aston Villa in Sheffield, by disposing of Burton Swifts, West Bromwich and Nottingham Forest, while Everton eventually lined up in the semis against Derby County at Stoke. 'Centre Forward', writing in the *Liverpool Review*, was more than confident: 'I expect to see one, if not both, of the Liverpool clubs left in the final.' Liverpool, certainly, 'went away in dashing style' and even had two goals disallowed against Villa. But in a 'rough and tumble forcible game' a 'fluky goal' from John Cowan followed by another from a corner that should have been a goalkick put the Reds unluckily on the back foot. Villa's Charlie Athersmith finished them off with a second-half 'classic shot' for a comprehensive 0–3 Reds defeat. Everton beat County 3–2 in the other semi, thus keeping their side of the Mersey bargain, but they fell, in turn, to Villa (2–3) at Crystal Palace in a coruscating final.

The failure of the Merseyside clubs to secure major silverware (though Everton did win the Lancashire Cup) despite paying high wage bills and attracting the highest aggregate crowds in England now provoked a very early example of something sports readers in the city and elsewhere would become very familiar with: the press questioning not only of the salaries of players but also their lifestyles, status and attitudes. 'Go Straight' was an editorial in the *Liverpool Review* on 27 March 1897 that rounded on the alleged 'don't care, get-what-we-can attitude' of professional players. Already, here was barely concealed nostalgia for the old days when 'the training the men got was at their daily work with a run around the parks at night-time'. Which meant, of course, that these past players had much more commitment and enthusiasm for the game than did the pampered full-timers of the present.

'Weak' football selection committees were also criticised for their alleged kowtowing to the stars and especially for 'allowing leading players to dictate as to who shall play in a team, or to say, "If you don't play so-and-so, I *can't* do my best (which often means *won't*)."' Early footballers needed managing and motivating as much as later celebrities did. Club committees were also alleged to offer illegal financial inducements to their stars when footballers should actually be seen primarily as *workers* – as simple employees. 'This is not right. A football player, like a mechanic or a professional man, should always give his best services to his employer at the stipend mutually agreed upon.'

Here were the first real press arguments for much more discipline and control over football affairs for the likes of Liverpool's Tom Watson. When Everton lost to little Rock Ferry in the final of the Liverpool Cup in 1897, the 'richest club in the country' was urged by the Liverpool press to appoint a 'team manager' who should 'with the trainer, have full charge of the team'. Instead, the Everton board decided they knew best.

LOCAL HEROES OR IMPORTED STARS?

But a more powerful theme in the local press was the growing public debate about local versus imported players. Letters to the *Liverpool Review*, for example, suggested that the major football clubs might better look to local leagues for their new signings. They certainly provoked a strident response from Centre Forward on 22 May 1897, who argued that possibilities for success for the major Merseyside clubs in late-nineteenth-century Liverpool already depended on *rejecting* just this sort of parochialism in selection:

> I am at one with the letter writers that every effort should be made to unearth good, local men ... But to stick to local players whether they are up to form or not would ruin any club in existence ... Everton and Liverpool have built up their football following by good, scientific football. You could not fill the Everton and Liverpool teams with local players and still keep in the league, and we would soon see these two fine organisations drift to the level of minor local clubs.

As these sorts of exchanges developed and became more heated, it also became increasingly clear that there was a strong public preference, even in cosmopolitan Liverpool, for English players rather than for Scots, Irish and Welsh professionals. A press survey of the 16 teams in the First Division in October 1897 revealed that 97 out of 176 top players (55 per cent) were English. Liverpool actually had six Englishmen, Everton only two and Bolton Wanderers a bare one. 'The prevalent desire of the football public is not necessarily for purely local talent,' argued 'Goodison Park' in a letter published on 8 July 1897, 'but there is a widespread wish that more *English* players should be signed by our local clubs . . . It is surely but reasonable that professional English clubs should consist, for the most part, of English players.' Another letter complained that club officials were ignoring public opinion on these matters and that certain football officials were already 'being busy on the rummage up north'.

No prizes for guessing who was rummaging. On one such trip, Liverpool's Tom Watson signed right-winger Bob Marshall from Leith Athletic, though George Allan had unaccountably moved the other way, having been sold to Celtic for just £50. His goals would be sorely missed. Watson also signed a large number of younger players as part of a new longer-term plan to develop the club. There is no evidence, however, that new president John Houlding brought back football players with him from Russia. He had recently travelled there, looking ceaselessly for ways of bettering Liverpool life, and the Liverpool FC president did offer some typically eye-catching 'hard-headed and political' lectures in the city in order to publicise his eventful trip.

LIVERPOOL BEAT THE BLUES, AT LAST!

After a jittery and winless start to the new season, in September 1897 a great moment finally arrived: Liverpool's first Football League win over rivals Everton. Thirty thousand fans – of all types – crammed into Anfield, with local supporters complaining about the lack of transport to the stadium. 'I waited nearly an hour opposite St George's Hall,' claimed one, 'and then only got a chance brake.' The *Liverpool Review* reported that, 'The spectators came from everywhere and they represented all kinds and conditions of men, youths, boys, yes, and women and girls. For hours there was intense excitement.' So great was the crowd pressure at Anfield that twice the pitch-side barriers gave way, leading to stoppages in play.

This was, indeed, a rather heated affair, producing 'blind and unreasonable partisanship' in the crowd, which only intensified after Jack Taylor gave the visitors an undeserved lead after 25 minutes. The raw-boned and stocky new Liverpool signing Daniel Cunliffe and then Joe McQue replied for the Reds before the break. From this point on, only Harry Storer's 'champion form' in the Liverpool goal kept the hosts ahead, until a Frank Becton goal finally secured the points. Brave, confident and reliable goalkeepers, with skilled feet and hands such as Storer had, were especially important at a time when keepers could wander some way from their goal and grab the ball. This victory was a marvellous moment for Houlding, McKenna and Watson, and for all Liverpool fans. But in late October it was clear that Everton were determined to have their revenge at Goodison Park. They got it, too, by 0–3, after Becton was injured early on, thus making him 'practically useless' for the rest of the match. Ten-man Liverpool were reportedly 'never in the hunt' due to rugged Everton's 'questionable tactics'.

The 1897–98 season produced consolidation but no improvement in Liverpool FC's fortunes: a modest ninth place in the league, with a long injury list and a struggle for goals. But the following 1898–99 season began to show Tom Watson's astute influence to near full effect, as Liverpool avoided injuries and began to prepare for imminent Football League successes by challenging for the league and FA Cup Double. They were destined just to fail, controversially, in each. Tom Watson had obviously been given the green light by the Liverpool committee to make new signings, because a few key players arrived in 1898, mainly again from his favoured Scottish hunting grounds. But first there was a highly unusual football signing: at right-half Rabbi Howell was the first full-blooded Romany traveller to play as a professional footballer in Britain and to be capped by England. Born in a caravan, the son of a tinker, Howell was a small and wiry half-back with good speed and stamina who had won a championship medal with Sheffield United in 1898 before leaving the club under a disciplinary cloud and moving to Liverpool for £200. He stayed at Anfield until 1901, but, like many players, his career was cut short by injury.

A new full-back, the exotically named General Stevenson, signed from Padiham near Burnley, and Hugh Morgan, a skilful and canny forward, arrived from St Mirren to bolster the Liverpool attack. From Hearts, Liverpool signed John Walker, a dribbling right-sided attacker with a penchant for long-distance shooting, and Tom Robertson, a talented and elusive left-winger, for a combined fee of £350. Both would become Scotland internationals and would be key figures in Liverpool's first championship team in 1901. Robertson and Morgan would finish top league scorers for the club in 1899 – but with a paltry ten goals apiece. But all of these new arrivals, impressive as they were, were overshadowed by the era-shaping Liverpool signing of the nineteenth century. In May 1898, a fair-haired 20-year-old Scot, Alexander Galloway Raisbeck, signed for Liverpool for £350. It was a steal.

Raisbeck was born in Dolmont, Stirlingshire, one of seven brothers, and he had worked in the mines as well as playing professionally in Scotland for Hibernian. He had helped Stoke avoid relegation in the Football League Test matches of 1898 before, inexplicably, returning north of the border. Perhaps the Potteries club could not afford the required fee to sign the Scot? Maybe family demands drew him northwards once more – Raisbeck would eventually father an impressive 14 children. Maybe the great man was just waiting for a club with the potential of Liverpool to approach him? At 5 ft 10 in., Raisbeck was tall for his day and showed quite brilliant timing in the air. His speed, aggression and precision in the tackle and in defensive recovery were legendary. He also boasted huge stores of stamina in supporting forwards and was restless in his covering for defenders. In short, he was the perfect attacking and defending centre-half, an absolutely outstanding all-rounder, possibly the best ever to play for the club over an extended period, service which brought him two league titles. He also kept his feet admirably on the ground, being a noted amateur bowler and once remarking that he would be happy to return to a collier's life if things went badly for him in football. In volume four of Gibson and Pickford's *Association Football*, published in 1908, Raisbeck was profiled, justifiably, as one of the 'Giants of the Game':

> His great forte as a half-back is a dashing, breezy versatility. He is like an intelligent automaton, fully wound up and warranted to last through the longest game on record. To watch him at play is to see a man pulsating to his finger-tips with the joy of life. Swift, rapid movement, fierce electric rushes are to him an everlasting delight. One would think that he had discovered the secret of perpetual motion. He keeps on and on and never flags.[7]

Raisbeck sacrificed Scotland caps for the sake of Liverpool matches in the club's near-Double year of 1899, and this temporary rejection of his national team might explain his miserly final tally of just eight caps (seven v. England) in an era, admittedly, of few international matches. (Alan Hansen was also poorly treated by Scotland more than 70 years later.) No English player was allowed by the rules of the Football League to resist the call-up from England.

The Liverpool team under McKenna and Watson would certainly be built around Raisbeck for much of the next decade. In an era in which the 2–3–5 formation became the dominant system of play, the centre-half was the fulcrum or pivot of the team. He had to be a multi-skilled jack of all trades, a defender and an attacker, a fierce leader as well as a creative inspiration. Not without reason did the great Austrian football writer and intellectual Willy Meisl describe the early centre-half in football as 'the most important man on the field'.[8]

LOCAL BRAGGING RIGHTS

The Football League expanded again in 1898, this time to thirty-six clubs in two leagues of eighteen, with the rising New Brighton Tower joining the group of league clubs from the Merseyside area. This league expansion actually prevented a mutiny. Raisbeck's club at the time, Stoke, and opponents Burnley had publicly stated their plan to draw their final Test match with each other to ensure that both clubs were promoted. The clubs' players spent the match kicking the ball aimlessly into the crowd. Fortunately, the two victim clubs, Newcastle United and Blackburn Rovers, were promoted anyway due to the increase in the size of the league. But it was the end of the controversial Test matches to decide promotion and relegation issues – at least for the time being.[9]

Glossop North End was one of the two clubs automatically promoted in 1899, with Glossop thus becoming the smallest town ever to be represented in the First Division – they lasted just one season. Also, Second Division Grimsby Town sensibly proposed a different-coloured shirt for goalkeepers in 1898, but their idea was rejected by the league – it would eventually be agreed 11 years later, in 1909.

Big-spending Everton were reported to have laid out a whopping £5,787 on new players in 1898–99, but it was Liverpool that started the new season with a bang, a 4–0 home rout of The Wednesday in front of a reported 18,000 crowd. The *Liverpool Review* was also in good form, soon sermonising about the lot of professional players. It quoted one who allegedly said, 'When a player signs a professional form he literally sells his body and figuratively his soul.' And what of the early show by what the *Review* called 'Tom Watson's pets'? (This namecheck for the Liverpool manager was a very early admission of the new man's influence and his worth at Liverpool Football Club.) It was, the paper observed, 'faultless in every particular'. Moreover, 'It is evident that the Liverpool men are no "paper" artists this season. There is no question about their capabilities and apparently there is no doubt about their desire to try.'

For their part, Everton's average home crowds would now be overtaken for the first time by those at Aston Villa. But for big matches – for derby matches, for example – Goodison Park could still be stretched near to its limits. On 24 September 1898, 'with everybody on the tiptoe of excitement . . . the population of a large town' turned out to see Liverpool triumph at Everton 2–1 in a match that hit no great technical heights. 'A good sprinkling of blue jackets [sailors] mingled with the crowd,' reported the *Daily Post*. Proudfoot scored early on for the Blues, with the Scottish reserve utility forward Alex McCowie replying for Liverpool. The visitors got in front courtesy of a penalty awarded by the eagle-eyed referee Lewis against the uncompromising Blues full-back Walter Balmer, who had to be quietened in his protests by the Everton captain. McCowie doubled his tally from the spot. The Liverpool defence was 'the best department on the field' as Everton tried to respond but ran out of time. The 'snowy fronted stands' set against the emerald turf and the music of an 'excellent band' added to the visual and aural attractions of the occasion for local reporters. It was Goodison Park in full bloom – and stormed by the men from Liverpool Football Club.

Following this buoyant result, inconsistent Liverpool struggled to a 0–0 home draw with Notts County before embarking on a spell of three consecutive losses, including a 1–2 defeat to Burnley at Anfield. This result relegated Watson's team to the lower half of the table. Four early matches had brought Liverpool six points, followed by four more producing just one. But by December 1898 things had changed, once again, in this topsy-turvy season for the club's loyal supporters. They were offered the seasonal present of a return of five points from three away matches. By early January 1899, Liverpool had moved up to fourth place on a run of nine matches that had produced six wins and just one loss. 'Tom Watson must be a genius,' commented a relieved and impressed *Liverpool Review*. 'He can almost turn ice into fire.' Watson might have needed this trick at the home match against Stoke on 4 February. In a fierce snowstorm, during which the rolling football gathered snow, the visitors succumbed 1–0 in the kind of game 'that not only pays, but is pleasing and pretty to behold'. For their admirers, this victory in adversity meant that 'Liverpool remain the wonder and admiration of the football world'.

THE 1899 FA CUP SEMI-FINAL FIASCO

By March 1899, the Liverpool press was even able to allow itself the luxury of speculating on the possibility of the Anfield league and FA Cup Double. Liverpool now lay second in the table to Aston Villa and were preparing to play Sheffield United in the FA Cup semi-final in Nottingham. The local press priority seemed to be to bring home the FA Cup rather than the league title. Everton, after all, had already returned the league crown to the city, but the national FA Cup had never resided on Merseyside. At West Bromwich in the FA Cup quarter-finals, the Reds had ridden their luck, scoring two fortunate early goals and then hanging on for dear life. But hang on they did, defensive resolve again to the fore.

The decision to play the resulting Liverpool–Sheffield United semi-final in Nottingham, rather than at nearby Fallowfield, puzzled the Liverpool press. The Manchester venue was 'a decided sell', despite the chaos that had occurred at Everton's 1893 final. A moderate crowd of 35,000 showed up to the first encounter, a 2–2 draw. The first replay was at Burnden Park and still could not separate the teams in a 4–4 extravaganza, by which time Manchester was indeed calling. But it turned out to be a predictably unsatisfactory afternoon in the Fallowfield bowl – one of dangerous chaos and confusion.

The Fallowfield stadium was sited in a semi-rural setting and was designed to host athletics and cycling events, not major football matches. Its single stand could accommodate only 15,000 people, and the sightlines elsewhere – and stadium security – were abysmal.[10] Even before kick-off, some spectators had rushed the gates and crossed the running track, and thousands more poured onto the ground to line the touchline, many of them from Liverpool. Few could see, and barriers were smashed and piled up around the perimeter for fans to stand on. But the match kicked off, nevertheless, and Liverpool scored a goal through George Allan between two disallowed United 'goals'. Soon, the handful of policemen present were fighting to control groups of frustrated spectators, and after a short period members of the crowd invaded the pitch in front of the goals. The players and officials left the field for the first time. Police reinforcements eventually arrived, allowing the teams briefly to return at 4.53 p.m., with the intimidated and demoralised Sheffielders 'about as eager as snails'. At 5.18 p.m., referee Kingscott seemed to abandon the match, at which point, said the Liverpool press, 'the crowd goes clean off its head. Chaos develops into riot.' But by 5.22 p.m., the police had done their work, once more, and the players and officials came back on to finish the first half – which ended at close to six o'clock, some two hours after kick-off.

But that was the last any spectator saw of this doomed tie. The officials and police deemed the situation too dangerous to continue, leaving the Liverpool pressmen to rage that the Reds had been 'robbed of a goal' scored legitimately and possibly of a place in the FA Cup final. They were also concerned that gate receipts, which had exceeded £1,400, would be destined mainly for the coffers of a calamitous FA in a 'match that never was'. At least people from Liverpool could teach neighbouring Mancunians something about 'how to build football grounds, how to behave ourselves on them and how to play football, too'. But Liverpool's chance had already been stolen from them. Their stability restored, the Sheffield club came out on top in the final (third) replay, at Derby County, by the only goal. Liverpool would have to wait another 15 years to make their first FA Cup final appearance.

CHASING A FIRST LEAGUE TITLE – AND CHOKING

Back in the league, meanwhile, Everton v. Aston Villa was identified in the Liverpool press as a match that the hosts might be willing to 'throw' to ensure that their near neighbours floundered in the league race. In fact, the fixture ended honourably, at 1–1. Villa were also suspected of 'squaring' their matches against West Bromwich and Notts County, indicating the levels of suspicion around the results of top football matches at this time.

A 'rousing, exciting match . . . full of remarkable incident' between Liverpool and Newcastle United at Anfield on 3 April 1899 finished 3–2, producing 'terrific plaudits' from a reported four trainloads of visiting Geordie fans. The 23-year-old Wellingborough-born Bill Perkins made his debut in the Liverpool goal, having just signed from Luton Town. He joined Blackpool-born Jack Cox, a dribbling, sometimes over-elaborate flying winger who could play on both flanks. Cox had been signed by Watson for the title and FA Cup run-in. The winger had real talent and was something of a dietary and fitness fanatic, despite what was described darkly as an 'active' social life. The doomed George Allan, meanwhile, was injured, reducing Liverpool to ten men, and the home team went behind twice. But each time the depleted home squad responded with an equaliser before getting their noses in front to claim two vital points 'to save their championship bacon. It was a glorious game.' And it was a glorious Liverpool victory against the odds.

A 2–0 win against Blackburn Rovers meant that Liverpool, uniquely in the history of the Football League so far, would face their final league fixture at Villa Park locked at the top of the table on 43 points with their hosts. Free-scoring Villa needed only a draw to claim the title on goal average. Liverpool would end up scoring only 49 goals in 34 league matches, compared to Villa's 76. There were some other bad omens. Villa had already destroyed Liverpool by three clear goals at Anfield in October, and whilst new Reds goalkeeper Perkins had seemed deceptively 'cool' against Newcastle and Rovers, perhaps his demeanour was actually more a sign of catatonic nervousness. Local reporters on Merseyside were hopeful more than expectant, but they were sure of one thing: 'They may best us at cup winning, but the Villa people can't teach us anything about cheering.' This seemed like thinly veiled resignation before the off. Nevertheless, Tom Watson had taken his squad away to sunny St Anne's near Blackpool for a week's preparation. At 1.30 p.m. on Saturday, many of the 41,357 fans were already heading towards the Villa stadium for a 3.30 p.m. kick-off and the season's grand finale.

An eager Villa started like a train. Liverpool looked like an outfit exhausted by their season's endeavours and disappointments. After four minutes, Billy Garraty headed Villa in front, and then their experienced forward John Devey 'sent in a lightning shot which completely beat Perkins'. Soon after this dagger, Villa men Smith and Wheldon combined before the latter shot into the corner of the Liverpool net with the uncertain Perkins 'making a feeble attempt to save'. Now

Villa Park was in a state of pandemonium, and a 'bully' involving a large number of players in front of the Liverpool net eventually broke the ball to Jimmy Crabtree, who netted for number four, followed by Wheldon again for 0–5 to Villa. By half-time! Some seventy-seven years later, another famous championship-chasing Liverpool side would also turn around at Villa Park having conceded five first-half goals. But this catastrophe must have seemed to Tom Watson and Liverpool in 1899 as if their potentially wonderful season was collapsing about their ears.

At half-time, reported the *Daily Post*, the Midlands band poignantly played 'Au Revoir'. It was 'goodbye' all right for Liverpool's title dreams, and it was a disastrous end to a season of great promise, though no further goals were conceded. Even the *Liverpool Review*'s wry comment that 'we would rather have the Villa beat us than any other team because they invariably play a sportsmanlike game' rang hollow in the face of this slaughter. But Tom Watson knew that this defeat was a temporary glitch. He would return, soon enough, with a championship team of his own.

THE USES – AND ABUSES – OF VICTORIAN FOOTBALL

The next season (1899–1900), Liverpool slumped to tenth place in the league, with Villa retaining their hard-won title. Who could measure the mental and physical impact on Watson's men of what had gone before? Liverpool began the new campaign disastrously, with eight straight league defeats, a top-division record that still stands. After this awful start, so much of what followed was actually close to title form. This was the clue that things were about to go very well for Watson and his men as football became a much more civilised sport. Apeing the comments often made today about 'new' football compared with its tougher versions in the 1970s, in *The Windsor Magazine* in 1899 the great gentleman sportsman of his day C.B. Fry wrote:

> It is the barbarian in us that loves football. The game is exceedingly civilised and scientific nowadays . . . In olden days the sport was nothing but a free fight; now it is, as it were, a very refined form of the same. Indeed the game has become almost too refined. It was at its best when just entering upon its civilised stage, before there were quite so many rules and regulations.

In an editorial on 6 May 1899, the *Liverpool Review* worried at the condition of two-thirds of the football audience for the modern version of the sport – the working-class artisans, men who might be moved to spend seven and sixpence of a weekly wage of thirty shillings on a single trip to Birmingham for a football match. Is the game, 'admirable as it is, worth the time and money and thought he expends upon it?' the *Review* asked. But then there were also the positives of football – its contribution to local pride and to the lives of working people. The paper had its own quite strange and rather eclectic list of the sport's key strengths, which might have had some wider support in the city of Liverpool at this time:

> It supplies an agreeable topic for rational conversation, and it circulates money. If it dis-employs and distracts labour, it employs it and recreates it also. It encourages the instinct for manly endeavour and discourages femininity and namby-pambyism. It inculcates a respect for muscularity and places a heavy discount upon cowardice and funk. Hence, the love of football indirectly strengthens the virility of the nation and makes its masculinity a force . . . These, you will agree, are more than enough to counteract the evil that is in it.

So, football was, in this account at least, a force for improving the local economy and the masculine base of the national stock – important matters at the time of the Boer War and challenges to the British Empire – and it guarded against the supposed veiled dangers of homosexuality. This was quite a list. By 1901, a total of 339 teams and possibly in excess of 4,000 men played football in the Liverpool area, helping to reaffirm local masculinities, community identities and solidarities.[11] Football also primed the local economy, of course. On this last point, as the city of Liverpool lurched uncertainly towards the twentieth century, its sea-faring businesses were certainly doing well out of the war in South Africa: 60 vessels had been chartered for transport, with profit 'getting towards a couple of millions'. But football – and, it must be said, the Liverpool police – seemed helpless to curb the 'empty headed noodles' and the 'hordes of roughs' who were involved in the fancy dress, drunken rowdyism and other 'disgraceful scenes' that took place during the city-centre celebrations on New Year's Eve in 1899. It was noted that the presence of hundreds of inebriated young children, 'bare footed and black faced gamins', meant that 'every slum seems to have vomited its inmates into Church Street' as the new century approached. As reformers eagerly pointed out, there would be a grand total of 4,107 arrests in the city for drunkenness in 1900 to welcome in the new century.

But this sort of arch and contemptuous press coverage of the city's poor was distinctly lacking from discussions of the behaviour of local *football* crowds. Indeed, when Liverpool fans cheered distant news of Lancashire neighbour Bury's FA Cup final win during a routine 1–0 Anfield victory over Nottingham Forest in

April 1900, it was deemed locally to be a signal of 'what unselfish people we are'. There were also other signs of local self-preening. 'They want a tower in St John's Gardens as a memorial to the Liverpool war heroes,' one local newspaper letter writer remarked in June 1900. 'But why? We are all heroes in Liverpool.' However, in July 1900, the *Liverpool Courier* warned that not all local folk were made of the same right stuff. There was a new form of sharp practice reported in the city: a workman calls upon the 'lady of the house' offering coal at an absurdly low price. Two shillings is asked for, and is given, on account – the man (and his coal) disappears. Like it or not, street smartness has always been one of the necessary survival tools on the Mersey.

Football sometimes seemed almost similarly self-serving. The game's leaders used a 'cold, calm business tone' to argue in 1900, for example, against the pooling of gate receipts to help the weaker league clubs survive. 'When wages are cut down and something is done to make each team really representative of its own city,' commented the *Liverpool Review* testily, 'the Football League will be still more assured of a very long and lusty life.' Liverpool Football Club was in no mood to share its profits. Instead, Tom Watson and John McKenna put its cash towards some shrewd signings for the new campaign. A combative left-sided forward with a booming shot, Charlie Satterthwaite, arrived from Burton Swifts in November 1899 and added much needed direction, bite and aggression to the Liverpool frontline. Cheshire man and wing-half Charlie Wilson also arrived to offer the club reliability and continuity in what would be 40 years of devoted service, first as a player, then as a scout and trainer up until the Second World War. But the New Brighton Tower forward Sam Raybould was the real jewel, a key playing find for Tom Watson and a vital figure in Liverpool's title wins of 1901 and 1906. Chesterfield-born Raybould had not really set the Wirral football world alight, and he seemed like a pretty ordinary 25-year-old utility forward when he first signed for Liverpool for a hefty £250 fee in January 1900. But appearances were deceptive.

Of course, the public-school men at the FA still considered transfer fees in sport to be vulgar and 'unsportsmanlike', and they had recommended a maximum charge for the transfer of a player at this time of a puny £10. The Football League management committee effectively and sensibly ignored them.[12]

At goal-starved Liverpool, Raybould soon found his shooting boots, and eventually he would manage 128 goals in 226 appearances, including a goal at Goodison Park only 30 seconds into his derby debut. He also managed a pre-Second World War club record 31 goals in 33 league starts in 1902–03 and was a formidable replacement for Harry Bradshaw. Moustachioed and lean, Raybould was also quick and brave, a willing worker as well as a reliable goalscorer. 'When

Raybould gets the ball anywhere near the half-backs,' purred the *Liverpool Mercury*, 'there are stormy times ahead for someone.' And yet the robust Raybould could attract no support from the England selectors, despite his league-title heroics for Liverpool. But, frankly, could Tom Watson and the club's followers care less?

THE FIRST LIVERPOOL CHAMPIONSHIP, 1900–01

Tellingly, Liverpool had won nine of their last eleven league matches to end the first season concluded in the 1900s. They took off from the same place in September 1900, trouncing Blackburn Rovers 3–0 and then West Bromwich 5–0. In these victories, Raisbeck was 'ever prominent with head and feet', and the physical and spritely Satterthwaite showed 'his special penchant for being among the bruises'. Notoriously shy full-back John Robertson, meanwhile, a recent signing from Stoke, was showing 'sound defence' and thus 'ingratiated himself in the favour of the spectators'. But the big change at Anfield was the scoring of more goals: against WBA, for example, 'the visiting backs were run to a standstill' and were taunted as Liverpool's wingers 'flashed along in exhilarating style'. The new man Raybould was 'the pivot of every attack'. This was a dimension of Tom Watson's Liverpool persona that the Merseyside public had not yet seen – and it was thrilling and uplifting stuff.

Against Everton at Goodison Park in September 1900, however, it was much tougher going in a 1–1 draw, a match played in filthy conditions. It was the sort of no-quarter-given contest designed to bring the very best out of Alex Raisbeck, who dominated proceedings as 'the prominent figure in every movement whether of attack or defence'. The *Liverpool Mercury* was astonished by the Liverpool man's all-round commitment and ability, an Alan Hansen and Steven Gerrard combined. 'Now taking the ball clean from an opponent's toes, now urging on his forwards with a well judged pass, now darting to the assistance of his backs and checking many a dangerous rush. Always when danger threatened or opportunity presented itself was the light-haired Scot.' When Liverpool lost 1–2 at home to Tom Watson's old boys Sunderland on 29 September 1900, the 'fully employed' Raisbeck was 'the only one among the backs who appeared able to check the rapid rushes of the visitors', as home goalkeeper Perkins 'saved his side from utter collapse'.

The talented Wales international Maurice Parry replaced the injured Raisbeck when Liverpool beat Bolton Wanderers 2–1 in the next home league match, but the replacement inevitably paled by comparison with the great man (as any reserve would). Unlike Raisbeck, Parry 'lacked life, his passing was slow and his tackling feeble'. The bionic Satterthwaite, meanwhile, was carried off after colliding with the Wanderers keeper John Sutcliffe in scoring Liverpool's winning goal, but, typically, he recovered for the Reds' trip to Notts County. He eventually played only 21 league matches, mainly because of injury. The match in Nottingham produced a potentially shattering 0–3 loss for Liverpool, even with the mighty Raisbeck reinstated. Which all meant that the Reds stayed second in the league table behind leaders Nottingham Forest.

It was probably on 10 November 1900, in front of 18,000 fans at Anfield, that the locals really began to believe that the league crown might actually be a possibility for Tom Watson's Liverpool. The visitors that day, Aston Villa, were chasing a hat-trick of league titles, but a 5–1 Liverpool victory, based on the 'persistency and untiring effort' of the home side, destroyed the Midlands men, who eventually limped home just above the relegation slots. Tom Robertson, charging down Villa's right flank, was the pick of the home men as he 'flashed along the touchline to the corner flag' to set up three goals, including the fourth, a sumptuous volley from Raybould so that Villa keeper Billy George 'could only feel the waft of the air as the ball crashed past him'.

But Liverpool still struggled for consistency, and although in December the legendary Sheffield United heavyweight keeper Fatty Foulke 'had to save repeatedly' to help his club stay afloat at Anfield, it was enough for United to chalk up a 1–2 defeat for the Reds, despite another Satterthwaite goal. After twelve eventful matches, Liverpool had fallen back to fifth place, four points behind Forest and with four defeats already as dark stains on their record.

It was the sort of form to dim even the positive economic news on Merseyside in the new century. Plans for the world's largest warehouse had been recently drawn up for the Stanley Dock – the port of Liverpool was still booming, if facing an increasingly uncertain future. It might also have driven some of the club's supporters to the sort of blasphemy and street cursing that meant that at the Liverpool workhouse in December 1900 a censor was appointed to vet the songs being prepared by inmates for a Christmas entertainment for the nurses. Or perhaps it might have driven some Liverpool supporters to try the exotic Bavarian Münchener beer and Löwenbräu lager that was already being widely advertised in the *Liverpool Mercury*. British ale was off the menu for some; at the time, a scandal about the poisoning of beer with arsenic had resulted in prominent court cases. Meanwhile, more discerning folk in the city might even have chosen an evening out with the young Winston Churchill. The future prime minister was speaking at the city's Philharmonic Hall in November 1900 about the rights and (less probably) the wrongs of the Boer War.

In December 1900, with Alex Raisbeck once more in 'capital trim', despite being choked by a 'very disappointing exhibition of football', a single goal by Jack Cox at Anfield was enough to see off the then FA Cup holders Bury in the league. Raybould, 'clean through' in the second half, had obviously left his shooting boots elsewhere. On 22 December, the Reds, away at league leaders Nottingham Forest, held on for a 0–0 draw in front of a 10,000 crowd, although Raybould again had 'an open goal, but shot over the bar'. Towards the end of the contest, the home goal was reported to be 'hotly besieged'. This improvement in Liverpool's form was carried on into the new year, when Stoke were despatched 3–1 on a 'treacherous surface' at Anfield. Much more of this and the club's fans would be making good use of the improved tramway service in the city, which meant that people who lived in the Parliament Fields, Smithdown Road and Edge Hill areas of the city would no longer have to travel into the centre of town to get an overloaded tram back out to the Anfield stadium. Nevertheless, letters soon followed to local newspapers about the new problem of tram overcrowding caused, it was alleged, by 'poor conductoring'.

Now a real local test. 'Everything else pales into insignificance today,' trumpeted the *Liverpool Courier* on 19 January 1901. It was derby day at Anfield. But a 'terrible downpour of rain' turned the ground into a quagmire and threatened to ruin Liverpool's entire season in front of an estimated 18,000 fans. The match kicked off 15 minutes early, in fading light, just to ensure a finish. It was tough luck on those ticket-holding customers who came to the stadium on time! Jack Taylor scored for Everton after 20 minutes, and Raybould might have replied had the ball not stuck in a pool of water in conditions described as 'frightful'. Jack Cox, 'who up to this had been practically idle, pounced upon the ball like a greyhound' and scrambled in the equaliser for a 1–1 score at half-time. The sodden and muddied teams reappeared in fresh kit after the interval, and the two captains, Raisbeck and Settle, evidently discussed the possibility of abandoning the match, as did the officials. But the crowd cried, 'Play the game!' It was best not to invite a riot so play continued. Centre-half Tom Booth headed in for the visitors, and this time there was no reply: 1–2. Disaster!

Three days after this sporting 'tragedy', the whole nation would join Liverpool football fans in mourning. Queen Victoria had finally passed away. In the city of Liverpool, as elsewhere, 'sad-eyed groups packed the pavements' and 'the anguish of the community was terrible indeed'. But this public grief for royalty was actually short-lived in the city. Next morning, reported the *Liverpool Review*, with some admiration, 'the city of Liverpool went about its business pretty much as if little or nothing had happened'.

The Rugby Union and the FA reacted immediately and patriotically to the monarch's death, in the latter's case by postponing all forthcoming FA Cup ties. This irked the more pragmatic men at the Football League, because the gesture promised future fixture congestion. All league fixtures were also postponed on

2 February, the day of the old Queen's funeral. Liverpool would have no match now until their rearranged FA Cup tie with Notts County on 9 February and then a league fixture with Bolton Wanderers on 16 February: they lost both, scoring no goals. A 'display of ineptitude' was how the *Liverpool Courier* described the Reds' limp FA Cup exit. Wingers Cox and Satterthwaite, the newspaper complained later at Bolton, 'hardly seemed to understand each other'. Liverpool were now drifting to midtable oblivion and apparently out of title contention. With the passing of Queen Victoria – who had defined an astonishing era in British history – seemed to slide any fading Liverpool FC hopes of winning football silverware in 1901.

And yet there was still hope. This faltering at Bolton would be the last Liverpool league defeat of 1900–01. As a shipment of 'wild beasts' was exported out of the city by steamship from Cross's famous menagerie on Earle Street, and Dr Lasker, chess champion of the world, visited the city of Liverpool to lecture at the Central Chess Club on North John Street on the crucial question of the king's gambit, there followed a twelve-match unbeaten Football League run for Liverpool Football Club, nine of them victories. This sequence took the Anfield club from eighth place to league champions. And what looks suspiciously like what we might now call 'mind games' were not beyond the wily Liverpool manager Tom Watson. He strived to take every advantage to secure the club's first league title.

In March 1901, a letter from Watson was read out at an emergency board meeting called at Manchester City. In it the Liverpool manager denied a claim that a Reds director had said loudly before the meeting of the two clubs that all the opposition had to do was to contain the great City winger Billy Meredith. 'The rest are no good.' City duly collapsed. Was it Watson who was behind this psychological ploy? It was certainly a devastating aside, one probably designed to dissolve the morale of fragile opponents. The Liverpool manager was certainly a deep admirer of the brilliant Meredith. In 1906, when the Welshman signed for Manchester United, Watson told him, 'Why didn't you come to us; we'd have given you the docks?'[13]

Liverpool conceded just two goals in their last ten league fixtures, with ex-New Brompton full-back John Glover covering for John Robertson at right-back and the Welsh Methodist teetotaller 'Long Legs' Maurice Parry doing the same brilliantly for Wilson at half-back. John 'Sailor' Hunter filled in up front when needed for the injury-troubled Satterthwaite. Bill Perkins (in goal), Bill Goldie and winger Tom Robertson were the league title ever-presents with 34 league starts, but Dunlop, Raisbeck, Cox and Raybould all played more than 30 times, with the reliable John Walker stuck just behind on 29. The consistent form of this core of players – and avoiding injuries – was the crucial factor in this final charge for the title. Liverpool's 1901 favoured title-winning XI lined up like this:

Liverpool FC, league-title winners, 1900–01

Perkins

Robertson (J)   Dunlop

Wilson   Raisbeck   Goldie

Cox   Walker   Raybould   Satterthwaite   Robertson (T)

Narrow wins, first at challengers Sunderland and then at home against Wolves, with Satterthwaite again in the wars and hobbling, started off this title sequence, with a 'clever victory' by 2–0 in 'very greasy and treacherous' conditions at Aston Villa to follow. As we all know, momentum means a lot in football, and this Liverpool squad and their manager now seemed to have it in spades. But a 1–1 home draw against The Wednesday, following a misjudgement by Perkins of Fred Spikesley's header for the visitors, slowed down the upward surge. Raisbeck's absence in favour of the England v. Scotland clash at Crystal Palace on 30 March as Liverpool faced Newcastle United threatened more lost points. Instead, with Dunlop authoritatively assuming the captaincy, replacement Sailor Hunter came up with two vital goals in a 'businesslike' 3–0 victory. No other Liverpool players were on international duty that day: this group was a *team*, not a collection of stars. Incidentally, things got no better for Newcastle. At the club's next match – versus title-chasing Sunderland – there was rioting as locked-out angry spectators stormed the palisades. Sunderland fans pulled up the goalposts, and the police baton charged the 'rough elements' in scenes of chaotic violence reminiscent of the very earliest wild days of the Football League.

In the calmer waters of Anfield, meanwhile, on 8 April 1901 in a match that 'might possibly decide the question of the championship', Liverpool squeezed past Notts County 1–0. It was one of so many crucial narrow victories. Cox centred, Pennington fumbled and, with 15 minutes to go, Johnny-on-the-spot Raybould 'tipped the leather into the net amidst a hurricane of cheers from an intensely excited crowd'. The Reds were now five points behind leaders Sunderland but with three games in hand. The title was actually in reach.

Manchester City were next to be put to the sword at Anfield, with two goals for Robertson, while an overly exuberant Cox was 'penalised for an exhibition of rugby play' and the off-form Raybould was merely a 'broken reed' in attack. A 0–0 grind at rugged Bury followed, but then, unusually, defender Goldie scored from a 'beautiful shot' in the next home fixture against Nottingham Forest.

This after Cox's first-half opener had been 'cheered to the echo' and Forest had been conveniently reduced to ten men through injury. Winger Cox had now contributed ten crucial goals and numerous assists in the campaign.

The expectant Liverpool directors had enraged the Merseyside press – and their neighbours Everton – by resisting FA attempts to bring the 1901 FA Cup final replay between Tottenham and Sheffield United to Goodison Park on the same day as the vital Liverpool v. Forest league fixture. They claimed, not unreasonably, that staging the final across Stanley Park might have deleterious effects on the Anfield attendance. The 'cloven hoof of commercialism', the *Daily Post* called the Liverpool objections; 'mean and unpatriotic' offered the *Liverpool Review*, who saw this move as the craven actions of businessmen, not visionaries or even football enthusiasts. Had the Liverpool board acceded to the FA's request then the city of Liverpool might have seen the destination of the FA Cup and the Football League title decided on either side of Stanley Park on the *same* afternoon. The city of Liverpool might even have hosted future FA finals. As it was, the city would never again host an FA Cup final or a final replay – and Liverpool Football Club would have to grind out its first league title in the club's last match of the 1900–01 season, in the West Midlands.

For Liverpool's final league fixture, away at already relegated West Bromwich Albion in front of a miserable crowd of 2,000 at kick-off and around 4,000 at the end, 'The weather was far from favourable and greatly affected the attendance,' reported the *Daily Post*. Merseysiders continued to arrive long into the season's final match. In 1947, and again in 1976, Liverpool would return to the Black Country to win Football League titles. But surely in 1901, unmotivated, resigned and weak WBA would simply collapse in the face of the champions-elect? Nothing could be further from the truth. Liverpool were at strength, with Parry in for Wilson their only concession to injury. A win was needed to be sure to secure the title from Sunderland, but it was the hosts who began as if their very lives depended on the outcome. It was typical of the English way.

The Liverpool goal 'was kept in a perfect state of siege' in the first half, at least quelling any fears that this fixture might have been 'settled' in advance. Eventually, the visitors got a foothold, and a shot from Raybould slithered out of goalkeeper Joe Reader's grasp. John Walker was there to bundle the ball in for an entirely undeserved half-time Liverpool lead. Now it was all about the Reds digging in and seeing out time. As the minutes ticked down, 'Liverpool worked hard to the finish to maintain their great advantage,' reported the *Daily Post*. The visitors held on 'and amidst a scene of excitement and enthusiasm, they left the field champions of the league for the season 1900–01'.

It had been a stupendous final run-in by any measure: 21 points won out of a possible 24 and no defeats, even if it was a rather scruffy and nervous end. The final title-winning margin was a comfortable two points, with Liverpool winning nineteen, drawing seven and losing eight of their thirty-four matches for forty-five points. Raybould had contributed seventeen precious goals, but Alex Raisbeck had been the standout talent. The Scot had helped prevent many more goals against Liverpool at the opposite end.

'Long before 11 o'clock last night,' reported the *Daily Post* on 30 April 1901, 'a large concourse of people assembled in the Central Station' to welcome their league champions home. A fife and drum band struck up 'The Conquering Hero' as the train drew in, and disembarking players were lifted onto the shoulders of the 'many thousands' of jubilant fans present. A few ambitious admirers even tried to lift aloft the rather portly Tom Watson 'but no arms were long enough to grip his girth and no muscle strong enough to lift him up'. They had the correct man all right: 'Owd Tom' had done his stuff and was recognised locally for it. It had taken just nine short years for a declining John Houlding to finally square matters with his Everton detractors. How sweet this first league triumph must have been for all the ex-Evertonians at Anfield – Houlding and Barclay – and also for McKenna. And, of course, for the marvellous man from the north-east, Tom Watson, Liverpool Football Club's mainly forgotten first great football manager.

CHAPTER 3 REFERENCES

1. Pooley, 'Living in Liverpool: The Modern City', pp. 241 and 244
2. Milne, 'Maritime Liverpool', p. 278
3. Carter, *The Football Manager*, p. 43
4. Carter, *The Football Manager*, p. 31
5. Carter, *The Football Manager*, p. 45
6. Young, *Football on Merseyside*, p. 59
7. Quoted in Young, *Football on Merseyside*, p. 68
8. Quoted in Wilson, *Inverting the Pyramid*, p. 22
9. Inglis, *League Football and the Men Who Made It*, p. 44
10. Inglis, *Made in Manchester*, p. 62
11 Preston, 'The Origins and Development of Association Football in the Liverpool District *c.*1879–*c.*1915', p. 174
12. Inglis, *League Football and the Men Who Made It*, p. 46
13. Harding, *Football Wizard: The Story of Billy Meredith*, pp. 61–2

4

AS MANY DOWNS AS UPS
The Topsy-Turvy 1900s

POST-TITLE STRESS

'It is a pity,' wrote a scribe in the *Liverpool Review* of 31 August 1901, on the brink of another new football season, 'that the managers of Liverpool Football Club cannot be prevailed upon to provide some music to while away the time previous to the match commencing.' Talk about being ahead of its time. Roll on the era of today's Anfield stadium music man George Sephton. The newspaper wanted an ode, or even a symphony, for the new Football League champions from Liverpool. And everyone wanted to see this Liverpool team play. A letter writer to the local press, who signed himself W.H.B., was already warning about the likely 'overcrowding' of tram cars to the stadiums in the city and the 'shock' that awaited any new fan when they first experienced the dangerous enthusiasm for the sport both inside and outside Goodison Park or Anfield. 'I myself have been carried off my feet many a time for fully a hundred yards,' he reported. 'Outside the Liverpool enclosure,' he went on, 'once I was lifted up and did not alight on terra firma again until I found myself inside the ground.' He recommended more self-restraint among supporters and a queuing system for the turnstiles.

Within weeks of his letter, something rather more chilling on the same front was reported in 1901 by a Reds fan calling himself simply 'A Footballer'. Before the derby game in September at Anfield, he recounted, the pay boxes were soon closed at the Oakfield Road (Kop) end, producing a rush of fans towards the Anfield Road entrances. On the terraces at that end of the ground, it 'suddenly felt as if all the juice was going to be squeezed out of us. Word came that the entrances were being rushed and for a time we were like sardines in a box and literally panted for breath.' Accounts like this rarely made it into the press, though pretty much all 'shilling fans' would have had similar stories to tell.

Most people had anecdotes about 'almost' being injured or about being crushed or discomforted at a football match. It was remarkable that serious accidents at English football were so relatively few in number, given the size of crowds and the intensity of the 'football fever'. Stadium facilities in Britain at this time were still basic at best, and mechanisms for counting supporters into stadium areas or for ensuring their safe exit were either crude or non-existent. At least fans could still escape onto the pitch in emergencies. Eventually, though, some poor souls would surely pay the ultimate price. They did so: in Glasgow just a few months later at a Scotland v. England home international match at Ibrox in April 1902; at Burnden Park, Bolton, in 1946; and at Hillsborough in 1989. British football had often been warned, but it didn't always seem to listen.

On the pitch, and in a pattern that characterised much of the next two decades, Liverpool Football Club now slumped from title winners to midtable also-rans. Perhaps taking the players to Paris as a reward for winning the title dulled their senses for its defence? Only one win in the club's first ten league matches – including a 2–2 Anfield draw with Everton – signalled that trouble was ahead. Loss of form and especially the impact of injuries played its part. Just fifteen players had filled all but five first-team slots in the title season. Now Tom Watson was forced to call upon 24 players in a squad that between them could muster only 42 goals in 34 games, a miserable 14 goals away from home. Only Derby County scored fewer goals.

At Everton in January, it was a 0–4 drubbing for Liverpool, and it was expected the Blues would 'do' for the Reds in the first Merseyside FA Cup derby, on 25 January 1902. The *Liverpool Mercury*, forever hopeful, wondered if the tie might not 'awaken the champions from their somnolence', while the *Daily Post* complained that local rivals should simply not be drawn together at this early stage in such a prestigious competition. It suggested a novel form of regional 'seeding' to replace the 'old fashioned' open draw of the FA. This would require two hats: one containing clubs from the north and the other clubs from the south. 'This would give fair play and avoid clashing.' Predictably, the proposal fell on deaf ears in London.

The *Liverpool Courier* reported on Tom Watson's frustrations with the Liverpool injury count but also on his resolution that 'We are not giving in. The men we have are as fit as can be and they mean to play for all they are worth.' There was also an insight into the club's preparations at their Lytham FA Cup base: 'Walking, sprinting, football training and hot baths', with billiards to follow in the evening at the local Working Man's Institute. The Liverpool chairman William Houlding and the other club directors 'showed their interest in the team by paying them periodical visits'. Despite this, all was set fair for an

Everton victory. However, in 'vile' weather in front of around 25,000 huddled souls, 'the revival of Liverpool was remarkable', with the home side dominating the exchanges in a hard-fought 2–2 draw. 'If the team does as well at Goodison and shoots a bit straighter,' argued the *Daily Post*, '[Liverpool] will come out of the test all right.'

A reader wrote to the *Liverpool Courier* to complain about the behaviour of 'roughs' in the Oakfield Road area of Anfield who 'amuse themselves by playing so-called football in the open street and, moreover, are often heard to be making objectionable remarks to any of the public who happen to be passing by'. These young tyros were probably encouraged by the weather for the derby cup replay, which was much improved. After 40 minutes of sparring, home full-back Walter Balmer mis-headed a Raisbeck free-kick past the unsighted Blues keeper George Kitchen, who 'making a wild kick missed the ball, which rolled slowly into the goal'. This rather comical and welcome clanger was 'greeted wildly' by the Liverpool supporters present. After a 'rather prolonged' interval, Everton's Sam Wolstenholme deliberately handled, and from the ensuing free-kick Sailor Hunter advanced to score for the Reds with a 'beautiful long shot'. There was no reply forthcoming from a jaded Everton.

As the *Daily Post* put it, it was a result that 'staggered most people', but it was only a temporary respite for Liverpool. Southern League club Southampton – on their way to their first FA Cup final – dumped the Reds 1–4 in the next round. Liverpool lost only two more matches (twelve) than did second-placed Everton in the league in 1901–02, but they won only ten in total, fewer than any other club. A lack of penetration saw them draw 12 times, including at eventual champions Sunderland.

The signing in March 1902 of right-winger 'Graceful' Artie Goddard from Glossop promised more consistency and more attacking threat – the marvellous Goddard played more than 400 times for Liverpool, scoring 77 goals. Cox moved to the left to replace the transferred Tom Robertson, and in 1902–03 ten outfield players each mustered at least twenty-seven league appearances, a return to some of the stability of the title season. But there were two other main reasons why Liverpool climbed back up to fifth spot. The first was a change in playing philosophy, which meant a little more risk-taking and attacking football, an approach that produced more wins (17) but also more defeats (13) than in the previous season. The second was the fantastic form of Sam Raybould, 31 goals in 33 league matches and a club record 32 for the season (also netting in a 1–2 FA Cup loss to Manchester United). It was also noticeable that the early Scottish leanings of the two Merseyside clubs were now being balanced by more English influences.

PAYING FOR SUCCESS – AND KING JOHN'S CURTAIN CALL

A good example of the decline of the Scottish influence came when Liverpool and Everton played out a 0–0 draw in April 1903 – notable for Raybould's 'wild marksmanship'. The *Liverpool Review* wrote that 'at least fifteen out of the twenty-two performers were born below the Border, a truly striking observation on the present predominance of English football'. And, we might say too, a sign of the declining influence on the playing and recruitment side at Liverpool of Honest John McKenna. The Liverpool man would be a future vice chair of the players' union, and he was now also serving the Football League. McKenna had been a bitter opponent in 1900 of a new FA rule that limited the maximum weekly wage of professional footballers to £4 (£208 per year) and a plan to ban the payment of bonuses. This meant that top professional footballers were well rewarded but not excessively so; officially, they now earned wages commensurate with lower-grade professional men, about twice the wage of skilled workers and clerks and just under twice the wages of foremen and supervisors.[1]

Unofficially, the earnings of many top players – including those at Liverpool – were simply not contained by the £4-a-week wage limit. The retain-and-transfer system in England effectively tied players to their clubs and under-the-counter payments were rife. What right anyway did the FA have to interfere in the private business of Football League clubs? By 1904, the league was effectively back in control of the players' wages issue, but it refused to abolish the maximum wage and, frankly, why bother? The richer clubs had long worked out ways of rewarding players surreptitiously. The Wales star Billy Meredith would later agree that the 'secret of success' behind Manchester City's 1904 FA Cup win was that 'the club put aside the rule that no player should receive more than £4 a week'. He estimated that City had paid £654 in bonuses: 'The team delivered the goods and the club paid for the goods delivered and both sides were satisfied.'[2]

In 1906, Manchester City lost almost an entire team, including Meredith, on match-fixing charges in an investigation that also revealed that some of the club's players had been receiving at least £6 a week in wages since 1902. According to the Liverpool FC directors, the Anfield players who won the 1900–01 league title were paid even more, a basic £7 a week. With bonuses, this figure could reach £10 a week – more than double the permitted maximum.[3] The smaller league clubs, of course, were probably very thankful for the constraints on costs promised by the maximum wage, thus producing in the boardrooms of the football elite a 'silent conspiracy in which subterfuge became the accepted norm'.[4]

If it was assumed that the 0–0 result with Everton in April 1903 meant another corner had been turned for Liverpool Football Club, then a rude awakening lay ahead. Liverpool's goals dried up, and the club's confidence and defensive meanness almost completely disappeared. So too – not entirely coincidentally – did its founder and long-time leader. At 7.15 a.m. on 17 March 1902 in Cimiez in the South of France, after a lengthy illness, the remarkable John Houlding died in his 69th year. The Everton club acknowledged King John's huge role in establishing the *two* major professional football clubs in the city by flying flags at half-mast and having the Blues team wear black armbands as a sign of respect on the occasion of his passing.

Houlding's death followed hard on the heels of that of the local philanthropist and great Liverpool Liberal politician William Rathbone, who was honoured by a funeral cortège a mile long and a wreath sent by Florence Nightingale in recognition of his work on district nursing. But the great John Houlding also had his own strong claims to good local works: with the aged poor of Everton and the homeless young, for example; on improving sanitation for the least well off in the city; in the Liverpool mayoral office, fighting against the 'murderous protests' of local temperance supporters; and, of course, in establishing Merseyside professional football on both sides of Stanley Park. Many people from 'humble backgrounds', as well as the nation's football cognoscenti, attended his funeral. 'He had no pretence to inspired genius,' remarked the *Liverpool Courier*, perhaps a little too unkindly, 'but had abiding faith in diligent, painstaking work.' More importantly, in the words of the *Liverpool Mercury* on 24 March 1902, 'His place can never be filled and the Liverpool club is staggering under one of the heaviest blows it has ever received. The future of the Anfielders seems far from reassuring now that their leading spirit has passed away.'

LIVERPOOL FC AFTER JOHN HOULDING

Houlding's death and the loss of his steely influence *did* hit Liverpool FC hard. But on the pitch it was also crucial that forward Sam Raybould missed the first 19 league games in the 1903–04 season through injury and that no one stepped in to fill the resultant goals vacuum. Moreover, new defensive recruits John Chadburn and Fred Buck proved failures at Anfield, though the latter, at just 5 ft 4 in. tall, remarkably went on to play at centre-half for WBA in the 1912 FA Cup final. Like Chadburn, the locally born amateur centre-forward Syd Smith played the opening two Football League fixtures, scoring in the first and attracting good press in 'a most promising exposition of the soccer code'. But he was then unceremoniously ditched by the perfectionist Watson.

The uncomplicated but reliable Nottingham man Alf West was signed to play right-back in November 1903, but by then much of the damage had already been done – including five straight Liverpool defeats at the start of the campaign. Even Alex Raisbeck was moved to full-back as Watson sought a foothold, and a 2–2 draw with Everton in October offered some hope, though the *Daily Post* was little fooled, commenting that Liverpool 'must have played a little above their form and the probability is that they will not again this season be seen to such advantage'. These proved to be wise words. A 2–5 hammering at Stoke followed – Stoke would finish one point above Liverpool, in safety – with even the saintly Raisbeck being roundly criticised by the *Liverpool Echo* for his panicky defending. The Anfield team was now at rock bottom and praying for a signing. 'Surely,' asked a plaintive *Daily Post*, 'the resources of Mr Tom Watson and his directors are not so beggarly as they appear?'

A further run of eight matches without a win around Christmas 1903 and then another 2–5 hammering in the return derby at Everton on 1 April 1904 seemed to have all but killed off Liverpool. When a struggling Stoke, rather suspiciously (for Reds fans), won at a canter at Goodison Park of all places, the game was really up for the 1901 champions. A new signing from Sunderland for £500 in February, inside-right Robbie Robinson, offered plenty of future promise, and he began to score goals immediately he arrived towards the back end of the season. But wins at home to Bury and then at Blackburn came way too late to swing things around for Liverpool. With Everton comparatively lording it in third place, it was ignominious relegation for their near neighbours just three years after title glory – what a come down. Old rumours were now ominously reported again in the *Daily Post* in April 1904 questioning the very future of the club without its founder, predicting that if Liverpool were indeed relegated 'it would sooner or later drop out of existence as the owners of the land at Anfield intend to build on the ground . . . It would surprise nobody if the rumour was correct this time.'

Following John Houlding's death, the ownership and control issues around the club – including around the Anfield stadium – still needed to be resolved. It was a crisis not unlike the 2010 version. But Liverpool Football Club homeless? In May, the *Liverpool Review* could not resist producing the words of an imagined sporting operetta, featuring a mournful Tom Watson, who summed up the club's gloomy predicament when he supposedly sang:

> McKenna's not smiled for a week,
> He thinks we'll sail off in a sloop.
> We're all without fable,

Dressed in crepe and sable.

In the Second they've placed us

They've gone and disgraced us.

Because – and I have it on the very best authority –

We have all been drowned 'in the soup'.

'In the soup' and downbeat Liverpool Football Club may have been, but they were far from down and out. The 37-year-old goalkeeper Teddy Doig, recruited from Sunderland for 150 quid in August 1904 – still the club's oldest signing – gave the Liverpool backline the confidence it had so palpably lacked when the club had been demoted. Doig, a trained boxer, could punch a ball to the halfway line and he soon struck up a rapport with the early Kop. Given that relegation-threatened Middlesbrough paid Sunderland a record £1,000 fee for Alf Common in February 1905, it could hardly be argued that Tom Watson was trying to 'buy' the Anfield club out of their problems. 'Bee', the *Liverpool Echo*'s football correspondent, said of Watson on Owd Tom's death that, 'He had signed more cheap and good players than any secretary in the world.' It was not a bad commendation. In fact, the Liverpool manager/secretary was convinced that he had the core of a squad that was capable not only of running through the Second Division but even of challenging again in the First. Not for the first time, Watson showed his sound judgement.

Complaints abound today about the alleged chasm in playing quality between the Premier League and the Championship, but the lack of real depth in the early Football League was also very plain to see. The demoted Liverpool stormed to the Division Two title in 1905, dropping just two points in their first thirteen matches and scoring ninety-three goals in losing only three times in thirty-four matches. Twenty-year-old Bootle forward John Parkinson offered vital goalscoring support to both Raybould and Goddard: the three players scored sixty-three league goals between them, Parkinson scoring twenty in just twenty-one league appearances, including a hat-trick in an 8–1 demolition of Burslem Port Vale. The only opponent Liverpool failed to beat in the league was the also promoted Bolton Wanderers, not that the club's supporters were always convinced by the Reds' form. Against Lincoln City in January 1905, the Anfield crowd produced 'ironical cheers' and 'a continuous roar of derision' as the home players struggled to find their promotion form. Maybe fitness was the problem, because when the Reds were drawn to play First Division table-topping Everton at Anfield in the FA Cup in January 1905 eight of the home players weighed in at over 12 st., compared to only three Evertonians. Almost a century before it became commonplace to focus on such matters, an amateur statistician reported to the *Liverpool Courier* that Everton had the best of the 1–1 Cup draw on corners (7–3) and throw-ins (50–46) won. The Blues had also forced sixteen goalkicks from Liverpool, compared to taking seven of their own. Everton won the replay but were reported to have been 'distinctively lucky' to have done so.

A few weeks later, on 22 February 1905, a public meeting was held at the Carlton Hall on Eberle Street to start finally to plan the post-John Houlding era for the Liverpool club. Every season bar one since Tom Watson had been made manager, Liverpool FC had made a profit. Chairman Edwin Berry told the meeting that the club had £700 in the bank and was financially stable, but also that, 'In name it [LFC] was a limited company, but practically it was a one-man show.' Out of 3,000 existing Liverpool shares, the Houlding family held 2,000. This needed to change. The club debt to the late John Houlding was £10,000, with a further £5,000 bank overdraft guaranteed by the Houlding family. William Houlding had approached the board, said Berry, to put the club 'on a more popular basis, so that it would really belong to the people'. Houlding had agreed to give up the 2,000 family shares and to wipe out the debt if the club agreed to relieve him of the bank-loan guarantee. Other existing shareholders, it was reported, had also agreed to give up 50 per cent of the money they held in the company. It was a new beginning. A share issue was agreed for 1906 of 15,000 shares at £1 each and, supposedly, a more 'popular control' of the club with much more public accountability would be established.

Liverpool FC could now purchase the Anfield ground from Orrell and the Houlding estate. With this last point in mind, a shareholder, Fred Perry, suggested that the club consider installing a cycle track around the pitch, a move that would be supported by the National Cyclists' Union. Chillingly, Edwin Berry promised that the Liverpool board would give the matter serious consideration, but it never came about. There were no big money men behind the new Liverpool. The local businessmen of modest means who fronted the new share issue were: William Houlding; John McKenna; Alexander Nisbet, a relieving officer; John Ramsey, a bookkeeper; John Dermott, a tobacconist; William Evans, a cashier; and Albert Edwin Berry, a solicitor's clerk. Relatively little of this assumed 'spread of control' to put the club in the hands of local people was actually in evidence in the years that followed, as the club's board quickly established a lasting dominance in share ownership. Football supporters who were dubious about the role of football club directors might have been amused by article number 45 of the Liverpool FC 1906 Memorandum of Association, which read, 'If any member is a lunatic or idiot he may vote by his committee or other legal curator.' Football club directors and shareholders as lunatics – surely not? The new Liverpool board had already assembled plans to redevelop the ground, given some reasonable stability on the field – which meant, minimally, staying in the First Division.

CHAMPIONS AGAIN

The formation of FIFA in 1904, a new international body for the administration of football, spoke eloquently enough of football's widening global horizons. But the home countries generally kept their distance from the new body in case it diminished the influence in world football of the British. An expansive Liverpool FC had at least voted for the domestic growth of the Football League in 1905, from thirty-six clubs to two divisions comprising forty clubs. This produced 38 league fixtures, although most top clubs also still played lucrative friendly fixtures and local and regional cup matches, bringing the total fixture load for the elite up to around 60 or even 70 matches in a season.

This minor expansion in the league programme also helped to air differences of opinion about the Football League's real ambitions and future status: was it to remain a largely regional competition for selected members, or did it have true national aspirations?[5] Woolwich Arsenal was the only southern club in the First Division, having been promoted there in 1904, though the strong performances of both Tottenham Hotspur and Southampton in the FA Cup had shown the obvious and growing strength of the rival Southern League. Major structural changes lay ahead.

The game itself was also changing, becoming less brutal and slightly more 'scientific', with systems of passing play now replacing aspects of the more traditional 'kick and rush' tactics. Tackling was still central, of course, and the brawny British shoulder charge was certainly not outlawed. But the charge was now permissible only if it was deemed to be neither 'violent nor dangerous'. England international William Bassett wrote in 1906 of the new flexible approaches to playing the game that 'the one-style team is not the successful team . . . if forwards cannot adapt themselves to all conditions they are not likely to be permanently successful'.[6] Liverpool would have to look to their mettle.

They began their return to First Division football with the veteran Doig in goal, but in October 1905 Tom Watson invested £340 in what would later become Chesterfield's factory for goalkeepers by signing Sam Hardy for the task. This was a brilliant piece of managerial business – Hardy was a magnificent keeper – and Watson was seldom beaten to the transfer punch. Later, a telegram about a Reds transfer target sent from a Liverpool scout to Watson went astray. It landed instead in the lap of the press, and the player was lost to Leicester Fosse. The next day, Watson changed the Liverpool telegraphic address to the distinctive 'goalkeeper' in order to rule out any more costly communication mishaps.

'Safe and Steady' Sam Hardy became the England goalkeeper from 1907, collecting 21 caps, and he displayed 'a rare, quiet competence', becoming an imposing fixture in the Liverpool defence for the next seven seasons.[7] Watson was pressed so rapidly and so decisively into the transfer market because Liverpool lost five of their first eight matches back in the top flight, conceding twenty goals in the process, including a 2–4 defeat at Goodison and a 0–5 humiliation at Aston Villa. The *Daily Post* certainly had it right when reviewing the Reds' defensive inadequacies during the events of a 'bewildering rapidity' at Goodison Park, where 'the multitude who on Saturday, by their numbers and enthusiasm, demonstrated the amazing influence which football exercises over the British peoples'. On the early condition of Liverpool FC, it opined that, 'West might work like a Trojan and Raisbeck be as ubiquitous as a sprite, but with a disheartened custodian [Doig] and full-back [reserve Murray] the game was up.' In stepped new signing Sam Hardy, and Liverpool never looked back.

Reds forward John Parkinson had broken his wrist in the opening match against Woolwich Arsenal, and he would play only nine times in the league. But with the rock-solid Hardy now on board, only 26 goals were conceded in the 30 Liverpool league matches that followed. Chester-born centre-forward Joe Hewitt had signed for Watson from Bolton Wanderers back in January 1904 for £150, but now he got his chance with an extended run alongside Sam Raybould and ended up top scorer with 23 goals. He supplied his entire life to Liverpool Football Club. After playing 164 times for Liverpool, scoring 71 goals, Hewitt later served the club as a coach, club steward and even press-box attendant over a 60-year period. From Stoke, Watson filched hard-working left-half Jimmy Bradley in September 1905, and the new man played 31 times in the league in the 1905–06 title season and 185 times in all for Liverpool, another typically astute signing. From 21 October 1905, when they played Nottingham Forest, Liverpool took 20 points from the next 22 on offer, and they were chasing the title rather than fighting relegation, as had been initially feared. The typical Liverpool XI in 1905–06, in 2–3–5 formation, was this one:

Liverpool FC, league title-winners, 1905–06

		Hardy		
	Dunlop		West	
	Parry	Raisbeck	Bradley	
Goddard	Robinson	Hewitt	Raybould	Cox

Of these players, Dunlop, Raisbeck, Parry, Raybould and Cox were all men who had survived from the 1900–01 title campaign. Cox had almost left Liverpool for Fulham, only to be forced to stay at Anfield, fortuitously, on a technicality following the late intervention of the FA. Of the dual title winners, arguably Dunlop, Raisbeck and Raybould all have a good case for consideration for inclusion in the club's greatest team of all time. Goddard was also a fantastic servant, and even the occasionally inconsistent Cox was considered 'the fastest left-winger playing today'.

The grey-haired Dunlop, a 'powerful punter' with great stamina, had made his debut in 1895 and ended up playing at the club for 15 seasons. Dunlop was a real leader, Watson's cohering figure in the 1905–06 Reds dressing-room, and he was a fair musician who would entertain the Liverpool players when they were away from home preparing for major cup ties. In his benefit-match programme in 1906, it was said that 'there was never one who, year in year out, has given such wholehearted service as Dunlop has to Liverpool'. It was a fitting tribute to a totally committed club man.

By December 1905, when Notts County were hosted at Anfield, according to the *Football Echo*, Tom Watson's work was apparent to all. 'The attitude from start to finish was excellent . . . The Reds were engaged in a very pretty attack which showed off the scientific methods of the Liverpool front line to perfection.' Liverpool were top of the table with a 2–0 victory, and they rarely looked like conceding their advantage. In March 1906, it was Middlesbrough's turn to suffer at Anfield, clouted 6–1, with local reserve forward 'lively Jack [Carlin] of Wavertree' helping himself to two goals. According to the by now near-poetic *Liverpool Echo*, this was a performance of 'such dash, such virile shooting, feeding and racing' that 'the Reds were in excelsis'. Not to be outdone on the poetry front, the *Daily Post* said more simply, 'The Reds were standing on velvet.' What could stop this title charge?

Actually, a 0–3 league defeat next up at Notts County came as quite a jarring shock to the Liverpool system. There was little poetry, and not even too much pretty prose, here. But a stirring 2–1 win at title rivals Preston North End, with utility man Tom Chorlton grabbing a priceless goal, put Liverpool back on track for two forthcoming derby matches: one in an FA Cup semi-final at Villa Park on 31 March, the other in a league meeting at Anfield on Good Friday. Liverpool had certainly been favoured by good fortune in the FA Cup draw, comfortably beating Leicester Fosse, Barnsley, Brentford and Southampton all at home, conceding only one goal and thus avoiding any First Division Football League opposition. Now here was another opportunity for the Reds to strike for a possible league and FA Cup Double. Everton, on the other hand, had been uncompetitive in the league and so could focus strongly on the cup.

Because of its inclusiveness and history, the FA Cup was still seen in 1906 as more of a national 'championship' than was the Football League. But injuries kept key men Cox and Raybould out of the Liverpool line-up, and the first real signs of tiredness had also started to show in the Anfield ranks. Two Everton goals within two minutes in the second half settled it. The second, from Hardman, drifted in past a 'fascinated' (transfixed) Hardy and resulted from the keeper dropping the initial strike, having 'kept out a dozen worse shots'. A goalkeeper, alas, is always remembered for the key mistakes, not his great saves. 'There was more excitement and sensation merged into ninety seconds,' said the *Daily Post*, 'than the whole ninety minutes. It was all over with the Reds then.'

Liverpool sought some revenge for this grave FA Cup disappointment in the vital league derby fixture on 13 April, and with Everton fans keenly anticipating the FA Cup final, a much larger than normal holiday crowd of 33,000 turned up for the contest, some of whom forced the gates and spilled onto the pitch. 'The referee and officials had great trouble in placing the encroaching crowd,' reported the *Daily Post*, 'so that the touchline and corner flags were clear enough to proceed with the game.' This excited supporter disruption went on throughout the match, and as Everton advanced in the first half 'Hardy, who was impeded by some of the spectators, emerged from his charge to clutch the leather from Young'. Sam Hardy was usually unflappable, immovable, but the intruding spectators, who now assembled in 'deep ranks' along the touchlines, had definitely ruined his concentration. He dropped the ball again following this easy save, with Everton's Jack Taylor on hand to net the gift. This error gave the Blues an undeserved – and a crowd-assisted – half-time lead.

It took fully 25 minutes even to get the game restarted because of further 'difficulties' with the crowd, but in one of Liverpool's 'hot attacks' in the second half Taylor fouled Parkinson in the penalty area, and Alf West converted from the spot 'amidst terrific acclamation'. Rival spectators now held their breath and struggled to keep each other off the field of play. Liverpool continued to press, but there would be no more goals – or pitch invasions. It was probably fortunate that things remained even at one-all so that all spectators could return home peaceably, honour satisfied on both sides. As a result of the shared spoils, Liverpool were still top, and a confident Everton now faced fancied Newcastle United in the FA Cup final. Local 'Dicky Sams' were beginning to think of Merseyside football glory once more: a league and FA Cup Double, different clubs, one city, one big party.

At bottom club Wolves on 14 April 1906, the hosts put up a 'capital fight' against the prospective champions Liverpool, but in a 'rough and tumble' scrappy match 'class and training told its inevitable tale'. With the injured Raybould and Cox now out for the season, goals by Hewitt and Goddard sealed the Reds' win. But it was nearer the Liverpool goal that the victory was really forged. 'The half-back line showed splendid confidence in their own ability,' judged the *Daily Post*. 'Neither Raisbeck, Parry nor Bradley ever for a moment lost their heads.' Nor had they done so for most of the campaign.

In the penultimate round of fixtures, Liverpool lost away to Bolton Wanderers, 2–3, with the last ten minutes 'almost painful as each side attacked in turn'. But it was of no matter. The pressure of the chase also told on the Anfield club's closest challengers, Preston North End, who lost 0–2 at Sunderland on the same day and thus conceded the title to Liverpool. When the sheepishly defeated but triumphant Anfield men arrived back at Exchange Station at nine o'clock that night, they were met by 'several hundreds of enthusiasts who cheered the players lustily and escorted them to their waggonette'. Ordinary travellers were reported to have joined in the celebrations when it was reported to them that the league champions were back in town. Inevitably, the Sandon Hotel waited for a party that continued long into the misty Merseyside night.

A HOUSE DIVIDED AGAINST ITSELF

In reviewing Liverpool FC's extraordinary recent history, the *Football Echo* of 17 April 1906 referred delicately and quixotically in a 'comment' column to Tom Watson's relegation year as a 'quaint experience'. It was a nice touch. But the author also had no doubt that the Liverpool manager 'has worked indefatigably all the time, and to a large extent the success now achieved may be ascribed to the excellent spirit which he contrives to infuse into the team'. It was true that the Watson 'of the iron nerves' had not gone in for signing star players or for recruiting an over-large squad that might risk festering discontent. Liverpool FC were a very tightly knit group: most of the players lived very close to the Anfield stadium, between Breckfield Road and Oakfield Road. Raisbeck lived at 16 Elsie Road, Parry and Dunlop on Arkles Road. Sam Raybould lived on Lyon Road, James Bradley on Thirlmere Road and Arthur Goddard on Walton Breck Road.

Words of praise were also saved for club trainer Bill Connell and even the Anfield groundsman. The wily Connell was soon featured in the local press endorsing 'Zam-buk', a skin cure for cuts and bruises. The *Echo* trusted that ticket prices would not be increased next season 'when the new ground, which is to be started within a week, is in readiness'. Typically, club chairman Councillor Edwin Berry commented that the Liverpool club was looking to sign only 'class men' (not simply class *players*), and it was noted that Liverpool 'have fewer players on their list than any other club in the First Division'. Maybe this was part of their success? The *Liverpool Echo* further pointed out that in 1905–06 'every position has been filled by a tryer, and there are not more than three outfield brilliants [by which it meant Raisbeck, Bradley and Dunlop]. It is collectively that the Reds were superior to opponents.' This was indeed a championship win in the typical Liverpool Way.

This left only the ritual of a title celebration for Liverpool and their supporters to see out at home against Sheffield United (a valedictory 3–1 win) in a now largely redundant fixture that was scheduled, nevertheless, for the same kick-off time and day as the FA Cup final at Crystal Palace. Significantly, when news of Everton's FA Cup-winning goal finally reached Anfield, 'This was the signal for tumultuous cheering, which did not subside for several minutes.' Unlike some of their Blue rivals, Liverpool supporters seemed genuinely pleased at their neighbours' – and the city's – success. The crowd that welcomed the Everton party back to Lime Street later that night was reportedly 'immensely good-humoured, and partisans of both Liverpool and Everton clubs shared alike in the enthusiasm'. At the civic reception that followed for Everton at Central Station, Liverpool FC directors were present to hear the lord mayor say that the city was in a position no other had experienced and that 'at least half [only half?] of the male citizens of Liverpool were sympathisers with the game of football'. He argued that there was no ill-feeling in the rival camps and 'trusted for years to come there might be a good feeling between the two clubs and that they might work together in harmony and good fellowship'.

It was a nice idea, this cosy football bond, one born out of a moment of near-unique twin football success for the city. But it was unlikely to last, and no fan of either club was liable to apologise too much for that. As a correspondent to the *Evening Express* put it on 26 April 1906, perhaps just a little *too* bleakly:

> Actually, healthy rivalry cannot but have a beneficial influence, but I fear that generous, kindly rivalry is sadly lacking in the ranks of our local clubs. The partisanship is bigoted: too many of each club's supporters are utterly intolerant of the other club's merits; each set of followers are carping critics of the other side. In short . . . we are a house divided, against itself.

For the *Daily Post*, a combination of 'stout hearts, good constitutions and a determination to overcome difficulties' had aided Liverpool in surviving their horrendous start to 1905–06, although this sounded perhaps more like the making of a resolute mountaineering club rather than that of a champion football team.

It was certainly some achievement to come back from the foothill depths of 1904. Two titles in two seasons: from Second Division champions to champions of the Football League in a matter of months. Indeed, it had been a tumultuous six years for the club and for Tom Watson: league champions in 1901; twelfth; fifth; relegated; champions of Division Two; and league champions again in 1906. 'Roller coaster' seems a modest description. In a speech at the first AGM of the 'new' Liverpool FC in June 1906, Watson (to loud laughter) twinkled that the club 'had always been [one] of ups and downs'. He trusted that 'they had finished with the latter, and that upwards was their future motion'. There followed a loud crescendo of applause.

Today, of course, few top manager–coaches would have survived the shock of a mid-period demotion and still be in office to make this kind of cheeky little observation. But this was a different age, and this Liverpool board believed in their manager, who, in turn, believed in his players. In any case, there were few authentic football managers in the game in 1906 and, while crowds harangued players and referees, there was certainly no media-induced sacking culture to identify and harass them. Average gates at Liverpool in 1905–06 at 17,736 exceeded those at neighbours Everton (15,920) for the first time, though receipts at Everton still beat those at Liverpool. The total balance available at Anfield in June 1906 amounted to a very healthy £3,360. The champions had (officially at least) paid their players £4,440, less than Everton's £5,270, and wages made up about 35 per cent of gate-receipts income – happy days indeed. With the promise that the new Anfield stadium would be 'considerably altered and improved' and would be 'one of the best equipped in England' by September 1906, good times surely lay ahead again for Liverpool Football Club. You think?

THE END OF A STADIUM ERA

Before the remodelling of Anfield in 1906, the Liverpool stadium was made up, like most others of the time, of irregular timber crush barriers, unterraced earth and ash slopes, and very basic iron and timber flat-stand roofs covering wooden bench seats. There was, as yet, no complete outer wall to offer either definition or convincing security. The chimneys of John Houlding's Stanley House home could clearly be seen from the uncovered Kop as they jutted out over the modest Anfield Road covered terrace.[8] This was no haven of early modern comfort or prestige, and it was hardly a fitting home for the 1906 Football League champions.

Not that the situation for local football in Liverpool was much better. In 1908, the city had a maximum of 81 football pitches for use by local clubs compared to 360 in Manchester. This situation led to local campaigns to better resource the woeful participation side of the sport on Merseyside.[9] But the early years of the new century would produce something of a revolution in building design, technology and engineering. Iron was replaced by precision-made standardised steel for stanchions, stairways and beams, for example, and also, crucially, reinforced concrete was used to replace the sometimes unstable fire-risk wooden structures in buildings, including football grounds.[10]

As professional football expanded at an astonishing rate in British cities, so the new club owners sought ways of increasing stadium capacity and improving customer comfort, and also of maximising returns on their investment. The brilliant young Scottish engineer Archibald Leitch was a revolutionary figure in stadium design. But he had the horrifying experience of attending the Scotland v. England match at Ibrox Park in 1902 when the 'flimsy and insubstantial' wooden stands he had designed collapsed before his eyes. Twenty-six people were killed and five hundred and sixteen injured. Scotland fans, oblivious to the scale of the disaster – there was no public address system in operation – chaired off a home hero, the future Liverpool recruit Teddy Doig. The devastated goalkeeper was clearly in tears.[11] Unsurprisingly, Leitch was emotionally drained by these events, but he was also determined to use the new advances in technology and materials to build bigger and safer stands at British football grounds. He moved the family home to Blundellsands, just north of Liverpool, in 1909, having worked with both the Liverpool and Everton clubs in the redesign of two of the premier football grounds in England.

On 25 August 1906, the *Liverpool Echo* provided an enticing glimpse of what would be the new Anfield, designed by the precocious 31-year-old Leitch, with its walled-in 'fancy brick setting', large exit gates on all four sides, raised pitch (by five feet) and its extended 'elevated terrace consisting of 132 tiers of steps, which will afford space for something like 20,000 spectators'. Only the Anfield Road end would survive unaltered. This new development constituted an extraordinary vision of the new, modern era of British sport. The original plans laid out in June 1906 had also included a roof over the Spion Kop, newly named by sports editor of the *Liverpool Echo* Ernest Edwards. But this cover would not be added until 1928 and by a different architect, local man Joseph Watson Cabre. The topmast of the SS *Great Eastern*, one of the world's first iron ships, had been salvaged when the ship was broken up, and it was floated up the Mersey. It was then hauled by horse to the Anfield ground, where it had first been raised inside the corner of the Oakfield Road outer wall in 1891, presumably to signal the city's connection with the sea and seafaring.[12] The new stadium incorporated the mast, and it remains outside the Kop to this day.

'The entire scheme [of 1906–07],' the *Echo* continued, 'is modelled on a new departure from what football grounds are generally supposed to be and when completed will provide ample space for about 60,000 visitors.' This improbable projected figure seemed astonishing. It dwarfed the official Anfield capacity in 1905 and, crucially, was larger than that at Goodison Park. The jewel of the Leitch plan was to resite the then current main stand (opened in 1894) to the Kemlyn Road side of the ground and replace it with a completely new structure, combining a seated area with a standing paddock in front. It was Leitch's first football stand made in reinforced concrete, and it was lauded by building-design experts for its 'elastic strength' and 'durability'. It was probably the first of its kind in Britain. The curved gable of the new main stand would be the characteristic Leitch signature for Anfield until it was replaced by a much more functional and ugly flat roof in 1970.

Impressed and alarmed in equal measure by the imposing Anfield redevelopment, in 1908 neighbours Everton hired Leitch to rebuild their own new main stand to keep pace with their rivals across Stanley Park. A journalist duly described the new 80-ft-high Goodison Park monster edifice as the 'Mauretania Stand', after the world's largest ship.[13]

Sadly, the league champions Liverpool could not match in their performances the obvious grandeur of their new surroundings. Perhaps the players missed the greater intimacy and hostility of the old stadium? Whatever the reasons, after a scrambled first-day home win against relegation candidates Stoke, there followed two draws and five consecutive defeats in the league for Liverpool, including a 1–2 home loss against Everton. Third from bottom with four points from eight matches, the *Liverpool Courier* deemed that 'drastic action' would have to be taken to resurrect a campaign that so far had brought 'no credit to an organisation with the strength and resources of Liverpool'. Problems clearly lay at both ends of the pitch: up front 'chance after chance was thrown away', while at the back an unusually uncertain Sam Hardy 'shared . . . the demoralisation of his colleagues. He is not altogether blameless.' With a small squad, serious injuries to Dunlop, West and Parry all contributed to growing defensive uncertainty, while in the forwards Joe Hewitt lost both fitness and form, and no one came in to replace his vital goals. Left-sided attacker Bill McPherson, signed for £200 from St Mirren in August 1906, eventually contributed a useful ten goals in twenty-eight league games.

By the middle of October 1906, with a trip to Bury in the offing, the local scribes concluded, not unreasonably, that Liverpool's form had been 'atrociously disappointing'. The directors (no mention of Tom Watson here) took a 'strong step' by leaving out Cox from the forwards, and the tide turned for the champions with a 3–1 win, which showed some of the 'dash and spirit' previously lacking. Gone was the current pattern of possession and pressure without the finish, and in its place was the penetration of old, with Raybould weighing in with two familiar goals. The next eight matches brought six Liverpool wins and just two defeats, and included a 6–1 home mauling of Preston and a 'perfect farce' of a 5–1 Anfield victory against an eight-man Notts County. The visitors had left-back Jack Montgomery ordered off for flooring Raybould and two men carried off.

Liverpool had now climbed to seventh place, six points behind leaders Everton. By the time the squad took to their Christmas quarters in Southport, facing three games in five days, hopes were even high of another title challenge. But instead it was five goal-less Liverpool performances that followed, four of them defeats, and a slide down to 14th place. 'Unless some revolutionary alteration is seen,' said the *Liverpool Courier* after a January 1907 0–2 reverse at Blackburn, 'the team is certain to drop still lower and further besmirch the reputation of league champions.' New man McPherson 'was unable to do the right thing at the critical moment', while some truly great Liverpool players of this era were now obviously in decline. 'Bradley was the best of a very moderate trio of halves, and Raisbeck the worst . . . an accurate pass was rarely seen among the whole team.'

After this drought, there were goals galore at the Sunderland v. Liverpool fixture on 19 January 1907, ten of them, in an amazing 5–5 draw. But Liverpool had been 4–1 up at half-time, succumbing later to some very dubious offside and penalty decisions by a poor replacement referee that let the 'kick and rush' Wearsiders back into the match. Later, in March at Aston Villa, another referee, a Mr Mason, was delayed by rail problems, as was the Liverpool left-back Tom Chorlton. The match at Villa Park was delayed by some 15 minutes, with an obviously embarrassed Chorlton taking the pitch only after the late start in a sorry 0–4 Liverpool defeat. With Liverpool ejected from the FA Cup by eventual winners The Wednesday, some pride was at least salvaged for the Reds in a scrappy 0–0 draw with Everton at Goodison Park. But only one win in the last eight league fixtures (and this against relegated Derby County) meant an unceremonious slide down to a final 15th position. 'It is doubtful that such a disastrous month as April has ever been experienced,' opined the Liverpool press.

The local post-mortems pointed to injury and loss of form as the key factors in the slump, which meant that 'the team had to be constantly reshuffled, fore and aft'. West and Dunlop were sorely missed. The latter's replacement, Percy Saul, signed from Plymouth Argyle, was 'erratic' before eventually finding his feet. This chopping and changing was the exact opposite of the approach in the title year, when the same reliable Liverpool team seemed to play match after match. But the crucial figure here was really Raisbeck, who had shown poor form at the start and had missed matches later through injury. The *Daily Post* on 29 April 1907 was troubled:

> Raisbeck is beyond comparison. Raisbeck has been for years the Liver's lucky star – a great, outstanding personality, not only in his team but in the football firmament . . . Without Alex Raisbeck Liverpool would have to be born again, so to speak. That the redoubtable half-back may regain health and strength during the recess is the earnest prayer of everyone. It is, however, probably a subject which will cause the executive most serious deliberation.

In September 1907, the *Liverpool Echo* noted Raisbeck's absence from the Liverpool line-up once more, 'as one never likes to even contemplate what might happen in his absence'. This was no serious injury: Raisbeck was suffering from a rather strong dose of diarrhoea. But he would play only twenty-three league fixtures for two goals in 1907–08, with defender Dunlop restricted to just two appearances. The inestimable Raybould had also now been sold to Sunderland, with Joe Hewitt taking over the main striker duties and scoring a decent 21 league goals – no one else got into double figures. Inside-forward Charlie Hewitt joined from Spurs for £75 in August, which was one year later than he had hoped. His Anfield career was short enough – just 16 matches. Hewitt had joined what was once a great team that was now winding down, it seemed – one shored up, but not improved, by bit-part signings like his own.

'HURRAH FOR THE REDS'

The *Liverpool Echo* on 7 September 1907 came up with a different and novel explanation of Liverpool's sudden fall from grace – a *lack* of Scots: only one, McPherson, had played in a recent match. 'This is a transformation indeed,' said the *Echo* wryly, 'but one unattended with success.'

One Liverpool fan, a W. Seddon from Tuebrook, even came up with a rallying song, 'Hurrah for the Reds', which appeared in the press on 31 August 1907, aimed to rouse the team and the club's fans. Were Liverpool fans already singing collectively at matches? Certainly, Manchester City supporters were singing odes to their favourites, especially Billy Meredith. And supporters 'borrowed' songs and catchphrases from the music hall at this time – Sheffield United fans sang the drinking song 'The Rowdy, Dowdy Boys', for example.[14] It seems likely that the strong 'performance' culture and oral tradition on Merseyside would have produced early local versions of their own songs at football, though the evidence is actually quite scarce. In an FA Cup replay at Barnsley in 1914, the *Liverpool Echo* reported that Reds supporters had 'transposed the song of 1906 and made it "Aye, Aye, Lacey scored the goals".' So singing does seem to have been going on in sections of the home crowd at Anfield at around this time. Mr Seddon's early 'masterpiece' certainly hints at a great oral tradition around support for the Reds, one that is still evident more than a century later. It went:

> Hurrah for the boys to play the game
> Hurrah for the Reds
> Hurrah for the boys, there's none can tame
> Hurrah for the Reds
> There's Hewitt and Mac to lead the attack
> With Hardy to hold the fort, boys
> There's Goddard and Cox and Raisbeck the fox
> And more to the good old sorts, boys
> Hurrah! Hurrah! Hurrah! Hurrah!
> Hurrah for the Reds.

This typically stirring anthem might even have been behind an early 2–0 home win against Blackburn Rovers in September, in which the referee was 'as blind as justice', according to the *Football Echo*, for disallowing a 'lovely, perfect' home goal by Joe Hewitt. The Rovers were themselves encouraged 'by some Blackburn choristers on the Spion Kop'.

In November, the *Echo* claimed that it was quite justified to complain about the class of football recently served up by Liverpool, which had been 'of the poorest description', and even a 6–0 home rout of Notts County had served up first-half fare that was full of 'wild tackling, totally inaccurate passing and dreary football'. These were high standards indeed. Fortunately, Joe Hewitt was 'in rare trim', dishing up a hat-trick past visiting keeper Albert Iremonger. Liverpool were now sixth after 12 matches, a 4–2 victory at Everton comfortably on board. But the Reds were already nine points behind early leaders Manchester United. Inconsistency was the only reliable here, and by an early kick-off on Christmas Day the Reds were on the slide once more, losing 1–4 at home to newly arrived Chelsea.

After this latest defeat came a signal about the precarious economics of the sport and the lowly status and power of professional players. Rather than return home to their families, the Liverpool squad, astonishingly, was required by the club's board to travel immediately to play Woolwich Arsenal at distant Plumstead in a Boxing Day *friendly* match (2–2). Presumably, this trip was agreed simply for a cut of the gate. The Reds caught a train to London at 4.05 p.m. on Christmas Day, 1907, after the home thrashing by Chelsea. One can only imagine the atmosphere in the team's carriage. The *Echo* duly noted that 'more than one of the players objected to this unnecessary addition to an ordinarily long programme'. But there was no comeback – these employees simply did their job.

What was the highlight of the rest of this forgettable season? What about Liverpool seven, runaway league-leaders Manchester United four on Wednesday, 25 March 1908? 'Eleven goals for sixpence!' the *Echo* crowed about an evening fixture for which 'atrocious weather' limited the crowd to fewer than 10,000 souls. 'Yesterday the Redbreasts were brilliant,' wrote a local scribe – although this particular moniker for Liverpool FC had no possible hope of catching on. Ted Doig, temporarily back in the Liverpool goal for Sam Hardy, had a poor time of it, but his teammates revelled in the heavy going. Joe Hewitt, Bill McPherson and Robbie Robinson shared the goals as Liverpool climbed to seventh in the table. Alas, it would get no better. Indeed, by the time Aston Villa had inflicted a 1–5 hammering in April, in a tight league Liverpool were just three points off the relegation places. Ronald Orr, a chunky, small and direct Scotland international inside-left, had made his reputation at recent champions Newcastle United, and Liverpool now snapped him up in April 1908 for £350 as an insurance against the drop. He was good value, too, scoring against Villa and claiming a total of five vital goals in his seven appearances as the season leaked away. Praising the uncomplicated new signing, the *Echo* asked, rhetorically, in closing, 'Do we not overestimate the value of dribbling and rather undercut the praise for good, hard, well-directed shots?' Stylish play or results by any means? The debate would continue.

ANFIELD TROUBLE – ON AND OFF THE PITCH

Orr's admirable 20 goals in 33 league matches could not save the following 1908–09 season from being another mediocre campaign for the Reds, topped off by a 2–3 second-round home defeat in the FA Cup to lowly Norwich City. The failures to beat Everton at Anfield were also now beginning to stack up; a 0–1 loss in October meant no Reds victory in the Merseyside derby so far that century. But in the spring and summer of 1909 much larger issues were on the horizon – the possible further expansion of the Football League and potential players' industrial action. In March 1909, the Southern League suggested an amalgamation with the

Football League in order to produce a 60-club national league, comprising the current First Division and two Second Divisions, north and south. The Football League (which already housed six 'southern' clubs) rejected the proposal, partly, it was argued, because some league officials feared that it was beginning to lose its provincial character and spirit and to assume 'too much of a London complexion'.[15] It was only after the First World War that the idea of a league competition for football really chimed fully with wider cultural, social and economic developments in Britain around the concept of the 'national'.

Despite the historically strong links between drink and football, the game at this time was also put forward by its supporters as a boon to the temperance movement. An FA official argued that in Liverpool dock workers tended to 'rush home from work and hand over their wages before going to the match' whereas in the summer months there was a tendency for them to 'spend their money before they reached home', often in a pub.[16]

On the players' front, the Football League continued to oppose the FA's rule 31, which prohibited the payments of bonuses to players. But the FA retorted that dangling money to induce players to win matches was degrading and confirmed the view that business had overtaken the sport. It was a classic stand-off between the league professionals and the FA amateurs. The new players' union, led by representatives of the 1908 league champions, the already glamorous Manchester United, sought protection and strength in this dispute by affiliating with the Federation of Trade Unions in 1909. This move so appalled both the FA and the Football League at a time when strikes and riots were becoming a common feature of industrial Britain that they promptly withdrew their recognition from the players' union. Far from backing down, however, the players threatened to strike, only withdrawing at the eleventh hour as clubs assembled squads of amateurs ready to fulfil fixtures. A number of top Liverpool players even refused to re-sign their contracts. Public support for the players – and the union members' resolution – began to fade. In April 1910, the rule on the payment of bonuses was finally amended, but rule 30, restricting the maximum wage to £4, remained. What clubs wanted to pay their players in bonuses was now down to them, and professionals could still not initiate their own transfer. In effect, the clubs still held all the cards.[17]

The following season (1909–10) produced storm damage to the Anfield Road stand, which cost some £1,500 to renovate. Manchester United were about to unveil their own 80,000 capacity Edwardian 'super stadium' at Old Trafford in 1910, and so the stadium advances on Merseyside would soon be overshadowed by their regional rivals. On the field, Liverpool were a highly creditable second in the league, losing out to a superior Aston Villa, with 78 goals scored. It was important that the Reds upped their game, according to a journalist for the *Cricket and Football Field* on 5 June 1909, because 'spectators nowadays will pay only for the best article'. This improved league performance more than counteracted a 0–2 first-round FA Cup exit at Bristol City.

Tom Watson was slowly rebuilding, breaking up the 1906 Liverpool championship team. Both West and Dunlop were effectively gone, and in 1909 Watson brought in half-back James 'Head Up' Harrop from Rotherham as a possible future replacement for the incomparable Raisbeck. Harrop matched Raisbeck in his intelligence, if not in his all-round game. The Liverpool legend was eventually sold to Partick Thistle in June 1909 for £500, but he would return later to give further service to the club.

The highly capable Harrop stayed at Liverpool for four years before moving on to star for Aston Villa in the 1913 FA Cup final. The feisty Scot John McDonald replaced Cox on the left-wing and offered high-quality crosses at pace. His compatriot, inside-right Jimmy Stewart, signed from Motherwell, produced 18 goals in 37 league matches in his first influential season. But the main reason for the Liverpool league revival was the form of a local man, Bootle-born centre-forward Jack Parkinson, who had made his debut at the club back in 1903. Parkinson had since struggled with injury, but he now grabbed his chance with both feet. Eight times he scored more than two goals in a league match in 1909–10, including four in a 7–3 Anfield drubbing of Nottingham Forest in April. Parkinson and Orr scored the goals that satisfyingly beat league-champions elect Aston Villa at Anfield on 30 April 1910, the closing day of the season, but it was too little, too late to affect the title outcome.

The Villa match also publicly revealed the very real hooligan potential of the Liverpool crowd, especially if it was aroused by perceived unfairness on the pitch. From the evidence we have, football crowds at this time seem to have been made up mainly of slightly older male sections of the 'respectable' working class, though there were younger fans, female supporters and also some middle-class followers, too, especially in the Anfield seats. Hooliganism at football at this time typically involved low-level incivilities, such as pouring beer on rivals, running onto the pitch 'for a laugh', pelting the visiting mascot with fruit or peel, gambling, jostling, and general rowdiness on streets and in local bars.[18] But these latest incidents in and around Anfield for the visit of Villa were of a rather different order. Their source was injury to the Liverpool goalkeeper Sam Hardy, who dislocated his wrist after an ugly collision with the long-serving Villa centre-forward Harry Hampton.

Hampton was a man who, due to his 'dashing propensities', according to the local press, already had an 'unenviable reputation' in the city. This meant that the England international enjoyed putting himself about on the pitch. Reds fans started 'booing, hooting and yelling' for Hampton to be sent off, and referee Ibbotson threatened to halt the match. Liverpool captain Artie Goddard appealed to the crowd, 'owing to a stone thrown from the spectators striking [Villa forward Joe] Bache above the eye, necessitating the attention of the trainer'. When matters eventually calmed down, Goddard went in the home goal, and Robbie Robinson 'worked himself to a standstill' in order to secure a famous Liverpool victory. But then the fun really started, as the *Evening Express* of 2 May 1910 reported:

> At the end of the match the brake conveying the Villa players to the city was followed by a yelling crowd of youths and boys who pelted the occupants for some considerable distance. The brake was stopped and one or two of the ringleaders marked out. There was some sharp scuffling and Hunter, one of the Villa players who had accompanied the team to Liverpool, received a severe blow to the face. In a few seconds the police arrived on the scene.

Fights such as this between visiting players and local spectators were unusual, but the *Evening Express* also noted the recent 'disgraceful barracking' at Anfield of the injured Notts County full-back Bert Morley. Missiles had also been thrown by the Liverpool crowd at the Sheffield defender Bob Bensen. It was agreed that this sort of incident 'is getting the Anfield ground an unenviable reputation'. In reply, a correspondent calling himself 'Anfielder' showed little remorse, assuring the *Evening Express* that Liverpool supporters would not settle for the 'laxity of certain referees' in ignoring illegal tripping.

There seems to have been no FA action taken as a result of these street assaults – the main incidents took place away from the ground, after all. But they marked out the real risks sometimes posed to visiting players and officials at Liverpool and elsewhere when locals were roused by perceived wrongdoing. Ironically, rival fans might have been rather less at risk at this time.

SEE-SAW LIVERPOOL

At the club's AGM in June 1910, the Liverpool board reflected on the union 'agitation' of the previous summer and reported that the club was 'in a healthier position, so far as feelings between directors and players were concerned, than for years'. It was also announced that 'an appeal for money to meet the demands of summer wages met with a generous response'. Fans would have to dip into their pockets once more. Total income was £12,931, and income over expenditure stood at a healthy £4,435, with average home attendances up from 17,660 to 21,620 (thus overtaking Everton once again). The chairman remarked that the quality of the football seen at Anfield during the season had been 'most creditable', adding that 'those who had witnessed the memorable match against Newcastle United would never forget it'.

It is strange that matches between Liverpool and Newcastle should crop up as items of note over the next 100 years. But this meeting, on 4 December 1909, was a rare classic. 'One of the most remarkable games in the history of the league,' argued the *Liverpool Courier*, 'and certainly the most sensational that has been witnessed in Liverpool.' Albert Shepherd had scored four times before half-time for the then league champions Newcastle, who led 2–5 at the break. But the visitors were 'simply overwhelmed' in the second half. Goals from Parkinson and Orr revived Liverpool. 'When Orr equalised from a scrimmage the crowd nearly went frantic with delight. Newcastle were absolutely outplayed.' Goddard headed the late winner for a quite breathless 6–5 home win – and there could well have been more goals.

After this brief promise and excitement, the years leading up to the First World War were eventful ones for the city, if very disappointing ones indeed for Liverpool Football Club. League finishes of 13th, 17th (saved from possible relegation in 1911–12 only by a late run of four victories in the last six matches), 12th, 16th and then 14th in 1914–15 were hardly what the Anfield board and the Liverpool public had expected, especially after pushing Villa so close to the title in 1910. Until 1913–14, neither were there lengthy FA Cup runs for Liverpool to offer its supporters compensation for lack of success in the league.

Meanwhile, in the city of Liverpool, as in other great British cities, unemployment and claims for better wages and working conditions for working people continued to ravage communities and dull the senses as national strikes were now threatened and public disorder erupted. Even as the new 'skyscraper' Royal Liver Building was regally unveiled on the Merseyside seafront in August 1911, strikes by local dockers and other transport workers in Liverpool brought the British Army onto the streets of Merseyside to keep order. Eighty thousand people turned out in Lime Street to demonstrate, and the Riot Act was read as crowds refused to disperse. Word spread: the *New York Times* on 17 August reported that bread supplies in Liverpool were almost exhausted and that soldiers now bivouacked at Edge Hill had been ordered not to shoot over the heads of rioters but to aim their guns at 'apparent ringleaders' of the mob. Two unarmed local men were shot dead as crowds attacked vans conveying striker prisoners to Walton Prison. Liverpool streets around the Vauxhall and Scotland Road areas, always simmering with tribal enmities and the privations of poverty, suddenly came to the boil, too, hinting at the underlying tensions in the city.

After this tumult eventually subsided, the effects of growing unemployment in the city lived on. 'The reading room adjoining the museum in William Brown Street is not a cheerful place to visit,' reported the *Evening Express* on 3 May 1912. 'There is a suggestion there of slowly dying hope. Persons of all ages are to be found there, from boys who dream of the world of work as a pleasant land . . . to old men, grey, haggard and disillusioned.' More uplifting perhaps was the sight of the construction, early in 1913, of the extraordinary white Palace of Industries building on the Edge Lane Hall Estate for the Liverpool Exhibition of that year. In 1906, the Street Betting Act had outlawed betting on public streets in Britain, but gambling was as rife in Liverpool as it was in all major British cities, and arrests were frequently made of people who were attempting to organise coupons for football betting, either on the street or out of their own homes. It seemed to many commentators as if the legislation revealed a class bias by effectively criminalising popular working-class leisure. It offered 'one law for the rich and another for the poor'.[19]

Meanwhile, the laws of football continued in their own refinement. In 1912, goalkeepers were reined in to handling inside the penalty area only, and in 1913 defending players were required to retreat ten yards from free-kicks. On 12 May 1912, the players of Swindon Town FC spent the evening at the Empire Theatre and the Adelphi in Liverpool before sailing on the SS *Ortega* the next day for an eight-match tour of Argentina. Football was increasingly an international sport, one that the English professed to both spread and dominate. The Merseyside press reminded its readers accordingly that cosmopolitan Everton Football Club had already played 22 times abroad and had yet to be beaten.

At the Liverpool FC AGM in May 1912, a brave shareholder complained that results for the club had actually been better in 1906 when less money had been spent on signing players. Chairman John McKenna replied that he thought the directors could hardly be blamed for spending *more* money on players today than six years ago. Another shareholder argued that there should be 'less experiments with veteran players' while yet another asked why Harrop, Hardy and John McDonald had all not been re-signed, to which the chairman replied that owing to what had happened last season – when Sam Hardy had apparently refused to move to the area – Liverpool 'were going to insist in future that their players should reside in the district'. The chairman now asked, rather defensively, whether any supporter in the meeting could point to a club with *more* honours after such a short history. One shareholder responded sharply, and to loud laughter, 'Has any club had a more see-saw existence than what the Liverpool club has had?'

What exactly was wrong with Liverpool Football Club during this period? Its 'old failing', according to the *Evening Express* in 1913, was not converting chances. 'Liverpool's forwards should know that goals count,' it argued, helpfully. 'A good motto for forwards: Get Goals!' As a remedy, the Wexford-born Ireland international left-winger Bill Lacey was signed from Everton in February 1912 in a swap deal the Blues would live to regret. Lacey added pep and goals to Liverpool for the next 12 years. And yet it was long-term, mainly *defensive*, recruitment for the new era that continued apace, a Tom Watson policy that would herald much better days for the club soon after the war.

In September 1910, Bolton-born right-back and future Liverpool and England captain Ephraim Longworth made his debut for Liverpool, the first of 490 consistently excellent appearances in peacetime and at war for the club. On 31 May 1912, the *Evening Express* reported that a Bootle-born full-back or wing-half, Walter Wadsworth, had also signed professionally, having 'last season assisted Ormskirk with distinction'. The fearless 'Big Waddy' would prove a crucial figure and local leader in the dual championship-winning team of the 1920s. Scottish left-sided defender and dead-ball specialist Donald McKinlay signed in 1910 from a local club in Glasgow, an inspired Watson discovery this one, a man who went on to give Liverpool 19 years of near-unblemished service.

With Longworth and Wadsworth, McKinlay became the club's new defensive shield in the early interwar years. Finally, on New Year's Day 1913, those Liverpool supporters who had stilled their hangovers sufficiently to travel to Newcastle would have seen the first glimpse, in a 0–0 draw, of the final defensive cog for the new Liverpool of the 1920s. Guarding the visitors' goal that day was a young goalkeeper who would become a legend, the brusque and brilliant Irishman Elisha Scott. It was reported later that young Scott had an injured (possibly broken) arm but chose to play this match nevertheless. Newcastle United instantly offered Liverpool £1,000 for the goalkeeper. The offer was turned down. In goal, at least, the Reds' future could reliably take care of itself.

But back in the present, Liverpool's star had sunk low enough for the team to be accused in a letter to the *Fulham Times* in March 1913 by the Fulham and Woolwich Arsenal director H.G. Norris of lacking the necessary 'desire' when losing at home to relegation-threatened Chelsea. In short, Norris sniffed a fix. New Liverpool club captain Ephraim Longworth responded with indignation. In a rare interview given in the *Evening Express* on 5 April, he expressed his disquiet that Norris should have 'led the man in the street to infer that the

Liverpool players deliberately lay down and allowed the other side to win . . . There is not an atom of truth in the suggestion.' The FA and Football League inquiry that followed could also find no proof, even if there were certainly plenty of poor performances by Liverpool that season to choose from – an aggregate league loss to Sunderland by two goals to twelve, for example.

THE GREAT LIVERPOOL FOOTBALL SWINDLE

Just two years later, on a rain-soaked Manchester afternoon on 2 April 1915, Liverpool players incontrovertibly *did* help to fix a match, a sensational 0–2 defeat at Manchester United, which, this time, threatened to send Chelsea down. The ensuing inquiry resulted in four Liverpool players, Jackie Sheldon, Tommy Miller, Bob Pursell and the wonderfully named tough-tackling Scottish half-back Tom Fairfoul being suspended. But the post-war expansion of the league to 22 clubs meant Chelsea escaped the relegation places after all. The suspensions for the Liverpool players were eventually lifted soon after the end of hostilities. With no summer wages in the offing because of the war, the players involved from both sides had bet heavily on a 0–2 result, and once this score had been reached – and to the consternation of the sodden crowd – the co-conspirators began to kick the ball into the stands. Jackie Sheldon missed a penalty and another Liverpool forward was bawled out by a teammate when he almost scored near the final whistle.

This was 'undoubtedly the worst scandal to afflict the league in its twenty-seven seasons', and it perpetuated rumours about payment for strange results, especially given the wage restraints on players.[20] But Liverpool FC and its followers could, at least, reflect on the club's first FA Cup final appearance, in 1914, after more than 20 years of trying. And most people's concern was now focused on the much greater, and much more deadly, 'game' that now lay ahead.

CHAPTER 4 REFERENCES

1. Taylor, *The Leaguers*, p. 115
2. Harding, *Football Wizard*, p. 97
3. Taylor, *The Leaguers*, p. 102
4. Inglis, *League Football and the Men Who Made It*, p. 54
5. Taylor, *The Leaguers*, pp. 10–11
6. Taylor, *The Association Game*, p. 89
7. Young, *Football on Merseyside*, p. 79
8. Physick, *Played in Liverpool*, p. 54

9. Preston, 'The Origins and Development of Association Football in the Liverpool District *c.*1879–*c.*1915', p. 187

10. Inglis, *Engineering Archie*, p. 34

11. Inglis, *Engineering Archie*, pp. 21 and 23

12. Inglis, *Engineering Archie*, p. 89

13. Physick, *Played in Liverpool*, p. 55

14. Taylor, *The Association Game*, p. 95

15. Taylor, *The Leaguers*, p. 14

16. Tischler, *Footballers and Businessmen*, pp. 134–5

17. Inglis, *League Football and the Men Who Made It*, pp. 73–4

18. Russell, *Football and the English*, p. 62

19. Chinn, *Better Betting with a Decent Feller*, p. 203

20. Inglis, *League Football and the Men Who Made It*, p. 96

5

THE FIRST FA CUP FINAL
1914 at the Palace, and Then War

THE ROAD TO THE 1914 FA CUP FINAL

The FA Cup final had its brief visits in the nineteenth century to the north – to both Manchester and Liverpool – and then a stopover at Old Trafford for the 1915 'wartime' final. But from 1895 right up until 2001, when it moved briefly to Wales, the FA Cup final found its resting place in London, despite its many northern critics. Early sports historians commented approvingly when the final returned to Crystal Palace in 1895. 'It is good that the Cup Final is played in the great Metropolis again, for however much our cynical provincial friends may effect to despise "Lunnun" and Cockneyism, there is no denying that London is the place for a great sporting battle.'[1] Certainly, going down to London in the spring was a popular trip for the football 'hordes' and alleged sporting 'barbarians' from the north and the Midlands. For once a year, at least, they could look ahead to teaching their so-called betters from down south a thing or two about 'footy', supporter styles and having a rollicking good time.

But Crystal Palace was a rather strange place to host the FA Cup final, its last, in 1914. The Palace was no less than a Victorian pleasure garden in the suburb of Sydenham that housed an inadequate pitch and pretty terrible viewing facilities for spectators. It was overlooked by an odd array of sights and amusements, including the glass structure of the Crystal Palace itself and also the forbidding 'Switchback' fairground ride. This seemed more like a venue for a sunny family day out with the children than one set up to host the world's premier football club fixture to the satisfaction of its mainly cloth-capped and beer-fed visiting partisans from the provinces. After the war, in 1920, the final would move briefly to Stamford Bridge before English football had a stadium suitable for staging its major club occasion. And even in 1923, *managing* the game's premier event at the new Empire Stadium at Wembley initially proved quite beyond England's football authorities.

In the context of English national life, the FA Cup final manages to combine several important messages at the same time: about sport and male working-class culture; about a shared national ritual in a familiar calendar of sporting events; and about a constitutional link between sport, the British people and the royal family.[2] The 1914 FA Cup final was the first one truly to signal the increasing respectability of the English game and also the new nationwide reach of professional football. The King, George V, would attend the final for the first time. This public royal sanction for association football, the people's game, even led *The Times* to conclude on 27 April 1914 that perhaps the old divides between amateurs and professionals, between the humble sixpenny or 'bob' terrace supporters and the 'toffs' in the stands, could finally be laid to rest:

> Professional football of the best kind is no longer regarded as a spectacle only suited for the proletariat . . . The fact that the King himself has attended a Cup Tie and shown a keen interest in its vicissitudes . . . will, let us hope, put an end to the old snobbish notion that true-blue sportsmen ought to ignore games played by those who cannot afford to play without being paid for their services.[3]

What *The Times* did not yet know, of course, was that all these ingrained class and social divisions – and more – would soon be dragged up again by the national and local press when the Football League refused to halt the league programme as war began to engulf Europe later that same year. But Liverpool's quest in 1914 was to capture the FA Cup at last, and the Reds' journey to the final began, inauspiciously enough, on a heavily sanded Anfield pitch in January against a determined and rugged Barnsley, the 1912 FA Cup winners. The Yorkshire club fielded seven of their cup-final heroes, and it showed. Although Lacey squeezed a long shot under the napping Jack Cooper in the Barnsley goal before half-time, the visitors more than deserved their equaliser, a George Travers shot that rattled in off the underside of the crossbar. 'Liverpool were fortunate to draw,' concluded the *Liverpool Echo*, which now feared the worst in the replay.

At Barnsley, Travers soon kicked Robert Pursell, the cultured Liverpool left-back who had been recruited from Queen's Park in 1911, 'and a fighting pose was adopted by both players'. Referee Bamlett stepped in to show that he was like this contest – hard. All FA Cup finalists, it is said, need luck en route to the final. Liverpool had theirs here – in boatloads. The 800 Liverpudlians who had made the trip to south Yorkshire saw their keeper Kenny Campbell assailed by 'beefy shots' from all sides, but he remained defiant, and when Lacey again sent Cooper diving the wrong way in the 89th minute it was clear that it was Liverpool's day.

A home draw against distant and mysterious Gillingham was Liverpool's reward. A 'genuine crush' occurred before the match at a windy Anfield, which saw the Kemlyn Road stand full and closed long before the start, causing a 'grievance' among visiting fans, who, the *Echo* remarked sniffily, 'did not seem used to finding their way around in a big crowd'. Forget the patronising treatment; it took the home team more than eighty minutes to break through the Gills' defence, and then Lacey and Robert Ferguson, a stylish Scottish half-back who had been signed two years before from Third Lanark, both struck to end the debate.

For the third-round trip to West Ham on 21 February 1914, according to the *Football Echo*, there were a few flighty overnight Reds in tow – Liverpool were 'followed at midnight' in their trip to London 'by a fairly large crowd of supporters'. After heavy rain, the Boleyn Ground pitch was a mudheap, having only a few patches of green at each corner flag. The visiting pressmen also wondered at the extremely tight walling-in of the East End ground because, for a forward player with some pace, 'a collision with a cement wall is not inviting'. Tom Miller, a physically robust centre-forward recruit from Hamilton Accies in 1912, scored the Liverpool goal immediately after the half in a tough 1–1 draw that was full of good football, especially given the conditions. The *Echo* noted, in passing, that both West Ham and Burnley were now 'shilling gates', but it reassured its readers that Liverpool understood well the harsh economics of the Merseyside area, that they had had 'wonderfully generous support from the city throughout the season and will not dream of raising the prices of admission'. Here was a hostage to fortune if ever there was one.

How would people in work and school in Liverpool attend the daytime midweek rematch? The *Echo* had some streetwise doggerel to explain exactly how these tricksters might excuse their way to Anfield, part of which read:

There'll be grandmothers to bury,
At the Anfield Cemetree [sic]
And lots of sudden illnesses,
Next Wednesday at three.
There'll be reams of lies on paper
Special Spion Copper Crammers
There'll be lots of French leave taken
For the fun'ral of the Hammers

REDS

A crowd of some 43,729 eventually squeezed into Anfield, and thousands were turned away by officials who 'wisely decided they could not take any risks'. The capacity of a pre-war football ground was something of a movable feast and clearly down to local interpretation. Many matches played to audiences that were well under – or over – the official limit, depending on the willingness of club officials and the crowd to allow more customers to be squeezed onto the terraces. The *Liverpool Echo* commented that supporters could also move to all parts of the ground, meaning that the take up of space was highly uneven. 'The Spion Kop in some parts is crowded and in other parts could stand more spectators.' One thing was clear: such was the appetite for the game in Liverpool in 1914, as the *Echo* averred, 'The schoolboy nowadays is not au fait if he does not have a complete knowledge of football matters.' Liverpool cruised this cup reunion by 5–1, and the packed Anfield stadium played its part – and not for the last time – because, for the *Echo's* correspondent, 'The surroundings had some of the Hammers upset. Spion Kop's thickly populated crowd frowned down upon the visitors and they have previously had no frown like it.'

Crowd frowns or no frowns, promise or no promise, FA Cup ticket prices were not frozen at Anfield. Dream again – this is business. For the fourth-round home tie with Queens Park Rangers on 7 March, prices *were* raised and some local supporters threatened a boycott. But how often do fans ever vote with their feet? In the event, the Kop was closed at 2.20 p.m. for a 4 p.m. kick-off, and the large crowd was in beered-up, boisterous form, judging by the oranges playfully used as missiles before the start. Liverpool had met 'curious clubs' in its FA Cup run so far, agreed the *Liverpool Echo* – it meant, of course, mainly feeble southern non-Football League clubs – but 'nothing weaker has been tackled than Queens Park Rangers'. The visitors first tried the physical stuff and then resorted to the 'one-back' offside trap, but nothing worked for them. The 5 ft 6 in. tricky winger John 'Jackie' Sheldon had been bought by Tom Watson from Manchester United in November 1913, and it was he and centre-forward Tommy Miller who got the goals here in a 2–1 win. This was the height of their Liverpool careers: within 14 months both men would be banned after the Manchester United 'fix' fiasco.

Twenty-eighth of March 1914: a London FA Cup semi-final for Liverpool and also the university boat race. The *Echo* pressmen thought that the japes of the Oxbridge student spectators compared very poorly with the dignified demeanour of northern and Midlands football fans in London for the match: 'Their hustling and mad-brained tricks were a disgrace to civilisation and the top-hat brigade.' The cup experts and holders Aston Villa were overwhelming favourites to win through at White Hart Lane. Villa even had the esteemed ex-Red Sam Hardy in goal, a man who had left Anfield back in May 1913. The London press certainly gave Liverpool no chance at all, and Tom Watson was so enraged by this slur that he delivered a 'storming speech' to his men that they should show the football public that this Liverpool side was, indeed, 'on the man'. A 2–0 scoreline for the Merseysiders registered an underdogs' glorious triumph. 'The surprise of the season,' as one national newspaper put it. The 'big-timbered' Liverpool unit was slow to get started, but it soon moved into gear. And it was not one of Hardy's 'safe and steady' afternoons. Instead, he needlessly conceded the corner from which Glaswegian forward Jimmy Nicholl scored the first of his two goals of the afternoon for Liverpool. Like many other players, Nicholl's short football career at Anfield was effectively ended in 1915 by the war. Bill Lacey, especially, tormented and teased his old comrade Hardy for the remainder of the contest, which Liverpool dominated.

When news of Nicholl's goals and Liverpool's win eventually filtered through to the reserves' Central League match being played on the same afternoon at Anfield, it was reported that 'scenes unprecedented in the history of the club were witnessed between players and spectators alike'. Joy was unconfined as the match was stopped dead and players and people in the crowd gleefully hugged each other. Back in London, the victorious Liverpool players had no time even to put on their coats and collars before pouring excitedly into taxis bound for Euston to catch the last non-stop train to Liverpool. At Lime Street, they were exhausted but ebullient as the club's supporters and players mingled and contemplated something quite unique in Liverpool Football Club's short history: an FA Cup final appearance at last.

THE KING'S BIDDING

'We are authorised by the Earl of Derby,' reported the *Daily Post* solemnly on 18 April 1914, 'to state definitely that the King has signified he will be present at the final contest for the Football Association Cup at the Crystal Palace.' Excitement gripped Merseyside, though it was also made clear that, in these troubled times, the monarch might not even be able to stay to present the cup and medals. Tom Watson would be there, of course. And he also had a novel idea to satisfy those supporters who could not make the trip for this first royal 'Lancashire final', which would pit Liverpool against Burnley. Why not replay the match later, in Liverpool, for charity? So, arrangements were made for Burnley to visit Merseyside to play soon after the final and for the FA Cup to be paraded at Anfield, regardless of who had won it. From today's perspective, it seems like an extraordinary suggestion.

Did such a strange proposition mean that Tom Watson was worried, or was he super-confident? He was certainly concerned about a knee injury to his steadying captain, the Derbyshire born half-back Harry Lowe, who had made his debut for Liverpool back in 1911. According to the *Liverpool Echo*, the club trainer Bill Connell 'doesn't get full publicity when the deeds of Liverpool are mentioned. He has his men in perfect trim and gets the last ounce of energy out of them.' Connell was optimistic (he was paid to be), and he told the *Post* that a specialist had ensured that Lowe 'will be certain to play'. On the very eve of the match, it was reported in the city that Lowe 'has improved wonderfully, and is expected to be quite fit'. Was this pre-match bravado, or possibly even time-honoured football subterfuge? In fact, like Bob Paisley in 1950, the Reds skipper Lowe would miss the 1914 FA Cup final – he was replaced by Bob Ferguson. This late change might well have swayed the outcome by a fine margin towards Burnley. Liverpool's opponents had been promoted into the First Division only in 1913 and had finished 12th to Liverpool's 16th in 1914, so compared to Aston Villa they were no FA Cup or league giants. After their semi-final showing, Liverpool, at odds of 4–6, were widely expected to win this London meeting.

Unusually, Liverpool chose to base their FA Cup final players' camp down south, in Chingford, while Burnley remained closeted up north, in Lytham. Light training only was the order of the day for the Liverpool squad, including 'sprinting and ball punching', while the Reds players were reported to have 'spent a lot of time on the golf links'. The Liverpool outfield men had had no practice at all with a football during their entire week in Essex, save for a few 'accidental' minutes on Thursday afternoon 'when a ball came in their way as they were going for a stroll in the forest'. Even under the visionary Tom Watson, the team was expected to benefit most from rest and starvation of collective practice with a ball. It was the way of the times and the way of the English, a people who were generally dismissive of too much practice and coaching, the preserve of Continentals. Bill Connell had replied with a world-weary shake of the head to the *Liverpool Echo* scribe of 24 April 1914 who thought that ball practice was 'the one essential in the course of training prior to an important cup tie'. The inscrutable Connell reminded the Liverpool press that:

> When the boys beat the Villa they had not seen a ball for a week. Their football was good enough, eh? They relish the sight of the ball on the Saturday, and they have had such a hard time latterly that it is necessary to take measures to get their full stamina. A team of men like I have under my control do

not want training in the full sense of the word. They simply want to keep the muscles lissom and the wind and limb sound. The course of training this week will be simple . . . For the moment, 'ball lost' is the order.

The Liverpool players would be expected, magically, to click into gear, hungrily find their best game and invent their own tactics as the match developed. Tom Watson had special words of praise in the build-up for young McKinlay and full-back Sam Speakman, a local man, both of whom were 'reserves who did not grumble and were as delighted as the rest of the team as if they had played in the ties'. These were true Liverpool club men, McKinlay especially – he would go on to epitomise the very heart of Liverpool Football Club after the war. Watson would tell his players that Burnley were 'a good sporting side and if they won the day he would be the first to heartily congratulate them'. But there was no doubt that he expected Liverpool to win the 1914 FA Cup.

The Reds would certainly not want for support at the Palace: on Friday evening alone, 12 special trains carried Liverpudlians down for the final, and an estimated 170 special trains in total would reach the metropolis, ferrying the majority of the 'below par' 72,778 crowd to their destination. Thomas Cook & Son confirmed that all previous records had been broken concerning the number of passengers who had made arrangements to travel to London from Liverpool. Some fans would, clearly, do whatever it took to make the journey, even if they lived outside the city and struggled for cash. William Hatton, a shed-man from Wigan, for example, ended up in court on 22 April 1914 for stealing copper and brass from a railway shed. His defence was that his £1-a-week earnings were not a living wage and that he had 'arranged a trip to London for next Saturday's English cup final and . . . having paid his fare found that he would have no money left to spend when he got to London'. The bench was not made up of football supporters: Hatton was fined ten shillings and costs were imposed.

The 'travelling village' from Merseyside, as the *Liverpool Echo* described it, was argued to scotch the views of those predicting that the meeting of two Lancashire clubs 'would not create a great deal of enthusiasm'. A reporter for the *London Evening News* commented later that this meeting did not strike the imagination of the ordinary football fan and that 'I cannot remember any final that has created so little interest, except possibly in Lancashire'. It was seen as two modest, midtable northern clubs playing in the game's southern showpiece.

Many of the earliest travellers from Liverpool were reported to have been working all night, so they planned to catch some sleep on the train. Portraits of the Liverpool team and players were stuck to carriages that were sometimes crammed with groups of 15 or 16 supporters who did not want to be separated. The *Echo* produced souvenir cardboard hats for supporters which said 'Cap them in the Cup'. Some fans came with facsimiles of the cup stitched to their coats, while others brought sandwiches loyally wrapped in red-and-white paper. They had also packed 'not a few well-filled bottles'.

The *Daily Post* of 25 April 1914 also described the 'pandemonium' around Lime Street station on the Friday evening as supporters departed and reported that a popular souvenir for the trip was a black-edged card grimly headed 'In Memory of Burnley', which contained a verse of triumphant doggerel on the demise of the East Lancastrians and how Liverpool had:

> Rushed them and pushed them, until they were sore,
> And beat them all hollow, as they'd oft done before.

Was all this crowing too early? On the chaotic station platforms:

> Red button bouquets, red hats, red jackets and red flags besprinkled the crowd, and as if these were not enough to show how the wind was blowing in regards to the prospects of the match, corncrake rattles were rung with hideous sound. Shouts of 'Liverpool forever!' were heartily endorsed and passed around. It was very seldom that the name of Burnley was mentioned.

In London on the day of the final, according to the *Echo*, 'the Lancastrian was the predominant personality: "John Willie" was everywhere' and the 'best of good fellowship' prevailed when bleary-eyed rival supporters passed each other in the West End to the general astonishment of the 'solemn Londoner'. Hundreds of 'four-in-hand' brakes carried visitors through the London streets, and a fleet of about two hundred motorised omnibuses was chartered to take supporters sightseeing. But these enthusiastic northern excursionists had some act to follow. An extraordinary crowd in excess of 120,000 had seen Aston Villa play Sunderland in the 1913 final at Crystal Palace, many of them having no view at all of the pitch. Perhaps the FA authorities were basing their match preparations on this latter figure, because the *Daily Post* carried details of the food that would be set aside to feed the masses from Lancashire at the Palace. The FA seemed to assume that every single spectator would dine lavishly at the final. Compared to today's stodgy fast-food football diet of pies, sausage rolls and burgers, this seems like a feast. The 1914 FA Cup final football menu included:

75 rumps of beef	30,000 rolls and butter
80 loins of mutton	75,000 slices of bread & butter
250 fowls	25,000 buns & scones
150 hams	1,500 dozen bottles of minerals
12,000 sandwiches	48,000 slices of cake
2,500 veal and ham pies	6,000 pastries
1,000 dozen bottles of beer	2,000 gallons of beer

The men from the north also exercised a characteristic determination not to be taken for a ride by the 'sophistication' of the capital. Even in 1914, the notion that London and the FA might try to exploit its guests seemed well founded for those who visited from the provinces. Spectators had to pay a shilling for admittance to the Palace pleasure grounds, for example, before gaining access, at an additional cost, to the football stadium. Most visitors grumbled at this double whammy, effectively a London football 'tax'. But then they conceded later that a once-in-a-lifetime sight of the famous glass monument might have been worth the extra money after all.[4] Following all this paraphernalia and exhausting build-up, the match itself was a huge disappointment, at least to the people from Merseyside. Liverpool lined up, without the injured Harry Lowe, in familiar 2–3–5 formation:

Liverpool FC, FA Cup final team, v. Burnley, 1914

Campbell

Longworth   Pursell

Fairfoul   Ferguson   McKinlay

Sheldon   Metcalf   Miller   Lacey   Nicholl

The versatile Wearsider Arthur Metcalf had joined Liverpool from Newcastle United for £150 in May 1912, and he had been top scorer for the club in season 1912–13. But injury then intervened, and he played only ten league matches, mainly at inside-right, in the 1913–14 season. He was preferred in the cup final to another north-easterner, but a less consistent goalscorer, Bill Banks.

On a warm afternoon, there was pre-match entertainment from the bands of the Irish Guards and the First Liverpool Regiment in front of a 'perspiring crowd'. The First Liverpool Regiment, based in Aldershot, had volunteered to play before the final, and all members of the regiment wore the Liverpool team favours on their sticks and in their caps, which was, according to the *Liverpool Echo*, 'quite unique in the history of the British Army'.

'WHAT A BERNARD SHAW SHAME!'

The *Daily Post* focus in its match report in 'perfect Palace weather' was on a popular Reds theme: 'Cleverness without finish counts for nothing.' Liverpool had plenty of the play all right, but Miller 'muddled several chances' as the Merseysiders pressed right up until half-time to break the deadlock, when Tom Watson could get to work once more. As the players rested and anticipated the second half at the sweltering Palace, back at Dingle Park, where South Liverpool were entertaining Tranmere Rovers in front of 18,130, a spectator prankster changed the local scoreboard to show Liverpool to be leading Burnley 2–0 at half-time. This news caused some of the crowd to throw their hats and walking sticks in the air and even to perform somersaults along the touchline. Only later did they realise the cruel hoax, and when the real state of affairs was announced 'an audible murmur of disappointment ensued'.

After half-time, Burnley began to have more of the ball and soon scored the crucial and only goal in a move that was 'bewilderingly sudden'. A throw-in on the right was crossed to inside-left Teddy Hodgson, who trapped the ball and flicked it gently to ex-England and Everton forward Bert Freeman. Freeman was undoubtedly a class act, a man who had scored 61 times in just 88 appearances for the Blues. No doubt he enjoyed flashing this volley past Liverpool's Kenny Campbell, 'who did not even see the ball'. At Goodison Park, where Everton and Liverpool's reserves were clashing, cheers and cries of 'Good old Burnley' and 'Good old Freeman!' rang out from the home sections when the score was announced. A Liverpool man wrote later to the *Echo* to point out that Evertonians had not long ago barracked the same Freeman and to complain about this 'disgraceful display of partisanship'. (What else did he expect?) It was a great cup-final goal, no question, and the Reds were stunned. But they later rallied and 'the last moments of the struggle were all in favour of Liverpool'. But a 'chance shot' from Donald McKinlay missed its target, and it was all over.

The *Daily Post* man was apparently close enough to events to report that the King had said a sympathetic 'hard luck' to the 'blushing Scotsman', the Liverpool captain Ferguson, as he picked up his loser's medal. In a later editorial, the *Post* rehearsed the greeting of the terrible news of the Reds defeat on the streets of Liverpool when a local 'urchin' was reported to have responded to an *Echo* newsboy's comments on the scoreline with the extravagantly despondent (and rather educated) outburst, 'What a Bernard Shaw shame!' One thousand supporters turned out to welcome the Liverpool party home on the Monday, but there was little time to commiserate – the Liverpool players had to rush directly to Anfield, where they were playing Sheffield United that very evening in their final league fixture. What was planned as a huge celebration turned, instead, into a sullen 2–1 victory. There was still no FA Cup for Liverpool.

When the FA Cup trophy eventually *did* come to Anfield on 29 April, for the Theatrical Gala charity match against Burnley that had earlier been agreed by Tom Watson, hundreds of boys poured over the front of the Kop at the end of the match to get a better look at the silverware. In their enthusiasm, they knocked over an Anfield salesboy who was carrying cigarettes, chocolates and cakes in a basket for sale to supporters. They pounced. When the poor seller emerged from under the ensuing scrum, his basket – like Liverpool's trophy cabinet – was pitifully empty.

Looking ahead to the summer and to the awful prospects of war, the *Post* sagely suggested that, 'A nation which wastes time over football is likely to last longer and do more enduring work in the world than a nation in arms.' These were wise words, indeed. But the English game was about to face one of its biggest battles yet.

'PLAY UP, PLAY UP AND PLAY THE GAME?'

English football's so-called 'crisis season' of wartime football in 1914–15 has been described as one of the most damaging in the sport's history.[5] Lacking guidance from the British government, the outbreak of the Great War on 4 August 1914 meant that the whole of British sport faced difficult decisions about if and how to proceed. Broadly speaking, amateur sport halted its activities immediately in order to face the enemy square-on. But, with its wider responsibilities to its employees and customers, professional sport tried to continue. Inevitably, these different routes attracted strong comment, especially along the lines that the sports professionals were essentially in conflict with both patriotic and properly sporting values. Class prejudice was also strongly in play here, especially given football's roots in the working-class, urban communities of the great industrial cities and towns of the north and the Midlands. The Footballer Battalion was eventually formed in December 1914, as national press coverage of football became more and more hostile. But this move looked, to many, like a mere public relations exercise, and by March 1915 it was reported that just 122 out of 1,800 professional players had come forward to join the military.[6]

In August 1914, the Football League management committee, with a strong 'over by Christmas' mentality in play, was preparing for the new season almost as if life was proceeding as normal in Britain and the rest of Europe. With no national conscription in force, in September the men from the league were close to publicly describing football as some kind of 'magical potion' that would act as an 'antidote' to war. The management committee even claimed it would be a 'national calamity' if league football was curtailed.[7] A reader's letter to the *Daily Post* on 3 September 1914 commented, acidly, that until he had read the league's manifesto, 'I had no idea . . . that these matches would stir up the patriotic spirit.' The British public seemed not quite so sure, as gates fell by more than 50 per cent, and the Football League instigated reductions on players' wages and a central fund to which all clubs contributed to try to keep the financially worst-affected members afloat.

In Liverpool, club chairman John McKenna, who was also president of the Football League, announced that the club's players had agreed to contribute 2.5 per cent of their wages to the War Fund for the rest of the war, and Will Cuff, the Everton secretary, promised that equipment would be secured to allow rifle practice during the club's training sessions. McKenna was, without doubt, a brilliant advocate for Liverpool and the league. 'He talked like an American,' said one player of an earlier dispute. 'He quoted figures, income, expenditure, gates and liabilities that simply floored those who imagined the clubs were rolling in wealth.' Honest John was, indeed, a master servant of the management and economics of the sport and of his local club, and although both loved and feared equally he had few airs and graces: he lived modestly in a terraced house in Anfield even when he was chair of Liverpool and president of the league. A fierce opponent of gambling on sport, his brusque exterior and straight-talking demeanour masked an even temperament and a man who was happy to mix with all classes of people. Making arrangements for wartime league football in the face of national criticism was not likely to ruffle him. Remarkably, he remained president of the Football League until the day of his death on 22 March 1936, when he was 81 years old.[8]

Tom Watson was also squarely behind wartime football. He reassured the local press on Merseyside in September 1914 that 'our boys have been anxious that they should be trained from a military point of view, and they and we welcome the league's decision [to carry on playing and ensure players train for national service]. We shall soon have the league's views carried into fact.'

Meanwhile, the amateur Liverpool Rugby Football Club (and the RFU) had adopted a demonstrably different stance. A Mr E. Roper from Liverpool RFC told the *Daily Post* proudly on 1 September 1914 that 'between fifty and sixty of the club's players . . . had joined the forces, and there was not a player left'. This revelation made footballers look like war-dodgers. Judging at least from the letters to the *Daily Post*, public opinion in Liverpool towards football's stance – and thus to the local clubs – was hostile enough. 'Is it not

The men who made Liverpool Football Club. Clockwise from top left: John Houlding, early Everton man and Liverpool FC founder; John McKenna, Irish stalwart of Liverpool FC and of the Football League; Joe McQue, a scorer in Liverpool's first-ever Football League match in September 1893; and Tom Watson (with hat, and with Reds goalkeeper Sam Hardy and defender Tom Chorlton), peerless architect of the first two league-championship wins in 1901 and 1906.

J. McQue.   J. McCartney.   A. Hannah.   S. H. Ross.   M. McQueen.   D. McLean.   J. McBride   A. Dick (*Trainer*).
T. Wyllie.   J. Smith.   J. Miller.   M. McVean.   H. McQueen.

The 1892–93 Liverpool FC squad, a formidable-looking bunch of men. Later Reds manager and director Matt McQueen stands out (back row, centre right). These were the men who started the long Liverpool Football Club journey at Anfield.

The first Liverpool league championship-winning squad in 1901, kitted out in regulation-length shorts. Liverpool would slump and be relegated in 1904, before winning the league title again, under Tom Watson, just two years later.

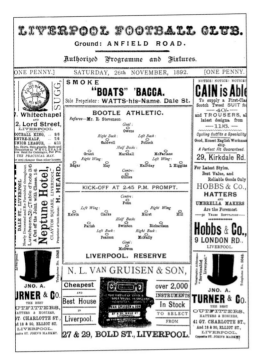

A very early Liverpool match programme, for a local derby clash between the Reds reserves and Bootle Athletic in 1892, advertising 'Boat's 'Bacca'.

Harry Bradshaw, Reds forward from the 1890s, a predator who scored a crucial Test match goal against Newton Heath in 1894 to get Liverpool promoted to the First Division.

A quick exit from the Kop, *c.*1900. Note the still prominent mast of the SS *Great Eastern*, the handy tramlines and the long tradition of early leavers.

The city of Liverpool in 1908. Dockers were said to 'rush home from work and hand over their wages before going to the match'. They watched 'the Redbreasts', as the local press then dubbed Liverpool FC, at Anfield.

A 1908 press illustration of a Liverpool home game. With no photographers to call upon, local newspapers had to use the skill and imagination of an artist to get the story across.

Immortalised on a collector's card, the bustling Sam Raybould, Liverpool's record goalscorer in 1902–03.

OGDEN'S CIGARETTES.

A. G. RAISBECK.

Alex Raisbeck, defensive linchpin and attacking pivot for Liverpool, the driving force behind the club's first league titles in 1901 and 1906. He returned to Anfield as a scout after the Second World War.

The prince of full-backs, England international Ephraim Longworth, 18 years a Liverpool player from 1910 before joining the club's coaching staff.

The Liverpool squad of 1910. The craze for the wild moustache had clearly passed by now and the club's players suddenly began to look like modern footballers.

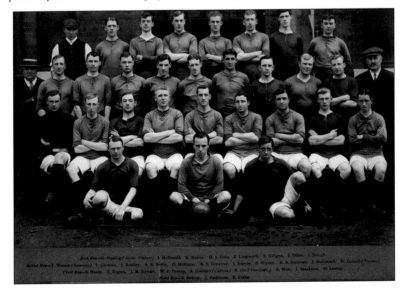

A rare view of the 1914 FA Cup final at Crystal Palace. Even the presence of the King could not save Liverpool from defeat and a 51-year wait for cup success.

The historic Liverpool squad that won back-to-back league titles in 1922 and 1923. Trainer Bill McConnell is in the middle row (far left) with manager Davie Ashcroft front left and secretary George Patterson front right. The fearsome Jock McNab is to the left of the goalkeepers and the hunched genius winger Bill Lacey shows off his sharp centre-parting (front row left).

WADSWORTH, Liverpool

A Reds collector's item featuring Bootle-born Walter Wadsworth. Wadsworth, who flattened a bandsman at Sheffield in 1923, was a feared opponent in Liverpool's 1920s championship teams.

Donald McKinlay, brilliant Reds captain and loyal servant for two decades from his signing in January 1910, a man who cared more about playing for his beloved Liverpool than winning caps for Scotland.

A hot ticket: a menu card for the Liverpool championship dinner at the Midland Adelphi, 1923. It would get even hotter: Liverpool FC now faced 24 long years without winning a major trophy.

Harry 'Smiler' Chambers, later chased by the taxman, provided the goals for Liverpool's title-winning teams of 1922 and '23.

LIVERPOOL ASSOCIATION FOOTBALL CLUB

English League Champions
Division 1. Season 1922-23.

COMMEMORATION DINNER

HELD AT THE
MIDLAND ADELPHI HOTEL
LIVERPOOL

Chairman — W. R. Williams Esq
27th JUNE, 1923.

H. CHAMBERS
LIVERPOOL

England international and Liverpool captain Tommy Bromilow, the midfield brains behind the championship sides of 1922 and '23 and also a tonic advertiser – a nice little earner back in the early '20s.

South African forward Gordon Hodgson wowed the Kop from 1925 and he became a mainstay of the inconsistent inter-war Liverpool teams.

The incomparable Elisha Scott, an authentic Kop hero of the 1920s and '30s, a man who often preferred to talk to the Liverpool crowd rather than his own defenders.

enough to make one despair of his race?' blustered one correspondent. 'Apart from withdrawing the services of scores of trained athletes, it encourages thousands of supporters to withhold their own.' Another letter accused the league of the 'prostitution of a noble sport' and suggested that entirely new leagues be formed of players aged between 16 and 19 and of those under 16, and that the government should 'commandeer . . . playing grounds for drilling purposes, preferably for artillery regiments'.

Football followers in the city were rather more supportive of their clubs. When a poor Liverpool side lost 0–5 at home to Everton on 3 October 1914, for example, the crowd was well over 30,000 and was 'in high spirits and its colour scheme was deeply tinged with patches of khaki'. Lord Derby – a local dignitary and Tory football supporter, and a man who had survived a devastating political put-down from Lloyd George that 'like a cushion, he always bore the impression of the last man who sat on him' – now came up with the novel idea of a 'census' of the crowd at football in Liverpool, ostensibly in order to demonstrate the potential contribution to the war that could be made by the Merseyside football audience. Survey cards were handed out to the players and supporters at the Liverpool v. Manchester United 1914 Boxing Day 1–1 draw.

The Liverpool FC minute books for the time show that the club was committed to pay half the wages of any player who joined up under Lord Derby's scheme. The *Liverpool Echo* of 29 December 1914 reported that out of a healthy crowd of 27,015 at Anfield, 1,453 were soldiers and 3,044 boys, and that elsewhere the custom of free admission for soldiers had reduced receipts at some clubs by a reported 80 per cent. 'Maybe football clubs will have to ask these sporty soldiers to assist them in the late months of the season,' argued the *Echo*, 'by paying half-price for admission.' The ravages of war were soon apparent: when Liverpool played Preston at Anfield on 22 October 1917, out of a crowd of 15,422 some 3,345 (22 per cent) were soldiers, including 1,769 who were wounded.

Lord Derby was probably better at running his various estates than he was at doing research. Out of 16,000 census cards distributed at the match, only 1,034 were returned by men, but they made interesting reading nevertheless. From the replies, 308 supporters were too young, too old or married and so were ineligible to enlist; 144 were in the type of work that prevented them from enlisting; 335 were unfit; 31 were already enlisted; 10 were unsigned. This meant that there were around 206 supporters present who were eligible to enlist. Extrapolated to the whole crowd and allowing for a sprinkling of female fans, this could mean around 5,000 potential recruits – who, instead, said the critics, were watching football.

On 23 April 1915, the council of the FA finally announced a formal suspension of all football for the next season, a decision that meant that 1915 league champions Everton would end up holding the title for the next five years. Strangely, the Blues would also win the last league title before the Second World War, in 1939. In July 1915, the Football League finally suspended the league competition, but the management committee agreed to come up with a regional form of the sport so that there might be football played throughout the country to maintain national morale.

REGIONAL FOOTBALL AND THE BLIGHT OF WAR

Perhaps it was a sign of the sheer cultural and economic power of the sport on Merseyside that the *Liverpool Echo* on 20 July 1915 felt able to heartily endorse the league's determination to allow the game to carry on in a new, reduced format, with expenses only allowed for players who trained sparingly, on Tuesday and Thursday nights. Local firms that offered players employment were given complimentary tickets in return. In other northern football heartlands, such as Blackburn, Newcastle, Sunderland and Middlesbrough, and in many of the Midlands' strongholds, it had been decided not to play football during the war. 'They are entitled to their opinion and their stand. We respect people who have theory,' argued the *Echo*, tartly. 'But, sirs, the backbone of the army is what may be termed "football inclined", and I say emphatically that we ought to play football for their sakes, if for no other.' John McKenna, on behalf of both Liverpool FC and the Football League, said, 'We feel we owe a duty to the game and to those who perforce must stay at home.' The city of Liverpool was determined to play on and buck the trend elsewhere.

Money was certainly tight in the war years. In August 1915, the Liverpool club doctor was offered only half his fee from the previous year, and Bovril halved their payment to the club for exclusive rights to sell sweetmeats inside Anfield. Also in line with general cuts, the Liverpool minute books reported that 'it was decided that Mrs Lilly's offer of eight shillings for washing and repairing players' clothes be accepted'. The minutes also show how all major financial decisions at this time – on policing, admission charges, advertising and match programme rights – were made in direct consultation with neighbours Everton. When Liverpool told the Goodison board in August 1915 that they now planned for the 'non-issue of intoxicants in the boardroom' as an economic measure, the resident Everton Methodists received the news with 'distinct pleasure' and said that such moves would be 'strongly supported' across Stanley Park.

Liverpool FC received many requests for financial assistance at this time, including a begging note from ex-keeper Joe McQue, who was sent a 'nice letter' in reply stating, sorry, the club could not help. A letter received at Anfield in December 1915 asked for 'comforts' for an ex-player Harold Fitzpatrick, who was now a prisoner of war. The chairman instructed that 'two parcels of groceries be purchased from Coopers at about 10–6d each'. One was sent immediately, the other held back 'in case Fitzpatrick is heard of again'.

In February 1916, the Anfield stands were insured against air attack, and in September of that year the still-banned Jackie Sheldon asked if he could attend the Reds home match v. Burnley. He was admitted free as a wounded soldier but was told sternly by the Liverpool board that 'he must not go near the dressing-rooms'. He did better, at least, than local 'lady footballers' who were raising money for the war effort. They asked for the loan of a room at Anfield in December 1917 – and were, of course, refused.

The regionalised football competition that was played in the war years was often chaotic – Liverpool were late arriving for the club's first match, for the fourteen-club Lancashire Section Principal fixture, at Bolton – but the core of the Reds' league squad remained. And there was even a decisive home win at last (4–1) to celebrate against a depleted Everton, in November 1915. A ten-match supplementary tournament filled in the months of April and March 1916, though, inevitably, crowds fell substantially compared to the league average of 24,315 who had watched Liverpool in the 1913–14 season. Later, restrictions on transport and fuel also added to the problems of completing wartime fixtures.

THE PASSING OF OWD TOM

In all this confusion and disturbance brought by war, perhaps it was in some ways a blessing that the great Sunderland and Liverpool football man Tom Watson was spared the cannibalising of the Football League format and the teams that played in it. On 5 May 1915, the much loved Owd Tom died suddenly of pneumonia and pleurisy. His death came barely a week after he had been attending a South Liverpool v. Liverpool match and had complained to friends about 'feeling odd'. The Liverpool board wrote later to Tom's wife of the 'irreparable loss' they had sustained by Watson's death, which was overshadowed somewhat by news of the sinking of the Liverpool-registered SS *Lusitania* on her maiden voyage and the anti-German rioting and vandalism in the city involving 'wreckers and looters' from Seaforth to Garston that followed. This meant that all Germans and Austrians were soon advised to leave the city. But it was still very clear, even through this haze of war-induced violence and hatred in Liverpool, that, as the *Football Express* put it with some understatement, 'the football world has lost one of its ornaments'.

Watson, undoubtedly, was, as the *Echo* described him, 'perhaps the most popular figure in the association code of professional football', a man who had 'no enemies' but had a genius for signing good players at low cost. He had not only guided Liverpool to league titles and promotions, but he was also intensely affable, and he had had an unusually wide vision for the sport in an age when the English football establishment was unsure about how to respond to the spread of football around the world. 'Bluff, hearty, jovial, fond of a joke, could tell one in spasms, and was always prepared to listen to one,' mused the *Liverpool Echo* on his death. The *Liverpool Express* reasoned that the late manager had the capacity to attract recruits to the Liverpool club by the power of his sheer geniality, although trips to sign favoured players did not always work quite as planned. Watson enjoyed telling a story of a scouting trip to Scotland that led to the Liverpool party following the player concerned to the dynamite factory where he worked, only for them to be chased by navvies armed with the company's products. They thought the intruders were employer's agents.

'During the summer season, Mr Watson was in the habit of spending his holiday abroad,' recalled the *Echo*, 'and he had a distinct influence in popularising the game on the Continent.' In fact, Watson had just planned a trip to the USA to assess football there. He was also a regular church-attender and a keen local bowls man, typically acting for a spell as the president of the Liverpool Bowling Association. But what had made Watson so unique in football was his huge network of trusted contacts in the game, which aided so much in his famed 'talent tracing'. As one newspaper put it, 'Tom, as a manager, must have had the record for signing on men he had never seen.' Watson also had an assured capacity to bend the press to his will. 'Bee', the *Echo* football writer, recalled that Watson had insisted to him that newspapers should always 'encourage' football and had argued that it was difficult to convince the press that the game was not 'the blackguardly thing some supposedly good folk believe it to be'.

At his funeral at the Anfield Cemetery, paid for by the club, hundreds of supporters and the English and Scottish football world turned out in large numbers to pay their respects, including all the Liverpool club directors: Messrs John McKenna, John Asbury, W.R. Williams, A. Worgan, R.L. Martindale, T. Crompton, E.A. Bainbridge and W.C. Briggs. There were rather narrow limits to the club's generosity, however: it was reluctant to contribute towards the cost of a headstone for Watson's grave. There were more than one hundred wreaths at the funeral, which 'represented all the leading football associations', and seven former Liverpool players, including Alex Raisbeck and goalkeeper Ted Doig, as well as the great Liverpool trainer William Connell, acted as pall-bearers. The sport – and the city of Liverpool – agreed that it had lost one of its early greats.

LEARNING TO FLY

Football during the war continued without Tom Watson, and with no new Liverpool football manager to replace him. It would be five years before a 'football man' would step into the role. Because of the general economic problems in the game, each club was now required to pay 20 per cent of its wartime gate money to the visitors, a practice that was unimaginable before 1914 but now became the economic mainstay of English football for almost 70 years. Wartime matches were reduced to 80 minutes in length, but the minimum cost of admission was actually increased, from sixpence to ninepence, following the introduction by government of an entertainment tax in October 1917 – it would cost Liverpool FC some 37 precious shillings to repaint the headstones advertising the new prices at Anfield. In January 1918, there was more ground expense as the Liverpool board decided to move the official club entrance, from Walton Breck Road to Anfield Road.

In these straitened times, flexibility was the watchword. The nearby Southport club, for example, was allowed by the Football League to rename itself Southport Vulcan because of its support from a local factory, thus becoming still the only club in the history of the Football League to have an overtly commercial name.[9] In 1919, Leeds City were expelled from the Football League for violating wartime regulations and withholding information regarding the payment of players, and the league management committee actually sanctioned proposals from the owner of Huddersfield Town, Hilton Crowther, to move his club to play at the now defunct Leeds stadium, unless fans in Huddersfield could raise the necessary funds to buy Crowther out. They did so, thus ensuring that Town did not become, in 1919, England's first professional 'franchise' football club.

In March 1919, Arsenal were also gerrymandered into the First Division of the Football League ahead of other, more deserving cases, allegedly because of the friendship between Liverpool's John McKenna and Arsenal's powerful chairman Sir Henry Norris. Money and power talked, and the London club became the first and only Football League club to gain such a promotion for reasons other than merit – they have never been relegated since. These were very extraordinary football times indeed.

When Liverpool Football Club eventually resumed its 42-match league football programme in August 1919, the Reds voted for the southern challengers

Chelsea and Arsenal to make up the new numbers in the enlarged First Division. The city of Liverpool, meanwhile – like London and parts of South Wales – had been badly scarred by 'race' riots in the summer, with the *Liverpool Echo* on 6 June 1919 unsympathetically describing the erupting local black communities in the city as 'distinct foreign colonies' and their separateness from the mainstream as 'partly a check against the pollution of a healthy community by undesirables'. *The Times* of 10 June 1919 reported that a large body of police requisitioned by the city authorities to quell disturbances on Merseyside soon got into their stride: 'Whenever a negro was seen he was chased and, if caught, severely beaten . . .' The next day the south end of the city was in turmoil, 'the streets filled with thousands of excited people'. According to the *New York Times* on 4 August 1919, the city was given over to more disorder, consecutive nights of 'riot and pillage' in the face of strikes and local food shortages. Troops were drafted in as the local police went on strike and mobs gathered in Scotland Road and raided stores on London Road. Local children continued their work after dark. Other rioters targeted beer-bottling plants in Tariff Street and Love Lane and were confronted by armed soldiers who shot some of the offenders. The routine treatment of the city's poor and of Liverpool's long-standing ethnic-minority communities was finally beginning to come home to roost.

Compared to this kind of serious social and economic unrest, football in the city had a veritably easy ride. True, Liverpool FC still had no manager, but what it did have was the core of a potentially great team, built mainly by the late Tom Watson. The capable Kenny Campbell was still in goal, even though he had asked for a transfer back to Scotland in 1915. But Elisha Scott, the young Irishman recruited by Watson for free from Belfast, was now getting rave reviews in the Liverpool reserves. At the club AGM in June 1915, Scott was mentioned by name by John McKenna as the player whose performances had rescued Liverpool's season. The backs were the impressive Donald McKinlay and Ephraim Longworth, and also included in their reserve ranks was the skilful, but slight, St Helens-born right-back Tom Lucas. The half-backs included the improving Bootle enforcer Walter Wadsworth – whose winger brother Harold had also joined the club – and a very talented left-sided link player from Liverpool, the brilliant Tom Bromilow, a man who had been invalided out of the army because of septic poisoning.

Jock McNab, a raw, young tough-tackling Scot, also began to make small waves at Liverpool in 1920 – he would do plenty more later. In the forwards, there was Bill Lacey and the rehabilitated right-winger Jackie Sheldon, Preston-born marksman Dick Forshaw and a versatile and reliable – if sometimes injury-prone – forward, Harry Lewis, a Birkenhead-born inside-forward who had scored freely for Liverpool in the war years. Harry 'Smiler' Chambers, a trained shipworker who had spent his war service in Ireland playing as a guest for Distillery FC and Glentoran, was now back with Liverpool and determined to make a name for himself as a goalscoring centre-forward. Most of these men would be key figures in taking Liverpool Football Club back to the very top of the Football League in the early 1920s, even as social division, depression and hardship wracked the city.

Before the 1919–20 season began, Eph Longworth, the Liverpool captain, unusually gave a long interview with the *Echo* on the issue of the working lives of professional footballers. This came about mainly because players had typically worked during the war and then had played football on Saturdays. This made some critics doubt the need for full-time professional football players at all. Longworth argued that in this period of climbing post-war unemployment, most footballers had decided, patriotically, that 'it would not be playing the game to stay on in our positions'. He also pointed out that wartime football had meant less competitive play and much less travelling – all this would change again as 'the pace of play in the coming season will be swifter than for four years'. Matching playing professionally with working in industry during the week would inevitably take its toll on a man's strength and was an idea, Longworth suggested, that came from people 'who have never spent more than an afternoon at a training ground'. It was a spirited and articulate defence of his profession.

Even with players becoming full-time once again and increasing their pre-war wages by 50 per cent, the new season was not entirely without its teething problems, as the nation and its people struggled to recover from the privations of war. All club expenditure had to be accounted for: Liverpool had a cash balance of just £175. Director Tom Crompton was even required to report to a full board meeting in October 1919 that he had successfully purchased a set of new balls for the club billiard room. The occupational status of professional players was hardly improved by the war. In September, Liverpool's footballers asked the board for two complimentary tickets for each home match. The Anfield hierarchy barely blinked in formally regretting that this request 'could not be agreed'. The Liverpool minute books also show that in June 1919 the club paid Sunderland a fee of £100 to move their fixture at Anfield from 26 April to Christmas Day. But generally the war habit of playing the same club home and away on consecutive weeks was maintained by the Football League.

Liverpool's home midweek fixture with Arsenal on 1 September 1919, in front of a poor crowd, was much delayed because of the late arrival of the referee, which meant the match 'was finished in semi-darkness'. When Liverpool later visited Chelsea in October a breakdown on the tube meant that many people were still pouring into Stamford Bridge well after kick-off. In the same month, the *Football Echo* commented that travel even within Lancashire was prohibitive.

'The inaccessibility of Burnley from Liverpool is proverbial,' the newspaper observed. 'Today's journey, its stoppings and changes, showed that improvements in the matter of railway facilities is still far to seek.'

Liverpool had started the new era slowly and the club had had an especially disappointing October and November. But they battled to an encouraging 0–0 draw at Goodison just before Christmas. The return fixture at Anfield on 27 December was a red-letter day in the club's history – the first Football League victory over the old enemy at Anfield since the previous century – since 1899 to be precise.

By now football had begun slowly to recapture the imagination of an increasingly enthusiastic and demonstrative Merseyside public, one that was desperately attempting to escape the recent traumas of conflict. A massive crowd of 49,662 gathered at Anfield to witness a famous 3–1 derby home win. The *Liverpool Echo* noticed a change in the match atmosphere and in the character of the local football crowd, warning, 'There was a need for more crush-barriers [at Anfield], more effective barriers and many more police, together with some honourable stewards . . . The wonder was the game was finished, for the crowds at the corners swung inward to the playing space as soon as ever there was an exciting piece of play in the vicinity.' The main home excitement centred on the utter solidity of Longworth at the back against the 'very big men' at forward for Everton and two goals from Tom Miller that followed an early score from Harry Lewis.

In a news feature headlined 'Is Football a Lost Art?', the *Evening Express* on 24 January 1920 also detected an alleged new post-war hedonistic focus among football supporters in the city, in the sort of complaint that might have easily been heard 80 years later:

> One only has to mingle with the crowd and listen to their comments to realise that it is the excitement rather than the finer points of the game which are generally appreciated . . . [It is] fair to admit that the pace at which matches are now played has never been surpassed . . . The old-fashioned dribbling, finessing forward of 20 years ago is a very rare type today. The impression left in an old stager's mind is that in modern football, particularly in forward play, everything has been sacrificed to speed.

Also sensing change, the dean of Durham argued in the press that 'association football has been pretty well ruined by the betting upon it', but an ex-international player, the Reverend Kenneth Hunt, saw only changes for the good, arguing that post-war football 'has replaced tendencies that were far more vicious. It was the greatest challenge to the public house on Saturday afternoons. Football provided for the masses the recreation and excitement they obviously needed.'

How exactly were players recruited to conjure up this excitement produced every week at Liverpool FC? Well, the decision-making Liverpool board meetings at this time had a very simple structure. They were weekly and dominated by numerous reports from members of the public, scouts and Liverpool directors on prospective players. Club officials could, seemingly, be dispatched to the distant south coast, Scotland or Ireland on the flimsiest basis of a letter of recommendation about a player from a scout, supporter or onlooker. In December 1919, ex-player Matt McQueen joined the Liverpool board – it required special FA permission for an ex-player to join these gentleman ranks – and he at least offered some recent practical expertise in player assessment and recruitment. There were stock phrases used by Liverpool directors at this time to describe watched players: 'worth another look'; 'will not suit us'; 'on the small side'; 'showed much promise'; 'club would not part'; 'could not recommend him'. There seemed little discernible structure to these scouting visits and most were to local non-league clubs where Liverpool clearly hoped to pick up bargains, largely at random.

On many occasions, scouting trips proved to be so much wasted time. Communication difficulties made precision rather difficult. Fancied players were injured or omitted from teams, or matches were simply moved to other venues without notice. In October 1920, for example, Matt McQueen and a director travelled to watch a player at Atherton only to find that the fixture they planned to watch was being played at far-away Darwen. Liverpool board meetings also dealt, variously, with: the medical needs of players; fixture changes; financial and stadium matters; letters from the FA and other bodies and individuals; requests for charity fixtures or for use of the club stadium; and pleas for donations. They invariably ended with the naming by the board of the selected first team and reserve teams for the forthcoming club fixtures. These selections were then boldly written out in the minute books. If the board meeting was held before the busy Christmas or Easter holiday periods, complete teams might be chosen and written down in advance for *three* first-team Liverpool matches, irrespective of player form or the opposition. In the absence of a dedicated team manager, only injuries or illness could lead to late omissions and last-minute call-ups.

NEW BEGINNINGS

On New Year's Day 1920, Archibald Salvidge, the arch-Conservative leader of Liverpool City Council, spoke publicly of the urgent need for local renewal in the city, because 'Liverpool is engaged upon problems of reconstruction, which are colossal'. The government committee appointed to assess the health of British men in the wake of the First World War reported on the condition of 66,000 men from Liverpool and remarked on the high levels of TB in the city and the poor physique among 18 to 20 year olds. Some local males were described as 'old men at 38'. The *Evening Express* argued that the city of Liverpool was too old-fashioned, much behind 'Cottonopolis' (Manchester), and that people in the city were 'stodgy and slow and too conservative'. This might have been partly why, in February 1920, in an extraordinary development, the blue-chip retail giants Harrods finally ditched well-advanced plans to open up a proposed nine-storey £750,000 Liverpool store in Church Street because of disagreements with Liverpool City Council. The proposed investment duly disappeared, so a huge post-war branding and retail commercial opportunity, which would have had an impact on the city for decades to come, was lost.

In the arena of popular leisure, the Liverpool Parks and Gardens Committee now agreed to allow an experiment with evening dancing in Stanley Park during the summer months. But on the streets the struggle for popular leisure was never-ending. In 'an apparently new departure by the police', two youths were hauled in front of the Liverpool stipendiary magistrate in January 1920, charged with the offence of playing football in the street. 'It seems a remarkable thing,' argued the perplexed magistrate, 'that boys should be arrested for playing football.' Later in the same month, Henry Ainsworth, a fitter, was fined £61 for printing football coupons and dispersing them in the city. The FA thanked the Liverpool magistrates for suppressing this 'menace to the game'. Meanwhile, a young Manchester entrepreneur called John Moores and his partners were experimenting with a new football pools business that would help shape the Liverpool economy and the national public consumption of football for the next 50 years.

A winning sequence for Liverpool FC in January and February 1920 followed the December defeat of Everton, and it pleased new Reds manager, the Irishman David 'Little Dave' Ashworth, an ex-referee and coach, just five feet tall, who had been recruited in June 1919 by the Liverpool board as a safe pair of hands from Stockport County. Ashworth was no Tom Watson, but he shared Owd Tom's love of humour and tall tales – he was a 'great teller of Lancashire dialect stories'. He also liked to relieve the tedium of long railway journeys for pressmen and players with his dry wit. But Ashworth was a bundle of nerves during matches, claiming never to have seen a penalty kick taken in his entire career as a manager for fear of its outcome.

He would soon be opposed in the city by Harry Makepeace, Everton's first secretary–manager. The *Evening Express* commented on 10 August 1921 on this new trend in city football towards younger player–coaches and managers, which, it argued, would mean that quality young players would now find it easier to make their way inside the local clubs: 'Too often a young player of promise is picked up by the league team and because he does not develop with sufficient speed he is allowed to go. Now, when a youth shows skills, he will be encouraged and helped to master the game by the club coach.' Was this modernisation at last?

For the visit of Liverpool to Luton Town in the FA Cup in January 1920, 'the big railway fare prevented the visitors from having a large contingent with them', reported the *Evening Express*, 'but the mascot was in evidence in a variegated suit, dancing to his heart's content and well, too'. Later, at Bolton, 'the [Liverpool] mascot was again in full bloom'. But was the Reds mascot present, one wonders, when on 26 February 1920 the future Anfield great Elisha Scott finally made his post-war Liverpool reappearance? We can only guess. Scott's restart with Liverpool came after an injury and an operation, and at Notts County in a 0–1 defeat Scott had no chance with the County winner. But when Harold Hill got in a useful shot in the second half, the *Football Echo* reported, prophetically, that 'the Irishman caught it like a master'. By 9 March, perhaps sensing what the future held for him, the loyal Kenny Campbell asked again to be placed on the transfer list in order to be able to return to Scotland. Scott was immediately promoted to the Liverpool first team. By 3 April 1920, a 3–0 demolition of Derby County, Liverpool were yet to concede a single league goal at home that year.

A fourth-round 1–2 away FA Cup defeat in March to eventual finalists Huddersfield Town did not dampen club spirits. The build-up to the tie in the *Evening Express* also revealed details of the physical make-up of this emerging Liverpool team. Only two players, the departing Campbell and Walter Wadsworth, reached 5 ft 11 in. in height and everyone else was below 5 ft 9½ in., including Lucas, Sheldon and Harold Wadsworth, who all measured around the diminutive 5 ft 6 in. mark. Only one player, the chunky 5 ft 9 in. Irishman Bill Lacey, weighed in at over 12 st. This was no powerhouse of a football team, even for the 1920s. Nor was entertainment always guaranteed from them. When Liverpool struggled past lowly Sheffield Wednesday at Anfield on 10 March 1920 by a 1–0 score, in characteristically humorous style the 'home crowd became so fed up that they started shouting for the Wednesday'. These Reds supporters might have given thanks that they were not Chelsea followers: the London club defender Jack Harrow sportingly missed a penalty kick *on purpose* in March 1920 when he agreed with his Notts County opponents that their alleged handling offence was accidental.

Jackie Sheldon badly broke his leg near the end of the campaign, but Liverpool finished off a highly promising effort by overtaking Sunderland into fourth place after a 1–0 last-match victory at Roker Park. This was the first season when Liverpool's John McKenna, on behalf of the Football League, began the tradition of presenting the league-championship trophy to the winners on the field – it was to prove just in time for his beloved Liverpool Football Club to benefit from the new arrangements. The *Liverpool Courier* astutely identified some of the core strengths of this emerging post-war Liverpool side:

> Undoubtedly, Scott, Longworth and McKinlay won the game. Scott made good saves when only good ones would prevent a goal, but the backs were brilliant . . . both tackled with confidence and judgement and kicked perfectly. In the middle, W. Wadsworth was a very effective power . . . Only a leader who uses his brains would have headed [the] goal, as did Chambers.

Consolidation followed around this strong group of players in 1920–21, another Liverpool finish of fourth in the league behind champions Burnley – but ahead of Everton in seventh place – and a dull second-round FA Cup defeat at Newcastle United. Liverpool conceded fewer goals (35) than anyone in the First Division and did not concede a penalty throughout the entire season. But only Smiler Chambers and a fast and brainy centre-forward signing from the north-east, Dick Johnson, made any real impression on the scoring charts. Liverpool were slowly building their strength and consistency from the back, and it was about to pay off handsomely.

Also paying off was pressure from the players' union for a wage increase for its members. Attendances and the cost of living were rising after the war, but even the union must have been surprised when, in March 1920, the maximum wage was doubled by the league management committee, to £9 a week, and made payable over the whole 52 weeks, not 39 weeks and training weeks as before. The Football League also expanded from 44 to 66 clubs by incorporating the Southern League as a new Third Division, before adding another 20 clubs in 1921–22 to form regionalised third divisions, North and South, and including Southport, Tranmere Rovers and Wigan Borough from Merseyside and the surrounding area. Now, for the first time, the Football League could really claim, as the FA Cup had done before it, that it was a premier football competition and a truly *national* one.

These had been difficult years. The debate about whether to play in the war had been a damaging one for football, although in Liverpool public opposition had been more muted. Tom Watson had been lost, but the Reds were rebuilding on the back of his excellent work and had a new manager. It did not know it

THE FIRST FA CUP FINAL

yet, but Liverpool Football Club was preparing to be the first club since The Wednesday in 1902–04 to win back-to-back Football League championships. More importantly, Liverpool FC would be the first truly *national* Football League champions of England.

CHAPTER 5 REFERENCES

1. Quoted in Hill, 'Rite of Spring', p. 87
2. Whannel, *Fields in Vision*, p. 3
3. Hill, 'Rite of Spring', pp. 91–2
4. Hill, 'Rite of Spring', p. 104
5. Taylor, *The Association Game*, p. 119
6. Taylor, *The Association Game*, p. 120
7. Inglis, *League Football and the Men Who Made It*, p. 93
8. Inglis, *League Football and the Men Who Made It*, pp. 80–2
9. Inglis, *League Football and the Men Who Made It*, p. 98

6

THE ROARING TWENTIES
Liverpool Back on the Title Trail

THE LAST STAND OF HONEST JOHN McKENNA

For what would prove to be a memorable 1921–22 season, there were more changes afoot at Anfield. The entire playing area was returfed and a concrete wall was built to replace the old wooden palings around the pitch. Fortunately, Anfield was not as tight a location as the local press had claimed the Boleyn Ground at West Ham to be. In fact, a passage down each side of the ground measuring 8 ft wide and 5 ft at each end was added to the site, which tacked on between 5,000 and 7,000 new places to the existing stadium capacity. Moreover, 'ambitious ground improvements have already been projected', promised the *Evening Express*.

The Liverpool ground was beginning to catch up with developments elsewhere, not least those just across Stanley Park. But the Liverpool club could still do much more to improve its rudimentary stadium management and also perhaps its public relations. Early in 1922, a merchant, Robert McCulloch of Wavertree, sought court proceedings to sue the club for three shillings after he paid for two seats that were no longer available on his admission to the stadium. This was no occasional mishap before reliable numbered seating was established: the court heard that 'many other claims are pending'.

But there was a real bombshell to hit Liverpool before the start of this momentous season. It was the summer resignation from the Liverpool board of 'the sheet anchor of the club', John McKenna, after 29 and a half years' unbroken service. McKenna resigned at the Liverpool AGM in the summer of 1921, ostensibly because the club's major shareholders had decided to vote off the board ex-Liverpool favourite Matt McQueen, who had been McKenna's own nomination to the Liverpool administration 18 months before. McKenna had clearly had enough of this sort of malarkey at club level and he had plenty already on his plate as president of the league. The Liverpool shareholders, McKenna complained, 'seem to have quite failed to recognise the ability and genuine hard work done by these men on behalf of the club. I am certainly not going to be a party to it.'

McQueen would soon return to the Reds board, but this was a sad end to relations between McKenna and the club, especially since Liverpool also announced at the same AGM just the sort of progressive and money-saving policy the Irishman favoured – the running of a Liverpool third team or 'A' team for amateurs and local young professionals which would play at Sutton Lance Lane, Wavertree, managed by chief scout Charlie Wilson. This was aimed at 'fostering talent, which undoubtedly abounds in this area'. As the *Daily Post* reported it on 6 July 1921:

> The club had taken this step with the object of nursing young players. Present transfer fees were prohibitive and they [the Liverpool board] did not feel justified in spending large sums in acquiring players who might, or might not, prove successful.

In fact, the high transfer spending of Sunderland in the new season would provoke much wider discussion in the game about limiting the number of transfers, perhaps to one major signing per club, per season.

This innovative new Liverpool scheme might have been just made to attract talented local players, such as the Michael Owen-like waif John Hallows, a 15-year-old Chester-born 8 st. orphan who was much in the local sports news. He was described by the Liverpool press as 'the finest centre forward for his age in the country'. Hallows, reportedly a potential 'gold mine', had scored three hundred goals in just three years of junior football in the area – but he would not make it into the Liverpool system at Wavertree. Instead, Hallows played briefly for West Bromwich Albion and then turned out 164 times for Bradford City in the 1930s, scoring a tidy 74 goals. Nevertheless, this type of planned prudence in producing local young players was exactly typical of the new Liverpool FC approach that had been developing under the wily Tom Watson. The club was not – and never would be – about 'buying' success, despite Watson and John McKenna's early raids on Scotland for playing talent.

SEEING OUT THE BAD TIMES?

On 21 August 1921, the Liverpool minute books report that, 'It was decided that the duties of the manager be to have the full charge of all players and trainers on the books of the club and that all matters appertaining to the players be under his control.' Here was a clear statement of managerial status and duties but one which stopped short of the key issue – selecting the Liverpool team.

One promising player who was disappointed not to be offered a contract by Liverpool in 1921–22 was the talented amateur Ted Ray. Instead, Ray did what most Liverpudlians do for free: make people laugh. He went on to become a nationally known professional comedian and performer. Ray very probably made much more in earnings than did the professional football players he had so wanted to emulate. A First Division manager at this time revealed that top players at his club earned, on average, around £6 5s a week in 1921–22. The First Division clubs would have to find a reported £531,208 in first-team wages for the 613 First Division players employed.

With this new local focus from Liverpool FC, it was also widely hoped at this time that the *economic* situation in the city – and even relations between Protestant and Irish Catholic communities on Merseyside – might be changing, too. Liverpool's Orangeism had penetrated the civic culture of the city more than in any other city in Britain, including Glasgow.[1] But unlike in Glasgow, it had made relatively little impact on the support for, or the 'meaning' of, the two major football clubs, despite Liverpool FC's Protestant roots. Both clubs supported similar charities, and both Liverpool and Everton signed players irrespective of their religious background. This might well have been partly because of the unusual origins of the clubs and the fact that neither served a specific geographical area of the city, thus guarding against the sort of territorial tribalism in football seen elsewhere. Liverpool FC's early Orange administration might have caused it to be labelled the city's Protestant club and Everton's earlier north Liverpool base might have contributed to its soft identification as the Catholics' team in the city, but for most people on Merseyside these descriptions were simply that – labels. People in the same families often supported different clubs – and do today – irrespective of creed or religious affiliation.

If the city of Liverpool and its surrounding area was suffering from the impact of national recession, then it was also trying characteristically hard to show that it might just party through the bad times. In July 1921, for example, applications were made to build *seven* new cinemas in and around the city centre, with Liverpool FC director Edwin Berry behind the proposed 1,700-seat giant £200,000 Rialto development at the corner of Upper Parliament Street. But ultimately these were difficult days for this sort of popular leisure expansion, and within six months Arthur Williams, the managing director of a number of Liverpool picture houses, was asserting that 'the cinema, like many other trades, is going through a very bad time'.

In sport, a summer baseball match between England and Wales on Stanley Park in 1921 attracted a crowd of 4,000, and a fierce debate now took off in the Liverpool press about the local demand for Sunday sport in the city's parks. Some letter writers described Liverpool on Sundays as 'old fashioned' or even 'the city of the dead'.

The core identity of the city was also under attack, because in a controversial lecture delivered locally Robert Gladstone argued that the Liverpool liver bird was actually a grossly misleading copy of the seal granted to the city by King John and that it should really be an eagle. 'The corporate seal of the city is an atrocity,' he went on, with apparently little care for local sensibilities. 'Its design is ludicrous and its motto gibberish.' His view was clear enough.

THE FA'S KNIFE IN WOMEN'S FOOTBALL

A crowd of 9,000 people attended a match involving the famous Dick, Kerr's women's football team in Southport in August 1921. Perhaps because of its popularity, on 5 December the women's game was effectively banned by the FA due to alleged 'irregularities' in managing funds raised by women's charity matches during the war. In Liverpool, the FA decision provoked a strong response. A furious Mr Cecil Kent wrote to the *Evening Express*: 'Why have the FA got their knife into girls' football? . . . Are their feet heavier on the turf than men's?' A Mr J.H. Harrison, who ran Suggs' Amazons, a women's works team from Liverpool that had planned to play a Boxing Day game in Bootle, argued, 'Surely this is for the players to decide. The girls merely play against each other on equal terms, and if they think it is a suitable game to play that ought to settle it.'

Liverpool would clearly not give up women's football so easily, and a well-attended women's 'international' match was staged after the ban, at the Stanley Athletics Ground, Fairfield, in March 1922. It was refereed by Everton defender Dickie Downs and was fought out between England (Dick, Kerr's) and France (Olympique de Paris). The teams were hosted before the fixture at a lavish dance in the Adelphi ballroom by the mayor and mayoress of Liverpool. But this women's contest drew little support from the Merseyside press. An *Evening Express* editorial on 30 March 1922 argued, 'Nothing more likely to injure the dignity of womanhood could be devised. Nothing less likely to inculcate a respect for femininity among boys and youths could be imagined.'

The vehemence of general male opposition to women footballers should not surprise. After all, football had been developed as a tough and physically exacting working-class diversion in cities such as Liverpool. Football was a male retreat from the constraints of home and, in the 1920s, a refuge from an increasingly uncertain future for men.[2] Older women now had the vote, and a speech in Wallasey in the early 1920s by a Miss S. Midgley argued that it was as 'humanly natural' for women to desire wealth as it was for men. Maude Roydea from the Victorian Women's Settlement in Liverpool even suggested in a lecture that ambitious young girls were already asking why they needed husbands at all and why should they not have children outside marriage.

In short, the post-war world – including the world of sport – was transforming fast. Many Liverpool men were threatened by the pace and direction of change. 'Backlash' letters to the local press were all too common, such as the one from 'Elkay' suggesting a night-time curfew on women in Liverpool. Or 'Strap-hanger' to the *Evening Express* in January 1922, who argued that women workers should be required to show a special pass on Liverpool trams. For Merseyside men, seemingly under attack from all sides, the prospect of women taking over their beloved football was probably just a step too far.

BUILDING FOR THE LEAGUE TITLE

The 1921 census revealed Liverpool's population to stand at an impressive 803,118, an increase of 6.5 per cent. Liverpool and Everton were attracting around 70,000 people on average every fortnight to football in the city, even when times were hard, so demand for football was clearly still very high. Everton actually *raised* seat season-ticket prices in 1921, from 35 shillings to £2 10s, and George Patterson, Liverpool's secretary, used the local press to inform Liverpool club members in August that their tickets should now be collected from the Anfield office 'without delay as the number is limited'. Meanwhile, Sunderland, Liverpool's first opponents in the new season, announced that it would *not* be issuing season tickets at all this term because of fears about the effects of the recession on attendances.

'Liver', the football writer of the *Evening Express*, travelled to see Liverpool lose 0–3 in front of 40,000 fans at Roker Park, and, surveying the streets of Wearside, he announced himself to be 'greatly impressed by the large number of men who were apparently idle . . . They did not appear to have any work to do.' He really need only look on his own doorstep: 5,000 men demonstrated outside the Liverpool town hall for the right to work in September 1921. In October, unemployed protesters in the city outside St George's Hall fled with their leader Robert Tissyman into the Walker Art Gallery, where they were locked in and then roundly beaten by the Liverpool police. The Liverpool unemployed in the 1920s proposed boycotting both local pubs and football matches at this time as a form of protest about the lack of work locally, thus suggesting that at least some of the jobless might still have been attending matches at Anfield and Goodison. But there was also little doubt that the rise of minimum entrance from sixpence to ninepence in 1917 and then to one shilling after the war probably meant that regular attendance at football was beyond their means and even that of some skilled workers.[3]

Writing to the *Evening Express* in 1921, a Mr D.C. Williams from Smithdown Road had a futuristic answer to Liverpool's growing unemployment problem: employ idle men on public works to dig a road tunnel under the Mersey. It was just a thought – but it would have to wait. Instead, work would begin in the autumn of 1922, offering employment for some, on a 27-mile £3-million arterial road linking Liverpool to Manchester.

Away from these sorts of social and political tensions, Liverpool Football Club's playing ranks were bolstered for the new campaign by the emergence from local football in Garston of forward Danny Shone, a short and stocky left-footed player with real promise, who soon won Red hearts by scoring his first goal for the club against local rivals Everton. St Helens-born right-half and England cap John Bamber also started against Sunderland, but he would soon lose his place, briefly, to Seaforth man Frank Checkland, who gave way, in turn, to the gritty fighter and Scottish midfield enforcer Jock McNab. Cyril Gilhespy, an outside-right bought from Sunderland, also briefly made a splash. But the most important new man at Anfield was certainly outside-left Fred Hopkin, signed from Manchester United for a hefty £2,800 fee in May 1921.

The balding Hopkin was no manic goalscorer – only 12 goals in 360 appearances – but when he finally broke his Liverpool goal duck at Anfield after 70 matches, against Bolton Wanderers in March 1923, amidst the excitement a fire broke out in the Anfield Road stand, reportedly because some straw had been ignited by a discarded cigarette butt. The *Liverpool Echo* reported that the fire brigade could be heard 'hacking away at the goal-stand' as the match continued and smoke blinded the visiting goalkeeper. Hopkin was hard-working and quick, and he provided plenty of ammunition for men who knew better where the goal was, characteristically dropping on his right knee and looking for suitable targets when crossing the ball.

The *Echo* had praised the 'courage' of the Liverpool directors for fielding the 'enthusiastic and ever ready' local man Shone at Sunderland, but the 0–3 reverse in the north-east was an early shock. That the future England international Sunderland's Charles Buchan congratulated Elisha Scott on his 'thrilling saves' in the besieged Liverpool goal was a nice touch, and Hopkin shone on his debut in his left-side forward combination with Chambers. It emerged later that Tom Watson had almost brought the brilliant Buchan to Liverpool back in 1910, after agreeing a fee of £750 with the Leyton club. But by the time the cautious Liverpool directors had agreed to pay this sum, the price for Buchan had risen to £1,000 in a seller's market. Despite Liverpool's best efforts to scrape the money together, Sunderland stepped in first to clinch the deal. It would not be the only time a Liverpool manager would be frustrated by his board – almost 90 years later Rafa Benítez would have similar complaints. Certainly Liverpool's slide after 1906 might well have been arrested by Buchan's arrival, but the history of the game is chock full of these ifs and buts.

Bizarrely, the *Liverpool Echo* blamed the shot-shy display from the Liverpool forwards at Roker on their training on the spongy, lush new Anfield turf, where 'the ball drags a lot when driven'. In the return, Liverpool won 2–1, relying heavily on goals from Wales international Billy Matthews and Dick Forshaw, and, again, on Elisha Scott to save brilliantly from a goal-bound Buchan header. Liverpool would not lose again in the league until 26 November, at Middlesbrough, winning seven and drawing seven (all by 1–1) of the next fourteen matches. It all seemed a little 'safety first', but manager Ashworth's approach was effective, and by the time of the first derby match on 5 November 1921 Liverpool's 'rock-like' defence had conceded only 11 league goals in total. Both matches against Everton were tough 1–1 draws, though after the Goodison stalemate the *Evening Express* reasoned, 'I think the most biased Evertonian will admit that Liverpool were the cleverer eleven.' In the return at Anfield, Tommy Bromilow starred – 'England has no finer,' argued the *Echo* – and the irrepressible Elisha was reported to be in 'jubilant mood'.

Was there a little football bias about in the city of Liverpool? Each of the major clubs had their own press correspondent and point scoring was common in the daily sporting press. But a letter from a 'common spectator' to the *Evening Express* on 17 November 1921 complained about the 'Blue spectacled' football reporting in the local press and also, caustically, about the high-handed criticism from reporters that standing football supporters were blocking the scribes' view of the match:

> As to spectators, including myself, who pay our money to see the match getting in the way of our noble pressmen, we will have to see about getting the mounted police to guard the press box and also hire a band to play them into their seats. How would my critic like to fight to work each morning?

Liverpool finally threw off their shackles for all to see in a 4–0 home defeat of Middlesbrough in November, where Bromilow, according to the *Echo*, was 'again the star half-back of the day. He accomplishes everything by pure skill.' Danny Shone also won plaudits for a hat-trick and a 'capital game throughout', and in the return the following week the forward had a goal unluckily disallowed for offside, with Liverpool already 1–0 up. The visitors slid from a likely win to a 1–3 defeat but then set off on another 15-match unbeaten run in the Football League until the middle of March 1922.

In December, as Liverpool rode high and clear at the top of the league table, neighbours Everton languished at fourth-bottom and were reported to be 'worse off than at almost any period in the club's history'. As Everton struggled, even Liverpool's reserves were attracting attention from other clubs. The deposed Ephraim Longworth's request for a transfer was refused, and England half-back John Bamber was reported to have drawn a bid from an unnamed club of a very tempting £7,000. The Reds had no need to sell, and the retain-and-transfer arrangements meant that Bamber could not choose to leave. He stayed, to play an important back-up role in the Liverpool FC league-title successes that followed.

'THIS INTENSE SOLIDARITY' – THE 1921–22 LEAGUE CHAMPIONSHIP

Into the new year in 1922, even the generally supportive *Evening Express* admitted that Liverpool had been 'lucky' to take a point at Newcastle United on 2 January, relying inevitably on 'some wonderful saves by Scott'. The home pressure was obviously intense: the contrary Liverpool goalkeeper was sternly warned twice by the referee for time-wasting. 'But,' said the *Evening Express*, 'I would ask what team does anything of note in a tournament like the league without enjoying some luck?' It was a fair point.

After a drawn FA Cup tie at Sunderland that was 'full of hair-raising situations', influenza ran through the Roker side that came to Anfield for the replay in front of a record midweek crowd of more than 46,000. This type of sickness was no trifling matter: 25 people died from influenza in Liverpool in January 1922 alone. On the left-wing, Hopkin was irrepressible for Liverpool, 'beating man after man' before setting up Forshaw in a 5–0 demolition. The Liverpool crowd laughed contentedly as the tiny Harry Lewis marked the imposing Buchan, 'a case of the long and short of it'. Lord Derby visited the Reds dressing-room after the game to congratulate the bubbling hosts, who were now starting to believe that this really could be their year.

With Tom Lucas strongly challenging the unsettled Eph Longworth for the right-back slot and often replacing him, the England man suddenly resigned as Liverpool captain. The directors quickly appointed Donald McKinlay in his place. A letter from 'RPW' from Dingle to the *Evening Express* on 18 January 1922 highlighted some of the local concerns among Reds supporters about morale in the squad, even with Liverpool comfortably heading the league table from Burnley. He wanted Longworth restored to the team to 'stop rumours of discontent', and he wondered 'if it is a record for league leaders to have such a poor total in the goals-for column'. Liverpool had lost only two matches, but in seventeen out of twenty-five league games thus far Liverpool had scored only one goal or fewer. 'Having watched every home game this season,' the writer continued, 'I would like to ask the directors are they making the best use of the talent at their disposal.' RPW wanted, as a minimum, full-back Donald McKinlay's dead-ball expertise moved up into the forwards: 'We "specs" roar for Mac whenever a free-kick is to be taken near the opponents' goal.' This appeared to be a rather radical suggestion. Liverpool seemed to be close to winning the league title, but were they winning over their own supporters?

There might have been too much caution and even a little disharmony in the Liverpool ranks, but this paled into near-insignificance when compared to the growing unrest at a rapidly fading Everton. The Blues were dumped 0–6 at home in the FA Cup by Second Division Crystal Palace and would eventually slump to 20th in the First Division. When Aston Villa were hosted by the Blues in January 1922, Everton players Sam Chedgzoy amd Stan Fazackerley complained bitterly at half-time about the barracking they had received from their *own* supporters. Fazackerley, a £4,000 buy, was later suspended by the Everton directors for 'disobedience to orders'. By contrast with this shambles, when Liverpool's players attended the Liverpool Stadium for boxing entertainment in January before the club's forthcoming home FA Cup tie against West Bromwich Albion they enjoyed a 'big rally' from local sports fans.

This public adulation proved to be of little help: Liverpool lost 0–1 to WBA in front of 49,332, who paid £3,050. The result was attributed by the *Evening Express* on 30 January to 'the lack of a first-class centre-forward' at the club. Two local brothers who were unlikely to be moved by this shock Liverpool loss were James and Robert Yates. They were otherwise engaged, arrested for stealing a Singer car from outside the Anfield stadium during play. Liver, however, saw some time-honoured consolation in the Reds defeat when he admitted, 'The double is definitely off. Perhaps, after all, it is as well. I don't expect the directors to agree with me in that, but competition is so keen nowadays that it is well nigh impossible to win the cup and head the league in the same season.' Liverpool were four points clear of Burnley in the league, but no team had done the Double since Aston Villa in 1897, in the first decade of the Football League. It was generally agreed that talent was so evenly spread in the game, and that the league programme was so penal, that winning both trophies was beyond even the strongest outfit.

Meanwhile, in early February 1922 police teams from Bootle and Chester played a charity football match at Hawthorne Road for the benefit of Liverpool's unemployed, with Walter Wadsworth, Dick Johnson and reserve Liverpool goalkeeper Frank Mitchell acting as the officials. It was a small sign at least of local football solidarity with those in dire need. What else could the clubs do? In Barrow, where the unemployed had been allowed to attend football matches free of charge, near-riots had broken out.[4] Frustration and anger was also routinely spilling out now into local football, in what has been described as the 'crisis' of 1919 to 1922, which saw the local game purportedly blighted by an upsurge in 'free fights', betting and bad language.[5] The FA gave regular warnings around this time about alleged 'rough' play and poor discipline in local football. When Bootle St James and Bootle Rovers met on the North Recreation Ground in February 1922 – in a case that was becoming familiar in and around the city – John Nolan, a supporter acting as a linesman, assaulted the referee Ernest Ellis and ended up in court. The chair of the bench commented, 'It was very essential in the interests of the sport that it should be carried on in an honourable manner. It was a most disgraceful thing to assault a referee.' Ill-discipline seemed rife, but public facilities were at least expanding for local football in Liverpool at this time, from 154 corporation pitches in 1921 to 172 by 1930.[6]

Back in the rather more tightly controlled professional football ranks, title-chasing Liverpool won 2–0 in the league at a snowy Birmingham, with two goals from Smiler Chambers. When Chambers scored his late second goal after a run of 'spirit and dash' by Longworth, who was replacing Donald McKinlay, it was the first occasion in the campaign that the Reds had scored more than one goal away from home. The *Evening Express* began to wonder at these comparative riches and if Liverpool supporters were 'inclined at the moment to get ready for jubilation'. This was even with 15 games left – including both meetings with main rivals Burnley. David Ashworth, Liverpool's manager, now had to work hard to keep the club on track by denying potentially destabilising rumours that regional foes Manchester United were trying to sign two of the club's reserves. This news came out just as Falkirk in Scotland paid a record fee of £5,000 to West Ham for England international forward Syd Puddefoot – talent was moving north, not always coming south. Despite Everton's free-spending reputation, ten players in the club's A team in the Liverpool County Cup semi-final were actually locally born.

With a free Saturday on 18 February 1922, and having been reportedly 'inundated with offers to play', the Liverpool directors 'very wisely', according to a Liverpool newspaper, resisted the temptation to arrange a friendly fixture. It was agreed that 'first team men should take advantage of the holiday'. Liverpool's England internationals – John Bamber and Tommy Bromilow among them – would get a further rest because the proposed France v. England fixture was cancelled, highlighting deep schisms in the new international football order. The still-amateur French association had objected to England's plans to field professionals in their ranks. At least the England men would get their chance to play eventually. By contrast, the Liverpool minute books show that the Anfield board routinely turned down requests from Ireland for the release of the players Lacey and Scott as 'impossible'. These men missed international caps as a result.

It was the clear-thinking Liverpool chairman Walter R. Williams who was behind the unusually commendable Reds restraint not to arrange additional fixtures to fill in free weekends. He had first been elected to the chair in 1919, and he would later be followed into the Liverpool chairman's seat by his son Samuel, thus confirming the family ethos at the club first established under the Houldings. Williams was presently recovering from illness, which gave a chance for the *Evening Express* on 10 February to reflect favourably on his role and the general good work and good sense of the current Liverpool board:

> The Liverpool club is directed by a body of gentlemen who work smoothly and amicably together. Mr Williams holds the reins with rare tact and judgment and much of the present season's success is due to the chairman's wise guidance on all affairs appertaining to the welfare of the club. Mr Williams is never happier than when his team is doing well.

And Liverpool continued to do well. Another narrow home win (1–0) against Birmingham in a poor display on a hard and slippery pitch in which even the saintly Scott 'made the crowd hold its breath' when he dropped the ball stretched Liverpool's lead to five points. 'JC', a reporter in the Manchester-based *Sporting Chronicle*, pointed out the most admirable – if not exactly the most exciting – decidedly *British Isles* features of the Liverpool title assault:

> Look at Liverpool's record and it will be seen that in 13 matches – nearly 50 per cent – they have not forfeited a goal at all. Since December 3rd they have lost four goals in 12 matches . . . It is this guardianship of the goal, this intense solidarity, which discourages opponents and wearies them. But there in Elisha Scott stands the most complete and the surest keeper of the day.

[Liverpool have] a pan-Britannic defence, including England [Longworth], Ireland [Scott], Scotland [McKinlay] and Wales [Parry], almost the best of the four nations. I am not forgetting Bromilow the artistic tapper; Wadsworth the worker; and McNab, the big Scottish bustling intervener. But the stalwarts of the four nations come to final grips. Not even by implication do I intend to detract from the craftsmanship of Lacey, the dash of Hopkin, the thrustfulness of Forshaw and the calculation of Chambers, but it is the pan-Britannic guard which so often decides the issue.

This is a very astute summary of the team but also of some of the traditional Liverpool Football Club British strengths – much of the same combination of complementary Celtic and Anglo qualities would be discussed in the press and by fans over the next 80-odd years. The strongest Reds formation for this title-winning season, in classic 2–3–5 formation, looked like this:

Liverpool FC, league-title winners, 1921–22

Scott

Longworth (or Lucas)   McKinlay

McNab   Wadsworth   Bromilow

Lacey   Forshaw   Lewis   Chambers   Hopkin

The obvious positives here were the solidity and security of the Liverpool back three, the sheer power and consistency of the half-backs, the trickery and work ethic of the wide players, plus Bromilow's organisation, intellect and creativity in the centre, and the goals of the bow-legged Chambers. The only real weakness was at centre-forward, where neither Lewis nor the Garston youngster Danny Shone truly convinced. Elisha Scott was, unquestionably, the greatest goalkeeper of his day, probably the best of all keepers before the Second World War. He was a perfectionist, routinely berating his defenders for their failings, and his later duels with Everton's Dixie Dean would become the stuff of legend as the 1920s rolled on. But just one description, taken from the season, shows Scott's real worth to the 1921–22 Liverpool team. It is not from a spectacular win, not a dazzling show or even from a crucial fixture. It is taken instead from a crucial, ground-out 0–0 draw at Blackburn Rovers in March 1922.

Liverpool were collectively off colour at Blackburn, no question. They had Gilhespy and the Welshman George Beadles filling in for Lacey and Lewis, and it was not working out. But Scott simply refused to buckle behind this general incoherence, as press accounts from the time confirmed. 'Elisha Scott saved some remarkably fine shots,' said Liver for the *Evening Express*. 'The Irish keeper was cool and collected throughout and at the finish had never turned a hair. His display gave one the impression that no matter what the rest of the side did, he would not fail.' This was typical Scott, irascibly succeeding individually when the collective threatened to break down. The return at Anfield showed another side of his sheer bloody-mindedness. This time he led the exasperated Blackburn forward Johnny McIntyre a merry dance, which ended with 'Scott circling round and round bouncing the ball with McIntyre after him' and his beloved Kop, of course, in gales of laughter.

Ephraim Longworth, the 'prince' of full-backs, right from his Liverpool debut in October 1910, had been noted for his 'raking stride' and for his unshowy excellence in both tackling and distribution. His kiss-curl hairstyle belied his reliability and toughness and also his leadership qualities, which were recognised by his selection as captain of both Liverpool and England. Longworth formed a formidable defensive partnership with Donald McKinlay, another leader, who won two caps for Scotland in 1912 but deserved more. McKinlay would play centre-half and all the left-sided positions in his 19 years at the club, and he ended up scoring 34 priceless goals, as if to show his game was not all about impenetrable defence. These great men were hardly glamorous figures: the Scot had his false teeth broken at a match in Blackpool in 1923, and he had to apply to the club for them to be repaired. Wadsworth and McNab were both hard nuts at half-back – the latter, especially, could be relied upon to 'leave a foot in' when it was needed. The Bootle man Wadsworth was also a ruthlessly committed tackler who liked to fly the ball forward quickly and was a dead-ball specialist of some repute. He was also a man who could be notoriously abrasive with his own supporters as well as the opposition. He often brusquely rejected requests for autographs, and in December 1923 Wadsworth assaulted a bandsman after a match in Sheffield but was excused by the Liverpool board because of the 'great provocation' he had endured.

Wadsworth and McNab left much of the fancy half-back work to Tommy Bromilow, the slim passing genius and the brains of this Liverpool title team. Here was a complete master of the true arts of half-back play, a man who, unlike his combative midfield partners, scorned physical contact and was also a true sportsman, the first choice of many good judges for any match to be played without need of a referee.[7] With the goal-shy Hopkin and the dark-haired Irishman Lacey forcing things wide and serving up chances for Chambers and Forshaw, this was a new Liverpool team fit to challenge the Reds title winners of 16 years before. When Liverpool destroyed Arsenal 4–0 in February, with a Forshaw hat-trick, it was Hopkin who did the real damage. 'He controls the ball like a juggler and his dribbles are a delight to witness.' Tellingly, too, according to the *Evening Express* – and like almost every one of this Liverpool team – he was also 'not frightened to give or take a hefty charge'.

WINNING UGLY IN THE HOME STRETCH

In early March 1922, Liverpool became 'more than ever the capital of Wales', or so crowed the local press when England took on the Principality (the Rose v. the Leek) at Anfield, with Bromilow and Chambers both in the England party. Then, on 18 March 1922, a real Football League shock: a Liverpool home defeat, 0–2 to Bolton Wanderers. There was serious mitigation, however: Chambers, Bromilow and Lacey were all selected to play for the Football League against the Scottish League on the same day, so it was a much weakened Anfield unit that fell prey to its first league defeat since 26 November.

How odd was this? Here were the prospective league champions potentially undone by the selections and scheduling of their *own* league body. It seemed like a bizarre state of affairs indeed. Only at a conference held in Liverpool on 7 January 1931 between the national associations and the Football League would real progress finally be made on the staging of international and representative matches that clashed with league fixtures. But more bad news was to follow for Liverpool sympathisers in 1922: an immediate 0–1 defeat at relegation-threatened Arsenal. Tellingly, the match ball was replaced right after its drunken flight path took Baker's surprise shot wobbling past Elisha Scott. 'Have Liverpool started on the toboggan?' asked a worried *Liverpool Courier*.

Calm was briefly restored, however, with a 3–1 Liverpool win at Bolton, while Burnley lost at Cardiff. Spurs were now lurking in the wings. Liverpool were prepared to fight and to win ugly if necessary, as they had been all season. The home favourite Vizard was 'incapacitated' by McNab in the first half, and the Scot was then 'heckled by the crowd throughout the game'. Or more accurately he was heckled for his remaining time on the pitch, because the sometimes brutal McNab was eventually sent off for tangling again with the already stricken Vizard.

These results stretched Liverpool's lead to six points once more. By 6 April, the lead was seven points with a match in hand. It might be needed after Liverpool, without Tommy Bromilow (who was on England duty), slumped 0–4 at Oldham. But the Reds were all but home and dry with a 1–1 draw at closest rivals Burnley on 14 April – the otherwise magical Bromilow even missed a penalty. A 5–1 Liverpool home win against Cardiff City followed on 15 April, including a hat-trick for Smiler Chambers and an extraordinary swerving cross-shot by Bromilow. Two footballs were lost in the Liverpool stands during this latest procession, and while the arrival of a third was awaited a wag in the home crowd threw on a small rubber ball, creating 'hilarious laughter' off and on the field. Everton shareholders, meanwhile, were not smiling: they were busy circulating venal letters claiming that the Goodison board had spent £30,000 on transfers and had done little more than make the club a 'laughing stock'.

The crucial Liverpool home league fixture with Burnley now loomed on 17 April 1922 – three vital matches would be played in four days, all teams simultaneously selected in advance and handwritten in the minute books by the Liverpool board. Anfield was crammed for the visit of Burnley. 'It was necessary at various points in the ground,' reported the *Evening Express*, 'for the spectators nearest the wall to climb over and there was quite a ring of enthusiasts on the grass around the pitch.' Played in bright sunshine on a holiday Monday afternoon, the affair was end to end, with both Scott and Burnley's Dawson called upon to make early saves. Then Lacey passed to Chambers, who neatly tricked the Burnley defence and 'shot the ball like lightning into the far bottom corner of the net', beating Dawson comfortably. Liverpool continued to play 'storming football' and were good value for a 1–0 lead at the half. In the second period, Scott twice saved brilliantly from visiting forward Bob Kelly but could not stop George Richardson from equalising. The home crowd audibly gasped at this setback, and with the match leaking away, and Lewis struggling with a suspected face fracture from a flying boot, it looked as if Liverpool would have to wait at least another week to claim the title.

But up stepped the reinstated Ephraim Longworth, defensive master, now goal-maker. 'He suddenly took it into his head to retain possession and dribble down the field,' wrote the *Evening Express*, as if the England man had briefly lost his mind. 'Veering into the centre he looked for a likely opening. The full-back was brought down, however, and as he lay on the ground he managed to push the ball to Forshaw.' Seventy-eight minutes had passed.

The willowy Dick Forshaw was consistency personified. A man picked up for free in 1919 on one of the club's erratic scouting missions, he would be the only player to play in all eighty-four league matches in the two Liverpool championship seasons in the early 1920s, scoring a priceless thirty-six goals. He would go on to win another league title with Everton in 1928, the first player to win titles with both of the top Merseyside clubs. Here he picked up the loose ball and carefully placed it past the exposed Dawson. Both he and the prostrate Longworth were then 'promptly mobbed by their colleagues'. With

Oldham Athletic beating Spurs, no one could now catch Liverpool with three matches still to play.

To the victors, they say, come the spoils. Not necessarily in football. It might not surprise people to know that while 1922 champions Liverpool earned £32,852 in receipts for winning the title, ninth-placed Chelsea made more: £34,043. But commercial opportunities were becoming more available to the top football players in the 1920s, though not quite advertising the sort of luxury items we see today. Tommy Bromilow soon appeared in the pages of the Liverpool press, for example, advertising Phosperine, a well-known cure-all for chronic exhaustion and everything else, from sleeplessness to malaria. 'Today,' Tommy and his advisers told the great British public, 'football calls for a greater amount of physical exertion than ever on account of the marked increase in the speed of the game and the extension of the league programme.' He was right, of course. And Tommy's own exquisite sporting skills stretched much wider than to football: in July, playing in local cricket for Bootle Extras, he scored 131 blissful runs against Wavertree CC.

With the football pressure now released, Liverpool lost to both Cardiff and at home to West Bromwich Albion, with the Kop barracking Albion's ex-Everton man Stanley Davies and potentially tarnishing, according to the local press, the fact that 'Liverpool crowds have in the past gained the reputation of being very fair'. But Albion were beaten away 4–1 in the final league fixture, so Liverpool racked up fifty-seven points, six clear of Tottenham and eight ahead of Burnley. Everton hung on to their First Division place, just above relegated Bradford City and Manchester United. Forshaw and Hopkin had played every league game for the Reds in the 1921–22 season, and Bromilow had missed only due to international call-ups. Liverpool had used 22 players in all but had relied on a core of 14 and, crucially, had suffered no major injuries. Only Middlesbrough had called on fewer players. If truth be told, the championship had been nailed on well before Christmas, won on the basis of defensive strength, teamwork and goalkeeping magnificence.

The Charity Shield match with FA Cup-winners Huddersfield Town was played on 10 May 1922 at Old Trafford, and 'in a match that had not been advertised as it might have been' around 8,000, mainly Liverpool, supporters turned up to see the championship trophy presented to the club by the familiar figure of John McKenna. How bittersweet this must have seemed to the man who had done so much to help build the Liverpool club. How ironic, too, that the very early birth pangs of the football video replay suggested that Town might not even have been worthy FA Cup winners to play in this match. The Topical Film Company had filmed the 1922 final and, in a special showing for journalists, had slowed the pictures down sufficiently to show that 'in the cold, impartial record of the film camera' in the crucial penalty incident that decided the match there was 'little doubt' that both Hamilton of Preston and Smith of Huddersfield were at least a yard *outside* the penalty area. It would be more than 40 years, of course, before slow-motion replays were common in the English game. More than 80 years after this first controversy, the game is still debating the proper use of video technology.

David Ashworth and trainer Bill Connell, as well as the Liverpool players, received medals, and John McKenna's presentation speech at Old Trafford was barely audible over the 'hubbub' made by the club's supporters. Club chairman Walter Williams said in reply that he hoped that Liverpool would now win the elusive FA Cup another season. Typically, too, every key member of staff from Anfield, from the assistant groundsman and helpers to the chairman, participated in the presentation. 'No one was forgotten, and it was a kindly thought on the part of the directors to see that they all shared in the triumph.'

When the Liverpool players reached Exchange Station on their 'joy ride' from Manchester at around 10.30 p.m., there was a big crowd to meet the team. The Everton Terrace Boys Band turned out to welcome the players, and captain McKinlay could not avoid the revellers. 'Donald tried to walk to the "chara",' reported the *Evening Express*, 'but he was picked up and carried in triumph out of the station. One trembles to think what would have happened had last night's match decided the championship.' The players retired for their celebrations, as they had done back in 1906, to the late John Houlding's Sandon Hotel. Looking ahead, they might have had one thought in their minds: could winning the elusive FA Cup in 1923 be any more difficult than trying to retain the Football League title?

CHAPTER 6 REFERENCES

1. Belchem and MacRaild, 'Cosmopolitan Liverpool', p. 327
2. Holt, *Sport and the British*
3. Taylor, *The Association Game*, pp. 137–8
4. Inglis, *The Football League and the Men Who Made It*, p. 126
5. Fishwick, *English Football and Society*, p. 19
6. Taylor, *The Association Game*, p. 128
7. Young, *Football on Merseyside*, p. 105

7

'WHERE'S LIVERPOOL?'
'Top of the League!'

CIVILISING THE GLOBE THROUGH FOOTBALL

The Liverpool players' 'reward' for winning the 1922 league title was a summer tour to stifling Italy – to play their erstwhile title rivals Burnley! The Liverpool board accepted a £100 payment and all expenses paid by their hosts to make the trip. Players were given a royal ten shillings expenses a day. The two clubs even travelled together to Stresa and stayed in the same hotel, with their exhibition match planned for the city of Milan. Making money was behind the venture, no doubt. Tom Bromilow wrote a column for the Merseyside press, informing the Liverpool public about the unusual events and sights from abroad. Little reached Britain about the development of football on the Continent, of course, so this was all entirely new and exotic material for the Merseyside sporting public to chew over. It made grim reading.

In 'terrific heat', and with buckets of water scattered around the pitch to aid with rehydration, the match in Milan (which was won 0–1 by Burnley) was frequently reduced to walking pace, and 'a certain section of the spectators showed their disapproval by some hooting and booing'. This surprised the visiting players, especially since an estimated 25 per cent of the 10,000, mainly Italian, crowd was female. Bromilow was not much impressed by the 'typical' Italian spectator, though it was hard to know whether the local reaction to English football was a result of cultural difference, the effects of the heat or simply poor British technique. 'What an excitable people these Italians are!' said a bemused and disapproving Bromilow. 'Whenever a possible chance presented itself and the shooter failed, he was greeted by a combination of howls of derision or disappointment . . . The players took no notice.'

A week later, on 6 June 1922, when Liverpool played a combined Italian team from Tuscany and Ligne in a 2–2 draw, cultural differences were to the fore once more. The match teetered on the very brink of disintegration after an Italian was barged and fell heavily, breaking an arm in the process. Things immediately kicked off. Never, said Bromilow, had he played in a match in which the opposition had shown 'such recklessness and disregard for the rules. I have never played in such a game wherein so much hacking, kicking and pushing was tolerated. In fact, the home side indulged in everything except biting. They would not play the game properly, nor would they allow us to.' This was a common English complaint of the time and later, of course – 'foreigners' who did not really know the game or its standards or who failed to match up to the physical challenges of the British. These sorts of accounts and experiences would colour the football relationship between Britain and other Europeans for many decades to come. As respected northern football commentator W. Leslie Unsworth told *Evening Express* readers on 17 June 1922, these football trips abroad were no beano, no joy, for English teams. They were undertaken only out of a sense of national duty. 'Foreigners focus on the science, tactics and niceties,' he wrote, 'but they still have a great deal to learn in the matter of showing the sporting spirit. We need more visits to "educate" the Continentals.' It was the British leading the way, once more.

These deep-seated ideas and prejudices about 'foreigners' and their unsuitability for football were unquestioningly reinforced by a series of fictional football stories carried in the Liverpool *Evening Express* at this time. In one, published on 21 October 1922, entitled 'Team of All Nations', an ex-British serviceman called Sam formed a football club to try to bring people of the world together in post-war harmony. Inevitably, his plans were doomed to failure. The team was made up of unreliable Swedes and Egyptians, and a Spanish goalkeeper who 'you could smell a mile [off]' and who pulled a knife when dropped from the team. Also involved was Mass Tull Dixon, a 'coal-black coon' on the wing who was psychologically destroyed when teammates smashed his banjo. Finally, an effeminate French player, Hyacinth Bourget – 'he has some flower' – ridiculously challenged a love rival to a duel. What was the moral of this mess, drawn out for the Liverpool readers of the *Evening Express*? That 'football's essentially a game for Britishers. These foreigners ain't got the right temperament.'

WORLD IN MOTION

Elsewhere in the summer of 1922, the Liverpool press was reporting on an exciting but unstable world. The violent blackmailing and robbing antics of British racecourse gangs fascinated the popular press closer to home. So, too, did the news from the Postmaster General that it was 'quite possible' that every village in Britain with more than 2,000 people would presently have a telephone call office. Sir Henry Norman, vice-president of the Wireless Society, reported that all homes would soon have receiving sets and that the city of Liverpool was especially well placed as it was near a designated broadcast command centre.

Not that too many Liverpool *voices* were ever likely to be heard on the new wireless. They had that unmistakeable nasal combination of English, Irish, American and Welsh influences that was a mile from received English. Could the Liverpool dialect be described at all as Lancastrian, asked the *Evening Express* on 10 May 1922? 'Not Liverpool. Liverpool is everything BUT Lancastrian . . . The Liverpool twang must remain outside the pale. It is distinctive, indescribable and absolutely un-Lancashire. Liverpool is altogether *too* cosmopolitan.'

The closure of the famous Reynold's Waxworks in Lime Street now signalled the end of an era in the city. Nine out of ten visitors to Liverpool had attended the gory attractions of the waxworks in its heyday, but it had long fallen out of public favour. Instead, 40,000 £1 shares were offered for sale to local people in the new futuristic 1,500-seat Sefton Picturedrome, which was to be built to the south of the city centre. Meanwhile, the Midland Adelphi hotel proudly announced 'dances for every evening of the week during the season' and it was reported that 'large, eager crowds have been present each evening'.

The really big news story in the area, however, was a much more troubling one. It was about the new port extension at Southampton, which directly challenged Liverpool's supremacy in port cargo and distribution, having already stripped the declining Merseyside port of much of its major passenger transport custom by sea. A spokesman for the White Star Line offered reassuring words on Merseyside about the city's 'favourable' geographical position for cargo work, but there were also plenty of stern warnings about the apathetic and conservative Mersey docks and Harbour Board and the risks for Liverpool of poor and declining facilities if she should 'tarry on the road to progress'. The dangers were clear enough, and they were accentuated by the news that Manchester was soon to open a new air terminal, offering daily flights to London and Continental connections to Paris, Amsterdam and Berlin. Too much of the employment in Liverpool derived from trade through the port. The city had fallen behind in many ways and would fall still further – the halcyon days of the Merseyside docks were already over.

It was enough to drive locals to drink – and other drugs. A 'Mrs E' told the *Liverpool Courier* that recently on Church Street she had noticed an unfolded piece of blue paper lying on the pavement with the word 'COCAINE' printed on it twice in black ink. There seemed little subterfuge here. In nearby New Brighton, however, the locals were at a peak of excitement about something rather more wholesome and certainly less addictive: they were preparing to stage the World Cycling Championships of 1922 between 28 and 29 July. Adding to this sense that the Merseyside area was a world centre for *sport* and not just football in the 1920s was the fact that leading Liverpool swimmers gave exhibitions for the public at the local baths in Garston in south Liverpool in 1922. Among them was multiple record-breaker Hilda James, one of the four Garston swimmers who had made up most of the team of six swimmers who had competed for Great Britain in the 1920 Olympic Games in Antwerp. As the *Liverpool Courier* proudly reported, Garston – and only 15 years after the local baths were completed – was now 'world famous in swimming'.

TITLE CELEBRATIONS – AND 'GOING IN' FOR THE FA CUP

Back out of the pool and into the shark-infested waters of professional football, Blackburn Rovers proposed a sensible move back to 'random' rather than the back-to-back fixtures favoured in the Football League in order to increase variety and reduce 'needle' between players. But the proposal was turned down by the league management committee. The FA was soon complaining about 'rough' play in league matches in 1922–23, precisely because clubs were meeting again instantly in competitive combat. The Scottish FA suggested a new offside law: a 25-yard line across the pitch beyond which no forward could be offside. This was designed to counter the 'three-defender' law that currently operated and that had helped make Liverpool so solid defensively. Again, it was turned down, though this debate about offside would not disappear.

Liverpool FC announced a £30,609 credit balance for the 1921–22 season. Players' wages and bonuses reached £12,477, about one-quarter of total income. Entertainment tax creamed off almost £10,000, and Anfield season tickets, it was announced, would retail for £2 10s to watch the English champions next season. They would not want for takers.

At a special dinner attended by 276 shareholders and held by the Liverpool club at the Midland Adelphi hotel in June to celebrate the title win, 14 members of the 1905–06 team who were invited to attend turned up. The great Alex Raisbeck and his colleagues challenged the current Liverpool title-winning squad to a match – at tug of war! Raisbeck reiterated the now familiar Liverpool mantra that the club should now 'go in for the cup'. Three of the 1906 squad – Alf West, James Bradley and Sam Raybould – were 'owing to the present trade depression, faring none too well', and the Liverpool board voted to give £50 to each of them to aid their recovery. It was a nice touch, but it also smacked perhaps too much of charity. It was certainly not a gesture that would solve the difficulties of three of the club's best servants, with almost five hundred and fifty Liverpool games between them. 'The directors' action, I am certain,' said 'Cri' of the *Evening Express*, 'will be approved by all supporters of the Reds, while it is an incentive to players and clubs of today.' The truth was that very few football clubs cared much for their old warriors, no matter what their campaign medals might be.

The 1922 Liverpool title-winning players were all presented at this event with a gold watch – a traditional employer's gift to his willing workers. Chairman Walter Williams agreed that the players 'were gentlemen on and off the field. A happier and more united family all round, directors, players and staff, could not be found anywhere.' Liverpool Football Club in this period did seem a particularly unified ship, especially compared to strife-torn Everton. Williams also spoke out against the Football League's reduction in players' wages – to £8 per week maximum – and against large transfer fees, arguing that paying £4,000 for a player would be a worse policy than 'signing players they believed would fit into their present condition'. In reply to his chairman's words, club captain Donald McKinlay said, modestly, that speech-making was no game of his. But he expressed gratitude for the 'generous and sporting way' in which the directors had met the players. He then mentioned the main aim for the new season: 'We will do our utmost to win the English cup.'

'THEY COULD WIN ANYTHING'

Some of the extra income derived from the Liverpool championship win of 1922 was ploughed back into the club to further improve the Anfield ground. Concrete walls and steps were built at the back of the Kop, costing £4,500, and plans were announced for a revolutionary new triple-decker stand, a so-called 'hat-trick' stand, for the Anfield Road end, with the club 'deciding that as they cannot extend they must build up'. It was innovative but overly ambitious, and the stand was never constructed. But a new boys' pen *was* added, to the right of the press box on the Kemlyn Road side, to be entered from the Anfield Road end of the stadium. The enclosure was formidable, running half the length of the stand and built to accommodate some 4,000 boys. It seems almost unimaginable today, reflecting both a determination to tap into young support and early concerns about youthful misbehaviour. It was surrounded by iron-spiked railings to dissuade any younger supporters from trying to join the general crowd. It would later be much reduced in size and relocated to the Spion Kop. The club's plan was clearly to reduce nuisance and pitch encroachment, as well as recruit more, younger supporters, so the Liverpool directors put out a clear message through the local press that 'they would be glad if all boys who attend the game would make for this enclosure'. Was football really such a bad thing for a boy's education? The *Liverpool Courier* joked lightheartedly on the issue of 'how football crips the young':

TEACHER: Can you do arithmetic?
BOY: Yes, sir.
TEACHER: What's 2 and 6?
BOY: Half-a-crown.
TEACHER: Where's Liverpool?
BOY: Top of the league!

Liverpool manager David Ashworth was also hopeful of more first-team success, and why not? 'We ought to have a very good season,' he reasoned. 'There is perfect harmony from the boardroom to the dressing-room and that goes a long way.' He also had forward Dick Johnson back from a serious knee injury to add a little more substance to the Liverpool attack, and all the key members of the title team remained fit and well. Why not another championship, then, or even a run in the 'pimpernel' FA Cup, as the chairman had described it? Johnson certainly started well in a 5–2 season opener against Arsenal: two goals in the first five minutes and a hat-trick overall in front of 40,062 of the faithful. Arsenal's defence was 'in a tangle dealing with Liverpool's long passing and the triangular work of the Reds'.

But at bogey ground Roker Park – where Liverpool had played and lost in that stadium's opening match back in 1902 – there was another defeat, in gruelling circumstances. Under leaden skies, with a heavy ball and with darkness approaching, the referee decided there was no time for half-time, so the teams did not leave the field at all. In December 1922, a match between Blackburn and Stoke was abandoned with four minutes to go because of darkness. The satirical magazine *Punch* had noted that on the opening day of the league campaign, the press complained about players kissing a goalscorer. 'It is noticed, too, that nobody ever kisses the referee.' Not here, not today. In the gloom and on sodden turf, a heroic Elisha Scott saved again and again – playing against Charles Buchan always sparked the Ulsterman's interest. Scott produced one 'masterpiece' save from a drive by Jock Paterson. But the home centre-forward would not be denied, and the visitors left pointless, with a single goal against. At Arsenal, soon after, it was another wet, 'horrible' day for football, with no goals in open play and Liverpool's Walter Wadsworth conceding the deciding penalty kick – and another loss.

It had been a poor start for the champions Liverpool, no doubt about it. But a Wednesday evening return meeting with Sunderland in dry conditions at Anfield produced a 5–1 home win and sparked a run of seven wins in eight matches, enough to get Ashworth's men back to the top. 'It is a tribute to the efficiency of W. Connell, the Anfield trainer, that the Reds invariably outstay and outpace the opposition in the second half,' commented the *Liverpool Courier*. It was true that Liverpool often scored in the second half, and Chambers, Forshaw and Johnson were all in the goals against Sunderland. Everton were then downed twice in one week (there *were* attractions, after all, to these back-to-back fixtures). Liverpool had only won four out of twenty-two games against Everton at Anfield since the great split of 1892, but, according to the *Courier*, 'the days have gone by when the old jibe was that Liverpool only had to see a Blue shirt to be mesmerised into inactivity'.

The paper was right. This time all the mesmerising was done by Liverpool in the club's fourth five-goal haul in just nine league matches, with only one defeat, 0–2 at old adversaries Burnley. In East Lancashire, 'Bromilow was not up to his usual standard', and Elisha Scott, for once, missed a cross, leaving Weaver an easy finish. After the match, it was revealed in the *Liverpool Echo* that Scott, Johnson and Wadsworth had all received letters offering a £10 bribe to lose to Burnley. These 'honest players' had 'instantly' reported the matter to the Liverpool committee. Scott was also later asked to 'let his side down' at a match at Newcastle. 'Only a lunatic,' counselled the *Evening Express*, 'would take such an attempt seriously.'

Everton FC had already hit the big screen in 1922: footage of their home match against Newcastle United had been advertised as the *Evening Courier* film on show at various times at the Scala cinema in the city and on at the Futurist later in the week. This seems like a precursor to the Sky TV pub offerings 80 years later, but who would want to watch it? At Anfield against Everton, more than 50,000 fans paid record receipts of £3,200 to see Williams put Everton ahead by half-time, but Bill Connell's fitness regime soon had Liverpool roaring back. With his shirt outside his shorts, the urchin McNab was outstanding, including a trademark 'unnecessarily heavy foul on Hart which drew a stern warning from referee Andrews'. The veteran Everton goalkeeper Tommy Fern had a bleak time of it, at fault with at least two of the five goals that followed, including a hat-trick from the uncontainable Chambers. 'Longworth,' said the *Liverpool Echo*, 'was a study in enterprise. He was ceaseless in his work, he was everlasting in his sure punts and he had ideas of marching forward, like a king going forth to war.' It seemed like last season all over again, Liverpool already top and Everton struggling among the paupers at the bottom.

But tragedy also struck at this match, because Charles Newman, a forty-six-year-old butcher and father of five, fell and was killed on leaving the Kop, after hitting his head on one of the new concrete steps. A collection for the dead man was held at the next Liverpool home match, raising £94 7s for his family. Liverpool director Edwin Berry reported that inasmuch as Newman 'was not in very affluent circumstances', the club would also bear all the expenses of the fan's funeral. Was there any assumption of guilt in play here? Another director and head of the Liverpool FC grounds committee, Walter Cartwright, was instructed by the board to take up the matter with the club's insurers 'in case of any claim made for compensation', and he was soon inviting in the local press to show them the installation at Anfield of 17 new crush barriers around the ground. The unfortunate Mr Newman missed Liverpool winning 1–0 at Goodison Park, with his team having resorted to shameless time-wasting following Johnson's early goal and injuries to Lacey and Chambers. The Reds repeatedly hoofed the ball into the mainly Everton crowd. Lacey was 'almost useless' in the second half, but he stayed on the field, thus aggravating an injury that would keep him out of the next 12 league matches. Sportingly, Everton also held a collection for the deceased man Newman, which realised £26, and two Liverpool directors contributed £10 each to make, with fan subscriptions, a total of £158 for his widowed family. It was another sign of the close relations between the Liverpool clubs, and between supporters and the clubs in the city.

As the 1922 autumn British general election rumbled along in the background, and as Mussolini announced in Italy that the Fascist military command had assumed the direction of affairs at the recent Milan location for Liverpool FC's 1922 summer tour, the Anfield club, with the willing Gilhespy replacing Lacey at right-wing, continued to collect victories and points in domestic competition. Not even a 0–3 reverse at Cardiff in October could move them from the top of the table. This was a pathetic Liverpool show in South Wales, one that produced just one visitor's corner and provoked an acid poem, allegedly from the pen of a furious Elisha Scott:

> Twinkle, twinkle little star
> How I wonder what you are
> Wheel 'em in and wheel 'em out
> Cardiff three, Liverpool nowt.

Also in October, the Football League introduced forms for use by clubs to assess the performance of referees: they would be put to good use over time. Research at the time suggested that English players now dominated the top Football League clubs: in the First Division one hundred and eighty-two players were English, forty-three Scottish, ten Irish and just seven Welsh.

The experiences of ex-Everton star Joe Clennell, who played for Cardiff but still lived in Liverpool, also brought to mind more recent cases of very affluent professional players as potential crime victims. Clennell's Liverpool house was burgled while he was playing football and while both his wife and his servant were out of the home. Clearly, top footballers in the 1920s could lead pretty well-appointed lives, even if this meant they combined their football with other work. Liverpool's Walter Wadsworth, for example, had apparently blossomed as a manufacturer of superfine wax polish. It seems that the residences of some football players were obvious and easy targets for local criminals from quite early on and that some top players often lived some way away from the site of the club to which they had been transferred.

A 4–2 Liverpool victory at Tottenham in November 1922 had a Spurs director commenting that if the Liverpool team could keep up this standard of play 'they could win anything' and the *Evening Express* drooling over a brilliant Liverpool second-half spell 'when they would surely have beaten any opponents in the world'. The return match was much less impressive, a dull 0–0 draw that meant that 'suddenly the little boys who shout "1–2–3–4" do not look as debonair as usual'. But even vocal young Liverpool partisans like these were likely to show their respects at this time for the requirements of Remembrance Sunday. The Great War had been over only four years, and a press reporter recorded Liverpool local football's impressive response to the salute for the war dead. A morning match was in heated progress on the White Star Athletic Ground in Wavertree on the due date. But at the signal for the minute's silence at precisely 11 a.m., the players stopped rigid on the pitch in the middle of an attack and all the spectators immediately removed their hats and dipped their heads. Football had learned a lot since the controversy of 1914.

TITLE GIANTS OR A BUNCH OF 'ROUGH HOUSES'?

When Liverpool beat Aston Villa 3–0, also in November, Villa's own 'bad boy', England half-back enforcer Frank Moss, reportedly 'went about the field giving the Liverpool players a fearfully good time'. Unsurprisingly, the return match at Villa the next week had 'rather too much red light about it'. Liverpool won 1–0, moving two points clear at the top, but it was a crude affair, a 'too robust game', claimed the *Liverpool Courier*, with too much 'man before the ball at Villa Park'. A 'hack' by Moss on Chambers 'made the latter momentarily lose his head . . . Hopkin grabbed him.' The formidable Walter Wadsworth got into the bad books of the crowd 'by his heavy work and restless kicking . . . Wadsworth was too reckless in his interventions and must need to curb himself in this direction.'

McNab and Wadsworth could match anybody if things got rough in midfield. Only a miraculous late save by Scott from a 'headlong dive' kept Liverpool ahead after Chambers had scored just before half-time.

This contest at Villa was just the kind of wild tussle that later led Everton's Dixie Dean to describe the Liverpool team of this period as 'no more than a bunch of rough houses'. He probably had a point, but the truth was also rather more complex than that. The Liverpool teams of the early 1920s could certainly play – Bromilow, Hopkin and Forshaw were all refined footballers. The great Charles Buchan had also said of Walter Wadsworth that he was the most difficult half-back proposition the England forward had ever faced: 'You never know what he's going to do next. He's so unorthodox and seems to "get there" without disclosing his intentions.' But Liverpool could also mix it compared to the 'prettier' approach of Everton and others – they were formidable at 'practising a resolute cohesion', as one commentator delicately put it, when they needed to.[1] This sort of toughness and sheer will to win was the basis of dual league champions. But was the sporting ethos fast disappearing from English football? Was all this alleged aggression and ruthlessness, and also the money at the top end of football, ruining *all* levels of the sport?

This seems to have been a constant media theme of the day, what with champions Liverpool getting into ugly scrapes, FA Cup tickets for the 1923 final at the new Empire Stadium announced to be priced from a hefty five shillings and Hull City keeper Billy Mercer bloodying a fan's face by hurling a stone into the crowd at Barnsley.[2] A junior local club in Liverpool, Earle FC, even wrote in its own magazine, *Goalpost,* that 'referees are constantly being booed and are the object of many an unsportsmanlike and unnecessary remark'. Nationally, the *Daily Herald* argued, 'Ninety-nine spectators out of a hundred go to a football match, not so much to see a sporting game as to see their team win by hook or crook . . . the truth of the matter is when money comes in, sport goes out.' But Cri, the local Liverpool football reporter for the *Evening Express,* replied evenly and sensibly that this view that football was sliding into anarchy was actually 'tosh'. He contended that professional players in the city were 'sportsmen to their fingertips' and that 'league soccer is not a money-making business. It takes most clubs all their time to meet their obligations.' Liverpool Football Club also had another league title to win.

CHASING ANOTHER DOUBLE – BUT LOSING A MANAGER!

The night before Liverpool won 1–0 at Newcastle in December 1922, the visiting players and journalists went to see a Charlie Chaplin-style comedian perform in a theatre revue built around a gormless character called 'Dick Johnson'. The Liverpool man of the same name was 'unmercifully ragged' by his teammates the next day – but he played well enough and saw Chambers athletically volley the winning goal from his high pass. In the return match, a shock 0–1 defeat, the Newcastle forward Tommy McDonald, a Scot, won a chase with Ephraim Longworth to a penny thrown from the Anfield stands. The visitor kept it 'firmly clasped in his left hand until the conclusion of the game'. He then handed it to a United director who had it gilded and made into a brooch for his wife, engraved with the date and score of Liverpool's first home loss of the season. But it had started life as just a penny.

Liverpool, shaken but not stirred, now faced three matches over Christmas 1922 in just four days: Forest (away) on Saturday, 23 December; Oldham (away) on 25 December; and Oldham (home) on Boxing Day. When a letter writer complained to the *Evening Express* about Christmas Day football, Cri pointed out that these were pretty much the only games that shopkeepers and assistants and other similar workers could actually attend. The debate about Christmas football was thus ended before it had really begun – at least for now.

There now followed a real bolt from the blue: Liverpool FC, via secretary George Patterson, announced that the club manager David Ashworth would be 'released from his engagement' with Liverpool, 'which does not expire for a few months yet so he can take up duties as the manager of the Oldham Athletic club'. In short, in the very middle of an already thunderous season, Ashworth was asking to leave prospective league champions Liverpool for a relegation fight in Oldham – which he would ultimately lose. There was no mystery here, 'no friction whatsoever' between Ashworth and the Liverpool board, though the Liverpool FC minutes of 28 December 1922 show a rather cold approach to the whole business: 'All moneys, keys, etc., belonging to the club to be returned to the secretary before leaving.' The Stockport man's wife and daughter were both invalids, and Ashworth simply wanted to live in the family home in Stockport rather than in digs in Liverpool, as he had been doing. Oldham were willing to pay very well to recruit their man. But the Liverpool press pointed out that Ashworth had been in charge of a 'ready-made team' at Anfield so he had had 'no necessity to join in the feverish search for players which makes the lives of so many managers a burden to them'. The Liverpool manager was giving up a lot.

Ashworth was no builder of a side or of a specific ethos in the manner of a Tom Watson, and his departure also probably signalled the extent to which the Liverpool directors had assumed, once again, direct selection responsibilities following Watson's death. But this shock departure was still a blow, and it would surely affect the Liverpool players, who had to play Ashworth's new club Oldham *twice* over the coming days! In fact, Liverpool won both matches, thus effectively sending Athletic down before their new manager had even arrived to take charge. On 26 December, it was Elisha Scott's turn for a benefit match – although the Irishman would play at Liverpool for another 12 years. As always, the club asked for volunteers to act as collectors with buckets. The papers reported that 'a fine collection is taken'.

The effects of Ashworth's departure on Liverpool were immediately apparent – with Dick Johnson injured, the adventurous Jock McNab volunteered to play at centre-forward on Boxing Day in an 'extraordinary experiment'. McNab even tried a 'pantomime somersault' to try to reach a wild Hopkin cross. The Liverpool directors were thinking outside the box, all right. But the Reds were four points clear of Sunderland going into the new year, and an advert was promptly placed for a new Liverpool manager in the *Athletic News* and the *Sporting Chronicle*, applications to 10 Cook Street by 15 January. Unusually, the Liverpool directors at their board meeting of 28 December put on record their appreciation of the 'splendid performances' of the Liverpool team during the holiday matches. Meanwhile, Little Davie Ashworth would have few chances at Oldham to enjoy what he really liked about the game: three-goal leads, so 'then he can puff on his pipe – from which he is seldom separated – in peaceful tranquillity'.

Liverpool's FA Cup campaign without David Ashworth would begin at home against Arsenal. The Londoners prepared in brine baths in Southend while Liverpool retired to Rhyl for some bracing Welsh sea air. Arsenal played Dr Jimmy Patterson, an amateur, on the wing in a dour 0–0 draw at Anfield, but at Highbury Liverpool turned it on in a 4–1 replay win. In a high comedy moment, the home keeper Robson was chased by a stray dog while carrying the ball and then kicked the ball straight to Johnson – who scored. As did 'Sharkey' Chambers – a strange new moniker, this one, for the Reds forward. Elisha Scott hotly disputed a penalty awarded against him for punching the bustling Turnbull on the back at a corner, but Scott saved the kick anyway. Ephraim Longworth had cleverly packed the Liverpool players along the line of the penalty area immediately behind the kicker to offer abusive comment and to restrict his run-up. The FA took note and eventually (in 1937) introduced the restraining arc on the penalty area to offer proper clearance for spot-kickers. It remains the last official change to pitch markings.

In unfamiliar stripes and back in the league at Middlesbrough later in January 1923, Liverpool's Jock McNab took 'strange exception' to his pen picture in the Boro programme, which had been provided by a Liverpool journalist. It had described the midfield man as an 'unspeakable Scot. Stutters when talking and is hard to follow by word or deed for, indeed, he is dashing and the best shot of the lot, though half-back.' Liverpool chairman Walter Williams lodged an official complaint, though much worse could have – and had – been said about the fierce McNab outside the city. Liverpool won 2–0, with home keeper Williamson to blame for Chambers' low shot finding the net. Liverpool had now taken 22 out of the last 26 league points and looked unstoppable in the title race. The usual question was now raised: could this actually be the year for an FA Cup and league Double at Anfield?

CHAMPIONS AGAIN – BUT FRUSTRATED IN THE CUP

As neighbours Everton tried to spend their way out of a crisis with a £10,000 transfer spree, so nearby Chester FC held a fans' crisis meeting early in 1923 as the club's overdraft doubled in the face of falling crowds. The latest Liverpool beneficiary, meanwhile, was the captain Donald McKinlay, a true and loyal leader who was 'no martinet' but instead was happy to listen to the opinions of other players and to 'see that justice is done'. McKinlay was no public speaker either, and he had few interests outside the game except his family. 'Ask him about his little girl,' the *Evening Express* suggested, 'and Mac will wax quite eloquent.' Asked about the possibility that he might play for Scotland again, McKinlay replied with the sort of direct assurance and fortitude that has marked out the Liverpool club's best servants for more than 100 years. On 25 January 1923, he told the *Evening Express*, 'Red is my colour. I'll play for Liverpool as long as they will have me. I don't want to play for anybody else and when I pull off the red shirt for the last time I expect I will finish with football, at any rate as a player.' Jamie Carragher had his role models to follow: the magnificent McKinlay was true to his word, playing his last-ever Football League match – for Liverpool against Aston Villa – on 1 September 1928. The defender was part of a Liverpool team that was more solid, more reassuringly predictable, than even the 1922 equivalent. It read, pretty much on a weekly basis, in its traditional 2–3–5 formation:

Liverpool FC, league-title winners, 1922–23

Scott

Longworth   McKinlay

McNab   Wadsworth   Bromilow

Lacey   Forshaw   Johnson   Chambers   Hopkin

Only Lacey (twelve missing league matches from October to December 1922, mainly replaced by Gilhespy) and Wadsworth (five matches missed in March 1923) would suffer anything like an extended run of absence for injury during the season. The form of Longworth had seen off Lucas at full-back, and Dick Johnson had made the previously problematic centre-forward position his own.

This consistency of selection, the experience gained from the previous season's success and the relative absence of injury would all contribute considerably to Liverpool maintaining the league title in 1923. But could they win the cup? Drawn to play at Wolves in the FA Cup on 3 February, Bill Connell had the Liverpool players away at Rhyl, once more, kitted out in flat caps, collars and with golf clubs on the local course. The *Evening Express* praised the psychological work of the Reds trainer, who fully 'understands human nature as applied to football' because 'though his velvet glove may conceal the proverbial iron fist, Bill never needs it'. Who says modern methods were not used in the past? The modest Connell, for his part, praised his players' 'great spirit of unselfishness and cheery optimism'. Managerless Liverpool now sent club secretary George Patterson to Bradford to sign cover for Tommy Bromilow and the great Elisha. The Liverpool man came back with Algernon Wilkinson for goalkeeper and utility man David Pratt. Sadly, the wonderfully named keeper would never play for Liverpool before being sold to Blackpool – Scott could never be dropped or rested. But the ex-Celtic man Pratt became a useful Reds squad player in the years that followed.

Liverpool FC – and the club's fans – were quite outstanding in a 2–0 win at Molineux. 'The Anfield club has followers the like of which most clubs would be proud of,' said the *Liverpool Echo*. 'They are loyal to the core, and their vocal efforts would put some army camps to shame. There was a vocalian company behind me at Molineux, and their chants were stunning the natives.' This latest FA Cup win was a 'fine stroll', according to the *Evening Express*, and 'a great day out ended up with a fight out of Lime Street, where another enthusiastic crowd gave the players a strenuous welcome home'. Liverpool were also in 'invincible form' at home to West Brom, where a 2–0 league victory courtesy of goals by Forshaw and Johnson could easily have been 22 but for the display of the veteran visiting keeper Hubert Pearson. A win pocketed, the Liverpool directors even went into the away dressing-room to congratulate the Albion man after the game. A Midlands letter writer to the *Liverpool Echo* compared Liverpool to Preston North End in their prime, gushing that 'Liverpool were simply great'.

Clear in the league as title holders, dominant in the FA Cup, a wonderful team ethic and everybody fit and playing to their maximum: it was not a bad outfit for an incoming manager to take over. Matt McQueen and two other ex-Liverpool players were reputed to be in the final three for the job, and it was McQueen who was chosen, some consolation for his humiliation at the hands of the Liverpool shareholders back in 1921. McQueen had refereed after his playing career had ended, up until the First World War, and had then been co-opted onto the Liverpool board in 1919. He still lived in Anfield, and despite his inexperience in this sort of job he was well known and trusted by the Liverpool board, who admired his understated qualities of leadership and integrity and his intimate knowledge of the club. He frequently scouted players for Liverpool and was brought in as manager essentially as a line of communication and a buffer between the board and the dressing-room. Not that McQueen did much shouting himself, because when the *Evening Express* went to interview the new man the reporter had to overcome McQueen's obvious diffidence – it was the first press interview Liverpool's new young manager had ever given in his life. What was the difference between today's Liverpool and the great teams McQueen had played in almost 30 years before at Anfield? On this point there was no hesitation. Any previous Liverpool goalkeeper, said McQueen with real feeling, 'was not anything like as clever as Scott'.

Sheffield United at home in the FA Cup in round three looked like an invitation for Liverpool and Matt McQueen to progress gently towards possible Double glory. Would their new manager inspire a great Reds performance? Instead, he brought crashing disaster, a 1–2 defeat in front of 51,859 spectators crammed into Anfield. Chambers' early goal was never enough as Liverpool spluttered and finally capitulated to their moderate guests – who also later thumped the Reds 1–4 in the league at Bramall Lane just to show that this was no fluke result. This shuddering FA Cup setback at least meant that it would not be Liverpool and its supporters who would be caught up in the crowd fiasco that symbolised the chaotic first Wembley FA Cup final in 1923. And despite back-to-back 0–1 losses in March, to Blackburn Rovers and Manchester City, Liverpool's league form continued mainly to hold up.

A sequence of five straight league draws in a crowded April after the hammering at Sheffield might be taken as a sign of a nervy Liverpool finish, or else a tired stumble by some struggling veterans up the home straight. Perhaps the team was missing Ashworth's guiding hand? But it could also be reasonably read as a dip in form and a loss of edge due to the lack of any really threatening pressure from below. There was no credible title challenge from Sunderland or Huddersfield Town, or from any of the other chasers, including Everton, who had now clambered up to fifth place. When Liverpool drew 1–1 at home to Huddersfield on 21 April, Chambers equalising a quickly taken Town free-kick, Sunderland's same-day loss at Burnley simply confirmed what had been apparent since Christmas: that Liverpool would easily retain the Football League title, this time with two games to spare and ultimately by a crushing six points.

There was just one more party piece for the rather spoiled Liverpool crowd to enjoy before the season's end – a beaming Bill Lacey excelling in goal and keeping an Anfield clean sheet in a 1–0 home victory, with Chambers scoring against the already relegated Stoke. Elisha Scott had picked up a thigh injury in front of John McKenna, representing the Football League. When the trophy and medals were presented, according to the *Liverpool Echo*, McKenna said that the Anfield club was noted, above all, for consistency and that given the 'strenuous character of today's games there could be no doubt that Liverpool's performance stood high above anything else that had occurred'. Most of the cheering crowd heard little of this praise. Nor did they hear the ebullient Walter Wadsworth say to McKenna, 'See you again next year, sir!' The modest Matt McQueen absented himself so he would not receive the manager's medal that was really not of his deserving. He had tinkered admirably little with the winning formula he had been bequeathed, and he was mainly directed in his management duties by the Liverpool board.

Walter Wadsworth, with an eloquent little speech in his best Bootle accent, presented the Liverpool backs and former captain and current captain, Longworth and McKinlay, with a miniature cup on behalf of the players and staff as a tribute to their service, leadership and sheer playing quality. It was a touching moment and typical of the respect players in the Liverpool squad held for each other. The club got permission from the Football League to give presents to the players to the value of £25 each – about three weeks' wages. Chambers had contributed 22 league goals in 39 appearances and Forshaw 19 in 42, but it was in conceding only 31 times in 42 fixtures and losing only once at home that the championship was really won.

'There were mounted police outside to ensure there was no Wembley nonsense,' said a scathing *Liverpool Echo* in its conclusion to the day's events. The newspaper was reflecting, of course, on the recent farce at the white-horse Wembley final. Altogether 'it was a memorable day in the history of the club'. Double league champions: it sounded wonderful. Where next for Liverpool – and indeed for English football? Change, as always, was lurking just around the corner.

CHAPTER 7 REFERENCES

1. Young, *Football on Merseyside*, p. 106
2. Huggins and Williams, *Sport and the English*, p. 18

8

THEY SHALL BE OUR TEACHERS
The First Internationalisation
of Liverpool FC

LADY LUCK – AND A NEW FOOTBALL AGE

The kind of luck needed to win consecutive league championships in an age in which money was much less the key divider between football clubs than it has since become is unlikely to last long. So it was with Liverpool Football Club under its new manager Matt McQueen. Indeed, McQueen's own personal luck was also to turn bad, painfully and cruelly so. Injuries beset the Anfield club on and off the field in 1923–24, as if in payback for the relatively clean bills of health for the title-winning seasons before. Added to this, McQueen and the Liverpool directors could not quite bring in the high-quality replacements that had been common currency when Tom Watson had been at the club. Some key Liverpool players of this period were now ageing, but why try to fix what ain't broke? Bill Shankly faced the same question almost 50 years later. This eventually meant a problem for the high-tempo, aggressive game built around the traditional 2–3–5 formation initially perfected by Watson that had brought Liverpool so much recent success. In 1923, Ephraim Longworth was approaching 36 years of age, Donald McKinlay was 32, Billy Lacey 34 and Walter Wadsworth 33. 'Can the Liverpool veterans rise again to a new challenge?' the *Liverpool Courier* asked, hinting strongly that it already feared it knew the answer.

This kind of continuity and loyalty at least meant that Liverpool could hang on to their values and vaunted team spirit, so that when the club reached the Lancashire Cup final later in the new season the club invited all its staff to attend, plus ex-manager Davie Ashworth, and also insisted on presenting a full benefit cheque of £650 to the departing Harry Lewis. As the local press agreed, 'Such little acts of forethought speak well for the camaraderie of the team and officials.' But the game was also moving on, finally ridding itself of the shackles of the First World War, even if a major global economic depression was brewing. Manchester City, for example, had opened a vast stadium at Maine Road with new creature comforts, reportedly capable of holding an astonishing 90,000 people. Football spectators were beginning to demand much more for their shilling. New, more 'scientific' tactical advances were also slowly emerging on the pitch, despite the continued British focus on aggression and physicality. Ironically, these developments abroad were actually led by an Englishman, Jimmy Hogan. The deep-thinking Hogan had, briefly, returned from football coaching on the Continent to live in Liverpool after the war, and he worked as a dispatch foreman for Walker's Tobacco. Sadly, his huge talents were not sought out by Anfield. Hogan's futuristic visions of preparation and coaching, and of new systems of play, were little supported among any of the hardened working-class professionals or football-club directors in England. But his early teachings on the importance of technique and tactics, using chalk on a blackboard, heavily influenced the so-called *Wunderteam* of Austria and helped produce the 'Danubian School' of football that radicalised the traditional Scottish passing style and would lead the rest of Europe into modern approaches to football play.[1]

Not that the English football hierarchy was much impressed at all with the Continental game. Writing in the *Football Echo* on 18 December 1924, the Football League's powerful Charles Sutcliffe, an ardent anti-European and a man known variously in the English game as either 'the brains of football' or the 'football dictator', told the people of Liverpool how little he thought of the Continentals from Belgium whom he had just seen play limply against an English team.[2] 'I have no desire,' said Sutcliffe, 'to see another game with Continentals in this country.' FA secretary Stanley Rous confirmed later that in the English football hierarchy well into the 1930s, 'There was a sense of natural superiority, a smug feeling that all was right in our enclosed world and others had nothing to teach us.'[3] The English still had a lot to learn about developing their international ties through sport.

The new, more subtle approaches to the game were led in the 1920s and 1930s by the extraordinary Herbert Chapman, the educated son of a Yorkshire miner and ex-bare-knuckle fighter. Chapman was only a moderate player, but he did show an early knack for the spectacular – and for predicting the future – by playing in bright yellow football boots.[4] Huddersfield Town, under Chapman, won the FA Cup in 1922 and then three league titles in a row following Liverpool's Double, from 1924 to 1926, two of them under the Yorkshireman.

Following on from the strides made by Liverpool's Tom Watson, Chapman was probably the first British football manager to have complete control over the entire running of a football club. He also revolutionised player preparation and football tactics, though few British managers were actually able to follow his lead in the 1920s. When Huddersfield beat Liverpool 1–3 at Leeds Road on 10 November 1923, their style and the result was widely interpreted by the British press as a crucial shift in the balance of football power in England. The move was from the physicality and strength of the Anfield title-winners to the altogether faster and more skilful approach of the Yorkshire club.[5] Within a year, Bee in the *Liverpool Echo* was commenting on Liverpool football (with admirable partisanship *and* honesty) that 'we have become slothful, stereotyped, rutty in our thought and manner of play'.

English football as a whole certainly needed change. On 22 November 1924, a female correspondent to the *Football Echo* signing herself 'Play the Game' complained about the negativity of the current offside law in football (*three* defenders required between forwards and the goal). Teams playing the so-called 'one back' tactic – thus continually catching forwards offside – had meant that 'games are simply ruined from a spectators' point of view'. When the home football associations, via the International Board at FIFA in 1925, amended the offside law to just *two* defenders, a flood of goals initially resulted in league football. But the new law change also led directly to more strategic defensive tactics: the 'third back' or the W–M formation. This change made the traditional centre-half much more of a defensive player rather than the versatile half-back do-everything pivot, such as Liverpool's Alex Raisbeck.

LEFT-BEHIND LIVERPOOL?

Chapman joined Arsenal in 1925, and by the early 1930s his new counter-attacking W–M formation was fully established. Full-backs now marked wingers, rather than the inside-forwards: wing-halves watched the inside-forwards, rather than opposing wingers; centre-halves played deeper and marked the centre-forward rather than acting as a team pivot; and inside-forwards dropped deeper, too, rather than supporting the centre-forward. In funnelling back and allowing opponents to 'come on' to Arsenal and then striking them on the break, Chapman, according to the *Daily Mail*, had become the modern controller of a football machine, 'the first manager who set out methodically to organise the winning of matches'.[6]

Following the Chapman revolution on and off the pitch in England, the clubs from the south would now pose much more of a threat between the wars to the commanding traditional giants of the north and the Midlands. Was Liverpool Football Club simply falling behind at this seminal moment in the sport's development, lacking both foresight and, especially, tactical and managerial innovation? It looked like it, because initially the club persisted with 2–3–5, though, more simply, Liverpool also lacked a reliable forward to build on the good work of Harry Chambers in the early 1920s.

In the first season after the change in the offside law (1925–26), Liverpool scored more goals (63 up to 70), but the goals-against column also moved up, from 55 to 63. Champions Huddersfield Town scored 92 goals and fifth-placed Sheffield United a thumping 102. Even relegated Manchester City scored 89. But Everton's new star forward Dixie Dean was the man to plunder goals in this more open era, scoring by some estimates a staggering century of goals in all competitions *on his own* in season 1927–28, when the Blues won the league title. Sixteenth-placed Liverpool scored 84 league goals in total.

At Anfield there was little obvious adaptation to the new era. But long-term injuries to key figures – especially among the forwards – undoubtedly hit Liverpool hard in the mid-1920s, and they also affected the form of other players who had been so vital in bringing title success to Anfield. The cultured Forshaw, for example, had contributed nineteen crucial goals in 1922–23, but he could now manage only five in thirty-nine appearances in 1923–24. Even Harry Chambers was reduced to just thirteen goals in thirty league appearances, and *all* of Johnson's goals disappeared in 1923–24 – he made only two league appearances because of injury.

IN THE GRIP OF A CLERICAL TYRANNY

All this change was still ahead when in the summer of 1923 the Liverpool directors held an unusual board meeting on the train from Merseyside to Llandudno on 3 August and decided on an early version of corporate ticketing for the new league champions. Two complimentary season tickets were allocated to: the Bank of Liverpool; the Royal Liver Company; the chief constable and his deputy; and HM Customs and Excise. Even the Reds players – double league champions after all – were finally allocated two complimentary tickets for each home match. By 1929, there would be the first authentic steps towards identifiable corporate hospitality at Anfield. 'Mr Cherry is appointed as steward in the refreshment room,' the Liverpool minute book entry reads, 'and a commissionaire [is to] be engaged at the entrance to ensure that no one is admitted without refreshment tickets.' Keep the riff-raff at bay. Later, the Reds chairman Walter Cartwright might have welcomed ticket-only access, because in October 1929, while returning by train from another Reds defeat at Leicester City, a travelling companion – presumably a fellow director – made a 'serious allegation' concerning his integrity. After an apology was given, Cartwright cooled down and was given a vote of confidence by the board. But his Liverpool team was already struggling.

In the city, meanwhile, in the early 1920s, a 'beautiful and vastly improved' Clayton Square shopping precinct, 'a magnificent pile of buildings', was promised by the Liverpool Estates Committee as part of continuing modernisation. This was in line with a policy, reported in the *Evening Express*, to make Liverpool 'a more attractive city to visit, a greater centre for shopping and amusement, a cheerier, more cosmopolitan sort of a place than ever'. It could have been the 2008 Capital of Culture talking.

In 1923, three young Manchester entrepreneurs led by John Moores were experimenting with distributing football pools coupons outside Merseyside football grounds. They had borrowed the idea from Birmingham, where the pools business had failed. Their Littlewoods football betting business would eventually provide thousands of jobs for Liverpool women.

Betting was frowned upon locally in the 1920s, not least because the patently 'dull' city of Liverpool was still held in the iron claw of religion. It was also no closer to getting Sunday sport for working people. In July 1923, Liverpool City Council turned down, by 60 votes to 25, another motion to allow the playing of Sunday sport in the city's parks. Alderman Austin Harewood described Liverpool as being 'in the grip of clerical tyranny'. Perhaps the Merseyside clerics were simply underestimating the positive power of football. In 1923, the *Evening Express* reported that a Bradford man, Percy Bottomley, who had lost his capacity for speech after being blown up in Germany in the Great War, suddenly found his voice again during a local football match in the city. He blurted out, 'Leave it, it's mine!'

ACCIDENTS WILL HAPPEN?

The Liverpool Football Club players were rather less hamstrung by tradition and restraint than were the city's authorities. Three of them – Dick Johnson, Harry Chambers and the reserve Welsh full-back Ted Parry – only narrowly missed serious injury as the new season began when the motorcycle sidecar they were riding in was hit head-on by a car. Early road transport had its risks. This was not the only – or the worst – Liverpool FC traffic mishap of the new campaign. In November 1923, half-back Jock McNab suffered serious facial injuries requiring 17 stitches when he hit the windscreen of the taxi cab he was travelling in when it collided with a car after midnight. His injuries kept him out for 12 league matches. Life could be dangerous for footballers in the 1920s. Later in the same year, Tommy Ball, the Aston Villa centre-half, was tragically shot dead by his neighbour and landlord in Perry Barr after an on-street argument. Liverpool played Villa soon afterwards in an eerie atmosphere at Villa Park in which both sides wore black crêpe armbands.

When Liverpool opened the new campaign against West Bromwich Albion on 25 August, they 'failed to show the sparkle' of the previous season, and worse, Dick Johnson, a key figure, broke down with a serious knee injury. Patchy form followed, though Johnson's replacement Jimmy Walsh showed up well, ending as top scorer with 16 goals. The visit of the prime minister and Lord Derby to Anfield on 3 November could produce only a 1–1 draw with Chapman's rising Huddersfield Town, and Liverpool had already settled into the midtable obscurity from which they would never escape. Matt McQueen and the Liverpool directors' response was hardly earth-shattering: they signed Joe Keetley, a 23-year-old forward from Third Division Accrington Stanley. Keetley managed two goals in his nine starts, but the Reds were soon in a goal drought. In nine league matches across November and December 1923, Liverpool managed only five goals, with five straight losses.

By this stage, Johnson, Lacey, Longworth and Bromilow had all been missing for lengthy spells due to injury, and only five of the Liverpool title-winning team contested a turgid 0–0 draw at Villa Park in November. The Liverpool press accused Villa of having the 'most partisan of all supporters' and of being schooled missile-throwers. Elisha Scott was a past expert at riling the Villa faithful. Here, the Liverpool goalkeeper was 'subject to a great deal of vituperation and was nearly hit by something thrown by one of the crowd'. In December, Sheffield United warned their own fans about bad behaviour after a Liverpool player (probably Walter Wadsworth) was 'grossly insulted as he walked off the playing pitch' at Bramall Lane. But Liverpool's real problems were *on* the field. On 27 December 1923, after a defeat at Newcastle United, a *Liverpool Courier* headline – also reflecting the rise of new harsher media values and reporting style – read, simply, 'Liverpool going from bad to worse'.

Things could not get much worse, certainly not for the unfortunate Matt McQueen. While scouting for players in Sheffield, the Liverpool manager was hit by a car, suffering serious leg injuries in the collision. What was it with the Liverpool staff and road accidents all of a sudden? By February 1924, septic poisoning had set in, and the great Liverpool player and manager had to have a leg amputated. The club paid McQueen's medical bills amounting to £100 2s 6d. Already knowing his fate, McQueen bravely and jauntily wrote to Cri at the *Evening Express* on the subject of Liverpool's improving form. 'I say old chap, the Reds are doing all right now, eh?' This voice sounded more like a country squire than that of the Liverpool boss. McQueen promised that 'if everything goes on with my "baby" as desired', he hoped to meet the Reds players at the FA Cup final at Wembley in April. Neither Matt McQueen nor Liverpool Football Club would make it to Wembley intact. Worse, Liverpool was now without many of its best players *and* its stricken manager.

On 8 January 1924, the *Evening Express* reported that Liverpool FC was on the brink of a full-scale crisis. 'With manager Matt McQueen in hospital and more than a full side in the hands of the doctor, chairman Mr W.R. Williams, his fellow directors and secretary George Patterson are at their wits end to know what to do for the best.' Did the best it could do involve signing Hector Lawson from Rangers? Lawson was the Scotland understudy of Alan Morton, the renowned middle-class, teetotal international wing genius. Lawson was snapped up on the uncertain premise that anyone capable of stepping in for Morton must himself be a very good player. Sadly, Lawson was not.

'BOUNDLESS AND UNENDING INSPIRATION'

Hope flickered eternal in the FA Cup, especially after Liverpool dispatched Bradford City at Anfield and then turned over cup holders Bolton Wanderers on 2 February 1924 in a 4–1 away upset that bore all the hallmarks of a club heading for Wembley. Five football-special trains had departed Liverpool for Bolton, but still hundreds of Reds fans were left disappointed and stranded at Exchange Station. Walsh was the obvious Liverpool hero on the day, with a superb hat-trick, but it was McNab who was 'the talk of the match'. Bolton's Jimmy Seddon (who later coached at Liverpool) was injured and off the field for most of the second half. Serious match injury shaped so many crucial football encounters before substitutions were sanctioned.

A big crowd waited to greet the Liverpool squad at Exchange Station, but the players cleverly 'escaped' the throng into a party at the Exchange Hotel, also attended by John McKenna. Honest John wanted so much for *his* Liverpool to lift the FA Cup. Chairman Williams spoke warmly of the loyalty shown by players during these difficult times, and Donald McKinlay mumbled some thanks before saying, 'I reserve the rest of this speech until the return from Wembley.' Belief was already growing.

Why not? With injured players returning, and form and results picking up, the omens seemed better for Liverpool. Being drawn away to Southampton in late February 1924 did not deter hundreds of Reds fans from catching the quarter-past-midnight train on Friday evening, to arrive at 7.30 a.m. on the south coast for the day's festivities. Liverpool might have been a little windy about the tie, because directors Cartwright and Troop complained in advance to the FA about seats being 'too close' to the goal-line at one end of the ground. A tight 0–0 draw included the usual 'miraculous' save from Scott, this time to keep out forward Art Dominy.

At Anfield, for the Wednesday-afternoon replay, local workplaces must have been short-staffed, because thousands of locals were left locked outside, and 'enthusiasts' in the corners of the ground climbed the concrete walls to sit around the pitch. There was the first report at Anfield of what the *Evening Express* described as the 'rather dangerous' practice of supporters passing children over their heads to the front of the crowd. The Southampton mascot, clad in red and white, amused the locals with his wild dancing, while Liverpool supporters inflated hundreds of red balloons in an early show of FA Cup football carnival. One visiting supporter, squeezing in late, comically caught his coat in a closing entrance gate and missed the entire first half as a result. In a match of 'accidents', which had both Donald McKinlay and Southampton's Fred Titmuss hospitalised with head injuries, Liverpool's ten men beat off the Saints 2–0 in a scrappy encounter. It was 'poor football', admitted half-back Tommy Bromilow unapologetically later, 'but both sides were upset by the accidents'.

The Liverpool minute books reveal that a Mr Kay was given permission by the club in February 1924 to produce a booklet about its history, with 750 copies to be given to the club free of charge. Was it ever produced? Also, Liverpool and Everton agreed to play a historic exhibition game as part of the celebrations at the new Wembley Stadium in 1924, with the clubs sharing 50 per cent of the receipts. It would have been a Merseyside coup, but the proposed match was cancelled at the last minute because of the poor state of the Wembley pitch. 'If there was a greater and larger spirit in Liverpool than in other towns,' commented Member of Parliament T.P. O'Connor during the festivities at Wembley, 'it was largely because Liverpool was always in touch with the boundless and unending inspiration of the rolling ocean. The sea was really the mother of Liverpool . . . It was the great cosmopolitan site of banter and exchange, and through it passed the production of every land.' The mythologies of the city of Liverpool and the deep origins of its unique character clearly ran very deep.

DREAMS DASHED

The rather maligned borough of Bootle began to rise to the challenge of poor facilities for local football when on 4 September 1924 the *Daily Post* reported that the local authorities had bought from the Earl of Sefton, for £7,416, a 30-acre site near Captain's Lane to be developed along the lines of Stanley Park and to include 20 football pitches. It was indeed, as the local chairman of the parks committee put it, the 'cheapest bargain Bootle has ever made'. For the best part of the next 50 years, these 'pleasure fields', as they became known locally, would serve Bootle football enthusiasts. But the men in Bootle were the lucky ones. Early in 1925, following the FA ban on women's clubs, the *Football Echo* reported, 'Lady football teams have, by now, hardly got a kick left in them.' Meanwhile, the emergency committee of the Liverpool County FA reported that offending local footballers increasingly refused to give their real names to officials and that its 'duties in dealing with players sent off the field are as onerous as ever, and if the proceedings of this committee were ever published, it would be an eye-opener to the general public'. Harsh times in local football.

Snowstorms gripped much of Britain by the time the 1924 FA Cup quarter-finals approached on 4 March, but not in Saltburn on the north-east coast, where elderly Liverpool director Edward Bainbridge was, as usual, travelling with the Liverpool players and officials as they prepared, using the hydro-baths of a local hotel, for their crunch FA Cup meeting with Newcastle United. The simple committee structure of the largely self-selecting Liverpool board at this time divided up responsibilities for its various directors between ground issues, finance, the playing side, etc. Chairman Williams and directors Cartwright, Crompton, Wood and Troop all travelled up from Exchange Station on Friday afternoon to finalise the Liverpool team, with Mr Astbury indisposed and Richard Martindale looking after the Liverpool reserve side. The Martindales were to become another of the great Liverpool Football Club supporting families, with Richard briefly becoming the club chairman in 1924. His son Robert Lawson Martindale was co-opted onto the board in 1931.

Some Liverpool supporters also left a freezing Merseyside for the north-east in high spirits and lively red-and-white fancy dress, the best wishes of comedian George Robey (playing at the Olympic Theatre in the city) ringing in their ears. The Red half of Merseyside was buzzing with Wembley anticipation, convinced it was their time. But it was all so much hot air, because, according to the *Evening Express*, 'Liverpool never approached within a mile of their proper form' in a drab 0–1 defeat. As the visitors slumped, Jock McNab, typically, began using 'robust methods' to try to quell outside-left Stan Seymour, drawing the anger of the locals and also a stone from the crowd, which hit him on the back of the head. The deciding goal (whisper it very quietly) was an Elisha Scott mistake. A McDonald header from 12 yards out bounced awkwardly at the goalkeeper, who could only flap jerkily at it with his left arm, scooping the ball high into the net. It would be Newcastle United, not Liverpool, who would go on to win the 1924 FA Cup. With this latest cup exit, the Reds' season was all but over, despite just one defeat in the last 11 league matches, for a respectable finish in 12th position.

A LONG TIME COMING

It must be difficult for modern football fans to contemplate that a club such as Liverpool could play 16 seasons and go fully 24 years without winning a major title or even reaching the final of a national competition. And yet that was the situation that faced the club from the mid-1920s to the late 1940s. The FA Cup seemed perpetually out of reach, with only a run to the sixth round in 1932 offering any sort of real promise for a second final appearance. The FA Cup is notoriously quixotic, of course, with club officials and supporters often complaining about the vagaries of the draw. This Liverpool team could hardly claim ill-fortune, however: from 1929 to 1934, for example, the Reds were knocked out of the FA Cup five times after having been drawn at home in the tie. 'Considering the city of Liverpool has been in football since its infancy,' wrote Ephraim Longworth in his regular column in the *Football Echo* on 2 January 1925, 'the fact that we [Everton and Liverpool] have won the cup but once is a standing disgrace to us.' The failure of Liverpool FC in the FA Cup in the period leading up to the Second World War can probably best be explained by three things:

1. Self-induced anxiety
2. The decline in the club's own high standards, especially in forward play
3. The relative rise of the strength of the game in the south and particularly *outside* of its traditional early strongholds.

Between 1925 and 1939, Liverpool lost in the cup no fewer than eight times to clubs from outside the main northern and Midlands centres, including twice to Cardiff City (1928 and 1930) and twice to Arsenal (1927 and 1936). There were also defeats to Southampton (1925), Fulham (1926), Chelsea (1932) and even to lowly Second Division Norwich City in a third-round embarrassment in January 1937. This was now truly a national game and a national competition.

In the Football League, the picture was barely brighter, with only two top-five finishes for Liverpool (fourth in 1925 and fifth in 1929) and three brushes close to relegation (eighteenth in 1934, nineteenth in 1936 and eighteenth again in 1937). By the mid-1930s, some Liverpool supporters were beginning to blame the club's general approach to the new systems of play as the prime reason for its poor performances. After a crushing 2–9 loss to Newcastle United in January 1934, for example, 'Red Hot' wrote to the *Liverpool Echo* to say he was 'disgusted with their play of forwards [half-backs]. If it is orders to play that type of football, then the sooner they forget the W-formation the better.'

'Springbok', from Wallasey, noted that after an hour the score at St James's Park stood at 2–2, and he argued that:

> It is obvious . . . that Liverpool exaggerate the W-formation . . . It means the inside men become extra half-backs; that it leaves only three forwards in attack. The inside men have too much work: they are compelled to defend and attack. The result is generally a pronounced falling off in the second half: they tire. No wonder Liverpool are suffering from a preponderance of injuries. The inside men have double the work to do.

The Reds had difficulties adapting to the new offside law and new playing styles. Meanwhile, neighbours Everton seemed to have few such problems. Being inspired, initially, by the Birkenhead-born bombshell Bill Dean, the Blues mocked Liverpool's mediocrity by winning three interwar league titles, in 1928, 1932 and 1939, and one FA Cup, in 1933. Most Evertonians would probably accept their club's shock relegation for one season in 1930 – scoring 80 goals but conceding 92 – in return for these triumphs. Certainly, most Liverpool supporters, one suspects, would have done so.

THE (SOUTH) AFRICAN INVASION

The Liverpool minute books for the mid-1920s show that the club's directors were working feverishly to sign players, and they were even adopting a more 'scientific' approach to player recruitment and preparation. On 29 December 1925, for example, 'the manager was instructed to keep a book with the heights, weights and ages of all players, amateurs and professionals'. This looked like progress of sorts, and it echoed work at Melwood later under Bill Shankly. In September 1929, the club even purchased an Electrical Massage Machine from Good Bros for £30 to quicken up player recovery. The Liverpool directors and scouts travelled ceaselessly, scouring for cheap talent, though the board decided that the north of England, Scotland and Ireland were the best areas to pick up Liverpool players – the club had no southern scout at all until the mid-1930s. They did pick up occasional bargains: the wily Matt McQueen talked Aberdeen down from £4,500 to £1,750 for ace centre-half James Jackson, for example. A young S. Matthews in Stoke City reserves was also watched and noted but was never the subject of a bid. Liverpool did sign centre-forward Sam English from Rangers for a weighty £8,000 in 1933, not realising how mentally blighted the Northern Irishman had been by his fatal on-pitch collision with the Celtic keeper John Thomson two years earlier. But Liverpool also missed out on many star players – goalkeeper Frank Swift and genius inside-forwards Patsy Gallagher and Alex James were examples – because the Anfield board simply refused to pay substantial transfer fees, or else the player concerned refused to come because of the uncompetitive rewards on offer.

Both Walter Wadsworth and Harry Chambers now had serious income-tax problems and wanted transfers away from Anfield, as the club agreed in 1925 to buy a 'parking ground for motors immediately behind the new stand'. Many players – like most fans, of course – could barely afford their taxes, never mind buy a car. By 1931, soil was used to replace the cinder border behind the goalmouths at Anfield to reduce incidents of missile-throwing, and major boxing matches were now being staged at the stadium for a suitable fee. The footballing Brazilians of Botafogo wanted to come to play Liverpool in 1932 – but asked for £350, too much cash – and the club settled instead for a sequence of exhibition home fixtures against top Viennese clubs. These were all early signs of the modern football world approaching. As, indeed, was a letter sent to Elisha Scott reported in the minute books on 27 January 1927. A local bookmaker contacted Scott saying that he stood to lose £6,000 if Liverpool beat Derby County. He offered the Ulsterman £50 to ensure Liverpool lost by two goals. The fixer promised to meet Scott at Lime Street Station to pay up, wearing a trilby, spats, white scarf and red rosette for identification. He ended his note with a warning: 'Do as I say Elisha and don't let me down, for God's sake.' Liverpool beat County 3–2 and the police turned up at Lime Street, but there was no sign of Scott's correspondent.

On 1 October 1924, Liverpool had turned out a strong mix of first-teamers and reserves to play a touring amateur representative team from white South Africa. On paper it looked like a gentle training exercise for Liverpool – it was anything but. The Africans won 2–5 in a blistering exhibition of technique and movement, 'one of the most enjoyable games ever witnessed on the ground'. The *Daily Post* saw the drubbing as 'a lesson for English players', an exciting alternative to dominant British approaches, which still required that the ball be passed slowly within the team and then to the wingers, who tried to outwit the opposing half-back before crossing. The South Africans played a much more direct and central game, one sprinkled with the 'back-heel touch' and an approach of 'simple methods of passing and by the upwards pass'. For Bee in the *Liverpool Echo*, the South Africans were nothing less than a revelation. 'We must learn our lesson afresh,' he advised. 'They shall be our teachers.'

Bee made much of the way in which the visitors, by 'taking the ball as it comes, moving it to right or left', had speeded up the game. They accepted passes first time without trapping or 'deadening' the ball, as was the traditional

British way. The *Daily Post* reasoned that this unusual style was due to the 'hard pitches' in South Africa but anticipated that supporters in England might reject this fast, more direct, approach to football. 'Perhaps English crowds are the barrier; they so like to see a ball worked and to see a player become tricky.' The *Post* also noted the athleticism and maturity of the South Africans compared to Liverpool players, despite the relative youth of the visitors. 'The goalkeeper, a tall and keen fellow who has reach, anticipation and a safe pair of hands, is only 20, but he looks more like 35. The inside right is only 19, but plays like a seasoned professional.' These 'mystery' players were the Transvaal men, and future Liverpool signings, Arthur Riley and Gordon Hodgson.

At the Adelphi Hotel reception held after the match, John McKenna for the Football League highlighted the beneficial effects that English teams touring South Africa had had on African football, though the final tour record in Britain was actually very patchy: played twenty-five matches, won ten, lost fifteen. But the Liverpool board had seen enough – perhaps the best – of the touring party, and by December 1924 had made groundbreaking offers to three players. According to the *Cape Argus*, 'They regard Riley as the most promising goalkeeper in England, Brunton as one of the best backs now playing football, and Hodgson as the best inside-right in the country.' It was the physicality, as well as the cleverness and pace, of the South Africans that really attracted the Liverpool directors – and their cheapness. The distinction drawn in British law between the colonial and the foreigner was helpful. As the former, the South Africans were British subjects who were free to enter and settle in the home country.[7] Brunton never made it to Liverpool, but both Riley and Hodgson signed – for just £90 travelling and hotel expenses, and no transfer fees, of course – and once this English-speaking Empire route was effectively opened up, so were scouting networks and more South Africans followed between the wars to the familiar and welcoming territory of Anfield Road.

By the early 1930s, 'Liverpool were qualifying for some kind of record by their trade with South Africa', with at least six South Africans on the club's books by the start of the 1933–34 season and sometimes only two Englishmen, talented Bootle-born goalscoring winger Alf Hanson and Newcastle-born full-back Jack Tennant, in the side.[8] These African recruits would include Lance Carr, a Johannesburg-born left-wing flyer who later moved to Bristol City, and Harman van der Berg, another outside-left. Liverpool's sudden internationalism was startling, and these South Africans soon knew that they had come to a truly football-mad place. A social survey conducted in Liverpool in 1934 found that 15,000 to 20,000 adult males now played the game 'fairly regularly' in the city alone.[9]

This early batch of 'foreign' signings in the 1920s and early 1930s was actually a fantastic piece of business for the club. The big and powerful, if rather ungainly, Hodgson (241 goals in 377 appearances) was the main forward spark for Liverpool and the club's regular top scorer for much of the next decade. On making his first-team debut against Manchester City in February 1926, the very muscular Hodgson impressed. He was comfortable at either inside-right or centre-forward and authentically two-footed in a period – and in a culture – in which this remained an unusual trait. But a local scribe commented that 'a little more speed . . . would send up his stock a great deal'. Hodgson established a partnership of 'perfect understanding' between 1927 and 1929 with the Gillingham-born winger and ex-dockyard worker Dick Edmed, a man who later scored for Bolton *against* Liverpool in May 1932 in a terrible 1–8 Reds humiliation.

The Liverpool minute books show that in April 1926 Hodgson was allowed to return to South Africa and that he was 'very doubtful' of ever returning to Liverpool because of family problems. But Hodgson *did* come back, and by October 1928, when he scored three goals in a 4–4 draw at Highbury, the *Evening Express* was able to sum up the forward's strengths: 'He may appear clumsy, but he makes the fullest use of his 13 st. weight in bullying the opposing defence. His height is a distinct advantage in intercepting centres from the wing with his head and he is most deadly in his shooting with either foot.' After the South African had ploughed through a hapless Burnley defence in an 8–0 drubbing at Anfield over the Christmas period in 1928, the *Evening Express* even argued that 'Hodgson is becoming almost as much a hero as Dixie Dean as a thrustful leader of attack . . . The demoralisation of the Burnley backs was largely due to the relentless bustling tactics of the Liverpool leader.' Typically South African, Hodgson was also a broad-shouldered cricketer of some note for Lancashire CCC, but he eventually won three caps at football for England, his adopted country. In 1930–31, Hodgson would need every inch of those broad shoulders for his football work, scoring a then record 36 league goals in a rather ordinary Liverpool side.

Hodgson was joined at Anfield in 1933 from Germiston Calies by Berry 'Nivvy' Nieuwenhuys, a tall, loping right-winger with deceptive pace and a fierce right-foot shot who made 260 Liverpool appearances over 14 years, including 15 in the 1946–47 championship season. 'Nivvy' had penetration and directness, and, like wingers today, he enjoyed using his strength and height in the air at the back post against smaller full-backs. He could also work back, thus showing the novel demands on wingers in the new W–M era of the 1930s. He effectively sealed his relationship with Kopites in his first full match, in September 1933, by scoring at Anfield in a 3–2 derby win over Everton. 'It was an uncommon home debut,' enthused the *Liverpool Echo*, 'because he got a goal, gave [made] a goal and not only introduced new methods to the public, but also showed that he could lend a "surprise item" by falling back and taking the ball from an unsuspecting Everton forward.' It was a perfect start for the South African.

Goalkeeper Arthur Riley, a pragmatic, brave and reliable number one, had been signed, of course, as cover and the long-term replacement for the ageing Elisha Scott. When he filled in for the injured Scott at Leicester in October 1927, the *Daily Post* wrote, 'Riley, in any other side, would be the senior goalkeeper and Liverpool are fortunate to have such a deputy for Scott. He made some remarkable saves.' Riley actually seemed to have displaced the wonderful Ulsterman by the late 1920s, before losing his own form in 1931 and allowing the 37-year-old Scott back into the side. Riley was also briefly challenged for his place in the Liverpool goal in the mid-1930s by the Durham-born Alf Hobson and also the Cape Town man Dirk Kemp, another Anfield recruit from Africa. In these turbulent years of transition for defenders and for Liverpool Football Club, it is true that the unfortunate Riley often faced a barrage from the opposition. These included a 1–6 last-day thumping at Old Trafford in May 1928; an embarrassing 0–6 home defeat by Sunderland in April 1930; a 0–7 loss at West Ham in September 1930 – though the *Evening Express* insisted that 'it was doubtful if he had a chance to save any of them' – and a 1–8 mauling at Bolton Wanderers in May 1932, after which the *Liverpool Echo* correspondent reported, 'I have never seen [Liverpool] play worse . . . Goals came like hailstones; it took all my time to keep tally with them.'

In September 1934, when Arsenal repeated this 1–8 dose, the *Echo* wrote, 'Riley's was a sickening job. There is not the slightest charge against him.' Finally, in November of the same year, the final straw: Liverpool lost 0–8 to bottom club Huddersfield Town when 'Riley kept the game from a cricket score'. This era was clearly a time for forwards and for goals – and no goalkeeper was entirely safe from its effects. When Liverpool were humiliated 2–9 by Newcastle United on New Year's Day in 1934, it was the ailing hero Elisha Scott who was in goal, rather than Riley. The Ulsterman, improbably, gave 'a display of heroic proportions', according to the devoted *Liverpool Echo*. Despite these various beatings, 338 Liverpool appearances in goal confirmed the original judgement of the directors and the Liverpool manager made back in 1924 that in the young Arthur Riley Liverpool had secured a fitting heir – albeit from an unexpected quarter – to the great Elisha.

THE COMFORT OF STRANGERS ON THE COVERED KOP

By 1928, many of the core members of the Liverpool championship side were either already gone or were now well on their way out of Anfield. Dick Forshaw was perhaps the most spectacular departure, in March 1927, because he not only joined local rivals Everton, but he also scored on his debut for the Blues and then – a real dagger this to the heart of any Reds fan – he won a league championship medal in his first full season at Goodison Park in 1928. Ephraim Longworth, especially, had been a remarkable leader and servant to the Liverpool club, but it was perhaps a sign of their stretched loyalty to favoured players – and of Liverpool's current travails – that Ephraim continued to play in the First Division when well past his best. In his final appearance for Liverpool, a 0–2 defeat by Birmingham on 27 April 1928, the *Daily Post* remarked that it was 'only natural that he was beaten for speed'.

On 15 February of that year, another local favourite, manager Matt McQueen, had finally given in to his health problems and resigned. The Liverpool board reasoned that *they* could continue selecting the team and recruiting players, and that the club secretary George Patterson could easily pick up the rest of the managerial tasks, thus saving on salary costs. Patterson kept the secretary–manager job until 1936. It was another sign of a lack of focus and the penny-pinching at the club, and that Liverpool had failed to see the importance of what had been recently happening in the era of Herbert Chapman on the coaching and management side of the game. In 1928, there was also a major restructuring of the Anfield training staff: Bill Connell retired but continued to scout for Liverpool; and Charlie Wilson took over as trainer, with Ephraim Longworth and Joe Hewitt as his assistants. All three men had played for Liverpool.

In 1932, Maurice Parry, another ex-player, was briefly appointed as 'coach' at Anfield – a barely heard-of role – but he lasted only a year. The board decided it needed no coach, instead instructing the Reds training staff that 'more ball practice be given to the players' while the trainers awaited the arrival of a 'ball board'. Robert Lawson Martindale was the director who seemed keenest on modernising the playing side of the club, registering his frustrations at the slow pace of change and conferring with the people at the Adelphi Hotel gym in February 1933 before fitting out Anfield with a rowing machine, wall bars and a weightlifting bench. Off the pitch, in the mid-1930s the entire Liverpool club was administered by one full-time salaried staff member, George Patterson, one man on a weekly wage, J.C. Rouse (the secretary's assistant), and a lowly clerk, Mrs Hilda Riley, who was paid £2 per week. It was a 'corner shop' arrangement.

On the occasion of the official opening of the new £38,000 Joseph Watson Cabre-designed roof over the 28,000-capacity Spion Kop at Anfield for the home match v. Bury on 25 August 1928, VIP guest John McKenna congratulated the Liverpool board on providing more covered accommodation than any other club in the Football League. But he also offered a word of advice to the Liverpool directors: 'Stay your hands in the matter of further improvements of the ground and devote your finances, energy and intelligence to creating a *team* worthy of its splendid ground accommodation.' Was anyone listening?

The Crosby-based Watson had been a surprise choice for the Kop project – he worked mostly on private houses and religious restorations. The new construction was the largest such structure in England, measuring 425 ft wide and 80 ft high, but its new roof could not disguise the dangerously poor terrace design and the limited circulation routes on the Kop, which would mean routine injuries for fans and give rise to the time-honoured tradition of some male Kopites being forced to urinate where they stood at half-time.[10] From the start, the covered Kop was a highly social space – chanting and also betting among its members were soon established. The Kop catered mainly for male, working-class supporters, with the 'toffs' or the 'mobs', as some Kopites called them, located in the stands and the Paddock.[11] Nevertheless, the *Liverpool Echo* made much of this supposed new luxury in spectator provision, which included roof glazing that was 'wire-woven, to protect the spectators from broken glass if someone raised the roof shouting "goal"'.

Such opulence – and it was added to by the grand erection of a franchise tea stall on the Kop in September 1929. 'To be in keeping with the glorious new stand,' the *Echo* continued, with an eye on gentrification and the young confection-sellers who paraded their wares inside Anfield, 'they might put gold knobs on the goalposts and the chocolate boys should have their hair water-waved and scented.' The match programme for the Bury fixture carried an artist's impression of a proposed new double-decker stand at the Anfield Road end of the ground, which carried the distinctive criss-cross balcony design of Archibald Leitch. But the playing success at Anfield said to be needed to raise the funds for the new development never came.[12]

As a Football League man, McKenna might have been expected to stress prudence, structures and planning over signing new players and a thirst for immediate success. But then McKenna was no ordinary Football League official, at least not as far as Liverpool Football Club was concerned. When he was club secretary at Anfield, he recalled he had but a shed for his office. 'Those people who pay their shilling to go on the Spion Kop,' said the new Liverpool chairman Mr T. (Tom) Crompton at the grand opening in 1928, 'have really been the backbone of the club. Wet or fine they have loyally filled their places and it has given great satisfaction to the directors to now make them as comfortable as possible with every protection against inclement weather.' McKenna responded, in turn, 'No one knows better than I do that we cannot live in the past, but I think that the past should at least be an inspiration for the future.'

The *Liverpool Echo* reporter also ruminated on the contradictions of the opening of this wonderful new structure, which implied that everything in the Anfield garden was lovely, while angry voices rang out from the Kop claiming, 'So-and-so, you are a **** twister!' 'There are times,' the *Echo* continued, '[when players] catch sight of the culprit and would like to take the law into their own hands – and also the culprit's neck!' In fact, there would be many occasions under this grand new roof when Liverpool supporters would run out of patience with their often ragged team. But only twice in this troubled period, in 1935–36 and 1937–38, did Liverpool lose more than five league matches at home – the Kop was obviously a factor in this, and it would be for decades to come. But the Reds frequently struggled to win more than five matches *away* in a season, managing only two away victories in the near-calamitous 1935–36 season. After the undreamed-of success of consecutive league titles in the early 1920s, it had been a troubling period in this part of the footballing district of Liverpool 4. Worse was to follow. The Liverpool fans had their newly covered Kop at last, but they were about to lose a local folk hero, and arguably the club's greatest-ever player.

CHAPTER 8 REFERENCES

1. Wilson, *Inverting the Pyramid*, pp. 25–9
2. Inglis, *The Football League and the Men Who Made It*, p. 110
3. Rous, *Football Worlds*, p. 90
4. Carter, *The Football Manager*, p. 50
5. Page, *Herbert Chapman*, pp. 126–7
6. Wilson, *Inverting the Pyramid*, p. 51
7. Taylor, *The Leaguers*, p. 234
8. Young, *Football on Merseyside*, pp. 130–1
9. Jones, *The Social Survey of Merseyside*, p. 291
10. Physick, *Played in Liverpool*, p. 58
11. Kelly, *The Kop*, p. 16
12. Inglis, *The Football Grounds of Great Britain*, p. 210

9

LISHA! LISHA!
Elisha Scott and the Liverpool Kop

THE SCOTT AND DEAN SHOW

As Liverpool Football Club struggled collectively after 1923, the aura around the club's remaining great individual talent, the Irish goalkeeper Elisha Scott, continued to grow stronger, even when most of the 93 league goals that Liverpool conceded in 1931–32 were put past the great man. This mythologising accelerated as Scott's duels with Everton's Dixie Dean offered an alternative focus for a generation of Liverpool supporters who were now pretty much starved of FA Cup and league-championship prospects. These two great rivals were made for each other, and they were undoubtedly good for football business in the city at a time when, frankly, Liverpool were struggling to be even vaguely competitive with the near neighbours. Mr Justice Charles at the assizes in Liverpool was a football man and a great admirer of Elisha Scott's goalkeeping. When they met, according to a *Liverpool Echo* story in 1934, the exchange was typical of the rather taciturn and obtuse Scott, and also of his disregard for fripperies or even praise:

> Said Judge Charles, 'I think it is very wonderful the way you keep goal.'
> 'Och,' said Scott, 'I'll be better a year from today.'
> 'How do you make that out?' asked the judge.
> 'More experience, see; more experience, see,' said Scott.

Bill Dean did not lack confidence or experience. He scored nine times against Scott in their eight derby meetings, and few forwards had a better record against the Ulsterman. Not that Elisha Scott – a man with his very own Kopite chant of 'Lisha, Lisha' – was intimidated by Dean, or by anyone else. Not even when Dixie sent the Liverpool keeper a tube of aspirin and a warning note to his

Wallasey home before every derby game. In reply, Elisha good-naturedly taunted the Everton forward in the tunnel before each derby meeting with, 'You'll get none today, you black-haired bastard.'[1] A journalist of the day famously described Elisha Scott as having 'the eye of an eagle and the swift movement of a panther', and the pugnacious and lethal Dean agreed that Scott was 'the greatest goalkeeper I have ever seen'.

When Liverpool first scouted Scott as a teenager, the report came back that he was 'as raw as meat', but he already had both presence and courage. Dixie highlighted the biggest strength of the Liverpool man to be less his shot-stopping capacities than his early preparation and fearless 'point-blank charge' to meet a forward head-on. A determined and fearless moving goalkeeper, even at a modest 5 ft 9 in., was a threat in the corner of the eye of any forward. The Liverpool keeper was 'never still', reasoned the Everton icon Dean. 'As soon as the attack against him crosses the halfway line, watch Scott jump.' Another journalist commented, 'To the end he could leap to the high ones like the magnificent human stag he was.' On 19 September 1931, Dean did finally manage to get his Anfield hat-trick with Elisha in goal. It was scored in a deadly nine-minute spell in a 1–3 Liverpool defeat. The Everton man then cheekily bowed three times in front of the foaming Kop and, predictably, received a volley of 'choice language' in reply. Elisha Scott was in a rage.

By this time Elisha, the younger brother of another Irish international goalkeeper, William Scott, had become especially well known, as the *Liverpool Echo* put it later, for his 'sallies with the crowd, his looks of despair at some forwards – or his own side – his shrill cry "rate" [meaning "right"] can never be forgotten by followers of the club'. Scott very willingly and very publicly *communed* with the Liverpool supporters, said the *Echo*. 'They have heard him; he holds conference with them; he chats and back-chats; they hear his opinion about positions and positional play. He was built in with the Kop!'

By now, this vast standing terrace had already established its own highly distinctive identity. Its members furiously thrashed rattles adorned with club colours, abused the carriers of the pitch-side blackboards that noted team changes, bawled wildly at referees and rival players, and lustily sang along with the brass-band players before matches. 'Yes, We Have No Bananas' was an early Kop favourite. The terrace had few airs and graces. Jean McDonald, as a 12 year old, was, unusually, taken by her father to the Kop in the mid-1930s, when, 'There were no ladies' toilets or anything like that.'

Scott loved the earthy male humour and the bawdy irreverence of the Kop. During home matches, he was usually furious with the Liverpool defender Jimmy 'Parson' Jackson, a former Clyde shipyard worker, a church elder and devout Christian, who had studied Greek and philosophy at Cambridge University and would be ordained a Presbyterian minister in 1933. In August 1947, Jim Jackson, now a reverend and a Liverpool man through and through, would officiate at the funeral of the former Liverpool chairman W.H. (Bill) McConnell.

Jackson was the son of a professional footballer, but by no stretch was he an obviously 'typical' British professional. He was certainly a mile away from the brusque Scott in both background and temperament. Jackson was a scrupulously fair, intelligent, big-hearted, determined and versatile defender, a Liverpool captain who played 224 times for the club, usually at either right full-back or centre-half. The largely working-class, strongly Irish-flavoured Kop sided unconditionally with its heroic and volatile – and often expletive-ridden – Irish goalkeeper. The club centre-half, by way of contrast, represented brushed-up, staid authority. Jackson would go on to have many an even-handed tussle with Dixie Dean in his long and honourable Liverpool career, but few would be as painful as Dean's hat-trick match at Anfield in 1931. Jackson's chief crime was that he was the man who had allowed Bill Dean to humiliate Elisha in front of his own people – and in fewer than ten excruciating minutes.

The abrasive Scott (like his friends on the Kop) thought that Jackson was far too gentlemanly with opposing forwards and that he should have tried more to 'rough up' Dean. He bawled this out in no uncertain terms in front of the Kop. The sensitive Jackson was distraught and shocked by the goalkeeper's industrial language, confiding in an amused Bill Dean, 'William, I never want to play in front of *that* man again.' Ironically, Dixie, the Liverpool goalkeeper's most-feared opponent, seemed more Elisha Scott's personal cup of tea than were his own defenders. After derby games, regardless of the outcome, the two great internationals would retire to the Lisbon pub in Victoria Street, where they could discuss the outcome. As the world raged around them, the notoriously penny-pinching Scott would be hunched quietly over a bottle of Guinness with Dean nursing a pint of bitter, oblivious to all except their own professional friendship forged in the intense heat of battle. Both men, tough as old boots, would be amused to learn that today the Lisbon is firmly on the Merseyside gay-and-lesbian pub circuit.

FOOTBALL – AND FA CUP – DEPRESSION

In January 1932, the Merseyside clubs were drawn together in the FA Cup third round at Goodison Park, the first FA Cup derby since 1911. The *Industrial Survey* of 1932 predicted that 'a vast problem of unemployment would weigh upon Merseyside for many years', and throughout the 1930s unemployment in the area remained above 18 per cent, double the national average.[2] So this FA Cup meeting was an effervescent local tonic to dispel some of the gathering industrial gloom.

Everton were favourites, and the Liverpool team contained only Elisha as a survivor from the great years of the 1920s. But the visitors still had some reputable performers – and were reassuringly chock-full of Scottish men. Scott's place in goal was now increasingly challenged by Arthur Riley. Jim Jackson played at the back, and Gordon Hodgson was the key Liverpool man up front. Willie Steel, an intelligent Scottish full-back, replaced the more attack-minded Runcorn man Robert Done on the left side, and it was he who accompanied Jackson and fellow countryman 'Tiny' Tom Bradshaw, a strapping 6 ft centre-half in the Liverpool backline. Bradshaw had played in the 'Wembley Wizards' Scotland team that had thrashed England 5–1 in 1928, but, perversely, this had proved to be his only cap. He had been signed by Liverpool for £8,000 from Bury in 1930 and eventually clocked up some 291 Liverpool performances.

At right-half, Tom Morrison, another Scot, made over two hundred and fifty appearances for Liverpool but won no senior trophies and scored only four goals for the club – a consistent rather than a dynamic contributor in a fallow Liverpool period. Something similar could probably be said of the superior Scotland international at left-half, Jimmy McDougall, a man who skippered his country twice and, like Ray Kennedy many years after him, was originally a forward who was converted by the club to a left-sided midfield player. Between 1928 and 1937, the stocky and cultured McDougall was consistently first choice at Liverpool, making 338 league starts in total. Another Scot, Danny McRorie, played against Everton on the right-wing, having temporarily replaced the more established Lancastrian favourite Harry Barton, who switched to centre-forward alongside Hodgson. At inside-forward was yet another Scottish recruit, the bald-headed utility forward David Wright, who was standing in for the injured Archie McPherson, a clever but rather goal-shy inside-left. Completing the line-up at outside left, and along with 'Tiny' Bradshaw the only ever-present for Liverpool in the 1931–32 season, was Chester-born Gordon Gunson, a precision crosser and the man who scored the crucial equalising goal against Everton that helped keep Liverpool in the FA Cup.

In the new W–M formation, the still-unnumbered 1932 Liverpool FA Cup side lined up like this:

Liverpool FC v. Everton, FA Cup round three, 9 January 1932

Scott

Jackson   Bradshaw   Steel

Morrison   McDougall

Hodgson   Wright

McRorie   Barton   Gunson

Football attendances had been hit hard in the city by a combination of the economic downturn and inconsistent form, especially from Liverpool. In 1927–28, the Reds averaged just a fraction under 30,000 for league matches compared to champions Everton's 37,461. In Everton's single season in Division Two, in 1930–31, Liverpool's average crowds just bettered those at Goodison, with both clubs touching a little over 26,000. But by 1931–32, at the height of economic depression, Liverpool's average crowds, for a tenth-place league finish, had slumped to a post-war low of 22,742, with crowds at champions Everton up again, to 35,451. In the years leading up to the Second World War, only in 1933–34 did Liverpool's average attendances top those at Everton, although little divided the teams in terms of league performance at this time, until Everton won the league title again in 1939.

During this period of severe economic difficulty, people who could not afford to attend at Anfield would simply stand outside the ground to savour the atmosphere and, on hearing a roar inside, would chant 'Who scored?', awaiting the inevitable reply.[3] When the Pilgrim Trust reported on unemployment in Liverpool in 1938, it noted that unemployed men who could not afford the shilling entrance fee used to turn up on Saturday afternoons just to watch the crowds going to the match.[4] On 9 January 1932, the *Evening Express* captured well the real sense of occasion and the symbolic importance generated by the FA Cup meeting between the Merseyside clubs, especially in the midst of so much local economic uncertainty and poverty. Three policemen were reported to be on the roof of the Goodison Road stand to monitor the heaving crowds. Many people in the city clearly still had money to spend on association football and its various, gaudy paraphernalia, as the local press reported:

> Rattles swung vigorously kept their owners warm, while all kinds of Red and Blue favours were being sold by vendors who met with a ready sale. These favours ranged from red and blue roses to celluloid dolls dressed in red and blue, names of star players being stamped on them. The crowds

were boisterously cheerful. 'All seats now guaranteed' was one catch-phrase they shouted. Some of the fans wore blue or red bowlers and sashes of similar colours.

There was a great demand for hot tea and coffee which was supplied by the shops in the vicinity . . . By 1 p.m., thousands of spectators were already in the ground but still they came. Crowded tramcars arrived every few minutes, while motor-cars, taxi-cabs and omnibuses set down hundreds more. A strong force of foot and mounted police marshalled the crowds. They were happy crowds. What was a bump or a push on a day like this?

Evertonians were happier still when after just 15 seconds of the contest the talismanic Dean scored against a strange-looking Liverpool 'in their somewhat vermilion-coloured shirts'. The Liverpool captain Bradshaw had been a doubt all week, with doctors attending his pleurisy, and it was his misunderstanding with Morrison that let 'the Blue Devil' Dean in to beat Elisha Scott with a left-footed shot via the inside of the near post. But the Reds defender gathered his men about him in heroic fashion, aided, of course, by 'Parson' Jackson and the astonishing Reds keeper Scott. Gunson got Liverpool's first-half equaliser after the ball broke to him following a rather aimless free-kick taken by the fouled McRorie. Now came the turning point. 'With the score at 1–1,' reported the *Evening Express*, 'Dean delivered one of his best headers. It looked all over a goal, but Scott, who had advanced from his goal, clutched at the ball with the keenness and quickness of a cat and held it.' How many times had Scott saved Liverpool? With 15 minutes left and Everton increasingly nervous and under pressure, Gunson and Wright combined to release Hodgson, whose 'task was easy and pleasurable for a man of his size'. The South African shrugged off two defenders to score robustly past Ted Sagar in the Everton goal. 'Never was a scorer so pounced upon by his own men,' reported the *Evening Express*. The scenes that followed were 'fifteen minutes of full-blooded cup-tie enthusiasm', but Liverpool survived intact. At the final whistle, 'roars nearly wrecked the roof of the stand'.

After the match, Everton captain Dixie Dean graciously crossed to the celebrations at Anfield to personally congratulate Scott and Liverpool in a short speech in which he also thanked the Reds for 'beating some of the best clubs in the league' that season, so aiding Everton's latest (and ultimately successful) league-title challenge.

Could it be the FA Cup *at last* for Liverpool? How many times had their supporters had similar hopes? The lord mayor and lady mayoress followed the Reds to Second Division Chesterfield in round four, where ground attendance records were broken and red balloons and rattles were much in evidence. It proved to be Harry Barton's match. The makeshift Reds centre-forward was 'like a greyhound out of the leash'. By half-time, Liverpool led 3–0, all three goals scored by the Liverpool flyer who simply had too much pace for Chesterfield's lumbering defenders. He scored a fourth, too, in a 4–2 stroll for the visitors. Next season it would get even better for Barton, a hat-trick from the wing in a 7–4 Anfield derby extravaganza against Everton.

A home tie against First Division Grimsby Town was Liverpool's – and Barton's – reward, but it proved a tense battle. Town played 'splendid football', according to the *Daily Post*. The Reds needed encouragement – 'in this case the crowd unmistakably carried the victory to the home side, after a struggle by Grimsby against fate and her curious tricks'. It was the Kop to the rescue once again. When Gunson hurtled in to head the winner from a cross by Wright and ended up standing enmeshed in the back of the Kop goal, 'it created a crush in the Spion Kop and many injuries for those caught in the jam'. Cup-cursed Liverpool were in the FA Cup quarter-finals once again, this time to face a moderate Chelsea at home.

The eyes of the British sporting public were on Anfield – or at least they *could* have been: Liverpool refused permission for 'cinematographic photos' to be taken of the contest. Both Paramount Pictures and British Movietone wanted to film but for no fee. Liverpool FC simply locked the cameras out. The Merseyside sporting press was at yet another pitch of FA Cup excitement, but it was all to no avail once more. Chelsea's Hughie Gallagher was just too cute at centre-forward for the towering Bradshaw, the latter colliding with Chelsea's Harry Miller and cutting an eyebrow as Gallagher pounced on a cross 'in the last breath of the first half' for the crucial first goal. Liverpool then panicked, its 'wild, erratic attack' crying out for more composure in a frenetic second half. But Chelsea scored again on the break, and Liverpool's best opportunity to win the FA Cup before the Second World War would intervene had gone. This was also effectively Elisha Scott's last chance of FA Cup glory. Everton would win the FA Cup in 1933, beating Manchester City 3–0 in the final.

ELISHA SCOTT'S 'MATCHLESS' KOP

After the lame 1932 FA Cup exit to Chelsea, the much-abused Liverpool shareholders seemed finally to be shamed into some action. Clause 66 of the Articles of Association of 1906 allowed the Liverpool directors to replace any retiring or deceased director with someone of their own choosing. The board was a self-selecting members' club. Uniquely, 83 disgruntled Reds shareholders now called for an extraordinary general meeting to demand that new Liverpool directors must be elected at an AGM. One shareholder, Tom Sayle, also demanded that each of his colleagues receive a copy of the Articles of Association and the name and number of shares held by each shareholder. The board decided it could not entertain this final request and voted to 'pledge ourselves individually and collectively to use all our power' to re-elect retiring board members. But from then on, at least the election and re-election of Liverpool board members would be done in public in front of shareholders – although the process was still very tightly controlled by the existing board.

Also in 1932, the *Liverpool Echo* sent the fearless Bee onto the Spion Kop – it seems Everton had no equivalent terrace spectacle to scrutinise – in order to gauge local sentiment and assess the knowledge and varied make-up of these partisan Reds supporters who had such a strong affinity with their cultish Irish goalkeeper. Bee's mission produced one of the first early pieces of journalistic anthropology on football fans. It offered real insights into the inner life of one of the great pre-war football terraces. The account was presented rather as investigative journalists in the city had earlier penetrated local gangs or else explored desperate communities pierced by poverty and disease. 'I climbed the steps of the Kop,' the piece began, apprehensively, but then:

> Here was loyalty, here was belief; here was a trusting nature; they cursed the directors for having missed the Cup boat; they had commentaries on all phases of play, players, press and from their unequalled view they reckoned they saw things that the people in other parts of the ground could not hope to see. Yes, the Kop is the home of the loyalists.
>
> Two women were there, one in chocolate brown and another daring to wear a blue hat, a tricky thing of beret design, but the colour scheme did not seem to be quite inviting, as she was in the Anfield ground. Two swarthy sons of Ireland came beside me. They had come to see the MA of goalkeepers, Elisha Scott. One wore a black velvet beret and a film face that suggested a Valentino. He was plainly of Basque extraction and was silent as the grave . . .
>
> Where I had expected slashing attacks on players, I found praise and kindness. The kind way they talked of the players astonished me. True, Liverpool were playing better, but these were embittered partisans who could hardly forgive a Cup defeat. They were an object lesson to me . . . Their sportsmanship was a great feature; their language was fit and proper, and they treated the players encouragingly and in a sporting manner. Anfield's all right if they can keep this man at their back. They have tantalised him, he says, by some of their movements, but he's loyal to the core and he goes on talking his matches, debating his matches. This spectator is matchless.

This sort of approving media coverage only added, of course, to the early mystique and reputation of this great football beast. Watching football from here was no longer about simply taking one's place on just any goal-end terrace, a man lost in the crowd. The Kop itself was a performer, a football forcing ground with a membership of tens of thousands and a disarmingly fearsome goalkeeper as its spiritual leader. The Liverpool defence had Elisha Scott, and behind Scott there was the priceless Kop. How could the club be in such a slump with these unique assets?

In 1932, J.G. Hickling, the secretary of Huddersfield Town, argued that with 7.30 p.m. kick-offs under lights, the game could easily 'double the followers of football', with club bank overdrafts becoming a thing of the past.[5] But both the FA and the Football League were dubious in a climate of economic downturn, and, like most innovations in the English game, it would take another 20 years for this one to really catch on.

Meanwhile, despite the Kop's obvious intelligence, loyalty and support at this time, Liverpool continued to struggle horribly. At the end of the 1932–33 season, there was a player clear-out at Anfield, with 16 professionals placed on the transfer list. The totemic Scott even wrote to the club's directors saying that he was considering retirement – he had been complaining about pay, had been slack in training and Arthur Riley was back in the Liverpool goal. In the league in 1933–34, it was a disaster, with Liverpool at one stage going thirteen games without a win and looking certainties for the drop. It was Gordon Hodgson (who else?) who came to the rescue in March 1934, scoring a hat-trick against Middlesbrough in a 6–2 win and all four goals against Birmingham in a 4–1 victory. The South African forward was beyond value for Liverpool now, and Harry Hibbs, the England goalkeeper, described Hodgson as 'the greatest shooter he had ever known'.

But things were still in the balance when the Reds – without Elisha Scott – visited Hillsborough on 21 April, even though the home club 'looked upon Liverpool with a friendly eye'. Liverpool were slaughtered by Wednesday's football, but the home team could not get a lead that would stick. At 1–1, replacement keeper Arthur Riley suddenly came into the picture. 'He had not had his fingernails cut or he would not have stopped a ball from crossing the line,' said the *Echo* reporter. 'That save will always remain in my mind as the save that kept Liverpool from the Second Division.' This moment possibly changed the course of a club's entire history. Bootle-born Alf Hanson (unfortunately christened Adolph) then scored Liverpool's improbable winner with a 'cross-grained drive' to keep the Red Men just about afloat for another season. Saved from the drop by Elisha Scott's replacement and a man called Adolph. What next lay in store in the 1930s, in this 'morbid age', for Liverpool Football Club?

FACING THE UNTHINKABLE – ELISHA SCOTT LEAVES LIVERPOOL

The royal opening of the Mersey tunnel in 1934 symbolised the slow upturn in the economic fortunes of the city of Liverpool. The tunnel was fundamental to improving local transport links for a new generation of businesses that might bring a wider range of much-needed employment to the Merseyside area. But the diversification of Liverpool industries over the next decade should not be exaggerated. The Liverpool University-based social scientist David Caradog Jones argued in 1934 that the industrial landscape of Liverpool 'was very easily sketched', and this remained the case for many years to follow.[6] On 16 January 1934, the Liverpool Football Club directors decided they should each have a special card granting permission for their entrance to the car park from Anfield Road. Club officials would now have more and more special privileges to mark them out from ordinary spectators.

These new arrangements might have been a red-letter day for the club's directors, but the date 18 April 1934 was certainly more important for most Liverpool football supporters. The Merseyside press announced what many Reds fans probably thought was unthinkable: that Elisha Scott, fast approaching his 40th birthday, was 'not wanted' by Liverpool and that he must look for another club. Even given Scott's advanced age, it is difficult to think of a more contentious proposed transfer in the entire history of Liverpool Football Club. This moment certainly compares with Bill Shankly's shock retirement announcement 40 years later. In 1928, Everton had first asked about Scott but were rebuffed. In January 1930, the Liverpool minute books show that the club had actually secretly accepted an offer from Everton of £5,000 for the keeper. As luck would have it, the Ulsterman injured an ankle and the proposed deal was called off, thus avoiding a local earthquake. But four years later this parting of the ways looked like the real thing – and Everton were involved once again. The *Echo* saw this development as a 'shock' to the supporters on the Kop, who were losing both 'an institution' and one of their own. But it also reasoned that supporters should not go 'off the deep end' in their opinions about the break in a long chain. This breach with the past had to come sooner or later. The *Echo* might have saved its breath. A reader's letter of 19 April 1934 signed 'Red' was typical of the local response:

> To say that the action of the Liverpool directors in relation to Elisha Scott is a bombshell with violence to his countless admirers in this city is to put it very mildly. Not only is it a knockout blow to the team but what is even more important, the *coup de grâce* delivered by the directors to the most loyal and wholehearted band of supporters to be found wherever the game is played.

I submit they have alienated that great-hearted crowd who have cheered and 'gagged' their best beloved star and idol during all these years.

Another emotional letter writer, who signed his missive 'Disgusted' and had it published on 24 April, saw the whole process as demeaning, both to the club and to a great servant who was still needed:

> To think, the one and only Elisha should have to submit to the indignity of a transfer is unthinkable, especially as it is being proved week in and week out where the weakness is. He is the world's best. The 'owld man' could do for me if he came out and played in goal on crutches.

Some of this was just rhetoric, a product of frustration. Scott's brilliant career with Liverpool stretched back to before the First World War, and he was the last link to the 1920s championship years, but he was now also well past his best. What really hurt was the idea that this Liverpool icon, possibly the club's greatest-ever footballer, would now be sold on by the Liverpool board, just like *any other player* might be.

These sorts of feelings intensified when it was mischievously intimated that *Everton* might be the club interested in signing Scott. In fact, the Ulsterman wrote two letters to Bee of the *Liverpool Echo* on this matter, the first saying, 'I think the loyal Anfielders are upsetting the directors more than you and me. If you know of any Second or Third Division club wanting a goalkeeper, I am prepared to go to them.' The second took a very different tack: it stated that discussions had been ongoing and that Scott had actually been prepared to sign for Everton that afternoon for £250, 'but, unfortunately, there is a hitch. I don't know what for.' The Liverpool board had stepped in as a flood of letters from the club's supporters made their views clear: letting the great Elisha go was one thing but letting him go to Everton was tantamount to writing a collective suicide note. That deal was off. Instead, Scott eventually returned to Ireland as player–manager for Belfast Celtic, winning the Irish league championship seven times between 1935 and 1941.

Because he was injured, Elisha missed the season's closing fixture at Anfield against Manchester City, but a microphone was set up in the Main Stand for his goodbyes. It was a poor crowd, the stadium barely one-third full. Was this a protest from Liverpool supporters against the board? The Liverpool chairman Walter Cartwright, another from the Liverpool 'family' of administrators and who was followed into the role later by his son Harold in the late 1960s, told the crowd that the club would honour the full share of Scott's accrued benefit.

'Scott has taken the view that football is a young man's game,' he continued, 'and it was his own desire to make room for a younger man.' The Kop then howled its unhappiness when a young supporter broke the spell by running onto the pitch to get a better view of matters. The intensely private and obviously emotional Scott then spoke in his distinctive Belfast growl. 'We have always been the best of friends and shall always remain so. I have finished with English association football. Last, but not least, my friends of the Kop. I cannot thank them sufficiently. They have inspired me. God bless you all.' A generation of working-class men had grown up with this stooped, wiry figure guarding the Liverpool goal in front of them, risking life and limb. And now it was all over. Many hardened men were in tears. It was, indeed, the end of an era.

The brilliant Elisha Scott was never forgotten by those Liverpool supporters who had grown up with him on the Kop during his 468-match Liverpool career. When the great goalkeeper died some 25 years later, in 1959, floods of letters reached the offices of the *Liverpool Echo*, all packed with memories of Scott and of his unique relationship with the Liverpool fans. Where was such togetherness now, they asked? One recalled a popular local story about a complete stranger who had stopped Scott and launched into a long conversation outside Anfield in the 1930s. Eventually, a perplexed Elisha asked the man, 'Do I know you?', to which his new friend indignantly replied, 'You ought to. I threw the ball back to you from the Kop last Saturday!' Billy Liddell and later Kenny Dalglish would both become great Liverpool idols, but, arguably, neither would have the affinity with ordinary Liverpool fans once enjoyed by the incomparable Elisha Scott.

SURVIVING THE POST-ELISHA ERA

With a new bunch of recruits, Liverpool tried to turn things around in the post-Elisha Scott period. The Liverpool minute books tell us that in 1934 the Reds board resolved that 'In all future cases of players being secured for a transfer fee an independent medical certificate and birth certificate be obtained'. Too many players in the past had been found later to have lied about their age and their fitness. These new Liverpool men included two full-backs to try to stem the flood of goals flushing past Arthur Riley. The elegant, sweet-passing Stoke-born England right-back and captain Tom Cooper was signed from Derby County for £7,500 in December 1934. He followed in another England man, the cultured left-back Ernie Blenkinsop, who had come from Sheffield Wednesday for a £5,000 fee in March. Here, it seemed at last, was a full-back pairing with the potential to replace the great Longworth and McKinlay partnership of the 1920s.

Bob Savage, a tall and strong right-half, stepped up from the Liverpool reserves, and Cheshire-born Fred Howe came in from little Hyde United to bolster a forward line that, apart from Hodgson, had lacked presence and devil for years. When Liverpool memorably thumped an injury-hit Everton 6–0 in the league in September 1935, with the largely one-footed Howe scoring four times, the *Liverpool Echo* exhorted, 'Let us encourage Howe and believe he is the centre we have so long looked for. We have stared into the past 25 years for a leader.' A week later, Liverpool lost 0–6 at Manchester City but then put seven goals past Grimsby Town. Who could manage this contrary team?

Despite the best efforts of Howe and the South Africans, Carr and Nieuwenhuys, there was to be no Liverpool renaissance in the late 1930s. The exhausted Gordon Hodgson was sold to Aston Villa in January 1936 for £3,000. Goals conceded by Liverpool were reduced, but just 17 league goals scored away from home in 1935–36 told its own sorry story. And while Liverpool and some of the other northern giants of the past struggled in the 1930s, so Arsenal began to fly the flag for professional football in the south of England, bolstering traditional north-south antipathies and adding fuel to suggestions that southern successes on the field of play increasingly reflected material inequalities off it.[7]

Arsenal were also the national darlings of the new age of broadcasting about football, but Liverpool FC would continue to be one of a number of league clubs who would be staunchly opposed to live broadcasting or to allowing newsreel companies ground access. But in other ways club communications were improving. In 1935–36, for example, Liverpool FC produced its own one-penny, red-fronted match programme for the first time, finally breaking away from the weekly black-and-white effort that had been jointly issued with Everton. By 1938, the programme price had doubled to twopence, but there were also cover photos and lively features for the committed to enjoy. The club's minute books reveal that by March 1939 a home crowd of 18,380 produced programme sales of 2,805 – about one in six fans bought one. By 1950, the club was pressed to issue warnings about supporters buying 'pirate' programmes on sale outside the ground (early fanzines?) as official sales rose to 25,000 before the post-war paper shortage in 1951 halved the print run.

A promising if fragile young Liverpool-born inside-forward called Jack Balmer now began to get a few first-team starts, and he impressed good judges, as did the versatile future England international Phil Taylor, who was bought in from Bristol Rovers for £5,000 in March 1936. We would hear more about these two men later. Notable, too, was the signing from Manchester City for £8,000 of a stylish young Scottish half-back called Matt Busby. Busby was a converted inside-forward who lacked the pace to play higher up the field, but he was technically excellent and a cultured thinker and distributor, a true leader at half-back. Like so many players, Busby's playing career would be severely curtailed by the war. The Liverpool board agreed that it had paid an 'extremely high figure' for the half-back but that it had acted wisely and had 'laid something in for the future' of the club.

John McKenna, the remaining original founder of Liverpool FC, finally died on 22 March 1936 in Walton Hospital, Liverpool, aged almost 82. He had devoted his entire life to football. In his last few years, the strictly anti-gambling McKenna had seen tensions grow between the Football League and the Liverpool-based Pools Promoters Association. The pools companies relied on access to league fixtures for their business, which now attracted an estimated six or seven million punters. But the Football League management committee was still morally opposed to any sort of match betting. In February 1936, the crunch finally came, and the Football League refused to confirm the weekend's fixtures. Chaos ensued, with confused football supporters, and even parliament, siding with the pools companies. Eventually, the league backed down, deriding claims from John Moores of Liverpool's Littlewoods Pools that league representatives *had* talked about demanding 'exorbitant' amounts of money in possible payment for exclusive access to fixture lists at an earlier meeting. In the end, the public outcome was that the Football League refused to accept any payment from the PPA for sole use of the fixtures, and the pools companies continued to make their huge profits. In effect, it was like football throwing cash away.

MANAGING THE COUNTDOWN TO WAR IN A CAR WITHOUT PETROL

On 14 July 1936, the Liverpool board advertised for a football manager who might better understand the emerging modern game. Fifty-two applications were received. The club recruited, from Southampton, George Kay on £600 per annum and a £250 bonus for finishing first or second in the league. He brought with him trainer Albert Shelley. The Liverpool board even resolved to build a manager's office for the first time, erected by Tyson and Co. for £63 in 1936. However, the issue of a new 'boss' was typically discussed at the 1936 Liverpool AGM *not* in terms of the importance of bringing in an experienced and influential football manager, but of releasing George Patterson from his residual management duties 'because the value of secretarial work was growing enormously'. The main question from the AGM floor revealed how little the manager's post was valued by shareholders: would the appointment of a new manager involve the payment of an extra salary?

The Manchester-born Kay had spent most of his playing career with West Ham United, and he had captained the Hammers in the first Wembley FA Cup final, in 1923. Kay certainly knew the game, and he was sympathetic to players, even if it was difficult to describe him as a 'tracksuit manager'. Kay insisted on always wearing a collar and tie, in order to identify with the board and club officials above rather than with the dressing-room below. This may explain why he favoured 'left-wing' politics but also sent his two sons to Winchester public school. But Kay was a good talker and motivator, and he could get close to professional players. Matt Busby, for example, was greatly influenced by Kay and the way he managed to treat his players at Liverpool with loyalty and consideration, compared to the brutality of the regime Busby had experienced at Manchester City. Busby also saw how the pressures of the job eventually got to Kay, who was often seen 'shouting, beseeching – wringing his hands, holding his head in apparent anguish, and making an excellent attempt to head and kick every ball in the match' from the trainer's bench.[8]

George Kay had more to say on transfers and tactics on the pitch, and perhaps he also had a little more luck than some previous Liverpool managers had, because it was Kay who sat in the manager's chair at Anfield in the summer of 1938 when the club made its best signing for almost 30 years – and for no fee. A slight 16-year-old winger called Liddell scrawled his signature on the dotted line as an amateur. On 17 March 1939, he signed professional forms on £3 a week in the Liverpool A team. Here was a future Reds hero to take over the mantle from the departed Elisha Scott.

The son of a Scottish miner, Liddell had played both rugby and football at school, and he had considered careers in both the ministry and in accounting while playing soccer for Lochgelly Violet for 2s 6d expenses. When Partick Thistle fatally hesitated over taking Liddell, it was Matt Busby who rang George Kay suggesting that Liverpool take a look at the boy.

Soon after, Liverpool's Scottish scout Johnny Dougary visited the Liddell home with an offer. 'Willie, how would you like to live in Liverpool?' Chairman Bill McConnell and George Kay then visited and offered Liddell's parents two assurances: they would provide 'homely' accommodation for young Liddell, and their son would be able to continue his studies for accountancy. The deal was done. 'Willie' would live with the widow of Ted Doig, the ex-Liverpool and Scotland goalkeeper. Liddell recalled later how the very different characters of the two men who came to Scotland – men who each had an intense love of Liverpool Football Club – did the necessary convincing. 'Mr McConnell, quick and volatile, Mr Kay, inclined to introspection and slower to make up his mind, made a wonderful pair, the one the ideal foil for the other.' The inspiring, fast-talking local man McConnell especially impressed Liddell with his rags-to-riches story of a Liverpool-crazy youngster, shirt hanging out his pants and holes in his shoes, blagging his way into Anfield as a boy. After many years at sea, McConnell eventually became the proprietor of restaurants and dockside canteens in the city before becoming a director and then the chairman of the football club he loved. Manager George Kay impressed the caring Liddell in a rather different way:

> If ever a man gave his life for a club George Kay did so for Liverpool. He had no other thought but the good of Liverpool during his waking hours, and also during many of his nights. He told me often of the time he had lain in bed, unable to sleep, pondering over the manifold problems that beset every manager, but which can be a curse to the overly-sensitive or excessively conscientious ones.[9]

As football writer Percy Young put it in relation to the Billy Liddell capture by Liverpool, 'One man does not make a team, but one outstanding personality can do much to fix the positive image of a team.'[10] Liddell would define the post-war era for Liverpool, but in an early A-team game at Blackburn in 1939 he suffered a 'badly injured knee' in a horrible collision with concrete posts sited too close to the pitch. The Reds board heaved a huge sigh of relief as their new prospect slowly recovered. Reflecting the traditional relations between a club board and players at that time – but also the essential decency of Liddell as both a man and an employee – in 1960 Tom Williams, chairman of Liverpool, said about the Scot, 'Whatever he has been asked to do he has done willingly and with good grace, content with the knowledge that even if it was occasionally not just what he would have preferred, it was for the good of Liverpool Football Club, which has always been his primary aim.'[11] Billy Liddell was a wonderful servant for Liverpool Football Club and the club's best post-war footballer for at least three decades.

Despite this crucial signing, George Kay would have his work cut out. Liverpool's form continued to oscillate alarmingly. After a three-goal loss to Second Division Norwich City in the FA Cup third round in January 1937, it was too much for many. Later in 1937, Kay tried to sell arguably the club's best players, Phil Taylor and Matt Busby, to raise funds for transfers. A letter from 'Paddock Mug' to the *Liverpool Echo* called on the entire board to resign and asked why Liverpool had spent thousands of pounds on full-backs when 'the pace of modern football was beginning to tell its tale' and 'when forwards were the urgent need'. Another letter writer, who signed off as 'No Work, No Pay', asked if the new Liverpool manager was 'restricted from purchasing much needed players', which would be like 'expecting a chauffeur to drive a car without petrol'. He wondered why the club's players were not sacked, because they were 'not worth their wages'. Players on the maximum wage at this time would have earned £386 per annum, about double a skilled worker's or a clerk's salary.[12] Yet another Merseyside letter writer argued that 'they [the board] have done nothing right' at Liverpool for some time and that Anfield Road lacked 'discipline'. It was a Liverpool Football Club low point, no doubt about it.

Bizarrely, Liverpool began their FA Cup campaign of 1938 in highly unusual red-and-white hoops against Crystal Palace, and in February 1938, after yet another FA Cup capitulation, this time at home to Huddersfield Town, the *Evening Express* reported on innovative plans among a group of Reds fans who wanted public feedback on an idea for the formation of a Liverpool Football Supporters Club. Meanwhile, Fred 'Bullet' Rogers, a tidy, blond Cheshire-born centre-half or right-half, played thirty times in the 1938–39 season, with young Balmer and the increasingly impressive Matt Busby being the two ever-presents in the Liverpool team.

'Prospects are brighter than for a long time,' commented the *Echo* in May 1938 about Liverpool's supposed recent progress. This was more in hope than expectation. Albert Shelley had replaced the ailing Charlie Wilson, and he, the manager and a number of directors even attended an FA training course in Leeds in 1938 as the new approach to coaching in England slowly began to take hold in the ranks of professionals. The message from club chairman Will Harrop in the first match programme of 1938–39 was an idealistic call for supporter patience: 'We cannot command success . . . Never forget the players are not machines and they are not machine-made, and to err is human, to forgive divine.' But when, on 1 October, the Merseyside clubs met for the Goodison derby, won by Everton 1–2, it was a sense of denial about the possibility of war that was very much in the air: a special performance of the national anthem took place to mark the return of Prime Minister Chamberlain from Munich. English club footballers touring Germany were among the few who could see a nation gearing up for war. At least Liverpool managed to drag themselves up to a respectable 11th-place finish in this final league table before the conflict began in 1939. But they had to look a long way upwards to see neighbours and rivals Everton, reigning supreme as champions again.

On 6 May 1939, the 'international situation', as it was now euphemistically called in the press, was said by the *Echo* not to interfere with Liverpool's post-season plans to tour Sweden. But the Liverpool club became the first in Britain to announce that all its players, the manager George Kay and assistant secretary Jack Rouse were to join the Territorial Army as a unit: 'A grand example to the remainder of the football world.' Albert Shelley had to treat the players' feet for blisters after route marches in ill-fitting army boots.[13] These seemed like strangely mixed messages from Anfield as the country now prepared for war.

The band struck up 'Auld Lang Syne' on 6 May 1939 as Manchester United and Liverpool players left the field at a final league match of 'intense dullness', according to the *Daily Post*. 'It would certainly be a hardening off process,' said the *Echo*, not wholly convincingly, in assessing the forthcoming TA military training period for the Liverpool players. 'They would certainly be 100 per cent fit for the start of the new season – if any!' Of course, at this precise moment no one could say exactly when the world's oldest football league might restart. Or, indeed, exactly *which* Liverpool Football Club it would be that arose again from the ashes of war.

CHAPTER 9 REFERENCES

1. Keith, *Dixie Dean: The Inside Story of a Football Icon*
2. Belchem, 'Celebrating Liverpool', p. 38
3. Liversedge, *Liverpool, We Love You!*, p. 22
4. Mason, 'The Blues and the Reds', p. 20
5. Taylor, *The Leaguers*, p. 259
6. Milne, 'Maritime Liverpool', pp. 264 and 270
7. Russell, *Looking North*, p. 255
8. Carter, *The Football Manager*, pp. 71 and 79
9. Liddell, *My Soccer Story*, pp. 28–9
10. Young, *Football on Merseyside*, p. 131
11. Liddell, *My Soccer Story*, p. 9
12. Taylor, *The Leaguers*, p. 115
13. Rippon, *Gas Masks for Goal Posts*, p. 9

10

FOOTBALL LIFE DURING WARTIME
Surviving the Conflict and Emerging Stronger

WAR STOPS PLAY

At the AGM of the Football League in 1939, the main agenda items were, to say the least, varied. Elliptical goalposts were made standard at all Football League grounds, though they would keep square posts for many years in parts of Scotland. It was also made compulsory that players wore numbers – though when Liverpool played Walsall in the FA Cup in January 1947 the Third Division Midlands men were recklessly numberless (Reds player Bob Paisley was also kicked by a fan when leaving the field). The league had finally caught up with some of the pre-war ideas of Herbert Chapman. But much more substantive problems now loomed in the sport. Professional players would get numbers on more than their shirts in 1939 – they would also be on their call-up cards.[1] When war was finally declared on 3 September 1939 and the assembly of large crowds was banned by the Home Office, the Football League remembered the painful controversy of 1914 and this time went immediately onto a war footing. They dusted down the arrangements for regional competition that had been formulated during the First World War.

There had been time for just three normal league fixtures in the 1939–40 campaign, with the 19-year-old Liverpool-born Cyril Done, an uncomplicated and direct forward presence, reportedly putting 'pep' into Liverpool's attack by scoring his first Football League goal in a closing 1–0 win against Chelsea at Anfield. Many of the Liverpool players in the forces had been on military duty until the early hours of that Saturday morning, and the band at the match played 'old time' war songs, with the teams coming out to the winsome strains of 'It's a Long Way to Tipperary'. At the end, Liverpool stood fourth in the embryonic league table for 1939–40 – who could have guessed what was going to happen in the rest of the season? Then, Britain's foes in Europe called 'time' on Football League action. For how long, no one knew.

The players' union agreed that in matches played for charity during the war their members would play without remuneration, and on 16 September 1939 the *Evening Express* reported that the local police authorities had given permission for the Merseyside clubs to play in a 'sectional competition'. All players' contracts were cancelled, although, crucially, clubs still held the registration of players and crowds were initially restricted to 15,000. It was agreed that the players be paid 30 shillings a match, raised to £2 in 1943. The players' union claimed it was a licence for clubs to profiteer.

Liverpool warmed up for the new challenge with friendly matches against Chester and Blackburn Rovers. The trip to Ewood Park was typically eventful for the time. Five Liverpool players made it to Ormskirk Station and were then joined at 2.10 p.m. by George Kay and Jack Rouse. Liverpool director Ronnie Williams went on ahead to Blackburn in his car to tell Rovers that the visitors would be late. But his vehicle broke down. Other Liverpool players eventually arrived from military duty and the match kicked off, considerably delayed. Wartime football would often be a chaotic affair. Apparently unaffected, Liverpool won 5–0 at Rovers – and the score could easily have been doubled.

When the regional football competitions began, they were deemed a success, attracting not far short of 200,000 spectators on the first weekend. But this was still less than one-third of normal gates. Anfield crowds fell dramatically if the opposition was weak, but the story was the same elsewhere. Twelve clubs, including Liverpool, lined up in the strangely titled Western Division, and just fewer than 5,000 supporters, sprinkled with khaki, saw a broadly familiar Liverpool line-up defeat Stockport County 3–0 at Anfield in the first fixture. Despite the reduction in competitive football, the vigilant Football League still found plenty of vital things to do, of course. Liverpool FC were fined in 1939–40, for example, for admitting juveniles for fourpence, instead of the minimum charge of sixpence. It was something short of a hanging offence in the circumstances.

The careers of a whole generation of football players and staff were hugely affected by the war. By June 1940, Liverpool announced it could no longer pay salaries to its staff, and manager George Kay was placed on £4 per week with a week's notice. He was given a cash float of £50 for 'emergencies'. Bob Paisley, a dour but highly productive left wing-half who had been recruited from Bishop Auckland, impressed in pre-war Liverpool trials, and he played 32 times for Liverpool in the early years of the war. But from 1941, Paisley was abroad with the British Army, making his return to play for Liverpool only in September

1945. Meanwhile, George 'Stonewall' Jackson, the Everton full-back, played for both of the major Merseyside clubs, including, during emergencies, as a goalkeeper. He once played in goal for wartime Liverpool against Everton in a 3–1 Reds win, an example that shows both the flexibility necessary for wartime football and also the essential lack of competitive edge now involved, even in local derbies. Small clubs crammed with guest players routinely beat the game's giants. Young talent still shone through, however. In March 1940, manager George Kay described Liverpool's 18-year-old trainee chartered accountant Billy Liddell as 'the best thing that has come out of Scotland in the past ten years'. The coltish Tom Finney, England's equivalent of Liddell, also made his senior debut for Preston, at Anfield in August 1940, against a Liverpool team that boasted a star guest, Stan Cullis, at centre-half.

Several Liverpool players were promoted in the forces even before the fighting began. The South African goalkeepers Arthur Riley and Dirk Kemp, for example, were made sergeants in the 9th King's Liverpool Battalion. Tom Cooper, Willie Fagan, left-back Bernard Ramsden and the tall and elegant Reds left-half Tom Bush were promoted to lance corporals. Billy Liddell joined the RAF as a navigator and ended up serving in Canada, Bob Paisley became a desert gunner in the Royal Artillery, while Phil Taylor and Jackie Balmer were learning to drive tanks and Willie Fagan became a trench mortar expert.[2] Later, full-back Ted Spicer, a lieutenant in the marines, was promoted to captain after capturing a German NCO who turned out to be a football international!

Among those who were initially employed in reserved occupations, Berry Nieuwenhuys managed to find work on nights as a driller on Merseyside, mainly so he could continue to play golf during the day. 'Nivvy' had an interesting war. He had his jaw broken while guesting as a player in January 1943. As an RAF flight-sergeant, he was later decorated for his work with the Czech Fight Squadron. Then the wily South African captain of Liverpool was suspended for life (later rescinded) by the Football League for asking other clubs for more than the regulation £2 fee for wartime appearances. Liverpool had six players decorated for war service, including a Military Cross for the amateur Len Carney.

CELEBRITY FOOTBALL FOR WAR HEROES

The limits of the regulation football training and pre-war preparation of players in England was soon revealed by the fact that as the game settled down in the war years it was widely considered to be of better quality and to be at least a yard faster than its pre-war counterpart. The extra fitness showed in those players who were now marched and generally exercised on a daily basis in the Armed

Forces. But great sportsmen are also not immune from the very real dangers of war. Tragically, the stylish Reds full-back and regimental policeman Tom Cooper lost his life on 25 June 1940 when his motorcycle was in a head-on collision with a bus near Aldeburgh. He was the only Liverpool FC fatality during the conflict. Only Crystal Palace and Wolves contributed more than the 76 players in total from Liverpool FC who gave wartime service.

As the war dragged on, players turned out for their clubs whenever possible, but it all depended on where they were stationed and whether they could get leave. They could play for other clubs within a reasonable distance, with the consent of the club that held their registration. But this system was open to abuse, with star guests often replacing other willing players at the last minute. In February 1942, for example, the brilliant Irish international Peter Doherty travelled to Blackpool to watch Liverpool play, and he casually called into the Reds dressing-room before the match to chat with friends. He was immediately asked by George Kay to turn out for Liverpool, with Leeds United's George Ainsley cruelly being told to step down.

Clubs could also seemingly track down international footballers, even in camps of thousands of men. A youthful Bill Shankly later recalled being approached by Norwich City, and he played under the false name 'Newman' for the Canaries in January 1943, scoring twice in an 8–4 win against an army XI in front of 484 people.[3] But it was clearly a risk to have valuable professional players turning out for local clubs in uncertain conditions. Cyril Done, Matt Busby, Phil Taylor and Jack Balmer all played for the same works team to keep themselves fit and all suffered serious knocks. Liverpool's prize asset, Billy Liddell, stepped into a pothole on a pitch at Bridgnorth in 1943 and suffered serious injury just above the ankle. The damage might have ended Liddell's league career before it had even begun.

Liverpool finally gave in to the broadcasters when the BBC agreed to pay five guineas to cover the second half of the Liverpool v. Blackpool match on 14 February 1942 – the Reds lost 1–3. But, as the Liverpool minute books tell us, 11 years later it was conservative Liverpool FC who proposed a resolution to the Football League 'deploring the action of the FA in granting permission for the televising of the whole of the FA Cup final on 2 May 1953'.

Another way of trying to get wartime crowds interested in 'big name' recruits as guest players was to sign up unlikely star names from other sports. In 1944, Liverpool Football Club registered the world heavyweight boxing champion Joe Louis, then aged 30, but manager George Kay seemed reluctant to select the fighter to add punch to the Reds attack. As the *Evening Express* pointed out in October 1939, in wartime football 'names will still count in the matter of players, but not so much in the matter of clubs'. But, to be fair, there was plenty going on to deter even the most determined football fan from attending wartime football matches: air-raids, for example, often caused long delays to kick-offs, especially if some players were also ARP (air-raid protection) wardens who then had to report for duty.

Amazingly, the Liverpool football ground avoided suffering major war damage, though the strategically important city of Liverpool suffered substantially in the Blitz. Much of the national focus on the bravery of the British people, however, largely ignored Liverpool and other provincial cities (causing some resentment in the north) and homed in on London instead. But many Liverpudlians responded to the privations of war with typical innovation and energetic creativity. Almost anything – including, it was rumoured, Spitfire parts – could be found offered for sale in pubs in the city, and as the war and its misery progressed it became clear that 'the whole of Liverpool was beginning to feed and clothe itself on the black market'.[4] Football was also important in raising the national morale, especially after the initial shock of war slowly began to diminish. A letter to the *Evening Express* on 4 January 1940 commented, for example, that football in Liverpool was 'spirited and skilful to a high degree' and that 'football is a valuable asset to the home front and deserves the support of all lovers of our characteristically British game'. A survey by Mass Observation in 1940 found that 65 per cent of pre-war football supporters were not attending matches because of a variety of wartime reasons, but by 1945 the sport's followers were beginning to flood back to matches in Liverpool and elsewhere around the country.[5]

PLAYING FOR BRITAIN

In front of generally very modest crowds, Liverpool finished second to Stoke City in the 12-club Western Division in 1939–40. The really exciting news from the Reds camp was that on New Year's Day 1940 the 17-year-old Billy Liddell made his debut at Anfield against Crewe Alexandra and scored after just three minutes, a low header from a Nieuwenhuys cross in a 7–3 victory. When Liverpool won by the same score at Manchester City a week later, the *Evening Express* correspondent noted the outstanding 'brilliance' of the 'amazingly cool' Liddell and thought the Scotsman was 'the most promising young winger I have seen in years'. Here was potential already being realised. 'He is becoming two-footed and . . . uses his brains and has complete control over the ball,' enthused the *Express*. 'He had a direct hand in five of the Liverpool goals.'

The fact that the young Liddell seemed comfortable with either foot was entirely unusual in the English game in 1939 – as, indeed, it is today. Once, at

Preston North End, the winger lined up for a free-kick with his right foot but at the last moment the wind blew the ball across to his left. Without hesitating or changing stride, he struck the ball with his left instead, and it thundered past the bemused keeper. How could you stop him? In 1942, Liddell scored on his enthralling Scotland debut in a 5–4 win over England, and by 1943 the *Evening Express* was already describing Liddell as 'irresistible'. In September 1945, when Liverpool beat Everton 2–1 at Anfield, the Reds' fast, long-passing style overcame Everton's more intricate short-pass build-up, and the newspaper was simply in awe of the Scotsman. Liddell was 'unpredictable, like a flash of lightning, and the essence of versatility. Liddell . . . has everything.' The winger had destroyed Everton, scoring the first goal and terrorising the visitors' defence. 'Liddell,' said the *Express* with just the slightest trace of hyperbole, 'is one of the greatest, if not *the* greatest, all-round forwards in football.'

In 1946, Billy Liddell's immense talents were recognised internationally when he was selected to play in a Great Britain v. FIFA match at Hampden Park to celebrate the re-entry of the home countries into FIFA after the war and to raise money for the ailing international football body. The Great Britain forward line of Stanley Matthews, Wilf Mannion, Tommy Lawton, Billy Steel and Liddell is still argued by many good judges to be the greatest array of British forward talent ever assembled on these shores.[6] A crowd of 135,000 watched as the British XI thrashed FIFA's select 6–1, thus probably perpetuating the mistaken view in these islands that Britain was, inevitably, best at football and that it was great wingers rather than the tactical advances being made elsewhere that would really shape the modern game.[7]

In 1940–41, Liverpool played in the extended Northern Regional section, which listed the standings by percentage of 36 northern clubs that had played between 16 and 38 matches each, including local and national cup fixtures. Liverpool finished a mediocre 16th in a highly volatile competition, which produced results as varied as a 9–1 Reds win over neighbours Chester and a 6–4 victory over New Brighton, as well as two heavy defeats at the hands of Preston North End. Everton were played six times by Liverpool in the season to lift crowds, producing only one Liverpool win and four defeats. For the next three seasons, the Northern section was divided into two competitions for different numbers of clubs. These were staged, broadly speaking, before and after Christmas.

Liverpool actually finished top of the second Northern section in 1942–43, having ended up second to Blackpool in the first section. After beating Bolton Wanderers 4–0 at a one-quarter-full Anfield on 1 May 1943, the *Evening Express* congratulated the club on a 'really brilliant season' in which, even with these modest crowds, Liverpool had commanded 'a support as good as any – and better than most'. It credited everyone at the club, from chairman Robert Lawson Martindale down to each member of the ground staff. Manager George Kay was also praised as being a man who had taken on extra tasks and 'has had his finger on the pulse throughout the season . . . handling both managerial and secretarial duties with an amazing energy and conscientiousness'. In the two-legged Lancashire Cup final that followed – played for the prize of four saving certificates for each winner and two for every losing player – Manchester United won easily at Anfield in the first leg. This left Liverpool with a 1–3 deficit to make up at Maine Road. Jack Balmer scored a brave hat-trick in Manchester, but it could only produce an honourable 3–3 draw for Liverpool in the leg and thus no Lancashire Cup or savings-certificate extravaganza.

A SQUAD FIT FOR PURPOSE?

After the war, football gradually began to shake itself into recovery mode. In July 1945, less than three months after VE Day, Liverpool became the first senior English club to play on German soil after the hostilities, in two matches against British Forces teams. The Reds returned with a smart set of new red shirts, reputedly made of material previously used to make Nazi flags. In 1945–46, the Football League staged its transitional return to a forty-two-match programme in the shape of northern and southern versions of the league, with 'only' six guest players allowed. Liverpool, apparently returning to its moderate performances before the war, finished a disappointing 11th. The 1939 league champions Everton were threatening ominously once again, finishing second to Sheffield United. A version of the FA Cup returned, too, played over two legs, with the Reds easing past Chester in the third round. But then, with 5,000 Liverpool supporters travelling to Bolton in the next round, including in dozens of corporation double-decker buses, the visitors dominated the match but collapsed 0–5. Without the unavailable Liddell for the second leg, the Reds clawed two goals back, but that was all.

Bob Paisley, out of uniform at last, played 25 times in the transitional league in this rehearsal for real football combat the following season, and Fagan, Liddell and Jack Balmer combined well at forward to score 56 out of Liverpool's 80 league goals. Something important was clearly developing at Anfield. 'Beyond a shadow of a doubt,' concluded the *Evening Express* in August 1943, 'the war break has not impaired their abilities.' Young players were coming through strongly, gaining useful experience without the usual pressures brought by titles and relegation, large and demanding crowds, and the sheer treadmill of a normal league campaign. The backbone of a quietly impressive post-war Liverpool side was beginning to emerge at Anfield, out of the confusion and unfulfilled promise of the late 1920s and the 1930s.

Ideas about 'new beginnings', thus connecting with the prevailing national post-war sentiment of reform in Britain, were also prominent at the offices of the Football League in 1945. What about a British League or a new League Cup competition, members of the management committee were asked? Both were turned down. Everton (and others) wanted the FA Cup to be played over two legs from then on. But this money-spinning idea, designed to protect the larger clubs from early cup embarrassments, was again rejected. Radical proposals to modernise football, for example by having four up and four down in the league, were also put to the management committee. These notions especially incensed Ronnie Williams from ever-watchful Liverpool FC, who replied sternly, 'What was wrong with football [before the war]? Were the public dissatisfied?'[8]

Liverpool's regular and most impressive performers during the regional competitions in the Second World War included the very competent north-east goalkeeper Alf Hobson. Winger Berry Nieuwenhuys was still a fixture and he had been joined by future Wales international full-back Ray Lambert, a laid-back but highly consistent defender who would make 341 senior appearances for Liverpool. Club captain Willie Fagan and wing-half Phil Taylor, plus Liverpool-born right-half George Kaye and the emerging young forward talents of Jackie Balmer, Billy Liddell and Cyril Done were also prominent. Done scored an impressive 122 goals in just 103 wartime appearances from 1941 to 1944 before a broken leg cracked this rich spell. There was also an imposing and intelligent young centre-half from Liverpool, Laurie Hughes, who was beginning to make his mark. Though regularly troubled by injury himself, 'Big Lol' was a consistent and football-playing defender who would go on to parade his skills at international level for England in their ill-fated World Cup campaign in Brazil in 1950. He figured in all matches there, including the infamous 0–1 England defeat to the USA, which probably cost him his international career. Among this group of war 'veterans', the core of a new Liverpool title-winning team was slowly beginning to crystallise.

PLAYERS WANTED – MUST HAVE CHAMPIONSHIP POTENTIAL

There were still a few problem positions to attend to in order to produce the new Liverpool XI. The club even advertised for players: 'Particulars of age, height, weight and clubs played for (mark envelope "Trial") to be sent to George Kay,

Liverpool 4.'⁹ The South Africans Riley and Kemp were no longer options in goal, for example, and Alf Hobson would soon drift down to South Liverpool. So Cyril Sidlow was recruited by George Kay for £4,000 in February 1946 from Wolverhampton Wanderers. Sidlow's career had barely got off the ground at Molineux before war had intervened. But this Wales international was a good shot-stopper, and he was one of the few goalkeepers who had begun to explore throwing the ball out to half-backs and defenders as a more accurate means of holding onto possession. Just in his 30s, Sidlow was a generally mature and stabilising figure at the back, making a good combination with the emerging young centre-half Hughes.

At right-back the very spritely and tough Scottish defender Jim Harley, a war hero, stepped in to replace the much mourned Tom Cooper, and he briefly picked up his nascent pre-war partnership with Yorkshire-born left-back Barney Ramsden. When Stoke City hosted a sprint competition for £100 at the Victoria Ground in August 1944, the lightning ex-commando Harley – who had won the famous Powderhall Sprint as an 18 year old – took part. The elegant and cerebral Phil Taylor had taken over from Matt Busby, who was now finished with Liverpool at right-half. The brilliant Scot Busby might well have stayed much longer at Anfield, and he could even have changed the course of football history if Liverpool had made more positive noises about his possible management prospects there. Instead, Liverpool stuck with George Kay and offered Busby a five-year coaching contract. But Manchester United stepped in with a management job, and Busby took his chance at Old Trafford. It clearly riled the Liverpool board that Busby chose to leave the club, because an invitation for him to play in a farewell exhibition/benefit match was later withdrawn.

That pugnacious half-back Bob Paisley (very much part of Liverpool's glorious future, of course) was finally back from his foreign manoeuvres to play on the Liverpool left. The reinstated 'Nivvy' shared the right-wing slot with the clever Blackpool-born Harry Eastham, and they now partnered the prodigious Jack Balmer at inside-right. Balmer was a great cross-field passer, a man of real talent, but he split Liverpool supporters because of his deep reluctance to tackle. Balmer's footballing uncles had sensibly warned him to protect his ankles for his future health. Cyril Done and Willie Fagan shared duties at inside-left, with the precocious Billy Liddell outside. Bill Jones, a reliable and versatile defender, and Eddie Spicer, a tough-tackling full-back, made up the main Liverpool squad. Which left the crucial centre-forward berth to fill – it had been a problem position for Liverpool for the past 20 years. The Reds looked to the north for their man. They were not disappointed.

KING ALBERT

The powerful and speedy red-haired twenty-seven-year-old Geordie centre-forward Albert Stubbins, a former shipyard draughtsman, had had a good war – twenty-nine wartime hat-tricks and five-goal hauls on five occasions. This man could score goals for fun. Jock Dodds, from Blackpool and later of Everton, was one of the few British forwards to score more wartime goals. Stubbins was powerful and fiercely quick but also 'dainty', unpredictable and exciting, hardly attributes that had characterised recent Liverpool centre-forwards. Stubbins could bring a ball under control immediately from any height, and he could bind together a forward line and bring other players into the game.

Ironically, Stubbins had no real intention of leaving his native Newcastle United. In fact, he had grand plans to open a business there after he stopped playing, and his family was well settled in the north-east. That is until *both* of the Merseyside clubs came up with their record offer for him of £12,500 in September 1946. Stubbins was, famously, watching a film in the Northumberland Street News Theatre when a message flashed across the screen that he was to report to St James's Park right away. He loped off in his size-11 shoes to find that United had accepted the offer: no wonder the post-war Newcastle struggled so hopelessly to win league titles. Albert would need to keep hold of his formidable football boots: in the post-war gloom, professional players struggled to get a pair that fitted, and Bob Paisley even played in boots of different sizes.[10]

So, all that needed to be decided by Stubbins was *which* Merseyside club to join. With no official differential in wages to worry about, on the face of it this selection might have seemed fairly obvious. Everton, after all, were 1939 league champions and had won the FA Cup in recent memory. All Liverpool's league successes were more than 20 years ago, and the Anfield men had *never* won the FA Cup, the holy grail at Newcastle. But because he had made no plans to move and had had little time to think, and perhaps because he feared causing offence by being seen to make a choice, Stubbins tossed a coin to decide which club to speak to first. It came down in Liverpool's favour. It was the most important coin toss in the club's history – at least until Liverpool's European escapades began in the 1960s. The silver-tongued Liverpool chairman Billy McConnell probably convinced Stubbins to come to Anfield by offering him a club house – much sought after following the war – and assuring him that he could live in Newcastle later to look after his business interests. There would be ructions about this in time. But for now Liverpool had paid out big money and had its goalscoring centre-forward at last.

The war had turned football upside down, but it had survived. Even the Littlewoods Pools company (based in Liverpool) had offered up its premises and turned its hand to printing call-up papers and the production of parachutes and barrage balloons during the conflict.[11] It could now hope to get back to employing women checkers in the city and making a tiny number of winners reasonably rich while making vast profits. But for millions of people, sitting checking the pools coupon on a Saturday evening would also signal a return to some kind of normality.

One player who was probably looking forward to the resumption of serious sporting rivalries at last, with a smile of satisfaction that was likely to be rather wider even than those of his Liverpool colleagues, was full-back Jim Harley. He had been sent off in the very last official league fixture played in the 1939–40 season, versus Chelsea at Anfield. Would the game's guardians catch up with him six years on? He need have no fears. Not even the normally nitpicking FA was willing to carry a suspension over this sort of period. So Harley was free to start the new campaign with a clean slate. He would play only four matches before injury cut him down and would finish with seventeen league appearances in total. But he played a significant part, nevertheless, in what would prove to be one of Liverpool Football Club's greatest-ever seasons.

CHAPTER 10 REFERENCES

1. Inglis, *The Football League and the Men Who Made It*, p. 165
2. Rollin, *Soccer at War*, pp. 15–16
3. Rollin, *Soccer at War*, pp. 45–6
4. Rollin, *Soccer at War*, p. xi
5. Belchem, 'Celebrating Liverpool', p. 44
6. Rous, *Football Worlds*, p. 96
7. Wilson, *Inverting the Pyramid*, p. 86
8. Inglis, *The Football League and the Men Who Made It*, p. 169
9. Taw, *Football's War and Peace*, p. 52
10. Taw, *Football's War and Peace*, p. 61
11. Reed, *Football and Fortunes*, p. 20

11

1946–47, CHAMPIONS AGAIN
George Kay and the Willie
and Albert Show

DANGEROUS GROUNDS AND ARMCHAIR FANS

For most people, the return of league football to England in August 1946 signalled the return to aspects of what passed for normal life after the war. But times also remained incredibly hard. The Liverpool-based football-pools business had continued at a lower level during the war years, but it was now back to full throttle: between ten and fourteen million people did the pools in Britain in the 1940s, and by 1950 Liverpool employed around 18,400 people in the industry, 17,000 of them women. In this sense, football engaged with almost every British household in some way. But many of these small-time pools gamblers were probably just too poor to be among the one million weekly football spectators who would now attend Football League matches as the game moved towards its post-war peak.[1]

And there were plenty of desperately poor people about on Merseyside. In January 1947, for example, the *Evening Express* reported that, with coal rations exhausted and the 'big freeze' of that year really starting to bite, families in Bootle 'are burning books, rags, old wooden toys and bicycle tyres in an attempt to provide warmth and heat for cooking purposes'. Power cuts were a norm in 1947 as the fuel crisis deepened. No wonder a writer who had left the city six years before told the *Express* that Liverpool looked 'drab and dismal, a gloomy, dusty film seems to have grown over the streets'.

Gangs of teenage 'desperados', aged from ten to fifteen years, were routinely rounded up for appearances in Liverpool courts at this time, usually charged with petty gas meter break-ins or else bouts of shoplifting. Meanwhile, on Boxing Day night 1947 three Liverpool men broke into the safe at Anfield Road hoping to steal £4,000 in match receipts from the fixture against Stoke

– but they found just £72 instead. New post-war concerns now regularly expressed in the Liverpool press included that of troublesome 'youth', while in 1947 Birkenhead 'teen-age' girls (another new idea) were offered 'expert tuition in charm' by the local youth-welfare service, including in dress sense, hairstyling and deportment. Even in these grim times, a new world for the young was already coming.

The minimum admission charge for football in the war years had been increased to 1s 6d, but with a reduction in Entertainment Tax this was reduced again to 1s 3d – though superior standing areas kept the 1s 6d charge. The maximum wage for players was increased from £9 to £10 – though only 5 per cent of professionals actually received the maximum, despite the post-war boom in gates. A motion to the league management committee in February 1947 that players' wages be further increased to £12 was supported by only six clubs, one of which was Liverpool. Liverpool's average home gate in the last full season before the war was 31,422, but in 1946–47, as the club fought for the Football League title even in these hard times, it would rise to 45,732, eclipsing Everton by almost 5,000 per home match. Only Newcastle United had larger average crowds in the Football League, though for some time it looked like fixtures would not be completed due to the foul weather and a government ban on midweek football to save energy and to guard against absenteeism. In March 1947, James Fay, the players' union secretary, even suggested playing games in midweek behind closed doors to get matches completed. Instead, Football League fixtures would bleed into high summer in the most unimaginable of circumstances.

With large, enthusiastic football crowds would also come the need for greater regulation and improved facilities to meet the new demand, though such lessons seemed difficult to learn. In March 1946, 33 people were crushed and killed at Burnden Park in the type of stadium disaster that had actually threatened throughout the entire history of the English game. Admirably, the Liverpool press called for instant change: a new licensing regime for sports grounds; capacities of sports stadiums to be assessed, section by section; and for ticket-only matches to be introduced. As the *Evening Express* aptly put it on 11 March 1946, even after six years of daily sacrifice in war 'the thought that men and women should be suffocated and trampled to death in the atmosphere of sport is distressing beyond words'. People in Liverpool, of course, would have these words come back to haunt them more than 40 years later.

But throughout the late 1940s and early 1950s there would be a succession of 'near misses' at Anfield and elsewhere, when sometimes hundreds of people were injured on the terraces or else were forced to leave the stadium – sometimes well before kick-off – because of the risk of excessive crushing. Hundreds climbed in over the outer wall of the Kop. In December 1946, when Liverpool played Wolves, for example, the *Football Echo* reported:

> There was some ominous swaying of the crowd in the corner between the Spion Kop and the Main Stand, and just after the second goal the police and ambulance-men helped out about 30 spectators onto the cinder track and shepherded them down the players' exit. One or two of the more elderly ones had to be supported.

In October 1948, a 'constant stream' of supporters left before the Liverpool v. Middlesbrough match 'and there were a number of stretcher cases'. Goalkeeper Cyril Sidlow remembered a Christmas Day fixture in 1950 during which streams of people were led onto the Anfield track – including a young woman carrying a baby in her arms.[2]

On 31 December 1949, a Mr O'Gorman from Amity Street in the city wrote to the *Football Echo* to register a public protest after 200 or 300 fans out of 58,757 had elected to get out of Anfield before the match kicked off against Chelsea 'rather than risk injury of excessive crushing'. He wrote, 'Hundreds inside had to fight their way out . . . The condition at the Kemlyn Road corner of the ground made another Bolton Wanderers disaster imminent.' A club record 61,905 crowd was ruthlessly shoehorned into Anfield for a fourth-round FA Cup tie against Wolves in February 1952. The message was simple enough: clubs would do pretty much anything to satisfy demand, and football grounds in England remained occasionally unstable, potentially dangerous places as a consequence. Anfield was no exception from any other venue in that respect. No comment came from the club about this, or any other such complaint, beyond a general plea that supporters in the ground should close up spaces on the centre of terraces and let latecomers in to ensure safety and good order. It was a case of negligence without punishment.

Despite such concerns, the growth of television as a popular medium in the early 1950s helped in 'nationalising' the sport of football and to spread its influence. Liverpool would finally reach the FA Cup final again in 1950, but perhaps the 1948 final between Manchester United and Blackpool signalled the birth of the modern game for fans. Ticket touts reportedly asked for – and got – 20 times the cover price for tickets as northern supporters poured into London in what would become a familiar annual scalping ritual. But it was the television coverage of the 1953 'Stanley Matthews' final, in which Blackpool recovered to beat Bolton Wanderers 4–3, that is often regarded as the key moment when the 'traditional' English game moved into the new media era. The nation now increasingly gathered collectively in their millions around the 'telly' every May to watch the FA Cup final as part of a great national ritual that confirmed the 'national community' of British people and their families, as well as the symbolic closure of yet another winter season of sport.

Television, radio and the expansion of the sporting press would also help people keep more 'connected' with their local clubs, especially as working-class communities were dispersed from around the old city centres to 'overspill' housing estates because of the damage inflicted by war. It was estimated that 148,000 people in Liverpool fitted this 'overspill' category, and they were dispersed throughout the 1940s, '50s and '60s, some of them first into 3,500 new 'pre-fabs' in and around the city, and then to an outer ring of city-corporation housing estates in Kirkby, Halewood, Huyton and Speke. The growth rate of these outer estates was incredible: the first house in Kirkby was built in 1952, but by 1965 some 52,000 people lived in the area.[3] Travelling by tramcar or walking to home matches at Anfield, as many people had done before the war, would increasingly no longer be an option in this new era of post-war urban redevelopment and cultural change in which the private motorcar would all too soon become king.

FUELLING FOR THE FOOTBALL LEAGUE

'Tomorrow,' wrote the *Liverpool Echo* on 30 August 1946, 'sees the start in England and Wales of what promises to be the biggest boom season soccer has ever known.' The war years had produced, according to this account, only 'ersatz soccer', but here was the real thing once again in all its gory glory. The *Daily Post* – messing about with its figures slightly – predicted 'the greatest season in its sixty-year history' for English league football. Some people in the game wanted promotion and relegation to be suspended for two or three seasons while clubs 'settled down' again following the strains and disruptions of the previous six years. But the Football League pointed out that all clubs were in the same boat, and what had the 42-game transition season been about if not getting the clubs attuned to the new demands?

George Kay cleverly took his team out of 'ration city' Liverpool to North America in the pre-season, mainly to get some high-quality food into his players. In 1945, the Liverpool chairman Billy McConnell had been on a Ministry of Food mission to the USA to study catering, and he knew very well the value of good nourishment to athletes. The Reds players put on an average of half a stone during the trip, with Liverpool averaging seven goals a game in a ten-match unbeaten tour. But it was not all plain sailing. 'Played under lights and the ground rough and poor,' George Kay wrote in a telegram about the match against Falls River FC. 'Lights not effective in the night game: spectators a bad lot.' Liverpool were hosted by Branch Rickey, president of the Brooklyn Dodgers, who seemed willing to offer British footballers £20 to £25 per week to join the new American Professional Soccer League.[4] Although the players still looked like scrawny scarecrows when the Reds eventually won the league title in 1947, both the chairman and the Liverpool manager would highlight the 'good food our boys had in America' as a key reason for the club's immediate success. Who says attention to diet for footballers was an invention of the 1990s?

Cheekily, on their return from North America Liverpool made an offer straight off for Everton's unsettled England international Joe Mercer, just to stir the local pot. Mercer was at serious odds with Everton manager Theo Kelly about his injury problems, and he had asked for a transfer. There was no believing for a moment at Anfield that the Goodison club would sell an England captain to their near neighbours and keenest rivals. Liverpool's enquiry might even have been a bit of tit for tat for the Elisha Scott affair back in 1934. In any event, Mercer eventually joined Arsenal for £7,000, but his connections with Liverpool Football Club did not stop there. Mercer continued to live in Hoylake, and he trained at Anfield during the week, travelling down to London at weekends for Arsenal home matches. This arrangement of having players from other clubs training with rivals was not unusual, and the Mercer situation continued right up to the 1950 FA Cup final meeting – between Liverpool and Arsenal.

THE WILLIE AND ALBERT SHOW

Liverpool began the first post-war league season slowly but steadily as the team, without Billy Liddell, who was still with the RAF, scored a last-minute winning goal by Len Carney, the little-used 31-year-old ex-local amateur, and claimed both points at Sheffield United. But a confidence-draining home loss to Middlesbrough followed, with Laurie Hughes scoring a classic own-goal header. The new post-war impatience of football supporters was already apparent as 'a hurriedly called meeting of Liverpool fans . . . assembled outside the club's offices . . . with the object of calling upon the directors to make quick team changes'.[5]

It was the Anfield clash with a strong Chelsea side on 7 September that showed the real potential of this new Liverpool team. Charlie Ashcroft, an England B international, deputised for Sidlow in goal, but it was no coincidence that Bob Paisley and Billy Liddell both made their post-war debuts on Liverpool's left side, Liddell offering searing pace and goal threat backed up by Paisley's tenacious tackling and precocious long throw-ins. Bob Paisley was a committed and aggressive player, often using the shoulder charge to barge opponents off the play so that his more skilful centre-half Lol Hughes could pick up the ball unmolested and send Liverpool off on another attack. These three players – Hughes, Paisley and Liddell – complemented each other perfectly down the Liverpool left. The Chelsea match ended up as a 7–4 home win, but, as the *Evening Express* reported, it could have been many, many more for Liverpool, who led 6–0 on 50 minutes and whose forwards 'made the Chelsea defence look absolutely inept on occasion'. Liddell (2), Fagan (2) and Balmer all scored, as did Bill Jones, a long-serving 'play anywhere' squad man who appeared twice for England and got two goals here as a forward. He would move back into a more defensive role later in the campaign. Jones also proved his intelligence and adaptability when he returned to work for the club in the 1960s as a scout.

The Reds' new star signing, centre-forward Albert Stubbins, was a hard man to second-guess. He was reported 'missing' by the *Daily Post* when he failed to meet Liverpool club staff off a 10 p.m. train from Newcastle on 13 September 1946. Had he decided to join manager Theo Kelly at Everton after all? Waiting journalists, manager George Kay and the Liverpool captain Willie Fagan all searched the train compartments with amused press hounds, but eventually they tracked the elusive Stubbins down to the Hanover Street Hotel. Liverpool had booked a room there for their new man, and not expecting a reception committee and little recognised on Merseyside he had simply slipped off the train and into the night. The centre-forward would soon learn about the intensity of interest in the game and its stars in the city of Liverpool. Stubbins brought more than a touch of glamour to the city. Assailed by autograph hunters, he was later taken by the Liverpool party to the Adelphi Hotel, where he stayed the night and where 'he answered a battery of questions with all the composure of a Hollywood film star'.

Stubbins missed the trip to Manchester United, where Liverpool were painfully reacquainted with Matt Busby in a 0–5 win for the home side. There was other mitigation. Sidlow was still out, Liddell again missed, awaiting demobilisation, and Jim Harley was soon a passenger, seriously injuring his left leg, which meant he would miss much of the season. The *Evening Express* complained in January 1947 that three key Liverpool players – Liddell, Sidlow (still not demobilised either) and Hughes – were effectively still part-timers and that this was affecting the Reds' early cohesion. Notwithstanding these handicaps, Liverpool were, it was agreed, 'completely outclassed and outplayed' by this 'devastating' United outfit. Better was to come at Bolton, with Liddell back and Stubbins on debut in a 3–1 win. 'This is the best forward line I have ever played in,' said the grateful new Liverpool centre-forward to the club's blushing chairman Billy McConnell immediately after the match. 'I am only sorry I could not give you more than one goal.' Scoring on debut and still apologising? It was music to any director's ears. And it was also exactly the type of goal the club had signed Albert Stubbins to score: a head-on from Nieuwenhuys, and the centre-forward latching on and shrugging off two defenders before driving the ball right-footed past Wanderers keeper Stan Hanson.

The *Daily Post* marked the debut qualities of Stubbins as 'good timing, a long stride and an almost nonchalant style', but it also asked that if Stubbins was worth his huge fee then what price Cyril Sidlow, 'who makes victories possible'? It was a point well made, especially as goalkeepers' transfer fees would remain resolutely below those of top forwards in England for decades to come. In this new sporting world, sports journalists now even got the occasional interview out of players after matches to spice up their copy. Not that there was too much controversy here. 'Thanks,' said the new man Stubbins evenly to congratulations from waiting local press men. 'But I promise you I'll do better.' The red-headed Albert already seemed far too good to be true.

But if Albert Stubbins was to deliver some of the extra goals that Liverpool needed – eventually he would score 83 in 178 matches for the club – it was the Presbyterian Scot Billy Liddell who provided the essential speed, guile and bite down the left side that marked out this Liverpool team as exceptional. On occasion, the 24-year-old was simply unplayable – but Everton were alert to his tricks for the Anfield 0–0 derby meeting of 21 September that followed. With Phil Taylor playing 'delicious football' in the middle of the field, Liverpool chairman McConnell said he thought it was the best local derby game he had seen for some time, though most supporters saw a different match. The *Daily Post* used the convenient imagery of war to suggest that some of the younger players on both sides were 'shell-shocked by the atmosphere, the pace and the urge to play a hero's part'. The truth was that two well-marshalled defences and the 'snappy, non-stop worker' on Liverpool's left, Bob Paisley, had easily managed the attacking threat from both units in a frenzied 0–0 encounter. Although Stubbins had failed to score, and might even have been feeling the weight of his great fee in his feet, he also produced many 'bright things'. The Liverpool supporters, so the local press commented, 'will always be glad to have his relief from the drab, stereotyped methods common to so many of our players'. In short, this draw was a disappointment but no disaster.

'LUCKY' LIVERPOOL

Berry Nieuwenhuys was now approaching 35 years of age, and in a newish, young Liverpool team he was beginning to look a little like yesterday's man, short of real pace and guile, certainly compared to Liddell and Stubbins. He was a player who signified the disappointing pre-war Liverpool past, one laced with too many so-so South African imports, rather than a possibly brighter post-war, mainly British, future.

Supporters noticed his decline: time catches up with even the greatest of footballers, especially when fans have been starved of entertainment for six long years. They were certainly much harsher and quicker now in their judgements. 'Spectators at Anfield,' reported the *Daily Post* on 30 September 1946, talking about the treatment of Nivvy, 'have a bad habit of verbally marking a man and they trouble a player by reason of their alleged humour.' The tall winger got his own back on the Anfield knockers by scoring a header from a Liddell corner against Leeds United in a 2–0 Liverpool canter in the autumn sunshine. But one good week would not be enough: Nivvy was replaced in the next game by Harry Eastham, a sometimes overcomplicated but popular wing-man from Blackpool. Jack Balmer scored the other goal, Albert Stubbins missing a penalty, his first blot.

These were really complaints from Reds supporters in a time of relative plenty, rather than those signifying potential famine. It was a fact confirmed by the 6–1 Liverpool tanning of Grimsby Town that followed in Cleethorpes. Billy Liddell ran half the length of the field 'at lightning speed' to add to Stubbins's opening goal, and then the second-half flood gates opened, with all the key Liverpool forward men of this campaign – Stubbins, Liddell, Balmer and Willie Fagan – getting goals. Balmer was clearly offside but sensibly netted before checking. 'The referee,' reported the *Liverpool Echo*, 'bore the brunt of the Grimsby barracking.' The Reds were up to fourth place after this rout. 'The best thing Liverpool have done all season,' was the *Daily Post*'s smug verdict. The Liverpool managerial 'brains trust' then had a late-night discussion about tactics with journalists in a Redcar hotel before the 2–2 draw at Middlesbrough – it was truncated by a local resident's complaints about loud voices in the night. Perhaps this interruption meant they had only had time to talk about the *first* half, because Billy Liddell put Liverpool two goals up by the break, only for the Boro to reply with second-half goals from Fenton and Dews. 'I was thankful when the final whistle blew,' confessed the home manager David Jack. But it was still only one point for Liverpool in a contest they had all but wrapped up after forty-five minutes.

Stubbins missed the home match against Charlton, allowing Cyril Done a start at centre-forward – and a goal – in a 1–1 draw in front of 51,127 spectators. Sam Bartram allowed Done's header from a Lambert cross to squirm over the goal-line. In the second half, even the switch of Fagan and Liddell to allow the Liverpool star to roam more effectively from his restricting left-wing channel could not pin back a gallant Charlton. The key man for the visitors was their on-field leader Don Welsh, who scored an excellent equalising header after 58 minutes. Welsh would resurface at Anfield five years later as George Kay's replacement in the management seat, but here he was stealing a valuable point rather than the Liverpool manager's job. Cyril Done held his place for the visit to Huddersfield on 9 October, replacing the injured Willie Fagan, who was out for three months with a strained Achilles tendon. Billy Liddell missed out because of international duty, his stand-in being an able reserve, the South African Bob Priday. The ex-Southport man Ray Minshull made his debut by replacing Wales's Sidlow in goal. He was 'absolutely faultless'. But the real star turn was Cyril Done, with a 'brilliant' hat-trick, scored after Town had taken the lead. Balmer took over penalty duties from Albert Stubbins, but he also missed from the spot before scoring in open play. It was Liverpool's fourth goal in a commanding performance. The win was set up by the doughty Bob Paisley, 'the best intermediate on view', according to the *Evening Express*. It was a show of Anfield strength in depth on a potentially difficult day. 'Lucky Liverpool,' argued the *Express*, 'to have such excellent reserves to take the places on international days.' It was either luck or else good management.

STUBBINS FINDS HIS HOME SCORING BOOTS

Albert Stubbins – all £12,500 of him – had still not scored at Anfield, so the winning goal he produced against relegation-bound Brentford on 26 October 1946 was a relief as well as a guarantee of two hard-won points. Billy Liddell sped up the Liverpool left and crossed low to Stubbins, who beat the stubborn Brentford goalkeeper Joe Crozier low down in the left-hand corner after 50 minutes. The Liverpool man was given a 'tumultuous cheer' by the locals. But although the Reds were supported by 'trainloads of fans, including a contingent of schoolboys' next up at Blackburn Rovers, they had to settle for a goal-less draw in East Lancashire. Billy Liddell was at last playing for the club again as a civilian. Liverpool now lay in third place, two points behind early leaders Blackpool. Manager George Kay, a thinker and a boss who cared about the well-being of his players, announced he would be taking his squad to Buxton around the fixture with Derby County on 16 November for some country air and relaxation. This was designed 'to help tone them up for the hectic holiday rush and the FA Cup ties ahead'. It was good management and a sensible strategy in a long season. It would also pay handsome dividends.

The experienced Jack Balmer sometimes lacked the commitment and confidence that a full England cap might have brought, so George Kay and the players made him Liverpool's captain in the home game against Portsmouth to give him a boost. More good management – and it worked. The inside-forward would stay captain. Against Portsmouth, he scored a hat-trick in a 3–0 win and then set off on an astonishing record league run of scoring ten goals in three matches, while scoring in six consecutive league games. At Derby on 16 November, it was all four in a 4–1 win, including 'one of the best goals he is ever likely to get', according to the *Liverpool Echo*, drifting to the right past four defenders and then cutting back his shot into the left-hand corner. Harry Eastham did a 'Matthews trick' in dribbling to make the fourth so adeptly that another Balmer hat-trick in the 4–2 home win over Arsenal on 23 November was no longer a surprise. Balmer scored from a penalty before Arsenal responded to lead 1–2. But Billy Liddell (who else?) dragged Liverpool back into the contest with a 'scintillating run', before flicking off the outside of his right boot to Balmer, who instantly finished in the top corner.

The *Football Echo* compared the wild Anfield celebrations at this equaliser to those at Everton when Dean had scored his stunning 60th goal back in 1928. 'Rarely has an Anfield goal given so much joy. Liddell's part was as great as that of the scorer.' When Balmer got his third goal – and a Football League record three hat-tricks in consecutive matches – it produced 'the biggest cheer Anfield has ever known in its long history'. Stubbins wrapped up the scoring before some post-war professionalism from the home team, of a kind that might well have pleased the wily Elisha Scott from a generation before, annoyed local scribes. 'It was a great pity,' opined the rather pious *Echo*, 'that Liverpool employed time-wasting tactics right at the finish, putting a blemish on the match. Arsenal were trying and playing right to the end.'

Perhaps these were the early signs of a new approach to playing league football, one more directed at winning matches, come what may, rather than just entertaining. Supporters certainly seemed more demanding, quicker to condemn. But Liverpool supporters could say they had both good football and points: twenty-seven goals in ten games, seven wins, no losses and top of the table. The test would come at close challengers Blackpool on 30 November, when 'thousands of followers of Anfield made the trip by car, coach and train. Favours and rattles and whistles added to the atmosphere.' Blackpool led through a stunning volley from McIntosh, but Balmer equalised on 35 minutes, his low, slow shot from the right-corner of the penalty area bobbling gently onto the left-hand post – and in. Jimmy Blair scored again for Blackpool, and the game seemed up when Stan Mortensen flicked in the third from close range on 87 minutes. But Cyril Done scored right from the restart, setting up a frantic finish in which Liddell 'flashed the ball inches wide of the post amidst tremendous excitement'.

It was a 2–3 loss, but Liverpool were still joint top with Wolves on 24 points. The Wanderers just happened to be the next visitors to Anfield.

The Liverpool team against Wolves was the standard one in a very loose version of the W–M formation, with Harley and Fagan both injured. With the exception of the versatile Bill Jones – who would fill in brilliantly later for both Lol Hughes and Barney Ramsden – and the fading Berry Nieuwenhuys, this was, broadly speaking, the team that would win the 1946–47 league championship for Liverpool. It was a highly competent Liverpool side rather than a truly great one, one lit up by Billy Liddell on the left. There was no one of the quality of Alex Raisbeck or Elisha Scott, nor full-backs to match Dunlop, Longworth or McKinlay from earlier Liverpool eras. There was no star wing-half or inside-forward schemer of the Tommy Bromilow type from the early 1920s, either. Neither Balmer nor Done were really classic inside-forwards in the W–M tradition. Phil Taylor certainly had a touch of class at half-back, and Bob Paisley did have something of the Bill Goldie about him from 1901 or even the bite of Jock McNab from 1923 – but without the Scot's occasional indiscipline. This pair complemented each other well.

Liverpool FC, league-title winners, v. Wolves, 7 December 1946

Sidlow

Lambert   Hughes   Ramsden

Taylor   Paisley

Balmer   Done

Eastham   Stubbins   Liddell

Albert Stubbins had much of Sam Raybould's instinct for goal in the early Liverpool title teams, and Jack Balmer was undoubtedly a very clever player, some argue one of Liverpool's best ever despite his obvious lack of bravery. These were quality forwards, no doubt about it, but not quite Liverpool's greatest. Lol Hughes had some of Walter Wadsworth's defensive presence and comfort on the ball. But there was no one on Liverpool's problematic right flank in 1947 to match, say, a Jack Cox from 1901 or a Bill Lacey from 1922. Instead, much of this Liverpool team's creative threat came from down the left, where the dynamic Billy Liddell would often push inside if he was getting isolated on Liverpool's left-wing.

Some of this relative weakness in the 1947 side was about to be highlighted. Liverpool could do little to promote their 1947 league title cause against Wolves at Anfield because, frankly, it was a horror show: a home thrashing by their closest rivals in front of 52,512 people, most of whom had expected something quite different. It was the sort of 1–5 home defeat, in fact, that had manager George Kay tossing and turning in his bed, looking too hard and too long for solutions, damaging his brittle health. The Wallasey-born Dennis Westcott, formerly of New Brighton, a rapid centre-forward who scored goals at every club he played for, got four for Wolves, all of them in the first half. Liverpool crumpled to a side for whom forwards Pye and Hancocks were constant threats to a nervous home defence. Hughes and Sidlow were on different wavelengths for once, as long balls straight up the middle accounted for three goals. Mullen scored a fifth after a slip by the Liverpool centre-half, who had a truly miserable day. A late Jack Balmer penalty was all the deflated Reds could manage in reply.

RESILIENCE NEEDED – NOT YET FOUND

After two crushing defeats, one week later things looked different again in the fog and then driving rain at Sunderland on 14 December, in a 4–1 Reds win. Scorer Nieuwenhuys was back to add some experience and stability on the right, and Bill Jones was in for Ramsden. 'Liverpool back to their best,' was the *Football Echo*'s verdict, with the adaptable Jones 'a complete success' at the back and 'the wing-halves in brilliant form'. At home against Aston Villa on 21 December 1946, fog intervened again, delaying the arrival of the visitors until ten minutes before kick-off. The disorientated Midlanders then faced a heavily sanded pitch and icy, bare patches for a repeat 4–1 home result, with Paisley 'playing brilliantly' and Balmer (2), Stubbins and Nieuwenhuys all on the scoresheet, as they had been in the north-east. Liverpool now trailed Wolves by two points. But it would have seemed to George Kay and the Anfield board that they had survived a rocky spell and were back on track as the Christmas fixtures approached. How wrong could they be? Five defeats in the next six matches – that's how wrong.

The first of these losses came at Stoke City on Christmas Day – what a rotten way to spend the holidays. Tom Bush, a strapping centre-half who had been at Liverpool since 1933, got a rare start for the injured Hughes. Bush was blackly lucky, because he witnessed a masterclass. Stanley Matthews utterly outshone Liddell, his centres providing Steele with two goals, one in each half. Stubbins scored a header with eight minutes to go, but it was only a consolation. The next day, Boxing Day, the same men met at a different venue. But Matthews brought his tricks again, even more of them and more dastardly ones. 'A slimly built, wasp-waisted, wan-looking winger stole the show,' said the *Daily Post*.

'When they walked off, Stanley Matthews' kit was cleaner than any, although he had done twice as much with half as little effort.'

'Go to him!'

'Tackle him!'

'Don't be frightened of him!'

This was the crazy advice reportedly hurled down from the Liverpool terraces, but 'Matthews was the complete footballer in this game', no less than a 'football mesmerist'. To commit yourself against Matthews on this sort of day was to risk ridicule, no matter what the crowd bawled for. Fans who saw it never forgot this exhibition. Matthews in the clear on the deputising Minshull lobbed the goalkeeper exquisitely but onto the crossbar, and Steele missed a gaping net from the rebound. But one great player and dollops of good football cannot alone guarantee success. You also need luck. The prosaic Nieuwenhuys in comparison had already headed Liverpool in front (something as mundane as heading was below Matthews), and with five minutes remaining the otherwise anonymous Stubbins sealed a thoroughly undeserved Liverpool win with a left-foot shot.

Good managers are not fooled by wins such as this one: they prepare for the worst, and it was coming. Four Liverpool league defeats in a row followed, broken only by a 5–2 thumping of Walsall in the third round of the FA Cup and a 2–0 win over Grimsby in round four. For Liverpool's training preparation for the Walsall match, the *Evening Express* reported that the 'shooting box in the old car park was kept busy', while for the visit of the Mariners the presidents of both the Italian and French football federations were present at Anfield. Who were they spying on? The *Daily Post*, meanwhile, reported that the huge post-war crowds (and shamefully poor player wages) had reduced Liverpool's £28,000 overdraft to virtually nil, and another 50,961 hopefuls contributed to the cause when they came to see Sheffield United escape with the points from Anfield. The unfortunate Ray Lambert handled for a penalty and then diverted a Nightingale shot past Minshull, thus sandwiching a Stubbins equaliser. Chelsea, inspired by Tommy Lawton, then defeated Liverpool 1–3 at Stamford Bridge, and when Lol Hughes was injured off at home in a rough encounter with Bolton Wanderers the writing was on the wall for yet another Reds defeat, this time by 0–3. 'If there were a sliding tackle championship,' commented the Wanderers acidly, 'Liverpool would win it.'[6]

The late-January 1947 headlines in the Liverpool press were 'Warmer in the Antarctic' and 'All Britain Shivering in Coldest January Spell for Many Years'. People were skating on all the park lakes in the city. The corridors of Anfield were certainly trembling. So it was a snow-covered Goodison Park that hosted a quiet and sporting derby encounter, woken only by Everton's Wainwright heading past Sidlow in the 58th minute. It was a bleak Liverpool house, indeed.

INTO THE BLEAK MIDWINTER

Liverpool were now down to fourth place in the league, five points behind leaders Wolves. And worse news was that there was also something of a national sentiment building behind Wolves for the title in 1947. The great England half-back Stan Cullis was planning to retire, his prime playing years stolen by the war, and this was his last chance for some silverware after the disappointment of the 1939 FA Cup final Wolves lost to Portsmouth. Liverpool still had to play Wanderers again, of course, but the meeting would be at Molineux.

The roots of the Reds' problems were clear enough. The young defender Hughes had begun to lose his nerve, and Jack Balmer had gone off the boil. Fagan and Cyril Done had been missing through injury, and Liddell had lost some form over the holidays. The half-backs were struggling to compensate. Were Liverpool tired, despite all that rest and early good food? At Leeds United, where the ball dragged in the snow and there were drifts on the wings on a near-unplayable pitch, Willie Fagan was back and created a goal for Stubbins, the one Liverpool man who had kept on scoring during the crisis, even though the local press now saw him as 'more a creator of chances than a taker'. But an equaliser from Grainger 'sent the 25,000 spectators joyful, as if it had been a cup final goal'. No matter: red-headed Albert delivered again on 85 minutes. Liverpool were back on the league rails.

Was there no ridding of this snow? The winter of 1947 was as severe as anyone could remember, and some clubs resorted to using former prisoners of war to help clear snow from their pitches.[7] Liverpool beat Derby County at home 1–0 with a welcome goal from a limping Jack Balmer in frosty conditions in the FA Cup. For the first time, a standing area of Anfield, the paddock, was made all-ticket for this match after a belated safety campaign by the local press. The same tactic might soon be tried for Liverpool's younger fans, it seemed. 'The club asks the lads of the boys pen to keep their orange peel to themselves,' warned the *Evening Express* on 7 February, 'or else other arrangements will be made for boys in future.' Complaints had already been made in the local press about booing and cries of 'Send him off' from these 'young hooligans'.

Only the one-inch cushion of snow on an iron-hard Anfield pitch allowed Liverpool v. Grimsby Town (5–0) to take place in the league on 12 February 1947. No snowballs were reported, but there were plenty of good signs here. Liddell was back on song, creating goals from powerful runs and accurate crosses. Cyril

Done scored a hat-trick as a result, and Willie Fagan continued his comeback from injury with two goals. The pressure on Jackie Balmer to score was thus relieved, and he could begin to relax back into his best form. This was the theory. 'The great mystery at Anfield,' admitted the *Football Echo* on 22 February 1947, 'was how Huddersfield could take the ball up to goal so frequently . . . and still fail to score.' On the usual icy, slippery pitch, Liverpool at last made use of Bob Paisley's unusually powerful throws. Paisley's long delivery persuaded Cyril Done beyond the Town defence in this match, and the big man unselfishly passed to Stubbins, who evaded the slithering visiting defenders to score the only goal. 'This was Huddersfield's most unlucky day,' said the Liverpool press. But don't good teams make their own luck?

Two hard-fought 2–1 Liverpool wins followed in the league – against Blackburn Rovers at home and in desperate blizzard conditions at Portsmouth away – and Liverpool had clawed their way back up to second place in the table with eleven games still to go. But they were still four points behind Wolves, and Blackpool, Stoke City and Manchester United were also challenging. What a title fight!

However, for the Merseyside press it was still the FA Cup that had all the romance. This was the competition that really grabbed the public's attention. Another home FA Cup draw, which brought Birmingham City to Anfield in the sixth round, had begun to get the city buzzing again about Liverpool Football Club's 'missing' FA Cup. Such was the local interest, the Liverpool directors decided to make this meeting the first-ever all-ticket league or FA Cup match on Merseyside, with the ground capacity limited to 51,911. It took a while for Reds supporters to get used to the idea: most ticket applications by telephone came from the crew of ships who would be in port when the match took place. One optimistic letter from a ship asked for '500 tickets for the Kemlyn Road Stand'. Chairman Billy McConnell warned supporters to check on the source of their tickets because counterfeiters were at work in the city, and on the day of the match an *Evening Express* reporter was offered a pound for a five-shilling ticket.

Because of transport problems, not all of the 12,000 ticketed Birmingham fans arrived in Liverpool to join in their chant of 'One, two, three, four, five', but the match will always be remembered for a remarkable goal from hat-trick man Albert Stubbins, a near-horizontal diving header in the 66th minute on bone-hard ground, scored from a fiercely driven Billy Liddell free-kick. Bob Paisley was also knocked unconscious when competing for a header, and he moved briefly to the right wing to replace Willie Fagan to clear his head. The Liverpool players secured their £8 FA Cup win bonus when Balmer added to the Stubbins three, for a comfortable 4–1 victory.

MORE FA CUP MISERY

Prospective league champions Liverpool were drawn against Second Division Burnley in the 1947 FA Cup semi-final. Burnley had conceded just seven goals in twenty-eight matches but this looked a sure-fire route to Liverpool's second final and, surely, its first and long overdue FA Cup win. And it was quite a sporting weekend, because on its first Saturday run 300,000 people watched the 100–1 shot Caughoo win the Grand National at Aintree by 20 lengths. But the FA Cup meeting at Ewood Park would prove a bizarre affair. How would people reach the match? There were no football-special trains allowed by government, and restrictions on transport and fuel were severe. Many Burnley fans resigned themselves to *walking* the 14 miles to Blackburn, while in Liverpool 'bicycles were hastily overhauled by hundreds . . . and the "one-made-for-two" was a common sight in Blackburn'. Some Liverpool supporters were forced to travel to Lancashire a day in advance and spent the night wandering the Lancashire town's streets until first light. 'From dawn onwards,' reported the *Evening Express*, '[these men] made the streets of Blackburn ring with incessant chatter and the inevitable clamour and whistles.' Counterfeiters made detection easy for once – they had misspelled 'competition' on their fake tickets.

These devoted travellers and explorers then faced a largely open, overcrowded stadium so that 'the pouring rain forced spectators to use handkerchiefs and newspapers for head covering'. Many were carried out injured or exhausted. It must have tried the keenest of supporters, this gruelling test of their devotion. The 'reward' for the 52,700 crowd was a suitably damp squib 0–0 draw, with Liverpool's Ray Lambert the 'immaculate defender' on the pitch and Burnley's negative game plan working, with tough defenders Woodruff and Atwell assigned to try to quell the spirits of Billy Liddell. Comedian Robb Wilton led Liverpool's post-match reception, but there was really nothing to smile about. The Reds were now edgy and facing a trip to Maine Road on 12 April to resolve this troublesome matter.

Before that there was league business to attend to. Liverpool squared up to three matches in four days over Easter, and Paisley (ankle), Jones (groin), Liddell (thigh), Stubbins (leg bruising) and Harley (thigh) were all doubtful for the visit to Preston. Lacking at centre-half, George Kay might possibly have turned to the Dutch giant Jan van Albert, who had turned up in Liverpool to much hoo-ha in order to appear in a 'freaks' review at the Shakespeare Theatre. But, fortunately, Laurie Hughes was back from injury and the Scot Tom McLeod, an army man, made his debut at centre-forward in a much changed Liverpool team that dogged it out for what would prove to be a crucial 0–0 draw. The next day, against Blackpool at Anfield, George Kay made *nine* changes – Rafa Benítez did not invent rotation. But despite leading 2–0, Liverpool eventually went down to the odd goal in five and were now fully five points behind Blackpool and four adrift of Wolves with only eight league games left. The Reds were now a 100–1 shot for the title, according to the *Daily Post*. It looked like the end of the league challenge and that everything would have to hang on the FA Cup. But against Preston at home on 8 April Liverpool dug into their reserves and won 3–0. Bill Shankly missed a penalty for Preston after Liverpool captain Jackie Balmer tipped off Minshull that the kick would go to the goalkeeper's left – it did.

A few players had made a case for inclusion in the Liverpool FA Cup replay team – Eddie Spicer and Laurie Hughes among them – but the Liverpool directors stuck with the XI who had played at Ewood Park, with Fagan on the right wing, Harley at right-back and Jones at centre-half. Hopes were high on Merseyside. So much so that three twelve-year-old members of a juvenile gang ended up in a Liverpool court on 10 April after stealing food from Islington shops and running away from home. In the letter they left for their parents, they said they were headed for London 'so they will be there for the cup final'. Alas, Liverpool Football Club would not be. With so little time to complete any replay, the Burnley directors agreed to play an extra *hour* if it were needed to split the clubs, but the Liverpool board refused. Were they confident, or afraid?

Burnley set out to defend and frustrate Liverpool from the outset, and it proved a successful ploy. The crucial goal came on 80 minutes, the usually reliable Sidlow missing a punch from a corner and Harrison driving home the loose ball for Burnley. This felt like the final FA Cup blow, especially for the now terminally ill childhood Reds fan, Liverpool club chairman Billy McConnell. The day also got a little worse for 42-year-old James Haughey of Epsom Street, Liverpool, who was later arrested for being drunk and disorderly in the city, saying, 'I had a few drinks when Liverpool lost.' He was fined by a possibly Everton-leaning magistrate. Little Burnley had foiled Liverpool in the latter stages of the FA Cup for the second time.

RUNNING ON EMPTY

On the day they should have been playing in the FA Cup final, 26 April 1947, Liverpool Football Club were instead grinding out a 2–1 league win at Aston Villa, with goals from Willie Fagan and the 25-year-old ex-Prescot Cables right-winger Bill Watkinson, who would replace the injured Cyril Done in the last six league matches of the season. Results had favoured Liverpool in the league, so that when Albert Stubbins scored the single goal from a Liddell cross to beat the blue-shirted Manchester United at Anfield on 3 May local press headlines predictably declared 'Stubbins' Goal Worth 4 Points'. For the *Football Echo*, 'there was more than a shade of spike and spirit' about this contest. The league table now read:

TEAM	PLAYED	POINTS
Wolves	37	53
Manchester United	39	51
Stoke City	37	50
Liverpool	38	50

A Stubbins hat-trick in a 3–1 win followed at FA Cup-winners Charlton Athletic, keeping Liverpool in the hunt. Painfully, two of the girl Dagenham Pipers had paraded the FA Cup before the start at the Valley so that the Liverpool players and supporters could get a look. While title rivals Stoke City chose this strange moment to agree to the transfer of Stanley Matthews to Blackpool, the Liverpool board tried to make their intentions clear by agreeing a record fee of £15,000 for Morton's Scotland international forward Billy Steel. Predictably, negotiations broke down with the player before a scraped 1–1 Reds draw at lowly Brentford. 'Paisley's tackling was deadly,' according to the *Football Echo*, '[but] Liverpool did not show the necessary devil.'

Liverpool were now left with two tricky away fixtures to complete their season, at depleted Arsenal and Wolves. Bob Paisley would miss both with a knee-ligament strain. The Reds were level with Stoke City on fifty-three points and were just one point behind Wolves and Manchester United. Any one of these four clubs could still win the title. Liverpool's brave 2–1 win at Arsenal ensured the trip to Molineux would at least be meaningful. Liverpool were now two points ahead of Stoke, and one ahead of Wolves and United. George Kay – who, incredibly, missed some closing Reds matches to scout players – had moved Bill Jones forward to replace Fagan in the last ten minutes at Highbury, and two Liverpool goals had resulted. It was a masterstroke. But with Stoke City having two games left and a superior goal difference to Liverpool – and not due to complete fixtures until 14 June – even a Liverpool win at Wolves on 31 May would not yet decide matters.

On 2 June, in the week of the Epsom Derby, the *Daily Post* commented, not unreasonably, that 'football in June seems out of place'. The *Liverpool Echo* reported, 'The Reds produced speed, stamina and classic football to sweep Wolves off their pedestal at Molineux.' In the blistering summer sun – 91 degrees in the shade, with the officials refereeing in white tops, no blazers and soft shoes

– Wolves 'had four scoring chances to Liverpool's one'. But it was a 'picture goal' by Jackie Balmer and a brilliant dash half the length of the field by Albert Stubbins for the second that won the day in a famous 2–1 Liverpool win. A tearful Stan Cullis was inconsolable later, but there could be no Liverpool celebrations yet. A win by Stoke City at Bramall Lane in two weeks' time would still scupper everything. After all their hard work – seven wins and one draw in the last eight league matches, five of them away from home – Liverpool Football Club would win the 1947 Football League title only by waiting.

There were no Anfield officials in Sheffield on 14 June 1947 to ensure fair play. After all, Liverpool were playing a delayed Liverpool Senior Cup final against Everton at Anfield on the same summer evening. One Reds player had to be smuggled into Anfield that evening to avoid the police, who had questions to ask about alleged tax evasion.[8] In Sheffield, it was a story highly typical of English football and the resolute British football professional. Sheffield United had nothing to play for, except pride and a £2 bonus, and yet they battled like demons in a deluge that threatened to swamp the pitch. Stoke City, searching for their first league title, simply could not cope on the shifting, unstable surface. Their hopes, according to the Stoke *Evening Sentinel* on 16 June, 'crashed on the rock-like defence of Sheffield United'.

The news of Stoke's eventual 1–2 defeat, delivered over the PA by director George Richards, was greeted with scenes of extraordinary joy back at Anfield, where supporters watching the Reds pound Everton invaded the pitch in wild celebration. Later, Sir Francis Joseph, president of Stoke City, said that it might be strange to some people abroad that a country in crisis, so short of coal and short of production, should focus so intently nevertheless on a mere football match. But this devotion to sport was essential to the 'British character'. Had not Drake completed his game of bowls with the sails of the Armada in sight before setting off to rout the Spanish?

To commemorate this dramatic title win, the Easton Press published a pamphlet entitled *The Sport's Spectator's Story of Liverpool Football Club* for 1s 6d. As a tilt at the club's history so far and a summary of the current players' strengths, this publication had its moments – and its faults. It noted that others depicted this 1947 Liverpool as the 'Crazy Gang' – an inconsistent mix of the very good and the very bad. Albert Stubbins was described as being 'very tall, very gentle', Bob Paisley as having a 'riotous tackle' and Willie Fagan as having 'a nonchalance that makes his work stand out'. Bill Jones, it argued, 'could be the best back in the world'.

It had certainly been an extraordinary season, the final poignant act of which was for the ailing Billy McConnell to leave the Radium Institute, where he had been a patient for five weeks, to collect the championship trophy from the offices of the Football League and transport it respectfully to Anfield in an open-topped taxi. It was a life-long dream of his to hold the Football League trophy for his club. Later, Liverpool FC cancelled a proposed 400-person championship celebration dinner scheduled for 8 August, because on 7 August 1947 the former butcher's boy and Liverpool supporter, and a director since 1929, died at the age of 59. It was a cruel moment for his family and the club, but there was a smile in Billy McConnell's heart.

Several thousand people attended McConnell's funeral at the Anfield cemetery, where he would join Tom Watson and many other Liverpool greats in rest. He had done his duty for his club and for his people – the Liverpool supporters. When fellow Reds director and ex-chairman Walter Cartwright died in October 1947, after 27 years' service, the much reduced Liverpool match programme was printed in black, not the now familiar red, as a mark of respect. Now a new generation would have to pick up the Anfield reins to face the challenges which surely lay ahead.

CHAPTER 11 REFERENCES

1. Fishwick, *English Football and Society*, p. 122
2. Taylor and Ward, *Three Sides of the Mersey*, p. 66
3. Murden, 'City of Change and Challenge', p. 396
4. Taw, *Football's War and Peace*, p. 72
5. Taw, *Football's War and Peace*, p. 93
6. Taw, *Football's War and Peace*, p. 171
7. Inglis, *The Football League and the Men Who Made It*, p. 178
8. Taw, *Football's War and Peace*, p. 221

12

THE ALMOST SEASONS
The Double Frustration of 1950

POST-TITLE BLUES

You have to be a very special football team indeed to follow on a league title win and then show exactly the same levels of commitment, endurance and skill necessary to do it all again just a couple of months later, when all your key rivals – and others besides – begin again from exactly the same place you do. The psychological strength required alone is enormous. So it was tough for Liverpool to maintain the same emotional levels, especially after the amazingly draining and late end to season 1946–47 and also the early death of their popular and influential club chairman. It must have been harder still when only 11 players in a tight group of 16 who had made a major contribution to winning the league title received a championship medal. This strict policy on medals was an example of Football League parsimony to the nth degree. Incredibly, Spicer, Done, Nieuwenhuys, Ramsden and Eastham all missed out. Barney Ramsden, especially, had played 23 times in the league in the title season, but the full-back had also upset the Liverpool board by saying he wanted to leave for the USA and get married there. The Liverpool directors simply turned down his request, but he left in May 1947 anyway. He was out of the team (and the medals). The Reds started the new season slowly, and came with a rush at the end of it, but 11th position was no satisfying follow-up for a club that had been so close to winning the league and cup Double in 1947.

What is it they say in football and life about standing still meaning that you are actually moving backwards? George Kay had certainly moved things on in the title year by pursuing his keen interest in player diet and by holding 'tactics talks' with his players before matches. There was little of this going on before the war. Kay was, according to the late Bill McConnell, 'the greatest manager in football' and player Cyril Done later described him as 'the Shankly of his day', though Kay actually had little of the Scot's confidence and charisma. Was the English game slowly waking up to innovations elsewhere at last? England finally had a national team coach in Walter Winterbottom, but, discussing tactics, 'Pilot' in the *Evening Express* admitted that some people in English football still 'try to dismiss these talks as so much rubbish'.

So maybe Liverpool under the kindly but usually unsmiling George Kay had a measurable advantage here. In December 1949, Kay attributed the post-war Liverpool success to the 'willing cooperation of all players in pre-match practical workouts and theoretical discussion and to their excellent coordination of tactics on the field of play'. Others had different views, pointing to the strength and knowledge of the experienced Liverpool backroom staff of Albert Shelley, Ephraim Longworth and Jimmy Seddon – the last named had played for the Bolton team that had beaten Kay's West Ham in the 1923 FA Cup final. Kay stayed in his office, chain-smoking, during much of the week, surfacing only at weekends, so he left much of the daily work at Anfield to his trusted coaches and trainers.

All this talk about tactics and theory was still rather foreign to English football. In fact, the Liverpool trainer Albert Shelley thought that football in the 1920s was as good and as fast as English football in the 1940s, and that training and coaching methods in the two periods were not hugely different. He had support from Eph Longworth, still on the Liverpool ground staff and 'for his years the fittest man I have ever seen', according to Albert Stubbins. The latter wrote later in the *Football Echo* about the real differences between Liverpool and elsewhere in the 1940s. 'Although coaching is much more in evidence than it was in 1939, I have met several first-class players who think that if a man is a natural player he doesn't need coaching.' Players at Liverpool were probably getting more coaching and certainly more tactics now than at most other English clubs, though that was still saying very little compared to some developments in football abroad.[1] George Kay probably had a little more autonomy in team affairs than most other football managers of his day, but he still had to submit his team suggestions for discussion and revision by the Liverpool board at its weekly meeting. He was not his own man.

A NEW POST-WAR LIVERPOOL?

Another north-west football club, Blackpool FC, with the saintly Stanley Matthews now in their ranks, was not about to stand still either. In the summer of 1947, the Tangerines promised to build a 'Wembley of the North', a stadium capable of holding a startling 150,000 people, because 'Lancashire is the home of football'. Of course, no northern ground could ever really rival the allure of Wembley. And what other events might be held there to make it pay its way? The so-called northern Wembley remained a dream.

Nor was the city of Liverpool easily accepting that its best years were now in the past. Firebrand local Labour MP Bessie Braddock, for example, kept the city in the national news headlines by irreverently 'dancing a jig' on the floor of the House of Commons during an evening debate and ending up exhausted in Winston Churchill's chair. A town-planning exhibition in Radiant House, Liverpool, in the summer of 1947 promised that the post-war 'new' Liverpool would share some of Mrs Braddock's brio by becoming more like a pre-war Paris or Berlin in its activities, architecture and design. Sure, the Blitz had destroyed 6,500 houses, 1,500 commercial buildings and 400 factories/works in the city, but this destruction offered a 'great opportunity' for social and design experimentation and innovation. Lewis's department store, it was announced, was to be restored on Ranelagh Street at a cost of £1.2 million, and Blackler's store was also to be rebuilt and modernised. Here was a start for the new Liverpool. The war was not a gloomy trough in the city's fortunes, as some people seemed to believe. But the city of Liverpool's economic future, and also its core thinking about approaches to popular culture and working-class leisure, would really have to change – and change fast – to make this sort of ambitious vision work, even in part.

A public vote among local electors in Liverpool in 1947 had finally swayed the reluctant Liverpool City Council on the vexatious issue, locally, of allowing Sunday cinema. But in August – and even after the Archbishop of York had said publicly in July that he saw 'no harm in playing amateur football on a Sunday' – Thomas Parry, a mill worker from Timpson Street in Liverpool, was actually fined by magistrates for playing a pick-up game of football on a Sunday on the Lower Breck Road recreation ground. The Liverpool religious protagonists were still at large in the city, it seemed, and mainly in charge. Youth workers in Liverpool and Birkenhead were also concerned about the capacity of the local authorities to deliver in the new era on 'boom' sports such as football. Where would the budding Liddells and Balmers *play* their early football in the city? They claimed that 'more than a thousand' Liverpool boys would be denied the opportunity to play organised football in the late 1940s because of a post-war shortage of pitches and facilities in the area.

There were other key post-war shortages afoot and also some notable changes of habit in the city. Huyton MP Harold Wilson, the president of the Board of Trade, for example, controversially said that there were still barefoot children in Liverpool streets in 1950, while the County Licensing sessions noted that since the war 'it is now usual for men to take their wives out for a drink'. A census of licensed premises in Liverpool found that one local pub had one thousand customers crammed inside because of a shortfall in the number of suitable venues in the city. Barefoot children crushed by poverty and wandering around outside overcrowded Merseyside pubs? It could have been Victorian Liverpool all over again.

While the Everton team manager Theo Kelly said that he wanted his club's supporters to look to the past and revive the traditional Everton nickname 'The Toffees', Liverpool Football Club's new chairman Ronnie Williams also wanted change, but of a very different kind. Liverpool had had real problems allocating tickets throughout the FA Cup run of the previous season. Demand always outstripped supply, and safety problems at Anfield pointed in the direction of more all-ticket affairs in future. Some Liverpool directors probably secretly dreaded reaching a major final because of the potential problems of coping with local ticket demand – shades of Athens 2007. Williams called on the league management committee to lobby the FA for a rise in the number of tickets allocated to the FA Cup finalists. Here was a popular move for all football supporters but not for football administrators – there was no seconder for the Liverpool motion. Williams and Liverpool were met, instead, by bland assurances that the league would 'review' the situation, but nothing much changed.

The players' maximum wage was finally raised to £12 in the winter (£10 in summer), though there were still no simple answers (nor questions asked) about exactly *where* all the money in the sport was going. It was not being spent on players' wages or on stadiums, that was for sure. Billy Liddell still worked in his accountancy firm, including on Saturday mornings before home matches before catching the number 26 tram with Liverpool supporters up to Anfield. He also supplemented his football pay by doing some reporting for the BBC's new *Sports Report* programme. Liddell had a key to the local BBC office in the city and was instructed to catch a tram and let himself in on a Saturday evening to deliver his material 'in the event of anything newsworthy occurring at Liverpool's matches at Anfield'. It seemed a pretty wide brief.[2]

As football crowds continued to grow, so did the number of clubs now trying to get into the Football League. Twenty-seven applied for four possible places in 1947, including South Liverpool and the interestingly named Annfield Plain (from Wearside). But because this was the first season after the war, the league decided to keep all existing clubs on board, without even taking a vote. So there would be only one Anfield, and only one Liverpool, in the Football League after all.

LIVERPOOL FC ON THE SLIDE

Berry Nieuwenhuys was now finished at Anfield, effectively signalling the end of that era of the Liverpool South Africans, but everyone else stayed, with Bill Watkinson holding his place on the right and the post-war 'Holy Trinity' of Balmer, Stubbins and Liddell all starting the early league matches in 1947–48. But Liverpool struggled to score goals and won only three of their first twelve league matches – though one of these was a 3–0 canter at Goodison Park in September. By Christmas, this inconsistency had already ruled out a title challenge. By the end of January 1948, relegation looked more likely: the Reds went five matches without a goal and took just one point from seven games. When they lost 0–3 to Burnley in a violent rainstorm on 17 January 1948, even the lack of a change strip was blamed for their capitulation. Burnley had exchanged their sopping wet outfits for dry and warm shirts at half-time. Jackie Balmer reported that the Liverpool players 'could not move' because of the sheer wet, cold clamour of their sodden cotton shirts. They had no change strip. Anfield attention turned, urgently, to acquiring more clothing coupons – and ideally, of course, the FA Cup.

After comfortably defeating Nottingham Forest at Anfield, Liverpool were drawn away in the cup against Manchester United in the fourth round. But United still had no use of the bombed-out Old Trafford after a long period of homelessness. The tie was switched to Goodison Park, where forged tickets and boys and men climbing the stadium walls kept the local police honest. Tens of thousands were locked outside. A Merseyside record crowd of 74,721 (many more sneaked in) saw Liverpool slide irresistibly to a 0–3 deficit at half-time and out of the FA Cup. So, when Everton played at home in the FA Cup (v. Wolves) on 31 January 1948, Liverpool played at Anfield in the league (v. Portsmouth) in an unusual case of a Merseyside football-fixture clash. This double booking was generally to be avoided, not only because of logistical problems for the police, but also because of the grounded suspicion in the city that a large number of people still attended *both* clubs' home matches. The evidence on this occasion seemed quite strong, if not entirely conclusive. Everton drew a gate of 72,579, while Liverpool could attract only 23,097 to another 0–3 disaster. Liverpool were certainly on a poor league run, and in dire form, but their previous home-match attendance (without a similar Everton distraction) had been a very respectable 48,665. The question raised here was: could as many as 20,000 people in the city be regular watchers of *both* Everton and Liverpool?

With a choice of local matches, it certainly looked as if quite a large number of football supporters in the city might well have been not so highly committed to a specific club at all. They might have opted, instead, for the better-quality contest on the day. But an Everton shareholders' meeting in November 1949 suggested something rather different: a voice from the floor argued that Reds followers were routinely coming across to Goodison Park when Liverpool were away to jeer the struggling home favourites in blue. No one had made the same suggestion about Everton fans coming to Liverpool for the same purpose. Liverpool letter writers to the *Liverpool Echo* insisted that this was an aberrant handful and that most Liverpool supporters 'were sorry to see Everton in their present plight'. But there might well have been plenty of 'overlap' at this time between membership of the Liverpool and Everton crowds. At least at Anfield any new supporters would now have some decent information and entertainment to rely upon: the Automatic Telephone Company agreed to install loudspeaker equipment at Anfield for £300 for season 1948–49. With their club sliding down the Football League table, the Liverpool directors reportedly offered Newcastle United £18,000 for the clown prince himself, Len Shackleton, but the forward rejected the move to stay in the north-east, eventually joining Sunderland for £19,000.

Instead, Bevin Boy Kevin Baron (Bevin Boys were wartime mining conscripts) occasionally figured for Liverpool at inside-forward, but it took until 6 March 1948 for his club's first league win of the year to come, with the Reds hovering uneasily in nineteenth place in the First Division table. The victims were Huddersfield Town, downed by four Albert Stubbins goals and an impressive debut by left-winger Ken Brierley, a £7,000 purchase from Oldham, with Billy Liddell shunted over to the right-wing to make way. Stubbins had received a threatening letter before the meeting with Town warning him his leg would be broken if he went near the visitors' goal. Typically, it merely made him more determined than ever to score – but where would he get *four* legs to break? It would get better still for Brierley, grabbing a goal in a 4–0 drubbing of Everton at Anfield in the 80th league derby in April, as Liverpool finally raised their game to finish with eight wins in the last eleven league games and just one loss, to Aston Villa.

ALBERT DOCKS

In August 1948, an outbreak of interracial rioting near the Rialto Cinema and on Upper Parliament Street in the south end of the city stunned Liverpool, as it had done in the past and as it would do again in much more spectacular fashion some 33 years later. Sixty people ended up in court on this occasion, most of them 'coloureds', as the local press insisted on calling black Liverpudlians. The tensions here, on the surface at least, seemed to be about local 'turf wars' between young white and black men. But the defence also challenged the role of the Liverpool constabulary in these incidents, claiming that 'the defendants were badly knocked around by the police'.

Racism and systematic exclusion and absence underlined these outbursts from Liverpool's long-standing (and long-suffering) black population: in education, employment, law and order, leisure, and sport. Why should football be any different? Black Liverpool faces were almost entirely absent in roles inside the two major football clubs (and everywhere else in England). Despite the recent (white) South African connection, neither Liverpool nor Everton had yet signed a black player or had a black member of staff. There were few signs either that black spectators had yet made a visible place for themselves inside the supporter cultures of either Liverpool Football Club or Everton. Would they have been welcomed if they had?

As this court case continued in the Liverpool press, it was a different type of absence that caught the eye of the local sporting public. Liverpool's star signing Albert Stubbins had failed to report back to training and had not re-signed for Liverpool, as every footballer had to do annually. This was almost unheard of. It transpired that Stubbins was tending to his business affairs in Newcastle, and he claimed that the late Liverpool chairman Billy McConnell had agreed that the centre-forward could live and train in the north-east in order to manage his businesses while still playing on Merseyside. The new board said no, so Stubbins then asked for a transfer. Again the board said no and offered to help the forward find a sweets and tobacconist business on Merseyside. Liverpool held Stubbins's registration, so he could not play for another club, but nor was he playing for Liverpool. He was replaced by the underrated Liverpool-born Les Shannon, who later had a successful career as a wing-half at Burnley.

This was a state of impasse that lasted until mid-October 1948, when the Liverpool directors agreed to purchase the house Stubbins had bought in the north-east and that their record signing could now live in Newcastle and that he should train at Gateshead FC. When Stubbins played in a warm-up in the Central League, a reported 20,000 turned up to welcome back the prodigal son. His first-team reappearance at Anfield on 23 October, 13 games in, seemingly added about 15,000 supporters to the gate to see the Reds crush Middlesbrough 4–0. Although Liverpool Football Club had a policy that its players should live in or near the city, most Reds supporters and much of the press on Merseyside seemed to side with Stubbins in the dispute, though Liverpool supporters might also have been sore at the Reds board about a rise in stand ticket prices at Anfield, from 2s 9d to 3s and 3s 6d.

Albert never recovered his earlier Liverpool form, almost certainly because he spent so little preparation time with his teammates. By 1951, Liverpool were trying to offload him to Middlesbrough, but Stubbins refused to leave, and the remainder of his career was frittered away. Stubbins was intelligent, respectful and well liked locally, and he had a thoughtful regular column in the *Football Echo*. He was no typical troublemaker or disruptive, pointing out that all his conversations with the club on this matter 'have been conducted without the slightest acrimony'. He was also well aware of the special bond that existed between the players and supporters at Anfield. 'Liverpool players are important in one respect,' he told *Echo* readers on 13 November 1948. 'We don't receive poison-pen letters which occasionally drop in on clubs in other parts of the country. They are a cowardly form of attack on players who usually don't mind honest criticism.' The affair was a painful lesson for the Liverpool board.

It was easy to see why the club had eventually been forced to accede to Stubbins. Without their forward pivot, Liverpool's goals had almost completely dried up: just four in a nine-match spell before the great man's return. But even with Stubbins back in harness, and with Jimmy Payne, a crowd-pleasing Bootle-born right-winger, emerging to offer guile and threat on the touchline as the putative 'Merseyside Matthews', Liverpool could find no consistency or real goalscoring potency. Indeed, many Liverpool supporters thought that the gentlemanly Stubbins never regained his original spark for the club because of this interlude and that he was kept on by the Liverpool board way beyond his peak or original commitment to the club as Liverpool began to slide towards relegation trouble.

Captain Jack Balmer ended up as top scorer with just 14 goals from 42 league matches, with Cyril Done weighing in with 11. 'Stork' in the *Liverpool Echo* identified another problem – Liverpool, he suggested, was becoming a long-ball team. 'More construction is needed in the half-back line – the lifeblood of a successful football team. Pumping the ball up the middle and chasing it will not do.' To be fair, Stubbins was plagued by injury after his late start to the season – perhaps this was due to his lack of pre-season preparation and the quality of his training at Gateshead? It was difficult to imagine that either George Kay or Albert Shelley were happy with the situation as Liverpool's season petered out to a midtable finish and elimination from the FA Cup by Wolves.

THE MODERN WAY

In the summer of 1949, full-back Tom Liddell – brother of Billy – joined Liverpool from Lochore Welfare in Scotland. Sadly, the brothers were never to play together for the club. Tom would certainly struggle to better Ray Lambert, 'a sure kicker of any sort of ball' and Liverpool's youngest-ever schoolboy signing at 13 and a half – at least before modern football academies began to trawl around for kids young enough to watch TV cartoon shows. But in 1949, Liverpool were beginning to refine their approach to recruiting young local players. 'Prior to the war,' opined the *Liverpool Echo*, 'much lip-service was paid to the nursery system.' Now things were getting much more serious, as transfer fees were rapidly rising (Everton had recently offered a staggering £25,000 for England man Wilf Mannion).

In August, the Liverpool club held public trials at the Anfield nursery ground in Prescot. But in contrast to the 'open house' approach of before the war, when literally anyone could turn up and have a trial, triallists were now confined to 'youths who have been vetted by the club's official scouts or recommended by friends of the club who have seen them in action'. This was a more rational selection process, one designed better to sift the wheat from the chaff and to establish a constant process of assessment of young players in local leagues and in the seven hundred and fifty amateur football clubs that the Liverpool County FA said existed within twenty miles of Liverpool town hall.

Other clubs were also starting to be more 'scientific' in their general approach, for example in their assessment of the opposition. 'Ranger' from the *Football Echo* noted that Bolton officials came to Anfield in 1949 to watch Liverpool play before the clubs met in a league fixture. 'Once upon a time,' he confirmed, 'this sort of preliminary investigation used to be reserved solely for cup-tie opponents.' No more. Some football clubs were now beginning to take opponents into account in planning their playing strategy. Liverpool were also beginning to play around a little with player numbering and positioning, many years before it became de rigueur. Much of this caper centred around the role of Billy Liddell, who was regularly switching now between centre-forward, right-wing and left-wing to offer the team some spark. But generally he wore the number 11 shirt wherever he played. Cyril Done recalled later how much confusion this sowed in opposition ranks when England captain Billy Wright of Wolves tried to work out before an FA Cup tie exactly why Done (9) was playing on the left-wing while Liddell (11) lined up in the middle. Who was Wright to mark?[3]

Other, perhaps less welcome, signs of the more 'modern' vision of the post-war game now came in the shape of some early product marketing around the Merseyside clubs. Unofficial Everton and Liverpool ties in club colours could now be purchased locally (price 7s 6d). More interesting was the brief appearance of the *Echo Magazine* and in it the connections already being drawn between football and sex. Here, as early as 20 August 1949, actress Virginia Mayo, 'owner of Hollywood's loveliest legs', was pictured in a bikini alongside a hastily sketched-in football and set of goalposts. The actress was 'fit and raring to go when the kick-off sounds' trilled the *Echo* commentary, heralding decades of similarly cheesy money shots to welcome every new league season in the tabloids in England. It was the type of local feature that was actually the precursor to *The Sun*'s later page-three dolly 'fan' of the 1970s and beyond.

Another noticeable post-war media development was the increasing local press intrusion into the family lives of star footballers. In September 1949, for example, the *Echo* began, briefly, to carry a regular feature on star local football players at home with their wives and children. This was an entirely new departure, and its main focus was on the 'ordinariness' and the wholesome nature of footballer family life. Cyril Sidlow was one of the first to figure from Liverpool, snapped with his children Rita and David as he was undertaking some woodwork as a hobby at home. Bob Paisley later featured, seen around the piano and also studying his books for his physiotherapy qualification. Billy Liddell's wife and new-born twin boys were covered later in the press at the christening of the new arrivals. These were hardly provocative or overly glamorous player profiles, but they were the very early signs of the British media's – and the British public's – increasing fascination with the lives of top footballers away from the playing field, an interest that would eventually coalesce – much later, of course – into a focus on football players as fully fledged local and national celebrities.

THE INTERNATIONAL ORDER – AND LIVERPOOL'S 'KICK AND RUSH' MERCHANTS

As the new football campaign got underway in England, Liverpool's Albert Stubbins was soon bemoaning not only the dearth of young British football talent, but 'the shortage of good old-fashioned steaks' as the sort of fuel needed to build up the stamina of young players. George Kay liked to take the Liverpool players to Birkdale, north of the city, before home matches for sea air, rest and good food. The Liverpool sporting press was also looking ahead to the World Cup finals in 1950, where England would be competing for the first time. This growing 'internationalisation' of the game had already been reflected in the city in 1948 in an audacious (and unsuccessful) bid by Italy's Roma to sign the brilliant Everton centre-half Tommy 'T.G.' Jones and in 1949 by the visit to Liverpool of a team of barefooted Nigerians to play at South Liverpool under floodlights. In 1950, there was the arrival of the 'tip-tapping style' of AIK from Sweden in a guest match at Anfield. Liverpool FC were also invited by the Colombian government and that country's top clubs to tour the South American country in the summer of 1950, but the trip was eventually called off after FIFA objected that the major clubs in Colombia had broken away from the national federation and were thus operating as a rebel league.

Although Liverpool had experienced lights on their North American tours, floodlights were still not permitted in the Football League and few people in Liverpool – or Britain – seemed to see them as part of the future of the sport. Certainly, Liverpool were way behind a number of other English professional clubs in seeing the potential of floodlit play, first trying out lights in a friendly at Watford in November 1954 and even refusing to play Accrington Stanley competitively under lights in the event of an FA Cup replay as late as January 1956. The visiting Nigerians, it was argued archly by the *Liverpool Echo*, would obviously be advantaged by playing under lights because 'their natural vision tends to be sharper than ours in the shades of night'. A gathering of 13,007 at Holly Park saw a 2–2 contest that brought 'almost unceasing gasps of amazement from the crowd at the Nigerians' speed or powerful barefoot shooting'. Their frightening pace, reported the *Echo*, 'by comparison would make some of our senior players resemble rheumaticky old cab-horses'.

The Swedes from AIK visiting Anfield were notable for something rather different: compared to English teams they made hardly any 'full-blooded clearances'. Players and coaches from around Britain came to watch this fixture. Few people in Liverpool would have seen top Continental footballers close up like this, of course, and the Swedes showed a very modern face of football, the importance of which would only really register with Bob Paisley and his staff at Anfield more than 25 years later: they *kept* the ball rather than simply hoof it out of defence. 'They made practically every pass with the inside of the foot,' commented the startled *Echo*, 'and they were remarkably accurate in all they did. When the full-backs or wing-halves found the way blocked to making good use of the ball in a forward direction, they were not above turning around and started a passing move towards their *own* goals.' These were strange tactics indeed to British eyes in the 1940s.

These were international football visits to the city in the late 1940s that highlighted real differences elsewhere, but did they point to obvious British failings? The Swedes thought that the forthcoming World Cup finals were more important than club football, while Everton manager Cliff Britton was sure that many English players 'do not train half as hard, or as seriously, as Continental sides'. But passing *backwards*? And likening British players to knackered old cab-horses? This kind of criticism must have seemed a little harsh in the autumn of 1949, because with Eddie Spicer in at left-back and Willie Fagan returned, and with Payne and Baron now fixtures on the Liverpool right, the Reds made a solid start to the new season – six draws and two wins in the first eight matches – which then blossomed into a fantastic nineteen-match unbeaten run, a modern league record at that time for the twenty-two-club First Division, beaten only by Leeds United in 1973–74. At Arsenal in September 1949 in a 2–1 win, Liddell and Stubbins simply tore the Gunners apart. 'Liverpool were so much on top,' said the almost disbelieving *Liverpool Echo*, 'that they indulged in all manner of artistries.' When woeful Everton, by contrast, lost 0–7 at Portsmouth at around the same time in front of the bemused comedian Arthur Askey, the Liverpool funnyman remarked, 'If you see a body thrown on the pitch, it's mine.'

With Everton's current travails and Liverpool's wonderful form, October 1949 must have seemed to the *Football Echo* like the ideal time to start a letters page for supporters' comments 'in response to numerous requests'. It soon disappeared again, but the early months of the postbag were sure to have been dominated by gripes from Goodison Park – Everton still seemed like the senior Merseyside club in terms of its coverage in the local press. But it was an open enough forum to capture complaints from a 13-year-old Bootle schoolboy that the boys' pen at Anfield was already a jungle in which 'the older boys bully the younger ones and push their way to the front'. There were also claims from Liverpool fans that the club's traditional style of play had been misrepresented and maligned by their opponents. The *Echo* agreed, arguing on 12 November 1949 that to label this current successful Liverpool side as 'kick and rush merchants' was a harsh judgement. 'Liverpool's speedy and direct methods of play demand just as much science, accuracy and skill as the close-passing moves of sides who prefer the more old-fashioned type of game.' Liverpool, the *Echo* argued, was actually playing a faster, more modern style of football compared to the failing, more laborious methods from across Stanley Park. It was a new angle on a very old and crude Merseyside debate about supposed Anfield graft and perspiration versus Goodison Park craft and inspiration.

After Liverpool had thumped Manchester City 4–0 on 5 November 1949, with Liddell, Brierley and Baron all scoring, *Echo* letter writer 'Red Well-Wisher' highlighted what many people in the city already clearly saw as the unremittingly positive media focus on regional rivals Manchester United. This was almost a decade before the Munich disaster would make United a focus for national sentimental attachment and some 30 years before relations between United and Liverpool fans deteriorated dramatically, for largely the same reasons. 'If there is a better team playing at the moment I have not seen it,' Well-Wisher wrote of Liverpool's current form, 'and I have seen the darlings of the press, Manchester United, who can do no wrong apparently.' Media darlings or not, by the end of November 1949 Liverpool were three points clear of Busby's United.

Even after losing 2–3 at Huddersfield on 10 December, thus finally ending the record unbeaten league run, the Reds were still clear at the top. Not that this was much to get the Liverpool press too excited, not with the FA Cup coming around again and with Liverpool Football Club still searching for its first FA Cup triumph.

THAT FATEFUL FA CUP, AGAIN . . .

In the FA Cup third round, Liverpool drew 0–0 at old rivals Blackburn Rovers on a 'sheet of mud' at Ewood Park before defeating Rovers 2–1 at Anfield in a Wednesday-afternoon replay in front of 52,221 supporters. No wonder government and local businesses were so ambivalent about football – were *all* these supporters really granted time off work to watch this fixture? Five thousand people had applied for the two thousand seats on sale for Anfield after season-ticket holders, shareholders and visitors had all had their slices of the total 7,400 seats on offer. Perhaps more seats would have been a good idea, because five minutes before kick-off people were being led out of the paddock again for fear of being crushed. For those who stayed, goals by Payne and Fagan – the latter looking suspiciously offside – replied to Edds' volley 'at lightning speed' for Rovers.

This win lined up a fourth-round home meeting with Third Division South club Exeter City. The visitors from Devon took the plaudits for a 'terrier show', punctured only by Kevin Baron's scrambled goal on 44 minutes. Three more goals in the last ten minutes – one for Smart for Exeter – settled a 3–1 win in which all the breaks went Liverpool's way. An Exeter fan wrote later to the *Liverpool Echo* with thanks on a 'happy day and a clean game', but he also pointed to the 'novelty' of a city that still had working trams – the very cheek of it.

Almost 60 years ahead of his time, the FA chairman Brook Hirst suggested in February 1950 that FA Cup semi-finals be played at Wembley, a proposal that brought only contempt from Ranger in the Merseyside press: 'London is not the hub of the football universe.' The idea was discreetly dropped. A record 27,833 crowd saw Liverpool scrape through round five, 2–1 at Third Division North's Stockport County. As usual, the lower-level club looked to pack in as many supporters as humanly possible for a mouth-watering, money-making tie such as this one. Partly as a result, a fence collapsed during the first half, which had Reds supporters spilling onto the touchline. But it also confirmed that 'there were likely to be a few more spectators [inside], for some people had climbed a wall into the ground so had got in "on the nod"'. A Liverpool supporter wrote later to the *Echo* that he was 'disgusted' at the County arrangements and that 'fully 3,000' paying customers inside had been unable to see the game. Fifteen minutes after kick-off, local police let out hundreds of paying spectators who simply had no hope of getting any sight of the pitch.

Ranger argued later for standing season tickets to help sort out ticket allocations and ground regulations for cup ties such as this one as the best way to avoid another Bolton tragedy. One male supporter in Liverpool wrote, 'Women are a contributing factor to overcrowding,' but he also pointed out, gallantly, that 'they are entitled to go to see the Reds or the Blues'. The overwhelming popularity of football was clear, but clubs were poorly regulated and barely accountable. With little in the way of organised supporters' campaigning, club officials seemed to care little about this type of spectator maltreatment, and there were no complaints for Stockport from the Anfield boardroom. These early departing Reds fans were at least spared a frantic Liverpool performance in which everybody, bar the referee, agreed that Phil Taylor had brought down veteran Scotland international Alex Herd from behind for a nailed-on home penalty, not given. This was before Willie Fagan scrambled the ball past goalkeeper Bowles on 57 minutes following a Liddell cross. Rain had now turned the pitch into a bog and the ball into a sodden cannonball – Arsenal had recently returned from Brazil with a waterproof laceless football, but a drowning England was not yet ready for this type of space-age technology. With 20 minutes left, Albert Stubbins showed his class at last: a run from halfway was finished decisively by him after his first attempt rebounded back off the Stockport keeper. Herd scored a late consolation for brave County, who frankly deserved more.

'Although the Cup is Liverpool's main objective,' reported the *Liverpool Echo* on 15 February 1950, 'they have a great chance of winning the championship.' The league title was definitely treated as a secondary goal, but a 2–1 Liverpool league home win against ten-man West Bromwich Albion, courtesy of keeper Sanders effectively punching into his own net with three minutes remaining, kept the Reds on top. 'If Liverpool's luck continues as it has recently,' commented the tongue-in-cheek local press, 'they will be a good bet to win the league title, the cup, the Grand National, the boat race and the Statue of Liberty from America.' But luck deserted Liverpool at Middlesbrough with a crashing 1–4 defeat that allowed Manchester United to go top by goal difference. Blackpool's visit to Anfield on 4 March in the sixth round of the FA Cup did not promise goals on this scale: the Tangerines had conceded only 23 in 23 league games. But the absence of the injured Stanley Matthews added somewhat to home confidence, and the Liverpool programme 'hoped' that the community singing before the match, conducted by invitation by Wembley's Mr Philpott, 'will not affect the Spion Kop's roar'.

Visiting Blackpool supporters – the Atomic Boys – joined in the fun by bringing a live duck painted tangerine as their mascot, which was described later by Liverpool supporters as 'the funniest turn since silent picture days'. But it failed to stop Willie Fagan scoring, following a 19th-minute corner, with 'a cute and most deliberate right-foot effort', the ball being gently passed into the opposition net. Within six minutes, though, Laurie Hughes had handled at the other end, and Sidlow could only palm Stan Mortensen's penalty into the side of the Liverpool net. At this stage, 'Blackpool's shots so far outnumbered Liverpool's, by ten to one.' But the Reds held on, with a draw looking the likeliest outcome until, with nine minutes left, Jimmy Payne hared up the left wing. Instead of crossing, the clever Payne delayed and carefully passed the ball inside to the lurking Billy Liddell, who 'slewed it with his right foot beyond the dismayed Farm'. As Kopites celebrated, there followed more FA Cup cheer. 'Roars and cheers greeted the news, which spread like lightning around Anfield, that Everton too had won [2–1 at Derby County].' So much, then, for those who still argued that Reds fans wanted to see the Blues damned.

THE GREAT MERSEYSIDE FA CUP SEMI-FINAL – AND TROUBLE IN MANCHESTER

Could it actually be a Merseyside FA Cup final at last, fifty-eight years after the great 1892 split that produced two intense rivals out of one seed? Sadly, the FA showed no sense of history, drawing the Liverpool clubs to meet in a Maine Road semi-final – and on Grand National weekend to boot! The owners of the Aintree course, the Topham family, appealed to the FA to change the match date but to no avail. With Arsenal playing Chelsea in the other contest, it was the first time in almost eighty years of FA Cup action that two clubs from the same city were competing against each other in both semi-finals. An exodus to Manchester was promised from Merseyside – 400 motor coaches and 30 football-special trains were booked for travel. Some people – including relatives of the players – spent most of one day queuing for train tickets simply to get to Manchester. But how was Liverpool FC to sell these prized match tickets?

Despite objections from residents, some 60,000 Merseyside supporters queued outside the respective stadiums for their chance, some staying out overnight to make sure they got a ticket. As the ticket offices opened, supporters on both sides of Stanley Park panicked and one hundred spectators were injured in the ensuing stampedes, with six of them hospitalised. Tension and tempers were definitely rising on Merseyside as the great football conflict approached. In the days before the match, the Fitzsimmons brothers from Spellow Lane, Edward and Michael, were accused of assaulting a George Kelly from the city after the latter had made a 'jocular remark' about the Liverpool v. Everton semi-final. This incident wasn't that funny: the unfortunate Kelly risked losing an eye from his injuries.

Everton went to Buxton for three days' relaxation and light training before the match, but Liverpool stayed at home until Friday before leaving for Alderley Edge in Cheshire. 'Match of the Century for Merseyside Folk' was how the *Football Echo* headlined the meeting on 25 March 1950. Future Blues manager Harry Catterick would play for Everton, but would Bob Paisley play for Liverpool? With the versatile Bill Jones showing solid form at both half-back and in defence, there was a broad hint in the local press that even a fully functioning Paisley might not now be in the optimum Liverpool FA Cup team. 'Most of their followers feel that had [Laurie] Hughes been fit and Jones available to cross to left-half,' said the *Echo*, 'the side would have gained in strength.' As it turned out, Hughes was unfit with a cracked little toe, so Paisley played – and scored – in a match that the Reds dominated in the spring sunshine, forcing fifteen corners to relegation-threatened Everton's five.

After 30 minutes, Everton keeper Burnett punched a Payne cross only as far as the advancing Paisley, who lobbed the ball back into the danger area. Billy Liddell jumped cannily with Burnett and the distracted Blues full-backs, but none of them made contact as Paisley's hopeful punt leaked into the Everton net. At first, the local pressmen assumed that Liddell had got the final touch, but it was Paisley's goal, aided by Billy's quick thinking. Now Baron especially but also Jimmy Payne continued to stretch their opponents on the Everton left, and Liverpool's half-backs – the stylish Phil Taylor, the terrier Paisley and the ice-cool Jones – made a nice balance and controlled proceedings. Everton's Eddie Wainwright prevented a corner on 62 minutes, though it looked as if it might have crossed the goal-line. Better for him that it had, because in saving the kick he inadvertently fed the ball to Liddell. Bad move. Billy could smell his Wembley day out, and he scored low at the far post from an acute angle – 2–0 to Liverpool. Liddell also hit a post late on in a comfortable Reds victory in which Cyril Sidlow 'has never earned his money so easily'.

Off the pitch in Manchester, things, clearly, hadn't been quite so easy or so orderly, even in this so-called 'Golden Age' of generally good behaviour from English football spectators. A reduced crowd limit made possible by ticketing had prevented excessive crushing, but outside Maine Road it had been a very 'lively' afternoon. A letter in the *Football Echo* from 'Fairplay' of Kenyon Road, Liverpool, for example, a man who said he was no 'crank' and that he enjoyed himself 'among the lads of the Kop' as well as 'under the clock at Goodison', described the kind of eventful trip to Maine Road that could have occurred at any time in the ensuing 30 years, and beyond:

> I was ashamed of being a native of Liverpool. At one time there were three fights going on around me, among so-called sportsmen. Later, I saw two youths knocking the stuffing out of one another and on going to the bus station saw the sorry spectacle of a Manchester bus conductor with a black eye, caused through one of our 'supporters'. On the journey into town some youths were bragging about what they had 'pinched' . . . and were using obscene language . . . I do hope those folk who are going to Wembley behave in a reasonable manner.

But this was no time to anticipate Wembley. Liverpool now had *seven* vital league games to play before the final – and they also had to make special training arrangements for the captain of their FA Cup final opponents Arsenal. Local man Joe Mercer was currently training at Anfield. Move him out? Not a bit of it. Liverpool simply asked Mercer to train in the afternoon, and they provided the Arsenal half-back with a goalkeeper for shooting practice and an outfield player to help with his ball work. These were different times, indeed – politely helping out your direct cup-final enemies seemed perfectly reasonable. Three consecutive Liverpool league wins – against Manchester City, Charlton Athletic and Burnley – revived the Reds' title hopes, as the club now wrestled with methods of allocating the 12,000 FA Cup final tickets without inducing the sort of chaos and injuries that had characterised the semi-final distribution.

Rather than risk more queuing and mayhem, Liverpool asked supporters who wanted a ticket to send in a plain postcard containing just their name and address. A public draw would then be made for the three-shilling Wembley tickets. The scope for trickery was obviously considerable here: there were no limits on how many postcards supporters could submit, or indeed on who might send them in. An avalanche was expected, and an astonishing 170,000 cards were reported to have arrived at Anfield. This scheme made methods used for European Cup final ticket allocation for Athens 57 years later seem entirely plausible by comparison. To rule out accusations of possible foul play in the postcard selection, the club even recruited two blind boys from Birkenhead and Belle Vale to make the draw. Most people, of course, missed out via this route and tried others, no matter how desperate. In nearby Colwyn Bay, for example, Gordon Jones's tobacconist shop was swamped with North Wales Reds enthusiasts after one of his female customers heard the proprietor talk about the 'cup final' tickets he had for sale and then spread the word. Jones was actually talking about the Cookson Cup final, between Colwyn Bay and Colwyn Boro. He was fortunate to escape intact from the angry and confused scenes that followed.

BACK TO THE LEAGUE

The condensed run of Easter fixtures started to take its toll on a Liverpool club now chasing the league title and FA Cup Double again. A tired and bedraggled side faced the holiday match at Newcastle without Paisley (thigh), Lambert (groin), Balmer (knee) and Sidlow (sciatica). At 0–2 on Tyneside, a concussed Albert Stubbins was helped off by Albert Shelley after a heavy collision, and Liverpool collapsed to a 1–5 defeat. But they were still third in the table and only one point off leaders Sunderland with four games left to play, though one of these remaining matches was carelessly blown in a 0–1 home loss to Burnley. Missile-throwing in this match by frustrated locals led to an FA admonishment and warning notices being posted at Anfield. But other clubs at the top were also losing, so everything was still possible.

Arsenal, meanwhile, had no such worries. They were busy giving a trial to a completely new FA Cup final strip in their league matches: gold, white shorts and gold socks. Both clubs had to change for the final under FA rules, so Liverpool decided on white shirts and black shorts, wearing the club badge for the first time. Not that this was a useful option against Fulham, who drew 1–1 at Anfield, with Billy Liddell missing on international duty. With two league games left, Liverpool were now one point behind new leaders Portsmouth, but other clubs were in contention and results now needed to go Liverpool's way for any title attempt to work out. The next league match was Portsmouth v. Liverpool on 22 April, and it still had the ring of a possible 1950 league-championship decider.

The bluff George Kay managed to persuade the FA to allow him to take his Liverpool players to Wembley en route to the Portsmouth match, just over one week before the cup final. This was unprecedented stuff, with Cyril Sidlow quipping that the final should be easy pickings for the respective goalkeepers – there were no goalposts up at the Empire Stadium as the Liverpool party got a feeling for their future surroundings. But was this Wembley trip also a distraction before a potentially crucial league match? Was it another sign of the absolute priority Kay and the Anfield board now placed on winning the elusive FA Cup?

At Portsmouth, Kay wanted Liverpool to try out their FA Cup final kit (another distraction?) but he discovered after arriving on the south coast that Liverpool could not play at Wembley in their usual red-and-white socks. The

FA had meant that the *entire* kit must be changed for the final. Liverpool had travelled south with their white kit but with no change of socks, and Kay wanted this to be an authentic rehearsal for the following week, so he sent Albert Shelley off to a sports outfitters in Portsmouth. The trainer returned with the only set of football stockings he could find: blue-and-white hooped ones. Liverpool wore them at Fratton Park and would thus play their first FA Cup final for 36 years sporting the colours of their closest rivals. Did this seem like bad karma at all?

Minshull was a late replacement for the struggling Sidlow (thigh muscle) at Portsmouth, and Paisley and Payne were both out, but Laurie Hughes was fit – which was potentially bad news for Paisley, even if he recovered for the FA Cup final. Lambert and Albert Stubbins were OK to start in a tightly contested and tense first half, which ended goal-less, even though the pace of Portsmouth's wingers was troubling the visiting full-backs. On 52 minutes, Albert Stubbins scored for Liverpool, a shot from a centre by Liddell. Was the impossible actually possible after all? This dream lasted ten minutes, by which time Reid had equalised with a header from a cross from Harris. Liverpool's main hope Billy Liddell looked exhausted now, 'a shadow of his normal dynamic self', and Liverpool had no reliable forward outlet as the pressure began to pile on their defence. Finally it told. With nine minutes left, Froggatt headed the Portsmouth winner from Scoular's precise cross. Defeat at home against Huddersfield Town in the final, meaningless, league fixture would follow and took Liverpool down to eighth place in a tightly packed final table. But this finish hid the real story of this valiant Liverpool 'Double' campaign, which remained alive almost until the final fixtures of the season.

THE SHAMBLES OF WEMBLEY 1950

After scoring a semi-final goal against Everton, Bob Paisley was left out of the 1950 Liverpool FA Cup final team. But it was no real surprise locally, certainly not to the *Echo*'s Ranger, for whom Paisley was 'the obvious twelfth man' if all other contenders were fit. Bob had played 23 league fixtures in a season troubled by injury; Bill Jones had played 26 games, admittedly many at centre-half, but Jones was also more mobile and certainly a more flexible half-back at that stage than Paisley. The rest of the Liverpool cup-final team pretty much picked itself – the ageing Jack Balmer was now well behind Kevin Baron in George Kay's eyes, and Cyril Done had played only 14 league games. Everyone in the side selected by Kay for Wembley had played more times in the league than the distraught Paisley had managed in the season.

For the kindly George Kay, this sort of tough decision contributed to the stress the manager habitually suffered, and he was taken ill before the final. He turned up at Wembley pasty-faced and drawn on what should have been one of the greatest days in his managerial career. Paisley's omission was a sad personal footnote to a generally distressing Liverpool experience, and he said graciously later that facing up to missing the biggest game in his career steeled him as a manager to making difficult selection decisions of his own.[4] Bob Paisley certainly thought seriously about leaving Liverpool in 1950 after missing out at Wembley. But his omission was probably not quite the injustice it was obviously felt to be by his family and some supporters. And Bob Paisley would be remembered for becoming a truly great Liverpool football manager more than he would for having been a very capable and unconditionally loyal Liverpool footballer.

Arsenal, capably managed by Tom Whittaker, pinned their Wembley hopes mainly on experience, fielding one of the oldest teams ever to play in a Wembley final thus far: George Swindin in goal, Wally Barnes, the Compton brothers and Joe Mercer were all highly seasoned professional footballers. The Arsenal team averaged 31 years of age and had eventually finished sixth in the league, above Liverpool, although they had spent almost the entire campaign in their wake. The heavy pitch and unseasonably cool conditions would suit the veteran Gunners, who were in form, as they would be able to play the final at a pace that suited both their style and make-up.

Before the war, the TV viewing figures for FA Cup finals were no higher than 10,000 to 12,000 people, but by 1950 the number of licensed sets had risen to 386,750, meaning that this was probably the first FA Cup final to be seen on British television by an audience of more than 1 million people.[5] For the first time, people who had not actually attended the match could hold an informed opinion on its incidents and outcomes.

The post-war fashion was to treat the FA Cup final as 'just another match', so Liverpool eschewed any special training regime for Wembley, and although George Kay valued tactics he didn't want his players, as he put it, to be 'cluttered up with a mess of theoretical ideas' that might make them seize up on the day. Accordingly, the Liverpool party travelled to Oaklands Park, Weybridge, for the last 48 hours before the match. But their arrangements were not quite as watertight as they might have wished. The hotel they had chosen was unusually crowded – who was making the bookings here? – and trainer Arthur Shelley and Reds inside-forward Kevin Baron found themselves bumped onto camp beds in the hotel ballroom, 'the only place where beds could be fitted up for them'. Young Baron would therefore play in the biggest game of his young life having slept the night before in a public space on a put-up bed alongside the club trainer. It seemed more like Sunday-league stuff than thought-out preparations for a historic Liverpool FA Cup final appearance.

Liverpool FC, FA Cup final team, v. Arsenal, 29 April 1950

Sidlow

Lambert   Hughes   Spicer

Taylor   Jones

Baron   Fagan

Payne   Stubbins   Liddell

Proud Arthur Shelley's spirits were certainly not dampened, either by the heavy London showers or by his own pre-final sleeping arrangements – he turned out for his day of a lifetime as Liverpool trainer in a striking, if rather slightly incongruous, outfit of red shirt and trousers and a cream linen jacket. The wives and relatives of players dressed in their own finery who had opted for uncovered seats to be closer to the action would rue the decision – it poured with rain, making the whole day an even more miserable affair for the defeated masses from the English north-west. The 5.50 a.m. Saturday train from Lime Street had transported probably the youngest fan on the whole trip from Merseyside, almost three-year-old Eric Stubbins, who carried a pair of clogs and a red teddy bear hoping, no doubt, that his dad might do the trick for Liverpool and for these people around him who were breaking out beer at breakfast time. The press on Merseyside carried pictures of the semi-official Liverpool mascot in London, James Phillips of Speke Road Gardens, dressed in all-red and hoisting a bell, while ticket touts were out in force: three-shilling tickets were fetching forty shillings on the capital's streets and top seats were going for £10 or more. But it was not only hard cash that was changing hands 'down south' in a still austere Britain in which the north was especially badly hit. The *Evening Express* reported that there was more than money on offer for tickets. 'In one café a black marketeer produced a box of American nylons. At a coffee stall another opened a suitcase full of bottles of scotch.' If only Reds fans had known what was in store for them, such treasures might even have been tempting.

Before the match, as the massed bands played and the community singing rang around Wembley Stadium, a Liverpool supporter dressed in white shirt and red shorts evaded the 500 stewards on duty and raced onto the middle of the pitch, shook hands with the Wembley conductor and then, typically, briefly conducted the crowd himself. The Liverpool supporters stirred, glad of a diversion from the soaking most of them were enduring. Meanwhile, inside the bowels of Wembley Stadium, players from both sides were retching with nerves in the bathrooms. Liverpool's Billy Liddell, a religious man and later a lay preacher, was sitting in the toilet for another reason. He was saying a prayer to help him get through the match and to ask for the safety of all the participants, a ritual he had performed before every major football match in which he had played since he was 16 years of age.

The rain and the lush thickness of the Wembley grass meant that Arsenal's footballer of the year and Anfield lodger Joe Mercer had to spin the coin twice to get it to lie flat for the choice of ends and kick-off to be decided. These players had seen so little grass on a football pitch for months, and now they had this greasy carpet to master. Mercer shook Phil Taylor's hand warmly and looked directly into the Liverpool man's eyes. Here was a player he had spent comradely years with on many a cold and dank training day at Anfield, not anticipating for a moment that they might actually meet here in deadly opposition in the most important club match of all in English football. Now they must put all friendship aside, like good professionals.

FINAL DESPAIR

In the opening exchanges, the players of both sides slithered around on the shiny green surface, but it took Joe Mercer's Arsenal only 17 minutes to settle down and to take the lead, a knife to Liverpool's nervous heart. A corner was only half-cleared by the Liverpool defence, to be returned instantly by Logie for the unmarked Reg Lewis to swivel and score from about ten yards. On the flanks, Liverpool were being buffeted and dominated, with Payne out of the game and the Reds' key danger man Liddell struggling on the sodden turf but also getting a pre-meditated roughing-up from the rugged Scottish half-back Alex Forbes. Loud Liverpool boos attached to Forbes whenever he got possession or hacked at Liddell, but the Liverpool man got little protection from Bedfordshire referee Henry Pearce, an official who reportedly changed his whistle every six weeks. He showed little sign of using it judiciously here. The Arsenal veterans coldly and professionally 'played' the referee and continued to dish it out to Liverpool's creative players, meaning it was difficult for the Reds to get any meaningful foothold in the contest before half-time.

For a period just after the interval, Liverpool actually pressed forward with some belief and purpose, and Payne finally came to life with a header to force a 'wonder save' from George Swindin in the Arsenal goal. Billy Liddell then embarked on a mazy run to beat three defenders, but he was squeezed out before he could shoot. This was much better; a Liverpool equaliser was potentially in sight. Moreover, a team that comes from behind often has the necessary momentum to accelerate past their shocked and doubt-ridden rivals to victory. But after 62 minutes, a clinching second goal arrived for Arsenal, Cox to the free man Lewis once again and another clinical finish. Liverpool could not come back from this deficit, not in these conditions and not against this sort of experience and confident resolve.

So a man who knew Anfield and its staff very well would climb, after all, to the royal box to pick up the 1950 FA Cup. But it would not be a Liverpool player, and his shirt would be a sweat-plastered golden yellow, rather than a rain-splattered Liver-birded white. The next morning, Arsenal captain Joe Mercer knocked on the door of the hotel room of Albert Stubbins to commiserate with his friend – and to play on the floor with his young son Eric. It was typical of Mercer to care like this for his fellow professional. This was a scene from a more sporting era, and it was a memory that stuck with the curiously detached Stubbins rather more than the match itself.[6]

On the Sunday after the final, the Liverpool party went to Brighton to relax before returning to Merseyside on the Monday afternoon. Liverpool's defeated return to the north was a hugely emotional occasion. Even hardened hacks seemed visibly moved by the bond expressed between the club and its supporters in such times of loss. 'All the way from Lime Street Station to Anfield,' reported the *Liverpool Echo*, 'cheering crowds up to ten deep lined the route and made one's ears ring with their cheers, rattles, bells and what-nots.'

The players went to Anfield, where a junior match was in play, to be rapturously received by the 30,000 crowd present. A further 20,000 people had gathered in Town Hall Square to reassert their ties with the club and its players in a season that had come so close to producing a near-unique achievement, but which had now been reduced to so much ashes. 'I doubt whether any club in the country can possibly possess such a fine bunch of supporters as Liverpool,' said the *Echo* proudly. 'No wonder Hitler's hordes couldn't break the spirit of Merseyside, in spite of all their efforts.'

This might have seemed like so much hyperbole, but it was only nine years or so since Liverpool had been blitzed, and the war remained a powerful and painful memory. But it was also a cohering one for almost every adult in the city. The language and idioms of war and football are also near-constant cellmates in English football parlance, even today. English football professionals are often ranked by their performance in the trenches, which can apply either to a muddied foreign football field or else to the bloodied ditches of France and Belgium. These are the brave warriors, the comrades upon whom you must rely for your profession or your life, the troops of both sport and war. The *Echo* was quite within its rights to draw upon other images of community suffering and mutual support to explain this emotional bond.

Despite their ultimate failures, this post-war group of Liverpool players had shown their mettle by winning a league title and also coming close to the Double *twice* in four years – in 1947 and in 1950. But their collective time was now coming to an end, and George Kay, his managerial successors and the Anfield board would have to build a new Liverpool, albeit on these sturdy foundations. But their attempts to do so would attract some sharp local criticism and the sorts of metaphors that are of a kind also connected to times of war: lions led by donkeys was one of the suggestions made. As football historian Neil Carter has argued, at this time in the English game 'boardrooms were riddled with complacency and characterised by staleness and immobility, with shares generally passed on to relatives and friends'.[7] This image of a lack of dynamism fitted the 1950s Liverpool Football Club perfectly, and its supporters would have to wait a while for inspiring new leaders to emerge. The football people of the city who had assembled to cheer and weep, simultaneously, in Town Hall Square in May 1950 did not yet know it, but some very difficult and perplexing years lay ahead for Liverpool Football Club in the next painful decade.

CHAPTER 12 REFERENCES

1. Wilson, *Inverting the Pyramid*
2. Keith, *Billy Liddell*, p. 104
3. Taylor and Ward, *Three Sides of the Mersey*
4. Keith, *Bob Paisley*, p. 47
5. Inglis, *League Football and the Men Who Made It*, p. 184
6. Taylor and Ward, *Three Sides of the Mersey*, p. 85
7. Carter, *The Football Manager*, p. 82

13

THE ROCKY ROAD TO GLENBUCK
The Bleak 1950s

MEN WITHOUT MASTERS: THE PASSING OF GEORGE KAY

Did Liverpool Football Club enter the new decade on a high after almost achieving the FA Cup and league Double? Initially, the signs were good. Reds players Bob Paisley, Cyril Done and goalkeeper Ray Minshull even appeared as authentic football celebrities on a 'spontaneous and unrehearsed' Radio Luxembourg quiz-panel show against local rivals Manchester United in December 1950. Surely this confident Liverpool team was on an upwards spiral? But no. Actually, Liverpool Football Club was on a severe downslope: it had an ageing team, a spent and ailing manager, and a lacklustre board that displayed no real ambition and drive. Within four years of appearing at Wembley in 1950, the club was relegated.

Losing its chairman Billy McConnell through illness in 1947 had certainly robbed Liverpool of one of its most dynamic and forward-looking figures on the board, and losing the services of its manager George Kay through illness in 1951 further damaged the crucial infrastructure and the deep football know-how that had existed inside the club since the mid-1930s. Key players had also declined or left the club, or else retired in the normal process of team renewal. Albert Stubbins faded very badly from his marvellous years in the 1940s, and crucial men from all core segments of the team – Sidlow, Fagan and Balmer, to name but three – would all soon be gone and would not be effectively replaced.

Only one man saw out much of the decade with the sort of commitment, loyalty, quality and sheer will to win that had symbolised the great Liverpool teams of the past. For 11 full seasons after the war, and save for international duty or injury, Billy Liddell's name was pretty much the first on any Liverpool team sheet, irrespective of manager, board shenanigans or fixture. His number and position might have changed over time but never his passion, honesty and focus for his only football club. Certainly, playing in the Second Division was no shame or hindrance to Liddell, just as long as he could pull on the red shirt of Liverpool. No other club ever seriously attempted to wrench him from Anfield, such was the strength of his allegiance and the manner in which he virtually defined the Liverpool club on the pitch for two decades. Only an Alex Raisbeck or an Elisha Scott could have done the same. Indeed, these three football players were the unquestionable greats from the pre-Bill Shankly Liverpool – from the league championship teams of the early 1900s, the 1920s and the 1940s, respectively. They would also walk, unassisted, into any team selected from those who have represented the Liverpool club. (Sadly, by 1954 five of the great Liverpool team of the 1920s – Chambers, Wadsworth, Lucas, McNab and Johnson – were all dead.) One championship medal and a single loser's medal in the FA Cup was barely reward for Liddell for the routine but extravagant brilliance he showed selflessly for Liverpool in his then record 534 appearances for the club.

In January 1951, Liverpool manager George Kay finally retired due to illness after 15 years at Anfield. He had been in hospital for some time, suffering from stress and nervous exhaustion caused by the job. He died on 19 April 1954 as the club he loved was also ailing and falling into the Second Division of the Football League. There was little side or polish to the man, who was a good friend to his players, a very human confidant for them almost as much as a boss. He was someone who found it painful to make hard but necessary decisions about their futures. Worst of all, every important football match for Liverpool was a war of nerves for him. He would frequently start games relatively detached in the grandstand but then would end up on the touchline, pacing out meaningless yardage, making every tackle or pass and wringing his hands with tension. As the *Liverpool Echo* put it about Kay on his death, 'Bitter irony that he should lose his zest for living, and finally his life, through strain and worry imposed by his association with the game he loved.'

The Liverpool board continued, without fuss or a manager, for five months while Kay was in hospital, connecting with the players via Albert Shelley. But in January 1951, Kay told the board from his hospital bed that he 'felt he would never be able to return to his duties', and out of more than 40 applicants (including a young Bill Shankly) in March 1951 Liverpool finally appointed the ex-Charlton Athletic forward Don Welsh to the role. Welsh had been manager at the Third Division South's Brighton and Hove Albion, without exactly pulling up any trees, but he had also played for Liverpool at centre-forward as a guest player during the war, scoring 42 goals in 41 appearances. The Liverpool board knew and trusted him. He was also young enough (just forty) to offer a good link between the boardroom and the Liverpool players, and he was seen as something of a tracksuit moderniser, but not one who was too headstrong or had too many of his own ideas. And, best of all for these cautious, parsimonious Liverpool directors, he was cheap.

The thinking inside Anfield was that Welsh could learn how to manage a top football club by relying on the wisdom and experience of the Liverpool board. As the *Liverpool Echo* supportively put it, 'If two heads are better than one, then nine directors and a manager must be better still.' It was a view, certainly. Welsh believed in the typical English virtues of strength and power, and he was something of an upbeat, extrovert joker and athlete, a man who liked to get up in fancy dress and to walk on his hands in hotels and the dressing-room, challenging others to do the same. He made training more interesting, with much more ball work and different exercises, so this much was an advance on what had gone before.[1] Liverpool also appointed a qualified physiotherapist to work on the players' fitness for the first time.

When the Liverpool chairman George Richards welcomed Welsh and introduced him to the Liverpool players, he left the new man and the squad in no doubt as to exactly why he had been brought to Anfield. 'Mr Welsh's career as a player entitles him to your confidence,' he told the staff, 'and I trust that in the not-too-distant future he will lead you to Wembley.' It was the FA Cup again.

REBUILDING – TOWARDS RELEGATION

With Albert Stubbins now generally out of sorts or else injured much of the time and Jackie Balmer in decline, in the new Don Welsh era Liverpool plainly and urgently needed to recruit quality goalscoring forwards to support Billy Liddell in this crucial exercise. The demand that young players do national service in the forces at this time offered a further complication in signing younger men. Lowly Sheffield Wednesday splashed out a world-record £34,500 on Jackie Sewell in 1951 – and were promptly relegated. Liverpool's record purchase remained the distant £12,500 spent on the suddenly unproductive Stubbins. The Liverpool club had been involved in more than a dozen major transfer negotiations for forwards since 1946, pretty much all of which had mysteriously fallen flat. What was going on here? Was the Liverpool board deliberately aiming impossibly high at unfeasible targets – Shackleton, Mannion, Steel, Hagan among them – merely to give the impression locally that they were trying hard to make big-money signings? This was one prominent theory. Another was that the board was unwilling to meet the substantial fees demanded by clubs. The Liverpool minute books suggest the Anfield transfer strategy was that Liverpool directors typically asked rival directors what was the lowest figure they would accept for a player – and then offer substantially below that figure as a bargaining stance. Unsurprisingly, this was seldom a successful tactic.

The club often trotted out the line about its responsibilities to shareholders as well as supporters, and the Liverpool board seemed quite unwilling to speculate in order to accumulate. Another theory was that the board would not offer the necessary 'extras' required to sign top players in those days. Because of the constraints of the maximum wage and the black-market hangover from the war, the transfer system was widely assumed to be bent. Maybe the strait-laced men from Anfield just refused to play ball with players and clubs on this score? When Don Welsh was accused by the FA in December 1954 of offering a £100 inducement to the Droylsden centre-half Lomas to sign for Liverpool, rather than take it in their stride the Anfield board was shocked and appalled by the accusation. As the *Liverpool Echo* put it, 'Liverpool are determined not to take part in any "under the counter" business.'

The Liverpool board had regularly tried to assure the club's supporters that it would only sign the right men at the right price. Chairman George Richards, for example, said, 'The search for good players still goes on. The board are prepared to pay top price for men of proven ability when they are available for transfer.' But the local press became increasingly dubious: 'That age-old formula has been trotted out so many times now that folk are becoming rather cynical about the effort to sign new players of experience.' But the Liverpool board was also generally cosseted from hostile public opinion, even when the team was playing below what was expected or required. The Merseyside press was largely friendly and supportive, and the club's supporters had a tradition – unlike at Everton – of near-unquestioning loyalty to the Liverpool board, manager and players. More importantly perhaps, the Liverpool club directors had a vice-like control over the club's shares. These men held overlapping duties and responsibilities in local businesses, public office and in high levels of local politics, invariably in the Liverpool Conservatives. They ran a very tight ship indeed, one that brooked little or no internal dissent or external opposition.

This last point meant that since the Liverpool shareholders mini 'revolt' of 1932, there were seldom difficult or 'unharmonious' Liverpool AGMs or even contested director elections at Anfield, as there frequently were over at Goodison Park. When a Liverpool club servant was deemed to have 'fallen out' with other key board members – perhaps after an unusually high level of trading in shares, as happened in 1955 to ex-chairman and director for 24 years Ronnie Williams – the unfortunate man who opposed the usual consensus was simply frozen out with minimum fuss or discussion. 'An odd question or two has been asked from time to time, usually in apologetic tones,' recalled the *Liverpool Echo* of the typical Anfield AGMs of the time, 'but rarely has anything approaching a spanner been thrown into the works.' Indeed, it was difficult to remember a single emergency general meeting successfully called by any group of shareholders in the entire history of the Liverpool club thus far. The nature of share ownership there, as well as the ingrained culture of the club, simply prohibited such a potentially dynamic move from taking place.

In July 1953, for example, after a quite awful season in which Liverpool had finished seventeenth in the league and had lost in the third round of the FA Cup to little Gateshead, there was barely a whimper at the AGM. The *Liverpool Echo* reported, 'Many a church choir meeting has produced greater dissension and more bitterness than Liverpool's annual gathering of shareholders.' For once, the board was divided on who should replace the deceased director R.K. Milne, but the most that club chairman George Richards could bring himself to say on the matter was that the board was 'not undivided'. As Ranger put it:

> Altogether, this was another 'All pals together' meeting, without a dissenting voice, apart from the gentleman who doubted the genuineness of the board's unanimity. There was not even a question about the prospects for next season, which was rather surprising. Nobody felt bold enough to insert a discordant note into the happy and cheerful atmosphere.

Seldom did the Liverpool directors come to an AGM in any way publicly split or disunited because 'domestic affairs, team problems, and any other matters on which there has not been unanimity . . . have always been kept private, which is right and proper'. This was the much vaunted and historic 'Liverpool Way' in action, of course, an approach to directing the club that could be traced right back to the autocratic rule of John Houlding and that ran through the 1920s and 1930s. Don't do your dirty washing in public. But it also must have been immensely frustrating to some Reds supporters in the 1950s to have so little response to how the club was performing, and it made the club's directors almost completely unaccountable – except, of course, to themselves. Only very occasionally did the directors' veil slip, slightly, as it did at the 1954 post-relegation 62nd Liverpool AGM, when a shareholder called Parker asked whether potential opponents to the election of Harold Cartwright and Chief Inspector J.W. Morris to the Liverpool board had been dissuaded from standing by the club chairman Alderman Will Harrop. The chairman was alleged to have told them, 'You have no chance. If you withdraw now, you might have a chance next year.' This was typically the way in which contested elections were avoided. Harrop, of course, was affronted and vehemently denied the charge, and the meeting moved quickly on (Parker himself was later quietened because he was soon elected to the board). Someone then enquired about Albert Stubbins, who was said still to be registered with Liverpool. The directors responded, evenly, that the man who had won the league title for the Reds in 1947 would 'never play for the club again'. It was business as usual.

A GLOBAL GAME, BUT A LOCAL CRISIS

Club director T.V. Williams, who had joined the board in 1948, was a man with a little more vision than other directors. It was Williams who decided that Liverpool now needed its own training ground, and he orchestrated the purchase of land in West Derby for the purpose, bought from a local school. But beyond building a new boundary wall, the Liverpool board was unwilling to spend much cash on the new facilities at Melwood. Williams was also the key figure in appointing Bob Paisley as second-team trainer and budding physiotherapist when the rugged wing-half retired at the end of the relegation season in 1954. Paisley could instinctively judge a footballer's body as easily as many working-class men from Durham could weigh up racing animals – dogs, horses or pigeons.[2] The kindly but shrewd ex-Manchester City man Joe Fagan followed Paisley onto the Liverpool backroom staff in 1958.

Liverpool's slide into football obscurity was masked somewhat by Everton's own relegation in 1951, but by 1952 the writing was probably already on the wall for the Reds. Liverpool went 23 weeks – from 13 October 1951 to 22 March 1952 (10 matches) – between home league wins. Some old-stagers were still doing their stuff – Liddell, of course, and Bill Jones had been in 'scintillating form' in defence, while Ray Lambert continued to be 'a tower of strength' at full-back. Reserve goalkeeper Charlie Ashcroft had finally been given his chance, but he did not always convince. However, when the Yorkshireman Russell Crossley replaced him in goal in 1953, Spurs' full-back Alf Ramsey scored over the new goalkeeper's head from a free-kick near the halfway line. Injuries to other stalwarts such as Paisley (wrist), Hughes (ligaments) and Taylor (cartilage) were serious disruptions as Liverpool limped to a final 11th-place finish. By April 1952, Jack Balmer had been offered an Anfield coaching job, Cyril Done had been released, and Sidlow and Fagan were on the transfer list. In May 1952, Liverpool met Everton in a 'thrill-packed' Liverpool Senior Cup final – a competitive derby game at least – won for Liverpool by a goal from Welshman Mervyn Jones, a man so small that Bob Paisley had once asked him in a team-photograph group whether he could see over the football he was carrying.

The Liverpool board finally bought to try to plug the goals gap up front by bringing in the bruising Sammy Smyth, a 27-year-old Northern Ireland international from Stoke City, for £12,000. It wasn't exactly the 'statement' signing that Reds supporters had been calling for, and Smyth had been signed only after the 1953 FA Cup deadline because fog had interrupted plans for the Liverpool directors to meet with the player. But the new man's goals in three crucial league matches won in February 1953 helped save the club from relegation. His forced omission from the third-round FA Cup tie at lowly Gateshead, and the fact that the Liverpool board could find no place for Stubbins, which, for the *Daily Post*, 'surprises few', was probably decisive. Liverpool slipped miserably out of the Cup, 0–1, in dense fog and on a typical early FA Cup pitch that was 'almost the consistency of plasticine'.

Later in 1953, national hero Stanley Matthews won his FA Cup-winner's medal at last with Blackpool, a new young queen took her place on the British throne and, appropriately, *women's* football was poking its head above the parapet once more in the Merseyside area. At the Tower Ground, New Brighton, in July, for example, Manchester Corinthians played Dynamo Women of Cheshire in a charity game. Later, Preston's Dick, Kerr's took on a London Select at the Stanley Track in Prescot Road in aid of Liverpool City RLFC. Women footballers had not simply disappeared since 1921 after all. Local Sunday footballers in the city might as well have disappeared: they were still locked out of Liverpool parks. 'One would almost think they were engaging in crime instead of healthy sport,' complained a correspondent to the *Liverpool Echo* in July 1953. People in the city who had been relocated to the 'salubrious and well-planned' outer Merseyside estates of Kirkby and Speke were rather happier with their lot, according to the *Echo*. They were finding 'a whole new joy in their surroundings and the pure air saves no end of cleaning'. This optimistic message rather simplified – and probably misrepresented – the real experiences of many of those who had been yanked out of tightly bound city neighbourhoods and plonked miles away in areas with no shops and little in the way of infrastructure.

In Durban, South Africa, meanwhile, a Liverpool and Everton football social club was set up for expats – an astonishing 18 Scousers turned up for the first meeting. A Liverpool-born singer, Lita Roza, had a number-one British hit in March 1953 with the unlikely '(How Much Is) That Doggie in the Window?', and stylish 'zoot suits' made their first appearance in the American-obsessed city of Liverpool, as some young people began to earn decent wages at last following the austerity years after the war. Robert Lawson Martindale, Liverpool FC director and chairman of the Liverpool magistrates, was soon talking in court in 1953 about 'gang warfare' and 'knife gangs' in parts of the city that would continue to exhibit the same sorts of tribal problems more than 50 years later. He was one of four justices of the peace on the Liverpool board, which was still dominated, of course, by Conservatives and Freemasons, but also by local men with a strong sense of civic duty. Certainly, Liverpool FC continued to exhibit a reasonable sense of public community responsibility and attachment. The annual pre-season first team versus reserves practice match in the 1950s, for example, regularly produced between £600 and £800 in receipts for distribution between 30 or more local charities. Also, between 20 April and 9 May 1953 Anfield staged a staggering 16 local community, schools and charities football matches and finals, all virtually free of charge. But not everyone could be taken on board. In March 1955, for example, the application by a Mr Lott of Aigburth Road to be admitted to matches in his invalid carriage was refused – facilities at Anfield simply did not permit disabled access of this kind.

Robert Lawson Martindale valued both public service and responsibility, and it was he who urged the Liverpool board to cut its own cloth in February 1953. He issued a list of alleged director excesses, including quaffing champagne, high lunch bills and poorly monitored expenses. Predictably, the board threw out most of his suggestions, but at least it ended the tradition of holding Liverpool board meetings over a groaning lunch at the Adelphi Hotel. They would now take place at Anfield or at a director's workplace.

George Band, from Bebington on the Wirral, would have had little time for this sort of high living: this local man looked after the radio equipment and food supplies on the Sir John Hunt-led expedition that famously conquered Mount Everest in 1953. George briefly became something of a local hero on Merseyside, and, in the 1950s, for a man who was not a footballer or an embryonic pop star this was quite a trick. The year 1953 certainly felt like a good one to be British again – but not, perhaps, to be either a Liverpool or an Everton football supporter.

GOING DOWN, AT HOME AND ABROAD

Liverpool embarked on a marathon six-week tour of the USA in the summer of 1953, which seemed to drain them fatally for the new campaign. After losing 0–4 at Newcastle in September, Ranger said sternly, 'It is a rather sad story I have to tell, but the time is now for true criticism and Liverpool at the moment do not promise any great things for the future.' How true this would turn out to be. Gloom hung over the entire Anfield area. During training in the car park in November 1953, a Mrs Morris of 35 Lothair Road was hit by a stray football and had her false teeth broken – the club had to fork out £22 to repair them.

Actually, incurring injury was one of the very few ways that females could get any sort of payment out of Liverpool, because there were few real employment opportunities at Anfield for women in the early 1950s. Even when the club advertised for a shorthand typist in February 1954, the club minute books show that the board insisted that the word 'male' was firmly and prominently inserted in the ad to put off any unwanted applicants.

As Everton started to tear up the Second Division at last, Liverpool meekly propped up the First. A 0–6 defeat at Charlton saw 'Liverpool in the depths', according to the *Daily Post*. There were rays of hope, nevertheless. Centre-forward Louis Bimpson from Rainford was something of a raw reincarnation of Cyril Done, and he scored all four goals as Liverpool saw off Burnley at Anfield in September to end a run of eight league matches without a win. Correspondent Leslie Edwards in the *Daily Post* still saw a downside to the victory. 'I can imagine no more frightful place for the light-fingered than this huge terrace mound,' he said of the Kop. 'Rabid and highly elated supporters might almost be sledge-hammered without knowing it.' But there would be only three more Liverpool league wins for the Anfield faithful (and local pickpockets) to celebrate before the middle of March 1954, when it was already too late to avoid the drop. 'Have they signed him yet?' the *Post* suggested was the question on all Liverpool lips in October 1953 as the club sought a transfer saviour. 'Too many players have grown old too quickly. Do not players want to come to Anfield, or have the club been slow moving?'

The truth was that the Liverpool board did not want to spend anything approaching big money, and the new Reds manager Don Welsh had neither the personality nor the independence or experience to press for new blood of sufficient quality. John Atyeo, a £20,000, 6-ft, 21-year-old centre-forward from Third Division Bristol City, was briefly a target, but even he escaped the Anfield net. He might have baulked at Liverpool's doomed position at the bottom of the table. Atyeo burned brightly very briefly and then disappeared without trace. By December 1953, Eddie Spicer had badly broken his leg and retired from the game, and even Liverpool's 16-year-old mascot David Goodman was in hospital – he missed an incredible 5–2 Reds victory over cup-holders Blackpool at Anfield, in a run of one league win in nineteen games. It was 'the turn-up to beat all turn-ups', the press reported. Or maybe not . . .

On the national football stage, on 24 November 1953 Ranger, speaking confidently of the forthcoming international match between England and Hungary at Wembley, said, 'It is an old English custom to belittle our own skill and magnify that of the opposition. Maybe it springs from our own innate modesty.' Or maybe the English just had a lot to be modest about. This was typical national hubris, and over the next few days Ranger, like many others in the British press and inside the English game, would have to eat plates of humble pie – with cream on it. England lost for the first time at Wembley, savaged 3–6 by the kind of sheer skill, pace and movement that English football supporters and players had rarely seen. Ranger now recalled the Englishman Jimmy Hogan's coaching work with the Hungarians – the Magyars had learned everything from us, after all – before suggesting that the FA should finance their own squad of full-time players rather than periodically 'loan' them from clubs. 'Professional football' in England, he argued on 26 November 1953, 'has degenerated into a lazy and indolent life for all but the few really conscientious players.' Suddenly English football seemed outmoded and inept. 'The unpalatable fact is that 50 per cent of players have neglected the need to master their craft from A–Z. For years a lot of paltry and aimless stuff has been put before the long-suffering spectator in the guise of first-class football.'

It was hardly surprising that the general technical quality of the English game had suffered. While the Continentals were already talking about 'science', tactics and variety in player preparation, the English approach to training was still incredibly basic, drawing largely on the brutal fitness regimes learned in the forces during the war. It was aimed at producing stamina and strength for the long slog ahead more than at developing ball skills. Training at Liverpool was a case in point. Monday was the day off training, while Tuesday was spent at Melwood on exercises and perhaps with a brief practice match. Wednesday and Thursday were usually Anfield days, spent endlessly lapping the pitch under the eagle eyes of Albert Shelley and Jimmy Seddon, while on Friday the players were back at Melwood in spikes for some sprinting and speed work. If it rained, the players would slog up the covered terraces or else they would do some basic gym work. There were still very few practical or creative activities undertaken with a football in training, and nothing at all on set-pieces.[3] The Liverpool directors routinely reported to board meetings on the hundreds of players they scouted by referring mainly to their size, physique and weight of kick. These were among the reasons why the top English clubs were also vulnerable to FA Cup defeats by the lower orders. There was little technical or tactical advantage higher up the English football food chain that had been generated by superior coaching.

The English would never really learn the full lesson of 1953. Decades later, managers of English clubs were still doubting what we could learn from football cultures abroad. And there could be no doubt that 'paltry and aimless' was a good description of Liverpool's current form. The Reds eventually called on 31 of their large group of 44 professional players for the 1953–54 league campaign, a sure sign of trouble ahead. Among these, however, was a skilful, balding

Liverpool-born inside-forward called Jimmy Melia, a man who never quite won over the whole Liverpool crowd but who would be a key figure in eventually dragging the club back into the big time. The 23-year-old Geoff Twentyman, a rangy and intelligent half-back or centre-half, a leader and briefly the Liverpool captain, joined for £10,000 from Carlisle United in December 1953. He would return to the club in the late 1960s as a coach and scout under Bill Shankly. Alan A'Court, a sparky Prescot-born left-winger with a fierce shot, now began to figure, and he would prove an undoubted star in a weak Liverpool team, playing three times for England in the World Cup finals in 1958, while his club was still rooted in the Second Division. A'Court actually stayed long enough at Anfield to play in Liverpool's first-ever tie in Europe, against KR Reykjavik in 1964. Forward John Evans and a 'dainty and stylish' full-back Frank Lock signed jointly from Charlton Athletic in December 1953 in a Liverpool spending spree totalling £12,500. The Reds even went to bitter rivals Manchester United to sign another full-back, Tom McNulty, for £7,000, but it was money poorly spent. These latter signings made a less than long-lasting impression – Liverpool continued to slump.

Early in 1954, things finally began to overheat among the club's long-suffering supporters. On 2 January, a Reds fan got onto the pitch at Anfield and wrestled with the Bootle-born Bolton Wanderers goalkeeper Hansen at the Anfield Road end after a goalmouth melee towards the end of a 1–2 defeat. The player suffered a split lip in the assault, and a section of the crowd stayed behind outside the ground afterwards to carry on the argument, as Hansen was slipped out by the back door. Imagine the hoo-ha this sort of thing would produce today!

An older supporter, John Roberts from the Isle of Man, wrote to the *Daily Post* on 6 January summing up what many Reds supporters probably thought about the current Liverpool:

> When they last went into Division Two it was because they lacked money. Today they must be fairly well off. I think the way the club has been run in the past couple of years has been scandalous. To start this season without a single decent signing to replace the old faithfuls was shocking and an insult to their most loyal supporters.

By 1 March 1954, when Liverpool went down 1–2 at Aston Villa, even Billy Liddell had lost heart and the scoring touch, supplying only six league goals in the season. The *Daily Post* reported that Liverpool officials 'profess themselves surprised that the press and their followers have been so kind; that the criticism of the side has been so tempered'. Well they might.

By 5 March, Liverpool were reported to have circulated to all clubs that they were prepared to receive offers for players in all positions. (Did they mean Liddell, too?) It looked like a closing-down sale. Still, 'the crowd was full of encouragement' and a remarkable 46,074 turned up for the 'must-win' home match against Huddersfield Town – which was lost 1–3. 'Of all the games Liverpool have played over the past 50 years,' said the *Daily Post* glumly, 'this one rates as the heaviest of black borders.' Nine league games were left, but Liverpool were already effectively stranded, ending half a century in the top division, even though four of their nine league wins that season came in April. This run included a victory at Maine Road, their first away win in 24 attempts. George Kay passed away just as the First Division last rites were also being read for Liverpool Football Club. 'In a hydrogen-bomb age,' mused Leslie Edwards wisely in the *Daily Post*, 'should we really worry too much about the prospects of no First Division club in the city next year?' He had no need to worry too much, at least not about football: Everton were already on the up escalator and moving out of the second rank, even as Liverpool crashed down.

SECOND DIVISION WOES – AND A RECORD LEAGUE DEFEAT

Don Welsh was now at the end of his first three-year contract, with an unimpressive record, but he was instantly reappointed. After all, he was doing the Liverpool board's bidding without complaint. He told his directors, not unreasonably, 'We have too many players growing old together.'

Things got only a little better at the lower level. By the end of December 1954, Liverpool already had ten away defeats and no away wins at all in the Second Division. After 20 matches, they had 20 points and were just midway. In one comic moment, Liverpool beat Middlesbrough 3–1 in front of just 26,749 at Anfield on 4 December. When the Reds were awarded a penalty, Boro keeper Rolly Ugolini left his goal for the penalty spot to ask Billy Liddell if he wanted a bet on whether he would score. The Kop hooted. Billy growled that the keeper could have any money on it he wanted – and scored.

English clubs were now starting to acquire lights, awaiting a relaxation of league regulations. Liverpool finally got theirs in the autumn of 1957 at a cut-down price of £12,000. On 10 December 1954, meanwhile, the *Liverpool Echo* previewed the club's forthcoming league visit to Birmingham City with the businesslike headline 'Liverpool Visit Birmingham in Search of Elusive Away Win'. Were they joking?

Ken Rudham, Liverpool's third South African goalkeeper, had now pushed his way in front of Ashcroft, and Lock and Ray Lambert had teamed up at full-back. Brian Jackson, a southerner ex-schoolboy international who had been brought in from Leyton Orient, was now playing on the right wing with the Bishop Auckland amateur George Wilkinson behind him at right-half, taking advantage of the fall of the 1947 trio of Taylor, Jones and Paisley. He accompanied the long-serving Laurie Hughes and also Geoff Twentyman at half-back. Eric Anderson, a Manchester-born lightweight inside-forward, offered what help he could to Evans and Liddell. Future international Alan A'Court patrolled the left-wing.

This was the uncertain XI that travelled apparently with some hope to Birmingham. In the event, Liverpool lost 1–9 at St Andrews on 11 December 1954, the club's record league defeat. The explanation offered – though it seems grossly unprofessional – was that Liverpool staff had misread the frost-bound Birmingham pitch and so players wore the wrong boots in the Midlands. Nothing at all was said about the scale of the defeat in the Liverpool minute books or the need to change policy. Perhaps the defeat never happened? Amazingly, most Liverpool supporters seemed resigned, rather than angry, at this capitulation, though there was some public angst on Merseyside at this latest humiliation. As 'Fed Up' told the *Football Echo* on 18 December 1954:

> Liverpool's debacle at Birmingham calls for a full inquiry. They are going from bad to worse, and I fear for the future. Don't ask us to keep on cheering, we haven't the heart. They have no reserves of any promise.

The Liverpool directors made their own point by saying (apparently without irony) that 'the result should not be taken too much at face value'. In fact, they decided to field the same 11 players in the next league fixture, against Doncaster Rovers. This match was also lost, but by only 1–4, so this was obviously an improvement. After Birmingham, a supporter had asked the teetotaller Billy Liddell why he had had 'one over the eight' on Saturday, and Liddell also heard of Reds supporters who went to bed on hearing the result and stayed there all day Sunday. During a Merseyside v. Birmingham amateur boxing match at Byrne Avenue Baths a few days later, a count of nine against a Birmingham fighter brought from a wag in the audience the observation, 'There's nine back for Liverpool!' This was black humour of the most desperate kind, because this was surely Liverpool Football Club at its lowest twentieth-century ebb. When the Reds played Ipswich Town at home on Christmas Day 1954, only 24,073 bothered to turn up, suggesting both public disillusionment in Liverpool and changing social habits. Christmas Day was increasingly a family day to be spent at home, not freezing and despondent at a football match. It would finally disappear as a day for football in England in 1958.

As if to add insult to injury, Liverpool were drawn to play Everton at Goodison Park in the FA Cup on 29 January 1955. It looked like more certain gloom for Anfield. Few could have predicted the outcome, a remarkable 4–0 win for Liverpool. The unexpected victory came after the Reds sprung Everton's offside trap following a helpful telephone call to Anfield from a supporter who had noticed that the Blues always advanced up-field at free-kicks to play their opponents offside. Notably, it had taken the unsolicited advice of an observant Kopite to get the Reds to consider any kind of set-piece practice, and it paid off in spades here. Everton collapsed in the match after being so brutally exposed. Sadly, Huddersfield Town had no such foibles or weaknesses and comfortably beat Liverpool next round up. A 2–2 draw when hosting Birmingham in the league at Anfield in May 1955 restored a little more lost respect. But a chaotic 1–6 Reds defeat to promotion-chasing Rotherham in the season's last league match showed just how much there was still to do to get Liverpool Football Club out of the Second Division.

FROM THE DEPTHS OF DESPAIR

In the summer of 1955, two men who would see the club into a brighter future, T.V. Williams and Sydney Reakes, began to assert themselves much more prominently on the Liverpool board. They hinted at a change of policy and direction for the club at last. Tom Williams, a former postman, had been a keen supporter of Liverpool all his life, and he had watched the club from the Kop as a young man. Williams was a long-standing shareholder who had been approached earlier to be a club director He had decided then to focus on his growing cotton-broking business but was now retired and in his late 60s. He did not lack energy or ambition. It was Williams who would provide the historic link between McKenna and John Houlding and Bill Shankly, as Liverpool Football Club finally threw off its 1950s gloom.

In February 1956, on the death of Will Harrop (another man who had been unchallenged as a director of the club for 30 years), Williams would become Liverpool FC chairman for a period of crucial transformations. But before all that, Liverpool had a contest in the annual director elections for once. When Harrop was asked by a Reds shareholder why this had happened, he replied, to general surprise, 'It was felt that the possibility of a change of directors on the board might do the club good.' Finally, the closed shop was opening. Clifford Hill, another director, said that he was willing to forego the directors' box to watch the A or B teams, or even the Liverpool youth team, if it would help build up the first team. This seemed like revolutionary stuff, though it actually turned out to be more like evolution.

Tom Williams argued that in offering his leadership, Harrop had sacrificed 'football's greatest honour' – the possible presidency of the Football League – for the sake of Liverpool FC, and he added this warning: 'Four years ago the writing was on the wall . . . If there is a member of this club, from the chairman down to the youngest ground boy, who does not pull his weight then we will sweep him out of the way. We mean to keep it that way.' For the sometimes slapstick Liverpool manager Don Welsh this kind of language must have sounded either like a declaration of war or else an assurance that he would now be given the financial ammunition he had previously lacked – although Will Harrop confirmed, wearily, that the club had no intention of paying 'fantastic' prices for 'ordinary' players. It seemed unlikely, in any case, that Welsh was in a position to demand big-money signings from his employers. In fact, his comments on the general failings of Liverpool players sound eerily like the sort of thing that all drowning football managers dredge up to say in mitigation today. 'Players are money conscious instead of playing conscious,' he told the Liverpool board in 1955. 'There are so many interests provided for them now that they do not practise as much as boys used to a generation or two ago.' But he was not talking here about a stocky and pugnacious little Liverpool-born left-back Ronnie Moran, who was now pushing himself into the Liverpool first team and who struck such a level of consistency and resilience that he would miss only six matches in five seasons beginning with 1955–56.

With Moran shoring up the Liverpool left side and the club's league shirt now carrying the distinctive liver-bird club badge for the first time – most clubs would wait until the 1960s or '70s to adopt club crests on their shirts – Don Welsh managed to get the Reds back into promotion contention again in 1955–56, with a 7–0 home win against fancied Fulham the highlight. The Reds made it up to third place in the table. But for the local press Liverpool – like their manager – generally 'lacked subtlety and craft', and two losses against Doncaster Rovers (again!) in March and April 1956 probably finished off their chances – and also finished off Welsh.

Liverpool Football Club was a very large and well-supported enterprise in Division Two in the 1950s, and the size – and occasionally the behaviour – of their travelling support, with little to cheer on the field, sometimes threatened to overwhelm local police forces. The visits to Doncaster were obviously among a number of lively away affairs at this time. Rovers fielded future stand-up comedian Charlie Williams at centre-half, one of the few black players in the

English game in the 1950s. A letter to the *Liverpool Echo* from James Corish from Doncaster on 4 April complained of Liverpool racism, claiming that Williams had been 'reviled by a loud voice snug in the crowd; this being coupled with the colour of the player's skin'. A knife was reportedly thrown at the Doncaster keeper from the visitors' end, and local letter writers to the *Echo* were generally alarmed about the actions of 'filthy-mouthed, beer swillers' from the city and worried that 'several Liverpool fans [were] ready to fight – literally – over their team'. Another letter, this time from 'Ever Red', a Liverpool fan, reported on 'the element of sheer, savage hooliganism among some of our supporters'. It was a warning.

Two years later, in March 1958, when Liverpool lost 1–2 in the sixth round of the FA Cup at Blackburn, there were much more serious and widespread disturbances. Shop windows were smashed, goods stolen and police officers attacked before and after the match. The police used truncheons to deal with troublemakers, and eighteen Liverpool men eventually appeared in court, with four sent to prison, after what one local commentator described as 'the worst case of hooliganism I have ever seen in Blackburn'. Much of this kind of thing was the result of sheer frustration, of course, but it also seemed to echo wider developments in youth culture in Liverpool and elsewhere at this time. Drinking and public-violence offences began to soar in the city and around Britain in the late 1950s. In June 1956, for example, a 'teddy boy brawl' occurred in a Wallasey cinema, and on 11 June Bootle was said to have 'declared war on teddy boys' after a very large street fight in Strand Road ended up with a rack of local offenders in court. The message seemed to be that post-war British life was rapidly changing and that English football was not immune to some of its more difficult consequences.

On 4 May 1956, the inevitable happened. The *Liverpool Echo* reported that Don Welsh had finally resigned, noting, 'During his period at Anfield he has not had a free hand with the selection of the team and this, no doubt, is one of the reasons for his recent unhappiness with the club.' Welsh had no more to offer. 'As everybody knows,' he told the press, 'team selection at Liverpool has always been a board affair and there we have not always regarded things in the same light.' In an era in which other clubs were now giving rather more responsibility and independence to their managers, the Liverpool board was clutching inertly to its historic right as employers and owners to have the final say. Tellingly, there were no traditional messages of thanks to the outgoing manager in the Liverpool minute books. When discussing a new incumbent, Billy Liddell was mentioned, of course, but Welsh's replacement indicated that little would actually change. Phil Taylor was a well-liked ex-player who was now a coach at the club.

But the board described his appointment as that of a mere 'liaison man' in the dressing-room. Taylor became the acting Liverpool manager on a wage of £18 per week – a saving of £12 a week on Welsh. The club's board, it was announced, reserved the power to have 'the final say in all matters of importance affecting the success and well-being of the club'. It was not a formula that was likely to succeed in either the short or the longer term.

But some things did change: a 'shooting box' was bought for Melwood for £140, and a short-wave therapy machine was purchased for £400 to treat players' injuries. A four-yard-wide cinder track was also laid out at Melwood to aid with speed training. Taylor had undoubtedly had an impact. New, solid players also arrived at Anfield, but all within Liverpool's strict budgetary regime – and none with a schemer's flair or a goalscorer's golden touch. Right-back John Molyneux moved across from Chester for £4,500, for example, and he was a consistent presence in the Liverpool defence for the next six years. Dick White, a versatile defender who could play full-back or centre-half, came in from Scunthorpe for £8,000 in November 1955 and would eventually play a key role in dragging the Reds out of Division Two. Tommy Younger, a chunky Scotland international keeper, joined from Hibernian in June 1956 for £9,000, and the hard-tackling, fierce-shooting England right-half Johnny Wheeler came in from Bolton Wanderers for the same price.

These last two players were the first sizable signings of the new Taylor era but not much had really changed at the club. Liverpool remained competitive in the Second Division, but team selection still seemed too haphazard and overly cautious to guarantee promotion. In a vital match against Leicester City in February 1957, for example, the *Daily Post* pointed out that Liverpool had fielded three centre-halves – White, Twentyman and Hughes – and lost. Later that month, on a snow-bound Anfield pitch in the FA Cup against Manchester City, Billy Liddell famously 'scored' an equalising 'goal', but just after the referee had blown for time. In the ensuing confusion, many spectators left the tie sure it had been drawn. The occasion certainly made a big impression on one young Kopite that day: the Anfield-born youngster Tommy Smith dreamed on the terraces that his time would eventually come – as indeed it would – at Liverpool Football Club.

As Liverpool struggled to get out of the English second tier, the game around them was now evolving fast, and they were in danger of falling irreparably behind. In April 1957, a 'slow and listless' Liverpool played 'almost entirely without fire and fight' and lost limply 0–3 at Sheffield United, thus condemning the Merseyside club to yet another season among the also-rans. Tellingly, in the same week the English title holders, Manchester United under Matt Busby, were playing in a newish competition, the European Cup, against the Spanish champions Real Madrid. The great Welshman John Charles was also leaving Britain to sign for the Italians from Juventus for a fee of £10,000. Leslie Edwards in the *Daily Post* railed against this embryonic British player drain and the 'pittance' that even top English players were still paid – £17 was now the maximum wage – compared to their Continental equivalents. This meant that in England 'technicians of the highest class [were] set to work with labourers with the proviso that they should receive labourer's pay'.

In August 1957, the Liverpool players briefly made their own point about the criminally low earnings of English professionals by refusing to pose for pre-season photographs unless they were paid for doing so. But they were soon brought into line again as humble employees rather than the sporting stars some of them were. Leslie Edwards, nodding vigorously at Anfield, also called for a new charter for football managers in English football, saying, 'If a manager contracts to manage, he should be given absolute authority over the team, leaving directors to direct.' No one was listening. But at least Phil Taylor had now been confirmed as the permanent Liverpool manager, for what it was worth.

The last tram operating in Liverpool, the 293 from Pier Head to Bowring Park, made its final journey at 5.55 p.m. on 14 September 1957. The city was finally moving to a new, modern and flexible bus service to meet the anticipated needs of 1960s commuters. There were few signs that the same forward-looking processes of modernisation might soon waken Liverpool Football Club from what appeared to be its interminable post-war slumbers. However, something *was* about to happen at Anfield that would actually change the entire history and direction of the club. But first there was just a little more pain to endure.

SLOW TRAIN COMING – FROM WORCESTER

Modernisation and change in any domain brings risk and the unmetered threat of the unknown. So it was that in February 1958, in a terrible accident at Munich Airport, the guts were wrenched out of a great young Manchester United team challenging in Europe. These were British pioneers who threatened to dominate European club football. Eight players died. As the crowds slopped through the slush-sodden streets of Liverpool 4 to the Second Division Liverpool v. Charlton match on 10 February, according to the *Daily Post*, 'Men's minds were still very much on the Munich tragedy, and the hush that descended on this so boisterous ground when the black armbanded players lined up for the two minutes' silence was almost uncanny.' Liverpool Football Club even offered United the services of two Anfield players to help tide the Old Trafford club over the next few months, a neighbourly lesson from the past for the present.

The long shadow cast by Munich lifted only very slowly from the English game, in what was to prove another generally disappointing season for Liverpool. Chairman T.V. Williams told the Liverpool shareholders that 'the Liverpool Football Club was his sole concern and his whole life', but he had little solace to offer supporters regarding the club's fourth-place finish in the second tier of the Football League. Accordingly, the 1958 Liverpool AGM was typically heavily stage-managed and characterised by a feeling of 'philosophic resignation' – it was over in just 45 unrewarding minutes. Williams also sent an open letter to club shareholders and fans defending the club's (lack of) spending policy and reminding them of the responsibility that the board had to shareholders as well as supporters. It cut little ice, locally. 'Success breeds success, as Wolves and [Manchester] United have proved,' pointed out a Mr A. Mercer in a letter to the *Football Echo*. 'It is high time this great city of ours came out of the wilderness.'

The signing of Jimmy Harrower, a stylish inside-forward bought from Hibernian for £11,000, had at least given the Reds midfield a little more craft – if no more pace – but Liverpool made their, by now usual, unpredictable and inconsistent start to the new league season, playing 'bash-ball' in an opening 3–3 home draw with Grimsby Town and losing 1–2 at Sunderland, with a local young winger Johnny Morrissey getting a rare outing. Significantly, the Reds still relied on the ageing and slowing Billy Liddell for league goals, but Jimmy Melia now weighed in with 21 in 39 matches to lead the field for once. A 0–5 thrashing at Bill Shankly's Huddersfield Town on 4 October 1958 was probably the siren call for Phil Taylor. Some of the Liverpool directors knew and liked the tyro Scot Shankly, and they had noted how he had completely turned around Town, bringing in and improving young future internationals such as Ray Wilson and Denis Law without lashing out on large transfers. In August 1957, Huddersfield had drawn 1–1 at Anfield but should have won, their 'solid, smooth-looking and young' team comparing favourably with a very stodgy Liverpool. Back at Leeds Road, the men from Yorkshire had now quite wrecked the Reds, who were a goal down within a minute and never recovered. After ten matches, Liverpool under Phil Taylor were midtable and going nowhere. The Liverpool board even held a secret emergency meeting after the Terriers' rout, deciding that the club needed more discipline and more experienced coaching support to firm up the current lax Liverpool regime – and, possibly, another new team manager.

After the Huddersfield debacle, a run of eight straight league wins in December and January 1959 actually carried Liverpool up the table to second place, and this might even have saved the beleaguered Liverpool manager his job if it were not for the events of 15 January 1959, the most notorious in the club's, so far unfulfilled, FA Cup history. As the Soviet Union launched the first human being into space, gales and icy storms lashed the English north-west at the start of 1959. The desperate weather welcomed to Liverpool the tough Scotsman Reuben Bennett as the club's new chief coach. Liverpool had actually wanted to appoint Bill Nicholson to the job, but Nicholson had since accepted the team manager's job at Spurs. So the Reds turned to Bennett, who was claimed to be the best coach in Scotland. The Scot had been a sergeant major and physical-training instructor during the war and had been a goalkeeper with Hull City, Queen of the South and Dundee until 1950, then trained and managed Ayr United. Deciding that management wasn't his bag, Bennett had returned to coaching, at Motherwell and Third Lanark, before throwing in his lot with Liverpool.

Tommy Younger described Bennett as 'a quiet unassuming fellow with no regard for publicity'. This reticence was one reason why Bennett had given up on his early football-management ambitions. He was known as a 'believer in a strict training schedule obeyed to the letter', and Bennett became famous with later Liverpool players for his near-deranged hard-man insistence that training grazes could best be cleaned with Brillo Pads and that rubbing a kipper on bruises had its own special medicinal qualities. Albert Shelley would now take care of the treatment room and stores, and Bob Paisley would become the first-team trainer in his place. Phil Taylor's role in coaching and training was much reduced as a result of these changes. He was not consulted on the Shelley demotion or the Bennett appointment, and the move was a clear comment by the Liverpool board on his struggling regime and its supposed failings.

The signs were probably bad when the Liverpool FC Supporters Club premises were broken into early in the new year in 1959. The thieves, obvious music lovers, took a radiogram as well as cash and spirits. But the FA Cup was soon around again to lift local hopes, and 66–1 cup long shots Liverpool were confident, even when they were drawn, banana skin-like, to play away to Worcester City of the north-west section of the Southern League. Where *was* this place? City were already cup giant-killers that season over Millwall. But the Reds were confident, even though Billy Liddell was injured and would be missing his first FA Cup tie for Liverpool since he'd turned professional. Phil Taylor and the board had been brave enough to drop the slowing Liddell for the first time during this current campaign, though the decision had gone down badly with many of the club's frustrated supporters.

Worcester skipper and ex-Manchester City captain Roy Paul and his manager Bill Thompson had watched Liverpool, and they claimed to have identified weaknesses that their own team could exploit. But there seemed little doubt that the major advantage the non-leaguers would have over their league opponents was the very poor state of the sloping George's Lane pitch. 'It is in a mess,' said Thompson, happily. The pitch, according to the *Liverpool Echo*, was 'like iron, a bare, brown board of a surface'. Terrible pitches were part of the folklore of the FA Cup, of course, the graveyard of the elite. A late bid to thaw this icy slab of earth for the due date of 8 January failed, under the wary eyes of manager Taylor and his assistant Bob Paisley, with many of the 4,000 travelling Liverpool fans already on their way down to the south-west. Here at least was a little breathing space.

The match was rescheduled for a Thursday afternoon, and Worcester officials and volunteers spread eleven and a half tons of salt on the pitch to guard it against frost and, no doubt, to try to get the contest on while the weather was as filthy and inhospitable as possible. Certainly, the snow, fog and freezing conditions all around the West Midlands area made it look quite impossible to stage a football match. Only referee Leslie Tirebuck – and the entire Worcester City staff, of course – thought that the rutted, grassless, horribly salted pitch was playable. In short, this was a major football accident waiting to happen, in front of 17,000 gawping ambulance-chasing spectators.

The home team played the dreadful pitch perfectly, banging long balls forward with no pretence at all of trying to play any sort of constructive passing football. By contrast, Liverpool 'tried to play too much football', according to the *Echo*. The more direct approach of the hosts immediately unsettled the visiting defence, which panicked into giving away a goal after just nine minutes. A long ball from Gosling spooked Molyneux, who misplaced his backpass beyond the immobile Younger. A tottering Dick White then tried to retrieve the situation but succeeded only in directing the ball into the path of Skuse, who scored into an empty net. It was all the encouragement the hosts and their supporters needed. At 0–1 at half-time, the Liverpool players were already carrying plenty of cuts and bruises, and Twentyman was struggling with a more serious leg injury. Phil Taylor looked drawn and helpless. It was not the happiest of Reds dressing-rooms.

But help was at hand. Worcester's part-time players now began to get just a little afraid of actually *beating* this historic Football League club. So Liverpool began to make some second-half chances, which Melia and A'Court lamentably missed, while Twentyman hit the Worcester crossbar. Then, with just ten minutes left, another 'amazing combination of mistakes' in Liverpool's defence brought about a second home goal, the killer blow. Both Melia and White had chances to clear before Knowles got away for Worcester on the right wing and crossed low and hard. The retreating White – in the middle of a nightmare, clearly – trying to clear behind, could only blast the ball high into his own net over the helpless Younger. A controversial Liverpool penalty, which Twentyman converted, set up a storming finish that almost had the lot: premature pitch invasions, missile-throwing, constant whistling and a bundle of near-misses – but no more goals. Liverpool were out of the FA Cup, overturned in a town that had never – and probably would never – host a Football League club. It was a very difficult message to swallow.

BEWARE THE MAN FROM GLENBUCK

'A small fire is put out by the wind but a great fire only grows greater'

Anonymous

Phil Taylor was already effectively a dead man walking when the passing away of Elisha Scott in June 1959 reminded all older Liverpool supporters of some of the great title years and the many impressive Liverpool teams of the past. Bert Slater was the latest Liverpool goalkeeper, recruited from Falkirk, with Tommy Younger going in the opposite direction in June 1959. Slater was agile but small for a goalkeeper, and not since Scott himself and Cyril Sidlow just after the war had the club really had a goalkeeper to give confidence to the rest of the Liverpool defence. It again simply showed up the value of the great Elisha and what Liverpool supporters were missing compared to the club's greatest days.

The Liverpool board ritually reported an annual profit (of £3,178) in the summer of 1959 and said that it had offered 'an open cheque for the best player in Britain [generally assumed, in fact, to be £40,000 for Middlesbrough's Brian Clough] but his club would not accept it'. But even the local press was now running out of patience. 'Despite the oft reported statement that Liverpool will not baulk at paying top prices for top players, there is still no action.'

The club was rather luckier in their local scouting activities. And this really was luck rather than the result of some coordinated recruitment strategy laid out by Liverpool Football Club. The ex-Reds defender and club scout Bill Jones was casually watching a local football match in Cheshire when he spotted an outstanding 20-year-old goalscoring forward who had strength and incredible shooting power, a raw talent who had somehow evaded the usual networks of the professional clubs. He immediately put Liverpool onto the case, and the young man concerned signed professional forms at Anfield in July 1959. Occasionally, these good solid football professionals are late developers or else they are initially missed by scouts because they have fears about their lack of speed, poor character or dubious physical attributes. But this case was rather like those inert and incompetent book publishers who would foolishly fail to see the magic of Harry Potter. Jones had struck real gold. He had uncovered a hidden gem, a deadly, hard-running and dedicated forward and a future World Cup-winner, no less. Bill Jones had discovered, for his old football club, the selfless and brilliant Roger Hunt.

Hunt seemed like a natural. He immediately adapted to the tough environment of professional football, and he scored four times in his first five senior outings for Liverpool, from September 1959. Here was the type of goalscorer the Liverpool board had spoken about for so long, and he had arrived – as they had always dreamed he would – free of charge. How ironic for manager Phil Taylor that he would have so little time to work with Hunt and to benefit from the buckets of goals he would score for Liverpool. Because despite his new young star's contribution, when a listless Liverpool drew 1–1 with Portsmouth at Anfield on 24 October 1959 in front of a paltry crowd of 21,075 they were already nine points behind Second Division leaders Aston Villa.

On 28 October 1959, two letters to the *Liverpool Echo* summed up local feelings. Mr K. Dickenson from Belper Street, Liverpool 19, wrote, 'The blunders made by the board in the past have put the team in a dangerous position. A drop to the Third Division is a real possibility. We followers of Liverpool have never had it so bad.' A Mr G. Unwin of Kingsthorne Road, Liverpool 24, agreed, saying, 'Never in the history of the club have their local supporters' spirits and enthusiasm been at such a low ebb. We see no optimism or hope for the future in the present team.' This was bleak stuff, indeed, even for the darkest Liverpool years of the 1930s.

Fortunately, Everton were hardly tearing up the First Division, either. So how do you cheer up your most despondent supporters in times of need? How do you get the local crowd behind you once again? Easy: you sign up the iconic hero of your bitterest local rivals.

The mop-haired, erratic and occasionally terrific 29-year-old Blues centre-forward Dave Hickson had publicly reported himself to be 'not in love with playing for Everton any more', having been dropped by his manager Johnny Carey just once too often. Evertonians howled with disappointment and anger. Hickson wanted to stay in the city, so Liverpool Football Club stepped in, and after some soul-searching and haggling – and to the horror of most Evertonians – Hickson signed for the Reds for that magic figure of the then unofficial Liverpool transfer limit of around £12,000. Liverpool supporters were triumphant. An expectant 49,981 – a 20,000 crowd 'bonus' – turned up to see Hickson trash the Second Division leaders Aston Villa with two goals in his debut in a 2–1 Liverpool win. To rub in this neighbourly larceny, Kopites called Hickson 'the Red Dean' at

Anfield and put it about that thousands of Evertonians had followed their new man across Stanley Park to Liverpool. This felt much better. But the mercurial Hickson was inconsistent, and he had no magic wand, so when Liverpool lost 2–4 at modest Lincoln City in November the letters and grumbling began anew, increasing the pressure on Taylor and the Liverpool board once again. Liverpool had won only six out of seventeen league matches. In the Empire Theatre in Liverpool, comedian Arthur Askey described his new show in November 1959 as 'this indescribable and varied act'. It could easily be applied to the manager's job at Anfield. Change had to come. On 18 November 1959, the *Liverpool Echo* announced what many people had expected to happen since the backroom appointment of Reuben Bennett: Phil Taylor had resigned as the manager of Liverpool Football Club.

Despite all Taylor's problems, this seemed like a strange time to press him to leave his post, especially with both Hickson and Hunt so recently brought on board. Taylor informed the local press that it was the strain of the job that had finally told on him, that he was 'very tired at times' and that 'I have never tried to cause anyone any trouble, and I must say few have caused me concern'. It was the usual apologetic tone from a man who had been uncomplaining but who had never been given the full power of his own office. The Liverpool board announced that they would be interviewing candidates and that applications should be sent to the club's registered office, because stamped letters might alert the press to the locations of those who applied. The board seemed paranoid about the press and the possibility that the club's business might be discussed prematurely in public. But Huddersfield's Bill Shankly was already the man they had in mind. They might well have said as much to Taylor to get the old Liverpool servant to go amicably.

Shankly had first been contacted by the board when Liverpool had appointed Don Welsh back in 1951. But he would not accept the Liverpool directors picking the team, so he was rejected as a candidate. The board now wanted – and got – the Huddersfield manager, not because of Bill Shankly's independence or charisma, but rather because the Scot was beginning to develop the sort of managerial reputation the Liverpool board liked: he was a man known for capably running and reviving football clubs on shoestring budgets.[4] Growing media criticism of football directors was also paving the way for the independent modern football manager.

Always a man for making bold entrances, Shankly introduced himself to the Liverpool players by strutting into the Anfield dressing-room like the American gangsters he loved to imitate and saying, 'Some of you boys have been here too long.'[5] It was a challenging rather than a consensual start, but actually his bark was much worse than his bite and very little changed very quickly at Liverpool on the personnel front. Indeed, Tom Leishman, a long-striding left-half replacement for Geoff Twentyman, who had left to become player–manager at Ballymena United, was signed for £9,000 from St Mirren by T.V. Williams and Syd Reakes between the resignation of Taylor and the appointment of Shankly. The Liverpool board was clearly not going to give up on its powers to sign and transfer players that easily. This new relationship between an ambitious, charismatic, media-friendly young firebrand of a manager and a Liverpool board that some felt was still mired in the attitudes and values of the past would be something worth watching. Liverpool Football Club was about to be awakened from an often desperate nine-year slumber.

CHAPTER 13 REFERENCES

1. Taylor and Ward, *Three Sides of the Mersey*, p. 92
2. Keith, *Bob Paisley*, p. 69
3. A'Court, *My Life in Football*, p. 16
4. Carter, *The Football Manager*, p. 88
5. A'Court, *My Life in Football*, p. 70

14

BILL SHANKLY AND THE
NEW LIVERPOOL

Or How the Liverpool Board Finally
Learned How to Spend Money

'AMONG FOLKS OF MY OWN KIND'

Right from the start, Bill Shankly's brand of exuberant west-of-Scotland popular socialism and collective ambition and the rather penny-pinching, cautious individualism of the English high Conservatives in the Liverpool boardroom were a potentially toxic mix. But the new manager actually liked the Liverpool chairman Tom Williams, and rather than seek out confrontation Shankly, initially at least, simply sought to establish a very different identity for himself inside Liverpool to the 'employee' or 'servant' tag that had been hung like a millstone round the neck of both Welsh and Taylor and many before them. For one thing, Shankly had chosen to have no contract for his £2,500-per-annum position, saying confidently, 'If I cannot do the job, it is up to the people who employ me to do as they wish.' Here was an audacious and principled stand right from the start. For another, Shankly wanted the freedom to manage, precisely the arrangement denied to the men who had gone before him. The Liverpool board swallowed hard, but it would have to get used to this new direction. Shankly especially wanted to establish a sense of personal ownership of the Liverpool project, mainly in two ways: first, through his sheer devotion to the club, its supporters and to the sport – few men *lived* football as Bill Shankly did, few dedicated themselves so totally to the game to the exclusion of family and friends; and, second, by his very practical determination to improve the basic infrastructure of the Anfield stadium and the Liverpool training ground.

When Shankly filled in forms at hotels and elsewhere that asked for details of his place of residence, he often wrote 'Anfield' in the space provided. It felt to him like he lived in the football stadium he had now adopted. Accordingly, he soon started to deal with the Liverpool ground as if it was his own home, a place that 40,000 or more personal and valued friends might be expected to visit every fortnight. So it had to be kept properly spruced up and habitable. He got the Liverpool directors to pay for a pipeline to ensure all the toilets in the ground could be flushed and the pitch could be watered, and he soon had the apprentices and the Liverpool ground staff busy painting walls, staircases and crush barriers. He and Bob Paisley were often discovered by the Liverpool directors – he probably engineered the meetings – late at night inside Anfield painting the toilets or passageways. Paisley even built the dugouts at Liverpool when the traditional box for the brass band sited under the main stand was no longer needed.[1] All this was part of the contract that Shankly felt he had made with the working-class people of Liverpool: to offer them better facilities at the club, facilities that had been allowed to diminish because the Liverpool board had refused to spend on players or regular upgrades.

Another way in which the new manager tried to keep his bargain with local people was to involve them more inside the club by rebuilding the strong bond that used to exist between the club staff and local supporters when Tom Watson and the late Elisha Scott were all-powerful at Liverpool. In many ways, Shankly's presence and style began to epitomise the sort of intimacy that Scott had once engendered with Kopites.

Although the *Liverpool Echo* initially described him, insanely, as 'not a man with the gift of the gab', Shankly actually communicated his enthusiasm and commitment for Liverpool Football Club very well through the local press, which had been starved of decent copy on this score during the troubled recent regimes. Shankly was built for the television age. But he also wanted to maintain the grounded links between players and 'ordinary' people in the city, something that would risk strain with the lifting of the maximum wage in 1961. This was one of the reasons why Shankly liked to invite in local workers, such as Liverpool's dustbin-men, to play football matches against his young apprentices. This was more than simple practice. The message was that no one should be outside the scope of the club and that no player should ever get beyond his station in relation to the people who funded their careers – the manual workers of the city of Liverpool. 'I knew that, by and large, the people who produced that [Kop] roar were men just like myself who lived for the game of football and to whom football was their abiding passion,' Shankly said later. 'I knew that no matter what trials lay ahead I would be at home among folks of my own kind.' He had mixed with passionate Liverpudlians at boxing promotions in the city. Shankly knew about the sheer desire and sporting potential in Liverpool.

Shankly was depicted, cartoonishly, in the local press as a 'sergeant-major with the human touch', the kind of manager who made 'wild claims' about some of his players: he said that Denis Law was 'the best thing on two feet', for example. This was part of the new manager's famed motivational technique, which he later used to 'big up' his Liverpool players and rubbish the opposition, no matter their status. He used to tell his hard men at Liverpool, his leaders on the pitch, 'Don't take any shit from anyone,' and he warned the Scots who came to the club – and he brought in many – never to soften up and never to lose their working-class Scottish accents. He wanted his imports to be proud and impervious to temptations in a city reawakening with the hum of pop culture and youth consumption.

Shankly was suspicious of the new coaching regimes then being established at the FA in the wake of the country's international failings. Simple methods, talent and practice were what really mattered: pass to the nearest red shirt and move for the next pass. This might sound like typical mulish British opposition to modernisation. But the Scot was no simple traditionalist, no blind flag-waver for the British way above all others. As the *Liverpool Echo* put it on 15 December 1959, Shankly's approach would be a real eye-opener to those Liverpool supporters who had been raised on an outmoded and now mundane diet of rough-and-ready British playing styles:

> Shankly is a disciple of the game as played by the Continentals. The man out of possession, he believes, is just as important as the man with the ball at his feet. Continental football is not the lazy man's way of playing soccer. Shankly will aim at incisive forward moves by which Continentals streak through a defence, when it is closed up by British standards. He will make his players learn to kill the ball and move it all in the same action, even when it is hit at them hard and maybe awkwardly; he will make them practise complete mastery of the ball; he will ensure that whatever else they may not learn, it won't be the fundamentals of good soccer.

Notwithstanding the weird journalistic double negative used here, this was quite an agenda, but one pretty clearly stated. It was also an ambitious programme for a club that was still locked in the middle of the English Second Division. In line with Continental standards of professionalism, Shankly suggested flying his team to long-distance away games, such as at Plymouth, and he liked to have modern technology in the treatment room for work on his injured players, even if none of the Liverpool staff seemed quite sure how to use it. Some of this approach could also be applied in new Melwood training regimes, which prioritised much more ball work, the playing of small-sided games and five-a-sides, and the use of punitive training boards arranged into a square to build up control, passing accuracy and stamina.

It had its effects, this new regime. Club captain Ronnie Moran said Liverpool would have soared out of the Second Division much earlier with Shankly involved. He said he learned more in the first three months of Shankly at Liverpool than he had in the previous seven years. New signings were also astonished at the fitness levels demanded under Shankly, Reuben Bennett, Bob Paisley and Joe Fagan. 'No team will field fitter men,' promised Shankly. 'They will all go flat out for 90 minutes.' They did.

Bill Shankly's first competitive match in charge of Liverpool was at home to Cardiff City on 19 December 1959, and 27,291 came to see it – the new manager obviously paled as a crowd draw compared to ex-Everton man Dave Hickson. Shankly desisted from picking the Reds team, leaving that to Bob Paisley. But when right-back John Molyneux cried off with boils on the shin, it was Shankly who decided that the current reserve full-back – the young Welshman Alan Jones – be promoted automatically into the first team. The inexperienced debutant was rinsed in a 0–4 defeat. A 0–3 loss at Charlton immediately followed. But then Shankly found his feet, with six wins and two draws from the next eight league fixtures. A poor run in March 1960 killed off any possible promotion hopes, including a 4–4 draw with Aston Villa after Liverpool had led by four goals – fitness again. A striker strangely called Linnecor then scored a hat-trick in a 1–3 Anfield defeat by Lincoln City (making it an unlikely league double over Liverpool for the Imps). The *Liverpool Echo* reported on the sadness in this match of seeing Billy Liddell 'once the lion of Anfield . . . left out in the cold so often as a player whose active days are numbered'. It was almost as if the great man Liddell had to sign off as a Liverpool player before the new era for the club could begin under the man from Glenbuck.

LIFE AFTER LIDDELL

The demise, finally, of the 1940s and '50s home-based Liverpool hero Liddell – a man whose whole career had been based on modest wages and just two days' training a week to fit in with his accountancy work – corresponded almost exactly with the 1960s consumption boom, the rise of televised sport in Britain, the lifting of the maximum wage and the start of the emergence of football players as authentic sex symbols and televised national celebrities. Liddell's last Liverpool game, for example, would come only a couple of years before the debut of George Best at Manchester United, but the two men looked decades apart in terms of their respective styles and their attitudes to the sport and life. The world was changing again – and fast. The FA even sanctioned Sunday league football at last in 1960, and the Football League Cup was added to the professional football roster in England in the same year. In 1960, too, the city of Liverpool was also announced as one of the host cities for the 1966 World Cup finals.

In the Liverpool press, meanwhile, flashy advertising for home goods and services – cars, televisions, twin-tub washing machines, bank loans, hi-fidelity music systems, 'luxury' underwear – now challenged news stories for space. In November 1960, the first bona fide pop acts started playing at a little-known Liverpool nightclub called the Cavern.[2] Soon its local products would stun the world. An upstart supermarket company called Tesco made a £2-million takeover bid for John Irwin and Sons grocery stores in the north-west, American-style skyscraper blocks appeared on Merseyside, and more were planned. This was the modern world.

By April 1960, still in his first season and with promotion no longer an issue, Bill Shankly could begin to experiment with some of the young talent he was beginning to scrutinise at the club. He had watched plenty of reserve and A- and B-team football already at Liverpool, and now he wanted to throw some youngsters into the first team to see if they could swim. Liverpool-born left-back Gerry Byrne's career was one of those that was hugely affected by the new manager's arrival. Byrne had been transfer-listed and unwanted under Phil Taylor, but now he was in the Liverpool first team under Shankly, heading for league and FA Cup medals and eventually a place in the 1966 England World Cup squad. So, too, was the just 18-year-old right-winger Ian Callaghan from Caryl Gardens, Liverpool, who was also en route to a record 857 appearances for Liverpool Football Club. Callaghan played brilliantly and received a standing ovation on his debut, a 4–0 Anfield walloping of Bristol Rovers.

The stocky Liverpool-born wing-half Bobby Campbell was also getting his chance, though he would later make his name in the game more as a football manager than he ever would as a player. In June, Shankly managed to wring a record £13,000 out of the Liverpool board to buy Kevin Lewis, a 19-year-old right-sided goalscoring winger/forward from Sheffield United, and then in August 1960 he brought in Gordon Milne, another record at £16,000, a polished and tough little right-half who joined from Preston North End. Shankly had been a neighbour of the Milnes, a football family, and he had watched this kid grow up to become a 'right-living, right-thinking boy. He neither smokes nor drinks.' Here, already, were the beginnings of the new Liverpool.

At the suddenly interesting 1960 Liverpool AGM, Bill Shankly 'played a blinder', according to the *Liverpool Echo*. The new manager said that he felt he had the full support of the board and that he thought a 'new chapter had begun at Anfield'. He called on the supporters and shareholders to 'forget the past . . . all the hard luck stories. I am sure success will come much sooner than some people anticipate.' No one had ever heard a Liverpool manager talk like this at an AGM, at least not since Tom Watson before the First World War. There was real applause at the boldness and style of the manager's delivery. Here was a Liverpool boss, at last, who was definitely his own man. Maybe this was real change, a new future? There would still be ructions, of course, especially when the Liverpool board tried to buy and sell players, thus provoking Shankly to threaten to resign on a number of occasions. But things did seem to be changing at Anfield. Even the Reds supporters had a voice of sorts now at the Liverpool high table: a Solly Isenwater spoke from the floor for the newly formed Liverpool Shareholders Association, though he raised only minor issues: ticket prices for OAPs and had Liverpool by any chance bought a copy of the film of Real Madrid's extraordinary 7–3 destruction of Eintracht Frankfurt in the 1960 European Cup final at Hampden Park?

To puncture this excitement just a little, Liverpool reported a loss of £4,918 due to a fall in attendances that was attributed to wider social and cultural processes connected to rising car ownership and televised sport. Football was now part of the 'entertainment business', and there had even been talk in football circles in 1960 of a possible British 'super league', while television coverage of floodlit English and European football was now a very live and present issue. Liverpool's average home gate had held up pretty well for a club in the Second Division, in the light of all of this, at 30,269. But even in the relegation season of 1953–54, First Division home gates at Anfield had averaged 40,488, which meant a 25 per cent fall in crowds over six years. English football as a whole had been losing supporters, year on year, but everyone at Anfield knew that a promotion campaign and a return to First Division football would bring some of the crowds back to Liverpool. Could this enthusiastic young Scot, a man who liked boxing, hard-man American cinema heroes and wilfully short holidays up the north coast in Southport and Blackpool, really work the oracle?

It wouldn't happen right away. Billy Liddell's final competitive match for Liverpool was at centre-forward in a 0–1 home defeat against Southampton on 31 August 1960, when the great man was clearly 'out of touch'. It looked as if Shankly might even have given Billy this final competitive league game at home to say goodbye to the Anfield crowd. The new manager admired Liddell as a great Scotland international, and he was not beyond a touch of sentiment in deserving cases. But without Liddell, who would offer Liverpool a spark? When a labouring Reds side beat Scunthorpe at home 3–2 on 18 September, it was a 'lifeless, uninspiring, untidy display', and there was slow handclapping on the Kop. A crowd of 38,789 then turned out on a filthy Liverpool night to salute Liddell in his testimonial match, launched by a magnificent 16-page *Liverpool Echo* souvenir in which Danny Blanchflower best described the Scot as 'a wonderful, stirring, awesome force, liable to erupt at any moment'. The club would never see his like again.

With Billy now celebrated and gone, and after a poor start in the league, Liverpool went on a 14-match unbeaten run to take them up to second place behind Sheffield United at Christmas, until a 0–1 defeat at Rotherham on 28 December broke the spell, with police climbing into the crowd at the end 'to deal with a fight between rival supporters'. When Liverpool lost at home 3–4 to Middlesbrough on 2 January 1961, with a brilliant Brian Clough scoring twice, police ended up patrolling the goal areas after the visiting goalkeeper Appleby had been struck in the face by a coin thrown from the crowd. Liverpool's crowd problems had not disappeared.

Sunderland had just too much know-how for the Reds in the FA Cup a few weeks later, and it would prove another near-miss in the league for Liverpool, confirmed when Norwich City downed Shankly's men 1–2 at Carrow Road on 17 April 1961. Liverpool finished third again, behind Ipswich Town and Sheffield United. But things were finally taking shape. Byrne, Lewis and Hunt were all now established in the Liverpool first XI, and Milne and Callaghan were gradually being eased into first-team football. This was real progress, a talented young player base already established. Bert Slater in goal and Dick White at centre-half both played 42 matches, and John Molyneux played 39 at right-back, but 58 goals conceded were too many advantages lost for the Liverpool coaches and manager to endure. Dave Hickson scored a respectable 16 goals in 33 matches, but he lacked the real pace and cleverness needed to help open up rival defences in the modern era. Bill Shankly had much still to do to get his squad in the sort of shape he wanted.

GOODBYE, CRUEL WORLD

'In my opinion, Liverpool can, and will, be one of the leading 12 clubs in the country.' This was Bill Shankly talking in 1960 at the Liverpool Football Club AGM. What was he thinking of? Today, this kind of claim would seem ludicrously unambitious coming out of Anfield. But in the early 1960s, these words, thunderously spoken in that characteristic west-of-Scotland growl, at least offered Reds fans a brighter football future. Here was some hope, at last, of a release from the icy wastes of a barren decade. They believed in Bill Shankly, and he fed upon their energy and hope. So did club captain Ronnie Moran, to whom Shankly had cleverly written a long letter explaining his approach to management before even coming to Anfield. The President of the Hungarian FA, Sandor Barcs, seemed less sure about the talents of British football managers. He had scoffed at club training in England in August 1960, saying that many British coaches 'still seem to be living in the age of your dear old Stephenson, who invented the steam engine'.

Liverpool Football Club had certainly seemed to be locked in the Dark Ages during their post-war slide. They had been conservative, unimaginative and rigid, both on and off the pitch. It was a team poorly led, cheaply recruited and badly selected by the club's directors. Training facilities at Liverpool were abject. This was quite unlike the set-up at dashing and successful Manchester United, where its brilliant, recovering young manager Matt Busby had already been in charge for more than a decade. Liverpool had been stuck in the outdated training doldrums, shamed in their shambolic training ground and its holed and ragged austerity training kit, under the 'nice' but deferential and undemanding Phil Taylor and his predecessors. But here was real change. The new Melwood coaching team – Reuben Bennett as head coach, Bob Paisley as first-team trainer and Joe Fagan as reserves trainer – was hard-nosed, but it was also young and dynamic and full of imaginative work and new ideas. It just needed a whirlwind, a catalyst such as Bill Shankly, to galvanise and release them from the clutches of the inert Liverpool board. And now he had arrived.

Reuben Bennett was the fitness man. He pounded out merciless laps at Melwood with the players, building up their reserves of strength and mocking the freezing cold weather. Joe Fagan had been recommended to Liverpool by Harry Catterick, who was then manager at Rochdale, and Bill Shankly had once tried to sign him as a player for Grimsby Town. He was kindly, a listener, but also a very sharp football man and a good coach. But Bob Paisley was to be the key backroom character. Bob had grown up at Anfield, of course, and had studied physiotherapy towards the end of his playing career. The Liverpool directors got him informal access into Merseyside hospitals so that he could study the mechanics of the human body close up. He was one of the few trainers in the Football League in the 1950s to have any kind of medical training, a major step-up from Albert Shelley's shambolic cursing and cold-water-bucket treatments. Paisley even managed to get the club to buy some of the latest heat and sonic equipment for the treatment of muscle injuries. It was a little like bringing the vestiges of science to bear on otherwise primitive communities.

The first of these machines was known enigmatically at Anfield simply as 'the Electric'. Many injured players were so reluctant to try it out that Paisley was happy to trial it on the pet dogs of people passing by Anfield.[3] Suspicion of being consigned to the Anfield treatment room and its supposed barbaric practices would survive well into the 1980s.[4] Paisley had some of the same communitarian, northern-village, working-class values of his new manager, if little of Shankly's communication skills and chutzpah. Paisley often compared the physiology and mental make-up of top football players to thoroughbred racehorses. He thought they had a common athletic 'edginess', and Bob became very well known among the players for his intuitive capacity to diagnose injuries from simply watching them stand or walk, much as he would sum up the runners in the paddock for the 5.15 race at nearby Haydock Park. Great footballers implicitly trusted their bodies and their careers to him, and Liverpool developed a deserved reputation as a club whose footballers simply did not get injured – or at least hid their injuries well.

Paisley was no great talker or motivator – Shankly did all of that stuff. Frankly, Bob's musings were near-incomprehensible to most. And he was no trusted counsellor for the players – this was Joe Fagan's job. But Bob did have to keep the impact of the local nightlife on Liverpool's players in check, a generally uneven contest. And he even had to paint out the white Adidas stripes on the players' boots – no English club yet had endorsements with any kit manufacturers. But most of all Bob was a dispassionate and quietly brilliant assessor of footballers, focusing on their mental and physical make-up equally, making sure that Liverpool Football Club recruited men who were courageous winners as well as having a physique that was up to the brutal task of playing large numbers of high-tempo, intensive British football matches. Players could only show their worth to Liverpool if they were out on the pitch. Famously, Shankly believed that footballers who were injured were being disloyal to him and to Liverpool Football Club, and he found little time to sympathise or even to talk with them. 'Good players don't get injured,' he liked to say.[5] Indeed, it is generally assumed that Liverpool had fewer injuries than most other clubs at this time, in part because players had real difficulty in telling Shankly, face to face, that they were incapacitated. Better to play on in pain and hold your place than to have to tell the man from Glenbuck that your body had let him – and Liverpool Football Club and its fans – down.

This kind of backroom collective expertise – the core of the later famous Liverpool 'boot room', of course – was a more than useful legacy for the relatively inexperienced Bill Shankly to inherit. It was one offered up to him by the much criticised Liverpool directors. He had to concede that Tom Williams and his colleagues had at least chosen the club's backroom staff incredibly well, even if they were often hopeless at selecting and signing players. Shankly reported in the local press that, in time, he and his coaching team had 'reorganised the whole training system' at Melwood. First, gone were the rag-arsed training outfits. Were these professional footballers or tramps? 'Every phase and detail was planned,' said Shankly, 'so we could move swiftly from one function to another.' After about a year spent eyeing things up, checking on all the club's players and facilities, 'everything changed', said the young Roger Hunt. 'Suddenly, everyone seemed to be walking about with a new sense of purpose.'[6] Alan A'Court noticed a sea change, too, but only after Shankly had carefully sized up the job. 'In no time at all, both Anfield and Melwood were buzzing with an electric atmosphere. It was rather as if you were on board a powerful new racing car and he had just switched on the engine.'[7]

Gone was the disorganisation and easy-going atmosphere at Liverpool training. Notes were taken and kept on the effectiveness of different training routines, and players were graded and trained in groups because, as Shankly put it, 'different players require different exercises and quantity of training'. No eating facilities were built at Melwood, because Shankly wanted his players to cool down on the coach journey back to Anfield before they ate. These daily coach trips also helped to bolster banter and team spirit. This was mainly informal but actually very advanced football thinking in England for the time, the sort of detailed preparation designed to help the Liverpool coaches 'size up the requirements of individuals to reach and retain peak fitness'. There was not a sign of Stephenson's *Rocket* steam engine in sight.

Shankly's approach to playing the game was best described by the phrase 'continuous movement'. It came from his old Huddersfield boss Andy Beattie, who had stressed the importance of instant control and moving the ball quickly. The emphasis was on organised fluidity within a team structure: players being constantly available for the next pass and having the highest possible levels of fitness. Shankly was not interested at all in set-pieces; he thought they were static and ugly and too dependent on luck and players' instincts. So Liverpool never practised them. When the team did try out something for free-kicks in a match situation, it invariably ended up in chaos. Shankly was keen on psychology and tactics but not on how the coaching men from the FA taught mental preparation and the new theories of the game and its systems. He barely lasted a couple of sessions on FA coaching courses at Lilleshall. He hated the new technocratic language of football, of 'overlapping full-backs' and the 'penetrative through-ball'.[8]

THESE NAMES MADE NEWS

Standing — Mr. W. Harvey Webb (director), Freddie Hopkin, A. G. Whitehurst, Gordon Hodgson, Charlie Wilson, Elisha Scott, Jimmy McDougall, W. Miller, the late Mr. W. H. Cartwright (director).
Sitting — Dave Davidson, Dick Edmed, James Jackson, Donald McKinlay (captain), Tom Morrison, Tom Bromilow

Liverpool FC in transition: the 1928–29 squad. Gordon Hodgson and Jimmy McDougall (either side of Elisha Scott) were key figures. The intemperate little master Scott and defender James 'Parson' Jackson (three from left, front row) were not always on the same wavelength in Liverpool's creaky back line into the 1930s.

The globalising game: an urbane-looking Liverpool squad in transit for the tour to Sweden in 1939 under George Kay (far left). Matt Busby is sixth from left, just behind the blond Tom Cooper, who would be a fatality of the war. Strange football times beckoned during the conflict.

A young – and decidedly Goth-looking – Bob Paisley gets stuck in on the Anfield car park just after the war.

Walking off the effects of war: Liverpool players troop around Anfield during a less-than-strenuous 1940s training session.

'Film star' post-war centre-forward Albert Stubbins tracks his son, Eric. The toddler also travelled to Wembley in 1950 and was comforted by winning captain (and Anfield interloper) Joe Mercer.

Billy Liddell greets the locals on Liverpool's title-preparing 1946 summer tour of the USA. The Reds only went stateside to get some decent food – and it did the trick.

Willie Fagan (in the suit), Albert Stubbins (centre), a rather dubious-looking Billy Liddell, and the ailing Reds chairman Billy McConnell (far left) finally claim the league-championship trophy of 1947. The title came only after a lengthy wait to see off Stoke City's challenge.

Jackie Balmer, Liverpool's captain just after the war, enters the fray under the ever-watchful eye of the bizzies. Not everyone's hero, perhaps, Balmer was undoubtedly a great Liverpool post-war goalscorer under manager George Kay.

Up for the Cup. Blackpool's strange 'Atomic Boys' meet the Liverpool faithful, sixth round of the FA Cup, 4 March 1950. No dressing up the fact that Liverpool won, 2–1.

The defeated 1950 Liverpool cup-final squad manage to secure a piped entrance and a fluffy mascot – but, crucially, no FA Cup.

The Liverpool dressing-room in the early 1950s. FA Cup final despair came before the slide into the Second Division began. From left to right: Ray Lambert, Kevin Baron, Laurie Hughes, Bob Paisley, Jimmy Payne, Bill Jones, Eddie Spicer, Phil Taylor and Billy Watkinson.

Selling the *Echo* outside the Kop in 1957. Football grounds in the '50s were often inhospitable and potentially dangerous places.

Roger Hunt's goals helped Liverpool out of the Second Division and were crucial to the successes of the 1960s.

The comfort of strangers: stricken Reds winger Alan A'Court is offered tea and sympathy by the humorously concerned patrons of the Kop.

All quiffed up and somewhere to go, the stylish new Liverpool begins to take shape. Manager Bill Shankly (rear) amongst his men before a Reds training session in 1962.

The FA Cup at last, after 73 hard years of trying. The 1965 triumph (2–1) over Leeds United is celebrated by the Liverpool players – with pints of milk and a fag.

The Reds off to conquer Europe in 1965 – but Bill Shankly was duped by Helenio Herrera and Inter Milan.

Bill Shankly says his long goodbyes in 1974. His was no easy passing for Liverpool, but his apprentice Bob Paisley took over the mantle and won three European Cups.

Jimmy Case and Phil Neal get some serious kissing action on the 1977 European Cup, in Rome, the start of a run of European successes under Bob Paisley and then Joe Fagan.

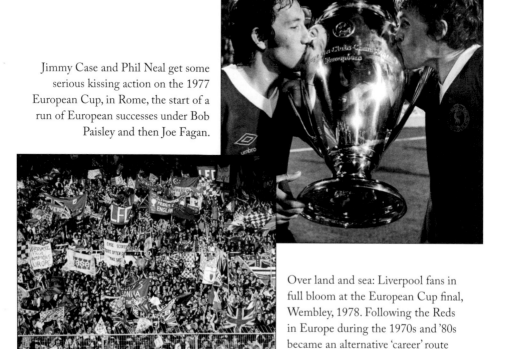

Over land and sea: Liverpool fans in full bloom at the European Cup final, Wembley, 1978. Following the Reds in Europe during the 1970s and '80s became an alternative 'career' route for many in the city.

The healing after Hillsborough: Liverpool drew 0–0 at Goodison to get restarted and then beat Everton 3–2 in an emotional first all-Merseyside FA Cup final in 1989.
A tragic year – and for much more than just football.

Liverpool Football Club greats, past and present: the extraordinary Billy Liddell meets the brilliant Kenny Dalglish.

The new global Liverpool. But could Steven Gerrard, Fernando Torres, Dirk Kuyt and others finally deliver that elusive Premier League title? (© Getty Images).

Magnetic discs representing opponents would be theatrically swept off a metal pitch-board in team meetings at Melwood, the Liverpool manager aping frustration that he could find nothing positive at all to say about these pitiful rivals or that he was wasting his time even trying. The tenor and style of his own football team talks he attributed to his early coal-mining experiences, which had taught him that brashness or humour could relax men for the physical and dangerous task at hand. Many of the players in the Liverpool dressing-room came from the same, northern manual working-class roots as the people from Glenbuck.[9]

A pre-match tactical session at Liverpool properly evoked the comradeship and cod-democracy of the past: football matches in England were peacetime battles to be won by skill, fortitude and brave hearts – and through trust in your own ability and in your teammates. Toughness was central to all this: poor or uncommitted opponents had 'a heart as big as a caraway seed'. Whenever his own football 'hard men' were growing cocky or showing weakness, Shankly would simply throw photographs of real-life American gangsters onto the dressing-room table, saying that *these* guys had it really tough – they could be shot for making mistakes.[10] There was little room for fancy tactics or any consciously planned strategy. In 1962, Shankly told the *Liverpool Echo*:

> It is not my function to stand in front of a blackboard haranguing the lads.
> A tactical session is more like a good discussion group in the Forces, with
> me as the officer leading it . . . I start the ball rolling, but anybody who has
> anything to say knows that he is expected to say it.

The Second World War had been over for some 17 years, but its influence – in the wartime training and fitness regimes established for young men and the uplifting spirit and camaraderie ingrained in the Forces and that could still be experienced in national service – was hugely formative for Bill Shankly and Bob Paisley and for other football men of their generation. Its impact and memories lingered long as a contributing feature of coaching in the British game. Even in the brash and brand-new 1960s, most young footballers in England still had to complete their two years in the Forces before they could commit themselves entirely to their professional clubs. But who could say what a football future might hold without the threat or the remnants of war?

There were certainly some free-thinkers on the subject still around at Anfield. 'Nothing is more certain than in time we shall see a European league established,' confided Billy Liddell in his newly published autobiography. 'In another decade or so, rail and coach travel will be as outmoded as stage-coaches are today.'[11]

This sort of visionary 'blue sky' thinking was clearly not always exactly right on the button: players never did travel to European fixtures in helicopters that disembarked them inside the stadium as the saintly Billy had predicted. But the retiring Liddell had certainly seen part of the future. Within four years, Liverpool Football Club under Bill Shankly would be travelling to Iceland to begin a rollicking adventure with Europe's football elite that would last for much of the next four decades. It would eventually bring five European Cups and other European baubles back to Anfield. Few people in the early 1960s – except perhaps Bill Shankly himself – could have predicted that. But first he would have to convince the notoriously frugal Liverpool board to start spending big money. As it turned out, he would receive help to deal with this once-intractable problem from a rather unexpected source.

HEY, BIG SPENDERS

Bill Shankly and his staff now had to drag the Reds out of the English Second Division – and the Liverpool board, kicking and screaming, out of its transfer-fee torpor. Littlewoods Pools man and Eccles-born Blues supporter John Moores had taken over as chairman at stumbling Everton in 1960, promising to pump big money into the Goodison club. Moores was true to his word, and after appointing Harry Catterick as manager in 1961 Everton won their first post-war league title in 1963, mainly on the back of the new chairman's free-spending. But the Moores family also held shares in Liverpool Football Club, and John Moores was a bridge partner of the Reds chairman T.V. Williams. Moores gently chided Williams about Liverpool's parsimonious transfer spending. He thought the Anfield club had to show a little more initiative and willingness to take risks in its transfer dealings if it wanted to progress.

John Moores decided to place his own nominee, Eric Sawyer, on the Liverpool board. The shrewd Sawyer was in charge of accounts at Littlewoods, and he became the financial director at Liverpool in 1961, with a mandate from Moores to start loosening up the Anfield purse strings. John Moores was no commercial mug. He was a man of expansive vision and some daring who told the *Football Echo* in December 1960 that he had even tried to bring the Hungarian master Ferenc Puskás to Everton in the 1950s but had faced opposition to his plans from the conservatives at the FA, the Football League and the Home Office. The lifting of the maximum wage in 1961 and the challenges from the players' union to the retain-and-transfer system that would finally succeed in 1963 promised more movement of top British players to football clubs that were free-spending, ambitious and progressive. Everton would buy more than their fair share of stars in this new age for football. But Moores wanted to see both of the major football clubs in the city of Liverpool become successful and competitive in this new television and marketised era for the game. After all, the turnstiles at the Glasgow clubs Rangers and Celtic, and at City and United in Manchester, rattled best when these bitter local rivals were both winning and snapping at each other's heels. In a period of dramatically falling gates in England, having Liverpool FC near-dormant in the Second Division and apparently refusing to pay top dollar for top talent was simply bad for football business in Merseyside. This was felt even across Stanley Park at the Football League champions-elect from Goodison Park. Something had to change.

The modern Liverpool FC transfer revolution finally began in the spring of 1961, some 15 long years after the title-winning capture of Albert Stubbins from under Everton's nose in 1946. Sawyer and Moores were right behind the new Anfield buying policy, helping to steer it through. Before the transfer deadline, Liverpool had again offered £40,000, plus a £10,000 promotion bonus this time, to Middlesbrough to sign star centre-forward Brian Clough. But the bid was again rejected; Clough would move to Sunderland. Frustrated, Bill Shankly then spotted a small item in the Scottish sports press early in May 1961. The story said that Motherwell's young Scotland international Ian St John was being made available for transfer. He blinked. St John was a deep-lying centre-forward who positively bristled with intelligence, youthful aggression and energy. He was a man Shankly had been tracking for close on two years in the hope that one day he would become available. The Motherwell forward might be better even than Brian Clough – and he was a Scot.

But signing Ian St John for Liverpool would cost. The manager first phoned up the Motherwell secretary to ensure this was no set-up. He then collected Syd Reakes and Tom Williams to check that his own club was in big-spending mode. He wanted no sticking points on money, though Shankly actually had no experience of big-money signings before coming to Liverpool. The biggest transfer deal he had been involved in elsewhere was for just £4,000. The trio then drove in Reakes's Rolls-Royce to watch St John play against Hamilton Academical that same evening, sweeping into Fir Park like land-grabbers. At half-time, the clubs' respective directors went into negotiations, and just after midnight a deal was struck. Charlie Mitten, the manager of Newcastle United, had been sniffing around the Scottish centre-forward, but he turned up too late to start an auction. Ian St John and his wife Betsy, meanwhile, sat outside the boardroom whispering like nervous patients in a surgery waiting room.

The young Scot did not finally agree to sign for Liverpool before the couple had been driven to Merseyside and shown a club house under construction in 'salubrious' Maghull, where they might live in comfort with their new baby. The areas of Maghull and West Derby were regarded as close enough to Melwood for players to make it into training, even without a car. Seeing what the club had planned was enough. The St Johns were living in a pokey flat in Motherwell, and the £1,000 signing-on bonus Liverpool had promised to pay him would buy a new Vauxhall and some furniture. The Anfield board had finally learned to bend the rules a little.

Although a full international, St John was still playing part-time football in Scotland, and while Liverpool was a Second Division club it was one that had big plans – and a fast-talking, utterly charismatic Scottish manager who wouldn't take no for an answer. St John also knew and admired Reuben Bennett from his Motherwell days, so Liverpool Football Club seemed something like a home from home to him.

This signing was a sea change in Liverpool's post-war fortunes and particularly the club's intent. Above all, the brash, young Ian St John symbolised the arrival of the 1960s at Anfield. He had the swagger and the confidence to challenge authority, and the irreverent youthful style that underpinned wider social changes in Britain, and which would soon produce a wonderful surge of working-class musical creativity in the city. On the pitch, St John produced real verve and invention – and the sheer devil that had been missing from the Liverpool team for a decade or more. Off it, he was at the forefront of many of the illicit adventures involving the club's players in the new fleshpots and nightclubs at home and abroad. Bob Paisley would soon be on his case.

Not that his new club was offering St John anything like the wages now reportedly available elsewhere. Unlike at some other clubs, where selected international players were immediately moved from £20 to £100 a week after the lifting of maximum wage, Bill Shankly wanted all of his players to be locked onto the same basic wage in order to maintain a common purpose and a sense of natural justice – it was a nod to his strong belief that 'team spirit was a form of socialism'. Shankly had picked up his political ideas, and the importance of local togetherness and a sense of community, from his early years in the village of Glenbuck, and especially from the effects on local people of the privations of the General Strike (when Shankly was just 12 years of age).[12] Keeping all players' wages level was also a way of keeping costs down, of course, and of making more money available to him for transfers. Wages paid to players by Liverpool rose to £35,595 in 1961–62 compared to £29,635 the previous season, suggesting that players' salaries at Anfield rose by around 17 per cent in the first season of the lifting of the maximum wage, hardly the catastrophe some clubs might have feared at a time when the wages of manual workers were also rising.

The brash and ambitious Ian St John was rather less politically minded than Shankly, and he told the local press on signing for Liverpool, 'I like money. Who doesn't?' In fact, the Saint later reported that, depressed by his low early wages, he had once been involved in negotiations to fix a match for cash in Scotland but the deal was called off. He now happily accepted the new arrangements at Anfield and its crude equality principle.[13]

So, at the very moment that the USA was sending its first man into space, Liverpool Football Club also seemed to be sailing into orbit. 'Boy, what a ride!' the Yankee spaceman Alan Shepard told the world's press in blaring front-page headlines that week. It could easily have been Bill Shankly enthusing to his new signing and his prospective Kop worshippers about the glorious Liverpool future he was now planning for them all. Shankly had more than doubled the club's previous transfer record by getting the Liverpool board to spend £37,500 on a little-known Scottish steel-mill worker. Eric Sawyer had clinched the deal by telling those fellow Anfield directors who wavered, 'I don't see, if we have real ambition, how we can afford not to do it.' This was precisely the sort of 'spend to accumulate' philosophy that the club seemed to have been resisting for much of the 1950s. Sawyer was willing to back Bill Shankly's judgement all the way.

The league fixtures were already done, but on 8 May 1961 Liverpool faced Everton in the Liverpool Senior Cup final, and St John made his debut. A crowd of 51,669 turned up to watch a thrilling and bruising encounter. According to the *Daily Post*, 'Some of the tackling was out of this world and certainly well out of the rule books.' It was a good test. The new Liverpool man was up against Brian Labone, a player who was fast emerging as one of England's toughest and best young centre-halves. St John confused and then terrorised him, completing a hat-trick in the last minute of a hugely promising 3–4 Liverpool defeat. Shankly at least had something positive to take to the 1961 Liverpool AGM, where he blamed the accumulated tension of seven years of trying for the latest Liverpool promotion failure. 'What a tonic it was to see him [St John] play against Everton in the Senior Cup,' Shankly said, sparkling at the memory of his new man's debut. He knew promotion was now in reach.

But the members of the Liverpool Supporters Association who were present at the AGM displayed an unusual 'underlying annoyance', arguing that the Liverpool board had, as normal, acted too little, too late, and that it should be condemned for its inaction and latest promotion failure. For once, the usually unflappable Tom Williams lost his temper. He rose to his feet and bellowed, 'Rubbish!', claiming that the Anfield directors had travelled hundreds of miles in the season to look for new players. He was agitated and angry, especially having been pressed by Eric Sawyer so recently to lay out a cool £37,500 for a new untried centre-forward. A Mr Adler then jumped up from the floor and shouted that this was no way for the chair to talk to the club's shareholders, and he called for a vote of no confidence in Williams. This was real drama.

Meanwhile, Bill Shankly looked on, both intrigued and impressed: these supporters had guts as well as loyalty. It was the first real sign of a direct challenge by the club's followers to the Liverpool board, but Adler could get no seconder for his resolution. The meeting eventually calmed down, with Williams, Syd Reakes and Clifford Hill all being re-elected unopposed. The storm had quickly blown over, but it was probably the most exciting – and the most disharmonious – AGM in the entire history of the club as a limited company so far. At last something was brewing at Liverpool Football Club.

HEADING FOR PROMOTION

Bill Shankly now had the front-end and the middle of his new team pretty much sorted out. Ian St John would be the perfect foil for Roger Hunt, a man to link up defence and attack, but also a centre-forward who would score his share of goals. The Saint had once scored a hat-trick in 150 seconds in Scotland. But the deep-lying St John would not deprive Hunt of the vital penalty-area oxygen – the space – the inside-right needed to complete his own deadly work. Kevin Lewis or the young Ian Callaghan would deliver the bullets from the right wing, and the England international Alan A'Court was a more than reliable provider on the left. In midfield, Jimmy Melia was clever and consistent, a goalscoring, balding little general, and Gordon Milne would grow into his work on the right. The experienced, long-striding Tommy Leishman would be the defensive anchor, balancing on the left side for Milne's inexperience.

At the back, the Reds full-backs Gerry Byrne and Ronnie Moran were rugged and solid enough – Byrne was not allowed to tackle in the training five-a-sides on Fridays at Melwood because he was just too brutal and people were liable to get injured. But the Liverpool defence still lacked a pivot and a leader, a real physical presence. The young Jack Charlton was an early target. Shankly had also tried to tap up Leicester City's Scotland captain Frank McLintock for the role, even dragging him out of the club banquet on the night City lost to Spurs in the 1961 FA Cup final. McLintock declined, joining Arsenal instead. Bill Shankly typically rubbished the Scot for his audacity – and stupidity – and he turned his attention to Scotland once again, carrying with him Eric Sawyer's best wishes and the once little-seen chequebook of Liverpool Football Club.

Ron Yeats was from Aberdeen, but he was a Rangers fan. In junior football at 14 years of age he had been converted to centre-half from left wing-half, and the growth spurt that followed confirmed him as a left-sided defensive stopper rather than the sort of guy who stepped out from the back, as an Alex Raisbeck might or as Alan Hansen was to do brilliantly a decade later for Liverpool. Yeats had happily worked on shifts as a slaughterman from 15 years of age, and he enjoyed the toughness and the camaraderie of the job – it certainly paid more than part-time professional football ever did in Scotland. When he signed for Dundee United in 1957, he typically went to work at 2.30 a.m. on Saturday mornings, clocked off at 11 a.m., grabbed a few hours' sleep and then played football. After just twenty-eight United appearances, Yeats went on to do two years' National Service in the Royal Army Service Corps, including captaining the British Army football team in a match against Liverpool. Bill Shankly took note.

But when Shankly and his directors first travelled to Dundee to discuss a deal for the huge centre-half, they were greeted with what the manager later called an 'arctic reception'. But they persisted, and when his club recalled Yeats to Edinburgh in July 1961, saying that a 'big' English club wanted to sign him, the centre-half dreamed, naturally, about Manchester United, Arsenal or Spurs. He knew nothing about Second Division Liverpool or their slightly deranged Scottish manager. But his managers at Dundee United had always been grimy and insecure, only just above the shop-floor culture of the Tannadice dressing-room. By contrast, Liverpool's Bill Shankly had the glossy, almost corporate or even film-star air of a man really going places. Here was a man who had his red ties specially made for him in Germany. Shankly made a big first impression on Ron Yeats when they first met:

> I always remember this: he was a lovely dresser: lovely suit and tie, and white, white teeth. That really impressed me. And then he's walking round me, I can hear him at the back of me and he says, 'Jesus Christ, son, you must be about seven feet tall!' And when he comes back to the front, I said, 'No, I'm only six foot two,' and he said, 'That's near enough fucking seven foot to me!' I thought, there and then, I *like* this man.[14]

Shankly talked up the Hollywood looks and especially the sheer size of Ron Yeats into the defining feature of his new £30,000 signing by inviting journalists to marvel at the supposed immense scale of his 23-year-old centre-half. It was psychology, of course, more than anything else. Yes, 6 ft 2 in. was big, but it was hardly super-giant class. Yeats was also broad and powerful, but there were plenty of other big men in the English game, and the Scot's scoring record for a big centre-half was actually quite unimpressive. Nor was he a great shouter or a natural organiser on the pitch – he was deceptively quiet and reserved, a rather gentle man. But Shankly wanted opponents to *feel* that this guy was huge, a colossus; he wanted them to fear Yeats for his physique and his alleged bullying temperament before they even saw him lining up against them. Generally, it worked. Ron Yeats certainly made people sit up and take notice. Liverpool director Syd Reakes was so excited about the signing of 'Big Rowdy' that he insisted on doing all the driving himself back from Edinburgh with no stops, not even for a cup of tea.

Now Shankly had his new side – Byrne, Milne, St John, Hunt and Yeats were the core – and he was almost completely in charge of it. At last, some 47 years after the death of Tom Watson, probably the last man to have some real freedom in team selection at Anfield, Liverpool's directors would talk, from now on, mainly about the stadium and the club's finances and not about Liverpool's players or the team set-up. There would be no more weekly submitting of the proposed line-up to the board for its approval and changes. Molyneux was out, and Dick White was immediately moved by Shankly from centre-half to right-back. With Byrne, Yeats and Tommy Leishman also regularly in the Liverpool team, this was now a physically imposing but mobile new defensive shield. The age of the Reds' first-team squad had also been reduced radically from that under Phil Taylor in 1959 – Byrne, Yeats, Milne, Hunt, St John, Lewis and Callaghan were all in their early 20s or younger. In the Liverpool reserves, there already appeared the names of Tommy Lawrence, Chris Lawler, Alf Arrowsmith, Gordon Wallace and Tommy Smith. They were talented and hungry, all these men, and they also had skill and toughness. It was as if the modern game had suddenly arrived at Anfield in the boardroom, on the training ground and on the pitch all at the same moment. A combination of shrewd buying, the fruits of the club's youth policy and a lucky break in spotting Roger Hunt in local non-league football had produced a team and a club that no longer looked at home in Division Two of the Football League.

The truth of it is that Liverpool Football Club completely routed the clubs in the Second Division in season 1961–62. It was a profoundly unfair contest, almost embarrassingly easy right from the start. The *Daily Post* said that the new post-maximum-wage era would mean that 'it will be no use for managers to ask civil servants and teachers and engine drivers in the ground to be patient. They've been patient long enough, thank you.' There was little need for patience at Anfield. After a crushing 3–0 defeat of fancied Sunderland in August 1961, the local press reported that 'football was reborn at Anfield last night' and ran headlines reading 'Liverpool's Finest Team for Many Years'. A 5–0 pounding of Leeds United followed, with a first Roger Hunt hat-trick, some 71 matches into his Liverpool career. Hunt would score three more league hat-tricks in that season alone – the signing of Ian St John had released him to ransack defences with goals. The Merseyside press reported that the presence of Ron Yeats had 'bolstered the defence almost beyond belief' and that St John was 'an artist . . . full of ambition'. In honour of the new forward, the Kop had begun to sing its first real modern song in anger: 'When the Saints Go Marching In', adapted later to 'When the Reds Go Marching In'.

By the end of November 1961, there were only two Liverpool league defeats to report, at Middlesbrough and Derby County. No team would win at Anfield during the season, and only three took league points there, though it would take two goals in the last two minutes to save the home record against Charlton Athletic on 30 April. Liverpool were now unbeaten in the league at home since 31 December 1960, a real fortress. Even the club's reserve and B teams were unbeaten at home. The Reds were already clear, destined for promotion, despite the hiccup of two consecutive losses in Yorkshire over Christmas, to the Uniteds from Leeds and Rotherham, respectively.

But Shankly wanted more. In March 1962, Everton and Liverpool both bought new Lancashire-based goalkeepers in the same week, Liverpool signing Jim Furnell from Burnley for £18,000 and Everton splashing out even bigger money on the erratic but entertaining Gordon West from Blackpool. Furnell, as it turned out, was just keeping the gloves warm for the young Tommy Lawrence, who was growing up in the club's reserves. Liverpool conceded only one goal in three tough FA Cup meetings with Preston North End in February 1962, but it was the *only* goal, scored by a dashing left-winger called Peter Thompson. Bill Shankly was impressed.

Bert Slater had conceded only 27 goals in 29 league matches, but Shankly had decided, ruthlessly, that his keeper was just too small to really dominate his penalty area, and the Burnley reserve Furnell went straight into the Liverpool first team. With Ian Callaghan now in for Kevin Lewis on the right wing and Ronnie Moran filling in for Dick White at full-back (Gerry Byrne had moved across to right-back), the 'new' Liverpool was now in full bloom, and this was beginning to look increasingly like a group of players who would not only win promotion as champions, but could actually achieve something in the First Division, too. And then – who knows?

Liverpool FC, Second Division champions, 1961–62

			Furnell			
	Byrne	Yeats		Moran		
		Milne	Leishman			
Callaghan	Hunt		St John	Melia		A'Court

With seven games left and five points clear, and with one game in hand over nearest chasers Leyton Orient, it looked like a clear run-in, a formality. Roger Hunt had already smashed Gordon Hodgson's 36-goal league-scoring record in a season for the club – he would eventually end up with 41 goals in 41 appearances – and he had just scored on his full England debut, against Austria. Later, 'Sir Roger' was presented with (and he valued) a canteen of cutlery by the Liverpool Supporters Club for his achievements. But 'real life' then took a hand, once again, when a deadly smallpox outbreak in South Wales meant that Liverpool's fixture at Swansea was postponed in early April. This meant that promotion was finally clinched only on 21 April 1962 in a constant downpour against Southampton at Anfield, with two goals from the returning Kevin Lewis, who was filling in at centre-forward for the occasionally hotheaded and currently suspended Ian St John. The Saint had typically sneaked into the ground to watch proceedings, even though the FA ban barred him from Anfield.

There were still five league fixtures left – including the entire Easter programme – but Liverpool's promotion had been an open secret almost since the early exchanges. Liverpool would end up eight points clear of Orient and, tantalisingly, on ninety-nine league goals scored. The Southampton team gallantly made a rather sodden and bedraggled guard of honour for Liverpool as the teams left the field, and one soaked pitch-invader plonked a red-and-white hat and a kiss on a bemused Ron Yeats's head. Tom Williams and Bill Shankly both tried to make speeches from the Main Stand, but the Liverpool PA system was so poor and the supporters so excited that no one could hear them. The players got showered while the Kop repeatedly chanted, 'We want the Reds.' The players even tried to do a lap of honour in mufti, but it lasted about 20 yards before they were mobbed and forced back into the players' tunnel. The fans had to feast, instead, on dressing-room photographs in the next day's newspapers, showing the players and staff drinking champagne out of crockery mugs: a nice touch this one, the sporting artisans getting just a little taste of the high life. At the front of the shot, a proud Bill Shankly was beaming.

When the Second Division trophy was finally presented at Anfield after the lucky home win against Charlton Athletic, in the crowd was a list of past Reds greats, including Fred Hopkin, Eph Longworth, Bill Jones and Jim McDougall. Six-year-old Reds mascot Leslie McCann was also present, as he had been at all Liverpool's matches, home and away, that season. But pride of place went to the 80-year-old Joe Hewitt, a man who had served the Liverpool club for more than 60 years. As Ron Yeats held the trophy aloft, Joe had a discernible tear in his eye. The old warrior's hand tightened around a small object that he had carried carefully in his pocket that day: it was his 1905–06 Liverpool league-championship medal.

It had been 12 long years since Liverpool had last appeared at Wembley and 15 since the last Liverpool league title, in 1947. But all that achievement seemed like it was from quite a different age. This, after all, was the 1960s, a period in which attacks on the 'old order' in Britain came from all directions, including comics, television and politics, as well as from sport.[15] Even Billy Liddell and his ilk already seemed consigned to Anfield history, alongside Joe Hewitt and all the other Liverpool greats. The message from Bill Shankly and his team was that there would be no more Liverpool gloom in the second rank of the English game. All that darkness was over. The club had sleepwalked into this dreadful slump, led, largely, by its own directors. It had taken a stimulus from local rivals Everton to refloat the Liverpool vessel. Now the Reds had the wind in their sails again and an ambitious manager for whom nothing seemed out of reach. 'A trip to Wembley,' hazarded Leslie Edwards in the *Liverpool Echo*. 'That is the next mission, I would think, on Shankly's list of priorities.' It would take Shankly three more years to achieve that elusive Liverpool FA Cup target – and we all know that a lot can happen in football in three years.

CHAPTER 14 REFERENCES

1. Smith, *Anfield Iron*, pp. 30–1
2. Leigh, *The Cavern*, p. 86
3. A'Court, *Alan A'Court: My Life in Football*, p. 84
4. Kennedy and Williams, *Kennedy's Way*
5. Taylor and Ward, *Three Sides of the Mersey*, p. 96
6. Ponting and Hale, *Sir Roger*, p. 19
7. A'Court, *Alan A'Court: My Life in Football*, p. 70
8. Taylor and Ward, *Three Sides of the Mersey*, p. 97
9. Bale, *The Shankly Legacy*, p. 70
10. Taylor and Ward, *Three Sides of the Mersey*, pp. 99–100
11. Liddell, *My Soccer Story*, p. 16
12. Bowler, *Shanks*, pp. 8–9
13. St John, *The Saint*, p. 62
14. Quoted in Williams, *The Liverpool Way*, p. 100
15. Sandbrook, *Never Had It So Good*, p. 567

15

EE-AYE-ADDIO, THE FA CUP AT LAST!
Liverpool FC at Wembley
and in Europe

LOST AND FATALLY ADRIFT

On 24 April 1962, spoiling the Liverpool Second Division promotion party somewhat, local thieves on Merseyside returned to check out a familiar target. Safe-blowers stole £4,000 of match takings from a safe sited in the Anfield office of the then Liverpool FC club secretary Jimmy McInnes. These persistent crooks had finally got a decent result out of Liverpool Football Club, and the conscientious McInnes felt the loss personally, as if it was somehow his responsibility. It was typical of the man. The diminutive Scot had played 51 times at left-half for Liverpool after signing from Third Lanark in March 1938. In line with the club's 'family' policy of recruiting ex-players, he had joined the administrative staff at Anfield after the war. McInnes would have seen the chaos around distributing FA Cup tickets in 1950. He had been club secretary since 1955 and had seen his responsibilities grow. He was a kindly, undemonstrative man, a university graduate who dealt with his duties quietly but efficiently. In the backwaters of the English Second Division, with few sell-outs or all-ticket events to deal with, the role of a club secretary promised a reasonably uneventful life. Not so in the top flight.

But in the next three years under Bill Shankly, Liverpool Football Club rocketed from being a marginal outpost rooted in the domestic second tier to being one of Europe's major football clubs with top players and a celebrity manager. This happened in a city that had suddenly become a magnet for global attention for both its music and its football. The Liverpool club probably underestimated the strain placed on its backroom staff by some of these rapid changes. As we have already seen, the club also had an unfortunate reputation for penny-pinching in some of its policies and appointments, and in its provision of administrative support. Even its top players were earning no more than £35 per week as a basic wage as the club began to win league titles and the FA Cup and compete in Europe from the mid-1960s.[1] Cost-cutting was an established part of the club's identity.

In the middle of 1965, these pressures would already have become acute: Liverpool played in the European Cup semi-final for the first time and in the FA Cup final within a matter of days, so the demands on ticketing and other connected matters in these pre-computer days would have been quite out of proportion to anything the club had previously dealt with. The pressures behind the scenes were intense. His wife, Joan, said later that McInnes had been 'worried and overworked for a long time'. He worked 12-hour days and often stayed all night at the ground on a camp bed. He had 'months and months' of backlog of work to get through. The precise circumstances of what happened next are unclear, beyond the fact that McInnes and his small staff were stretched enormously – ironically, by Liverpool's sudden, extraordinary success. This is what everyone in the club had been striving for since the war. But it is the backroom staff that typically bears the brunt of supporters' anxieties, expectations, complaints and demands in these times of plenty. What we do know is that on 5 May 1965, four days after Liverpool had finally managed to win the FA Cup after seventy-three years of gut-wrenching trying, a distressed and exhausted Jimmy McInnes walked to the silent darkness at the back of the Spion Kop and under a hut at the Archway turnstile hanged himself. He was just 52 years of age. It was, to put it glibly, a very tragic end to an unprecedentedly glorious period of Liverpool Football Club success.

MOVE ON UP

With promotion assured back in 1962, and Bill Shankly acting as both bold figurehead and club cheerleader, Liverpool's average league crowds jumped in the 1961–62 season from 29,608 to 39,237, just below Everton's seasonal average of 41,432. This was actually Liverpool's largest average crowd figure since 1953–54 – the club's last season in the First Division. But the general football-crowd trend in England was still decidedly downwards. More than 41 million paying customers in the post-war peak season of 1949–50 had dwindled to just under 28 million in 1961–62. Four and a half million football supporters had been lost to English club football even since 1960. European club football and concerns about rising hooliganism were already part of this wider picture.

A conservative and hidebound Football League was another – that there was no need for the sport to modernise or change appeared to be its position. This seemed an extraordinary stand to take, especially considering what was happening to youth culture and general patterns of consumption in Britain, not least in the city of Liverpool itself. The Cavern, in the city centre, had been a jazz music venue since 1957, and the poet Adrian Henri thought that the Liverpool of the late 1950s was a site for exotica, which 'seemed to me like Paris in the 1920s'.[2] But 1962 was the year that Liverpool really started to become a national and then international centre for pop music, with the Cavern as its beating heart. The Beatles emerged to national prominence, to be followed by a shoal of Liverpool music acts, and the Cavern even offered the decadence of lunchtime beat-music concerts in 1962 for those 'hip' enough to get access. The 'Fab Four', of course, were regular early performers, allegedly clocking up 275 Cavern appearances alone in the early 1960s.[3] The city itself also seemed to be in relatively resurgent form, with the docks enjoying a temporary revival in international trade, though the still overwhelming dependence of the local economy on the fortunes of the port continued to make Liverpool vulnerable 'both to the structural decline of its service and manufacturing specialisms and to downturns in international trade'.[4]

A Football League survey in April 1962 identified some of these themes of rising incomes and growing consumer choice in accounting for the relative decline of active football-club support. The report highlighted greater prosperity but also uncomfortable league grounds and defensive football, as well as pressures from women for their husbands and boyfriends to spend more time with them and their children on Saturdays as the key reasons for falling attendances. Pop music offered a leisure outlet for young men and women away from their parents that had very different things to offer from standing on open terraces in the rain. But Joan Kennedy of Anzio Road in Huyton resented the underlying assumption here that women had no place at football in Liverpool or elsewhere. She wrote angrily to the *Echo* on the matter on 27 April 1962, criticising the sport for its chauvinist attitudes:

> Women don't like to be left out, as they feel they are when their husbands and boyfriends go off alone or with their pals to football matches. Why not encourage the girls and women to go along and watch, instead of discouraging them . . . Girls can be just as enthusiastic as men about football.

In June 1962, the *Liverpool Echo* reported on a new local enlightenment. 'It seems there is sufficient interest to form a Liverpool ladies football team in the city.' But it was a false alarm. In fact, it would take almost another 30 years for football in England to really take the role of women in the game seriously, either as players or spectators. By that time (in the early 1990s), near-terminally damaged finances, hooliganism and terrible stadium disasters – with Liverpool supporters as both perpetrators and victims – had finally forced the sport's hand to modernise, with satellite television now increasingly pulling football's purse strings. But a series of official reports on restructuring football in England in the 1960s had been rejected by the heads-in-the-sand Football League. The English game would continue to plough its traditional furrow, even as crowds tumbled. The single international triumph for the England national team – at Wembley in the World Cup final of 1966 – masked many deeper problems that were festering in English football at this time, both on and off the pitch.

None of these issues troubled Liverpool FC in 1962, of course. The club and its supporters simply contemplated life back among the sport's elite. Some football clubs, ill-resourced and small, just manage to scrape into the top flight and see a year in the spotlight as a bonus before sliding back into obscurity. It happened to Second Division runners-up Leyton Orient, promoted behind Liverpool. Some clubs go up on the back of an already ageing side that is past its peak – achieving promotion is the very apex of their ambitions. Still others lose their best players or their manager to other clubs *because* of promotion. Others spend wildly once promotion is achieved. None of these cases applied to Liverpool in 1962. Bill Shankly had built a new young team at a big club with a large and enthusiastic fan base. He now had a supportive board that was not quite so afraid to spend big money, and his ambition was to win the FA Cup (as soon as possible), the league title and, ideally, the European Cup.

As a starter, he won a local bauble when Liverpool beat Everton 1–0 in the Liverpool Senior Cup in May 1962, with a 30-yard 'missile' free-kick from Ronnie Moran deciding matters. All wins against Everton were valuable, and Shankly would never, ever lack for confidence or for a memorable one-liner aimed at the Goodison Park club. When World Cup-winner Alan Ball signed for Everton in 1966, the Liverpool manager phoned him up to welcome him to the city. 'Congratulations, son,' said Shankly. 'You'll be playing *near* a great side.'

At the celebratory Liverpool AGM that followed in 1962, chairman Tom Williams warned the club's occasionally disorderly young supporters about their behaviour, saying, 'Do not let yourself be carried away by the excitement of the moment.' He might have better addressed his remarks to his occasionally excitable Scottish manager. An iridescent Bill Shankly sparkled with a story about the 'cauldron' Anfield had now become and about how, not being the coolest of people himself, he had recently been paid a wonderful compliment by a visiting manager. This rival boss was, in contrast with Shankly's animation, calm 'almost to the point of contrition'. Shankly paused for maximum effect now, eyeing up his Liverpool AGM audience. What *had* the rival boss said to him? Shankly continued his story, reporting that the visiting man had nodded toward the Kop before growling to the agitated Shankly, 'You're worse than those people on the terraces.' The Liverpool manager beamed with pride at the memory of the moment as his audience laughed approvingly. The Scot, as he liked to say, was among his own people.

But the Liverpool board was not yet completely cowed by their manager. They moved the winger Johnny Morrissey on to neighbours Everton for £10,000 in August 1962 – and to a league title, of course – behind the manager's back. Shankly was furious and had to be persuaded not to walk out. The board finally agreed to do no more deals without the manager's approval, and there were no other major arrivals or departures at Anfield when the Reds returned to the top level. This inaction might have been a mistake. Liverpool's proud undefeated home league record could not even survive the club's first match back in the First Division, a 1–2 home defeat to Blackpool. In fact, there were four Liverpool defeats in the first seven top-level matches, though a 2–2 draw at Everton in September steadied any shredding Anfield nerves.

The step-up had already proved too much for wing-half Tommy Leishman, who was now dropped and later sold back to Scotland for a small profit in January 1963. In came a silky left-sided wing-half from Glasgow Rangers for £20,000. Willie Stevenson was a brilliant passer, if a sometimes reluctant tackler, a man who was just about holding up the great Jim Baxter at Ibrox, so he was keen on joining the Liverpool project. But Willie 'Stevo' did not lack in confidence. Like Graeme Souness, who would follow him later into Liverpool's midfield, Stevenson had more than a touch of the grand stylist about him, preferring cognac and snappy, expensive suits to beer and the knitwear favoured by the 'peasants' in the Liverpool squad. When Peter Thompson arrived to play on the Liverpool left, Stevenson told him, 'Just stay out on the wing and I'll supply you with everything. In fact, I'll make you an international if you're good enough.' It was a long way from Billy Liddell, but the famed Liverpool dressing-room banter of the modern period had already begun.

Stevenson's arrival on Merseyside coincided with the promotion of the Lancastrian–Scotsman goalkeeper Tommy Lawrence to replace Jim Furnell. The stocky and awkward Lawrence hardly fitted the photofit of a modern keeper: he was neither tall nor particularly agile. He was even known affectionately by Liverpool fans as 'the flying pig'. But he was brave, solid and reliable, and he also had some of Elisha Scott's alert reading of the game. Lawrence was quickly off his line whenever he spotted danger, confidently sweeping up anything that got behind his defenders, even straying out of his penalty area to deal with local alarms. He could use his feet as ably as most outfield players, and he helped to revolutionise the traditional goalkeeping role because of the way he knitted his job in with those of his outfield men. Reds defender Tommy Smith, not a man to impress easily, thought Lawrence was probably the greatest goalkeeper in the world in the middle of his time at Liverpool. Enough said.

The winter of 1962–63 was a particularly bad one, the worst since 1947, with Liverpool occasionally training on the dog track at Lower Breck Road because of frozen pitches at both Melwood and Anfield. But these new men, Lawrence and Stevenson, made an almost immediate difference to results, with Liverpool setting off on a nine-match winning streak in the league in November 1962, conceding only five goals in the process. Shankly was in ebullient mood, telling the national press in November 1963:

> There are a lot of very ordinary sides in the First Division and Liverpool were far from ordinary when they came into it. Now the penny has dropped, there is no reason why they shouldn't keep on doing well. They might do even better if so many of their opponents were not obsessed with negative soccer.[5]

This winning league run was ended only by bogey side Leicester City on 2 March. Leicester also later saw off the Reds in an FA Cup semi-final at Hillsborough in 1963 and were described by football historian Percy Young as having played 'the most imaginative football seen in a cup tie for years'. Imaginatively dull, perhaps: Liverpool had more than thirty attempts on goal compared to City's three. It was a match that echoed the one-sided 1947 semi-final Liverpool defeat to Burnley, and it only confirmed Shankly's fears about defensive football. England goalkeeper Gordon Banks resisted everything Liverpool threw at him that day, as City parked the bus and banked on snatching the vital single goal and then holding on. It worked and reduced a distraught Ian St John to tears.

In the league, meanwhile, champions-elect Everton also shut up shop in a 0–0 draw at Anfield in April 1963, as Liverpool briefly threatened a title challenge following a 5–2 Easter thumping of Spurs. But three days later, in the rematch at White Hart Lane, came a result more reminiscent of the roller-coaster 1930s than the Bill Shankly years. Liverpool were crushed 2–7, a slippery Jimmy Greaves scoring four times. This reverse seemed to sap the young team's resolve, as the Reds rapidly slipped out of contention, with only one win secured in the last nine league matches. As the season dribbled away, Shankly experimented with Gordon Wallace, a young Scottish forward, Alan Jones, a Welsh schoolboy international right-back, and Bobby Thompson, another Scottish defender who Shankly had brought in from Partick Thistle for £7,000. None would have a future at Anfield. The robust and quiffed Manchester-born forward Alf Arrowsmith would promise to do much more until injury cruelly struck him down in August 1964.

SILENT KNIGHT

But the emerging new Liverpool star for the future, briefly seen at this time, was a young, technically gifted centre-half and England-schoolboys captain called Chris Lawler. For his first Liverpool match, deputising for Ron Yeats against West Brom in March 1963, Lawler took two buses to get to the ground. When he got off at Arkles Lane, he was bemused by how few people were milling around the stadium. He suddenly realised that the Liverpool crowd was already safely inside, awaiting his debut.[6] The quiet and considered Lawler was initially frustrated by the lack of first-team opportunities behind Ron Yeats, and he even asked Shankly for a transfer, before becoming a regular at full-back in the 1964–65 FA Cup-winning season. This confronting of the Liverpool manager took some courage. Lawler's footballing skills were unusual for a tall defender, and so was his scoring record of 61 goals in 549 Liverpool appearances. His clever footwork and his predatory strikes at corners and from headers on diagonals for Liverpool attacks would rescue his manager and teammates from many a prickly situation.

Eighth place in the First Division was a respectable finish in 1963, but it hurt that Everton were champions, and Shankly knew that he was so close to producing a title-winning side. Kevin Lewis's Liverpool career was now effectively over, because Ian Callaghan was established on the right wing, and 29-year-old Alan A'Court's football world was also about to shatter when the Liverpool board sanctioned a £37,000 bid for Preston's outrageously talented left-winger Peter Thompson in August 1963. The slowing A'Court was immediately relegated to the Central League team, playing in front of a few hundred anoraks as Thompson played all 42 matches in the 1963–64 title season. There was no room for sentiment here, and, like most players of the time lacking an agent or anyone to advise him on a future move, the international A'Court simply languished in the reserves as his career dribbled away. He eventually left for Tranmere Rovers.

Meanwhile, the new man Thompson thrilled his manager, who saw him as a modern, if occasionally over-elaborate, version of Tom Finney. The Liverpool crowd also fell in love with Thompson's trickery and his sinewy runs and crosses. He was the perfect balance for the more direct and hard-running Ian Callaghan on the Liverpool right. What a pair of wide players. 'Cally' could run night and day. With Arrowsmith available to cover for injury in the forward positions and the ghostly Lawler ready to do the same defensively, Shankly knew that if he could steer clear of injuries his squad was capable of challenging for the title in 1963–64. And so it proved. He also had the setting for success. In 1963, the old Kemlyn Road stand was demolished to be replaced by a cantilevered new structure seating 6,700 spectators at the incredible cost of £350,000. Liverpool Football Club was going places.

THE LEAGUE TITLE – AND INTO EUROPE

The real signal that Bill Shankly was finally where he wanted to be, with the squad and board he craved and with real prospects of winning the sport's biggest prizes, was that in August 1963 he finally signed a contract at Liverpool for the first time. The agreement was for five years. He told the *Daily Post*, 'I suppose it is the modern trend to have agreements such as this, and I have simply fallen into line.' It was well known that ambitious Nottingham Forest had been making overtures to the contract-free Shankly, so the Liverpool board, not unreasonably, wanted to tie their man down. The move also offered some greater general stability to the club and more security to the Liverpool boss. Shankly had begun to identify strongly with the Liverpool people – and they with him.

The Liverpool and Everton football clubs were both riding high after some years in the wilderness, and the city's musical success had brought the world's press to Merseyside. The Beatles' many imitators and protégés in the city meant that on 3 October 1963 the BBC screened a nationwide documentary called *The Mersey Sound* and that for a fifty-one-week period, between April 1963 and May 1964, there would be a recording by a Liverpool artist at number one in the national pop charts. With a new Labour government soon to be formed and headed by ambitious local MP Harold Wilson, it felt like Liverpool was at the very centre of a radical shift in generational and class politics and was the key place for popular culture in Britain – and perhaps the world. It was exciting to be a part of this shimmering Liverpool cultural scene, which was now very different from the rather austere provincial backwater the city had sometimes appeared to be just a decade earlier.

Bill Shankly was a Labour man, of course, but he was no great lover of glamour or pop music. Instead, the Scot preferred a quiet game of cards or else ballads by Jim Reeves, Tom Jones and Ray Charles to going out or to listening to the racket produced by Liverpool's pop groups. But Shankly also recognised and enjoyed the energy of the city and its people and the public focus they now attracted. His players regularly mixed socially with local pop stars, and some of them had begun to exude some of their confidence. Shankly was well attuned to the demands of the 'performance culture' favoured by the city's emerging stars in music, comedy and football. He was something of a comic performer himself. It was no surprise to him that the BBC's first match on its new Saturday night BBC2 TV football highlights show *Match of the Day*, on 22 August 1964, was screened from Liverpool – where else? Only 75,000 armchair viewers watched on TV as the Reds beat Arsenal 3–2, but it was a start. The club's younger fans were singing Beatles and Gerry and the Pacemakers pop songs on the Kop, thus defining the new links between the three key modern cultural domains of youth, football and music.

Shankly had no desire at all to produce a glamorous team, of course. This was not his way, and football was too important to be showy. Anyway, Manchester United along the East Lancs Road were already dominating in the razzle-dazzle stakes. No, why leave the city of Liverpool when you had built a young team and when signs of regeneration and well-being were all around and everyone else seemed so desperate to move there? Bill Shankly signed his new contract and prepared for his assault on the league title.

The Liverpool league-championship win of 1963–64 was eventually almost as definitive, almost as predictable, as the Second Division triumph had proved to be in 1962. But it did not start that way. In August 1963, Liverpool lost consecutive home matches to Nottingham Forest and Blackpool, and then lost at home again to West Ham United in mid-September. What had happened to the so-called Anfield fortress? By the time Everton visited Anfield on 28 September 1963, the Reds had accumulated just nine points from nine league matches, but two Ian Callaghan goals were enough to see off the champions from Goodison and to kick-start Liverpool's season. Not that Leicester City could be shaken off – another 0–1 home defeat followed to the East Midlanders. But a string of league wins, and a 6–1 Boxing Day home trouncing of Stoke City, revived Liverpool's title hopes. Liverpool would eventually lose eleven league matches, but they drew only five, thus securing a relatively high number of league wins at twenty-six. Losing the derby return to Everton 1–3 in February seemed like a painful blip rather than a defining moment, and by the time Liverpool lined up against Second Division strugglers Swansea Town at home in the sixth round of the FA Cup on 29 February 1964, having already dumped Arsenal in the fifth round, it even felt like a Liverpool league and cup Double might be possible once again. It was daft – and possibly distracting – thinking.

Every team has its FA Cup day, and this was Swansea's. Their goalkeeper, Republic of Ireland international Noel Dwyer, had an inspired match – and bucketfuls of luck. When he dived the wrong way under the Liverpool siege, the ball simply hit his legs or else the post or the bar, or a loitering, absent-minded defender saved him. When Ronnie Moran stepped up to take a Liverpool penalty kick, it was almost ordained that he would miss. And he did. Liverpool could do little else to avoid the 1–2 defeat that resulted, arguably the club's second-most humiliating FA Cup exit after Worcester City in 1959. But at least it meant that the league could now be the sole focus.

Relegation-threatened Ipswich Town paid for the Swansea debacle with a 6–0 thrashing at Anfield. The goal-snatching rocker Alf Arrowsmith, who was replacing the injured Jimmy Melia, was prominent, scoring two of the goals. His contribution would prove vital in the title run-in: 15 league goals in 20 appearances. It also signalled the end at Anfield for the little midfield general Melia, as Shankly now sought more of a power game – and more defensive cover – from the central areas.

The 1964 league title was decided – as many had been before – during the crowded Easter programme. In nine days, between 27 March and 4 April 1964, Liverpool defeated title-challengers Tottenham Hotspur twice, bogey side Leicester City at Filbert Street and eventual league runners-up Manchester United 3–0 at Anfield, scoring eleven goals in this period and conceding only two in the process. Roger Hunt scored a brilliant hat-trick at White Hart Lane in a 3–1 win, and his combination with the burly Arrowsmith gave Liverpool an attacking edge they had previously lacked. No one could match this burst of points-collecting. A comprehensive 3–0 win away at Burnley on 14 April 1964 set up the home match against Arsenal as a potential title decider, with a further three fixtures still outstanding. Roger Hunt had an ankle injury, but he kept it from Shankly and played in what turned out to be the key fixture. Had George Eastham scored a penalty to equalise St John's early goal, the result might have been different. But Liverpool stormed away instead, Peter Thompson scoring two goals in a 5–0 rout. From 7 March, Liverpool had scored twenty-seven goals in nine breathtaking league matches, conceding only three. They were worthy champions.

Winning football matches, rather than settling for draws, had been the key to the Liverpool triumph. Six players – Lawrence, Milne, Hunt, St John and Thompson – had played forty league games or more. The Liverpool-born Phil Ferns had spent most of his Liverpool career since September 1957 playing second-team football, but he had filled in capably for both full-backs and for Willie Stevenson, playing 18 league matches and claiming an unlikely league-championship medal. Roger Hunt and Ian St John between them had scored 52 of Liverpool's 92 goals. Liverpool lost two and drew one of the 'dead' fixtures they had left – the club's players have never shied away from celebration – so their final points tally was fifty-seven, four clear of Manchester United. The margin could have been much greater.

Virtually this entire 1960s Liverpool side had now been raised or bought by Bill Shankly, and the following season would offer two main targets: an extended run in the European Cup – Liverpool's first season in Europe – and a real tilt at the FA Cup. His team was young and hungry for success, but the Liverpool squad was small and lacking in experience in key areas. Arrowsmith's critical injury and Gordon Wallace's failings left a hole at inside-left. The slim Scot Bobby Graham threatened to fill it after scoring a hat-trick on his league debut against Aston Villa in September 1964, but he seemed fragile and inconsistent and never quite gained Bill Shankly's trust.

Geoff Strong, a versatile forward from Arsenal who could also play in midfield and defence, was brought in for £40,000 in November, and his arrival hinted at Shankly and Bob Paisley's thinking. Perhaps one of the inside-forward berths should involve a much more defensive role than had previously been supposed? Liverpool's full-backs were caught up in marking wingers – most clubs played two wide players – and for all Ron Yeats's dominance in the air, he could be caught on the ground by a fleet-footed forward, especially on his weaker right side. One was likely to come across more skilful and more intelligent forwards in Europe. Maybe asking Strong – or someone like him – to play more defensively from the inside-forward position might allow more cover and pace across and behind the Liverpool defence? It could also mean skilful attacking full-backs, such as the emerging Chris Lawler, could get forward much more effectively. Detailing four players to defend most of the time was not necessarily a defensive move if it released your full-backs with width and your wing-halves to do more attacking. This was the theory of it.

But everything had to be proved out on the pitch, not in the boot room. Liverpool struggled to defend their league title: eight defeats and only four victories in the first fifteen matches in 1964–65 told the story. This run included a humiliating 0–4 home reverse to Everton. The club's focus was elsewhere – on the Continent, to be precise. The Reds were late into Europe compared with some of their English rivals, and it was difficult to balance priorities at home and abroad, even though the European Cup was played in an unseeded straight-knockout format. The Liverpool European adventure finally began with a 5–0 win in Iceland, part of an 11–1 aggregate walkover against little KR Reykjavik in September.

There followed a much stiffer task against the Belgian champions Anderlecht, who included in their number the prodigious inside-forward Paul van Himst, arguably Europe's best young player. Before the home leg, Shankly came up with not one but two innovations. First, that Liverpool would wear an all-red strip for Europe from then on, ditching their white shorts and red-and-white socks. Psychologists have long argued that the colour red offers a positive advantage to its wearers. Why not all red? Long before the kit manufacturers began to see profit in producing exclusive European kits, and rather as Reds supporters did when they came back from Europe with stylish new gear, this strip would also signal a new chapter in Liverpool's development as a fully European club. Second, Shankly wanted to get his defensive, tough young tyro Tommy Smith into the Liverpool team, perhaps to shadow the dangerous van Himst.

Shankly was worried about the technical ability and the pace of the Belgians against a possibly exposed Ron Yeats. The number 10 shirt was available, but he wanted to try Smith out in the new defensive position he had discussed, alongside the Scottish centre-half. Shankly consulted Yeats and St John – an unusual practice in itself – and then opted to field Smith as his number 10. His new role and his strange numbering was as confusing to the Liverpool public as Billy Liddell's role had been playing centre-forward while wearing the number 11 shirt in the 1950s. But the Liverpool formation was also different, much more of a 4–3–3 system, with Smith defending, St John dropping deep to work with Milne, and Stevenson and the wingers supporting Roger Hunt. If Liverpool got on top, St John played further forward in a 4–2–4.

The new system worked perfectly against the Belgians at Anfield, with Liverpool strolling the first leg, winning 3–0. A relaxed Ron Yeats even got on the scoresheet. In Belgium for the second leg, Liverpool sat back and risked being overrun, but Tommy Lawrence was inspired in goal, and Roger Hunt even stole a winner in injury time to clinch the match and the tie.

With the fearsome Tommy Smith now firmly in the Liverpool first team and quickly acting like a veteran, Liverpool's league form picked up. But Manchester United were already stretching away at the top, so the cup competitions became the key Reds targets in 1965. West Bromwich Albion away in the third round of the FA Cup was a tough enough assignment without Ron Yeats picking up the ball in the penalty area after he heard a whistle, only to see the referee pointing to the spot for handball. Bobby Cram missed the kick, sparking Liverpool to a 2–1 win. The Reds were even luckier at home in round four against the bottom Fourth Division club Stockport County, grinding out a horrible 1–1 draw courtesy only of a last-second goal-line clearance by Gerry Byrne. Almost uniquely, Shankly had missed the match on a European Cup spying mission in Germany. When a customs officer told him the score on his return to England, the Scot assumed the official was mad.

As if trying to make good – and also recalling the horrors of Worcester City – Shankly now came up with some 'magic' footwear for the replay, which was fought out on a frozen and rutted pitch. These rubber-soled, cleated boots (possibly picked up while he was abroad in Germany) allowed Roger Hunt to score two goals to see Liverpool through the replay. Ian Callaghan was the unlikely hero at Bolton Wanderers in round five, with a late headed winner in a very hard-fought 1–0 victory. Only really dedicated Reds can recall Cally headers for Liverpool. The FA Cup was in sniffing range once again, but how often had this been said about Liverpool in the previous 70 years?

Before all this, Liverpool faced the Germans from FC Cologne – nicknamed 'the Billy Goats' – in Europe. In two classic European meetings, the Reds held Cologne scoreless in West Germany on 10 February 1965 and then waited until 17 March for the return – a Liverpool blizzard had ruled out an earlier meeting – but could not break through the visitors' defence at Anfield. Without penalties to turn to, a third match in neutral Rotterdam in front of almost 48,000 mainly locals saw Liverpool take a 2–0 lead before the Germans replied with two goals of their own. Extra time produced no more returns. These two clubs could not be separated on the pitch in over three hundred minutes of football, and UEFA apparently preferred the toss of a disc over any kind of test of football acumen to resolve this epic contest. It seemed like a farce, a gross dereliction of duty, but the clubs were stuck with it. As had happened at the 1950 FA Cup final, the first toss agonisingly came up stuck in the mud and indecisive. But it was Liverpool who 'won' through when the disc was re-tossed and eventually came up 'red'.

As the players celebrated, Bill Shankly shook his head and quietly walked over to the Cologne bench to commiserate with his opponents. He told the opposing coaches that this was no way to decide such a hard-fought and evenly balanced European Cup tie played over a 42-day period and that there was no real honour for his own club in proceeding in such fashion. Shankly himself would be on the losing side of a coin toss in September 1968, when Athletic Bilbao went forward in the European Fairs Cup at Liverpool's expense. Inter Milan now lay waiting in the European Cup semi-final.

Liverpool were also still alive in the FA Cup, having held old adversaries Leicester City at Filbert Street in round six and winning through at Anfield with a lone Roger Hunt left-footed goal on 72 minutes, following a run and cutback by the dynamic Ian Callaghan. Hunt's low shot, sweetly hit in a very even contest, followed the striker as he wheeled back to the centre spot, such was the ferocity with which it rebounded from the goal stanchion. All this meant that, three days after playing an emotionally and physically draining European Cup extra-time match in Holland, Liverpool now faced a young and talented Chelsea FC in the FA Cup semi-final at a muddy Villa Park. The London club was managed by the flamboyant and outspoken Tommy Docherty, another potential headache.

Shankly and Paisley were certainly concerned about the impact of Rotterdam on their team, and they also wanted to unsettle Chelsea with new tactics if they could. Tommy Docherty had definitely surprised the Liverpool management by inviting Ron Yeats and Ian St John round to the Chelsea man's Dutch hotel room right after the Cologne match for a few late-night beers. Enraged, Shankly and Reuben Bennett managed to track the party down and ordered the Liverpool men back to the official party before laying into 'the Doc'. It was ostensibly an innocent affair, based around Docherty's Scottish links and his supposed access to spare FA Cup final tickets, the holy grail for players. But drinking abroad with the opposing club manager a few days before an FA Cup semi-final? And being offered cup-final tickets by him? Well, the press would have a field day today, and the meeting was seen in some quarters as being a prima facie case of bringing the game into disrepute. You could see their point.

After flying direct to their Birmingham base and ordering a couple of days of almost complete rest, the Liverpool coaching staff decided to advise the players to temper their typical, all-action style and try to play more conservatively, easing their way into the contest before trying to pick Chelsea off. This might conserve Liverpool's energy levels, but it was a strange way indeed to approach an FA Cup semi-final, which tended to be the most 'British' of all football contests, one played at a frightening pace on a usually worn or muddy surface. And Shankly had already, typically, spiked his own players by producing in the Liverpool dressing-room just before the match a copy of Chelsea's presumptuous FA Cup final brochure. He might even have printed it himself. This sort of contempt for his players deserved, nay demanded, a response, he told his team. In any case, with warriors such as defenders Eddie McCreadie and Ron 'Chopper' Harris in the Chelsea ranks and Tommy Smith and Gerry Byrne lining up for Liverpool, this was never likely to be a quiet or a restrained affair. In English FA Cup semi-finals, even the most talented sides have to 'earn' the right to play, which invariably means sticking your foot in and establishing dominance and respect.

After a little over an hour of just this sort of sparring, stopping a few inches short of out-and-out violence, one of the real creatives in the match, Liverpool's Peter Thompson, made the decisive play. Willie Stevenson and Thompson had their usual grinding relationship on Liverpool's left side: Stevo wanted more help defensively from Thompson and the ball delivered more quickly from the flank; Thommo chided Stevenson for lacking the pace to offer more support in attack. They were constantly at each other. It was exactly the same sort of left-sided griping that would later characterise the fractious partnership between Alan and Ray Kennedy under Bob Paisley. What was it about these Reds left-footers? Shanks loved Thompson, but even he criticised the winger occasionally for not getting the ball into the box early so that Hunt and St John could take advantage of a defence not yet set. And what about coming inside and shooting now and again? Thompson had a fierce shot in both feet, but he seemed so consumed with humiliating his full-back and dancing down the line that he seldom went for goal himself. But today he did so, cutting inside for once, to near the angle of the six-yard box and firing past a startled Peter Bonetti. The Red half of Villa Park, still steaming from the rain and the heat generated by thousands of alcohol-enhanced bodies, erupted. When Ian St John cleverly 'bought' a penalty from the furious Ron Harris on 79 minutes, the only other surprise was that it was Willie Stevenson who silently grabbed the ball and took the kick. No one disputed it, even though it was the only penalty the Scot ever took for Liverpool, a moment of supreme confidence and willingness to take responsibility. (Remember Steve Nicol in Rome in 1984? A less happy memory.) All's well that ends well. Liverpool Football Club were through to their third FA Cup final in 73 years of trying.

WONDERFUL, WONDERFUL WEMBLEY

Liverpool now stumbled to the end of their league programme with four consecutive defeats in April and just one goal scored. Chelsea had their revenge, of sorts, in a 0–4 reverse for Liverpool at Stamford Bridge, with Gordon Milne crucially picking up an injury that would rule him out of the rest of the campaign. In the club's last league fixture, at already-relegated Wolves (which Liverpool won 3–1), Wallasey-born forward John Sealey played and scored in his only ever game for Liverpool, in an unrecognisable Reds team that also included one-match-wonders defender Tom Lowry and England schoolboy international wing-half Alan Hignett. It was one of the very few occasions that Shankly ever rested or rotated players in an era when the FA came down hard on clubs that failed to field their strongest team in all fixtures. He had some cause: Liverpool had played a remarkable ten league matches in April 1965. The Reds eventually finished a respectable and exhausted seventh in the league, but a mile behind champions Manchester United and second-placed Leeds United, who they now faced in the club's third FA Cup final.

By 1965, the city of Liverpool's brief but ecstatic reign as world 'Beat City' was probably already over. The Beatles had left the city for good, and the UK was now swamped by original US musical imports and increasingly challenged by the rise of hippy culture in San Francisco and elsewhere.[7] But it still felt wonderful to be a Liverpudlian in the mid-1960s, and the links made between local pop culture and football glory were everywhere to be seen in the city in the build-up to the 1965 final – even though, ironically, relatively few pop stars from Merseyside at this time had any sort of real allegiance to either the Liverpool or Everton football clubs.[8] Bill Shankly was even on BBC radio's *Desert Island Discs* in the week of the final, and he chose many of his and the Kop's – and all Liverpool's – favourite songs. It was great build-up work, and it added to the manager's aura. The programme was played on the bus on the way to Wembley, to the mock groans of the players. The manager also arranged for a second bus to follow immediately behind the first, just in case the Reds' vehicle broke down.

For fans and players, Liverpool's European football adventure had also added a splash of colour to a generally black-and-white domestic football landscape. Incredibly, to modern sensibilities at least, the FA Cup final of 1965 would be pretty much the only chance for anybody inside or outside the city who was not an active fan to see this Liverpool team play 'live'. There was little live broadcasting of European football yet, save if an English side reached the final of a club competition. So the FA Cup final remained a very special event, one marked by supporters in the Red half of the city by the ritual dressing of houses with home-made rosettes and favours, and souvenir pictures from the *Echo*, stocking up with bottles of beer and drawing the curtains in mid-afternoon in order better to lock out the world for a few hours and to filter the shades of a grey Wembley day on a small black-and-white TV screen. Only 12,000 Liverpool supporters would get tickets for the final; Liverpool's average home attendance in 1964–65 was over 41,000. Wembley seats and terrace places were reserved by the FA, instead, for the worthy but non-partisan staff and volunteers of County FAs drawn from around the country. In short, fanatical football supporters, the lifeblood of the game, were still generally treated by the administrators of the sport like so much rubbish and mere terrace-fodder.

Before the match, Frankie Vaughan and Jimmy Tarbuck were both in the Liverpool dressing-room, keeping the players relaxed. Ron Yeats was very confident Liverpool would win: he had spent weeks practising what he was going to say to the Queen. Nessie Shankly sat excitedly in the stands; it was her first-ever Liverpool match. Shankly gave the players a rousing pre-match speech about being willing to 'die' for the supporters, perhaps sensing some tiredness, but, frankly, the 1965 FA Cup final was pretty unremarkable – except, of course, for the result.

Liverpool FC, FA Cup-winning team, 1965

Lawrence

Lawler   Smith   Yeats   Byrne

Strong   Stevenson

Callaghan   Hunt   St John   Thompson

Leeds United were on the rise, a tough, talented and cynical team under manager Don Revie, orchestrated by Bobby Collins, Billy Bremner and Johnny Giles in midfield and held together at the back by Jack Charlton and Norman Hunter, an almost mirror-match for Yeats and Tommy Smith at Liverpool. Leeds also had a left-winger, the black South African Albert Johanneson, who offered some of the pace and trickery of a Peter Thompson. Liverpool missed the injured Gordon Milne, Geoff Strong filling in at right-half in the new flexible 4–2–4 formation.

Maybe the two teams just cancelled each other out at Wembley? Neither club had yet to win the FA Cup – meaning additional pressure – and Liverpool's recent programme had been torrid. Both teams played conservatively, in Liverpool's case a little more justifiably because after just three minutes full-back Gerry Byrne broke a collarbone in a collision with the hard little Collins. Injury jinxes were not at all unusual at Wembley, and the stricken team invariably ended up defeated. This fact was not lost on Bill Shankly. The obvious thing – the compassionate and the losing thing – to do now was to bring the defender off or else strap him up and move him to the left-wing for nuisance value only. But Byrne was tough enough, and he could still run reasonably freely, albeit holding his arm across his chest. Johnny Giles was no conventional right-winger, and Shankly reasoned – drawing on an example from his own playing days with Andy Beattie – that if Byrne soldiered on in defence sheltered by Stevenson, the best player on the field, then Don Revie and the Leeds players might not even notice his weakness.

None of the other Liverpool players knew about the injury until half-time. Reuben Bennett spent the whole match with his eyes glued on Byrne, nervously chain-smoking on the Liverpool bench. He and Gordon Milne sheltered from the rain by draping training tops over their heads like a couple of troubled nuns. They need not have worried. The Leeds coaches missed a trick and made no attempt to play on the damaged Liverpool left side. In a very tight contest, it was the sheer bravery of Gerry Byrne that probably won the first FA Cup for Liverpool. Bill Shankly certainly thought so. He said later that the man who was all but transferred out of Anfield in the late 1950s 'should have had all the medals to himself'.[9]

After a dull, goal-less 90 minutes, incredibly it was the overlapping, injured Byrne who got to the Leeds byline to pull a low cross back early in extra time, cutting out both Sprake and Charlton but finding a stooping Roger Hunt, who headed unerringly in. This score was surely enough to win what was proving to be an arduous battle. But within eight minutes, Leeds were level, an unsaveable snapshot from Bremner. This was not in the script. But back came Liverpool, Callaghan sprinting down the right, this time to cross for St John to head in spectacularly. There was no coming back from this place. Leeds United were spent, and it was no disgrace to lose this contest. This was a truly exceptional Liverpool team, after all, one that would sweep to the league title again in 1965–66 using only fourteen players, and two of those would play only four matches between them.

After all his rehearsals, Ron Yeats forgot his speech for the Queen. Instead, the monarch said, 'It looked hard,' to which the exhausted Scot answered simply, 'It was.' The winners' photographs later captured the sport in its traditional guise and yet already in transition: the Liverpool players, still in their red shirts, dutifully filling the FA Cup with milk as part of some sponsor's agreement, while a hollow-cheeked Geoff Strong slyly cupped a dressing-room cigarette. Bill Shankly reflected later on the public perception of this Liverpool side and how they were still undervalued in some quarters:

> Because of our fitness and the pressure we put upon the opposition, the teams we built came to be called 'Powerhouse'. We were strong, that's true, but we didn't get the credit we deserved for the skill in the team . . . People said we were mechanical though 'methodical' would have been a better word. At least we knew what we were doing. They said we were predictable. Well, I think anybody who is unpredictable is a waste of time. Being predictable is not too bad . . . Our players worked for each other, not for individual honours, and by working unselfishly they still won the glory of being selected for international matches. Everyone at the ground worked for a common cause. The manager trusted the players and the players trusted the manager.[10]

There was Shankly's native socialism, once again, and it reached downwards into the club's supporters. The celebrations in Liverpool when the FA Cup was finally brought back to Anfield dwarfed anything seen in the history of the club – of any English club. An estimated 250,000 people turned out to cheer and sing Beatles songs and 'You'll Never Walk Alone' and to see their heroes parade the FA Cup. The trophy had only once been seen inside Anfield, and that was more than 50 years before. It had been brought there, of course, by Burnley in 1914 for a charity match after Liverpool had lost to the East Lancashire club in the final. But now it was Liverpool's to parade by right. And all those great players from the past who had tried so hard to bring the FA Cup back to the city for Liverpool – Raisbeck, Raybould and Cox from the 1900s; Longworth, McKinlay and Lacey from 1914; Scott, Bromilow and Chambers from the 1920s; Liddell, Stubbins and Balmer from 1947 – they were all equally honoured now. They could all rest, contented at last. Liverpool Football Club had finally reached their historic goal. After so many ifs and near misses, after so many hard-luck stories and broken promises, after so much disappointment, Liverpool Football Club had finally won the FA Cup.

LOCKED OUT IN MILAN

And maybe the Liverpool story in the year of 1965 should have ended right there, with the club's first FA Cup win. It would have made a natural and wonderful conclusion to an epic journey that spanned almost three-quarters of a century. But there was still a place in the European Cup final to play for in a semi-final against the mighty Internazionale of Milan. Sadly, this contest left a terrible taste in the mouth after the glories of Wembley. Inter were managed by the Argentinian Helenio Herrera, 'Il Mago' (the wizard), the man who claimed to have invented the modern version of the defensive sweeper system *catenaccio*. Herrera had been something of a shadowy figure from the start: he allegedly changed the date on his birth certificate in Buenos Aires. He was an authoritarian boss who insisted on controlling everything a football manager could possibly control, including, ideally, the match officials. He was accused by some Italian players of running their entire lives and experimenting with pills with his junior squads, and it was constantly suggested in Italy and elsewhere that he habitually rigged big matches, including a European Cup semi-final against Borussia Dortmund in 1964.[11] He was certainly as much a cod psychologist as Bill Shankly, who called Herrera, simply, 'a remarkable little fellow, a cut-throat man who wanted to win'. He underestimated the South American.

At Anfield on Wednesday, 4 May 1965 for the first leg, Shankly insisted that Inter take the field first, which they did to a monumental howl from the Kop of such volume and vehemence that it almost blew the visitors back inside the Main Stand. He then instructed his wounded warriors Milne and Byrne to parade the newly won FA Cup around the ground to further stoke the crowd. Anfield was now at boiling point. The Reds emerged into a swirling torrent of emotion, and they tore into their opponents. The Italians simply could not compete with the energy and pace of Liverpool. Hunt scored an early stunning volley from Callaghan's cross, but Mazzola equalised after ten minutes, following a slip by Yeats. And yet Inter seemed troubled by Liverpool's attacking frenzy, something they had never faced in Italy.

The second Liverpool goal, from Ian Callaghan, came from a complex set-piece move the Reds had practised in training. When St John scored the third goal with no further Italian reply, Bill Shankly was convinced that he now had a decisive lead to take to Italy, though today the away goal scored by Inter would be regarded as a precious cargo to take back home. Nevertheless, many Reds supporters regard this 3–1 victory as the team's greatest-ever display and the club's most atmospheric home night.

Herrera said magnanimously later that Inter had been beaten before but never so comprehensively *defeated* as they had been that evening. Shankly could see his rival was shaken, and he was even alleged to have cheekily asked Herrera for tips on Liverpool's likely final opponents, the Portuguese side Benfica. Sympathetic Italian journalists smiled at this, but they remained unconvinced. Even if Liverpool could outplay Inter again, they warned the Liverpool camp starkly, 'You will never be allowed to win.' Of course, they were right.

Near Lake Como, before the second leg, the Liverpool players were kept awake in their hotel by church bells and rowdy locals, but it was on the field, in front of 76,000 witnesses, where things seriously began to fall apart. Inter's lazy midfield genius Mario Corso started things rolling, scoring directly from a controversial free-kick, which Liverpool claimed was signalled as indirect, after just eight minutes. It was the start the Italians needed and the one Liverpool had feared. And within a minute, Liverpool's entire night's work and more at Anfield was wiped out after Joaquín Peiró illegally stole the ball out of Tommy Lawrence's hands as he prepared to kick it downfield and scored the second. This was a circus goal, not even allowed in parks football. Incredibly, the Spanish referee Ortiz de Mendibil allowed both goals to stand. Liverpool were shattered, bowed by this perceived injustice.

Fachetti's goal in the second half, Inter's third, was a brilliant irrelevance. De Mendibil was later implicated in the European match-fixing scandal reported in the *Sunday Times* in 1974, but Inter Milan escaped any punishment or even any serious investigation concerning the outcome of the tie. As Italian journalists had known it would be, the outcome of the match had been shaped by Inter's darkest desires. The proceedings were an affront to Bill Shankly and his innate sense of fairness. He was desperate to win football matches, but not like this. Liverpool's hard-headed, socialist muse had been frustrated by the arch dictator and South American football manipulator Herrera.

The great Scottish manager would have his European successes with Liverpool, but to his considerable frustration he would never win the European Cup – or even come this close again. The trophy, instead, was to become the property of another great Liverpool Football Club manager, one who was already being schooled in the sometimes devious ways of the European football hierarchy by sitting quietly on the Liverpool bench alongside the Glenbuck master. Although it seemed unimaginable at the time, the boot-room apprentice Bob Paisley would rule football in the grainy 1970s even more decisively than Bill Shankly had shaped the game in the 1960s.

CHAPTER 15 REFERENCES

1. St John, *The Saint*, p. 121
2. Du Noyer, *Liverpool Wondrous Place*, p. 101
3. Leigh, *The Cavern*, p. 117
4. Murden, 'City of Change and Challenge', p. 405
5. Keith, *Shanks for the Memory*, pp. 127–8
6. Young, *Football on Merseyside*, p. 168
7. Du Noyer, *Liverpool Wondrous Place*, p. 96
8. Williams and Hopkins, *The Miracle of Istanbul*, chapter 8, pp. 191–6
9. Shankly, *Shankly*, p. 102
10. Shankly, *Shankly*, pp. 103–4
11. Wilson, *Inverting the Pyramid*, p. 188

16

NOTHING BUT BLUE SKIES
Bob Paisley in Charge at Anfield

BILL SHANKLY'S GAP YEARS

Winning the 1965 FA Cup was the end of a grand quest at Liverpool Football Club, a moment of closure on a fabulous story that had started with John Houlding and John McKenna when they established the club out of their struggle with the Everton board back in 1892. Winning the cup had become the club's obsession ever since the first Liverpool Football League title had been claimed in 1901. The early 1960s also signalled the start of the modern history of Liverpool Football Club, the precursor to a period of near-constant success in the 1970s and 1980s that is still unique in the history of English football. Seventy-three years without a senior cup win of any kind was followed by a period of seventeen years when the club barely went a season without claiming knockout silverware. In the mid-1960s, the Liverpool club arguably had the best manager and the best backroom staff in the English game. It also had a seasoned group of players who were talented and still ambitious, a stadium that was both feared and respected at home and abroad, and supporters who were feted around the globe.

By now, the great Liverpool Kop, suddenly influenced by pop culture, had become something of a celebrated international institution, with documentary film-makers from around the world patiently queuing to crawl pretentiously over its rituals as anthropologists might examine distant and strange tribes. John Morgan from BBC's *Panorama* had proclaimed the Kop in 1964 to be 'as rich and mystifying a popular culture as any South Sea Island'. Local Liverpool football hooligans – often hidden by the international tributes flowing out for the choirs of Anfield – would soon be moving from the Kop's tumbling ranks to the Anfield Road end in pursuit of more satisfying action closer to rival supporters. The writer Arthur Hopcraft described the Kop, brilliantly and affectionately, in 1968 as a 'soft-sided crane grab' that dangled its members for minutes on end and a 'monstrous, odorous national pet' that it would be a cruel act of denial to kill off.[1] Despite the changes wrought by youth culture and new supporter styles, the Kop was essentially still the terrace that had bonded so powerfully with Elisha Scott in the 1930s. It had another 26 memorable years to breathe its friendly fire at opponents as a standing conference on the quality and commitment demanded of Liverpool Football Club on the field.

The Kop's spiritual leader Bill Shankly, meanwhile, was to add another FA Cup and two more league championships to his Liverpool roster, as well as blazing the trail in Europe. But progress would be uneven for the great Liverpool impresario. In England in World Cup year 1966, when Portuguese, Brazilians, Hungarians, North Koreans, Russians and West Germans all came to play football in the city of Liverpool, Shankly's own team stormed, virtually unopposed, to another league championship. Remarkably, nine Liverpool players completed forty or more league appearances in the season, with only injuries to right-half Gordon Milne threatening the Reds' shape and serene progress. In the 1966 European Cup-Winners' Cup, Liverpool overcame the Italians from Juventus and, on a drink-fuelled semi-final night that had Scots in disorder on the Anfield Road end, the Celtic side that would win the European Cup in 1967. The Reds would now face the West Germans from Borussia Dortmund in the final on a wet Thursday night at a one-third-filled Hampden Park.

This was quite possibly the most competitive year in the entire history of this rather unloved European tournament, and it is the only notable competition entered by the Liverpool club at home and abroad that it failed to win at some stage (later FIFA inventions for television, such as the Club World Championship, need not detain us here). Dortmund were formidable opponents, no doubt about it. The German side contained a core of the players who would face England in the World Cup final at Wembley in three months' time. One of them, the dynamic blond forward Sigi Held, scored the opening goal on a quite filthy Glasgow night. The Liverpool equaliser, scored by the struggling Roger Hunt, came from a cross after Peter Thompson had run the ball over the byline, undetected by the linesman or referee. But, unfazed by this setback, the Germans would not be denied, and in extra time Libuda floated a brilliant 35-yard lob over the stranded Tommy Lawrence to win the trophy for the men from the Ruhr.

This unexpected defeat in the club's first European final seemed likely to be a blip in what would surely be a procession of titles and cups for Shankly and his team. But instead it announced a mini-drought: no Liverpool trophy for seven years. What happened to the Liverpool machine, to Shankly's indomitable trailblazing? A number of factors probably collided here. First, both of the major

Manchester clubs and also Leeds United noticeably upped their game in the late 1960s (United won the European Cup in 1968), and Everton and Arsenal also had spells of real excellence that brought league titles to both and a Double for the Londoners in 1971. Arsenal beat a transitional Liverpool side in extra time to win the FA Cup. The First Division was competitive again. Second, Roger Hunt's bountiful years as a world-class striker – and his partnership with Ian St John – were coming to an end. Liverpool's goals began to dry up as a result. Most clubs would struggle to replace this quantity of goals, and Liverpool were no exception – it was no easy task to replace a man of his quality. Third, some of the players brought in by Shankly and his contacts to score goals and freshen up the team were simply substandard. Ex-Red Geoff Twentyman (and his distinctive trilby hat) had returned to Anfield in 1967 as the club's chief scout, and it took him time to hit his straps. Despite the spending binge sanctioned by chairman T.V. Williams in the late 1950s, Shankly knew that he would have to shop around for young talent once again. 'Liverpool successful by the cheapest possible way,' as he put it. It seemed like a return to the old unsuccessful ways of the past.

Local journalist Simon Hughes later wrote a book based on Twentyman's scouting diaries, which lists the key things the new man looked for in prospective Liverpool players. The first was a 'clean kick'. As Twentyman put it, 'I've never looked twice at any prospect who couldn't kick the ball properly.' Next was passing ability, followed by pace and attitude, and then craft and brains.[2] This was the complete package. His first recommendation to Shankly to stop the scoring rot at Anfield had all of these qualities. He was the free-scoring forward Francis Lee from Bolton Wanderers. Lee might have made all the difference, but the little man was never signed by Liverpool, probably because of his price in an auction. Instead, Lee inspired Manchester City to European and Football League titles, while Liverpool went into a mini-slump. Bobby Graham, Tony Hateley, Alun Evans, Jack Whitham and Phil Boersma were all tried up front and all failed to replace Sir Roger or to ignite Liverpool.

The final reason for this mini black hole in Shankly's time at the club was the manager's excessive loyalty to his players. His signature names of the early 1960s, St John, Yeats, Thompson and Hunt, were still in the Liverpool first team as the 1970s arrived. A turning point of sorts was reached on 21 February 1970 when Liverpool lost 0–1 at lowly Second Division Watford on a muddied heap in the sixth round of the FA Cup. This campaign was no 'slump' season – the Reds eventually finished second in the league to Leeds United in 1970. But Shankly had targeted winning the FA Cup to get his team moving once again, and he had finally run out of patience. Lawrence, Yeats, St John and Thompson were all dropped – Hunt had already been discarded. Only the winger Thompson survived to make any kind of impact in the season that followed.

St John had also been omitted earlier in the season, and he took his exclusion especially badly. His manager had been unable to face probably his favourite player with the news that his time at Anfield was finally coming to a close. The Saint knew he was on his way out for sure when Liverpool's assistant secretary Bill Barlow doled out a scraggy club turkey to him at Christmas, gleefully telling the Scot that the plump birds were being saved for 'first-teamers only'. St John left to play in South Africa, spitting feathers.[3] The 'family' club could also ruthlessly punish those who had once been its nearest and dearest.

REBUILDING – FOR RETIREMENT

With the great 1960s Liverpool side at last disbanding, and with the help of his scouts and advisers, Bill Shankly set about building his second dominant Liverpool team. In came the talented but impetuous 20-year-old Larry Lloyd to replace Yeats. Roger Hunt noted astutely that Lloyd's willingness to bring the ball forward on his strong left foot added to the confidence and forward momentum of this new Liverpool.[4] Alec Lindsay, a deceptively talented but ungainly ex-pig farmer left-back from Bury, displaced Geoff Strong, and Alun Evans, an inconsistent 19-year-old striker from Wolves, replaced Hunt. The awkward but effective lighthouse and cod poet John Toshack also joined from Cardiff City for a tidy £111,000 in November 1970, and he went on to form vital scoring partnerships for Liverpool over the next eight years. Steve Heighway and Brian Hall were also recruited, two amateur forwards and university graduates who had initial problems convincing hard men such as Tommy Smith that they cared just as much about winning professional football matches as he and all Liverpool supporters did. Heighway was cerebral, coltish, long-striding and direct; Hall was earnest, busy and combative. Both would offer Liverpool service after their successful playing careers were over. The latter inadvertently entertained the Liverpool dressing-room and his manager by turning up for training at Melwood wearing the conductor's outfit he wore while earning some extra cash as a student working on the Lancashire buses.

Soon after these arrivals, a scrawny and dodgy-permed young Kirkby kid with bird's legs called Phil Thompson started putting his hand up to be selected in and around the Liverpool defence. He would become a key figure in the new era, a modern, ultra-moaning version of Tommy Smith. A European Cup defeat to a cultured, quick-passing Red Star Belgrade in November 1973 convinced the Liverpool coaching staff that the days of the British-style stopper centre-half were finally over. Larry Lloyd had been the bridge. Footballing centre-backs, men who could read the game, keep the ball and pass it, would now be required in the modern era, especially in order to progress in European club competitions.

Surprisingly perhaps, the Liverpool manager's only real concession to his beloved Scotland during this period of rapid change was the recruitment, in July 1972 from Nottingham Forest, of the high-stepping midfielder Peter Cormack, who added class and goals to this department – and also a Scottish voice to the Liverpool dressing-room. Cormack bravely (foolishly?) stepped in at Melwood one morning when Tommy Smith and new man Lloyd locked horns in a typical training-session ritual testing of the balls of the new recruit. The intervening Scot came out worst.

All these men played their part, but Bill Shankly constructed his new vision for Liverpool around three other key signings, all of them Englishmen, all of them bargains. The Liverpool scouting network really earned its corn here. Barrow-born left-sided defender Emlyn Hughes first attracted the attention of the Liverpool scouts in Blackpool's reserve team, and Bill Shankly was especially impressed by the physical presence, sheer competitiveness and cold-eyed nerve of the youngster. He even offered £25,000 for Hughes straight after his Blackpool first-team debut. It was rejected. Later, Shankly watched Hughes as he fronted up to a hostile crowd and intimidation from Chelsea players and their manager Tommy Docherty in a violent FA Cup tie in which Peter Osgood broke his leg tangling with the young defender. The Liverpool boss had seen enough. In March 1967, he agreed to pay £65,000 for the full-back. That night, and driving atrociously as usual, Shankly famously scolded a traffic police officer who stopped his car whilst the manager was ferrying his new signing back to Merseyside. What was he doing, this doltish plod, asked Shankly? Did he not know he was holding up a 'future captain of England'? The sheepish Emlyn Hughes was just 19 years old.

Initially, Hughes replaced the graceful Scot Willie Stevenson on the left side of Liverpool's midfield. His leadership, confidence, boyish enthusiasm and immense power made him an instant crowd favourite at Anfield – and a truly great Liverpool player. For his arm-flapping, head-down, all-action running style, the amused Liverpool crowd affectionately christened Hughes 'Crazy Horse', a label that stuck throughout his career. With this young tyro at its heart, Shankly's Liverpool won the league title again in 1973 (the first of four at Liverpool for Hughes), beating Arsenal and Leeds United to the punch. The club also won the UEFA Cup in the same year, the first time in Liverpool's history that two major trophies were claimed in the same season. Hughes was later successfully converted to centre-back to counter the pace and cleverness of European forwards. Under Bob Paisley, and with the club now tightening its grip domestically and abroad, Hughes won more league titles, in 1976, 1977 and 1979. Under Hughes's inspiring captaincy, Liverpool also won the UEFA Cup again, in 1976, and consecutive European Cups in 1977 and 1978. These achievements, and a personal Footballer of the Year award in 1977, were the crowning moments of Hughes's glittering football career at Anfield.

But, for all his qualities, the effervescent 'Yosser' could also show just too much brass neck on occasions for the barrack-room Liverpool squad. He thought a lot of himself in a team with plenty of competing talents and some egos. The self-promoting Hughes urged Bill Shankly to replace the then Reds captain Tommy Smith with someone younger – the doting Shanks took note. Tommy Smith was incandescent with rage. So, in 1974 it was Emlyn Hughes, not the loyal and abrasive Smith, who hoisted the FA Cup for Liverpool after the 3–0 Wembley rout of a limp Newcastle United. It was to prove to be Bill Shankly's last great Liverpool FC occasion, and Smith never forgave the manager, or Hughes, for this act of personal treachery. Occasionally, when they played together later in Liverpool's defence, the two men refused to communicate directly – Hughes asked centre-half Larry Lloyd to 'tell that fat bastard to pass the ball'. Smith could also be heard congratulating under his breath any opponent who had managed to lamp his defender colleague. The message was that great teams seldom get along in *all* departments.

Skegness-born 18-year-old goalkeeper Ray Clemence was bought by Shankly, just after Hughes arrived, from Scunthorpe United for a paltry figure of around £18,000 in June 1967. Shankly watched Clemence more than any other player before signing him. It was a major scouting coup and one of Shankly's best-ever signings for Liverpool Football Club. Clemence was working at his summer job, hiring out deckchairs on Skeggy beach, when word first came through that Liverpool and Bill Shankly were interested in signing him. Even as a young man, Clemence was self-possessed, a smart guy, and he was unsure that he really wanted to swap first-team football in the Third Division for a couple of seasons (or maybe more) playing in front of one man and his dog in the Liverpool reserves. But Shankly was undeterred, and he poured it on, telling the young keeper that Tommy Lawrence was an elderly 30 years of age and on his way out of Anfield (Lawrence was actually 27 and in his prime for a goalkeeper). Shankly assured Clemence that he would very soon be between the Liverpool posts, possibly playing in European finals for the recent European Cup-Winners' Cup finalists. In fact, the new man would have to wait two and a half years to make his senior Liverpool debut, after the Watford FA Cup debacle. There was no discussion at all about salary when Clemence agreed to sign. Shanks simply told him he would be 'well looked after'. For the Liverpool manager, all this young keeper needed to think about now was that he would be playing for the greatest football club in the world.

Clemence was agile and supple but not huge for a goalkeeper – he was under 6 ft tall and under 13 st. But he was an excellent decision-maker and a good and very vocal defensive organiser, a man who demanded – and usually got – excellence from his back four. His concentration levels were immense, something that was vitally important. The Liverpool goalkeeper had to stay 'in the game' even when he was getting little real match action as the Reds in the 1970s started to dominate their rivals. He usually came off the pitch mentally drained, even if Liverpool had played almost the entire match in their opponents' half. His sweeping behind the backline (he starred as an outfielder in training) and his distribution from hand or foot were first class, and he hardly seemed to make any mistakes – or to get injured. For eleven Liverpool seasons, from August 1970 until May 1981, Clemence missed only six league matches and ended up with six hundred and sixty-five major domestic and European appearances for the club. In 1978–79, he helped the team achieve the greatest defensive record in forty-two-game Football League history – Liverpool conceded just sixteen league goals, only four of them at Anfield. Clemence was also a bubbly character in the Reds dressing-room, a very positive and intelligent influence, attributes that aided him in becoming the England goalkeeping coach after he retired as a player.

The third key Shankly signing for this period was, of course, the forward Kevin Keegan. This future international and honed national sporting product – a precursor of the Michael Owen England figure – also came from Scunthorpe United, in May 1971 for around £33,000. The Liverpool manager later described the deal, proudly, as 'robbery with violence'. Keegan was recommended to Shankly by his old mentor Andy Beattie, whom Shanks now employed as part of Geoff Twentyman's scouting network. Beattie had been tracking Keegan for 18 months and was bemused that no other club had even registered an interest in him after 124 Scunthorpe appearances. Had he missed something? Absurdly, some good judges thought Keegan lacked courage. As soon as Bob Paisley saw him, he told Shanks to start preparing to woo this new talent. Other suitors eventually stirred, but Keegan signed just as Liverpool were about to lose the 1971 FA Cup final to Arsenal.

The new recruit went with the Liverpool party to Wembley and was personally devastated by the defeat. Fagan, Paisley and Shankly raised collective eyebrows. This was some commitment already to the Liverpool cause. Not that the signing made a big splash – Keegan's first Liverpool wages were little better than those he had been on at little Scunthorpe. Bill Shankly had given Keegan the 'move to a big club like Liverpool and the money will follow' speech he had worked on with Ray Clemence, and the youngster had lapped it up. But this was no deception on the Liverpool manager's part, no politician's spin or wind-up. Shankly passionately believed that his younger players should properly appreciate their rise up the ranks, and he needed to know that they were playing from the heart for Liverpool Football Club, not for their pay cheques. He need have no fears about Keegan. The two men actually became very close, Shankly as a kind of father figure and mentor to this rapidly uncoiling ball of football energy, as he had once been to the young Tommy Smith.

Although he was lacking a little in natural ability compared to other top forwards, and initially short on confidence, in the late summer of 1971 Keegan was first to everything in training at Melwood and impossible to track or predict; experienced Liverpool defenders were being given the run-around by a kid they had never even heard of. He was a demon to impress, with terrific acceleration, and he was incredibly fit and vibrantly enthusiastic, another Emlyn Hughes. Shankly was worried about a shortage of goals and pace in the Liverpool side – his forward recruits were not delivering – so he promoted Keegan directly into the Liverpool first team in August 1971. This was virtually unheard of: a raw recruit from the English Fourth Division being thrown in without any of the detailed Anfield grooming and reserve-team apprenticeship. It looked like desperation, and the manager certainly needed a boost. Keegan was crying out for a chance, and he did not disappoint. Again, like Michael Owen, his sheer naive exuberance seemed to unhinge even experienced defenders. Keegan simply never gave up. He teamed up instantly with the tall Welshman John Toshack and was to become the attacking fulcrum of the Liverpool team for the next six years, replacing at last the successful Hunt and Ian St John forward partnership of the 1960s. Keegan starred in the club's second FA Cup win, in 1974, and in the first European Cup triumph under Bob Paisley, in Rome in 1977. He also became one of the first British players in the modern period to have an agent and was the first to leave the Liverpool club to develop his career elsewhere – with Hamburg. It was a very early marker of where the European trade for footballers might eventually end up.

TOO LONG GONE

With these key signings in place, and Bill Shankly apparently in his pomp again and marked for a long stay and more trophies at Liverpool, new man John Smith (as chairman) and Peter Robinson (as all-seeing club secretary) gradually became the new driving boardroom and administrative forces around the club in the 1970s and beyond. For 17 years, between 1973 and 1990, Liverpool's 'dapper businessman chairman' Smith, a brewery sales director and deputy chairman of an electronics firm, and also chairman of the Sports Council between 1985 and 1989, ran the club not just as the traditional Liverpool 'family' concern but also as a tight and cohesive administrative and business unit. Gone for good (or so we thought) was the era of lack of leadership and focus and the endless chairman re-elections of the 1950s. Smith and his board, with Robinson close at hand, worked hard on raising the necessary cash for player recruitment to try to keep the club among Europe's elite. They also worked diligently on the important modernisation of the Liverpool stadium. The new Main Stand, seating 8,600 and with 2,150 standing in the paddock below, and a modern floodlighting system were officially opened on 10 March 1973, during the club's eighth championship season. All seemed set fair for the next great Liverpool advance.

And it duly came, with the league title won again in 1973 and the club's first European trophy, the newly named UEFA Cup, won by narrowly defeating Borussia Mönchengladbach 3–2 on aggregate over two legs in May. Inspired by Keegan, Liverpool had demolished the West Germans 3–0 in the first leg at Anfield, but not before a washout first attempt at the fixture was abandoned, leading Shankly to change his original selection and bring in John Toshack to terrorise the German defence in the air. Liverpool were truly outclassed and pummelled in the return, only just holding on to the 0–2 scoreline that won the trophy for their manager and the Liverpool hordes.

Liverpool FC, UEFA Cup-winners, 1973

Clemence

Lawler   Smith   Lloyd   Lindsay

Callaghan   Cormack   Hughes   Heighway

Keegan   Toshack

But frustration would follow for Shankly in the European Cup against Red Star Belgrade in the autumn of 1973, and the Liverpool manager so wanted revenge for his 1965 humiliation in Milan. Would it ever come? Not now, because almost without warning, the great man Shankly, the Glenbuck visionary, resigned on 12 July 1974. The glorious 12th it was not. But why go now? He was only 61 years of age, not old at all for a football manager. His new side, playing a flexible 4–4–2, had recently won in Europe and had clinically dismantled Newcastle in the 1974 FA Cup final, practising just the sort of football he had always preached: passing, movement and power combined. Liverpool supporters had even invaded the Wembley pitch to kiss his feet. Why throw all this away, with players he had developed, such as Hughes, Keegan, Clemence, Thompson, Hall and Heighway, still young and hungry? There are many theories about his Liverpool departure but very few clear answers.

Shankly had certainly dragged Liverpool into the modern era. He was made for the new age of television sport, and he had established the right of the club's manager actually to manage at Anfield without undue interference from the board. His identity was now interwoven with that of the club. The story hit so hard in Liverpool that people on the street either refused to believe it or simply gawped at the news – they just couldn't take it in. This was because Shankly had also become part of the city's mythology; he was so much more to local citizens than a mere football manager. His values and principles extended well beyond the dressing-room. It is not too much to suggest that Shankly had become something of a modern local exemplar of a kind of lived socialism. Many ordinary people had memories of him in this respect: looking for unemployed supporters outside grounds where Liverpool played to offer them match tickets; paying the train fares to away matches of down-at-heel Reds fans; attending, unannounced, the funerals of committed Liverpool supporters whom he barely knew; or even helping to carry the weekday shopping of elderly people in West Derby Village.[5] Again, images of the great Elisha Scott come to mind, in terms of feelings of attachment to and identification with local people. Indeed, Tom Watson, Elisha Scott and Shankly form a chain of continuity in this respect. Shankly would also frequently turn up unannounced at supporters' birthday parties or social events on Saturday evenings with one proviso only: that he had to be home in time to watch *Match of the Day* on TV. This was no ordinary modern football boss. When he told his players he was going to retire, the impact was so enormous that his captain Emlyn Hughes openly sobbed – much to Tommy Smith's disgust.

It is true that Shankly was something of a serial resigner. He often offered his resignation to the Liverpool board at the season's end, depressed by impending inactivity and seemingly needing confirmation that he was still valued and wanted at the club for another season. Until then, the club's directors and staff had always easily talked him out of leaving, and this summer role play had grown into something of an annual ritual. But now his backroom staff at Anfield had grown in stature – the famed Liverpool boot room had European experience and a collective voice that was separate and different from Shankly's own. If the Scot really did want to go this time, it was not quite the disaster it might once have seemed. His assistant Bob Paisley could conceivably step up, ably supported by a coterie of hardened professionals, which now included Ronnie Moran, on the Reds coaching staff. And not everyone in the Liverpool boardroom appreciated their manager's open disdain for the doings of football-club directors. Some of them would not be so sad that their attention-grabbing manager was on his way. Not that loyalty counted for much: Peter Robinson intimated soon after Shankly had departed that if Bob Paisley failed to win a trophy or to keep Liverpool in football's elite in his first season, the club would very probably be looking for a new manager again. This was business.

Bill Shankly had been under the media spotlight at Liverpool for 15 years, and the intense pressure of constant performing had also begun to tell. He once described football management as 'a soul-destroying job' and rightly rated the most important quality of a manager as being 'the natural ability to pick a player'. Its lack would unseat many pretenders who followed him. He was no simple romantic. 'Managing a football club is like drowning,' he once told Tommy Smith. 'Sublimely peaceful and pleasant once the struggle is over.'[6] Shankly knew that his utter devotion to the game had been hard on his family, and especially on his long-suffering wife Nessie. All those away trips and deathly scouting nights away from home.

He probably really did think for an instant that he should spend more time with the other people in his life who loved him unconditionally. But it also looked as if he was deeply uneasy with his decision to retire from the game almost as soon as his resignation was reluctantly accepted. Often, a difficult life-changing choice once taken produces a sense of profound relief, a weight lifted from one's shoulders. There was very little evidence of that here. There was only confusion and regret. Significantly, Shankly had named no successor, and he looked as if he missed football and his day-to-day involvement at the club right from the very moment he left it. Had he expected the Liverpool directors to do even more to try to keep him? Had he wanted a public uprising to demand that he take charge again? He later wrote, 'It was never my intention to have a complete break with Liverpool.' But no new manager could have survived easily at Anfield with the ghost of Bill Shankly loitering in the background. And there seemed little realistic prospect of the Glenbuck socialist being invited to join the still very conservative Liverpool board. That would have been a recipe for disaster.

THE MANAGER OF THE MILLENNIUM

A terrible decision had now been made. Although Liverpool Football Club owed a huge debt to Bill Shankly, it also had to move on, to get behind the new manager Bob Paisley. The club was bigger and more important than anyone, and the old boss could not be allowed to haunt the Reds training ground – it had to be all or nothing. All of this caused misunderstanding, unhappiness and tension. There were accusations that Liverpool FC had dealt badly with its great modern leader. Shankly himself seemed bitter, and he clearly felt rejected by his old club. He even suggested that Everton was warmer towards him now than was the Anfield hierarchy, and Evertonians certainly enjoyed propagating the myth later that the Liverpool club and its supporters had soon 'forgotten' Shankly's contribution.[7] They ought to check out the Kop today and look for similar Harry Catterick flags at Goodison Park.

The truth was much more banal: the Liverpool club had not pushed Bill Shankly out, far from it. But once his decision was confirmed, the matter had simply been dealt with as ruthlessly and as professionally as Shankly himself had often dealt with great footballers who had passed their peak of usefulness to Liverpool Football Club. It might have seemed callous, but, as always in football, the future was all that mattered now.

Partly because of all this shock, sadness and uncertainty, Bob Paisley began his managerial regime at Liverpool as probably the most reluctant Liverpool incumbent since George Patterson had been pressed to take over back in the 1930s. His choice as Shankly's successor was both inspired and unusual in the English game: assistants did not naturally become managers when their bosses departed. He told his players, 'I don't particularly want the job, but someone's got to do it.' It was hardly Churchillian rhetoric, no rallying call to arms. But then Bob was no public orator. He led by example and by sound decision-making, rather than by fine words or native psychology as Bill Shankly might have done.

Few of the players could understand Bob's north-east mutterings anyway – about 'doins' and 'what's its' and 'jag down there' – but they respected him. 'Bob was great at not giving players problems,' as Alan Kennedy later put it, rather backhandedly.[8] In other words, he kept things simple and trusted his players. And plenty of things were in Bob Paisley's favour. He knew the club and its staff inside out, and the players and coaches were all behind him. Most football managers take over a club because the last man has been sacked and left the business in a mess. Nothing could be further from the truth: Liverpool were riding high with a good young core of players. Shankly had just added to it by buying the bulky and disillusioned forward Ray Kennedy from Arsenal for £180,000, a player Paisley later converted into a mobile and brilliant goalscoring left-sided midfielder, although Kennedy was ultimately a man dogged by demons and illness. Bill Shankly had left Liverpool Football Club in fine fettle.

Paisley also made some astute early signings of his own, directed by Twentyman and the Liverpool scouts. In October 1974, he recruited a versatile, authentically two-footed defender from Northampton Town called Phil Neal for £66,000, initially to replace Alec Lindsay on the left but eventually to substitute for Chris Lawler on the right. It was a bargain. Joey Jones, a raw young leg-biting Welshman, would come in a year later from Wrexham to briefly hold sway on Liverpool's left side. The 23-year-old Neal was like a top golfer, according to Twentyman: he was able to chip, drive and weight a ball perfectly, and on both flanks.[9] He was simply the most consistent and most reliable outfield player in Liverpool's history. In ten seasons – four hundred and twenty league matches – between August 1975 and May 1985, Neal missed precisely one league match for Liverpool, an injury incurred in a meeting at Manchester United in September 1983. Neal is the only Liverpool player to win four European Cups, and he played in five finals, while also winning eight league championships. He became the ever-present defensive rock of the Bob Paisley era, a wonderful servant, without doubt one of the club's greatest-ever players.

In, too, came Terry McDermott, an expat from Kirkby, a 'Duracell' midfield player who had somehow ended up at Bury and then in the north-east at Newcastle United. Many thought Paisley had wrongly spent £175,000 on Terry Mac in November 1974 when the Scouser initially struggled to get into Liverpool's team. But the new man later came to the fore with his ceaseless running and brilliant goals, and all this with a 'reluctant' attitude to training and weirdly obtuse match-day preparations. Terry Mac liked a drink – many of the Liverpool squad did – he ate all the wrong things and he also liked watching the horse racing in the players' lounge until 2.40 p.m. on match days, then dragging on his kit and tumbling out onto the pitch like any Sunday-league footballer might. The Liverpool coaching staff accepted his idiosyncrasies, as long as he continued to produce where it mattered: on the pitch. For six great seasons he did.

Paisley and his boot-room men, ex-reserve team player Roy Evans, Reuben Bennett, Joe Fagan and Ronnie Moran, spent a year settling in, and, despite Peter Robinson's warning, they were allowed their time. There were no trophies in this first season, but second place in the league in 1974–75 was just enough to keep the Liverpool board off his case. The directors (for once) knew what they were doing. The title returned to Anfield in 1975–76, and so too did the UEFA Cup, Liverpool seeing off both Real Sociedad and Barcelona from Spain before overcoming Club Brugge KV in a hard-fought two-legged final.

By now, a tough-tackling young midfielder by the name of Jimmy Case had signed from South Liverpool and was making waves among Liverpool's opposition – and sometimes in local bars and clubs, too, with his chief partner in crime the unpredictable Ray Kennedy. A flame-haired, sometimes chaotic, local attacker called David Fairclough was also trying to force his way past Keegan and Toshack into the Liverpool team. He was, more usually, making an impact as a substitute. Fairclough's chances of making a real splash at Anfield diminished still further when the hard-working England and ex-Everton centre-forward David Johnson was brought in by Paisley from Ipswich Town in August 1976. With Clemence securely in goal and Hughes by now partnering Phil Thompson or Tommy Smith in the middle of a more mobile Liverpool defence, Jones and Neal at full-back, and Case, McDermott and Kennedy all established in midfield with the evergreen Ian Callaghan – an astonishing survivor from the 1959–60 season – Bob Paisley's first Liverpool team had begun to take some shape. The flyer Heighway or Johnson accompanied Keegan up front. In just three years, Paisley had built on the Shankly legacy and produced a new, more flexible side. He would now manage to do what even his great mentor had been denied in Milan in 1965: win the European Cup.

WE'RE ON OUR WAY TO ROMA

The path for Liverpool to the 1977 European Cup final may look simple enough compared to today's marathon: Crusaders, Trabzonspor and FC Zurich (in the semi-final) were all comfortably put to the sword. But the campaign really took off in the quarter-finals, when Liverpool were drawn to play the French champions St Etienne, who had been cruelly and unjustly beaten in the 1976 final by Bayern Munich. This was a real test. After losing 0–1 in France, Liverpool faced an uphill task at Anfield when Bathenay equalised Kevin Keegan's early goal with an unstoppable long-range drive. Now two goals were needed – a situation calling out for heroes. Ray Kennedy had already scored a second goal for Liverpool in a pulsating match of high quality played in a frenzied atmosphere before substitute David Fairclough was summoned, once again, to replace the ineffective Toshack. Liverpool players marvelled at the Bionic Carrot's capacity to score goals from the substitutes' bench. But Fairclough was less sure this was a blessing. He hated the super-sub label – he wanted to start in the team. Now, put clear on the left of the French defence, he scored the crucial goal with six minutes remaining as the home crowd went wild. It was a coming of age of Liverpool in the major European competition, a memorable occasion but also a signal of intent. This was now an experienced and hardened European unit, real contenders for the top European club crown.

FC Zurich were casually brushed aside in the semi-final, but before the Rome final could be contemplated there was another league title to wrap up, with three nervy (or was it boredom?) draws in May closing the final gap ahead of Manchester City to just one point. Liverpool also survived in the FA Cup, playing in a luckily drawn semi-final to Everton at Maine Road before demolishing the Blues 3–0 in the replay. This meant that, four days before playing the biggest match in the entire history of the club, Liverpool would meet Manchester United at Wembley in the small matter of the FA Cup final. There had been no season for any English club like this one, and none to test the marital status, pockets and employment records of the club's mainly working-class supporters in quite this fashion. Plenty of Liverpudlians set off to Wembley and then carried on going to Italy – why bother driving back north? Even the Liverpool Treble seasons that followed in 1984 and then 2001 lacked the intensity of this climax. Who could catch their breath? And in the end it proved just too much for the players. In a scrappy match, United prevailed 1–2 at Wembley. The Reds now had to lift themselves for their European Cup final chance at last. Once again, the Germans from Borussia Mönchengladbach lay in wait. It proved to be an unforgettable occasion.

The 1977 European Cup final is probably mostly recalled for Kevin Keegan's headline contest with the West German international defender Berti Vogts, or Tommy Smith's bullet-headed second goal (later remembered, to no great fuss in Liverpool, by a father-of-three Scouser on a reality TV show as simply 'the greatest moment of my life'), or Phil Neal's nerveless penalty conversion to finally clinch the 3–1 win. But for those who were there, this was also a fantastic cultural experience for the people of Liverpool, one to match and then easily surpass the 1914, 1950 and 1965 great supporter flows from the city to London for FA Cup finals. Small knots of Liverpool fans had travelled with the club around Europe, but this was the first great epic European journey for a mass of Liverpool supporters – an estimated 25,000 travelled to Rome, using every conceivable route and form of transport, every possible excuse for missing work (think back to all those midweek Reds cup replays in the 1930s) and every means of raising cash for the trip. Merseyside pawnbrokers and moneylenders were even better-used than usual for a few weeks in May 1977.

Liverpool FC, European Cup-winning team, v. Borussia Mönchengladbach, 25 May 1977

Clemence

Neal   Smith   Hughes   Jones

Case   Callaghan   McDermott   Kennedy

Keegan   Heighway

This was the era before cheap flights, so these supporters were no sophisticated and experienced adventurers. Nor were they members of the sort of well-padded, mixed-sex global contingents that later followed the Reds to big finals abroad. This was a pasty-white crowd of mainly working men, pretty much all of them from the city. Many of them afforded this arduous journey about the level of preparation and respect typically demanded for an overnight stop in south London or for a football visit to Bristol in the distant south-west. Plenty of people from Liverpool (including the author) made a gruelling five-day round trip by coach to be there, with no overnight stops. Other young 'scallies' set out for this adventure in vans and by train with only the clothes on their backs, a little (British) cash in their pockets, a plastic bag full of sandwiches and possibly an apple (a vain nod, this last provision, to the importance of dental hygiene).[10] Most of these supporters got to Rome and into the Olympic Stadium and had the time of their lives in the process. But hundreds of Reds got there and then slumped in the city or even outside the ground, the worse for drink, ticketless or simply exhausted and confused by the whole process of being abroad and making it to this distant, glorious place. It was a fantastic Liverpool affair.

The Liverpool anthem for this great trek was more lyrical and inventive even than the 1965 Liverpool FA Cup final songs and the chants that had so charmed the British media or indeed any of those that had been popular in the city in earlier periods of the football fever. To the tune of 'Arrivederci Roma', the following rang out from every bus, boat, plane and van that carried Reds southwards across Europe:

> We're on our way to Roma
> On the 25th of May
> All the Kopites will be singing
> Vatican bells they will be ringing
> Liverpool songs we will be singing
> When we win the European Cup

The extraordinary party in Rome after the 1977 final involved Reds supporters and the players together. These groups were still broadly drawn from the same stock, drank (and got drunk) in the same pubs, had pretty much similar lifestyles and diets, and footballers had not yet moved into the sort of wage brackets that later had them sealed off behind tinted-windowed cars the size of small armoured trucks. But this was also the period for the emergence of new terrace rivalries about clothes and attitude in English football support, initially out of the north-west. There had been signs of this at the FA Cup final against United

– young Scousers had effeminate wedge haircuts and wore straight jeans, cords and Adidas trainers rather than the home-made punk or disco styles, or the flares that had gone before.[11] After Rome 1977, a flood of foreign sports gear started piling into Merseyside from similar trips, the more obscure, expensive and exclusive the better. Suddenly, the act of wearing sports clothing and trainers in the city was no longer just about sport. These new outfits were all signs of class distinction: about 'hardness', style, capacious consumption, club loyalty in following the Reds to far-flung locales and bringing parts of the world back to the great seaport of Liverpool in time-honoured fashion. This gear was also useful to flaunt in the face of less-favoured, more domesticated, rival football supporters. Who the fuck are *you*?

Eventually, discussions of the nuances of supporter style would make the pages of music and football fanzines in Liverpool – Pete Hooton's *The End* was positively forensic in sniffing out terrace fakers and Merseyside woollybacks – as well as fashion magazines and colour supplements. Supporters' styles even became the subject of PhD theses. It was the time of the casuals and the well-turned-out mob, and for seven years, at least, this sort of performance culture at football at home and especially abroad was hugely enjoyable, frequently anarchic, and occasionally dangerous and violent fun for those involved – and for others. And then, after Brussels in 1985, when Liverpool played in their fifth, disastrous, European Cup final, the whole business of travel for football abroad became something quite different.

PAISLEY'S LIVERPOOL: TAKE THREE SCOTS

With the club's first European Cup now safe on Bob Paisley's mantelpiece, Kevin Keegan immediately left Liverpool Football Club for Germany. The old football sage from County Durham barely blinked. Bill Shankly had built his first great Reds team around three Scots – Yeats, St John and Stevenson – and his second around three key Englishmen. Now Paisley looked to the north again to construct his new post-Keegan Liverpool. Again, he brought in three brilliant, highly intelligent Scots, a crafty intellectual balance for Paisley's native, intuitive football mind. These were men who would rule the Liverpool dressing-room, run his team on the field when tactical adjustments were needed and also lead from the front if the Reds needed to scrap. It would be the last time the English would drain Scotland for some of the world's best football talent, because the Scottish game would now dry up in the face of cultural change and global competition. It was also the end of a great tradition on Merseyside for recruiting groups of 'Scottish professors', one that had stretched back over a century and had been central in establishing Liverpool as a football club more than 80 years before.

A slightly gawky young Scottish midfielder called Alan Hansen had attended trials at Liverpool as a 15 year old in the summer of 1970. He had been rejected. Hansen's laid-back attitude and lack of pace had not impressed the Liverpool coaches, showing just how capricious the process of finding real football talent can be. The Scot was much brighter than most young players (and probably the club's coaches), and he wasn't even sure that he wanted to be a professional footballer at all. He was well educated, enjoyed golf more and got very nervous before big matches, despite looking outwardly calm. He had other options. Nevertheless, Hansen signed professional forms for Partick Thistle in December 1973, and as he grew taller his manager Bertie Auld insisted he play centre-back, a position Hansen hated. Hansen kept on pushing up from the back into midfield at Partick, and this combination of positional dexterity, defensive assurance and ball-playing invention eventually attracted English interest. Most club scouts thought that the Scot was too weak and took too many liberties to play in England. But Geoff Twentyman, for Liverpool, wanted defenders who could play at home but also in Europe, where opposing forwards needed to be outwitted more than bludgeoned into submission. Not that he was overly impressed with Hansen. 'Gives the impression,' he wrote in his scouting diaries, 'that if faced with quick forwards would struggle.' Nevertheless, in May 1977 Liverpool invested £100,000 in the 21 year old – it was a steal. Hansen filled out physically and became stronger mentally. In his defensive ability, intelligent game-reading and comfort on the ball, Hansen was arguably the best defender the club had recruited in 70 years. Hansen played 618 times for Liverpool, strolling to a first European Cup-winner's medal at Wembley in 1978 and then replacing Emlyn Hughes for good in the Liverpool team in the 1978–79 season. His calm, unflustered defending meant that for the next 13 years, if Hansen was fit, he was in the Liverpool side, no question. He often played when he was not. He was part of the on-pitch Scottish brains trust that effectively ran each section of the successful Liverpool team for Bob Paisley and his coaches until the mid-1980s.

In the midfield department, the Scot who ran things for the new Paisley generation was a haughty natural leader, a football aristocrat and a superb technician. Graeme Souness was signed from Middlesbrough for £352,000 in January 1978. The Edinburgh-born Souness had a very flaky disciplinary record as a youngster – he had trouble controlling his natural aggression and his overwhelming cockiness. But under Paisley and his coaches he managed to rein things in, combining some of Ian St John's irreverent brio and cleverness with the uncompromising toughness of the soon-to-depart Tommy Smith. He forged these potentially toxic qualities into a stocky frame that lacked a bit of pace but wanted little for self-belief and skill, and that had an utterly ruthless will-to-win mentality. Politically, Souness represented the antithesis of Bill Shankly's native socialism – the idealism of the 1960s would soon give way to the brute greed and selfishness of the 1980s in Britain. The Liverpool midfield man had a taste for money, champagne and beautiful women, and he had little time for the collectivism espoused by the west-coast Scots. But on the pitch and at the training ground, the two football men would have made a great partnership.

Souness openly mocked lesser rival players, and he soon assumed Tommy Smith's alpha-male role of 'testing' new Liverpool recruits on the Melwood training ground. His demanding standards could also be cruelly punishing in match situations, especially for his less-talented teammates. For many years, he taunted left-back Alan Kennedy, who had been brought in by Paisley from Newcastle United in August 1978 for a record fee – Souness derided the defender for his lack of style and precision. Souness's leadership, his passing and his imperious game management were his real strengths. But also right up there was his cynical determination to get the job done for his club when others might have wavered. He would do most things to win. In 1984, in a European Cup home semi-final first leg against a dangerous Dinamo Bucharest, a frustrated Souness assaulted the Romanian captain Movila, who suffered a broken jaw as a result. Liverpool struggled home 1–0. The visitors were outraged and promised bloody revenge in the second leg. The local police even seemed to be in on the act, and other Liverpool players were clearly affected by this Eastern European threat. But the unflustered Souness was quite beyond intimidation, and he fearlessly governed the match as boots flew, Liverpool winning 2–1.

This sort of trial by fire was good preparation for the final in Rome in 1984, where the home club AS Roma were eventually beaten on penalties. Fittingly, the Liverpool captain who lifted the trophy was a jauntily moustachioed and beaming Graeme Souness, a man peerlessly leading his club through all-comers once again. Always ambitious and hungry for new experiences – and for big pay days – the Liverpool captain departed to play in Italy soon after, but he would return later to Anfield in much more difficult times.

Up front, the final brilliant Scot of the Paisley era was someone many good judges argue is the club's greatest-ever player. He certainly rivals Alex Raisbeck, Elisha Scott and Billy Liddell, who would all have good claims to the title. The Glasgow-born striker Kenny Dalglish left Celtic for Liverpool as a 26 year old in August 1977 for a record fee between British clubs of £440,000. Dalglish had already won four Scottish league titles and four Scottish Cups, a fact often forgotten amidst the acclaim about the flood of cups and titles and the European honours he amassed while at Liverpool as both a player and a manager. His departure from Scotland and his later successes at Anfield even helped forge powerful links between the Liverpool and Celtic clubs, connections that were movingly visible after the Hillsborough disaster in 1989, when Dalglish was the stricken Liverpool club's manager.

Like Alan Hansen, Dalglish had once been a teenage triallist at Anfield (in August 1966), but his unremarkable physique and lack of speed counted against him for the demanding Liverpool coaches under Bill Shankly. By the time he returned to Anfield 11 years later to fill the number-7 shirt vacated by Kevin Keegan, he had developed into the complete European forward. He was collected and deadly in front of goal yet unmatched in his selfless work around the pitch for his teammates. His ego-free passing and his determination to keep the ball and play the game simply was straight from the Shankly and Paisley textbook, and his will to win was enormous. All this meant that Dalglish had more self-confidence than Hansen, but he lacked some of the taunting bravado and disrespect for opponents of Souness. When Bob Paisley had looked at his most vulnerable as the Liverpool boss – when his touchstone forward Keegan left for Germany – available and ready to sign for Liverpool Football Club was a player right in the Keegan mould but someone who was an even *better* player than Bill Shankly's adopted forward 'son'. Was this good fortune or simply great football management? Whatever the answer, Dalglish improved more modest players simply by bringing them into the game and flooding them with confidence. There was no greater sight for Liverpool supporters than the way this private and shy man's boyish, blond features lit up with unconstrained delight after he had scored or helped fashion a Liverpool goal in his 515 outings for the club. And there would be plenty of occasions to admire that smile.

Dalglish was also a magnificent reader of the game, near-flawless in his capacity to hold the ball up using his fantastic balance, awareness and lower-body power. Wise coaches spotted a real strength: the Scot had a 'big arse', and he used it brilliantly to make both time and space. He could then concentrate on threading through exquisitely weighted and invariably sublimely timed passes to his strike partner, in later years the nerveless and gauche Welshman Ian Rush. There have been few, if any, British players in the history of the game who have been more complete or more courageous. And who in Britain has ever better 'seen' a football pitch – the various angles and outlets it offered – than Kenny Dalglish? He seemed to be two, or even three, passes ahead of most opponents, making up for his half-yard lack of pace.

Moreover, when Liverpool Football Club was at its lowest ebb after the tragedy at the Heysel Stadium in 1985, banned from European club football and with its supporters unfairly reviled around Europe, it was Dalglish who stepped up as player–manager to pilot Liverpool to the club's only league and FA Cup Double, in 1985–86. He also offered incredible dignity and leadership in 1989 when the Hillsborough tragedy struck. Along with a select group of others – John Houlding and John McKenna, Tom Watson, Alex Raisbeck, Elisha Scott, George Kay, Billy Liddell, Bill Shankly, Bob Paisley, T.V. Williams, John Smith and Peter Robinson – Kenny Dalglish has claims to be remembered as one of the greatest servants and architects of the Liverpool club, both off and on the pitch. He is one of the modern proselytisers of the Liverpool tradition and mythology. He is, in short, a truly great Liverpool football man.

Once these key signings were in place, the merciless Liverpool dressing-room banter and vaunted team spirit were orchestrated around these three imperious Scottish lairds. They had willing followers: Liverpool-born Jimmy Case and stick-like defender Phil Thompson were talented and fearless competitors, a crucial ingredient in the subtle chemistry necessary to produce a great side. Bob Paisley and his men retained the European Cup in 1978, defeating old rivals Club Brugge KV at Wembley, with Dalglish scoring a delightful winning goal. At home, only Brian Clough, the Shankly-like young manager at Nottingham Forest, occasionally got the better of Bob and Liverpool.

This new Paisley team then produced arguably the greatest-ever season by a club in 42-game Football League history. In 1978–79, Liverpool won the league title at a canter, conceding only 16 goals and winning 30 matches. Included was a 7–0 virtuoso Anfield thrashing of a Spurs team containing two recent Argentinian World Cup winners. Apart from the Shankly men, Ray Clemence in goal and Steve Heighway occasionally in attack, this was now Bob Paisley's team, one completely revamped in five years from the side he had inherited. Four players – Clemence, Neal, Ray Kennedy and Dalglish – played all forty-two league matches in 1978–79; Souness missed just one.

Liverpool FC, league-title winners, 1978–79

		Clemence		
Neal	Thompson	Hansen	A. Kennedy	
Case	McDermott	Souness	R. Kennedy	
	Dalglish	Johnson/Heighway		

When the nerdy Welsh teenager Ian Rush arrived to play his part, from Chester in May 1980, it eventually solved the problem of who was the best striking partner for Dalglish. The poorly dressed and fragile Rush initially failed to fit in at Anfield: he struggled to score in the reserves and was the butt of the savage Liverpool dressing-room piss-takes from the Scottish mafia.[12] He looked like a hick from the North Wales sticks, and Rush soon wanted to leave Liverpool Football Club and these bastard big-heads who were running the club's social and drinking cultures and ruining his life. Maybe Paisley was wrong about the Welshman's talent and his mental strength after all? But once Rush got settled and started to shoot back at the Anfield comedians, it positively rained goals for him at Liverpool, with Dalglish as the main provider. Rush had little grace or style on the pitch, either, but this hardly mattered. His pace and clinical finishing were breathtaking, and he was also now a willing member of the Reds' formidable drinking cliques. When Liverpool played in midweek at Middlesbrough in May 1980, another league championship already won, most of the players had been out celebrating in a local pub on the afternoon before the match.

With these two Celts in harness, a recent Anfield striking tradition was continued – Hunt and St John in the 1960s, Keegan and Toshack in the 1970s, Dalglish and Rush in the 1980s – and Liverpool Football Club now seemed likely to be as unstoppable in the 1980s as they had been for most of the 1960s and 1970s. But although success on the field would continue, things off it would not be quite so simple.

JUST FOLLOWING BOB

To prepare for the new decade, there were changes afoot at Anfield. Despite Liverpool's successes under Shankly and then Paisley, the economics of the sport were already changing in a way that made it impossible to fund European and domestic success largely on the basis of income from normal football activities. In 1980, the Main Stand paddock at Anfield was seated, and in 1982 seats were placed in the home area of the Anfield Road end. These improvements resulted in a new ground capacity of 45,600 and scope to raise more admissions cash but with little provision at all for corporate customers – now standard at the larger European clubs. As stadium guru Simon Inglis pointed out, 'Anfield was still lagging behind other leading clubs in terms of executive boxes and was still often too small to cope with demand.'[13] A more visionary, a more expansive, club board might have remedied this situation during the good times, but Liverpool was caught in a positive cycle of playing success, and the board understandably wanted to invest its resources on the pitch. Britain's top players wanted to come to the club, and Liverpool's supporters would probably have opposed spending on facilities for a business class as an affront to the club's established traditions and its relationship with its core customers. Why change direction when things were going so well? In the long term, of course, this relative lack of investment in the commercial infrastructure of the club was probably a mistake.

Not that Anfield stood still on the commercial side. In July 1979, Liverpool became the first major British football club to attract shirt sponsorship, a £100,000 deal with the Japanese electronics firm Hitachi, the sixth-largest manufacturing company in the world. While still a player, Bob Paisley had predicted that footballers would become human advertising hoardings and earn huge salaries – it looked like this was coming. Liverpool certainly needed the cash. The club's turnover in 1978–79 was £2.4 million, but profits were a miserly £71,000, an accounting situation that Reds chairman John Smith described as 'absurd'. A local journalist reported around this time that Liverpool FC was 'virtually bankrupt'. The first-team squad was dragged abroad to play money-raising friendly matches whenever an opportunity presented itself, even in the middle of a taxing set of league fixtures.

Smith had some tough messages to get across about the finances of the club and the game at large. 'While we are very successful in football terms,' he told the *Liverpool Echo*, 'in economic terms we are broke. Clubs like Liverpool cannot exist on the money coming through the turnstiles alone. Costs are going up all the time. Wages are high – and rightly so – and we have to use every avenue to increase our income.' Football League secretary Alan Hardaker warned that English football at the turn of a new decade was in danger of 'bleeding to death'. Sport would have to change to survive was the message here, while Liverpool FC's main concern – and certainly that of its supporters – was that everything should remain the same.

Another European Cup followed for Paisley and his team in 1981, in a rather forgettable final against a tepid Real Madrid in Paris settled by a single goal from Alan Kennedy. In typical style, the players left the official celebrations and took the trophy around the Paris nightspots for more drink-fuelled fun. The club's supporters were also on a mission. They were greeted by water cannons and riot police, and some of them did not exactly cover themselves in glory, ignoring bar bills, raiding local stores and stealing tickets from alarmed Spaniards as well as from local touts. Plenty of Liverpudlians got in without tickets, an early and serious warning to UEFA that was ignored because no terrible disaster ensued. Things were going seriously wrong on the Continent concerning visits from English fans, but because there was no mass brawling

– at least not involving Liverpool supporters – no one in the VIP zones was picking up the messages about growing danger at these showpiece finals.

Soon after this latest triumph, the South African-born eccentric Zimbabwe goalkeeper Bruce Grobbelaar replaced the departing Ray Clemence in Liverpool's goal, thus reviving memories of Liverpool's South African recruitment policies of the 1920s and 1930s, but also pointing ahead to the future globalisation of the sport in England. He would play 628 games for the club and was also the focus, later, of a major match-fixing accusation. Craig Johnston, a perky if rather disorganised South African-born winger raised in Australia, also arrived in 1981 from Middlesbrough. Johnston was a prodigious worker, if a poor crosser, but he helped the club lift five First Division titles in the 1980s, and he played admirably in the Liverpool European Cup-winning team of 1984. He retired at 27 years of age to turn his cluttered mind to matters other than football. Both of these international players arrived with Liverpool FC at the very height of its post-war powers, clawing in league and European titles, and even dominating the domestic League Cup competition.

Reduced to mere statistics, Bob Paisley's record in major competitions over his nine years as Liverpool manager still looks outrageous. It comprises three European Cups, six league titles, one UEFA Cup and three League Cups. Only the FA Cup escaped him. He had that one losing final, in 1977 against Manchester United, when Liverpool might have been excused for being consumed by their forthcoming first European Cup final. It was the only one of eleven visits to Wembley as a manager or assistant with Liverpool that saw Paisley end up on the losing side. Liverpool under Paisley also established a then record sequence of 85 home matches without defeat in all competitions between January 1978 and January 1981. As a manager, he had matched – many would argue, surpassed – the achievements of Bill Shankly, though there would be no knighthood for Shankly or for Bob Paisley as there would be later for others when football became gentrified and politically more significant. When he finally left the club that he had served so loyally since before the war, Paisley simply returned to his carpet slippers and TV horse racing in his modest Liverpool home. He had no airs or graces and no ambitions beyond serving the club and its followers. When he finally handed over the managerial reins to his assistant Joe Fagan in the summer of 1983, Liverpool Football Club were league-title holders and League Cup winners, after having beaten Manchester United 2–1 in the Wembley final. As Bill Shankly had done nine years earlier, Bob Paisley had not only produced an astonishingly successful Liverpool team, he had handed something impressive and stable on to his immediate successor.

Two versatile defenders, the silky smooth Mark Lawrenson, signed from Brighton for £900,000 in August 1981, and Steve Nicol, a supremely consistent purchase from Ayr United in the same year, had been recruited by Paisley to add to Liverpool's all-round defensive strength. The attacking and alarmingly tough Irishman Ronnie Whelan had also stepped up from the Reds reserves, alongside a bustling and bossy little Liverpool-born midfielder, Sammy Lee. All of these men became long-serving international-quality recruits to the Liverpool cause.

As it had often seemed for Paisley – deceptively so – it sometimes appeared as if the new manager Joe Fagan simply had to pick the 11 men for the Liverpool team in the 1983–84 season and then let them play. Fagan certainly seemed relaxed and at ease in his new role. Sometimes the players seemed to be organising things for themselves, with the staff rubber-stamping their regal progress. This transforming Liverpool side was both experienced and hungry for more success. And what a first season it was for Fagan – a European Cup win in Rome, the first Merseyside Wembley final in the 1984 League Cup – though it would take a Maine Road replay and a Graeme Souness goal for Liverpool to see off Everton – and another Liverpool league title: *three* unprecedented trophies in one season. Could it possibly get any better at Anfield? As it turned out, the answer was emphatically no – not for the city of Liverpool, not for Liverpool Football Club, not for English football.

INTO THE DARKNESS

With a neo-liberal Conservative government now in power in Britain from 1979, stressing the bleak doctrine of market forces, and with the port of Liverpool haemorrhaging global influence and jobs with few signs of local regeneration, the city and its people struggled for a foothold in the new world order. But having experienced the good times in the 1960s, the new generation of resourceful and expectant young people in the city were in no mood now to accept the 'no future' mantra played back to them from London in the 1970s and 1980s. Some rebelled, during the violent 1981 street disturbances in Toxteth or via the work of Militant politics, which took hold in the Liverpool City Council; others took the music option by forming pop and rock bands and living on the dole or sampling the good life; still others decided to have their own adventures by setting off to see the world by following Liverpool Football Club across Europe and living off the land to fund their trips.

In this dark economic period for the city, the anti-Thatcher Alan Bleasdale TV drama *Boys from the Blackstuff*, shown in 1982 but which the writer began in 1978 during the Callaghan Labour administration, featured Liverpool footballers, including Sammy Lee and, ironically, the right-leaning Graeme Souness. In some ways, it was possibly the club's most 'political' statement since the gentle nod to the 1930s' unemployed and the 1960s' 'socialism' years of Bill Shankly. Bleasdale's darkly humorous TV series *Scully* in 1984 also showcased members of the Liverpool squad, especially Kenny Dalglish, and it had as its central theme the view that only football could offer an escape for young men in the city. Liverpool could boast a glorious past but for many it now faced a depressingly empty future.

There were some obvious rewards and real potential costs involved in taking the European football adventures route out of this local inertia. These included the petty (and some more serious) thieving and 'free' train travel often involved in these outings; the occasional disorder and fighting that took place – though fans of some other English clubs at this time were much more disorderly than Liverpool fans – and the counterfeiting and the mass 'bunking in' that sometimes threatened fan safety inside grounds on European trips.[14] It also seemed more than mere coincidence that while the Liverpool trip to the 1981 European Cup final had been a pretty chaotic and disorderly affair, young inner-city black Liverpudlians, echoing events in the city in 1919 and 1948, were involved in their own street uprisings later that summer. In fact, young working-class men from all ethnic backgrounds in Liverpool wanted rather more from their lives than what was currently on offer from the powers that be.

Local-born forward Howard Gayle had actually become the first black man to play for the club in the same year, 1981 – he had performed heroically for a depleted Liverpool in the European Cup semi-final against Bayern Munich. Was this the long-awaited breakthrough, the vital new connection between football and the city's estranged black communities that would break down some of the old divisions? In fact, Gayle would make only five first-team appearances in the seven years he was registered with Liverpool, being frequently frustrated by the culture of the club and by Paisley and the Liverpool staff's lack of comprehension about the importance of this courageous black Scouser's background. Liverpool Football Club seemed, in Gayle's eyes, determined to make invisible his proud racial heritage.[15] The Reds coaches just wanted to talk football. It was, arguably, an old Liverpool story of exclusion and division, albeit in new sporting clothes.

Howard Gayle was no longer in the Liverpool first-team picture (or anywhere near it) as Joe Fagan prepared for his first European Cup final as Liverpool manager in 1984. His team was assured and confident, even though the opposition were local favourites AS Roma.

Liverpool FC, European Cup-winning team, v. AS Roma, 1984

Grobbelaar

Neal   Lawrenson   Hansen   A. Kennedy

Johnston   Lee   Souness   Whelan

Rush   Dalglish

This was a tense, tactical affair, the Italians seemingly nervous in front of their own supporters on such a major European football occasion. A 1–1 draw resulted, Liverpool taking the lead through Phil Neal before holding on for a penalty shoot-out after an equaliser from Pruzzo. Fagan had done little preparation for this outcome – though it must have looked like a distinct possibility. He probably thought – as many coaches in England still do – that penalty shoot-outs were a lottery and barely worth practising for. In the brief session he had organised in training for penalties, few players took it seriously and most had missed the target. Now everything rested on the penalty spot. Fagan selected his five penalty-takers on the pitch from those who showed willingness or were too slow to scurry away, and then decided the order. But young substitute Steve Nicol grabbed the ball and, ignoring his manager's and teammates' pleas, strode off to take Liverpool's first penalty. He missed, spectacularly. No problem: Neal, Souness and Rush all scored for Liverpool, while Grobbelaar's strange wobbly-legged antics induced two nervy Italian misses. Alan Kennedy had scored in open play in Paris to win the 1981 trophy for his club, but the left-back could barely have expected a repeat show. However, he had been chosen for the final Liverpool penalty. He closed his eyes, shot low and goalkeeper Tancredi dived the opposite way.

The players' night's work was over, but for the Liverpool supporters in Rome things would now take an alarming and dangerous turn. Italian knife gangs lay in wait in the dark grounds outside the Olympic Stadium, with the Rome police typically inert and inept. The Italian way in these matters is to attack the legs and buttocks with blades and to throw bottles and bricks indiscriminately. It was a dangerous chicken run, a horrible gauntlet that ensnared the inexperienced, as well as the streetwise and those willing and able to fight back. The hospital cases that resulted – it was remarkable no visiting fan was killed – meant that there would be a bounty to be paid next time Liverpool Football Club met Italians in Europe. So when the Reds reached the European Cup final again, in 1985 in Brussels, this time against the northern Italians from Juventus, it was clear that for this event to go off smoothly and safely it would require a well-appointed stadium, good and efficient policing, and a sensible approach from all of the club's supporters. Sadly – and fatally – it turned out that something was badly lacking in all three of these departments. Liverpool's great 20-year run in Europe, stretching back to 1965, was about to come to an abrupt and unimaginable end.

CHAPTER 16 REFERENCES

1. Hopcraft, *The Football Man*, p. 189
2. Hughes, *Secret Diary of a Liverpool Scout*, p. 6
3. St John, *The Saint*, p. 204
4. Lloyd, *Larry Lloyd: Hard Man, Hard Game*, p. 62
5. Gill, *The Real Bill Shankly*, pp. 124–5
6. Smith, *Anfield Iron*, pp. 278–9
7. Corbett, 'Shankly: Forgotten Man'
8. Kennedy and Williams, *Kennedy's Way*, p. 102
9. Hughes, *Secret Diary of a Liverpool Scout*, p. 179
10. Kirby, 'Rome, 1977', p. 27
11. Hewison, *The Liverpool Boys Are in Town*, p. 13
12. Williams, 'Ian Rush', pp. 173–4
13. Inglis, *Football Grounds of Britain*, p. 220
14. Allt, *The Boys from the Mersey*
15. Hill, *Out of His Skin*

17

AT THE DARK END OF THE STREET
Heysel and Hillsborough

SLIDING INTO CHAOS: THE HEYSEL DISASTER

In the depths of a national economic depression that was affecting Merseyside especially harshly, the Liverpool Football Club playing project was also perceptively starting to slide in 1985. The great enforcer Souness had gone and Kenny Dalglish was coming towards the end of his brilliant service for the club as a player. Ian Rush would soon leave for an unfulfilling stay in Italy. Their replacements were simply not of this stature – who could be? Paul Walsh, unusually for Liverpool a southerner, was an average forward only, signed from Luton Town, a man who flitted in and out of games but had little of Dalglish's assurance, guile and intelligence. John Wark, a loping goalscoring Scottish midfielder from Ipswich Town, had something of the Ray Kennedy about him without ever reaching those classy heights, and Kevin McDonald, another Scot and a left-sided ball-carrier bought from Leicester City, was a one-paced workhorse who occasionally showed flashes of something close to exceptional.

The only really exciting capture at this time was a Dane, Jan Mølby, an Ajax graduate who joined in 1984 and who stayed for 12 years and 260 appearances. Foreign players were still something of a novelty in the English game, and big Jan was something else again. Mølby, a central midfielder, had mobility problems from the outset – he would fit perfectly into the Liverpool dressing-room drinking club – but no one could doubt his exquisite touch, technique and luscious passing ability. His weight of pass was near-faultless, but his weight was a real problem. Mølby was astounded at how little Liverpool worked on tactics. He asked the coaches at Melwood how he should play and fit into the Liverpool system. They looked at him blankly and shrugged, saying just do what you did at Ajax. Mølby had much of what Graeme Souness had, except, crucially, athleticism and that unquenchable Scottish desire and willingness to turn to strategic violence when it was needed in Liverpool's cause. The Dane had real quality, but Mølby could not manage a potentially anarchic English football match as Souness once could.

Liverpool were eclipsed by a rising Everton in the league in 1984–85 and lost in a replay to Manchester United after an utterly poisonous atmosphere in an FA Cup semi-final in April. The English game was run through with nasty hooliganism, but a real spectator darkness revealed itself here as rival supporters exchanged obscenities and missiles and fought running battles outside Goodison Park. Few Reds supporters present could remember quite this level of bile and disorder, even at this combustible contest. Thankfully, the rounds of the European Cup in 1984–85 produced little of this sort of frenzied hatred (or competition) as Liverpool sauntered through to another final, dispensing with opponents from Poland, Portugal, Austria and Greece on the way. This was not Europe's elite: the Greeks from Panathinaikos were casually dismissed by a 5–0 aggregate in the semi-finals. But the formidable Italian champions Juventus now lay waiting in the final, in the Heysel Stadium in Brussels.

There were probably three reasons to be surprised (as well as appalled) at the terrible events that occurred in Brussels on the evening of 29 May 1985. First, that it had taken so long for what was happening in and around English football supporters abroad in the 1980s to produce a tragedy, and possibly fatalities, on this scale. There was a toxic combination already in play here: just too much drink; English and local mobs in xenophobic disharmony; idiotic and sometimes cowardly Continental policing; ticketless supporters determined to see it through; inept UEFA decisions and responses; and poor stadium security. These had all threatened on many occasions to produce a stadium disaster like this one. And now it had finally and tragically been delivered, live on international television.

The second surprise was that it was *Liverpool* supporters who were the key figures involved. After all, Reds fans had travelled extensively on the Continent for 20 years, and there had been plenty of minor dust-ups since with local lads, shopkeepers and bar owners around Europe. As people's lives in the city were getting harder, with joblessness booming, things had also been getting noticeably wilder, more desperate, at finals and major football matches, a fact evidenced in different ways by events in Paris in 1981, Rome in 1984 and Goodison Park against United in 1985. Something bad was probably on its way, and there was the usual routine disorder and thieving going on in Brussels on the afternoon of the match. But – and it is a small defence only – Liverpool supporters had expressly not been involved as instigators in any of the kind of major hooligan incidents on the Continent that had been provoked by other English supporters elsewhere.

Indeed, the hooligan credo for Liverpool abroad had its own highly distinctive features. It was based largely around street style, robbing, ticketless travel and ground access, and, yes, fighting, but usually when it was unavoidable and almost always small scale and away from the ground. There was no Liverpool record abroad for provoking major disturbances, mass combat with the local police or stadium wrecking. The Liverpool hooligan tradition – and one certainly existed – was largely instrumental rather than expressive. Exceptions might be made for clashes with Manchester United but few others. No one, not even among the club's most aggressive followers, was remotely interested in establishing Liverpool Football Club's international hooligan credentials through this or any other kind of major 'incident' abroad. This was one reason why local people in the city reacted so vehemently later to media suggestions that Liverpool and its people were somehow brand leaders in this sort of sporting barbarity. Nothing, in fact, could have been further from the truth.

The third reason to be surprised was that UEFA had seemingly learned so very little in almost 20 years about football supporters from Liverpool, because ticket security and the condition of the Heysel Stadium were shambolic. What were the organisers expecting for this contest: a crowd of sober, unexcited and uncommitted athletics fans? There were no recognisable turnstiles in some places, and parts of the stadium outer barriers were easily dismantled. Well before the disaster happened, the hapless Belgian police had already lost control. Like it or not, to a bevvied-up ticketless Scouser's eyes these ridiculous arrangements were actually an insult – as well as an open invitation. They were just asking to be abused, and abused they roundly were. Reds supporters poured in over turnstiles as ticket checks began to disappear. Who was really to blame here: those desperate, passionate and ticketless Reds supporters for possibly endangering their own lives and those of everyone else present? Certainly. But if you know that stadium security might be a problem, you do not produce the exact opposite of an effective strategy. You do not choose a truly terrible venue and the worst possible administrators of it for Europe's most important club fixture and simply hope that everything turns out all right. UEFA were supremely culpable for what happened next, along with the Liverpool fans involved and the inept Belgian authorities. UEFA would also be culpable again 22 years later in 2007 in Athens, though Liverpool supporters, more than any other, should surely also have learned their own lessons by then about the sanctity of stadium safety.

The details of what happened are these: Italian supporters, mainly from Belgium, had bought tickets to a supposed 'neutral' terrace, sector Z, next to an area housing Liverpool fans and separated from them only by what looked like chicken wire and a handful of police. The Liverpool sections, boosted by the ticketless, were fuller than this area, which seemed to Reds fans to be far from neutral: it housed Italians, seemingly in the Liverpool end. Some anger about the treatment of Reds in Roma the previous year might have fed resentment on this score. Before the match, missiles were exchanged and then Liverpool fans began dismantling the fence that divided these sections. This was followed, from around 7.20 p.m., by a 'charge' towards the Italians through the by-now ragged fences as Reds fans started pouring through.

The Italian supporters in sector Z – many of them 'family' fans – now panicked and rushed to their right, towards an exit away from the red invasion and trouble, as Liverpool supporters hugged in triumph at claiming this Italian territory for their own.[1] And in banal terms, the whole thing had been an enactment of typical English territorial rites at a football ground, the kind of incident that is usually sorted by the British police before ever reaching this stage. But here the mass movement in a confined space of terrified Italians caused a wall at the side of the terrace to collapse under the weight of their alarm. Thirty-nine supporters were crushed or suffocated to death, thirty-two of them Italian, but only two from the city of Turin itself.

The Liverpool players were sheltered in their dressing-room only yards away from this unfolding horror. They had heard the terrible rumble of the collapsing wall and the screams of panic outside. Alan Kennedy, who was in Brussels but not in the Liverpool playing squad, was now charged with going out to see what had happened and with relaying the awful news back to the dressing-room. He saw lifeless bodies and very angry and distressed Italians. He feared for his own safety. Back with the Liverpool players, he talked vaguely about 'crowd trouble'. Some players wanted to know what had happened, others wanted to stay completely focused on one of the biggest football occasions of their lives.[2] They all knew something very serious had occurred but, frankly, hooliganism was part of the cultural fabric of the English game. A few players – Bruce Grobbelaar among them – claimed to have realised the enormity of what had happened and expressly did not want to play. In the end, they all had to do their job.

The Liverpool supporters in the crowd had seen the disturbances and the ensuing panic, and the kick-off delay told them something pretty extreme had happened. But many had no idea that people had been killed in the disturbances.[3] Amazingly, the match eventually took place, 'for safety reasons', kicking off at 9.40 p.m. The Belgian police feared anger and frustration would turn to more violence between the rival fans if the match was abandoned. Perhaps more amazingly still, although television executives knew about the fatalities, the TV coverage continued in a near-funereal atmosphere. When Juventus eventually scored the winning goal from a penalty that was erroneously – or generously – given, the scorer, the current UEFA president Michel Platini, was widely criticised in Italy for the 'bad taste' of his wild celebrations.[4] He claimed not to have known people had been killed. Later, the Italian internationals Paolo Rossi and Marco Tardelli blamed the 'confusion and chaos' of the evening for the Italians' misjudged joyous response. It was Juve's first European Cup win in the worst possible circumstances.[5] But in truth all the Italian team and their officials celebrated in the same way. After the trophy was presented in the privacy of the Juventus changing-room, the players even came out to do a lap of honour, and some 50,000 Juve followers in Turin celebrated the win until the early hours of the morning.

Back in Liverpool, some returning Reds supporters crassly blamed the police and the Belgian authorities for the deaths, and any shame that was felt very soon gave way to anger and counter-accusations from club chairman John Smith and others about who was really involved in the trouble. But no convincing evidence was ever presented that there was some kind of right-wing infiltration of the Liverpool contingent, and no case was made along these lines by the official inquiry that followed. It seemed instead that a relatively minor case of drunken hooliganism (by English standards at least) had been allowed to escalate out of control in a stadium and with a police force that were simply not fit for purpose. But at home, the British press turned on the city and on the English game with a barely concealed mixture of venom and glee. Merseysiders were uniformly vilified. Later ingenuous accusations from Evertonians about Liverpool hooliganism abroad were especially distasteful.[6] In fact, later publications by Everton's so-called 'top lads' revealed – to no great surprise – that the Blues had pretty much exactly the same sort of rabble-rousers and hard-cases adventuring abroad as those who practised it from across Stanley Park.[7] Hooliganism in the 1980s was not a Liverpool Football Club problem, it was an *English* problem.

Twenty-seven supporter arrests (60 per cent from Liverpool) were eventually made on manslaughter charges, and after a trial in Belgium in 1989 fourteen Liverpool followers were given three-year convictions for involuntary manslaughter. Most of them were from the city. The UEFA secretary-general Hans Bangerter was rightly found guilty of negligence, and gendarme captain Johan Mahieu and the secretary of the Belgian FA Albert Roosens were charged with manslaughter and 'massacre' – each were given six-month suspended sentences. The Belgian government collapsed in July 1985 when the interior minister refused to resign over the affair. Recognising that serious spectator disorder was a general problem involving English supporters abroad, all English clubs were now banned from

European competition for an indeterminate period – including the 1985 league champions Everton. The English game was in shame.

But perhaps what was really shameful here was the treatment of the Heysel dead and their families. Neither Juventus nor Liverpool seemed to want to focus on their needs or their memory. Most of the dead were not from Turin, so mourning and solidarity there was distressingly limited. Juventus immediately displayed the European Cup, despite relatives of the dead saying that the trophy was stained with blood. Liverpool Football Club seemed unable or unwilling to take at least some responsibility for the disaster, and there were no proper memorials set up at either club's stadium. Nor was there serious discussion about compensation or even public regret for what had happened. Only when Liverpool finally played Juventus again in the European Cup in 2005 was culpability finally publicly accepted on Merseyside. Juve ultras at the match at Anfield unsurprisingly turned their backs on the Kop's belated apologetic mosaic. Here was some closure of sorts at least on a highly damaging and disreputable episode in the club's wonderful history.

KING KENNY TO THE RESCUE

Liverpool FC and its followers were now the official pariahs of European football. But not only was the city reviled internationally for its supposed depravity and poor spectator behaviour, the local job market was plummeting and Merseyside was rapidly de-populating, too: between 1971 and 1985 employment in the city fell by some 33 per cent. As one local commentator put it at the time, 'Liverpool looks to be the Jarrow of the 1980s.'[8]

As the recession kicked in hard and hooliganism thrived in England, so football crowds in the city and elsewhere fell. Once-mighty Everton averaged below 20,000 in 1983–84, and even Treble-winning Liverpool could only manage an average of just under 32,000 in the same season, including a league gate of just 20,746 against Watford on 1 February 1984. In Liverpool's case at least, this fall in crowd numbers was partly down to ennui; the club's supporters were becoming blasé about winning titles. Who was to challenge Liverpool's domestic dominance? In fact, in the aftermath of Heysel the club's crowds actually improved in 1985–86, even as they fell elsewhere in England. Some Reds supporters certainly stopped attending because of their revulsion at what had happened in Brussels, but it was also as if many local people had found another struggle. They were determined to get behind the embattled club again and reaffirm its traditionally positive bonds with the communities of Merseyside. A group of local Reds fans also started a new national supporter body, the

Football Supporters Association, to give supporters a stronger collective voice in the sport and to raise the public profile of non-hooligan fans. It was the start of the fightback on the terraces and in the stands against the press and the European and English football establishment.

As Liverpool FC tried to rebuild on the pitch in these very difficult circumstances, bravely and with great dignity Kenny Dalglish took over as player–manager, leaning on Bob Paisley for advice and the much mythologised Liverpool boot room for his philosophy: give the opposition very little and get as much out of them as you can. Dalglish turned to the Joe Fagan signing Jan Mølby as the player he might shape his new team around. The rotund Mølby was hardly built for the typical high-tempo exchanges of the English game, but what he lacked in mobility he more than made up for in technique. His penalty-taking was also near-faultless. Dalglish brought in Scouser Steve McMahon, a hard-tackling midfielder, from Aston Villa to offer balance and support for Mølby, Kevin McDonald and Ronnie Whelan in Liverpool's midfield. Jim Beglin, a one-paced but reliable Irishman, had also replaced Alan Kennedy at left-back by this time, and the gangly Gary Gillespie was brought in as centre-back cover from Coventry City. Alan Hansen, for one, was sceptical about the new squad; he had been part of great Liverpool teams in the recent past, and he thought this group was miles off a championship outfit. It lacked depth and some quality, but the combination worked as Liverpool set off on a run that would produce 34 points from the last 36 on offer. Fittingly, it was Dalglish himself who scored the goal at Stamford Bridge that won the 1986 league title for Liverpool, over runners-up Everton. And in a memorable first all-Merseyside FA Cup final in 1986, after falling a goal behind a Jan Mølby-inspired Liverpool stormed back to win 3–1. Everton's bogeyman Ian Rush scored twice to seal his club's first league and FA Cup Double. It was a fantastic response on the pitch to desperate adversity and ill-judged policy off it.

Liverpool FC, FA Cup-winning team, 1986

Grobbelaar

Nicol	Hansen	Lawrenson	Beglin
Johnston	Mølby	Whelan	McDonald
	Dalglish	Rush	

Gillespie, the ex-Oxford United midfielder Ray Houghton and Scouse striker John Aldridge would now all figure strongly in the 'new' Liverpool being reconstructed by Dalglish. Aldridge, especially, was delighted by his new dressing-room drinking partners, but he was also a first-class finisher, a man who had fought his way up the football food chain. But the two key new Dalglish recruits here were the England international forwards John Barnes and Peter Beardsley. The arrival of the middle-class, Jamaican-born Barnes from Watford for £900,000 in June 1987, the first regular black first-teamer at the club, stirred predictable emotions – and some racist hostility – in the city. But his wing-play was sublime. He had the strength, touch and pace to defeat almost all defences, allied to a thunderous shot and wonderful crossing ability. Barnes was the most direct and effective goalscoring winger at Liverpool since Billy Liddell, and he became almost as popular with the new generation of the club's support as the Scot had been in the 1950s. His popularity only increased on Merseyside when he was criticised for his disappointing shows for England. His general acceptance and celebration at Anfield signalled some progress at least on the historic racial exclusivity at the club.

Peter Beardsley's qualities were rather more prosaic but no less effective. Beardsley lacked the reliable technique and strength of Barnes, but he was boyishly enthusiastic, inventive and hard-working, almost in equal measure. Together, he and the ex-Watford man, allied with the unerring finishing of Aldridge, energised a new attacking Liverpool: eighty-seven goals resulted in the league in 1987–88, including five in a rout of close rivals Nottingham Forest on 13 April 1988. Some judges argue this to be the best league football performance by the club at home since the war. Praise indeed. Liverpool cantered to the league title in 1988 with ninety points and only two defeats. Lacking the additional pressure from Europe only seemed to make the Reds even more dominant at home. But another domestic league and cup Double was prevented in the FA Cup final when a brutal Wimbledon team (and bad luck) intimidated Liverpool to a shock 0–1 defeat. The old master of planned violence Graeme Souness was probably growling displeasure and contempt somewhere at this sorry Wembley capitulation by the club he had once ruled.

HILLSBOROUGH, 15 APRIL 1989

In the following season, Arsenal would dramatically wrench the league title from Liverpool on goal difference in the final minute of the final league match between the two clubs at Anfield on 26 May 1989. The Liverpool team (and its supporters) was emotionally and physically drained: this was the club's eighth match in twenty-three days, including a charged 3–2 extra time Reds FA Cup final victory over Everton. It was, by any measure, a ridiculous and punitive programme, but placed in its context it was even crueller than this. This was the latest finish by date to a Football League season since Liverpool under George Kay had snatched the title ahead of Stoke City back in June 1947. But the weather in 1989 had been fine. The reason for the delay was much more tragic than mere snow and ice, as it had been just after the war. It was due to another terrible disaster involving the Liverpool Football Club, this time at the Hillsborough Stadium in Sheffield. There, neglect and mismanagement by South Yorkshire Police caused the deaths of 96 Liverpool supporters as a result of events on 15 April 1989 near the start of an FA Cup semi-final meeting with Nottingham Forest. The club and the city were thrown into a vortex of mourning and the defending of its own victim supporters as a result.

As all football supporters should now know – though shamefully many still seem to have different views – the police in Sheffield failed to monitor the Liverpool crowds effectively both inside and outside the ground. Liverpool supporters had been delayed arriving because of roadworks on the M62 motorway, and the Leppings Lane end of the ground had too few turnstiles to properly process these delayed fans in time. The police responded to overcrowding outside by opening an exit Gate C to allow supporters entry, but they then failed to direct arriving Liverpool fans to less crowded pens in the Hillsborough Stadium. As a result, supporters walked into already overcrowded and fatally penned terraced areas of the stadium, where the deadly crushing took place. The police now failed again. The match was halted by referee Ray Lewis at 3.06 p.m., but the police did not respond appropriately or quickly enough to obvious signs of distress among Liverpool supporters who were trapped beneath the police control box in overcrowded pens that had perimeter gates that would not open under crowd pressure. Desperately escaping Reds supporters were even returned to the killing pens because the police initially interpreted crowd panic and suffering as a pitch invasion or the result of hooliganism. In the confusion, only one of the forty-four ambulances that responded to the disaster call was allowed by the police into the stadium. Its crew was overwhelmed by the number of Liverpool supporters requiring treatment on the pitch. The police then compounded all these gross errors by their later disgusting treatment of bereaved families and their attempts to smear Liverpool supporters in a repellent attempt at a cover-up in the national press, viciously led by *The Sun* newspaper.

Historically, as we have seen, English football had long displayed too little care in its treatment of football fans. In the 1950s, grounds were dangerous places that were poorly regulated, and it was only good fortune and the care that supporters showed for each other that had avoided similar disasters since the 1946 tragedy at Burnden Park, Bolton.[9] The 1980s in Britain was a harsher social and economic climate altogether, and football crowds were more volatile, less consensual and rather less caring. Some commentators argued that Hillsborough was symbolic of a general attack by the British state on working-class people in Liverpool and elsewhere.[10] More convincing were those accounts that suggested that the disaster was attributable to a planned general deterioration of public facilities in Britain, a development that had also brought a range of recent disasters on public transport, as Tory policies had prioritised the private sector and devastated areas such as Merseyside.[11] It was difficult to avoid the conclusion that the deaths were also connected to deep-seated problems in terrace cultures and poor relations between some football fans and the police. After all, the Sheffield ground was argued to be one of England's best-appointed stadiums, but this seemed mainly because of the way it was designed to deal with potential hooliganism. The English game had gone down a fatal route and was routinely treating *all* its customers as potential threats.

As the city of Liverpool mourned its huge loss and responded angrily to suggestions that its people, rather than the public authorities, were once again at fault, the Anfield stadium soon became a vast shrine containing flowers and mementos in memory of the dead. The Liverpool players and officials, and the manager Kenny Dalglish and his family, undertook the draining responsibility of attending funerals of dead supporters. Sometimes they attended a number on the same day. The FA discussed abandoning the FA Cup for that season, and the Football League also considered its options for Liverpool FC. Halting the season might have been a sensible response to the scale of the disaster. But after a relatively short period of time, followers of the clubs involved and even some bereaved families seemed to want the league and the FA Cup competitions to continue. Accordingly, after almost three weeks of playing inaction taken up mainly with grieving and showing appropriate respect for the dead, and amidst febrile public debate about where responsibility for the disaster really lay, the Liverpool team played out an emotional friendly match at Glasgow Celtic and then a 0–0 league draw at Everton on 3 May to restart their league campaign. Local followers of the two clubs – some of whom had become rather distanced after the impact of Heysel – were now brought together once again in a communal celebration of their common bond as Merseysiders.

Liverpool then completed their league fixtures, winning the next four to set up yet another league-title bid. They also defeated Forest 3–1 in the replayed FA Cup semi-final at Old Trafford and then Everton 3–2 at Wembley in the final. In the frenzy of the occasion, ticketless supporters tried every means of gaining illegal entry, and fans of both teams invaded the fence-free Wembley pitch, but there was no violence. Removing pitchside fences and converting terraces at major stadiums to seating areas were the key structural outcomes of the official inquiry into the Hillsborough disaster. But at least as important were the new ways that were established of managing football supporters inside grounds. Under a new, more rigorous stadium-licensing system, the police would no longer be responsible for the general organisation of football grounds or for the spectators in them. Instead, football clubs would now be in charge of arrangements for supporters inside grounds, and the police would deal specifically only with matters of hooliganism. A new rhetoric, not centred around issues of control, now began to emerge around football stadiums in England: the job of the new generation of stadium managers, stewards and senior police officers was to ensure, above all else, the safety of their customers. It was a step in a new direction for the national game at last.

The various Hillsborough family supporter groups in the city have since been frustrated by their attempts to make accountable those who were at fault in Sheffield. The inquest into the deaths of supporters insisted that only events up until 3.15 p.m. on 15 April should be considered, even though there was evidence that many of those who died were still alive beyond that point. A private prosecution brought later against senior police officers involved was abandoned when it was decided that the chief superintendent in charge on the day, David Duckenfield, was unfit to face charges. He eventually retired on medical grounds on a full pension. In 1996, the Liverpool supporter and scriptwriter Jimmy McGovern wrote a 90-minute drama-documentary about the disaster and its aftermath, *Hillsborough*, which was screened across the ITV network. It drew huge acclaim for clarifying what had happened, but it also seemed to some critics to present a highly sanitised version of existing football culture in 1989.

Partly as a response to the frustration and sense of injustice felt locally over Hillsborough, over the past 20 years Liverpool supporters have ingested the disaster, the public response to it and the campaigns that have followed as part of the identity of the club itself. For some Reds, this new set of cultural meanings around 'the 96' and the club are even comparable to Celtic FC's historic social heritage and FC Barcelona's socio-political Catalan agenda that proudly proclaims Barça to be 'more than a football club'. No match at Anfield today is complete without the distribution of 'Justice' and 'Don't Buy The Sun' stickers, and on 6 January 2007 for the first six minutes of the televised FA Cup tie against Arsenal the Liverpool Kop displayed a mosaic demanding 'The Truth' about the disaster and Reds supporters repeatedly chanted 'Justice for the 96'. On the 20th anniversary of the disaster in 2009, an extraordinary and unprecedented 28,000 people turned up to hear the Anfield service and to heckle government minister Andy Burnham (an Everton supporter). The British government finally agreed in July of that year that thousands of secret files pertaining to the events in April

1989 be released for public scrutiny under the auspices of a new Hillsborough Independent Panel. Despite this latest development, 20 years on 'the truth' about Hillsborough seemed, for those involved, as distant a goal as it had ever been.

THE LAST GAME?

Back on the football field, on the evening of 26 May 1989 Liverpool Football Club now faced a fresh and determined Arsenal, a club that was obviously outside the Merseyside bubble about Hillsborough and that had been eagerly contesting the league title with few extraneous distractions. This final contest was a strange affair indeed. Liverpool supporters were divided about whether claiming a second league and cup Double would be a fitting memorial to the dead or an insult to those who were still directly suffering because of the impact of Hillsborough. The team seemed caught in the same dilemma, and on some occasions it can be more difficult to defend a position of relative strength rather than be required to go out decisively to win a football match. In the event, Liverpool never really got going, and the Anfield crowd had difficulty responding with the required level of urgency to lift their team's performance. How important was winning yet another league crown, anyway, given what had happened?

As a result, a committed Arsenal pilfered the title by winning 0–2 at Anfield, with future Liverpool man Michael Thomas scoring the decisive and dramatic last-minute goal that eventually divided the clubs. Arsenal won the title only by scoring more goals (73 to 65) than Liverpool. In the directors' box, even as the winning shot ballooned in the net behind Bruce Grobbelaar, Liverpool club secretary Peter Robinson calmly rang down to the Anfield kitchen to get the post-match champagne provided by the sponsors redirected to the visitors' dressing-room.

The Kop was still a standing terrace that night – it would eventually disappear in 1994 – and thousands of Liverpool supporters stayed on to sit on its great steps to applaud the new champions and watch the Arsenal celebrations. Some thought that the wild reactions of the visitors mirrored the distasteful Juventus celebrations of 1985, but this was certainly unfair. And many Liverpool supporters were glad to applaud Arsenal as champions, because the outcome avoided the dilemma of quite how to react to a Reds title win that would have felt like so much ashes in the mouth given the circumstances. Liverpool fans were instead left to reflect soberly on the enormity of what they and their football club had been through over the previous six weeks, and indeed over the past four years. These terrible experiences had probably bonded supporters to the club even more firmly. It had been an emotionally draining journey, with many wonderful highs on the pitch but punctuated by unimaginable, desperate lows off it.

In 1989, the world was changing. Just a few months after Hillsborough the Berlin Wall was breached and Communism went the same way as the Liverpool dominance of European football was heading. Some authors suggest that Hillsborough and this deciding match at Anfield was the key turning point in the post-war history of the sport, the defining moment that moved the game on from its local roots, traditional stadiums and partisan masculine rituals, all of which had given English football both its historic cultural meaning and also deeply scarred it in the hooligan era.[12] There might be something to this idea. After all, Nick Hornby's manifesto for new football, *Fever Pitch*, reached a climax with Arsenal's title win and then went on to sketch out the new, more civilised world for the game. Certainly, the media coverage of those who tragically died at Hillsborough – the sons, daughters, husbands and friends – meant that football supporters would now be more likely to be seen through the prism of the family rather than the usual hooligan lens.

And there was still time in this period of rapid transition for one more Liverpool league title – the 18th – to be collected in 1989–90. By then, the stylish but vulnerable Swedish international Glenn Hysen and the rugged West Midlander David Burrows were in defence, and the still irresistible John Barnes was scoring 22 league goals in 34 appearances. But the cracks were also finally starting to really open up in Liverpool's previously near-invulnerable make-up.

Liverpool FC, league-title winners, 1989–90

Grobbelaar

Nicol Hysen Hansen Burrows

Houghton McMahon Whelan Barnes

Beardsley Rush

Liverpool manager Kenny Dalglish reported later on the enormous stress that had been involved for him in the club's return to a 'creepy' Hillsborough to play a league match in November 1989. Liverpool lost 0–2, but few in the Liverpool party wanted to dwell on the result or too long in Sheffield.[13] Crystal Palace were thrashed 9–0 by Liverpool in the league at Anfield in September, and Swansea City were later thumped 8–0 in the FA Cup, so this Reds side could still turn it on and destroy poor opposition. But in the FA Cup semi-final at Villa Park in April 1990 – and this was perhaps the real turning point for the Liverpool team – the rapid but inexperienced Crystal Palace attack made Liverpool's defending look threadbare and inept for once. This shock 3–4 defeat for the Anfield club was a shuddering sign of future struggles to come.

Alan Hansen was now clearly at the end of his wonderful Anfield career, and Kenny Dalglish had started to look strained and drawn in the manager's seat – God knows, he had been through more than any football manager should be forced to endure. The era of the great historic Scottish influence at Liverpool was at its close. Indeed, Liverpool's period of dominance of English football was effectively over. Even as the Reds thrashed Coventry City 6–1 in the last match of the 1989–90 season, with John Barnes and the erratic Israeli striker Ronnie Rosenthal rampant, there was already a sense that this amazing run – eleven league titles and six second-place finishes in eighteen seasons since 1972–73, plus numerous cups won at home and abroad – could not go on. Only a finish of fifth place in the injury-hit season of 1980–81 stood out as a relative failing, and Bob Paisley had still won the European Cup for Liverpool in that year. This fantastic league-and-cup record for one club was now at the end of its supernatural cycle. And English football was about to change radically to try to escape from its recent nightmares.

OLD ROUTES, NEW DIRECTIONS

The depleted and troubled Kenny Dalglish had wanted to resign as manager of Liverpool Football Club in the summer of 1990. He was worn out by the events of the past five years, but especially those of the previous twelve months. He also wanted to buy shares in the club he loved. He was able to do neither. The Liverpool board insisted that he continue as manager and said that there were no shares available, not even for 'King Kenny'. But by Christmas 1990 the huge strain of what had gone before was obvious, and the Liverpool boss was clearly ill and having trouble making decisions, the crucial area of any football manager's job. His signings for Liverpool Football Club had also started to lose their previous assurance and quality: players such as Steve Harkness, Don Hutchison, Jimmy Carter, Nicky Tanner and David Speedie simply could not match the men who had made the club so dominant in the previous two decades. His scouts were letting him down. Also, the sleeping English giants at Arsenal and especially Manchester United had finally got their acts together. There would be no more Liverpool cakewalks in the league. A crazy 4–4 fifth-round FA Cup replay at Everton in 1991, when the manager dithered over making changes as the match see-sawed in front of him, was the moment he chose to make his announcement to resign.

Rather like Bill Shankly before him, Dalglish hinted later that had Liverpool waited over the summer of 1991, while he rested and got his mind straight, he might have returned refreshed and ready to continue in the job. But, as was the case back in 1974, there is seldom time for reflection in football, and – again like in 1974 – Liverpool Football Club felt that they had continuity assured in a more-than-adequate replacement for Kenny. It was one of his old Scottish buddies, the former midfield organiser at Anfield Graeme Souness, who now stepped forward. Souness had been a successful, if controversial, managerial figure at Glasgow Rangers, and the Liverpool hierarchy thought that he would bring back the old reassurance and swagger of the 1980s. But the game had moved on. Kenny Dalglish eventually re-emerged at cash-rich Blackburn Rovers, claiming a Premier League title there as manager in 1995 as Liverpool under Souness, and then Roy Evans, continued to struggle.

Crucially, all this emotional upheaval, disruption and uncertainty for Liverpool Football Club also happened at a critical moment in the development of the modern English game. Liverpool had fallen behind the rest of English football in the 1920s because of tactical inadequacy and in the 1950s because of boardroom penny-pinching. Now it would fall behind again, mainly because of a reluctance to embrace change and because of the baggage of the awful disasters that had so engulfed the club. The old boot-room competitive advantage would no longer work in this new age. The aftermath of Hillsborough had produced an agenda for stadium modernisation in Britain, but it was also a moment when the game itself was completely reconstructed and repackaged in England. This came with the birth of the brassy new FA Premier League in 1992, the rise of satellite TV as a major new funder for English football, and the globalisation of the elite levels of the English game made possible by new technology and new marketing and communication techniques.

'New' football had its doubters, of course, as fans found their voice: Liverpool's excellent local fanzine *Through the Wind and Rain*, for example, routinely poured scorn on the sport's commercial excesses and its empty new promises. Liverpool Football Club had been efficiently and cleverly run by T.V. Williams and later by John Smith and Peter Robinson in football's 'old times'. But the club was hardly best placed now to ride this new commercial and communications wave, especially as it had been immersed for a number of years in the consequences of dealing with two terrible spectator tragedies and focused on avoiding change rather than embracing it. It also lost its guiding figures and some of the crucial domestic advantages it had enjoyed over its close rivals of being continuously involved in European club football. English clubs were banned from Europe for five years, with Liverpool being excluded for six, returning to European action in the UEFA Cup in 1991–92. The glorious boot-room days of Shankly, Paisley, Fagan, Bennett, Moran, Evans and Dalglish were over. Just as the club had lost momentum because of the managerial innovation of Herbert Chapman, and had done so again because of post-war conservatism, now it was falling behind as the game's commercial arm was undergoing a period of rapid and radical revolution.

Liverpool Football Club had, understandably, stressed continuity and stability in its golden years, rather than the sort of transformational and dynamic processes of adaptation that seemed to be required in the new future for the game. One sign of this was that after being regularly thwarted by its local residents and neighbours in its ground redevelopment plans, the club was only able to open its very first executive boxes in August 1992, when a second tier was finally added to the existing Kemlyn Road stand at a cost of £8.5 million. The new Centenary Stand was officially opened on 1 September 1992 – 100 years to the day after Liverpool's first match at Anfield. Suddenly, for things to stay the same in terms of maintaining Liverpool's playing dominance at home and abroad, everything else would have to change.

To be fair, in terms of his policies and his general approach to club management, Graeme Souness was much less of a continuity candidate for the Liverpool manager's job than he might have at first appeared. For example, he lacked the loyalty and the communitarian values of the Shankly/Paisley dynasty. He had left Liverpool in 1984 simply for more money in Italy. He was no Liverpool disciple, and he was a player who was respected rather than loved at Anfield. Dalglish was adored. But Souness came back to the club, supposedly, with a winner's mentality. He rightly realised that Liverpool Football Club urgently required modernisation. He recognised, too, that it was in danger of ossifying by resting on past glories when the world of football was changing so fast. He also thought that some of the club's older stars – John Barnes and Ian Rush among them – were now past their best and obstructing necessary change. Souness altered the Liverpool training regime to finally break the boot-room traditions – players would no longer change at Anfield and travel by coach to Melwood – and he stood accused by some Liverpool supporters and players of trying to alter too much, too soon. The truth was that he took over at probably the most difficult time in the club's recent history. Any new manager might have had difficulty turning Liverpool around at this precise moment, but Souness hardly helped himself, either, with his style of management or his chosen personnel.

In fact, Graeme Souness turned out to be a very poor man-manager and a surprisingly weak judge of players. Some of his key signings – Dean Saunders, Paul Stewart, Nigel Clough, Torben Piechnik, Neil Ruddock and the positively lumpen West Ham skinhead Julian Dicks – were simply not up to past Liverpool standards. The cartoonish Dicks liked to drink two cans of

Coca-Cola before playing matches, and he had regular run-ins with Ronnie Moran during training ('I used to row with Ronnie every day,' he said). Reds coach Steve Heighway clearly thought Dicks was not a typical Liverpool player and refused to talk with him. When Dicks was later dropped to the club's reserve team, the depressed defender got drunk in local pubs in the afternoon before matches.[14]

In the past, senior Liverpool players had made sure that the drinking cliques at Anfield never obstructed the professional responsibilities of the players and also contributed to team spirit. Now the attitudes and values – as well as the football ability – of some of these highly paid new recruits were very questionable. Because of all this gross unprofessionalism, Souness also risked squandering the talents of a rising group of excellent youngsters – the Dalglish signing Jamie Redknapp and two irrepressible and brilliant Scousers, loping winger Steve McManaman and nerveless striker Robbie Fowler among them – as he tried to shape the club for the new era.

An FA Cup final win for Liverpool over Sunderland in 1992 briefly stayed local protest. As George Kay had done in 1950, a pale and drawn Souness attended at Wembley only after a serious illness and hospital treatment. He also faced further fan criticism for crassly selling the story about his illness to the locally hated *Sun* newspaper. A weak sixth-place finish for Liverpool in the new FA Premier League in 1993 – some 25 points behind winners Manchester United – caused further rumblings. It had been preceded by a near-comical UEFA Cup-Winners' Cup exit to Spartak Moscow in November 1992, which had already revived serious doubts about Souness's long-term Anfield future. In the summer of 1993, most Liverpool supporters confidently expected (and hoped) that Souness would be sacked, but with the Liverpool board dithering and divided under the new Liverpool chairman David Moores, a personal friend of the manager and many of the players, Souness managed to hang on. It was a stay of execution only. After a bright start to the 1993–94 league season – but with Liverpool out of Europe once again – things predictably began to deteriorate, and early on in 1994 the critical loss occurred. It was a shattering home defeat to Bristol City in an FA Cup replay. Even the hard man Souness realised that he could not survive this latest lapse, and he resigned before he was sacked.

THE RETURN OF THE BOOT ROOM

Souness was replaced – perhaps reluctantly – by Roy Evans, a boot-room product and a man who could claim 20 productive years' service on the Liverpool coaching staff. Evans was a calmer, much more reflective influence than was Souness, and he vowed to bring the traditions of the Liverpool Way right up to date and, by doing so, to lead the club to a better tomorrow. His personal lineage at the club reached back, reassuringly, to Bill Shankly, and he relied on advice from old Anfield servants, including Tom Saunders, a man who had spotted and raised young talent for the club for many years. The traditional boot-room references delighted the Liverpool fans, but again it looked, possibly, like a return to the past when the future now looked so different for English football. And did the rather kindly Evans really have the necessary ruthlessness of a Shankly or a Paisley to make tough decisions and drive Liverpool on in a new commercial era in front of the all-seated, more pacified, Kop?

With ex-Reds player Doug Livermore, Ronnie Moran and a rejuvenated John Barnes promising a modern version of the traditional Anfield brains trust, Roy Evans constructed a novel and attractive 3–5–2 playing system that briefly threatened to win Liverpool the league title once again in the mid-1990s. With a new, young future international goalkeeper David James and a flexible back three made up of Mark Wright, John Scales and Phil Babb, and flying wing-backs Jason McAteer and Souness signing Rob Jones, it was a slowing John Barnes who now cleverly directed matters from a more withdrawn midfield position. Jamie Redknapp provided some midfield finesse, Steve McManaman offered brilliant wing-play – but in a mazy new channel *across* the pitch – and the left-footed Toxteth urchin genius Robbie Fowler scored goals, seemingly hundreds of them.

This new Liverpool under Evans passed and kept the ball superbly, albeit sometimes at the expense of penetrating weaker opposition and killing off matches. A McManaman-inspired League Cup-final win against Bolton Wanderers in 1995 offered much future promise of returning more silverware to Anfield. Perhaps this renewal of the boot-room ethos was going to work after all? But then Evans helped murder his own dream by making a major mistake, the sort of gaffe that Shankly or Bob Paisley seldom, if ever, made. These earlier bosses checked the character of prospective signings with their scouts as much as they did their football talent. Evans failed to remember this lesson. He signed, for a then record Liverpool fee of £8.5 million, a player whose main focus was palpably not the future of Liverpool Football Club. Evans's new recruit was congenitally programmed to think only about himself, not his teammates, nor his supporters or his employers. The talented, but ultimately corrosive, Stan Collymore joined Liverpool from Nottingham Forest in June 1995. His signing turned out to be the equivalent of a managerial suicide note.

Depending upon who you believed, Collymore was either a football manager's dream or his worst nightmare. He was a player with undoubted ability but also many personal demons that were fully revealed only after he retired as a player. Stan could be brilliant or truly awful, and he often combined these two opposing traits in the same match. But more importantly, Collymore, like an invisible virus, was a stone wall guarantee eventually to destroy the collective unity in any football dressing-room he inhabited. He was the antithesis, in fact, of a 'typical' Liverpool player. According to Robbie Fowler, Stan was 'fucking hopeless' in terms of his attitude to other footballers and building the necessary collective ethos of a successful football dressing-room. He scored 35 goals in 81 appearances for Liverpool, a more than tidy return, but his performance in almost every really significant match that he played for the club was poor, sometimes irresponsibly so. Moreover, he eventually alienated both Fowler and McManaman, his key forward partners. In an era when players' wages soared, Collymore wilfully challenged the authority – and eventually the self-respect – of his caring and much abused manager.

Nevertheless, Liverpool threatened again in the league under Evans in 1995–96 before finally falling away. But the Reds had also powered to the FA Cup final in 1996, fuelled by Fowler's goals, where they met Manchester United. By now the club was haunted by press tales of player excess and a lack of discipline in the dressing-room – the Liverpool 'Spice Boys'. This was unfair on Evans, and the stories were often exaggerated, but it was also clear that the current squad lacked the cold-eyed professional focus of earlier Liverpool sides. This was the infamous 'white suits' final, of course, when the Liverpool players looked both ridiculous and disrespectful in their pre-cup final outfits, and then simply failed to perform in an insipid contest, subsiding to Eric Cantona's late goal. Stan Collymore, Evans's signature signing, was predictably substituted at Wembley, as he would be at half-time in a spineless Reds performance as Liverpool collapsed 0–3 in the UEFA Cup-Winners' Cup semi-final against Paris St Germain in April 1997.

Stan Collymore's brief and unsatisfactory Liverpool career was now effectively over, a football talent carelessly thrown away. He had also done for the manager who had so mistakenly trusted him. A new local star, the much more committed and electric Michael Owen, was about to burst on the Liverpool football scene. Sadly, Roy Evans's entertaining and sporadically promising time as manager of Liverpool Football Club was coming towards its inevitable end. The Liverpool board was about to turn to Europe to try to revive its fading league-championship dreams.

CHAPTER 17 REFERENCES

1. Sampson, 'Brussels, 1985', p. 203
2. Kennedy and Williams, *Kennedy's Way*, p. 205
3. Reade, *43 Years with the Same Bird*
4. Foot, *Calcio: A History of Italian Football*, pp. 328–40
5. Jackson, 'The Witnesses'
6. Corbett, *Everton: The School of Science*, p. 261
7. Nicholls, *Scally: The Story of a Category C Football Hooligan*
8. Murden, 'City of Challenge and Change', p. 428
9. Ward and Williams, *Football Nation*, pp. 16–24
10. Scraton, *Hillsborough: The Truth*
11. Taylor, 'English Football in the 1990s'
12. Cowley, *The Last Game*
13. Dalglish, *Dalglish: My Autobiography*, p. 179
14. Blows, *Terminator: The Authorised Julian Dicks Story*, p. 202

18

CONTINENTAL DRIFT
The New Liverpool Technocrats

THIS IS THE MODERN WORLD

odernisation in English football towards the end of the 1990s increasingly meant looking towards the Continent for inspiration, science, creativity and discipline. These sorts of themes had come and gone in the English game, in one way or another, since before the Hungarian defeat of England back in 1953. But now the new money in English football and a relaxation of the English-are-best mentality meant that club directors were capable – and increasingly willing – to sign up their key men from abroad. They looked for recruits for positions both on and off the field. The previously unknown Arsène Wenger's cerebral coaching success at Arsenal for a while seemed like a signal for the future for almost every top English club. Roy Evans and his staff at Liverpool knew best the English game, of course, and the Bootle-born man had recruited largely British players – his Continental buys had not always been a success.

The club was still well known in football circles for its drinking culture (as was Arsenal before Wenger cleaned it up). Post-match drinking for Reds players had seemed fine in the 1980s, when Liverpool were dominant and the press and supporters were compliant, but now it was beginning to appear outdated and self-indulgent amidst increasing talk about diets and computer analysis of body fat and player performance. The club's supporters were also asking questions about the alleged lack of professionalism at Anfield, where players seemed to be allowed just too much leeway. The Liverpool teams produced by Evans were attractive, sure, but they also indulged in over-passing and had a mental soft centre in critical matches.

Evans's latest major signings to address some of these failings included the hard-nosed England international midfield player Paul Ince and the German European Cup-winner Karl-Heinz Riedle in the summer of 1997. The manager finally lost faith in his 3–5–2 team shape, and in both Collymore and John Barnes, in preparation for a move back to a more conventional 4–4–2 formation, with the ex-Manchester United man Ince supposedly adding the missing steel. The young Michael Owen, every mother's dream, was helping out with the goals while also contributing to the traumas of the 22-year-old injury-hit 'veteran' Robbie Fowler, who was already being written off in some quarters. But was this move back to a more familiar playing system really radical enough to turn things around at Anfield? Owen scored 18 league goals in his first full season, but Liverpool could do no better than third place in the Premier League in 1998.

Perhaps more of a European influence at coaching or managerial level at the club could help get Liverpool back on track and also help Evans develop his management skills? Perhaps a partnership of the old boot room and the new Continental science could finally do the trick? It might also rid the Liverpool dressing-room of some of its bad habits acquired under Souness and not dealt with effectively by Evans. The Liverpool board, and Peter Robinson in particular, scanned the Continent and came up with just the man for the proposed job-share – the French youth academy architect, disciplinarian and confirmed Liverpool Football Club admirer Gérard Houllier.

This was a risky strategy. At the very top level of the game, the Frenchman's record was actually quite patchy, including a last-minute failure to take the French national team to the 1994 World Cup finals. And going for joint football managers – one an Englishman steeped in the Liverpool tradition, the other an internationally known learned French coach, best regarded for developing youth players for the French Football Federation – was never likely to work at Anfield or anywhere else in England. Roy Evans did not want it. But at least it avoided the unpleasantness of sacking the Liverpool manager. The club rarely fired the top man – it was bad form, not the Liverpool Way. The co-manager role would give Houllier a heads-up inside the club before the inevitable outcome of him taking over the first team on his own.

At least Houllier had studied and lived in the city of Liverpool as a trainee teacher, and he loved the traditions and cultures around the club. He liked the working-class fans in the city, the way the terraced houses of Anfield folded around the stadium, and the bond between the supporters and the team, which he likened to the importance of the pass on the pitch. He had respect for what he called the 'Liverpool imaginary'.[1] Here was a boot-room man in French clothing. Or so it seemed.

Houllier's arrival corresponded with the move to Anfield of one of the architects of the cash-cow Premier League, Liverpool fan Rick Parry, after Peter Robinson picked his moment to leave. Parry was a restless advocate of constant change in the game, and he knew Liverpool had suffered in comparison with the recent commercial development of Manchester United. He also knew that the club would have to finance a new stadium to keep up with its competitors. As far back as 1990, a joint all-seated stadium to house both major Merseyside clubs had been proposed on Kirkby golf course at a cost of £125 million, backed by Liverpool City Council. The clubs were scornful, of course, but almost 20 years later Everton were looking again at Kirkby as a location, and neither club would be much advanced in their individual ambitions for stadium relocation. Liverpool FC, for example, were facing a bill of more than £400 million for a venue for which they still had no funding while their rivals had all moved on. But Parry was also wary of the real dangers of going down an ultra-commercialised route for Liverpool Football Club because of the history and values of the club and its cultural importance in the city. In 2002 he said:

> I hate to use the word 'brand', but it's the word that fits. The great thing that Liverpool had never done was to prostitute the brand. And that is terrific. There is a paradox for Manchester United that they are simultaneously the most loved and the most hated brand of all, which is kind of tough from a commercial perspective. The 'brand values' that we have developed for Liverpool, well, the key word for us is 'respect'. In the 1970s and '80s, we were not loved by everybody, but there was always a respect for Liverpool, and that's a value I think is very important.[2]

Liverpool was now a global club, a 'brand' with new markets to serve. The impact of the Internet, club merchandise and satellite TV meant rethinking the whole concept of the fan and seeing the club as an international concern.

Parry favoured the appointment of Gérard Houllier because he liked the attention to detail and the urbanity and strong principles of the new manager, and Parry believed that the Frenchman understood the cultural significance of the Liverpool Way. Houllier thought Parry was the kind of ethical moderniser he could work with. Both men were determined to revolutionise the general approach to organisation and discipline inside the club, and to modernise tactics and player preparation at Melwood. And there was much to do.

THE MEN FROM THE CONTINENT (1)

Gérard Houllier did not like what he saw at Anfield when he arrived in 1998: too much drinking and ill-discipline; too little training tailored to match situations; a training ground that needed rebuilding and modernising; and too little emphasis on scientific preparation in terms of diet, the use of computer technology and specialised coaching. Liverpool had fallen behind its competitors once again. He also thought that Roy Evans was too close, too friendly, with the Liverpool players, some of whom had just too much to say about training and tactics. A manager needed to maintain his distance from his team to properly exercise his authority. In contrast to the great Liverpool dynasties of the recent past, Houllier interpreted players who spoke out of turn as showing a lack of respect. Many would remark later that the new Continental presence at Liverpool lacked something in personal security, but nothing in ego.

Gradually, Houllier asserted himself and his new approach at the start of the 1998–99 season, and in November 1998 Roy Evans realised that this attempt at joint authority could never work in a British football club where players needed to know exactly who the boss was. One Liverpool manager favoured rotating his players, the other sticking to a winning team in the Shankly and Paisley tradition. What exactly *was* the Liverpool policy? After a dressing-room bust-up following a European tie in Valencia, like the honourable man he is Roy Evans took the hint and resigned. Liverpool had finished in the top four in each of his four seasons in sole charge, had won one trophy and played in another major final. With Houllier in lone charge for much of 1998–99, the club slumped to seventh place.

Now the Frenchman acted decisively. He brought in ex-Red Phil Thompson to add some local knowledge and steel, and he started to clear out the players he couldn't work with or who challenged his approach. These included Ince, error-prone goalkeeper David James and defenders McAteer, Wright and Babb. Out, too, went the very moderate foreigners Bjørnebye, Kvarme and Leonhardsen. In a more costly loss, Steve McManaman also opted to join Real Madrid on a Bosman free transfer, the first in England. Houllier began building a new Liverpool team around an emerging core of young local talent he could mould, including the forward prodigy Michael Owen, the young Bootle-born defender Jamie Carragher, the clever midfielder Danny Murphy, and eventually a brilliant youth-team starlet who was beginning to make local waves, a man called Steven Gerrard. Local hero Robbie Fowler seemed truculent and less convinced by the new manager, and was therefore a much more marginal figure.

From abroad for the 1999–2000 season, his first in sole charge, in came the key signings of defenders Sami Hyypiä and Stéphane Henchoz, Dutch goalkeeper Sander Westerveld, fragile but skilful Czech forward Vladimír Šmicer and the excellent German international defensive midfield player Dietmar Hamann.

An elusive but limited African forward Titi Camara and a mysterious young Croat midfielder Igor Bišćan later added a touch of the exotic to this otherwise solid group. It was a mass internationalisation of the Liverpool Football Club playing staff, just as the club's board had hoped and anticipated it would be. The stylish Finnish centre-back Hyypiä and Didi Hamann were the key figures here – powerful and reliable and technically excellent, they would provide much of the Liverpool backbone for the coming campaigns.

This new Liverpool under Houllier was highly functional rather than exciting, with the emphasis on a prosaic brand of counter-attacking football that had little of the romance or style of the Roy Evans era. It was sporadically effective, but it could also be incredibly dull. The new manager also began to insist on the tactical rotation of his squad. It was the end of the period when the sign of a typical Liverpool championship team was six or seven players who had played every league and major cup match. Liverpool's regimented play also contrasted wildly with much of the more sophisticated football now played by Wenger's Arsenal. But Liverpool were broadly competitive in 1999–2000, and the signing of the brawny young England forward Emile Heskey for £11 million from Leicester City in March 2000 was supposed to confirm the club's inevitable passage into the Champions League places. But Heskey had problems settling and scoring, and his presence seemed to unsettle, rather than inspire, his new club. With Fowler now deeply at odds with his manager, the Reds suffered a late-season goal drought and collapse, five winless and scoreless league matches. So it would be the UEFA Cup only for Liverpool in season 2000–01 after all. What an unlikely bonus this turned out to prove.

Landing the experienced German international full-back Markus Babbel on a free transfer in 2000 looked like good business for Houllier, and signing Nick Barmby from Everton kept the local sports scribes happy: Barmby was the first direct Liverpool signing from Everton since Dave Hickson in the 1950s. But the most important Liverpool capture for the 2000–01 season, in a flurry of transfer activity, was a Scot. How fitting. The Coventry City veteran Gary McAllister looked like a retirement case, a man recruited by Houllier mainly to coach, and the midfielder sensed the 'negative vibes' in the camp about him when he signed. But McAllister actually became a key player in an incredible Treble season. He gave the previously stodgy Liverpool side more cleverness, flow and direction from the centre of the field, crucial ingredients. Moreover, the seemingly ageless McAllister would assure himself of a permanent place in Red hearts by scoring an astonishing 44-yard match-winning free-kick against Everton at Goodison Park in a vital Easter 3–2 league win.

Before that, the Reds had stumbled to a League Cup final victory in the

Millennium Stadium in Cardiff, on penalties, over gallant Birmingham City. Michael Owen was left out of the final, while Robbie Fowler scored a stunning goal. Then, after having a peculiarly leisurely route to the later stages, Liverpool – or, rather, two-goal Michael Owen – returned to Wales to positively steal the 2001 FA Cup by 2–1 from under the noses of a dominant Arsenal. This time a crestfallen Fowler was omitted. It was a return to winning ways at last, a triumph for the insight, discipline and hard work of the Liverpool board and for Houllier and his staff. But could it last?

In the league, Liverpool were inconsistent, but they also produced some notable victories: two league wins over Manchester United and a Gerrard-inspired 4–0 rollicking of a classy Arsenal at Anfield, for example. Abroad, the club were also steadily progressing in the UEFA Cup, but making few friends along the way. In the fourth round, the Reds won 2–0 in the Olympic Stadium in Rome, both goals from Michael Owen, which meant a 0–1 loss at home in the second leg against Roma was a very decent result. After they beat Porto in the quarter-finals, next came an especially defensive semi-final display in the first leg in the Nou Camp in Barcelona that produced a ground-out 0–0 draw. It was an excellent result for a side inexperienced at this level, but the manner of the performance saw the Reds accused by some of the European football cognoscenti of 'murdering' the game. Houllier could care less. No one in the Liverpool 4 district complained when McAllister scored the only goal from the penalty spot in the second leg to take Liverpool through.

After all these lean years, it was difficult to take all this in. In this extraordinary season, Liverpool had won two domestic cups already, were still on course to qualify for a chance to win the European Cup once again and were in the club's first major European final for sixteen years – an opportunity to atone at last for all those terrible memories of 1985. And this was Houllier's team, an international combination rapidly rebuilt with a Scouse heart and a new Scottish professor as its brains. What an occasion it was. Fresh from snaffling the FA Cup from Arsenal's grasp, Liverpool now faced the Basques from Alavés in the 2001 UEFA Cup final. On paper, this might have looked like easy meat, and Liverpool were clear favourites. But the Spanish side had destroyed Kaiserslautern 9–2 on aggregate in the semi-finals, so tough competition and goals were on the menu. Tens of thousands of Liverpool supporters made the trip to Dortmund on a damp Ruhr night, a new generation of European football explorers. The flags and songs there made it seem just like old times. But the trip also lacked some of the excesses and the aggression of the 1980s – some hard lessons had been learned.

Liverpool FC, UEFA Cup winners, v. Alavés, 16 May 2001

Westerveld

Babbel   Henchoz   Hyypiä   Carragher

Hamann

Gerrard   McAllister   Murphy

Owen   Heskey

Alavés fans, in their first European final, were charming and hopeful, while Liverpool supporters were, well, just glad to be back on the big stage once more. The city of Dortmund perhaps owed Liverpool a victory after the 1966 Cup-Winners' Cup fiasco, and so it proved. But *what* a struggle! It did not look that way after sixteen minutes, when the Reds were two goals to the good, scored by Babbel and Gerrard. Alavés looked inexperienced and vulnerable, but they came back almost immediately with a goal of their own, from Alonso. Game on – enough to stir Michael Owen to win a penalty, converted by McAllister, who else? A score of 3–1 at half-time ought to have been enough to see this through, but Sander Westerveld was showing the arrogance and sloppiness that would soon cost him his Liverpool career, and danger man Moreno scored twice to level things at 3–3. When a frustrated Robbie Fowler came on for Heskey after 65 minutes and scored with a sublime right-foot shot, most Liverpool supporters would have settled for this romantic ending. But instead Alavés replied again with their third headed goal, from Jordi Cruyff. A final that began as exciting and adventurous was now in danger of just looking defensively naive.

The ridiculous mechanism of the 'golden goal' would now decide this UEFA Cup final. Just three minutes from the end of extra time, as the TV companies were gleefully preparing for penalties, a slithering headed own goal from Geli, after a McAllister free-kick, finally settled matters. Not that many of the Liverpool players knew the rules – they took their signal that the game was over from the Liverpool crowd's delirious response.

The reborn McAllister was voted man of the match in the final (he was man of the season for Liverpool), and there was still time for the Reds to thump Charlton Athletic 4–0 in the final league fixture to clinch a Champions League spot. It was an astonishing return on all four fronts. Gérard Houllier had confounded his critics, who had worried at his management style, conservative tactics and rigid formations. He deserved huge credit in the face of some opposition.

Not everyone even at Liverpool FC – even now – was convinced. Robbie Fowler was the focal point for this group of dissenters. The Scouser hated the new regimentation of it all. He was 'sick to death' of the lack of enjoyment in training and on the field, and the fact that no banter and play-acting was allowed in the camp any more. Even the Liverpool greats of the past would have missed these vital ingredients. Robbie had his sympathisers: Johan Cruyff, the guest of honour at the UEFA Cup final, was no lover of Liverpool's long-ball tactics. He whispered conspiratorially to the striker at his medal presentation, 'Don't let him get you down. You're too good.'[3]

Fowler also despised the way the new manager treated his players like schoolchildren and was depressed by the sheer dullness of many of the new foreign recruits. 'I want the players to be nice,' said Houllier, 'to be good people, to have respect for each other but also respect for the girls in the canteen or the kit manager. I think if you are a nice man, you are a nice player.' This kind of thing was a necessary riposte to the era of Dicks, Ruddock and Collymore, but it also offered a picture of a rather sanitised and authoritarian culture inside the dressing-room. A low point was reached when the young French full-back Grégory Vignal was found sobbing by players in the car park when illness had frustrated his chances of a first-team debut. This was the last straw to some of the local men: a first-team Liverpool player *crying* in front of his teammates! Things had gone too far, and Fowler was bemused and disillusioned. He knew this stage of his Liverpool career was over.

TOTAL ECLIPSE

Emboldened by his successes and lauded by the Liverpool board, Houllier prepared for the new campaign by signing Polish international goalkeeper Jerzy Dudek to replace Westerveld, the veteran Finnish forward Jari Litmanen and a young fitness fanatic, Norwegian left-back John Arne Riise. Liverpool's first match back in Europe's elite club competition after 16 long years away was a tepid 1–1 draw against Boavista. It took place in an eerie Anfield on 11 September 2001 while the rest of Europe looked westwards to the United States. The Twin Towers still smouldered in New York City. No one quite knew that night what lay in wait for the world. Less importantly, no one knew, either, that a different kind of fate would soon strike down the Liverpool Football Club manager near the top of his game and thus change the whole trajectory of his project at Anfield.

Illness hit the Liverpool boss hard, as it had done Liverpool management men before him. Matt McQueen in the 1920s, George Kay in the 1950s and Graeme Souness in the 1990s were all victims of serious illness or accident during their Anfield tenures. Houllier would now have to be added to this list: he suffered a damaged aorta at a match v. Leeds United at Anfield in October 2001, and the Frenchman spent much of the 2001–02 campaign in hospital recovering from serious heart surgery. Nevertheless, Liverpool, under the authority of Phil Thompson and with Steven Gerrard and Jamie Carragher offering on-field leadership, reached the quarter-final of the Champions League and amassed 80 points in the league to finish second only to Arsenal. The players seemed devoted to their recovering leader, and with a little more careful investment surely the ultimate success in the league and Europe would come to Liverpool?

An apparently restored Houllier signed Milan Baroš, a spritely and youthful but essentially heads-down Czech international, and the much coveted Senegalese international pair El-Hadji Diouf and Salif Diao as his final pieces. In, too, came midfield-man Bruno Cheyrou, who joined Liverpool from Lille with glowing references. But critically for the future of their French manager, all of these players, ultimately, failed the test at Anfield.

With Houllier back fully in charge, after a fine 12-match unbeaten league start in 2002–03 Liverpool slid down the table, and they made little progress in the Champions League. The manager fiddled relentlessly with the team. 'Asking Houllier to do nowt,' said keen Reds observer James Lawton in *The Independent* on 16 December 2002, 'to let a group of players grow organically rather than by constant Dr Frankenstein surgery, seems to be too tall a requirement of a passionate, hyperactive man.' He had a point. But the Reds still managed to defeat Manchester United 2–0 in the 2003 League Cup final, some reward in a difficult season that had started to raise new doubts about whether Gérard Houllier could secure the really big prizes for his supporters and players.

Since his illness, Houllier had seemed much less decisive and much too thin-skinned, showing ever-darkening concern about media comment, especially from ex-Liverpool players. Rick Parry certainly thought that the manager had become obsessive, had changed in character, since his heart problem. The quality Australian winger Harry Kewell joined Liverpool from Leeds in July 2003, but the manager had also put his store in recruiting young Continental players at 'bargain' prices, such as Florent Sinama Pongolle and Anthony Le Tallec, who seemed lightweight and ill-suited to the English game. By November, after a run of defeats, his captain Steven Gerrard was already admitting to the press that after just 13 matches Liverpool Football Club could not win the 2004 league title. A pall of paranoia had suddenly settled over Anfield, the manager stalking its corridors like a man plagued by demons. Houllier seemed increasingly lost and befuddled in a fog of statistics, which he now spewed out at every press conference. Journalists had begun to see past his urbanity and were now questioning his managerial capacity – even his sanity. Another Champions League place won in season 2003–04 could not disguise the fact that many of the club's supporters were also losing faith in their manager. Liverpool collected only 60 league points, 30 behind the champions Arsenal. Suddenly, this grand French march seemed to be heading nowhere, and the manager knew it. After brief discussions with the Liverpool board in May 2004, Houllier left the club.

THE MEN FROM THE CONTINENT (2)

On the surface, the new Liverpool manager, the Spaniard Rafa Benítez, seemed very much like the departing Gérard Houllier. He was a technocrat, a coach with no great playing record, a man who laid great store on preparation, tactics and discipline. He favoured scientific assessments of players, and defence more than attack. He liked to keep a rather cold distance between himself and his squad, and he also favoured rotation to keep its members fresh. Unlike Houllier, however, he had enjoyed some club management success in one of the toughest leagues in Europe, twice winning the Spanish title and in 2004 also taking the UEFA Cup with a Valencia side that he had largely inherited.

Despite this incredible recent domestic and European success, Benítez was available because he had fallen out with his employers. They had insisted on the Spanish club model: that the director of football should recruit players who the coach (in this case Benítez) should then prepare. Benítez much preferred the English model, in which the manager chooses his own players and then moulds them into a winning unit. Don't buy me a lamp when I ask for a table, summed up his frustrations with the director of football at the Mestalla. He was glad to leave Spain.

Aware of the growing tensions at Valencia, Liverpool chief executive Rick Parry had rushed to sign up Benítez a matter of days after Houllier had departed. The new man had barely been to Liverpool, but he liked what he was hearing from Parry and his chairman David Moores. He would have the freedom – and the funds – to build his own team with no board interference. He could also bring his Spanish coaching team.

Make no mistake, this signing was a major coup. Benítez was arguably the most prized young coach in Europe at the time, but he knew little about managing in England, where another new young foreign manager, José Mourinho, was already making huge surfer's waves at Chelsea. Winning the Premier League crown would be more difficult than ever. Benítez immediately faced the qualifying rounds of the Champions League (a context in which he excelled), the hard yards of the Premier League (of which he had no experience at all), domestic cup football in England (which he seemed to ignore) and threats from the club's star player and local symbol Steven Gerrard that the young Scouser was leaving, right away, for rivals Chelsea. Clearly, it would not all be plain sailing for the new manager.

Gerrard eventually agreed to stay on at Liverpool, but Michael Owen left – for Real Madrid. The unknown Antonio Núñez joined Liverpool from Madrid to smooth the Owen deal. It was a difficult start. Benítez recruited, in Owen's place, Luis García, a talented if lightweight forward from Barcelona's reserves for £6 million, and also the £10 million 22-year-old midfielder Xabi Alonso from Real Sociedad. Alonso was a quality passer, a game-organiser not unlike Jan Mølby, but a man with much more mobility and tackling verve than the Dane. A man with one name only, Josémi, was also recruited from Málaga in Spain to play right-back, but he never convinced and was soon replaced by a late Houllier signing, the solid and consistent Ireland international defender Steve Finnan. Benítez was also stuck with Djibril Cissé, a forward Houllier had agreed to sign for a then club record fee of £14 million from Auxerre. Cissé was flaky and temperamental, the kind of forward who probably had the look of a pacy, powerful and daunting man in the French League, but who was bullied and clobbered by most British centre-halves he faced. It was a final Houllier mistake that effectively tied the new manager's hands. Benítez tried to loosen the binds in January 2005 by signing Fernando Morientes, a great striker in Spain but half a yard and some courage short for the game in England. Morientes also enjoyed too much the company of physiotherapists.

Initially, Benítez struggled in the league: he tried to rotate his squad in places it should not (and could not) be rotated, underestimating the capacity of any Premier League side at home to mug Liverpool – especially if his own team was stuffed full of still half-baked foreign recruits. It was a lesson the new manager found difficult to learn, especially as Arsenal, Manchester United and the recently funded Chelsea were all candidates now to win the league title. He would also need to learn the importance to English club supporters of the FA Cup: he fielded a weak Liverpool team at bleak Burnley in the third round in January 2005, and the Reds crumbled to a 0–1 reverse, young French full-back Traore scoring a comical back-heeled own goal. There was a near-hysterical reaction in the city to this humiliation and early calls for the manager's head. Better progress came in the League Cup, in which Liverpool eventually made it to the final in 2005 before losing out 2–3 to Mourinho's Chelsea. This rivalry was stoking up nicely: the flamboyant Portuguese versus the unflappable Spaniard – and it had a few miles to run yet.

In contrast to his league travails, Benítez excelled in the European arena, where he had more time to prepare tactically for a specific project in a setting he felt comfortable with and where he was less likely to come up against the sort of bludgeoning approach he was routinely encountering in the British game. There, physical force could smash up well-laid tactical plans. But he still ended up at the rear of the group-stage table in 2004–05, with Liverpool needing to beat the Greeks from Olympiacos by two clear goals at Anfield in the last match to be certain of qualifying for the knockout stages. Actually, Liverpool could barely have chosen more hospitable travellers – the Greeks had rarely secured a decent European result away from home. But the Brazilian master Rivaldo curled home a first-half free-kick, meaning Liverpool now needed three goals in reply and with a team full of inexperienced young players. They got them, the extraordinary Steven Gerrard completing a famous second-half comeback with a rocket past the hopelessly stranded Nikopolidis in the Greek goal.

Next up, Liverpool eased past the Germans from Bayer Leverkusen before an emotional couple of meetings loomed with Juventus, the first time the clubs had met since the terrible events back in 1985. Liverpool and its supporters tried to make their public apologies to the Italians at Anfield, before squeezing through with a 2–1 lead, courtesy of Hyypiä and Luis García, to take to Turin. In Italy, what looked like a tough task proved much hotter off the pitch than on it, with the Reds comfortably holding on for a near risk-free 0–0 draw. Returning from injury, Xabi Alonso was outstanding in organising Liverpool's resistance. It was much the same story at Stamford Bridge in the first leg of the semi-final v. Chelsea, which pitted Benítez against the self-proclaimed 'Special One'. Liverpool played for – and got – a cagey scoreless draw, hoping that the Anfield crowd might subdue a star-studded Chelsea back in the district of Liverpool 4. And this proved to be a magnificent tactical victory for the Liverpool manager over the two legs, little Luis García scoring the famous early 'goal that never was' at the Kop end and then the entire Liverpool crowd screaming cacophonously until the final whistle sounded.

There had been many, many wonderful football occasions at Anfield in the previous 113 years, of course: to celebrate the championship in 1906 against Sheffield United; the joyous scenes for the match against Stoke for another title in 1923; the news reaching Anfield from afar that the Reds had won the league again, in 1947; the 5–0 rout of Arsenal in 1964 to win Shankly's first championship; Inter Milan in 1965; Fairclough's European Cup night against St Etienne in 1977; the 5–0 destruction of Nottingham Forest in 1988; two amazing, gut-wrenching 4–3 evening Premier League matches with Newcastle United in the 1990s; and Gérard Houllier's emotional return from illness as Liverpool beat Roma 2–0 in the Champions League in March 2002. But surely there was nothing quite like this night. There was nothing like the noise and the celebrations and the pinch-yourself-is-it-really-happening exchanges around the city that followed. Twenty years on from the disgrace of Brussels, astonishingly, Liverpool Football Club was back in the European Cup final. There could never be another football night like this one – could there?

THE MIRACLE OF ISTANBUL

Of course, every Liverpool supporter has their own story to tell about Istanbul 2005: where we saw it; how we got there; what we did afterwards in the middle of the night; how we had all given up all hope at half-time. Everyone who was there will remember the chaotic organisation at a stadium built, literally, in the middle of nowhere. How lucky were UEFA that Liverpool won this final, thus deflecting criticism about the European body's continuing contempt for its customers? This epic contest against AC Milan was simply the most dramatic of all European Cup finals, possibly the greatest-ever major final, one that straddled Asia and Europe. It kicked off on one day and finished on another, and had just about *everything* in between. There have even been half-decent books written about this single match.[4] It was a game that raised all the difficult and controversial questions that had been simmering about the Liverpool manager. Should he be considered a tactical genius for turning around a three-goal half-time deficit against one of the best club sides in Europe? Or a stubborn fool for his hubris in making a huge tactical error, one from which he was eventually rescued only by the heart and unwillingness to accept defeat shown by his players? The debate will continue as long as this match is talked about.

Liverpool FC, European Cup-winning team, v. AC Milan, 25 May 2005

Dudek

Finnan (Hamann 46)   Carragher   Hyypiä   Traore

Gerrard   Alonso   Riise

García   Baroš (Cissé 85)   Kewell (Šmicer 23)

There is not much doubt that the vaunted Liverpool manager did err by leaving out Didi Hamann, his most experienced midfield defensive player, from Liverpool's starting line-up for the 2005 Champions League final. This move was so unexpected that when Hamann heard Benítez announce the side, he wondered why *Xabi Alonso* had been left out: the German's mind had blanked the fact that it was *his* name that was missing from his manager's team sheet.

This match had seemed like an unfair contest right from the start because Milan was stuffed with seasoned international stars – Cafu, Seedorf, Shevchenko, Pirlo, Maldini, Crespo, Gattuso, Kaká, Stam – while Liverpool were inexperienced greenhorns by comparison, especially without Hamann. The usually cautious Benítez had seemingly tried to outwit his rivals, who were expecting a dour Liverpool performance focused on counter-attacking. Instead, the Spaniard dispensed with his midfield shield and played the fragile Australian winger Harry Kewell, who had only just returned from injury. It was a typical piece of Benítez conceit, and this tactical gamble failed on all fronts. Kewell broke down in the first half, but Benítez stubbornly stuck to his favoured pattern by bringing on the attacking Czech international Vladimir Šmicer rather than his German midfielder. This woeful mistake simply compounded the manager's earlier selection blunder.

Without the experienced Hamann, Liverpool had no means of coping with the movement of the peerless young Brazilian Kaká, in a match that was far too open for Liverpool to manage. Milan scored in the first minute through Maldini and then ripped through the Reds for a 0–3 half-time lead, with two goals from Crespo, fashioned by Kaká. This looked like humiliation, a possible record scoreline in a major final. This was what some of the fans and key Liverpool players were now thinking: how to face their mates back home. What exactly happened at half-time remains contentious today. Did the Milan players celebrate prematurely, so provoking a murderous response from Liverpool? Did the defiant singing of the Liverpool fans raise the Reds' spirits to launch an irresistible second-half assault? Did Benítez rouse his men to a recovery of Lazarus proportions with a touch of tactical genius and some motivational inspiration? Or did none of these things really happen? Did Liverpool simply decide to 'have a go' at Milan in a typical piece of British football bloody-mindedness, just to see what might transpire when they had nothing left to lose?

Initially, at least, the Liverpool dressing-room seemed to be both devastated and chaotic. The players were in shock. The manager's first plan was to bring on Djibril Cissé for the outclassed Traore, to try to attack his way back into the contest. Who knows what might have happened next if this strategy had actually been followed? The young French full-back was already heading for the shower when it was discovered that the right-back Steve Finnan was injured, so Traore was reinstated. He played a blinding second half. Then Benítez decided to bring on *both* Hamann and Cissé, until it was pointed out that Liverpool now had 12 players in their new system. Some much needed clarity now struck home. Cissé would stay on the bench and Hamann *would* come on; Jamie Carragher would move to the right of what was effectively a back three, with Šmicer supporting in defence when needed. Gerrard would push further forward to support his attackers. At last this looked like a tenable plan, one to offer some scintilla of hope in a hopeless situation. Nobody in the Liverpool camp really believed it would work – except, perhaps, the great unwashed, the Liverpool army of despairing spectators.

But when Benítez restored the German Hamann at the interval, it looked too late; Milan continued to attack, and it seemed like they might score more goals. Benítez had essentially asked his players to try to score and then 'see what happens'. So much for scientific Continental tactics: Liverpool needed some old-fashioned British grit to unnerve their opponents and get back into this uneven contest. They also depended upon the fantastic support of the Reds fans, who just refused to give this up. Captain Steven Gerrard, inevitably, led the charge. Remarkably, Liverpool scored three times – Gerrard, Šmicer and Alonso – in six astounding second-half minutes. 'Six minutes' carries major symbolic importance for the Liverpool club, of course: in 1989, the disastrous Hillsborough FA Cup semi-final lasted only that long. Now the phrase 'six minutes' would have an additional, more joyous, meaning for a new generation of Liverpool supporters.

Visibly rattled, Milan, for all their international experience, could not reply. Dudek, the Liverpool goalkeeper, a modest Catholic man from Polish mining stock, saved point-blank from Shevchenko near the end of normal time and said later that some divine intervention had aided his resistance. Perhaps it also helped him deal with the mental torment of the penalties that followed? He did not need much help. Milan were drained, agog at the Liverpool fightback – it was the usually deadly Shevchenko who missed the vital kick. Liverpool Football Club had come back from the dead to win their fifth European Cup – their first under a foreign manager and with a largely foreign team. It was a miracle, aided from above, some wags claimed, by the Anfield Holy Trinity of Shankly, Paisley and Fagan. But without their two current Scouse rocks, Jamie Carragher and Steven Gerrard, and without the club's extraordinary supporters, none of this would have been remotely possible. Which left one key question: did Liverpool win the 2005 European Cup despite or because of the actions of their manager? Was Benítez inspired or just lucky? In football, history is written by winners.

STILL CHASING A DREAM

What could possibly follow this? Another severe bout of 'Gerrard is going' anxiety in the summer of 2005 and ambitions for winning the Premier League title, of course. In some circles, the Liverpool manager might have been nominated to join the Liverpool greats because of what happened in Istanbul, but he would never be fully accepted into the pantheon until he had conquered *all* the domestic peaks. He climbed another one in 2006. A small mountain, Peter Crouch, was brought in to help him, an unlikely stretched-out target man. Bolo Zenden also arrived, an experienced Dutch midfielder whom the manager tried, unsuccessfully, to sell to the Liverpool crowd by describing him as 'Middlesbrough's best player'. Momo Sissoko was signed up, a destructive Malian midfield player who Benítez had worked with in Spain and who achieved some brief cult status in Liverpool 4. But his poor technique was a vital flaw. Arriving too was a highly promising young Danish central defender called Daniel Munthe Agger from Brondby, though injury blighted his start with the club. Finally, there was even a romantic return to Liverpool for Robbie Fowler, a local folk hero who had been dispatched by Houllier to Leeds United in December 2001 for a crazily inflated £12 million fee and whom Benítez now embraced as a veteran forward option with impeccable Liverpool credentials. All these men had some quality, but some were too late in their careers and none of them were out-and-out successes at Liverpool.

As European champions, Liverpool contested FIFA's invented Club World Championship tournament in Japan in December 2005. The club had lost twice in Japan in the old World Club Championship (in 1981 and 1984) and had barely taken the matter seriously. In 1981, Bob Paisley warned his players to avoid bookings in the fixture because of their impact on much more important league matches. Things had changed in 20 years. Benítez showed something of his deep commitment to the club, and also his rather icy emotional baggage, by staying with his team in Japan even after news of his father's death in Spain. This tournament was a shabby event that intruded badly into the English League season and was palpably more important to the club for marketing purposes than because it had any serious football worth. But who would baulk at the title 'World Champions'? Liverpool lost 0–1 in the final in Yokohama to the South Americans São Paulo. Back in the real football world, meanwhile, the Reds eventually finished behind Chelsea and Manchester United in the Premier League, scoring a paltry 57 goals in the process, despite their new strikers.

But there were compensations. The Liverpool manager out-thought José Mourinho again in an FA Cup semi-final win at Old Trafford on 22 April 2006, immaculately sculpted by Luis García, which led to another Steven Gerrard-inspired dramatic final win in Wales, this time on penalties in the 2006 FA Cup final after a pulsating 3–3 draw with the luckless West Ham United. By now Gerrard was sorting out his gremlins, and he was assuming the mantle of one of the club's greatest-ever players, routinely dredging his team out of seemingly impossible situations, carrying inadequate colleagues and scoring vital goals.

He had every quality – power, technique, vision and coolness in front of goal – even if, as a shy man, he sometimes seemed to lack self-belief. Gerrard was also helping his manager stave off difficult press interviews. Saving the penalty kicks in Wales in 2006 was new Reds goalkeeper Pepe Reina, the Spanish son of a goalkeeper, brought in to replace the heroic – but occasionally slipshod – Jerzy Dudek. Indeed, what had also been astonishing about the 2005 Liverpool European Cup win was that it was the swansong for a group of players recruited under Houllier who had played vital roles in the final. Šmicer, Baroš and Dudek had all left the club immediately after Istanbul, and Hamann and Traore were reduced to minor roles.

In the summer of 2006, Benítez was offered yet more funds for transfers by the Liverpool board, if not (as he liked to point out) the vast sums afforded to those in charge at the two clubs that had just bettered his team in the league. In came Craig Bellamy, an unruly and unpredictable Welsh forward; Fábio Aurélio, a talented but brittle Brazilian full-back Benítez knew from Spain; Mark Gonzalez, a Chilean international winger the manager had chased for two years but who was quite unsuitable for the English game; Dirk Kuyt, a reputable and hard-working striker from Holland; and – a quite startling signing this – the very mundane right-sided forward Jermaine Pennant from the equally ordinary Birmingham City. The superior Argentinian international water-carrier Javier Mascherano joined later in the campaign, on loan from West Ham, to add defensive solidity to the Liverpool cause. He would eventually cost £17 million to keep. Collectively, these players did not seem to be signings designed to build a title-winning team, and although Liverpool again finished third in the Premier League in 2007 they now trailed by 21 points the title-winners Manchester United.

Benítez's counter to local criticism about continuing league failings was again in Europe, where the Reds comfortably saw off PSV Eindhoven, Bordeaux and Galatasaray in the Champions League group stages, won sensationally in Barcelona after Bellamy and Riise had publicly fallen out before the match, the former using a golf club as a preferred weapon, and then thumped PSV again to set up another meeting with Chelsea in the semi-finals. Remarkably, Rafa Benítez outsmarted José Mourinho for a third consecutive occasion in knockout play, with Liverpool winning 4–1 on penalties after each club had secured a 1–0 home win. Pepe Reina in Liverpool's goal was beginning to show all the class and assurance his manager had identified in him, and he was a demon to beat in penalty shoot-outs. But, alas, there was no happy ending, because in a near-chaotic setting in Athens, against the old enemies from 2005 AC Milan, Liverpool eventually lost 1–2.

The Milan side of 2007 was older and definitely weaker than it had been in 2005, which suggested, therefore, that the same might also be true for Liverpool. But a more ambitious approach from Benítez might well have brought another European Cup victory for the Reds, despite the flaws in the 2007 Liverpool squad. The perpetually underperforming Pennant got into great positions but failed to deliver, and leaving Peter Crouch on the bench for seventy-eight minutes, by which time Milan had established a crucial one-goal advantage, was certainly not the cautious Liverpool manager's finest hour.

The reputation of Liverpool's support was also later dragged through the mud by UEFA because of ticketless intrusions into another poorly organised venue. In short, it was business as usual in the European governing body. Two European Cup finals in three years was handsome compensation for failings in the league. But by now things happening off the field at Anfield were beginning to cloud the Liverpool manager's vision of his rightful place at the club. In fact, these developments in the Liverpool boardroom seemed to threaten the entire future of Liverpool Football Club.

CHAPTER 18 REFERENCES

1. Hopkins and Williams, 'Gérard Houllier and the New Liverpool Imaginary'
2. Williams, *The Liverpool Way*, p. 153
3. Fowler, *My Autobiography*, p. 298
4. Williams and Hopkins, *The Miracle of Istanbul*

EPILOGUE

THERE MUST BE SOME WAY OUT OF HERE
The Liverpool Ownership Crisis

THE MONEY GAME

Liverpool Football Club had now acquired an ambitious international manager who seemed imperious in Europe, if rather less certain at home. But the economics at the club still lagged behind developments on the field, and the ailing remnants of the Littlewoods empire could no longer provide the cash to build a new stadium and fund the team. In their search for finance to build a stadium on nearby Stanley Park, club chairman David Moores and chief executive Rick Parry had been keen to try to conserve as much as possible of the cultural heritage, the administration and the 'family ethos' of the Liverpool club. Ideally, the Liverpool Way built patiently over many generations of essentially conservative (and often Conservative) club stewardship, would remain intact and relatively unsullied. But despite this ambition and Liverpool's complex mix of parochialism and historical 'openness' as a city, the realisation that investment in Liverpool Football Club was now being sought from all corners of the globe made some fans – especially locally based supporters – understandably uneasy.

Back in May 2004, the billionaire prime minister of Thailand, Thaksin Shinawatra, had offered a £65-million investment for a 30 per cent stake in the Liverpool club, while a 'hostile' counter-offer of a reported £73 million had been placed on the table from local building magnate Steve Morgan to buy outright control of the club. Both offers were eventually rejected, Shinawatra's possibly because of rising public unease among fans about his alleged human-rights abuses in Thailand. Morgan's offer was at least made up of more local capital, but it was claimed by the Liverpool board to 'undervalue' the club. Morgan also, undoubtedly, posed a threat to the future at Liverpool of both Moores and Rick Parry.

In the light of the obvious difficulties involved in finding suitable new investors or owners for the club, other avenues were also tentatively explored by Liverpool, ones that stressed the local affinities of the club much more clearly. There had been discussions below the surface for some time on the potential for a shared stadium with neighbours and eternal rivals Everton FC. The Goodison Park club were also eyeing several potential sites for relocation (including the vacant King's Dock on the city's waterfront). Predictably, there continued to be vehement objections raised to the idea of a shared stadium from many diehard fans and elements within both club boardrooms, who viewed the proposal as little short of sacrilegious. More prosaically, a shared stadium would cut potential profits as well as costs, and where would the near-destitute Everton club come up with their share of the capital required for such a venture?

More than two years of searching later, Liverpool still had no new investment capital. Then a consortium representing Dubai International Capital (DIC), an arm of the Dubai government and ruling family, reportedly offered a total of £156 million for the purchase of all existing Liverpool shares, plus funds to cover debts and the building of a new stadium on nearby Stanley Park, a total package of around £450 million. The Liverpool board seemed keen to accept the Dubai bid, despite further human-rights concerns. However, just two months later, in February 2007, two American sports and property tycoons, Tom Hicks and George Gillett Jr, men who had never worked seriously together in business, raised the offer for the club to £5,000 a share, or £172 million, plus promised funds for a new stadium. The DIC group had earlier sneered that the 'soccer-phobic' Gillett would not know Liverpool FC from a 'hole in the ground', but it was now publicly furious at the sudden collapse in negotiations, describing the Liverpool board as 'dishonourable' and the club as 'a shambles'.

Liverpool chairman David Moores now had the onerous responsibility of weighing up the pros and cons of the American and Middle Eastern options. He eventually decided to take the plunge and agreed to sell his controlling stake to the US entrepreneurs. Rick Parry was quick to deny that Moores was being swayed by the increased offer for the club shares, saying: 'The price is not a factor in David Moores's mind. He is not after cash for himself, absolutely not. Be assured, the only thing David Moores is concerned about is the club being in the right hands for the future. You can be certain he has done his homework carefully and will make a decision in the best interests of the club.' Moores, himself, was determined to make it clear that he was selling up only to secure the long-term future of the club: 'When you have a decision to make like this and you are so desperate to see the club go into the right hands, then you have to be comfortable with whatever you decide.'

Moores would certainly be 'comfortable': he stood to raise his own cut of the club buyout by some £8 million, to a reported £89.6 million. He was also installed as honorary life president of the club in recognition of his decade-and-a-half service, and he was charged to act as something of a nominal 'boardroom delegate' for astonished Liverpool fans. David Moores might well have favoured passing on his Liverpool shares to the Americans for reasons other than profit. After all, these were two identifiable sports benefactors from across the Atlantic, people who understood the global sports business and who had money to invest, but who also had the club apparently at heart. These might have looked a better bet for a city with strong business and cultural links to the USA than a faceless and rather 'alien' corporate government body from the Middle East. And David Moores was hardly the first football-club chairman in England in the new era to profit from the sale of a club.

But what is more significant is that this profiteering seemed like a complete reversal of the history of the patrician and custodian local funding for Liverpool Football Club. Indeed, it seemed like an inversion of the entire Moores family project of long-term investment in the Merseyside football clubs and in the city of Liverpool itself over more than 70 years. This was a business deal typical of the new age of global liberalisation, one that plainly traduced the core tenets of the Liverpool Way. It was certainly unlikely to endear David Moores to Liverpool fans in 2007, even to those who approved, initially at least, of the American investment over that offered by the men from Dubai.

FISTFULS OF DOLLARS

Two American billionaires, Tom Hicks, owner of the Texas Rangers baseball franchise and the (US) National Hockey League's Dallas Stars, and George Gillett Jr, owner of the Montreal Canadiens and formerly of the Miami Dolphins, had cobbled together in just two months an unlikely alliance to secure a reported £470-million funding package, via a loan from the Royal Bank of Scotland, to buy Liverpool Football Club and to allocate some £215 million to begin work on a new stadium. Hicks, a Texas acolyte and former business partner of President George W. Bush, had made his fortune from raising private equity to fund multimillion-dollar corporate takeovers. Liverpool Football Club was suddenly in the hands of the sort of global sports capitalists who made no secret of their financial motives, their ignorance of 'soccer' or their ambitions to model this highly atypical English football club, commercially, along the lines of an NFL franchise. They openly highlighted the attractions of English football's booming TV monies, the growing Internet income streams for the English game, expanding markets for the Liverpool club in South-East Asia and in South America, stadium naming rights and even their plans for introducing American-style 'bunker suites' into the proposed new Liverpool stadium: underground 'living rooms' where corporate elites could dine in plush splendour and watch banks of TV sets before taking an elevator ride to their match seats. This seemed like 'Americanisation' writ large.

And yet local resistance on Merseyside to this cultural, as well as corporate, takeover of one of the city's core institutions was, for some commentators, surprisingly muted to say the least. This apparently benign reception for the Americans on Merseyside was mainly for four reasons. First, a realist resignation now existed among most Liverpool supporters that in the age of open borders non-local financing was inevitable for any football club with serious pretensions to be competitive for titles at home in England and in Europe. More knowledgeable (and, perhaps, more cynical) Liverpool fans could even make the appropriate historical connections here, about the origins of the club and the commercial hard-headedness of one of its great cultural leaders of the past, as 'Real Deep' told readers of *Through the Wind and Rain* in 2007:

> Haven't we been a plaything for the rich from day one, when we were formed, not for sporting reasons, but to fill a recently vacated Anfield and provide the owner John Houlding with a steady stream of income from both paying customers at the game and the sale of beer in the nearby hostelry? And *he* imported a whole troop of Scottish mercenaries to fill the team. [Bill] Shankly, if he ever stops spinning in his grave (to listen to some people), was quick to threaten to resign when not offered enough money in the transfer market . . . He was also happy to advocate a move away from a dilapidated Anfield.

Second, the cosmopolitan 'city of the sea' of Liverpool was no stranger, of course, to global cultural exchange or, more specifically, to American cultural and commercial investment. Indeed, for much of its history Liverpool had looked west to Ireland and the United States for guidance and inspiration on identity issues more than it had to other English cities. Near its height in the early years of the twentieth century, the port at Liverpool had provided direct employment for up to 60,000 people in the city, much of it in trade involving North America. Even before the First World War, Americans were envied in Liverpool for their supposed modernity and stylishness, and American fashions were imported by Liverpool tailors, who regularly copied clothes brought in by seamen from the eastern seaboard of the USA. Later, this maritime connection

– seamen on the passenger services to the USA were known locally as 'Cunard Yanks' – also fed directly into Liverpool street idioms and language, nightlife and music, with 'the most American of English cities' acting as a site of feverish transatlantic cultural exchange of a sort that allowed the city to take the lead in pop music in the world during the 1960s. In short, the city of Liverpool already had ingrained American sensibilities and sympathies well before Tom Hicks and George Gillett strode into Anfield early in 2007 with their 'good ole boy' homilies about 'tradition' and 'heritage' and their promises to make Liverpool FC the most successful football club in the world. Given the city's distinctive history, the possibility of transatlantic investment and exchange in football did not strike most of its citizens as an especially alien or threatening intrusion.

Third, allied to their obvious commercial savvy, the new Liverpool co-owners were experts in 'selling' themselves to the Liverpool supporters in the set-piece press conferences that followed. They showed little of the arrogance of the Glazer family at Manchester United, for example, who seemed to believe that money was its own explanation for their actions and who had made little attempt to engage with Manchester United fans. 'They are very private people,' said Tom Hicks of Malcolm Glazer and his family. 'I have owned sports teams for 13 years. I gave up my privacy a long time ago, and it is easier for me to be open about these things . . . He showed us how not to do it.'

With the Merseyside press acting largely as enthusiastic cheerleaders, crucially, the general assumption was that the Liverpool buyout would *not* involve the kind of leveraged deal that had loaded more than £600 million worth of Glazer debt onto the Manchester club. Indeed, in the offer document for the Liverpool club the Americans had made it very clear that any loans taken out to secure the deal would be personally guaranteed and that payment of any interest 'will not depend to any significant extent on the business of Liverpool'.

The new owners also cleverly, and rather humbly in this charm offensive, played back to the Liverpool club's supporters some of the familiar and comforting rhetoric about the club's past. 'We are custodians not owners of the franchise,' Gillett said, thus combining the Victorian Britain of John Houlding with the language of late-modern American sport and both reassuring and alarming Liverpool supporters simultaneously. It was left to David Moores to admit, 'I don't think we have maximised our world brand and hopefully they [Gillett and Hicks] will help us get into these areas where we have fantastic fan bases.' And it was George Gillett who coyly told the same group of journalists on 6 February 2007, 'I don't think it's appropriate for Tom or I to try to convince the fans today that we understand the history, the support or the legacy anywhere as well as they do. What we would try to say to the fans is that we have respect. Respect is the way we feel about the history and the legacy of this franchise [sic] . . . I am still learning about the club but I will get it into my blood in every way I can.'

Finally, another familiar device skilfully employed by the Americans and their advisers to mask some of the bleak economics of the deal was the notion of the Liverpool 'family'. The friendly Moores family dynasty – that had followed other Liverpool boardroom families – would now be seamlessly replaced by a transatlantic equivalent, made up of the Gilletts and the Hickses. This message about 'respect' and 'family values' was strongly reinforced in words and images in a commemorative booklet issued by Liverpool FC, carrying pictures of the American buyers and their adult sons at Anfield. It was almost as if the club had been acquired through marriage by some august royal family from a superior and distant culture. Gillett's son Foster would even come over to work inside the club on a day-to-day basis on an executive level with Rick Parry, while Tom Hicks Jr would join the club board. How, exactly, this arrangement would pan out remained a moot point, because it seemed full of potential tensions and conflict. By the end of the 2006–07 season, there were already reports that, smelling who now held the club purse strings, Liverpool manager Rafa Benítez had started to bypass Rick Parry and was talking directly to Foster Gillett in order to expedite transfers and other matters. Parry was now the self-appointed guardian of continuity and the main defender of the 'Liverpool Way' inside the club, but he was already starting to look increasingly and disturbingly isolated in the new Liverpool ownership structure.

THE BACK OF LOVE

This was the background against which, in May 2007, Liverpool had reached the European Cup (Champions League) final for the second time in three years. By the autumn of 2007, it had become clear that the American owners would have to renegotiate a new financial package worth £350 million with the Royal Bank of Scotland and the American investment bank Wachovia in order to pay off their original loans and raise cash to begin work on the Liverpool stadium. Revised plans for the new stadium insisted upon by the new owners had considerably increased its price, so proposals to raise a further £300 million for the funding of the new ground would now have to wait until 2009. Worse, despite their initial denials, the Liverpool owners now reportedly wanted to load the whole of the original acquisition debt of £298 million onto the club's balance sheet, thus replicating core aspects of the Glazer deal at Manchester

United. Gone was the earlier talk about 'respect' and the 'tradition' and the 'heritage' of the Liverpool club. Instead, Hicks chose to compare the purchase of Liverpool Football Club to that of a breakfast cereal company. 'When I was in the leverage buyout business, we bought Weetabix and we leveraged it up to make our return. You could say that anyone who was eating Weetabix was paying for our purchase of Weetabix. It was just business. It is the same for Liverpool: revenues come in from whatever source, and if there is money left over it is profit.'

The first element of the refinancing package was finally agreed in January 2008, with £105 million of the debt saddled on Liverpool and £185 million secured on a holding company, Kop Investment LLC, held in the tax havens off the Cayman Islands and in the US state of Delaware. These were the routine machinations of global capitalism in full flow. The Americans increased their personal guarantees, mainly in the form of credit notes, to around a reported £55 million. This suddenly looked like very deep financial water and not the sort of deal that Liverpool fans – or Moores and Parry – had anticipated. Added to this, a very public row over transfer funds between manager Rafa Benítez and Tom Hicks in November 2007 mobilised Liverpool spectators squarely behind the manager and against the new owners, sparking fan protests. By January 2008, any debates there might have been over the 'politics' of foreign ownership at Anfield had, for some fans, effectively been replaced by a stark pragmatism: broadsheet newspapers carried pictures of Kopites holding up a large home-made banner reading 'Yanks out, Dubai in. In Rafa we Love'. This position hardened still further when it was revealed that Parry, Hicks and Gillett had all secretly met with ex-Germany national coach Jürgen Klinsmann to discuss the managerial position at Liverpool should Benítez's position at the club become 'untenable'. The mood was changed decisively with this revelation. Moreover, despite repeated promises given by the new owners – and this was the main reason, after all, why the club had sought large investors – no visible progress had yet been made on building the proposed new Liverpool stadium.

Finally, as rumours began to circulate early in 2008 that DIC were considering a new £500 million offer for the club, it was clear that Hicks and Gillett were no longer in direct communication with each other nor could they agree on the future of Liverpool Football Club. Gillett looked as if he might be willing to sell his share of the club, possibly to DIC, while Hicks publicly demanded the resignation of the 'failing' Rick Parry. Parry would soon leave as the club began to look like a laughing stock and its borrowings were reported to be some £313 million. David Moores was pronounced to be 'disgusted' at Parry's treatment, and he retired from the Liverpool board in June 2009, saying he was 'heartbroken' at how the new owners had treated the club. At the same time, Merseyside MPs called for the British government to resist an application from the Americans for a loan of £350 million from the majority government-owned Royal Bank of Scotland. Liverpool Football Club, once a model of conservative and unobtrusive stability in the English game, suddenly seemed to be impossibly split, rudderless and constantly in the public eye. Public protests organised by the Spirit of Shankly group continued to occur in the city into the 2009–10 league season, as the Liverpool owners were reputed to be looking for new Middle Eastern investors in the club.

IN TORRES WE TRUST

Despite all this hugely distracting background noise and lack of focus and direction off the field, the Liverpool manager Benítez had soldiered on and had continued to strengthen his team and his squad by bringing in a number of differential quality signings in the summer of 2007. Yossi Benayoun was among them, a skilful and intelligent Israeli wide midfielder. Benayoun had real ability, some speed, mental strength and loads of energy – and he could also score goals. He was the signing Liverpool should so obviously have made when Benítez brought in the soon to be discarded Pennant. The Israeli might even have helped secure a second European Cup for Benítez in 2007.

The much-hyped but pedestrian Brazilian midfield man Lucas Leiva joined from Grêmio in Brazil, having won the coveted Bola de Ouro (Golden Ball) for being the best young player in the 2006 Brazilian championship. He would take time to settle – perhaps he never would. Ryan Babel, another highly rated young star, joined from Ajax for £11.5 million, and he could score extraordinary goals. But the forward seemed destined to be better known for his 'romps' with serial Liverpool 'WAG' Danielle Lloyd than he would be for incisive and courageous play for his club. He lacked technique and heart and seemed destined, at best, for the fringes of the Benítez project.

But the signature signing was the £20-million capture of the Atlético Madrid centre-forward Fernando Torres on a six-year deal in July 2007, with Luis García joining the Madrid club. Benítez had built a successful team at Valencia without a major goalscorer, but his Liverpool side had lacked this sort of flexibility and range of goal contributors. Peter Crouch scored only in spurts, and Dirk Kuyt had reinvented himself as a right midfielder when goals had evaded him in England. So the manager brought in a man who pretty much guaranteed front-end goals. Torres was already a major football figure in Madrid, a man who had been made Atlético captain at 19, so he had some maturity and a sense of responsibility to the collective as well as the necessary selfishness of an authentic frontman. He also had power and threatening pace and was a brilliant finisher. He had turned down a move to Chelsea in 2006, and the only question mark was how he would stand up to the sheer physicality of the English game. Could he stay fit and committed in the hurly-burly of the English Premier League? He showed some early signs that at home, with Liverpool on the front foot, he could be consistently lethal, while away from home he sometimes lost a little enthusiasm if defenders were allowed to buffet him and Liverpool were under the cosh. But this is carping about a player with such talents.

In his first season, and playing in concert with a supporting Steven Gerrard, Torres showed exactly why the Liverpool manager had signed him and why he had joined Pepe Reina and Xabi Alonso as one of Benítez's three gold-standard Liverpool signings. Torres scored 24 goals in 33 league games, the first Red since Robbie Fowler to score 20 or more in the league, and a record for a debut season for a foreign striker in England. In February and March 2008, he became the first Liverpool player since Jackie Balmer in 1946 to score consecutive Anfield league hat-tricks (v. Middlesbrough and West Ham). When he scored the home winner v. Manchester City on 4 May 2008, Torres equalled Roger Hunt's club record of scoring in eight consecutive league matches at Anfield.

The Madrid man ended up by scoring 33 goals in 46 matches in all competitions in his first season, and he could now already be added to the post-war list of truly great Liverpool goalscorers that included Hunt, Rush, Fowler and Michael Owen. This was all good news, of course, but the fitness of Torres seemed an enduring problem. And wider doubts about Benítez and his policies persisted. The manager was at odds, for example, with the club's youth policy, even though Liverpool academy director Steve Heighway had managed to produce *two* recent FA Youth Cup-winning sides out of the Liverpool youngsters. These two men clearly cared little for each other and had very different views on youth team football. Heighway wanted to raise mainly local talent in a caring and supporting environment, and he thought that some of his young stars should have been getting more of a chance in the Liverpool senior squad. How else could you offer incentives to local young players? Benítez, however, wanted to recruit globally and thought the academy was producing sub-standard products ill-prepared for the intensity of the Premier League. Heighway soon left the club, muttering darkly about the loss of important Liverpool FC traditions.

Another low point – and these doubts never fully went away – was when in February 2008 a rotated Liverpool side, excluding Torres and other senior players, abjectly lost 1–2 at home in the FA Cup to the modest Championship club Barnsley. This kind of submission – an invitation to defeat in a competition the club had spent years trying to win – was intolerable for Liverpool supporters who were hungry for more success at home. Benítez seemed to care little for the domestic cups, and his raft of expensively recruited young global squad members seemed little better than the local men who had been patiently raised by Steve Heighway. A number of these imports – the £2-million Argentinian centre-back Paletta among them – represented appalling squander. Later, however, in a generally fretful season, the money-well-spent Fernando Torres almost got Liverpool to another Champions League final with an equalising goal at Stamford Bridge (where else?) in the semi-final second leg in 2008, but at last it was the turn of Chelsea to slide past the Reds to reach the final, only to be defeated in Moscow by Manchester United.

THE TRIALS OF RAFA BENÍTEZ

The Liverpool manager had now assembled his talented Spanish spine – a great goalscorer, a sophisticated midfield organiser and a world-class goalkeeper. Also his key English midfielder Steven Gerrard seemed truly settled for the first time, and the Scouse Carragher was solid at the back. Benítez had signed some centre-back cover in the shape of Martin Škrtel from Zenit St Petersburg in January 2008 for £6.5 million, and the manager was given more money to invest in the summer of that year. At last this was looking like a real championship squad in the making. Some judicious recruitment now and Liverpool would surely run the others very close. But Rafa's spending in 2008 was mysterious and his targets proved, ultimately, to be self-destructive. In some strange ways, chasing the very competent and model professional Gareth Barry from Aston Villa was analogous to Roy Evans signing Stan Collymore in the mid-1990s, because it would eventually have the same sort of corrosive impact on the Liverpool team. Barry was highly rated and an excellent team player, but Benítez crassly let it be known that he was willing to sell the pivotal Xabi Alonso to bring in the Villa man. Not only did it seem like poor management to try to offload his key midfield organiser, but all this took place long *before* Barry was a confirmed capture, and in the end the England international stayed in the West Midlands. Predictably, Alonso decided he would leave Liverpool when the next chance came – which was for Real Madrid in the summer of 2009 for £30 million. Steven Gerrard, for one, was 'devastated' by Alonso's departure.

Benítez compounded this error by signing, for an inflated £20-million fee, Robbie Keane from Spurs to replace the disillusioned and little-used Peter Crouch, then wondering how to fit the Irishman into his Liverpool side. The manager seemed almost immediately unimpressed by what he had bought, and he started to leave the new man out, even after impressive performances.

Stripped of any confidence, the intelligent Liverpool-supporting Keane returned to White Hart Lane soon after for a hefty loss. This left a title-chasing Liverpool squad with little experienced forward cover for the fragile Fernando Torres in the second half of the season. Left-winger Albert Riera joined his Spanish international mates at Anfield, but he had already tried – and failed – to make it in England at Manchester City. Riera seemed to lack pace and a little heart, omissions not recommended in the Premier League.

Finally, Liverpool's first-ever Italian signing, international left-back Andrea Dossena, joined the club from Udinese for around £7 million in July 2008 as a direct replacement for John Arne Riise. On paper, this looked like good business: the top Italians are usually very good defenders, men with a cynical edge. But Dossena seemed to have little of what competent defenders needed in England: he lacked speed, good positional play, height, power and tackling ability. He seemed slightly better going forward than defending, but he also struggled for a decent final ball. Had the Liverpool scouts even been watching the right man? The Italian soon became despondent and virtually sank from view. When Glen Johnson arrived at Anfield in the summer of 2009, it was noted that the England international picked up Dossena's number-2 shirt and the Italian was allocated the rather marginal number 38. He returned to Italy in January 2010.

Despite these problems and misjudgements, this was very nearly a great Liverpool season, and very nearly the league title at last. Benítez still struggled in the domestic cup competitions – falling to Everton in the FA Cup – but in the Champions League there were two famous wins, home and away, against a tepid Real Madrid before Liverpool fell again to Chelsea, despite a 4–4 draw at Stamford Bridge. Only two league matches were lost by the Reds all season, unluckily at Tottenham and predictably at Middlesbrough, where the Reds manager fielded a quite incomprehensible line-up for such an important fixture, including a debut for a raw young French-born Moroccan forward Nabil El Zhar. Liverpool lost 0–2, and Middlesbrough were eventually relegated. Against the other three top-four sides, Liverpool were actually unbeaten, defeating both Chelsea and Manchester United home and away, with the latter being crushed 4–1 at Old Trafford. This sort of away resilience in difficult locations was a major improvement on recent Benítez seasons. But injuries to Torres and an inability to break down the defences of moderate opposition at Anfield cost Liverpool dear. Another extraordinary 4–4 draw, this time at home to Arsenal in April – with the excellent Andrei Arshavin scoring all four goals for the visitors – effectively ended the title race. It was a sobering thought that what Liverpool had spent on the meek and unproven Ryan Babel was very close to what Arsenal had paid for the Russian captain. Meanwhile, Manchester United were now level with Liverpool on 18 league titles won.

A MAN FOR ALL SEASONS?

After six full seasons at Anfield, assessments of Rafa Benítez still varied wildly on Merseyside. For some, his tactical awareness and his achievements in 2005 and 2006 put the manager almost beyond criticism. The duplicity and instability of the new Liverpool owners was also argued to have put the manager in an impossible position; it had on occasions certainly deflected anger that might otherwise have been aimed at the Liverpool boss. For others, Benítez remained just too cautious and too uneven in his judgement of players to ever forge a title-winning squad at Anfield. His substitutions and player selection still mystified. In season 2009–10, Liverpool seemed to have a first XI capable of beating any in the Premier League, but they lacked the sort of depth and squad balance that was now necessary to be truly competitive across a number of fronts. Back-up forwards recruited by Benítez, such as the Ukrainian Andriy Voronin, did little to excite Liverpool fans or suggest that the Liverpool boss yet knew what was required to make a convincing top-level squad in England. How much had really changed at Anfield since 2005 when the manager first came to the city on the bounce from Valencia? Most of those players who now made up the crucial fringes around the Liverpool first XI were Rafa Benítez signings. The new economics of English football also meant that clubs such as Manchester City, Aston Villa and Tottenham would be strongly challenging for top-four places in 2009–10. Things were getting more difficult.

'Big Four' net transfer spending 2004–05 to 2009–10 (millions)

	2004–05	2005–06	2006–07	2007–08	2008–09	2009–10
Liverpool	-31.05	-23.4	-32.85	-23.3	-6.45	-4.95
Chelsea	-87.6	-32.1	-37.7	-13.5	-6.8	-22.0
Manchester United	-20.3	-13.5	- 2.9	-24.0	-33.1	+66.5
Arsenal	-2.55	-5.0	-0.7	+19.9	-20.75	+31.0

Source: Sunday Times, *25 October 2009*

The claims from Benítez that he had simply been outspent by all the other top clubs since 2004 were challenged by the facts. The evidence was that Abramovich's Chelsea was the only major club in England to have outspent

Liverpool over the Benítez era, by £186 million to £122 million, and that Benítez had spent an average of £20 million over income for each season he had been in charge at Anfield. Manchester United's net spend over the same six-season period was just £27 million (after the 2009 sale of Ronaldo), and Arsène Wenger at Arsenal had actually made a net *profit* on deals over this period of around £27 million. What was also different about Benítez was that he had signed a total of 23 players who had cost a fee of £3 million or less, hardly any of whom had succeeded at the club. This attempt at shrewd investment was actually mostly money wasted, and Liverpool were reported to have had as many as sixty-two professional players on the club's books at one stage.

A group stage exit from the Champions League and a crucial failure to qualify for the 2010–11 Champions League also counted against the Spaniard. So too did an attitude to away fixtures that had begun to border on the paranoid. At around 3.45 p.m. on Thursday, 3 June, what had seemed increasingly inevitable finally happened: after six seasons in charge, Rafael Benítez was sacked by the Liverpool board, paid off with a promised £6 million booty.

Few could doubt Benítez's commitment to Liverpool Football Club or indeed the huge problems he had recently faced in managing successfully under his uninterested, absent American owners. But in the end, it was his judgement of players, his incapacity to build and keep a balanced elite squad, Liverpool's increasingly inert showings away from Anfield and perhaps Benítez's personal difficulties in relating effectively to top professional footballers that were his undoing. Xabi Alonso had once said about Benítez that few players really 'enjoyed' being managed by him, but they instantly missed his influence when he left. Perhaps that would be Liverpool's fate and Benítez's legacy: free, for now, from the paralysing disappointments of the recent past, but also facing an increasingly uncertain future in highly unstable times.

In the summer of 2010, Liverpool was at another of those crucial junctures in its eventful history. Having finally moved on, in 1998, from the Anfield boot-room legacy represented by Roy Evans to the age of the foreign technocrat, but with no league titles to show for their adventure, the new Liverpool executive of managing director Christian Purslow and chairman Martin Broughton now had a doubly tough task. They had to sell the club to a rich and responsible buyer *and* recruit a credible new manager. Some foreign talent was briefly reviewed, but the eventual Liverpool solution was to combine in one man some traditional British stability and football knowhow with a convincing Continental veneer.

Roy Hodgson, a 62-year-old multilingual English coach, had done more than Rafa in 2010 by taking lowly Fulham to the Europa League final and he was tipped in some quarters as a likely successor to the faltering Fabio Capello as the next England manager. Hodgson had no Champions League or Premier League title pedigree to talk about, but he had successfully coached abroad and was widely respected in the game and by journalists. He also promised a release from the rather austere man-management approach of Rafa Benítez. Hodgson was something of a football intellectual – he had once compared his career to a painting by the abstract modernist Russian artist Wassily Kandinsky – but he was also more likely than Benítez to put a caring arm around players who needed it and to offer press conferences filled with more than the banalities typically served up by the Spaniard. Finally, Hodgson promised to deliver rather more interesting football. It was a surprisingly sensible managerial choice, one that gently harked back to the more successful traditions of the club.

The avuncular and likeable Hodgson certainly had plenty on his plate. Key Liverpool players were said to be unsure about staying at Anfield and the new Reds manager would have to cope with the financial uncertainty that still mired the club: its debts had risen to over £351 million. Hodgson would need to recruit new coaching staff at Melwood, while rooting out some of the unwanted buys made by Benítez and getting the Liverpool Academy functioning effectively once more. He would need to sell players to bring in his own selections. To all this patient and necessary work would be added the uncomfortable fact that nearly every Liverpool supporter would be crying out immediately for trophies. It was another new direction in the search for what 30 years ago had seemed like the norm: Liverpool football club as league champions. It was difficult not to wish this decent man at the pinnacle of his career a reasonable period of tolerance and a fair wind; he would surely need it.

THE BEST-EVER LIVERPOOL TEAM?

So, how can we wind up this astonishing football story so far? Perhaps by musing about which players, over the entire history of the club, might make up its greatest team. This selection is made much more difficult by the differences between the eras in which these great Liverpool players played. How do you sensibly make comparisons? After all, the brilliant Billy Liddell spent much of his Liverpool career playing in the Second Division. Surely, some will argue, all the real Liverpool greats played in the 1970s and '80s, when the club won title after title and trophy after trophy? Perhaps this is true. Certainly, players of the stature of Souness, Neal, Clemence, Keegan, Rush and Barnes would get into many current Liverpool supporters' best Liverpool side. They all have strong cases, and they all are very close to being in mine.

But the only way to attempt, with any seriousness, this type of entertaining parlour game is to examine, historically, the impact of players from across different eras. We need to look at quality, of course, but also the relationship of players with the Liverpool fans, the longevity of their service to Liverpool Football Club and the opposition they face from other Liverpool greats in their respective positions. That is exactly what I have tried to do here, balancing the whole history of the club against that great period of 1970s and '80s Liverpool dominance.

By looking at the club in this way, it is quite possible to come up with something of an 'alternative' – but I would claim plausible – great Liverpool team to the one that is usually picked by most commentators and supporters today. That is what I have done here – just to get the arguments started. I have selected one current Liverpool player, Steven Gerrard, who seems to me to have been as influential and important over the past decade as any player has been at the club in any period of its existence. Other recent players – Sami Hyypiä, for one – also have their supporters, and Fernando Torres might yet become a Liverpool great. I have selected Bill Shankly as manager over Bob Paisley simply because the former built great Liverpool teams out of the depths of the Second Division in 1959, while the latter inherited and built upon a winning formula. The side set out below can play in a 4–2–4 or a 4–4–2 formation. The dates included here refer to their periods as players at Liverpool Football Club. Have fun with this selection – it might differ a lot from your own.

Liverpool FC's greatest-ever team? 1892–2010

Manager: Bill Shankly; Asst: Tom Watson

E. Scott
(1912–34)

E. Longworth   A. Hansen   E. Hughes   D. McKinlay
(1910–28)   (1977–90)   (1967–79)   (1910–29)

A. Raisbeck   S. Gerrard
(1898–1909)   (1995–)

I. Callaghan   K. Dalglish   R. Hunt   W. Liddell
(1960–1978)   (1977–91)   (1959–69)   (1939–61)

BIBLIOGRAPHY
Sources and Useful Reading

A'Court, A., *Alan A'Court: My Life in Football*, The Bluecoat Press, 2003

Allt, N., *The Boys from the Mersey: The Story of the Annie Road End Crew*, Milo Books, 2004

Allt, N. (ed.), *Here We Go Gathering Cups in May*, Canongate, 2007

Bale, B., *The Shankly Legacy*, Breeden Books, 1996

Belchem, J. (ed.), *Liverpool 800: Culture, Character and History*, Liverpool City Council and Liverpool University Press, 2006

Belchem, J., 'Celebrating Liverpool', in Belchem, J. (ed.), *Liverpool 800: Culture, Character and History*, Liverpool City Council and Liverpool University Press, 2006

Belchem, J. and MacRaild, D., 'Cosmopolitan Liverpool', in Belchem, J. (ed.), *Liverpool 800: Culture, Character and History*, Liverpool City Council and Liverpool University Press, 2006

Blows, K., *Terminator: The Authorised Julian Dicks Story*, Polar Publishing, 1996

Booth, K., *The Father of Modern Sport: The Life and Times of Charles W. Alcock*, The Parrs Wood Press, 2002

Bowler, D., *Shanks: The Authorised Biography of Bill Shankly*, Orion, 1996

Carter, N., *The Football Manager: A History*, Routledge, 2006

Chinn, C., *Better Betting with a Decent Feller: A Social History of Bookmaking*, Aurum Press, 2005

Collins, T., *Rugby's Great Split: Class, Culture and the Origins of Rugby League Football*, Cass, 1998

Corbett, J., *Everton: The School of Science*, Macmillan, 2003

Corbett, J., 'Shankly: Forgotten Man', in *Observer Sports Monthly*, November 2009

Cowley, J., *The Last Game: Love, Death and Football*, Simon and Schuster, 2009

Dalglish, K., *Dalglish: My Autobiography*, Hodder & Stoughton, 1996

Dohren, D., *The Ghost on the Wall: The Authorised Biography of Roy Evans*, Mainstream Publishing, 2004

Doig, E. and Murphy, A., *The Essential History of Liverpool*, Headline, 2003

Du Noyer, P., *Liverpool Wondrous Place: Music from the Cavern to the Coral*, Virgin Books, 2004

Fishwick, N., *English Football and Society: 1910–1950*, Manchester University Press, 1989

Foot, J., *Calcio: A History of Italian Football*, Fourth Estate, 2006

Fowler, R., *My Autobiography*, Macmillan, 2005

Gill, K., *The Real Bill Shankly*, Trinity Mirror Sports Media, 2006

Hale, S. and Ponting, I., *Liverpool in Europe*, Carlton Books, 1992

Harding, J., *Football Wizard: The Story of Billy Meredith*, Breedon Books, 1985

Hargreaves, I., Rogers, K. and George, R., *Liverpool: Club of the Century*, Liverpool Echo Publications, 1988

Harvey, D., *Football: The First Hundred Years – The Untold Story*, Routledge, 2005

Hewison, D., *The Liverpool Boys Are in Town: The Birth of Terrace Culture*, The Bluecoat Press, 2008

Hey, S., *Liverpool's Dream Team*, Mainstream Publishing, 1997

Hill, D., *Out of his Skin: The John Barnes Phenomenon*, WSC Books, 2001

Hill, J., 'Rite of Spring', in Hill, J. and Williams, J. (eds), *Sport and Identity in the North of England*, Keele University Press, 1996

Holt, O., *If You Are Second You Are Nothing: Ferguson and Shankly*, Macmillan, 2006

Holt, R., *Sport and the British: A Modern History*, Oxford University Press, 1989

Hopcraft, A., *The Football Man*, Cox & Wyman, 1968

Hopkins, S. and Williams, J., 'Gérard Houllier and the New Liverpool Imaginary', in J. Williams et al. (eds), *Passing Rhythms: Liverpool FC and the Transformation of Football*, Berg, 2001, pp. 173–94

Huggins, M. and Williams, J., *Sport and the English: 1918–1939*, Routledge, 2006

Hughes, S., *Secret Diary of a Liverpool Scout*, Sport Media, 2009

Inglis, S., *The Football Grounds of Great Britain*, CollinsWillow, 1985

Inglis, S., *Football Grounds of Britain*, CollinsWillow, 1987

Inglis, S., *League Football and the Men Who Made It*, Willow Books, 1988

Inglis, S., *Played in Manchester: The Architectural Heritage of a City at Play*, English Heritage, 2004

Inglis, S., *Engineering Archie: Archibald Leitch –Football Ground Designer*, English Heritage, 2005

Jackson, J., 'The Witnesses', *The Observer*, 2 April 2005

Jones, C.D. (ed.), *The Social Survey of Merseyside Vol. 3*, Liverpool Corporation, 1934

Jones, S., *Sport, Politics and the Working Class*, Manchester University Press, 1988

Joyce, M., *Football League Players' Records 1888 to 1939*, Soccer Data, 2004

Keith, J., *Shanks for the Memory*, Robson Books, 1998

Keith, J., *Bob Paisley: Manager of the Millennium*, Robson Books, 1999

Keith, J., *Billy Liddell: The Legend Who Carried the Kop*, Robson Books, 2003

Keith, J., *Dixie Dean: The Inside Story of a Football Icon*, Sport Media, 2005

Kelly, S., *Idle Hands, Clenched Fists: The Depression in a Shipyard Town*, Spokesman, 1987

Kelly, S., *The Kop: The End of an Era*, Mandarin, 1993

Kelly, S., *Rotation, Rotation, Rotation*, Heroes Publishing, 2008

Kennedy, A. and Williams, J., *Kennedy's Way: Inside Bob Paisley's Liverpool*, Mainstream Publishing, 2004

Kennedy, D., 'Class, Ethnicity and Civic Governance: A Social Profile of Football Club Directors on Merseyside in the Late Nineteenth Century', *The International Journal of the History of Sport*, Vol. 22 (5), 2005

Kennedy, D., 'Locality and Professional Football Club Development: The Demographics of Football Club Support in Late-Victorian Liverpool', *Soccer and Society*, Vol. 5 (3), 2004

Kennedy, D. and Collins, M., 'Community Politics in Liverpool and the Governance of Professional Football in the Late Nineteenth Century', *The Historical Journal*, Vol. 49 (3), 2006

Kennedy, D. and Kennedy, P., 'Ambiguity, Complexity and Convergence: The Evolution of Liverpool's Irish Football Clubs', *The International Journal of the History of Sport*, Vol. 24 (7), 2007

Kirby, D., 'Rome, 1977', in Allt, N. (ed.), *Here We Go Gathering Cups in May*, Canongate, 2007

Leigh, S., *The Cavern: The Most Famous Club in the World*, SAF Publishing, 2008

Liddell, B., *My Soccer Story*, Stanley Paul, 1960

Liversedge, S., *Liverpool: From the Inside*, Mainstream Publishing, 1995

Liversedge, S., *Liverpool, We Love You!*, Soccer Books Limited, 1997

Lloyd, L., *Larry Lloyd: Hard Man, Hard Game*, John Blake Publishing, 2008

Lupson, P., *Thank God for Football!*, Azure, 2006

Lupson, P., *Across the Park: Everton FC and Liverpool FC Common Ground*, Sportsmedia, 2009

McGregor, W., 'The League and the League System' (1906), in Leatherdale, C. (ed.), *The Book of Football: A Complete History and Record of the Association and Rugby Games*, Desert Island Books, 1997

Macilwee, M., *The Gangs of Liverpool*, Milo Books, 2006

Macilwee, M., *Tearaways: More Gangs of Liverpool 1890–1970*, Milo Books, 2008

Marne, P., 'Whose Public Space Was It Anyway? Class, Gender and Ethnicity in the Creation of Sefton and Stanley Parks, Liverpool: 1858–1872', *Social and Cultural Geography*, Vol. 2 (4), 2001

Mason, T., *Association Football and English Society 1863–1915*, Harvester, 1980

Mason, T., 'The Blues and the Reds: A History of the Liverpool and Everton Football Clubs', *The History Society of Lancashire and Cheshire*, No. 134, 1985

Matthews, T., *Who's Who of Liverpool*, Mainstream Publishing, 2006

Milne, G., 'Maritime Liverpool', in Belchem, J. (ed.), *Liverpool 800: Culture, Character and History*, Liverpool City Council and Liverpool University Press, 2006

Munck, R. (ed.), *Reinventing the City? Liverpool in Comparative Perspective*, Liverpool University Press, 2003

Murden, J., 'City of Change and Challenge', in Belchem, J. (ed.), *Liverpool 800: Culture, Character and History*, Liverpool City Council and Liverpool University Press, 2006

Nicholls, A., *Scally: The Story of a Category C Football Hooligan*, Milo Books, 2002

Overy, R., *The Morbid Age: Britain Between the Wars*, Allen Lane, 2009

Page, S., *Herbert Chapman: The First Great Manager*, Heroes Publishing, 2006

Pead, B., *Liverpool: A Complete Record 1982–1990*, Breedon Books, 1990

Physick, R., *Played in Liverpool: Charting the Heritage of a City at Play*, English Heritage, 2007

Ponting, I. and Hale, S., *Sir Roger: The Life and Times of Roger Hunt*, Bluecoat Press (undated)

Pooley, C., 'Living in Liverpool: The Modern City', in Belchem, J. (ed.), *Liverpool 800: Culture, Character and History*, Liverpool City Council and Liverpool University Press, 2006

Preston, T., 'The Origins and Development of Association Football in the Liverpool District *c.*1879–*c.*1915', PhD thesis, University of Central Lancashire, 2007

Reade, B., *43 Years with the Same Bird: A Liverpool Love Affair*, Macmillan, 2005

Reed, P., *Football and Fortunes: The Inside Story of the Littlewoods Football Pools, 1923–2003*, Brahm Ltd, 2003

Rippon, A., *Gas Masks for Goal Posts: Football in Britain During the Second World War*, Sutton Publishing, 2005

Rollin, J., *Rothman's Book of Football Records*, Headline, 1998

Rollin, J., *Soccer at War: 1939–45*, Headline, 2005

Rous, S., *Football Worlds: A Lifetime in Sport*, Faber and Faber, 1978

Russell, D., *Football and the English: A Social History of Association Football in England, 1863–1995*, Carnegie Publications, 1997

Russell, D., *Looking North: Northern England and the National Imagination*, Manchester University Press, 2004

St John, I., *The Saint: My Autobiography*, Hodder & Stoughton, 2005

Sampson, K., 'Brussels, 1985', in Allt, N. (ed.), *Here We Go Gathering Cups in May*, Canongate, 2007

Sandbrook, D., *Never Had It So Good: A History of Britain from Suez to the Beatles*, Abacus, 2006

Sanders, R., *Beastly Fury: The Strange Birth of English Football*, Bantam Press, 2009

Scraton, P., *Hillsborough: The Truth*, Mainstream Publishing, 1999

Shankly, B., *Shankly*, Book Club Associates, 1977

Smith, T., *Anfield Iron: The Autobiography*, Bantam Press, 2008

Taw, T., *Football's War and Peace: The Tumultuous Season of 1946–7*, Desert Island Books, 2003

Taw, T., *Football's Twelve Apostles: The Making of the League: 1886–1889*, Desert Island Books, 2006

Taylor, I., 'English Football in the 1990s: Taking Hillsborough Seriously?', in

Williams, J. and Wagg, S. (eds), *British Football and Social Change*, Leicester University Press, 1991

Taylor, M., *The Leaguers: The Making of Professional Football in England, 1900–1939*, Liverpool University Press, 2005

Taylor, M., *The Association Game: A History of British Football*, Pearson Longman, 2008

Taylor, R. and Ward, A., *Three Sides of the Mersey: An Oral History of Everton, Liverpool and Tranmere Rovers*, Robson Books, 1993

Tischler, S., *Footballers and Businessmen: The Origins of Professional Football in England*, Holmes & Meier Publishing, 1981

Ward, A. and Williams, J., 'Bill Shankly and Liverpool', in J. Williams et al. (eds), *Passing Rhythms: Liverpool FC and the Transformation of Football*, Berg, 2001

Ward, A. and Williams, J., *Football Nation: Sixty Years of the Beautiful Game*, Bloomsbury, 2009

Whannel, G., *Fields in Vision: Television Sport and Cultural Transformation*, Routledge, 1992

Williams, G., *The Code War: English Football Under Historical Spotlight*, Yore Publications, 1994

Williams, J., 'Ian Rush', in Stead, P. and Williams, H. (eds), *For Club and Country: Welsh Football Greats*, University of Wales Press, 2000

Williams, J., *Into the Red: Liverpool FC and the Changing Face of English Football*, Mainstream Publishing, 2001

Williams, J., *The Liverpool Way: Houllier, Anfield and the New Global Game*, Mainstream Publishing, 2003

Williams, J. et al. (eds), *Passing Rhythms: Liverpool FC and the Transformation of Football*, Berg, 2001

Williams, J. and Hopkins, S., *The Miracle of Istanbul*, Mainstream Publishing, 2005

Williams, J. and Llopis, R., *Rafa: Rafa Benítez, Anfield and the New Spanish Fury*, Mainstream Publishing, 2007

Wilson, J., *Inverting the Pyramid: A History of Football Tactics*, Orion Books, 2008

Wilson, J., *All Change at Anfield: Liverpool's First Five Seasons*, Now and Then Publications (undated)

Young, P., *Football on Merseyside*, Stanley Paul, 1963

INDEX

BOOKS BY CARLOS FUENTES

WHERE THE AIR IS CLEAR

THE GOOD CONSCIENCE

AURA

THE DEATH OF ARTEMIO CRUZ

A CHANGE OF SKIN

TERRA NOSTRA

THE HYDRA HEAD

BURNT WATER

DISTANT RELATIONS

TERRA
NOSTRA

TERRA NOSTRA

CARLOS FUENTES

TRANSLATED FROM THE SPANISH BY

MARGARET SAYERS PEDEN

AFTERWORD BY MILAN KUNDERA

FARRAR • STRAUS • GIROUX

NEW YORK

Library of Congress Cataloging in Publication Data

Fuentes, Carlos. / Terra nostra. / I. Title.

PZ4.F952Te [PQ7297.F793] 863 76-18238

FOR SYLVIA

CONTENTS

I. / THE OLD WORLD

II / THE NEW WORLD

III / THE NEXT WORLD

AFTERWORD 779

Esch Is Luther

by Milan Kundera

What does that old spook want . . . ?

Goya, Los caprichos

Fervid in her fetid rags. It is she, the first

False mother of many, like you, aggrieved

By her, and for her, grieving.

Cernuda, Ser de Sansueña

Transformed utterly:

A terrible beauty is born . . .

Yeats, Easter, 1916

TERRA NOSTRA

CHARACTERS

THE LORDS

FELIPE, *the Fair, married to*
JOANNA REGINA, *the Mad Lady*
FELIPE, *El Señor, son and heir to the former, married to*
ISABEL, *La Señora (Elizabeth Tudor), his English cousin*

THE COURT

THE JESTER *at the court of Felipe the Fair*
GUZMAN, *secretary and chief huntsman to Felipe El Señor*
FRAY JULIAN, *painter and miniaturist*
FRAY TORIBIO, *astrologer*
THE CHRONICLER, *poet and court scribe*
PEDRO DEL AGUA ⎫
JOSE LUIS CUEVAS ⎬ *doctors*
ANTONIO SAURA ⎭
FRAY SANTIAGO DE BAENA
THE BISHOP
THE INQUISITOR OF TERUEL
GONZALO DE ULLOA, *Comendador of Calatrava*
INES, *his daughter, novitiate*
MILAGROS, *Mother Superior*
ANGUSTIAS ⎫
CLEMENCIA ⎬ *nuns*
DOLORES ⎪
REMEDIOS ⎭
AZUCENA ⎫
LOLILLA ⎬ *maids to Isabel, La Señora*
THE DWARF BARBARICA, *companion to the Mad Lady*

THE BASTARDS

THE PILGRIM, *son of Felipe the Fair out of Celestina*
DON JUAN, *son of Felipe the Fair out of Isabel, La Señora*
THE IDIOT PRINCE, *son of Felipe the Fair out of a she-wolf*

THE DREAMERS

LUDOVICO, *student of theology*
PEDRO, *peasant and sailor*
SIMON, *monk*
CELESTINA, *peasant girl, witch, and procuress*
MIHAIL-BEN-SAMA, *wanderer*
DON QUIXOTE DE LA MANCHA, *knight-errant*
SANCHO PANZA, *his squire*

THE WORKERS

JERONIMO, *blacksmith and husband to Celestina*
MARTIN, *son of serfs from Navarre*
NUÑO, *son of a foot soldier of the Moorish frontier*
CATILINON, *rogue from the streets of Valladolid*

THE MEDITERRANEANS

TIBERIUS CAESAR, *second Roman Emperor of the*
Augustan line
THEODORUS OF GANDARA, *his secretary and counselor*
FABIANUS
GAIUS
PERSIUS } *sexual entertainers to the Emperor Tiberius*
CYNTHIA
LESBIA
PONTIUS PILATE, *Roman Procurator of Judea*
THE NAZARITE, *minor Hebrew prophet*
CLEMENS, *slave*
THE GHOST OF AGRIPPA POSTUMUS
THE JEWISH DOCTOR *at the Synagogue of Toledo*
THE SCRIBE OF ALEXANDRIA
THE MAGUS OF SPALATO
THE GYPSY GIRL OF SPALATO
DONNO VALERIO CAMILLO, *Venetian humanist*
and bibliophile

THE FLEMISH

THE MISTRESS *of the Beguine Monastery, Bruges*
SCHWESTER KATREI, *possessed Beghard*
HIERONYMUS BOSCH, *painter and adherent to the Adamite sect*
THE DUKE OF BRABANT

THE INDIANS

THE LORD OF MEMORY
THE LADY OF THE BUTTERFLIES
THE FAT PRINCE
THE WHITE LORDS OF HELL
THE LORD OF THE GREAT VOICE

THE PARISIANS

POLLO PHOIBEE, *sandwich man*
CELESTINA, *sidewalk painter*
LUDOVICO, *flagellant*
SIMON, *monk, leader of the penitents*
MME ZAHARIA, *concierge*
RAPHAEL DE VALENTIN, *man-about-town*
VIOLETTA GAUTIER, *consumptive courtesan*
JAVERT, *police inspector*
JEAN VALJEAN, *former convict*
OLIVEIRA, *Argentine exile*
BUENDIA, *Colombian colonel*
SANTIAGO ZAVALITA, *Peruvian journalist*
ESTEBAN *and* SOFIA, *Cuban cousins*
HUMBERTO, *deaf-and-dumb Chilean*
CUBA VENEGAS, *Cuban torch singer*
THE VALKYRIE, *Lithuanian benefactress*

I

THE OLD
WORLD

FLESH, SPHERES, GRAY EYES
BESIDE THE SEINE

Incredible the first animal that dreamed of another animal. Monstrous the first vertebrate that succeeded in standing on two feet and thus spread terror among the beasts still normally and happily crawling close to the ground through the slime of creation. Astounding the first telephone call, the first boiling water, the first song, the first loincloth.

About four o'clock in the morning one fourteenth of July, Pollo Phoibee, asleep in his high garret room, door and windows flung wide, dreamed these things, and prepared to answer them himself. But then he was visited in his dream by the somber, faceless figure of a monk who spoke for Pollo, continuing in words what had been an imagistic dream: "But reason—neither slow nor indolent—tells us that merely with repetition the extraordinary becomes ordinary, and only briefly abandoned, what had once passed for a common and ordinary occurrence becomes a portent: crawling, sending carrier pigeons, eating raw deer meat, abandoning one's dead on the summits of temples so that vultures as they feed might perform their cleansing functions and fulfill the natural cycle."

Only thirty-three and a half days earlier the fact that the waters of the Seine were boiling could have been considered a calamitous miracle; now, a month later, no one even turned to look at the phenomenon. The proprietors of the black barges, surprised at first by the sudden ebullition, slammed against the walls of the channel, had abandoned their struggle against the inevitable. These men of the river pulled on their stocking caps, extinguished their black tobaccos, and climbed like lizards onto the quays; the skeletons of the barges had piled up beneath the ironic gaze of Henri de Navarre and there they remained, splendid ruins of charcoal, iron, and splintered wood.

But the gargoyles of Notre-Dame, knowing events only in the abstract, embraced with black stone eyes a much vaster panorama, and twelve million Parisians understood finally why these demons of yesteryear stick out their tongues at the city in such ferociously mocking grimaces. It was as if the motive for which they were originally sculptured was now revealed in scandalous actuality. It was clear the patient gargoyles had waited eight centuries to open their eyes and blast twaa! twaa! with their cleft tongues. At dawn they had seen that overnight the distant cupolas, the entire façade, of Sacré-Coeur appeared to be painted black. And that closer at hand, far below, the doll-sized Louvre had become transparent.

After a superficial investigation, the authorities, far off the scent, reached the conclusion that the painted façade was actually marble and the transparent Louvre had been turned to crystal. Inside the Basilica the paintings, too, were transformed; as the building had changed color, its paintings had changed race. And who was going to cross himself before the lustrous ebony of a Congolese Virgin, and who would expect pardon from the thick lips of a Negroid Christ? On the other hand, the paintings and sculptures in the Museum had taken on an opacity that many decided to attribute to the contrast with the crystalline walls and floors and ceiling. No one seemed in the least uncomfortable because the Victory of Samothrace hovered in mid-air without any visible means of support: those wings were finally justifying themselves. But they were apprehensive when they observed, particularly considering the recently acquired density in contrast to the general lightness, that the mask of Pharaoh was superimposed—in a newly liberated perspective—upon the features of the Gioconda, and that lady's upon David's Napoleon. Furthermore: when the traditional frames dissolved into transparency, the resulting freeing of purely conventional space allowed them to appreciate that the Mona Lisa, still sitting with arms crossed, was not alone. And she was smiling.

Thirty-three and one half days had passed during which, apparently, the Arc de Triomphe turned into sand and the Eiffel Tower was converted into a zoo. We are confining ourselves to appearances, for once the first flurry of excitement had passed, no one even troubled to touch the sand, which still looked like stone. Sand or stone, it stood in its usual location, and after all, that's all anyone asked: Not a new arrangement, but recognizable form and the reassurance of location. What confusion there would have been, for example, had the Arc, still of stone, appeared on the site traditionally occupied by a pharmacy at the corner of the rue de Bellechasse and the rue de Babylone.

As for the tower of M. Eiffel, its transformation was criticized only by potential suicides, whose remarks revealed their unhealthy intentions and who in the end chose to play it cool in the hope that other, similar jumping places would be constructed. "But it isn't just the height; perhaps even more important is the prestige of the place from which one jumps to his death," a habitué of the Café Le Bouquet, a man who when he was fourteen had decided to kill himself at the age of forty, told Pollo Phoibee. He said this one afternoon as our young and handsome friend was pursuing his normal occupations, convinced that any other course would be like yelling "Fire!" in a movie theater packed with a Sunday-evening crowd.

The public was amused by the fact that the rusted structure from the Exposition Universelle was now serving as a tree for monkeys, a ramp for lions, a cage for bears, and as a very heavily populated aviary. Almost a century of reproductions and emblems and references had reduced the tower to the sad, but really affectionate, status of a commonplace. Now the continual flight—dispersion of doves, formations of ducks, solitudes of owls, and clusters of bats, farcical and indecisive in the midst of so many metamorphoses—was entertaining and pleasing. The uneasiness began only when a child pointed to a passing vulture that spread its wings at the very top of the tower, sailed in a circle above Passy, then flew in a straight line right to the towers of Saint-Sulpice, where it settled in a corner of the perpetual scaffolding of the eternal restoration of that temple to watch with avarice the deserted streets of the Quarter.

First, Pollo Phoibee brushed a strand of blond hair from his eyes, then ran the fingers of one hand (for he didn't have two) through his shoulder-length mane; and finally he leaned out of his sixth-floor rooming-house window to salute a summer sun that like every summer-morning Paris sun was supposed to appear borne on a chariot of warm haze, attended by a court of street perfumes—the odors the sun king disperses in July different, of course, from those distilled by the moon queen in December. Today, nevertheless, Pollo looked toward the towers of Saint-Sulpice, reviewing in his mind the catalogue of accustomed odors. But as the vulture settled onto the scaffolding, Pollo sniffed in vain. No freshly baked bread, no scent of flowers, no boiling chicory, not even damp city sidewalks. He liked to close his eyes and breathe in the summer-morning air, concentrating until he could distinguish the scent of the tightly closed buds in the distant flower market of the Quai de la Corse. But today not even cabbage or beets in the nearby market of Saint-Germain, no pungent Gauloise or Gitanes, no wine spilled on straw or wood. Not a single odor in the whole of the rue du Four—and no sun appeared on its customary vehicle of haze. The motionless vulture faded from sight amid billowing black smoke issuing like a blast from a bellows from the towers of the church. The enormous vacuum of odors was suddenly filled with foul and offensive effluvium, as if Hell were discharging all the congestion from its lungs. Pollo smelled flesh . . . burned fingernails and hair and flesh.

For the first time in his twenty-two summers, Pollo closed the window and hesitated, not knowing what to do. But he would scarcely realize that in that instant began his longing for the visible symbol of liberty provided by that always open window—night and day, winter and summer, rain and thunder. He would scarcely identify his unaccustomed indecision with the feeling that he and the world about him were irremediably growing older. He would not likely overcome that feeling with a swift question: What's happening? What is it that forces me to close my free and open window for the first time . . . ? They must be burning refuse; no, it smelled of flesh, they must be burning animals.

An epidemic? Some sacrifice? Immediately Pollo Phoibee, who slept in the nude (another conscious symbol of freedom), entered the stall with the portable shower head, listened to the noisy drumming of water against the white-enameled tin, soaped himself carefully, sudsing with extra attention the golden pubic hair, raised his only arm to direct the stream of water onto his face, letting water dribble through his open lips, turned off the tap, dried himself, and left the small and impeccable confessional that had washed him of every sin except one, that of innocent suspicion; forgetting to prepare any breakfast, he slipped on leather sandals, drew on khaki-colored Levi's and a strawberry-colored shirt, glanced swiftly around the room where he had been so happy, bumped his head against the low ceiling, and ran down the stairs, ignoring the empty, abandoned garbage pails on each landing of the stairway.

At the entresol, Pollo stopped and with his knuckles rapped at the concierge's door. There was no answer, and he decided to go in to see if there was any mail, a most unlikely possibility. Like the doors of all concierges, this was half wood and half glass, and Pollo knew that if the self-absorbed face of Madame Zaharia did not peer from between the curtains, it was because Madame Zaharia was out, but since she had nothing to hide from the world (this was her favorite saying: she lived in a glass house), she had no objections to her tenants' coming in to pick up the infrequent letters she sorted and left tucked in the mirror frame. Consequently, Pollo decided he could go into that cave of bygone gentility where the fumes of an eternal cabbage stew misted over photographic mementos of soldiers twice dead and buried, once beneath the soil of Verdun, now beneath a film of vapor. And if his earlier indecision had controlled Pollo Phoibee's spirits when, like a warning of disillusion and old age, he had noticed the absence of summer smells, now to enter the concierge's room in search of a most improbable letter seemed to him an act of primordial innocence. Absorbed in this sensation, he entered. But the physical reality was more novel than his new mood. For the first time he could remember, nothing was bubbling in the kitchen, and the photos of the dead soldiers were limpid mirrors of useless sacrifice and tender resignation. Even the odor had evaporated from Madame Zaharia's room. But not sound. Lying on her sagging bed, upon an eiderdown covered with the blooms of ancient winters, the concierge—less preoccupied than usual—was choking back a gurgling moan.

Many suns will pass before Pollo Phoibee condescends to analyze the impression provoked by Madame Zaharia's condition and posture: which cause and which effect? Perhaps it would be possible to propose, without the authorization of the protagonist, that the terms of his matutinal equation had been inverted: the world, irremediably, was growing younger—and decisions had to be made. Without stopping to think, he ran and filled a pail of water, he lighted the flame of the burner and set the water to boil on the stove, and with a blend of atavistic wisdom and simple stupefaction he gathered towels and tore strips of sheets. The same thing had happened too many times during the past thirty-three and one half days. With his teeth Pollo rolled up the sleeve of his one good arm (the other sleeve was pinned over his stump), and knelt between the open, febrile thighs of Madame Zaharia, ready to receive the tiny head that must soon appear. The concierge uttered a sputtering howl. Pollo heard the water boiling; he lifted the pail from the flame, threw the pieces of sheet into it, and returned to the foot of the bed to receive, not the expected head, but two tiny blue feet. Madame Zaharia moaned, her belly was gripped by oceanic contractions, and Pollo's stump throbbed like a piece of marble longing for the companionship of its mate.

After the breech birth had been effected, and once Pollo had spanked the babe, cut the cord, tied the umbilical cord, disposed of the placenta in the pail, and mopped up the blood, he did certain things in addition: inspected the infant's male genitals, counted six toes on each foot, and observed with amazement the birthmark on its back: a wine-red cross between the shoulder blades. He didn't know whether to hand the baby into the arms of the ninety-year old woman who had just delivered it or to take charge of it himself, care for it, and carry it far from possible contamination and death by asphyxia. He chose the second; in truth, he feared the ancient Madame Zaharia might drown or devour her so untimely son, and he walked to the antique gold-framed mirror where the concierge customarily inserted, between the glass and the frame, the few improbable letters addressed to her tenants.

Yes. There was a letter for him. It must be one of the official notices that arrived from time to time, always inordinately late, for the almost total collapse of the postal services was a normal fact in an epoch when everything that a hundred years earlier signified progress had ceased to function with either efficiency or promptness. No chlorine purified the water, the mail did not arrive on time, and microbes had imposed their triumphal reign over vaccines: defenseless humans, immune worms.

Pollo leaned closer to look at the envelope and noticed that the letter bore no recognizable stamp; gripping the newly born infant against his chest, he slipped the letter from the frame. It was sealed with ancient, grimy sealing wax; the envelope itself was old and yellow, as the writing of the sender seemed old, and curiously antiquated. And as he took the letter in his hand a few quivering drops of quicksilver rolled across it and dropped onto the floor. Still clasping the child, Pollo broke the ancient red wax seal with his teeth and extracted a fine, wrinkled sheet of parchment, as transparent as silk. He read the following message:

"In the *Dialogus Miraculorum*, the chronicler Caesarius von Heiterbach warns that in the city of Paris, the fountain of all knowledge and the source of the Divine Scriptures, the persuasive Devil inculcated a perverse intelligence in certain few wise men. You must be on the alert. The two forces struggle between themselves not only in Paris but throughout the world, although here the combat will seem to you more acute. Chance has determined that it was here you would be born, spend your youth, and live your years. Your life and this time could have coincided in a different space. It does not matter. Many will be born, but only one will have six toes upon each foot and a wine-red cross upon his back. This child must be baptized Iohannes Agrippa. He has been awaited through long centuries; his is the continuity of the original kingdoms. Further, although in another time, he is your son. You must not fail this duty. We are expecting you; we shall find you, make no effort to look for us."

This extraordinary missive was signed *Ludovico* and *Celestina*. Astounded by this reversion from the death he had smelled in the smoke of Saint-Sulpice and divined in the zealous vultures to the life he held in his single arm and believed to have extracted but not introduced, as the letter so mysteriously indicated, Pollo had no time to reread it. Twice he shook his head in negation: he knew no one named Ludovico or Celestina, and he had never slept with the ancient woman. He dipped his fingers in the bloody water, sprinkled a few drops on the head of this infant as exceptional as recently born, and in accordance with what the letter had requested, he murmured: "Ego baptiso te: Iohannes Agrippa."

As he did so, he winked an eye in the direction of the robust poilu killed in some forgotten war of trenches, tanks, and mustard gases who was the ephemeral, the certified, the only husband of the aged Madame Zaharia; he placed the child in the arms of the startled old woman, rinsed his hand, and without a backward look left the room with the satisfaction of a duty well done.

Truly? He opened the heavy street door onto the rue des Ciseaux, that imperturbable narrow little street that for centuries has stretched between the rue du Four and the Boulevard Saint-Germain, and he had to struggle against a new alarm that threatened anew his wish to enjoy this glorious July morning. Was the world growing younger? growing older? Pollo, like the street itself, was partly bathed by the sun but partly in deserted shadows.

The open doors and sidewalk tables and chairs of the Café Le Bouquet, usually filled with the faithful, looked inviting, but the mirrored wall behind the bar reflected only orderly rows of green and amber bottles, and the long copper stripping showed only light traces of hastily smeared fingerprints. The television had been disconnected and bees buzzed above the cigarette showcase. Pollo reached out his hand and directly from the bottle drank a gulp of anise. Then he searched behind the bar and found the two large posters advertising the bar-café-tobacco shop. He thrust his head between the panels and adjusted the leather straps that joined across the shoulders. Thus outfitted as a sandwich man, he returned to the rue du Four and without concern walked by the open and abandoned shops.

Buried in Pollo's young body, perhaps, was an ancient optimism. Sandwiched between his posters, he was not only doing the job for which he received his modest stipend. He was also adhering to a code according to which, when the subway has been stalled for more than ten minutes and all the tunnel lights go out, the proper thing to do is continue reading the newspaper as if nothing had happened. Pollo Ostrich. But as long as none of the things that had happened to Madame Zaharia happened to him (and considering the times, who was going to stick his only hand into the fire?), he saw no reason to interrupt the normal rhythm of his existence. No. Just the opposite: "I still believe that the sun rises every day, and that each new sun announces a new day, a day that yesterday lay in the future; I still believe that, as one page of time closes, today will promise a tomorrow invisible before and irrepeatable afterward." Immersed in these reflections, Pollo did not notice he was walking through thicker and thicker smoke. With the innocence of habit (which inevitably is solidified by the malice of the law), he had walked toward the Place Saint-Sulpice and was now prepared to parade before the faithful, the usual café customers, the posters that fore and aft covered him to the knees. His first thought when he saw he was surrounded by smoke was that no one would be able to read the words recommending the choice of the Café Le Bouquet. He looked skyward and realized that not even the four statues on the Place were visible; nevertheless, they were the only witnesses to the publicity posters trussed upon Pollo, and entrusted to Pollo. He told himself, idiotically, that the smoke must be coming from the mouths of the sacred orators. But not even Bossuet's teeth, Fénelon's lips, Massillon's tongue, or Fléchier's palate—aseptic stone cavities all—could be the source of that nauseating odor, the same stench that had been so noticeable at the window of his garret room. What accentuated it now, more than proximity, was the beat of unseen marching feet his ear first located on the rue Bonaparte. Soon he realized what it was: the sound of universal movement.

Smoke enveloped him, but someone besieged by smoke always believes there is clean air about his own body; no one trapped in haze feels he is devoured by it. "I am not become haze," Pollo said to himself. "The haze simply swirls around me as it surrounds the statues of the four sacred orators." From smoke, but also toward smoke, Pollo extended his only hand, then immediately drew it back, frightened, and thrust it behind the panel that covered his chest; in that brief instant his outstretched fingertips, invisible in the smoke, had touched other flesh, fleeting, naked . . . other flesh. He hid the fingers that remembered and still bore the traces of a film of thick oil almost like butter: other bodies, invisible but nevertheless present bodies . . . swift, grease-covered bodies. His only hand never lied. No one had seen him, but Pollo felt ashamed for having been afraid. The true motive of his fear had not been the casual discovery of a quickly moving line of bodies marching toward the church in the obscuring smoke, but the simple image of his only hand, his outstretched hand, devoured by the smoke. Invisible. Vanished. Mutilated by the air. I have only one. I have only one left. With that recovered hand he touched his testicles to assure himself of the continuance of his physical being. Higher, far from his hand and his genitals, his head whirled in a different orbit, and reason, again triumphant, warned him that causes provoke effects, effects propose problems, and problems demand solutions, which are in turn, by their success or failure, converted into the causes of new effects, problems, and solutions. This is what reason taught him, but Pollo didn't understand the relation between such logic and the sensations he had just experienced. And he continued to stand there in the midst of the smoke, exhibiting his posters for no one to see.

"Don't be too persistent, it's annoying, counterproductive," the *patron* had admonished him when he contracted for his services. "A turn or two in front of each competitor's, and away . . . alley-oop . . . off to a new spot." Pollo began to run, far from the Place Saint-Sulpice, far from the smoke and the stench and that contact; but there was no escape; the smell from Saint-Sulpice was stronger than any other; the odor of grease, of burned flesh and fingernails and hair stifled the remembered perfumes of flowers and tobacco, of straw and wet sidewalks. He ran.

No one will deny that in spite of an occasional slip our hero basically is a dignified man. The awareness of that dignity caused him to slow his pace as soon as he saw he was approaching the Boulevard, where, unless everything had changed overnight, the usual (for the last thirty-three and one half days) spectacle awaited him.

He tried to think by which street he could with least difficulty reach the church, but they were all the same; down the deserted rue Bonaparte and rue de Rennes and rue du Dragon, he could see the compact mass of heads and shoulders on the Boulevard Saint-Germain, the crowd lined up six-deep, some perched in trees or sitting in the temporary stands they had occupied since the previous night, if not before. He walked along the rue du Dragon, which was, at least, the farthest from the spectacle itself, and in two long strides had overtaken the owner of the Café Le Bouquet walking toward the Boulevard with his wife, who was carrying a basket filled with bread and cheese and artichokes.

"You're late," Pollo said to them.

"No. This is the third time this morning we've gone back for more provisions," the *patron* answered condescendingly.

"You two can go right up to the front. What luck!"

The *patronne* smiled, looking at the sandwich boards and approving Pollo's fidelity to his employ. "More than a right. An obligation. Without us, they'd die of hunger."

"What's happened?" Pollo would have liked to ask. "Why are two miserable tightwads like the two of you (that's the truth, I'm not complaining) going around giving away food? Why are you doing it? What are you afraid of?" But, discreetly, he limited himself to a "May I go with you?"

The owners of the café shrugged their shoulders and indicated with a gesture that he could accompany them through the ancient narrow street as far as the corner. There, Madame placed the basket on her head and began to call out: "Let the supplies through, make way for the supplies," and the *patron* and Pollo forced a path through the festive multitude jammed between the house fronts and the police barricades set up along the edge of the sidewalks.

A hand reached out to steal one of the cheeses and the *patron* clipped the scoundrel on the head: "This is for the penitents, *canaille!*"

The *patronne*, too, rapped the joker on the head. "You! You have to pay. If you want a free meal, join the pilgrims!"

"That really tears it!" Pollo muttered. "Did we come here to laugh or cry? Are we dying or being born? Is it the beginning or the end, cause or effect, problem or solution? What are we living through?" Again reason proposed the questions, but the film of memory, swifter than reason, rolled back in time to a cinema in the Latin Quarter . . . Pollo walking with his employers, carrying their supplies along the rue du Dragon . . . Pollo remembering an old film he'd seen as a child, terrified, paralyzed by the meaningless profusion of death, a film called *Nuit et brouillard* (fog, the smoke from the Place Saint-Sulpice, the haze pouring from the vulture-guarded towers), night and fog, the final solution . . . cause, effect, problem, solution.

But now the spectacle burst before his eyes, interrupting his pensive, nostalgic, fearful mood. Circus or tragedy, baptismal ceremony or funeral vigil, the event had revived ancestral memories. All along the avenue, people were decked out in peaked Liberty caps that protected their heads from the sun; there were tricolor ribbons for sale and assortments of miniature flags. The first row of seats had been reserved for a few old ladies, who, quite naturally and in respect to certain well-known precedents, knitted ceaselessly, commenting on the groups passing before them, men, boys, and young children carrying banners and lighted candles in broad daylight. Each contingent was led by a monk wearing a hairshirt and carrying a scythe across his shoulder; all of them, barefoot and exhausted, had arrived on foot from the diverse places identified by their gold- and silver-embroidered scarlet banners: Mantes, Pontoise, Bonnemarie, Nemours, Saint-Saëns, Senlis, Boissy-Sans-Avoir-Peur. Bands of fifty, a hundred, two hundred men, dirty and unshaven, boys who could scarcely drag their aching bodies, young children with filthy hands, runny noses, and infected eyes, all of them intoning the obsessive chant:

> The place is here,
> The time is now,
> Now and here,
> Here and now.

Each contingent joined the others in front of the Church of Saint-Germain, amid the hurrahs, the toasts and jokes of some, the sepulchral fear and fascination of others, and the occasional scattered, drifting choruses repeatedly singing the stirring *La Carmagnole* and *Ça Ira*. Antithetically and simultaneously, voices demanded the gibbet for the poet Villon and the firing squad for the usurper Bonaparte; they advocated marching against the Bastille and the government of Thiers at Versailles; they recited chaotically the poems of both Gringore and Prévert; they denounced the assassins of the Duc de Guise and the excesses of Queen Margot; paradoxically, they announced the death of the "Friend of the People" in his tepid tub and the birth of the future Sun King in the icy bed of Anne of Austria. One cried, "I want a chicken in every peasant's pot on Sundays!"; another, "A marshal's baton in every knapsack"; over here, "get rich"; over there, "all power to imagination!"; and one, a sharp, ululating, anonymous voice drowning out all the others, shouting obsessively, "O crime, what liberties are committed in thy name!" From the rue du Four to the Carrefour de l'Odéon, thousands of persons were struggling for a favored spot, singing, laughing, eating, wailing, embracing, pushing, exhausting themselves, joking among themselves, crying, and drinking, while Time flowed into Paris as if toward a roaring drain, and barefoot pilgrims took each other's hands to form a double circle before the church, an enormous circle whose extremes touched, to the north, the Gallimard bookstore and the Café Le Bonaparte; to the west, the Deux-Magots; to the south, Le Drugstore, the Vidal record shop, and the Boutique Ted Lapidus; and to the east, the church itself, towering and severe. An escaped prisoner and an Inspector of Police timidly raised a heavy metal manhole cover, could not believe what was happening before their eyes, and disappeared again, lost in the black honeycomb of the sewers of Paris. A tubercular courtesan watched with languor and disillusion from behind the closed windows of her high-ceilinged apartment, closed her curtains, lay back upon her Empire couch, and in the shadowy room sang an aria of farewell. A young, slim, febrile man, dressed in a frock coat, top hat, and nankeen trousers, strolled along, indifferent to the throng, his attention fixed on a piece of skin of wild ass shrinking upon the palm of his hand.

Pollo and his employers reached the corner of the Deux-Magots and there, according to agreement, Madame handed the basket to her husband.

"You go on, now," he said to his wife. "You know they won't accept anything from a woman."

Madame faded into the crowd, not without first musing: "Something new every day. Life is wonderful these days."

Pollo and the *patron* walked toward the double circle of silent pilgrims, who were beginning to disrobe, and as the two men approached with the basket, those nearest looked at each other without speaking; they suppressed an exclamation, probably joy, and fell to their knees; with humility, heads bowed before their two providers, each took a piece of bread, a piece of cheese, and an artichoke, and still kneeling, heads still bowed, and with sacramental piety, broke the bread, savored the cheese, and peeled the artichoke, as if these were primary and at the same time ultimate acts, as if they were both remembering and foreseeing the basic act of eating, as if they wished never to forget it, wished to inscribe it upon the instincts of future generations (Pollo Anthropologist). They ate with increasing haste, for now, whip in hand, a Monk advanced toward them from the center of the circle. Again bowing their heads before Pollo and the *patron*, the pilgrims finished removing their clothes, until, like all the other men, boys, and children who formed the double circle, they were clad only in tight jute skirts falling from waist to ankles.

In the center of the double circle the Monk cracked his whip and the pilgrims in the first circle, the internal one, fell, one after another in slow succession, arms spread, face down upon the ground. The impatient, distracted, and excited murmurs of the crowd diminished. Now every man and boy and child standing behind those who had prostrated themselves stepped over one of the prone bodies, dragging their whips across them. But not everyone in the enormous circle lay flat, with arms outstretched. Some had adopted grotesque postures, and Pollo Catechist, as he glanced around the circle, could repeat, almost ritually (for haven't we been educated to know that every sin contains its own punishment?), the cardinal expiations demanded by fists clutched in rage, an avariciously grasping hand, those bodies sprawled in green isolation, the unrestrainedly plunging buttocks, the stuffed bellies bared to the sun, lolling heads propped upon lifeless hands, the prideful poses of disdain and self-esteem, the gross mouths, the greedy eyes.

As the Monk walked toward the penitents, a blanket of silence descended over the crowd: the whip cracked first in the air and then against those fists and hands and buttocks and bellies and heads and eyes and mouths. Almost all choked back their cries. One sobbed. And with every whiplash the Monk repeated the formula: "Rise, for the honor of sainted martyrdom. Whoever say or believe that the body will arise in the form of a sphere, with no resemblance to the human body, be he anathematized . . ."

And he repeated the formula as he stopped only a step away from Pollo before an old man clenching and unclenching his fists, an old man whose stooped shoulders were covered with gray hair. With every blow on the penitent's livid hands, our young and beautiful friend shivered and bit his lips; he felt that everyone in the dense crowd was shivering and biting his lips, and that, like him, they had eyes for nothing but the Monk's whip and the old man's flailed hands. Yet a force stronger than Pollo made him look up. And as he looked, he met the Monk's eyes. Dark. Lost in the depths of his hood. An expressionless gaze in a colorless face.

For the last time the Monk lashed the clenched hands of the old man so visibly containing his fury, and repeated the formula, staring directly at Pollo. Pollo no longer heard the words; he heard only a breathless, timbreless voice, as if the Monk were forever doomed to that breathless panting. The Monk turned his back to Pollo and returned to the center of the circle.

The first act had ended; a noisy roar surged from the throats of the crowd: old women clicked their needles, men shouted, children agitated the branches of the plane trees where they perched. The same Police Inspector, lantern held high, continued his pursuit of the fugitive through the rat-infested labyrinths of black water. In her shadowy room, the courtesan coughed. The thin and febrile young man clenched his fist in desperation: the wild-ass skin had disappeared completely from the palm of his hand, as life flowed from his liquid gaze. A new whiplash, a new silence. The penitents rose to their feet. In his hand each held a whip, a cruel instrument ending in six iron-tipped thongs. The Monk intoned a hymn: Pollo could scarcely hear the first words: "Nec in aerea vel qualibet alia carne ut quidam delirant surrecturos nos credimus, sed in ista, qua vivimus, consistimus et movemur."

The initial words of the celebrant were expected; whether thirty-three days and twelve hours old or new, never heard or ancient, they were received with the same amazement, bathed in the same aura, as when this hooded man had first sung them, standing in the center of the double circle of penitents lines up before the Church of Saint-Germain. It seems that on that extremely distant occasion the spectators had stood in silence until the end of the hymn and then had run to buy all the Latin textbooks in the Quarter's bookstores, for the most informed among them barely knew that *Gallia est omnis divisa in partes tres.* But now, as if they all knew somehow that the opportunities for the purely oral excitement of every performance would necessarily become fewer, or at least less exalting, the crowd immediately erupted into shouting and weeping as the Monk chanted the first words.

This echoing wail, this long loud lament was passed from voice to voice, it died out on one corner, was resuscitated at the next, was muffled in a pair of hands, and recovered between breaths . . . It was one vast onomatopoetic bell, prayer, poem, chant . . . a sob in the desert, a howl in the jungle. As they chanted, the penitents looked to the heavens; the Monk exhorted them to prayer, to piety, and warned against the terror of the days to come; whips snapped against naked shoulders with a rhythmical crack interrupted only when a metal point dug into a penitent's flesh, as now happened to the young man whose flying hair formed a black aureole against the sun, who yelled above the anticipated howl of the crowd, the moaning of his companions, and the chanting of the Monk. Added to the crack of leather against skin was the tearing of metal upon flesh, and this robust young man, trapped in the perpetual rhythmic, circular movement of the flagellants, struggled to remove the iron dart from his thigh; gouts of blood stained the paving stones of the atrium; and at that moment Pollo thought the young man's skin was not actually dark but greenish, swollen, and inflamed. He saw a flash of agony in the protruding green eyes of the wounded flagellant, whose olive-colored forehead was as hard as a breastplate, crisscrossed with throbbing veins and trickles of cold sweat.

The news of the self-flagellation spread from mouth to mouth until it exploded into a moving ovation, a blend of compassion and delight. Pollo turned away from the spectacle and walked toward the Place Furstenberg, opening a path through the crowd with the posters that were his breastplate, the sails of his useless windmill. And as he walked away from the abbey that was also the tomb of the Merovingian kings, that had been burned by the Normans, reconstructed by Louis VII, and consecrated by Pope Alexander III, it was too late to see the flagellant's arms reaching out to him, as he muttered through clenched teeth in a Spanish-accented French: "I am Ludovico. I wrote you. Didn't you receive my letter? Don't you remember me?"

The Place Furstenberg was untouched. Pollo sat upon a bench and admired the symmetrical arrangement of blooming poincianas and round white street lamps: an island of calm, a place privileged to convey the belief and to engender the belief that no time had passed. He clamped his hand over one ear: so Paris was a dream; the *patronne* had been grateful; life had become marvelous; things were happening; the desperate routine had been broken. For her (for how many others?), things again had meaning; for many (for her too?) there was vision again in existence, vibrations with everything that, unlike life, identifies life. He could see the Monk's lips moving, his words drowned out by the roar from the spectators and the flagellants. Pollo had no proof that the man with the dead eyes had really said what he was attributing to him now, sitting here on the bench in the Place Furstenberg; he didn't understand the corollaries to this extremely simple proposition: in Paris, this morning, an ancient woman had given birth, and a *patronne* had found life enchanting. This average, chubby, adorable *patronne* with her rosy cheeks and tight-knotted bun; vile, greedy, dull *patronne*, counting every centime that came into her coffers. What frightening force, what terrible fear, had brought her to this new generosity? Pollo looked at his only hand, at the traces of the grease so obstinately clinging to his palm, congealing in the creases of the lines of life and fortune and love and death. That film he had seen as a child . . . night, fog, the meaningless profusion of death, the final solution. Pollo shook his head.

"It's time to be practical. It is mathematically exact that this morning I walked among several thousand spectators. Never before at one time have so many people been able to see the advertisements for the Café Le Bouquet. But it is also true that no one noticed them. My posters could not compete with the spectacle in the streets, and so the day when most people could have received the impact of the publicity so desired by the *patron* turned out to be the day when fewest people were disposed to be seduced by an advertisement. Neither the number of the crowd nor their lack of interest is my fault. Ergo: it doesn't matter whether I walk among the crowds or through the most deserted streets."

Quod erat demonstrandum: Cartesian Pollo. This reflection neither cheered him nor disheartened him. Furthermore, clouds were building up in the west and soon would be speeding to meet the sun, which was traveling in the opposite direction. The beautiful summer day was about to be spoiled. With a sigh, Pollo rose and walked along the rue Jacob, neither too slowly nor too fast, preserving a kind of impossible symmetry, displaying the profile of the sandwich boards in the windows of the antique shops, stopping from time to time to admire some display of trinkets: gold scissors, antique magnifying glasses, famous autographs, miniature dictionaries, little silver bookmarks in the shape of fists, a cloth or a mask worked of feathers with a design of dead spiders in the center. It was so serene on this street that his spirits were almost calm again. But as he saw himself reflected in the shop window he asked: can a one-armed man ever be truly serene? Pollo Mutilatum.

He stopped before an abandoned kiosk exhibiting dusty, yellow newspapers, he read some of the more provocative headlines: Urgent Meeting of Geneticists Called by WHO in Geneva, Madrid Mysteriously Deserted, Invasion of Mexico by U. S. Marines. He realized that the clouds were gathering more swiftly than he had expected and that in the narrow canyon of the rue de l'Université the light and shadow were changing with the regularity of heartbeats. It's light from the clouds and shadow from the sun, Pollo repeated, or maybe it's someone making jokes with the old tin pan in the sky. No, it isn't; that isn't the smoke from Saint-Sulpice stagnating somehow over the Place Furstenberg. That smoke was filled with ash, but this promises water. Pollo walked down the rue de Beaune to the Seine, murmuring the words of his baptismal poem (for when he was born it was no longer the fashion to baptize with an obsolete saint's name, but rather to choose a name from a book of poems). This poem had been written by a mad old man who had never learned to distinguish between political treachery and raving humor; he was a man who detested equally mimicry of the archaic and avant-garde ingeniousness, who would not accept a past that had not been nourished in the present or a present that did not comprehend the past, who confused all symptoms with all causes: "Bah! I have sung women in three cities. / But it is all one. / I will sing of the sun. / . . . eh? . . . they mostly had gray eyes, / But it is all one, I will sing of the sun."

There they were, all along the Quai Voltaire, the young women and the old, the fat and the thin, the delighted and the inconsolable, the serene and the distressed, lying on both sides of the street, some propped against the parapets of the quay, others huddled close to the buildings, all alternately illuminated and obscured by the swift play of clouds and July sun. July . . . murmured Pollo . . . in Paris everything happens in July, always . . . if you collected all the calendar pages of all the past Julys, you wouldn't miss a single gesture, a single word, a single trace of the true face of Paris; July is the anger of the crowds and the love of couples; July is paving stones, bicycles, and a lazy river; July is an organ-grinder, and many beheaded kings; July has the heat of Seurat and the voice of Yves Montand, the color of Dufy and the eyes of René Clair . . . Pollo Trivia. But this is the first time that a July announces the end of one century and the beginning of another (the first time in my life, I mean . . . Pollo Pubescent), although deciding whether 2000 is the last year of the old century or the first of the new can lead to confusion and arguments. How far away is December, and the January that will dissipate all doubts and fears!

July, and the sun, that enormous, free, and fervent reflecting ball revealing with every successive blink of its eye that the city is open space, the city is a cave. And if Saint-Germain was all confusion, here, as in Saint-Sulpice, there was only silence punctuated by soft sounds: the marching of bare feet in the Place echoed in soft weeping.

Everywhere the eye could see, from the bridge of Alexandre III in one direction to that of Saint-Michel in the other, women lying on the sidewalks were being assisted by other women. The unique miracle at the house of Madame Zaharia had become the collective miracle of the quays: for here women of all ages, shapes, and conditions were giving birth.

Pollo Phoibee picked his way among these women in labor, trusting somehow that some of them might be in the mood to read the advertisements on the boards thumping against his knees and thighs and, once present contingencies were overcome, find themselves disposed to visit the advertised café. But it is true he had very few illusions along that line. Swathed in sheets, bathrobes, and towels, stockings rolled to their ankles and skirts raised to their navels, the women of Paris were giving birth, preparing to give birth, or had just given birth. Those who had already delivered were eventually removed by the makeshift midwives who had assisted them and who immediately prepared to attend the new arrivals waiting in line along the two bridges. Pollo asked himself: at what moment would the midwives themselves become the ones giving birth, and who would assist them but those who either had delivered or were about to? And if the miracle of Madame Zaharia were not exclusive but generic, would the old women knitting socks and fussing with their peaked caps at the Saint-Germain-des-Prés spectacle already have had their moment, or was it still to come? In any case, all the rooms facing the river had been emptied, and the new mothers, with their babes, were led to them as soon as they had passed the obligatory interval between the birth, the modest celebration of the new arrival, and a brief rest in the open air.

But these administrative details were not what made Pollo uneasy as he threaded his way among the prone figures, repressed moans, and gurgling of infants; it was the glances the birthing women directed at him. Perhaps some, the youngest, might have taken him for the possible father, who surely at that very moment was celebrating with the flagellants at the Church of Saint-Germain; some glances were hopeful, some disappointed, but as is the way with things, the hopeful ones turned into certainty of deception, while the disappointment yielded to false expectation. Pollo was sure that not a single one of those newly born infants was any of his doing; and the women who could see his mutilated arm were also sure, for one can forget or confuse anything except copulation with a one-armed man.

Some infants lay on the maternal breast; others were waved away in anger or fear by their mothers and grudgingly held in the arms of the midwives; the beatitude of some young girls and the resignation of some of the thirty-year-old women, however, were not the common denominator in this new spectacle of Paris-in-July. Many of the young girls of marriageable age, and the more mature, probably married, women, seemed as puzzled as numbers of the elderly among them; their expressions communicated a certain slyness . . . and amazement. These aged women, some dignified, straight as ramrods, some stooped as a shepherd's crook, little old ladies until yesterday engrossed in their memories, their cats, their television programs, and their hot-water bottles, those parchment-skinned octogenarians who hobble through the streets grumbling at passers-by, ironclad relics who stand about all day arguing in markets and in stairwells, all of them, all the formidable, the hair-raising, and the dearly beloved female gerontocracy of Paris, smacked their gums and winked their eyes, undecided between two attitudes: whether, in bewilderment, to question, or whether to feign a secret knowledge. Pollo had only to look: he could tell that none of these women knew the father of their infants.

As he advanced along this frontier between astonishment and slyness, some old women reached out to touch our hero's leg; he sensed that one of the ancient ladies had let it be known to her neighbor that he, the blond, handsome, if slightly crippled young man, was the unacknowledged father of the swaddled infant the old harpy was shaking in the air like a rattle. The chain of gossip was about to form, and its consequences—Pollo suspected with terror—would be unequaled. The scapegoat. The Lynch law. *Nuit et brouillard. Fury. Mother Joan of the Angels. The Ox-Bow Incident.* Pollo Cinémathèque. The accusing stare of the little old lady paralyzed Pollo; for an instant he imagined himself surrounded by a pack of betrayed women, the old, the mature, and finally the young, all rushing at him, kissing him first, running their fingers through his hair, pinching and scratching him, each convinced that it was with a one-armed man, only with a one-armed man, they had made love nine months earlier, invoking his mutilation as proof of a singular fertility, demanding that he acknowledge his paternity; blind, furious at his every denial, driven by the need for a propitiatory victim, tearing off his clothes, castrating him, ceremonially, communally eating his balls, hanging him from a post, claiming up to the very end that he was the one, when in all sincerity—although with great astuteness—he could only repeat: "I'm just me, just me, a poor crippled young fellow earning a difficult livelihood as a sandwich man for a neighborhood café. That is my one destiny; humbly and gratefully, I swear to you that is my only destiny."

He had the sang-froid to return the stare of the decrepit old woman who was insinuating that he was the father of her child. Pollo's stare transfixed the old thing, caused her to frown and sadly shake her head. Weeping and sniveling, chin trembling, she pressed the infant to her raddled lips; stupidity and terror welled in her eyes. For, without actually planning it, as he looked at her, Pollo had willed a single image, one exclusive and overwhelming image, to pass through his mind; and that vision was necessarily the opposite of the present inordinate procreation. In his mind Pollo had projected the film of a row of grease-covered, barefoot men, veiled in smoke, penetrating into the frightful stench of the church watched over by the birds of prey: Saint-Sulpice. And as he projected that image from his mind to his eyes and from his eyes to hers, he added one idea: the final solution . . . rigorously programmed death. Then he told himself he wasn't sure of that, that he'd only invented it, merely remembered the unifying symbol of the film; his real intention had been to project to the old woman a terrifying image related to the immediate situation, something emanating from the earth, and pinning her down to the very sidewalk where she lay.

No one will ever know whether Pollo truly communicated anything to the old woman, but that isn't important. What he wished was not to test his telepathic powers but to free himself from any memory or intuition about Saint-Sulpice, now converted by his imagination and cinematographic memories into a cathedral of crime, a death chamber. He felt relief at having transferred, having bequeathed, the image to the old woman, the image, perhaps the fate, of death. But he wondered, is it the young who pass death to the old, or do the old bequeath it to the young? To some few good men, disorder is the evil. Such simple convictions allow them, in exceptional situations, to find peace where none seems to exist. This concept made Pollo's head spin: implacable order ruled at Saint-Sulpice—along with an absolute absence of good—whereas terrifying disorder reigned on the Quai Voltaire, but there was no evil there, unless life had adopted the features of death, or death the semblance of life. Facing Pollo across the sidewalk lay the Pont des Arts, an iron structure linking the quays of the Institute to those of the now transparent Louvre. The bridge stretched from the restrained tumult of this open-air maternity ward (it would be raining soon, and then what?) across the boiling, noisy anarchy of the waters. In the midst of all these signs of catastrophe the bridge stood as a lonely landmark of sanity. Impossible to know why the women crowded the other accesses to the quays and ignored this one. Some unknown rule? Free choice? Fear? The fact is that no one was crossing the Pont des Arts; consequently, that bridge shone in solitary stability.

Pollo felt the need to find the dead center of a city thrown off balance, its scale pans tipped by an excess of smoke and blood. He climbed the steps of the bridge, but could not believe his eyes; he could see the Seine, flowing toward the Ile de la Cité that split its waters; he saw the glassy outlines of the Louvre, and the corona of the storm above the truncated towers of Notre-Dame. The transformations which had seemed like ominous portents now seemed insignificant details: mist lay upon the river, veiling the ruined barges; the city's skyline was once again visible in the crystal-clear air and glowing light, captured in a band of glass and gold between the land and the hovering storm.

A girl was sitting halfway across the bridge. From a distance, against the light (Pollo ascending the steps leading to the Pont des

Arts), she was a black dot on the horizon. As he walked closer, Pollo started to fill in the outline with color: the hair caught back in a long braid was chestnut, the long smock violet, and her necklaces green. She was drawing on the asphalt surface of the bridge. She did not look up as Pollo approached, and he added to the description: firm skin delicate as a china teacup, a turned-up nose, and tattooed lips. She was drawing with colored chalk, as hundred of students had done through the years, reproducing famous paintings or inventing new ones to solicit aid from passing pedestrians to pay for their studies, or a trip, or a ticket home. In other times, one of the joys of the city had been to walk across this bridge reading the chalk letters "Thank you" written in all the languages of the world, to hear the clinking coins, and the guitars at dusk accompanying the students' ballads of love and protest.

Now only this one girl was drawing, absorbed in the banality of her uninspired depiction: from a black circle radiated colored triangles, blue, garnet, green, yellow; Pollo tried to remember where he had only recently seen a similar design. He stopped before the girl, and the thought passed his mind that her lips were much more interesting than her drawing: they were tattooed with violet and yellow and green snakes, capricious flowing serpents that moved as her lips moved, determined by that movement and at the same time independent of it. The tattoo formed a separate mouth, a second mouth, a unique mouth, perfected and enriched by the contrasting colors exaggerating and underlining every glimmer of saliva and every line inscribed on those full lips. Beside the girl was a large green bottle. Pollo wondered whether the painted lips would drink its wine. But the bottle was made fast with an ancient, imprinted, and virgin red-wax seal.

One round drop, then a larger one, then yet another, fell upon the drawing. Pollo looked toward the dark sky, and the girl looked at him; as he watched the sky, his first thought was of the design being erased by the rain, and his second, inexplicably, of a sentence that had been running through his dreams for several days, unuttered until this very instant. The tattooed lips moved, and spoke the words he was thinking: "Incredible the first animal that dreamed of another animal."

Pollo's impulse was to flee; he looked back toward the quays: there was no one there; obviously the intensifying rain had forced the midwives and their patients to seek refuge. Staring at the sign Pollo had so ineffectually displayed all morning, the girl mouthed words as if she were reading what was written on it. The young cripple relaxed; his newfound calm changed to pride; Pollo wished his employers could see him now; if only they could see him now. No one, ever, had read with such seeming intensity and with such gray (eh?) eyes the advertisement for Le Bouquet; Pollo puffed out his chest; he had justified his wages. Then he exhaled; he'd been acting like an idiot. You had only to look at the girl's eyes to know she wasn't reading that innocuous advertisement. Now it was raining steadily, and the girl's vulnerable design was trickling toward the river in spirals of dark color; surely the letters of his sign were similarly streaked; nonetheless, the girl, frowning in concentration, and with an indescribable grimace on her lips, continued to read.

Now she rose and walked toward Pollo through the rain. Pollo stepped back. The girl held out her hand. "*Salve*. I have been waiting for you all morning. I arrived last night, but I didn't want to inconvenience you, although Ludovico insisted on sending you the letter. Did you receive it? Besides, I preferred to wander awhile through the streets alone. I am a woman [she smiled]; I like to receive my surprises alone and the explanations later, from the lips of a man. Why do you look at me so strangely? Didn't I tell you I would come today to meet you? We made a vow —don't you remember?—to meet again on the bridge this very day, the fourteenth of July. Of course, the bridge didn't exist last year; we dreamed there should be a bridge on this spot and now, you see, our wish has been fulfilled. But there are many things I don't understand. Last year all the bridges across the Seine were of wood. Of what are they made now? No, don't tell me yet. Hear me to the end. I'm very weary. The trip from Spain is long and difficult. The inns are crowded, and the roads are more dangerous every day. The bands of pilgrims are advancing at a rate that can be explained by only one fact: the aid of the Devil. Terror reigns from Toledo to Orléans. They've burned the lands, the harvest, and the granaries. They're assaulting and destroying the monasteries, churches, and palaces. They are terrible: they kill anyone who refuses to join their crusade; they sow hunger in their wake. And they are magnificent! The poor, the vagabonds, the adventurers, and the lovers are joining them. They have promised that sins will no longer be punished, that poverty will erase all guilt. They say the only crimes are corrupting greed, false progress, and individual vanity; they say the only salvation is to rid oneself of everything one possesses, even one's name. They proclaim that each of us is divine and therefore everything belongs to all of us. They announce the coming of a new kingdom and they say they live in perfect joy. They are awaiting the millennium that will begin this winter, not as a date, but as an opportunity to remake the world. They quote one of their eremite poets and sing with him that a people without a history is not redeemed from time, for history is a pattern of timeless moments. Ludovico is their master; he teaches that the true history will be to live and to glorify those temporal instants, and not, as until now, to sacrifice them to an illusory, unattainable, and devouring future, for every time the future becomes the present instant we repudiate it in the name of a future we desire but will never have. I have seen them. They are a tumultuous army of beggars, fornicators, madmen, children, idiots, dancers, singers, poets, apostate priests, and visionary eremites; teachers who have abandoned their cloisters and students who prophesy the incarnation of impossible ideas, especially this: life in the new millennium must eradicate all notions of sacrifice, work, and property in order to instill one single principle: that of pleasure. And they say that from all this confusion will be born the ultimate community: the minimal and perfect community. At their head comes a Monk, I have seen him: an expressionless gaze and a colorless face; I have heard him: a timbreless, breathy voice; I have known him in another time: he called himself Simón. I have come to tell you of this, as I promised. Now you must explain the things I don't understand. Why has the city changed so? What do the lights without fire mean? The carts without oxen? The women's painted faces? The voices without mouths? The Books of Hours pasted to the walls? The pictures that move? The empty clotheslines hanging from house to house? The cages that rise and descend with no birds inside them? The smoke in the streets rising from Hell? The food warmed without fire, and snow stored in boxes? Come, take me in your arms again and tell me all these things.''

The girl knew him. Because of his occupation, Pollo was recognized every day by everyone in the district, but the girl's recognition was different. He had never been truly recognized before. All about him, throughout the city, children were being born and men were dying: in spite of everything, each child would be baptized and each man would be laid to rest with his own name. But it was not the children being born or the men dying, or the flagellants and pilgrims and crowds at Saint-Germain, that attracted this girl's attention, but all the normal, everyday, reasonable activities of Paris: the cages rising and descending with no birds within them. Pollo watched with fascination the calligraphy of those lips that had just spoken: this girl has two mouths, with one she speaks perhaps of love; with the other . . . not hatred, but mystery; love against mystery, mystery against love; idiotic to confuse mystery with hatred; one mouth would speak the words of this time; the other those of a forgotten time. Pollo took a step backward, the girl followed. Wind fluttered her violet smock and the rain bathed her face and hair, but the tattooed lips were indelible, moving silently.

''What's the matter? Don't you recognize me? Didn't I tell you I would return today?''

Be he born or dying, he was Pollo; he was baptized Pollo and would be buried Pollo; the young cripple, the employee of the Cafe Le Bouquet, the sandwich man; Pollo from A to Z. Here . . . look . . . where could that book of poems be? Where does it say my name is Pollo? Written by an old madman who confused all symptoms with all causes. The Poet Libra, a Venetian phantom, Pound, exhibited in a cage, a recluse in an American asylum. Gray eyes, eh? The gray eyes of this girl recognized him; but her lips formed, soundlessly, a different name: "Juan . . . Juan . . ."

Who was being born? Who was dying? Who could recognize a cadaver in one of the newborn infants on the quays of the Seine? Who is it who's survived to remember me? Confused, Pollo asked himself these questions; he had only one possible recourse in deciphering the enigmas. He would try to read the words written on the sandwich boards and thus find out what the girl had been reading with such intensity: but the words were written so that the public could read them, not he, and as he twisted his head to try to decipher them, fighting against the whirling wind that blew his long hair into his eyes—twice blinded, by wind and hair—fighting the threat of being engulfed in that odor of burned fingernails, fighting the tactile memory of grease and placenta, fighting against the meaningless words he had uttered, words dictated by a memory of resurrections, ego baptiso te: Iohannes Agrippa . . . Pollo slipped and lost his balance.

And the girl, through whose eyes had passed the same questions, the same memories, the same survivals—as detailed in her memory as generic in his—reached out to steady Pollo. How was she to know the boy had only one arm? She grasped empty air, her hand scratched by the pins of the empty sleeve . . . and Pollo fell.

For an instant, the sandwich boards seemed like the wings of Icarus, and a soaring Pollo saw the flaming Paris sky, as if the struggle between light and clouds were resolved in an explosive conflagration; bridges floated like ships in the fog, the black keel of the Pont des Arts, the distant stone sails of the Pont Saint-Michel, the gilded masts of the Pont Alexandre III blazing corposant. Then the blond and handsome youth plunged into the boiling Seine; his shout was muffled in the implacable, silent fog, but for an instant his only hand—white, emblematic—was visible above the water.

With one hand the girl clung to the iron railing of the bridge, and with the other she tossed the sealed green flask into the river; she prayed that Pollo's hand would grasp the ancient bottle; she tried to peer through the almost motionless mist to the water; she hung her head.

She stared down at the river for several minutes. Then she returned to the center of the bridge and sat down again, legs crossed, straight-backed, letting the wind and rain play with her hair as her spirit drifted into indifferent contemplation. Then through the storm a pale white light descended toward the bridge; the girl raised her head but immediately buried her face in her hands. The light, a white dove, settled upon her head. But the moment it alighted, its white plumage began to fade and streak in the rain; as the dove revealed its true color, the girl repeated silently, over and over:

"This is my story. I want you to hear my story. Listen. Listen. Net-sil. Netsil. Yrots ym raeh ot uoy tnaw I. Yrots ym si siht."

AT THE FEET OF EL SEÑOR

It is told:
Since the previous night his alguacil had been installed in the mountain shelter with all the accouterments. Huntsmen and hounds, carts and baggage, pikes and harquebuses, hangings and horns, lent a festive air to the inn. El Señor arose early and opened the window of his bed-chamber to enjoy better the radiant sun of this July morning. The village nestled in a forest of6 live-oak trees, extending into a cool glade that disappeared at the foot of the mountains. The sleeping valley lay in shadow, but the rising sun shone between the knife-edged peaks.

Guzmán entered to tell El Señor that the plans for the hunt had been made. The hounds had been to the mountains. The tracks and signs indicated that a hart was somewhere on the ridge, a stag that had been hunted before. El Señor tried to smile. He stared at his chief huntsman, who lowered his eyes. Satisfied, El Señor placed his hand on his hip. When this man—who was both his lieutenant and his secretary—had previously come to tell him, prudently and respectfully, what game was in the forest and where the chase would lead, El Señor had found no need to feign a haughtiness that was natural to him—although it is true he used hauteur to conceal his true feelings for the sport: a mixture of aversion and indifference. But when the deputy told him they would be hunting a hart that had been run before, El Señor did not hide his feeling. Calm, and secure, he could look Guzmán in the face, smile, even sigh with a touch of nostalgia. He recalled his youth in this country. The heat would lead them, hart and hunter alike, to the most beautiful parts of the mountain, where water and shade alleviate to some degree the harshness of the sun on the open plateau.

El Señor ordered that more dogs be readied, for the summer day is long and it is the beasts that tire most quickly; he said, too, that water should be loaded onto the mules, that they should calm the ardor of the dogs and run them through the coolest, greenest places. The chief huntsman, still facing El Señor, bowed his way from the room; the Liege, as he again approached the window, immediately heard the horn summoning the gathering for the hunt.

Following the storm, the day will be clear. The receding tide laps at the shoreline. A brigantine has for a long time lain in the cleft where a dry stream bed leads to the sea. A tattered standard catches the wind and flutters between the rocks. Motionless fog lies over the water, blurring the horizon. The only beacon along the coast has been extinguished during the storm. They say its keeper embraced the dog who is his usual companion and that the two lay down beside the howling fire in the chimney.

When the horn sounded the departure for the mountain, El Señor, on horseback, joined his huntsmen. Dressed entirely in green and wearing a short hooded cape of Moorish style and making, he arrived at a light trot. His company followed on foot and on horseback, the servants with tent, spade, billhook, and pickax, should it prove necessary to spend the night in the field. El Señor told himself that all would go well: the brilliant dawn promised a swift, sure hunt, and a return to the mountain pass with the first evening shadows, followed by a well-deserved nocturnal celebration at the inn where his alguacil had already set out several kegs of red wine, and where they would sing ballads and consume the savory entrails of the hart. In their game bags his personal servants carried flint and tinder, needles, thread, and diverse curatives. In accordance with custom, El Señor murmured a prayer, and looked with affection at his favorite dog, the large white mastiff Bocanegra, who preceded the ten huntsmen. Each of the men carried a lance in one hand and with the other checked the straining dogs chained to wide iron collars displaying gleaming heraldic devices and the dynastic motto *Nondum*. When they reached the foot of the mountain, El Señor stopped and looked sadly at the dried vines and the surrounding basalt hills. He remembered his hopeful anticipation of the morning, the imagined ride through the green lands of his youth. It is true that every mountain has four faces, and one tends to know but one. And the saying says that even the best of leaders can lose his way, but El Señor did not dare protest in the name of nostalgia, or countermand an order under the guise of being misled; his chief huntsman was not the kind of man who made mistakes; clearly, the hart had chosen the arid face of the mountain, not the rivulets and bosky groves of El Señor's childhood. His vision, that of the flowering landscape, was superseded by another: an arduous ride under a burning sun across the bluffs and gulleys of the mountainside, hoping that time and strength would permit them to reach the higher vantage point that promised a third prospect: a refreshing view of the sea.

Almost no one visits this area of the coast. Sun and storm, both equally cruel, dispute this domain. When the heat rules, sea spray sizzles as it splashes upon the hard-crusted earth: no man's foot can bear the heat of the fine black sand that penetrates, and desiccates, the strongest leather breeches. The stream bed dries up like the skin of an ailing hawk, and in its meanders agonize the ruins of ancient shipwrecks. The beach is an oven with neither breeze nor shadow; to walk along it, one must fight the suffocating weight of this sun-drenched terrain. To walk this beach is to wish to escape from it, climb the baking dunes, then mistakenly believe it possible to cross on foot the desert separating the shore from the mountain range.

But the desert is as unmarked as the hands of a cadaver, all lines of destiny wiped clean. Everyone knows the stories of shipwrecked men who have perished here (for only disaster can lead a man to this remote territory), turning in hopeless circles, fighting their own shadows; inveighing against them because they do not rise from the sand; imploring them to float like cool phantoms above their owners' heads; kneeling, finally, to straddle and strangle those implacable ghosts. The brains of the ill-fated melt in this heat, and when that butter-yellow sun no longer rules the coast, the tempest reigns in its stead to complete the task.

A world of spoils awaits the hapless man, still another man who, almost defeated by the sea, hopes to find salvation here: empty coffers and demagnetized compasses, skeletons of ships and carved figureheads recarved by wind and sun to resemble broken phalanxes of petrified squires, a desolate battlefield of statue and shadow: tillers, tattered banners, and sealed green bottles. Cabo de los Desastres, it was called in the ancient maps: the chronicles abound in notices of galleons from the Spice Islands, Cipango, and Cathay sunk with all their treasure, of ships vanished with all hands aboard, their crew of Cadizmen as well as captives of the wars against the Infidel, master and servant made equal by the catastrophes of fate. But as if to compensate they also speak of sailing vessels battered against these rocks because lovers were fleeing in them. And if not the chronicles, then superstition, often an unacknowledged source of the former, says that on stormy nights a flotilla of caravels, more spectral than the fog enveloping them, passes by here, their mainmasts flaming with St. Elmo's fire, illuminating the livid faces of captive caliphs.

Four men on horseback and eight on foot had returned with the exhausted hounds, confirming the news: this hart had been hunted before. Guzmán, fingering the moustache that fell in two thin plaits to his Adam's apple, stood in his stirrups and issued commands in rapid succession: ready more hounds than usual, and use only four dogs for each foray; the hunters must be very quiet and strongly discipline their dogs so their growling will not alert the hart.

From his saddle, El Señor pondered the paradox: the timid hart requires more precautions than the pursuit of a courageous, if ingenuous, quarry. Innocent movement, cautious cowardice. Fear is a good defense, he said to himself as he rode forward under the sun, his face hidden beneath the sheltering hood.

They unleashed twelve dogs to cover the mountain and locate the hart's territory; riding beside El Señor, Guzmán told his Liege that the hart was seeking new feeding grounds but because it was summer any new feed would be found in the haunts of the previous summer: where there was water. "It will be easy, Sire, to follow the only stream bed in this arid land and find where the water collects in marshy ground." El Señor nodded without really listening, then cautioned himself he must be more alert . . . his indifference, the burning sun . . . Guzmán still waited for an answer, and as El Señor studied the bronzed face of his chief huntsman he realized he was awaiting not only the practical answer his present duties required but also another, more intangible response involving hierarchy: Guzmán had suggested what should be done, but El Señor must give the order. The Liege reacted, and told his deputy to prepare a replacement of ten dogs for the moment when the first dogs, flews frothing, should return from the search. Guzmán bowed his head and repeated the order, adding a detail El Señor had overlooked: a band of men should immediately climb to a high position where they could oversee the whole operation in silence.

He pointed to this one, that one, another, until he had selected ten men. A mutter of protest rose from the huntsmen chosen to form the party that must climb still higher. When he heard the rebellious murmuring, Guzmán smiled and raised his hand toward his dagger. El Señor, flushed, checked the movement of his lieutenant, who was already caressing the hilt in anticipation; he stared coldly at the men, who felt themselves diminished by an order to fulfill a task that held no danger. Their barely veiled expression of rancor changed now, revealing the anticipated fatigue of that climb to the highest, most rugged parts of the mountain, and also their dejection at not being able to kill the hart they would be the first to sight but the last to touch.

Angered, El Señor spurred his horse toward the band of rebels: the action alone was sufficient; they hung their heads and ceased their muttering. They avoided looking either at each other or at El Señor, and from among them Guzmán chose three men he could trust; those three lined up their sullen fellows and posted themselves one at the head, one in the middle, and one at the end of the line, like guards leading a chain gang to garrison.

"Do not take the crossbows" was Guzmán's final order. "I see too many impatient fingers. Remember, this hart has been hunted before. I want no sound of voices. I want no shots fired. Signal only with smoke or fire."

El Señor no longer listened; he continued up the hard-baked mountainside, displaying nobility in his attitude, although to himself admitting indolence. That rebellious muttering, immediately quelled by Guzmán's actions and his own presence, had drained him completely. Then his eye caught the majestic outlines of the mountains, and as he fingered his reins, he reminded himself that he was here to give a rest to his powers of judgment, not to make them more keen. How many times, as he knelt before the altar or walked about the cloister, had the memory of the obligation he was now fulfilling interrupted his most profound meditations. He spent more time secluded than he should: he needed to be in the field performing heroic feats to be witnessed and remembered. But until now he had always managed to dominate his natural inclinations; he had always given the order for the hunt before Guzmán had to remind him of it, or before his wife's ennui yielded to mute reproaches. And to El Señor's pragmatic reasons, his wife had contributed another of purest fantasy: "Someday you may find yourself in danger, some animal may threaten you. You must not lose the ability to take physical risks. You were young, once . . ."

More judicious now, El Señor consciously exaggerated his noble attitude and gallant posture to gain respect. For long hours in the saddle beneath the burning sun he would not ask for water, so that his vassals might feel the strength of his royal presence, so that when he was once again in prolonged seclusion they would ignore the counsel divulged from mouth to mouth, dark mysteries, imagined disappearances: has our Liege died, has he secluded himself forever in the holy sanctuary, has he gone mad, does he permit his mother, his wife, his deputy . . . his dog, to govern in his stead?

Squinting, he peered up the mountainside. The lookouts, forbidden the use of horns, were excitedly signaling the sighting of the buck. The hounds were brought up from the rear; they would follow the scent of the prey sighted by the men high on the mountain. As they passed by his side, straining but silenced by their handlers, El Señor could sense the trembling strength of their bodies, compounded by restraint and enforced silence.

The hounds raised a light cloud of dust and soon were lost from sight in the rough terrain. El Señor felt lonely, his only company the mastiff Bocanegra, following him with sad small eyes, and the faithful guard of men who, like the dogs and the men stationed on the mountainside, were panting to participate actively in the hunt—but whose duty obliged them to stay behind El Señor, to carry the bags with the curative agaric and mistletoe.

Then, unexpectedly, the sky began to darken. El Señor smiled: he would have respite from the terrible heat without having to ask for relief; all the planned maneuvers of his chief huntsman, as definitive as the authoritative voice in which he had ordered them, would be reduced to naught by the fortuitous change of weather, by the willful caprice of the elements. Double relief, double pleasure; he admitted it.

In this way the storm completes the labors of the sun and the sun those of the storm; the one returns burning bodies, unable to advance a hundred feet beyond the dunes, to the sea; the other offers the ruins of its shipwrecks to the devouring sun. The blond and beatific youth might lie there forever, unconscious and abandoned. Half his face is buried in wet sand, and his legs are licked by soul-less waves. His arms and long yellow hair are tangled with kelp; his widespread arms resemble a cross of seaweed, or one covered by a clinging ivy of iodine and salt. The visible side of his face—eyebrows, lashes, and lips—is covered by the black dust of the dunes. Tattered dun breeches and strawberry-colored doublet cling wetly to his skin. Crabs skirt his body, and someone watching from the dunes might say this is a solitary voyager who like so many before and after him has prostrated himself to kiss the sandy beach, to give praise . . .

"What country is this?"

If outward bound, he will kiss the foreign soil he never thought to encounter beyond a stormy, interminable sea expected to end in the universal cataract. If returning home, the voyager will kiss the prodigal earth and whisper his exploits to her, for there is no better partner than she in these dialogues: the adventures of the pennon he carried into battle and on to new discoveries, the fortunes of armies and armadas of men, like him exiled and liberated by an enterprise that although undertaken in the name of the most exalted sovereigns was secured by the humblest of subjects.

But this traveler still dreams he is struggling against the sea, knowing his efforts are in vain. Gusts of wind blind him, spume silences his cries, waves burst over his head, and finally he mumbles he is a dead man, deposited in the depths of a cathedral of water; a cadaver embalmed with salt and fire. The sea has yielded up the body of this survivor, but it has confiscated his name. He lies there upon the sand, his arms tangled in kelp, and from the heights of the dunes watching eyes discern through the ragged shirt the sign they wish to see: a wine-red cross between the shoulder blades. A face buried in the sand, outstretched arms. And a fist clinging—as if to a lifebuoy—to a large green bottle, rescued, like the youth, from extinction.

Rain drums upon the canvas tent. Inside, seated on his curule chair, El Señor is stroking Bocanegra's head, and the mastiff looks at him with those sad bloodshot eyes, as if revealing in that gaze the eagerness for the hunt that fidelity to his master forbids him. Bocanegra may be condemned to domestic company, but he nevertheless wears an iron breastplate and heavy spiked collar. El Señor strokes his favorite dog—short silky hair, smooth skin—and imagines how that sadness would disappear were the mastiff, accustomed to watching the other dogs depart as he remained by his master's side, solicited for a different hunt: perhaps, sometime, El Señor might ride too far ahead, lose his way, be attacked. Then Bocanegra would know his hour of glory. From his eternal position at his master's feet, he would rise and follow the scent of his master's boots to the farthest gully of the mountain and with a savage bark rush to his defense. Once the father of El Señor had been attacked by a wild boar; his life had been saved solely by the fine, fierce instincts of the dog that was always by his side, which sank its ferocious canines and spiked collar into the eyes and throat of the boar—already wounded, it must be acknowledged, by rutting rivals.

At times like these, El Señor repeated that story to the mastiff as if to console him with the promise of a similar adventure. But no, it wouldn't be on this occasion. Guzmán knew his office well and had ordered the tent raised in this narrow gorge, the hart's only exit from his haunts in the marshy little valley. All afternoon the servants of his personal guard had been cutting brush and madroño branches so that, if the rain let up, El Señor could sit in a blind higher on the mountainside and watch the outcome of the hunt; other servants, with picks, had set up the tent in the gorge so that if it was necessary El Señor could spend the night on the mountain. No, Bocanegra, it wouldn't be this time. But perhaps it was also true that when the opportunity for risk and valor presented itself the domesticated mastiff, his instincts forgotten, would not know how to respond.

It was raining. The snares Guzmán had ordered set up close to the tent were soaking wet. Cords and strips of linen cloth sealed off the narrow stream bed the driven hart must enter—where he would meet his death at the feet of El Señor. Guzmán had placed the greyhounds in position. Guzmán had situated the horses that must await the end of the hunt. Guzmán had stationed the men that were on foot. If the hart attempted to change its course it would run into the lines and cords; in turning from them, it would fall into the hands of the hunters.

"Guzmán knows his office well."

El Señor patted his mastiff's head, and as the dog moved, the spikes of the studded collar scratched his master's finger. Quickly El Señor put his finger to his mouth and sucked the blood, praying it would stop, don't let me bleed, a bit of good fortune, just a light scratch, don't let me bleed like so many of my forebears dead from the bloodletting of wounds never healed; he tried to concentrate upon an immediate recollection in order to block out that ancestral memory: yes, the men who had been on the verge of rebelling that morning. There was no reason the incident should continue to upset him. Guzmán had merely demonstrated he knew his office well, an office he performed in the service of El Señor. It was natural he should choose from among the lowest ranks the men who served as lookouts; no others would lend themselves to such an unrewarding task. What he could not accept, because it could not be explained, was the fact that it was the most unpretentious men who showed signs of rebellion. But neither he nor his deputy could possibly be responsible for that; and after all, the brief uprising had been instantly quelled. Nevertheless, the question remained unanswered: why was it these most humble men, raised from nothing in their villages to a station in the palace, placed in a situation that was clearly an improvement for them, why was it they who muttered through clenched teeth and tried to evade a responsibility that they of all men should know they were chosen for in the first place? Wasn't pride a privilege to be enjoyed by the enlightened, and those of noble lineage? Why did men who were nothing and who had nothing protest once they were given something? El Señor did not dwell upon this enigma beyond a well-remembered maxim of his father the Prince: Give the most beggarly of the beggars of this land of paupers the least sign of recognition, and he will immediately comport himself like a vain and pretentious nobleman; do not dignify them, my son, not even with a glance; they are entirely without importance.

For the moment, the party of lookouts high on the rocky mountainside would have to suffer the rain. The fog would blind them, and their voices would be twice silenced, once by their orders, and again, by nature: a wind that could drown the most penetrating blast of a hunter's horn could certainly muffle the shouts of these rough mountain men. Perhaps they would be thinking of their Liege, who had for one moment deigned to look at them, who without words had destroyed them with a glance. Perhaps the men were cursing, imagining El Señor's privileged position, a site chosen so that he more than any other could experience the supreme pleasures of the hunt: watch the hunters leave, direct the progress of the hunt, determine whether there were any miscalculations and how they might be remedied; preside over the entire process and then enjoy its culmination. And it would be he who assigned the rewards and punishments of the day. If missing the excitement of the hunt had caused those men to climb the mountain with such reluctance, then surely they would be imagining anything except that El Señor—sheltered from the rain in his tent, his only wound the accidental scratch from a spiked collar—was also suffering the anguish of the wait, that he like them might be unaware of the progress of the hunt. El Señor wrapped his scratched finger in a linen handkerchief; it was barely bleeding, it would heal; this time I will not die, I thank you, my God. Had those rough men seen him sitting with his dog inside the tent it is possible they might have muttered anew: the family line has lost its taste for hunting, which, after all, is but a practice game of war; perhaps the smoke of the sacristy and the soft life of devotion have exhausted the vitality of their leader, and he is leader only because he knows more, can do more, risk and bear more than any of his subjects. Were that not so, the subject would deserve to be the chief, and the chief would be the servant. And when El Señor dies, who will succeed him? Where is his son? Why does La Señora constantly announce pregnancies that never reach port safely but always founder in miscarriage? These were the murmurings in the mountains and the inns, in forges and tile kilns . . .

Suddenly the mastiff Bocanegra scrambled to his feet, displaying short, thick claws. His collar and breastplate shone in the feeble light of the tent; the dog slipped beneath the canvas and, barking, ran off into the night. But El Señor did not want to think of anything now, not even the reason for his mastiff's strange behavior; easier to close his eyes behind the handkerchief-bandaged hand, easier to sit alone, his thoughts subdued; better to drift off into a milky vacuum than dwell on memory . . . surprise . . . premonition. He murmured a prayer in which he asked God whether it was sufficient, if God and his vassal El Señor found there was any pleasure in the hunting and killing of a hart, that the vassal, even though he not feel it, reject such pleasure for the greater glory of his Creator.

"It is he," says the man, sure he recognizes certain identifying marks on the body of the shipwrecked youth lying below on the beach.

He and his men spur their horses forward and plunge down the dunes, raising blinding clouds of black dust. Their horses whinny as they near the prostrate body; the horsemen dismount, walk forward, and encircle the body, their footsteps resounding like whiplashes as they stride through pools of tepid water. The horses snort nervously at the unfamiliar scent, and seem to sense intuitively the fear behind the armor of that deep, strange sleep. The slow, silent sea, warm and muddied from the storm, laps at the shore.

The leader kneels beside the body, runs his fingers over the blood-red cross; then, grasping the boy beneath the arms, rolls him over. The youth's lips part; half his face is blackened by sand. The man with the long, plaited moustache gestures, and his men lift the youth to his feet; the bottle drops from his grasp, and returns to the waves. The youth is dragged to one of the horses and thrown across its back like a prize of the hunt. His arms are lashed to the saddle trappings and his lolling head presses against the animal's sweating flank. The chief issues a command and the company rides up the dunes and gains the flat rocky plateau extending toward the distant mountains.

Then through the dense fog they hear a sound like the rowels of spurs or metal striking against rock: following the sound appears a litter of burnished ebony; four Negroes strain beneath its weight as they advance toward the party of men leading a horse with a body across it.

A bell tinkles inside the litter and the blacks stop. Again the bell tinkles. The porters, with a concerted groan, hoist the palanquin with powerful arms and deposit it gently upon the desert sand. Exhausted by their efforts and the humid heat following the storm, the four naked men fall to the ground and rub their streaming torsos and thighs.

"Up, pigs!" shouts the man with the plaited moustache; as the horseman raises his whip to lash the porters, he communicates his fury to his mount; the horse rears and pitches in a nervous circle around the litter. The four Negroes, whimpering, get to their feet; their yellow eyes are filled with glassy anger, until a woman's voice speaks out from behind the closed draperies of the litter: "Leave them alone, Guzmán. It has been a difficult journey."

The horseman, still circling, still flogging the blacks, shouts above his horse's snorting: "It is not well for La Señora to go out accompanied only by these brutes. The times are too dangerous."

A gauntleted hand appears between the curtains. "If the times were better, I would not need the protection of my men. I will never trust yours, Guzmán."

And she draws the curtains.

The shipwrecked youth believed he had been embalmed by the sea; blood pounded at his temples; he squinted through half-opened eyes; the sight of this fog-shrouded desert was perhaps not too different from what he would have encountered on the floor of an ocean of fire, for as he fell from the ship's forecastle to the sea, he couldn't see the waves he was falling toward, only the blazing corposant above him: the St. Elmo's fire at the top of the mainmast; and when he was tossed unconscious onto the beach, he was wrapped in dense fog. But now, as he opened his eyes, the curtains of the litter also opened; instead of sea or desert or fire or fog, he met someone's gaze.

"Is it he?" the woman asked, looking at the youth, who stared in turn at black eyes sunk in high cheekbones, brilliant eyes contrasting with a face of silvery paleness; she looked at him, not realizing that from behind a web of sandy eyelashes he was watching her.

"Let me see his face," the woman said.

The youth saw clearly now, saw the sure, arrogant movements of this woman swathed in black reclining in her litter, looking very like the nervous but motionless bird reposing on her gauntleted wrist. The man with the plaited moustache grasped the youth's hair and jerked his face upward for the woman to see. The youth's lusterless eyes caught the impatient movement of her head, framed by the high white wings of a wimpled headdress.

She raised her arm, covered in a full, puffed sleeve; as she spoke, her pointing finger ordered her Negroes: "Take him."

The sound of panting echoes through the desert, an infinite breathiness that seems to come from the fog itself; then a swift, trembling body, a flash of a huge white dog that growls and throws itself against the leader's horse; for a moment the chief is stunned; the dog leaps at his legs, drives the spikes of his collar into the belly of the man's rearing, whinnying horse; the leader pulls his dagger from his waistband, tugs at the reins to control his mount, and aims a vicious, slashing blow at the dog's head; the dog's collar scratches the man's fist, and the dog whines and falls to the ground, his sad eyes staring into the eyes of the forgotten voyager.

At nightfall an exhausted El Señor entered his tent, slumped into his chair, and drew a coverlet around his shoulders. The rain had stopped, and for several hours the servants had been out looking for Bocanegra, but instead of following the trail of the fugitive dog, the hounds stupidly circled the tent, as if the scent of their master's dog were inseparable from that of the master. Finally El Señor, heavy of heart, resigned himself to the loss of his mastiff—and felt even more chilled.

He had begun to read his breviary when Guzmán, his sweating face and stained clothing showing signs of the prolonged hunt, parted the flap of the tent and advised El Señor that the hart had just been brought to camp. He apologized: the rain had altered the tracks; the hart had been chased and killed at some distance from the site reserved for El Señor's pleasure.

El Señor shivered and his breviary fell to the ground; his impulse was to pick it up, he even bent forward slightly, but like a flash Guzmán was kneeling before his Lord; he picked up the book of devotions to hand to his master. From his kneeling position Guzmán, as he looked up to proffer the breviary, for an instant looked directly at El Señor, and he must have arched an eyebrow in a manner that offended his Liege; but El Señor could find no fault in his servant's celerity in demonstrating his obedience and respect; the visible act was that of the perfect vassal, although the secret intent of that glance lent itself, and all the more for being ill-defined, to interpretations El Señor wished both to accept and to forget.

Guzmán's wound grazed the wound on El Señor's hand; the handkerchiefs that bound them were of very different quality, but the scratches caused by a spiked collar were identical.

El Señor arose and Guzmán, not waiting for his Lord to express his intention—would he continue reading? would he come out to the fire?—already held the Biscayan cloak in his hands, ready to assist his master.

"I did well to bring a cloak," El Señor commented.

"The good huntsman never trusts the weather," said Guzmán.

El Señor stood motionless as his chief huntsman placed the cape about his shoulders. Then Guzmán, bowing deferentially, again lifted the tent flap and waited for El Señor, face hidden beneath the hood, to step out to the blazing bonfires. El Señor left the tent, then paused before the body of the hart stretched on the ground before his feet.

One of the huntsmen, knife in hand, approached the hart. El Señor looked at Guzmán; Guzmán raised a hand: the huntsman tossed his dagger and the lieutenant caught it in the air. He knelt beside the hart and with one swift, sure motion of the hunting knife slashed the throat from ear to ear.

He cut off the horns and then slit the skin above the rear hoofs, breaking the joints to expose the tendons.

He rose and ordered the men to hang the hart by its tendons and skin it.

He returned the knife to the huntsman and stood watching; between Guzmán and El Señor hung the cadaver of the hart.

The men slit the hide of the animal from hock to anus, and from there in a line down the middle of the belly. They spread open the gash and removed the bladder, the stomach, and the entrails; they threw these organs into the bucket filling drop by drop with the hart's blood.

El Señor was grateful for the double mask of the night and his hood; nevertheless, Guzmán was observing him in the wavering firelight. The huntsmen cut open the chest to the breastbone and removed the lights, the liver, and the heart. Guzmán held out his hand, and the heart was handed to him; the other viscera plopped into the bucket of blood with a sound identical to that of the beating of El Señor's troubled heart. Unconsciously, El Señor clasped his hands in a gesture of pity; Guzmán caressed the hilt of his dagger.

The head was severed at the back of the neck, and although the task of quartering the hart continued, El Señor, in the flickering firelight, could see only the head, that stupid-looking, that slack-jawed, that excruciatingly pitiful head deprived of its crown. The dark, glassy, half-open eyes still simulated life, but behind them, triumphant, lurked the specter of death.

Now several huntsmen cut the tripe into small pieces, toasted them over the fire, then dipped and stirred them in blood and bread. And if previously only the hart's body had separated El Señor from his lieutenant as they skinned, dehorned, and quartered the animal, now there was a world between them. The blood and bread and tripe were brought to the bonfire; the huntsmen stood in a circle around the blaze, along with the hounds that had participated in the hunt. With one hand the men restrained the dogs; in the other they held their hunting horns. El Señor's traditional position of eminence had for the moment been preempted by the excitement and confusion. The distraction of the nervous, panting hounds and the men's absorption in the double task of managing dogs and horns would have allowed the Liege to slip back to his tent and renew his pious reading without anyone's being the wiser, but he knew there was still one formality demanding his attention. An order, a casual gesture, and the huntsmen would blow their horns in unison, signaling the ritual end of the hunt.

In that obscurity to which he'd been relegated, El Señor started to give the signal, but at that very moment the huntsmen blew their horns. The ringing blast from those great curved instruments shook the night, a hoarse lamentation seeming not to fly but to gallop on iron-shod hoofs across the hard-baked drum of the earth to the mountains from which it had been torn. Although El Señor had never given the signal, the ritual had been fulfilled. It was too late. He stood stupefied, his unheeded gesture frozen in mid-air. He was thankful Guzmán was not beside him, grateful he was engrossed in the activity that absorbed them all, that he had not seen the startled face, the half-open mouth whose ritual command had been fulfilled—without word or gesture of the Liege.

At the sound of the horns, the hounds had strained forward to be fed, their greedy muzzles and trembling loins illuminated in the glow of the firelight. Surrounded by the ravenous pack, Guzmán dangled the hart's entrails at javelin tip, high above their heads. The hounds snapped and leaped. Maddened by the deafening horn blast and their own natural savagery, they were a flowing river of luminous flesh; their tongues were sparks flashing against a sweating, happy Guzmán, javelin held high, feeding the hart's entrails to hounds that would relish the treat and greedily await the next hunt. El Señor turned from the spectacle; he was obsessed by an infinite and circular thought.

As the dogs smeared their muzzles in blood and charcoal, Guzmán, with the point of his knife, traced a cross on the heart of the stag, then deftly divided it into four portions. He chuckled dryly as he tossed one portion to each point of the compass; the huntsmen laughed with him, well pleased with the day, and with every spirited gesture of the chief huntsman; thus exorcising the evil eye, they shouted: to Pater Noster, to Ave Maria, to the Credo, and Salve Regina.

"Sire," said Guzmán, as finally he approached El Señor. "It is Your Mercy's pleasure to distribute the rewards and punishments of the day."

And he added, smiling, grimy, wounded, exhausted: "Do it now, for these men are tired and wish to return as soon as possible to the shelter."

"Who was first at the kill?" asked El Señor.

"I, Sire," replied his chief huntsman.

"You returned just in time," said El Señor, cradling his chin on his fist.

"I don't understand, Sire."

Thoughtfully, El Señor toyed with his thick lower lip. No one could realize that the Liege's eyes, hidden beneath the hood of his cape, were examining his lieutenant's boots and that upon them he observed traces of the black sand of the coast, so different from the dry brown mountain dirt. For the first time, Guzmán noticed on his Liege's hand the wound that was the counterpart to his own, and irresolute and perturbed, he hid his hand. Reward and punishment? El Señor and Guzmán thought simultaneously: For whom? They thought of each other and of themselves, of the dog Bocanegra, and the frustrated and rebellious band of lookouts.

A woman's hand awakens him, caressing his face, wiping away the damp black grains of sand. The youth awakens a second time, dozes, made drowsy by the motion of the swaying litter where he lies captive among silken pillows and ermine coverlets, brocade curtains, and a deep and aggressively feminine perfume, a scent the youth can see at the same time he inhales and sees the color black.

He knows he is lying in a moving, luxurious, fantastic bed. A woman's soft hand strokes him without ceasing, but from where he lies he sees her other hand, gloved in a rough and greasy gauntlet on which perches a bird of prey. The youth's eyes and the sunken eyes of the bird lock in an unswerving gaze, but if the youth drifts between sleep and wakefulness, the hawk's stare is unvarying, hypnotic, as if an artisan had set two old, worn, blackened copper coins in the head of the bird; and in that gaze are two timeless numbers. The furious falcon is motionless, stiff, its legs spread to better grip its mistress's gauntlet. The purchase of the bird's feet on the woman's wrist is such that its claws seem an extension of the greasy fingers of the glove. One would think it a Maltese statue, it is so still; only the tiny bells fastened to its tarsi indicate movement or life; their jingling blends with other persistent metallic sounds of iron buckles and metal dragging along the road.

The youth turns his head toward the woman who caresses him, sure he will see the silver-pale face he had glimpsed that morning between the curtains of the litter, the woman who had asked who he was, who had looked at him not knowing she herself was watched. But black veils hide the features of the woman in whose lap he rests . . . sleeps . . . wakens. La Señora (so the brutal man who had tied him across the horse had called her) is a statue in black: brocades, velvets, silks; from head to foot she is swathed in veils and draperies.

Only her hands indicate her living presence; with one she caresses the youth's face, brushes away the sand; the other sustains the motionless bird of prey. The shipwrecked youth fears the question she must ask: Who are you? He fears it because he does not know the answer. Lulled within the cushiony perfumed litter, he realizes he is the most vulnerable man in the world: he cannot answer that question; he must wait for someone to tell him "You are . . ."—to reveal an identity he must accept, no matter how menacing, disagreeable or false it may be—or remain nameless. He is at the mercy of the first person who offers him a name: alone, lulled by the motion, he thinks, he knows. But in spite of the thick fog clouding his senses—sleep, motion, perfume, the hawk's hypnotic gaze—the touch of those soft fingers on his face and forehead keeps him awake, permits him to cling to lucidity as the falcon clasps the gauntleted wrist of La Señora. The youth's feeble argument, reinforced by the fact he has no other, is that if someone recognizes and calls him by name, he will recognize and name the person who identifies him, and in this act know who he is: who we are.

Consoled, very softly he brushes the cloth of the woman's skirt; he is content for a long while, but when he feels almost overcome once more by the swaying, the perfume, and fatigue, he reaches toward the veils covering the woman's face.

She screams: or he believes she screams; he does not see the mouth hidden behind the veils, but he knows that a cry of horror has shattered this dense atmosphere; he knows that as he reaches toward her face, she screams; but now everything happens simultaneously: the litter stops, he hears heavy, moaning voices, the woman thrusts the hawk's ungainly head toward his face and the bird rouses from its heraldic lethargy, its bells jingle furiously as La Señora's hand—once caressing, now rapacious—brutally covers his eyes, he barely glimpses behind the parted veils a mouth displaying teeth filed sharp as the spikes of a hunting dog's collar; the hawk strikes at his neck, tender from the sun and salt of fiery seas, and against his flesh he feels the icy humors exhaled from the heavy curved beak; he hears the words of that shout congealed in space, entombed in the oppressive luxury of the litter; a shout that claims and claims again the right of every being to carry a secret to the grave. And the young prisoner cannot distinguish the breath of the falcon from that of the woman, the bird's icy beak from La Señora's sharp-filed teeth as the pinpricks of tenacious hunger sink into his neck.

That night a crippled, bleeding Bocanegra limped into the inn. His arrival spoiled the huntsmen's celebrations. They ceased their drinking and their singing:

> How sad and long the day, oh,
> How poor the rich may be,
> To sadness I'd say nay, oh,
> His castle I'd gainsay, oh,
> Today a roof of hay, oh,
> Seems fairer far to me,
> Yes, fairer far to me.

Quarrels were interrupted and loud talk stilled; astonished and uneasy, they all stared at the fine white mastiff with a gaping wound on his head, his paws stained with the black sand of the coast.

The dog was led to El Señor's quarters, where the Liege ordered him to be treated. Now, in the candlelight, the servants at last had reason to open their bags. El Señor knelt on his prie-dieu, placed his opened breviary upon it, but turned his back to the black crucifix that accompanied him on all his journeys; he watched the servants, who had first wished to carry the dog to the courtyard, considering it not entirely proper to treat him in the master's bedchamber. El Señor said no, they must tend him there; reluctantly, the servants bowed to his superior will. The Liege's presence would inhibit their excited comments about this event, their improbable versions of what had taken place.

Once again, kneeling and silent, El Señor asked himself whether unbeknownst to him the servants were secretly rebellious, whether from their humble condition they demanded something more than the favor of their Lord, more than the duties that gave them greater rank than any servants in the land. But in the flurry of activity the servants forgot their indiscreet discontent, and their master his discreet conjectures.

One servant removed the dog's hair from around the wound; he cleaned and then stitched the wound with a formidable thick, squared needle, careful to fasten a little hide and a little flesh with every stitch. The wound was closed with the heavy thread, pulled not too tight, and not too loose. Then the first servant withdrew various curative powders from the bag to apply to the wound: oak leaf, palm bark, blood of the dragon tree, burnt sorrel and hordeum, medlar-tree leaf, and pennyroyal root. The second servant dampened heated handfuls of oakum fibers, wrung them well, and placed them over the powders, while the third placed a dry layer over the first, binding it finally with a strip of cloth.

The servants left behind them a sad and whimpering Bocanegra, and a dozing El Señor kneeling on his prie-dieu, his head resting on the velvet armrest, giddy from the foul stench of the powders and smoking kettles, and the metallic taste left (in the air) by the dog's blood, and (on the floor) the traces of dark coastal sand where you lie, returned, your own twin, your new footprint upon your ancient footprint, your body for a second time outlined on the sand that a body like yours abandoned this morning when the sea abandoned you; you are lying on the same beach, outspread arms entangled in seaweed, a cross between your shoulder blades, clutching a large green sealed bottle, your old and your new memories erased by storm and fire, your lashes, your eyebrows, your lips covered by the sand of the dunes, as Bocanegra whines and El Señor in his sleep obsessively recalls the day of his triumph and repeats it to the dog; but the dog wants only to learn the terror of the black coast, while El Señor wishes only to justify his return, tomorrow, to the palace he had ordered on the very same day to be constructed in honor of his victory.

VICTORY

The fortified town fell following a ferocious battle. The news was carried to the camp; within the hour he was entering the conquered city; now, in his memory—black and brilliant as the cuirasses of his German mercenaries, turbid and liquid as the lakes surrounding the besieged borough—arose tumultuous images of the devastating battle he had waged against heresy in the lowlands of Brabant and Batavia. In earlier times, in Spanish territories, El Señor's remote ancestors had combated and vanquished the Waldenses and Insabbatists; now their obstinate descendants, with their train of supporters and Jews who had renounced their conversion to Catholicism, had found refuge and a land propitious to their resurgence in these North Countries that had traditionally harbored heretics. There, like moles from their tunnels, they gnawed at the foundations of the Faith, whereas in León and Aragon and Catalonia these same people showed themselves in the light of day, proclaimed their beliefs with Luciferian pride—and so were more easily persecuted.

Looking at the flat contours of these Low Countries, El Señor mused that perhaps their very flatness demanded that men hide, and move with caution, while the ruggedness of the Iberian landscape stimulated men's honor and pride, animated them to rise to heights inspired by their rugged mountains, to shout their defiance from the peaks and openly join the unarmed legions of the blasphemous, as Peter Waldo, a merchant of León, had done; he had publicly preached poverty, censured the riches and vices of ecclesiastics, established a secular church where everyone, even women, had the right to officiate and to administer the Sacraments, a right they denied to those priests they considered unworthy; they fled from the temples, saying it was better to pray in one's own home, and on these principles Peter Waldo organized a dreadful rabble called the Insabbatists, because as a mark of poverty they wore shoes with a thick wooden sole and with a coarse leather strap across the instep; and following the teachings of their heresiarch they said they were rich because they had renounced all worldly goods; they were called the Poor Men of León, who lived on charity and rejected the inheritance of property, and among them there was no "mine" or "yours," and they called Rome covetous and false and wicked, rapacious wolf, crowned serpent, and many disciples were attracted to their mystic austerities; they allied themselves with the heretical Cathari and the rebellious Provençal troubadours, who said that the human body was the seat of pain and sin and that the earthly consolation offered by Jesus Christ and His saints was of no worth, either in life or at the hour of death; they believed that the natural sinfulness of the human body should be exhausted during the course of life on earth, and that thus it would be purified and worthy to meet the divine gaze of Heaven. Don Pedro el Católico had zealously eradicated this Waldensian heresy and the tenacious uprisings of the Poor Men of León. El Señor remembered his ancestor's words and repeated them now to himself: "Be it known that if any person, noble or plebeian, discover in our kingdoms any heretic, and kill or mutilate him or divest him of his goods or cause him any other harm whatsoever, he must not for that be punished; rather, he will enjoy the benefit of our grace."

Black, brilliant, turbid, liquid memory of the present: the heretics were well supplied with stores inside the walled city built upon a small hillock and encircled by a deep moat; it was additionally protected by its swampy lakes, as the heretics were protected by the inciting Brabantine and Batavian dukes who set their temporal authorities against the divine authority of Rome, claiming Caesar's portion for themselves instead of God; in this way they freed themselves from the payment of tithes, kept in their own coffers all proceeds from the sale of indulgences, and favored the merchants and usurers of the gray Nordic ports; and too, El Señor smiled bitterly, the heretics, akin to Waldensian austerity and Catharistic sin, but who now called themselves Adamites, had ended up in the service of the sins they claimed to combat: greed and riches and power. That alone was enough to justify this war against heretics and princes who had rebelled against Rome, and merchants faithful only to their overflowing treasure chests. Give me strength, O God, to combat them in your name and in the name of the Christian power bequeathed me by my warrior father.

"Follow always the example set by your father," his mother had told El Señor since he was a child. "On one occasion he slept thirty successive days in his armor, thus uniting the sacrifice of the body with the battle of the soul." El Señor, entering the city he had conquered by siege, considered himself worthy of such a dynastic inheritance: later he would remember tremulous images of faces blasted by powder, raw and mutilated flesh, eyes and hands torn away by crossbow and cannon on the sites where these novelties had been employed; there was similar cruelty where the struggle had followed ancient seignorial custom: chain mail driven into flesh by heavy ax blows, eyes burned raw by enemy-thrown quicklime: the combat of body against body, mount against mount; horsemen killed not by enemy action but by concussion when their helmeted heads struck the ground; men drowned in the attempt to cross the lake in their heavy armor or dead of heat stroke inside their creaking cuirasses; men run through by El Señor's swordsmen after they had fallen and were struggling like overturned turtles in their heavy armor. Maneuverability, on the other hand, was the rule of war in the troops of El Señor, who had brought with him Spanish infantry—Asturians and miners, by origin—to dig and sap and act as rear guard once the light cavalry, the strategic weapon of victory, had descended upon the heavily armored phalanxes of the heretic-protecting Duke; the victory had been won by the mercenaries recruited among the Germans of the Upper Rhine and the Danube, mounted forces most effective in this new style of warfare—effective, that is, as long as they received their wages, for otherwise the risk was great that they would desert to the enemy; these German reiters fought with the pistol, a new weapon invented in the Italian village of Pistoia; five or six of these light arms assured stunning mobility in skirmishes, confusing and unsettling at the first encounter the massed enemy cavalry, whose horses were slowed by armor and the disproportionately long lances of the troops. As their armor and trappings were all of black, these mercenaries were called the Germans of the Black Band.

The victory belonged to them, but also to El Señor's cold and lucid martial ingenuity—inflamed by faith, cooled by the science of warfare learned from his father. Once its heavy cavalry had been destroyed, the enemy barricaded itself inside the city, protected by tall towers and projecting bastions, a deep moat, and the waters of the river that branched into many smaller channels to form small lakes and swamps about the city walls. But El Señor overcame this natural defense: observing the cumbersome cavalrymen drown in river and swamp, he had utilized the boats along the shore, formerly used to transport foot soldiers, to construct a surer, swifter crossing; gunwale to gunwale he lined up the boats and filled them all with earth; the clever Germans obtained information from fishermen about places a man could wade across the lake in waist-deep water: light, light at all costs, the advance upon the besieged city, give every horse a measure of oats, captains and horsemen must do without the service of their squires, maneuverability, the enemy has lost four flags in the battles outside its walls, we must entrench ourselves in that lost ground, mobility, set broad planks across the river, mark a route through the swamp, the enemy lies in ambush, cuts down trees we might use as refuge or hiding place in the woods along the river, for man and tree are easy to confuse by night, the mills are turning, mills driven by horsepower, water mills, windmills, praise God, the wind is rising, and a strong wind means a swift-spreading fire, the Germans thunder across the causeway of boats, the infantry follows across planks and tightly bound branches, straw huts in the false village outside the walls burst into flame, the enemy constructs ingenious trenches, deep inside, low outside, now black smoke engulfs the besieged city, they cannot see us but we can see the buttresses of the wall, now, Asturian miners, dig a honeycomb of trenches so we can reach the moat about the city, mine the bastions with powder so rotten that like the dead it must be carried in shrouds, now, from the side of the river lost by the enemy, fire the cannon, tower after tower falls, rampart after rampart, don't hold back now, days pass, the city resists the siege but we can smell what is happening inside: the stench of death; deserters leap from the ravaged towers into the lake, our vanguard sees the city fathers expelled, they come to us and tell us: We are peaceful burghers, the Duke and his heretics force us to work like slaves repairing the walls, if we refuse we are flogged in public and if we are recalcitrant we are hanged, and if we do not accept his terms we are thrown from the city into the hands of the enemy, for the Duke considers this a worse punishment than the whip or the gallows, and we can tell you that although the city is without provisions or arms it is not lacking in courage, and it will defend itself whether with stones or arrows or caldrons of boiling pitch, for there are many archers and many strong arms, but no cannon or culverin or ordnance; El Señor ordered his troops to shield themselves against the falling stones and to assure their positions beside the battered walls and crumbling towers inside temporary shelters, and thus protect themselves from both defenders and attackers, from the stones and arrows of the Duke as well as the cannon and crossbows of El Señor; he ordered his German cavalry to position themselves outside the city's rear gate, then the mines were exploded, the towers demolished, the artillery finally breached the wall, and shouting and yelling, El Señor's troops entered the terrified city: the Duke and his heretics fell back and attempted to escape, but with pistols and daggers the Germans awaited them, fearful squadrons—the black splendor of the Rhinelanders' cuirasses and the coppery refulgence of those of the Danubian mercenaries; with pistol and dagger they fell upon the heretics; the Germans shot and slaughtered, the Spanish shoveled and exploded, and at exactly one o'clock in the afternoon a captain of the Banner of the Blood planted his flag on the ruins of the highest tower, opened the gates, lowered the drawbridges, and El Señor rode into the city.

He expected a triumphal reception, if not from a populace accustomed to wars and indifferent to interchangeable lords, or from soldiers equally available to either side, at least from his own troops. But instead, as he advanced through the narrow streets, from the windows overhead, clouds of feathers and storms of loose straw rained down upon him and upon his caparisoned charger.

Seeing a captain of his troop emerging from one of the houses, El Señor shouted to him: "What is happening? What does this mean?" The captain, his face flushed, told El Señor that his Spanish soldiers were ripping apart the beds in search of the gold they had heard this Northern race of misers and usurers hid beneath their pillows; had the inhabitants still been there, the soldiers would happily have thrown them from the windows, but they had fled in fright, perhaps leaving their savings behind. At least, that's what the soldiers hoped. Don't they know that this is a Crusade of the Faith and not a war of spoils, El Señor asked his captain. Don't they know that of all the Princes of Christendom the Pope named me Defensor Fides and charged me with the eradication of this Flemish heresy? The captain shook his head. Crusade or no, the men engaged in these wars are hired soldiers, Sire, and they don't fight for pleasure or for sacrifice; they fight because war is their profession, and it doesn't matter to them whom they fight as long as they get their wages and their spoils. If he wanted a crusade, El Señor should enlist the peasants of his domains, but those peasants knew only the plow; they couldn't manage a sword—much less a crossbow or a firearm or the big cannon that gave us the victory, praise God, and thanks to His providence it will not be said of us, as it is of unsuccessful armies, that the throne of military honor rests upon the triumphs of one's enemy. Resign yourself, Sire; accept the dishonor of the sacking, for it is proof of victory; the honor of the vanquished serves only as food for worms and flies.

The captain walked away, and that afternoon neither flowers nor terrified burghers rained down upon El Señor from the windows overhead, only stuffing from gutted pillows and mattresses. And dogs devoured the bodies of the dead in the streets, not the worms and flies the captain had invoked. Gripped with rage, El Señor stopped before the great Cathedral and directed a crossbowman to throw open the portals of this magnificent Gothic temple, the ancient tomb of martyrs, and a collegiate church; he ordered the church bells rung, he would convene a grand *Te Deum* in honor of the victory against the enemies of the Faith. The crossbowmen seemed nervous, even aggrieved; some covered their faces, whether to hide their laughter or to shield against the stink of the bodies piled high in the atrium, it would be difficult to judge. As El Señor watched the soldier open the Cathedral doors, he said to himself, knowing he could never, he must never, reveal an instant's doubt: "Always that moment of uncertainty between the order and its execution . . ."

When the doors were opened, he himself was forced to cover his nose and mouth with a gauntleted hand; from inside the Cathedral came a foul excremental odor that mingled with the stench of the dead heaped in the street.

Laughing, shouting German soldiers and horsemen were running up and down the naves; some were defecating at the foot of the altar, others were urinating in the confessionals, and dogs wandering in and out of the temple, not satisfied with the banquet of human carrion in the streets, were lapping up the vomit of the drunken troops. Even before El Señor gave the order, his crossbowmen made a brusque and aggressive movement, prepared to expel their companions from the Cathedral, arrest them . . . or perhaps they intended only to advise them that El Señor was standing watching from the shadow of the threshold. But El Señor signaled them to stop; then, irresolute, he stood toying with his lip.

Surely his duty was first to discipline the crossbowmen who had not prevented the profanation, and second to punish the profaners themselves. But he felt a stronger, a mortifying, impulse to linger behind one of the columns in a dark corner of the Cathedral. With a gesture, he ordered his men to leave him in the Cathedral. He listened to their reluctant footsteps, and then the great doors closed and El Señor was alone with a feeling of personal defeat that more than offset the satisfaction of the great military victory of this day; the anonymous captain was mistaken, it would be better for honor to derive from the triumph of the enemy if such dishonor was the fruit of victory. He rested his head against the column; he was overcome (are you listening, poor Bocanegra) by the repulsive odors and raucous noises of the German mercenaries who had won the day for the Faith.

It was difficult to see clearly what was happening by the altar; the guttural accents of a black-clad horseman stood out above the base and drunken voices. Everyone stopped to listen, and after he had finished speaking in his Teutonic tongue, his companions shouted "Long lives!" and "To the deaths!" They retrieved their swords and their cuirasses, the copper of the Danubians and the black that gave the name to the Rhenish band, thrown carelessly in the heaps of stinking excrement, black and copper, at the foot of the altar; and in the thick darkness the assault began, sword against sword, Rhinelander against Austrian, the Black Band against those in copper armor, shouting insults, threatening death, and howling in agonistic ecstasy, and as I could not see them clearly, Bocanegra, I closed my eyes and remembered similar profanations in the past; I imagined that this monstrous din and nauseating stench might have accompanied earlier scenes: the French crusaders in Hagia Sophia, where they had sat a whore upon the throne of the Patriarch and drunk from the sacred ciboria, all the while singing obscene rondelets; and I recalled the taking of the temple of Jerusalem by Christian horsemen who rode through the sacred nave in blood up to their knees; but that was the blood of infidels, Bocanegra.

Leaning against the column, he felt infinitely weary. The victory had drained him. Him, yes, but not the warriors; they'd not had enough, and the battle was continuing inside the Cathedral; those German reiters were far surpassing the obligations of their mercenaries' salaries. He stood there a long while, eyes closed, secretly fascinated (yes, Bocanegra, I can tell you) with the spectacle God had visited upon him, he was convinced (I am convinced), to dilute the pride of military victory, to propose that the victory of arms be set aside and that instead we recall the unending battle for the salvation of souls. For what was this war but the struggle between Christianity and these heretics who had found refuge beside the icy Northern Seas, against the last Waldenses and Cathari, who now called themselves Adamites, who disguised themselves under the name of the father Adam and claimed to live as God's first creature lived before the Fall?

"Since there is nothing worse than our world, Purgatory and Hell do not exist; because man's nature is sinful, and since that nature is acquired on earth, it is here that sin must be purged; man fell because of sensuality, therefore he must infernally exhaust himself in sexual excess to cleanse himself of every vestige of this bestial tendency; then he will be purified, and when he dies he will become one with the Celestial Body; we deny, therefore, that Jesus Christ and His saints come at the hour of death to give solace to the souls of the just, since life is pain and no soul leaves this earth without great pain; and we maintain that as compensation no soul retains any awareness or memory after death of what it loved in its Age. So be it."

These words coming from the darkness surrounding El Señor turned his blood to ice. At first he thought the speaker was one of the three buried there who had been martyred by Nero; then as he looked toward the silent sepulchers of Gaius, Victoricus, and Germanicus, he imagined it must be the very darkness speaking.

"Adam was the first Prince of the world, and when he came into his kingdom he had an intimation of his destiny: Adam, the first commandment of your religion is this: your flesh will sin today so that tomorrow you will be pure of soul and may conquer death. Your body will not be resurrected, but if it has been cleansed by pleasure, your purified soul will unite with God's, and you will be God, and like God your soul will have no memory of the time lived on earth. But if you have not fornicated you will be doomed to Hell, and be reincarnated in the form of a beast until with a beast's instinct you expend what you were unable to vanquish with the intelligence of a man."

As El Señor peered into the shadow, he discerned the figure that spoke these things. He could distinguish the figure from the shadow, but shadowy still was the figure; the face, hands, and body of the unknown were cloaked in a habit dark as the ecclesiastical space (my dream intensifies the shadow); before the trembling, victorious Liege, the speaker affirmed:

"From Lyons to Provence and from Provence to Flanders, men's bodies are inflamed with the Truth, and neither your arms nor your victories will prevail against them. Our succession of homilists is older than your line of princes; we came from Byzantium, roamed through Thrace and Bulgaria, and by unknown roads reached Spain, Aquitaine, and Toulouse; your ancestor Pedro el Católico ordered our homes burned and destroyed our Books of Hours written in the language of the people, and he took for himself the castles of the rich who had joined our crusade of poverty; your ancestor Don Jaime el Conquistador submitted us to the tortures and persecutions of the Catalan and

Aragonese Inquisitions, and of our devastated Provence the troubadour could only sing, 'Would that he who sees you now have seen you once!' You believe that today you have finally defeated us. But I tell you that we shall outlive you. Beneath the cold moonlight in remote forests where your power cannot penetrate, bodies are coupling in cleansing pleasure so that they may reach the heavenly kingdom free from sin. Neither prison nor torture, neither war nor the stake, will prevent the natural union of two bodies. Look there at the altar and see the destiny of your legions: excrement. Look deep into my eyes and you will see the destiny of mine: Heaven. You cannot prevail against the gratifications of an earthly paradise that combines the pleasure of the flesh and the act of mystic ascension. You cannot prevail against the ecstasy that is ours when we enjoy the sexual act as it was practiced by our parents Adam and Eve. Sex as it was before sin; that is our secret. We realize fully our human destiny so that we may free ourselves eternally from our burdens, so we may become souls in a heaven that ignores earth; and in so doing, we also realize our celestial destinies. Your mercenary legions will not prevail against us; you represent the principle of death, and we the principle of procreation; you engender corpses, and we, souls; let us see which multiplies more swiftly from this time on: your dead or our living. You can do nothing. Our free spirit will live on the far shore of night and from there we shall proclaim that sin is nothing but the forgotten name of an impotent thought, and that innocence is the pleasure with which Adam, once he knew himself to be mortal, fulfilled his destiny on earth.''

"Where do you come from?" El Señor managed to ask.

"From nothing . . . *nada*," the shadow replied.

"What is nothing?"

"Our father, Adán."

"Who are you?"

"I am not."

"What do you want?"

"I want not."

"What, then, do you possess, that you show yourself so proud?"

"I possess nothing, which is everything, for in poverty lies absolution from sin. Only the poor can fornicate in a state of grace. Greed, on the other hand, is the true corruption, the final and utter condemnation. Nothing I have told you would be true if it were not done in poverty. Such is the precept of Christ."

"Not his precept but his counsel."

"Christ was not a courtier; he taught by example."

"Can you, a sinner, compare yourself to Christ?"

"I am more like Him than any luxury-dulled Pope."

"The Church has answered you and men like you with two weapons: Franciscan poverty and Dominican discipline."

"The Antichrist in Rome knows very well how to dissemble, and how to use half measures to distract from what should be fully accomplished."

"Regardless of what you say, you could learn something of humility from the Franciscan, for your pride cannot be easily reconciled with your poverty; and from the Dominican you could learn system and order, for your dream is not consistent with action."

"My action is poverty: I would offend the Dominican; my dream is pride: I would not be congenial with the Franciscan."

"Where is it you are going?"

"To absolute freedom."

"And what is that?"

"A man who lives according to his own impulses, who makes no distinction between God and his own person. A man who looks neither ahead nor behind, for a free spirit knows neither before nor after."

"What is your name?"

The specter laughed. "The Nameless Wilderness."

And the specter approached so close that El Señor could feel its warm breath, and a burning hand touched his.

"You thought you had destroyed us today. Be grateful that is not true, for if you defeat us you defeat yourself. You think you have won the battle? Look at the altar; look at the troops that routed us in the name of Rome, the crowned serpent. Look. Fight against the true powers of the earth, not against those of us who promise pleasure and poverty in life and purity and forgetfulness after death. Come with us, with us who have nothing. We are invincible: you can take nothing from us."

"In the name of God, who are you?"

"Try to remember. Ludovico. Do you remember? We shall meet again, Felipe . . ."

And for an instant El Señor could see two glinting green eyes and hear loud laughter; he dropped to his knees behind the column, hoping to close his eyes if they had been open, or open them if everything he had seen had been a dream; the shouting inside the Cathedral grew louder, and mockery and boisterous laughter outstripped even the loathsome odors. El Señor reached out in the darkness; the specter was not there.

The only light that night came from the sparks of clashing blades; the copiously sweating comrades were waging a battle to the death; the day's meager victory had not sufficed to consume their energies; that poor victory, won by mercenary soldiers over heretics who proclaimed the paradoxical divinity of sin and the eventual riches of voluntary poverty, was ending a second time in this pagan celebration of blood and excrement before the altar of the crucified Christ, and, crossing himself, El Señor could believe that the instincts of the Assyrians were everlasting and inherent in the blood of man, that the Whore of Babylon sat upon all thrones and all altars, and that theological benevolence lied when it affirmed that all a soldier need do to reach Heaven—even without the intermediary step of Purgatory—was to perform well the duties demanded by his office: war, war against the true heretics, those who had won the battle against the excommunicants only to profane the Communion altar! War, war against the warriors! But with what arms? I alone? Unarmed battle against the arms that had won the day for Christ the King? I alone? The pierced side of Christianity was bleeding; Jesus, God, and true man, born of the Blessed Mother, the always virgin Mary who had conceived without knowing man: I prayed quietly, Bocanegra. The odor of blood was joined to the stink of excrement, urine, and vomit, and to the clatter of swords, the sound of ciboria rolling in the aisles.

Then they tired; they fell asleep before the altar, along the naves, in the confessionals, the pulpit, behind the shrine, beneath refectory cloths. Only one drunken, humming soldier, crawling on his hands and knees, showed any sign of life. The others seemed dead, as dead as those on the field of battle. With his hands, the crawling soldier shaped a mound of excrement at the feet of the crucified figure on the altar. Did he laugh or cry? No one knows. It was the end of El Señor's vigil. There was no light that night? For El Señor, yes: the excrement shining like gold at the feet of the agonized Christ. The brilliance of that common, anonymous offering disturbed El Señor's secret prayer.

Over and over he repeated a verse from Ecclesiastes, *Omnis Potentatus vita brevis,* and in his own life this night he wished to verify it: gold from the entrails of the earth, excrement from the entrails of man, which of the two gifts was the more worthy in the eyes of the Creator who had created both? Which was more difficult to obtain, to offer, to recompense?

Trembling, sobbing, incapable of distinguishing between what he had seen and what he had dreamed, El Señor left the Cathedral and in this last hour of a long night walked through the empty streets of the conquered city toward the ruined bastions. He climbed to the tower where the Banner of the Blood had been set in pulverized sandstone. He looked out over this Low Country dotted with windmills and sheltered by compact clusters of low woods, soft, undulating flat land stretching beneath the light of a pale moon toward a North Sea whose icy, untamed waves regularly invaded them.

As he left the Cathedral, he had longed for the silent companionship of the moon. But when he saw it he knew again he was incapable of judging whether perhaps the brutal mercenaries of the Upper Danube and the Rhine had intuitively made the maximum, the priceless offering of their blood and waste to God Our Father, incapable of understanding whether the true sacrifice of those soldiers had been made there before the altar or earlier during the battle. He thought of the profaned temple and in that instant he swore to erect another, a temple to the Eucharist, but also a fortress of the Sacrament, a stone chalice that no drunken soldiers could ever profane, the marvel of the centuries, not for its luxury but for an implacable austerity and a stark symmetry whose divine severity would have frightened even the hordes of Attila the Hun, the Scourge of God, and it was those hordes, and that cruel chieftain, who were the ancestors of the barbaric Germans who had today won the day for the Faith.

Standing beside the flag fluttering in the stormy gray breeze of the dying night, looking out toward the windmill-spiked fields of Flanders, there amid the debris of the round fortified tower with no company but the silent moon, El Señor uttered these words, his statement of purpose in founding his inviolable fortress of the Eucharist: Recognizing the many and great beneficences we have received from the Lord Our God and every day receive from Him, and recognizing how He has been called upon to direct and guide our deeds and affairs in His holy service, and to help sustain and maintain these kingdoms within His Holy Faith, which by doctrine and example of the religious servants of God is conserved and augmented, and so that likewise they may pray and intercede before God for us, and for our fathers who came before and those who will follow us, and for the good of our souls, and the continuation of our Royal Estate, I shall erect a vast edifice, rich, holy, decorative, beneficial, the eighth marvel of the world in rank but the first in dignity, a retreat for spiritual and corporeal recreation, not for vain pastimes, but a place where one may devote himself to God, where every day divine praises will be sung with a continual choir, with prayer, alms, silence, study, and letters, to confound and shame all heretics and cruel enemies of the Catholic Church and all the blasphemers who with impiety and tyranny have leveled Thy temples in so many lands. Amen.

And as El Señor spoke this prayer aloud, he removed the Banner of the Blood with his own hands: the campaign would end here, the victory would serve as an example, the mercenaries' armies would penetrate no further into these Low Countries, their villages and crops devastated by fire. Let this example be sufficient; El Señor kissed the ancient banner that had served as the ensign of his father's victories, and in truth he prayed so that his father's wandering soul might hear him: Father, I promised to be worthy of your heritage, to do battle as you had done, to declare my presence in the fires of forts and villages in lands unsubmissive to our power and that of God, and like you to fight and sleep thirty successive days in armor; Father, I have fulfilled my promise, I have paid my debt to you and to your example, now I must pay my debt to God: I shall never again go to war, my blood is weak; I am exhausted, Father, forgive me and understand me, Father: from this time forward, my only battles will be battles of the soul; I have won and lost my last war of arms.

He threw the flag of victory into the moat of the conquered city: a yellow and red bird, it floated an instant upon the ashy waters and then sank to join the armed corpses of the conquered.

"And you, my faithful Bocanegra, what are you dreaming? Where were you today when you escaped my presence? Who wounded you? What do you remember, dog? Could you tell me things, as I have you?"

With no intent of hurting him, El Señor softly patted the dressing covering Bocanegra's wound. The dog howled with pain. In this recollection of danger he returned to the coast, to the black sands.

WHO ARE YOU?

Weary waves caress your bare feet. Gulls skim across the water and you can believe it is their tranquilizing chatter that awakens you. You can also imagine that the warmth of the sand where you lie is that of your own body, that it had awaited you, was held for you alone: the darkest convolution and the most recent wound in your consciousness tell you you have been here before. You touch your burning throat and raise your head from the sand.

First you look close around you: the flotsam of many disasters returns a different gaze, sterile and opaque; only a green bottle, buried in the damp sand and, like you, licked by the sea, shines with something that your hunger and thirst would like to identify as a life of its own. A sealed bottle that may contain something to drink; you realize that the shine you attribute to the bottle originates only in your starving gaze; you pick up the bottle, you turn it, shake it, but it contains no liquid, only something like a twisted whitish root, some repulsive tail, perhaps a twist of tightly rolled paper; weakly, you toss the bottle back into the waves, and again look about you, this time into the distance.

The sun is beginning to set behind the dunes. But on the skyline you perceive a long row of figures passing between you and the sun. Dark outlines, silhouette after silhouette, plodding slowly and silently. Little clouds of dust raised in their passing whirl and disintegrate in the light of the setting sun.

You hear—perhaps you hear—a wordless hymn, guttural and somber. The marchers move with lowered heads as if each of them, even those who are unencumbered, even those who are riding, were carrying a heavy burden. You cannot count them; the procession stretches, uninterrupted, from one extreme of the dunes to the other. Clearly, what you hear is a persistent, rhythmic drumming. You raise your arms and beckon. You shout, and more than greeting, your *Salve* implores help. But no sound leaves your throat. You stand and brush the sand from your body, you run toward the dunes; your feet sink in deep soft sand, you progress with difficulty, you will never be able to make the climb, it seemed so close from the beach, so easy to gain . . .

Sand cascades onto your head, choking you, blinding you, deafening you; you breathe sand. And yet you can see the insects working their hidden tunnels in the dunes, insects that at your stumbling, desperate step skitter like grains of gold in a sieve; filled with gratitude, you are alert to the marvels of the earth; the earth lives, even in the tunnels of the most despicable insects. You do not know how you came here. But an instinct that has been awakened with movement tells you you have been saved and that you should be thankful. Someone shouts to you from the heights of the dune; a dark arm waves to you; a rope strikes your forehead; you hold on with all your strength, and open-mouthed, eyes tightly closed, you are dragged up through the sand. You are exhausted. At the top of the incline, arms seize you and try to pull you to your feet. Each time, you fall again beside the halberds the soldiers have left lying in the sand. Your legs are numb. The procession has halted because of you. The soldiers grumble reprovingly. They hear the sound of a penetrating voice and hesitate no longer. They leave you lying there on the ground, your dry, sand-caked tongue protruding from your mouth, and the caravan renews its route to the rhythm of the drummer.

You watch the figures pass, blurred, reverberating, spectral: fatigue blinds your eyes. Behind the troop of halberdiers follow two officials on horseback, and behind them, many people riding mules laden with coffers and large kettles, wineskins, and strings of onion and pimento. The muleteers drive their animals, whistling through toothless gums, and a garlic sweat glistens on their scarred and barely healed cheeks. You watch the passing parade: barefoot women balancing clay jugs upon their heads; men in straw hats carrying long poles on which are impaled the heads of wild boars; a party of huntsmen leading suspicious dogs; men in hempen sandals, two by two, supporting poles upon their shoulders from which hang spoiled partridges and worm-infested hares; modest palanquins bearing women with protruding eyes and women with deep-set eyes, women with rosy cheeks and women with parchment-dry skin, all breathless from the heat, all fanning themselves with their hands, and even the dry-skinned ones trying to dry with handkerchiefs the perspiration streaming down their faces toward paper-and-parchment-stiff wimples fastened beneath their chins; more elaborate palanquins occupied by men of wise aspect whose eyeglasses slip down their noses or are suspended from black ribbons, men with salt-and-pepper beards and with holes in their slippers; hooded monks intoning the lugubrious hymn you heard from the beach, at last you can decipher the words—Deus fidelium animarum adesto supplicationibus nostris et de animae famulae tuae Joannae Reginae—their shoulders bearing the weight of palanquins carrying priests oppressed by heat and by their own humors of urine and incense; then two skittish horses drawing a leather carriage with closed curtains, and behind that, pulled by six slow-paced horses and accompanied by another guard of halberdiers, the great funeral coach, black and severe, like a vulture on wheels. And inside the coach, bolted to the floor, the coffin, also black, its glass carapace capturing the light of the setting sun like the glittering shells of the insects that live in the sandbanks. You saw them. I want you to hear my story. Listen. Listen and I will see for you.

Behind the funeral coach follows a tortuous, writhing retinue of beggars, contrite, sobbing, swathed in dark rags, their mangy, scabrous hands offering empty soup bowls to the dying sun; at times the most daring run ahead to beg a scrap of the rotten meat and are rewarded with kicks. But they are free to come and go, run ahead, fall behind. Not so another throng encircled by a crossbow-armed guard, painfully dragging themselves forward, women dressed in long, torn silks, hiding their faces behind a bent arm or behind cupped hands, dark men with dark gazes, painfully choking back scraps of a song caught in taut throats, other men with tangled beards and long dirty hair, dressed in rags, in pain, attempting to hide the round yellow patches sewn over their hearts, and in the midst of this multitude, staring at the heavens, a monk humming they must be converted by the eventide, they will hunger like dogs, they will surround the city . . .

And behind the beggars and the captives marches a page dressed all in black and beating on a black velvet-covered drum a slow deliberate rhythm like the sound of the feet and wheels and iron-shod hoofs upon the sand. Black breeches, black leather shoes, black gloves holding black drumsticks: only the page's face is alight, like a golden grape in the midst of so much blackness. Firm, fine skin—you are sure; once you have seen the page you truly see again, your sight no longer clouded by obscuring sound—upturned nose, gray eyes, tattooed lips. He is staring directly ahead. The leather tips of the drumsticks define (or only recapture) the solemn chant floating above the procession, Joannae Reginae, nostrae refrigerii sedem, quietis beatitudinem, luminis claritatem, the overall chant of the procession that competes with and drowns out the secret chant the monk hums amid the captives . . . they will hunger like dogs, they must be converted by the eventide.

You have so feared that someone would ask "Who are you," knowing you cannot answer, that now you do not dare, for fear of another's fear, to ask the same question of the page with the tattooed lips marching to the muted rhythm of the drum. At first, kneeling there in the sand, the sea behind your back, you felt confused, and you watched until the caravan passed you by; then quickly you arose, the long line is disappearing in a cloud of dust, creating the illusion (accentuated by the long, moribund shadows) of a distance that belies time; for a moment, you think you might never again recapture—are you still dreaming on the beach? have you dreamed of another shipwreck, death by drowning, burial in the sea?—the company of that long parade, at once funereal and festive, with its onions, halberds, horses, palanquins, beggars, Arab and Hebrew captives, palanquins, hymns, coffin and drummer.

You rise to your feet and race to catch up with the last figure in the cortege, the black-clad page, who does not turn to look at you, who continues to march to the rhythm of the drum, who is perhaps challenging you to ask "Who are you," knowing that you already know he knows you fear to ask the question and receive the response. You run as if the distance that separates you from the caravan could be measured in time and not in space. You run, but all the while continue to address that part of you you do not know. What a fool you are; it's been centuries since you've seen your face in a mirror; how long has it been since you've seen your twin image? How can you be sure? Perhaps the storm that tossed you upon these shores erased your features, perhaps the corposant burned your skin and the waves tore out your hair, perhaps the sand wounded forever your eyes and lips. Storm and sword; corposant and worms; waves and dust; sand and ax. You extend your seaweed-entangled arms: how can you know what appearance you present to the world, how the world may see you, shipwrecked, orphaned, poor, dear wretch.

The drummer does not turn to look at you, and you do not dare ask him anything. Again you touch his shoulder, but he is indifferent to your appeal. You run before him and his eyes look through you as if you did not exist. You leap, you growl, you fall to your knees, you rise again, you wave your arms wildly before his eyes, but the imperturbable page continues on his way and again the cortege leaves you behind.

Now you run parallel to the procession and the dunes; you run past the drummer, past the Moslems and the Jews, past the beggars and the mounted halberdiers, and in a swift movement, unforeseen by the mounted guard, you leap onto the funeral coach and in that instant glimpse beneath the glass carapace a bed of black silk, cushioned and decorated around all four sides with black brocaded flowers, and you see the bluish figure reclining there: great staring eyes and skin the color of a plum; a prognathic profile with thick parted lips, a medallion upon the silk shirt, a velvet cap; the halberdiers swoop down upon you, seize you by the neck and arms, throw you to the sand, a blow from one of their iron weapons splits your lower lip; you taste your own blood, you smile, idiotically satisfied with this proof of your existence; the preceptor monk of the captives also approaches, gesticulating madly, runs to where you lie in the sand, claims you for his train: "What is your name?" You cannot respond, the monk laughs, what does it matter.

"He will say his name is Santa Fe or Santángel, Bélez or Paternoy, but of course he is a Jewish pig, a convert, he will not admit even that, he will say he is a true Christian, but I can see the face of a heretic Jew, converted, but returned to his faith, I see his hungry dog's face and I say he belongs in my train, we will make him taste the rotted flesh of pig and see whether he likes it or whether it sickens him, I see the face of a convert pig, a false Christian, a Judaizing animal, he stays in my train, in my train . . ."

Until now the beggars had paid no attention to you, surely because you are so like them, but now the monk is calling you pig they pause, they sniff an entertainment, violence, smelling your blood with more acuity than the monk. They wink at one another biliously, they suck their withered gums, shake their lousy heads, point to the diversion, drive their poles into the sand and run to where you lie, prostrate and bleeding, ringed by halberdiers, the zealous monk leaping about you, and over the heads and between the legs and embracing the waists of the soldiers and shouting into the ear of the monk, they stare at you, spit at you, shake their clenched fists at you.

"Who is he?"

"From a wrecked ship, they say."

"No, a heretic, this monk says . . ."

"Hey, you, Santurde, look down on the beach . . ."

"Anything there . . . ?"

"No."

"I say yes."

"I see coffers and bottles and pennants."

"Is the ship's cat on the beach?"

"I say no."

"Any man on the beach?"

"I say no."

"No survivors, man or cat, whatever's down there's ours."

"They say his ship was lost."

"I say we beat him to death."

"Anything's there belongs to him."

"Kill him, I say, fucker. If there's no man or cat survived, it's ours! That's the law."

"They say he's a heretic."

" . . . a pig."

" . . . a captive."

"Who needs another mouth to feed?"

"Who gives a fig if he's a son of Allah or of Moses; we never hear the end of that. Kill him!"

They pull their poles from the sand and brandish them in the air, they stick them between the monk's and the soldiers' arms and legs, guffawing, shrieking toothlessly, spitting, they threaten you, kick you, curse you, as the halberdiers drag you through the sand, the beggars grumble and the monk returns to his flock of prisoners, and you are dragged toward the small, slow-moving carriage with the drawn curtains.

MONOLOGUE OF THE

LADY VOYAGER

"Señor caballero, whoever you may be, please remain quiet, and be grateful. You have gone too far. You hoped to pardon your indiscretion by attributing it to a youth still untaught in respecting another's mystery.

"The mystery of other individuals, señor caballero, is ordinarily grief we neither share not understand.

"Keep silent and listen.

"Do not attempt to draw the curtains and look at me.

"Keep silent and listen . . .

"No! Do not attempt to look at me! I say that for your good more than for my own.

"I do not know who you are or where you are going.

"What I am telling you now will be forgotten the moment we part.

"And that will be true even though you live a thousand years more trying to recall it.

"It would be useless; we voyage only by night; you are unaware of the exception that permitted you to meet us by day; I have always feared that an accident of this nature might be placed in my path; praise God that not a glimmer of light can penetrate this carriage; the curtains are thick, the glass is sealed with lead and painted black; it is a miracle, señor caballero, that one can breathe in here, but I need very little air; that which enters during the day while I rest in the monasteries and the servants clean my carriage is sufficient.

"Light and air. Those who need them are those who still cultivate the deception of their senses. First of all, señor caballero, I shall tell you this: long centuries of exhortation have taught us that we can trust only in our five senses. Ideas flourish and swiftly fade, memories are lost, hopes are never fulfilled, sentiments are inconstant. The senses of smell, touch, hearing, sight, and taste are the only sure proofs of our existence and of the reflected reality of the world. That is what you believe. Do not deny it. I have no need to see you or hear you; but I know that your poor heart is beating at this instant because of the aspiration of your senses. You would like to smell me, touch me, hear me, see, perhaps kiss me . . . But I am not important to you, señor caballero; I interest you only as proof that you yourself exist, that you are here, and are master of your own senses. And if I demonstrated the contrary . . .

"Who are you? I do not know. Who am I? You do not know. But you believe that only your senses can verify each of our identities. In exchange for your senses, in order to conserve them in all their precious distinction—which for you is actually the vain and voracious affirmation that life was created for you, not you for life—you would sacrifice me without a second thought: you continue to believe that the world culminates in you, do not deny it; you continue to believe that you, you yourself, poor señor caballero, are the privilege and the sum of all creation. That is the first thing I want to advise you: abandon that pretense. With me your senses will be useless. You believe you are listening to me and that by listening you can act upon me or against me. Stop for an instant. Don't breathe, for there is no air in this carriage. Don't open your eyes, there is no light. Don't attempt to hear; I am not voicing the words I am directing to you. You do not hear me, you cannot hear anything, no sound can penetrate the sealed glass of this carriage, not even the hymns I have ordered to be sung, not even the drum that announces the anguish of our passage . . .

"We have left our homes and we must pay the price of such prodigious behavior: the home is prodigal only if we abandon it in search of the abandon we are denied by its customs. Exile is marvelous homage to our origins. Oh, yes, señor caballero, I see that you too are traveling without direction. Perhaps we can accompany one another from now on. Time has lost its rhythm; this is the first occasion I have voyaged by day, and that explains two things. That we met by chance. And that now we must continue our wandering until we recapture all the moments lost in the accidental encounter: until night once again comes to an end. The councilman must appear very confused. His duty is to keep time with the hourglass he carries constantly beside his knee (Didn't you see him? He is traveling in a modest palanquin; his eyeglasses slip down his nose), but yesterday instead of falling as usual from the upper into the lower, the sand inverted the process, defied the natural laws and would have filled the upper glass in an hour if the unhappy councilman, who is antagonistic to marvels, had not instantly reversed the hourglass to assure the normality of its measurement.

Normality! As if the origin of the world, the alternation of light and darkness, the death of the grain so that the wheat may grow, the body of Argus and the gaze of the Medusa, the gestation of butterflies and gods, and the miracles of Christ Our Lord were normal. Normality: show me normality, señor caballero, and I will show you an exception to the abnormal order of the universe; show me a normal event and I shall call it, because it is normal, miraculous.

"From that time, as in the beginning, since the councilman reversed the hourglass, we have been governed by the revolutions, appearances, disappearances, and possibly by the immobility of the stars; we cannot know, perhaps the stars explode, are born, live and die like us. but perhaps, too, they are but congealed witnesses of our wanderings and agitations. We cannot control them, señor caballero. With that you will agree. But continue to believe that you can control your senses; you will not attempt to control the waxing and waning of the moon. We can maneuver an hourglass we can hold in our hands; we cannot make the disk of the sun revolve. But now we do not know whether we have lost or gained a day. There is no solution except to await the next sunrise and then renew our routine, approach a monastery, ask for hospitality, spend the day there, leave by night . . .

"But the sun does not penetrate these painted windows of my carriage. I am at the mercy of my servants. We are dependent upon their seeing the sun. I will not be aware of it. I do not want to be. Every dawn we shall come to a different monastery. Swaddled in rags, I shall descend from this carriage and they will lead me to a windowless cell, then to the crypt beneath the earth; then back to the carriage again, always in shadows . . . We must take care, señor caballero; we are at the mercy of their deceit. They can pretend that they have seen the sun. They can take advantage of our constant appetite for darkness. You saw them this morning; they are not people to be trusted. They behave as they do from habit, you see; but habit affects only individuals. I, señor caballero, live by heritage. And that affects the species.

"It is not that they are bad people. On the contrary, they serve me devotedly, beyond even ordinary demands. But they must be weary. We have not paused since we fled from that convent. They must believe I have imposed this march on them as punishment for their mistake. The horses are probably frothing at the mouth. The feet of the muleteers are probably badly wounded. The food has probably spoiled. By now perhaps neither Moors nor Jews, not even the beggars, will accept our hares and partridges. How my poor sheriffs and ladies-in-waiting must be sweating!

"Poor ladies! Permit me to laugh; if you desire, imagine my laughter, for your ears would hear only an indignant howl: poor ladies, indeed! I have been deceived, sir, I have been deceived; we arrived at that convent at dawn; I am in the hands of those who serve me; without them I cannot take a step; it is they who must prepare everything, see that we want for nothing, my son is generous and has placed at my command all that you have seen, a guard of forty-three halberdiers and their officers, a majordomo, a councilman, controllers, doctors, treasurers, servants, wine stewards, a sheriff, eight ladies-in-waiting and fifteen duennas (Oh, señor caballero, permit me to laugh, do not be startled by my laughter), fourteen valets, two silversmiths and their apprentices, eighteen cooks and their scullions; the preceptor monk, and thirty-three captives, the false converts from Mohammed and from Jewry, for in this manner my son El Señor, in the course of my wanderings, assures all the villages in Spain that we are steadfast in our combat, that we are tearing out the root of those accursed beliefs, and thus stills the voices that murmur against us, insinuating that all this filth, pretending false conversion, has placed itself in the councils of the kingdom and there debates and disposes in our name; no, let them all see the tenacity of our persecution of the tenacious infidels and how I amuse myself by leading both Jews and Arabs, who despise one another, for it is commonly known that the Jew steals from the Arab and the Arab kills the Jew, and here all are mixed together and humiliated and without any anticipated end to their afflictions amid muleteers, messengers, rough horsemen, hunters, valets, and pensioners, my thirteen priests and a drummer-and-page; everything you have seen and also someone you have not seen: Barbarica, my Barbarica, my faithful companion, the only woman I allow in my presence; you cannot see her because she is very tiny and as she has a most unpleasant defect she insists upon traveling inside a wicker trunk . . . Señor caballero, what more could one expect of filial gratitude, I who have never asked but one thing, I who willingly would wander these roads alone, bearing my burden on my back, I who without need of this procession would travel from town to town and from cloister to cloister, dressed in sackcloth, begging charity and shelter, contenting myself with the little I could importune: solitude, nakedness, and darkness, by night and by day. I alone, bearing my burden on my back. If I had strength, if it were physically possible . . .

"That is my desire. Balls and gallantries are not for him, or luxuries and childbirth for me. The merriment has ended and we are alone. I ordered burned all the clothing he had touched; I ordered that in the courtyard they make a pyre of our bed, and although first I wished to remain to my death dressed as I was at the moment I learned of his, until my skirts fell from me in shreds and my slippers grew thin as paper and my undergarments came unstitched of their own accord, later I decided to change my clothing one final time and to wear forever this habit of patched and mended rags. But you can see for yourself; they swaddled me in black rags, they do not allow me to see or breathe, and now I am unable even to undress myself. I had wished differently. I wanted only to eat what was indispensable, bread moistened in water, perhaps gruel, very rarely chicken broth. I wanted to sleep on the ground.

"Can all the sordidness possible to humanity, sir, compensate for the vacuum left by death? I wanted sordidness, I lived with sordidness. But since my son insists on it, I am now dependent upon this scrupulous service in my travels. My rules are simple. You would be surprised, you, señor caballero, who seem to wander through the world with no beast of burden to bear your sorrows and without even a rough pair of leather breeches to protect you from the stones and thorns, you would be surprised, I tell you, at the way the most simple dispositions are complicated the moment they are set apart by ceremony. In the end, the ceremony is converted into the substance, and the marrow of the matter becomes of secondary importance.

"Every evening at dusk they transport me to my carriage; they always draw the curtains and seal the doors and windows; they have the horses hitched in pairs; the black coach rolls behind my carriage; the torches we need to light our way are lighted; we travel through the night; every dawn the monks and a few halberdiers approach the nearest monastery and, with humility and authority, ask for shelter against the unbearable sun; as always they convey me, swathed in rags and carried by the soldiers, to a bare room; after me they bring the body of my husband; they prepare the Requiem Mass; they advise me of the hour, the Mass is celebrated; they leave me there at the foot of the catafalque, my only company my faithful Barbarica; again at dusk they come to get us; the voyage is renewed once the obolus has been paid to the monks.

"Let my grief be respected. Let my solitary company with death be respected. Let no woman approach me! None, except Barbarica, who is hardly a woman and who can awaken no passion or jealousy. I hear their footsteps, their women's footsteps, women's voices, rustling taffetas, crackling crinolines, high-pitched laughter, sighs of intrigue; the walls of the convents moan with the voices of love; the hollow walls howl with indecent gratifications; behind the door of every cell some woman weeps and cries out her pleasure . . . Let no woman dare! I tolerate everything, señor caballero, this costly company my son has imposed upon me, the violation of my declared desire to be anonymous, the mockery of my supreme intent of sacrifice: a poor woman, naked and hungry, widowed and solitary, in rags, dragging along the roads her heavy burden wrapped, like herself, in the sackcloth of beggarhood. I accept everything . . . except the presence of a woman. Now he is mine, mine alone, forever.

"The first time I kissed him again, señor caballero, I had to break the seal of lead, the wood, the waxen cloths enveloping him. I could, at last, do what I would with that body. They had been generous and lenient with me. Let no one oppose her in anything, let no one do anything that might cause her discontent; do her will and protect her health, and little by little she herself will be convinced of the necessity for burying the corpse: that is what they murmured with their stupid air of compassion.

"Locked within my castle, I could, at last, do as I wished: part the fur cape, rip the silken shirt (like this, señor caballero, like this), tear the medallion from his chest and the velvet cap from his head; I could remove those brocade breeches (like this, Barbarica, like this) and the rose-colored hose and know whether it was true what was said about him, murmured in bedchambers as well as in anterooms, kitchens, stables, and convents, son mary estoit beau, jeune et fort bien nourry, et luy sembloit qu'il pouvoit beaucoup plus accomplir des oeuvres de nature qu'il n'en faisoit; et d'autre part, il estoit avec beaucoup de jeunes gens et jeune conseil, qui et l'oeuvre luy faisoient et disoient paroles en présens de belles filles, et le ménoient souvent en plussieurs lieux dissoluz . . . Because I had to know whether it was true; I had known him only in bedchambers as black and dark as this carriage, señor caballero, at the time of his choosing and his pleasure, with no warning, with no words, no light, almost without his touching me, for he only looked upon and allowed himself to be seen by the courtesans in innumerable villages and the country girls with whom he exercised his seignorial right; he took me in the dark; he took me to procreate heirs; with me he invoked the ceremony that prohibits to all chaste and Catholic and Spanish couples any delight of sight or touch, or any prelude or prolonged contentment, especially in the case of a royal pair, whose hurried coupling has no reason but to fulfill the strict laws of descendancy; do you understand, señor caballero, how one's senses can be suffocated by such ceremony, how we can be left with no domain but that of incorporeal imagination? Only now that he is dead, I alone can see him, I can see all of him, motionless and subjected entirely to my caprice, night after night in our hollow of cold stone, with no adornment, not even a prie-dieu.

"I sent for the learned gentleman and apothecary Don Pedro del Agua so that he could correctly remove my husband's entrails and all the other organs except the heart, which Señor del Agua himself recommended should be left in the body; he cleansed the cavities and incisions with a brew of aloes, alum, wormwood, caper, and lye that he boiled according to his art, adding the first spirits drawn from the still, strong vinegar, and ground salt. When the body was well cleansed, he left it to dry for eight hours in two bushels of ground salt. Then he completely filled the body cavities with powders of wormwood, rosemary, sweetgum-tree sap, benzoin, alum rock, cumin, water germander, myrrh, lime, thirty twigs of cypress, and all the black balsam the body would hold. When the cavities were filled, Señor del Agua closed them, sewing them with the fellmonger's stitch, and then, except for the head, face, and hands, he anointed the cadaver, using an aspergillum to sprinkle the body with a mixture of distilled substances; turpentine, rosin, benzoin, and acacia. Then he immediately swathed all the anointed portions in bindings saturated in a liquor made of gillyflower, sweetgum-tree sap, wax, mastic, and tragacanth. Then Dr. del Agua left, affirming that my husband would be preserved without suffering the offensive ravages of time. And so I made him mine.

"I have had even the altars removed and have ordered the windows painted black so that every chapel we visit is identical to the service it lends. Even the royal catafalque seemed an offense to the severity I desired, requested, and obtained. The purple mantle that covered his body, the silver ornamentation on the coffin, and the ornate crucifix were a mockery; the four candelabra, an insult; the light on the candles, a flickering offense. They said to me: Señora, in life he loved luxury and gaiety. Remember, you yourself gave birth to a child one evening while a ball was being held in the courtyard of the palace of Brabant; while your husband was pursuing the girls of Flanders you felt the pangs of birth and went to hide in the privy and there we found you and there was born your son, the present Señor. The midwives arrived just in time, for the umbilical cord was strangling the infant, his suffused face was blue with asphyxia and he was bathed in blood. So it was related. Now I shall reject the excesses of such pomp and I shall find motive for life in the spectacle of embalmed death, as before in the act of giving life to my son I nearly knew death; like Rachel, I could proclaim to my son, filius doloris mei, and to the world, the sons of maternal pain are inclined to happiness. I kissed the bare feet of this swathed and spice-filled spoil, my husband, and the silence was sudden and absolute.

"One must close one's ears with wax, señor caballero; one cannot live with one's eyes closed, one's ear involuntarily sharpened, telling oneself that soon one will be hearing the squeaking of the coffin lid, the movement of a tortured body, the hollowness of invisible footsteps, the slow regeneration of features, the crepitating growth of a dead body's hair and nails, the rebirth of the lines erased from the hands of a cadaver that lost them at death as they had acquired them at birth; no, señor caballero, deaden your senses; as I have told you, there is no other solution if one wishes to be alone with the one one loves. Dr. Pedro del Agua went away, and I did not know whether to thank him or curse him for his diligence. I was absolute mistress of an incorruptible body, one that maintained the semblance of life, but one that for that very reason could be mistaken for other men; women would see only a handsome, sleeping man. Don't you hear them? It's the women! Yes, I cursed the science of Señor del Agua; he had restored my husband with the appearance that had been his in life, and with the promise of corporeal incorruptibility; but he had taken from me the one thing I might have called my own: a corrupt cadaver, foul flesh, dust and worms, white bones that belong to me . . . ! Do you understand what I am telling you, señor caballero? Do you know that there are moments that cannot be measured? Moments when everything becomes one: the satisfaction of a fulfilled desire along with its remorse, the simultaneous desire and fear of what was, and the simultaneous terror and longing for what will be? No, perhaps you do not know of what I am speaking. You believe that time always advances. That all is future. You want a future; you cannot imagine yourself without it. You do not want to provide any opportunity to those of us who require that time disintegrate and then retrace its steps until it come to the privileged moment of love and there, only there, stop forever. I embalmed Prince Don Felipe so that, as he looks like life, life may peacefully return to him if my undertaking be fulfilled, if time obey me, move backward, return unconsciously to the moment when I say: Stop, now, never move again, neither forward nor backward, now! Stop! And if that undertaking be frustrated, then I have faith that my husband's resemblance to life will attract to his body another man capable of inhabiting that body, eager to inhabit it, to exchange his poor mortal shell for the immortal figure of my incorruptible husband.

"You look at me with scorn; you believe I am mad. You know how to measure time. I do not. Originally because I felt I was the same; later because I felt I was different. But between before and after, time was forever lost to me. Those only measure time who can remember nothing and who know how to imagine nothing. I say before and after, but I am speaking of that unique instant which is always before and after because it is forever, a forever in perfect union, amorous union. Do you think you feel my hands upon your lips, señor caballero? I laugh, I soothe you, I caress your head. Quickly, Barbarica. Do not try to touch me, señor caballero. In spite of everything, in spite of everything, you see, we each possess a unique body; because they are different they are immediately adversaries. One lifetime is not sufficient to reconcile two bodies born of antagonistic mothers; one must force reality, subject it to his imagination, extend it beyond its ridiculous limits. Soon, Barbarica; he will never return, this is our only opportunity, hurry, run, fly, go, return, little one! I am attempting to breathe to the rhythm of the body, to imitate the body, young man; I always concentrate in this imitation all the lassitude of my own body and all the edge of my mental powers so that you do not encounter any resistance; so that I may hear the other breathing, I myself cease to breathe; that hushed breath will be the first sign of my desire and of the return; if there was the slightest distraction, that sign might escape my notice; you must understand, if I move, I shall not know whether he, whether you, has begun to breathe again. I have stilled all sounds, except that of the chant that is my sorrow and the drum that is the beating of my heart. Embrace me, señor caballero, sleep (you, he) embracing your mortal twin and perhaps this morning (we voyage only by night, I in the sealed carriage, he, you, in the black coach) you will speak in your dreams, and his dream will be different from the two-become-one I have dreamed of.

"In that case, I will have to kill him again, do you understand? Death must, at least, make us equal; dream, even though a shared dream, would once again be the sign of difference, of separation, of movement. Truly dead, with no dreams, inside death, made equal by the total extinction of death, inanimate, identical, neither the dream of death nor the death of dream to separate us and provide a channel for separate desires. An exchange of dreams, señor caballero. Impossible! I shall dream of him. But he will dream of other women. We should be separate again. No, señor caballero, do not draw back. I swear I shall not touch you again. It is not necessary. Did you hear, Barbarica? It is no longer necessary. Lying upon him (him, not you, you no longer feel anything, isn't that true?), I trembled and wept to prevent our dreams from becoming separate and thereby separating us, but I could not prevent it; within the quietude of the two embraced bodies I felt a swift withdrawing, and in order to hold him with me, I caressed his entire body, my husband's reclining body, with my tongue. My tongue tastes of pepper and clove, sir, but also of the worm and aloe.

"I imagined that the only thing I could truly possess was a silhouette. I caressed myself. I thought of the man sleeping beneath my weight in the shared coffin. I felt new. The first wave reaching the first shore. The decision to create a city upon the earth: to raise an empire from the dust. I kissed the eternally parted lips. I imitated that voice: I always imitate it, tomorrow will be today and today will be yesterday; I imitated the immobility of the dust and the stone that confiscate our movements of love, desperation, hatred, and loneliness. I brushed my cheek against the castrated hoarfrost where my husband's sex had beat, the virility I had never seen, neither alive nor dead, for although Dr. del Agua extracted before my view the corruptible viscera, he turned his back and stood between us the moment when he severed the already corrupted sex of my husband. He was other and he was the same. He spoke, he moved, only when I dreamed of him; I was his mistress, his nurse, his wife, forever, but only in the realm of thought. Dr. del Agua's efforts had been in vain; I could have buried my husband because I could possess him only in memory. I thought about this, and I made a decision; I asked Barbarica to lash me with a whip, and she, weeping, beat me. I had thought only of myself, but I was only one branch of a dynastic tree.

"I watched my husband sleep; he was called the Fair, and oh, he was fair. Perhaps sleep was but the ultimate channel for his scandalous presence. A black cat devours you each night, Felipe, father, husband, lover: *La reyna no tenia sano el juyzio para governar.* No, the Queen did not have sound judgment to govern, only to love, love with desperation, in death and beyond death. Our houses are filled with dust, señor caballero, the houses of Castile and Aragon; dust, sound, tactile sensation. Don't you hear those bells that are restored to the wholeness of a solitary dream before they are returned to their essential state of reverberation? *La reyna no tenia sano el juyzio para governar. La reyna* has abdicated in favor of her son, the Benjamin of this tearless Rachel, sure that the son will continue the task of the mother and will govern for death. Don't you hear those hymns announcing what has already happened? Deus fidelium animarum adesto supplicationibus nostris et de animae famulae tua. . . . *La reyna,* the servant of God, has died, señor caballero; she is again one with her poor Prince, ungrateful and faithless in life, grave and constant in death.

"*La reyna* is dead. Nothing more appropriate than that one dead person should care for another. The Queen is now responding to the summons of her son, who has constructed a tomb for his ancestors in the garden of a demolished castle, converted into a dust and plaster plain by ax and pick and hoe, by calcining ovens and great lime basins white as the ancient bones of royalty at this very instant converging upon their final fatherland: the Spanish necropolis. We shall arrive amidst dust, ashes, and storm, we shall listen in shrouded silence to the Responsory for the Dead, the Memento Mei Deus, and the antiphonal Aperite Mihi; we shall recall the ancient stories:

"Our Lord the Prince, may he rest in glory, had played very strenuously at ball for two or three hours in a cool location before he became ill, and without covering himself he had cooled off from the exercise. On the morning of Monday he awakened with a temperature, with the little bell-shaped piece of flesh we call the uvula very thickened and swollen and slack, also the tongue and palate to some degree, so that he had difficulty swallowing his saliva or speaking. They applied the cupping glasses to his back and neck, and with that he felt some relief. His chill came upon him that day, and the doctors were in accord that he should be purged the next day, Tuesday. But, first, he died.

"Ah, señor caballero, you will say it is laughable to drag throughout the whole of Spain the body of a Prince who died of a catarrh and who in life was as cruel and inconstant, as frivolous and as shameless a womanizer as any of those scullions who follow in my train. El Señor my husband was so irrepressible that only yesterday, in spite of my order that in every village we enter the women must remain in their houses, as far removed as possible from the cortege of my handsome husband, fate—as if the Prince Don Felipe still attempted to indulge his appetites from the depths of the penumbra that envelops him—led us to a convent of Hieronymite nuns, who upon our arrival carefully shielded their faces from me, sending as representatives in their veiled stead several miserable, beardless acolytes who lend their services there, and not only at the hour of Holy Mass, you may well imagine!, so that these nuns did not show themselves until after the coffin had been installed in the crypt; and then, fluttering like black butterflies, as cunning and voracious as cats in heat, the nuns swooped down upon my grief, mocked my presence, and, as in life, adored my husband.

"Butterflies? Cats? No, they were daughters of Phorcys and Ceto with the heads of slick serpents; Medusas of penitents' cells; abbesses with stony stares; Circes of sputtering candles; nuns with inflamed eyelids; mystic Graeae with one common eye and one single sharpened fang for all the aberrant multiplicity of their bodies; novices with tangled gray hair; Typhoeuses of the altars; Harpies strangled with their own scapulars; Chimerae sweeping down in concerted attack from the crown of crucifixes to press their parched lips upon the dead lips of my husband; Echidnae exhibiting swollen white breasts of poisonous marble; see them fly, señor caballero, see them kiss, feel, suck, cuddle in the hollow of scraggly wing, part their goats' legs, sink in their lionesses' claws, offer their bitches' bottoms, their damp nostrils quivering and sniffing at the remains of my husband; smell the incense and the fish, señor caballero, the myrrh and the garlic, sense the wax and the sweat, the oil and the urine, now, yes now, let your senses awake and feel what I felt: that not even in death could my husband's body be mine. See the white-coifed flight and the aspiration of yellow claws, hear the sound of spilling rosary beads and splitting sheets: see the black habits engulfing the body that belongs to me! To the convents he so infamously profaned returns the body of my husband, there to be profaned, for there is not a woman in this kingdom who does not prefer the dead caresses of my whoring Prince to the inexperience of a living, beardless acolyte. Pray, nuns; reign, *reyna.*

"We fled from that confusion, from those intolerable contacts; and that was why you chanced to meet us on the road in daylight. Señor caballero; no one will say it is laughable to do what I do: possess a corpse for myself alone, in death if not in life; such was my undertaking and now you see how it was frustrated by the vulgar appetites of my embalmed husband and of those buttocks-waggling nuns; but if not to me that body shall belong to our dynasty; we shall die together, but not our image upon the earth. The perpetual possession of and perpetual homage to the Very High Prince whose body I bring with me is mourning, yes, and is ceremony, but also it is—believe me, I know, I do not deceive myself, they call the ultimate limits of my lucidity madness—play and art and perversion; and there is no personal power, even ours, that can survive if to strength is not added the imagination of evil. This we who possess everything offer to those who have nothing; do you understand me, poor dispossessed soul? Only one who can allow himself the luxury of this love and this spectacle, señor caballero, deserves power. There is no possible alternative. I bequeath to Spain what Spain cannot offer me: the image of death as an inexhaustible and consuming luxury. Give us your lives, your sparse treasures, your strength, your dreams, your sweat, and your honor to keep our pantheon alive. Nothing, poor gentleman, can diminish the power based upon the meaninglessness of death, because only for men does the fatal certainty of death have meaning, and only the improbable illusion of immortality can be called madness.

"It is sad that you will not live as long as I, señor caballero; a great pity that you cannot penetrate my dreams and see me as I see myself, eternally prostrated at the foot of tombs, eternally present at the death of Kings, insanely wandering through the galleries of palaces yet to be constructed, mad, yes, and drunk with grief before a loss that only the combination of rank and madness can support. I see myself, dream of myself, touch myself, señor caballero, wandering from century to century, from castle to castle, from crypt to crypt, mother of all Kings, wife of all Kings, surviving all, finally shut up in a castle in the midst of rain and misty grasslands, mourning another death befallen in sunny lands, the death of another Prince of our degenerate blood; I see myself dry and stooped, tiny and tremulous as a sparrow, dressed like an ancient doll, in a loose gown of torn and yellowed lace, toothless, whispering into indifferent ears: 'Do not forget the last Prince, and may God grant us a sad but not odious memory . . .'

"A true gift does not admit equal recompense. An authentic offering rises above all comparison and all price. My honor and my rank, señor caballero, prevent my accepting anything in exchange which could be considered superior or even equal to my gift: a total, final, incomparable, and uncompensatable crown or body. I am offering my life to death. Death offers me its true life. At first, being born, I believed I was dying, although unknowing I was born. Later, dying, and knowing, I have again been born. This is my gift. This is the unsurpassable offering of my cult. No, my work is not perfect. But it is sufficient. Now rest. You will forget everything I have told you. All my words have been spoken tomorrow. This procession is moving in the opposite direction from that you know how to measure. We came from death: what kind of life could await us at the end of the procession? And now, because of your perverse curiosity, you have joined us. Notwithstanding, let no man speak evil of my largesse. For you, señor caballero, I have a gift also. They are awaiting us, señor caballero, we have an appointment. Yes . . . Yes . . ."

REUNION OF SOUNDS

Silence will never be absolute; this you tell yourself as you listen. Forlornness, yes, possibly; suspected nakedness, that, too; darkness, certainly. But either the isolation of the place or that of forever embraced figures (you say to yourself, señor caballero) seems to convoke that reunion of sound (drum; squeaking carriage wheels; horses; solemn chant, luminis claritatem; the panting of the woman; the distant bursting of waves upon the coast where you awoke this morning, again in another land as unknown as your name) which in the apparent silence (as if it were taking advantage of the exhaustion of your own defenses) builds layer upon layer of its most tenacious, keenest, most resounding insinuations; the silence that surrounds us (señor caballero, she says to you, her head resting upon your knees) is the mask of silence: its person.

You cannot speak; the lips of the lady voyager silence yours, and as she kisses you you are repeating her words, unwillingly you repeat: "Make no mistake, señor caballero; it is my voice, and they are your words issuing from your throat and mouth." You speak in the name of what she, her body resting upon yours, summons. Like her, you are inertia transformed into a conduit for energy; you were found along the road; you had a different destiny; she separates her lips from yours and you feel too-tiny hands upon your features; they seem to be drawing, tracing, the contours of the face that belongs to you but which you have never seen. The fingers are minuscule, but heavy and rough. They seem to hold colors and stones and feathers that they arrange upon your face, as your former face disappears with every stroke of those moist fingertips. The fingernails scrape against your teeth as if filing them. The plump palms pass through your hair, as if spreading a dye, and as they touch your cheeks, those tiny hands create a beard light as a canary's plumage; surprised, you rub your jaw. Those strange fingers, so removed from the voice of the woman who seems remote from it, work upon your former skin, and suddenly the monotonous and changeless rhythm of the drum ceases, only the wail trapped behind the clenched lips of the captive Moslem can be heard; then that chant, too, dies. She warned you; in the silence you can hear your hair and fingernails growing, your features changing; the tutelary lines of your palms are erased, rerouted, reborn.

"My husband's body is mine only in the realm of thought; I give it to you, señor caballero, for you to inhabit, not in the name of my love, but of our power. Such is my offering. You can neither reject it nor make an offering in return."

You are immersed in something you can only call nothingness. In spite of it all, the drum had been a message from the external world, a thread to rescue you from the impenetrable darkness of the carriage; similarly, so was the dislocated Moorish chant seeking flight toward sacred Mecca. The drum was: the beating of a heart (professionless, possessionless señor caballero). The drum was: the heart of death (Didn't I tell you, señor caballero, that Dr. Pedro del Agua extracted all the viscera except the heart?). You were listening all the time, not realizing; and once you realize what you are hearing, it is too late; its unaccustomed sound is replaced by tumultuous presences. Then: pandemonium, babel, clamor, hullabaloo, brouhaha: for the first time since you were thrown inside it—you know neither how nor where, such was the combined menace of the beggars and the halberdiers—the carriage stops.

The door of the carriage opens, or rather, light in a riot of white blades pierces the carriage and a woman's loud wail is heard over the shouts of the crowd and the jabbering gibberish of the astonished halberdiers, who whirl in their tracks, weapons in hand, not knowing whom to attack or whom to defend but instinctively alerted to a danger which because it is intangible is all the more menacing; over the noise of the monks, as incredulous as astounded, running toward the carriage, flapping like windmills in the wind; over the babble of deceitful ladies-in-waiting, who forgetting to maintain their fragile disguises drop their perukes and raise their skirts to reveal twisted, hairy legs; over the song of the beggars, who kneeling around the carriage sing the *Alabado*, praise to the Sacrament, for as the beggars are always closest to the funeral coach they are the first to see the miracle; and over the finally released shouts of the Arab, who had restrained his song: at last, the soul is One, One is the soul, the ancient Averroës died, but not his science!, and over the sound of the Moorish woman, who hides her unveiled face with her hands and croons: the hearts of the fallen reveal a great marvel, to Spain and her realms has come a great evil; the Jews, more circumspect, murmur among themselves: sephirot, sephirot, All emanates from All, and All emanates from One, thirty and two are the roads to Adonai, One is the God, but three are the mothers who give birth to the emanations, three mothers and seven doubles: the Cabala spoke, and hearing them the delirious preceptor monk cried out, I was right, I was right, the Judaizing reverted pig slipped through my thin fingers, he climbed upon the royal carriage, he bewitched Our Most High Queen, he made her prisoner of his philosophy of transformations while I wished to make him prisoner of our truth of unity, the

Infidel transformed himself into a snake and a bird, a unicorn and a cadaver, for the Christian is but an image of the Creator who is One and although the Christian be born, suffer, and die he is always one, one, one, not two, not three, not seven, but one, and scullions drop the rotted hares and run to hide among the squat bushes beside the mountain road, and notables tumble from litters suddenly abandoned by bearers, and clay jars break shattered upon rocks, for here all is confusion and babble and buzz and beside you in the carriage a bundle whitened by the glaring sun of this summer afternoon trembles and hides her face behind a cascade of rags, helped by a chubby-cheeked dwarf who watches you through acrid, puffy eyes, smiling a toothless smile.

The woman orders with a new wail: "Take him! Don't let him escape!"

For you have leapt from the carriage, poor wretch, searching for the gray eyes of the drummer amid the throng of terrified servitors, who look as if they were participating in a hecatomb. Finally the halberdiers find an outlet for their energies and, deathly afraid, prepare to detain you: the miracle glows in the innocence of their eyes. They have not known what to do; they sniffed danger, they heard the woman's voice; they were grateful for the ferociously shouted order; they prepared to fulfill it; but when they saw you they hesitated, dumfounded, as if you were untouchable; only a new order from the woman traveling in the leather carriage has impelled them, terrified, to seize you.

You do not resist. Returning your gaze, you have just seen the only serene eyes in this cortege of madmen. You ignore the beggars who are beginning to kneel around you, trembling, heads lowered, stretching out their hands to touch you as they would a saint, murmuring words soliciting your favor: the same beggars who shortly before wanted to beat you to death in order to steal any remains from your shipwreck.

Two maids lift the woman wrapped as always in the rags hiding her face, and lead her thus veiled to the funeral carriage. The dwarf descends from the leather carriage, tripping and stumbling; she wears a dress of red brocade much too large for her, sleeves turned up, skirts caught up in a thick roll about her waist. The throngs of servants and companions open a respectful path to the invalid and the dwarf; you trail behind them, receiving no such respect.

They pause beside the black coach. A horrendous silence descends. The maids assist their bundle, helping her approach the glass of the coffin fastened to the coach floor. Fleetingly, two slits of eyes glisten through the rags, but now the woman does not cry out. Following the silence there is an incredulous exclamation, and as the beggars had done before, all those present fall to their knees around the funeral coach. They have all seen the same thing. A corpse dressed in the clothing you wore this morning when the waves tossed you upon the shores of the Cabo de los Desastres, clothing that would be unremarkable were it not that it had been ravaged by fire and sea and sand; they say the tattered dun breeches and strawberry-colored doublet cling, still damp, to the dead flesh resting in the coffin of black silk, cushioned, decorated around all four sides with black brocade flowers, beneath a carapace of glass. And upon the face (is the face the same face?) a cloth or mask of garnet and yellow and green and blue feathers; and in the place of the mouth, a circle of spiders. The broken arrows that form the nervure of the mask rest upon the neck, temples, and the forehead of the cadaver no longer that of the Very High Prince and Lord dragged from monastery to monastery by his widow: formerly only the beggars and captives had seen this miracle, now the courtiers and servants of the lady traveler also see it.

And before such convincing evidence everyone begins to stare at you, poor caballero, flogged, dragged through the sand, thrown into the sealed carriage; and as their astonishment is so great they force you to examine yourself, touch the velvet cap that smells of benzoin, the medallion resting on a silken shirt redolent of aloes, to look at the rose-colored hose, and the fur cape still retaining an aroma of clove; amazed, you rub a jaw covered by a new beard you sense is golden. Everyone is kneeling around you, only the rag-swathed Lady sustained by her maids remains standing, while her vast company of halberdiers and notaries, cooks and scullions, sheriff and deceitful ladies, cross themselves and chant prayers of praise, and the Jews murmur: sephtori, sephtori, All is emanation and the world is transformed, and the Arabs grasp the opportunity to praise Allah and to ask themselves whether this portent bodes good or ill for them. The dwarf kneels also; with a grimace of false respect on her chubby face she crosses herself, but when she notices the multicolor stains on her tiny hands she quickly hides them among the folds of her voluminous dress.

Still not revealing her face, the Lady says: "My son will be happy to see you." And she orders her servants: "I want to kiss the feet of the Prince."

And they lower the bundle they hold to your feet and she kisses them and now you alone are standing, the honored caballero who doesn't know his own name or his own face, and fears now never to recover them, and before you, you see the black-clad drummer with the gray eyes and tattooed lips, and from those intently staring eyes and those moving but silent lips you read—a moment before you fall, fainting, stranger to yourself, enemy to yourself, enemy to your new body, overwhelmed by the black invasion of the incomprehensible, your former, although unremembered life, battling against your new and unsought mortal shell—the single message: "*Salve*. We have awaited you."

But as night falls, in this confusion of sounds, mute are the words of the drummer, resonant those of the invalid voyager, the wandering phantom that found you along the way, bring him here, bring him to my carriage, march, march, we shall not stop again, our painful pilgrimage has ended, they are awaiting us, the sepulchers are prepared, sheriff, notary, halberdier, without pause, march, toward the Pantheon of Kings erected by my son El Señor Don Felipe, there we shall find repose, the living and the dead, march, away from the coast toward the high plains, toward the palace constructed from the heart of the mountains, identical to the mountains: to our tombs, all.

THE WORKERS

Where are the rockrose shrubs where we used to shelter our flocks, eh? Martín smiled and sank his hands into the lime basin, glancing at his two companions, who were preoccupied with slaking the lime. Where will they find succor and shelter now in time of storm and wind and snow and all the other misfortunes we know so well? Nuño started toward the lime kilns, and Catilinón said they'd done a good job, and that it would last well. Martín felt the lime burning his arms and withdrew them from the tank.

As they walked, they cleaned their arms and hands on their chests and shirt fronts, passing the day laborers, who were sinking the foundations until they touched solid ground and then throwing the excavated dirt outside the enclosures. It was one o'clock in the afternoon and time to rest and eat. Martín shouted this to the laborers on the crane, as if his voice could be heard in the midst of all the commotion on the platforms and scaffolding.

"Hup!"

"Easy!"

"Pull, now!"

"Hold it, there!"

"Stop!"

"A little over, there!"

"Back!"

"A little more!"

On this very spot there had been a spring that never went dry, Martín smiled again, and beside it the woods that were the only refuge for the animals, winter and summer. Catilinón winked his eye and guffawed. "Ah, but you're in such a state now, my pretty, we'll never have pleasure of you again!" And everyone laughed heartily with him.

All the stone was carved at the quarry; at the work site and in the chapel one could scarcely hear the ringing blows of the hammer. Martín and his friends ate in one of the tile sheds, seated on bricks;

then they bade each other farewell and Martín walked to the quarry; he ran the back of his hand across his mouth and picked up his chisel. The supervisor walked among the workers, repeating with kindness and gentleness the specifications for this particular work, for these lands had never seen its equal and it was difficult for the old shepherds converted into stoneworkers to construct a palace conceived in the mortified imagination of El Señor; as the supervisor continually reminded the workers, El Señor wished to offer to Heaven some noteworthy service for favors and intercessions performed. Round the columns very carefully, said the supervisor, and Martin applied his chisel with care; easy now, smiled the estate master, just two light taps of the hammer, no pit marks, no rose or chip or bump anywhere; so Martín had only to smooth it a bit with fine chisel strokes; in that way it was smooth all over. Martín looked up at the pounding sun, missing the rockrose, the flock, and the spring that never dried either in winter or in summer.

Later he walked to the stream bed that drained the quarry, where several day laborers were cutting stone from the vein and carting it out in hand barrows. Although it was not his work, Martín helped them load the rough-hewn blocks he would later chisel and polish. He nodded to Jerónimo, who was in charge of the quarry forge; better than anyone, this bearded man knew how to sharpen iron tools, how to set the wedges and sheath the iron tools with steel edges to protect them from the ruinous blast furnace. Even so, only yesterday he had been accused of oversharpening the tools. That meant the loss of a day's wages. It doesn't matter, Jerónimo told Martín; we just do our jobs the best we can; the supervisors do theirs by finding defects where there aren't any; they're parasites, that's their condition, and if from time to time they don't criticize some error, soon they themselves would be criticized for not doing anything.

At four-thirty in the afternoon they all ate a plate of chick-peas with salt and oil, and Martín calculated the time. It was midsummer. It was still two months before winter work hours began. Now during the long fatigue of the sun they must resign themselves to their own. From Santa Cruz in May to Santa Cruz in September a man must come to work at six in the morning and work continuously until eleven, and from one in the afternoon until four, and then, as they were now, cease work for a half hour, then return at four-thirty and continue until sunset. But in July the sun never sets, Catilinón said, laughing; he could already see himself in Valladolid with his little pouch full of wages saved to spend through the long, nightless summer, going from eating house to eating house, matching his sure pleasure against his unsure fortune. Martín spat out a mouthful of sour and masticated chick-peas at the lime worker's feet and said that at five ducats every three months he'd be lucky if he got as far as Burgo de Osuna, where every morning the oxen left, pulling their granite-laden carts, and bearded Jerónimo rapped the clownish Catilinón on the head and told him that in addition the oxen were more sure of their food than any rapscallion dreaming of city eating houses, for the beasts had hay and straw and rye and wheat aplenty, and in addition had provisions for two years in advance, and that there was also an order to deliver two thousand bushels of bread annually to the monastery and an equal quantity for any poor that might pass by; but for them? no provision at all when this work was ended, not even if they became the homeless poor, and as for that scamp Cato, he shouldn't get any ideas, he'd be returning to Valladolid exactly as he'd left, to live the same way he had as a child, hanging about under stairways and fighting with the dogs for scraps of food. Well, at least there's scraps, Catilinón answered with another wink, and hunger sharpens your wits, so a man can get by; poulterers throw chicken heads and feathers into the street; butchers slaughter their animals in their shop doorways and let the blood run down the street, and lacking for wine, the blood's not bad watered a little, and there are always pigs running loose, and fishmongers toss what they don't sell into the street. Fishmongers, grumbled Jerónimo, toss what's rotted into the street, what those able won't buy, and you, Catilinón, you're a born fool, bound to die of the Great Pox in cities swarming with madmen delirious from pure hunger, and why can't you just be happy with your work here, Nuño added, at least we'll be eating more than dirt and with luck the end of this job doesn't seem to be anywhere in sight, maybe our sons and even our grandsons will be working on it. And Catilinón wiped a crocodile tear from his eye and said: Give me money, not counsel, and if I'm to be a fool I choose to be foolish like the fool from Perales, who while he was servant in the convent got all the nuns pregnant, and I don't want to end up like Santa Lebrada, you know what happened to her, that sainted rabbit put on her habit and went out to do a good deed, but for all her toil she was boiled in oil, and worse, she was fricasseed, for we're all screwed from the start and alive only by a miracle, for let's see, now, how old was your brother, Martín, when he died, and your father, Jerónimo? and let the shortness of life console and unite us, brothers, and stinking water and damp rooms as well, for either here or in the city we live the same, here or there, a bit of light, a lot of smoke; beasts or men, there's but the one door for us all.

"You ask about my brother," Martín replied. "We were laborers in Navarre, in the kingdom of Aragon. The King promised us justice, the Lieges, too, who so zealously safeguarded justice—but for themselves, only to find more ways to oppress their serfs and pile so many more taxes upon our shoulders, in coin and kind, that several lifetimes wouldn't be long enough to pay. And since my brother was the oldest of the family and couldn't pay the debts we owed to our Liege, and as we'd contracted new debts with some of the villagers not as unfortunate as we were, the Liege demanded the debts he was owed, and he informed my brother that in these lands the Liege could treat his vassals well or badly, according to his whim, and take away their belongings when it pleased him and deprive them even of their names, and there was no King and no statute that could protect them. And as my brother could not pay he took refuge in the church, and the Liege denied him even that asylum, and when he captured him he reminded my brother that we, the poor of the land, had no rights, whereas the Liege had the right to do as he wished, kill us, and choose the manner of our death: hunger, thirst, or cold. And as a warning to the slaves, our Liege ordered my brother killed by hunger and thirst and cold, and in the worst of winter he left him upon a little hillock, naked and surrounded by troops, and after seven days my brother died on that hill— of hunger and thirst and cold. From a distance, we watched him die, and there was nothing we could do. He became like the earth, hungry, thirsty, and cold; he became one with the earth. I fled. I came to Castile. I hired out for this work. No one asked me where I came from. No one cared to know the name of my land. They urgently needed laborers for this construction. The Liege of my land orders death for all who flee. I made myself one of you, exactly like you, and hoped no one would recognize me here.''

"Fighting against the Moors and defending the frontiers, we at least earned the right to abandon our Liege, if we left him our property; thus, from the Liege's chattel we could become the King's villager, and the Liege cannot seize us in royal territory; that's why I came here,'' Nuño said.

"Your land was very far south,'' Martín sighed.

"And yours far to the north,'' smiled Nuño.

"North and south, it doesn't matter,'' murmured Jerónimo. "Our lives have very little value, for the life of a Jew is estimated at two hundred days' salary, and that of a laborer at only one hundred.''

"I say you're all fools,'' laughed Catilinón, "and everything you say is laughable, pointless; you've been more concerned with your dignity than with your life, while others just like you who have been obedient and submissive have courted favor and in the end were freed, even earned their right to be called gentlemen.''

"And do you know what it cost them, churl?'' Martín answered in a rage. "The Liege's right to mount their virgins. Accepting the fact that marriage between two serfs is not permanent and that a family is not even a family—for the father has no authority, since the Liege owns our land, our lives, our honor, and our deaths. Yes, even the serf's corpse belongs to the Liege.''

"Patience and obedience,'' Cato winked cockily, "for those who don't flee or rebel or dispute with their Lords pass from serfs to vassals, from vassals to laborers, from laborers to landholders, and there's always a way to a fortune for the person who knows where to look.''

''And what will your road be, poor Catilinón, for here we all chew the same chick-pea, we all cook with the same measure of oil, and every man of us washes with the same square of Castile soap.''

And cock-of-the-walk Cato crowed: ''A man like me would make a good servant for some high Lord. And a servant sees his Liege mother-naked, and hears him when he shits.''

The old man who tended the forge sighed, rose, and declared: ''When my father came to these lands he was so poor and desperate that he sold himself as a serf to El Señor's father. He had to present himself at the church with a cord around his neck and a maravedi coin on his head to signify his lowly rank. El Señor promised him protection, a job, and land to work. But now the land no longer yields any fruit; we might as well sow in the sea, for the land's going bad on us and God and his saints seem to have fallen asleep; brothers, we'll have eaten up our own livelihood in this construction, and in so doing we'll have dried up the land that once nourished us. We need to think about what's going to happen in the future, and forget what's gone before.''

ALL MY SINS

He sees him kneeling on his prie-dieu, his hands folded upon the velvet armrest and his dog drowsing at his feet. He will spend the morning contemplating the man contemplating the painting.

The painting: Bathed in the luminous pale air of Italian spaces a group of naked men with their backs turned to the viewer are listening to the sermon of the figure standing in front of a small stone temple in the angle of an enormous empty piazza whose rectilinear perspectives fade into a gauzy, greenish, transparent background. Everything in the figure of the orator bespeaks his identity: the sweet nobility of his bearing, the white drapery of his tunic, the admonitory hand with the forefinger pointing toward Heaven; the blend of energy, pain, and resignation upon the face, the straight nose, thin lips, the chestnut-colored beard, the golden highlights in the long hair, the clear forehead, the very fine eyebrows. But something is lacking and something is overdone. The head is not encircled by the traditional halo. And the eyes are not directed toward Heaven as they should be.

El Señor buried his head between his interlocked hands and over and over repeated (each word amplified by the preceding word, because in this crypt the echo would be inevitable): Should anyone say that the formation of the human body is the work of the Devil and that conception in the maternal womb is diabolical, then anathema, anathema, anathema it be.

Thrice he struck himself upon the breast and the mastiff growled uneasily. Blows and growls echo hollowly against the arches, walls, and bare floors. El Señor, coughing, wrapped himself in his cape and repeated the three anathemas.

The painting: The eyes are not directed toward Heaven. Cruel, or elusive, bearing the secret of a different sign, too close or too distant to what they seemed to observe, not visionary as one might expect, not generous, not inclined to sacrifice, unaware of the fatal denouement of the legend, sensual eyes, yes; eyes for the earth, not for Heaven? These eyes stare at the naked men and they are staring too low.

Hidden behind a column in the crypt, Guzmán could have said what El Señor was thinking as he beat his breast; he was thinking he shouldn't be kneeling there examining a painting in order to examine his own conscience, he should be actively employed in hastening the construction that, for one reason or another, was unduly behind schedule. The various processions ordered by El Señor were on the road; the scouts and messengers had reported seeing them approaching the palace, dragging their heavy burdens over bare mountains and wooded mountains, along the coastal roads, stopping at inns, sheltered among the pines, abandoned in mastic-tree thickets, mired down along the highways, but advancing inexorably toward the place appointed by El Señor: the mausoleum of the palace. And here was El Señor, with eyes and energy only for the supposed mystery of an Italian painting.

Even the growling of the dog Bocanegra could be interpreted as a reproach against its master. Hadn't it been he who had dictated unequivocally: Construct with all haste?

The palace: Above and outside on the vast surrounding plain, blocks of granite were piled high. Sixty master quarriers were working the marble, and oxcarts laden with new stones were arriving every moment. Masons, carpenters, smiths, weavers, goldsmiths, and woodworkers had set up their workshops, their taverns, and their huts on the flat field beneath the burning sun, while the original constructions were being raised beside the chestnut grove, the last refuge on plains and mountains devastated by the fury and urgency of building this edifice ordered by El Señor Don Felipe upon his return from the victory against the heretics of Flanders: the ax had felled forever the pine groves that had been intended to shelter the palace against the extremities of summer and winter. It's true, thought Guzmán, that El Señor had said, "The woods will guard against the cold northerly winds of winter, and zephyrs and west winds will cool us in summer." But even more true was the fact that today the stripped lands could offer neither; the good intentions of El Señor and the exigencies of construction had not been compatible. And El Señor, always enclosed in the crypt, was unaware of what had happened.

El Señor coughed; his nose and throat felt very dry. He resisted the temptation to seek a glass of water from the room beside the chapel, preferring to discipline himself, fingering the leather pouch filled with holy relics he wore tied about his neck. And his thirst was soothed by the thought, constantly in his mind, that behind every immediate material expenditure lay the inexhaustible riches of eternal life; he was constructing for the future, yes, but also for salvation, and salvation knows no time; salvation is not just an idea, he murmured, it is another place, the life eternal we must all attain, for men's lives cannot be counted by years but by virtues, and in the next life white hairs do not crown the head of he who has lived longest but he who has lived best; yes, the life eternal that we must all attain, but also an eternity that is mine by both natural and divine right. It is a very small thing to leave behind some tangible evidence of that certainty, this palace dedicated to the Most Holy Sacrament of the Eucharist.

"For doesn't everything testify that eternal life will be mine, my imperfections, but also my persistence by word and deed in being pardoned, the discipline I impose upon myself, rejecting all indulgence of the senses, war, hunt, falconry, carnal love, as well as the construction of the fortress for the Eucharist? I concede my sins, but with greater devotion I concede that he who is not mortified cannot be a Christian Prince, but I know that frailties, expunged with penitence, do not arouse God's ire, not even their memory. Will the life eternal be denied to him who not only fulfills the penitences of all men but who also, because he is the Prince, would deprive his subjects of all hope if in spite of everything he were condemned at the final judgment?"

To know this (he said to himself; or the vassal who was observing him said it for him) was almost to know himself immortal. El Señor rejected this arrogant notion; he looked at the disquieting eyes of that Christ without a halo and murmured: "Confitemur fieri resurrectionem carnis omnis mortuorum."

The painting: The Christ without a halo, standing in the angle formed by the temple walls, looks at the naked men whose backs are turned to the viewer. The arcades of the vast, clean, open piazza are contemporary, characteristic of the new airy architecture of the Italian peninsula; the diligent eye might note small flaws in the painted marble floor, minute cracks, scratches, shoots, and sprouts of grass; the piazza is of the age. But from what age are the scenes in a background lost in the distance of deep perspectives and echoing a remote chorus to the protagonists on the proscenium of this sacred theater—a Christ without an aureole, and a group of naked men? Minute, remote scenes, lost in time, the profound perspectives of this painted space distance those scenes, convert them into remote time.

El Señor flung himself upon the polished granite floor, his arms spread in a cross; and on the back of his cape the yellow embroidered cross recaptured what little luminosity was shed by an altar intricately carved and ornamented to house the monstrance from which this isolated light originates; light shimmers on a jasper plinth shot with golden veins, on columns so fine and hard that no tool, not even the best-tempered steel, had been found that could cut them; they had been cut and polished with diamonds. El Señor's forehead was resting on an icy floor which, like the light, seemed enormously remote from the parched ground and all-pervasive sun overhead; above this crypt and chapel lay dry dust as hot as ashes. At the far end of the extensive sacred space, an uncompleted stairway began an ascent that was to lead to the burning plain overhead. His head pressed against cold granite, feverish images El Señor preferred to forget raced through his mind. And he did forget them, by contemplating the unfinished stairway behind him, and thinking about his immediate duty: to bring this construction to a conclusion, but to avoid the Greek arrogance of an Alexander who ordered that Mount Athos be cut and carved in his own image; here, in Spanish mansions imitating those of Heaven, day and night the same, one might continually engage in the occupation of angels, with continuous prayers one might pray for the health of Princes, the conservation of their estates, one might mitigate divine ire and justly deserved rage against the sins of man; such, in this hour, was the supplication of El Señor, for his mind could not conceive of separation between religious and political affairs, knowing as he did that of all the virtues that regulate human actions the queen of all is prudence; and that among the varieties of prudence, the one that best serves a Prince is politics: St. Basil laments that some defame politics under the improper appellations of artifice and cunning, and never perceive that acts of cunning and of artifice are daughters of the deadly prudence of the flesh, not of the spirit, for from spiritual prudence derives the life and peace of kingdoms. To this peace, now—the cunning of his youth, the artifices of the flesh, the simulations of war, behind him—El Señor aspired in his humble prayer. And what better mark of the union of prudence and politics than to construct a monument, which means, after all, "something to remind"; monumentum dicitur, eo quod moneat mentem?, according to the words of St. Augustine. And this being so, can there be any true monument that does not convert political prudence into religious glory, since no man who takes counsel in this life loses the eternal?

The painting: In the sixth month the angel Gabriel was sent from God unto a city of Galilee, named Nazareth, to a virgin espoused to a man whose name was Joseph, of the house of David; and the virgin's name was Mary. And the angel came in unto her, and said, Hail, thou that art highly favoured, the Lord is with thee. She was troubled at his saying, and the angel said unto her, Fear not, Mary: for thou hast found favour with God. And, behold, thou shalt conceive in thy womb, and bring forth a son, and shalt call his name Jesus. He shall be great, and shall be called the Son of the Highest: and the Lord God shall give unto him the throne of his father David: And he shall reign over the house of Jacob for ever: and of his kingdom there shall be no end.

The palace: The emissaries have traveled throughout the continent commissioning the treasures that, by contrast, will enliven the somber majesty of the palace under construction. Either already obtained or still on the road, waiting in improvised storerooms or about to arrive on beasts of burden, everyone knew that the iron grillwork was forged in Cuenca and the bronze balustrades in Zaragoza; that the gray, white, green, and red marbles were extracted from veins in Spain and Italy; that the bronze altar figures were cast in Florence and those for the mausoleums in Milan; that the candelabra arrived from Flanders, and the censers and crosses from Toledo, and that the altarcloths, surplices, albs, purificators, Rouen and Holland linens, and India silk were embroidered in Portuguese convents. El Señor covered his face with the wounded hand bound in a linen handkerchief embroidered by the Holy Sisters in Alcobaça. The religious paintings had been painted in Brussels and in Colmar, in Ravenna and in Hertogenbosch. And the painting he had spent the morning contemplating had come from Orvieto. People were talking: Hertogenbosch, the evil bosk where the Adamite sects had celebrated their Eucharistic orgies, transforming each body into the altar of Christ and each carnal coupling into redeeming Communion. Orvieto, no one denied it, was the ancient Etruscan Volsinii conquered by the Romans and converted into Urbs Vetus, site of a black and white cathedral, and fatherland to austere, sad, and prolific painters.

The painting: And Joseph also went up from Galilee, out of the city of Nazareth, into Judea, unto the city of David, which is called Bethlehem, to be taxed with Mary his espoused wife, being great with child. And so it was, that, while they were there, the days were accomplished that she should be delivered. And she brought forth her firstborn son, and wrapped him in swaddling clothes, and laid him in a manger; because there was no room for them in the inn. And there were in the same country shepherds abiding in the field, keeping watch over their flock by night. And, lo, the angel of the Lord came upon them, and said unto them, Fear not; for, behold, I bring you good tidings of great joy, which shall be to all people. For unto you this day is born in the city of David a Saviour, which is Christ the Lord. When Herod the king had heard these things, he was exceeding wroth, and sent forth, and slew all the children that were in Bethelem, from two years old and under, but behold, the angel of the Lord appeareth to Joseph in a dream, saying, Arise, and take the young child and his mother, and flee to Egypt. And they were there until the death of Herod: that it might be fulfilled which was spoken of the Lord by the prophet, saying, Out of Egypt have I called my son.

The dog Bocanegra could move his bandaged head with his accustomed nervousness, but not his ears. And perhaps the fresh wound, the roughly stitched flesh, and the pressure of the compress made him doubt his own instincts. Lying by his master's side, he looked toward the nuns' choir loft hidden behind a high iron chancel.

Guzmán was watching from a place of concealment behind a column, counting on the knowledge that the dog was familiar with his scent and fearful of his hand. And behind the intricate grillwork of the choir loft, La Señora will spend many hours watching without being observed. At first the mastiff's muffled growls had disturbed her, but finally she told herself that Bocanegra's fear must be the result of something he had seen rather than fear of anything unseen. Like the dog, La Señora was watching her master, stretched out upon the floor, face down, his arms spread in a cross, his lips murmuring professions of faith, with the light from the altar reflecting on the embroidered cross on his back. Like her husband, La Señora was motionless, but she stood erect, more erect than ever (Guzmán wished to penetrate the invisibility of that chancel), more conscious than ever (because no one was watching her) of the value of a gesture and of the intrinsic dignity of a posture; she was enveloped in shadow, and once again she regretted the fact no one was witnessing her magnificent picture of majestic ire. She, too, was looking at one of the background scenes in the painting.

The painting: Then cometh Jesus from Galilee to Jordan unto John, to be baptized of him. But John forbad him, saying, I have need to be baptized of thee, and comest thou to me? And Jesus answering said unto him, Suffer it to be so now: for thus it becometh us to fulfil all righteousness. Then he suffered him. And Jesus, when he was baptized, went up straightway out of the water: and, lo, the heavens were opened unto him, and he saw the Spirit of God descending like a dove, and lighting upon him: And lo a voice from heaven, saying This is my beloved Son, in whom I am well pleased.

La Señora stroked the bald head of the hawk clinging to her gauntleted wrist, free of its bells and relieved from the heat by a light breakfast of water and the heart of a deer; La Señora herself had fed the bird before coming, as she did every morning, to the choir loft, where she could observe her husband waste another morning—as he always did. But inevitably the moment arrived when the bird of prey, by his natural inclination, began to be uneasy in the darkness. Initially grateful for the shadows that saved him from the burning summer heat, little by little the hawk began to long for the light. La Señora stroked his head and body (Guzmán knew those gestures); the warm, dry skin of the bird suffered in summer; it was necessary to carry him to cool, dark places like these. Such would be her excuse (La Señora kept repeating) if someday the dog or El Señor should find her hidden in the nuns' choir loft.

Guzmán had warned her more than once that it is the nature of the bird to demand spaces where no obstacle is interposed between his rapacious gaze and the desired prey; great open spaces, Señora, where once he has sighted his prey, the hawk can speed toward it like an arrow. La Señora could feel in the palm of her hand the increased pulse in the bird's breast, and she became fearful that his instinct for action would overcome the passivity she demanded, and that yielding to his instinct, the bird would launch itself from its mistress's wrist and believing the darkness infinite would crash against the chapel walls or the iron grillwork and thus be either killed or crippled: Guzmán had warned her.

The painting: And Jesus went into the temple of God, and cast out all them that sold and bought in the temple, and overthrew the tables of the moneychangers and the seats of them that sold doves. And said unto them, It is written, My house shall be called the house of prayer; but you have made it a den of thieves. And to the scribes and Pharisees he said, Woe unto you! for ye shut up the kingdom of heaven against men. Woe unto you, scribes and Pharisees, hypocrites! for ye pay tithe of mint and anise and cummin, and have omitted the weightier matters of the law, justice, judgment, mercy, and faith! Woe unto you! for ye are like unto whited sepulchres, which indeed appear beautiful outward, but are within full of dead men's bones, and of all uncleanness. And to his disciples he said: Think not that I am come to send peace on earth: I came not to send peace, but a sword. For I am come to set a man at variance against his father, and the daughter against her mother, and the daughter-in-law against her mother-in-law. And a man's foes shall be they of his own household. And he that loveth father or mother more than me is not worthy of me. And he that taketh not his cross, and followeth after me, is not worthy of me. He that findeth his life shall lose it; and he that loseth his life for my sake shall find it.

As she felt that desperate throbbing, La Señora covered the bird of prey's head with the black hood, turned from the iron grillwork, the altar, and the painting, and accentuating the disparity between her shameful vigil and her lordly hauteur, slowly and silently, almost on tiptoe, her head held high, she climbed the spiral stairway and emerged into the blinding light of the flat ground where blocks of granite, boards, and tools were stacked.

The palace: The crypts, the chapel, and the choir loft were completed, and alongside them extended the nuns' cloister, El Señor's bedchamber, and a bare patio where stone arcades communicated with other rooms, which were in turn to communicate with the church proper, as yet not built. But in each room a double window was already installed—one stained glass, one solid like a door—designed to enable one to hear Mass from one's bed, if necessary, and to attend services apart from the religious community.

But until the plan was completed, to return to the cloister and her own room, La Señora, choosing not to pass through the chapel itself and ascend the monumental but still unfinished stone stairway, had to make a complete circle around the chapel, beneath the burning sun, through the construction and materials (and worse, in view of the workers), always with the hawk poised upon the greasy gauntlet and fondled by a pale hand; no one was aware what delight the woman derived from that tumultuous throbbing, from possessing such a fine bird, from that good hawk body—more flesh than feather—whose pulsing manifested the desire to fly, bells jingling, announcing his rapacious hunger, his consuming desire to swoop down upon his prey, talons sinking so deep and sure that not even the fiercest boar could free himself from that grip.

Every morning she would return to the chapel, accompanying from a distance the pain and professions of faith of her husband, El Señor. She would stroke the bald, hot, throbbing hawk. From the corner of her eye she would look at the painting brought (it was said) from Orvieto.

The painting: The naked men turn their backs to El Señor and La Señora to look at the Christ; El Señor looks at the direction of Christ's gaze and La Señora looks at the small, tight buttocks of the men. And Guzmán will look at his masters, who are looking at the painting. Disturbed, he will glance up toward the painting; the painting is looking at him.

Every morning, La Señora would return to her rooms, holding the bird, unaware that anyone might suspect the sensual delight that caressing the hawk's pulsing body afforded her. Lost in her pleasure, La Señora paid no attention to the palace laborers.

Martín, bent almost double beneath the weight of the stones, paused with his loaded hand barrow. He licked the sweat rolling down his temples and cheeks, mixed with the dust that powdered his eyelashes. Once again he saw the mirage seeming to float over the flat reverberating ground: the erect woman, her pace swift but deliberate, so firm and sure she seemed not to touch the ground, dressed entirely in black velvet, farthingale belling, the outer skirt dragging through the dust, the tiny feet barely visible, lace appearing and disappearing with that subtle, incorporeal movement, one hand pressed to her waist, the other extended to support the hooded hawk upon its perch on the greasy gauntlet, red-jeweled rings absorbing the unbearable heat of the sun in their bloody coolness, face framed by the high white wimple . . . Droplets of sweat stood out on La Señora's forehead; she withdrew the hand from her waist to wave away the flies, and entered the palace.

For a long while Martín stood doubled beneath the weight of the stones, captured by that vision, at the same time imagining his own rough and powerful body, tan and hairy, shirt open to the navel and stained with sweat, his square face shaved only on Sundays, his hands tough as pigskin. Then he shook his head and continued on his way.

The painting: And seeing the multitudes, he went up into a mountain; and when he was set, his disciples came unto him: And he opened his mouth, and taught them, saying, Blessed are the poor in spirit: for theirs is the kingdom of heaven. Blessed are the meek: for they shall inherit the earth. Blessed are they that mourn: for they shall be comforted. Blessed are they which do hunger and thirst after righteousness: for they shall be filled. Blessed are they which are persecuted for righteousness' sake: for theirs is the kingdom of heaven. No man can serve two masters. Ye cannot serve God and mammon.

El Señor, lying face down, arms opened, sobbed; he raised his head to look at that minute scene, only a remote echo in the great painting in the chapel; and believing himself alone, he cried out: Tibi soli peccavi et malum coram te feci; laborabor in gemitu meo, lavabo per singulas noctes lectum meum; recogitabo tibi omnes meos in amaritudine animae meae . . .

The painting: And as they came out, they found a man of Cyrene, Simon by name: him they compelled to bear his cross. And when they were come unto a place called Golgotha, that is to say, a place of a skull. They gave him vinegar to drink mingled with gall; and when he had tasted thereof, he would not drink. And they crucified him, and parted his garments, casting lots; And sitting down they watched him there; And set up over his head his accusation written, THIS IS JESUS THE KING OF THE JEWS. And the people stood beholding. And the rulers also with them derided him, saying, He saved others; let him save himself, if he be Christ, the chosen of God.

With no intent of hurting him, El Señor softly patted the dressing covering the wound of the mastiff Bocanegra. The dog growled, and sniffed at his torturer. Then Guzmán moved forward from the concealment of the column, and as he knew he would, the mastiff ceased his growling, retreated into silent fear, and with complete naturalness the vassal walked to the prostrated figure, stopped, leaned over, and, barely touching El Señor's outspread arms, murmured that such penitence was harmful to his health. El Señor closed his eyes; he felt utterly defeated, and at the same time aware of a voracious appetite.

He allowed Guzmán to help him to his feet and then lead him to the bedchamber constructed beside the chapel so as to enable him to attend services without moving from his bed, as well as to be able to pass directly (as now) from the chapel to the bedchamber, unseen by anyone.

Aided by his servant and followed by his dog, El Señor, lips parted, eyes expressionless, breathed heavily through his mouth; there was a finger's breadth between the upper and the lower lip. He complained of an intense pain that originated in his brain, but spread throughout his entire body; as he walked clumsily to rest against the doorframe of his bedchamber, he mumbled something Guzmán could not understand.

The painting: Now from the sixth hour there was darkness over all the earth until the ninth hour. And the sun was darkened, and the veil of the temple was rent in the midst. And when Jesus had cried with a loud voice, he said, Father, into thy hands I commend my spirit; and having said thus, he gave up the ghost.

Nevertheless, Guzmán pretended he understood; he nodded obsequiously, led his master to the bed, removed his cape and slippers, loosened his doublet, and unfastened his ruff.

El Señor, his mouth agape, looked about the room; he was lying upon black sheets beneath a black canopy in a chamber whose three walls were covered by black drapes and the fourth by an enormous map of dark and ocher hues; the only light was that of a chandelier so high that to light and extinguish it one needed a long pole with a crook on the end. Guzmán approached with a flask of vinegar in one hand and a small coffer in the other. El Señor caught himself with his mouth open; he tried to close it. He felt as if he were choking; Guzmán rubbed El Señor's hairless white chest with vinegar, rattling the pouch of holy relics tied around El Señor's neck; El Señor tried to breathe with his lips closed and to open his hand and move his fingers to reach out for the coffer. Guzmán would not speak another word; he never spoke except when absolutely necessary. At the back of El Señor's palate, the adenoids were atrophying and hardening more every day. Again his lips parted, and he tried to move his fingers.

With vinegar-damp hands, Guzmán prized open his master's fist; then he chose one ring after another from the coffer, placing on El Señor's ring finger the gold-set stone intended to prevent bleeding, and on the other fingers and thumb English bone rings to ward off cramps and spasms, and again on the ring finger, above the first ring, the most miraculous of all: a diamond ring in which was embedded a hair and a tooth of St. Peter; in the palm of that crippled hand he placed the blue stone that was supposed to cure gout; in the other he placed the green stone that would eventually cure the French malady.

The painting: And he took bread, and gave thanks, and brake it, and gave unto them, saying, This is my body which is given for you: this do in remembrance of me. Likewise also the cup after supper, saying, This cup is the new testament in my blood, which is shed for you. But, behold, the hand of him that betrayeth me is with me on the table, and dippeth with me in the dish.

For almost an hour El Señor gasped and trembled while his servant discreetly stood in the farthest and darkest part of the room. The dog had stretched out beneath the bed. Perhaps El Señor's repose was like that of an overly active dream; perhaps a waking nightmare is more fatiguing than all the happy and cruel activity of a war, either mercenary or holy; perhaps . . . I will not drink henceforth of this fruit of the vine, until that day when I drink it new in my father's kingdom. El Señor spoke in dead nasal tones; he demanded something to eat, immediately. Guzmán halved a melon lying upon a copper platter. El Señor sat up and began to devour it; Guzmán, after bowing with obeisance, rested one knee against the edge of the bed.

Their glances met. El Señor spit the seeds on the floor; Guzmán's nimble fingers searched through his master's thin oily hair; occasionally the fingers found what they sought, the louse was cracked between his fingernails and thrown on the cool tile floor as the master had thrown the melon seeds.

The palace: Patios would be added to patios, rooms for monks, servants, and troops would be added to the bedchambers of the original rectangle. A granite quadrangle, as wide as it was long, would be the center of the palace, conceived of as a Roman camp, severe and symmetrical; and in that center would rise the great basilica; the exterior would be a straight, severe castle with a bastion on each corner; within there would be a single nave, enormous, empty; and all four sides would be enclosed by a strong wall, so that from a distance the palace would look like a fortress, its straight lines fading into the plain and the infinite horizon without a single concession to caprice, carved like one solid piece of gray granite and set upon a polished stone base whose snow-white contrast would lend an even more somber air to the whole.

She could envision it from the double window that would someday overlook the palace garden, but which for the time being overlooked only the expanse of heavy, distant plains bound by granite mountains whitened like the bones of a bull beneath the double assault of deforestation and sun; like a mountain, this palace would be wrested from the mountain. And as she envisioned it, she repeated what El Señor had said on one occasion when he stated his wishes; he had never again had to repeat the words: with all haste construct a palace and monastery that will be both a Fortress of the Most Holy Sacrament of the Eucharist and the Necropolis of Princes. No ostentation, no celebration, no swerving from that implacably austere project. He had conceived it; now the army of workmen were executing his concept.

La Señora, staring at the monotonous plain from her room, was imagining with some alarm that her husband's wishes finally would be fulfilled; and she confessed to herself that secretly she had always believed, the world being what it is, that some chance, some unpredictable whim, or a very predictable weakening of will, would impose upon El Señor's master plan a few—not many, but all the more delectable for being few—concessions to the pleasures of the senses.

"Señor, may the shepherds come beneath my windows to shear their sheep, and perhaps to sing me a few songs?"

"We are not conducting a fair here, but a perpetual Mass for the Dead that will last until the end of time."

"Some baths, then, Señor . . ."

"The bath is an Arabic custom and will have no place in my palace. Follow the example of my grandmother, who wore the same footwear for so long that when she died it had to be pried off forcibly."

"Señor, the greatest of the Catholic kings, Charlemagne, accepted from the infidel Caliph Harun al-Rashid, without diminution of his Christian faith, gifts of silk, candelabra, perfume, slaves, balms, a marble chess set, an enormous campaign tent with multicolored curtains, and a clepsydra that marked the hours by dropping little bronze pellets into a basin . . ."

"Well, here there shall be no treasures but the relics of Our Saviour I have ordered to be brought here: a hair from His most holy head, or perhaps His beard, within a rich inlay, for if He said He loved the hairs of our heads, we should die for one hair of His; and eleven thorns from His crown, a treasure that would enrich eleven worlds; just to hear of such treasures pierces the soul, what will the actual seeing of them be! God's goodness, He who suffered thorns for me, and I not one for Him; and a piece of the rope that bound the hands or throat of that most innocent Lamb."

"Señor, I cannot imagine power without luxury, and the Byzantine court would be forgotten were it not for its artificial lions, its trilling mechanical birds, and its throne that rose into the air; and the Emperor Frederick was not in the least impious when he accepted from the Sultan of Damascus a gift of bejeweled astral bodies, moved by hidden mechanisms, that described their course upon a background of black velvet . . ."

"When one begins in that direction, Señora, he ends like Pope John, converting the pontifical palace into a brothel, castrating a cardinal, toasting the health of the Devil, and invoking the aid of Jupiter and Venus in a night spent playing at dice."

"A great King always wishes to be the wonder of the world."

"My asceticism will be the wonder of this age, Señora, and of ages to come, for when we are dead this palace will be dedicated throughout the ages to a perpetual Mass for the Dead, and every moment of the day and night there will be a pair of priests before the Most Sacred Sacrament of the altar, praying to God for my soul and the souls of my dead, two different priests every two hours every day; twenty-four priests daily executing a task as savory as prayer is not a heavy burden. This will be the disposition of my testament. The wonder of the world, Señora? Simon, that famous prince of the Maccabeans, wished to make eternal the memory of his dead brother, the prince Jonathan; to do this he ordered a sepulcher to be built beside the sea, so prominent that its funereal memorials could be seen from every ship, for it seemed to him that whatever he could tell of his brother's excellent virtues would be less than what strangers would learn, or what that mausoleum might mutely preach. Thus, I, Señora; except that it will not be sailors who see this funereal sepulcher, but pilgrims who venture to our high plain; and always, from Heaven, God and His angels. I want, I ask no other testimony.''

"You are speaking of the dead; I ask only a small adornment for myself . . . for the living . . ."

"The only adornment in this house will be the orb and the cross, the symbol of Christianity and of its triumph over pagan styles. Our faith is above any style. Here everything will be consistent. Somber. So that anyone who comes to this palace will say: 'When you have seen one column of it, you have seen them all.' ''

"Señor, Señor, have mercy; do not reproach my wish for beauty; ever since I was a child I have dreamed of having a tiny portion of that beauty created with trees and fountains and colored stone and delightful vistas that the Arab inhabitants left in your land from another time.''

"It is easy to see, Isabel, that you are English, or you would not yield in this manner to the temptations of the Infidel. We have spilled our blood in reconquering our Spanish land.''

"It was theirs, Señor, the Arabs filled it with gardens and fountains and mosques where before there was nothing; you conquered something foreign, Señor. . . ''

"Quiet, woman, you do not know what you are saying; you are denying the course of our destiny, which is to purify all Spain of the Infidel scourge, to eradicate it, mutilate its members, to be left alone finally with our humiliated, but pure, bones. Do you want to know what the only concession to sinful senses in this entire fortress will be? Look, then, atop this edifice I am constructing, the eighth wonder of the world, and you will see it crowned by golden spheres. In this way, as did my forebears upon reconquering the cities of the Moors, I will commemorate our victories for the Faith: see in those spheres the heads of the Infidel exposed to God's wrath.''

La Señora gazed sadly into the gathering dusk. She smelled something intolerably offensive; the offense was converted into an even more intolerable suspicion: she smelled the burned flesh, fingernails, and hair of a man.

The painting: And Jesus being full of the Holy Ghost returned from Jordan, and was led by the Spirit into the wilderness, being forty days tempted of the devil. And in those days he did eat nothing: and when they were ended, he afterward hungered. And the devil said unto him; If thou be the Son of God, command this stone that it be made bread. And Jesus answered him, saying, It is written, That man shall not live by bread alone.

Pressing his hands to his temples, El Señor asked: What is going on outside? Nothing, Guzmán replied; some miserable twenty-four-year-old youth was involved all summer in a vile affair with two thirteen-year-old boys, just here, in the rockrose thicket below your kitchen, and today he is being burned alive beside the stable for his wicked crime. Yesterday he demonstrated great repentance and regret; he said that to be pardoned even the angels must weep for their sins, and that his was the sin of angels, for he had committed one more diabolical that he would never confess. He said it, Señor, as if he wished to defy his punishment as much as the judges' curiosity, and he was condemned for what was known as well as that still unknown. You yourself signed the death sentence, do you not remember?

The painting: And Pilate, when he had called together the chief priests and the rulers and the people, said unto them, Ye have brought this man unto me, as one that perverteth the people: and behold, I having examined him before you, have found no fault in this man touching those things whereof ye accuse him: nothing worthy of death is done unto him. I will therefore chastise him, and release him. For of necessity he must release one unto them at the feast. And they cried out all at once, saying, Away with this man, and release unto us Barabbas: Who for a certain sedition made in the city, and for murder, was cast into prison. Pilate therefore, willing to release Jesus, spake again to them. But they cried, saying, Crucify him, crucify him. When Pilate saw that he could prevail nothing, but that rather a tumult was made, he took water, and washed his hands before the multitude, saying, I am innocent of the blood of this just person: see ye to it. Then answered all the people, and said, His blood be on us, and on our children.

El Señor looked at his cramped fingers, closed his eyes and said in a slightly stronger voice that the boy was right; yes, the saints, the very elect of God, wept, because they knew that not even angels may be pardoned without tears and without penitence; doubtlessly, God has special scales to weigh and to expiate the transgressions of all those who are inferior to Him; some for the crimes and punishments of men, and others for those of angels, whose codes we do not know; but one thing is true: only God is free; therefore, everything inferior to Him, not being free, sins, even a King or a seraph; yes, they sin by their mere imperfection.

He buried himself deeper in his bed and said that the clamor of the saints could be heard and they said: I have sinned only against You and before You I have done evil; therefore, there is no such thing as a secret crime; God is witness to evil even when it is but imagined; God is impassioned against sin, for all that is not God is culpable imperfection. For that reason, Guzmán, we have all sinned before God; for that reason, we will all be guilty before the divine tribunal. You ask me: Who has not thought evil? and you will have partially proved my assertion; I shall answer you: What living thing is not guilty simply by the mere fact that he exists? and I shall have proved it fully. Is it right that on earth we are innocent only if we have not been apprehended by law and judged by the courts? I have suffered in my lamentations and every night I have bathed my bed with tears; El Señor added, his head bowed, for You I shall review all my years and all my sins in the bitter solitude of my soul. All my years. And all my sins.

He tried to rise from the bed, but the pain in his swollen foot impeded him.

"Guzmán. Have I still time to pardon him?"

The servant shook his head. No, it was too late. The boy's body had been consumed by flames.

"It is true, Señor; we all sin against God; but only God has the right to judge the crimes of the mind, or, if it please you, the crime of existing. But it is the right of power to judge the crime of acts."

All my sins, murmured the man lying helpless in the bed. I shall be better tomorrow, he said to himself, tomorrow I shall be better.

"Need I remind you what day tomorrow is?"

El Señor shook his head and waved his vassal away.

"God be praised."

"God be glorified."

The palace: Along the only nave of the chapel, one wall interrupted by the door leading to El Señor's bedchamber and the other by the elaborate grillwork of the nuns' choir loft, await the open tombs, the rows of porphyry, jasper, and marble coffins, open, their heavy stone slabs resting against the tomb markers and pyramidal bases, each inscribed with the name of one of El Señor's ancestors, an Ordoño, a Ramiro, the Alfonsos and the Urracas, a Pedro and a Jaime, the Blancas and Leonors, the Sanchos and Fernandos, each slab and each marker engraved with one simple inscription beneath the name and the dates of birth and death, a different inscription for each body, many bodies reproduced in supine marble effigy, all the inscriptions linked together by a single thought: sin and contrition, sin and death. HE DID NOT DO THE GOOD HE DESIRED, RATHER THE EVIL HE DID NOT WISH, *Manifest were the works of his flesh, which were fornication, lewdness, and lust,* Peccatum non Tollitur Nisi Lacrymis et Paenitentia; Nec Angelus Potest, Nec Archangelus; *In his members was discovered another decree which struggled against the decree of reason; He was prisoner to the decree of sin, which was in his members;* he who placed all his happiness in music and vain and lascivious songs, in roaming, games, hunts, galas, riches, authority, vengeance, in the esteem of others— see him now: that brief appetite converted into eternal, irremediable rage, implacable dust; SWEET UNFORTUNATE QUEEN FREED BY DEATH FROM THE PRISON OF EARTHLY DEATH; The Sins of the Throne Are Seldom Single, Thus the Most Difficult to Forgive; O GOD WHO TAKETH AWAY FOR BETTERMENT; he was example of bad habits, bad customs, and sinister advice, those qualities that clothe the souls of the wretched, who for their pride are lions; for vengeance, tigers; for lust, mules, horses, pigs; for tyranny, fish; for vainglory, peacocks; for sagacity and diabolical cunning, vixens; for gluttony, monkeys and wolves; for insensitivity and malice, asses; for simple-mindedness, sheep; for mischief, goats; vainglory, and a brief life; DEATH RAN CLOSE BEHIND THE PAGES OF HIS HOPES TO MAKE OF THEM ASHES. And at the rear of the nave ascended the interminable and unterminated steps that led to the plain above, for by that broad stairway were to descend all the bodies at this moment advancing through mourning towns, through cities and cathedrals, escorted by priests, entire convents, and chapters of all orders. And only when they had arrived and were reposing in their tombs would the heavy slabs be lowered upon them; and the ingress from the plain to stairway, conceived only for this ceremony, would be forever sealed, along with the crypt, the nuns' choir loft, the altar of gold and jasper, the painting brought (it was said) from Orvieto, and the bedchamber of El Señor.

The painting: While we spake these things unto the disciples of John, behold there came a certain ruler, and worshipped him, saying, My daughter is even now dead: but come and lay thy hand upon her, and she shall live. And Jesus arose, and followed him, and so did his disciples. And when Jesus came into the ruler's house, and saw the minstrels and the people making a noise, he said unto them, Give place: for the maid is not dead, but sleepeth. And they laughed him to scorn. But when the people were put forth, he went in, and took her by the hand, and the maid arose. And the fame hereof went abroad into all that land.

Outside, the July sun never tired. There're enough people here to populate a city, said Martín, shrugging his shoulders, shortly after the dispersal of the throng that had gathered to witness the boy's death beside the stables: some were unloading iron ingots, some were rolling and plaiting esparto and cáñamo fibers into ropes and cables, cords and swirls; farther away an army of sawyers and carpenters was working, and closer by, beneath their awnings, upholsterers silently worked on their satin cloths, skeins of silk, fringe and cord. How the sun lingered above this desert-like earth! Martín looked at the earth as he drove the wedges into the wall of the quarry, trying to divine the hidden gardens and concealed rivulets in this fierce plain: leagues and leagues of rock, and such pale gold light that one could see every puff of dust for miles.

Jerónimo, Martín said to the bearded man pumping the bellows and then at intervals arranging the chain he had forged during the day, have you seen that woman? And the smith answered him with another question: Martín, do you know who the boy was they just burned alive?

ON THE BEACH

Summer storm clouds gather to the north of the beach on the horizon where the land meets the sea; and along the shoreline, at the meeting of sand and sea, a young man lies face down, his arms spread in a cross.

High on the dunes, watching eyes discern upon the naked body a sign they wished, and at the same time did not wish, to see: a blood-red cross between the shoulder blades.

THERE IS A CLOCK
THAT DOES NOT STRIKE

So El Señor, very early in the morning, and with great stealth, arose and threw on a heavy black cape. He was so practiced, so skillful in silently slipping from the bedchamber, crossing the chapel—without looking toward the painting brought from Orvieto—and reaching the foot of the great stairs, that this morning the dog Bocanegra, usually so alert, did not even stretch in his sleep as his master left, but continued to lie at the foot of the bed, head bandaged, a persistent smear of black coastal sand next to the wound and on his paws.

But this particular morning (El Señor has asked Guzmán to be sure to remind him what day it is; a boy has been burned yesterday at the stable beside the palace construction; the work of the palace itself is unduly delayed, while funeral carriages struggle through time and space to attend their rendezvous; Jerónimo has been punished for over-sharpening the tools; Martín has watched La Señora pass, the hawk upon her wrist; a young man lies face down, arms spread in a cross, upon the black sand) El Señor, before leaving his chamber, stops an instant with the cape in his hands and stares at the dog, wondering why Bocanegra slept so soundly. But he gave no import, no reply, to his own question. He preferred instead to have this fresh morning for himself, to enjoy the coolness of the high plains that compensated for the fiery blasts of the previous day, so removed from the grinding heat that would follow in a few hours. He left the bedchamber, crossed through the chapel, and reached the foot of the stairway.

What were considerations of the unusual behavior of a dog compared to those raised by this tremulous proximity to the uncompleted stone stairway? Looking up, he could count the thirty-three broad steps that connected the crypt to the flat ground of what had been the shepherds' grove. Broad stairs, well polished, smooth. What worker had polished them? What did he look like? What were his dreams? Where did these stairs lead? He pressed a hand to his brow: outside, to the plain, to the whirling, proliferating, sweating world; to an encounter with the laborer who had constructed them. He knew that well enough. Why did he always doubt it? Why did he always rise before dawn to see with his own eyes the state of this stairway conceived with the single purpose of accommodating the procession of seignorial coffins and the corteges that would accompany them to their final resting place? Why were his orders not fulfilled? Were they constructing with all haste? And why did he himself not dare ascend those stairs, preferring to look at them from below before beginning his long daily routine of prayer, reflection, and penitence?

Why did he not dare take the first step? A lost sensation, a fire in his blood, forgotten during the imperceptible passage from youth to maturity, was born again in his loins and breast, raced through his legs, shone in the luminous excitement of a rejuvenated face. He raised one foot to climb the first step.

He made a rapid calculation; it was still not four o'clock in the morning. First he looked at his own black slipper suspended in air. Then he stared up toward the top of the stairway. A night as black as his slipper returned his gaze. He dared; he took the first step; he placed his right foot upon the first stair and immediately the cool night turned to rosy-fingered dawn; he took the second step, he placed his left foot upon the first stair; the dawn dissipated into warm melting light, morning. At that moment El Señor's flesh, already exalted by his eagerness to achieve the next step, prickled involuntarily, and for an instant he could not distinguish between the shiver of pleasure and the shudder of fear.

Bocanegra ran from the bedchamber through the chapel toward the stairway; the thought flashed through El Señor's mind that perhaps his momentary doubt before the sleeping dog had, in some way, stirred the depths of his dream. But now a ferocious dog, sharp teeth bared, jaws slavering, was racing forward as if his hour to defend his master had at last arrived; he ran toward his master and his master, trembling, said to himself: "He doesn't recognize me."

But Bocanegra stopped at the foot of the staircase, cowed before the first stair, where El Señor stood, a figure diffused in the violent light falling from overhead: a solar column of light, a column of dust motes, El Señor. First the mastiff barked with fury, and El Señor could not separate that emotion from his own fascinated innocence; did the dog or its master realize what was happening? El Señor thought, I can't tell the difference between my trembling ignorance and the dog's ignorant fury. Bocanegra barked, he approached the first step, he fled as if the stone were fire; worse (his master observed closely): for the dog the stairway did not exist; the dog could not see the standing El Señor, yet he smelled his presence; for El Señor was not present at the time the dog was living, but rather in a time he had encountered by chance when he stepped onto the stairway; the fire died in his entrails, he could no longer believe in the resurgence of his youthful exaltation, he cursed the notion of maturity and its identification with corruption; he cursed the blind will for action that one day had distanced him and now separated him forever from the only possible eternity: that of youth.

"The apple has been cut from the tree, its only destiny to rot."

Then El Señor, poised upon the first step, committed the error of stretching out his hand to take Bocanegra by the spiked collar with the heraldic blazon inscribed in the iron. The dog growled, shook his head, and tried to sink first the spikes, then his canines, into the hand attempting to pull him toward the first step. The initial sensation that he was not recognized was followed in El Señor's soul by the certainty of animosity; the bellicose dog not only did not know his master, he saw him actually as an enemy, an intruder. He refused to share the place and the instant his master had invaded on the stairway. El Señor regarded the perspective of the crypt from the first step; the chapel, from the stairway to the altar in the background to the luminous Italian painting and the jasper monstrance, was a copper engraving. Instantly he was suffused with immeasurable rage; on the day of his victory he had sworn to erect a fortress of the faith that no drunken soldier and no ravenous dog might ever profane; yet at the very entrance of the space he had chosen for his life and his death, the space constructed for him and by him, here he stood defending himself against a dog that was, in turn, resisting being pulled toward the stairway; El Señor looked toward the distant lights on the altar and, with a jerk, ripped the bandage from the dog's head. Bocanegra howled heart-rendingly; the bandage had pulled the sandy scab from the wound.

Howling, vanquished, his head lowered and the bandage trailing between his trembling paws, Bocanegra retreated to the seignorial bedchamber. El Señor hesitated between ascending one stair more and returning to the granite floor of the chapel. He moved his right leg to ascend the second stair; but now that pleasureful lightness had once again turned to leaden weight. He was afraid; he made a half turn and placed his foot beneath the first stair, on the floor. He looked up: the sun had disappeared from the firmament, the dawn was again announcing its appearance. He moved his left leg and stepped completely from the first stair; again he looked up, toward the square of the heavens at the top of the stairway: the dawn had yielded to the night that had preceded it.

THE KISS OF THE PAGE

The page-and-drummer, dressed completely in black, descended from the dunes to the beach and knelt beside the shipwrecked young sailor. He stroked the damp head and cleaned the face: the buried half was a mask of wet sand; the cleaned half, however (murmured the page-and-drummer), was the face of an angel.

Startled, the boy awoke from his long dream; he cried out: he could not distinguish between the caresses of the page and those he believed he must have dreamed from the moment when he fell from the foredeck into the boiling waters of the sea; dreams of encounters with women in carriages; he feared that the avid lips and sharp-filed teeth of a young Señora would again sink into his neck; he feared that the wrinkled lips and toothless gums of an old woman bundled in rags would again seek his loins. With the eyes of innocence he stared at the tattooed lips of the page-and-drummer, and imagined that in those lips—like the field and the device upon an escutcheon, like the coat of arms and the wind upon a pennant—were blended the desirous mouths of the other two women; he decided the page was the women he had dreamed of resolved into a new hermaphroditic figure; if he were half man and half woman, the page would be sufficient unto himself, he would love himself, and these caresses with which he was attempting to console and resuscitate the young sailor would be either an insignificant or an infinitely charitable act, but nothing more. And if the page were a man, the youth would accept his affection as that of the companion long desired in his solitude and mortal danger. But as the page's tattooed lips approached his, he did not smell the heavy scent of sandalwood or fungus of the other women, but a perfume of the forest, of flaming brambles and dye baths in the open air. The page cupped the youth's face in his hands and placed his warm soft tongue between the youth's parted lips. Their tongues met and the youth thought: "I have returned. Who am I? I am reborn. Who are you? I have dreamed. Who are we?'' He believes he must have repeated it aloud, for the page answered him, whispering into the ear he was caressing: "We have all forgotten your name. My name is Celestina. I want you to hear my story. Then you will come with me.''

EL SEÑOR BEGINS TO REMEMBER

There was no anger in Guzmán's attitude, only the profound and silent contempt of one who knows his office and who scorns the errors of others; but emphasizing El Señor's guilt, Guzmán's contempt was disguised in the precision with which he attempted to remedy the hurt done the dog. The master, breathing heavily and scratching his jaw, has no time to notice either these details or what they might reveal of the disparity between Guzmán's actions and his thoughts. His attention is captured by a much more powerful fact: it is five o'clock in the morning, the sun is just rising, and the dog Bocanegra is being treated by Guzmán for an incident that had occurred one hour earlier when the sun was at its future zenith.

He glanced at the vassal, allowing him to proceed. Guzmán rubbed the dog's wound with olive oil to soothe the pain, then applied a thick coating of stale melted hog fat; finally he bound the dog's body to a board so he couldn't scratch himself, and said: "It would be better now for the wound to get air; it will heal more quickly that way.''

El Señor scratched his tickling ear and looked again. Guzmán had treated the dog and was kneeling before the hearth; he laid a fire and lighted it with oakum. El Señor sat upon his curule chair beside the fire, aware that Guzmán had again divined his desire: in spite of the fact it was a summer day, El Señor was trembling with cold. The flames began to play impartially upon El Señor's prognathic profile and the sharp angles of Guzmán's face.

"I must remind El Señor that today is his birthday. I must apologize for not having mentioned it sooner. But because of the dog's condition . . .''

"It is all right, all right," gasped El Señor, waving aside Guzmán's apologies. "It is I who should apologize, for my carelessness with the dog . . .''

"El Señor has no cause to concern himself with dogs. That is why I am here.''

"What time is it?"

"Five o'clock in the morning, Sire."

"You are sure?"

"A good huntsman always knows the hour."

"Tell me . . .Who constructed the stairway that leads from the chapel to the ground above?"

"All of them, you mean, Señor? Surely many; and none with a memorable name."

"Why have they not completed it? Soon the funeral retinues will be arriving; how will they descend to the crypt?"

"They will have to come around, Señor, around the grounds, through the corridor, across the patio, through the dungeon, the way all of us reach the crypt."

"You do not answer me. Why have they not completed the stairway?"

"No one dares interrupt the meditations of El Señor. El Señor spends almost the entire day kneeling or prostrate before the altar; El Señor prays; the work falls behind . . ."

"I pray? I meditate? Oh, yes, I recall, entire days, it all comes back to me . . . Guzmán . . . Would you wish to relive one day of your life, even one, to live it differently?"

"Each of us had dreamed of rectifying a wrong decision in the past; but not even God may change what has already taken place."

"And if God gave me that faculty?"

"Then men would see it as the gift of the Devil."

" . . . if God permitted me, at will, to walk into the past, revive what is dead, recapture what is forgotten?"

"It would not be enough to change time. El Señor would also have to change the spaces where the time occurs."

"I would grow young . . ."

"And this palace, so laboriously constructed, would tumble down like dust. Remember that five years ago this was a shepherds' grove and there was no building upon it. Ask God, rather, to speed up time; thus El Señor will know the results of his work, which are the results of his will."

"I would see them as an old man."

"Or dead, Señor: immortal."

"And if old, or immortal, I would only see in the future what I would see in the past: the flat plain, a building disappeared or in ruins, destroyed by battles, envy, or indifference; perhaps abandonment?"

"El Señor, then, would have lost his illusions; but he would have gained wisdom."

"You awakened a philosopher today, Guzmán. I prefer to maintain my illusions."

"As El Señor wishes. But time is always a disappointment; foreseen, it promises us only the certainty of death; recaptured, it makes a mockery of freedom."

"To choose again, Guzmán; to choose . . . ."

"Yes, but always knowing that if we choose the same as the first time, we shall live a pleasant routine, with no surprises; and if we choose differently, we will live tortured by nostalgia and doubt: was the first choice better than the second? It was better. In any manner, we would be more enslaved than before; we would have lost forever a liberty that chooses, whether well or badly, only once . . . ."

"You are talking more than usual, Guzmán."

"El Señor asked me to remind him what day it is. It is his birthday. I have thought, if he will forgive me, a great deal about El Señor. I have thought that to choose twice is to mock the free will that does not forgive our abuses and that, mocked, mocks us, shows us its true face, which is the face of necessity. Let us instead, Sire, be the true masters of our past and future; let us live the present moment."

"That moment is for me a long anguish."

"If El Señor consistently looks behind him, he will be turned into a statue of salt. In El Señor resides a sum of power much greater than his father's . . . ."

"At what high price! You do not know, Guzmán. I was young."

"El Señor has united the dispersed kingdoms; he has put down the heretical rebellions of his youth; stopped the Moor and persecuted the Hebrew; constructed this fortress that combines the symbols of faith and dominion. The usury of the cities that destroyed so many small seigniories renders homage to his authority and accepts the necessity for central power. The shepherds and laborers of these lands today are workers at the palace; El Señor has left them with no sustenance but their daily wage. And it is easier to take money from a wage than to collect bushels from a harvest, for the harvest can be seen in measurable fields, while wages are manipulated invisibly. Other great undertakings await El Señor, no doubt; he will not find them behind him, but ahead."

"If one could begin again . . . if one could begin better . . . ."

"Begin what, Sire?"

"A city. The city. The places we inhabit, Guzmán."

"El Señor would have to employ the same arms and the same materials. These workers and these stones."

"But the idea could be different."

"The idea, Señor?"

"The intent."

"However good it was, men would always make of it something different from what El Señor had intended."

"So I believed once."

"Forgive me, Señor, believe it still."

"No, no . . . Listen, Guzmán; take paper, pen, and ink; listen to my story. I wanted this on my birthday: to leave something tangible of my memory; write: nothing truly exists if it not be consigned to paper, the very stones of this palace are but smoke if their story not be written; but what story can be written if this construction is never completed? What story! Where is my Chronicler?"

"You condemned him to the galleys, Sire."

"The galleys? Oh, yes, yes . . . Then you write, Guzmán, write. Listen well to my tale . . ."

EL SEÑOR VISITS HIS LANDS

He arrived at dusk at the head of twenty armed men; they galloped through the mist-soaked fields, their swinging whips lopping off heads of wheat from the stalk. Some carried flaming torches and when they arrived at the hut in the middle of the plain they threw the torches on the straw-thatched roof and waited for Pedro and his two sons to be driven out like animals from a cave: light, smoke, beasts, men, all things have but one exit, El Señor had said before they rode out.

From his tall charger El Señor accused the aged serf of having shirked in his obligations as a vassal. Pedro said that was not the way of it, that according to the old laws he was to turn over to the Liege only part of the harvest and that he might keep some part to feed himself and his family and some to sell in the marketplace. As Pedro spoke he glanced from the blazing roof to his Lord seated astride the dun-colored horse, its skin freckled and wasted. Pedro's skin was like that of the horse.

El Señor asserted: "There is no law but mine; this is an isolated place, you may not invoke a justice long out of use."

He added that Pedro's sons were to be carried by force into his service of arms. And the next harvest must be delivered in its totality to the castle gates. Obey, said El Señor, or your lands will be turned into ashes and not even weeds will grow upon them.

Pedro's sons were bound and placed on horses and the armed company galloped back toward the castle. Pedro was left standing beside the blazing hut.

THE HEIR

The falcon struck blindly against the walls of the cell. "He'll pluck out my eyes, he'll pluck out my eyes," young Felipe repeated over and over, shielding his eyes with his hands as the disoriented bird swooped in flight, striking against the walls only to launch itself again into a darkness it believed was infinite.

El Señor opened the door of the cell and the sudden light increased the frenzy of the rapacious bird. But the Liege approached, holding out his gauntleted arm to the hooded bird, which settled peacefully onto the greasy leather, and as he caressed the warm wings and lean body, he guided the falcon's beak to the water and food. El Señor glanced at Felipe with an aggrieved air and led him to the great hall of the castle, where the women sat embroidering while minstrels sang and a jester cut his capers.

El Señor explained to his son that the falcon requires darkness for his rest and for his feeding, but not so much darkness that he believes he is surrounded by the blackness of infinite space, for then he feels he is master of the night, his bird-of-prey instincts are awakened, and he swoops off in suicidal flight.

"You must know these things, my son. It will be you who will one day inherit my position and my privileges, and the accumulated wisdom of our domain as well, for without that wisdom the privileges are but vain pretension."

"You know, Father, that I am reading the ancient writings in our library, and that I am a diligent student of Latin."

"The wisdom to which I refer goes far beyond the knowledge of Latin."

"I will not disappoint you again."

The conversation between the father and son was interrupted by the cavorting of the jester, who came toward them with a broad, smudged smile, saying in a low but at the same time grotesquely high voice—for this comedian also had about him something of the ventriloquist—we buffoons know secrets, and he who would hear more, let him open his purse. He danced away but at the height of his next leap fell, choking, bluish bubbles bursting from his lips, and died.

The music ceased and the ladies fled, but Felipe, guided by an impulse, approached the jester and stared at the malignant face beneath the belled cap. He thought he saw something decidedly disagreeable, disfigured, and degraded in that scarlet mask-like visage. Kneeling, Felipe embraced the jester's body, recalling the moments of pleasure he had afforded his father's court. Then he grasped the clown by the buckle of his belt and dragged his body through the passageways. He imagined how it had been, the jester doing things he did not want to do, mimicking, capering, juggling, rhyming couplets, offering secrets in exchange for money: whom was he imitating, whom was he deceiving, whom was he despising as he fulfilled his role with such ill will? For, yes, his inner life was revealed in death: he was not a likable person.

The two sons of the serf Pedro had been lodged in the jester's rooms, so that Felipe found them there as he dragged the body into the room and deposited it upon a wretched straw pallet. But the two youths believed, as they looked upon his well-cut clothes and graceful, almost feminine features, that Felipe was a castle servant, a page surely, and they asked him whether he knew what fate El Señor had in store for them. They spoke of escape, telling Felipe that some men lived in freedom, without masters, openly traveling the roads, singing, dancing, making love, and doing penance so that this world might come to an end and another, better one begin.

But Felipe seemed not to hear them; beside the body of the buffoon he had heard an infant's high-pitched cry. When the heir looked more closely he could see the body of a babe-in-arms, wrapped in coarse bedclothes and half buried in the straw beside the jester's body. He had not known the jester had a newborn son, but he did not wish to ask further, for fear of betraying himself before the two who had taken him for a servant.

"Let's escape," Pedro's first son said. "You can be of help to us since you know the ways out."

"Help us; come with us," said the second son. "The millenary promise is close at hand, the second coming of Christ."

"Let's not wait for Christ's return," said Pedro's first son. "Let's be free; once away from here we'll join the other free men in the forests. We know where they are."

THE FALCON AND THE DOVE

The tall Augustinian monk, his skin stretched taut over prominent bones, addressed the group of students in red felt caps, tranquilly repeating the consecrated truth: man is condemned before his birth, his nature corrupted for all time by the sin of Adam; except with divine assistance, no one can escape the limitations of this truth; similarly, grace may be obtained only through the Roman Church.

Ludovico, a young theology student, arose impetuously and interrupted the monk. He asked whether he had considered the beliefs of Pelagius, who judged that God's grace, being infinite, is a gift directly accessible to all men without the need for intermediary powers; and also whether he had examined the doctrine of Origen, who was confident that God's charity is so great it would pardon even the Devil.

For an instant the monk stood stupefied; in the next moment, he pulled his hood over his head, preparing to leave.

"Do you deny the sin of Adam?" he asked the student Ludovico with compunctious and ominous fury.

"No, but I do sustain that, as he was created mortal, Adam would have died with or without sin; I also sustain that Adam's sin hurt only Adam and not the human race, so that every child born of man is born without offense, as innocent as Adam before the Fall."

"What is the Law?" the tall monk exclaimed.

Raging, when his question met only silence, he himself answered: "The Synod of Carthage, the Council of Ephesus, and the writings of St. Augustine!"

Then the students, who had obviously prepared for the scene, simultaneously loosed a falcon and a dove. The white dove alighted on Ludovico's shoulder, while the bird of prey swooped, struck the monk's chest, then flew away over his head. The students laughed with pleasure as the monk fled the hall, his head splattered with the bird's droppings; this seemed a propitious moment to break a few windows.

THE WOMEN OF THE CASTLE

The two women had not yet finished dressing; they had been distracted by the bitch's whelping. They crouched beside the beast, the young girl caressing the pups as her duenna looked from the bitch's gaping and bleeding wound to the chastity belt shackled heavily between her own thighs. She asked the girl whether she felt well. Yes, the girl replied, well enough, no worse than any other month. But the duenna grumbled, saying it was woman's lot to bleed, to whelp like animals, and to have smothered beneath padlocks what the poets were wont to call the flower of the faith; well, so much for flower and so much for faith, lily she might be, but withered, called Azucena now more from custom than because she was baptized so, and her soldier of the faith, a poor smith of these parts, had turned the key on her and gone forth to fight the Moors, or maybe only to the offal heap to shit, begging the girl's pardon, the only certain thing being that a long absence breeds forgetfulness.

Then this same Azucena looked with tender eyes upon the young girl and asked whether she might ask a favor. The girl, smiling, nodded. And her duenna explained that when he died the jester had left a newborn child in his straw pallet. She didn't know its origin, only the buffoon could have solved that mystery. She had decided to care for the child in secret, but her breasts were dry. Could she suckle the infant at the bitch's teats?

The girl made a gesture of disgust, then smiled and finally said yes, smiling, why yes, but they must hurry and finish dressing and go to the castle chapel. There they knelt to receive the Sacrament. But when the girl opened her mouth and the priest placed the Host on her long, narrow tongue, the wafer turned into a serpent. The girl spit and screamed; the priest, enraged, ordered her to leave the chapel at once: God himself had been witness to the offense. No unclean woman may set foot within the temple, much less receive the body of Christ; the girl screamed in horror, and howling with rage, the priest answered her with these words: "Menstruation is the course of the Devil through the corrupt body of Eve."

Felipe loved this girl from afar; he witnessed the scene in the chapel, standing aside, constantly stroking his beardless, prognathic chin.

JUS PRIMAE NOCTIS

A great country wedding was being celebrated in the granary, with dancing, singing, and drinking. The newlywed pair, a ruddy-faced young smith and a pale, slim sixteen-year-old girl, were dancing; his arms were about her waist, her arms around his neck, their faces so close that from time to time their lips could not help but meet in a kiss. Then everyone heard the heavy hoofbeats in the yard outside and they were afraid; El Señor and his young sapling, the one called Felipe, entered, and without a word the Lord approached the bride, took her by the hand, and offered her to Felipe.

Thereupon he led his son and the girl to a nearby hut and ordered Felipe to bed with the bride. The youth resisted. His father pushed him toward the trembling girl. In his mind Felipe imposed upon this girl the features of the young Lady of the castle who had been expelled from chapel during the early Mass. Even so, that imagined face still did not excite him, but confirmed in him instead his profound conception of the loved one as something one may desire but may not touch: didn't all the youths and handsome minstrels tell only of the passion of parted lovers, of ladies adored from afar: didn't all of them dwell in ineffable distance?

El Señor pushed his son aside; he stripped off his own boots and breeches and fornicated with the bride, quickly, proudly, coldly, bloodily, heavily, while Felipe watched amid the smoke and stench of the cotton wick swimming in a basin of fish oil. The father departed, telling Felipe to return alone to the castle.

Felipe told the sobbing girl his name and she told him hers, Celestina.

THE LITTLE INQUISITOR

The student Ludovico had been brought before the Holy Office by the taut-skinned monk, and there the Augustinian informed the Inquisitor that the young man's ideas were not only theologically in error, they were, in practice, dangerous, for if they filtered down to the people they would corrode the effectiveness, even the existence, of ecclesiastical hierarchy.

"Less zeal, less zeal," the Inquisitor, a stooped little man wearing a cardinal's biretta, said in irritation to the monk. In contrast, he spoke sweetly to Ludovico, asking him to recant; he promised him everything would be forgotten. My design, the ancient man said, sucking his lips, is not to win battles with words but to convince the head and heart of man that we must accept the world as it is, and peacefully; the world we live in is well ordered and offers rewarding riches to those who accept their place in it without protest.

The impassioned Ludovico stood and asked violently: "A world from which God is absent, sequestered by a few, unseen to all who openly aspire to his grace?"

So the Inquisitor also rose, trembling like an aspen leaf, as Ludovico leapt toward the blue-leaded window and escaped across the red tiles of the Archbishopric city.

He slammed the window after him with such force that the leaded panes shattered at the feet of the monk and the Inquisitor, and the latter said: "Increase the accounts due the University *pro vitris fractis*. And do not bring me these foolish problems. Rebels grow tall with attention but are effaced by indifference."

THE PLAGUE

Cadavers lie in the streets and the doors are marked with hastily painted crosses. Atop the high towers yellow flags are whipped by a rancorous wind. Beggars do not dare to beg; they watch quietly as a man pursues a dog around the square, finally captures it and strangles it, for it is said that animals are the cause of the pestilence; the dye-stained water which formerly flowed from the dyehouses has dried up, now no one tosses urine and excrement from his window, even the hogs that once wandered loose through the streets devouring the filth have died; but the cadavers of cattle slaughtered at the slaughterhouse lie putrefying there, and fish thrown in the street, and chicken heads; and over it all the thick celebratory clouds of flies. The sick have been driven from their homes; they wander alone, finally joining their infected fellows among the piles of refuse.

Blackened bodies float in the river and black fish die on the contaminated shores. Open graves are set afire. One or two mournful orchestras play in the squares, hoping to dispel the heavy atmosphere of melancholy hanging over the city.

Very few people dare walk through the streets; when they do they are cloaked in long, heavy black robes, leather gloves, boots, and wear masks with glass-covered eyeholes and beaks filled with the oil of the bergamot fruit. The convents have been closed, their doors and windows sealed.

But a good and simple monk named Simón has dared go out, believing it his duty to attend and cure the sick. Before he approaches them, Simón dampens his vestments with vinegar and fastens about his waist a sash stained and thickened with dried blood and ground dried frogs. He turns his back when he must hear the confession of the sick, for the breath of the infected can coat the surface of a water jug with gray scum. The afflicted moan and vomit, their black ulcers bursting like inky craters. Simón administers the Last Sacraments, moistening the Host in vinegar and then offering it secured upon the end of a long wand. Usually, the dying vomit the Body of Christ.

The city is choking beneath the weight of its own refuse; in spite of the abundance of animal and vegetable detritus, greater still is the accumulation of decomposing bodies. Then the Mayor comes to Simón and asks that he go to the prison and speak with the prisoners to make them the following offer: when the plague is over they will be liberated if now they lend their services to work in the streets, burning the dead.

Simón goes to the prison and makes the offer, first warning the prisoners of the dangers they run; isolated in their dungeons they have escaped the sickness; once outside, collecting the bodies in the streets, many of them will die, but those who survive will be freed.

The prisoners accept the agreement proposed by Simón. The simple monk leads them into the streets and there the prisoners begin to pile the bodies upon carts. The black smoke from the funeral pyres asphyxiates birds in their flight; the bell towers become nests filled with black feathers.

CELESTINA

The thin pale bride took to her bed and lay there trembling day and night. Her bridegroom tried to approach her, but every time he came near, Celestina screamed, rejecting her husband's overtures. Then the young smith would bow his head and leave her in peace.

Once alone Celestina draws close to the fire, fed constantly to soothe the sick girl's trembling; she thrusts her pale hands into the flames, choking back her screams and moans by biting down hard on a rope. She continues this way, burning herself, biting the rope, burning herself, until there is nothing left of the rope but a wet string and her hands are one great running wound. When the virginal husband sees his wife's hands he asks her what has happened. She answers: "I have fornicated with the Devil."

THE FLIGHT

That night Felipe escaped from the castle with the two young serfs. All three hid in the nearby forest, breathing in its strong verdant embrace. They did not sleep, for Felipe had many questions to ask them, and the two youths, in great detail, told Felipe where he could find the armies of free men, the enlightened, the vagabond kings of the interregnum preparing for the second coming of Christ to earth.

As dawn approached, three of El Señor's hunters entered the forest, guided by large and ferocious dogs; Felipe climbed a tall pine and hid himself there, but the two sons of Pedro were hunted down and devoured by the mastiffs.

When the hunters had departed, Felipe descended from the tree and continued alone to the place described by Pedro's two sons. As night fell he heard music and he came to a clearing where naked men and women were dancing and singing: The divine essence is my essence and my essence is the divine essence, for every spark of creation is divine and reincarnation will be universal. Felipe thought of the bloody and dismembered bodies of his unfortunate friends; he took off his clothes and joined the dancers. He felt drunk, and like them, he danced and shouted.

SIMON'S FACE

The plague in the city has ended. The prisoners bury the last bodies and Simón the monk helps them. The yellow flags are struck while the monk joins the prisoners around a bonfire and they tell tales of the time they have passed together: they are friends.

There is a final brief silence. Simón announces to them that now they are free. Many have died, it is true, and sad; but those who live have won something more than life; they have won their freedom. They are drinking the last swallow from the wineskin when the Mayor and his halberdiers approach them. The Mayor simply orders his armed company to seize the prisoners and return them to the prison. The period of grace has ended. All the surviving prisoners will be returned to prison to fulfill the time of their sentences.

One of the prisoners spits in Simón's face.

IN THE FOREST

Celestina forsakes her home; she, too, wanders through the forest, bathing her injured hands in the fresh streams and eating roots and nuts. At night she sits beneath a great tree and fills with flour the little cloth dolls she carries hidden beneath her skirts; she caresses them, she presses them to her breasts, she invokes the Evil One and asks him to take her and give her a son. But she raises this supplication only when the sounds of the whistling, howling, moaning forest are most intense; only the forest must hear her.

One night, as two old men were returning from a distant fair, hot and excited, they heard her and parted the branches and watched her; when Celestina's passion reached an unbearable level, the two old men fell upon her and raped her, one after the other; but the pale thin girl, lost in the consuming intensity of her fantasy, was oblivious to their acts; perhaps she imagined only that her pleas had been attended, that a Devil with two tails had got her with child. The old men questioned the significance of the flour-filled dolls, then shrugged their shoulders, laughed, and destroyed them.

After the two old men had gone, Celestina lay exhausted and alone for a long while. Then she heard the sounds of music and singing coming toward her. She saw Felipe at the head of a vast horde of men and women dressed in hairshirts and carrying scythes across their shoulders. Felipe's heart turned over, for he recognized Celestina as the bride whom his father had one evening taken for himself. He knelt beside her, stroked her hair, and said to her: "Suffer no more. No one is going to punish you for your sins. Now poor souls like you may love and not be condemned for that love. Come with us."

He took Celestina's injured hands, and she answered him: "No, you come with me. I have had a dream. We must go to the sea."

The singing throng continued on its way; Felipe, who knew now that dreams may be real when no other course is possible, went in the opposite direction with Celestina.

THE BOAT

The aged serf Pedro had reached the coast and had set about building a boat. His arms were still strong and every time he looked at the sea he could feel his strength increasing. That morning, glancing from the sea toward the dunes, Pedro saw the monk Simón descending, covered in dust, his habit hanging in shreds. The monk asked Pedro: "Are you a sailor? Where will you be sailing?"

The old man told the monk that questions were unwelcome; if the monk wanted to go with him, he should get to work immediately. But before the two men had picked up their hammers and nails, the student Ludovico, in beggar's rags now, also appeared on the dunes; he, too, came down to the beach and asked whether he could join them on their voyage, for the boat could carry them far, very far, from here.

Ludovico joined in their labor, and as the day came to a close, Celestina, guided by her dream, appeared with Felipe, and both requested a place in the vessel. Pedro told them they could all accompany him, but on the condition that first they work.

"You, girl, tend to the cooking, and you, lad, bring us something to eat."

Pedro handed Felipe a sharpened knife.

THE CITY OF THE SUN

When they had finished their day's work, the five of them ate meat from the deer Felipe had slain and Celestina asked where they would be sailing once the ship was ready. Pedro answered that any land would be better than the one they were leaving behind. And Ludovico added that surely there were other, freer, more prodigal lands; the whole earth could not be one enormous prison.

"But there are cataracts at the ocean's end," said the monk Simón. "We cannot go far."

Felipe laughed. "You're right, monk. Why don't we stay here and try to change the world we know?"

"What would *you* do?" the student Ludovico asked. "If you had the power, what kind of world would you create?"

They all sat very close together, contented after their completed tasks and the savory food. Pedro said he envisioned a world where there were no rich or poor, a world where neither man nor beast would be governed by arbitrary powers. He spoke brusquely but with the voice of a dreamer who sees a community where every being would be free to ask and to receive from others the things he needed most, where his only obligation would be to give to others what they asked of him. Each man would be free to do what most pleased him, because every job would be natural and useful.

They all looked toward Celestina and the girl pressed her hands to her breast, closed her eyes, and imagined a world where nothing would be forbidden, where all men and all women could choose the person and the love they wanted most, for all love would be natural and blessed; God approves all the desires of all His creatures, if they are desires of love and life, not hatred and death. Didn't the Creator himself plant the seed of amorous love within the breasts of all His creatures?

The monk Simón said: "We can't have love until there is no more sickness and death. I dream of a world where every child will be happy and will live forever. No one will ever again fear pain or extinction, for when he is born into this world he will inhabit the earth forever, and thus earth will be heaven and heaven will be here on earth."

"But this," the student Ludovico intervened, "would presuppose a world without God, since in the world you have each imagined, a world without power or money, with no prohibitions, with no pain or death, each man would be God, and God therefore would not be possible. He would be a lie, because His attributes would be those of every man, woman, and child: grace, immortality, and supreme good. Heaven on earth, my friend monk? Earth without God, then, since God's proud and secret place is a heaven without earth."

Then they all looked to young Felipe and waited in silence. But the son of El Señor said he would tell his dream only after he had interpreted in turn what the others had just imagined.

PEDRO'S DREAM

You are living in your happy commune, old man; the harvests belong to everyone and every person takes and receives from his neighbor. The commune is a great island of freedom surrounded by the seas of serfdom. One evening, as you are peacefully contemplating the sunset from your reconstructed hut, you hear a great hue and cry. A man is brought before you; he has been captured, and is accused of stealing. He must be judged. He is the first man to have broken the laws of the commune.

You lead this man before your people assembled in the granary and you ask him: "Why did you steal, if everything here is held in common?"

The man asks to be pardoned; he did not know what he was doing; the excitement of the crime was stronger than his sense of obligation to the commune. More than by greed, since everything, it is true, belongs to every man, he was motivated by the lure of danger, of adventure, of risk; how can one overcome in a day the inclinations of a lifetime? He has returned to confess his guilt and to be pardoned. He has stolen something without value, something he found in the communal storehouse: a large green bottle, old, covered with moss and spider webs and sealed with very old wax. He had stolen to experience the exciting thrill of danger. But then he felt shame and fear, and fled from the commune. He fell into the hands of El Señor's soldiers. He was taken to the castle. And there, under torture, he revealed the existence of the commune to El Señor.

Contain your anger, old man, and disguise your fear, for you well know that your best defense has been invisibility; you know that El Señor will not visit you until the next harvest is collected, or until a wedding when he comes to take, by force, his rights as the Lord. For this reason you have forbidden anyone to marry before the harvest time, trusting that by then the commune will be sufficiently strong to confront El Señor. You ask the repentant man standing before you: Why have you returned when you could have remained with your stolen bottle under the protection of El Señor?

The thin man, his ankles raw from the torture ropes, answers you: "I have returned to do penance for my double betrayal: I have returned to fight in defense of my companions, for tomorrow the army of El Señor will march against us and will crush our dream . . ."

You ask him: Where is this bottle you have stolen? And he bows his head and admits that inexplicably El Señor took it from him. But he pleads: "I am a traitor and a confessed thief, but let me return and fight with you. Don't despise my poor bones."

You decide to pardon him. But the assembly protests: you hear voices demanding death for this man as an example to whoever might feel tempted to repeat his crimes. And there is more: many allege that if the man has returned, it is because El Señor plans to employ him as a spy within the commune. You argue heatedly, old man: not a single drop of blood must be spilled here; to yourself you say silently that, in the same way the thief and traitor could not change his instincts overnight, the multitude gathered here cannot suppress its own. The members of the commune defy you: once El Señor attacks, the spilling of blood will be inevitable; in fact, the time remaining before the fateful battle has been brutally curtailed. You point to the traitor's ankles, still bleeding from the torture: a man replies that this is an obvious stratagem of El Señor, so that, once pardoned, the traitor can remain in the commune and continue to inform against it. They accuse you of evading the facts, and several strong men hurry outside; soon in the warm summer night you hear the sound of the hammer and the saw.

Inside the granary your community first debates, then decrees: we will live in peace only when our rules of life are accepted by everyone; in the meanwhile we must set aside our own code of brotherhood and actively destroy those who do not deserve it, our enemies. You try to calm them, old man; you say we must live in isolation and in peace, with the hope that sooner or later our good example will spread; you say we must conquer with persuasion, not with arms. Your people shout in your face: we must defend ourselves, for if we're destroyed we can offer no example at all. You persist, weakly: we will negotiate with El Señor, we will deliver this harvest in exchange for the right to pursue our new mode of life. Then the assembly laughs openly at you.

The traitor is condemned to death and hanged that same night from the brand-new gallows erected in the middle of the commons. The people elect one of the carpenters to organize the defense; the new leader's first orders are to raise barricades in the fields; a popular army is formed and neighbor watches over neighbor to prevent future betrayals.

Old man: you are petitioned to remain in your hut; occasionally in the evenings young girls come to bring you flowers and honor you as the founder of the commune; but you do not dare ascertain what really is happening. The new leader has warned you that if you speak again, if you again repeat the arguments you expressed during the assembly, you will be exiled, and if you persist in debate outside the commune, you will be considered a traitor and murdered in broad daylight. From your window you can see the gallows erected in the commons. It seems to you that only the hangman and you are motionless, waiting, always waiting; the rest of an incomprehensible world races by before your eyes, and your ears are filled with the chaotic sounds of running horses, of weeping, of discharged harquebuses, and of fire. What is the source of the arms the members of the commune employ in their struggle against El Señor? You find out the day you see in the square the pennants and infantry of another Liege, a rival of your oppressor. Every day, men are hanged; you no longer know, you don't want to know, whether they are men of the commune or soldiers of El Señor. It is said (at times the sorrowing women dare communicate the rumors) that some members are opposed to the alliances that, under the guise of necessity, the new leader has effected with the noble rivals of El Señor.

Once the new leader visits you and says: "Pedro, I hope someday when we again live in peace we can raise a monument to you right here where the gallows now stands."

CELESTINA'S DREAM

Felipe took the girl's hand.

You've chosen me, isn't that true, Celestina? And I feel I've chosen you. Here, let's drink to our love. Together we'll work with our new friends to build the old man's ship; together we'll voyage to a new and better land. We've become good friends, we five, but you and I, my love, will make love beneath the stars as the ship softly breasts the waves of the unknown sea.

Ludovico the student is also our friend now; but every night, following the day's hard labor, as we drink and I look into your eyes he will try to hide his behind his cup; I can see my love for you reflected in his eyes.

We've no need for explanations, Celestina; soon every night Ludovico will lie with us beneath our covers; I love him like a brother and you love what I love; there will be no hatred, no suspicion, no jealousy, only satisfied desire, when I make love to you and then permit him to do the same.

At times you are assaulted by temptation and by doubt: "I am the only woman on board. It is only natural they both love me." But Ludovico's passion, his tender touch, even the newly minted words so different from his usual dogmatic expression, the beauty of the pleasure he gives and receives from you, all this tells you he loves you because you are Celestina, and that he could love no other woman. You are Celestina: you are mine: Ludovico is yours.

Then I begin to believe that perhaps my friend loves you more than I, Celestina, for he loves both you and me, or me through you; and you, because of your freely given loyalty to me, fear you are becoming too close to him and more distant from me. I love him, he is my brother; you must please me by loving him always more.

During the day, old Pedro stands at the helm while the monk prays and fishes. Ludovico and I perform the exhausting tasks; we climb the mainmast and ready the sail, we scan the horizon and at the sight of storm clouds prepare the crossjack, we sound and scrub and polish, and gaze interminably at the endless ocean from whose center we seem never to move, as if we were lying to. Our shoulders and hands touch constantly; we have learned to haul the ropes as one, to know the power and grace of our common muscles, for now we even walk like twins, as if the symmetrical distribution of our bodies' weight were essential to the equilibrium of the ship. And our bodies sweat together beneath the summer sun; our skin is dark, our hair bleached by the gold light of the sea. You, Celestina, are pale; you stand away from us during the day, in the shadows, salting down the fish and slicing the toughened loaves, alien to our active labor, alien to our cultured Latinist jests, morosely humiliated you cannot share in the wit and puns of the education we have in common, when Ludovico says to me: "Crinis flavus, os decorum cervixque candidula, sermo blandus et suavis; sed quid laudem singula?" And I reply, caressing the nape of his neck: "Totus pulcher et decorus, nec est in te macula, sed vacare castitati talis nequit formula . . ."

Now we come to you every night in order to be close to each other; I grow excited thinking of him, and then make love to you; he doesn't have to tell me he does the same. The long slow nights drift by; increasingly you are the vehicle of our desire, something to be possessed so we may possess each other. Finally one night you lie alone; we are together. The muscled sunburned bodies have fulfilled their desire, but frustrated yours.

Now you know, lying huddled apart from us, that if you attempt to satisfy your own desire you will wound me or hurt my lover, my brother. You look beyond that rhythmically moving coverlet to the place where the monk lies sleeping. You go and sit at his feet, and once again begin to stitch your little cloth dolls, and you feel a dark and distant urgency; you howl, Celestina, you howl like a lost bitch, and in the phosphorescent sea dew that moistens your lips seek the kiss of your only true lover, the Devil.

SIMON'S DREAM

When Felipe ceased speaking, the monk Simón shook his head no, and said: "You are mistaken. You have begun at the end. Before there can be true peace or true love, authentic justice or pleasure, sickness and death must cease."

Felipe looked into Simón's clear, pained eyes and remembered his father's dark and willful brow. And he said to the monk: "You, Brother Simón, have experienced the terrible plague you told us of today as we were eating; you saw men battle against death. But the only men who truly battled were your prisoners: they had been promised freedom. But in the perfect world that you imagine there will be no death. And without certainty of death, how can there be desire for freedom?

"Let me pause, good monk, and ask you to recall your city once again, this time without death. A child is born in the manorial castle; at the same time a child is born in one of the dark hovels of your city. All rejoice, the rich parents and the poor as well, for they all know that once their sons are born, they will live forever.

"The two male children grow. One excels in the arts of falconry, archery, hunting, and Latin; the other follows the paternal profession; he will learn to give shape to iron, to keep the ovens burning red, and to wield the powerful bellows. Let us say that the boy born and reared in the castle is called . . ."

"Felipe," murmurs Celestina.

"Yes, Felipe, we shall say; and let us suppose the young smith's name is . . ."

"Jerónimo," murmurs Celestina.

"Yes, let us suppose." Felipe continued: "Consider, monk, the iron apprentice; when he has reached his twentieth year he falls in love with a young country girl, much like Celestina, and weds her; but the night of the wedding the young Prince from the castle appears and takes the virgin for himself, invoking his inarguable seignorial right. Celestina's melancholy resembles madness; she forbids her bridegroom to come near her. The young smith fans the fires of hatred and revenge against me, Felipe, the young Lord.

"But both are immortal. He cannot kill me. I cannot murder him.

"We must find something to replace the death that neither can inflict upon the other.

"So for death I substitute non-existence. Since I cannot kill the young smith for despising me, or you, old man, for your rebelliousness, or you, Celestina, for your sorcery, or you, Ludovico, for your heresy, I condemn each of you to death in life. For me, you do not exist, I consider you dead.

"Look now, monk; look at your city peopled by my slaves, look at your walled city surrounded by my men and arms; listen to the steps of phantoms in my vast encircled cities. I have laid siege to the city. And I have entrapped each of you; not your immortal bodies, but your souls, mortal within immortal flesh.

"For this is the weakness of your dream, monk; if the flesh cannot die, then the spirit will die in its name. Life will no longer have any value; I shall have denied men liberty; they cannot exchange their slavery for death. They no longer have the only wealth an oppressed man can offer in return for the freedom of other men: his death.

"And I, monk, I will live forever, enclosed in my castle, protected by my guards, never daring to sally forth; I fear the knowledge of something worse than my own impossible death: I fear the spark of rebellion in the eyes of my slaves. No, I am not speaking of the active rebellion that you, monk, or you, old man, know and desire, although at times I also fear the simple, irrational murmuring of the multitude, the tides of living phantoms inundating my island, my castle, who, since they cannot murder their tyrant, convert him into one more of their infinite and anonymous company. No, monk, no: I fear the rebellion that simply ceases to recognize my power.

"I have not killed them; I have only decreed they do not exist. Why should they not repay me in the same coin? This will be the young smith's revenge; he can murder me by forgetting that I exist. You, monk Simón, walk among the spectral throngs of your city, vainly offering your useless charity and futilely seeking that spark I fear, for the immortal do not rebel unless the certainty of death is assured. They will kill me by forgetting me; my power will have no meaning.

"And so we will continue to live, you and I, I and they, repeating ceaselessly a few uncertain gestures that vaguely recall times past when we lived and fought and believed and loved and desired with the goal of either deferring or hastening death. We shall live, we shall live forever, monk, as the mountains and the heavens live, the seas and rivers, until, like them, immobilized, our faces will be lost, left to the obliterating powers of erosion and the tides.

"We shall all be sleepwalkers, you in your city, I in my castle, and finally I shall come out, I shall walk the streets and no one will remember me, no one will recognize me, as the stone fails to recognize the hill at whose feet it lies. We shall meet, you and I, but as we will both be immortal, our eyes will never meet.

"Only our fingertips will touch, Brother Simón; and our lips will foolishly utter the word 'flesh,' never 'Simón' or 'Felipe'; flesh, as one would say hair, stone, water, thorn.''

LUDOVICO'S DREAM

The student nodded gravely, considered, then shook his head no. No, he said to Felipe, your syllogism is false; the perfect world will depend upon my premise: a good society, good love, eternal life will be ours only when every man is God, when every man is his own immediate source of grace. Then God will not be possible because His attributes will be a part of every man. And man, finally, will be possible because he will no longer be ambitious or cruel; his grace will be sufficient unto itself, and he will love himself and love all creation.

Young Felipe spoke again, glancing from Ludovico's worried eyes to Celestina's somber, suspicious features. And he said:

I see you, my brother Ludovico, busy in your tiny student's garret, filled with the grace of God, convinced you are your own God, but obliged, nonetheless, to struggle against two implacable necessities. You feel the cold of this winter night, and the fire does not warm you, for the logs have been wet by strong November rains.

You wish your grace would spread beyond your body, beyond the narrow confines of your miserable little room, that it would overflow the limits of your serene spirit and subject the fires of earth and the rains of heaven to your will: you curse the same fires, the same rains old Pedro praises as he walks through the swampy fields toward the warm coals of his hearth.

You ask yourself, Ludovico: Can one separate the satisfaction of grace from the temptation to create? You ponder this question, shivering over your damp green firewood: Isn't grace worthless if it cannot dominate nature? God could have been content with eternal life, could have lived alone except for the companionship of His own grace; why did He feel the need to fill the void of that grace with the accidents of natural creation?

You are thinking about the Divinity before Creation. You see a solitary transparency surrounded by the black rays of that temptation to create: God imagines Adam, then declares himself insufficient. Unlike the sickly fire in your chimney, your brain is aflame, you imagine a piece of wood that would burn forever once it was lighted. Yes, that would be the material gift of grace, the practical equivalent to your divinity; then grace and creation would be one, and their name would be knowledge. Then, surely, master of gnosis, you would be God and God would be unnecessary since you could yourself convoke a new order, as God, unique, arrogant (and dangerously saddened to know He was insufficient, compelled), once did.

You learn the secrets of alchemy; you work for years, indefatigably; you grow old, stooped over dying fires, glutinous tars, and greenish oils, mixing, experimenting, coaxing the momentary flare, subduing the insistent flash, agonizing over a spark, exhilarated by a flameless aura, watching the St. Elmo's fire from the beaches, wandering through peat fields, distilling mustards and linseed oils, polarizing and magnetizing every combustible element known to man, and still others of your own invention, until your work is ended. Ah, how true the Biblical curse; neither grace nor creation alone would have granted you knowledge; science is not gratuitous; you had to add the sweat of your brow.

You have dedicated your life to pragmatic grace and now you can proudly show the results to the honorable council in your city. Some of the priests accuse you of practicing the black arts, but the burghers, who see in your invention a necessary reconciliation of faith and utility, override this clerical vigilance, and soon you are installed in a profitable workshop near the city, from which supplies of your incandescent firewood flow to peasant huts, lords' castles, and the ovens of the Guilds. No one need ever again feel the cold. You have triumphed over God's careless design: allowing wood to get wet when dryness is more useful, flooding the woods with winter's rain. The civilized world applauds you; it matters little that the vapors from your invention stain the firmament with a yellow cloud that settles into the valleys as a resinous bog. Grace, creation, and knowledge now are one in you; you have established the objective norm of truth.

Old and proud, saved by fame from the solitude and the questions that, were you alone, your forgotten grace—the original impulse to your creation and the solitary germ of your knowledge—might have posed, you ride through the countryside, basking in your renown, the gratitude of the populace, the usefulness of the gift you have bestowed upon them. That malodorous smoke issues from every chimney . . . from every chimney save one. Dumfounded, you dismount and enter that smokeless cottage.

There you find Celestina. She has grown old, too; she is truly a witch now, gray and wrinkled, sitting frostily before a bare hearth stitching her little dolls and stuffing them with flour. She is intoning a diabolic litany, in effect invoking the only companion to her solitude: the vacant intensity of her eyes reveals a true acquaintanceship with the being her voice is conjuring. In her solitude she too demands a contiguous presence, a shared wisdom.

Why do you not have a fire? you ask Celestina, and she replies she neither needs nor wants one; the smoke would frighten away her familiars and they would no longer come to her. You show your anger: woman, ignorant, superstitious . . . woman! but the truth is that your soul has now suffered the supreme insult: there is one being who fails to appreciate your offering to humanity, the tangible proof of your superior grace.

The wrinkled hag tries to read your face and finally cackles: "You know what you know; I know what you will never know. Leave me alone."

And you, old man, proud, wise Ludovico, return slowly to the city with a leaden heart and a deepening sense of decision. You denounce

Celestina before the ecclesiastical tribunal, and a few days later you go to the public square and there amidst the silent crowd you watch the halberdiers lead Celestina to the stake. The woman is bound to the wooden post and then the executioners set fire to the dry crackling wood at the feet of the recalcitrant witch. Your own invention, of course, is not utilized on this occasion.

NOWHERE

The three men and the woman sat a long while in silence after young Felipe stopped speaking. The youth himself sat staring toward the dawn sea; they had passed the night in conversation. And when the sun appeared, El Señor's heir thought he saw in the orb of day the dead jester's horrible grimace. Then he looked intently at Celestina and with his eyes asked her: "Please do not tell the others who I am." Celestina bowed her head.

The student Ludovico was the first to rise; with a sudden movement he seized an ax and before anyone could stop him (but no one wished or dared to stop him) he threw himself against the skeleton of the old man's boat and destroyed it, reduced it to splinters. Then, his face scarlet, he drove his ax into the black sands and murmured hoarsely:

"*Nowhere* does not exist. We have dreamed of a different life in distant time and distant space. That time and space do not exist. Madness. We must go back. Go back to your land, your harvest, and your serfdom, old man. Go back to your plagues and your healing, monk. Woman, return to your madness and your devils. And you, Felipe, the only one of whom we know nothing, return to your unknown. And I will go back to confront the torture and death that are my destiny. The Inquisitor of Teruel was not without reason: this is our world, even though it is not the best of all possible worlds."

Felipe remained kneeling beside the dawn waves. The others rose and walked toward the dunes. Finally Felipe ran after them and said: "Wait a moment, please. You have not asked me what my perfect world would be. Give me that opportunity."

The company paused at the edge of the high sandy ground, their silence interrogating the youth. And Felipe said: "Look. Utopia is not in the future, it is not in another space. The time of Utopia is now. The place of Utopia is here."

HERE AND NOW

And so Felipe led the mad young witch and the proud student and the honest serf and the humble monk back toward the city, and there he said to them: "There is the perfect world."

And their eyes opened to what they already knew, to shrieking, playing children, clerics selling indulgences, to the cries of street hawkers and the dragging steps of beggars, to quarrels among rivals and disputes among students, and also to sweethearts comforting each other, couples kissing in the narrow lanes, the strong scents of gin and bacon, roasting boar and frying onion; the hotchpotch of red-gauntleted, purple-robed doctors, purple-hatted, gray-cloaked lepers, scarlet-clad whores, freed heretics with the double cross embroidered on their tunics, and Jews with the round yellow patches over their hearts; pilgrims flourishing palm leaves returning from Jerusalem; pilgrims from Rome with St. Veronica's cloths covering their faces; pilgrims from Compostela with seashells sewn to their hats; and pilgrims from Canterbury with a drop of the blood of the priest, the turbulent Thomas à Becket, in a small vial.

But these accustomed sights, sounds, and smells were but the veil drawn across a world moving rapidly and silently from some unknown center, issuing from some subterranean force; this Felipe pointed out to his companions: the dances seemed the same happy dances, but they were different; one had only to look a little more closely to discover their secret design; clasping hands, people danced all together, the entire city tracing the patterns of a lively galliard, moving in the undulating contractions of a giant serpent, led by the fife and lute, the mandolins and psalteries and rebecs of a group of musicians; and suddenly, when the five friends joined hands to form part of that ribbon of dancers, they saw other signs of change, for monks were coming out of their monasteries and nuns from their convents and Jews from their *aljamas* and Moslems from their *alquerías* and magicians from their towers and idiots from their asylums and prisoners from their prisons and children from their homes, and men armed with garrotes and axes and lances and pitchforks joined them, and one of them approached Felipe and said: "We are here. At the time and the hour you ordained."

Felipe nodded, and many people climbed into the carts and others took the place of oxen and pulled the carts, while a horde of men dressed in frayed sackcloth, their bodies covered with crusted filth and scabs and ulcers, barefoot and hirsute, flocked into the city, dragging themselves on their knees like wounded cats, flagellating themselves cruelly as they chanted Felipe's words: "The time is now, the place is here."

And Felipe placed himself at the head of the crowd and cried: "Jerusalem is near!"

And the multitude shouted and marched behind him, following him beyond the walls of the city into the fields; and as they passed, the hordes burned and leveled the fields, and a leper, reaching out his sore-covered arms to the black clouds of smoke, said: "The Parousia is near, the Coming! Christ will return for the second time to Earth. Burn! Destroy! Let not a single stone from the past remain. Let not a single affliction from the past remain. Let the new age find us naked upon a barren earth. Amen."

Singing and dancing, the multitude advanced, scarring their knees and scourging their breasts; they attested that the river ceased to flow as they crossed it, and that its warm waters stood icy-still about their legs; that the hills flattened out before their march and the clouds visibly descended to touch the brittle crust of the earth and protect from the furies of the sun the new Crusaders of the millennium, the imitators of Christ, the prophets of the third Joachimite Age—the Age of the Holy Spirit—the exalted peoples living the last days of the Antichrist. This is what certain sweating monks proclaimed; the masses of Arabs and Jews following behind Felipe in this caravan muttered different things among themselves.

Then the singing, shouting children saw the castle resting beneath the low-hanging clouds, and they cried: "Is this Jerusalem?" But Felipe knew it was only his father's castle. He instructed the men to prepare arms for the assault, but when they reached the castle moat they found the drawbridge already lowered, the huge doors opened wide.

Silently, they descended from their carts. Children clung to their mothers' skirts. The flagellants dropped their scourges. Pilgrims from Rome peered from behind their Veronica cloths. Amazed, they entered the castle of El Señor, where a vast repast had been hurriedly abandoned; musicians' instruments lay in disorder beside the cold, ashy hearth; black blood and grease seeped from the cadaver of a decapitated deer; the tapestries hung motionless, although their flat ocher figures of glittering unicorns and hunters seemed to welcome Felipe's army. Then their amazement gave way to frenzied action; the crowd took up the wine flasks and the musical instruments, they seized the roast partridges and grape clusters; men, women, and children ran through the great halls and bedchambers and passageways, dancing, tearing down the tapestries and cloaking themselves in them, donning casques and caps and tiaras and birettas and steeple caps and airy gossamers; they adorned themselves in chains of gold and silver earrings, ceremonial medallions, even the emptied basins of oil lamps; they plundered every coffer, jewel chest, and casket that lay in their paths. Renegade monks offered indulgences to scarlet-clad whores in exchange for their favors, pilgrims from England mixed the blood of the saint with the blood of the wine, and a drunken cleric was proclaimed Dominus Festi and baptized with three pails of water, while during the height of the orgy a Brabantine heretic bellowed the catastrophes awaiting the world: war and misery, fire from the heavens and greedy abysses yawning at the feet of humanity. Only the elect would survive. Then the Jews rejected the plates of unclean suckling pig; the Moslems decided to swallow the pieces of gold they had found.

The celebration continued for three days and three nights, until everyone succumbed, overcome by love-making and lack of sleep, hysterical exaltation, bleeding wounds, by indigestion and by drunkenness. But during this frenzy—and its eventual attrition in mournful songs, renewed vows, and indolent gestures—the five friends first observed and then acted according to their own desires. Celestina and Felipe lay down together upon a soft bed of marten skins; the student Ludovico soon joined them, since in truth the three had thought of nothing else since El Señor's son had imagined the story of their love-making on board the ship that never sailed.

The two older men, Simón the monk and Pedro the peasant, slowly left the castle. Once beyond the moat they clasped hands, then set out on different routes; Simón said the sick awaited him in other unfortunate cities; Pedro, that it was now time to return to the coast and begin to build a new boat.

As Simón and Pedro bade each other farewell, the drawbridge very slowly began to rise; the old men paused again as they heard the sound of heavy chains and creaking wooden planks, but they could not see who raised the bridge. Each sighed and continued on his way. Had they waited but a few instants more, they would have heard the violent pounding on the other side of the raised bridge, now become an impregnable barbican; they would have heard desperate cries for help, and the heart-rending weeping of the imprisoned.

THE REWARD

When the slaughter had ended, El Señor's soldiers sheathed their bloody swords and returned to the soldiers' huts where they had been hidden during the long feast of the brief Apocalypse. Felipe had asked that the cadavers lie exposed for one whole day in the great halls and bedchambers of the castle; then, when the stench became unbearable, El Señor ordered that they all be burned upon a pyre erected in the center of the castle courtyard. Felipe also asked his father that Celestina and Ludovico be spared any punishment, because they had afforded him great pleasure.

"That pleasure is now a part of my education, Father, a part of the pedagogy not to be found in the Latin texts, the things you wanted me to learn in order to be worthy of my legacy."

El Señor approved what his son had done, for by his actions he had shown himself worthy beyond any doubt of the power that would one day be his. Playfully, he seized his son by the nape of the neck and murmured, with a wink of the eye, that perhaps it wasn't a bad thing that a father and a son should enjoy the same female. He laughed with prolonged pleasure and then, as a reward, he told Felipe he might have the thing he most desired.

"Father, I want to marry that young lady, our English cousin, who was reprimanded and expelled from the chapel by the vicar."

"You could have had that wish at any time, my son. All you had to do was ask."

"Yes, I know. But first I had to be worthy."

THE SILENT HOUR

It was the deepest, darkest night of the year; the guards were dozing and the dogs lay exhausted from being chained all day. That day El Señor's son had wedded his young Lady. In this silent hour Ludovico the student went to Celestina and told her to make ready, they must both flee the castle.

"Where will we go?" asked the bewitched young girl.

"First to the forest, to hide," the student answered. "Then we will look for the old man. He has probably returned to the coast to build another boat. Or perhaps we can find the monk. He is sure to be in some afflicted city. Come, Celestina; hurry."

"But we will fail, Ludovico, exactly as the young Liege told. I have dreamed it."

"Yes. We will fail, once, and then again, then still again. But every failure will be a victory. Come, hurry, before the hounds awaken."

"I do not understand you. But I will follow you. Yes, let us go. We will do what we must do."

"Come then, my love."

THE EXHORTATION

What do you expect of the future, my poor unhappy lad? Why did you leave your home, your distant but fertile fields where you were loved and protected? Why are you marching in this Crusade? What have they promised you? Listen, stop the dancing; do not excite yourself; why are you concerned, my son, why are you worried? Rejoin your friends; ask them to be silent, what an infernal din! No one can be rational in such circumstances, how can anything be understood; tell them to put down their fifes and bagpipes and drums and listen to me: the world is in order, it is well ordered; we struggled long and hard to emerge from the shadows; you young do not know what that was. Darkness, my children, barbarism, yes, the sacking, plundering hordes; blood, crime, and ignorance. It was with great effort that we came forth from that hell; more than once we fell back; more than once the sword of the Goth, the conflagration of the Mogul, and the horsemen of the Hun tumbled our constructs as if they were of sand. But look now: we have organized a space, we have created a stable order; look at the cultivated fields, look at the cities safe within their bastions, look at the castle on the heights and give thanks for the protection our Señor the Prince, like a good father, offers in exchange for our vassalage. Go back to your classrooms, my sons, what are you doing here? Go back to Bologna, to Salamanca, and to Paris; you will not find the truth accompanying this rabble, this mob of beggars and prostitutes and false heresiarchs: the truth lies in the teachings of the Church Fathers, and in the flower of their philosophy: the angelic doctor, Thomas Aquinas, who summed up for eternity all the wisdom of which the human being is capable; do not look for heaven in this orgy of sensuality and music and exultant doubts and heretical ideas, there are no heavens but those defined in the Elucidations: the corporeal heaven we see, the spiritual heaven inhabited by the angels, and the intellectual paradise where the fortunate shall stand face to face with the Holy Trinity. Young men: each of us has a well-established place on this earth; the Liege commands, the serf obeys, the student studies, the priest prepares us for the life eternal, the learned doctor propounds the inviolate truths; no, it is not true what you proclaim; it is not true that we are free because Christ's sacrifice redeemed us from the sin of Adam; it is not true that the grace of God is within the reach of every man without the intercession of ecclesiastical powers; it is not true that redeemed human flesh may savor its own juices, its own polished smoothness, its joyful contact with other bodies, without fear of sin, we cannot put aside the fact that, as today we throw ourselves with pleasure into bed, soon others will throw us into the tomb; it is not true that the New Jerusalem can be constructed on this earth; anathema be the teachings of the heretic Pelagius, defeated, thankfully, by St. Augustine of Hippo, anathema, too, the teachings of Origen the suspect, who, surely not without some reason, culminated his thought with the atrocious act of self-castration, and the teachings of Joachim of Floris, that tenebrous Italian monk, as well, for no man obtains grace without the Church, as Pelagian heresy would have; nor will a millenary kingdom be realized in the souls of all believers, as Origen speculated, nor will there be, as prophesied in the Joachimite madness, a place in space, a third age, that will be the sabbath and the pleasure of sorrowing humanity, and in which epoch Christ and His Church will be replaced, since the spirit will reign fully in their stead; it is not true that you are the bearers of grace, accompanied by this riffraff, barefoot vagabonds who burn the lands and harvests, stables and farms, who assault and destroy monasteries, churches, and hermits' cells, who steal food and clothing from devastated castles, who will not work, who contend they live in perfect joy, and who say they do all this to hasten the second coming of a Christ who must in truth be the Antichrist, and so a cruel and seductive tyrant—but a tyrant who may nevertheless be overcome, and for that reason one who is capable of bringing about the defeat of your millenary promise, of a kingdom-of-heaven-on-earth never to come about while Lords are masters of all and serfs masters of nothing. What confusion is this? You say the millenary kingdom will arise only upon a vacant, destroyed, and leveled earth, like that of the first day of Creation; but the Creation, my beloved children, was beyond history and thus cannot be repeated. And you add that only upon this demolished earth may the new Christ be received, a Christ who actually will be the conquerable Antichrist whose downfall will assure, oh yes, will assure that joyous era where the spirit will reign unfettered, not in an individual incarnation, but incarnate in all. But if that cruel and seductive tyrant should not be vanquished, but instead be perpetuated in a third age of weeping and terror and misery, embodying history, and with all his means enlisting those who do not understand that the act of Creation cannot be repeated, that its repetition would only disguise the original act, inscribing it forever in the same history they wish to negate, and thus provide the Antichrist the double weapon of the ability to act, masqueraded as the Creator, and also to reign with impunity as the Ruler—what then? Is this the way you say you are imitating Christ, whose reign will not be of this world, and whom we shall encounter only in Heaven when all time has come to an end, far from the earth, far from history, far from the eschatological delirium with which you are attempting to establish as a part of history everything that has no part in history? Do you truly believe that poverty erases sin, that communal property and the exaltation of sex and the sensuality of the dance and the rejection of all authority and the unrestrained life of vagabonds in the forest, on the beaches, and along the highways could supplant and even overcome the established order? Listen; stop your dancing, why do you not listen? Cease your singing, what infernal racket! How may I make myself heard? Damned sickness of St. Vitus, you are mad, you are sick; rest, go back to your homes, the carnival is over, the revelry cannot last forever: the disarmed crusades, the rebellious, aspiring soul, end in sacrifice upon funeral pyres in seignorial castles; forget your illusions, stop yearning for the impossible, accept the world as it is, stop dreaming! Yes! The Liege has the right to the first nuptial night, and his are the harvests and the honor and respect, and he is entitled to recruit for his wars and impose tributes for his luxuries; and yes, the Bishop can sell indulgences and burn witches and torture heretics who speak of Jesus Christ as if He were a purely human man, our equal . . . Do not doubt, do not think, do not dream, my unhappy sons; this is the world, the world ends here, there is nothing beyond the edge of the sea and whosoever embarks seeking new horizons will be but a miserable galley slave in a ship of fools: the earth is flat and this is the center of the universe; the land you seek does not exist, there is no such place! There is no such place!

And so a raving, ranting Simón wandered the streets of the cities of his time, cities stifled beneath the plague, buried beneath their own filth. Though they retained their pain, his eyes had lost their clarity forever; he was become a breathless, timbreless voice, an expressionless gaze, a colorless face.

ASHES OF THE BRAMBLES

"That woman . . . is it you . . . Celestina?" asked the youth sitting beside the breaking waves when the page-and-drummer's story had ended.

"I am also called Celestina," she answered.

"Why are you traveling in this funeral cortege dressed as a man?"

The page looked at the youth with sadness; her beautiful gray eyes asked: Still you do not remember me? Was the impression I left in your memory so weak? But the tattooed lips recounted another story:

I lived with my father in the forest. He used to say that the forest is like the desert in other lands: the place of nothingness, the place to which one flees, for in the world it was our fate to inhabit there were so many things one must flee: empty spaces will be our protection. He, and his fathers before him, my father told me, fled the world because the world was plague, poverty, war, and an early death. When I was eleven I wanted to know why; I never completely understood his answer. In the memory of his ancestors (I retained only images; they filtered through my memory, already filtered through the memory of my father) those plague-ridden cities, those wars and invasions, the chaotic hordes and orderly phalanxes, slavery and hunger, passed like diurnal phantoms. I never completely understood; as I have told you, all that was left to me were certain images and all of them spoke to me of the collapse of a cruel world and the slow construction in its stead of another world, equally cruel. Our life was very simple. We lived in an ordinary hut. I spent most of the year tending sheep. I recall very clearly the time of my childhood. Everything had a meaning and a place. The sleepy summer sky and the early frosts of winter; the sheep and the bleating; the sun was a year and the moon turned in a month; day was a smile, and night, fear. But I remember especially the autumn time; between September and December, my life was flooded with unforgettable odors; it was the time to gather ashes to use in washing, and also the time to collect the oak-tree bark I used in dyeing, and forest resins for making torches and candles; and honey from the wild honeycomb.

We lived an isolated life; my father, when we walked far from our hut, pointed out the ancient Roman roads and told me that those routes now overgrown with grass and torn apart by invasions were once the pride of the ancient empire: straight, clean, cobbled. We sold our honey and torches, our candles and dyes; I began to sew and to dye clothing that found buyers among the voyagers traveling the new roads— worn smooth, my father said, by all those trampling feet—between the fairs and holy places, ports and universities; in this way I learned the happy and distant-sounding names of Compostela, Bologna, Venice, Chartres, Antwerp, the Baltic Sea . . . And thus I came to know that the world extended far beyond our forest. Men on foot and men on horseback, beasts of burden as well as the carts of the merchants, all abandoned the ancient roadways that only linked one castle to another. The travelers told me: We are afraid to pass close by the fortresses, for the Lords invariably rob us, rape our women, and impose all kinds of taxes upon us. I asked my father: What is a Lord? and he answered: A father who does not love his children as I love you. I did not understand. I sold our honey and candles in exchange for clothing I then washed with the ashes and dyed with the bark, then exchanged again for onions and for ducks. And so I helped my father; together we tended our flock and later, after the time for shearing the lambs had passed, he would travel to the castle to deliver to our Liege bales of wool in exchange for his permission to continue living in the isolated forest. But, little by little, our forest became fraught with dangers.

I remember the first time I saw El Señor. He had never visited us, but one day he came to advise us that every Saturday from that time forward, except on Twelfth Night and Pentecost Eves, accompanied by priests and horsemen, by farmers and shepherds, he would devote to hunting and destroying marauding wolves and to setting traps for them throughout the district. I, who always had frightened away the wolves with bonfires and burning brands, could not understand the need for killing or trapping them. But my father said: "They want to come into the forest; someday even here we will not be able to live in peace and we will have to flee again, searching, for the harsh desert." But I recognized in the hard and fearful gaze of El Señor only the desire to assert his presence and the fear that someone, someday, somewhere, would fail to recognize him. This twelve-year-old girls understand, for we, too, fear that, when we cease to be girls and become women, people who have always loved us will not know us.

Then came the strangest event of my childhood. One clear spring night I was tending my sheep and in spite of the full moon and balmy air had built the usual fire to protect myself and protect my flock, when close by I heard the sound of an animal in pain. I picked up one of the brands, sure that a wolf was approaching; and so it was, except that the moan should have warned me: it wasn't a howl in the distance, or the approaching stealth I recognized in wild beasts; it was a very tender and painful moan, and it was very close by. I lowered the flame: the light fell on a large gray she-wolf, her ears pricked up and her eyes feverish. Ever since I had learned to speak I had learned, before anything else, the sayings about wolves, for they were our greatest danger; and in spite of the tameness of this wolf, I said to myself: even if a wolf grow old and lose its teeth, it's still a wolf. But the she-wolf showed me a wounded paw she'd hurt in one of the traps set by El Señor during the Saturday hunts and I, in a childish and spontaneous way, knelt beside her and took the paw she offered me.

The she-wolf licked my hand and lay down beside my fire. I saw then that her belly was great and that the beast was not moaning only from the pain of the wound but for a graver reason: I had watched my sheep give birth and I understood what was happening. I stroked the she-wolf's angular head and waited. Soon she was giving birth; imagine my surprise, young sailor, when I saw emerge from between the she-wolf's legs two tiny blue feet exactly like those of a human baby; I was doubly confounded by the fact that even when baby rams—the animals most inclined to the monstrous—are born, even with two heads, those two heads appear first, but the she-wolf was delivering a child, and that child was emerging feet first.

It was a boy; he was born quickly, hunched and bluish; I tried to take him, afraid for him, born as he was on the ground of the forest, amid brambles and dust and bleating sheep and tinkling bells that seemed to celebrate the event; only then did the she-wolf snarl, and she herself licked the baby and cut the cord with her sharp teeth. I touched my breasts and realized that although I knew a lot I was still a little girl; the she-wolf pawed the newborn infant to her teats, and suckled him. I saw then, upon the infant's back, the sign of the cross; not a painted cross, but part of his flesh; flesh incarnate, young sailor.

I didn't know what to do; I would have liked to take the she-wolf and her offspring to my father's house, but the moment I tried to separate them or pull them both from the brambles, the she-wolf again snarled and snapped at my hand. Filled with fear, astonishment, and uneasiness, I returned to our cottage. I told my father what had happened and at first he laughed at me and then he told me to take care; he repeated one of the sayings I tell you now: "When the wolf gets his fill of savage ways, he joins the priesthood."

Very early the following morning, I returned to the bramble thicket, but neither the she-wolf nor the child was there. I was afraid for them, and I cried. I prayed that the she-wolf would find a deep hidden den where she could protect the child; otherwise, both would die during the hunt the following Saturday. My father came to the place where it had happened, and when he, as I, found nothing, he said I shouldn't fall asleep again while I was tending the flock, for I had already seen that wolves can appear in dreams, and one day while I was asleep they might really appear.

In spite of all the distractions our forests offered—even though its limits were shrinking—I never forgot that strange event. I recall that more people passed by every year of my adolescence. I met students traveling to their universities; horsemen and clerics; jugglers, minstrels, drug sellers, sorcerers, itinerant workers, freed serfs, soldiers without employ, beggars, and barefoot pilgrims carrying long staffs with hooks holding bottles; all the travelers of the routes of our Christian empire. And farmers also passed by, complaining that they had lost their lands, or that they couldn't pay both the tribute demanded by their Liege and the taxes demanded by the cities that spread outside their walls, absorbing fields and forests for themselves. And I never stopped wondering if, in some manner as mysterious as his birth, the destiny of the child born and suckled of the she-wolf was not somehow tied to the destiny of all these people who now marched through the same brambles which had witnessed his birth.

And one day I had a new, although fleeting and incomplete. response, for it was the memory of a child who is beginning to remember. Months before the she-wolf's whelping, just now I remembered, some of El Señor's men rode by on horseback, announcing their presence with singing and banners and long-tailed monkeys hanging to the backs of the chargers; and among the servants of the castle, also clinging like a monkey, with his knees hooked around the saddle horn, came El Señor's jester, with his many-colored hose and belled cap; and this buffoon was dandling a very blond and very young child, laughing at the cool branches of our forest. This child, too, had a cross between his shoulder blades. The procession passed by quickly, and when I told this to my father, he laughed, and said that I was a very fanciful little girl, and that cutting a cross upon one's back with a dagger or branding one with a red-hot iron was an old custom of the Crusaders and a common occurrence among the pilgrims. But this was a very small child. If the buffoon and the child ever again passed through our forest, I would approach him and say, "I know him; I saw him born."

And if the forest had been converted into a much-traveled route (and how many new things my dazzled eyes beheld: caravans laden with coffers filled with crowns and swords and coins with Arabic inscriptions, chests filled with intoxicating spices from the Orient), it also had created its own dangers. Isolated before, now we felt closed in, not only by the wolves, but by the bandits who hid in the forest thickets awaiting passing travelers; and what is worse, by horsemen in ambush, former Lords forced into the forest darkness by the debts accumulated on their former domains. This my father also told me. They carried long knives; all they had been able to salvage from their disaster.

One day El Señor visited us again; he arrived on a dun-colored horse and told my father that, from then on, the products from the land and animals we had always paid him were not enough, but my father would have to pay with money for the use of the land on which he lived and grazed his flocks and dyed his cloth. My father replied that he neither had nor used money, but instead traded one thing for another. El Señor told us that rather than ducks and onions we should demand money for our bales of wool and our honey and dyes. "Have your astonished eyes seen, serf, the chests and coffers passing through this forest? Well, their contents are delivered into the hands of the merchants of the city and to buy them, to adorn my castle and clothe my women, I need money."

It was not this that disquieted my father, not the fact it destroyed our simple customs and confronted us with the problem of how we might procure money and the novelty of dealing with the merchants of the towns; it was the way El Señor looked at me, and the question he asked my father: "When will the girl be married?" For then he added; "Marry her soon, for noblemen are roaming this forest who have lost their lands, but not their taste for virgin girls; what's more, they are in a mood to avenge the loss of their seignorial rights, and as the people of the cities have organized the defense of their lives and possessions, such noblemen are taking advantage of the daughters of men like you, defenseless in the forest. In any case," laughed El Señor, "remember you must save her maidenhead for me, because I still have power, and I swear to increase it, whether at the cost of the burghers or the impoverished princes. Guard your girl from them all, shepherd; don't let it be said afterward that you allowed her to be ruined for both you and me."

He rode away laughing and my innocent father decided to dress me as a boy from then on, although later we learned that El Señor had died of the fever before I could marry or he could take me. Dressed in sackcloth and rough leather breeches, my hair cut like a lad's, I continued my work of dyeing and herding, and I became a woman. Several years went by; my father grew old and our lives changed scarcely at all. Until one day there appeared armed men from the Prince Don Felipe, heir to the lands and privileges of his dead father. Their mission was to gather all the boys in the forest for service at arms and as servants; they captured me in the oak forest that from my childhood had been my protecting habitation and took me with them while I reflected upon my thankless fate: whether dressed as a man or a woman, like misfortune awaited me.

When Prince Felipe saw me dressed like a shepherd lad he did not guess my true condition, although my features seemed to awaken something disturbing in his memory. I, I swear it, had never seen him before. The new Señor assigned me to the service of his mother, where the presence of women, I then learned, was forbidden. As a young shepherdess I had learned to play the flute and I let this be known to the head steward in order to entertain myself and as a distraction in my desire to live separated from the servants and soldiers, before whom I never disrobed. I was able to live in the quarters of the musicians, who were too occupied at night and early morning in sleeping off their drunkenness to notice me, and too busy during the day taking advantage of the funereal self-absorption of the mistress of the castle, constantly kneeling before her husband's embalmed cadaver, to steal provisions and bottles from the cellars. The mother of El Señor's son had forbidden all gay music in her presence, and although she respected my musical talents, she ordered me to learn to play the drum, for as she was living in continuous mourning she wished to hear only funereal sounds. And thus, when the elderly Lady began her long pilgrimage with her husband's corpse, she assigned me to the last position in the procession, dressed all in black and playing my drum, an announcement of mourning. La Señora, mother of the present Señor, does not admit women in her company because she is jealous of them all, as if her husband's cold dead flesh were still capable of the abuses that won him fame in life and from which, by my great good fortune, I was saved, although only to fall into this miserable condition.

But I have wandered from essential things, and I wish to bring my story to a close as night falls upon this beach. Only by a mistake that the mayor and the halberdiers will pay very dearly for, we entered yesterday a convent of nuns who wanted to take possession of El Señor's mummified body. And that is why, instead of traveling all night cloaked in the darkness the Lady prefers, we fled and are traveling by day. Thus I have found you. Now you must come with me.

"Who am I?" asked the shipwrecked youth. "Where have I come from?"

But the page had ended her story, and did not wish to answer him. She offered both hands to the youth, but he held out only one. With the other, impelled by some inexplicable fascination, he picked up a sealed green bottle, a piece of flotsam tossed by the waves onto this Cabo de los Desastres.

EL SEÑOR SLEEPS

El Señor had faltered in the midst of his narration, after recalling the affair with Ludovico and Celestina (imagined on the ship of the ancient Pedro, but actual in the bloodstained castle; more hallucinatory, nevertheless, the dreamed than the real). Guzmán had served him a soothing potion; and now, as he finished the story, repeating the exhortation of the monk Simón faithfully transcribed for El Señor by the Court Chronicler, the master asked for a second potion; Guzmán, ever solicitous, prepared it as El Señor murmured: "This is the story I wished to record on my birthday, which will also be the day of the second burial of all my ancestors. El Señor, may he rest in glory, was my father; and my name as a youth was Felipe."

"And the young Lady of the castle?" Guzmán inquired, as he offered the narcotic to his Prince.

"She is our Señora, who dwells here . . . ."

His lids heavy, he repeated, "Our Señora . . ." but could not finish the prayer; the sleeping potion had swept him to the depths of a heavy stupor in which he imagined himself besieged by eagles and hawks deep within a valley of stone. Sluggishly, he searched for an exit; but the valley was an open prison, a vast, deep jail with steep, sheer walls. One single distant unbarred window: the blue and mottled patch of sky high above, accessible only to the birds. And these birds of prey would soar high in the sky and then dive with rage to attack an abandoned and imprisoned El Señor, more heavy-limbed than fearful. And after wounding him, the eagles and falcons again soared to the heights. Immediately, without logical transition, he dreamed he was three different men, the three a single man although possessing three different faces in three distinct times; the three, always, captive in the stony valley with no exit but the sky. Dragging himself through sharp-pointed rocks of this frozen wasteland, he peered into the pupils of the first of the men who was himself and he could see, in one of the eyes of these alter egos, Pedro's sons mutilated by the hounds; and in the other pupil he saw himself as an adolescent protecting himself from his father's falcons. But the face of the first man that was he, through whose pupils these scenes were projected, was no longer the youth fleeing with the sons of the serf, or the youth fearful of the falcons, but the identical face of the man who one fateful day had threaded his way among the corpses of children, women, farmers, artisans, beggars, prostitutes, lepers, Jews, mudejares, penitents, heresiarchs, madmen, prisoners, and musicians led to their slaughter in the castle so that he, Felipe, might demonstrate to El Señor that he was worthy of inheriting the power of the older man.

Why did these painful images of a fearful youth persist in the eyes of the face that was both seductive and cruel? The dreamer could not answer his own question; he fled from the first man to encounter the third; he recognized himself now in the form of an ancient man dressed in black lying upon a large flat rock, his face turned to the sun; but the sun neither illuminated nor melted the waxen visage that repelled the light, and through its facial orifices crawled worms less white than the ancient's skin: from the ears, between the lips, through the nostrils, twisting and pullulating; and moist behind the milky concave curtain of the eyes, for behind the transparent cornea writhed a colony of tiny, threatening eggs.

He turned from the third man and lay down—he, the dreamer, the second man, the actual Señor, the prisoner of the profound sleep induced by Guzmán's potions—face down among the rocks; he opened his arms in a cross and begged forgiveness; but his dominion over measurable time had ended; he knew he would remain there forever, prostrate, mouth agape, breathing uselessly, prisoner of this palace of shattered rock, until the swallows built their nests in his open palms, until the falcons and eagles, in a false and unbelievable spirit of love for the species, no longer dived to strike: he, too, would be an eagle —a conquered eagle, an eagle of stone. "One wolf does not bite another," El Señor murmured in the prayer in his dream; he did not doubt the dark instinct of the relationships which in this jail of rapacious birds led him to think of other, of vulpine threats. Eagle and wolf, he murmured, wolf and lamb, swallow and eagle, spiritual lover and libertine, devout Christian and bloodthirsty criminal, punctilious student of the truth and unscrupulous manipulator of the lie, I am but one of you: a Spanish gentleman.

Lofty jail, icy sun, flesh of wax, charnel house . . . the dreamer sobbed: Where, my sons; to whom shall I bequeath my inheritance?

GUZMAN SPEAKS

In the tossing and turning of his nightmare, El Señor finally lay face down on the bed, arms opened in a cross. Guzmán circled about him, pacing always more nervously about the bed, as if El Señor's relentless sleep were a test of the narcotic prepared and administered by the vassal. And nevertheless he knew no more powerful drug than this mixture of the male and female blossoms, black and white, pepper and arsenic, of the mandrake, the tree with the face of a man. Only after his master lay face down in the customary position for prayers on the chapel floor, but also (Guzmán could not know that) imitating the posture he was that instant dreaming, so the postures in life and dream coincided, only then did Guzmán tell himself that he was master of El Señor's nightmare, as he could never be during the cruel penitential vigils. The impossible mask dropped: that of the Guzmán who knew how to cure dogs and train hawks and organize the hunt. He discarded that mask for what it was: a thin layer of flesh maintained—easily now, from habit—over his true features. Closer to the bone the true Guzmán was revealed: the expression recognized by the hounds, feared by the deer, and accepted as natural by the hawks; the rapacious profile that revealed itself to El Señor when the servant least desired: kneeling to pick up a breviary, withdrawing to fulfill a command.

Guzmán drew a long dagger from its sheath and held it over El Señor's back.

Here am I, he said to himself (to him), master of your sleep, master of your unconscious body, even if only to see you in sleep as you can never see yourself. If the value of a man is determined by the price promised for his murder, you, Sire, are of no value: no one would pay me to kill you. If I wish to murder you, it must be done without spilling a single drop of your blood or collecting a single maravedi. But you, if you knew my desire, how much would you pay for my death, Sire? And so our roles are reversed, for although you are everything, no one would give me anything for your death; whereas I am nothing, but for my death, to avoid your own, you would give everything.

Guzmán ceased speaking only to Guzmán: as he raised his voice, Bocanegra picked up his ears: Imbecile, you do not deserve your power; you will never even know that your sin was not in murdering the innocents but in wasting the opportunity to include your father and your mother and your sweetheart in the slaughter and thus build your absolute authority upon the absolute freedom of the crime: an ascension to power without the need of dynasty and without the pathos of being who you are merely by inheritance; you could have had a power free of any debt. You botched even your crime, poor stupid Felipe; you inscribed it upon the mortal line of your succession, instead of converting it into the uncompromised basis for your absolutism; that is the reason for your dissatisfaction, not remorse, but the mutilation you wrought upon your inner self. You aged mortally in the instant you presented your crime to your father, having killed your father's subjects. Did you want witnesses? Is that why you committed the error of pardoning the student and the witch? You will regret that; it is I, Guzmán, who tells you, you will regret that, because even an ignorant mountain bandit knows that one must never pardon an enemy, however innocent he may be; the pardon strips him of his innocence and turns him into an avenger. Did you want witnesses? You had me write your confession so that the events you recounted might come into being, because for you only what is written exists, and you understand no permanency but that of a piece of paper; bah, this very moment I could burn it; this very moment I could rewrite it, eliminate and add, write that you also murdered Ludovico and Celestina, and then you would yourself believe it, because it was so written; and if that man and woman should reappear you would only see two phantoms. Did you want witnesses? You are alone. Without witnesses, your crime would have been so absolute that only you and the world would have shared it; your witness would have been history, not the whimpering dog who hears your laments. Hear me, poor, suffering, sick little Felipe, aged before your time by your lacerating asceticism; I, Guzmán, tell you I am not what you believe or would like to believe, some upstart upon whom you can bestow minute favors that are supposed to seem enormous to me. It is I, Guzmán, who tells you this, not some bastard son of a bitch, but a Lord like you, although broken by debts. Not some scum covered with scabs and filth, but another Prince, although destitute. Not some young sneak thief from some dusty hamlet in Aragon, but a boy who like you had the opportunity to learn the arts of falconry and archery, horsemanship, and the hunt. Not some lout from Guadarrama turned highway robber, but a nobleman incapable of understanding or of holding back an invisible movement in which land, the base of all power, could be converted into insubstantial money, and where castle walls constructed for eternity would last a briefer time than winter's swallows; I, reduced to vassalage by a power with neither fortification nor cannons by the usurers, merchants, and miserable clerks of leprous cities. My fathers and grandfathers, Sire, fulfilled before your ancestors the ceremony of homage and thus entered a pact: our service in exchange for your protection. In this way, we would all maintain the fundamental principle of our society; no Lord without land and no land without a Lord. And we were maintaining the balance between strength and need; the power of the Liege in exchange for the protection and survival of the weak. And within this major pact, we entered a lesser—although for me, Sire, one no less important, reasoned, or vital: the service of noble vassals given in exchange for your protection would assure that we nobles would always be nobles and that the lower classes would be kept in their place, for the blood of the two is not equal, nor can their destinies be equal. But see me today, Sire, born a nobleman and become a servant—the blame is yours. You did not honor the treaty. Our service continued, but not your protection. You allowed the debilitation of the power based on the land, confronted with the power of commerce based on money. You undertook costly and distant campaigns against heresy, forgetting the counsel of the ancient Inquisitor to the zealous Augustinian: rebels grow tall with attention, but are effaced by indifference. You squandered your fortune in constructing a useless, inaccessible, austere mausoleum; the common man identifies power with luxury, not with death. Your guilty conscience led you to submit your interests to religion; the astute Prince subjects religion to his interests. But behind your sterile obsessions—heresy and necrophilia—a real world is growing, agitating and transforming everything. You left your noble vassals undefended; you were too much preoccupied with persecuting heretics and building sepulchers; we had to sell our lands, assume debts, close the workshops that could not compete with the city merchants, and sell our serfs their freedom. Faced with the power of the cities, you vowed to increase yours at our expense. We paid for your crusades and your crypts; you did not exterminate the heretics, for where one martyred rebel falls, ten spring up in his place; and you will not resuscitate the corpses of your ancestors; they will not accompany you in the solitudes of your governing. You have destroyed the grades of nobiliary authority between the Liege and the cities. So today there remain only two powers; that of the minor nobleman no longer exists. I, Sire, allied myself to what destroyed me; I passed over to the enemy lines so as not to be conquered by them; and I joined your service to enable myself to participate in both powers until this battle is decided; for it will be decided, Sire, have no doubt about that; and then I shall opt for the conqueror. What I am doing is called politics; choosing the lesser, the more secure, of two undesirable solutions. I, Guzmán, tell you that I learned to speak the language of the human rubble that constructs your palaces and hunts your boars; I, Guzmán, learned to control your peasants, to threaten and gratify them in turn; it was not my destiny to cut the heart from the deer and with this ceremony adulate those rowdies; I, Guzmán, converted by necessity into a knave, an informer, and for that reason cosseted by Lords who would be incapable of knowing what was happening in their domains if a Prince among bandits did not do it for them—and receive their favors for the task. I tell you this; I, Guzmán, like you, educated for divine and unending seigniory, but forced by circumstances to know the very temporal and profane sophistries with which these new men combat inherited power; I, Guzmán, capable, like you, of crime, not in the name of dynastic providence but in the name of political history. For to your faith in the hereditary continuity that makes of you a harassed accident of birth, these new men oppose the simple will of their own persons, with neither antecedents nor descendancy, a will that is consumed in itself, and whose dispersed potency is called history. I belong to both bands, my Lord; I am impelled to vengeance against them by the recollection of my seignorial youth, by the subjugation of my destiny by men of the cities who mock destiny, for theirs flows as swiftly as their ducats pass from hand to hand; I am impelled to vengeance against you by this question that I dare ask you only while you are sleeping: last of the Lieges, corrupt and crepuscular sum of the powers you wrested from the minor nobles but could not maintain against the great burghers, will your strength be less than that of a knave? And will you know less than a knave? But without the knave could you manage to be anything but a witness to the splendiferous sunset of your power? Our Señor . . . the last Señor. Bah . . . I shall mark my time patiently, I shall cure your dogs and order your hunts so that you maintain some semblance of your power; and I shall prepare for the inevitable contest between your power and that of the new men; if my will does not weaken and if fortune favors me, I shall be arbiter between both; and someday, have no fear, I shall govern in your name as governed the stewards of the indolent Kings of France.

THE DOGS

Guzmán walked around the sleeping body, still holding high the long knife, and a grieving and restless Bocanegra growled quietly; then Guzmán laughed and sheathed the dagger. He walked to the door and Bocanegra's growl rose to a ferocious pitch; he opened the door and took the leashes of several steaming, jostling, expectant greyhounds, along with vessels containing various compounds, from the hands of the faithful hunt attendants. He led the dogs into the bedchamber; Bocanegra, bound to his board, could not move, but he barked desperately; the other dogs approached to sniff him, as Guzmán called them by name: here, Fragoso; here, Hermitaña; down, Preciada; quiet, Herreruelo; here, Blandil. He took the forepaws of the swollen Hermitaña and rubbed her dugs and engorged black teats made tender by the overdue whelping; then he threw her on the bed of the sleeping Liege; he took the vessel containing a paste of ash and watered wine and briskly anointed the bitch's gaping genitals. Then with a burst of laughter he spoke to Preciada: "And how is my pretty little Preciada? How do you like going without food for a day? What sweet eyes she has, here . . . here."

He held out a portion of leavened dough and as the ravenous bitch ate, and before she realized, he had inserted three grains of coarse salt in her anus; then he unleashed Herreruelo, who went straight for the bitch's black hole, and excited by the trembling induced by hunger and the salt, mounted her and began pumping energetically, all on El Señor's bed. Then Guzmán called Blandil to the bed, fed him a mixture of human excrement and goat's milk, and the dog began to urinate on the bed while Herreruelo and Preciada fornicated, linked together like a monster with two heads and eight paws, and Hermitaña finally began to deliver her pups in her master's bed, one after another, and each one, born in the island of silk between the contracted paws and the warm muzzle, was licked clean by the bitch, who cut the cord with her teeth and then nuzzled the pups to her pulsing teats. Bocanegra barked, incapable, now the hour had finally arrived, of defending his master: Guzmán jerked three hairs from his tail and the great mastiff stopped barking, as if he were fearful of being expelled from his own quarters. The chief huntsman took Fragoso by the collar and dragged him to El Señor's curule chair where the master's clothing was scattered.

"Fragoso, good Fragoso, my beast," he murmured into the silky ear. "Smell the master's clothing, smell it well, that's a boy. Go get him, Fragoso, go at him, boy." Guzmán stimulated the dog, stroking its testicles and penis, and then unleashed him, directing him at the bed, where he leaped upon the person sleeping there drugged by the heavy vapors of the mandrake. Seated upon his Liege's wrinkled clothing in the curule chair, Guzmán observed the spectacle, laughing, master of El Señor's infinite dream.

"I know perfectly how to cure the dogs, but not El Señor. But what are your miserable amulets, Master Felipe, compared to my ointments of excrement and hog fat. When the hour arrives, you will not be able to save yourself, my fine Prince."

Then he looked at the crouching, suffering, confused, and resentful Bocanegra and said: "I know you, brute, and I know that you know me. You alone know what I really think, what I do, and what I plan to do. El Señor has no more faithful ally than you. Sad that you can do nothing to tell your master all you see and hear, what only you know; too bad, poor unhappy Bocanegra. Yes, we are rivals. Guard yourself well from me, for I know how to defend myself from you. You have the weapons, although not the voice, to be a menace to me. I, to combat you, have both weapons and voice."

In the depths of the walled valley, accompanied by a youth and an ancient, El Señor murmured prayers in which he asked three things: a brief life, an unchanging world, and eternal glory.

JUAN AGRIPPA

Enclosed; condemned to hear the sounds; every day, one day after another, the expected sounds, the day filled to overflowing with repetitious sounds that paralyzed every action except waiting and listening; the yearning for the exception, the accident of chance that would interrupt the monotony of the established sounds: matins, the cock's crow, the hammer, the wheels of the oxcarts coming from Burgo de Osuna, the smith's bellows, the shouts of the supervisors, the laughter of the water carriers, crackling fires in the taverns, deliveries of bales of hay and straw, the murmur of the looms, the screech of slate in the quarries, the hollow sound of tiles being broken and fitted, the barking of dogs, the wings of the hawk in flight, the cautious footsteps of Guzmán, the monotonous chant of El Señor's prayers, the orotund pealing of the evening bells. This is the accustomed, through every repetitious day; this is the first thing she would wish to interrupt, to disturb; but she comes to fear more the shock of an unexpected sound; the succession of known sounds is preferable; one can wait without waiting.

La Señora wept throughout the night; not from grief, that she would have rejected as unseemly, nor for a humiliation that she would know how to disguise with an exaggerated dignity of external bearing.

"He has been condemned. He will be burned alive beside the palace stables," Guzmán told her.

Slowly and with sensual pleasure, La Señora looked around the isolated luxury of her bedchamber, decorated from the beginning to contrast with the mystic austerity her husband had desired—and achieved. This corner of Arabia decorated in secret by La Señora with the help of Guzmán and the painter-priest Julián was far, still very far, from her ultimate aspiration: re-creating a Court of Love like the celebrated courts of Eleanor of Aquitaine in Poitiers and the gallant fairs celebrated in Treviso, the court of joy and solace where a Castle of Love had been defended by noble ladies against the assault of the rival bands of noblemen of Padua and Venice, the former dressed completely in black and the Venetians completely in white. But today in this chamber redolent of Chinese ginger, carnation, pepper, camphor, and musk, a major accouterment of pleasure was missing. La Señora accepted as the flaw in the luxury that, in order to maintain it, in order to dwell in it, from time to time it was necessary to abandon it, to summon the black bearers, climb into the heavily perfumed and curtained palanquin, position the falcon on her gauntleted wrist, and travel the desert, coastal, and mountain roads seeking the reborn prisoner; without him the luxuries of the bedchamber were but theatrical trappings, a dimensionless curtain, like the silken and gold veil that had belonged to the Caliph of Córdoba, Hisham II, and now adorned one wall of her chamber. Quite different destinies, in truth, thought La Señora: hers and that of her accursed mother-in-law, El Señor's mother; for while the one wandered hazardous roads searching for a renewed lover, the other wandered the same roads bearing the everlasting cadaver of an eternal lover.

Brother Julián, the palace iconographer, had endured many wakeful nights delicately tracing with minute brushstrokes on porcelain brooches the figure and place dreamed by La Señora: the place, the coast of the Cabo de los Desastres; the figure, a young man lying face down on the beach, naked, with a blood-red cross between his shoulder blades. Brother Julián was grateful for the potions of belladonna that La Señora furnished him to maintain his condition—lucid and dreamy, absent and present, remote and near, participant in the dream and the dream's faithful executor—while the monk's pale hand re-created the material lines of the dream fantasies communicated to him by La Señora. Looking at the drawing, the mistress kept to herself the ultimate meaning of the painter's art: the identity. Brother Julián, in his drugged trance, added minuscule details to the drawing, the six toes on each foot, for example, of the man presumed to be the victim of a shipwreck.

"Hexadigitalism is the privilege of those destined to renew their family bloodlines. Believe me, Señora, the sterility of your union is not your fault but the tariff accumulated by the family of El Señor, who, remember, is your second cousin. If you trace back a strict dynastic line, you will see that your common ancestors are reduced to a very small number. Every living man carries within himself thirty phantoms; such is the extant relationship between the living and the dead. Your line, Señora, goes back to only a half dozen incestuous brothers and sisters living for centuries in the promiscuous isolation of their castles, avoiding all contact with the mob and their pestilential menace; isolated, telling you the ancient stories of the birth, passion, and death of Kings. What is certain is that the price of extreme consanguinity as well as the excesses of extreme fertility are in the end enemies to dynastic continuity. Cambyses, King of Persia, married his sister Meroë and when she was carrying his child killed her by kicking her in the belly. See in this crime the ultimate in certain sibling relationships. And on the other hand, twins—a form of pregnancy as superfluous as redundant—have killed three great dynasties, those of the Caesars, the Antonines, and the Carolingians. Renew the bloodlines, Señora, seek neither sterile incest nor prolific births but love and its customs, which are the ways of passion that engender beauty and precision. Enough, Señora, of this attempt to deceive your subjects: the familiar public announcement of your pregnancy, hoping to attenuate the expectation of an heir, merely forces you to pretense: you must stuff your farthingale with pillows and imitate a condition that is not yours; then follows the equally familiar announcement of a miscarriage. Frustrated hopes are often converted into irritation, if not into open rebellion. El Señor, and you also, Señora, are beginning to suffer excessively for past legitimizations, for in our world custom makes law and a twice-repeated event becomes a custom. The rights of your dominion must be exercised continually or they will be lost. El Señor is no longer seen to wage war, to subdue, with the spilling of blood, any to whom it might have occurred to spill the blood of the powerful. And you are not seen to produce heirs. You must be cautious. Allay their discontent with one theatrical blow: fulfill their hopes by producing a son. You are the daughter of the happy English isle, Anglia plena jocis, and naturally you are unsuited to this Castilian severity. Wager everything on pleasure; combine it, Señora, with duty and you will win all the games. You may rely on me, whatever you decide; the only proof of paternity will be the features of El Señor that I introduce upon the seals, miniatures, medallions, and portraits that will be the representation of your son for the multitude and for posterity. I cannot change an infant's features, but I can emphasize in my icons the hereditary features of the supposed father, our Señor; I can erase the real features, whether they be those of one of your black bearers, of some common construction supervisor, or of the poor youth, your latest lover, condemned to die at the stake. And let us give thanks to God that he is dying for the secondary and not the principal crime. But to return to our concern: the populace will know the face of your son only through the coins bearing the effigy I have designed that are minted and circulated in our kingdoms; the ordinary citizen will never have occasion to compare the engraved image with the real face; he will never see your infant except from a distance, when you deign to display him from some high, remote balcony; and history will know only the effigy that I, following your will, leave to it. For, no matter how beautiful your offspring, I shall charge myself to mark upon his face the stigmata of this house: prognathism."

"You are right, Brother Julián. I should have allowed myself to become pregnant by that beautiful boy."

"Ah yes, he was truly beautiful! But think no more of him; he will be dead within a few hours. Better think of the new youth, the one of your dream."

"And what will his name be?"

"Juan Agrippa. Remember, six toes on each foot and a blood-red cross upon his back."

"What do the name and the marks signify?"

"That Rome still lives."

"How do you know these things?"

"Because you have dreamed them, Señora."

"I don't know whether the dream is completely mine; I don't know . . ."

"Some dreams can be induced, and some can be shared."

"You lie. You know more than you are telling."

"But if I told her everything, La Señora would cease to have confidence in me. I do not betray La Señora's secrets; she must not insist that I betray mine."

"It is true. Then you would cease to interest me."

La Señora and the miniaturist monk, both under the effects of the belladonna, stared at each other unseeing, their pupils dilated. In the pupils of the tall, fragile, blond, and bald cleric was revealed the image of an eternal empire, renewed and immortal throughout all the convolutions of blood and war, of bed and gallows; darkly reflected in La Señora's pupils was the chance event only, but not the continuity; the event was pleasure, the continuity the duty Julián wished to impose upon her; she saw, multiplied ad infinitum, the figure of the youth lying on the beach, and between his thighs she wished to divine the seed of pleasure as well as the seed of pregnancy; she did not know, actually, whether both could germinate at the same time.

"When?"

"Tomorrow."

"Tomorrow, against his will, my husband goes to the hunt."

"Even better; he will be distracted and absent-minded; and you will be able to go as far as the coast."

"Tell Guzmán to ready the litter, the hawk, and the Libyan bearers."

"He will want a guard to accompany you. It is a very lonely area."

"Let my orders be obeyed! And if your prophecies are true, Brother Julián, you will have pleasure."

"That is all a contrite and devout soul could ask."

BRIEF LIFE, ETERNAL GLORY,

UNCHANGING WORLD

When he awoke, El Señor attributed the filth of his bed to the attack of the eagles and the mockery of the hawks during his dream of the stone valley: bound to his board, Bocanegra dozed, exhausted. Captive in what he believed to be the physical prolongation of his nightmare, El Señor had no time to feel revulsion; the stench of the bedchamber, the inexplicable presence of the thick slobber, the tortured stools, animal placenta, and stains of urine and blood, semen and grease, were less compelling than the will to decipher the tripartite prayer that echoed through his dream like an airy refrain: Brief life, eternal glory, unchanging world.

Then he was struck by the recollection of the Cathedral profaned on the day of his victory: excrement and blood—copper and iron—of what were they signs? Inheritance or promise? Residuum or new dawn?

He sensed a flash of light; he turned his head; he saw himself reflected in a hand mirror resting against a water pitcher near the head of his bed. He saw himself, his mouth opened like a man yelling. But no scream escaped from that breathless, choking throat.

He picked up the hand mirror and hurried into the chapel, fleeing from the silent horror of the filthy bedchamber. In the chapel greater dangers existed, real dangers, dangers far removed from the intangible menace of his bedchamber.

Once there, he found time to question, once again, the Christ without a halo standing to one side in the painting brought from Orvieto. He received no response from the figure; then he walked to the stairway.

Mirror in hand, he paused at the first step.

He raised the mirror to his eyes, studying his image.

It was he. A man born thirty-seven years earlier: serene forehead, skin like wax, one cruel eye, one tender (both veiled by heavy-lidded, saurian eyelids), straight nose with flaring nostrils, as if compassionately amplified by God himself to facilitate the difficult respiration; thick lips, salient jaw, disguised both by the silken beard and moustache and by the folds of the high white ruff that hid the neck, separating the head from the trunk; above the ruff the head was poised like a captive bird.

El Señor gazed at himself and tried to recall how he had looked in his youth when he fled through the forest with the sons of Pedro and, with Celestina, reached the sea; how the wind had whipped his then curly hair and battered his bare chest; how the thorns had torn at his boots and the branches ripped his shirt; how strong his legs had been and how his sun-bronzed arms had glistened as he tugged at the ship's sail beside the student Ludovico; ah, to be young . . .

No longer was he that youth, but neither was he yet this man: watching himself in the mirror, he ascended the first step; and the change, although almost imperceptible, did not escape his keen attention, his secret proposal; the mouth was a bit more open, as if the difficulty of breathing had increased. He ascended the second step: in the mirror the network of wrinkles was more finely woven about eyes a little more sunken and hollow.

He climbed the third step, indifferent to the swift and inexplicable changes of the light, attentive only to the changing image in the mirror: the front teeth were missing now, and the mesh of wrinkles about the eyes and mouth had become impenetrable. He climbed the fourth step: his beard and hair were reflected white as an August cloud, white as a January field; the mouth, now agape, sought with anguish the never sufficient air and the bloodshot eyes recalled too much—and begged clemency for what they remembered.

He reached the fifth step, and it was only with a great effort that he refrained from retreating rapidly to the lower stair: the asphyxiated face in the mirror conveyed the image of the resignation that precedes death. His neck was bandaged, pus ran from his ears, and worms filled his nostrils. Already dead? Dead in life? To ascertain, he found the courage to climb the sixth step; the face in the mirror was motionless, and the neck bandages now shrouded his jaw.

He fled from that image, ascending; now it became difficult to penetrate the shadows of the mirror, to discern, after accustoming himself to the darkness of that reflection, that the bandages had been destroyed by the slow and persistent working of the worms, and the jaw itself consumed by the humidity and weight of the earth—but the mouth, closed at last, no longer pleaded for air. On the seventh step, he seemed to see several mirrors reflected in the quicksilver of his hand mirror, for the face was multiplied in successive whitish, silvered, phosphorescent layers as the flesh relinquished its privileges to bone. Only bone was reflected at the level of the eighth step, a skull that frightened him less than the previous apparitions, for why did it have to be his? How to distinguish one skull from all the rest, if death's booty is always the loss of one's face? He ascended rapidly: the skull persisted through the eternity of the four steps; but on the thirteenth, the prolonged darkness surrounding a glowing center of bones was dissipated.

In its place, a strange sky, at once opaque and transparent, like the metallic domed sky of solar eclipses—as if by the addition of layer after layer of white light a dense transparency was finally formed—clouded by the oval of the mirror; only then did El Señor realize, in retrospect, that the faces had not appeared in a vacuum, but accompanied by sounds he tried not to reconstruct: there were birds, yes, and footsteps, and the rustle of cloth; there were fragments of music too swift, too evanescent to be heard or judged; there were voices so low and thunder so loud that they could be recovered only in the reconstruction of memory; there was the sound of grass growing, close, very close, too close, and in the distance, bleating, neighing, braying, lowing, barking, howling, and buzzing. Again they existed only in memory; in that moment of nothingness even sound ceased, and what El Señor most mourned was the absence of the birds.

On the following step the domed sky parted; the metallic light disintegrated; but the gusts of wind and the flashing lights, resolved into hitherto unseen globes of color, into triangles of fire and columns of phosphorus, blocks of total terror and enigmatic spirals, obstructed his ability to place himself within that total space, fleeting and infinite, with no beginning and no end; El Señor mused that if his face had still existed—even if in the form of scattered, although reconstitutable dust—it would be the face of madness contemplating something without an origin and without an end; he recalled that the palace astrologer, Brother Toribio, had once spoken to him of Eridanus, the river of luminous sands in the heavens that flows beneath the scepter of Brandenburg illuminating the ramparts of the stars and vitalizing the tomb of the Phoenix: he felt as if he were falling from that cluster of flowing stars as upon ascending the next step he saw in the mirror the lush vegetating depths of a jungle where no sun penetrated, where not even the dense, petrified, archaic foliage of a dead flower moved; the flower acquired life, became aqueous, marine, plastic, undulating, only when he stepped onto the next stair.

In the center of the liquid and fleshy vegetation, again glowed a dot that, although unrecognizable, El Señor knew was himself. The dot was a white drop; he knew it had life, and desperately he willed it to be his. He climbed; the reflection again became murky; a sea of mud in the center of the night, the obverse of all medals, the horary of the moon, a palace of ashes, a recollection of rain, the first word, animals dreaming of themselves and of other animals and thus effecting the first breath of existence; dreamed, not created; creating themselves as they dreamed themselves.

Shivering, he reached the step he had been waiting for: a whitish being, hairless, amorphous, swimming in dark liquid. Now he advanced rapidly: here, connected to the body by a delicate web of veins and nerves, two egg-like lumps, shining but dormant, dominated the unformed fetus: the eyes; higher, the white body became covered with hair; the drawn-up paws began to move, as if wishing release from their prison; he heard a ferocious howl: suddenly all the lost sounds returned, the world again was echoing with laughter and waterfalls, waves and bird song, fires and marching feet, trumpets and whistles, rustling taffeta and scraped platters, the resounding blow of the ax and the blast of the bellows; but all that was reflected in the mirror was a newly born wolf cub; El Señor paused in his feverish ascent and with a growing tremor contemplated those eyes, one cruel and the other tender, that gaping snout gasping for air, those sharp teeth. Slowly, never taking his eyes from the vision in the mirror, he climbed. The wolf was full-grown now and it was running through fields that El Señor seemed to know, pursued by arms and men with insignia that El Señor recognized as his own: *Nondum, Not yet.*

Terrified, he threw the mirror from the top of the stairway and it shattered against the granite flooring in the crypt. Gasping, he ran down the stairs, crowned from above by the dyssymbolic light of refractory years; pursued by the past of his future, he threw himself face down, arms opened, before the altar; the steady light originating in the clear painted space of an Italian piazza illuminated the cross on his cape; the future lay behind him, half seen, for El Señor could not again review the totality of those thirty-three steps. His exhausted body called upon memorized words: "In my weakness I beseech your aid in my struggle not to be vanquished by the importunate and astute temptations devised against me by that most ancient of Serpents. But great is the battle of love; its powerful weapons are your beneficences that spread confusion in the hearts of the ungrateful. As the Holy Spirit says, the impious one, the evildoer, flees even though he not be pursued, for he accuses himself and is rendered pusillanimous and cowardly by his own crime. Oh, God, I know that the testimony of one's own conscience is a continual exhortation that cannot be ejected from one's house, or stilled. According to St. Paul, that conscience serves as glorious consolation to the Just, but is a continual torment to the ungrateful. Am I to be judged ungrateful, and not just? Am I to be judged impious, am I the evildoer, is that why you reserve these visions for me in spite of my intense devotion?"

Prostrate, weeping, choked by feelings of confusion and guilt, he rejected these ideas; but, unconsciously, he was seeking to reject the terrible duplicate memory: from this time forward he was doomed to recall both his past and his future. And that curse could not be the work of the Most Tender Lamb.

"The Devil endeavors with rabid fury to obstruct the holy exercise of my mental prayer. To this end this wily Dragon applies whatever means and whatever confusion his persistent and indefatigable malice can contrive; but when he cannot succeed, he changes his tactics and interjects his cunning deceits into the holy exercise itself. Oh, God, do not allow the Devil to take advantage of the intense fervor of my prayer; assure me in this moment, prostrate before you, my head filled with horrible visions, that my affection is no less pure, and assure me that my present state of abjection and forlornness will not serve the Enemy of God as an opportunity to sow the seeds of his accursed dissension; do not allow him to deceive my grieving soul, openly, invading every minute, every occasion, every place, invading the holy exercise of prayer itself. I do not know, my God . . . I question even whether the occasion of my penitence may be the Devil's greatest opportunity, for that venomous serpent strikes in silence; and there is nothing worse than his mind, for there is no good thought in it, and only that mind would unveil the picture of my future. You would not do so, you who have granted us the beneficence of not knowing what lies ahead, reserving for yourself that wisdom without which you would not be God.

You reserve for us only the certainty of death, not the where or the how or the why. Nor would you be God if you revealed upon our births the course and the final end of our lives, nor would we be your loving creatures if we knew: such intelligence may only be the false gift of the Evil One.''

The candles sputtered, and incense suffused the crypt; El Señor gazed with passion, anxiety, doubt, and surrender at the principal figure of the painting brought from Orvieto, and to that figure he directed his prayers: ''Liberate me, God, from vain complacency and hidden pride, from exaggerated pentitence, and from imaginary visions and false revelations. How may I distinguish the true interior voices, which are those of God, the supernatural and divine ecstasy and raptures in which a loving God communicates with my soul, from the methods of the Devil, who, in simian imitation of the works of God, attempts to counterfeit and mimic them? Let not my soul be deceived by imagining that God speaks to me and offers me visions when it is not God speaking but my own spirit and fevered imagination. I reject, I reject the hidden satisfaction and somber pride that leads me to believe that God is speaking to me; I accept that the Devil has feigned these raptures and ecstasies, that he has caused visions to appear to me, that he has taken advantage of the fact that my mind is but weak clay, and that if Your Majesty permits he may transform himself into the Angel of Light, appear even in the form of Jesus Christ himself. But then, oh, my God, how shall I distinguish the voices of the Creator from the voices of His Child, and these voices from the speech of the Devil we all bear within us because of the Fall of our first father, Adam? How? How? What does the doctrine offer to enable us to avoid that the moment of communication with God be converted into communication with the Devil? How do I distinguish Your visions from mine, and both of these from those of Lucifer? And how do I know whether I should accept, and suffer, and understand the Devil's visions, his demoniac fantasies, since you have permitted them, and for some reason from Your High Omnipotence you permit the Devil to act instead of crushing him forever beneath your Divine Foot? How am I to know?''

Dragging his body forward, he approached the altar, his arms still spread in a cross; with bloodless fingers he touched the great painting; his flattened fingertips traced the outlines of the figure of the Christ without a halo preaching to the naked men in the corner of the Italian piazza.

''The Chalice you hold, God, in your powerful hand, is filled with a mixture of tribulations and consolations, and only Your Divine Majesty knows and understands to whom and when it may behoove you to bestow either one or the other; you have filled my cup, oh, Jesus, with unequal measures and although my sparse fortunes serve to cloak my enormous afflictions, they are nothing—neither fortunes nor misfortunes—compared to the desire that enslaves me: oh, Jesus, allow me to achieve true union with you, the union of the spirit purged and purified of all sentiments of the base portion of the soul; thus I would no longer need occupy myself with governing and with war, with persecution of the heretic, with symbolic hunts; let me enjoy fruitive union with you, after which nothing I ever had or did not have in this life would matter; allow me to know the exceeding joy and delight of experiencing the immediate touch of divinity, and to remain intoxicated and annihilated in that enormous sea of softness and sweetness, transported beyond myself, borne entirely in my God and Lord, in you, Jesus Christ: far from this palace that emerged from and will return to stone; far from my wife, far from the demands of my dead but living father and my living but dead mother; far from what he, my father, asked of me, power and cruelty; far from what she, my mother, asks of me, honor and death; power and cruelty, honor and death. In your mysteries, Jesus, such unwanted duties of political legitimacy are dissolved and forgotten; in you, and not—as she believes—in the satanic black hole of the very virgin Señora, my wife.''

El Señor's eyes, at times wildly staring, occasionally suspicious—a warm gaze, a cold gaze—moved from the figure of the Christ of Orvieto to the transparent predella of the Sacrament, and from it, over his shoulder, to the rows of open sepulchers behind him awaiting the arrival of the Lords and Ladies and noble relatives, his ancestors: as each corpse would be contained within the sepulchral stone, so El Señor wished to be united with Jesus.

''I know that there are degrees within divine union, but you are free in all your works, even in regard to the Blessed, and like the spontaneous mirror you are, you may reveal yourself to a greater or lesser degree; manifest yourself to me, Jesus, in the state of passive union of the soul with God, in which are fulfilled the great mysteries written in the Holy Epistles of the dark Songs of Solomon. My happy soul longs like a bride to enter the Mystic Cellars owned by you, the Blessed Husband, where the purest and most holy love is the free-flowing wine that inflames and intoxicates hearts in sovereign love. Bestow upon me, Jesus, your most chaste and mysterious kiss, for I sigh for it like a virtuous wife. Your kiss is that precious Pearl without price. This is the innermost Kingdom of Heaven that you can communicate to me; let me know, my God, the flowery bridal chamber of the Divine Husband and the Paradise of your celestial delights. Contract binding matrimony with me in this my mortal life that you and I—that we both—may enjoy delicious consummation in the eternal felicity of Glory.''

Heavy sepulcher slabs, heavy bases in the form of truncated pyramids, carved effigies of the Señors, marble bodies of the Señoras, stone husbands and wives sleeping side by side in their beds of death, prostrate nobility awaiting the arrival of the corpses whose lives these pale statues represent, so natural they seemed hollowed from real bodies: witnesses to El Señor's prayer.

"Grant me your divine presence and Your divine touch and the sovereign encircling arms of the Divine Husband; I can live no more apart from you; grant me a brief life to hasten my nuptials with you; my inflamed anticipation can bear no more; grant me eternal glory where I will have no need to wait longer, wait, for nothing, where I need not despair of the resolutions effected by the tyrant Time; oh, my Jesus, when will it be! *Not yet, Not yet* read my dynastic devices, but I pray you: allow me to quit this unchanging world, more like its initial sin and pain, more like unto itself, the more it changes, and let me join with you in the delicious variability of a promised Heaven. Come, Jesus, come to me, come, come now, now, now . . ."

Then, still imploring, El Señor raised his head and saw that the figures of the painting were moving; he turned to see whether all the inanimate figures had taken on life, but only the naked men listening to Christ who had been standing with their backs to the viewer were now turning to reveal their faces to El Señor; behind El Señor the horizontal statues, the sleeping bas-reliefs on the slabs of the sepulchers, were still blind and unmoving; and the Christ without a halo who had been facing forward, preaching, began to turn away. The naked men had enormous, tumid, erect penises, red and shining, pulsing with blood and semen, and engorged hairy testicles, iridescent with pleasure; the Christ of the shadows displayed a blood-red cross between his shoulder blades, and a thick stream of blood trickled into the cleft between his buttocks.

El Señor screamed; he stretched out his hand and taking a penitential whip began to lash his back, his hand, his face, while the statues of his ancestors stared at him with blank eyes and inviolable marble skin. El Señor was bleeding now. Then he muttered between clenched teeth: "I do not want the world to change. I do not want my body to die, to disintegrate, to be transformed and reborn in animal form. I do not want to be reborn to be hunted in my own lands by my own descendants. I want the world to stop and to release my resurrected body in the eternity of Paradise, by the side of God. When I die, I do not want— please, have mercy—I do not want to return again to the world. I want the eternal promise: to ascend to the Kingdom of Heaven and there forget the unchanging world and lose for all time the memory of the life I led, forget that there is life on earth. But in order to reach Heaven, in order for Heaven actually to exist, this, my world, must not change, for only of its infinite horror, from that contrast, may be born the infinite goodness of Heaven. Yes, yes, the necessary contrast . . . . And it was for that reason that as a youth, darkly, not completely aware of what I was doing, I murdered those who dared offer me Heaven on earth; that was the reason, Father, Don Felipe, not because I had promised never to disappoint you again and to make myself a worthy heir to your cruel power; this is the reason, Mother, Doña Juana, not to consummate the nuptials of honor and death; yes, this is the reason, and that is why now I am growing old, and, consciously, I encourage evil on earth so that Heaven may continue to have meaning. Let there be a Heaven, God, your Heaven; do not condemn us to a Heaven on earth, to a Hell on earth, to a Purgatory on earth, for if the earth contains in itself all the cycles of life and death, my destiny is to be an animal in Hell. Amen.''

But neither the Christ facing away from El Señor nor the men with the throbbing erections nor the sepulchral statues awaiting the corpses of the thirty phantoms, his ancestors, were listening. El Señor realized that, and in fury he raised the whip: "Devil . . . Devil in disguise . . . You Devil, assuming at will the figure of other men, of phantoms, of the One God . . . Oh, cruel God, bestowing or withdrawing your gifts at will, permitting that Lucifer himself usurp your figure to deceive my poor soul . . . Show yourself to me, my God, let me know whether it is you who touch me or whether it is the Devil . . . Why do you submit us Christians to the severe test of never knowing, on the mystic heights, whether we are speaking with you or with the Enemy? Oh, you bastard Jesus, show yourself to me, give us one single proof that you hear us and that you think of us, one single proof! Do not humiliate me further, do not again proffer excrement as the mirror of my life, the excrement surrounding me at my birth in the Flemish privy, the excrement that encroached upon me at your altar the day of my victory against the Adamite heretics, the excrement that fell upon me this very morning as I slept; Son of shit, God of shit, how shall I know when you speak to me! Let me enjoy mystic ascension with neither doubts nor visions, for only in this epiphany may I resolve the conflict of my poor soul, captive here below of the debt of power owed my father and the debt of honor owed my mother and the debt of sensuality owed my wife: only by your side may I leave all that behind—but you do not wish to tell me whether by sacrificing power, honor, and sex I shall know you, or whether I am embracing the Devil!''

With a strength he would have believed impossible, El Señor arose and lashed at the painted bodies with his whip, imagining he had caused the very canvas of the painting to bleed; and then with fury he turned toward the back of the Christ whose shoulders were marked with the cross, but as he attempted to strike out, his arm was paralyzed; the whip writhed in the air with its own contractions as if it had become a black serpent; and the figure of the Christ was again turning, turning back toward El Señor, and the Christ was laughing, a sovereign laughter that resounded above all the doubts, all the desires, all the anger, all the terror, and all the humiliations of the Liege frozen like a statue, looking almost like another of the thirty sepulchers in this crypt, while the figures in the painting rotated, showing an infinite variety of forms.

And as El Señor's prognathic jaw strained forward seeking the rarefied air of the underground vault that was the center and the sum of his life, the lips of the Christ in the painting finally moved, and He said: "Many shall come in my name, saying: I am the Christ, and many will be seduced. And once again the Antichrists will emerge, and the false prophets; they will announce their coming with prodigious signs and they will execute false miracles, intending to falsely persuade the elect. The witness of St. John is true: and the Antichrists shall be many. But with the appearance of the one Antichrist, there will come many Antichrists. But only one among them will be the true Antichrist. You must recognize him. Through him you will find the salvation you have so long sought. You attempt to imitate me; the heretics you have persecuted also are inspired in the imitation of Christ. Fools! If I am God, my legend and my life on earth are unique and inimitable. But if I were merely the man Jesus, then anyone who wished might be like me. Why the devil, then, did I fall into the temptation of being born as a man and record my name in the annals of history, why did I live under the reign of Tiberius and the procuratorate of Pilate, why did I act in history and make myself its prisoner? Were it so, then more fool I, for true Gods preside over the irrepeatable origin of time, not its accidental course toward a future that has no meaning for a God. Resolve this dilemma. And furthermore, you are the bastard!"

PRISONER OF LOVE

The handsome youth gazed at her absently through dilated pupils as she moved back and forth, first arranging the perfumed pillows about his arms and beneath his head, then standing at a distance to stare at him with admiration, with gratitude; again she approached him, she kissed the sleeping nipples, trying to arouse them, her hands sought the hollow of his armpits, curling strands of blond, damp hair around her fingers; again, at a distance, she contemplated the youth lying upon her bed, completely naked, remote, surrendered to the power of the belladonna and the mandrake, unconscious of time or place or even the identity of the woman who was adoring him, who licked his navel clean with her tongue, who caressed his muscled belly, whose eyes closed as her lips kissed the bush of coppery hair crowning his dormant sex; then La Señora opened her blue eyes and hastily, timorously, with one hand she held the youth's hands and with the other she gestured toward the bedchamber, offering it to him.

"Take it, it's all for you; in all the pantheon constructed by my husband El Señor, this is the only luxury; and I amassed this luxury for you, waiting for you, desiring you in dreams and wakeful nights, in anger and in sadness, in deceit and in truth; I have always held you here, burning, clasped between my breasts and thighs, waiting, waiting; it is all for you, and without you it is nothing . . ." Her gesturing hand offered to the fair, semi-conscious boy the precious hangings covering the stone walls, the opened coffers filled with gold dinars and silver dirhems, Oriental rugs, barbaric goldwork, skins embossed with motifs from the Steppes, smoking censers, and crystal prisons enclosing gigantic flies and bees, spiders and scorpions—sterile, abulic, brutalized, sheathed in heavy copper, their shells encrusted with emeralds. She offered him this redoubt, this sumptuous lair won with deceit and bribery, won above all by the indifference of El Señor. She had pleaded: she wanted baths, she wanted to hear the song of the shepherds . . . He refused: the palace was a tomb of the living; she realized that, obsessed by and with death as he was, her husband would have neither time nor will to sniff out, to spy upon or pursue any living thing to its hiding place; she knew what Guzmán had told her was true: El Señor has faith only in what is written, not what is seen or told, and as long as no one records La Señora's bedchamber, La Señora may live in peace; she gave one of her necklaces to the man in charge of all the construction and a ring to the supervisor of the laborers; behind the curtains of her bed she had constructed a splendid tiled Moorish bath, and, like the most ancient synagogues of the desert, had her floor covered with white sand. El Señor dictated to Guzmán a folio declaring that in this palace the customs of Moors or Jews would not be tolerated and that, following his grandmother's example, every person in the palace should die wearing the shoes he had always worn. When Guzmán recounted this to La Señora she sighed; El Señor had only to consign something to paper and he believed it had an existence of its own; he would not bother again with these sensual minutiae. Beneath her pillows, La Señora had placed perfumed gloves, tiny colored pastilles, and little sacks filled with aromatic herbs.

The youth returned the pressure of La Señora's hand, freed his hand, and touched her arm. He saw the white sand that covered the chamber floor and saw in it the tracks of his own feet; he imagined he still lay on the coast, on the same beach where he'd been shipwrecked, now furnished, perfumed, adorned with skins and hangings. And the sand had changed color.

The youth moved his lips: "Who are you? Where am I?"

La Señora kissed his ear; she took an earring from one of the many nearby coffers and fastened it on the boy's earlobe; she performed this act with joy, concealing a certain perturbation welling up behind her joyful gesture; she had found him naked, dispossessed, on the beach of the Cabo de los Desastres; now she was placing an eardrop on his ear; perhaps with that single, simple, pleasureful act, she was imposing upon this man a personality and a destiny that, like the sands of the coast and of her chamber, were a clean sheet of white paper upon which nothing could be written, since all signs would immediately be erased by the waves and the wind, and by other footsteps; but the ear-ring hung now in the youth's ear, and La Señora was telling the boy that he was in a far-off palace where all spaces and all dwellings coex-isted in time, and that according to his pleasure he could imagine him-self in Baghdad, Samarkand, Peking, or Novgorod, and that she was both his mistress and his slave . . . A series of warring emotions flashed across the face of La Señora, mistress and slave; she asked her-self whether she was giving life to this man, now her captive in this rich room, or taking it away; whether she was diverting him from his true destiny by bringing him here, or whether, on the other hand, the man had been born for this moment; whether she assumed a power of creation similar to the divine; prisoners, both of them, enclosed, alone, face to face, would the young man end by being a copy of his mistress, or would she be the imitative servant of the absolute powers—until now untouched, erupted suddenly like the wings of a butterfly or an unexpected ray of light in a storm—of this young man?

She kissed the boy's lips, she placed her arms about his waist, she sighed, moved away from him, shrugged her shoulders when he re-peated: "Who are you? Where am I?"

"Pity me," La Señora replied, and sitting on the edge of the bed, she recounted the following story:

Still a young girl, I was brought from my native country, England, to the castle of one of the great Lords of Spain, who was my uncle. I came happily, for from the cradle I had been told stories of the land of the sun where the orange trees blossom and the fogs of my land are un-known. But here I found, as if the sun were a plague and the happiness it engenders in our bodies a sin, that the sunlight was shunned, was condemned to perish in deep dungeons, that granite walls were built against it, and that simple bodily gratification was subjected to the con-tritions of the fast, flagellation, and ceremonial etiquette. I came to long for the noisy vulgarity of the English; there drunkenness, the dance, insults, the pleasures of food and of carnal sensuality compen-sate for a climate of icy mists. Every night there were bonfires and ban-quets in my parents' mansion beside the river—both dead finally, he of cholera, and she from complications of childbirth. So I came to Spain; I was a proper child of English nobility with corkscrew curls and stiff white cotton petticoats. I was a little girl for a long, long time, my lover, my only entertainment dressing dolls, collecting peach pits, awakening late sleepers, and dressing up my duennas like the actors my father had taken me to see in London.

I believe I ceased to be a child one morning when I went to chapel to receive Communion; I was menstruating, and the moment the Host was placed upon my tongue it turned into a serpent; the priest reprimanded me before everyone and expelled me from the holy sanctuary. Listen carefully, my love; I still do not know how much evil that terrible event unleashed; I still do not know. Perhaps my cousin, the son of the Liege, my uncle, had loved me before that time, secretly; he has told me he watched me from afar that morning at Communion, already adoring me; I did not know. But I knew when I heard the order from the lips of his father several weeks later amid horror and crime, in the castle hall piled high with corpses that guards were dragging by the feet to a monstrous funeral pyre in the courtyard that for days infested the castle with its nauseous fumes. All I knew was that the slaughter of the rebels, the heresiarchs, the men and women who had been living communally, the Moors and Jews who had been deceived and led into a trap by the young Prince Felipe, had all been to prove something to his father: he deserved both his father's power and my hand.

I knew then I had to obey. I was going to be the wife of the heir and our wedding would be celebrated upon an altar of spilled blood. The ceremony took place; that moment signaled an end to all my games. The serpent that had surged from my impure tongue sank its fangs into me now, wound about my hands and feet, suffocated me and wounded me. I was the slave of those serpents: my duennas and my body servants took away my dolls, hid my costumes, discovered my hidden trove of peach pits, and forced upon me an endless and excessively strict schedule of lessons: how to speak, how to walk, how to eat . . . everything befitting a Spanish Lady.

I yielded to their customs. I became a prisoner of an obligatory symmetry of movement and demeanor. And after ten years of speaking in phrases prepared for every occasion, of learning to walk holding myself tall, stiff, with a hawk poised upon my wrist (symmetry of movement! As the country girls walk to the fountain with a water pitcher upon their head, so moved my falcon and I), of eating very little, a few mouthfuls, taken always with precisely held fingers and head erect, after all those years I was still as full of longing as I was innocent: but my hands were never, never again to play with my dolls, my legs were never to carry me in games around the costumed duennas, or my knees to touch the earth of the garden to bury my precious peach pits. I resigned myself. It takes a very long time to perfect bearing; that is what tradition is: choosing one of the many possibilities in life, maintaining it, cherishing it, disciplining it, excluding from it everything that would be an offense or menace. In this way we of the nobility are like the people, we have both endured a long time, and neither is inclined to change our customs every year. Tradition, Lords, people; this Brother Julián, my favorite friend who is the court miniaturist, explained to me.

I had no idea to what extremes protocol was to influence my life (my body forgetting everything it had learned naturally) until one day, while my husband was absent on one of his wars against rival Princes and protectors of heretics, I returned from an outing through some nearby gardens and as I was descending from my litter lost my footing and fell flat on my back upon the paving stones of the castle courtyard.

I called for help, because lying on my back, dressed in iron hoop skirts and billowing skirts, it was impossible for me to get to my feet by myself. But none of the menservants or the alguaciles or the duennas who came in answer to my calls, none of the many nuns and chaplains, stewards and priests, bearers and halberdiers—as many as a hundred gathered around me—held out a hand to help me to my feet.

They stood in a circle looking at me, uneasy and anxious; and the chief alguacil warned: "No one may touch her. No one may help her rise, if she cannot manage it for herself. She is La Señora and only the hands of El Señor may touch her."

In protest against such reasoning, I called to my maids: "Do you not dress and undress me every day, do you not dress and comb my hair for lice? Why can you not touch me now?" They looked at me, offended, and their injured glances said: "What happens within your chambers, Señora, is one thing, but what takes place before the eyes of the world is something quite different: ceremonial ritual." Again, dear heart, I longed for the freedom of my country, my merrie England. And I was sure that my destiny was to be worse than that of the English women pilgrims whose bad reputation had caused St. Boniface to prohibit female pilgrimages: most of them had strayed from the path, very few arrived still pure at their destination, and there is scarcely a town in Lombardy or France without a whore or adulteress of English race. But a thousand times worse, I tell you, was my destiny: a pilgrim ruined by etiquette and chastity, for both weighed heavily on my heart.

That afternoon passed; night fell, and only the most faithful chambermaids and roughest soldiers remained with me; the iron framework of my skirts creaked beneath my weight; I saw the stars move in the heavens, some more fleetingly than usual; I saw the new sun born, more slowly than on remembered days. The second day even my duennas abandoned me and only the halberdiers remained by my side, although at times they forgot who I was, or even that I was there, and they passed the time eating, urinating, and cursing there in the courtyard. I am stone, I said to myself resignedly; I am turning to stone. I ceased to count the hours. I imposed imaginary dawns upon the night, and I stained the day black. But the sun stripped the skin from my face and caused a dark fungus to erupt on my hands; it rained a night and a day, my powders and rouges ran, my hair and my skirts were soaked with rain. After the most unseemly delay, for the unforeseen event in ceremonial routine had petrified them with confusion, the duennas took turns holding great black sunshades above my head. When the sun came out again, I abandoned my modesty and loosened the ties of my bodice so my breasts might dry. And one night, mice sought lodgings in the ample cave of my tented underskirts; I could not scream, I allowed them to tickle my thighs, and to the most adventurous among them I said: "Mus, you have reached places even my own husband does not know."

Only my husband had the right to raise me from this position, first accidental, then ridiculous, and finally pathetic. But those arms have never taken me for myself, never! To whom, in that instant, was I speaking? No, I will not deceive you, my love: I was speaking to the most faithful of the mice, he who finally established his home in the hollows of my hoop skirt, for of course I considered him a better partner in conversation than my befuddled duennas or the pompous alguaciles or the inflexible halberdiers. I recalled the melancholy face of the man who was to be my husband—harsh and melancholy—the first time he had gazed at me through the eyes of love on that long-ago morning when I'd been expelled from the chapel by the priest. But what did I know of love, Mus? A few rather brutal things: that same morning a bitch had whelped her pups in my bedchamber; I had menstruated; my duenna Azucena was shackled by a chastity belt. What else did I know? What I had secretly read in Andreas Capellanus's book of honest lovers: that true love must be free, mutually shared, and noble; that a lowborn man, a common man, is incapable of giving or receiving such love. But above all, that love must be secret, my mouse; the lovers, in public, must not show signs of recognizing each other except in furtive gestures; the lovers must eat and drink very little; and last, I learned that love is incompatible with matrimony: everyone knows there is never any love between a husband and wife. My husband, mouse, had never touched me; was that actually proof that there is no love in marriage? So much so that husband and wife may never be united in their bridal bed? Or was it proof that like every true lover my husband loved me secretly and furtively, like you, Mus . . . like you, Juan? I told the mouse these sad things, and also this thought: my own mother-in-law, the mother of my husband El Señor, had known man's work only in the dark; my Spanish uncle, the Liege, had needed her only to engender princes. And I? Not even that; I, virgin as the day I embarked from my own country, from England. I could eat and drink very little in my absurd position; I lay in a secret and furtive posture, the posture of a true and honest lover . . . and only the mouse visited me night after night, nibbled at me, knew me . . .

And so I lay there thirty-three and one half days, my love; life in the castle resumed its ordinary ways; the duennas fed me from soup ladles; they had to grind my food in mortars, for I was otherwise unable to swallow it; I drank from the crudest wineskins, for anything else trickled down my chin; and when they brought my china pot the duennas shouted and shooed away the sly and cunning guards, although many times I was unable to contain my natural necessities before the chambermaids arrived, always at the same fixed hours, with no heed for my urgencies or desires. And every night, the furtive mouse visited me; he came out from his hole in my hoop skirts to nibble a bit more at the hole of my virginity. He was my true companion in that torture.

One afternoon, when I had ceased to count time, or imagine how my unwashed face must seem, or look at my stained skirts, my husband, at the head of the victorious troop, entered the courtyard. He had been informed on the road of my misfortune. But upon entering he passed me by and went directly to the chapel to give thanks, not even pausing to glance at me. I had sworn not to reproach him for anything; I had imagined he might be dead in battle and then my destiny, with no hands worthy of touching me, would have been to await my own death, lying in the courtyard, threatened by the elements until sooner or later, ancient or still young, I myself became an element: a pile of bones and hair under the sun and storm, with no company but that of the mouse. I could be lifted only in the arms of my husband, El Señor; if he was dead, I was dead; if he was dead, only one life would accompany me to the hour of my own death: that of a tiny, wise, silky-smooth, nibbling Mus. So how could I resist giving myself to the mouse, making a covenant with him, acceding in whatever he asked of me? Forgive me, Juan, forgive me; I did not know I was to dream you, and dreaming you, to find you . . .

Later my husband came to me accompanied by two youths carrying between them a large, full-length mirror. At my husband's order, the youths held the mirror before my face; I screamed, horrified to see that face I could not recognize as mine, and in that instant my thirty-three and a half days of grotesque penitence were totted up, and in addition to them, the humiliation my husband, El Señor, offered me with intentions that were mortal because they were eternal and eternal because they were mortal; in that moment, believing myself a virgin still, I lost forever my innocence.

I looked at my husband and I understood why he was doing this to me; he himself had aged, slowly, doubtlessly; but at that moment, upon his victorious return from still another war, the passage of time had become real, but something had happened of which I had not previously been aware: El Señor had returned from his last battle; I realized I was witnessing the moment of his aging, of his renunciation, of his dedication to the works of memory and death; I tried to recall, this time in vain, the visionary eyes of the slender youth in the chapel, or the cruel eyes of the man in the hall, the scene of the crime, who had felt worthy of me only because of that crime; the eyes now staring at me, as I stared at them, were those of an exhausted old man who in order that I might accompany him in his premature senescence was offering me my own altered image, dusty, without eyelashes or eyebrows, my nose sharp and trembling like that of a starving wolf, my scalp faded as gray as that of the mice who had visited me. I closed my eyes and wondered whether it was possible that from the distant fields of battle in Flanders El Señor, my husband, with the aid of the Devil and mischievous lemures, the specters of the dead, had contrived for me to stumble so ridiculously and fall on the courtyard paving stones with the purpose of making our appearances equally decadent when again we met. But El Señor's works were not those of the Devil, but rather divine dedication to Christian fervor; and if he had chosen God as an ally so that this might befall me, then in response I would choose the Devil.

Only then, after he had shown me my image in that dark mirror of horrors, El Señor offered me his hands, but I lacked the strength to take them and pull myself up. He had to kneel and for the first time take me in his arms and assist me to my own chambers, where the maids, on their own initiative and risking El Señor's displeasure—for him the bath was an extreme medication—had prepared a boiling bath. My husband disrobed me, helped me into the tub, and for the first time looked upon my body unclothed. I did not feel the burning temperature of the bath; I was paralyzed, numb. He told me that we would be leaving his ancient family castle and that we would construct in the high plains a new palace that would be both a mausoleum for princes and a temple of the Most Holy Sacrament. In this way, he added, he would commemorate the military victory, and also . . . He could not finish.

He fell to his knees, hiding his face with one hand, and said to me: "Isabel, you will never know how much I love you, and above all, how I love you . . ."

I asked him to explain; I asked with disdain, with arrogance, more than anything with rancor, and he answered: "Ever since that morning in the chapel when you spit out the snake, I have loved you so devotedly that I shall never be able to touch you; my passion for you is nourished by desire: I shall never be able, nor should I, to satisfy that desire, for once satisfied I would cease to love you. I was educated in this ideal; it is the ideal of the true Christian gentleman, and to it I must be faithful until death. Others may be faithful—and die for their faith—to the dream of a world without power, without illness, without death, a world with complete sensual satisfaction and of human incarnation of the divine. I, because I am who I am, can be faithful only to the dream of unrequited desire, constantly nurtured but never realized; in this way, comparable to faith."

I smiled; I reminded him that his own father, and with no small fame, had satiated his desires by claiming his seignorial right on a thousand occasions; with lowered head my husband answered that he, too, admitted his sins in that regard, but that it was one thing to take a woman of the lower classes, and a very different matter to touch his feminine ideal, the Señora of his heart; angrily, I pointed out that his father, though in the dark and without pleasure, had taken his, Felipe's, mother in order to beget an heir; how would he resolve this problem? Was he disposed to leave an acephalous throne? Bastards, bastards, my husband murmured several times, and in spite of his words, and in strange contrast to them, there amid the heavy vapors of my bath, he too removed his clothes before me for the first and last time, and it was now as if I held the same despicable mirror to the body of El Señor, and instead of observing the temporary ravages inflicted upon me by the intemperate weather, I could see the permanent dues his heritage had bequeathed him, abscesses, chancres, boils, the visible ulcers of his body, the premature debility of his parts. The boiling water wounded me, raising blisters on my back and thighs; when I felt it, I cried out and I begged him to retire. The moment demanded it, but also the future; I did not want my husband ever again to penetrate the sanctuary of my chamber; I knew that his shame at that moment would be the best lock on the door of my desired solitude, and that shame culminated in the words El Señor, my husband, said as he withdrew: "What thing could be born of our union, Isabel?"

Felipe withdrew with a gesture he hoped said more than the words that had been spoken: the frightful contrast between his words of ideal love and his loathsome body, his silence, asked me to draw my own conclusions, to deduce, to forgive. But I had not the strength for that. I left the bath, wrapped in sheets I walked through the vast galleries of the castle. Hallucinating, I saw a long row of my duennas who turned their backs to me as I passed. Their figures stood out against the light; they turned their invisible faces to the white leaded windows and I saw only backs cloaked by nuns' habits and heads covered by black coifs.

I approached each one, asking: "What have you done with my dolls? Where are my peach pits?"

But when I saw them in the light I saw that their habits covered only their backs; from the front, one could see their aged and obese, naked and feeble, varicose and wasted, hairless, yellowish, milky-white, purplish bodies; they laughed harshly; in their hands they held, as they would a rosary, clean and knotted roots like colorless carrots, and they offered them to me. My head chambermaid, Azucena, spit through broken teeth and saliva dribbled across her shimmering, enormous, purplish nipples; she said:

"Take this root; it is the magic mandrake that we have gathered from beneath the gallows, the racks, and the stakes of the condemned;

accept it in the place of your forever vanished playthings; accept it in the place of your forever postponed love; you will have no toy and no lover except this diabolical body born of the tears of the hanged, the tortured, and those burned alive; be grateful for our gift; we have had to expose ourselves to terrible dangers to obtain it for you; we shaved our heads and with the twisted gray hairs we tied one extreme to a knot of the root and the other to the collar of a black dog, who, frightened by the weeping of the mandrake, fled, and so pulled the root from the humid tomb that also was its cradle; we closed our ears with wads of oakum; the dog died of fright; take the root, cherish it, for in truth it is the only company you will ever know; care for it as you would a new-born child; sow wheat in its head and it will grow silken hair; insert two cherries in place of its eyes and it will see; place a slice of radish for a mouth, and it will speak. Do not be frightened of its livid, knotted body, or of its smallness; it will pass for the court dwarf; it will be your servant, your friend, and your seeker of hidden treasures . . . take it . . ."

Azucena placed the pale root in my hands, forcing my fingers to close around that obscene, palpitating tuber; I tried to drop her offering but the slimy surface of the mandrake stuck to my skin and, terrified, I fled back to my room, feverish, trembling, recalling my husband's desire and substituting for it another, real, alive, and tangible desire that exploded in my brain and coursed with fire through my breasts and belly, my sealed secret place, my arms and legs and back: a body, a body, oh, Señor, I have need of a body, a body for me alone, and my own; not a slobbery root, not a skillful and prudent mouse, not an ulcerated husband: a body. Feverish, maddened, I examined my naked, washed, clean, new body in the mirror of my chamber; I touched my body, and when my fingers reached the flower of my chastity I discovered I could insert one finger—rupturing the remains of a gnawed membrane—to the depths of my unschooled pleasure; I could not understand; I knew I was a virgin, I was a virgin, and yet all that remained of the sovereign portal of my virginity was a jumble of slender threads. Overwhelmed by sensation, I could stand no more; I fell on my bed, and dreamed; and from the plethora of my recent experiences was born a dream that was a memory; I dreamed you, and I remembered you; I saw you tossed face down upon a beach, swept by waves, your shoulder sealed with a purple-colored cross, the six toes and fingers of each hand and foot dug into the muddy sand; and as I dreamed you I remembered, born of the ashes of my ridiculous martyrdom, the pathetic visions of my husband and myself in that bath, the row of witches, the feel of the mandrake; when he died, the court buffoon had left a nameless child hidden in the straw of his pallet; the maid Azucena had found him, had felt compassion for him, had asked permission to suckle him at the teats of the bitch who had recently whelped; I recognized you; you returned; I dreamed you, shipwrecked on an unknown beach . . .

When I awakened, I told myself I would earn my sins: scarcely aware of what I was doing I called the court miniaturist, Brother Julián, who had afforded me my only moments of happiness in perusing his paintings, medallions, and seals, and by secretly providing me with volumes of the *De arte honeste amandi*: I stood before him, naked, and without a word he took up his brushes and painted the veins of my breasts blue, making the whiteness of my flesh even more startling; then the priest took me, and, finally, I lost my virginity. I rediscovered my lost nature. My dolls. My costumes. My peach pits. I was myself again; I was a child again. I mean, of course, that that was my first experience in the arms of a man. For as the priest made love to me with a preciseness of passion that used my body totally, I was becoming convinced I had earlier lost my virginity to a tiny nibbling beast. After our pleasure we both slept. I was awakened by faint noises. Something was moving beneath the sheets of my bed. Something emitting a fetid odor. A tiny mouse was huddled there; it peeped out from beneath the sheet, looked at Julián and me, hid itself again; a white and knotted root with the figure of a tiny person, almost a homunculus, crept toward our closely joined faces, disseminating sleep, desire, hallucination . . . Mandrakes grow beneath the gallows. Let us not weep for the dead: ashes to ashes, dust to dust. When we moved from the castle to the palace, I buried the mandrake here in the sand of this chamber. You, Juan Agrippa, I found on the sands of the sea.

Slowly La Señora disrobed. Without disturbing the youth's rest, calling him her little sleeping scorpion like the somnolent insects within the crystal boxes, murmuring that she had found her treasure of lost peaches, soft and wrinkled, the hard pits surrounded by savory, pulpous flesh, hanging like two ripe fruits from the tree of his golden skin; she licked that tree, kissed it, and when it was aroused, strong as a sword of fire and marble, burning cold, icy hot, she shifted and sat astride him, clasping him between her legs; she felt him penetrate the wall of black jungle, separate the moist lips, enter, soft and hard; so must the flames be that consume the condemned, she said to herself (to him), condemn me then, cast me into the flames of Hell, for I cannot distinguish between Heaven and Hell; if this is sin let my flesh know eternal salvation and eternal damnation; flame of flesh, devouring serpent of my black bats, son of the sea, Venus and Apollo, my young androgynous god, let me feel the pulsing of your stones beneath my parted welcoming thighs, stroke my buttocks, bury your finger, there, deep between them, part my lips wide, there, I feel it, play with my moist, silky hair, let me weave them with yours, there, I feel it, there, there, there, I die because I am not dying, there, there, strike deep your scepter, my true lord, grant me your great mandrake, my only root, be my body, and let me give you mine, give me your warm milk, yes, yes, now, give me . . . now . . .

Later, lying beside the new and handsome youth who from now on would be this room's inhabitant, trying to forget her former lover, La Señora whispered: Look at me carefully, for I am the only person you will see; I shall take that risk—that you may tire of me—but you will never leave this chamber, nor will you see anyone, speak to anyone, or touch anyone, except me; previously I wished to be generous, I permitted the boy chosen while I was attempting to find you, while I was searching for the incarnation of my dream, I permitted him, I tell you, to wander through the palace and even to go outside; I seduced him with my own desires; I caused him to dream of a different life, free from the strict moral and social prohibitions that suffocate us here, and he carried that freedom into the stable yards, to the stables and the kitchens; that is why he is dead, that, and because of the stupidity of wanting to leave behind him in a poem more than he was able to live; you are not going to die, my beautiful mandrake, you are going to live here with me, my blond mouse, here forever, although forever is a fleeting timepiece, alone with me even though you despise me, though I repel you, and it will be useless to pretend, for I shall know at what moment I cease to inflame you, the moment you begin to long for air and different company; perhaps that will be the moment when your seed begins to grow within my belly, and believing you were chosen for pleasure you reject the chains of duty; but I tell you now: you will only leave here, Juan Agrippa, when you are dead . . .

La Señora fell silent, startled again by the sounds and breathing seeming to emanate from the floor of white sand; something was growing there, something was scurrying swiftly, hidden, something was watching her, and from now on would be watching them. She saw only the captive youth, his dreamlike appearance, a trackless beach, an unmarked wall, receptive, hearing everything, saying nothing, listening to the responses to his obsessive questions, who am I? who are you? where am I? The youth named Juan opened one eye, and that eye, not needing words, communicated to La Señora: a man without a past begins to live the moment he awakens, hears, and sees; for him the world is whatever he first sees, hears, and touches; you, your words; I must accept the name and destiny you give me, because without them I have nothing and I am nothing; so you have wished it: and as I come to know you, do you not fear that I may be your twin, since I know no other reality but you?

And in that innocent eye, innocence born of a new birth from the sea, La Señora saw incredulity and doubt; Señora, you have told me a great deal, but you have not told me everything, and what you do not tell me, I must live for myself.

DISASTERS AND PORTENTS

And so things happened: Martín told Jerónimo, Jerónimo told Catilinón, Catilinón told Nuño, one whispering to another, Nuño in
Martín's ear, as they were eating their chick-peas or stirring the fires or
slaking the lime, wrapped in a dense cloud of smoke and dust that muted the tones of the uneasy, secretive voices sliced by the knives of the
sun of these high plains. First, a very simple thing happened: one of
the supervisors went to gather walnuts; he climbed the tree, was cutting a branch, and slipped; he tried to save himself by grabbing another
branch, missed, and fell to his death; and then some of the laborers
were working on the south façade of the great cloister when a journeyman fell from the scaffolding, and died from the fall; and then a carpenter fell from a crane in the small cloister beside the gates and was
killed, Nuño, he was killed, and that makes three in as many days; be
careful when you climb upon the crane, Catilinón, or your miserable
little store of savings will do you no good, you'll not be spending it
some summer night in the eating houses of Valladolid; but these things
aren't just happening to people, Martín, they're happening to things,
too; it's as if we were things ourselves, for whatever it is that's happening draws no line between a bramble hedge and a stonemason; listen, Jerónimo, hear how the wind is rising, blowing down scaffolding,
tearing tiles from the roofs, covering our meager supply of pond water
with a film of dust; someday, Martín, as the day is dawning, you will
sneak over to the flat hedged land where they plan to put the palace garden, and you watch La Señora look from the curtains of her room; you
will know her by the glitter of her earrings that at this hour of the morning are at the level of the sun and return the sun's dawning gaze; you
will watch her looking out at the hot dry crust and you try to see her
imagining a garden with cool, gurgling fountains, rosebushes and
stock and lilies, imagine Martín, her desire to part those eternally
drawn curtains and open her chamber windows to the early-morning
scent of non-existent honeysuckle, forgotten jasmine, and longed-for
honey locust, or her longing to lie upon her sweet-smelling bed hearing
and sensing the nearness, the sounds, and the fragrance of the garden
they promised when they brought her from her English fogs, when
they wedded her to our Señor, when they took her dolls and her peach
pits from her; how do you know all these things, Jerónimo?, her head
chambermaid Azucena told me when she came to ask me as a favor
that I, being the smith on this job, unshackle the chastity belt her husband, my apprentice, had girded on her when he left on the crusade
from which he never returned, and you, Jerónimo, what did you ask in
exchange for that favor, eh?, to play that her bosoms are two handfuls
of flax to be spun and then twirl your distaff in old Azucena's hopping

bunny, eh?, oh, shut up, Catilinón, why are you complaining?, everyone here's had either that old whore or her helper Lolilla, they've been fondled and diddled by all the workers, but they bring us gossip from inside and carry it back there from here; you'll look at that promised garden early some morning, Martín, you poor shitass, and then run away, afraid they'll find you in that forbidden corner of the palace we constructed for them, and you'll hope—with an anxiety so fragile, it doesn't seem to fit your rough body, an anguish so deep you can't explain it as you gaze at your plaster-coated hands—that that vision in silk and fine linens, our Señora, with the hooded hawk upon her wrist, will walk by—never looking at you—in her daily journey between the chapel and her chambers; listen, Nuño, the dust is going to settle, the sun's fatigue will find its rest; the storm is breaking on the granite peaks, it descends through mountain passes and pillars of rock, a gray and menacing figure with outstretched arms and moaning voice and avid fingers, it tears the brambles from a vineyard fence and tosses them onto the heads of the mules and horses; it demolishes a work shed where quarriers are working and kills one of them; then it drives us all away from our cranes and ovens and foundations, we abandon our pickaxes and bellows, we huddle together terrified in the tile sheds where bricks and slate and wood are stored, as if those materials could protect us against the fury of the storm and El Señor, because Guzmán suggests it, orders the Bishop to come out of his retirement, fat and old, barely able to officiate, never allowing himself to be seen; carried by palace monks in a palanquin, coughing, his hands livid, covering his face with a handkerchief, he is borne on their shoulders to the quarries, to the forges, the sheds, spitting phlegm into a batiste cloth and trying to subdue the wind with his shouts as the monks attempt to maintain the tall miter upon his head, his silver staff in his hands, the girdle of his alb about his vast, soft belly, and the dalmatic settled upon the rounded shoulders.

"The Devil is doing this to mislead us, but he shall not benefit from it, for we shall prevail and his wickedness will be revealed! Return to your work, men of God, my beloved flock, for the recompense of your hard labors shall be nothing less than Heaven itself! Vade retro, Satan, for you will gain nothing here! To work, to work, and then to Heaven, to Heaven!"

The Bishop raises his fingers toward the scudding clouds, and as if he had convoked it (you saw it, Jerónimo, for its light outshone your forges), a long-tailed comet appears in the sky, beautiful and great, its head pointed toward the lands of Portugal and the tail trailing toward Valencia; it races by with its long silvery mane and continues to shine in the night after the bearers have borne away the exhausted Bishop and we are still clustered together in the sheds, fearing to go out or to eat, for we don't know what significance to attribute to these portents, and all we can hear in the great silence of the night is the howling of a dog; a doleful, menacing howling that combines both rage and pain, that frightens us more than the storm or the comet or the deaths of our companions; and not only us, Martín, tempers are rising; there, inside, a supervisor quarreled with the journeymen and the architect with the overseer, and their quarrel was so heated that the girder on which they were standing broke and the first journeyman fell and was crushed to death upon the granite paving stones below; what do we know, Jerónimo?, only what reaches our ears, Catilinón, only what succeeds in penetrating the wax in our ears, that's all, what originates in those bedchambers that we will never see and sifts through the empty crypts and icy chapels by way of the cloister and courtyards and porticos and gates of this palace where, in spite of having constructed it with our own hands, you and I, Martín, would lose our way; all we know, day after day after day, is the site of a foundation or the area of a plastered wall, and then they give us five ducats for every window without our ever knowing what one sees when looking from that window, and eighteen reales for every door without our ever knowing where it will lead when it's opened, feeling our way with our hands, we see what we're building like the blind, but we will never know either how the entire palace looked in the heads of those who conceived it or how it will look when it's finished and inhabited by our Señores; I swear to you that we will never look outside from those windows, and I swear to you that we will never enter through those doors; and if someday the rosebushes that La Señora wants so much blossom in her garden, it won't be you who sees them; and in exchange for our feelings, Catilinón, they gave us five ducats not to see and eighteen reales not to hear; you think you're clever, Cato, but you're blind and crippled, and I wish to hell you'd fill that blaspheming mouth of yours with chickpeas: so shit on God, you filthy churl, but your curses fall on barren ground, and what you should do is pick the wax out of your ears; we hear the words spoken inside by way of the kitchens and the stables, words heavier and harder than the iron ingots we melt down here every day: a comet in summer means drought and the death of Princes; a comet under the sign of the Crab and in the house of Mars means misfortune; that's what Brother Toribio, the astrologer, said in there and we learned it through the passageways and stable yards and the mouths of Azucena and Lolilla, but you and I, Nuño, know only that we're afraid, and that the dog howls as if he wanted to tell us something, what is that you say, Martín?, that the dog doesn't want to scare us?, something else?, warn us?, what?, old Jerónimo, what do you believe he wants to tell us, you who have the fire of your ovens in your eyes, and in your beard the same burning red as your coals?, what does that dog say that frightens us every night running and barking through the passages and chapels, penetrating the nuns' cloister and frightening them to death, entering even the bedchambers of El Señor and the prelate, dragging chains and horns that blow by themselves, for so swift is the course of that unseen dog that we all hear it but no one sees it, none would fear it if it could be seen, that panting, stubborn dog, with an uncannily sharp nose, racing along an old and secret scent as if it were new, yowling as if every moment were its last; listen to it, all of you; you think the dog is telling us not to be afraid?, listen to what they're telling us, Nuño; you and I know that the comet disappeared yesterday, but that the storm is still crouching there, hidden behind its own veils, to deceive us; it is still there, leaden and restless, disguised as lowering clouds, obscuring the outlines of the mountains; that we know because we can see it; and we hear the dog running every night through the deserted galleries of the palace; but now we've been told that on the fourth night of the dog's forays the nuns, because they could hear it but could not see it, decided it was a phantom dog, a soul from Purgatory, the messenger of misfortune, the guide of the dead, and at midnight they gathered in the chapel beside the bedchamber— where El Señor was suffering from crushing headaches—beneath the gaze of the Italian painting and beside the sculptures of the royal sepulchers, and there they first began to pray, then chant, and finally to bark louder than the dog itself to still its voice, to trumpet louder than the horns it dragged behind it, to give themselves courage, or perhaps to be like the spectral dog, for they told us that in their raptures the pious Sisters, after crawling on their knees until they bled, began to lash each other with penitential whips and finally urinated—deathly afraid as the sound of chains grew louder—beside the columns in the sacred room, more frightened now of each other than of the dog, huddled together, clinging to one another, sniffing at each other's armpits and beneath the voluminous skirts of their black habits, weeping and moaning in ever decreasing volume until the chains and horns and the barking of the invisible dog filled all the space left vacant by the Sisters' fear; their mouths were still open, as if they were yawning, but no sound issued from them; the howling of the hound seemed to emanate from those gaping, benumbed, lipless mouths, raw slits in the flesh of their faces, like the mouths of vipers and mandrakes, Madre Milagros, for they say that snakes drag themselves, and they say that magic little men are born beneath the gallows, and we have an abundance of those in Spain, my happy-go-lucky Catilinón, a man who is born low will be lowborn no matter where he goes, don't forget: in Spain the worms don't eat the corpses, it's the corpses that devour the worms and so everything serves to fatten the vipers that in the end eat everything; see that you cry loud and long, Nuño, if you ever die on the gallows, for then your tears will engender the mandrake and you will have our offspring, poor miserable bastard.

"No one has died! No one has died! Why are you weeping so?"

Madre Milagros called to the Sisters; she did not fear the truth in their voices, rather the portent, for led by the young novitiate Inés, the Sisters had been slowly turning to face El Señor's bedchamber that opened directly onto the chapel so that he might, if he so desired, attend the Divine Services without moving from his bed; and the nuns cried and wept, staring toward the purple curtain behind which El Señor lay in Guzmán's arms, swooning, moaning, everything is excrement, Guzmán, it's all around me, it was there when I was born in the Flemish privy, it was there on the altar of my victories, and now, on this altar constructed to exorcise the horrors of the human body and condemn them to extinction, I smell the urine of these nuns; human excrescence is a tidal wave that will finally engulf me, Guzmán; I say this to Guzmán as well as to you, Catilinón, that a man who is a failure in his land will be a failure when he leaves it, but you've seen an example of that; common men, both of you, Guzmán has maneuvered things so he now has access to seignorial bedchambers while you, Catilinón, are as poor as dirt, and while he boasts of his successes, you, you miserable pup, you who arrived in this world without so much as two coins to rub together, you're still plotting and planning how to spend that pittance you've earned here, and that, you poor bastard, is what I call dressing in rags and giving away the rest to whores; and Madre Milagros exclaimed: No one is dead!, and El Señor trembled more violently, for now Guzmán had left him alone, enclosed in his four walls, three covered by dark hangings, the fourth by the ocher map of a world extending only to certain timorous boundaries: the Pillars of Hercules, Cape Finisterre, the mouths of the Tagus, and this wall of wailing flesh menacing him from the other side of the curtain, for El Señor (the rumor came through passageways, galleries, kitchens, stables, smoking tile sheds) feared that if the invisible dog was not located, the maddened nuns, either from fear or on the pretext of fear, would turn into an avenging mob: you, Señor, are responsible for our being here, we sought the peace of the cloister and you brought us to this ominous, dusty, desert place where we must live our lives surrounded by rough laborers, rude supervisors, and terrible workmen who polish and chisel all day at their granite with busy, restless fingers, by exciting, sweating leadworkers who melt down their ingots wearing nothing but a leather breechclout that barely covers their shame, by mares and mules fornicating before our eyes, crossbreeding to populate this plain with sterility; oh, yes, Señor, you removed us from the tranquillity we so desired to fill our thoughts with other, frightening desires: that our cell walls, that the palace walls that separate us might fall and that we might all come together, nuns and workers, in one great bacchanal of feeling, talking, drinking, belching, pinching, thrusting, and thumping beneath this burning sun; all that separate us from such promiscuous possibilities are a few unfinished walls: let the mares pump and the mules hump and the workmen's tools swell and the nuns be defiled; what have our eyes not seen, Madre Milagros, since you brought us to this desert of savage muleteers, far from the sheltered convents of our sweet homelands, Seville and Cádiz, Jaén and Málaga, Madre, see what happens when you bring a group of Andalusian nuns here to these arid heights, to this relentless heat, to this unremitting cold, and the most beautiful of all, Sor Inés, as beautiful as an olive grove in flames, her hair and eyes black as an olive, her skin white as a lily, her lips an overblown carnation, see her now, on her knees, howling like a bitch in heat, sniffing at armpits and peeing in the corners of the chapel—so deep and shadowed it looks more like a dungeon than a place of worship—of our Lord and Master, Liege of the Dogs, Lord of All Devils; why are we here, Madre Milagros, tell me, you who are our Superior; those terrible men who surround us by day and night, isn't it true they make you nervous, too?, the hubbub of their picks and cranes and forges and hammers drowns out our matins and hymns and vespers, our plaintive devotions; you, too, looked out of the corner of your eagle eye at the naked arms of the masons in the summer heat, the sweat trickling down their torsos, the hair of their armpits, the heavy weight of their breechclouts. Oh, Most Holy Mother Mary, cleanse us of these disturbing thoughts, quiet in our voices the howl of the phantom dog, bury in our breasts the sweet emblem of the Most Sacred Heart of Jesus, cover with a Carmelite scapulary our black throbbing triangles, draw a veil, Most Pious Mother, across that pagan painting that hangs above the altar of the Eucharist, we want never again to see men's legs, we want never to dream of men's bodies, we want never to have to gather together at night, slipping from our cells, sobbing, grievously distressed, beyond solace, knowing, but not speaking of, what is happening, seeking any pretext to remove the white starched nightclothes you apportioned us, to put on the heavy penitential hairshirts and the sackcloth that afford us the opportunity, in the exchange of clothing, to glimpse our Andalusian bodies, to divine our heavy oranges and sniff our black olives, oh, Mother, Mother Mary . . . Madre Milagros . . . what is this silence?, don't you hear?, don't you hear that there is nothing to hear?, don't you hear that the invisible dog has stopped howling? Madre! Madre!, what silence . . . and now, Madre . . . what new sound is that interrupting the silence?, whose loud, arrogant bootsteps are those advancing through the chapel?, what is that being dragged across the granite floor?, what sound is that of metal striking against stone?, passageways, kitchens, stables, Azucena, Lolilla; wake up, sleepyhead Cato, you may not owe a cent to any man, but he who would slumber and doze will never wear fine clothes; listen to what Guzmán said, knowing we'd hear; he knows everything, he's El Señor's chief huntsman, he says there are some greedy hounds that no amount of punishment can control, and this is their flaw; as soon as their handler lets them off the chain they are prone to pick up an old trail and bark as furiously as if it were a new one; they draw all the other dogs off the scent and when they follow the greedy hound they set up an uproar that confuses the huntsmen and endangers the hunt; such is the result of the sorrow and the excessive greed of this kind of hound; they want what they can never have, and so they die mad, mad of rage, and I tell you this, Jerónimo, so that you understand me, Martín, and listen, all of you, to what happened last night; all these restive nuns were in the chapel, sweet, luscious young Andalusians all of them, but none as ripe a plum as the one they call little Inés, Inesilla, haven't you seen her, Martín?, shit, Martín only has eyes for something he can never touch, La Señora, the untouchable, the sacred, why ask him?, only Nuño and I have eyes for Sister Inés, eh Nuño, for are we just to perish here, all suffering, and no whoring?, well look, would you, look at this crew of bleary-eyed jackanapes and bastards, but cool down, brothers, if it's consolation you want, remember that though the poor squire's horse may die on him, the rich squire loses his woman; we've all sidled up to that courtyard and those cells to look and to be looked at, to see whether we could catch a peep while those holy Sisters from Andalusia or Bilbao . . . or Turkey, who the hell cares, were undressing; those black habits don't drain the heat out of them or out of us either, especially when this cock-of-the-walk Cato raises his loincloth and flashes his stones for the little nuns; so they were all huddled together in that chapel we built beneath the earth, you remember?, with the crypt or dungeon with thirty-three steps leading up to the plain above, shouting like crazy women because of the phantom dog's howling, when Guzmán came in dragging the body of Bocanegra, El Señor's favorite dog, on a chain, all decked out as if for the hunt, with cords and tassels for the horns, the spiked collar with the arms and device of El Señor, his claws burned, his legs swollen; they say there were wounds on his throat and head, that he was dead as a doornail and that he smelled of all the unguents with which he'd been treated in life, pine resin, alum stone, cumin and juniper, paste of ashes and kid's milk: the dead dog smelled of all that, it had been a fierce mastiff they said, but as if he'd been infected, Catilinón, by the mortifications and sluggishness of El Señor, who always kept the dog by his side and never allowed him to go out to hunt, so he was dressed for it only then when he was dead, but instead of the hunter, he was the hunted; Guzmán stepped up onto the altar with the corpse of the dog in one hand and the still bloody blade in the other; he hung the mastiff from a railing and turned to the nuns: "There's your phantom dog. He won't howl again. Return to your cells. Respect El Señor's rest."

So, alleluia, their fears evaporated, their terrors ceased, it was the end of Babylon, and Pope Puffer and Panter went back to sleep, and we'll be returning to our basins, the quarries, the ovens . . . and the wind, Martín?, the wind's still blowing?, and the order, Jerónimo?, the order not to work today?, we're all supposed to go to the esplanade in front of the palace for a ceremony?, what ceremony?, who knows, some ceremony, a holiday, it must be a circus, maybe it's a troupe of puppeteers, who knows, anyway, a ceremony, and what a ceremony, with thunderbolts and lightning flashes that are seen, but not heard, same as the phantom that turned out to be El Señor's favorite dog, surely it was rabies, all those wounds smeared with pitch, careful, Catilinón, rabies are transmitted by foxes, don't go near anyone foxy; God has painted His heavens the color of slate and the storm is so near you can smell it in the earth, don't you smell the storm, Catilinón?, why do you think the dust is settling, as if sheltering, as if protecting, as if covering, its eyes with a gray sleeve? So, let's go, Nuño, Jerónimo, Martín, Catilinón, the dog wasn't a phantom, Guzmán demonstrated that, it was just a rabid dog, and even though he was El Señor's best dog, even though he died with El Señor's broad heraldic collar around his wounded neck, he ceased to be the favorite when he became rabid, you don't let a Jew or a pig or a rabid dog in your garden, and Guzmán killed him by driving a sharp blade into his neck, dead, stone-cold dead he is, dead as the youth who was burned the other day beside the stables, dead as the journeyman who fell from the scaffold and the supervisor who went to gather walnuts and the worker who splattered upon the paving stones, dead, all of them, and he who sighs over another's death wears a long noose about his own neck, Bocanegra is dead, hanging from the chapel railing, there won't be any more accidents now, they've killed the phantom dog that was the cause, the comet has disappeared, you'll see, everything's back to normal, everything, back the way it was before, hey, let's go, hear the clarion call and the voices singing, hurry, no, slowly, Catilinón, let's take our time, for at last we're going to see something with our own eyes, see, not be told, look, Nuño, look, Madre Milagros, have you told them?, one, two, three . . . thirteen, fourteen . . . twenty-three, twenty-four holy mendicants, two rows of Lords and noblemen, and eight Hieronymite nuns beside the chaplains and the chaplains beside the litters; just look what a long line, Madre, coming down from the mountain, Martín, look, they're raising the stilled dust, trampling the weeds, caught by the brambles, a long, interminable black line, Madre, they're cutting through the thicket and crushing even flatter the brush of this flat dry land, so different from our Andalusian gardens, here they come, Catilinón, through that rocky valley, avoiding the dangerous potholes; almost all have reached the esplanade, the procession is very long, behind the litters come mounted archers armed with lances and on the lances are tied streamers of black taffeta; be more circumspect, Inesilla, even if you're struck by lightning, don't be afraid of those black clouds, lower your eyes and forget that clouds bring rain and wind and thunder and lightning, no, Madre Milagros, the storm doesn't frighten me, I'm lifting my face to be washed by these heavy raindrops, to be refreshed after the terrible heat of this accursed plain you brought us to, far from our sea and the broad rivers, quiet, look how around each litter there's a splendid footguard and twenty-four mounted pages, count them carefully, carrying wax tapers, all of them wearing black mourning, even the trappings of the mules pulling the litters are black, but what's on those litters, Martín?, climb on my shoulders, Catilinón, look carefully, over the heads of the other workers and nuns and halberdiers and La Señora's duennas, look carefully and then tell me, I'm up, there, look, there's El Señor, all in mourning, standing in the palace entrance, pale, almost frightened, as if he expected to see himself in what he is seeing, and by his side, seated, is La Señora, Martín, La Señora, her face expressionless, dressed in black velvet, with the hooded falcon on her wrist, and behind her stands Guzmán, Martín, Guzmán, with the plaited moustache, one hand resting upon his blade, the same dagger he used to kill the dog Bocanegra, and yes, yes, Martín, El Señor is reaching out his hand as if he were looking for the faithful dog, but he's not there, but what is it we're seeing, Catilinón, quit all the quibbling and just tell me what's on those litters, they're bodies, Martín, bodies!, corpses, Madre Milagros, that's why we were all so frightened, that's why the dog was howling, because he smelled them approaching, because he knew more than we, and you said no one had died! those are dead bodies, Martín, on my faith and by my balls, they're corpses, some are skeletons, but they're all dressed up in rich clothes, black and red, with gold medallions, dressed-up skeletons, Martín, and some are mummies, still grinning, their hair still on their heads, now the halberdiers are lifting them from the litters and carrying them toward the tombs, Madre; be quiet, Inés, and look, here come four precentors dressed in capes, look, Martín, there's the fat Bishop again, blue in the face from coughing and gagging, and a gelding as well, they say, and he and all his ministers are wearing brocade, Madre, and the monks are singing the *Subvenite*, and I know how to sing it, too, but the wind . . . the rain . . . the decorations on the caskets are flapping in the wind, the wind will blow the dead away, they are our dead, daughters, El Señor's ancestors have arrived now, overcoming flatland and mountain, storms and deep pits, canyons and swampy grasslands to receive their final burial in this palace of the dead, all the dynasty, from the time of its foundation, the thirty ancestors on their thirty litters destined for the thirty sepulchers, the thirty phantoms of the dynasty that rules us, little Sisters, beneath the invincible motto, *Not yet, Not yet*, inscribed in the center of the abyss that is the very center of the coat of arms, *Not yet, Nondum, Nondum*; the first Señor, he of the battles against the Moors; the courageous Señor his son, who threw himself from the towers of his besieged castle upon the lances of Mohammed rather than surrender; the Arian King and his disobedient son whom the father ordered decapitated one Easter morning; the Señor who died of fire between incestuous sheets as he violated his own daughter, whose remains are eternally joined to those of her father, and their son and brother, who to avoid temptation dedicated himself to the collection of miniatures; the Señor who was an astronomer, son of the preceding Señor, who from the study of the minute passed to the investigation of the maximum, but as he did so complained that God had not consulted him about the creation of the world; the brave Señor who died of his sins, for his life was nourished by his virtues; and his Señora who fought like a lioness against the usurping pretenders; the Señor known as the Suffering, whether because of his spiritual pain or his well-known corporeal constipation isn't known, and his grandson, the taciturn and impotent Señor whose only pleasure came from sniffing the crusts of excrement he habitually allowed to accumulate in his breeches; and the young Señor, the murderer, who ordered his two brothers, his rivals, thrown from the walls, and who, as they died, summoned him to God's judgment thirty-three and a half days later, after which time this Señor was found dead in his bed, poisoned by the constant handling of a poisoned lead rosary; look at them, daughter, they are our wise and beloved masters and rulers; the cruel Señor who abandoned his legitimate wife for the love of a concubine and then forced the members of his court to drink his favorite's bath water; the abandoned Señora who fashioned a flag the color of her blood and tears, for a more worthy occupation for her widow-like state no one could propose, or she imagine, and that blessed banner of sorrows was carried into battle against impious Cathari heretics; and thus you are witnessing, Inesilla, little silly, how everything in this world is part of a greater plan, and how even the most insipid devotions have some purpose; and the harsh Señor who had statues erected on the sites of his nocturnal crimes, for he was given to sallying out at night, cloaked, to provoke street duels for no more than a knock-this-chip-off-my-shoulder, and then celebrated his murders by commemorating his victims in marble, until one night one of those stone arms fell on his head and killed him; and the virgin Señora murdered by one of her husband's halberdiers while she was praying, in order to assure her rapid passage to Paradise; the rebellious Señor who rose up in arms against his stepfather, the murderer of his mother, she who died in prayer; the seditious Infanta who in battling for the succession leveled plains, burned palaces, and decapitated loyal nobles; the Señor who employed all the days of his reign in celebrating his own funerals, thus considering his human servitude and making himself the equal of lepers who by law must observe their burials before they die, and so he lay in his coffin and intoned the *De Profundis*;

the Señor who was widowed at an early age and whose small sons were sequestered—it was soon discovered it was all the work of a Jewish conspiracy—for the famous Dr. Cuevas who attended the Queen was Jewish and the three heirs to the throne were kidnapped by Hebrews who later slit their throats by the light of the moon and manufactured magical oils from them, for which the King felt obligated to burn alive in the plaza of Logroño thirty thousand false Christians, in truth pertinacious Jews; see the little coffin, Inesilla, there is the body of a little child in it, symbolizing the three lost noble children; and El Señor's grandmother, our most chaste Señora, who never changed her clothing, for she said that in this way the Devil would never see what belonged only to God, and who on dying had to be pried loose from the stockings and shoes that had stuck to her flesh, and the mad Señor, her husband, the grandfather of our own Señor, who enjoyed boiling hares alive, who collected snow in his chamber pot and had his sugar dyed with ink: they say that one night as he was devoting himself to unspeakable pleasures he was strangled with a silken noose by four Moorish slaves; so they say; and finally, Inesilla, the father of El Señor, the whoring Prince whose body has been dragged by his widow, the Mad Lady, the mother of El Señor, through all the monasteries of this land drained by so many battles, by so much crime and so much heroism and so much injustice; here they will all find their rest, in these crypts of granite and marble, forever, daughter, forever, for this palace is a tomb and a temple and is constructed for eternity, but nothing is eternal, Madre Milagros, except the true eternity of Heaven and Hell, quiet, you're very impertinent for a novitiate, all these bones and skulls will never move from here, and the resurrection of the flesh, Madre?, and the day of the final judgment?, won't our Lords ascend to Heaven in the bodies they had in life?, accursed Inesilla, don't try to confuse me, you should be wearing bells, child of fun- and merrymakers, instead of the habits of our saintly order, are you trying to confuse me?, for the body in which we will be resurrected will not be the lustful body in which we died, but it will be a new Christian body, the same body, but renewed, reconverted by a second baptism in the temple of the Holy Spirit, repeat, my poor child, repeat, and then ask yourself, tollens ergo membra Christi faciam membra meretricis?, and recall the exhortation of St. John Chrysostom, "You have no right to defile your body, for it is not yours, but the temple of God, your Father," and recall also that the Holy Father in Rome has ordered denounced to the Inquisition all who hold that kissing, embracing, and touching to the end of carnal delectation are not mortal sins, remember that, but, Madre, I don't want to look at those repulsive mummies and skeletons, what I want to see are those wooden coffers with golden handles, lined with green taffeta and trimmed with silver gimp, don't you see them?, yes, my daughter, those house the relics of the saints and the beatified and others pertaining to the succession of our very illustrious Lords, but the weather is still gray and overcast, hey, Catilinón, what's in those boxes?, tell me, they're opening them now, Martín, I can see very well your shoulders make a good tower and now El Señor is walking toward one of the boxes which a monk is holding out to him and he's taking out a shinbone, do you hear, a shinbone, from the knee down, with part of the kneecap, with skin and nerves still hanging from a large part of it, and now El Señor is raising it to his lips, kissing it, and that, Jerónimo, and that was a flash of lightning that struck the bell tower and tore down part of the stonework, but look, there at the end of the procession, it's a small leather carriage advancing beneath the rain, surrounded by an exhausted multitude of halberdiers, cooks, alguaciles, ladies-in-waiting, and scullions carrying javelins with boars' heads impaled upon their points, strings of onions, dried pork, and tallow candles, and behind them, look, behind them, a funeral carriage, the last, the one that was missing, Inesilla, the one needed to complete the thirty bodies that must lie in the thirty sepulchers of this hall, the most ornate, the most embellished of the carriages, with all the fury of the rain pouring off its glass cover, they're stopping, Martín, who is coming now, Madre?, the procession is over, my habit is soaking wet, the cloth is clinging to my breasts, Madre, let's go change our clothing, let's go stand naked before the fire to dry, who's coming there?, four halberdiers are approaching to open the door of the leather coach, the storm is worsening, the corpses are being received in a terrible wind, the tabernacle is crashing to the ground, the wind is blowing the brocades of the caskets, look, Madre, look; look, Martín, a spark of fire high on the tip of the bell tower, just beneath the golden sphere, look, the sphere is blazing as if it held a fiery wax taper, and as the sphere blazes the chants burst forth, and the funeral bells, and the praise and psalms and the prayers of the multitude; the four halberdiers help from the small leather carriage a bundle in black, nervous, shaking, sobbing; yellow eyes shine from the rags and no one knows when the Mad Lady reveals her face whether those are tears or raindrops running down her dry cheeks; and behind that bundle wrapped in wet rags, you descend, beneath the storm, you, beatified, handsome, and stupid, you, in your velvet cap, fur cape, the golden fleece upon your chest, the rose-colored stockings, you, the resurrected Prince, fair, beatified, and idiotic, you, the usurping shipwrecked youth wearing these insignia and clothing, mere appearances, you, with the gaping mouth, the drooping lip, the prognathic jaw, the waxen stare, the labored breathing, and behind you stops the carriage of the dead wherein the youth found on the dunes lies in tattered clothing in the place of the whoring Very High Lord who died of catarrh after playing strenuously at ball, and who the following day was embalmed by the science of Dr. Don Pedro del Agua. They're calling you, Jerónimo, eh?, they need you, the lightning bolt has set fire to the bells themselves, the bells are fusing, are melting, and we . . .

"We've spent our lives constructing a house for the dead!"

THE MAD LADY

Shut yourselves in your cells, said Madre Milagros, all of you, and don't show so much as a hair of your head, bar your doors and cover your windows with cloth, El Señor's mother, the Mad Lady, wrapped in her black rags, carrying the corpse of her husband, and accompanied by some idiotic nobleman who, according to her, is her own husband revived, father of himself or son of himself or twin of her husband, El Señor's father, I don't know, I don't understand, I can't make any sense of it, Sister Angustias, Sister Clemencia, Sister Dolores, Sister Remedios, hide yourselves, children, for the Mad Lady cannot tolerate the presence of other women, even though they be nuns and novitiates devoted to the most chaste of devotions, betrothed to Christ, having already taken their vows, that isn't enough for her, she sees a threat in every skirt in the world, she fears that every woman has an ungovernable desire to rob her, if only for one night, of the husband who in life was so unfaithful that had he not died of fever from a catarrh he surely would have died of the French malady that poisons the blood and covers the body with chancres, is that why our Señor doesn't have children, Madre Milagros, because he inherited the malady and can't or because he can but fears he will transmit the infection?, all of you, be quiet, shhh, it's a heavy charge I've taken upon my shoulders in shepherding you Andalusian nuns, there's a contradiction for you, nuns from Seville, why, their breasts have budded by the time they're eleven and what they don't know they find out and what they can't find out they guess, shhhh, all of you, go to your cells and let me count you and bless you, you, Clemencia, and you, Remedios, and you, Dolores, and you, Angustiás, and . . . Inesilla, my God, where's Inés, Sister Angustias, she should be right here beside you in the cell next to yours, oh, that Inesilla, where could she be?, who knows, Madre Milagros, El Señor has ordered so many Masses celebrated, Low Masses, Requiem Masses, Pontifical Masses, sermons in all the cloisters and in every corner of the palace to commemorate the second burial of his ancestors, and Inesilla is so devout, so curious, you mean, and high-spirited, she wouldn't miss all the festivities, hush, Sister Remedios, these aren't festivities, you Andalusian girls are so irresponsible, this is funeral reverence we celebrate, ceremonies of tears and mourning, not Sevillian fairs, but listen, do you hear?, hide yourselves in your cells, do you hear the sputtering of the lighted tapers, the footsteps, the moaning?, what did I tell you, little Sisters of the Lord, servants of God, brides of Christ, go hide, for here comes the Mad Lady, hear the cart squeaking?, they are pushing her in her little cart, she's making the rounds of the entire palace to see whether all the women are securely locked up, look at them, Sister Clemencia, I'm looking, Madre Milagros, here come two halberdiers with lighted tapers, and a dwarf's pushing the little cart and within the cart is a motionless shape with yellow eyes peering out of the rags, and behind that a young man wearing a velvet cap and a fur cape—all accompanied by an icy blast of air—through the cloister, the stone galleries, the yellow plastered walls, that youth with the imbecilic air is running the tips of his fingers over the plaster bas-reliefs, the heart of Jesus, the wounds of Christ, oh, what a wind, Madre Milagros, and behind them are two priests perfuming everything with incense, and the Mad Lady looking at everything without a word, staring toward the little windows of our cells with those eyes of intense hatred, Madre, why is she in the little cart?, is she crippled?, shhh, daughter, shhh, the mother of El Señor has neither arms nor legs, when her husband died she lay in the center of the castle courtyard and said that a true Señora would not allow herself to be touched by anyone except her husband, and that as her husband had died, she would never again be touched by anything except the sun, the wind, the rain, and dust, for as those elements are no one, they are nothing, and there she lay for several months; her son, our Señor, said: Respect her will, give her food and water and attend her needs and keep her neat, but respect the will of La Señora, my mother, let her do as she will with her body and with her sorrow, and let this example of what the honor of a Spanish Lady is be known and praised; but she could have entered a convent, Madre, she could have flagellated herself, fasted, walked upon thorns, allowed them to pierce her hands and feet; but you are seeking logical solutions, Sister Dolores, and the Señora who is El Señor's mother is mad, and in her madness she decided to do that penance and no other; but her legs, Madre Milagros, and her arms?, you saw today, daughter, that shinbone that El Señor kissed, that member that he took from the coffer and then pressed to his lips, that is the leg of his mother, now a relic like that of a saint, conserved forever in these palace crypts alongside twelve thorns and a hair from Our Saviour's head, the shinbone almost as sacred as the hair and the thorns, but the Mad Lady had said that no one should touch her, and men understood, but not the beasts, and one evening her dead husband's dogs, being hungry for the hunt, for they had not been out of the palace since the death of their master, were taken for a turn by the huntsman Guzmán, as was his custom and his duty, but the mastiffs were restless, and by a stroke of bad fortune La Señora, the wife of El Señor, was having an entertainment that night, she had pleaded for it, begged her husband that they might again hear music and dissipate the long mourning in the palace, the musicians were playing horns whose sound could easily be heard through the windows opened to the spring; the hounds mistook the sound for the signal to the hunt, even for the attack, and they launched themselves, Guzmán being unable to restrain them, upon a strange quarry: it is believed that, perhaps all these things at the same time, they smelled the sweat and the flesh of their dead master in the flesh and sweat of the Lady lying in the courtyard, or that they were attracted by the scent of excrement and other filth on El Señor's mother's body, or that they confused the body of the Reyna with that of a trapped beast, and they fell upon her, growling and snapping, gravely wounding her extremities, while the Mad Lady, instead of screaming with pain, gave praise to God for this test and begged for the death that as a faithful Christian she could not inflict upon herself but nevertheless longed for and sought from God with the goal of being united with her very beloved husband; the gray spotted dogs were attempting to devour the mad Señora that night, incited by the horn of celebration that they thought sounded death, to the kill, until Guzmán fortunately had the idea of sounding his own horn to regroup and the mastiffs came to his call, setting the Lady free. El Señor tried to have her carried from that open-air prison, to have her tended and her wounds cured. But his mother, La Señora, insisted, she said that only her husband could touch her and thus her arms and legs wounded by the fury of the dogs began to swell, they never healed, and pus ran from her punctured, purple, pestilent limbs while the Lady mumbled prayers and prepared to commit her suffering body and contrite soul to the Creator of all things, God Our Father, shouting loudly that honor and glory are loss and not gain, voluntary sacrifice, and not avaricious hoarding, loss without possibility of recompense, loss because there is no richness in this world that can compensate for honor and glory, and that honor and glory are supreme!, she shouted that every night of that spring, until El Señor, her son, our present Señor, ordered some guards to violate his mother's, the Mad Lady's, express will, to lift her up by force, with fury and without respect, for the Mad Lady struggled with a ferociousness equal to that of the hunting mastiffs, she bit the hands of the guards, spit blood in their faces and invoked the Evil One to strike them dead with a bolt of lightning; but to no avail, she was carried to a bedchamber and there, although the doctors applied ointments and cupping glasses to the wounds on her legs and arms, it was too late, and they decided to amputate her limbs, which took place amid frightful shrieks which I heard, my sisters, which I heard, trembling with fear, listening to the words the Lady shouted as they chopped, oh, save me, Christ my Saviour, save me from the rage of these Jewish doctors come like rats out of their alleyways and hovels to mutilate me and then make impious use of my members, they are doctors of the Hebraic faith, look, look at those unnatural stars engraved upon their chests, they will boil my limbs in oil so that all good Christians die and they, therefore, inherit our riches: listening to the words that the Lady uttered before she fainted, while the saws were slicing her putrid flesh and splintering her fragile bones, I listened to how she gave thanks to God, finally, for subjecting her to this terrible test that again placed her in extremis, as she so desired, and just before she fainted she shouted: Honor through sacrifice, the height of my nobility is sustained not upon the possession of the ephemeral things of this world but upon their total absence, and what greater sacrifice or greater loss, excepting death, than this sacrifice of half my body, especially at the hands of these detested pigs who imposed even worse sacrifice upon Christ Our Lord. She retained, nevertheless, possession of her will. Look at her beady eyes, Sisters, see how arrogantly she stares at us, see how she tells us, never uttering a word, that we would not be capable of bearing what she has borne, see how she tells us that she has returned, mutilated, dragging with her a cadaver, in possession of a new being, of a new Prince, of a new youth, see her, there she goes toward the servants' quarters, parading her pride, telling us she has returned and that things will be as they were before, that death is deceit, that there is no possible decay when the will for loss is imposed upon the will for acquisition, she has returned; she's returned, Azucena, she's headed toward our corridors, she's coming to lock us up again, she's coming to take away the freedom that La Señora, El Señor's wife, enclosed in her bedchamber, indifferent to our coming and going, to all our quarrels and disputes, has given us; but not any longer, the Mad Lady's back, here she comes, pushed in her little cart, look, look, Lolilla, pushed by the dwarf Barbarica, that little monster's come back, too, that fat-cheeked, puffy-eyed, wrinkled little dwarf, look how the tail of her dress drags the floor, she's always insisted on wearing the old dresses of all the Señoras, even though they drag the floor and she has to roll up the sleeves on her short arms and gather them in a bunch around that belly tight as a drum!, didn't that dwarfish Barbarica dance around you, Azucena, didn't she leap and cavort around you, farting at will, didn't she show off in front of you wearing a cardboard crown, her face painted gold, the veins on her bare breasts painted blue, shouting "I'm a Queen, too, I'm a little Queen, a miniature Señora," and then fire off three quick blasts of her cannon?, didn't she?, they've come back, Azucena, they've come back, to our infinite bad fortune, oh, fateful day, oh, black day, this day on which the Mad Lady and her tooting dwarf returned to this palace, after we thought we'd been freed forever from that sinister pair, and look, look, Lolilla, would you look at what they have with them, a young man, he looks bewildered, as if he'd been clubbed over the head, as if they'd tossed him in a blanket till he couldn't move, either from the pain or the muddled brain, who knows?, look at him, he isn't really ugly, but the way he moves makes him seem ugly, as if he weren't really here, somehow, like a puppet, as if he were sick in the head, that shows, Azucena, that shows that if you try to bake your bread in a faulty oven, you can expect twisted loaves, he must be a son of St. Peter, one of those you can see right through even when he insists he's the nephew of some priest and then is knocked silly by the drubbing the priest gives him to keep the boy from calling him "Father," no, Lolilla, he's not the son of a cleric, no, have you forgotten what we saw when they burned that boy down behind the kitchens?, the new life from the tears of the condemned man?, the mandrake, Azucena, the mandrake!, and we told La Señora about it, about the tiny man born from the infamy of the stakes and gallows and racks, all the places where the men of our land die weeping, the pillory and the vile garrote, Azucena, the ashes of the boy burned alive!, oh, oh, oh, I knew it would happen, I knew it wouldn't be the young Señora who found it, but this mad old woman without arms or legs, this evil witch, she had to be the one to find it, and care for it until it grew to be a man, surely she suckled it with that Barbarica's milk, dribbling from her teats like milk from a mad nanny goat, unchecked and uncontrolled!, and what is it the Mad Lady's mumbling, Azucena, what is she saying?, where is her drummer?, she needs her black-clad drummer to accompany her, announcing her mournful passage through these halls, and what does that matter to us?, what matters to us is that this evil old tyrant's returned and she's headed toward the bedchamber of our Señora, our protector, our carefree mistress who so wanted to fill this somber place with joy and merriment, against the strict orders El Señor transmitted to us through Guzmán, to arrange gardens, to entertain herself with plays and courts of love and carrousels, who wanted the shepherds to return, to shear their sheep beneath her balcony, who wanted something entertaining to happen here, something besides our odious obligation to slick down the young Señora's hair with saliva when she's feeling drowsy, but now, not even that, for who knows how many days it has been since La Señora allowed us to enter her chambers, now we can't steal anything, no, not now, we've been had, and the tyrant's returned, here she comes on her little cart with her dwarf and her fool, shouting obscenities, that a true Señora has no legs,

"Do you know that? A true Señora has no legs!"

What do I know, Lolilla, what do I know?, the only thing we know is that this horrible old woman will shut us up, will send guards to lock us in our miserable little rooms, will take away everything we possess, everything we've managed to store away through the years, we won't be able to hide anything, that's what mandrakes are for, to discover hidden treasures, and so we won't have any treasures any more, the Old Witch will say we're thieving servants, and she'll deprive us of the dignity we've won as duennas and maidservants to La Señora and will turn us into scullery maids again, come on, Lolilla, yes, Azucena, let's run hide everything, let's put everything beneath a loose paving stone, everything we've sneaked from the chamber of the young Señora, the dolls, the peach pits, the silken stockings, the locks of hair, the worn slippers, the little sacks of dried violets, the colored pastilles, the insects dipped in gold that we make buzz around our breasts and our hairy mounds, all of it, all of it, let's hide it all very carefully, for it is our only inheritance, you tired old cunt, our only inheritance.

THE FIRST TESTAMENT

"Dip your pen in the inkwell, Guzmán, it's never too late to prepare oneself for a good death, to settle one's accounts with God, especially on the day—needing no mirror to verify it—I see my death reflected in that of my ancestors and I ask for myself that someday I may enjoy the repose I have procured for them. They are at rest, are they not, Guzmán?"

"Each has been placed within his own sepulcher, Señor. There they lie."

"I prepared everything, I planned everything so that the arrival of the thirty funeral litters would coincide with my birthday, so that the celebrations of life and death would be blended into one; one year less of life for me, one year more of death for them; but now, finally, we are all together, celebrating equally what we have in excess and what we need, for tell me, Guzmán, is it that they lack life or that I lack death? Do they suffer an excess of death or I an excess of life?"

"In my humble opinion, these dead are very dead, they have been for a long time. This is not the hour to weep for them, rather to make this ceremony a celebration of your life and power."

"I planned; I anticipated. So that all would arrive on the same day, the day of my birthday. But you saw, that wasn't the way it happened. The caravan was four days late."

"You demanded that the procession should be perfect, that all the bodies should arrive here together, at the same moment, not one on Tuesday and five Friday and three more Sunday; so that many were forced to wait in the foothills pending the arrival of the others, those that were delayed by accidents of the road, wrong turns, unexpected storms, perhaps unforeseen encounters, I don't know . . ."

"My will was not sufficient."

"The elements are invincible, Señor."

"Quiet. My orders were not sufficient. Four days of desperate waiting; four days during which other accidents occurred, other deaths, other storms that could have been avoided had they arrived on the day of my birthday. Bocanegra would not have died. You would not have killed him."

"Do not blame me for his death. He had rabies. He could not remain by your side. Does it make sense to save a dog and lose a Prince? Charity has its limits. Also sorrow, if we're not to become falsely melancholy."

"All right, all right, Guzmán; everything will again be at peace; the nuns will not be whirling madly outside my bedchamber; the workers will return to work and soon this, my life work, will be completed, the pantheon of my ancestors and the mausoleum for my own remains."

"Let us celebrate life, Señor; let us not anticipate the work of time."

"Place on me my bone ring, I feel a cramp."

"Let us go to your bedchamber where I can place your feet on a cushion and you can dictate to me in comfort."

"No, Guzmán, no; it must be here, here in the chapel, you seated before the lectern and I resting here on these icy stones, each of us surrounded by the thirty sepulchers of my ancestors; tell me, Guzmán, how did their remains reach this crypt if the stairway that was constructed for their use is still unfinished?"

"They had to come around the stables, through the kitchens and courtyards, galleries and dungeons, treading upon the damp leaves of the past winter accumulated in these subterranean chambers."

"Why is the stairway not finished?"

"I have explained; they feared to interrupt your devotions . . ."

"No, you do not understand what I mean; it should be complete; I ordered only thirty steps between the crypt and the plain above, one symbolic step for each coffin that was to descend to its tomb on this great day; why did they build thirty-three? I counted them, whom else are they expecting? How many steps will there be? There will be no more corpses, it's thirty, thirty phantoms, the number of my specters, Guzmán, not one more, nor one less, whom are they expecting?"

"I do not know, Sire."

"Who constructed the stairway?"

"I repeat, Sire; everyone, no one, they have no names. They're not important."

"If the corpses had been carried down the stairway . . . you do not know, Guzmán, you cannot imagine . . ."

"I know only what El Señor deems worthy to communicate to me and order me to do, Señor."

"Hear my secret, Guzmán; I have ascended that stairway; to go up those stairs is to ascend toward death. Coming down them, would my ancestors have descended toward life? Would they have been regenerated as I gradually decomposed in the mirror as I ascended? Would I now be surrounded by my living ancestors?"

"It is difficult for me to follow the reasoning of El Señor. May I ask again, let us return to your bedchamber, you will be more comfortable there . . ."

"No, no, it must be here where both of us can see and be seen by that painting they sent from Orvieto; we will speak to that painting, and finally, it will speak to us; I know it; unroll your parchment and place it upon the lectern; sit down, Guzmán, do as I ask, write, what I tell you will be told us by that painting, it will speak through my lips to give voice to its mute allegory."

"Señor: the storm calmed the din of summer on the plain, but it sifted coldly into the crypt as if here to await a premature encounter with winter; your teeth are chattering and your bones creaking, you are stiff with cold; permit . . ."

"Write, Guzmán, write, what is written remains, what is written is true in itself, for it cannot be subjected to the test of truth, or to any proof at all; that is the full reality of what is written, its paper reality, full and unique, write: In the name of the Holy Trinity, three persons and one All-Powerful and True God, Creator of all things . . . wait, Guzmán, what are we saying, what are we writing out of mere habit? Do you never doubt, Guzmán? Does a Devil never approach you and say, that wasn't how it was, it was not only that way, it could have happened that way but also in a thousand different ways, depending upon who is telling it, depending on who saw it and how he chanced to see it; imagine for an instant, Guzmán, what would happen if everyone offered their multiple and contradictory versions of what had happened, and even what had not happened; everyone, I tell you, Lords as well as serfs, the sane and the mad, the devout and the heretical, then what would happen, Guzmán?"

"There would be too many truths. Kingdoms would be ungovernable."

"No, something worse; if everyone could write the same text in his own manner, the text would no longer be unique; then there would be no secret; then . . ."

"Then nothing would be sacred."

"True, exactly so, Guzmán; and you would be right, kingdoms would be ungovernable, for upon what is government founded but the unity of power? And this unitary power, upon what is it founded but its privileged possession of the unique written text, an unchanging norm that conquers, that imposes itself upon, the confused proliferation of custom? The subject, acting, exists; the Prince, acting, is; custom falls into disuse, is exhausted, is renewed and changes aimlessly and chaotically, but the law does not vary, it assures the permanency and the legitimacy of all acts of power. And upon what is that legitimacy founded?"

"The law the Prince invokes is said to be a reflection of immutable divine law, Señor; such is its legitimacy."

"Then listen to me. You have never ascended that stairway, have you, Guzmán? You have not seen the changing reflection in a mirror . . . a mirror that . . . I don't know, I don't know, I don't know . . . I do not know whether it reflects the origin or the end of all things . . . or whether it tells me that all things are identical in their origin and in their end . . . but what things, Guzmán? What things? Please tell me, do you never doubt? Do you never imagine? For even though things are namable and countable and weighable, their Creator is unknown, no one has ever seen Him and perhaps no one ever will, the Creator has no number or weight or measure; we are the ones who gave Him His name, we wrote it, He did not tell it to us, He has never written His own name, not Allah, not Yahweh, or Ra or Zeus or Baal, which are all names that men have given the Creator, not names He has told us."

"Pardon, Señor; if what you have said is true, then may I take the liberty of believing that the name we give God cannot be sacred because it is not secret; and it cannot be secret because we need to know His name so that we may adore Him. A God worshipped in stealth is a thing of witchcraft, and that God must be a devil."

"You may take that liberty, but you reason badly, my poor Guzmán. You know a great deal about hawks and dogs, but very little about things of the soul."

"I am at your feet, Señor."

"Think, rather, that the name of God will always be secret and sacred, for no one but He knows it; and then an abyss opens between that mystery and the bad game we act out here, for I am where I am, and you are at my service, Guzmán, because I believe, you believe, and my subjects believe with us, that I am Prince by divine right; that God wrote my name so I might govern in His. Does God know my name while I am ignorant of His? What blind torture is this, and what injustice?"

"You give strange names to faith, my Lord. One believes in God, he does not try to prove His existence. If it consoles you, think that even if you cannot prove the existence of God, for God it is equally difficult to prove yours."

"Are you saying I should renounce my desire to know God?"

"I ask nothing of you, Sire; I hear you and accompany you. And I remind you that if we believe in God, God will believe in us."

"Do you know who was my listener and my companion before, Guzmán?"

"That would be vain pretension on my part; I serve El Señor, I do not spy on him."

"The dog Bocanegra. He heard everything that I am telling you today."

"Thank you, Señor."

"Write; do as I say."

"And if what is written endures, may I, with respect, ask El Señor why he has decided that I should hear and write what before only the dog—without understanding—was permitted to hear?"

"No, no, you may not. It is better that you simply write. I asked our Bishop here, on this very spot, in this crypt, whether he knew the Creator and he said no; in answer to whether he expected to know Him, he said yes, if the good fortune of death and resurrection carried him to be seated by God's side where he might see His face in the Paradise reserved for good Christians; now turn toward that stairway, Guzmán, look at it; I challenge you to climb it with a mirror in your hand, I challenge you; you will climb to the end and the origin of everything, but like me, you will not see the Creator in the mirror, and that absence, more than the announcement of our irremediable senescence, of our mortal death, will be what terrifies us; as you look into the mirror you, as I, will know only the most promiscuous solitude, for as I died I was alone, I did not see God, but I was not alone, if you can understand that, rather, surrounded by matter, absorbed by matter as if by a gigantic sponge; and the Being whom, according to the doctrine, I resemble, the Being who gave me life in His own divine image, did not await me at the end to guide me, to take me in and console me, to recognize me as I recognized Him, to prove finally my existence in His own, as our Bishop believes, to carry me with Him to Paradise; the Creator was not there, I was alone with living but mute matter and I did not know whether that was Heaven or Hell, eternal life or transitory death; and do you know why I have never seen Him? Because I suspect that the Father was never born, was never created; that is the question that neither our Bishop nor the learned Brother Julián nor the astrologer Brother Toribio nor our poor Chronicler, who imagined so many things, has ever been able to answer to alleviate my own imaginings and to buttress my well-tested faith: Who created the Father? Did the Father create Himself? Neither the dogma nor the Bishop nor the painter-monk's eagerness for conciliation nor the imagination of the Chronicler nor the stars of the astrologer could answer me; I answered myself: The Father was never born, was never created; that is His secret, His distinction, and only knowing this shall we understand why He was capable of creation: so that no one would resemble Him."

"Must I write all this, Señor?"

"Yes, and more: if you dare, as I did, ascend those stairs that do not lead, as our eyes deceitfully indicate, to the plain above but to the origins of everything, you can confirm it; yes, write, Guzmán, that there be written evidence; I have been to the beginning and I have not seen the Father born. Look upward, to the end of the stone stairs: look beyond the plain; what do you see?"

"The stormy light of this summer morning."

"Dare to ascend; take my mirror and tell me what you see in it as you ascend, as you pause on each stair . . ."

"Señor, don't ask that I repeat your sublime actions, which as they are yours are inimitable; who am I . . . ?"

"A mortal. And for that reason, like any mortal, you may know the dwellings of the Creator; yes, you may climb as I did, with Brother Toribio our astrologer, to the highest tower to look at the heavens through the glass that his invention has polished for the purpose of penetrating with the human eye the opacities of the firmament; I searched the heavens with the magical apparatus of the Chaldean and in no corner of the dome that embraces us could I encounter the likeness of the not-born Father; and, nevertheless, looking through those lenses, hearing the names that Brother Toribio gives to the celestial mansions, and measuring the distances he calculates between body and body, star and star, dust mote and dust mote, I saw that although the Father was not visible, the sky was not empty; I told myself that those spheres and those dissimilar particles were not the Father, but that they were visible proof of his creative origins. Although I thought also, listening to the explanations of Brother Toribio, that if his science was true, then it was also limited, for if the heavens are truly infinite, as the astrologer maintains, what the lenses showed me was only a finite part of that enormity; and if the heavens were infinite, the mystery of their lack of limits did not exclude the rule of the creative principle; in some place, at some moment, the first heaven was created; and once there was the first heaven, the succeeding heavens were derived from it, similar to the first, but more and more distant from it, until the reproduction of heavens, more and more pale, more and more tenuous, as happens with repeated copies, could be seen by us. With everything, even with Brother Toribio's lenses, we know only the last heaven, Guzmán, the most imperfect copy, the farthest removed from the original model although the closest to this earth we inhabit, and I fear that all the things of our earth are but the product of the creation closest to us but most distant from the Father who only indirectly created us, for first He created powerful angels who in turn created more and more inferior angels who in the end created us. We are the result of the uninterested caprice of a few bored angels who possessed only the strength and imagination necessary to invent human misery. But thus they fulfilled the secret design of the Creator: that man be what is farthest removed and least like the original Father.''

"The last act of creation was the creation of man and of the world, Señor; thus it is written in the Sacred Scriptures.''

"Which, because they are written, are; God save me from contradicting them . . . but not from enriching them.''

"Could God have been absent from the act with which He culminated the creation of all things?''

"You may still my voice, Guzmán; how shall you still my conscience?''

"I am writing this only because El Señor asks me . . .''

"Write, Guzmán; the last act of the creation was simply that, the last, not the culminating act, but an act of carelessness, of tedium, of lack of imagination; is it conceivable that the Father, being omnipotent, would have directly created this odious mockery we men are? If it were so, He would not be God, or He would be the most cruel of gods . . . or the most stupid. So realize that since it is we, and not God, who are the ones to give God a name, we who write His name, our sinful pride makes us believe and repeat that God created us in His image and likeness. Understand, Guzmán, what I wish is to purify totally the essence of God by freeing the Father Creator from the supreme sin, the creation of men; we cannot be His work, we cannot, no . . . Allow me to free God from the supreme sin that we attribute to Him: the creation of man.''

"Of whom, then, Señor, are we the work?''

El Señor was silent for an instant and then he took the hand mirror he had held as he ascended part of the thirty-three steps leading from the chapel to the plain; he looked into the sterile lake captured within the frame of satiny old gold scratched by many hands before those of El Señor, who today was its possessor without knowing how it had become part of his fortune, or who was its former owner, and he was at the point of losing himself in the rugged track of this new riddle: to return to the origin, not of the first and never seen God ignorant of the name that we give Him, of the ceremonies we perpetrate in His name, but of this object he held in his hand: this mirror, the descending line of its former owners, the maker of this beautiful utensil, useful only to see ourselves in and thus confirm our vanity or our desolation: the life of the mirror, of all the mirrors that duplicate the world, that extend it beyond all realistic frontiers, and to all that exists, mutely says: you are two. But if this mirror had an origin, it was crafted, and used, and passed from hand to hand and from generation to generation; so it retained the images of all those who had viewed themselves in it, it had a past and not only the magic of a future that El Señor had seen one morning as he ascended the stairs with the mirror in his hand.

"Look into my mirror, Guzmán," said El Señor, and the space of the mirror was transformed, echoing from heaven to heaven like a drum that with each thump of the hand reveals an earlier skin, and then another before that, and in each space revealed in the dissolving layers of its quicksilver allows a new voice to be heard, a voice of smoke, a voice of stars . . .

The mirror: What can we, we who are the last angels, we who have never seen God Our Father, imagine from our impotence? This we, the most humble delegates of Heaven, asked ourselves. And one of us, one who is anonymous among us, for in this our inferior heaven it is impossible to know whether we descended from other, superior angels or whether one of us was that superior angel, the fallen Lucifer, Lucifer himself, suggested to us: "Let us invent a being that will have the presumption to believe it is made in the likeness of God the Father."

"And so we were born, Guzmán."

"Señor, in order to find the truth, pray that Our Lord Jesus Christ grant you His favor and grace by virtue of the death and the passion He suffered, for the Most Holy Blood that He spilled on the cross for sinners . . .

"Yes, Guzmán, sinners, among whose number I confess before His Divine Majesty to be the greatest, in whose Faith I have always lived; I swear to live and die as a true son of the Holy Church of Rome, for whose Faith I have constructed this palace of paradoxes; its towers and cupolas rise impotently toward the heavens, aspiring to an encounter with the Father who has hidden His face from us, its rectangular lines imposed upon a level valley, its sad gray color, its perpetual dedication to suffering and death, have as their intent mortifying the senses and reminding us that man is small and that his power is but nothing compared to the greatness of the unseen Father; here, here in this stony austerity I caused to be erected, I say: we are the sons of Lucifer, and nevertheless we aspire to be the sons of God: such is our servitude and such is our greatness; look into my mirror, Guzmán, and write, write before the Devil dries my tongue, Father, Son, and Holy Spirit, one true God, and doubt, Guzmán, because neither Paul, nor Luke, nor Mark, nor Matthew ever had the audacity to say that Jesus was God: look into my mirror, Guzmán, look into it if you have the eyes to see and let its shifting quicksilver transport us to that hot spring afternoon in the Levantine; penetrate these mists of crystal and you will not see your own face reflected in them, look . . ."

The mirror: My dog is not well and I have neither the humor nor the patience for a prolonged trial of yet another of the all too many Judean magi who parade around announcing catastrophes and portents: the end of Rome, or the freedom of the Hebrew people; no, my sick dog and these crushing dog days and one informer more, one more among the spies I have placed, placed by the hundreds, in the councils of the Jewish nation; I shall pay the accustomed thirty pieces of silver; I, Pilate, could be any other, call me Numa or Flavius or Theodorus, I could fulfill my functions as so many other procurators have fulfilled them before me and will fulfill them after me, it is normal that I, one more judge, be judging one more of the magi who for centuries have repeated the same prophecies to false followers who for centuries have denounced them before us, the authorities desirous of maintaining secular order at any cost.

"Let us be reasonable, Guzmán, and let us ask ourselves why we have accepted as truth only one series of events when we know that those events were not unique, but common; that they are ordinary, multiplicable unto infinity in a series of plots that repeat into exhaustion: look at them, look at them filing by, interminably, century after century, in the glass of my mirror. Why, among hundreds of Jesuses, and hundreds of Judases, and hundreds of Pilates, did we choose only three upon whom to base the history of our sacred Faith? But also you must doubt these explanations, Guzmán, doubt the supernatural by explaining it rationally, but doubt also that which seems natural, seeking the magical, savage, irrational explanation, for none is sufficient unto itself, and each exists side by side, in the same way a God named Christ lived beside a man named Jesus: hurry, Guzmán, look at them, the two of them together, Jesus the man and Christ the God, see them in my mirror; the smoke is covering them, their images are being swallowed by time, no one remembers . . ."

"Señor, I would like to demonstrate my loyalty to you. Let us burn these words, for if the Inquisition should read them, all your power would not . . ."

"Do I tempt you, Guzmán? Do you feel, as you hold these papers in your hands, that you could barter them for my power?"

"I insist, Señor; let us burn them; let us put an end to this doubting . . ."

"Quiet, Guzmán, let me delight in this my hour of power by edging toward heresy, both punishable and unpunishable; punishable because it destroys a certain order of the Faith, that which through the chance and accidents of politics according to St. Paul, a persistently subtle coalescence of compromise and intransigence, has triumphed; unpunishable, truly, because heresy collects and recalls all the rich and varied spiritual impulses of our Faith, the faith that it never denies, but on the contrary multiplies, its magnificent opportunities to be and to convince. Pelagius, the conquered, is as much a Christian as Augustine, the conqueror: Origen, the castrated debtor, as much a Christian as Thomas Aquinas, the seraphic creditor. And if the heretical theses had triumphed, today's saints would be heretics and the heretics the saints, and none, because of it, less Christian. Let us struggle, not against heresy, but against the pagan and idolatrous abomination of the savage nations that do not believe in Christ: depending on how much they deny, they believe neither in His divinity nor in His humanity; we Christians believe in Him because we debate whether He was both divine and human, only divine, or only human; our obsession keeps Him alive, forever alive; write, Guzmán, write, erase from my mirror the monstrous image of Tiberius Caesar's procurator, blow on the glass, Guzmán, and cover with mist my accursed mirror so that I can no longer see the face of Pontius Pilate, the true founder of our religion, and his very real dilemma . . .''

The mirror: For I was the only one who knew the rivals, the son of God and the son of Mary, both led into my presence that burning-hot afternoon in Jerusalem. How was I to distinguish between them in the darkening shadows of this room whose cool stone and white curtains isolate me from the boiling heat of the desert spring, and how was I to hear them, so near the courtyard filled with swaying palm trees and bubbling fountains? Which of the two should die, the one who is called Christ and says he is the son of God, or the one who is called Jesus and says he is the son of Mary? Christ who asserts the humanity of His divine acts, or Jesus who proclaims the divinity of his human acts? This one who promises the kingdom of Heaven, or this one who promises the kingdom of the Jews? Which is the more dangerous, which must die, which· must supplant Barabbas on the cross? I must choose only one; it is equally hazardous to assassinate more than one prophet, or to liberate more than one thief; justice must be balanced so that it disguises the criminal nature of its decisions. But the one thing of which I am sure this afternoon is that my dog's illness, the summer weight of food in the belly, the shadows gathered to combat the heat, the external distractions of the clear fountains and the date clusters falling from the prodigal arms of the date palms, all weigh too heavily on my soul. I am sleepy. I am bored, and worried about the dog; this climate is not good for making decisions; one gets drowsy; the sea and the desert; Rome has extended her boundaries too far from her center, vigilance is becoming difficult, institutions are crumbling, becoming attenuated: who is going to ask me for an accounting? Who, in Rome, could be interested in this story?

''Guzmán: was our religion founded upon an error of the Roman police system? Anathema, anathema be whosoever divides between two characters or persons the words and deeds attributed to Christ-Jesus in the Scriptures, according one part to the man and the other to the God.''

The mirror: Which of the two did I condemn? Which of the two did I present before the people, murmuring: "Here is the man . . ." having decided that one of them was the man and the other the God; which of the two did I judge less dangerous, which of the two did I condemn? Confronted with two identical twins, two magi identically bearded, equally intense and eloquent and ravenous, how could I help but doubt? Which of the two? How was I to know? One would die upon the cross, and when I condemned him I believed that truly, and not only symbolically, I was washing my hands of the problem. The example of the death of the one would serve as a warning to the other and also to forewarn any Jewish prophets who were tempted to imitate him. How was I to imagine the subtle trap prepared by the two called Christ and Jesus? One would die, yes, on the cross, suffering; but the other, two days later, would play his part in the comedy of the resurrection. How was I to know that? And how, then, was I to know which of them died and which lived to be reborn in the name of the dead one? I shall only confess this to myself, in secret: Christ the God was crucified, He died; for if I, Pilate, did not condemn a God to death, then my life would have no meaning; I could kill a thief in the name of Caesar, but if I killed a God, the memorable glory is mine, only mine. It was the lifeless body of the God I ordered crucified, His forever useless body, that was thrown by His followers into the waters of the Jordan, with weights tied to the neck and ankles so that when it met the waters of the Dead Sea it would not float to the surface. But they needn't have worried, for the body disintegrated swiftly, became part of the mud and silt in the Valley of the Ghor; a hurried investigation I ordered so testified. And in exchange, Jesus the man—my spies told me: he was present at the death of his double, winking at John of Patmos and Mary his mother, and Magdalene the courtesan—was saved from the cross by a humanity that I deemed innocuous, and then he hid himself, with a handful of dates, a bottle of wine, and a large loaf of bread, in the tomb reserved for the victim, and he emerged two days later; but he could not then rejoin his mother or his lover or his disciples. This is what I had feared: that he would reappear, that he would renew his activities as prophet and agitator, mocking both the law of Rome and that of Israel, my indirect condemnation in turning him over to the Jews and the direct condemnation of the Jews in determining his crucifixion; yes, this would have broken the delicate equilibrium between the Roman and Jewish powers; yes, this simple administrative transaction, although it did not deserve to, would have come to the attention of my superiors in Rome; yes, that would have been the death blow to my career. That is what I thought two days following the death of Christ the God when His disciples announced that He had been resurrected. I was cautious; I waited before I acted. The disciples said that their master had ascended to Heaven. I breathed a sigh of relief; I had feared not an improbable miracle but the authentic continuation of the survivor's career of agitation in the lands under my jurisdiction. But if the actor of the death on the cross was now lost in the waters of the desert, the actor of the resurrection, for the purpose of making credible his ascension into Heaven, had the good judgment to lose himself in the waterless desert. From Egypt he had come, as a child; to Egypt he returned and there for many years hid in the dog-ridden, sandy alleys of Alexandria, mute, impotent, ragged, old, a beggar, rendered forever useless by his own legend, so that his legend might live and be spread through the voices of Simon and Saul; they say that when he was very old, his only opportunity to satiate his appetite for legend to become an aged wanderer, an ancient Jew without a country, without roots, he arrived in Rome during the reign of Nero, son of Agrippina and Domitius Ahenobarbus, and there was present, in the coliseums, at the death of those who died in the name of his legend. He, too, then, I condemned to death; the testimonial death of a wanderer who only could be present, unable to speak his name, at the death of those dying in his name or against his name. Hebrew pilgrim, I know you; you are Jesus the man, condemned to live forever because you did not die at the privileged instant of Calvary. I know because I accompany you, I am always by your side; I am condemned to be something worse than your executioner: your witness. The God died. You and I live, the phantoms of Jesus the man, and Pilate the judge.

"Condemned by the cruel, not-born Father to live forever, Guzmán, as the Father condemned Christ the God to eternal death, thus saving himself from the rebellious divinity of a new Lucifer; for what Pilate— from the ocher profundities of the painting from Orvieto, now reflected in the mirror—says is true: Christ the God was crucified, He truly died, abandoned forever, once His part in the play was enacted, by the phantom Father. And this is what Pilate did not know: that the omnipotent Creator could not tolerate the return to Heaven of a possible rival, of a new Lucifer who had known the detestable mysteries and needs of fallen humanity and who might contaminate the timeless, ambitionless purity of eternal Heaven; it was the Father who condemned the Son, Guzmán, not Pilate, not the scribes and the Pharisees; the Father abandoned, murdered, His Son; the Son of God could come to earth only to die on earth. Thus the Father saved himself, I tell you, from a rebel in Heaven; but he also spared himself the necessity of showing His own face: Jesus the man would represent Him forever, in His name, throughout history. And thus you must believe with me, Guzmán, that reason is the intermediary between God and the Devil, since neither the evils of the Devil nor the virtues of God would be as they are or would affect us without the aid of reason; if we accepted evil as fact and virtue as mystery, Guzmán, we would never rise above that, and then, do you understand me?, I would be born again from the belly of a wolf, I would be hunted in these same lands by my own descendants: I want the Heaven and the Hell that have been promised, Guzmán, I want to be condemned or saved for all eternity, I want that total non-existence that the Father denied the Son and the Man, Christ and Jesus, I do not want to return with claws and fangs and hunger to this world; I do not want my death to be the material guarantee of a new life, a second life, another life, but simply that: my absolute death, my absolute remission to non-existence, a hermetic absence of communication with all forms of life; this is my secret project, Guzmán, hear me: let us establish a hell on earth to assure the need for a heaven that will compensate for the horror of our lives; the horror we do and the horror that is done to us . . . Let us then doubt our Faith, always within that Faith, in order to deserve first hell on earth, torture, the stake, used against us as heretics, against the barbaric nations as idolaters; only in this way, by first liberating the powers of evil on earth, shall we someday deserve the beatitude of heaven in Heaven. Heaven, Guzmán: forgetting forever that we once lived . . . What did you do with my faithful mastiff Bocanegra?''

"Señor, I have explained. He had rabies."

"He never knew his hour of glory. He died without being able to defend me. He lived half awake, half asleep, drugged, at my feet. My poor faithful Bocanegra."

"He was the phantom dog."

"Do you mean to tell me that that was the glory he awaited so long? Is that why you killed him when he was dressed for the supreme hunt?"

"Perhaps."

"You killed him."

"It was my duty, Señor. He had rabies . . ."

"No one verified that but you."

"It was true; he was frightening the nuns, the workers; you saw the mad self-indulgence that overpowered the nuns; you yourself felt its menace; the Sisters and the workers were eyeing each other on the sly, Señor; they were becoming aroused; the contagion could easily have spread from the cloisters to the work sheds . . ."

"Ah, now that he is no longer here, I feel that the dog was my only ally, my only guardian . . ."

"He had become listless; he had lost his taste for the hunt."

"Did he at least die in God's grace?"

"He was a dog, Señor. What do we know . . . ?"

"Without pain? What do we know? Was he one of my ancestors? Is that why he was so close to me, tried to warn me against danger, never abandoned my side, never, except to protect me? Why did he run out that day from my tent on the mountain? When he returned, he carried the sand of the seashore on his paws, in his wound . . . Who wounded him?''

''He was a dog, Señor. He could not speak.''

''What was he trying to tell me, poor brute, poor, fine, supposedly fierce mastiff? Was he one of my blood? Have we buried here the lifeless body of a Prince dead for centuries, not knowing that at the same time we were killing, in my favorite dog, his resurrected soul, living, gifted—even though he no longer savored the blood of the boar—with high values, like fidelity, and unarguable adherence to my person? Tell me, Guzmán. Do not look at me like that, vassal, I am not reproaching you; write, write my testament: In the name of the always glorious, forever virgin Mary Our Lady, look quickly, Guzmán, watch what is happening in the painting from Orvieto . . .''

The painting: Mother of the carpenter's son, it all seems like a dream, I don't know where the truth lies, I don't know now, I never knew, I don't know whether I became pregnant by the carpenter, or by some lusty apprentice of that aged artisan, Joseph, to whom I had been wed still a girl, or whether by some anonymous voyager who stopped to ask for water for his camels and to tell me enchanting stories, I, married to Joseph the carpenter, I, the mother of the child . . . I, the true daughter of the house of David, not the carpenter. History will say the opposite, because it is written by men; I, the woman, the daughter of David . . .

''Look how the forms are changing, see how the figures are turning and walking forward and going in and going out as if in some elaborate altarpiece, see the child-become-man, see him in the company of the Holy Spirit that descends in the form of a dove to accompany him on the day of his baptism in the desert waters of the Jordan, see the fiery, flowing river crossing now from border to border of the painting, Guzmán, and doubt, imagine an impotent carpenter, and watch the tiny scene unrolling up there, on those rocks below that humble shed in one corner of the painting.''

The painting: He kissed me, all he did was kiss me, he told me that this was what marriage was, a few rough, panting, anguished kisses sterile as the roadways of Sinai, that is what he told me, but when he saw my belly swelling he repudiated me; I was of the house of David, I knew its ancient secrets, in us are united great wisdom, the liquid, flowing formulas of our rivers, the Nile and the Tigris, the Ganges and the Jordan, one single flux of ancient memories, of magical knowledge born by the shores of the waters where men founded their first cities, fourteen generations after the captivity of Babylon, one night I served hallucinatory philters to the unlearned carpenter and caused him to dream of the hovering, Priapic, subornable, Lucifer-like angels of the nearest heaven, the one all we women can see with our bare eyes, the corrupt heaven we have at hand, the heaven of bodies; in the stupor of his body I caused those false angels to visit the carpenter and in his dream I made him believe that I had been got with child by the Holy Spirit and that I would give birth to the son of God, the heralded Messiah, the descendant of David the King.

"Hear the raucous laughter of the angels, Guzmán, hear it echoing from heaven to heaven, down through the years that for the phantom Father are but an instant, until the not-born Father—see his perfidious triangular eye there in the upper center of the painting we contemplate as it contemplates us—becomes aware of the monstrous joke and in an instant of caprice endorses the joke by sending the dove."

The painting: Do you not see the light surrounding our bodies immersed in the river?, do you not hear the beating wings of an invisible bird, John?, baptize me, John, Master, I want to be a man with you, John, show me the road of life, John, my mother says I am the son of God, John, but beside you I feel I am only a poor Galilean, weak, human . . . too human, eager to taste the fruits of life, bored by so many hours of wearying Bible study, a discipline imposed by my mother, read, you must know everything, ever since I was a boy, astonish the doctors, you must play your part well, you cannot be a dull and ignorant man like your father, baptize me, John, bathe me, John, take me in your arms, John, in my blood are blended the ignorant humility of a carpenter and the proud wisdom of a race of Kings, tell me what I must do with this double inheritance of slave and King, John, help me lead the slaves and humiliate the Kings, John.

"See the dove, Guzmán, alighting on the head, yes, of the human, yes, too human, yes, Galilean, yes, the day of his baptism which perhaps was but the day of his sodomite nuptials with John the Baptist who was perhaps a handsome man who perhaps died, as the other day a boy died here, burned beside the stables, because of his heinous relations with the son of the carpenter and, as a consequence, because of the combined animosity of two women who desired him but could never seduce him: Herodias and Salome, the ancient and the young naiads of the court of Israel; look, Guzmán, see it in the painting: see how the figure of the Christ without a halo is approaching that of the man dressed in a brief tunic of animal skins, how they take one another's hands, how they embrace, kiss each other upon the lips . . . how the Baptist consummates his marriage with Jesus, what I ask for in my prayers, the divine embrace, the most chaste kiss . . ."

"Señor, for saying less, men have died in these lands, impaled upon a stake driven up their buttocks, tearing through their entrails, and exiting through an eye or a mouth, for your fables suggest a similar punishment . . ."

"Be quiet, and look; be quiet, and understand; look at Jesus, born of Mary and an unknown father, visited by a Christ sent from the phantom not-born Father; only after that baptism in the river do the two live together; a pragmatic Christ, Guzmán; hear Him . . .''

The painting: I shall do quickly what is to be done and at every opportunity I shall deny my terrestrial parents so that everyone may understand that my virtues and my miracles are not of this world, nor will they ever be, so I may offer to men the image of Tantalus, invite them to drink the water and eat the fruit that—the moment they stretch out their hand, or open their mouth—disappear before their thirst and their hunger.

"That is the joke, Guzmán; to recall to us His unknown and forgotten existence before there was any Heaven or creation, the phantom Father sends His impossible representative, places Him within the body of a son of a lowly Hebrew, offers the vain illusion of a virtue that reproduces that of a Father who was never born, Guzmán, who never knew what it is to tremble with fear, to sigh with pleasure, to desire, to envy, to scorn what he has and to undertake mad adventure for what he can never achieve, who never knew what it is to ejaculate, to cough, to weep, to evacuate, to urinate, Guzmán, the things that you and I and the monk and the Chronicler and the Bishop and the astrologer and the supervisors and workmen and smiths all do . . . the things we all do.''

The painting: Tremble with fear, sigh with pleasure, desire, envy, ejaculate, cough, shit, piss, weep, and, bound to such wretchedness, attempt furthermore to imitate me; but if, bound to passion as they are, to fragility and to the filth of the earth, they succeed, in spite of everything, in scorning what they have and in undertaking mad adventure for what they will never achieve, then yes, yes, in truth I say to you, not only will they imitate me, they will surpass me, they will be what I could never be, dung and courage, enamored dust.

"No, do not listen to that falsifier, Guzmán, it isn't true, Christ's cruelty is to demonstrate to us that we can never be like Him, the cruelty of excrement is that it makes equals of us all, and between the two cruelties we attempt to forge some personal differences that will give us an identity; that is what my mutilated mother does, and that false Prince she has brought in her train, that false heir, as false as Christ the divine was to the humanity of Jesus, in whose body he dwelt.''

The painting: As false as you, Jesus, are to my divinity as Christ: without consulting you I have appropriated all the blame, the defects and the needs of that body, your body, Jesus, chosen from among thousands; my Father has placed His phantom within your mortal flesh, oh, son of Mary, so He might offer to men the mirage of an impossible virtue; but the moment you feel the vinegar in your throat, I warn you; the moment you feel the thorns upon your brow, I shall abandon your body and leave you in the hands of human cruelty.

"Look at the painting from Orvieto, Guzmán, study its subtle movements, its subtle Italianate frivolities, look how a painting of pious intent is transformed into the scene of a drama of unforeseen entrances and exits, see how the fickle artists of the other peninsula have displaced the sacred representations of the ecclesiastical atrium with profane theaters of illusory spaces, curtains, arches, shadows, and fictitious lights, see how into the scene occupied by the man Jesus enters a double identical to him, how he embraces him, kisses him, see how the two bodies seem to blend into one another in order to perform the comedy of the master of mockery, the not-born Father. Multiply your doubts, Guzmán, tell all the possible stories, and ask yourself once more why we chose one single version among that pack of possibilities and upon that choice founded an immortal Church and a hundred transitory kingdoms."

"You are the head of one of those kingdoms, Señor; try not to lose it."

"I tell you to doubt, Guzmán: the human body of Christ was a phantom, His suffering and His death were mere illusion, for if he suffered he was not God, and if he was God he could not suffer. Doubt, Guzmán, and watch the performance that is taking place before our eyes, within the frame of that painting."

The painting: If I am God I cannot suffer; if I suffer I am not God; the vinegar and thorns are enough; now they will take me from the cell, they will lead me through the deep, shadowy passageways toward the great door where I must carry my own cross and painfully ascend that dusty hill seen so many times in my dreams, where they have raised, like the foundation of my destiny, two other crosses, miracles, miracles, now is the moment to concentrate all my powers of transfiguration, of convocation, of prestidigitation; if I could do it to fill the amphoras of Canaan with wine, to multiply the fishes, and to reverse the hours of Lazarus, why should I not do it now, now when my own divinity is in danger of escaping through the chinks of pain. As they gave me vinegar to drink, as they lashed me and crowned me with thorns, I avoided pain by thinking intently of a quiet, coarse, and therefore receptive man called Simon of Cyrene, invoking him to come to my side, intensely entreating with the same intensity I begged Lazarus to renounce the peace of death and accept the agitation of life through the simple recourse of suicide in death, entreating that Simon hear me from afar and be present at the hour and in the place with the necessary assistance; that afternoon I was conducted by guards through the dark and musty passageways that lead from the cells to the great Praetorian door, my gaze penetrated the darkness and to my nostrils came the odor of fish and garlic and sweat: Simon had heard me from afar, Simon, dressed as a simple vendor of foodstuffs, laden with vegetables and fish, had come to obey me, to take my place; I pretended to stumble, the guards lost their martial beat, stopped, turned back, started forward again, turned around, confused, beat me, beat and cursed the Cyrenian who had already taken my place, who was now carrying the cross while I carried the onions and dried salted fish; I offered them to the Centurions and was rejected; the procession continued on its way and I gave thanks for the blindness of the foreign masters toward an alien and submissive race, for although we could distinguish the face of each foreign oppressor, for our lives might depend on it, they see us for what we are: a mass of slaves without individual physiognomy, each indistinguishable from all the others . . . Later, that same afternoon, I was able to watch Simon, crucified in ignorance and in error; I was able to contemplate my own torture and death, for the Centurions, the apostles, Magdalene and Mary and John of Patmos believed that Simon was I; and as my eyes penetrated the light shifting between granular sunlight and stormy shadows, I saw Simon of Cyrene upon the cross, and I could not believe my eyes; in his agony, the quiet, ordinary man of Cyrene had assumed my features; the sweat and pain of his face were forever imprinted upon Veronica's handkerchief. And thus I, Jesus, upon the hill of Calvary was witness to the crucifixion of Simon, and this was my most miraculous, although my least well known, act.

"But look, Guzmán, how quickly the scenery of the painting is changing, the backdrop remains the same, but the clothing of the figures is changing, the set is being replaced, the invisible, cruel, and capricious artist is arranging his tale in a new order, he has prepared a new performance for us."

The painting: Neither divine nor miraculous: I am a Palestinian, a political agitator; I convince my companions and intimates that a mock martyrdom is absolutely necessary to our cause; we cast lots to determine who is to betray me to the authorities and who is to take my place when, as I foresee, I am condemned to death. The lots fall to Judas and to Simon of Cyrene. Our group is very small for reasons of security, mobility, and purity of convictions; but also because it is composed of men who physically are very similar. In this way we can disguise ourselves as one another, appear simultaneously in different places under the generic name of Messiah, and astound the ignorant and ordinary folk with false miracles carefully organized and executed not by one but by several of my companions, but always attributable to me, as I am the symbol of the rebellion and its intellectual author. Only in this way am I different from my companions; my mother forced me to burn the midnight oil reading the Sacred Scriptures; I articulated the spontaneous rebellion of my untutored companions and channeled, organized, and intellectualized it. I lament that Judas and the Cyrenian were those elected by chance. I would have preferred to lose Peter, the most insecure and the weakest among us all, or John of Patmos, too whimsical to be politically effective. But sentiment must not intervene in these decisions that are more important than our own personal likes and dislikes. Thus, along the road to the cross, we all follow behind a double prepared to give his life for me and for my cause; there we all feign tears and despair; pretending only to a certain point, it's true, for Simon of Cyrene is a good man and a loyal, although expendable, warrior; we feign tears and despair to deceive the authorities and to cement our subversive legend, and then all of us who are actors in the drama withdraw into the darkness from which we will emerge for a short time to perform the sacramental play of the individual insurrection of the slaves against the collective ethic of Rome and the weighty tradition of Israel. That afternoon on which the weather so opportunely collaborated with us, that afternoon begun in heat and sun and dust and ended in storm, that early darkness and the motionless violence of the stones, were necessary so that our rebellion might fly on the wings of a legend of sacrifice. Only from sacrifice are new worlds born. But men have always been sacrificed. So it occurred to me: sacrifice a God. The ancient gods and their divine history were born from human sacrifice. From divine sacrifice human history would be born. It was a very effective inversion, well worth the effort. My fate and that of my followers are not important. No one ever again knew anything of us. But there was no one who did not know what happened that afternoon on Golgotha. Our creation is called history.

"Doubt no more, Guzmán: the soul of Christ abandoned the suffering body of Jesus, who upon dying was again only the son of Mary and an unknown father. Write, Guzmán, write the principal section of my testament, dictated today, the day of the final burial of all my ancestors whom I shall one day join, write: In the name of the Holy Trinity, the Father, Son, and Holy Ghost who are one Being, unique, three names that are one essence, as the body, the intelligence, and the soul are the one essence of every man, and if we do not doubt the existence of this union, mysterious though it may be, why would we doubt the substantive union of our dogma: the intelligence of the Father, the body of the Son, and the soul of the Holy Spirit, like the Sun a unique substance that manifests itself as light, heat, and as the sphere itself: light, the Spirit; heat, the Son; and the sphere, the Father. So was the Son one day sent forth, like a ray of light; but doubt this, too, and believe in what this painting is telling us; I told you it would speak to us as we spoke to it, look at its space, suddenly empty, or invaded by a light so white it erases everything, blinds everything, converts everything into blackness, into absence of light . . ."

The painting: Because I am God I am unique; and I, that unique God, was the One who descended unto Mary the virgin and got her with child, and from her I was born, the only God who had never been born before: I, Father of Myself; I, Son of Myself; a unique, indivisible God, it was I who suffered and I who died, men crucified the one God, I, the Father.

"And so you will accept, Guzmán, that our Christianity bleeds because of simple arithmetic, and attempts to explain the inexplicable with the weapon of the Devil instead of forever defeating the Devil by denying the temptation of the rational, by drawing the fangs of the forbidden, by accepting that everything is magic, that everything is mystery, that everything is the intellectual liberty of the few—faithful, persecuted, eternally heretical, and eternally nonconformist: God's triumph, Guzmán, is that enduring, persecuted, and ever triumphant Christian community; Christianity exists because Jesus was defeated, not because Constantine triumphed; I know Nero's temptation, I sometimes dream it, I ask myself whether in order to strengthen my Faith there are not, in truth, more than two roads: to be either the persecutor or the persecuted . . ."

"You, Señor, ordered the unruly mob in your father's castle to be killed and you led your armies in crusades against the Waldensian, Abelite, Adamite, and Cathari heretics. Whom, then, did you persecute?"

"Ease my heavy spirit, Guzmán; perhaps that tiny community of true Christians is hidden in the souls of madmen and rebels, of children and lovers, those who live without need of me or need of the Faith . . . and by persecuting them and killing them, perhaps without knowing it I have strengthened that Faith."

"You are the Defender. Your battles, your escutcheon, and your laws so proclaim; and also a papal bull."

"Yes, yes, the Defender; seal my mouth, Guzmán, as you will put the seal to this my testament when it is completed, and repeat with me, now, this very moment, on your knees, the eternal truth: We believe in one God, a supernatural Father, the Maker, Creator, and providential Monarch of the Universe, from whom cometh all things, and in one Lord, Jesus Christ, His Son, a God procreated by the Father before the beginning of time, God of a God, totality issued from totality, unity of unity, King of a King, Lord of a Lord, the Word Incarnate, living wisdom, the true light, the way, the resurrection, the shepherd, the door, the essence, the purpose, power, and the glory of the Father; eternal image of the Deity, irreplaceable image, the unique image that no infidel can exchange for one of sullen stone and harrowing grimaces: Your image, Lord, is the sweet face of the Italian painting that stares down upon me as, kneeling, I praise your Name, and that image can be no other: God the Creator, divine Christ, most human Jesus, but only in that face consecrated by tradition, and never in the stone masks of savage idolaters; those who attempt to change your face, O God, shall see their works burned, torn down, destroyed by the combined anger and piety of my armies; never again will new Babylons arise to deform your sweet likeness, my God. Repeat with me, Guzmán, this credo, for if doubt transforms the dogma of the Trinity or stains the conception of Mary or separates Christ's divinity from his humanity or changes the most precious face of Jesus, endangered all by the heresies I have exposed for the purpose of exorcising them, then I would lose my power and it would be gained by madmen, rebels, children, and lovers; and it is not that they may not deserve it, no; it is that they would not know how to use it, it would be useless to them, and above all, a contradiction: once they had the power they would cease to be what they are: children and madmen, lovers and rebels. Better it be this, better it be I, better one single dogma, any dogma, than a million doubts and debates, whatever they may be. Now you must understand the reasoned order of my apparent lack of reason, Guzmán: all doubts are consigned to paper, dictated by me, written by you. They are there, and they will remain written; but they will remain in my possession, like black envoys of the luminous truth of the Faith, they will not be loosed and rained and carried and fluttered in the wind of temptation and the incoherent noise of mockery. Let us incorporate evil into knowledge, Guzmán, and it will be but a healthful contrast and warning to the life of truth and good. Write my words, Guzmán: evil is only that which we do not know; and only that which does not know us is evil; and it is that unknown and unknowing evil, unsubmitting, irreducible, not to be possessed even through the writing that is our privilege, which we must extirpate without mercy."

"Amen, Señor, amen."

"Peace, and an early death, Guzmán. Bocanegra was more fortunate than we; what we seek, he has already obtained."

"El Señor is unjust with me. I only fulfilled my duty, as I fulfill it now, by writing down El Señor's words."

"Truly, I am not reproaching you. Come, Guzmán, come nearer; let me tell you something, in confidence . . ."

"Señor . . ."

"That dog attacked me on the stairway . . . one morning . . . attacked me . . . he didn't know me . . . that's why I tore off his bandages . . . to defend myself from him . . . and you treated him, Guzmán . . . you were right; he had rabies. You treated him, not knowing; when you knew, you killed him . . . Loyal and efficient Guzmán; thank you, Guzmán, thank you for doing what is necessary, while I live in the realm of the imagination; thank you; I am not reproaching you . . ."

"Señor, I beg you; let us put an end to these words. Today is a memorable one; you have brought together all your ancestors in your own palace erected for that purpose; and, in so doing, you have raised your dynasty above any other in this land. Rest, Señor; your words are dictated by your soul's fatigue . . ."

"Guzmán, Guzmán, what intolerable pain . . . come, place the red stone in the palm of my hand . . . You see, my body pains me even more; Guzmán, do you never doubt?"

"If I had power, Señor, I would never doubt anything."

"But you do not have it, poor Guzmán; come, kiss my bone ring, kiss my hand, thank me for having taken you from nothing and given you a place in my service, in which you have risen, I recognize, by your own merits and well-proven abilities. Let me see what you have written . . . Where did you learn such a fine hand?"

"Although in straitened circumstances, I was able to spend a year in Salamanca."

"You learned a beautiful hand."

"Among other things, Señor. Students tend to be bellicose rascals. El Señor should be grateful that my defects are in the service of his virtues."

"Ah, yes. Come then, kiss my hand with respect and gratitude."

"I do so, Sire, I do so with great humility . . ."

"Do you know something, Guzmán? All you need do is show the Bishop this writing, alleging that it is a confession, and you can imagine that I would be brought before the Holy Office, judged and condemned to the stake; well, have no such hope; it would do you no good, however bellicose and rascally you may feel; they would not believe you, everything is written in your hand, yes, just so, sprinkle sand on the words to dry the ink, and even though they believed you and condemned me, Guzmán, it would not help you, for if you usurped my power . . ."

"Señor, you judge me harshly."

"Shhhh, Guzmán; for if you usurped the power in my name, you, or any man like you . . . I do not wish to offend you, but any man like you, a new man, you would not know what to do with power, you would go mad, you believe you would not doubt, but you would do nothing but doubt, the entire day, you would be riddled with doubt about what you had done and what you had allowed to be done, doubt establishes its kingdom between moral duty and political duty, there is no possible escape, none, Guzmán, thank heaven that you are a servant and not a master . . ."

"I do not complain, Señor . . ."

"But, hear me, one can retain power only when he has behind him a legion of murdering, cruel, incestuous, mad phantoms mortally damaged by the French malady and inclined to bleed to death at a scratch. What is there among men except exchange? And if some serve and others command, Guzmán, it is because some succeed in offering something for which the others have no response: something for which they can offer nothing in exchange. And who in this land can offer me anything in exchange for my thirty bloodless, corrupt, demented, incestuous, criminal, ill—ill even in death—cadavers, Guzmán, come here with me, look at them in their sumptuous sepulchers, see the grimaces and leprous bodies and infirmities and death's-heads and moth-eaten ermines, regard my thirty phantoms, their heads crowned in blood, their bodies brilliant with chancres and boils and wounds that never healed, no, not even in death. Who, Guzmán? Only I, Guzmán, only I can offer to myself the one gift that is superior, only I can say: this dynasty will die with me; hear me well, and now take my ring and roll the parchment carefully and seal it with the wax; obey me, Guzmán; do as I tell you . . . do it! Why do you stand there, motionless? Does it horrify you so to see such tumefaction? These are very old cadavers; there is neither stink nor fear in them.''

"But something is still lacking, Señor.''

"I tell you, nothing is lacking, in this testament I have left my doubt, my life, my anguish, and something more: a suspicion, that denies my uniqueness, a suspicion that whatever exists exists only because it is related to, circulates through, or eats into what we believed unique, turns uniqueness into a commonplace, a boiling quagmire, and the parallel suspicion that nothing is unique because everything may be seen and told in as many ways as men existed, do exist, or will exist. Is that not enough? Is there anything more to risk in my undertaking to rescue truth by accumulating in one place all the lies that refute it?''

"Only your signature is lacking, Señor, for without it, as you have said, and said rightly, these papers have no meaning. I could have written them myself, rolled the parchment and then sealed it with El Señor's ring as Your Mercy was dozing.''

"True, Guzmán, how am I to tempt you if I do not sign the papers?''

"El Señor must be equal to the challenges he proposes. Sign, Señor, here . . .''

"What do you really want, Guzmán?''

"Irrefutable proof of El Señor's confidence. Otherwise I cannot occupy myself in dissipating the dangers soaring around his head.''

"What do you mean? Everything is calm; the storm has passed; the nuns are quiet; the workers, I tell you, have returned to work; Bocanegra is dead; the cadavers lie in their crypts; the procession is over; now we are complete; now they may close forever the roads leading to this place; we are all here, united. It has been a memorable day. Nothing remains to be done. Nothing remains to be said. At least, that is my most fervent wish.''

"One day of glory, Señor! Many days of glory, for your dead have spread your renown throughout our land, not only today but during the weeks and months it took to form the corteges and begin their journey through mourning towns and cathedral cities, escorted by clerics, by the heads of all the orders, by entire convents that joined in the procession. All the land has seen your cadavers en route, lying within their litters draped and adorned in black, all for your glory, Señor. But this afternoon as the procession entered this uncompleted palace, upon hearing the funeral bells, the praise and psalms of the monks and the prayers of the multitude, as the Masses and sermons and funeral orations you ordered were celebrated in every corner of the palace, I had to ask myself, Señor, why nature seemed to oppose your design, eager to overthrow it; I saw a sign in that storm that in an instant divested the catafalques of their adornment, tore away the drapery, and allowed the wind to tip over the tabernacle and carry off the black ribbon clusters, ripping and tearing everything so badly that today the plain is covered with the remains of your dead's remains. Your corpses have been humbled by the storm. Now they lie in peace, but I believe that they will never again be the same; you have given them a second life, Señor, a second opportunity."

"No, no one shall have a second opportunity, neither the dead nor the living nor those who will never be born; all that I have told you would be in vain if it did not confirm in written words the wordless desire that pulses in every beat of my life: death, truly to be death, nonexistence, radical oblivion, and disappearance; my power is absolute because I shall be the last Señor, with no descendants, and then you and yours, with no need to denounce me, can do what you will with my heritage . . ."

"Señor, stand up, for God's sake, don't kiss my feet, I . . ."

"There will be no more wretched, defective sons forced to kill the dreams of others so that power may be transmitted from generation to generation, there will be no more . . ."

"Señor, Señor, stand up, here, lean on my arm, Señor . . ."

"Yes, let me sign, for if what I say is true, what does it matter . . ."

"Trust in me, Señor; you have constructed a house for the dead through the labor, accidents, and misery of the living; I have ears, Señor, I have eyes, and I have a good sense of smell; the storm is only nature's notice of what is happening in the souls of men; let me act, Señor; let me act against men, for, like you, I can do nothing against nature; let me work for you here in the place where the act of nature and the acts of men seem as one: this is the privilege you have accorded to us, the new men, the ability to act without the doubt that arises between morality and practicality; did the bells of the tower burn because they were struck by lightning, or because of a premeditated fire lighted by very human hands?"

"You doubt, Guzmán?"

"Señor: these fields are strewn with the black brocade flowers which the storm tore from the catafalques. At this very moment some stonemason or smith, the former shepherds of these lands, is walking through the arid fields picking up pieces of crape and thinking, remembering that they and their people were dispossessed, removed from their fields, denied their streams, their reserves of water exhausted, so that upon the ruins of the land could arise a funereal city. Let me work for you, Señor; and in my acts your will to conquer hell upon earth may encounter its best ally; and my services will finally be identified with the death and disappearance you so desire . . ."

"Guzmán . . . what are you doing? Why are you drawing that curtain? What is moving behind that curtain? Are we not alone, you and I? Who is it? Who is it, Guzmán, what are you showing to me, offering me? Who is it?"

"See, Señor, there is a witness who has heard everything."

"Who is it? Why is the hair so short? Is it a lad? No, the nightdress cannot hide the shape of her breasts, who is it, please?"

"Come to your bedchamber, rest, lie down . . ."

"What are you showing me? Who is this girl? What beauty, how white that lily skin, what eyes, like black olives . . . why have you brought her here? Who is she?"

"Rest, Señor; she will come to you; you need not move; she will do everything. Although a virgin, she is wise; and as you are who you are because of the life and death of those remains we buried here today, she is who she is because of the land where she was born . . ."

"Guzmán, what are you doing, I am ill, I am ill . . ."

"She is a broad, deep-flowing river . . ."

"Take her away, Guzmán, I am rotted . . ."

"She is the odor of damp geraniums and the zest of the lemon, come, Inés, come, do not be afraid, our Señor needs you, after such a festival of death, bodies demand the celebration of life, it is the law of nature, our Señor will give you all the pleasure you need, stop thinking about the journeymen and smiths and leadworkers, stop torturing yourself by imagining impossible love with the scum that works on this construction, lose your virginity in the arms of our Señor; come, Inesilla, you need El Señor and El Señor needs you, come, Inesilla, you know, you must allow yourself to become pregnant by our Señor . . ."

"No, Guzmán, no, haven't I told you . . ."

". . . for if El Señor cannot produce an heir, even if only a bastard, the mother of El Señor will impose her will, and will convince everyone that that imbecilic boy she has brought in her train is the true Prince, the providential sovereign announced in all the prophecies of the common people, the last heir, the universal usurper, the true son of the true father; fear your mother, Señor, fear her, for even mutilated as she is, a mere hulk without arms or legs, wrapped in black rags, she compensates for the missing limbs with intensity of will and the lucidity of her aged brain, I can see, Señor, and I can smell, and I already hear the sound of rebellion, the discontent because your Queen offers no legitimate heir, discontent that the Lady your mother might install an idiot as Prince; for either reason, rebellion . . ."

"Guzmán, do not betray my purpose; I do not want an heir, I must be the last Señor, and then nothing, nothing, nothing . . ."

"Choose quickly, Señor, there is no time: either sacrifice your desire for personal death and renew your life in the fertile seed of this young girl of the people, or once again face rebellion and the duty to repress it, as you did once before as a youth, again fill the halls of your palace with corpses; choose, Señor, renewed blood or spilled blood; and see, too, Señor, that what I am offering you refutes the lack of loyalty you suspect in me: I offer the continuity of your dynasty, Señor . . ."

"Why, Guzmán?"

"What would become of me in a world governed by children, lovers, and rebels? But enough; take this girl, quickly, let her slip between your black sheets, caress her, Señor . . ."

"Guzmán . . . the painting . . . what black space . . . the light has faded."

"Do not look at the painting, look at her flesh, Señor, could you imagine there was such softness in the world, you must touch her to believe it . . ."

"What a horrible voice . . . who is that speaking from the shadows of the painting . . . I don't understand . . . horror . . ."

"Lose yourself in your pleasure, Señor, and allow me to act for you. And if you are disposed to die, die in the arms of this maiden, spend yourself between her round thighs and give your soul to the Devil."

"Yes, let her come, let her come, bring her to me, Guzmán, let me touch her, let me . . ."

The painting: They always turn out the lights when I speak. I always speak in the darkness, when attention is focused elsewhere; no one has ever paid the least attention to me—and with good reason. A secondary character, a miserable Jewish carpenter who doesn't know either how to read or how to write, an honest workman who has always earned his living with his hands. They know nothing about that. They scorn my calluses and my sweat. But, without me, what would they sit on, what would they sleep on? Bah! They couldn't even sit down to discuss their idiotic problems or lie down to dream their equally imbecilic dreams. No; they turn out the lights when I speak because they are afraid of me. Afraid of the simple truth of a hairy, callused, ignorant old man, but a man who knows the truth; that's why they fear me and hide me as they would a shameful illness. Joseph doesn't exist.

The carpenter is happy with a good trencher of lamb, garlic, pepper, and wine. Perhaps it's true. I followed the steps of the Bastard and the truth is that I never paid too much attention to what he said or did because there were other more interesting things to see; at the last supper with all his cronies I spied on them from a distance; I couldn't hear what they were saying, not that it mattered to me; I was outside, lost among the dogs, the hangers-on and the passers-by, and looking inside I found it more interesting to watch what the cooks and the serving girls were doing; I was more interested in the braziers and their savory odors, in the platters of food and the bread and wine, than in the people being served. It's true; I'm always distracted by anything that tastes good, by anything that can be touched or smelled or chewed; I have no patience for the fancy words of that crew of geldings, for that's what they are: the only thing I really saw clearly was that Judas kissed the Bastard. That's proof he wasn't my son; would any son of mine allow himself to be kissed by a man? Bah . . . More and more lights are going out, they don't want to hear me, they're afraid of me. They've invented a personality for me that isn't mine; a quiet, ignorant old man who swallows all their lies, a shadowy figure on the edges of what's going on. They'd have a real laugh if they knew the truth: from the time he was a young man Joseph was a real hand with the girls, a braggart, a good eater, and a good drinker; anyone will tell you that, and if you believe I'm lying hear what they have to say in the brothels of Jerusalem, the taverns of Samaria, and the stables of Bethlehem, why, in that hay more than twenty wenches warmed by the burning days of the desert came to know me, they'd have died of the cold if it hadn't been for me; that's who I am, I, Joseph, and Mary and her family ought to be grateful to me for marrying her; I took her from a family that was having hard times but still very pretentious for all that, all her family putting on fine airs, although they were very happy to let an honest man who worked as a carpenter provide their food. Bah! And fine thanks I got from that twit of a girl. First it was no, don't touch me, I'm afraid, let me get used to it gradually, it hurts, not now, another night, and then one fine day I noticed that although she's supposed to be a virgin, she's pregnant, and I mean really pregnant, and what a wallop I gave her, and all the time she's swearing it was all because of some dove. Am I to take the responsibility for that? I, Joseph, a real man, cuckolded by a dove? Oh, I gave it to her, pow, and again, pow, and again . . . I left her; I went off to Bethlehem to look up some old friends, but she followed me and had her son there, and right away Miss Big-mouth began telling all the shepherds in those parts that her son was the son of God, and three clowns dressed up in turbans—magi and puppeteers by profession, and professional gossips as well—heard of it, and they took it upon themselves to carry the news to court and then . . . fury and fear from Herod, and children drawn and quartered all through Judea, and I on my way to Egypt to get away from the mess that witch had got me into, and she on a donkey right behind me, you can't abandon me now, what bellowing, and finally yes, I will be yours, take me, and the flesh is weak and she's very beautiful and so I fell for it. We had several more children in Egypt and after we returned to Palestine, but all her affection and care were for the Bastard, the others grew up wild as goats, dirty and running loose, but not the Bastard, no, all indulgence, and secrets all the time, and sorcery, and old rolls of papyrus brought from my in-laws' house covered with all kinds of useless stuff, and the boy stuffed with nonsense by the age of twelve, debating with learned doctors, Mister Know-it-all, full of silly ideas, delusions of grandeur, unbelievable pedantry, and then he goes off into the world and it was nothing but scorn for us who'd given him food and a roof over his head, I told you, woman, he's a good-for-nothing, he scorns us, he can't even say hello to us in public, he never says a word about us, he even counsels everyone to abandon his father and his mother, he's an unnatural son, and a liar besides, I've spied on him and I follow him, I watch while he makes a deal with Lazarus, a sick man from Bethany, so he pretends to die, and they bury him, and then the Bastard brings him back to life, and the whole thing arranged with Martha and Mary, the sick man's sisters, all pure intrigue, the sisters owe him a favor and that's why they agree to the comedy, and disciples hiding beneath the wedding table with baskets filled with bread and amphoras brimming with wine, and then, a miracle, a miracle, and I, forgotten, scorned, cuckolded, you think I'm not going to betray him?, you think I'm not going to give myself the pleasure of being the one, the very carpenter who with his old, callused hands, a simple man of the people, crude but honest, the one who held the saw and cut two planks and joined them together to make a cross and nailed them firmly so they would bear the weight of a body? Thirty pieces of silver. I'd never seen so much money. I hefted the weight of the pretty pouch as lost in the crowd of curiosity seekers I watched him die on the cross I had built. Do you hear me? I, Joseph, I . . . Bah! They always turn off the lights on me. I'm always talking into empty space.

THE PALACE IDIOT

Now the Mad Lady orders them to seat me in this stiff straight-backed chair, and she orders me to sit quietly while her servants throw a sheet over my shoulders and the barber in her retinue approaches with scissors and razors. But I am too young to need a barber, too beardless, I pull the two or three hairs from my chin with my fingers, pinching

them between my fingernails, it's a very simple process, all this ceremony isn't necessary; if it's ceremony they want, let them lend me a
mirror and I'll pull the hairs from my chin myself (and see myself for
the first time; my memory is very bad, I cannot remember my face; the
sea was too rough to reflect my image, and the fire of the corposant
blinded me as I fell from the mainmast; now they could at least be
good enough to hand me a mirror so that I could see my forgotten face
for the first time), but I see that their intention is not to shave me but to
do something more serious; the barber is clicking his scissors with gusto, with excessive gusto; he licks his lips, he bends over, he circles
about me, observing me, until the Mad Lady says, enough, do what
you have to do, and the barber approaches and begins to cut my long
hair; tufts of blond hair fall upon my chest and shoulders, fall upon the
cold floor of this chamber that according to that damned gossiping
dwarf will from now on be mine . . . my prison, the dwarf said. I
was led here by the Mad Lady, the dwarf, and the halberdiers, who
guided us with wax torches: we had to walk a long way (I am very
tired) through the galleries of this palace, hearing the murmur of feminine voices, doors closing, the whisper of nuns' coifs as they hurried to
their cloister, locks and chains, and water dripping down the walls, always lower, deeper, and if this were a ship and not a house I would say
they had brought me to the deepest part of a brigantine, to the brig, but
the Mad Lady calls this bare stone room with iron rings embedded in
the walls and a straw mat on the floor a bedchamber.

"Try to be comfortable here, you can come out only when I permit
it."

I remember nothing, not my face, not my life, only the St. Elmo's
fire on the mainmast, my fall into the sea, my miraculous salvation on
the beach, the passage of the procession across the dunes, the impulse
to save myself, to join those men, to know that I was alive and that
men would look after me, look after a poor shipwrecked youth who
had no home, no occupation, no memory: the most orphaned of or-
phans who had ever stepped upon these shores. I forget everything that
happens; by night I no longer remember what happened during the
day. Yes, perhaps I recall the things closest at hand, clothes, or the
most definitive things, death. But everything else . . . what happens
between the time one dresses and one dies . . . what is said and
thought between the time one puts on his breeches and the time he's
placed in his coffin . . . nothing of that. What is happening now,
yes. What is immediate, what happens during the day, before I go to
sleep, yes. We arrived here today as part of a procession, at the end of
a procession, the bells were tolling, there was a storm, the palace is
enormous and still uncompleted, there are many workmen, cranes,
piles of things, straw and tiles, blocks of stone, carts, smoke, smoke
everywhere, smoke that prevents one from seeing very far, that de-

ceives, that makes one believe that a corridor continues when in reality it ends, ends as empty space or continues only as dangerous planks, carelessly placed, the dwarf must be very careful as she pushes the Mad Lady in the little cart, the wax torches must illuminate very well, tonight we came close to killing ourselves, we came to the landing of a stairway, and continuing to descend (down, down, always down; this chamber must be in a very deep place, far beneath the rest of the palace, near the cisterns, for the plain is dry, whereas black water seeps through these walls), the dwarf, who must have very sharp vision— doubtlessly in compensation for her minute stature—shouted no, no, be careful, there are no stairs here, they've not been built yet, it's only a landing, it's open, be careful, and if she hadn't seen that there were no steps we'd have fallen off that open landing, yes, and now our broken bones would be lying at the bottom of some forgotten corner of the palace and our flesh would be food for rats and I wonder whether seeing the three of us dead—the Mad Lady, the dwarf, and me—would please the other persons who live here, and who are they?, and I realize I must be satisfied with this room that, whatever the Mad Lady and the dwarf say, is a jail, not a bedchamber. But I shall keep what I know to myself. And also I will tell them that it is a very fine chamber, very comfortably appointed, and I will allow the barber to cut my long hair and to take the razor, as he does now, and shave me, painfully, he's a clumsy brute, he wets my head with water and then quickly runs the razor over it, very roughly, without having first soaped it, and I can feel that he's cutting my scalp, and blood is rolling down my forehead and cheeks. The blood blinds me and I close my eyes, and I have a strange impression that is difficult to explain, I examine my thoughts, I know that I must never cross the Mad Lady and the dwarf, who are watching me with great contentment as the barber shaves my head, the Mad Lady is all satisfaction, her bilious eyes glowing like coals: all her life is there, gleaming, she is nothing but eyes, the dwarf, as she watches me, is holding a dove in her tiny little arms, stroking it, then suddenly I have a flash of intuition as to the role I must play here, I must not cross them, I must be respectful to them, they will treat me well, not as if I were a servant, no, I must not cross them, but others, yes, perhaps that's the very reason they will treat me well, they hope I will treat others badly in their name, an invalid Lady and a tiny dwarf, dependent upon me to convert their desires into actions, I begin to yell as if I were mad, I see that while they are shaving me the dwarf is playing with her dove, and I yell: I cannot bear this headache, relieve the pain, relieve my blood with the blood of the dove. The dwarf leaps toward me, shrieking with joy, not asking permission of the Mad Lady, and offers me the white bird; I take it and I seize the razor from the surprised barber, I plunge it into the smooth, white, quivering breast of the dove and when I see the blood staining its feathers I crown myself with the dying bird, I place its tremulous body upon my shaven and bleeding head and allow the blood to run down my face and blind me again, but now I refuse to close my eyes, I see the joy of the dwarf, who is leaping with pleasure, I see first the defiance, then the fear, and finally the proud acceptance of the Mad Lady, who exclaims: "The crown one fashions is the crown one will wear."

She understands that I understand. Then I am able to close my eyes and lick the sour taste of blood and remember, before I forget, for the day has been long and troubled and tomorrow in order to survive I shall have forgotten all that occurred today, how we arrived in the midst of the storm that tore the ribbons from the litters and the veils from the catafalques, how we descended from the carriage and prostrated ourselves before El Señor, who stood receiving the various companies, and how the Mad Lady orders me to kiss the pale hand and then the stinking feet of El Señor, her son, and she says to me: This is El Señor, my son; and to him she says:

"You should always have trusted me. I am the only one who has brought you a living person instead of a dead body. Do not bury in the black marble crypt reserved for my husband that corpse I bring with me; throw it into a common grave, along with the tavern keepers and criminals and dogs of your army of huntsmen: that body I have brought here with me is not that of a high Prince, your father, but a shipwrecked beggar. The true Señor, your father, was reincarnated in the body of this youth. See in him both your resurrected father and the son no one has given you: your immediate ancestor and your most direct descendant. Thus God Our Lord resolves the conflicts of privileged dynasties."

Now the Mad Lady enjoys the effect of her words: her son's increased pallor, the contained anger of the beautiful Señora seated beside El Señor with a hooded bird poised on her greasy gauntlet, the impotent gesture of the man standing behind them, who with such fury, but also with such futility, places his hand to his belt, to the handle of his dagger, but then has to settle for stroking his braided moustaches; how the Mad Lady's yellow eyes bore into my body prostrated at the feet of such high Lords before she says:

"One day you tore me from the arms of death, my son; you frustrated my will to die and join my most beloved husband. Today I thank you for that. You forced me to recover the past in my lifetime. Listen carefully, Felipe: our dynasty will not disappear: you will be succeeded by your own father, and your father by your grandfather, and your grandfather by his father, until we meet our end in our beginnings and not—as the sterile women who live with you, and despise you, would wish—in our end. Take good care of your dead, my son; let no one steal them from you: they will be your descendants."

As if he were obeying a ritual previously agreed upon, the halberdier supporting the trunk of the mutilated Mad Lady shifts her so that she looks directly into La Señora's face, but La Señora is not looking at the Mad Lady; rather, she is looking at me, and with an intensity, with an astonishment, that is also recognition; I would have liked to ask her: Do you know me, do you know me, do you know this shipwrecked victim, this orphan, this man without parents or any who love him, do you know me? But now La Señora was searching for something among the sea of faces at this ceremony. I follow the direction of her gaze, and more than meeting, it seems to transfix like a ray of lightning or a sword the gaze of a tall, blond, pale priest who moves away from the group and hurries into the palace. With the motion of her head—erratically tracing the sign of the cross in the stormy late-afternoon air—the Mad Lady blesses her son, El Señor; he seems almost asphyxiated, his thick lips move spasmodically, and he thrusts his enormous chin forward as if to capture any air escaping from his lungs. The Mad Lady smiles and orders them to take her to her rooms and there she joins me, the dwarf, and the halberdiers, who place her in the little cart that the dwarf begins to push along the passageways; there we go again, walking, it's no wonder I'm exhausted, the dwarf pushing the little cart, and I behind, past the cells of the nuns, who peer secretively from behind their veils and the hangings in their cells, past the bedchambers of the duennas, until we reach the bedchamber of La Señora, and I cannot understand why we enter the splendid bedchamber in this manner, with churlish fury, without knocking. The halberdiers guard the door, the dwarf pushes the little cart, the Mad Lady, with rapid movements of her head, looks from La Señora to me and from me to La Señora, the dwarf tilts her head to one side, jumps up and down twice, and then rushes at La Señora, pummeling her belly, beating her fists upon La Señora's bulging skirts, cackling wildly, as the Mad Lady says cuttingly:

"Enough of these silly games, Isabel; that bulge is false; there's nothing in your belly but wind and feather pillows. Enough of this announcing a false pregnancy, followed by an equally false miscarriage; your belly is as sterile as this devastated plain: enough, enough, it's no longer necessary; I have found the heir, I have brought him here: here he is."

I, the shipwrecked orphan? I, the heir? I expected to see in La Señora's face an astonishment equaling mine: but instead she pointed toward the bed and said: "Juan."

And naked, you rise from the bed redolent of spices and dried violets, you, a youth like myself, entirely naked, golden, with a faraway look in your eyes in which stupor is indistinguishable from forgetfulness or satisfaction.

"Turn around, Juan; show your back to this witch."

You slowly turn and show us your back and on it there is a blood-red cross, part of your flesh; I want to walk to you, to recognize you, embrace you, remember something with you, and you, as you look at me, seem astonished, of what I do not know, for an instant you seem to recapture something lost, to take a step outside that waking dream in which you move, impelled by the voice of the young Señora, perhaps, like mine, your spirit too struggles to recognize itself by recognizing me, I feel it, I feel the same hollowness in my stomach I felt as I fell from the mainmast into the emptiness of the ocean, perhaps you feel the same, I don't know, but La Señora paralyzes all of us with her words, directed to the dwarf: "Don't touch me again, you disgusting creature; you are beating my son."

"You lie, you are sterile, sterile, who sows his seed in you sows in the sea," shouts the Mad Lady.

Then, at a sign from La Señora, you turn sideways to us, you arch your back, you tilt your head backward, and we can see the priming of your great weapon, how it is gradually, smoothly, swiftly erect, enormous, so rigid its tip touches your dark, deep, warm navel.

Then, very calmly, La Señora says: "No, I am not sterile; it is your son, our Señor, who is sterile, sapped by the excesses of those remains that today we buried here in my palace, mine, poor Señora-mother, you've outstayed your welcome."

The Mad Lady screamed; with her voice she halted the dwarf, who had rushed toward the youth's huge, erect mandrake; La Señora has no need to laugh, she simply looks at me uneasily, I feel stupid, useless, dressed in these clothes that are not mine, the cape of moth-eaten fur, the velvet cap pulled down to my eyebrows, the tarnished gold medallion upon my breast, awkward, useless, disguised, envying the beauty and freedom and grace of that youth whom La Señora now commands: "Rest now, Don Juan; go back to bed."

Slowly the youth called Juan obeyed. He seemed asleep, eternally asleep, and La Señora, who must be the mistress of that sleep, stared with the icy gaze of a wild beast at the Mad Lady, at the dwarf, and me, and said: "When you returned this morning, I feared you, old woman, for a moment I feared you. I saw standing beside you a young man who looked very much like this one who sleeps with me. I thought you had stolen him from me. Then, when I ascertained that it was not so, I decided that fortune had been equally generous with the two women of this house: one youth for me, and another, very similar, for you."

She paused, smiled, and continued: "But now I see that anything you desire, anything you look upon, or anything your deformed, dwarfed little friend touches in your stead, turns into the image of yourselves: mutilation and deformity. Is this all your arts can convoke, Most Exalted Señora? A fool?"

I, mouth agape, I, the authentic fool: is this the role I must play? If I play it, will they treat me with affection, will they feed me from time to time? Will they, will they? The dwarf pushes the little cart, we flee from that place, far from the bedchamber of the young Señora and her young companion, I following the Mad Lady and the dwarf, understanding nothing, a true cretin, and now I am sitting here in this stiff chair, my eyes closed and a dead, no longer bleeding, pigeon upon my head: but I am bathed in blood, my face is covered with sticky blood, the sheet on my shoulders is a purplish mantle, and now the Mad Lady is enchanted, she seems to have forgotten her fit of temper, she bows her head and murmurs: "The imperial toga; the purple of the patrician. Praise be to God who in this manner manifests His signs, and make them concur and conform."

The stained sheet. My formerly blond hair now red with blood. What more can I do? The business of the dove was a good idea; the Mad Lady is very happy, perhaps if I continue to do mad things she will be even happier, less harsh with me, will allow me to go out from time to time, will forget her threat to keep me locked up in this hole; perhaps there are gardens in this palace and the Mad Lady will permit me to walk through them in the afternoon, no, from the bedchamber of the young Señora one sees no garden, only a dusty, dry, enclosed space, but that chamber is as beautiful as its mistress; how I hope they will transfer me to a room like that, her room brings long-lost memories, almost dreamed, I don't know, from distant lands, from lands where the sun is born, the East, yes, the East, the hangings, the perfumes, the skins, the tiles, everything in that chamber was almost a clear memory, a fearful and irrecoverable voyage, but the truth is that truly I must be a fool, a total fool, for I understand nothing; the dwarf whispers secretly to the Mad Lady: Take off his clothes, mistress, let's see if he too has that cross on his back, let's see if he too has a great stiff staff and a pair of great fat orbs like that impostor back there, let's see; but the Mad Lady pays no attention to her; she pays no attention because she fears something, then she recovers her dignity and authority and orders the barber and the menservants: "Bathe him, then put on him this long, black, curly wig, then summon the painter, Brother Julián, to come paint the miniature of the heir, the future Lord of all Spain."

The barber, as is their custom, holds the mirror before my face after they finish bathing me and fitting on the wig. Finally I recognize myself, finally I ask myself whether that stony figure, that pale, chalky face, that bewigged specter is really I, and I recall (for tomorrow I shall have forgotten) the golden beauty of the youth in the bedchamber of La Señora, asking myself why it is so upsetting to me to imagine that the youth's beauty might be mine.

HAWKS AND HAZARDS

Guzmán said to himself: "Something is happening that I do not understand. I must be prepared. What are my weapons? The great Lords have armies: I have only my dogs and my hawks."

He spent several days with the hounds and the birds, reviewing them, treating their ailments, refining his knowledge of them, preparing himself and preparing them for an event he could not foresee but that sent chills down his spine and kept him awake half the night now that he was sleeping on a straw pallet in the roost of the birds of prey. He asked the huntsmen who were under his command to mingle with the workmen, sharing bread and salt with them, and he asked them to listen sharply to what was being said in the tile sheds and at the looms. He remained in the place where the hawks are brought to be trained; he told himself that there, occupied in the elementary care a young hawk that is born small and with sparse plumage requires to become a bold, full-grown bird with fine plumage, he could await with laborious tranquillity what was to happen, he could think, think in the only way he knew how to think: occupied in an exacting task. He cared for the birds that had equal need: the eyas and the haggards. He trimmed the beak and claws of the young birds, and bathed them with water before attaching the bells for the first time so that they would become accustomed to them, and also so he would be able to hear them if the young falcons, so early are their rapacious instincts awakened, left the roost, became lost, or returned injured from their first forays. To avoid their languishing in captivity, he gave them good fare and offered them wood and cork to sharpen their beaks; he released rats, and sometimes frogs, so they might hunt within the confines of the mews. He stroked the dry, warm, young birds, and because it was summer refreshed them with beakfuls of water, for the dryness could make them hoarse and harm their craws and livers; he offered them small amounts of good food: the heart of a deveined sheep, the flesh of a lean rabbit, or the tenderest heifer, and then he listened to the huntsmen who night and day came to the roost to tell him: Yes, the storm is over now, but the rain strewed the spoils of the funeral procession across the plain; yes, the workmen are picking up the black brocade flowers torn loose from the catafalques; the fools are collecting them, carrying them with them, they are attaching them to their shirts and hanging them beside the sacred images in their huts, attempting to adorn their poor devotions; but the more malicious are making cruel jokes, they are saying that now only black roses will bloom on this high plain, only funeral carnations, and when they gather together to eat their chick-peas, they recall the rockrose, the streams, and the woods, and they say that even the climate has changed, that the summer is hotter and the winter cold-er since the trees were cut down, the valleys dried up, and that the animals had died and would die without the rockrose bushes to protect them.

Guzmán listened silently; he continued his precise tasks, dedicating the morning to the young hawks, taking care that they were kept in rooms that were not damp, in which smoke could not enter, rooms bathed in light, for the first rule of good falconry is to avoid complete darkness, thus preventing the swiftly flying hawk from confusing darkness with the limitless space of night, crashing into walls or beams, crippling or killing itself: as he repeated this rule to himself, Guzmán recalled the day, neither recent nor very distant, when he had presented himself to offer his services to El Señor, who demanded so many services to effect the rapid construction of the palace; and in order that his merits be appreciated, Guzmán, his head bowed before the master, a panting haste in his servile voice that made no attempt—just the opposite—to hide the urgent need for employment, enumerated in rapid fire the occupations he knew, and the rules of those offices, and El Señor listened calmly, and only when Guzmán said, Señor, your young falcons are badly attended, I have walked through the mews and I have seen they are crippled because someone has allowed them to confuse the confined darkness of enclosure with the great rapacious space of the night, only then did El Señor tremble as if Guzmán had touched an open wound, a live nerve, and only then had Guzmán raised his head and looked into El Señor's face. And Guzmán placed clods of turf in the mews for the hawks' rest, and the huntsmen came to tell him: Yes, the accidents have continued; no, the affairs of men have not calmed like the weather; it was not enough, Guzmán, that the storm abated when El Señor's dead were buried; it was not enough that the phantom dog was hanged from the railing in the chapel this morning; as the supervisors and the workmen were cutting stone in the quarry and removing earth to facilitate the process, an avalanche of earth from this fearful mountain fell upon them and buried them. And in the palace, asked Guzmán, in the palace, what is happening there? Nothing, silence, nothing, they replied.

In the afternoons, Guzmán attended the haggards; their talons, the bird's principal weapon in attacking and seizing its prey, split, fall out, and get caught in the cracks of their perches; Guzmán removed one aged bird from its perch and recalled its former glory, its talons are so hungry, so greedy, can be sunk so deep, become so embedded in the flesh of the boar or the deer, and the bird may so resist releasing its grasp, Señor, that only with great expertise can the talons be loosened without pulling them from the bird; but as they grow old, Señor, their talons—without exposure to either glory or danger—simply fall out, the falcons cling to their quiet perches and Guzmán listened as with a piece of turquoise he trims the broken talons of the old hawks, the wife of one of the laborers buried by the avalanche of earth came today, with scissors Guzmán cuts back the broken claws till he reaches the quick, the woman came in her terrible poverty, weeping, more dead than alive, through those fields, and Guzmán listened as he ground comfrey and the resin of the dragon tree, she came alone, unaccompanied, weeping, and Guzmán applied the mixture to the quick of the talon and bound the wound with a cloth of fine linen, weeping for her husband's death and attributing her misfortune to the fact that El Señor, had constructed a palace for the dead in the lands that had formerly belonged to the shepherds, and so great was the woman's poverty that she had no one who would help her carry her husband's body back to the village where she lived. Guzmán stroked the bandaged hawk and replaced it upon the perch. "Now you will rest there three or four days."

A gouty hawk: his prescription, mummified flesh from the apothecary. Laborer dead in a landslide: his prescription, burial at the site of your death, said Jerónimo, for only El Señor has the right to move his dead from the place where they died and bring them, accompanied by companies of guards and prelates, to a crypt of black marble: be satisfied, woman, leave your man buried on the very spot where he was overcome by bad fortune; we'll hold his wake right here. Who is Jerónimo? An old smith, the one who mans the forges; well, he isn't all that old, according to what he tells us, but he looks old because of his long beard and furrowed brow and disillusioned eyes. Jerónimo. And who else, huntsmen? And what else?

"A long absence breeds forgetfulness, my mother used to say, and it's a long rope that tugs at one who grieves over another's death. Forget the afflictions of others, we have enough of our own."

"Do you believe this life is worse than the one you left behind, Catilinón?"

"What I believe is that it's the local man who gets the ruined land. And if you don't like it here, why don't you go live in a city, Martín?"

"Because neither I nor any of mine ever had enough to pay our Lord what we owed him and thus be free to leave that land."

"Well, I say to you, Martín, that the land's abandoned us, and we've lost all our lands. We had some rights as long as we were a frontier against the Moors; we lost those rights, although we were promised protection, when the powerful Lords gathered the free lands under their sole dominion; we lost both rights and protection, in the end, when the greatest Lord claimed these lands from the lesser Lords in order to construct his tombs here. And what's left to us? A wage, as long as the work lasts. And then? Neither wage nor lands, and how are we to begin again?"

"You speak well, Jerónimo; but if we've nothing left, we've nothing to lose; all we have is a long life of pain, and death, at the end."

"That's mutinous talk, Martín . . ."

"And I speak following much deceit, Catilinón, and for many unquiet people who've been stripped of everything they had . . ."

"Well, your rope must be longer than the one that tugs at the dead laborer's wife; dead, there'll be no one to bury you, and alive, there's no one to look after you."

"And the burial of a Prince's bones costs more than all our lives put together . . ."

"And who'll be governing us when this Señor dies without leaving any heir?"

"Some foreign lady?"

"No, Nuño, but you can be sure there'll be a roar and hubbub among the nobles and clergy—the great Babylon of all Spain."

"But what can we do, Jerónimo, you know how it is with a whore or a crow: the more you wash them, the blacker they grow."

"You were born a blockhead, Cato, and you'll die a blockhead, and you'll never understand what it is to be a free man, or that we could govern ourselves."

"If you want to give me something, Jerónimo, make it money, not advice."

Who's Catilinón? A buffoon come from Valladolid, a rascal there and a good-for-nothing here, given to speaking in proverbs. Nuño? a laborer in the quarry, slow as an ox but stubborn as a mule, the son and the grandson of foot soldiers and farmers, a bad mixture, for those askari soldiers fought with the rebellious Urraca against her cousin and husband, Alfonso the Battler, and in favor of the laborers, against imposed taxes, and against the holdings of mills, vineyards, and forests by the monasteries, and since Doña Urraca was defeated, and the farmers lost the war, and the lands remained in the hands of the clergy and Lords, their resentment is deep. Martín? Be cautious there, he's so tough that quicklime doesn't strip the flesh from his arms, be cautious, he's Navarrese, from Pamplona, come here for this job, be cautious, those men did battle against the Moor but were just as happy laying ambush to the armies of the Most Catholic King Charlemagne who crossed the Pyrenees to defend Christianity; with the Navarrese, it's let's look after ourselves. Catilinón. Nuño. Martín.

Guzmán attended the falcons affected with hydropsy or diarrhea from having eaten damp or bad meat, from being kept in cold places, or from having swallowed feathers that had stuck in their craws through the hunter's carelessness. The birds thus affected secrete a warm, foul liquid that irritates and damages the liver and tripe. The bird's skin becomes dry, its thighs grow thin, it has no strength, its craw becomes engorged, it has a sorrowful aspect, ruffled feathers, and an insatiable thirst, Señor. Guzmán rattled off his words to insinuate himself with the Lord and obtain a place with him by enumerating his knowledge of birds and hounds, hunting and hawks' mews, and as he raised his head to look at El Señor, El Señor flushed, El Señor was humiliated; nevertheless, Guzmán knew from that moment that El Señor liked this humiliation. "Trust in me, Señor, count on me, Señor." Guzmán moved the sick hawks to dry perches made from the cork tree, and he prepared a new mixture of red powder, finely ground incense, and myrrh, what is happening in the palace?, nothing, Guzmán, all is silent, nothing, an odor of incense and myrrh issues from La Señora's bedchamber; an odor of warm, foul water issues from the Mad Lady's bedchamber, an odor of bad sleep and griped bowels issues from El Señor's bedchamber; nothing, Guzmán. As if each person had decided to remain alone in his chambers, forever, his body his only company, his body, huntsman?, what do you mean?, his own body, Guzmán, that's all; Guzmán smelled the reddish powder, the incense, and the myrrh: a young shipwrecked sailor, a foolish Prince, a nubile nun, each with his own body. Hadn't they been able to ascertain what he already knew, those loose-tongued huntsmen he had charged to find out? Valiant spies; the sailor, the Idiot, the nun. And I, I, Guzmán, with no one of my own, with no company but an old hawk with broken talons and a poisoned craw.

He made all his preparations, for something told him, something as sure and at the same time as vague as the first rapacious instinct of his birds, he must be prepared, as he had been earlier in preparing the death of the mastiff Bocanegra, and now that the greatest hunt of all was approaching, he must have the skins ready, the trappings, and the trimmings, he must have at hand the curved knife, the turquoise, the flat-and-convex file, the scissors, the irons, the awl, and the fetters, he must accustom the young hawks to wear the bells tied with jesses so artfully knotted that the birds can neither lose them accidentally nor pick them off themselves, though they be lost for many days in the field, searching, always searching, for big game? What? Who? A turbulent river, the river Guzmán.

"Great disorder breeds great order. Trust in me, Señor."

And he was extremely careful not to tell El Señor who he was, he, Guzmán, he told only his favorite hawk: Hawk, beautiful hawk, see these hands that care for you and feed you, those are not the hands of some boorish workman like those Martíns and Nuños, but the hands of an ancient line of Lords who sold protection to the Moorish kingdom of Al-Ta'if and thus amassed noble lands on the frontier that were then ruined by the combined enterprise of nature and men, but if it was by chance that a great plague killed half the population, it was the premeditated action of men that took advantage of our desolation, our lack of strong arms for labor, to ruin us: I owe my ruin to the laborer who feeling himself indispensable raised his normal salary five times over; I owe my ruin to the burgher who taking advantage of our sudden indigence bought up the lands of the dead at a low price; and the other ruin, the ruin of my soul, I owe to El Señor, who gave me shelter and humiliated me, kiss my hand, Guzmán, that's the way, with respect and gratitude, you think, Guzmán, but you think poorly, poor Guzmán, what would you do with my power if you had it?, what would I do, Señor?, what would we do, my angry hawk, what would we do? Let El Señor never know who I am, hawk, you must never tell him; let El Señor believe I am of his own making, let El Señor believe that the little I am, the little I have, I owe to him. You are my master, hawk, as you work, so shall I, and like you I shall soar to the heights from which I may wreak vengeance on all those who ruined me, hawk . . .

And last, he must try on the gauntlet made of the hide of a dog, test its roughness, for the bird cannot get a good purchase on a smooth gauntlet, grease it carefully, so that it is well covered with fat, and cut the tips of the fingers, for if one's own fingers are long they don't fit into the tips, which become very dry and hard, Señor. And trim the beaks well, over and over, one doesn't want the hawk to catch his beak in one of the holes of the bell, and die. And finally, take the hawks among the dogs with whom they must hunt, so they come to know them, and so that, feeling secure on Guzmán's wrist, and greedy for live prey, the hawk will eat amid the dogs, and never fail to recognize them, never forget them, so that the bird will know that his prey is not the dog but something else, but what?, a bearded smith, who seems old, a resentful quarrier, slow but stubborn, a rebellious Pamplonian; a clown from Valladolid, an imbecilic Prince who, did you hear, Guzmán?, the palace barber himself told me, crowns himself with bleeding doves; a Mad Lady in a little cart pushed by a babbling, ass-peddling, farting dwarf; a Señor who must be as ill in his soul as he is in body, for he moans as if something were eating at him that could as easily be the result of a thorny prayer as a trot with a spicy vixen. Oh, well, they are finding out something, the featherheads, and now, said Guzmán, stroking his favorite hawk, the situation is just reversed, for this time I possess the weapon—the hawk—but I am not sure of the prey; whereas before, I knew the prey—the faithful Bocanegra—but I was not sure of the weapon. It must be a weapon like this curved file, flat on one end and rounded at the other, so that it may be used two ways, for a man in my position, my fine hawk, must be the secret enemy both of those who have everything and of those who have nothing.

"Look sharp, hawk, my beautiful hawk, see how beautiful you've become, look how well I've cared for you; look sharp, nice and straight now, so you are one flowing line from your back to the tip of your tail, let me stroke your fine back and your wings, my hawk, those strong wings, your long slim throat; I tell you there is nothing in this world more beautiful than you, my companion, and I made you so, my beautiful, handsome, greedy hawk, look at that head, as flat and smooth as a snake's or an eagle's, my beautiful hawk, look at that jutting brow, those sunken, gleaming, yellow eyes, that slash of a beak, made spirited by the flare of the wide nostrils that give you the scent of the prey, my elegant hawk, my severe hawk, my fierce and gallant hawk, and it was I who gave you life, you who were born battered and small and scrawny, and it was I who trained you for the great hunt, remember me, remember Guzmán, my spirited hawk, my well-fleshed, beautifully formed hawk, remember Guzmán your true master, for your legal master is drowsing in bed with a novitiate, far removed from all my preparations, far from the difficult and rewarding and persevering office that formerly assured Lords a power and a rank granted them not by the mere fatality of birth but by the constant audacity of their actions, their valiant deeds, and by the noble knowledge of this office, amid hounds and falcons and arrows and sword blows and chargers; as I am your servant, you humiliate me, little Felipe, my Señor, you need do nothing, and yet you have everything; I shall humiliate you, Señor, my little Felipe, for today a servant knows how to do what formerly only Lords knew, hear me, my high, long, and full-breasted hawk, let me stroke you, again and again, my beautiful hawk, feel the hand of Guzmán, son of the Ta'if kingdoms where my Spanish fathers exploited the weak Moslem lords, where they placed all their faith in the prodigal land that produces on its own, where they lost faith in the cunning industry that creates riches where none existed before, where they acquired the conviction that the Spaniard governs while the Arab and Jew labors, for manual labor is not considered fitting for a don of Spain, only the riches acquired by exaction of fief and military tribute: let us not forget that lesson, hawk, you and I shall together win a kingdom with our hands and our wings, we shall not spare sweat or stain, or trust in the land or in the slave; and if not here, hawk, see for yourself in the mirror of our decadent Señor: new Spain will be ours, hawk, its only privileges those of the task well done, those who will not labor will become a nation of beggars, the powerful Lord will be he who labors most, and that will be our justice, hawk, a fitting justice, place upon my rough gauntlet your rugged, wide-spread claw, grip my greasy leather with your long slender toes, your beautifully rosy talons shading into blackest black, poise yourself upon my wrist with your feet planted firmly apart, and hear me, hawk, once you are upon the wrist of your true owner, I myself, stationed in a tree awaiting the passage of your victim, you must be prepared for the great hunt, you must swoop down upon the prey, conquering by the swiftness of your flight and killing in the clutch of your steely talons; and though your victim struggle, and thrash about, and fight against you, you, with your long tarsi, will take advantage of brush and scrub, making escape more difficult and allowing time for the arrival of your master and his dog. Noble bird; you shall be fed always on living or freshly killed animals;

I shall not give you less than you deserve, I swear it, I shall offer you living prey and you yourself shall kill it and be satiated on it. Faithful hawk: the traveler who returns and who is not recognized even by his wife is recognized by his falcon. El Señor no longer has his guardian, his companion, his dog; but I have you, and I shall not abandon you, my hawk; be prepared; I shall be present the day you soar into the heavens with the swiftness of a prayer and swoop down with the speed of a curse. You are my weapon, my devotion, my son, my luxury, the mirror of my desires, and the face of my hatred."

And yes, Guzmán, we thought we had seen everything, but we were bamboozled like little children and hoodwinked like fools, for the portents have not ceased, nor have the processions ended, as we believed; here's what happened: this afternoon, as the sun was setting, the fires in the forges dying, and the men leaving the quarries and gathering together to eat, the one called Martín, who has a reputation for sharp vision, saw a cloud of dust that descended from the mountain, and the one called Nuño, who has ears like a fox, added his ears to Martín's sharp eyes and between the eyes of the one and the ears of the other they came up with an impression that neither, reliant only upon eyes or ears, could have reached on his own, for oxcarts raise clouds of dust, and rumbling can often be heard in the mountains, even if it's only rockslides rattling down the ravines, that's enough, get to the point, now, I know, don't go for monkeys by way of Tetuán, yes, come, tongue, open the door, whatever else do I feed you for?, for they were descending the mountain through the valley, Guzmán, descending?, what was descending, huntsman, what?, another phantom?, another corpse?, come, man, never try to screw a catamite or rob a thief, I've paid you well—and I will continue to favor you with more than money, with promotions and good positions in the corps of huntsmen and later, perhaps, within the palace—first, paid you for several nights imitating the dog's howling that so frightened the nuns and upset El Señor, and now I'm asking you for exact news and not stammering and stuttering and certainly not stories about phantoms, for I am the one who takes care of phantoms, with my trusty blade, and they end up hanged for all their troubles, no, Guzmán, it wasn't phantoms, though that's what those ignorant laborers thought who gather every evening in the tile sheds to have their bite and to mutter, Guzmán, to curse and speak ill of us all, no , it wasn't a phantom, it was a drummer dressed all in black, surely some page was lost and left behind by the funeral procession, lost his way in the wolfsbane and arrived late, beating a steady drum roll, a very young page with gray eyes and flaring nostrils and tattooed lips, Guzmán, do you hear?, painted lips, all dressed in black, the cap, the cape, the breeches, the shoes, and even the drumsticks covered with cotton on the tips and black streamers attached to the sticks; and behind the drummer, Guzmán, came a young, almost naked man, wearing a doublet the color of crushed strawberries, dead with fatigue, and walking like a blind man with his hand resting upon the shoulder of the page leading him, a blond, slender, handsome youth, Guzmán, and on his back, through the torn doublet, Guzmán, we saw, we saw . . .

"Don't tell me, huntsman, I already know: a blood-red cross between his shoulder blades."

PORTRAIT OF A PRINCE

I feel very uneasy tonight; my body aches all over. I have a fearful pain right on my tailbone, just at the tip of my aching spine stiff from posing so long for this tall, pale, blond priest, who requests, with his eyes if not with words, the regal posture the Mad Lady demands of him in his portrait and from me in my life. But where have I seen this priest before? Yesterday, when we arrived? Before, in the life I cannot recall? Where? It is curious how I can remember words, but no events or people, at least until they become so deeply involved in my life that finally they are a part of my vocabulary and, because of that, take on substance and life, continuity and duration. If not, everything simply fades away, like this priest who is painting my portrait whom I swear I have seen before. The Mad Lady and the dwarf, no, they are no longer women to me, they are words, they have become words. My body aches, as if something, lost these many years, were about to take place . . . another body that was, or will be, mine. They permitted me to look at myself in the mirror; I did not recognize myself, nevertheless I have no other proof of my existence. Soon I shall have one more: the portrait this priest is so assiduously sketching with tiny brushstrokes, by order of the Mad Lady, upon an enameled oval.

"I want the portrait to have the immutability of the figure of the heir," said the Mad Lady. "I want the Prince to resemble no other living creature, Brother Julián; least of all, that impostor snuggled between adulterous sheets in this very palace."

The friar named Julián looked at me, inquisitively, as if he were asking me what instead he asked the Mad Lady: "Immutability, Most Exalted Lady? The portrait can adopt a thousand different configurations. Which do you desire: the image of he who was or he who is to be? And in what place do you wish him: in the place of his origin, that of his destiny, or that which he presently occupies? What places, what times, Most Exalted Lady? For my art, limited as it may be, is capable of introducing whatever changes and combinations Your Grace desires."

Then the Mad Lady leaned forward; her mutilated trunk, propped against the back of a leather chair, swayed, and only the rapid intervention of the dwarf prevented the disaster of a fall; the Mad Lady wished only to show the painter the enamel upon her bosom, the image, the profile, of her dead husband, a rigid profile, like that on an ancient seal, suitable for the minting of coins, gray, as gray as the undifferentiated space of the background; there is nothing to invent, said the aged Lady, everything is actual, we are the children of God, God is One, and his totality exists in all places, in the immensity of the firmament as well as in the reduced dimensions of this oval: it matters not whether you paint a portrait or a wall, Friar: the space your brushes cover will be the same as the space where we are now, and both spaces are the same as the universe, which is the invariable space of God's thought, accommodated equally in the largest or the smallest space, in a grain of sand and in the enormity of the broad seas; but come, hurry, paint, do not be proposing false problems.

The friar smiled and bowed his head, joining this action of respect with a serious investigation of the area of my feet, his courtly acquiescence to the demands of the Mad Lady blending into the continuation of honest artistic activity; he insisted on seeing me unshod, on carefully counting, his brush pointing to each one, the toes of my feet. In so doing, he took advantage of the fact that the Mad Lady had summoned a tailor and a bootmaker to make me a change of clothing and some boots, but if the clothing hung from me loosely, much too loosely, the boots were tight, too tight, and what could I do? I felt deformed in that footwear, bowlegged, and it seemed as if one leg were shorter than the other, and I gave the artisan a good kick with the toe of his own boots, till the rascal begged for mercy, making excuses, how was he to know that I had six toes on each foot?, why do you say that?, what is strange about that?, I have always had six toes on each foot, and exactly twelve toenails; I am infuriated; with great grimacing I order the servants to cut the boots into little pieces and to force the damned bootmaker to eat them like tripe, all of which was performed amid great shouting and other less civil noises from the dwarf, until the bootmaker ran vomiting from the room; the Mad Lady ordered the dwarf to be still, and showed me an open coffer filled with precious jewels and I was to choose from among them those that pleased me most for my personal adornment. I chose an enormous round black pearl; I put it in my mouth and swallowed it, which caused new merriment on the part of the dwarf, who handed me a chamber utensil so that when I felt the desire to defecate, the pearl could be deposited there with my evacuation, and between us the dwarf and I would charge ourselves with examining the excrement until we found the precious pearl; the Mad Lady nodded and said the pearl would be doubly precious for having passed through my body from mouth to bum, and that it would henceforth be known as the Pilgrim Pearl. And there was more, she promised she would give me clothing and more clothing so that I would never twice dressed in the same attire; I stared with avarice at the medallion that adorned her bosom, and as she perceived the direction of my gaze, she said that my likeness would be engraved upon precious stones, and my profile on all the coins of the land, and to that end they would use the image Brother Julián was painting at that moment; and smiling, the priest, still working, said: "Then see, Most Exalted Excellencies, how this image I am painting begins to be suffused with unforeseen desires, with pleasures and whims and humors not present in the unvarying original creation; see how I render not what is given but what is desired . . . For painting is a mental process."

But no one listened to him; the dwarf was already proposing that we write the Pope asking that he grant me the gift of the supreme relic: the foreskin from Christ's circumcision, then we would have everything; the dwarf guffawed, revealing her whitish, toothless gums, we would fill this chamber with relics, the ultimate relic, the piece of skin from the penis of the infant Jesus, we would fill the chamber with delights, with garbage, with talismans, with sumptuous clothing and superb tatters, curiosities, miniatures, we would celebrate magnificent banquets here, said the dwarf, as I nodded enthusiastically, gluttonously, with an increasing appetite to fill the chamber as full as I would stuff myself with pleasures; great banquets, the dwarf repeated, and the Mad Lady said yes, excess, expense, the most obnoxious ostentation: for that we had been born, that was why we were who we were, nothing would be too much to humiliate those who never may have, never should have, and never want to have anything, isn't it true, mistress?, isn't it true that our mourning is over?, that our weeping is ended?, yes, my faithful Barbarica, the Prince is again with us, our funereal devotion has ended, let there be luxuries, let there be excesses, look, said the Mad Lady, look, listen, make a good face for the painter, my boy, let him see you neither too happy nor too sad, put on a Prince's face; you will have a Prince's face when you understand me: I shall repeat to you the lessons I taught my son Felipe, our Señor, to educate you in the proper governing of these kingdoms, a man alone is nothing, I said to him when he was a child, each of us sitting beside the winter's fire, and now I say to you, an individual dependent solely upon his own strength readily succumbs, his life is spent in searching for what, once obtained, he must spend, only to begin once again to exhaust himself in the search; but not we, not we, because in the midst of the weaknesses of men who are alone, we, you and I, my boy, shall be like the world itself, single individuals represent only themselves, we shall represent the world, because we have created, with vices, powers, devotions, altars, hearths, battles, gallows, palaces, monasteries, the only immortal thing, the signs that last, the scars of the earth, what remains after individuals are forgotten: we have invented the image of the world; compared to fragile individual existence you and I will be the essence of existence, you and I are the sea and they the fishermen, you and I, Prince, are the veins of ore, and they the miners, they take sustenance from us, not we from them, they need us in order that their poor lives have meaning, they shall live from us and we shall live from ourselves, they go and we remain, they exploit, devour, and exalt us because they fear to die, whereas we shall not understand the meaning of death.

"Everything in excess, my boy, everything in excess to demonstrate that death has no meaning, that the powers of re-creation are much more vast than those of extinction, and that for every thing that dies, three are born in its place; the only thing that dies is that which dies as an individual, never that which is continued as a race. Quickly, Barbarica, order us a great dinner, I see the young Prince is fatigued, little eel pies and a great stew of pork, cabbage, carrots, beets, and chickpeas, and an infinite variety of sausages, red, and hot, and stuffed with onions, and naturally, order a hundred pounds of black grapes boiled in the copper caldrons to obtain the few grams of mustard we like to season our stew, run, quickly, order it, and return immediately, Barbarica, for the court painter has asked that you pose beside the Prince, that you appear in the second painting, a large one this time, on canvas, you standing, with the Prince's hand upon your shoulder, hurry back, Barbarica, men shall remember you, thanks to Brother Julián, our painter."

"They will remember me, mistress, Señora?" sighed the dwarf. "May I put on my pasteboard crown and my long cape so they'll believe that I am the Prince's wife, the miniature Queen?" How she laughs, beside me, that wicked dwarf, and more loudly as I laugh with her; easy as you please I lift her off her feet and swing her up in the air till I can bite one breast; I clamp my teeth upon one round, blue-painted teat until she howls with pain and then with pleasure, and finally the two are indistinguishable, and I nibble and I suck, never taking my eyes from the Mad Lady, who does not intervene, who looks at me as if a new idea were forming in her head, as if she were imagining a new project as she sees us, the dwarf and me together, embraced, what a pair.

"Who was it who kissed you in the carriage, who caressed you, who tore your shirt, who removed your breeches, who formed your new face with the soft, swift touch of her tiny, moist, painted, plump, magic hands? Who? Who was it invented your second face with the paints and cosmetics she carried hidden in her little wicker trunk? Who is it who's dying to touch you and suck your beautiful dingalingdong? Who? And please, never call me thus . . . dwarf, it sounds so ugly, call me what everyone else calls me, with affection, Barbarica, Barbarica . . ."

The dwarf whispers these words into my ear, then pulls away from my kissing and nibbling, her breasts marked by my teeth, she covers the tiny teeth marks on her blue-painted flesh, and runs from this jail, and I sit down amazed, more muddleheaded than ever, rapidly reviewing after listening to what she had said, forgive me, Barbarica, I had one face when I reached the shore, and in the carriage Barbarica had exchanged that face for another, then they had cut my hair and dressed me in a full, black, curly wig, and now the painter is imposing a fourth face upon me, renewed and different, and my true face was fading farther and farther into the distance, I have lost it forever, forever, and meanwhile Brother Julián continues his rapid painting.

My body aches. I hurt all over. Barbarica returns from ordering the meal, and climbs into the wicker trunk that serves her as a bed. Brother Julián has been impatiently waiting to begin the second portrait, and now he asks me to pose again, seriously. The priest sighs; the Mad Lady asks that he paint a third portrait of me, this time wearing the mask I had with me when I reached shore, where is it?, it had appeared upon the face of her husband's corpse, it was woven of brightly colored feathers, said the Mad Lady, with a center of dead spiders, that would be strange, new, incalculable, no one would know how to explain it, they would see my stiff, upright body, my throat and my cape and my hand upon my breast, my black breeches and my tight boots, but they would not see my face, they would have to imagine that, it would be covered by the mask of feathers I had brought with me from the sea when I was thrown upon the beach, and climbed the dunes to encounter my second destiny: the Mad Lady recalls all this, it happened a long time ago, I had already begun to forget, as tomorrow I shall have forgotten everything that has happened today; who recalls the most important moment of his life: the moment he was born? No one. I shall take care to tell that to the Mad Lady. But I speak only to myself, my words are within me, mine alone, the Mad Lady and the dwarf have never heard me speak, they probably believe I am mute, they have only seen me place bleeding doves upon my head, force the bootmaker to eat my raw boots, bite the teats of Barbarica. But where is that mask, a fifth face for me?, the ultimate folly, to mask myself, considering that I was already masked in my own flesh when I arrived here. The Mad Lady moves her head from side to side, disconcerted, searching; the painter sighs. The Mad Lady says that a painting of me with the mask covering my face would intrigue the chroniclers, no doubt about it. Where is the palace Chronicler? Have them search for him, bring him here, I want him to begin to write the true chronicle of the Prince's life. Let us establish immutability: she wants the signs of my identity to be multiplied, I, the heir, in paintings, engravings, coins, pearls, chronicles, let there be immutable awareness that I am who I am, the Heir Apparent of Spain, and no one else, least of all that blond stallion the wife of El Señor has secluded in her bedchamber.

The painter-priest sighs again; he says: ''The Chronicler is not in the palace. He committed an indiscretion and was banished to the galleys. If you so desire, I can tell you his story. Then you will be less aware of the passage of time as I finish the painting.''

And this is the story Brother Julián narrated, as the servants entered and prepared the stew on which we were to dine that night.

THE CHRONICLER

Feverish and ill, he wrote through the night; reduced to a tiny space in the depths of the prow of the reserve brigantine, he heard the groaning of the ship's skeleton, with utmost difficulty he held the inkwell upon one knee and the paper upon the other; the motion of the little stub of candle swinging back and forth before his eyes made him seasick, but he persisted in his wakeful task.

Along with the rest of the flotilla, the brigantine was sailing toward the mouth of the broad gulf, slipping among the islands. He did not know the nature of the maneuvers which the squadron was executing under the cloak of night so as to control the mouth of the gulf by dawn, thereby sealing the exit to the Turkish fleet aligned in rigorous formation far back in the gulf. But he felt certain that, whatever the agreed strategy, the following day would witness a fierce battle, frightful butchery, and little mercy for a humble oarsman like himself, removed that afternoon from the galley because of his feverish and unserviceable condition; ill or not, they would need all hands tomorrow to combat the formidable fleet of Islam, a force of a hundred twenty thousand men, including warriors and the crew of galley slaves.

One night, he thought, a single night, perhaps the last night. He was writing rapidly, the fever of his imagination adding to that of his body, made seasick by the dancing candle stub suspended before his eyes, its wax dripping upon the wrinkled parchment: a soul of wax, that I am, a soul of wax on which the continual motion of the world is imprinted, idea after idea. For the only thing that does not change is change itself, and not, as my most exalted Señores would have it, the stability that so consoles them on a medallion, in a sonnet or a palace, allowing them to believe that, everything considered, the world will end with them, that the world does not move, that the world will respect what is, without concern for what might be.

And so, simultaneously he recalled, he imagined, he thought, and he wrote, blessing the mercy accorded him in the remission of his pain. The respite granted because of his fever was not, nevertheless, gratuitous.

"No," the commander said to the galley slaves, "rather a demonstration of good faith that the oarsmen who perform well in this encounter will be freed from the chain. On the other hand, we captains of the Christian fleet know that the lack of similar magnanimity among the Infidels will assure that many galley slaves from the enemy armada will take advantage of the confusion of the combat to jump ship and swim for shore."

At any rate, he did not associate his night of grace with these maneuvers and calculations, nor did he differentiate his specific situation in this hour, exceptional although fleeting, from his larger destiny. Fortune had cast a heavy burden upon his frail shoulders; and to the uncertain question that he formulated as he wrote—Is it possible that a wrathful fate exceeds itself in persecuting me?—the answer, unfortunately, was as sure as it was affirmative. Of his family he remembered only oppression and debts; of his office, only lack of understanding and sleepless nights; of his masters, injustice and blindness. From all of it, necessity. Abundance, only in his imagination; too subtle to be spooned to his lips or cut with a knife. In this nocturnal hour, writing, he muttered to himself Friar Mostén's counsel: "As you wished it, so shall it be"; for, instead of limiting himself to dedicating his fictions, with their customary laudatory epistles and prologues, to the very exalted Señores who were his patrons, he concocted a great number of things in his imagination, and from invention passed to the documentation of the events he witnessed and of the world he inhabited, reaching a moment when he could no longer differentiate between what he imagined and what he saw, and thus he added imagination to truth and truth to imagination, believing that everything in this world, after passing from his eyes to his mind, and from there to pen and paper, was fable; in the end he convinced his Señores, who desired only chimeras from his pen, that chimeras were truth, but at the same time, truth was never anything but truth. See, thus, the mystery of all written and painted things, for the more they are the product of the imagination, the more truthful you may hold them to be.

Nevertheless, his was a very different scheme, and tonight he was putting it into practice with feverish haste; the swift flight of the hours, guttering away like the stub of the candle, announced the fatal battle of the coming day. Fatal for him whatever its outcome, whether death in combat, capture by the Turks, or liberation from the galleys (although he had little faith in this promise, since his crime was not an ordinary one, but of the imagination, therefore more severely punished by the powers that be than the theft of a money pouch), his destiny was to be neither envied nor extolled: shadow of death, shadow of captivity, or shadow of poverty. And that shadow he had always said and written was worse than the reality of poverty itself, the explicit situation, with no misconceptions, real and spacious as the Plaza of San Salvador in

Seville, where a legion of scoundrels could dedicate themselves to larceny, to contraband, to deceit and deception with no excise imposed, and with the broad satisfaction of knowing themselves to be the scum of the earth. The reality of poverty, not its shadow.

He said to himself: Then one is someone, as the farmer and the beggar are someone. In contrast, the impoverished nobleman, the surgeon's penniless son, the stepson for a fleeting moment of the halls of Salamanca, the heir to musty volumes wherein are recounted the marvels of knight-errantry, the orphaned son of the implausible deeds of Roland and the Cid Rodrigo merely exist, they do not live, and in that such a man is doubly accursed, for knowing what it is to be, he cannot achieve being, only existence, his head filled with mirages and his platter empty, existence, not life, maintaining the appearance of a nobleman though his leggings be tattered and frayed. The heir without his inheritance, the orphan, the stepson, merely exist in the shadow . . . like an insect. Poverty: he who praises you has never seen you. A battered beetle, an insect lying overturned on its hard, armorplated back, waving its numerous legs . . .

A different scheme, to cease to exist and to begin to be; a different scheme, paper and pen. This is what he was thinking as he wrote an exemplary novel that had everything and nothing to do with what he was thinking; paper and pen in order—at any price—to be; to impose no more or no less than the reality of the fable. The incomparable and solitary fable, for it resembles nothing and is related to nothing, unless it be the strokes of the pen upon the paper; a reality without precedents, without equal, destined to be destroyed with the papers upon which it exists. And nevertheless, because this fictitious reality is the only possibility for being, for ceasing merely to exist, one must struggle boldly, to the point of sacrifice, to the death, as great heroes and the implausible knights-errant struggled, so that others believe in it, so that one may tell the world: this is my reality, the only true and unique reality, the reality of my words and their creations.

How were they to understand this—those who, first, denounced him; second, judged him; and, finally, condemned him? He recalled, as he was writing a story for all time in the depths of the prow of a brigantine, one not-so-long-ago morning when he had walked through heaps of hay, tiles, and slate of the palace under construction, deploring, as he knew the former shepherds of the place deplored, the devastation wrought upon their oasis of rockrose and water by the necrophilic mysticism of El Señor. The Chronicler, on that not-so-long-ago morning, actually was attempting as he walked to imagine a bucolic poem that would please his Señores; nothing original, the thousandth version of the loves of Filis and Belardo; he smiled, as he walked, searching his mind for facile rhymes, flowery, bowery, rhyme, thine, sublime . . . and he asked himself whether his masters, when they summoned him for a new and delightful reading of the themes that were so comforting because they were so familiar, would accept the blending of the pastoral form with a singular nostalgia shared by the inhabitants of this devastated place, nostalgia that the Chronicler, because of that, considered more a temptation than a mockery; or whether, in truth, what they expected from him was not precisely that nostalgia, never accepted by them as such, but as a faithful description of an everlasting Arcadia. Did they not have, then, these Lords, eyes to see? Were they completely indifferent to the destruction that their hands wrought as their minds continued to find delight in images of clear, still streams, leafy arbors, and the trailing branch of the grapevine? Did they so mistakenly confuse nostalgia with fact, and fact with exigency? Perhaps (the Chronicler wrote) they were aware of their guilt and placated it with a secret promise: once the time of ceremony, of death, of inexorable constructing for death has passed, we shall re-create the garden; the dust shall flower, the dry stream beds will flow anew, Arcadia will again be ours.

The skeptical Chronicler shook his head and repeated quietly: "There will not be time, there will not be time . . . Once the flower is cut from its stalk, it never revives, but quickly withers; and if one wishes to preserve it, the best way is to press it between the pages of a book and, from time to time, try to sniff the remaining vestiges of its wasted fragrance. The tangible Arcadias are in the future, and we must learn how to deserve them. There will not be time, but they refuse to recognize that. Shoemaker . . ."

To your last: he returned to his quiet rhyming, and was linking the flowery with the bowery when he saw pass beneath the kitchen portico a youth whose beauty was in startling contrast to the smut and sweat that marked the other men who labored here. Not this youth, no; beautiful and golden, he was eating an orange, he displayed an extreme grace of movement that only the possession of luxury, if one is wealthy, or the contemplation of evil, if one is poor, produces; a sufficient pleasure in himself, capable of flowering either in this sylvan solitude or in the company of someone who expects, or even possesses, everything, would know when he met this youth that certain things can never be possessed unless they are fully shared. With rejoicing, the Chronicler thought he recognized in the youth who was savoring his orange the image his sterile pen required: the pastoral vision demanded by his masters, the figure of the shepherd lad crowned, like the ancient rivers of Arcadia, with salvia and verbena: the hero.

The youth passed by swiftly; happiness, wickedness, and deceit were in his gaze; he wiped his hand across his lips as he passed, perhaps because he was eating a juicy, flame-fleshed orange, or possibly because he had just kissed his beloved; either was justified by the secret satisfaction of his expression, the tempered, vibrant heat of his body. The Chronicler could at that very moment inscribe the words in his memory; he imagined a young pilgrim passing by this palace, the temple and the tomb of Princes, like a breath of young life, a carefree wanderer with that mixture of permanent astonishment and delicate disenchantment that the knowledge of other seas, other men, other hearths, gives a man; he was able to blend in the swift versifying of that instant the appearance of the sun and the appearance of this youth, naked, alone. The youth disappeared into the smoke of the palace kitchens; the Chronicler returned to his cubicle beside the stables, and sat down to write.

That was a Thursday; Saturday he read his composition before the Señores, Guzmán, and me, yes, I was there, I, the painter-priest who spent so many afternoons in the sweet, bitter, amiable, and quietly desperate company of the Chronicler, listening to his laments and interpreting his dreams: I, Julián, the gentle thief of my friend's words. And as I listened to him that Saturday as he was reading the poem to his masters, I did not know whether to look with amazement at my lost friend or to attend the growing plea for silence and warning of punishment in the eyes of La Señora, where the ice of fear and the fire of anger flashed in swift succession, the ice quenching the fire and then the fire inflaming the ice, both born of the icy heat in the convulsive breast of my mistress, the same breasts I had with my brushes one day painted blue, following the tracery of the network of veins with the purpose of making more startling the whiteness of her skin; eat, Most Exalted Lady, stuff yourself with sausage, my gentle Barbarica, suck the pork ribs, supposed Prince; I am aware that for some time now, engrossed in your gluttony, you have not been listening, I know that I am speaking only to myself; so it has been always: you eating while something important happens, not even realizing. I admired my poor friend's innocence, but I understood that his candor could be my ruin, for once someone pulled the loose thread the entire garment would unravel. Soul of wax, my candid friend had impressed in his poem more, much more, than he imagined; he had converted the fleeting vision of that youth, whom he had glimpsed eating an orange before disappearing in the smoke of the kitchens, into the foundation of his imagination, and upon it had raised an edifice of truth: I hear again the voice of the Chronicler, ringing with conviction, the habitual tones of despair stilled in the reading.

That voice described the handsome shepherd lad with greater exactitude than my own paintings; there was no doubt that it was he, the young pilgrim born with the sun, twin of the sun, so familiarly Spanish with the orange in his hand, so distant, so strange, so foreign in his gaze of disenchanted amazement: a hero here and a hero there, ours and not ours, relative and stranger, almost, one might say, a prodigal son: through the Chronicler he sang of Arabian oases, Hebraic deserts,

Phoenician seas, Hellenic temples, Carthaginian fortresses, Roman highways, dank Celtic forests, barbarous Germanic cavalcades; not an idealized shepherd, or an epic warrior, not a Belardo nor a Roland, the hero not of purity but of the impure, hero of all bloods, hero of all horizons, hero of all beliefs, having reached in his pilgrimage the bucolic carrousel of a Señora of a joyless palace, endowed with the pristine feelings that only nature, although all histories, had touched, and chosen by that Señora who, though she could have been any, could only be ours. Chosen for the pleasure of La Señora, led to a luxurious bedchamber, and there surfeited with love and other delights in exchange for his freedom to roam, at the end of the verse choosing to return to the byway, abandoning La Señora to time and oblivion.

El Señor seemed to understand none of this, experiencing, perhaps, only that vague, dreamy nostalgia the Chronicler, performing the function of his office, had wished to provoke; Guzmán suspected something, betraying himself by placing one hand on the hilt of his dagger, and nervously stroking his plaited moustache; La Señora envisioned it all, seeing herself thus depicted in a literary model, her love affair with the youth inadvertently revealed as the true model; I feared everything, but for other reasons. But the Chronicler believed only in the poetic reality of what he had created; any relationship that could not be reduced to the resolute struggle to impose his invented words as the only valid reality was as foreign to him as it was incomprehensible: candid pride, culpable innocence. And thus the strength of his conviction convinced the others of the documentary truth of what he was reading to us.

When he finished reading, the only sound to be heard was the weak and empty applause from El Señor's pale hands. The dog Bocanegra barked, breaking the icy tension of the moment—Guzmán's suspicion, El Señor's lack of comprehension, La Señora's outraged disarray, and my own fear. Only the Chronicler smiled beatifically, unaware of the passions loosed by his poem, sure only of the verbal reality created, and hoping to be congratulated for it; he was convinced that he had read us the poetic truth, he hadn't the least intimation that he had repeated aloud to us the secret truth. I moved with haste, I denounced the youth to Guzmán, accusing him, as was true, of having base relations with some kitchen lads barely entered into puberty, but keeping silent what I knew, and knew very well, for I had been the go-between who led the strange youth to La Señora's bedchamber, thus gaining the gratitude of my mistress on that afternoon of carnal despair after she had spent thirty-three and one half days lying in the castle courtyard with no arms worthy of assisting her, thus, in addition—except on one imperious occasion—saving myself the obligation of calming my mistress's desires: I do not like to break my vow of chastity, no, and to have to renew it again before a knowing Bishop who as he hears my confession dares look at me with disrespectful complicity: are we not all so?, do we not all do the same?, is it not fortunate that this vow of purity is renewable?, is not the Church magnanimous that it thus understands the weaknesses of the flesh? No, we are not all equal, nor shall I allow that the Bishop so believe. I am an artist. The pleasure of the flesh robs strength from my artistic vocation, I prefer to feel my sexual juices flow toward a painting, wash over it, fertilize it, realize it; the delights of the flesh castrate me, the delights of art satisfy me.

Yes, I concealed what I knew: that the shepherd lad who served as model for our Chronicler had alternated his sodomite afternoons with nights in the bed of La Señora. Guzmán communicated the crime against nature to El Señor, and El Señor, with no further formality, ordered the death of the youth, who was sentenced to burn at the stake beneath the kitchens of his sinful, although not unique, amours. I consulted with La Señora, convincing her that she should sacrifice her private pleasure to her public rank, and promising her, in exchange for her present sacrifice, renewed and increased pleasures in the future. "For the powers of re-creation are much more vast than those of extinction, Señora, and for every thing that dies three are born in its place."

From the Chronicler's cubicle, to which I had free access because of our frequent and delightful conversations, I removed some culpable papers in which my erudite friend related, mistakenly, the multiple possibilities of the judgment of Christ Our Lord at the hands of Pontius Pilate; I showed the papers to Guzmán, who did not understand their content but took me to El Señor, to whom I pointed out that in the guise of fable that narration evoked the anathematized heresies of Docetism, which affirms the phantasmal nature of the corporeal body of Christ; of the Syrian Gnosticism of Saturninus, which proclaims the unknowable and untransmissible character of a unique Father; of the Egyptian Gnosticism of Basilides, which has Simon of Cyrene supplant Christ upon the cross, and Christ becomes merely a witness to the death agonies of another; of the Judaizing Gnosticism of Cerinthus and the Ebionites, combated by the Father of the Church, Irenaeus, for declaring that Christ the God occupied only temporarily the body of Jesus the man; of the Patripassianist monarchism that identifies the Son with the Father; of the Sabellian variant that conceives of a Son who is emitted from the Father like a ray of light; of the Apollinarian heresy and of extreme Nestorianism, which attributes to two different persons the acts of Jesus and of Christ; and finally, of the doctrine of Pelagian freedom, condemned by the Council of Carthage and by the writings of the saintly Bishop of Hippo, which denies the doctrine of Original Sin.

"I shall be even more explicit, Señor; the fable is worse than the heresy it illustrates, for in one instance the most Pure Virgin, Our Lady, admits adultery with an anonymous camel driver; in another, Our Lord Jesus Christ declares that he is a simple political agitator of

Palestine; and, in the most evil of these examples, our St. Joseph declares himself criminally responsible not only for having betrayed our Sweet Jesus but for having built as well the cross that served as the rack of torture that redeemed our sins. And there is more, Señor. I investigated the palace archives; my suspicions were well founded: the Chronicler is a *marrano*, a pig, a filthy Jew, the son of converted Jews.''

But instead of being scandalized by the crushing weight of my most careful explication, El Señor asked me to repeat it, again and again; his eyes shone, his curiosity changed to delight, but delight did not give way to shock. I requested, as was natural, that the Chronicler be handed over to the Holy Office; El Señor waited a long while, his eyes closed, before answering me; finally, he placed one hand on my shoulder and asked this most unexpected question: "Brother Julián, have you never seen an uneducated soldier vomit and defecate upon the altar of the Eucharist?''

I answered no, not understanding the sense of his question.

El Señor continued in these terms: "Should I deliver you to the Holy Inquisition for having repeated these heresies?''

Hiding my alarm, I told him I repeated them only to denounce an enemy of the Faith, but that I myself did not sustain them.

"And how do you know whether the Chronicler has not done the same: merely recounted them, without approving them?''

"Señor, these papers . . .''

"When I was young, I met a student. He, too, believed that there was no Original Sin. He lived, fought, and loved (perhaps died, I do not know; one day I thought I had seen his ghost in the profaned Cathedral), because he believed that God could not have condemned us to misery even before we were born. Others died in the halls of my father's castle for believing what that student believed . . . but they were not redeemed by the grace of their thought. Not they, or those crude Teutonic soldiers who besmirched the altar of my victory. Imagine, Friar, that I had challenged those rebels and soldiers: explain in writing the ideas that move you to action, and you shall remain free; if not, you will be executed. None would have been capable of reply; none could have saved himself from death. On the other hand, the student and the Chronicler . . .''

This frail Señor seized my hand with great strength, squeezed my fist in his, and looked at me with terrifying intensity. "Brother Julián, we must have faith unto death in the values of our religion; let us condemn the idolaters and the infidels, but not the heretics, for they do not deny religion, rather they buttress it by revealing the infinite possibilities for combining our holy truths; let us burn the rebels who rise up against our necessary power in the name of a freedom that they themselves, should they obtain it, would be incapable of exercising, but let us not act against the heretics who in the saintly solitude of their intelligence fortify, unknowingly, the unity of our power by multiplying the alternatives of Faith."

"But you yourself crushed the Adamite heresy in Flanders, Señor, how then . . . ?"

"That heresy was a pretext employed by the Princes and merchants of the North in order to free themselves from the protection of Rome, and the payment of tithes and indulgences, and in order to name docile bishops who would work on behalf of the power of Mercury, not St. Peter. I acted at the behest of the Pope, not against the heretics, but against those who incited and manipulated them. Do you understand me, Friar?"

With the utmost respect, I bowed my head and then shook my head that I did not; I looked up, seeking my master's eyes; he was smiling with acerbic pity.

"But you, better than anyone, should understand. Theological skirmishes, Friar, are less dangerous than political ones. Political contention first debilitates me, but then forces me to act, whereas theological arguments divert and channel energies that otherwise would be turned against the government of these kingdoms. I know that the extent and the unity of my power removes very vast powers from the hands of men, but still, that men maintain reserves of uneasiness and strength that someday might menace me; I know that, Friar. I prefer that these reserves be spent in arguing whether Mary conceived without sin, whether Christ was God or man, rather than in discussing whether my power is of divine origin and if, in short, I am deserving of it. Heresy, then, is tolerable as long as it is not employed directly against power."

"Señor, the prelate who resides here in the palace might think differently."

"And who will show him these papers, tell me that, Brother Julián . . . who?"

"You would discourage those of us who try to watch out for your interests. The cause is clear: the Chronicler is a heretic, a Jew reverted to his beliefs . . ."

"And it is your wish that he be delivered to the Holy Inquisition?"

"It is, Señor."

"And you say you are safeguarding my interests? Is it your wish that I strengthen, by constantly offering it more jurisdiction, a power that I prefer remain marginal, expectant, dependent upon me, not I upon it? For if I nourish it, the Inquisition will grow at my expense. No, Julián. I prefer to be a little more tolerant in order to remain a little stronger. Our Chronicler does not deserve the renown you would accord him by prosecuting him before the Holy Office, nor do I deserve that for so slight a reason such a tribunal be aggrandized to the degree that someday it might impose its policies upon me. Always minimize your enemy, Friar, particularly if with that action you also diminish a dangerous ally."

"Most Illustrious Señor: you were not tolerant with the other criminal, the young lad who is to be burned beside the stables. Is sodomy a worse crime than heresy?"

"It is simply a crime that is condemned with horror by the Holy Bible and by common opinion. Let us suppose, Friar, that this youth, in addition to being a sodomite, were also a relapsed and heretical Jew. For which of his crimes would you judge him? For the crime that promised vexatious proceedings, complicated religious debates, and even worse judicial complications? Or for the crime whose punishment everyone would approve and expedite? Let us suppose . . . just suppose, I say . . . that this youth is not going to die for his true offense . . . Is it not considerably more convenient for everyone that he die for the false rather than the true crime?"

El Señor gazed at me sweetly, sadly, wearily. And his visage was one of such utter exhaustion that I shall never know whether or not he actually perceived my own state of agitation. I struggled to say something, but no words came to my defense. El Señor seemed to experience no similar difficulty, either ingenuously or by chance; or, perhaps with perverse calculation, he was touching upon all the points of my own involvement in the intrigue.

"Do you still paint, Friar?"

"That is my vocation, Señor, although minor and expendable compared to my greater vocation, serving God and serving you."

"Have you seen the painting in my chapel . . . the one painted . . . they say . . . in Orvieto?"

I trembled. "I have seen it, Señor . . ."

"You have doubtlessly noted the oddities and innovations within it?"

I stood without speaking; El Señor continued: "How would you have painted Christ Our Lord?"

I bowed my head. "I, Sire? As a sacred icon, unchanging since the beginning of time; a flat, fixed figure upon a nonspecific background, as befitting his eternity."

"The anonymous artist of Orvieto, on the other hand, has surrounded the figure of Christ with the atmosphere of the time; he has placed Our Lord in a contemporary Italian piazza and paints him standing before naked and contemporary men, speaking to them and looking at them. What does the artist mean in this manner to suggest?"

"That the revelation was not made only once, Señor, but that it is through new figures being constantly fulfilled for different men and different epochs . . ."

"Would you burn the painting in my chapel, Brother Julián? Is its creator a heretic?"

My head bowed, I shook my head. El Señor attempted to rise, but he was racked with a fit of choking. He put a handkerchief to his mouth, and these were his muffled, subdued words: "Very well. There is no more dangerous enemy to order than an innocent. Very well. Let him lose his innocence. Send him to the galleys."

The candle stub had burned out and the Chronicler had finished writing. Animated by an excitement that erased his fatigue, he arose and said: "Our souls are in continual movement."

And he added, first stroking, then tightly rolling the parchment: "Here I am master of myself: here I hold my soul in the palm of my hand."

He inserted the roll of parchment into a green bottle, tapped it with a cork, and sealed it with the still-warm drippings from the candle, crudely, but well, and placed it in the wide pocket of his slave's breeches, then climbed to the deck.

What a marvelous spectacle lay before his eyes! The Christian fleet, spread out in the mouth of the gulf, formed a huge semicircle of galleys, their pennants flying high and all oars held at the ready; they were facing into a strong wind blowing from the land; the sea was choppy. Sixty Venetian galleys formed the right wing of the crescent; sixty more, Spanish, the central core; and another sixty, from the Maritime Republics, closed the mouth of the gulf; in each galley three hundred galley slaves faced the sun and wind and sea, manning fifty-four enormous oars in each ship. Their guns were installed on the prow; each galley trim from stem to stern, from topmast to hold; the impression of order and symmetry was perfect. But as the Chronicler stepped onto the deck of the brigantine and saw the disposition of the battle lines, he had a moment for other sensations; he could smell the odors from the dark brown coast, the odor of sliced onion and the odor of bread fresh from the oven; and he observed in minute detail, grateful for this marvel, the flight of wild ducks above both armadas, indifferent, these free, guiltless birds, to the Christian standard being raised at that very moment, and to the Turkish pennant already waving deep within the gulf. And the Chronicler observed the rough turquoise-colored sea, the swiftly dissipating clouds, the limpid skies. He gave thanks, in short, for life.

As the standard was hoisted, the call to arms was also sounded, warning all the galleys; the Chronicler was aboard one of the reserve brigantines that along with the supply ships were standing at a distance so as not to obstruct the movement of the galleys, but were prepared to deliver troops and matériel to them; he heard the cannon blasts signaling the battle, and he saw how immediately both fleets moved into action, the Christian flotilla advancing toward the Turkish fleet trapped in the waters of the gulf, and the Turks advancing to the encounter with the Christians, their only alternatives to destroy the Christians, to perish, or to flee by land. The sun rose higher. The wind died down, and the gulf turned into a crystalline lake. Now the oarsmen had a less difficult task. A soft breeze was at their backs. Everyone, even those waiting in the reserve galleys and brigantines behind the central corps of the battle, knelt to receive general absolution, and to prepare to die. The flagship of the Turkish fleet fired the first cannon; kneeling, the Chronicler felt the weight of the green bottle in his pocket, and raising his eyes to Heaven he knew that one part of his life was ending and another beginning; farewell to the folly of youth, greetings to the age of extreme hazard: between the two ages, between the two moments, he found an instant to address himself to the clouds, to the sea, to the frightened ducks flying back to the brownish shores: "What Heaven has ordained, no human effort or wisdom can prevail against."

And thus he imagined himself to be at the true hour of his death, it could be this instant, or another slightly more remote; brief, nevertheless, was the time for anxieties to mount and hopes to flag.

Six Venetian galleasses, armed with cannon mounted on all sides, advanced to throw disorder into the Turkish ranks; the drums and bugles sounded to clear the decks for action, but even these strident sounds were drowned out by the fearful cries of the Moorish throng; the beaks on the prows of the Christian galleys, sawed before the battle, were pulled down, the great firearms belched smoke, inflicting great damage upon the Turkish ships, whose salvos, aimed above the obstacle of their own beaks, passed harmlessly over the Christian galleys. The Turks did not retreat, but sent formation after formation of galleys in their attempt to rout the wings of the Christian line, attack the rear guard, and gain access to the open sea; at noon the Turks launched a ferocious attack against the left wing, attempting to breach it and force its galleys, for fear of running aground on the sandbanks near the shore, to break ranks from the closed, crescent formation. The Turks were attempting to escape through that gap, when rough hands pushed the Chronicler toward a boat and from there to one of the galleys, and from there, without transition, into the merciless struggle between two galleys locked in combat like two animals in a definitive territorial battle for food and shelter. There was a steady hail of arrows, volleys from harquebuses, and shells; many ships were sunk, and others run aground; many Christians had fallen into the pantheon of the sea and many Moorish galleymen who had attempted to swim to shore were drowned among blazing ships and shellfire; the Chronicler in his position in the galley, clinging to his section of the oar, felt the shudder of the ship under a blast from a Turkish cannon; the prow was ripped away, exposing the tightly packed galley slaves and leaving them unprotected before an assault from the Turks who swarmed on board, granting no quarter; a small squadron rapidly arrived to defend them; they boarded the besieged galley and retaliated, blow with savage blow; the Chronicler, thrown to the deck, felt the open wound in his bleeding hand; with a strength he would not have believed possible he withdrew the sealed green bottle from his breeches and threw it into the sea. He watched the bottle, less swift than the salvos from the harquebuses, trace a slow parabola through the air and disappear from his sight before splashing into the water amid the smoke and fire and cannon blasts.

"Inexorable fates," he sighed, as he lost sight of the bottle that contained his last manuscript, the pages written under the certainty of misfortune and the uncertainty of life: inexorable fates, inexorable star, the manuscript would follow its course while the galleys were joined in combat, locked together at prow or gunwales or stern; the manuscript would float on, indifferent to the shouting, shots, fire, smoke, and laments; the bottle would be borne along in the currents of a turbulent sea, stained now with blood, the sepulcher of severed heads and arms and legs. The manuscript was this minute being washed away by the sea, master of its own eternal life, untouched by pike, lance, sword, fire, or arrow of this fearful combat; it would not perish in the holocaust, the crashing yardarms, masts, the flaming firebrands; and even the most desperate combatant, drowning this afternoon in the foaming sea, would cling to oar or trailing rope or rudder to save himself, but never to a green bottle containing a manuscript. And though its author should die at this very moment, the manuscript would never die.

"What is your name, lad?"

"What is yours, old man?"

"Miguel."

"And mine as well."

"It's a common name, of humble clay."

"You have to take the name of the land where you live, old man. Here, today, Miguel. Yesterday, in the melancholy oasis lost to us, Mihail-ben-Sama. The day before yesterday, in the tumultuous, teeming Jewish quarters, Michah. I fled the tumult before we were murdered; I fled the Andalusian oasis before we were defeated. I came to Castile to die."

"Did you know that, lad?"

"It was written. You can't flee the executioner forever. I thought I could avoid their persecution by living among them, that I would be invisible among them. You see that I was mistaken."

"You call them executioners? They were merely retaking what was theirs: Andalusia."

"What they took was ours. We created that land, we embellished it with gardens and mosques and clear fountains. Before, there was nothing. All races lived together there: look at my black eyes, old man, and my blond hair. All bloods flow in my veins. Why must I die because of only one of them?"

"Then you are dying for a lesser, not a principal, reason, lad."

"Which is which? And why have they locked you here in this cell with me? Why are you to die?"

"I am not to die. I have been ordered to the galleys. But possibly you are right. Perhaps I, too, am condemned for a secondary, not a principal, reason. Forgive me, lad. If I hadn't seen you one afternoon . . . walking amid the workmen on this job . . . savoring an orange . . . your lips so red . . . none of this would have happened. I wouldn't have written that accursed poem."

"It's all right, old man, don't blame yourself. If I don't die for one thing, I'll die for another. What can I do to change my mixed blood? And someday the Christian world will make a man pay for his Jewish blood. And then those kitchen lads, younger than I . . . I envied them. La Señora is a little more ripe than you might think. Race . . . boys . . . La Señora . . . what does it matter what the reason, it's my emotions and my pleasures that kill me, not men . . ."

"Do you envy youth? I envy yours."

"You do well to do so, old man. I carry all my secrets with me. With me, they burn at the stake. What shall you do with yours? It isn't too bad to die still thinking about what one could have been: I wouldn't like to die knowing what I was."

"Perhaps I shall imagine what you might have been, lad, and write about it."

"Good luck, old man, and goodbye."

The Chronicler moaned, touching his wounded hand, and in the midst of this fearful clamor, choking on the acrid odor of gunpowder, blinded by its murderous opacity, he saw the tattered pennants of Islam, the crescent moons, the defeated stars, and he himself felt defeated because he was fighting against something he did not hate, because he did not understand the fratricidal hatred between the sons of the prophets of Araby and Israel, and because he loved and knew and appreciated and wanted to save the merits of their cultures, although not the cruelty of their powers; he knew and loved the fountains and gardens and patios and high towers of al-Andalus, the nature that had been made more beautiful by man for man's pleasure, not for his mortification, as it had been at the necropolis of El Señor Don Felipe; surrounded by the inextinguishable fires of the galleys, thinking he must die, the Chronicler repeated a mute prayer that the peoples of the three religions might love one another and know one another and live in peace, worshipping the one unique God, faceless and incorporeal, the one all-powerful God, the name of the sum of our desires, the one God, sign of the meeting and confraternity of all wisdoms, all pleasures and recreations of mind and body; and believing himself to be mortally wounded, hallucinating from the vision of Turkish heads impaled on pikes and brandished with the victory cry, he remembered that lad with whom he had shared the dungeon the night before the youth's death and the old man's exile, he remembered him not as he truly was but as the Chronicler imagined him, the impure hero, the hero in whom all bloods and all passions flowed; in his delirium he imagined all the endless line of impure heroes, heroes without glory, heroes only because they did not scorn their own passions but followed them to their disastrous conclusion, masters of total passion, but mutilated and imprisoned because of the cruelty and narrowness of a religious and political rationale that converted their marvelous madness, their excesses, into a crime: pride . . . punishable, love . . . punishable, madness . . . punishable, dreams . . . punishable; certain he was dying, he imagined once again all the adventures of those heroes, all the transformations of those knights with frustrated illusions, the undertakings possible only in an impossible world where the external and internal faces of men are one, without disguise, without separation, but impossible in a world that masked both, one for appearing before the world and another for fleeing from it—the world mask, simulation; the escape mask, crime, passion forever separated from appearance: madmen and dreamers, ambitious and enamored men, criminals; he imagined a knight maddened by the truth of his reading, insistent upon converting that truth into a false reality, thereby saving it, and saving himself; he imagined ancient Kings betrayed on black and stormy nights of ignorance and madness by men and women more cruel than pitiless nature itself, which is only involuntarily cruel; and he imagined young Princes enamored of pure words, incapable of provoking the action or exorcising the death that reality reserves for dreamers; he imagined a profaner of honor and sacred convention, a hero of secular passion who would pay for his pleasures in the hell of the law he had denied so often in the name of free, common, and profane pleasure; he imagined couples consumed by love that was both divine and diabolical, for divine and diabolical would be a love in which the lovers no longer distinguished between themselves, the man being the woman and the woman the man, each the other's being, each one transfixed by a shared dream that defied the social convention of what is individual, separate, what is placed in the pigeonholes of condition, wealth, and family; he imagined a greatly ambitious man, trembling with cold, alone among the millions who populate the earth, alone, denied the presence of gods or men, separated from them, abandoned, the only channel for his energies that of attracting hatred and aversion toward the person of a nature that denies the size of his pride; and he imagined ambitious little men, resigned to their sensual mediocrity, their great dreams unachieved, already defeated, their illusions lost, wasted throughout their lives, like the traveler who leaves some part of his riches in every inn along the highway; power and riches, or murder and suicide: manners of accepting or denying a passion grown pallid; he imagined, finally, the penultimate hero, the one who realizes he is enclosed in the present, his past eclipsed, a past that no longer projects the shadow of the hero that the hero has previously called his future: Tantalus is the name of that hero, of all the heroes who have devoured their present in order to reach a dreamed-of future of madness, ambition, and love, never obtaining it because the future is a fleet phantom that will not let itself be captured; it is the hare, we the turtles; these heroes must turn their faces to the past to recapture what is most precious, what they have lost, what they cannot bring with them in the vibrant and desolate search for the passion forbidden by icy laws and demanded by fiery blood; desire possesses, possession desires, there is no exit, oh, heroic Tantalus of fragile ashes and vanquished dreams; the hero is Tantalus and his opponent is Time; the final battle: Time conquers, Time is conquered . . .

And believing he was dying, he imagined them all and lamented that now there would not be time to write about them; he had only been able to write about the last hero during a last night of grace granted his improbable stay on earth, and thus he had concentrated all his vulnerable life, all his sentiments of honest poverty, infinite misfortune, indiscreet pride, uncertain estate, sad rewards, and exhausted imagination, in repeating the first words of his last hero in that manuscript to which he had given his last night as he had just given the manuscript itself to the sea, to time to come, to men still unborn, thinking perhaps that with luck, someday, slimy and salt-pocked, carried from the white sands of this gulf, impelled by vast currents to darker seas, buried in the deltas of powerful rivers, dragged against the current by whirlpools that stirred the muddy bottoms, deposited finally in the dark beds of a lazy stream, fished from the water by the hands of a child, or a madman, an ambitious or an enamored man, by a man as ill and sad and persecuted as he, by another Jew in another land in another age of misfortune, beside other ruined palaces, beside other ashen tombs, the green bottle would be picked up, its seal broken, the manuscript extracted, read, and perhaps understood—in spite of the strange and ancient language of old Spain that Jews like this Chronicler had rescued, stabilized, given to be read and divulged in ordinary poetry—read, in spite of the crossings-out and the corrections in that spidery hand, further distorted by the pitching of the sea and fever and sadness the night before the battle; perhaps:

As he awoke (???—a man; a name; let whoever finds it put in the name; the lad who had been condemned to the stake was right: one must take the name of the land where one lives, old man, names of clay and dust and dreams) *one morning from uneasy dreams he found himself transformed in his bed into a gigantic insect* struck through: a different creature, perhaps mythic, a dragon, a unicorn, a griffon, a mandrake, the mandrake is found at the foot of gallows, of stakes, Miguel, do you hear me?, struck through a griffon, a salamander, no, better an insect, a cockroach, a hero, the final hero struck through). *He was lying on his hard, as it were armor-plated, back* (insect's shell, correction, eye, the shield of an ancient hero, shell a defense against being crushed beneath someone's foot) *and when he lifted his head a little he could see his dome-like brown belly divided into stiff arched segments* (abyss: struck through, correction, abyss, the center of a coat of arms, the navel of one's identity, abysmal, abysmally absorbed, sun of bodies) *on top of which the bed quilt could hardly keep in position and was about to slide off completely. His numerous legs, which were pitifully thin compared to the rest of his bulk, waved helplessly before his eyes. What has happened to me? he thought. It was no dream.*

I stopped. But they were dreaming, the Mad Lady, her dwarf, and the young Prince sleeping as if drugged following their copious dinner. They had heard nothing; they had understood nothing. Once again I remembered my lost friend whose dreams and literary plans I knew so well, having had continual discourse with him during the time he enjoyed the benevolent protection of our sovereign, that I felt capable of imagining what would have passed through his head when he was wounded, perhaps killed, in one of the fierce battles for Christianity. Yes. I picked up the enamels, the oils, canvas, and brushes, and silently stole from this prison, this bedchamber.

THE LAST COUPLE

Come, give me your hand, place the other upon my shoulder, pretend you are blind, do not stumble. I know the roads, all the roads, I grew up in the forest near the abandoned routes of the ancient empire, I traveled the new footpaths of the merchants and students and friars and heretics, I watched she-wolves whelp in the brambles, I collected honey and cared for flocks, come, I know this land, this land is mine, there is nothing in it that I either do not know or cannot predict, remember, or desire, let me guide you, we have already left the mountain behind, we are descending to the plain, smell the smoke of the bonfires and ovens, hear the sound of the carts, chisels, and cranes, come, follow me, hold tightly, my body is your guide, have faith in my body, young, handsome, shipwrecked sailor, we are exhausted, we have walked far since we left the sea that washed you up at my feet, beneath my waiting gaze, for I knew of your arrival, knew that that early morning you would be thrown upon the beach of the Cabo de los Desastres, and that is why my drumsticks beat a rhythm that took us to that very convent and not another, to that convent which I knew—because I know the land—was inhabited by voracious nuns avid for the flesh of man, as I knew that the Mad Lady, when she recognized she had been misled, would flee the place in the daylight, breaking the established routine, forgetting her own rule: we travel only by night, during the day we rest in the monasteries and worship my husband's remains; and so we would pass by the beach soon after you were tossed there by the sea, by life, by the history you carry with you, buried deep in the well of your corrupted memories. I, not you, knew you would be there, a man without a name, distinguishable only by the cross on your back; you reached that shore knowing nothing, and that is why you are the authentic traveler, the prodigal son, the unconscious bearer of truth, you, who know nothing, you, because you know nothing, you, who seek nothing, you, because you seek nothing . . . Place your hands upon my shoulders, walk behind me, do not look, let me play the drum, announce our arrival at the palace, now . . .

"It looks now as if it's all over," Nuño said to Martín.

"The storm's quieted now," said Martín to Catilinón.

"Now the workmen have returned to their jobs," Catilinón said to Lolilla.

"Now that idiot boy found by the Mad Lady is entertaining himself with Barbarica's buffoonery," Azucena said to Lolilla.

"Now that youth found while El Señor was hunting is lying in La Señora's bed," said Lolilla to a huntsman.

"Now we the huntsmen and halberdiers who have twice been to the beach swear, swear as God's our witness, that those two youths, the Mad Lady's and La Señora's, are absolutely identical," said the huntsman to Guzmán.

"Now a third youth is approaching, and he will probably be identical to the other two," Guzmán said to his hawk . . .

. . . now I am announcing with the black sticks of the black drum our arrival at the palace, with your hands upon my shoulders, walking like a blind man, you must let me guide you: don't look, don't look at the disorder on this dry plain, the tents of the taverns, the bodies crouched around the fires, the stream of black brocade flowers and torn funereal cloths, and rent tabernacles, the slavering jaws of the yoked oxen, the piles of tiles and slate, the blocks of granite, the bales of straw and hay, don't look, young sailor, do not look at this false disorder, do not open your eyes until I tell you, I want you to see the perfect symmetry of the palace, the inalterable order imposed by El Señor, by

Felipe, upon this gigantic, still-unfinished mausoleum, that is what I want you to see when you open your eyes; don't look now at the dumfounded peasants watching our arrival, don't listen to the cries of that woman kneeling beside a landslide where two lighted candles gleam palely in the daylight, don't look, don't listen, my handsome youth, body guided by my body, body saved by my body, the first thing I want you to see is the order of the palace, I want the first person you speak to to be El Señor: I want you to break the order of this place as you would shatter a perfect goblet of finest crystal; your eye and your voice will be like two powerful hands arrived from an unconquerable sea; my tattooed lips can repeat it all; my name is Celestina; my tattooed lips can repeat it all, my lips forever engraved with the burning kiss of my lover, my lips marked with the words of secret wisdom, the knowledge that separates us from princes, philosophers, and peasants alike, for it is not revealed by power or books or labor, but by love; not just any love, my companion, but a love in which one loses forever, without hope of redemption, one's soul, and gains, without hope of resurrection, eternal pleasure; I know everything, this is my story, I shall tell you everything from the beginning; I know the story in its totality, from beginning to end, handsome, desolate youth, I know what El Señor can only imagine, what La Señora fears, what Guzmán guesses; touch me, follow me . . .

"I had a nightmare: I dreamed that I was three persons," said El Señor.

"You and I, Juan, you and I, one couple, Juan," said La Señora.

"I alone, trembling with cold, I alone, without the presence of gods or men," said Guzmán . . .

. . . don't speak, don't look, you are blind, you are deaf; my knowledge is total, but incomplete, only you were lacking to make it complete, only you knew what I could not know, because my wisdom is that of only one world, this world, our world, the world of Caesar and Christ, a closed world, a sorrowful world, whole, seamless as a succubus, without orifices, contained within its memory of certain misfortune and impossible illusions: a world that is a flickering flame in a night of turbulent storm: of it I know everything; I knew nothing of the other world, the one that you knew, the one that has always existed knowing nothing of us, as we knew nothing of it; I saw you born, my son, I, I saw you born from the belly of a wolf; who, then, but I would be present as the circle of your life, begun one night in the brambles of a forest, closes; who but I on the beach where you awakened this morning, without memory, forgotten by everything, forgotten by everyone, except by the person who received your feet as you were born? Take your hand for one moment from my shoulder; check, do you have the map safe in your breeches, do you have the green bottle I saw you pick up on the beach? Good; again, forward; don't look; they are looking at us; they are coming toward us; they thought that the wonders had ended, they are looking at us in amazement, a page and a shipwrecked sailor: the pair that was missing; they are looking at us; they are leaving their taverns, their tile sheds, their forges; the weeping is quieting; we are walking forward, opening a path through the smoke and dust and heat, I, dressed all in black, deceiving them, giving the impression that my sex and my condition are other, not my own; you, tattered, your feet bare and bleeding, your hair rumpled, your eyes closed, your lips covered with dust. And then that bearded man—ruddy from the glowing coals, his chest sweaty, and his gaze prematurely old—drops his bellows, looks intently at me, approaches, opens a path through the throng, looks again, this time into my eyes, does not recognize my lips, but does recognize my gaze, holds out his hands, doubts, touches my breasts, falls to his knees, embraces my legs, and murmurs my name, again and again.

STAGES OF THE NIGHT

The night in Rome had seven phases, Brother Toribio, the palace astrologer, told Brother Julián, as he scrutinized the dark heavens above the high tower reserved for him by El Señor, and the other listened gloomily: *crepusculum*; *fax*, the moment at which the torches are lighted; *concubium*, the hour of sleep; *nox intempesta*, the time when all activity is suspended; *gallicinium*, the cock's crow; *conticinium*, silence; and *aurora*.

For each stage of the long night of our ancestors—so divided in order to prolong, or perhaps to shorten (it was impossible to know for absolute fact), the process of time—Brother Julián assigned one of the bedchambers of the palace still under construction to represent a different phase; in his mind, two figures, a pair, materialized in each chamber, arranged by the priest as a kind of game, or final combat, a tourney without appeal whose time would be regulated by those nocturnal phases, seven in number, a solemn, fatal, and consecrated number: "Choose seven stars from the sky, Brother Toribio . . ."

Seven stages of the night: seven stars?, seven couples? The night is natural, the painter-priest said to himself, and its division into phases a mere convention, as are too the names of persons; a person is a name or a noun, an action is a verb, conventions; the night itself would not know to label itself "night," even less know that it is inaugurated by dusk and closed by dawn; the stars are infinite, and to choose among them is another convention, the choice this time a matter of chance: Fornax Chemica, Lupus, Corvus, Taurus Poniatowskii, Lepus, Crater,

Horologium; neither did the seven constellations from among which Brother Toribio chose seven stars for Brother Julián's night know their names; when it came to naming seven pairs . . . would there be a sufficient number of men and women in this palace . . . in this world, to form them? For the roles of fate and convention, in matters regarding an encounter between two human beings, are insignificant beside the power of the will of passion or the passion of will. And thus the perfect symmetries conceived by intelligence never surpass the ideal of the imagination but instead succumb to the proliferating invasion of hazardous irrationality; one demands to be two in order to be perfect, but it is not long until a contingent third appears, demanding its place in the dual equilibrium, only to destroy it. But perfect order is the forerunner of perfect horror; nature rejects that order, preferring instead to proceed with the multiple disorder of the certainty of freedom.

Brother Julián remembered his lost friend, the Chronicler; he would have liked at this moment to say to him: "Let others write the history of events that are apparent: the battles and the treaties, the hereditary conflicts, the amassing and dispersion of authority, the struggles among the estates, the territorial ambition that continues to link us to animality; you, the friend of fables, you must write the history of the passions, without which the history of money, labor, and power is incomprehensible."

CREPUSCULUM

Many years later, old, alone, cloistered, El Señor would recall that this night, at the crepuscular hour, he had caressed for the last time the warm hollow of Inés's back, where in that animated sweetness, in that soft quiet spot of her body, he had found, and held in his hand, his true pleasure; the protuberant lip kissed the curve that transformed the delicious narrowness of her waist into the magnificent fullness of her buttocks, and he moved away from the novitiate's knowing body, a body that in spite of everything was still unknown to him; always he would ask himself—then and later, but always with the same feverish anguish, augmented perhaps by the swift passage of time that rushed toward the future while the memory of reality, of what could be verified because it had happened, ran backward, ceased to be tangible and sure to become spectral and doubtful, the past: who are you, Inesilla, a princess or a farm girl?, brought to me by Guzmán, delivered by Guzmán to my pleasure: are you the daughter of a merchant, a workman, or a noble?, how well the habit disguises one's origins, how well, the moment he dons the habit, the converted Jew, the heretical doctor, the son of miserable swineherds, disguises his condition; neither the armor of the soldier nor the ermine of the emperor disguises men as well, or to such a degree makes them equal, as the tunic of devotion. What lineage have I violated: the highest or the lowest?, what youth have I forever besmirched?, who is this, my subject?, more subjected than the peasant who delivers his harvest to me, more subjected than the vassal who pays me homage, or the worker who labors in my quarries; who is this subject of my sick flesh?, the sweet depository for the silver that flows through my bones?, the heir to my shameful afflictions?, who?, and to whom, in turn, do I deliver her that my very kingdom be overspread with that sick silver?, or are we condemned, she and I, to live together from this moment, secretly bound together, hiding our love as we hide our shared illness? In you, I have sinned, I have sinned knowingly, my unknown Inés; I did not want it, I did not wish it; Guzmán divined my weaknesses, the moment my will faltered; death surrounded me, my thirty corpses were less exhausted than I, I had dictated to Guzmán that spurious testament, imagining my death, and Guzmán took advantage of my awareness of death to offer you to me; who, even I, does not weaken when surrounded by so much death?, who does not fall into the temptation of affirming life, even though by so doing he poisons life, sickens it, and prepares it, though loving it, for death?, you came to me, Inés, like an offering of provisional life, to make me believe that I, a phantom, could without punishment, without affliction, without body, making love to a virgin; that I could possess you, Inés, more with terror of mind than with trembling of body; that I might imagine you, lying in the bed, only to consider that as today you lie in bed someday your body will lie in the tomb; and I succeeded, didn't I, Inés?; you have not closed your eyes one second, and to make love with one's eyes open is already to have one foot inside the grave, it is to spy upon the lesser death, the infant death, the servile death, that lurks behind the beauty of the rose; you have not sighed all the time we have been together, you have watched me with those wide-open eyes, however, you did not desire the irrepressible heat of your own body, your body that bursts into flame in spite of your cold will to know everything, to examine everything, to give yourself to me in order to know, not to take pleasure . . .

El Señor arose from the bed and wrapped himself in the dark green bedcover; he tried to hear, to see, to sense some sign of the normal passing of time. But his penetrating and avid eyes saw only proof of abnormality: the candles of the chamber instead of having burned themselves out had grown taller; the hourglass instead of having during all that time filled the lower glass showed the upper globe filled with tiny yellow grains; he looked at the vessel from which he had drunk during the long day and night of their love-making, the water that cleared the cobwebs from his throat; it was brimming full. And he thought, here am I, a man thirsting for marvels he wishes both to accept and to reject; such a disposition gives all the advantages to the marvels, for they can, as they are convoked, impose themselves, conquer, precisely because they have been summoned against the will; and magic prospers in negation.

El Señor picked up the hand mirror he had carried one morning as he ascended the thirty-three steps of the unfinished stairway, and in which on another day he interrogated the figures of the painting brought—he was assured—from Orvieto: he wished now to regard in it the man thinking these thoughts, as if the mirror might also reflect the semblance of thought, and a flicker of madness crossed his face; had not that same mirror fallen and shattered upon the stone floor of the chapel that dismal morning?, how, when, why did the fragments recompose between that morning and the day when he dictated his first testament?, did the shattered pieces join together by themselves, more desirous of their union in quicksilvery smoothness than El Señor himself to possess a single destiny and not a monstrous plural metamorphosis of youth into age into cadaver into dispersed, mutilated matter, dust   •
particles formed into antagonistic matter, reintegrated, formed again in the sperm of a beast, the egg of a she-wolf, in a resurrected birth, a new desire to nourish itself, grow, kill, die, an unending circle, immortal matter . . . without a soul.

He staggered toward the door of the chamber, he parted the tapestry that separated the room from the chapel, he looked toward the steps leading upward to the plain; raving, he asked, why was that stairway not completed?, why could his thirty corpses not descend there?, it was not completed, it was supposed to have only thirty steps, it would never be completed, it already had thirty-three, he raved . . .

"Accursed is a man who would govern so. He will lose everything if he cannot manage to maintain—with the same extenuating strength he employs to entreat his burning fantasy—an icy lucidity. Who would not exhaust his forces?"

From the bed Inés followed El Señor's movements with a slight movement of her head, round and thistly as the first figs of the Barbary coast, trying to deduce the meaning of El Señor's investigations, why his uncertain steps faltered as he walked around the bedchamber, why he looked at himself in a mirror, why he stood clinging to a tapestry; he looked at her looking at him with curiosity, he saw her shaven head, and with an uncontainable surge of affection he attributed to her an innocence that could only accentuate the degree of culpability of the acts in this cloister where mirrors and rites repaired unaided their scattered fragments; stairs, completed, were forever uncompleted; candles, as they burned, grew taller; water, as it was drunk, replenished itself; and hours, as they were spent, returned. El Señor felt that his body and soul had separated; the ax that had divided them was irrational time; to which of the thus divorced moments did his body belong, and to which his soul: to this moment, the one which with all too sufficient proof was skittering backward like a crab, toward fatal origins, the total consummation his mother the Mad Lady had announced, claiming to have arrived with the son of the father who at the same time would be the father of the grandfather; or to the moment which in spite of everything, with every step El Señor took through the chamber, with every slow and questioning turn of Inés's head, insisted on catapulting itself into the future?

"There is a clock that does not strike," El Señor murmured.

Then Inés—concentrating upon divining El Señor's thoughts, with no point of orientation other than his restrained curiosity as he stood before some candles, an hourglass, and a water pitcher—picked up the pitcher, contemplated it for an instant, and then poured its contents onto the stained and rumpled bed.

"What are you doing, for God's sake!" El Señor exclaimed; and as he observed the novitiate's action he felt that the shadow of madness flitted across his soul.

"I am cleaning the sheets, Señor; they are stained with blood."

Without putting it into words, Inés sensed that, like cisterns, hearts are rapidly emptied, but they fill very slowly, drop by drop. Like the cistern, she felt emptied; and emptied, conquered, and transformed. Her happiness, her curiosity, her nervous, childish, Andalusian innocence belonged to a remote past; yesterday, barely yesterday, giggling and shivering, she had stood with Sister Angustias looking at the bodies of the workmen. And now she knew that she must wait a long time before her body would again be filled. Her emotions were full, but she felt unsatisfied, used, defiled, with no freedom, no curiosity, no joy; she was not herself: "My self is not my own."

"Señor, I must go back."

"Where, Inés?"

"Do not ask me that; do not send Guzmán for me; I shall return . . . when I feel filled again. Filled, Señor, needed."

"I can send for you whenever I wish; I can order you . . . you cannot . . ."

"No; I shall come, if I come, at my own pleasure; you cannot force me; that would be a horrible sin."

El Señor knelt beside the bed and repeatedly kissed her hand; Inés, you are the innocent proof that time is turning back; sweet Inés, beautiful, young, soft, warm Inés with the olive-black eyes and skin like crushed white lilies; my youth has returned; we have spent twenty-four hours together, the time it takes to fill the hourglass, the time it takes a tall wax taper to burn itself out, the time it takes to drain a brimming water pitcher; you entered my chamber with the dusk; with the dusk you are leaving; how old are you, Inesilla?, eighteen?, twenty?, why were you not born earlier, ten, fifteen years earlier?, then we would have met in time, when I still was young; the two of us, you and I, Inés, young; we would have fled from this place, renouncing everything, with you I would have abdicated time before crime and inheritance collected their toll, we would have fled together on the aged Pedro's ship, we would have found a new land, together, now it is too late, because the end still has not come, how long it takes to come: there will be time only at the end, Inés, and then I shall be very old and you very different; now your presence and your youth are a mockery, a mirage that makes me believe that because I am master of this land, of labor and honor, I am also master of time, and can recover it at will, be young again, not fear death, offer my life to others, not their deaths; but that, at least now, cannot be, Inés, it cannot be; there is no salvation, for if time, instead of running forward to reveal to me the death I saw in my mirror as I climbed those unfinished steps, begins to run backward, then I shall fear not my death but my birth; then my birth will be my death; there is no salvation now, there will be none until dying I know whether I shall be born again, and once born know whether I shall again die; now there is no salvation: there is only a time that, however long it last, Inés, is never the same for two living beings, for no one is born at the precise instant another man or another woman is born; so I am alone . . . alone; the time of one man never coincides perfectly with that of other men; we are separated not only by years but by the unsynchronized and unique rhythm of our lives, my precious Inesilla, my beloved Inés; to live is to be different, only death is identical, only in death are we identical; and if this were not true, if death were only another form of being, then what?, would our guilt and our sorrows never end?, forgive me, forgive me, Inés, again, forgive me; absolve me, precious child, absolve me if you can; with you I have truly sinned; I have sinned against you; until I met you I had always asked myself, prostrate every day before the altar in my chapel, facing those carefully identified but unknown figures of the painting from Orvieto, what would be the unforgivable sin?; there must be one, one sin that will forever close to us the gates of Heaven; I wanted to know what it was, Inés, I imagined everything, every possible combination, scrabbling at the very foundations of our Faith like a devilish mole, suggesting to myself corrosive doubts that could undermine the basis of my power as it is recognized by the Faith, as a simple reflection of Faith, risking my power as I risked my Faith; I have tried by every means possible, do you understand, Inés, heresy and blasphemy, crime and cruelty, illness and culpable indifference, affirmation and negation, action and omission, to know the face of impardonable sin; to test myself, I tested everything I knew; what sin could never be pardoned?; but each of my sins found its own justification; hear me well, Inés, try to understand even though you will not listen: I killed, but power justifies that crime; I imposed my authority, but devotion is pardon enough for the sin of power; I spent hours and days in mystic humiliation, but honor, my own and that of God, excuses the sin of excessive devotion, which is in turn related to the sin of pride that engenders the crime that serves as the excuse for power that procreates devotion that seeks the pardon that, once again, culminates in honor—our salvation; by denying Faith one merely fortifies it, for Faith swells in proportion to attacks and doubts against it; one denies life, one levels a fertile plain and forces men who once earned their livings there to labor slavishly constructing a dwelling for death . . . and life is strengthened, finding a thousand reasons whereby it can thus assaulted affirm itself; and this very palace, constructed for death, does it not already have the life of all created things?, is it not like a gigantic stone reptile binding me in its jasper and mosaic coils, does it not possess a heart beating in its basalt breast that wishes to be heard, to affirm, to live on its own account, independent of the will of the one who conceived it and of those who constructed it? On the other hand, you . . . you are the unforgivable sin, the sin that cannot be pardoned either by crime or power or devotion or honor or pride or blasphemy or death; kill you, subjugate you, pray you, exalt you, insult you, kill you: all in vain; as is the abominable custom of human beings I have made love to you looking into your face—beasts, more wise, do not look each other in the eye during their fornication—facing you, I have sullied you, the more you consented, the greater the violation, facing you; I am lying here beside you, and you beside me, alone, alone in the universe, stripped of customs and motivations, the only relationship our own, yours and mine, you I and I you, and I have taken from you but can give you nothing in exchange, you and I alone, facing one another; but nothing more, I give nothing of the only things I am able, or fear, or have learned to give: not death, not subjugation, not sacrifice or pride; a man and a woman alone, together, their only offering to each other the draining coming together, sufficient, swift, eternal, gratuitous, impossible to transfer to any realm not that of its own instantaneity, its own pleasure, its own misfortune: Heaven and Hell, judgment beyond appeal, infinite pain and infinite joy forever united; anyone may call me to account for my acts, witch or astrologer, farmer or student, my wife, my mother, Guzmán or Julián . . . for any of my acts except this one, today, with you, an act that leads to nothing, consumed in itself, here and now, sufficient unto itself, enclosed in a circle of delectable flames, an act that originates in nothing and goes nowhere, and nevertheless the greatest pleasure and the greatest worth; it does not demand of us the calculation, the anxiety, the sustained will, or time of all the undertakings that promise us a place beneath the sun, and nevertheless, undemanding as it is, it is worth more than they, and is its own immediate reward. Is this love, Inés, this act that belongs to no one and to nothing but you and me?; have we consented to evil in order to experience good, and to good in order to know evil, alone, an act that affects no one except you and me and for which no one can demand anything of us, not even we ourselves, and if this is love and if love is such, Heaven and Hell, a cause sufficient unto itself, mutual sustenance, a hermetic exchange between two people, prison of enchantment, good and evil shared, then through which rent in Heaven, through which chink in Hell, through which crevice in the prison wall, Inés, will my individual, my unforgivable sin filter?, the sin that separates you from me and destroys the plentiful causes of love, linking love again to what would deny it: power and death, honor and death, devotion and death? I have given you illness in exchange for pleasure, while you have answered pleasure only with pleasure; I have involved you in the line of my corrupt blood, having denied that same evil to La Señora, my wife who is already of my blood, my cousin, out of horror of continuing a degenerate dynasty as well as nostalgia to maintain a juvenile ideal of love that may be desired but not touched; Inés, Inés, will you be what Guzmán said, new earth for my exhausted seed, will my corrupt seed be cleansed in your womb, or will my corruption impose itself upon your purity?, will I infect your very entrails, ravage your skin?; may I pardon myself by arguing that before I knew you I did not know I was to make love to you, Inés?; but that is not enough, is it?, that is not enough because love is like no other thing, and in no other thing may it be justified but in itself, nothing outside of love can save it although everything outside it can condemn it. Thus love is at once its own heaven and hell; but I have succeeded—knowing heaven and transforming it into hell—in separating Heaven from Hell, in giving all the powers to the abyss and denying them to Paradise, hoping, in spite of everything, that Heaven will take pity on me; do not abandon me, Inés . . . leave me, Inés, leave through that door that leads to my chapel and never return . . . never leave this chamber . . . go . . . stay . . . Inés . . .

With sweetness and strength, the novitiate withdrew her hand from the lips of El Señor. She arose from the bed; she donned again the rough sackcloth she had worn when she entered. She walked to the threshold that led to the chapel and there, sweet, distant, barefoot, she found words; words crowned her, transported her, possessed her; perhaps they were not hers, perhaps she was but the vehicle and they spoke through her tongue: "Señor, your race has made Heaven and Hell one. I want only the earth. And the earth does not belong to you."

El Señor would never, even before he knew they had been her last, forget Inés's words. He would repeat them to the end, until the moment when older and more ill than ever, astounded at his own survival but certain of his mortality, he again ascended the stairs of his chapel in search of the final light and truth.

FAX

Light the torch, huntsman, and lead me to the chamber of our Señora, Guzmán said: I do not know why this night, of all nights, seems the darkest I can remember; come, light up, it is the hour for torches, don't all the old sayings tell us that darkness follows the light, as the calm the storm, death, life, pride, humiliation, and patience, its reward? Come, light up, huntsman, for I already sense that our hour is approaching, and one must be prepared to seize the opportunity; I feel it; my bones tell me, and also the bodies of my hawks, quivering with eagerness; tell me, huntsman, did you follow my orders?, did you act while El Señor and the novitiate were sleeping?, did you reverse the hourglass?, did you fill the water pitcher and substitute new tapers for the burned ones? We must carefully govern our acts so that nothing be left to chance, for we have nothing to lose, you and I, and everything to gain, if we counter the calculation and might of new blood against the docile fatalism of exhausted blood; everything is change, huntsman; the man who knows how to see change and go along with it prospers; he who refuses to recognize it decays and perishes; that is the only unchangeable law: change; lead me with your torch, you will be rewarded; someone will need to take my place when I ascend to a more exalted position; who better than you, who knows so well how to serve me?, you, loyal servant and most faithful henchman; I know you, though I do not know your name—but even you don't know that; I know you as well as I know myself, for what I order, you execute, you are my right arm and my shadow: you know how to imitate a dog's howling beneath the echoing vaults of this palace; you know how to fill an empty pitcher in El Señor's bedchamber while our Señor sleeps away exhausted pleasures with the novitiate: I know you, and from this moment I put this challenge to you: be ambitious, huntsman; attempt in your turn to take my place; that will be the way to serve me loyally: scheme, plot, dissemble, rage against me as you serve me, or you will never have a name of your own but will be only an abject and expendable adjunct to the name of El Señor, who has his name because he inherited it, not because he earned it; and you and I, huntsman, we are going to demonstrate that one earns one's name, and that the only Señores will be those who acquire their names, not inherit them; I had no name either; I did not inherit a name, I earned it; Guzmán has a name today, though not as great as he would wish, or as great as someday it will be; so, huntsman, you must be both my partisan and my enemy, for only by being my adversary can you be my follower; that is what I want, that is what I demand of life among men: be my enemy, nameless huntsman, do not deny me that fealty, achieve your baptism with ambition, for the name given you at an inauspicious hour by your wretched parents has been forgotten by the world and you will earn your true name only in the history of men . . . if you know how to participate in it and excel, and in so doing, leave the trace of your person upon that history; struggle against me, huntsman, you and I both knowing, for if not, you condemn me to a life without risk, without opportunity to defend myself and affirm myself in the defense, and like the aged falcons, my claws will finally crack and split in idleness upon the perches of repose.

Guided by the torch, Guzmán halted before the door of La Señora's bedchamber; he ordered the huntsman to wait, torch in hand, outside; he entered without knocking and closed the door behind him; La Señora was sleeping, embracing the body of the youth called Juan; she smiled in her sleep and her smile spoke volumes: this is my man, this man is mine. Only these two, this pair, were honoring the hour of nocturnal repose, Guzmán said to himself: El Señor and the novitiate, lying apart, are each keeping an icy night vigil: he imagined Inés's naked feet, Felipe's naked hands, the icy stones of that cloister and bedchamber. Only this pair was joined in sleep, La Señora lying naked across the body of the youth.

"As if even in sleep she could possess him," Guzmán murmured with melancholy jealousy.

At his quiet words, and insistent stare, La Señora wakened with a start; when she saw Guzmán she covered her breasts with the sheet; the blond youth seemed to sleep; frightened, indignant, surprised, La Señora opened her mouth to speak, but Guzmán interrupted; she must choose: either she permitted herself the luxury of leaving her door unlocked, demonstrating thereby that she feared nothing and could be accused of nothing, or she bolted it like any other discreet burgher's wife as she allowed herself the luxury of adultery; she must choose.

"Do not look at me with such hatred, Señora."

La Señora pulled the sheet over the youth's head. "Your business had better be urgent, Guzmán."

"It is; so urgent it will not admit delay or ceremony."

And he told La Señora that the good huntsman has eyes and ears everywhere, in seignorial bedchambers as well as the taverns on the plain; for if the Señores were blind and deaf, either from choice or from apathy—Guzmán would not qualify which—their vassal, in proof of loyalty, would see and hear in their exalted names. See and hear, yes, but not act, for the second measure of loyalty owed the Señores was to inform them, and permit them to act with the authority that was theirs by divine right.

"Señora: we are not alone. We are not the only ones."

He smiled as he looked at the outlines of the figure he imagined sleeping beneath the sheet; this afternoon the third youth of this company has descended from the mountain to the plain. He is identical to the other two: the one you shelter here and the one your mother-in-law, the Señora, mother of El Señor Don Felipe, harbors in a dungeon. The three of them are identical, even to the sign they all bear: the blood-red cross upon their backs; identical, even in the monstrous configuration of their feet, for among them they can boast of sixty-six fingernails and toenails. Identical, different only because the persons who accompany them are different. I have ears, I have eyes: one youth is at the forge, one in a dungeon, and the third here in your bedchamber. One of them stares uncomprehendingly at his companion, who is probably his lover; her name is Celestina, or at least so she is called by the old smith of the palace. The other stares with dull stupidity, in which a tiny flame of horror begins to gleam, at his unsought companions: the one known as the Mad Lady, and Barbarica the dwarf. And this one? Is he still sleeping, my Señora? Are you desired by him, or detested? What do we know, Señora?

"He is my lover," said Isabel, with frightened arrogance.

And the youth named Juan, pretending to sleep beneath the sheet, silently repeated her words, and in silence listened to the continuation of Guzmán's discourse: one thing is certain, Señora, and that is that what we thought was a unique event when we found the shipwrecked youth that afternoon upon the beach of the Cabo, deceiving El Señor while he was hunting, is not unique at all; and this—Guzmán smiled again— offends my sense of reasonable coincidence. Why three? Why the cross? Why the six toes on each foot? And especially why, since the world is so wide and far-reaching, the three of them here? I have no time to answer these riddles. I have no arguments with which to answer magic, but I have actions aplenty. It is time to act, Señora, to act with the energy and determination that will skillfully unite the forces of fortune. We must take the initiative, you and I, Señora; I do not know what destiny holds in store for us if we allow events to unfold blindly; nothing good, surely; imagine an irrational encounter among the three youths come like phantoms out of nowhere, a mad old lady, a concupiscent dwarf, a catamite drummer-and-page who asks to be called by a womanish name and allows himself to be kissed and caressed by men; imagine an uneasy multitude whose words of rebellion have come to my ears, and a Señor with no vital strength who divides his time between mystic devotions and culpably lubricious interludes with the novitiates of this cloister who have taken the vows of chastity, confinement, and marriage with Christ. Can you and I, we two, eat of the stew of the ingredients simmering here? Do not let your eyes rebuke me, Señora; truly, my devotion to your person does not warrant that. But you think I am lying. You know your husband's body. You know he lacks vigor. But I speak the truth; there is one who has revived those dormant energies. It is not easy to confine a young and beautiful Sevillian novitiate in this somber cloister and expect her to dedicate herself to a life of shadows; like the air she will pass between the bars of her cell to play her role as harlot with the delight that comes only with the forbidden. And thus pleasure is not solely your privilege in this palace; your husband is pleasuring himself with a young girl who being a clever Sevilliana is not unaware that the vows of chastity are renewable. On the other hand, who will wash away the sins of my Señora? I speak the truth; but it does not matter. What is important is that El Señor has stored his coat of mail in chests filled with bran; he has lost, yes, this is surely true, the taste for war that, more than divine will, procured the throne for his grandfathers. El Señor, our master, is becoming mad: he is convinced that time has favored him, and that instead of advancing is running backward. He fears, therefore, his birth more than his death; but whatever happens, he fears his death, for he has not seen either Heaven or Hell reflected in the mirror of time, but rather, horrendous transformations of an eternity on earth: man into animal, and animal into man. In any case he fears the earth, which he does not deserve to inhabit. Do not be alarmed, Señora; I am not proposing a crime, that is not necessary. One day, as El Señor slept a deep sleep similar to death, I walked about his bed with my dagger held high above him; I could have killed him at that instant, but this thought stayed my hand: El Señor is already dead; all that is lacking, Señora, is that he be enlightened and interred. And who will succeed this sterile Lord? An imbecile fabricated by the madness of the Queen Mother? That lackluster lover lying beside you? A third usurper whose intentions, schemes, and means we do not know? Who?

La Señora broke her silence. "Guzmán, then?"

Guzmán, yes, Guzmán and La Señora, you and I, together; I the will, you the blood, and both destiny, he repeated, continuing his fevered plea; Señora, this palace has been constructed in the name of order, but today disorder threatens on every side . . . Guzmán attempted to recall to his mind's eye the naked figure of La Señora as she lay when he surprised her sleeping, her body intertwined with that of the youth called Juan . . . we know, you and I, how to take advantage of disorder and not lose ourselves in it . . . he struggled against the burning impulse to take La Señora in his arms, embrace that waist and caress those breasts, and beneath the sheet the youth named Juan felt the wave of that contained passion wash over him in a wordless challenge, a wordless longing to possess the woman that he, Juan, now possessed, and that he, Juan, did not know was his alone . . . these three youths are deceiving us, Señora, I do not believe in coincidence, it must be a plot, they must be conspiring among themselves, they are feigning a stupid apathy, like the cat pretending to doze so the mice will come out from their hiding places . . . mice, thought the youth called Juan, like the mouse that shares with me the sleep and love of La Señora, the Mus that traveled with her from the courtyard of the old castle of her torment to the bedchamber of the new palace of her pleasure, Mus, Mus, the one that crept into her flesh as Guzmán would like to penetrate the dark hiding place of the pale Señora . . . they thought, they desired, together, unknowing, Guzmán trembling, feverish, proud, standing before La Señora, so morbid and soft, so inciting, so hapless, what maddening contrast in the convergence of whitest skin and blackest hair that Guzmán had seen for the first time when, unannounced, he entered this chamber . . . let us not be led astray by the feigned disorder in the arrival of these three unknown youths, no . . . let me be led astray in your flesh, Señora, let me drive the shining silver of my arrow into the deep, final, black, lost, sweet heart of your carnation of milk and blood, fleece and honey . . . as I do, thought Juan, as I do, as Guzmán's awful, silent, unsatisfied wave of desire again washed over the white shadow hidden beneath the sheets . . . we must turn the true disorder that threatens us to our own advantage, the discontent of the workmen on this job, we must incite them, give wing to their displeasure so they do our work for us, so they clothe the revolt in the name of justice and popular rights, so they seize power and then, inevitably, lose it: then you and I can do everything a man and woman can do together . . . What I do, what they do to me, murmured Juan beneath the sheet, and he felt hidden like a mouse in his hole, like the mandrake root buried by La Señora beneath the white sands of this chamber; and he wanted to shout to Guzmán: Take her, then, if you want her so much, what's stopping you?, why don't you do what you want?, why do you speak and not act, Guzmán, does my presence immobilize you and terrify you more than you want to admit? Poor Guzmán, I am only a tiny mouse, a lifeless root, an orphan of the sea; do you want to kill me, Guzmán?

And as if she heard Juan's mute questions, La Señora asked: "And my lover?"

"Quick . . ."

"What would we do with him so that you and I might be together, Guzmán?"

"Señora, by night . . ."

"And what would you do that I might live without him?"

"My dagger . . ."

"Do you know me even the least bit, Guzmán? Do you know even the least bit who I am?"

"I have been of assistance to La Señora; I deceived our master to go with her to the coast and find this young castaway . . ."

"Yes, and thereby gained my confidence. Now you will lose it, poor Guzmán, and gain nothing in exchange."

"I served La Señora at the hour of pleasure; now I ask to serve her at the hour of duty; that is all."

"Would you take away my pleasure, this small sensual world that with such effort and such deceit I have succeeded in creating here?"

"The three youths must die . . . ."

"Do you know who they are?"

"We will find out later; for the moment, they are the mystery that threatens us. What we do not understand we must exterminate."

"I repeat: do you know who I am?"

"You and I, Señora, the will and the blood . . . ."

"You mean power, Guzmán? But the only thing that interests me is fucking the whole day long . . . poor Guzmán . . . ."

"I am a man, Señora . . . ."

"Hear me, Guzmán; I want an heir."

"I, Señora, I am a man . . . ."

"I am pregnant by this youth . . . ."

"It's a sorry heir you will have, then: the youth's apathy is like El Señor's; neither the passivity of pleasure nor the weakness of illness will be able to govern these kingdoms . . . ."

"He will be handsome, like his young father: I shall govern with him, Guzmán, with them, Guzmán, with my lover and our son, Guzmán. Do you see how my glorious plan excludes your pitiful hungers?"

"You will need me, Señora, you know nothing of the practical requirements of falconry, the hunt, war, controlling the rabble; you will not govern with pleasure and beauty, no; you will need me, I shall not be here, unless it is as I wish it."

"The world is full of men like you."

"Find them, then. Find someone able to take my place. There is no living soul in this palace who does not owe, fear, obey, or depend upon me—even if he does not know it."

"And who will live in this palace?"

"I do not understand La Señora."

"I said, who will live in this palace?"

"You and I, Señora, I am a man, let me prove it to you . . . ."

"Fool. You have not understood anything. Only my husband can live here. The rest of us are merely transients. The rest of us are but usurpers. You and I, you and all those you say you control here, all of them and even the palace itself would tumble down on us like sand castles without the presence of my husband El Señor. Fool. This is his palace; it was born of his deepest being, of his deepest need. He raises this palace in the stead of war, power, faith, life, death, and love; it is his, and for it he sublimates, and for it he sacrifices everything. This is his eternal dwelling: he constructs it for that, to live here, dead, forever, or to die here, living, forever. It is the same. Poor Guzmán. How can my husband see Heaven or Hell when the only thing he can see is this palace which is made of stone and which condemns him to stone?''

A trembling stone, the youth called Juan felt an icy sweat on his face and hands: prison of love, accepted, prison of stone, rejected; and his simple reasoning at this hour of the torches was: in a prison of love, I shall be love; in a prison of stone I shall become a statue. His rejection of the latter possibility was paralleled in an urgent plea, Guzmán, speak no longer, Guzmán, act; if you do not act now you never will and you will share the quality you scorn: the passivity you attribute to El Señor, and to me. Guzmán, embrace her, kiss her; come, Guzmán, to our bed. But instead Guzmán said only: ''Señora, you and I; Guzmán and La Señora; you and I, together . . .''

''No, wretch; no, clod; no, peasant; I and greatness; I and pleasure; El Señor and I; I and my lover; never La Señora and a common rogue, the dregs of pestilent cities.''

''Do not wound me, do not say such unpardonable things . . .''

''Return to the cellars of your servitude; call my black litter bearers: I would rather go to bed with them than with you; before I would go to bed with you, I would choose one of those laborers out there, in the kitchens, in the stables, in the lofts, one of the scullions or the mule drivers; go back there, Guzmán, go to your place, scum. And pray that I do not call my blacks, the mule drivers and scullions, to give you a good drubbing. For that is what you deserve, and not . . .''

La Señora crawled to the edge of the bed, staking her territory, dominating it, until she reached Guzmán's extended hands; she spit in his open, imploring palms.

''I and greatness, Guzmán; never you, you who know only ambition and cunning; I and my lover, or I and my husband; never you and I . . .''

Guzmán wiped the palms of his hands on his leather doublet. Now, implored Juan, the youth, now, Guzmán, don't let the words, the fury, the tears, the weapons of a woman overcome you, now, Guzmán . . .

''Is your cunning so limited? How have you dared to confide in me? I can denounce you; it is within my power to ask my husband this very night to send you to be tortured or beheaded, poor miserable, ambitious, wretched . . . lowest of the low.''

Now, Guzmán, wait no longer, I am choking, the sheets are suffocating me, they are drenched in sweat, they are my shroud, my winding sheets, save me, Guzmán, act now, take her, have her or you will never be master of yourself, please, Guzmán, save me as you save yourself, liberate your violence or it will turn to poison in your blood and you will seek revenge against us all for what you could not do to one woman, now, Guzmán, take her, choke her cries with your lips, don't speak, don't let her speak, dominate her or she will dominate us both, you and me, sully that womb with your foul lust, it is not my son that is germinating there, but the son of the mouse that makes its nest in this fraudulent bridal bed, act, Guzmán, for you, for me, Guzmán . . .

"La Señora forgets that the sword cuts two ways."

Juan moaned and closed his eyes, making doubly black the sepulcher of the bed.

"My husband tolerates everything; he can desire me only if he does not touch me; he has told me so; and he cannot touch me because his blood is poisoned; there is nothing he can do but tolerate everything. That is my certain if limited strength: he will tolerate everything."

"Because no one has told him anything. And even more: because no one has written it. He knows, only in secret. And silence is not the source of El Señor's authority, rather the declaration, the edict, the written law, the ordinance, the statute, the written word. El Señor lives in a world of paper; that is why those of us who know only the unwritten laws of action shall conquer."

Petrified Juan; Juan of stone; the statue Juan. Your words have defeated me, the young man said to himself; your words, Guzmán, have sealed my fate.

"My husband has what you will never have: honor . . ."

"A cuckold's honor, Señora?"

"Yes, Guzmán, see how far you can go; reach the limits of my tolerance, let me have the pleasure of collecting my due in one lump sum."

"You have already made me pay, Señora. There is nothing more you can do to me."

"And you, servant, do you expect to collect?"

Did you ask for a name, an identity, a mirror, a face, Juan, the day this man and this woman picked you up on the beach?, what are you thinking now, what are you asking yourself now, Juan?, shrouded in the sheet, your eyes closed, your hands cold, your head burning? And memory and premonition pulse as one in hands, eyes, and head. Pleasure and honor, honor and pleasure; when you were reborn in this land you said you would assume your identity from what you first saw in it after waking from your very long dream. So you arrived. You awakened. And you know. You listen to the little mouse gnawing in the heart of the bed.

"For El Señor, honor and paper are the same thing; the only testimony of honor is what is written. On the other hand, for us, for those whom you scorn so, such considerations have no value; neither paper nor honor mean anything; survival is all."

La Señora laughed. "You give a fine name to cowardice."

"El Señor knows and tolerates everything [Play your part, Guzmán, the moment for action has passed; how cold I feel, and suddenly I know that Hell must be winter: the longest winter of all], as long as there is no formal written accusation. Then his old habits are revived; then again he is the son of traditional procedure, Señora; then he is crime, honor, and the public act that is expected of him, as it was expected of his father and his father's father . . . everything in one, Señora: to El Señor, attitude is more important than substance.''

Guzmán was silent, because remembered visions were speaking to him and he was listening abstractedly; he recalled the ceremonial gestures that El Señor was wont to affect, as if to consecrate acts that were performed before El Señor had signaled permission . . . One night . . . on the mountain . . . by the campfire . . . as they were dressing the stag . . . as the heart of the animal was cut into four portions . . . La Señora was no longer listening; she was laughing at him and Guzmán prolonged his humiliation by the means for which he had just criticized El Señor: words; in response to words La Señora will laugh angrily, will walk around the sheet-covered body of her lover, will turn her back to Guzmán; acts, Guzmán?, why do you not take me, Guzmán, force me?; words, Guzmán?; shut up, servant, let disorder come, luck will carry my lover and me through; get out now, go, begone, do not insult my happiness further, it is enough: my bedchamber, my man, my possession; begone, and as you leave, remove the dog offal your boots have tracked onto the white sand of my bedchamber.

La Señora paused beside the body of her lover; she turned back the sheet, revealing the youth's hidden head, quiet, pretending?; impossible to know whether he truly slept, or merely feigned sleep; Juan: found on the beach, brought here, without consulting his wishes, to take the place of a foreign youth burned at the stake, Mihail-ben-Sama, Miguel-of-Life; brought here, silent Juan; he has never spoken a word, he is a body, he makes love, he makes love indefatigably, like no other man, a man, a body without words to extend its personality, bland, empty, expressionless eyes, clean as the sand of the bedchamber; anything might be written upon that sand, a name, Juan, my possession, mine, he was nothing, he was no one before he came here; he will be only what here he learns to be; I do not know whether he is sleeping, whether he hears us, whether he pretends not to be conscious, but even drowsing, what can be written upon that mind that is like a clean new whitewashed wall with not a mark on it, what can be written there except what he hears, sees, understands, and feels with me? Is this man my mirror?

''He will abandon you, Señora, like all the other youths who have passed, or who will pass, through this chamber. You give them what they did not have before, what they lacked; then they want to test it in the world, without you. Remember the one who died at the stake: he succumbed to the temptation of the world. The same thing will happen to the one lying here.''

''He will never leave.''

''He will leave; you are his wet nurse, and he will go out into the world.''

''So be it. Then through him I will be prolonged in the world.''

''Your payment will be solitude.''

''What we create is ours only after it is no longer ours. Can you understand that, servant?''

''The milk of your breasts tastes of gall, Señora.''

''You will never taste it.''

''Rather, Señora, think how others will come, you have nothing to fear, there is no contradiction, if this one leaves, others will come, there are plenty of youths; here there are three; do you plan also to take possession of the other two?''

''There is none like this one, and I would not exchange him for anyone. He is enjoying my weakness.''

''On the other hand, you and I, Señora . . .''

''Peasant. Clod. You have not justified your lack of respect in entering this room without notice. I cannot forgive that.''

''Close your door and lock it, Señora. The time of appearances has ended. Disorder has arrived. There are hearers. There are ears. Even the scullery maids and the halberdiers spy, run, tell, return, repeat. That is what I came to tell you. You must take precautions. And remember always who helped you find this lad, helped bring him here, deceiving El Señor and exposing himself to the most severe punishment. Why do you think he did it?''

La Señora laughed. ''Undoubtedly because you love me, Guzmán.''

''You know that?''

''It is of no importance. Anything you do out of love I accept as a service. Go ahead, denounce me, let us measure our strengths. And permit me to question yours. My lover is still alive, lying here by my side. You have not killed him. I am here, still untouched. You have not dared to take me. You talk a lot, but you do very little, you are a churl.''

Guzmán bowed his head and backed from the room; he swore to himself that whatever he did, whatever he had to do, he would never again let himself be tempted by that luminous, dark body; and that if ever he was tempted, it would be because, like El Señor, he had desired her body without seeing it or touching it, or even thinking of it. Desire it, but do not touch it; for a moment Guzmán felt himself a victim of the accursed chivalric code; no, by God, take, take without hesitation, immediately, yes, ravish what one desires. He was on the point of returning to La Señora's bedchamber. He was stopped by the taste of gall upon his lips, as if he had in truth drunk the milk of the woman's breasts. His soul was bitter and for a moment he hung his head, saddened and humiliated. But only the old and sick falcons would hear his pain.

"Quickly," he said to the huntsman who awaited him outside with his torch held high. "There is no time to lose."

CONCUBIUM

At the hour of sleep, Celestina was alone with Jerónimo in the forge, where the smith with the prematurely aged gaze, never taking his eyes from the woman, continued to forge the chains ordered by Guzmán: the ubiquitous and efficient Guzmán, who, when he was not personally attending El Señor or training hawks or curing hounds, wandered through the palace dungeons: Guzmán murmuring, stroking the plaited strands of his moustache: "Here there are luxurious marble prisons for the dreams of the dead, but not enough chains for the dreams of the living."

Jerónimo was close to Celestina, but also distant, while outside, Martín, Catilinón, and Nuño were feeding the weakened, mute youth who had accompanied Celestina here. Jerónimo felt close because he had recognized her and knew it was she, but distant, nevertheless, because he did not really recognize her, it was not really she. No one on the plain would sleep this night. The smith Jerónimo would keep the vigil of memory; looking at Celestina, he recalled the pale young girl whose hands had circled the neck of the ruddy, robust bridegroom on the day of their wedding in the grange, before El Señor and his son, the young Felipe, arrived to destroy—coldly, unfeelingly, disdainfully, and cruelly—the modest but ample happiness of the young pair. Jerónimo laid down the chains and approached Celestina, still dressed as a page, all in black. He took her hands in his and examined them for traces of that long-ago torture by fire, when the girl raped by El Señor repeatedly thrust her hands into the fire, biting upon a rope to bear the pain. But now he could not find the scars of those remembered wounds; he thought surely that time, for once merciful, must have erased them; in contrast, those painted lips were like a wound, as if on them time, once again merciless, had there recorded his sweetheart's pain and humiliation. He wanted to kiss those lips, but Celestina placed her hand upon his.

"It is you, Celestina; it is you, I am not mistaken?"

The youth led here from the beach, standing at the entrance to the forge illuminated by the weak fires of this late hour, watched Celestina parry the uncertain, irresolute kiss of the smith Jerónimo, who had not known whether to kiss first the ancient wounds of her hands or the new scars on the tattooed lips: he could not decide whether lips or hands more greatly merited the kisses of an old affection.

"Is it you, Celestina? Is it truly you? I am not mistaken? Many years have passed since you fled from that house, but you have not changed at all; you are the same girl I married, whereas I . . . look at me, I am an old man now . . . you are the same, aren't you?"

The page-and-drummer's fingertips still rested lightly upon the smith's lips, but Jerónimo, with a leonine movement, jerked his head away, seized Celestina violently by the shoulders, and said: "I have waited too long."

"But I was never yours."

"God united us."

"But I have belonged to others."

"That doesn't matter; I have waited years, many long years, for you; and your absence, woman, turned my waiting into patience; to-day it is my desire to change this humble patience into vengeance. You are Celestina, aren't you?"

" I am and I am not; I am she; I am another. Jerónimo, I do not belong to you."

"To whom then? That youth you brought with you?"

Celestina emphatically shook her head no, several times, and the youth moved sadly away from the threshold. Now in the hour of sleep, Celestina said no, I was not his, not in the way you believe; I thought I would possess him, but I was mistaken; when we lay together, the youth and I, one night on the mountain highway leading to this palace, naked beneath the stars, lying on the earth still warm from drinking in the July sun, impervious to the cold mantle of sudden night, I thought I would possess him; though he did not know who I was, I knew him, for I had taken advantage of the first hours of his sleep to break the seal of the green bottle and read the manuscript within, thus confirming that he was the same I had seen born, when I was a girl, from the belly of a she-wolf in the brambles of the forest; but then I fell asleep and when I awakened he had placed upon my face a mask of many-colored feathers, of bands of feathers radiating outward from a black sun, a center of dead spiders; and I knew I had discovered only half his secrets and that the other half I could know only by giving myself to him; still dressed as a page, I embraced him, fearing the passing of mountain muleteers who would see us and believe that two youths had given themselves to forbidden love, believing themselves alone in the night on the unpopulated mountain; slowly he disrobed me, slowly he covered my body with kisses, slowly he took me, made me his until my fingers clawed the cross upon his back and I cried out, from pleasure, yes, but also from horror, for I felt in the embrace of that youth a bottomless vacuum, as if when his flesh penetrated mine the two of us had hurtled into nothingness, fallen from some high cliff, were floating in air, captured in the cataract at the end of the world; my knowledge ended and his began there, in the center of the knot of love; forgive me, Jerónimo, but I must tell you everything; as I opened the windows of my flesh to him, I knew that he had been where no other man of our world had ever been; I am not sure whether I heard him speak or whether the soft pressure of his hands upon my buttocks spoke to me, or whether his warm breath in my ear recounted wordless stories, or whether in his fixed and tender and passionate gaze, when he drew his head back from mine to fully witness my pleasure, there unrolled a fragile parchment whereon were written the letters of a simple but incomprehensible message, serene in its certainty but terrifying in its novelty: voice, body, breath, gaze, probable dream, hands; everything about him was a cipher, a message, a word, the true and glorious news—not that which Christians have fruitlessly awaited century after century; no. Did I possess him? Did he possess me? I do not know, Jerónimo, and it does not matter; we were, perhaps, both possessed by the news my own body received as we made love, I and this youth found on the beach of the Cabo de los Desastres; for in love-making the youth's memory returned and what he remembered is this, Jerónimo: we were right, our youth was not mistaken, our love was not mistaken, old Pedro was right, his ship could have carried us to a new land, the earth does not end where you and I and El Señor believed; there is another land, far beyond the ocean, a land we do not know and which does not know us; this is what the youth told me; he knows, he has been there; he knows the new world, Jerónimo . . .

They stood silent a long while. The youth found on the beach had not heard them; he had rejoined the laborers; but as he raised his eyes he saw a profanation of the hour of sleep: a light was moving, interrupted but persistent, along the windows of the palace; it descended from a tower, proceeded along various passageways, then disappeared, growing fainter and fainter, into the lugubrious entrails of the building: Brother Julián, summoned with urgency, was hurrying, candle in hand, toward the chambers of the Mad Lady. Passageways, dungeons, kitchens, tile shed: Azucena told Lolilla, Lolilla told Catilinón, Catilinón, roaring with laughter, shouted it from the entrance of the forge to Jerónimo and Celestina, and left hurriedly to join La Lola in a haycart.

The smith said: "Death governs us. We are prepared to die to provide an opportunity to life."

"When?"

"As soon as Ludovico arrives."

"Will he be long?"

"He will be here this very night."

"You have taken twenty years to decide, Jerónimo."

"It was necessary to wait."

"They burned Pedro's hut, and killed his sons."

"They tore you from my arms on our wedding day, and raped you, Celestina."

"They led us to the massacre in the castle. Twenty years, Jerónimo. Why have you waited so long?"

"Our pain had to become everyone's anger. But you and your companion need not endanger yourselves with us. You can continue on your road, tonight, without stopping."

"No."

"We will act in your name too, Celestina; never fear."

"No; I have had my vengeance."

"When?"

"The very night of the massacre."

"But you and the student were saved by Felipe."

"And I poisoned Felipe. Not knowing, blindly, Jerónimo. As all those people were dying in the halls of the castle, I was destroying the young Prince as we were making love. I passed on to him the corrupt illness his father had passed to me when he raped me. The father poisoned me; I poisoned the son."

Jerónimo cradled Celestina's head against his breast; he feared the coming phase of the night. The man and the woman, chastened by the prolonged hour of sleep, lowered their voices.

"But your youth, Celestina . . ."

"Ludovico and Celestina fled the bloody castle that night. Each followed his own road, as before them the monk Simón and Pedro the peasant had followed theirs. Each had decided to be what Felipe had condemned them to be: conquered desire, frustrated dreams. None ever again heard of the others. I imagined the monk in pestilent cities, the serf building a ship by the shores of the sea, building it only to destroy it when it was finished and to begin again; I imagined Ludovico in his garret, receptive to the twin creations of grace and creation. I am sorry, Jerónimo; I was not able to envision Celestina with you again, adding harm to hurt."

"But that youth, you made love with him . . . you contaminated him . . ."

"He is incorruptible."

"But your bloom, your freshness; you are the same as the day we were wed in the grange."

"You must imagine why."

"There's not enough light, woman. You tell me."

"Wait. It still is not time. How long until the dawn?"

"Many hours. I wonder what is happening inside the palace?"

"Promise me one thing, Jerónimo."

"Whatever you say."

"That before you and your men enter the palace, you will give me one day of grace so that my companion and I may enter first. And one thing more, Jerónimo."

"Tell me, Celestina, I will do it."

"Remember the day of the massacre. If you find the gates to the palace open wide, beware, be on your guard."

And unexpectedly Jerónimo thought of Guzmán, who just the other day had come to ask the smith to place a new mirror in an old golden frame, to replace the broken glass; bad luck, you know, do it quickly; couldn't it be repaired; no, old man, look at the pieces, broken to slivers, take them, I give them to you, keep them or throw them away, perhaps they're worth a fortune, or more worthless than shit, I don't know . . .

NOX INTEMPESTA

At the hour when the augurs proscribe all activity, Brother Julián entered the dungeon inhabited by the Mad Lady, the Prince, and the dwarf Barbarica. He had to clear a path through the throng congregated there. With eyes still blinded and dazzled from stargazing with Brother Toribio, he sought the motionless torso and dizzying gaze of the ancient woman who had summoned him there with these precise directions: "Wear everything, the alb and dalmatic, the apron and the girdle, stole and cowl. And carry in your hands the missal you illuminated with your own hands."

What Mass did she mean to have him celebrate during the phase of *nox intempesta?* A path opened among the servants who were laying a table heaped with melons, watercress salad, omelets, pâté, suckling pig skewered on flaming lances, platters of bulls' testicles, tureens of jellied consommé, large plates of apple peel, scarlet tongue, pears, cheeses sprinkled with black seeds, and more: salted fish, young pigeons, pork tripe, huge roast geese, baked capons, francolins, and pheasants, timbale of pigeon, and toasted chick-peas: in short, all the delicacies of the Castilian table.

The dwarf was dipping indiscriminately into all the receptacles, stuffing her mouth with special morsels, her fat cheeks distended with food, and the Idiot Prince was lying in a corner alternately covering his ears and his eyes with his fists, his velvet beret slipping lower and lower over his forehead . . . what Mass was to be celebrated?

"All of them!" howled the Mad Lady. "The Mass of Masses! Solemn Mass and Low Mass, the Rosary Mass and High Mass, Good Friday Mass and ordinary Mass, capitular Mass, Advent Mass, the entire

Requiem: all at once, the Prayers at the Foot of the Altar, the Introit, the Kyrie, the Gloria, the Collect, the Epistle, the Gradual and the Alleluia, the Gospel, the Credo, the Offertory, the Lavabo, the Secret, and Preface, the Sanctus and the Tersanctus, the Canon and the Remembrance of the Living, the Consecration, the Elevation, the Anamnesis, and the Commemoration of the Dead, the Pater Noster, the Breaking of the Host, the Agnus Dei, the Communion, the Go-to-the-Devil, the Benedictus and the Last Gospel; Extreme Unction, the Anointing, the Impanation, and the Transubstantiation: everything, Friar, everything! Right here, right now, the Mass of Masses, because blood has met blood; image, image; inheritance, inheritance. There will be no more lies or delays or expectations or searches where there is nothing to be found: tonight the heir marries the dwarf, and you are officiating!''

All the Mad Lady's retinue was present: the halberdiers, the stewards, the alguaciles, the cooks, scullions, serving boys, wardens, muleteers, wine stewards, and false ladies-in-waiting, previously disguised so as to maintain appearances during the long funeral expedition through mountains and monasteries; now once again they were dignified black-clad Spanish gentlemen, their hands upon their breasts; even the beggars of her train were there; but there were men who were lower than the beggars, men who like the Idiot Prince sought the dark corners of this dungeon, demonstrating great familiarity with the shadows, and on their dark faces the pallor of prisons had not replaced the coppery hue of desert and sea.

"Only my drummer-and-page is missing!" the ancient Lady shouted. "I need the funereal drum to accompany the wedding of our heir!"

As they heard her, the laughing beggars began to drum upon anything they found at hand: walls, the stones of the floor, earthen pots emptied of their food, which the happy dwarf scooped up from the floor and shoveled into her gluttonous, lipless, toothless mouth, a pure moist orifice, chafed by excessive use, cured by the aseptic miracle of a mouth that like that of the buzzard becomes cleaner the more filth it devours; the Moorish prisoners intoned the high plaintive chants of the muezzin and secretly turned their faces toward the distant sacred oasis; the captive Hebrews, their lips tightly closed, throats vibrating, moaned the deep strophes of hymns learned in their Jewish quarters; the beggars rapped with raw knuckles upon their bowls, against the very back of the leather chair where the mutilated body of the howling Lady was propped upon her provisional throne, exposed to the fortunes of this greedy, drunken, rancorous, and vengeful crowd; the serving boys poured pitchers of red wine into copper cups and even the beggars permitted themselves the pleasure of making toasts and noisily slurping their wine in the presence of the Most Exalted Señora: men were there inferior to the beggars themselves—who, after all, considered themselves to be free men—and those were the captives who huddled in the corners and hummed and awaited, as they had learned from experience, the cruel rewards of the Christian feast.

"Look, look," the Mad Lady demanded of the terrified Prince, "I have brought you Jews and Moors, see them there in their corners, tatterdemalions, the very dregs of humanity, separated forever from the presence of God the Father and ineligible for the redemptive sacrifice of God the Son; look at them, at this moment of your wedding ceremony I want you to know our enemies, the enemies of our Faith, the object of your arrogant wrath, flesh for your prisons and fodder for your avenging sword; I have ordered them brought here to your wedding so that you may do to them whatever your sovereign will decrees; do not be compassionate: the garrote, the pillory, the rack, beheading, whatever you wish on this the day of your wedding, the stake—establish yourself in blood, my lover, son, husband, ancestor, and descendant; act quickly, give wing to your actions, indulge neither in repose nor impatience, for your time will be brief, and supreme; you are but the transition toward the resurrection of our breed, in you my husband has been reborn, from you will be reborn our father's fathers, our dynasty will regress toward its beginnings, our blood will be renewed: you shall marry my gentlewoman Barbarica. Steward! Place in the Prince's hands the sword of the battles against the Infidel; Barbarica, get up off the floor, stop stuffing yourself, roll your white nuptial taffetas tightly around your waist; Chamberlain!, place the crown of orange blossoms upon the head of the tiny Queen; Friar!, open your breviary . . . and let the ceremony begin!"

"Oh, mistress! Why are you crowning me with such riches? I have served you well, and I am the most faithful of your servants. But I do not deserve such happiness."

"I am thinking of my poor husband, Barbarica, and of all the women who desired him. Ah, what a mockery, what a fierce revenge, my little one!"

"Oh, mistress! Your worthy heir deserves something better than I."

"There is nothing better than you, I tell you, you are the only person I could bear to see married to the phantom of my husband. Let the whores, nuns, and peasant girls who loved my husband and were loved by him in turn writhe with envy; let them choke with rage when they see you, a little monster, a runty bitch, a misshapen fetus, in their place, you in the Prince's bed, you renewing the bloodlines of Spain."

"Oh, mistress! My body is too small to contain my joy."

"Grasp the sword hilt in your hands, Prince, do not falter; let it also be said of you: It was a propitious hour he girded on his sword; remove that grin from your face, Barbarica, more dignity, my gentle lady; and you there in your chamber beside the chapel, have no anxiety, my son, born of a sick father in a Flemish privy: the succession is assured, you now have an heir and an heiress, there is now a royal couple, Spain is saved, from this time forward there will be only fatal sterility or unfortunate monstrosity, now nothing will be born, or what is born will be irreconcilable, a step further toward our marvelous separation: let no one resemble us, let no one recognize himself in us, we are different, we are unique!, there is no possible interrelationship, there is none!, power must culminate in absolute separation or it is not worth the struggle, no one resembles us, no one may take a mirror and say, we could be you, no one, no one; and you, my barren Señora of the falsely bulging skirts, roll in your soft bed and on your floor of sand with your handsome lover, prefer the illusion of beauty and the mirage of pleasure to the insuperable power of that which resembles nothing else, that which is perfectly, definitively, immutably, heraldically unique; your pleasure and your beauty will disappear with time; fear time, watch it waste and bite and wrinkle and dry and gall and strip and rot and corrode; contemplate and fear the corrosive action of the years upon your defeated body and your stultified and envious mind, Señora; envy those of us who have nothing to fear because we have already been devoured by time, we are beyond its misery and we know that even time cannot ruin a ruin. This is where we live, in the abyss which is the very center, the blind spot, the motionless heart of the heraldic field. Glut yourselves, beggars; drink, alguaciles; eat, stewards; tremble, infidels; more dignity, Barbarica; clasp your sword, Prince; officiate, officiate, Friar; my monstrous couple against your handsome lover, Señora; my heirs against yours. Let the milk and blood flow; ooze nectars, seep odors.''

When the nuptial ceremony had ended, the Idiot Prince stood like a statue for a long while, his eyes staring into nothingness; Brother Julián stood with his head bowed; the dwarf disguised as Queen and bride tugged impatiently at the cape and doublet of her husband, and her eyes pleaded to the Mad Lady, tell everyone to go, please, mistress, tell them to get the hell out; this part is over, now my fun begins; in turn, the Mad Lady's eyes commanded silence and attention: frozen like a medallion that was both dead and alive, lacking any sense of animation, the motionless Prince compensated her for all her desiring, weeping, suffering, love, and hatred; in the Mad Lady's mind all the sovereigns of the past, all the dead of the present, and all the phantoms of the future were joined together, given substance, culminated in the figure of her heir: fabricated by her, animated by her, converted by her into this frozen statue.

Then the Idiot raised his arm, the long waxen fingers moved; he stared absently into the corners of the dungeon where the Moorish and Jewish captives huddled together; he extended his arm and for the first time he spoke: You are free, he murmured, you may go in freedom, rise, walk, leave here as free as the day you were born, return to life, let your hair and your beards grow, do not rend your garments any longer, cover your women's faces with veils, adore whomever you desire, be free in my name, please, get up and leave here; this is my will on the day of my marriage; leave here: you have been pardoned; leave us alone, my wife, the Lady, and me; leave this land; save yourselves . . .

The cock crowed. And before its distant sound died, it was revived in the melancholy strains of a flute.

"My drummer!" shouted the old Lady, bobbing her head like a nervous hen. "He's returned!"

But instead, amid the incredulous stares of the liberated captives and the rancorous stares of the beggars, who had expected something more in the way of largesse from the Prince, her wildly staring eyes met the eyes of a flutist squatting beside one of the dungeon walls. His eyes—with the unblinking stare of a mirror—were directed toward the Idiot Prince. But the flutist's eyes—groaned the ancient Lady—cannot see. They were clouded by the green opacity of blindness. And thus, in the upheaval of the Lady's emotions were blended in that hour—as the flutist blended into the crowd of captives and beggars—impressions of opulence and misery; she did not know whether this merriment, this wedding, these banquets, a musician's blindness, the captives' freedom, a Prince's will were a sign of poverty, or plenty.

GALLICINIUM

The smith's preternaturally old eyes gleamed, and outside, at the hour of the cock's crow, Celestina's young companion, drawn by an irresistible attraction toward the palace, walked along the side of the interminable construction until he stopped beside the high walls of an enclosed garden.

Once again La Señora traced the contours of the youth at her side; the air of the bedchamber was even heavier than usual, the odors of gum acacia blending with the aromas of exuded perfumes, and the captive breath of stock mingled with the secret exhalations of the little sacks hidden beneath the cushions that were also the habitation of the wise, silky Mus; the vapors from the tiled bath seemed to evoke a fine, almost imperceptible mist from the sand-covered floor. At this hour of the cock's crow La Señora's fingertips awakened the sleeping flesh of the youth; she thought her caresses were arousing him to the dawn, and to new love-making; she did not know that the youth called Juan had heard and understood everything during the hour Guzmán had spent in the chamber; but in this caress La Señora's swift touch performed a different function (and La Señora, even though she did not want to admit it, knew it; had not the diabolic little mouse told her—on her true wedding night as she lay upon the paving stones of the castle courtyard—that from that moment her diminished senses would double in power, extent, and anguish, seeing more, touching more, smelling more, tasting more, hearing more, heighten, as if by an unconscious drug, that secret pact between a virgin Queen and a satanic Mus crept in between her legs?); but the other youth could know none of this, he who was Celestina's companion, he was not the one with whom the little mouse had made its pact; and nevertheless, as he stood there beside the wall looking up toward La Señora's window, the third youth found on the beach felt as if invisible hands were caressing him, arousing him, summoning him . . . and then he leaned weakly against the wall, bathed in cold sweat, experiencing an anguish he knew was not his but that he longed to communicate with a cry of alarm to someone in danger, to a body that was not his but depended upon his as he depended upon it, a body both near and remote, intimate and strange: hands caressed both the body lying within their reach and the one not in their presence; as the flesh of the youth lying by her side was aroused there was a similar awakening of something forgotten until that very moment, forgotten since he had been found on the beach of the Cabo de los Desastres by La Señora and Guzmán; La Señora did not want to know what her touch elicited (in spite of the fact that the Mus that had gnawed away the thin membrane separating her from pleasure had warned her: You will feel more, Isabel, and therefore you will know more; but you will feel more than you know; you will delegate to me the wisdom procured by your senses; yours will be the pleasure and mine the knowledge; such will be our pact, concluded upon these icy stones in a courtyard on a night of gray clouds and black lightning; you will feel; only later, much later, will you know what you have felt, what you have done and undone with your fingernails, your senses, your eyes and nose and ears and mouth); and the youth called Juan, thus aroused by La Señora, remembered; and as he remembered he feared; and as he feared he imagined: he imagined, feared, remembered something that until that moment—buried in the drugged atmosphere of the chamber, lulled by the domination of another's senses, senses that monopolized all experience for themselves—had not again come to mind; also he asked himself, who am I?, and realized he asked that question for the first time since he had been borne in the litter along the deserts of the shore up to the high plain with La Señora, hidden behind her veils, and the heraldic bird of icy humors and proud, sleek head.

As La Señora moved closer to embrace the youth, he recalled with a rush of terror the last instant of his consciousness in the litter, when he had felt La Señora's breath upon his throat, when a face like a silvery moon had appeared between the parted veils and between parted red lips he had seen ferocious, bloody, greedy fangs . . .

"Do you want to see yourself, Juan? Do you want to know what you look like and, when you see, love yourself as I love you?"

La Señora held a mirror of black marble to Juan's face; as the youth penetrated its turbid depths he saw himself, naked; he recognized himself, and for an instant loved himself; the longer he looked, the more he loved himself, but as that love and that gaze were prolonged, a stern and rigid hatred rose from the tremors of self-love and crystallized in the form of a body; it was he, this image, this reflection, this shadow; he had no other proof of his existence, and on the beach his only certainty had been that he would become the name he was first called and the face he was first shown; it was he, his nakedness reproduced in the black mirror La Señora held before him, and that uncontestable self, always with the same features, the original face, was assuming the aspect of a woman; he saw his body, again in the same unchanging form, being clothed in La Señora's garments and then, like La Señora, lying upon its back on the paving stones of a courtyard; rain washed the body and soaked the clothing but did not wash away the assimilated man and woman in the mirror's image; when the sun reached its zenith the rain ceased; the shadow of Juan and La Señora's common body— La Señora with Juan's features, Juan with La Señora's clothing and hair and jewels—disappeared, and Juan choked back a moan; the mirror reproduced the death tremor, the reflected figure sighed its last sigh, and La Señora, who was he, surrounded by indifferent alguaciles and uneasy duennas and inquisitive halberdiers, expired in the courtyard of her torment; they died together, Juan and La Señora, with no arms worthy to assist them, the body of love abandoned by the master engaged in Flemish lands in his last combat of arms; they died at the same instant in the mirror, two souls inhabitating the same body died only for an instant; the mouse that had in turn inhabited La Señora's farthingale slipped swiftly between the corpse's legs, burrowed through the tangle of black hair, entered the slippery vagina, ascended through the entrails, devoured the heart of the dead figure, climbed to the eyes, the brain, the tongue, stained them with black urine, emerged through the mouth of the corpse, and the corpse breathed again; the shadow of the body reappeared and slowly lengthened toward the west, the movement in the courtyard, temporarily suspended, was resumed; the halberdiers renewed their coarse jokes, elbowing each other slyly, the maidservants held soupspoons to the mouth of the prone figure; it all happened in an instant, death passed without being seen, almost without leaving a trace; but in the hiatus between life, death, and resurrection, that body had been possessed, that pact concluded; the mouse restored life to the woman who was La Señora with the face of Juan: what would the woman give the satanic Mus in exchange?

The image in the marble dissolved. La Señora withdrew the mirror from before the youth's face. With a cry, he clutched his wounded neck; he imagined his own body, pallid and waxen, just as he had seen it in the mirror, dead in life, alive in death; and with a memory of lightning as dark as that at midday in the castle courtyard, a memory further awakened by the cock's crow, he repeated to himself the story La Señora had told him his first night in this bedchamber; he opened his eyes and searched in vain for the features of the little English girl who had entertained herself in dressing up the maidservants, playing with her dolls, and burying peach stones in the garden; he saw a mature woman by his side, almost overripe, poised on the hazardous, knife-thin edge of a ripeness depicted in contrasting areas of black and white, here the impenetrable blackness of the eyelashes, there the dazzling whiteness of the skin, here again the noxious darkness of the hair; not a step farther, not a minute more lest the equilibrium be broken and this Señora who watched over him here, made love to him, nourished him but was also nourished by him, would blow away like a statue of dust, disintegrate like a spider's web, cave in like a tunnel of sand, melt like the snows of spring, rot like fruit abandoned to the severity of the sun and rain and wind. (Do I nourish myself from you?, you the one called Juan Agrippa, according to Julián the painter-priest?, do I sink my teeth into your neck, suck your blood, without knowing, without will? I have wished only to love you, absorb you, touch you, kiss you, like any woman who desires her man, do only what any woman in love will do; I swear it, Juan, I did not know my fingernails and teeth do more, bite flesh, rake nerves, suck blood; for my body, for my ordinary body, Juan, what any woman wants would be enough, but my body is twofold, mine and that of my true master, the diabolical mouse that feeds from me as I from you; it kisses you through me, and through my flesh drinks your blood and through me makes love to you; poor Mus; it was so tiny and silky, so hungry, so industrious; it must envy your beauty, Juan, surely it wants to be like you: an angel . . .)

Like fruit abandoned . . . the youth remembered, again he summoned the image of La Señora lying in the castle courtyard, invaded by mice, skin peeling from the sun, body lashed by the rain, and he saw her at that moment convoking the last resort of the afflicted, the only being capable of saving her, the fallen Prince who could enter into a pact with her and promise her salvation in exchange for her submission to his mandates; he had known all this from the moment La Señora told him her story on the first day of his amorous captivity; but now, after looking into the black mirror, he knew something more: that La Señora was he himself, and that the pact effected with the Mus saved La Señora not only from her torment but from an actual although instantaneous death, fleeting because the mouse did not permit it to be prolonged into eternal death; that death, my God, was double: both hers and his; she had been saved from the torture of absurd ceremony and the anguish of unloved flesh, and saved also from death, along with the lover who was he, the young shipwrecked sailor with features identical to La Señora's; and thus he saw file before his feverish gaze the phantoms of the other youths who had preceded or would succeed him in this bedchamber; his ears were deafened with the sound of the forgotten footsteps of youths without name or number who had passed or would pass to the stake and the gallows through La Señora's bed-chamber, where their last years had engendered or would engender new subterranean creatures torn by night from their damp tombs and brought to the oasis of the palace, to this bedchamber of white sands and heavy perfumes and brilliant tiles and sumptuous brocades; for where could this chamber lead (Juan asked his awakened and fright-ened imagination) but to the tomb, from the tomb to this bed, and from this bed to the tomb, the only other avenues those of Hell: repetitious fate. He heard the crowing of the cock and told himself he did not want to be but another of that number, that legion of phantoms created like wax dolls from the love and hatred and dissatisfaction and desires of La Señora.

"Guzmán, Guzmán," Juan sighed sadly. "Guzmán, why did you not dare take her for yourself, why? Your man's body would have bro-ken the chain of phantoms. You could have saved me, Guzmán, I knew it, I told you, implored you in silence; you have condemned me, Guzmán, you have condemned me to be the twin of the woman who loves me so that she may love herself, and whom I love so that I may love myself; you have imprisoned me in a mirror, Guzmán . . . with her, like her . . . I am she, she is I . . ."

The first youth rescued from the sea countered La Señora's every ca-ress—the hands eager to insure their dominance and the passivity of the youth they possessed—with the question: Who am I?; the response was always the same: I am she, and if I am she, as I love her I love myself, and as I make love to her I make love to myself, and eventual-ly I shall not be able to answer the question: Who am I?, for this love will have forever destroyed my self, and he answered his jailer's every repulsive kiss with the burning strophes of a litany that defined him as it delineated her: in order to differentiate himself from her, he would be her equal, she would gain nothing of his true and secret self, she would derive from his beautiful and fecund and warm body only her own qualities, herself, and he would go into the world to be what she was in this enclosed chamber, a covetous and deficient woman, envi-ous, malicious, thieving, greedy, inconstant, the two-edged blade (Juan: "I fear, I imagine, and I try to recall my identity but I can iden-tify only with the first thing I see upon awakening, the only thing I know outside myself: I am you because the only thing I know besides myself is you), proud, pretentious, lying, garrulous, indiscreet, curious, lustful (Isabel: "I desire and I reject, I admit and I deny: you see yourself in me and that is my triumph, you despise what you see of yourself in me, and that is my sadness, you take from me what I am so you may be you, and that is my defeat, we are identified in one another, and that is our miserable truth"), root of all evil . . . who will tell of your lies, your deals and exchanges, your lewdness and your tears, your tumult and your daring, your deception and forgetting, your ingratitude and coldness, your inconstancy and your attestations, your denials and reconsiderations, your presumption, your depression and madness, your disdain, your chatter and your coercion, your greed, your fear and your audacity, your ridicule and your shame?, this woman, this woman (Juan: "Your hands are awakening me: I am you"), the vehicle of the Devil (Isabel: "I lie, I fear, I imagine; this youth is not I, he is you, Mus of the Devil, hymen-eater, you made use of me so that you could penetrate me and extract from me your desired image, your angel of light, your heart imprisoned within a body before the creation of the hells you inhabit"), discoverer of the forbidden tree, deserter of the law of God, inciter of men (Juan: "I am awake: I am you; am I a woman?"), seat of sin, weapon of the Devil, expulsion from Paradise, mother of sin, corrupter of the law, enemy of friendship, sorrow from which one cannot flee (Isabel: "Mouse, devil, fallen serpent who caused my fall, seek again your body of light, find the angel you one day were, possess it"), necessary evil, natural temptation, desired calamity (Juan: "I awake: I am you, are you a woman?, do I reflect you or you me?, are your attributes mine?"), domestic danger, sinful detriment, essence of evil (Juan: "Do you and I reflect another being?"), destroyer of manhood, tempest of the hearth, impediment to repose, jailer of life (Isabel: "But with me you would be neither you nor another; you would have neither face nor virtue nor defect; if you are not I, you are nothing except what passes through me; it is the same, regardless"), daily harm, willful dispute, sumptuous battle, invited beast, thirst for permanence, enveloping lioness (Juan: "The mirror, please, the mirror again"), embellished danger (Isabel: "Night, please, night again"), malicious animal, woman . . . this woman.

As he repeated the litany, the youth knew who he was: he was able to answer his own question; he identified himself with the woman; having plucked its fruit, he rejected the identification, and hoped that La Señora would do what she had to do, what he had begged and she had refused to do. La Señora took the marble mirror. Juan seized it from her grasp and held it to La Señora's face. In the mirror, as she looked at herself, La Señora saw Juan. She saw his slim body, the pattern of muscles in the torso, chest burned by marine sun, ocher arms, white legs; monstrous beauty: six toes on each foot; mysterious beauty: a blood-red cross upon his back: Juan's body, but from the neck emerged the head of a mouse; the crown of the body of love was the tiny, sagacious, mocking head of the Mus, darting eyes and twitching ears, gray fur and stiff whiskers, a damp, black, sensitive nose, a scarlet tongue, and greedy fangs. La Señora saw what she knew, and dropped the mirror upon the sand of the floor. He was she, and therefore other; he was other, and therefore he; he was himself.

"Everything that thinks, dares; everything that dares, thinks," said Don Juan.

With inexorable will, he cast La Señora from him, watched her tumble, hair flying, toward the edge of the bed, feigning incomprehension, weakened by the fear and the need to hide her terrible happiness (Isabel: "If I have triumphed, I have lost; if I have lost, I have triumphed"), momentarily defenseless, questioning, incredulous, knowing what she knew but rejecting that knowledge; bursting with self-awareness, obsessed by the resonance of his name, his destiny, his adventure, Don Juan arose from the bed; a cistern long empty, he was abruptly filled with the liquid vices and froth of an identity seized from the woman whose greatest fear and greatest desire was that she might lose him (Isabel: "My triumph and my defeat"), seized also from dream, words, the remote flow of origins, a long-dormant will awakened by the cock's crow with its faint promise of dawn and sun, a day of heat and risk, but also with its sad memory of betrayal; Don Juan walked to one of the walls; he tore from the wall a thick, opaque, luminous brocade woven of shadow and silver and wrapped it about him; he stared with mockery and scorn and pride at the Señora with the terrible lips and wild eyes, crouched like an animal, naked, on all fours upon the bed, black and white, at the point of rotting, at the point of crumbling into sand indistinguishable from the sand of the floor, contemplating the rebellion of her angel, her succubus, her vampire, with a mixture of apprehension and nostalgia, triumph and defeat, as if this was what she both expected and refused to accept, what she both feared and desired, something she remembered already, with resignation, and something more: the fatal return to this chamber, this prison and its caresses, already divined, expected. The youth walked with firm steps to the door of the bedchamber.

"Where are you going?" La Señora's voice could not express the contradictory complexity of her emotions, her words voiced a single attitude among the hundreds the Devil had set aboil in the breast of his serf. "You cannot leave here, you cannot; life is here, by my side (No, your life is outside; carry me into the world within your skin, carry my master, the diabolic mouse, into the world; bury his stiff, hairy tail deep in all the asses he and I can never possess, go, with your archangel image, to perform the work of infernal imagination; exist, fornicate, kill, deceive, satiate yourself for him and for me, Juan; break all the chains of chastity; free us, Juan; go and tell the world it is not we women who are the instruments of the Devil and thereby to be persecuted as witches and burned at the stake; demonstrate that a man may also be the incarnation of the Devil; free us, Juan; act so they forget us and persecute you; oh, how great is my triumph, Juan, how great my revenge upon men: my husband, El Señor; Guzmán, the humbled; the bishops and Inquisitors who if they knew of my actions would burn me before the greedy eyes of the workmen who would possess me merely by watching me die; oh, what triumph, Don Juan, you hide me and save me by acting for me in the world while I serve my true master in this secret chamber; go quickly, Don Juan, do the work of the Devil and the woman you embody in the world, go now, you have been born, but fear me because you carry with you my soul and my heart, you condemn me to the pursuit of a new lover to exorcise the loneliness of my bed); you cannot abandon me, Juan; you cannot survive alone; you lack will, you are mine; the man who leaves this room will encounter only death; you will encounter death (our life, Juan), only death."

"Death?" queried the erectly proud young man blazing now with his own light, burning cruelty in his eyes, master of his own words. "So remote a threat?"

With long strides and a mocking laugh he left the room, closing the door firmly behind him; he breathed in the cold, enclosed air of stone passageways; he walked with gusto and pride, dominated by an arrogance that in him, and for him, transcribed and attenuated all the attributes enumerated in the litany of woman: in the room next to La Señora's, the room where beneath loose paving stones they had hidden her dolls, peach stones, stockings, and locks of hair, Azucena and Lolilla heard the violent gust of wind—as if the brocade enveloping Juan were a sail impelling him across the seas of the palace—and peeked from behind their door; their mouths dropped open, their stares of amazement were returned by Don Juan's stony gaze; with him they laughed, and torn between fear and desire to be part of whatever was taking place, they slammed their door just as a laughing Don Juan threw his weight against it, and continuing to laugh, his arms spread in a cross, one hand on each side of the doorframe, allowed his man's smell, his man's laughter to filter through the cracks of the door, inflaming both of them with this inconceivable proposal: "Open the door; La Señora's lover can also be the servants' stud; down with doors; no more locks; pleasure is for all, or for no one."

He laughed again as he walked through the galleries of the palace, repeating his name to himself, Juan, Juan, Juan, desiring a mirror in which he might look at himself as a thirsty man becalmed upon the Sargasso Sea desires sweet water, wishing he could convert the granite walls of the palace into a mirror of vanities, a labyrinth of reflecting mercury; he spoke his name (and acted out before the silence and darkness of the stone the gestures and attitudes of all his names): greed and gluttony, inconstancy, two-edged blade, pride, gossip, lust, Devil's gate, seat of sin, corrupter of law, enemy of friendship, natural temptation, desired calamity, essence of evil, destroyer of womanhood, storm of hearths, sumptuous battle, invited beast, embellished danger, malicious animal: he, Don Juan; he, usurper of all the mirrors of all the women of the world.

And then he stopped. If not the mirror, then the mirage; at the end of the gallery a girl was leaning against the wall, a woman, in spite of the fact that with her closely shaven hair she resembled a lad; barefoot, dressed in rough sackcloth that for Juan's eyes could not disguise the fragile fullness, the round delight of her young, ripe, female form. Juan stopped. He placed one hand on his hip. He waited. She would come to him. She would come, fatefully, she would come in quest of the sumptuous battle.

CONTICINIUM

First, in the hour of silence, La Señora merely felt herself alone, abandoned, incomplete; defeated, she lay where she had been thrown upon the bed, listening to the fluttering wings of her restless falcon, thirsty—glutted with darkness—and hungry for the hunt; the sound of the wings awakened her from her lethargy; images of the hunt evoked by the hawk flashed before La Señora's half-closed eyes; quietly, sensing that pain would become despair and that despair then would circulate through her bloodstream as desire for revenge, she said to the hawk, offering it a wrist, on which the bird of prey obediently alighted: "Let me tell you a story, hawk. Selene, the moon, fell in love with a young hunter, Endymion; and as she was the lady of the night, she caused him to sleep; covering him with her white veils, she cloaked him in darkness, and thus, as he slept, she could kiss and make love to him at will."

The hawk's talons dug into its mistress's bare arm, but she felt no pain—pain of the flesh, no, pain of the soul; and the voice of her soul told her that the falcon's company would not be enough, but also that she could endure Juan's absence . . . The mouse . . . The mouse slept beneath the lover's pillow, he hid there, he crept from beneath the pillow every night to disseminate dream, desire, and hallucination. La Señora, her mouth half opened, her body swelling with expectation, fell upon the pillows with frenzy, threw them one by one onto the sand of the floor beside the accursed mirror. The frightened falcon fled from its mistress, fluttering uneasily. La Señora found the little sacks filled with aromatic herbs, the perfumed gloves, the colored pastilles. But not the familiar mouse.

"Mus . . . Mus . . ." murmured La Señora. "Mus . . ."

But nothing stirred in the perfumed early morning. This time the mouse did not creep out, look at her, and scurry back to its hiding place.

"Master . . . lover, my true lord . . . can you not hear me, Mus?"

Wildly, La Señora pawed through the pastilles, tore open the sacks, and strewed the herbs upon the sterile sand; as she bit the finger of each aromatic glove, she fancied she had discovered the mouse's new hiding place.

"Mus . . . have you forgotten your lover? Mus, have you so soon forgotten our wedding in the courtyard, how your tiny teeth nibbled my flesh, darling mouse, how you devoured my virginity, mouse, my love? Mus, I have fulfilled my pact . . . I delivered to you the body of my lover, Mus, I returned to you, poor tiny, scorned beastie, the image of the angel that once was yours . . . Mus . . ."

She buried her face in the softness of the bed. She understood, and as she understood, she wept. "You went with him, is that not so? The two of you abandoned me, is that not so? You used me in order that you might enter the body and soul of that youth . . . filthy mouse."

The hawk again alighted on La Señora's wrist.

She looked with hatred at the stupid bird that had understood nothing, had proved itself incapable of defending its mistress, of attacking the youth who carried off the mouse hidden in the folds of his brocaded cape.

"But what happened when Endymion awakened? Did he stay by Selene's side, or did he abandon her forever? I cannot remember how that legend ends, falcon."

The hawk, so confidently clinging to its mistress's wrist, shivered; La Señora carefully examined the rumpled sheets and found hairs from her lover's head and fingernail trimmings, which she piled into a little heap, stirred, held to her nose and mouth; she murmured incoherent phrases, and the bird of prey, accustomed to receiving solicitous attention and giving obedience in return, trembled and fluttered its wings, confused, sensing in its smooth, lean body that the normal order of things had been reversed, that in place of mutual fidelity there was now sudden menace; it fluttered desperately and lurched from La Señora's unsteady wrist, taking advantage of her intense concentration on the nail trimmings and strands of hair she held in the palm of one hand, the shivering bird launched into blind, nervous, suicidal but redemptive flight about the rich bedchamber, the oasis in this somber palace, striking against brocade-covered walls and ceilings embossed in Arab fashion, against closed windows and the door through which Don Juan had escaped; then La Señora rose from the bed and pursued the falcon, stretching out her arms, grunting, crouching, waiting for the bird to cripple itself as it flew into stone walls and fall upon the white sand floor; the sound of the fluttering wings sent ripples of terror through the chamber; the hawk's increasing fear would soon be turned against the Señora; forgetting the hours of faithful company, the falcon would see in her the enemy, its prey, which it should have seen in Don Juan and the falsifying Mus; and as it perceived its prey it would swoop down upon and seize La Señora's flesh in a fury of fear and incomprehension: its universe was crumbling; all the bird's habits, acquired by instinct and reinforced by Guzmán's application, faded with each thrust of frenzied wings; the hawk struck mercilessly against the windows and, wounded, fell to the floor; La Señora ran to it and the hawk pecked at its mistress, still attempting to defend itself, sinking it talons into the white flesh rejected by Don Juan; with one hand La Señora seized its beak, and with the other, covered its rapacious eyes, pushing its head into the sand, slowly, suffocating it, burying it in the sandy floor of the chamber, mercilessly strangling it as she muttered: "Domum inceptam frustra . . . frustrate the construction of this house . . . may this palace never be completed . . . domum inceptam frustra . . ."

Thank you, true Señor, true master of my soul, murmured La Señora as she opened the window of her bedchamber, you who did not refuse my call when I needed you, you who answered in the body of a mouse, slipped between my undergarments and crinolines during the nights of my torture and humiliation in the castle courtyard, you who with your sharp fangs divested me of my virginity and introduced me to pleasures forbidden by my husband, you who sent your young representative to my bed, you who were present when as I received the Host I spit it out in the shape of a serpent, not understanding that even then you had chosen me for your black works, you, the unknown, lurking, secret, insinuating power that guided my hands when as a child I buried my peach stones in the earth and dressed my dolls; and with all her strength La Señora flung the body of the hawk from her window; the inert body, its wings broken, its beak sealed, flew above the sterile space of the promised garden and fell beyond the wall. Thank you, Lord who governs tormented and evildoing lemures and the tormented exile of the wondering spirits of the larvae that punish the living thank you, Lord who gives me power to command the manes, disturb the course of the stars, limit divine powers, command the elements and threaten the very sun: astral body, I shall envelop you in a veil of eternal shadows; thank you for making me your servant and granting me your powers; thank you, master, fallen angel, black light, now I understand you, now I forgive you, you said that first I would feel and then I would know, such was our pact, you have not betrayed it, now I understand, I have had pleasure, now I shall have knowledge, no one, not you, not even the God whom you defy, may enjoy pleasure and knowledge at the same time, thank you, fallen angel, for revealing to me that my present body is but one more transformation among the thousands that I have, unknowing, lived throughout the centuries, not knowing that I have been woman, bird and she-wolf, child, butterfly, jenny, and lion, and that now, thanks to that youth who left here with you, I am pregnant by you and by him, for both of you fertilized me with your dark semen, and from my womb will be born the future Lord of Spain.

Smiling, she closed the window and walked to the foot of the bed, where the marble mirror lay amid herbs and pillows. She picked it up. She looked at herself in it. She saw nothing but dark bloodstains running down the glossy black surface, as if the stone were bleeding.

Dispirited, she hung her head.

"Not even this, master? You also deny me your son? This is how you inform me that I am bleeding again, that my woman's cycle has not been interrupted by the fecundation of my love-making with the youth called Juan? This is how you show me that in the period of the moon a woman's mirror is stained with blood?"

Her lips tightened. She told herself she could endure all trials, that she would overcome them with the arts of black magic inculcated by the Mus, she would not allow herself to be defeated, she would give thanks again, thank you, master, for teaching me the words of my powers, thank you for recalling to me words forgotten during the course of my metamorphoses, the words that define me through mutable time and the exhausted spaces of the world: saga et divina, potens caelum deponere, terram suspendere, fontes durare, montes diluere, manes sublimare, deos infirmare, sidera extinguere, Tartarum ipsum illuminare, thank you . . . The dead falcon fell at the feet of Celestina's companion, who stood contemplating La Señora's window, and La Señora, on the thrust of her new wings, followed the dead hawk through the same Castilian air on the membranous wings of the body convoked through age-old words of female sages and seers in the early dawn of time; flight, eager harmony in the black lance of her head, life in her fangs and phalanges, thank you, black light, fallen angel, who taught me these words through long nights in the courtyard, you have divested me of everything except words, but now words are everything for me, I can no longer nourish my dead life with the blood of the handsome youth I fed upon for you, Mus, but because of the power of words I shall now be able to nourish myself from death itself.

The bat, the winged mouse, Mus of the skies, traced a nervous arc above the plain and sought a new entrance into the palace through the crypts; veiled in mourning, the dying night guided it and sustained it in its flight.

Slow the heavens, suspend the earth's turning, stop the streams and dissolve the mountains, convoke the manes of Hell, defame the gods, extinguish the stars, illuminate the black regions of Tartar . . . invoking those powers, the blind bat, wings beating faster than the eye could perceive, guided by the proximity and remoteness of the mausoleums, entered into deep crypts reserved for El Señor's ancestors in his own private chapel.

When it felt the marble of a tomb, the blind winged mouse reassumed the body of La Señora, naked but defended against the cold of these tombs by heat of spirit; quickly, fearing that the coming dawn would rob her of her powers, sweating, excited, La Señora pried up the heavy stones of the tombs, with her hands she broke the glass panes of the sarcophagi where the royal mummies lay, and ripped away flabby nostrils, brittle ears, frozen eyes, powdery tongues, the dried members from several remains; she murmured curses and spells still unproved, for she did not know the true extent of the forces she invoked, mute forces of demoniac powers that God had given man immediately after this creation, nor did she know whether they would be fulfilled immediately, tomorrow, or many centuries later, for the power of the Devil is circular, a sphere divided by the line of time and thus a part of time, but it is also one hemisphere above and one below time, and thus removed from time; but someday, someday . . . if she could withstand the difficult tests to which her true master subjected her, if she did not falter in her prayers to the mouse who had crept in between her legs, if she maintained her absolute faith in the serpent she had spit out one morning as she received the Host, all she sought would come to pass:

may all those within this palace never leave it, may it be their eternal prison and eternal tomb, or if they leave it, may they carry it with them on their backs, as the snail his shell or Cain his crime;

may all men who wish to flee from this curse be transformed into beavers and terrified by captivity, may they devour their own genitals in the belief that they lighten their bodies in preparation for flight;

may Juan, captive within the palace, find within that prison the jail he most deserves, a jail of mirrors, a windowless prison;

and may any woman made pregnant by Juan be condemned to perpetual pregnancy, like an elephant bearing throughout eternity her heavy burden within an enormously swollen belly . . .

"When a man and a woman set sail with Venus, the only provisions they need are a lamp filled with oil and a chalice filled with wine; you and I have not even that; may our pleasure compensate for such poverty," Juan had said to the novitiate Inés as they lay down—the man dropping his brocaded mantle and the girl her harsh sackcloth—on a crude bed in the servant's room nearest the place of their meeting; and the ahs and sighs of love of the young pair blended with the squabbling of the servants Azucena and Lolilla, for the murmurs sifted through the fissures of the badly mortised stone separating these miserable rooms, and through the open windows of the July night; but they were completely compensated by their pleasure; Inés told Juan who she was, and asked whether he feared the furies of Heaven, and he replied: "That is a matter between Heaven and me. But believe me when I tell you that I fear neither Heaven nor Hell, nor the lycanthrope."

"Not even my father who is nearby in this very palace, waiting to speak with El Señor?"

"Never fear; someday he will invite me to dine."

"And do you not fear even El Señor?"

"Your blood is cold, Inés. El Señor was. I am. And he who says 'I was' is worth nothing, it is 'I am' that matters."

"And me, do you not fear me?"

Juan laughed: "Unfortunate the woman who places her trust in a man! Doña Inés, it is your gain that you are the first I found; but that is no reason you should deprive other women of the rightful claims they hold upon my heart."

"Your blood is cold, Juan."

Juan withdrew like a lizard from Inés's naked body, placing the palms of his hands against the wooden planks that served them as a bed and raising himself above her; through the open window they could hear the covetous giggles of the two scrubbing-girls-become-royal maidservants; Inés screamed with terror, she pushed away her lover's body, her tensed muscles slackened, with horrified hands she covered the sex Juan had just abandoned, the wound opened by El Señor and then enjoyed by Juan the same night had closed, she was again a virgin, inexorably the opened lips had closed, the hair knitting together into a mesh like steel wire, the teeth of chastity had come together, the flower closed its petals; Juan, laughing, his head cradled on his arm and the arm propped against a wall to support a body weak with laughter, said: "If either I or El Señor have made you pregnant, Inés, you will have to give birth through your ear . . . ."

Swirling his cape about him, Juan left the little room; he pounded on the door of the neighboring room, laughing at the excited giggling of Azucena and Lolilla.

La Señora, again transformed into a bat, flew several times from the crypts to her bedchamber, carrying each time in her mutilated phalanges a bone and an ear, a nose and an eye, a tongue and an arm, until from the parts stolen from the tombs she had formed upon the bed an entire figure of a man.

In her flight she feared the light of the coming dawn, the contrast of firmament against the increasing clarity of the sky; when her task was completed she contemplated, exhausted, her work; she admired the monstrous figure created from bits and pieces lying upon the bed: the nose of the Arian King, one ear from the Queen who stitched flags the color of her blood and tears; the other from the astrologer King who complained that God had not consulted him about the creation of the world; one dark eye from the fratricidal King, and a white one from the rebellious Infanta; the livid tongue of the cruel King who had forced the members of his court to drink the bath water of his concubine; the mummified arms of the rebel King who had risen in arms against the stepfather who had murdered his mother; the blackened torso of the King who died in flaming sheets; the skull of the Suffering and the shriveled sex of the Impotent King; one shinbone from the virgin Queen murdered by the King's halberdier as she was praying; another from her own mother-in-law, the Mad Lady, a relic of the sacrifice the mother of the present Señor had imposed upon herself after the death of her handsome husband, the whoring Prince and violator of country girls.

La Señora lighted her fire, over it she hung a caldron and threw into it Juan's fingernails and hair and then added the myrrh-like cáncamo, a tear shed from an Arabian tree, and the gum of the storax tree which coagulates and hardens like resin; she stirred everything together, waited until it boiled, and then poured the boiling, waxy mixture over the pieces of mummified flesh, anointing them, and joining the separate members into a human form. She waited for the wax to cool, looked at the new body, and said: "Now Spain has its heir."

"I smell something, I smell something," said the Mad Lady, sniffing nervously as she was wheeled in her little cart by the dwarf, who had stamped her feet and sulked and demanded to be taken to spend her wedding night in the magnificent crypt of the forebears; Barbarica and the Mad Lady, followed by a serene Idiot Prince, strangely indifferent to the two women, content with having freed the captives, an act the ancient Lady did not know whether to approve or condemn, but respected because it was the sovereign decision of the heir; nonetheless, she smelled something now that made her overlook both his idiocy and his need, an odor wafting in foul-smelling clouds through the galleries of the palace, the odor of putrescent flesh and burning bone and burned fingernails and wax that intoxicated the Mad Lady; "Where is it coming from, where is it coming from?, what is that nectar of new life?, who is doing these things?, why have I not been informed?, why do I have a service so vast and exact if no one knows to inform me of what is going on here? I must be alert, there are silent powers that may frustrate me, new blood for the banquet of time . . . no, old blood for the wedding with eternity, our world is now constructed to last until the end of the world, nothing must change it, I have done what needed to be done, hear me, Felipe, my son, aid your poor mother mutilated by honor and maddened by fidelity, nothing must change, not ever, you are right, Felipe, I ally myself with you, there is an heir now, banish those who would idolize nature, order the sacred tree to be burned, along with those who would search for God in nature, baptizing fountains, placing the cross upon rustic altars of branches and flowers, complete your palace, my son, enclose everything within it—sepulchers, monasteries, stones, and even the future palaces that may be constructed within yours—in a gray and infinite perspective, invent within the walls of your palace a replica of everything nature offers and enclose it all here, the double of the universe, enclose everything so that this be the true nature, not what merely passes for nature, not the nature that changes and dies, sows, germinates, grows, and flows, but a petrified nature of stone and bronze and marble that is ours, and within which our bodies are a miniature world: land, flesh; water, blood; air, breath; fire, heat; think on this, my son, in your chapel and in your bedchamber; think on this with the same intensity and pain St. Peter Martyr must have felt when the knife was buried in his skull, think on it so that our order may never change, so that things be as they have been conceived in our eternity: servitude, vassalage, exaction of taxes, homage, tribute, caprice, our sovereign will, passive obedience on the part of everyone else, that is our world, and if it changes we shall change; and if it dies, we shall die . . ."

At the mute explosion of the dawn the dwarf Barbarica, wrapped in her nuptial trappings, drunk and dyspeptic, farting and belching, climbing and clambering over the tombs of the forebears, shouted for the painter-priest to come record continuity: she was the Queen, only she, and upon each marble mausoleum, at the foot of each stone plinth, leaning against each bronze banister, the dwarf imitated what she imagined were the royal poses the illustrious Señores and Señoras and Princes and Bastards here buried had adopted in life.

The Mad Lady scornfully observed Barbarica's antics, she was completely silent, absorbed in the grandeur of the crypt; her gaze was lost in the gray perspectives of domes and colonnades that with unnatural attraction retained the dark wings of night that outside were already flying in swift pursuit of the last light of the new day. Inside, in contrast, the acid of the shadows was eating into the copperplate of the royal tombs. As her eyes were exactly like engraved metal, the Mad Lady first noticed only the general appearance of the crypt; only later, after they had adjusted to that darkness, the color without color, her eyes, like two prismatic engraving styli, bit into details: then she noted that the glass of certain sarcophagi was broken, the heavy stone slabs were pulled back, the tombs profaned, and she shouted to the Idiot to push her closer, and when she saw the profanation she screamed anew: curses, my own arms, my own hands, the relics of my sacrifice, are missing, the limbs embalmed by the apothecaries and learned doctors, who filled them with aloe and quicklime and black balsam; she shouted, she wept; the dwarf continued to swing from tomb to tomb, and the Idiot Prince, with an air of infinite weariness, removed his tightly curled wig, walked to the tomb of El Señor's father, the Mad Lady's husband, lifted the covering copper slab and there encountered himself, or at least some remains dressed in the clothing he had worn when he emerged from the sea: a tattered strawberry-colored doublet, and dun-colored breeches still stained with sand. The dwarf cackled, the Lady shouted with indignation, and no one was watching him; he could not remember (because his memory could not retain what vanished with each sunset) that the Lady when she arrived had asked her son that the body of the shipwrecked sailor be thrown into a common grave along with the cadavers of dead dogs, nor could he appreciate that it was only by a chance accident he did not question, since he could not even imagine it, that this dead replica of himself, vaguely familiar, lay in the tomb of the handsome and whoring Señor whose identity the Idiot had imperfectly usurped, as if some formula of the double metamorphosis had failed, as if traces and scraps of one had tenaciously adhered to the other. The dwarf cackled, the Lady shouted, no one was watching him.

The Idiot Prince climbed into the sarcophagus, lay down upon the remains of his own body, and sank into the corrupted flesh of the sailor who was himself; once again his flesh fused with the blood-red cross that stigmatized the cold depths of the sepulcher; once inside, he allowed the stone of the tomb to fall after him, and in the darkness he closed his eyes; he felt greatly relieved, in peace at last; now he could rest, wait, a long time, with no surprises, no need to decipher the enigmas that he in his doubling as sailor and Prince, true orphan and impostor heir was incapable of resolving; no need now to make decisions, to act out an expected madness or a certainty of approaching desperation, no need to free captives or crown himself with bleeding doves or swallow black pearls; he was freed from the duties of condemning or emancipating, of constructing his power upon the foundations of caprice. He closed his eyes, and slept within the tomb.

Celestina's companion entered the forge with the broken body of the strangled hawk in his hands. He showed it to the girl dressed as a page, and to the smith. Celestina took the dead bird and carried it to the entrance of the smithy.

"Give me hammer and nails," she said to Jerónimo, and he obeyed her.

Celestina placed the body of the hawk against the center of the doorframe, she extended the defeated wings and nailed the body and outstretched wings to the dry wood. The three stood mutely, witnessing the crucifixion of La Señora's bird. Then they heard muffled, dragging, infirm footsteps across the devastated plain; these steps were preceded by the plaintive strains of a flute.

AURORA

Like La Señora, Toribio, the astrologer-priest, dreaded the end of the night.

She dreaded its coming because she had still not completed animating the body that could assume or simulate life only during the hours of darkness. The astronomer dreaded it because then the stars would disappear from view, and not even the powerful telescopes he had constructed with such grave patience could return his darlings to him; for among all possible visions, he considered that of viewing the stars the one most to be trusted and desired.

La Señora, lying beside the cadaver she had only just fabricated from the skulls and scraps of the royal remains, cursed the lateness of Don Juan's flight, as it left so few nocturnal hours for forging a revenge she imagined circular, eternal, and therefore infernal. Brother Toribio, on the other hand, was preparing to greet the aurora (when it did arrive; not yet; there was still time to prove an experiment; what he needed was a witness) with praise that united the gratitude of his Christian soul for the miracle of a new day with the satisfaction of his *libido sciendi* that the new day proved the circular, eternal, and therefore celestial parentage of the spheres; and this joy compensated for his nostalgia for the night.

Thus where La Señora saw evil, he saw good; and where she saw good—in the vile fabrication that lay upon the black sheets beside her—he saw evil: he had always compared the dark science of his contemporaries and secret rivals with the witchcraft of the ancient sorceresses of Thessaly, who taking feet, hands, heads, and torsos from various sepulchers, ultimately created a monstrous Prometheus with no relation to true man; plotting their concentric circles, their excentric circles, and their epicycles, these false uranographers were incapable of discovering the shape of the earth, or its measure, for they knew everything about the infinite movement of the stars except the most simple and unique truth: that movement, all movement, is regular and invariable, the same for stones thrown by the creature's hand as for planets set in rotation by the hand of the Creator.

He was thinking these things as he fashioned a meniscus, concave on one face and convex on the other, resigning himself to postponing its use until the following night; then he would ask that fatal and eager night, never expecting she would speak or tell her own story, but hopeful that astride the mount of experience she would with a simple movement of her head sign the yes or no the priest's hypotheses deserved. Toribio put down the meniscus, picked up a piece of heavy paper, and patted it; he was impatiently awaiting the return of his comrade Julián, the painter-priest, urgently summoned by the Mad Lady.

La Señora patted the cold members of the human form by her side and put her lips to the mummified ear affixed with cáncamo to the dissimilar skull, for while in some places the Arabic resins had formed a flesh-like gray film, in others the bone shone through opaquely, like old silver; whispering into that ear La Señora asked her true master (multiplying his names, Lucifer, Beelzebub, Elis, Azazel, Ahriman, Mephisto, Shaitan, Samael, Asmodeus, Abaddon, Apollyon) whether, in truth, in the guise of a mouse, he had granted her that night of their secret wedding in the castle courtyard the powers of magus and seer, of slowing the heavens, suspending the turning of the earth, stopping streams and dissolving mountains, of evoking the manna of Hell, and extinguishing the stars so beloved by the wise Chaldean in the tower, Brother Toribio; if so, this was the moment to put them to the test, to animate gradually the rigid members of the heir she had constructed, for she knew now that this figure was the true fruit of her union with the mouse, and that possessed by him she could not be impregnated by Don Juan: let that livid tongue speak again; fill those mismatched eyes, one light and one dark, with flecks of light; now, please, Master and Lord, chief of Tartar, sovereign of the sulphurous hole of Acheron, prince of the shadows of Hades, you, king of Avernus, you who bathe in the waters of the river of fire but not in the waters of the river of forgetfulness, do not forget me, do not forget your servant, now, before the sun undoes the work of the shadows, make these parts rot again, return them all to dust . . . now . . .

"Hold this paper, Brother Julián," Toribio said when the painter-priest returned from his long night in the company of the Mad Lady, the dwarf, and the Idiot. "Hold this paper, punch a hole in the center with the point of this pin, and then hold the paper to your eye. Go out onto the balcony of my tower; hurry, for the dawn is coming. Look at the stars through the tiny aperture made by the pin. What do you see?"

"What do I see? That the stars have lost their aureole; they look very small . . ."

"And you realize, then, that their apparent size is an illusion created by their refulgence . . . ?"

"Yes; but I am not sure of what I see, Brother Toribio: I am tired; it has been a long night."

"Isn't it true that nothing looks as small as a star robbed of its light? And nevertheless, many of them are larger than this earth we inhabit. Imagine, then, how our earth must look—only one star among millions of other stars—from the star most distant from us; or imagine how many stars must fill the dark space between us and the most distant star. Can you believe, Brother, that our tiny star is the center of the universe? Can you believe that?"

"What I do not dare believe is that God designed the universe in honor of our earth and the miserable, cruel, and stupid beings that inhabit it. I have learned one thing tonight: men are mad."

The painter-priest offered several folded sheets of paper to the astrologer-priest, whose benevolent smile seemed to ask: You have only now come to that realization?, although his bowed head indicated a certain fear in response to the words of his comrade: "That is a conclusion I have tried to avoid, Brother Julián. I have never wished to imply that the great expanse of the infinite diminishes either God or man. You understand, that is something they would never forgive."

Julián looked at Toribio with affection; he had learned not to laugh at the slightly comic appearance of the astrologer, his tonsure encircled by wild, dark-red curls, and one perpetually wandering eye; he stood straight and tall, but lacked either grace or symmetry, and he always held one twitching shoulder higher than the other. Toribio accepted the folded manuscripts with respect; he had recognized El Señor's seal at the bottom of each page.

"Who gave you this?"

"Guzmán, just a moment ago, on the stairway that leads to your observatory. He asked me to read them and judge them."

Squinting his eyes, the palace astrologer approached a lamp of wax candles enclosed in smoke-blackened glass hanging from the beamed ceiling; he adjusted the light and with an eagerness belied by his outward casualness began to read the testament El Señor had dictated to Guzmán; he raised one arm and with a gesture at once forceful, gentle, and controlled he pushed the lamp, which described a wide pendulum arc above the heads of the two priests. One continued to read, while the other contemplated with exhaustion and surprise the arc described by the lamp.

"Watch carefully, and count," murmured Toribio, never taking his eyes from El Señor's folios, where the shadows cast by the lamp rhythmically shortened and lengthened. "Count your own pulse, Brother Julián, count carefully and you will learn, you will see, that each swing of this lamp takes exactly the same amount of time, always the same, whether the distance of the arc is great or small . . ."

Julián, counting his pulse, approached the astronomer: "Toribio . . . Brother . . . what can you . . . ? Tell me, do you know of anything that will cleanse me, purify me, of this accursed night?"

Toribio continued to read. "Yes. I know that the earth is in the heavens. Does that console you?"

"No, because I know that Hell is on earth."

"Do we ascend or descend, Brother Julián?"

"Our sainted religion affirms that we ascend, Brother Toribio, that there is no movement but that of the soul in its ascent, in search of an eternal good, which is above . . ."

Toribio shook his rust-red head. "Geometry knows nothing of good or evil, or of supremes or relatives, but it assures us we neither climb nor descend; we spin, we spin, I am convinced that everything is spherical and that everything spins in circles; everything is movement, incessant, circular . . ."

"You are describing men . . ."

"You have just discovered that men are mad; but mathematics is not mad; a hypothesis may be false if experience does not prove it; false, but never mad."

"Neither can the earth be mad, although the men that inhabit it are mad, and their madness is a movement like that you describe: incessant and circular, relentlessly returning to the same exhausted point of departure while they believe they have reached a new shore; and with this movement men wish to communicate their delirium to the earth. But the earth does not move . . ."

"You say it does not move?"

"How can it move? We would all fall, we would all be thrown into the emptiness of space . . . the immobility of the earth has to be the stabilizing factor for the agitated coming and going of its maddened populace, Friar . . . if the earth moved—in addition to the movement of men—we would all be thrown toward the heavens, Friar . . ."

"Did I not, just now, tell you that we are already in the heavens?" The astrologer laughed; he rolled up El Señor's papers and threw them on a table; he took Julián by the arm and led him to the balcony.

There Toribio picked up two stones of unequal size; he walked to the parapet and extended his hands beyond the edge, the smaller stone in his right hand and the larger in his left. "Look. Listen. I am going to drop the two stones at the same time. One is heavier. The other, lighter. Watch. Hear. Both will fall at the same velocity."

He dropped them. But neither friar heard them strike the ground. Toribio stared uncomprehendingly at Julián, his eyes, as always, vaguely out of focus.

"I heard nothing, Brother Toribio. Was this the miracle you wished to demonstrate? That your stones fall and strike the earth without making any sound?"

The astrologer trembled. "Nevertheless, they fell at the same velocity."

"We would have heard them strike; either one stone first, and then the other, or both at the same time; but we should have heard the sound, Brother, and we heard nothing . . ."

"And nevertheless, I swear to you by my Chaldean ancestors, they fell, and they fell together, at the same exact velocity, in spite of their different weights . . . even if they were caught by an angel! And they fell moved by the same force that moves the moon, the earth in its rotation, and all the planets and stars of the universe; should those two miserable and blessed stones not descend at a uniform velocity from this tower, then at this instant neither you nor I am alive; stones move because the moon moves around the earth, and the earth around the sun, as if in a stately celestial pavane; one impels another, one sphere affects another, indeed the entire universe, without a single imaginable fissure, without a single rupture in the chain of cause and effect; each is related to the other so that beginning with the revolution of each planet all phenomena are explainable and this correlation binds together so tightly the order and magnitude of the spheres and of their circular orbits and of the heavens themselves that nothing, Brother, do you understand me, nothing, can be changed in its place without mortally disrupting every other part, the very universe itself . . ."

"And you know all this because of the two stones you dropped that we did not hear fall?"

Toribio emphatically nodded yes, although his lips murmured: "I do not understand, I do not understand . . ."

And the rosy dawn crowned his head with pale flames but threw the bowed face of the astrologer into shadow.

"Brother Toribio: Joshua ordered the sun to stop in its course that he might gain the day in his battle."

"The Holy Gospels preach supernatural truth. Natural truth is of a different order. Everything is simultaneously uniform movement and persistent change . . . Change and movement, movement and change, without which the stars would be corpses on the highways of the night."

"El Señor, Brother Toribio, is like Joshua. Do not forget it. You have read the testament that the unlettered chief huntsman Guzmán could not have invented. You and I know how to read between the lines. El Señor desires neither movement nor change; he wants the sun to stay its course . . ."

"What battles can El Señor win now? Better that he invoke the powers of dusk and defeat."

"El Señor does not want change; and we are his servants."

"And, nevertheless, El Señor does change; and as he changes, he suffers, and as he suffers from change he decays and dies."

"Our poor Señor. Everyone says he is no longer the man he was. They say he was a handsome youth, audacious, also cruel. He led a rebellion against his own father so that he might more easily deliver the rebels into his father's hands. His own power is founded upon that slaughter, and because he has power he has been able to build this palace where you and I find protection and opportunity to read the stars and to paint icons . . . Do not forget that, Brother. Here you and I have saved ourselves from a dangerous world. What would have become of us were we not here? In what wretched workshop would you, a simple journeyman, be fashioning lenses?, I would be shoveling manure in the stables where I was born. Without the shelter of our sacred order and of the seignorial power that offers us the privileges of this palace, would you and I be able to paint and study, Friar?"

"Do not see in our Señor anything more than you observe in other men, Friar, in the universe itself. Perhaps in that way we may save ourselves from the dangers of the adulation of the court, and of being completely forsaken. There is nothing exceptional about El Señor except the accident of his birth. Everything else is a matter of components common to every thing and every person: violence originates force, force begets joy, joy is converted into forms, forms eventually harden, cool, decay, and die. And death is the violence that reinitiates the cycle."

"And suffering, Brother?"

"What suffering?"

"The same suffering you have been speaking of. The suffering that, as it changes, decays and dies."

"I was speaking generally, not specifically, about El Señor."

"Careful, Brother, nothing exists that is not made incarnate. And even in El Señor the suffering that, as you say, necessarily accompanies the passage from joyful violence to cold death must also be made incarnate. For our Señor is approaching death, the papers we have read tell us so. Death in life, it occurs to me, must be defeat and frustration, and this is the death, I suspect, that our Señor is living, although I recognize that I am incapacitated insofar as my ability to penetrate the secret motives of the decision that led him to create here in this palace and in those who inhabit it the perfect semblance of death. On the other hand, does the universe understand frustration? Tell me that, now that you are not only an astronomer but also a horoscopist."

Toribio returned slowly to the room filled with lenses, condensers, telescopes, ustorious mirrors, charts of the heavens, compasses, and astrolabes. He stopped, followed closely by the questioning Brother Julián, beside an astrolabe; he seemed to be admiring the graduated rule, gently he stroked the sights that marked the divisions of the metal sphere: he set the device spinning.

"No, it does not know frustration. The universe functions, and fully expresses itself, always."

"Is it pure force, then, pure realization, pure success, without the martyrdoms and beauties of joy, form, decadence and death? And if it is so, may I overcome with my painting the mortal norm El Señor imposes upon us? May I, with joy, form, decadence, death, and resurrection through martyrdom and the beauty of art, save myself from both the plenitude of the universe and the finiteness of El Señor, and thus establish the true human norm?''

Toribio spun the sphere faster and faster, murmuring: ''A force that accounts for itself . . . a force born of the perfect equilibrium of death . . .''

He looked at the painter-priest. ''Lightness is born of weight and weight of lightness; each expends in the same instant the benefits of its creation, each spends itself in proportion to its movement. And each, too, is simultaneously extinguished. All forces destroy themselves, but they also create each other; for them, death is mutual expiation and violent birth . . .''

With a deliberate, arbitrarily theatrical, gesture, the astrologer abruptly stopped the spinning of the astrolabe and added: ''This is the law. Neither your painting nor my science may escape the norm. But the paradox is that, by violating it, they create it: the law exists thanks to those who oppose it with the violent exceptions of science and art.''

Julián placed one hand upon Toribio's shoulder. ''Brother, in his testament our Señor dabbles in the most detestable violations of the law of God; he combines all the anathematized heresies . . .''

''Heresies?'' Brother Toribio's eyebrows rose, and he laughed. ''A good Spaniard is our Prince, and his heresies at times are nothing more than blasphemies . . .''

''Heresies or blasphemies, he discusses them, and allows them to run their course, exactly like our poor friend the Chronicler of this palace; poor Señor, too, for he cannot be sent to the galleys to expiate his sins. But I want to be charitable, Brother, and I ask myself, convinced by what you have just said, whether El Señor simply is not seeking, with pain, at a different level, the truths you say you have encountered through your telescope . . . Toribio, is El Señor too solitary? Could we not, you and I, for the good of all . . . approach him . . . ?''

''Do not be deceived. El Señor does not seek what we seek.''

''We, Brother?''

''Yes, you, Julián, you and your painting. Do you think I cannot see? That is all I do do, poor thing that I am, poor cross-eyed Chaldean: if I can scrutinize the heavens, I am entirely able to observe a painting, quite capable of going to El Señor's chapel and reading the signs of that painting they say was brought from Orvieto, perhaps so that the distance of the origin might also distance the painting and hide the real intentions of its creator . . .''

''Silence, Brother, please, silence.''

''Very well. But what I want to tell you is that there is no reason to pity El Señor, or to compare him to ourselves.''

''We have sworn obedience to him.''

''But there are many degrees of obedience, and above that of service to El Señor is the obedience you owe your art and I owe science; and above all, that we owe God."

"Silence, please, silence; El Señor believes that to obey him is to obey God; there is no room either for your science or for my painting in the two obligations that govern us."

"And nevertheless, in these papers El Señor doubts, and you believe that El Señor's doubt is similar to our secular faith."

"Yes, I believe that; obscurely, piously, I believe it . . . or at least I want to believe it."

"But it isn't true, Brother; his doubt is not doubt, his doubt is not our doubt; El Señor still lives in the old world, and truth may not be found among all those conceptual and analytical subtleties, distinctions, questions, and suppositions; these are the things you and I are going to leave behind forever: the words El Señor consigned to paper in these folios through the fervent hand of his lackey Guzmán are like a pile of bricks without cement or mortar to bind them; the least breath of air can tumble them, the cement is missing; their union is poetry and poetry is the lime, the sand, and the water of all things, poetry is logical knowledge, poetry is the fullness of human activity and creation; and poetry tells us, without El Señor's doubts and tricks of logic, that nothing is as audacious or sinful as El Señor believes, that there is nothing that is unbelievable, and that nothing is impossible for the profound poetry that binds all things together. Poetry is cohesion and coherence; your art and my science tell us, Brother, that the possibilities we deny are merely possibilities we still do not know. Condemn those possibilities, as has El Señor, and you give them the name of evil. Open yourself to them, and you will know the solidarity of good and evil, how they mutually nourish one another, and the impossibilities of dissociating them: can you split a coin in half and still call it a ducat? The only reason El Señor examines his doubts is to conserve an order; he places his trust in the fact that the truth revealed can withstand all assaults upon it, those of reason as well as those of imagination; believe that, Brother Julián."

"You and I, then . . . do we wish to destroy that order?"

"Now I am the one to say: silence, please, silence; let us simply proceed with our work, confident that the order of mathematics and the order of painting are, or in the end will be, identical to divine order."

"In truth, you have not answered my question."

"Allow me to answer in my fashion. Although nature, like the tormented Tantalus, has an insatiable hunger and thirst, nothing, basically, is destroyed; rather, nature creates a succession of new lives and new forms for her own nourishment; time destroys, but nature produces more rapidly than death destroys. In the depths of his soul, El Señor is opposed to nature; he opposes it, Brother, and this is the limited grandeur of his impossible combat; the earth wishes to lose life, desiring only constant reproduction: El Señor wishes to save his life, denying the increment of this holy terrestrial substance ordained by God. Not an inch further, El Señor has declared to nature, sequestering it forever within a parallel universe of stone and death: this palace. Who will denounce him for it if everyone, El Señor and you and I, are prisoners of the earliest and most ancient thoughts conceived by men in opposition to the cosmos? El Señor is the prisoner of the idea of a world designed by the Deity in a single act of immutable, irrepeatable, intransformable revelation; you and I are tributaries of the idea of a divine emanation which is in perpetual flux, realized by continual transformation . . . Yes, our poor Señor. He believes that, like creation itself, perfection is unfeeling, immutable, and unalterable.''

''Yes, I can see you are right. That is why he ordered the construction of this palace.''

''Then, like moles, ants, mice, and acids, like slow-moving rivers, like the wind, or the termite, you and I, allies of time and flux, must undermine his project from within so that the palace itself may suffer the imperfection of being alterable, generative, and mutable, for this is the law of nature, and there would be no benefits, but only misery, if the earth were one enormous pile of unfeeling sand, or one enormous mass of immutable jade, or if, following the flood, the frozen waters had turned it into an enormous crystal globe, perfect, but unalterable. Our Señor deserves to find himself encountering a Medusa head that would transform him into a diamond statue: he would find perfection there. But that may be his fear: to be transformed into something else, anything, even an eternal statue lacking life or movement.''

''But God is eternal, unchanging, as El Señor wishes to be; and God lives . . . He is . . .''

''Everything that is eternal is circular, and what is circular is eternal. My God, Brother! Do you not yet realize that this movement, this change, this perpetual regeneration means that God creates, creates unceasingly, animates everything, makes it spin for His greater glory, as if He wished to see His own creation from every angle, from every perspective, in the round, wished every conceivable view of the flowing marvels He conceives?''

''And you claim to have observed that movement, that order, in the heavens, to know when and where the stars are moving, how they are measured, and what they produce? Can you, therefore, deny that your pride is as great as El Señor's, for even though you will not admit it, you believe you possess the same genius as the Creator of the heavens?''

''I only believe that, having logically approached a comprehension of the structure of the universe, which God knew instantly and without temporal rationality, whereas we approach that comprehension step by step, and rationally, it would be ruinous to divorce the word of God from the work of God. The truth that astronomy demonstrates is the same truth already known to Divine Wisdom. Or do you believe that everything you see here should be destroyed, my charts, my spheres, my crystals, that I should cease to observe the heavens so that the divine presence might be made manifest without obstacles? Whom would my inactivity benefit? God, who brought me into the world so that I might know a fraction of what He has always known? El Señor himself, our temporal sovereign, who, in spite of everything, changes, suffers, and decays like every other living thing, and who needs that someone, although he would never say it, know the truth? Believe me, Brother; it is better that someone know these things, even if in silence; someday they can be, if not the accepted truth, at least an alternative to a policy of despair, or what is the same thing, repetition. And endless repetition changes the name of the despair that nourishes it; finally, Julián, it is called destruction.''

"Brother Toribio; I love you; you know that. I am merely saying what the Holy Office would say if it knew . . . if it knew that you affirm these things.''

"The partial knowledge of one man does not offend the total knowledge of God.''

"They would say that the center of the universe is the earth, the seat of Creation, the seat of humanity, and the seat of the Church . . .''

"Does it diminish the omnipotence of God to say that what God once performed can never happen again? Invert this negative proposition and you will understand what it is I do: little by little I identify human thought with divine thought, not with past thought, but thought that is taking place now; not with the design revealed one day, a simple initial act, but with its flow, its perpetual emanation and transformation.''

"You are looking into a deep abyss, and you make me dizzy.''

"I am not looking at the shadows of the cavern; I am bathing in the river. That is my desire.''

"May it also be your fear. For through that hole you have opened in the heavens our spirits may drain away from us, and if we lose our souls, what good will your frozen rhomboids and triangles do us?''

"The universe is infinite; perhaps we may lose what we consider our individual soul, and gain the soul of all creation . . .''

"Oh, my brother, and what if your discoveries carry you to this terrible, terrible conclusion: what if you discover that the divine order of the infinite is one thing, and the infinite order of nature something different? What if we discover that there are two infinites? Which would we choose, Brother?''

Toribio bowed his head and walked toward the table where the ustorious mirror stood. He did not speak for a long time. The day burst forth and the rays of the sun began to play upon the icy crystal. Finally he spoke: "I do not know what to answer."

"They will say that if the universe is ruled by its own laws, the powers of the Holy Father are not important, or those of powerful Señores like our own, or . . ."

The supplicant friar began to stammer; Brother Toribio spoke reluctantly. "I imagine nothing of this; no; that is what God does; it is God who made man mortal, for had He made him immortal, neither the world nor the presence of man in the world would have been necessary; man is mortal, therefore the world exists as the abode of mortality. Is this true, Brother?"

"They will condemn you, Brother; this is true: man was created immortal, in the image and semblance of God; and only because of Original Sin did he lose his divine attributes. Our religion is based upon these three stones: Original Sin, inherent corruption, and divine pardon. Destroy these foundations and you destroy the very edifice of the Church, which would then have no reason for being; for if man did not sin originally, then he is still God-like and can commune directly with God, without need for the mediating grace of the Church . . ."

". . . Was the proposal of creation to bind the feet and hands of man and then immediately condemn him because he cannot walk? No, Brother; for me, man's mortality is part of the divine plan of Creation; for me, dying is part of man's freedom, of God's loving paternity, and of the law of movement and change; these are my three foundation stones, it must be so; God made the earth in the form of a sphere and set it spinning in a uniform revolution with other celestial bodies that alter the earth and consequently are themselves alterable. If this is the eternal law of the universe, how could the law of the tiny man inhabiting a tiny planet be any different?, how?, how, Brother?, if the universe changes and decays and dies and is renewed, why would we be the exception? No, man was conceived mortal, he was born to die, and there is no inherent corruption in him, but rather corporeal and spiritual perfectibility."

"And if there is no sin or corruption, divine pardon is unnecessary. No, Brother! They will judge you, they will condemn you, they will force you first to retract, and then they will burn you, Brother; the earth does not spin as you say it does, or rise or descend, because above the earth is Heaven . . ."

"I tell you that the earth is in the heavens!"

". . . and beneath the earth is Hell, and it will not be you who crumbles the hierarchies of established truth."

"And nevertheless, man's death is the condition of his eternity."

Brother Toribio placed the face of the concave crystal of the ustorious mirror toward the sun, and the sun obeyed, casting its rays with fury upon the crystal. The friar placed the folios of El Señor's testament beneath the lens. Brother Julián ran to stay the hand of the uranographer: "Brother, what are you doing, what new madness is this? Guzmán will ask me for these papers, they bear the seal of our Señor . . ."

The sun's rays began to burn the papers, clustered together in the ring of the lens, a tightly bound fascine of fire. "Do not worry about Guzmán, he is an unimportant lackey; place the blame on me, Brother; say it was my carelessness, an accident . . ."

The smoldering, curling flames devoured the folios.

"You are right, Brother. I shall say nothing."

"Let these condemnable papers be burned, Julián, and the volumes of my library be saved. Look at them; their pages are in Arabic and Hebrew script. They could be considered more culpable than these dark blasphemies and foolish heresies dictated by El Señor to Guzmán, and delivered to you by Guzmán . . . under what pretext, by the way?"

"The same I used when I gave the papers of the Chronicler to him, which was how El Señor discovered these dissident heretics that today so delight and perturb him. Go, Guzmán, I told him, let El Señor see these papers, he will understand their contents. Guzmán said the same thing to me today. That he understood nothing. That I judge."

Julián looked at Toribio with great affection. "I shall say nothing."

The two friars embraced, and Toribio whispered to Julián: "I shall write nothing, as the disciples of Pythagoras wrote nothing. But not because of fear, oh, no, Brother . . ."

"You do well; believe that my spirit is relieved, knowing your resolution."

"But understand me: not from fear . . ."

And Julián, embracing his comrade, not seeing his eyes, but feeling in the encompassing embrace the trembling of the astrologer-priest, did not wish to ask: Are you weeping?, is it then because of pride since it is not fear?; but Toribio himself spoke: "Because of my scorn. There are more drones than bees in this world. I shall not reveal what I know to the mockery of mediocre men. I have spent much time, much love and care, in understanding a few things that for me are beautiful: I shall not expose myself either to the scorn or the mockery of miserable charlatans . . . Mockery, Brother: 'Look what this squint-eyed Chaldean has seen through his powerful crystals, with his celestial spectacles . . .'"

"Brother . . . sit down . . . wait . . . rest."

"I shall disclose nothing; we will wait. I shall disclose nothing, but neither shall El Señor. The sun will devour both his words and mine."

"And if El Señor himself asks an accounting of the destruction of his papers?"

"As is my courtly custom, I shall draw him a happy horoscope; there I shall demonstrate that the destructive sign of Scorpio determined the fatal loss of his testament. He will accept his unfortunate loss in exchange for the many false ventures that with eulogies and dithyrambs and comparisons to the gods and heroes of antiquity I shall announce to him. And that will be that, Brother. Come; let us go drink; let us go laugh . . . although he who laughs last, weeps first."

A pilgrim without a country, the son of several lands, and therefore the forgotten orphan of all lands, Celestina's companion, the blond youth with the blood-red cross upon his back, attempted to recognize in the feeble light of this dawn the place where he had been led; he walked to the foot of the astronomer's tall stone tower which reminded him vaguely of other buildings similarly oriented toward the stars. The youth's desire soared upward with that of the ascendant, supplicant tower. He looked about him; he saw the flat land of Castile, the calm dust of early morning, the even and shadowless silhouette of the mountains at dawn standing darkly against the first rays of the sun; he saw the swift passing of black horses, and the slow step of steaming oxen dragging carts heaped with straw, hay, and blocks of granite; with an early-morning flock of storks, he flew in search of a nesting site, he heard the cawing of the crows circling above the roofs of this interminable palace, he smelled the burned skin and dripping fat of a lamb roasting in some tile shed on the work site, and he listened to the first cattle bells of the day; he touched the gray stone of the tower and there, in spite of the recentness of the construction, his fingers felt an ancient and persistent sign of life, a hollow mysteriously worked in the stone, and in that sheltered place a tiny sprig of wheat was germinating. The pilgrim looked toward that land to which he had returned and asked himself whether it was so inhospitable that wheat was forced to grow in stone; and he tried to recall other fields, in another world he had known where tall green stalks grew bearing thick, flexible, hard, and yellow leaves, he thought of a different bread, the bread of the other world, the red and yellow grains.

He raised his arms above his head, he held his open palms to the sky, to the tower, not knowing as he did so whether he was praying, giving thanks, or attempting to remember; and in the instant he held his hands toward the dawn sky, two stones fell from the top of the tower, one large, the other smaller, the larger upon his left palm and the smaller on the right; the stones were cold, as if they had been all night in the cold night air; but as he closed his fists around them, the youth, excited by this miracle, quickly communicated warmth to them; the skies of Spain rained stones.

He returned to Jerónimo's forge, drawn by the soft, sad sound of a flute being played, with closed eyes, by the stranger arrived the night before, that strange, first night the pilgrim had spent in Castilian lands, one he would always remember, when lights moved unassisted along the passageways of the dark palace, when wheat grew in stone, when dead falcons flew from windows, and bats—he had seen it—soared back and forth above his head carrying mutilated limbs, shinbones, ears, skulls; when, finally, the skies rained stones.

The youth clutched the stones as if they were two precious jewels. He reached the forge where Jerónimo, Celestina, and the blind flutist maintained their vigil. Above the strains of the plaintive flute, he heard the footsteps of an armed company approaching across the plain. Jerónimo rose to his feet. Celestina took his arm.

"It does not matter," she said. "Let them come and take us with them. That is the reason my companion and I have come."

The flutist ceased his playing and cleaned his instrument, wiping it upon the tatters of his ancient doublet. The pilgrim kept the two stones in his hands as the members of El Señor's guard seized an unresisting Celestina; they approached the youth, and he, too, offered no resistance; he had known, since the night in the mountains when he had made love to the page-and-drummer with the tattooed lips, that he had come to this place in order to face a Señor and tell him what the pilgrim himself—though he knew it—was reluctant to believe.

THE SECOND TESTAMENT

"I . . I . . . by the grace of God . . . knowing, according to the doctrine of St. Paul the Apostle . . . what comes after that, Guzmán, what are the words dictated by our testamentary tradition?"

". . . how, following sin, it is ordained by Divine Providence that all men die in punishment of it. Señor, it is not time . . ."

". . . and as the goodness of our God is so full and great . . . how, Guzmán?, read it, read me what it says in the breviary . . ."

"That that same death which is punishment for our guilt is received by Him as due preparation of life, and we suffer it gladly . . . Señor, for God's . . ."

"Gladly, Guzmán? Have you seen my preternaturally aged members, my body sapped by the excesses inherited from those mummies and skeletons that the day before yesterday we entombed here for all time, the flame of my body that in spite of everything persists in igniting, and which must then be extinguished with penitence, words of repentance, flagellation, and unending nightmares . . . for I have no right to contaminate Isabel; true, Guzmán?"

"Do not vex yourself so, Señor . . ."

"If she became pregnant, Guzmán, what would be born of our coupling but another corpse, a monster dead before it was born, a tiny mummy destined to the cradle of the sepulcher, to be rocked in one of the crypts we have constructed here, is that not true, Guzmán?''

"And from your union with Inés, Señor, what will be born?''

"Evil; the unknown. Why did you bring her to me?''

"The unknown, yes. Perhaps good; chance; the renewal of your blood.''

"And patience . . . ? What do I say now? What does the dogma say?''

". . . and we come to our death with rational will, compelled not so much by the natural obligation of death, as to welcome it as transit and passage to eternal felicity and the well-lived life . . .''

"Doubt, Guzmán, doubt; look in my mirror; climb the thirty-three steps of my stairway and give the lie to dogma, affirm in opposition to the dogma that if we are resurrected it will be in ethereal flesh or in flesh different from that in which we live, are constituted, and move upon the earth; affirm, Guzmán, that if we are resurrected it may well be in the form of a sphere lacking any resemblance to the body we inhabit; deny, too, that on the day of final judgment resurrection will be simultaneous for all the men who have been born upon the earth, and that instead each will be resurrected in his time and his manner, from the bellies of she-wolves, from the coupling of dogs, from the eggs of serpents, from the indifferent union of the insects that infest stagnant waters; and by this reasoning we can believe, trembling, that the formation of the human body—in the womb of Isabel, in the womb of Inés, in the breast of my mother—is the work of the Devil, and that those conceptions in the womb of my mother or Inés or Isabel are the result of demons; yes, Guzmán, for if the first God—whom we do not know and who does not know us—created a first, perfect Heaven, there was no place in it for the imperfection of mortal men who are but the creations of Lucifer; Lucifer is the wound in the perfect Heaven through which Paradise seeps, the crack through which oozes the creation of something that is of no interest to an all-perfect and all-powerful God: men, you and I, Guzmán; take advantage of the birth of this new day to write my second testament; this I bequeath them: a future of resurrections that may be glimpsed only in forgotten pauses, in the orifices of time, in the dark empty minutes during which the past tried to imagine the future. This I bequeath: a blind, pertinacious, and painful return to the imagination of the future in the past and the only future possible to my race and my land. Do you understand what I am saying, Guzmán? Append, append these harsh formulas. This is my second testament.''

"Señor, there is no time now. And this second testament is unnecessary since you dictated another yesterday.''

"Append what I say. Yesterday I did not know Inés. Append. Add words to words. Will this palace survive? Should it not survive, let words serve as its continuity and reproduce the life that was lived within it.''

"So that dying we shall be faithful and loyal witnesses to the infallible truth that our God spoke to the first fathers: that sinning, they, and we their descendants, all would die . . .''

"False, Guzmán: God does not desire; God does not exist: God is but potential, He can do anything, but it serves Him naught, for He neither desires nor exists; He despises us; sin is being, sin is loving. Guzmán, Guzmán, what intolerable pain . . . come, place the red stone in the palm of my hand . . .''

"Have you finished, Sire?''

"Yes, yes . . . Guzmán, do you never doubt?''

"If I had power, Señor, I should never doubt anything.''

"But you do not have it, poor Guzmán.''

"And soon you shall not have it if you do not act against the dangers that threaten you.''

"I know well these dangers; they are the menace of a too-enlightened soul; they lurk about me here, in this chamber, in these galleries, in this chapel; I know them all too well, Guzmán; they are the dangers of the man who possesses both wisdom and power, irreconcilable gifts; I wish I were a brute like my murdering and warring ancestors who lie outside there in my crypt and chapel; to exercise power unaware; what relief, Guzmán, what profound peace, if only it could be so; the accumulation of time has added knowledge, doubt, skepticism, and the weakness of tolerance to the original deposit of power; that is the danger, can you not realize it?; I exorcise that danger with words, penitence, reason, and delirium; with sins, to the end of being pardoned . . .''

"Your danger lies outside, Señor, and only power can undo it.''

"Power? Again?''

"Always, Señor.''

"Was one crime not enough? Did I not fulfill my duties to power by basing it, that one time, upon the death of innocents?''

"This is vital, Señor; you must again act as God acts: not by being; not by loving; only by being able—power. You have said it yourself.''

"And I myself rejected it.''

"You cannot pay your debts with the words of your testament.''

"What are you saying? Everything belongs to me. The earth is mine; the earth is bounded, limited, by what I possess. Everything the land produces is mine, harvests, herds, everything is brought to my palace, delivered to my gates by vassals and serfs as it was to the gates of my fathers and my grandfathers . . .''

"Yes; your vassals still bring what they owe you under the old laws, but there are fewer vassals and less tribute, and the expenses of the construction are greater, and greater, too, the number of products that no longer pass through your hands. The cities, Sire . . . the cities today receive the greatest part of the riches . . .''

"But I continue to receive what I have always received: such is the law of my kingdoms . . .''

"Yes, and a good law it was when you received more than anyone else. But today, though you continue to receive the same, you receive much less than others. The cities, Señor. Almost everything today is taken directly from the fields to the nearest city instead of making the long trip to this palace, and from the city, merchants bring things here, and you must pay for them. You continue to receive what you have always received: so many head of cattle, so many sheaves of wheat, so many bales of hay. But you must now pay for things not due your sovereignty. Cadavers arrive here from great distances, but not the eggs, vegetables, bacon that are delivered to the markets of the burghers. These are no longer the golden times of your father, Señor . . .''

"What are you saying to me? Eggs, vegetables! I am speaking to you of death and sin and the resurrection of souls, and you speak to me of bacon?''

"Without eggs and bacon, one cannot speak of the soul. The world beyond the castles has changed, without your having realized it. Forgive my effrontery. The people constantly require less and less from you. People have invented their own world, without corpses, without sin, without the torments of the soul . . .''

"Then it did no good to kill them. Then heresy has triumphed. Then I am an imbecile. Is this what you are saying?''

"Señor, my devotion is to you alone, and it includes speaking the truth. I know nothing of theology. I only know that instead of working at your command and for the use of your kingdom, now men are producing things without your command, and selling them . . .''

"To whom?''

"To how many, you mean. Why, to buyers: whomever; they receive money; they use intermediaries; they specialize; there are new powers being formed not upon blood but upon the commerce of salt, leather, wine, wheat, and meat . . .''

"My power is of divine origin.''

"There is a greater divinity, if you will forgive me, Señor, and that power is called money. And the law of that god is that after debts are contracted, they must be paid. Señor: your coffers are empty.''

"What, then, is being used to pay the servants of this palace? The construction? The workmen?''

"Precisely, Sire; there is nothing left with which to pay them. This is what I urgently needed to tell you, once the ceremonies for the dead had been concluded. I did not want to bother you before that. Now it is my duty to inform you that the construction of the crypts for your ancestors, and the costly transportation of all the corpses here, have consumed everything that remained."

"But the riches within the palace; the iron railings forged in Cuenca, the balustrades from Zaragoza, the Italian marbles, the Florentine bronzes, the Flemish candelabra . . ."

"All still owed; nothing has been paid; your credit is great, but the moment for payment has arrived."

"What? Why are you holding my testament? What is that new paper?"

"A detailed listing of what is owed: debts with smiths, shipowners, butchers, carpenters, bakers, salt merchants, weavers, fullers, dyers, shoemakers—and look here, one of them is complaining that the youth who accompanied your mother forced him to eat the leather of his shoes; he asks indemnification for it; one must pay for such willful behavior—harness makers, drapers, vintners, brewers, barbers, doctors, tavern keepers, tailors, silk merchants . . . Should I continue, Señor?"

"But, Guzmán, everything used to be produced here in the castle . . ."

"There is no one now but the workmen constructing the palace and those of the religious orders, who serve death. There is honor. There is no money."

"And what do you propose, Guzmán?"

Guzmán walked to the entrance to the bedchamber; he parted the curtain separating it from the chapel. A stooped old man was standing behind the curtain. A short fur cape protected him against the cold of the early morning and the long night's vigil in the stone chapel; but the cape did not warm the rock crystal of his carved, avaricious features, or the blue snow of his eyes.

A cap of marten skins covered his head; his long, knotted fingers toyed with a silver medallion hanging upon his emaciated chest; his black breeches clung loosely to spindly legs. His toothless mouth was distorted into an obsequious smile; this old javel bowed before El Señor, professed his fealty, and thanked him for the honor of being received; he had waited many hours, all night, in that icy chapel, with no companion but the dead; it was a most sumptuous chapel, what had the balustrades, the marbles, the paintings, the sepulchers themselves, cost?; a fortune, doubtlessly, a fortune; the quality of the workmanship, the cost of the transport, then the installation, which was also very costly, no doubt . . .

No, he wasn't complaining about the wait; he had observed, he had seen; he had admired the great construction; no one except the royal servants knew what it was like inside; curiosity was high, as great as the fame of this interminable palace; and he had special reason to appreciate this place and he wasn't complaining of the fatiguing trip he had undertaken from Seville so that he might know it, so he might offer his service to El Señor and also know the place where his daughter, the rare fruit of a late marriage, was preparing to take her vows; strange girls, those of today, Señor, and his girl—instead of taking advantage of everything an aged father close to death and made rich by commerce and the moneylending arts could offer her—preferred to cloister herself in this palace; surely the old adage was right: when an old man has a daughter, if he's lucky, she'll pay him heed, but if she's inclined to madness, she's very mad indeed; and add to that fact that she's a Sevillian, then if she turns out all right, she's one in a million; well, the blood is tired, and the child of an old man is early an orphan; tired the blood, yes, but not the mind, especially if throughout a lifetime that mind has been sharpened, day in and day out, by the clever dealings demanded by the merchant's trade and by the evil called usury, which in truth is not an evil at all but an act of charity; but in any case, experience is the best teacher, and as a merchant I just go on my way, you know, not too much loss, not too much pay, though if I do say so, I've had a sharp nose when it comes to detecting when the price of metals is going up and when the price of salt is going down, and dealing accordingly with my colleagues on the Baltic and the Adriatic, for the merchant who doesn't know his lore closes his store; invest a little here, withdraw a little there, the coin of a miser is money that's wiser . . . a marvelous word, money, Señor; money . . . fondle it, sow it, and watch it grow, fertilized by commerce and manufacture, into a tree with great spreading branches, mining, maritime transport, the administration of lands, and loans to princes in need of funds for war, exploration . . . and the construction of palaces.

Ah, this palace should be completed, didn't El Señor think so?, it would be a shame to leave it half done, just a shell, looking as if the curses of Heaven had rained down upon it; it was El Señor's lifework, wasn't it, and it was for this he would be remembered in centuries to come; it was to erect this palace that he'd devastated the ancient Castilian orchard, turned it to dust, had removed peasants from their lands and shepherds from their hills, and put them to work as laborers in exchange for wages, very well, very well, and there's nothing I can teach you on this subject, Señor, you're aware that there's no reason the products necessarily should belong to the man who produces them, what good do they do him without the legs of someone to carry his produce to market for him, and the hands of a lender who can provide in case of a bad harvest, a storm, an accident, or overspending? We've been damned, Señor, and nevertheless I insist our mission is one of charity. And we've not always been well paid. In my long life I have known grandees of these Spanish lands who out of pure madness for

luxury and honor and appearances have after plowing their lands planted them with silver, as if the metal could sprout and yield new fruit; I
have known them to cook with candles of precious wax in order to impress their own scullions, and impress themselves; I have known them
at the end of a celebration to order thirty horses to be burned alive, for
the pure pleasure of the wasteful spectacle that allows them to believe
they are above the common mortal. And the worst is that they have at
times murdered the moneylenders who come to their aid. You see,
then, Señor, the demands and dangers of my miserable office.

In any case, let every whore ply her trade and every ruffian turn his
deal, the products must belong to those who encourage their production, transform them, increase their value greatly, didn't El Señor
agree?, times have changed, the codes of yesteryear no longer have
their old following, their old value; it used to be that illness and hunger
caused men to cherish hopes of the world beyond, but now a man can
work, Señor, dedicate his life to hard labor, and harvest his fruits right
here on earth, and in spite of low origins, know the favors of merit, if
not those of blood: money makes a man whole and when he has bread
his suffering is diminished: I live, Exalted Señor, from what I earn and
from the money I change; that will not impede me from serving you
and from sustaining with my tired old bones a power based on inherited rank. Do not judge me harshly; new times, new ways; the interdic-
tions of our faith, which have dealt so harshly with my office, belong to
a destroyed and sick and hungry world, Señor, to a stagnant world; the
sinful stigma cast upon the practice of usury by Christians forced Jews
to fulfill this necessary function; but if you persecute the Jews, who
will fulfill it?, and will an act of necessary charity be condemned when
pure Christians like myself practice it, Señor? Then my occupation
must be accepted as a sign of a strengthened and salutary faith which
promises two Paradises: one here and one beyond, one now and one
later: is this not an admirable promise? And finally, one must consider
that my sins, if they are sins, are compensated and perhaps even pardoned by the fact that my sweet daughter, my only heir, to whom, naturally, I shall leave all my money, is preparing in this very palace for
her permanent vows and her marriage with Christ.

So sooner or later, Señor, my copious wealth will have to pass
through the hands of the good nuns of your palace, for Inés, my daughter, will by then have made her personal vow of poverty. As a result,
what I am now more than disposed to lend you so that you can pay
your debts—at a modicum of interest, twenty percent annually—will
not only resolve your present but your future problems as well: my
money, thanks to Inesilla, will revert to El Señor's fortune, as the
girl—whom from the chapel I watched leave your bedchamber this
night—will again demonstrate her devotion to El Señor, in the same

way El Señor demonstrates his devotion to her father in a thousand little ways, for in dealing with El Señor a man will not have to come many times to the well, and anyone who comes to the aid of El Señor must surely receive something more than the ordinary moneylender's interest, for El Señor can make a gentleman of a flea, and permit me in December to enjoy the pleasures of May, and add honor to riches. You will emerge the winner, Sire, believe me, you will emerge the winner.

Now, if this gentleman can prepare the paper, the pen, the ink, the blotting sand, and seals, we can proceed to an agreement; I am cold, I am sleepy, it has been a very long night and in my long waiting, seated behind the chancel of the nuns, I have dreamed terrible dreams. Forgive my excessive loquacity; let us get on with it; it is getting late, let us get on with it.

El Señor, numb in body and soul, took the pen. But first, narrowing his glassy eyes, he asked: "If I may, I would like to pose a question to this gentleman: If your powers as a merchant and moneylender are so extensive, why do you accept mine?"

The aged moneylender bowed his head. "Unity, Sire, unity. Without a visible head, bodies are wont to be dispersed. Without a supreme power to which to appeal, we would devour each other like wolves. Thank you, Sire."

That morning Guzmán attended El Señor as he tended his sick falcons, with various ointments, brews, and infusions to ease the complaints of his prostrate master exhausted by ills too long held at bay which suddenly appeared, scourge in hand, and by sleeplessness, lovemaking, and the increasing horror of his conscience.

"Drink this, Señor"—Guzmán held the potion to his lips—"drink this grama tea that is an admirable remedy against difficulties of the urine and especially against those resulting from ulcers of the bladder, and let me rub your feet with this hot, damp bile of the wildcat, which soothes and assuages the pain of gout."

"Who opened the skylight, Guzmán? The room is filled with mosquitoes; it is summer, and as the ponds on this plain are dead water, mosquitoes feed there."

"Do not worry, Señor, I have placed a vessel containing bear's blood beneath your bed, and all the mosquitoes will gather there and drown."

"And I, I am drowning . . ."

"But, Señor, you should be happy; that aged Sevillian moneylender has given us new life, the palace can be completed; you must reward him; besides, he is the father of the novitiate, give him the title, at least, of Comendador; he is old, give him that pleasure before he dies."

El Señor moaned. "Who is that old man, who is he, really? Is he the

Devil, a homunculus come here to humiliate me, to offer me money in exchange for my life; but that is the most horrible sin of simony, does he want my soul in exchange for his money?''

"This is the way of progress, Señor, and the old Sevillian does not exercise a diabolic profession but a liberal one."

"Liberal? Progress?''

"Progress like that of the sun in its daily course, or of the corpses of your grandfathers to this palace, except that it is now applied to the ascendant road of an entire society; and liberal, Señor, as befits free men who are opposed to servility."

"But as the sun is born and dies on the horizon, so I conceive that this progress of yours will die of the same causes that engender it; and insofar as liberal is concerned, any serf that attempted to be liberal would run counter to the laws of nature; I do not know these words."

"The only knowledge is action, Señor."

"There is hereditary dignity, Guzmán, that cannot be bought or sold."

"There is the dignity of risk, Señor, one can live with and like either angels or the Devil, one may choose; knowing his limitations, one is free to ascend or descend."

"No, Guzmán, the only human hierarchy is based upon possession of an immortal soul and its patrimony in the life eternal."

"No, Señor, there is fate, there is fortune, and there is the virtue which constantly checks that hierarchy and transforms it; man is the glory, the mockery, and the enigma of the world, and the world is an undecipherable enigma either for man's glory or for his mockery."

"There is repression, humiliation, and sacrifice, in order to gain eternal life, Guzmán."

"There is passion, ambition, and desire to gain earthly life, Señor."

"Wisdom is revealed, Guzmán."

"Prudence is acquired through trial and error, Sire."

"The highest ideal is that of the contemplative gentleman meditating upon the Scriptures and the dogma of the Revelation, Guzmán."

"There are no absolute ideals, Señor, only secular prizes for a life of action."

"Truths are eternal, Guzmán, and I do not want them to change, I do not want that primary wisdom my family has conserved for centuries to be converted into an object of usury, to be debauched by men like that old man, a man so low he would sell his own daughter, and the multitude like him; I know them, Guzmán, I know their horrifying history, I recall the fate of the Children's Crusade that set forth to do battle for Christ in the land of the Infidel but instead fell into the hands of Hughes Ferreus and Guillaume Porcus, arms makers of Marseilles, who offered the children free transport to the Holy Land, but actually carried them to the barbarous coasts of Africa, where they sold the innocents as slaves to the Arabs. And will you tell me that I, too, have killed, Guzmán? Yes, but in the name of power and the Faith, or in the name of the power of the Faith, but never for money. And I suspect that he who dedicates his toil to money can be nothing but a falsifying Jew, a convert, a filthy pig, even though he bears the name of a pure Christian; the doctor who mutilated my own mother and almost killed her said his name was Cuevas, and he insisted he was a good and pure Spaniard until they discovered the prayer books and candelabra of Jewry in his house. Are you amazed by the confidence I place in you, Guzmán? Now you shall know: the Spanish nobility is infested with converted Jews, false faithful, and only among the people of your own low estate does one find today the old, uncontaminated Christian bloodlines. Do not tell me now, Guzmán, that you have allied yourself with the enemies of our eternal order . . ."

"Señor, for God's sake, everything I do, I do because of intense devotion to your interests . . ."

"But you believe that my interests can be reconciled with those of that band of merchants and moneylenders, simonists, enemies of the Holy Spirit?"

"They can and they must be, Señor; the new forces are a reality: dominate them or they will dominate you. That is my sincere counsel."

"No, no, I am right, our line ends here and now, the world may die with us but it will not change, the world is well contained within the limits of this palace, Guzmán; whom are you defending, on whose side are you?, tell me."

"Señor, I repeat, I serve El Señor, I advise him and I warn him that he must make use of the new powers so they do not make use of him: if you honor him with the title of Comendador, the aged moneylender will feel an obligation to honor and obey El Señor; at the same time El Señor can enjoy Doña Inés, and renew his blood, now that the seed is weary of growing in the same field; recognize the bastard and contravene the madness and intrigue of the Queen Mother who offers an idiot heir; and if not her madness, then the restlessness of the workmen who are sheltering a second pretender who arrived yesterday in the company of a page-and-drummer who is actually a woman, although dressed in the customary attire of a man, part of your mother's train; threat is added to threat, the designs of the women and the designs of the world are being joined, and if El Señor wishes somewhere to encounter the Devil, he may find him in the horrendous coupling of woman and the world."

"What are you doing to avert these threats?"

"What it is my place to do: order the arrest of the masquerading drummer and her young companion, and if El Señor authorizes, torture them."

"Why?"

"They went directly to the forge of the smith Jerónimo, and have remained there with all the grumbling workmen my men have heard and observed."

"A drummer who is actually a woman . . ."

"A Devil with tattooed lips, Señor."

"A youth accompanying her, you say?"

"Yes, identical to . . . to the young Prince your mother brought here, even down to the signs of a common monstrosity: six toes on each foot, and a blood-red cross upon their backs . . ."

"Twins, Guzmán? Do you know the prophecy?"

"No, Señor . . ."

"Twins always announce the end of dynasties. They are the excess that promises immediate extinction. And a swift renascence. Ah, Guzmán, why have you been so slow to reveal these things to me? Can these twins be the dual sign of the disappearance of my house and the foundation of a new line? Guzmán, do not torture me any more; enough; have the usurpers, the enemies to my uniqueness and to the permanence of my order, arrived at the very doors of my palace?"

"I am not torturing El Señor; I use the root, slim as chard and bursting with pungent liquor, of the turpeth-of-the-East, a name that meant 'quitcares' . . . and I am relieved of one care, knowing that finally El Señor understands the singular nature of the dangers threatening him . . ."

"Bring the youth and the disguised girl before me. Help me, Guzmán, the pain . . ."

"I am helping El Señor, who only tortures himself. And I shall take charge of averting the threats of which I have spoken . . . with El Señor's permission."

"Enough, enough, Guzmán, the only care you can relieve me of is this fear that things change, that the world can exist beyond the world contained within my palace . . . You must realize, Guzmán: I killed innocent people in order to assure the permanence of my world. Do not tell me that usury, money, debt, and a pair of unknown youths threaten that world; do not snatch away, Guzmán, my reason for being; do not destroy the very foundation stone of my existence; everything . . . here . . . within the stone walls of my palace; here my doubts; here my crimes; here my loves; here my ills; here my Faith; here my mother and her Idiot Prince and her dwarf; here my untouched wife; here, part of me and my palace, these two strangers whom you will bring before me; here my contradictory words, Guzmán, and also my vulnerability; I know I am contradictory, as are my profound Faith and the string of heresies I repeat, to test it, yes, but also to demonstrate to you, to myself, to no one, to everyone, to the very walls, for they have ears, that my knowledge is as certain as it is weak, that that *prisca sa-*

pientia, that fundamental knowledge, is not foreign to me, I guard it here, here in my head, here in my breast, Guzmán, adding light to shadow and shadow to light so that somewhere, in spite of and because of contradictions, the intelligence may exist that nothing is totally good or totally evil; that I know, although not everyone believes or knows or understands that I know it, and this is the privilege of the long continuity of my house upon this earth, with all its crimes and madness, that justifies everything, Guzmán, that is my wisdom, and everything that has happened has happened so that someone, one person, one single person, that I, may know it, and that, sadly, is enough; one cannot use that wisdom in governing, for then, you are right, he would lose his kingdom, although not the knowledge that good and evil are one and that each nourishes the other; I know that, although it serves me no purpose, but your usurer from Seville does not know it, or your grumbling workmen, nor do you yourself know it, Guzmán, for on the day you, any of you, sit upon my throne, you will have to learn it again, beginning from nothing, and you will commit the same crimes but in the name of other gods: money, justice, that progress of which you speak; none of you will have the minimal tolerance my awareness of madness, evil, fatality, impossibility, human frailty, illness, pain, and the inconstancy of pleasure assures us. Balance, a precarious balance, Guzmán: to burn a youth only for an obviously abominable crime, and for no other; to protect the life but punish the guilt of my Chronicler by sending him to the galleys as a cure for his innocence; to make myself blind and deaf to any other evidence. Who did the painting in the chapel? You would want to know Guzmán, if you saw, as I have seen in it, a culpable rebelliousness of the soul, but I know how to be deaf and blind and mute when the solution to one problem creates a thousand new ones. Look at that map on the wall: look at its limits, the Pillars of Hercules, the mouths of the Tagus, Cape Finisterre, distant, frigid Iceland, then the universal abyss, the shoulders of Atlas, the slow and deliberate turtle upon whose shell the world rests: Guzmán, swear to me that there is nothing more; I would go mad if the world extended one inch beyond the confines we know; if it were so, I would have to learn everything again, begin everything again, and I would know no more than the usurer, the workman, or you know; my shoulders, like those of Atlas, are tired: I can bear no more weight; nor is there room on my head for one additional fathom of sea or one additional square acre of land; Spain is contained within Spain, and Spain is this palace . . ."

"Look at me, Señor," said Guzmán, "look at me, understand me, multiply the number of men like me, and be assured. Spain can no longer be contained within Spain."

Quickly, huntsmen, said Guzmán as he left the bedchamber of the delirious El Señor, send an armed guard to the plain and bring to El Señor's chapel that drummer and her young companion; we will not rest a moment, so as not to allow our exhausted sovereigns a moment's rest; let our muscles and our tireless blood act so we will heap fatigue upon the heads and hearts of our Señores; what good and efficient confederates I have, who imitated the howling of Bocanegra and thus justified the death of El Señor's favorite dog, who took advantage of El Señor's diseased sleep to exchange burned tapers for fresh ones, fill emptied pitchers, and reverse the time of the hourglasses; from the common grave where it slept the eternal sleep with the cadaver of Bocanegra, they rescued the corpse of the sailor who arrived here in the coffin of El Señor's father, and they buried it in its rightful tomb to mock the plans of the Mad Lady; quickly, let us act, for our way is action and theirs the madness of irrationality; quickly, let us find the Mad Lady and tell her that the proclamation announcing the Prince and the dwarf as heirs to the crown will take place this very morning; and the huntsmen who have insinuated themselves into the ranks of the rebellious workmen, let them go to the quarries, the forges, and the tile sheds, and tell men like Jerónimo and Martín and Nuño not to fear, that I am with them, that the gates of the palace will be open to them when they decide to attack; and let the workmen know who the heir is, that it is the Idiot who will rule at the death of El Señor; and you, huntsman, go and tell the Sevillian moneylender that El Señor has favored him by granting him the title and the honors of Comendador, and after the Comendador has been informed of his appointment, let him know, huntsman, that his daughter the novitiate has been seduced and violated by La Señora's young lover, and go to La Señora and tell her that the same novitiate who seduced El Señor now has captive another prisoner of love, the youth we rescued from the beach of the Cabo de los Desastres; and as for El Señor . . . I myself shall inform El Señor, at the opportune moment, that that same youth is the lover both of the novitiate and of La Señora, his untouched wife; and I shall inform him that there are not two intruders here but three, and that all three are identical, not twins but triplets, ha, and we shall see—as that ingenuous, stammering, cross-eyed Chaldean in the tower would say to the no less ingenuous, although scheming, Brother Julián—what black prophecy this triangular, not singular, situation suggests to him; we shall have pleasure, huntsmen, pleasure, hubbub, and hullabaloo; count on Guzmán; from this adventure—happen what may—we shall emerge stronger, I in the forefront, and then with me you, my faithful companions; count on Guzmán.

NOTHING HAPPENS

La Señora resorted to every known means; she summoned the maid-servants Azucena and Lolilla and promised them pleasures and riches if they would conspire with her and steal from the palace kitchens the many supplies she needed to perform certain ceremonies; and they happily obeyed, for all these two desired was excitement and bustle and buzz, and doing these services for La Señora merely increased their excuses for tittle-tattle and for flurries of activity: go down to the kitchen, down to the stables, steal everything La Señora had asked, hide it beneath their underskirts, poke it into their bodices between their breasts, and before they delivered the herbs and the roots and the paste and the flowers, tell everything, amidst bellows of laughter, to Señor Don Juan, cloaked in the brocade drapery torn from the wall of their mistress's bedchamber; now he was lodged in the servants' room awaiting the return of the novitiate Doña Inés, who unable to endure his absence any longer would one day come, head bowed, knock on the door, and beg for a second night, a second deflowering to free her from her spell: a succubus made virgin again.

In the meantime Don Juan began to dally, alternately, at times simultaneously, with the scrubbing maids, who told him between giggles and belches, between sips of wine stolen as they stole the hog's fat, between mouthfuls of ham stolen as they stole the ground sugar, what La Señora was doing in her bedchamber of Andalusian tiles and Arabian sands, lying beside that fresh cadaver fashioned from scraps of the royal mummies that had taken the place in her bed formerly occupied by Don Juan:

She has prepared an ointment from a hundred grams of animal fat and five of hashish, a half a handful of cannabis blossoms and a pinch of ground hellebore root; she rubbed it on the neck, behind the ears, under the arms, on the belly and the soles of the feet, and on the crook of the arm—on hers or the mummy's, Lolilla?—her own, Señor Don Juan, on her own, and then she waited for the clock to strike eleven on a Saturday night of the new moon, which was yesterday; then she dressed herself in a black tunic and placed a lead crown on her head, and covered her arms with lead bracelets set with onyx and sapphire and jade and black pearls; then on her little finger she placed a lead ring set with a stone engraved with the image of a coiled serpent; she sprinkled the mummy with fumigating powders made from sulphur, cobalt, chlorate, chalk, and copper oxide; she has surrounded the mummy with seven wands made from the seven metals of the planets: gold of the sun, La Señora murmured; silver of the moon; mercury of Mercury; copper of Venus; iron of Mars; tin of Jupiter; lead of Saturn; in her hand she clutched a new knife from old Jerónimo's forge on the plain—and one after another she picked up the seven wands and thrashed the cadaver, shouting words in Chinese or Arabic or some language we couldn't understand:

"Peradonai Eloim, Adonai Jehova, Adonai Sabaoth," said Don Juan, "Verbum Phytonicum, Mysterium Salamandrae, Conventus Sylphorum, Antra Gnomorum, Daemonia Coeli Gad, Veni, Veni, Veni!"

"And nothing happened, Señor Don Juan, nothing; the mummy just lay there, stiff and stretched out on the bed; and La Señora fell exhausted to the sand."

She's asked us for more things, the servants said in unison, and then Don Juan asked them for a monk's habit, a prince's doublet and breeches, a white tunic and a crown of thorns, and when they went to gather the materials La Señora had demanded, Don Juan, in the hooded robe of a monk, came to the cell of the novitiate Sister Angustias; he listened to the wails from within and then quietly tapped on the door. The Sister opened the door, still on her knees, naked, and with a penitential scourge in her hand; her shoulders and breasts were bleeding. When she saw the monk, Sister Angustias bent over till her head touched her knees and said, Father, Father, I have sinned, free me from my evil thoughts, Father, I do not want to dream of the bodies of the men who work here, the supervisors, the ironworkers, the water carriers, the masons, and Don Juan stroked the girl's shaved head, helped her to her feet, embraced her tenderly, and told her she should suffer no more, that she should think instead how being in the convent made her supremely free, how since she could not marry she was free to love within the convent; she was not subject to the bonds of human law that restrict a legitimate wife to fidelity to one man, her husband, whereas a nun could be the delectable love object of all men, and with these arguments he led her to the bed of bare planks; tenderly he removed the shreds of her bloodstained nightdress and kissed the novitiate's bleeding wounds, and his lips caused both pain and pleasure; Don Juan consoled her, caressing her swollen breasts and the palpitating scapulary of hair between her legs, I will not love you forever, I am making love to you to make you free, to make you a woman; accept me so you may learn to accept all men without shame: I tell you I will not love you forever, Sister Angustias, come, Angustias, believe me when I say I love myself more than I could ever love you, and oh, how beautiful you are, how your wounds shine against your olive skin, and how it pains me, loving myself so much, to have to love you even for a moment, how I long for refuge and escape from self-love in your deep jungles and the rolling hills of your flesh, Angustias; liberate me; I am liberating you. Weep with pleasure, little nun, weep; beg me to return someday; I do not know whether I shall be able, for there are more women in the world than stars in the sky, and there will not be time to love myself in loving them all.

We took more things to her, Azucena and Lolilla said, we had to go everywhere, even to the monk Toríbio's apothecary in his stargazing tower, scurrying like mice through tunnels and stairways, passageways and dungeons, and she prepared a new ointment from fifty grams of the extract of opium, thirty of betel, six of cinquefoil, fifteen of henbane, a few grams of belladonna, the same amount of hemlock, two hundred and fifty grams of Indian hemp, five of cantharides, and then some gum tragacanth and ground sugar; look, Don Juan, Your Mercy, it's all written down here on this paper she gave us so we wouldn't forget the names; we had a hard time, but we spelled them out on the monk Toríbio's porcelain jars; and besides all that, she said in a loud voice that this time she would perform the ritual called . . . the clavier?, no, the clavichord, Azucena, no, the ritual of the Clavicle, Lolilla, the Clavicle, I know what she said; she took two candles that had been blessed and stuck them in the sand, and with a cypress branch—that's something else we'd got her, and it had to be cut by the light of the crescent moon—she drew a circle in the sand, stood inside it, and said:

"Emperor Lucifer, master of rebellious spirits, be favorable unto me," said Don Juan, "give to this inert form the mobility of the great Prince of Darkness, let that power surge forth from the great funnel-shaped Hell divided into seven zones each with seven thousand cells where seven thousand scorpions hide and a thousand barrels of peat bubble; send the Prince of Darkness to me with the dominions that are particularly his: knowledge, flesh, and riches, now that I invoke the words of the Clavicle, so powerful they may torment the Devil himself," said Don Juan, trembling and hiding in the folds of his brocade a temporarily aged, contorted, and intolerably pinched face: Aglon Tetragrammaton Vaycheon Stimulamathon Erohares Retrasammathon Clyoram Icion Esition Existien Eryona Onera Erasyn Moyn Meffias Soter Emmanuel Sabaoth Adonai, I convoke you, Amen."

And nothing happened, Señor Don Juan, nothing. The mummy still lay there stiff and stretched out on the bed; and the Señora fell exhausted to the sand.

During the scrubbing maids' next absence Don Juan dressed in the white tunic, stained it with his own blood, and placed the crown of thorns upon his head. And thus robed, by night he went to the cell of the Superior, Madre Milagros, and finding the door open, he entered with great stealth and found the sainted woman kneeling upon a prie-dieu, her hands folded in prayer before the sweet image of Jesus the Redeemer. On tiptoe, Don Juan silently approached until he stood between the divine image and the dazzled eyes of Madre Milagros; in the midst of the shadows he was the living incarnation of the Christ to whom she was directing her prayers. The devout woman choked back a cry that was almost a sob; Don Juan raised one finger to his lips, and with the other hand he stroked the Mother Superior's head and murmured softly: "Wife . . ."

Madre Milagros's eyes filled with tears, and her weeping betrayed a battle between incredulity and faith.

"Hail, you are filled with grace, the Lord is with you," Don Juan said sweetly. "Do not be afraid, Milagros, for you have found favor with God, and you shall conceive in thy womb and bring forth a son. He shall be great, and the Lord God shall give unto him the throne of his father David. And he shall reign over the house of Jacob unto the ages, and of his kingdom there shall be no end."

The confounded woman automatically repeated the words she had learned as a young girl: "How shall this be, seeing I know not a man?"

"Are you not wedded to me?" Don Juan smiled. "Did you not take a vow to love me?"

"Yes, yes, I am the bride of Christ, but you . . ."

"Look carefully . . . behold my tunic . . . behold my wounds . . . behold the crown of my torment . . ."

"Oh, Lord, you have heard my prayers, you have honored the most undeserving of your servants, oh, Lord . . ."

"Rise, Milagros, take my hand, come with me, the virtue of the Most High shall cover you with His shadow, come with me to your bed, Madre . . ."

"I am the handmaiden of the Lord; do with me according to your word."

And, Madre, Don Juan said in the bed of the Superior, the Lord honors those who are most deserving, and no one more than you, holy and beautiful, most fair and pure; pure, yes, Mother Milagros said, sighing, but not beautiful. I am an old woman, Lord, a woman thirty-eight years old; governess and shepherdess to this flock of young Sisters; no, Milagros, old, too, was Elizabeth, Mary's kinswoman, who believed she was barren but who gave birth to the Baptist who was called John; and shall I, too, give birth, Lord?, are you the Holy Spirit come down to visit me?; oh, Milagros, Madre Milagros, the duty and the honor of the elect has always been to be made fruitful by the Divine Spirit before belonging to any mortal man; I shall belong to no one but you, Lord, I swear it; then you will have a long wait, Madre, a long wait then; but I am the handmaiden of the Lord, do unto me according to your word.

Our mistress, Señor Don Juan, sent us out to the difficulty and danger of collecting animals, some within the confines of the palace, others in the nearest foothills; for some it was necessary to set traps, and at times we fled with terror before some stalking beast; at times it was necessary to spend the night waiting to hear the trapped cry of some animal, the two of us grumbling and complaining, Señor Don Juan, clutching each other in the shadow of huge rocks or holding each other tight from fear of the black forest, abandoning you those nights, longing for your so amiable company; we captured a kid and an owl, a dog and a mole, one black cat, and two serpents: when we were finally able to take these creatures to the bedchamber of La Señora, she had placed an inverted crucifix upon the mummy's bed which she had surrounded with red candles, ciboria she had made us steal from her husband's chapel, and Hosts made from black kale, and with her cypress wand she wrote in the sand the letter

	V
and then	I
	T
	R
and	I
again, and an	O

and finally an L and then she covered the mummy with a black sheet, and on the sheet there was a circle and a cross within it, and La Señora said it was the cross of Solomon; then she knelt and asked us to hold the kid very tightly by its horns, and exposing herself to an early death from its sharp hoofs, she kissed its ass and then, crazed, her forehead wrinkled by that tightly fitting crown, she plunged the knife we stole from Jerónimo's forge into its belly; and before the jets of blood stopped spurting from the kid, as if to startle fear itself, she jabbed at the owl's eyes, the dog's neck, the black silk of the cat, the yawning jaws of the serpent, and the scurrying figure of the mole which was trying to bury itself in the sand; the beasts defended themselves in their own manner, scratching, barking, digging, pecking, fluttering, writhing, but they had no chance before the awful fury of La Señora, who was screaming: Veni, Veni, Veni, as she slashed, slit, ripped, and disemboweled the beasts.

The sands of her chamber, Señor Don Juan, are still soaking up the spilled blood; La Señora, our Señora, scratched, wounded, and exhausted, lies amid the new corpses. We brought two serpents from the hills, but she killed only one, Señor Don Juan, help us; we do not want to go back to the mountain to look for more animals; that's a job for the master huntsman, Don Guzmán, and even he runs dangers among jackals and wild pigs, and we, poor little scrubbing girls, we're not good for anything but collecting lizard droppings, certainly not for finding the snake still hidden in the sands of La Señora's room, oh, oh, oh . . .''

But besides being so frightened we wet our underskirts, nothing happened, Señor Don Juan; the mummy still lies there, motionless;

and La Señora opened her window and is listening to the sad lament of a flute coming from the forges, the tile sheds, and the taverns on the work site.

With eyes of dark resignation, the Mad Lady regards the somber crypt and seignorial chapel; her resignation is a triumph; everything is as it should be; like precious metals, pain and joy, mourning and luxury, shadows and light are here alloyed; give them eternal rest, Lord, and may your eternal light illumine them, alleluia, alleluia; propped upon her little cart the aged and mutilated Queen was, on the other hand, paying no attention to the cavorting of Barbarica, who leaped from tomb to tomb, all profaned, so that every cadaver resembled her cruel and generous mistress, for one lacked an arm, another a head, that one over there a nose, this one an ear, and Barbarica could only murmur: Oh, my beloved husband, my poor foolish but handsome Prince, do not hide from me, why won't you come out and play with your tiny playmate?, come out of your hiding place, don't be cruel, you freed the unworthy prisoners on our wedding night, don't humiliate me while you've favored vermin crawled out of nasty Jewish and Arab hovels, don't deny me the great mandrake I so desire, don't let my wedding night go by without a prodding from your pike, don't make me believe you're a boy-loving sodomite, I offer you my bulging painted tits and my greatest prize, a purse of a normal woman's size, out of all proportion to the meanness of my other parts, oh, my little Prince, oh, my darling Idiot, who was it who took you from your beggarly state, from your sad condition as a tattered sailor, the day we found you on the dunes about to be torn apart by the crowd?, who was it who had brought in her wicker trunk the cosmetics, pomades, pencils, paints, and false whiskers that transformed your appearance?, who, my handsome Idiot? You could see nothing in the darkness of my mistress's leather carriage, you heard her but didn't see me or sense my presence; no, you didn't see or hear me, and you believed the hands that disrobed you were those of my mistress the Mad Lady, who has no hands, so it was my hands that removed your doublet and your breeches, and it was I who slipped from the hole in the floor of the carriage hidden by my wicker trunk, I who nimbly slipped out and ran between the wheels and the horses' slow hoofs to the funeral carriage, carrying your wretched clothes rolled into a bundle I had thrust in my bosom, and it was I who removed the clothes from the cold corpse of the Prince called the Fair, who in life was the husband of my mistress and the father of our present Señor, and in death was embalmed into incorruptibility by the science of Dr. del Agua, it was I who put your robber's rags on him and then ran back to the carriage of my Lady and dressed you in the cap and medallions, the fur cape and brocade breeches, the hose and slippers, belonging to the cadaver, and it was thus the miraculous transformation took place that caused such clamor and amazement among our following; and you owe to me the fact that you are a Prince and not a beggar; and I was rewarded, for my mistress gave you my tiny, pudgy, loving hand in matrimony; and you, who owe everything to my craft and my artifice, now want to deny me the pleasure of your beautiful dingalingdong between my chubby little thighs, oh, you wicked boy, oh, you rascal, why won't you come play with your poor Barbarica, your wife before God and man, come out where I can see you, come out where I can love you, you be my sweet pickle, come play with my pears, you darling idiot boy . . .

And, still babbling, the dwarf Barbarica came to the tomb reserved by El Señor Don Felipe for his father—the Fair, the whoring, Señor—and she was amazed to see that it was the only tomb with the stone still firmly in place upon the funeral plinth. Her strength was fed by desire, her short, chubby, baby-like body strained and struggled, and sweating and panting she moved aside the bronze slab; she shrieked, she crossed herself, she yowled like an alley cat and trembled like quicksilver, for in the depths of the sepulcher, side by side, lay two identical men, identically dressed and identically arrayed down to the most minute detail of rings and medals, and both were the Prince, her Prince, sleeping within this tomb like twins gestating within a stone womb, both resting upon the horrible remains of the Mad Lady's embalmed husband, still dressed in the ragged clothing of a sailor; two!, two!, my God, you redouble my pleasure, panted Barbarica, but you offer them only to take them from me, they are both dead; ah, the bitch that birthed them, ahhh, I shall die a virgin, ay, I must live my wedding night untouched, among men with cocks as cold as dead fish, the only procuress to remedy my ills death itself, ay, ay, ay, and the dwarf clambered into the tomb and kissed the lips of the embalmed Señor dressed in tattered sailor's garb; this first kiss tasted of aloes, and the lips were dead indeed; next she kissed the parted lips of one of the two identical Princes, and that kiss tasted of the dried blood of a dove; the dwarf jerked the cap from this Prince's head, saw the shaved skull, and knew he was the poor scramble-brained youth she had married, and her husband's bloody lips had the scent of madness and sacrifice, but not of life. The dwarf squinted one swollen-lidded eye, her upturned nostrils quivered; she smelled ordure; she remembered; she separated the legs and lowered the breeches of the Idiot Prince, her husband; her tiny hand poked through the greenish feces, she gagged, and kept repeating, oh, what a smell, it stinks to high heaven, but she continued to poke and paw through the Idiot's excrement until she found what she was looking for: the black pearl, the pearl called the Pilgrim, and she popped it between her bulging bosoms, after wiping it clean on the doublet of the sleeping youth, her—as yet unconsummated—husband.

Only then did she look with increasing curiosity and excitement at the third body lying in the tomb, the second Prince, identical to her husband who slept so soundly his sleep was twin to death, in the same way the youths were twin to each other; she kissed this Prince. And this kiss tasted of perfume, of sweet-scented herbs . . . and it was returned.

"He kissed me back," screamed the dwarf, "he did, he did, he kissed me back!"

Don Juan's hands seized Barbarica's waist, he tossed her playfully into the air like a doll, it stinks to high heaven, the dwarf laughed, it stinks to high heaven, she repeated as Don Juan raised her voluminous, bunched-up skirts; he tickled her tight little ass with one finger, and as he thrust his face between the dwarf's legs, he also laughed, saying, blessed Jesus, what a stinkus, blessed Jesus, what a smell, and a tongue that seemed to the little creature like fire and brimstone plunged into the swamp.

She sent us out onto the plain, Señor Don Juan, beneath the burning July sun, to search for a certain blind flute player, Aragonese by birth, who arrived a few days ago to take part in the meager festivities of the palace workmen, by playing his sometimes plaintive, sometimes happy, little tunes; by pushing him and overriding his mute protests, we brought him to our Señora's bedchamber, which he already knew through the stories of the poor Señor Chronicler sent to row in the galleys—and too bad you didn't have the pleasure of knowing him, Your Mercy, for he was a discreet and courteous man, and he would treat a scullery maid as well as a lady—and also from the accounts of Your Honor's predecessor in enjoying the favors of our Señora, the youth burned beside the stables for fiddling with too many bottoms: the kitchen lads' as well as La Señora's . . . though as you often say, and rightly, let every man take his pleasure where he may.

Our Señora ordered the blind man to sit upon the sand and play his wretched sad little flute; he was bald, dark-skinned and heavy-shouldered, dressed in crudely stitched, ragged burlap, and as he played he looked at everything out of sightless green eyes, bulging like two onions, seeing nothing; La Señora baptized the frogs we'd caught in the old wells and stagnant waters on the plain, and she forced black Hosts down the frogs' throats while with her left hand she made a reverse sign of the cross upon her trembling breasts, saying:

"In the name of the Patrician," said Don Juan, "of the Patrician of Aragon, now, today, Valencia; all our misery has ended, Spain; come, luminous angel, come to breathe life into this being I have formed, make him rise from the bed in the image of Lucifer, covered in sardonyx, topaz, diamond, chrysolite, onyx, jasper, sapphire, ruby, emerald, and gold, and accompanied by the music of this blind demiurge from the diabolical village of your Aragonese kingdom, Calanda, where hands beat on drums until the skin is raw, blood flows, and the very bone is splintered to insure that Christ will be resurrected in the full Glory of his Sabbath: so may this my Angel be revived; come, come, come, twin of God, fallen archangel, King of Spain.''

Yes, that's how it was, Señor Don Juan, exactly as you said it, although that wretched flute player surely is not from Calanda where the Holy Week celebrations are famous and pilgrims come from faraway places to witness them; considering his looks he must have come from Datos, Matos, Badules, Cucalón, Herreruela, Amento, or Lechón, for those are the most miserable of the villages of Aragon. Then, inflicting great pain upon herself, La Señora tore off one of her fingernails, howling those words you just spoke, Don Juan, and the blind flute player sat upon the red-stained sands amidst the day-old, already stinking cadavers of the sacrificed animals, and played his saddest, most plaintive tunes. Suddenly, as he heard La Señora's screams of pain, the flutist stopped his playing and said what you heard, Señor Don Juan, from where you were hiding behind the chamber door:

''St. Paul advised us that Satan is the God of this century. St. Thomas advised us that Lucifer desired beatitude before the time appointed by the Creator, desired it before anyone, wished to obtain happiness for himself alone, only for himself, and that was his pride, and that pride, his sin. God condemned him for his pride; that is why the haughty descend from him. The Most High gave powers of genesis to woman, and having it, woman felt she was the most privileged of all creation, for she could do what no man could do: create another being within her womb, and that therefore she was superior to man, who could fertilize but not reproduce. And woman decided that even this power of fecundation should be denied to man, and so she refused him her body and allowed herself to be deflowered and made pregnant only by God himself, or by a representative of God's spirit, before she would be touched by any mortal man. And mortal man felt even greater resentment at his mortality, for he lacked the power to produce another being, and woman was his only after belonging to God, to the Spirit, to the Priest, or the Hero designated by God to continue in the female's womb the responsibility of creation. And so man took revenge on woman by making of her his whore, by corrupting her, so she was no longer fit to be the vessel for divine semen. And man despised his children, for if they were the children of God they were not his, and if they were the children of whores they were not worthy to be his. And man murdered his detested children, sacrificed them, his children, for they were also the children of the prostitute who first had given herself to the Hero or the Priest acting in the name of God, or he devoured them, in order to nourish himself from the sacred essence that God had stolen from man and granted to woman and to her offspring. And so the mother protected her child, knowing that the father would not live in peace until he had murdered it, and she saved it, as with Moses, by entrusting it to the waters. And for all this, man blamed woman as being Lucifer's representative on earth; and believing that woman is the seat of the diabolical pride that desired happiness before its rightful time and that anticipated the common beatitude that men may achieve only on the day of final judgment, the Council of Laodicea prohibited woman from officiating in the Mass. Man took shelter in material power in order to negate the spiritual powers of woman. Woman thus became Satan's priestess, and through her Satan regains his androgynous nature and becomes the hermaphrodite imagined by the Eremites and seen in the Hebraic Cabala: and it is from the Devil that she acquires the knowledge transmitted on the day of the first Fall, for Satan fell before Eve. Bury the fingernail in the sand, Señora, and worms will be born from it, and great hail will fall in summer and terrible storms will be loosed upon this land."

"How, if you are blind, do you know I tore out my fingernail?" our Señora asked between tormented sobs.

"Everything done in a visible manner in the world may be the work of demons," the flutist replied." Only the invisible is the work of God, and therefore demands blind faith, and offers no temptation. Señora, if you desire the blind to see, slice the eyeball with a razor at the precise moment a cloud cuts across the circumference of the full moon; then night will become day; water, fire; excrement, gold; dust, breath; and the blind shall see."

"I have no desire to create worms or to unleash storms. The Chronicler spoke of you one day, and also my poor executed lover knew you, the youth called Miguel-of-Life. I know your name."

"Do not repeat it, Señora, or your efforts will be in vain."

"I know your powers. They spoke of that. But it is not hail in summer I want of you; I want the body that lies upon my bed to acquire life."

"Then do what I have told you, and the Devil will appear."

And so our Señora, trembling and subdued, the oil-anointed dagger in her hand, approached the cadaver fabricated from the scraps of the dead, and the Aragonese flutist closed his enormous green eyes and began to play. La Señora also closed her eyes, and at that very instant, with a single slash, she cut the staring white eye of the mummy; a thick black liquid ran down the silvery cheek of that motionless monster, Señor Don Juan. But aside from that, nothing happened; the mummy still lies there, stiff and stretched out on the bed; and La Señora again falls exhausted to the bloody sand, this time beside the corpse of the owl, and recriminates the flute player, casting his impotence in his face, calling him mendacious, a liar; where is the Devil?, the rites of the man from Aragon are worthless, the Devil did not appear to aid La Señora and to give life to the horrible cadaver of cadavers, and meanwhile the flutist smiles and spends his short breath in playing lugubrious little tunes.

"Poor Señora; she does badly to seek with such eagerness and such painful invocation what is already near, just across the passageway, something even her maidservants can see," Don Juan said, casting aside his brocaded mantle and revealing himself before the two awe-struck scullery maids, who embraced one another as they looked upon him and ran to huddle together in the farthest corner of the room, for they had never seen him naked and had dallied with him only in the darkness, and now they saw him, chest covered with sardonyx, his waist bound by a chain of diamonds, his arms painted gold, his sex garlanded with a rosary of pearls that disappeared between his buttocks and fastened over one hip, his legs sheathed in jasper, his wrists adorned with sapphires, his ankles with chrysolite, his neck with rubies. This their bedazzled eyes beheld, but finally Azucena saw something more, as this splendid man, unparalleled among mortals, whirled about, and that was the six toes on each of his feet and the vividly purple cross upon his back; laughing, Don Juan strode from the room; the scrubbing maids crossed themselves again and again, and as they watched him leave they knew he would never return, and Azucena said to Lolilla: It's him, it's him, the child the court jester abandoned twenty years ago, the one I took in, nursed at the teats of our young Señora's bitch, before her marriage to El Señor, I recognized him, he's mine, my lover, my son, I was his wet nurse, his true mother, until the day of the horrible slaughter in the castle when I feared for his life, feared that with the monstrous signs of his back and his feet he would be confused with that mob of heretics, Moors, Jews, whores, pilgrims, and beggars that overran us that day, even the children in that procession were slain by the knife, but I saved him, I placed him in a light basket and tied it and cast it into the river where it would drift downstream towards the sea, sure that someone would pick him up and care for him, and now he has returned, he has been my lover, he has promised to marry me, you, too, Azucena?, but that's what he told me, you lie, Lolilla, as God is Christ and Christ is God, you lie, that's what he told me, no, me, don't you lay your lowborn hands on me, you filthy hag, I've had about enough from you, slut, let me go, you squeezed-out old bag, I'll gouge out your eyes, you cheap little ass-peddler, I'll yank out your mane, baggage, why, you spawn-of-a-bastard-Moor, I'll tear your heart out, ay, ay, ay, my eye, my leg, you've got claws like iron, you tramp, but I'll ram a pike up your ass and out your snout that'll turn you inside out and rot your bloody bowels, you itching, snitching, butt-twitching, son-of-a-bitching old whore, oh, let go my hair, ay, get off me, oh, my knee, I swear I'll kill you, no, I'm going to kill you, you cunt-sir-ass-sir-anyway-at-all-sir old hump, stinking trollop, I'll knock the snot out of you, you troublemaking, double-talking, double-dealing, sneaky-slimy-snaky strumpet, why you hairy-chested, spindle-shanked bawd, I'll kill you, I'll straighten out those crossed eyes for you, I'll bash your brains against a rock, yagh, yagh, yagh . . . ! Oh, look what you've done to us, Don Juan!, all because of you, Don Juan, come back to us, Don Juan!, oh, Señor Don Juan, you are nothing but a woman's whore.

Don Juan returned to the crypt and chapel where he had left Barbarica, exhausted from pleasure, in the arms of the Idiot Prince, the two of them asleep in the sumptuous tomb of El Señor's father. He walked toward the little cart where the Mad Lady sat, and if the maidservants' terror had been awesome when they saw him naked and bejeweled, the Mad Lady's simplicity was now entirely natural; she greeted the young gentleman before her dressed in the velvet doublet, the fur cape, the cap and breeches and medallion of the embalmed Señor.

"You've come back at last," the Mad Lady said serenely.

"Yes. This is our place."

"Shall we always be close to each other?"

"Always."

"Shall we rest now?"

"Yes."

"Are we dead?"

"Yes, both of us."

He lifted the old woman from her little cart, carried her very gently to a niche carved between two pilasters, and very sweetly placed her there, her white head and black-clad torso propped against the icy stone of the wall. The Mad Lady seemed content; her eyes followed Don Juan as he walked away, stopped beside the great mausoleum of the old woman's husband, and lay down upon the stone slab. He lay half reclining, his head resting upon his right arm: he was the living crown of the funeral tomb. He was the perfect and chaste youth the old woman had adored in her obsessive dreams of love and death, the resurrection of the past and the transfiguration of the future. Now, at this instant, in a present the Mad Lady wished to hold captive forever, beneath these arching domes, in this crypt, the dream was a reality, and the youth who represented her husband, her lover, and her son lay half reclining, resting on his right arm, as he gazed with fascinated pride into a mirror that an inattentive visitor might mistake for a book.

For a moment, the aged Señora feared that both of them—she in her niche, looking at him, and he, half reclining upon the slab of the sepulcher, looking at himself—had turned to stone and had thus become forever a part of this sumptuous cave of tombstones, pedestals, truncated pyramids, funereal epitaphs, and carved stone bodies, the reproduction of the remains of all the descendants of this house. A shiver, an icy doubt, ran down the Mad Lady's spine; she knew until now she had dreamed, and that she had been dreaming in life; but from this moment, placed by Don Juan in her niche in this chapel, she would believe she was dead, for now she dreamed she was living.

And that night in his tower the Chaldean, Brother Toribio, said to the painter, Brother Julián: "Brother, if you believed in them, I would tell you that Devils are wandering around my tower, for henbane and belladonna, betel and hellebore have disappeared from the stores in my apothecary; it must be thieves."

GAZES

El Señor summoned his court, making use of Guzmán, who in turn availed himself of his faithful and anonymous band of huntsmen; he summoned all and all responded to the summons to gather in the subterranean chapel. Only La Señora remained in her bedchamber, intent upon instilling life in the mummy fashioned from bits and pieces of royal cadavers, exhausting the formulas of diabolic invocation, and in her turn counting on no one and nothing except the assistance of the uncouth serving girls, Azucena and Lolilla, and the obscure words of the blind Aragonese flautist. In contrast, many were gathered in El Señor's chapel: hidden behind the tall latticework whose shadows turned their faces and habits into a pattern of white honeycombs were Madre Milagros, the nun Angustias, Sister Inés, and all the Andalusian novitiates; the fat Bishop was there, reclining on a litter borne by mendicant priests, perspiring, wiping his brow with a lace handkerchief and followed closely by an Augustinian monk with cadaverous features; the Sevillian usurer, wearing his marten-skin cap, was quick to prostrate himself before El Señor and thank him for the title of Comendador that afforded him the opportunity to enjoy May in December and add honor to riches; and the astrologer Brother Toribio had been summoned to read the signs of this event through which El Señor hoped to decipher all past enigmas and then place them in the horoscope with the assistance of the walleyed, red-haired priest.

And Guzmán gazed upon it all, knowing that once the court had been assembled his huntsmen would scatter across the plain and communicate to the workmen on the site—Nuño, Jerónimo, Martín, Catilinón—the false, although entirely probable news: the Mad Lady had had her way; our Señor has proclaimed the Idiot and the flatulent dwarf his heir and heiress; it is this obtuse and deformed pair that soon will govern you, for the degenerate, mystic, and necrophilic El Señor, his energies lost forever, his love for the hunt, for warfare, for women—the sap of power—forever forgotten, will soon abandon his mortal shell; look what awaits you if you do not rebel now: generation after generation of idiot monarchs, bleeders prone to the French malady who like vampires will derive from your eternally robust but eternally servile blood what little strength they can possess. Do you dream of restoring your ancient rights as free men?, do you dream of a justice that will defend you against the power of the Señores?, do you dream of a statute that will free you from both the caprice of the castle and the usury of the cities?, do you dream of a contract that will permit you to give and receive with equity? Then look at El Señor, and if you think his reign has been harsh, imagine what that of the dwarf and the Idiot will be, and of the monstrous offspring such a pair will engender, and you will know that your lamentations can only increase and be prolonged endlessly unto the consummation of the centuries.

And the painter-priest Julián gazed at everything through different eyes, lost among the multitude of monks, alguaciles, stewards, councilmen, duennas, officials, majordomos, and comptrollers called before El Señor. For him this first gathering of the members of the court in the private chapel was like the inauguration, the unveiling, of the great painting that Julián, with the assistance of the Chronicler, had convinced El Señor had come from Orvieto, the fatherland of a few austere, melancholy, and energetic painters, but which in truth the priest, painter of miniatures, inflamed with rebellious ambition, had executed with patience and stealth in the deepest dungeon of the palace, fearing that his work's novelty, the audacious rupture from the symmetrical aesthetic demanded by orthodoxy—so that the works of man might coincide with revealed truth—would be so obvious that it would be Julián's destiny to join the Chronicler in cleansing himself of the guilt of the worst of all rebellions: not Cain's: fratricide; but Lucifer's: deicide.

This is what he feared, although secretly he was offended that no one paid any attention to the painting, no one scrutinized it, or even anathematized it. Was its message so veiled? So diaphanous and terse and hidden was its criticism (or perhaps its decisiveness, its judgments—thought Julián—if one considered the Greek origin of a word whose destiny he would not dare prognosticate) that to discover it would demand an investment of attention and time that none of those here present was prepared to make . . . or lose? Would the slow contamination, the inevitable corrosive power of the figures there arranged, arranged thus in order to shatter the sacred order of Christian painting, take so long to have effect? A central and uncontaminated deity surrounded by two-dimensional, unrelieved space, immune, too, to all temporal condition.

"That is the law."

Brother Julián was tempted to open a path through the indifferent crowd, the throng of palace sycophants, to reach the altar, approach the painting, and trace his signature with thick brushstrokes in one corner of the canvas. He was tempted, but he resisted; not because of physical fear, but rather, moral suspicion. He was restrained by a vague reflection, the residue of his conversation in the tower with the astrologer: if the universe were infinite it would have no center, not the sun, not the earth, not the powers upon the earth, and certainly not an individual person and his pretentious scrawl, *Julianus, Frater et Pictor, Fecit,* and furthermore his spirit might seep away through that signature; let there be no center to in infinite universe which lacks a center. Julián stood apart, airily spiritual, illuminated, because of its paradoxical nearness and immobility, by a sudden communion with everything that was outside himself or his body or his consciousness; he himself posed the opposite response to his own argument: then if there is no center, everything is central and thus, as he gazed at it, he could understand the painting he had created and say to himself, confused, but assured:

"No one put his signature to the towers of Milan or Compostela, the abbeys of Apulia or the Dordogne, the stained glass or domes of our Christian kingdom; and I must do honor to the anonymity of those artists and speak with them the new truths, never sacrificing the ancient virtues; paint an Italian piazza with profound perspective flowing like the time in which men are born, in which they mature and perish, and flowing like the unrestricted space in which men are fulfilling the designs of God: here are houses, doors, stones, trees, real men, not the unrelieved space of the revelation or the hourless time of the original fiat, but space that is place, and time that is the scar of creation. Blind men: can you not see my Christ without a halo, facing a corner of the painting that is thus prolonged beyond its limits to invent new space, no longer the space of oneness, the invisible and invariable space of the revelation, but the many and different places of a constantly maintained and renewed creation? Poor blind creatures: do you not see that my Christ occupies a corner of specific but in no way finite space in my painting, and that in that precise, ex-centric positioning, Christ is eternally his own center in relation to the dimensional circle I have drawn, and that the naked men are standing in a real Italian piazza, and thus instead of illustrating a theme they are protagonists of an event, and that their center does not coincide with the center Christ displaces, do you not see that what is important is not a central or ex-centric placement which ceases to exist if the center, being everywhere, is nowhere, but that what is important is the relationship between two distinct essences, divine and human, and that the bridge between the two is their exchange of gazes? Blind, blind: I paint so that I may see, I see so that I may paint, I gaze at what I paint and what I paint, when painted, gazes at me and finally gazes at you who gaze at me when you gaze upon my painting. Yes, Brother Toribio, only what is circular is eternal and only the eternal is circular, but within that eternal circularity there is room for all the accidents and variations of the freedom that is not eternal but instantaneous and fleeting: my Christ elects to gaze, freely, instantaneously, and fleetingly, at the men's bodies, whereas the men gaze at the world, the space and the time surrounding them, and it is this world that gazes at Christ and thus, as everything is related through the gazes, everything divine is human, and everything human, divine, and the true halo forming an aureole above them all is the pale and transparent light—no one's and everyone's—that bathes the space of the piazza. Blind men!

"My signature would mutilate the prolongation of the space that should extend, as one gazes, to the right and left of the canvas, behind, above, and beneath it, and also in a second perspective, the one that flows from the canvas toward the spectator: you, we, they. Let my figures gaze beyond the painting that temporarily emprisons them. Let them gaze beyond the walls of this palace, beyond the plain of Castile, beyond the taut bullhide of our peninsula, beyond the exhausted continent we have damaged with greed and lust, with numberless crimes and invasions, and saved, perhaps, with a handful of beautiful buildings and with elusive words. Let them gaze beyond Europe to the world we do not know and that does not know us, but which is no less real, no less space, and no less time. And when you, my figures, also grow weary of gazing, cede your place to new figures that will in their turn violate the norm that finally you will consecrate: disappear, then, from my canvas and let other representations occupy your place. No, no, I shall not sign, but neither shall I be silent. Let the painting speak for me."

Hidden behind the tall chancel, Madre Milagros also gazed at the painting, but all her attention was centered on the white-clad Christ with the bleeding brow: it was he, it was he, the very one who had come to her that unforgettable night and claimed her for himself, and the Mother Superior was not surprised by the absence of a halo above that figure, for no light had crowned the Christ who had made her His wife. Madre Milagros sobbed; now she would not have to pray imploring the Saviour's presence; now she knew where she could find Him: here, in this chapel, in this painting; all she had to do was come here in secret, by night or at dawn, and touch the figure of the Christ in the painting and He would descend to her, Milagros, the chosen, and would again take her upon the most sacred of beds, upon the bed of the altar itself, on this very altar. Madre Milagros sobbed, and quietly beat her breast, oh, unworthy woman, oh, prideful woman, why would the Lord come to me again after having done so once? Why would He not instead visit other women and confer honor upon them as He honored me? Pride, pride, and I presuming to think of coming here to see Him and touch Him and make love with Him, presumption, He would not remember me, He would turn his back upon me, pride, pride, torture me no longer, Serpent, I am afraid to return here because I am afraid the Lord my God will turn His back upon me, will banish me from His presence, will scorn my pleas and punish my presumption, my honor; my honor?, no, my pride, I became a nun for the sake of honor, to guard it and keep it, and because there was no man whom I considered worthy of my bed or for whom I would change my name, only to become the bride of Christ, for the sake of honor, no man will stain it, not even Christ the Saviour, forgive me, forgive me, sweet Jesus, but I do not love you, I do not love you, why did you come to me and make me yours?, I loved you while you were unreachable, incorporeal, and therefore the most perfect object of a love beyond human fetters, beyond the bonds of honor, pride, presumption, or the fear of being scorned, I no longer love you, Christ, I loved a sweet and pure image, I cannot love a real lover, forgive me, Lord, forgive me . . .

Different was the gaze of the nun Angustias, who was not engaged in scrutinizing the painting above the altar, but in scrutinizing the figures of the monks gathered in the chapel, and in guessing which was the man who had at last assuaged her hungers and her lacerations and given her in exchange the unknown pleasure and pulsing freedom of desiring more and more and more, but desiring now with the security of knowing she could have, have, have, have love, yes, but not a child, no, that was what she feared now, her trembling face hidden behind the iron fretwork of the nuns' choir, oh, monk, if you made me a child you will not have given me pleasure with the freedom you promised, and pleasure without freedom is not pleasure at all, oh, monk, you took advantage of my delirium, of my shame, of my hunger for a man, oh, monk, if you have made me pregnant I will have to say that your child is the work of the Devil, and I will have to kill him at birth, before you yourself kill him, for you and for me, monk, I pray that you gave me only freedom and pleasure, not obligation, for it would be our mutual triumph so to have conquered the two laws that bind us—marriage outside the convent and chastity within—and be free, monk, free, to continue to make love with impunity, you to as many women as you desire, and I to as many men . . . No, I do not love you, monk, but I shall love the pleasure and the freedom you have taught me. May you do the same.

And where should the novitiate Doña Inés look, she who found so many points of interest among the motley throng? There, making his way toward El Señor, was her aged father, the usurer, the marten-skin cap in his hand obsequiously extended in a sign of respect more toward El Señor than to this sacred area, chapel and tomb; there was El Señor himself, seated upon a curule chair at the foot of the altar: there was Guzmán, who had one night led her to the nearby bedchamber of El Señor. Everyone was there except the one she sought: Don Juan, he who had given her the pleasure El Señor was unable to give, but also a scourge: the flower opened by Don Felipe had been enjoyed by Don Juan and then closed again; who had condemned her to this punishment?, who could secretly have desired such misfortune?, who was it who wished that she belong to no one, or who wished that she belong to him alone? She did not understand, her head whirled, her eyes were unfocused, seeing nothing, until her gaze, with vague and tortured dreaminess, wandered along the rows of royal coffins raised upon truncated pyramids the length of the chapel, and lighted upon him, it is you, Don Juan, the half-reclining, chaste youth resting upon one arm, it is you, oh, yes, it is you, I would know you anywhere, my lover, oh, it is you and you are stone, you are a statue, a statue has made love to me, I invited a stone statue into my bed, that is my curse, I have made love with stone, so what is to prevent me from turning into stone myself?, and if we are both stone . . . I see it now, then of course we shall be faithful to each other, you, Juan, and I, Inés, you have blood like ice, I knew it, I told you so: do not fear my father, do not fear El Señor, fear no one, Don Juan, because no one can kill you, one cannot kill a statue, one cannot kill death; Doña Inés's fingers clung to the grillwork of the chancel and with a stony gaze she stared intently at the stony figure of her lover lying motionless upon the stone sepulcher. And when you and I are stone, Don Juan, the entire world will be stone, stone the rivers, the trees, and beasts, stone the stars, the air, and fire: creation will be a motionless statue, and you and I its unmoving center. Nothing moves now. Nothing. Nothing.

And while Doña Inés's gaze of stone was directed only at what she believed to be the stone figure of Don Juan, Don Juan merely feigned immobility; that was easy for him, he recognized it as one further attribute of his person: a will of iron that allowed him to simulate the most delicious impassivity. Not one nerve of the semi-reclining figure upon the stone slab moved, and like Inés, everyone present at this ceremony convoked by El Señor thought he was a statue. The youth did not even blink. With indifferent eyes, indifferent to the confused ceremony about to begin without any perceivable cause, insofar as those present could note, Don Juan, remote, unconcerned with the reunion of the court, disguised as a statue and disguised, too, by the shadows, gazed toward the painting in the chapel: for the first time he gazed at the painting that dominated El Señor's private chapel, and as if in a mirror saw himself in the Christ without a halo, a Christ, like him, on the periphery; it is I, it is I, someone knew me before I knew myself, why did someone paint my image before I arrived here, why?, why?, that painting is . . . more than the heart of La Señora, more than the eyes of Doña Inés, more than the jewels of Lucifer, my mirror . . . Oh, that painting, why was I so long in seeing it?, how I wish I had first seen myself in it and not in the mirror of La Señora that held our superimposed images; it is no wonder I so easily deceived the Mother Superior and enjoyed her favors; it is no wonder that I deceive all women, for each always believes I am someone else, a husband, a lover, a father, a Saviour, and each loves someone else in me; who will love Don Juan for himself, not because she believes he is someone else and that she is making love to someone other than him, a husband, lover, monk, Christ himself, but never Don Juan . . . never? Azucena and Lolilla love me because I promised to marry them, Madre Milagros because she believed I was the Divine Spirit, the nun Angustias because she confused me with her confessor, no one has recognized me, no one has loved me . . . except Inesilla, for only she knows who I am. And I do not love her, because no woman interests me unless she already belongs to a lover, a husband, a confessor, to God; no woman interests me if as I make love to her I do not stain another man's honor; no woman interests me if my love does not liberate her. I shall never love any woman forever, I love her only to make her a woman, and Inés is already a woman, Inés does not belong to El Señor, who deflowered her; El Señor is master only of this palace of death; Inés is the only one who loves me because she is already mistress of herself, and if my logic is correct I cannot love her, for then someone like myself would come to take her from me; I shall insult the honor of other men, but no man shall insult mine, for I shall have none, no honor and no sentiments; and if a scrubbing girl, a novitiate, a Queen, or a Superior should bear my child it will not be mine, it will be the child of nothingness and I shall condemn it to nothingness; I shall devour my children, castrate them, stab them to death; the nourishment of the ordinary man, honor and fatherland, hearth and power, is forbidden me; I have no nourishment but women and their offspring; I shall eat the cunt of the women and the heart of the children, and Don Juan will be free; he will sow disorder, he will inflict passion where passion seemed dead, he will break the chains of divine and human law; Don Juan will be free so long as a slave to law, power, hearth, honor, or fatherland exists upon this earth, and be captive only when the world is free . . . never.

And the brand-new Comendador, the Sevillian moneylender, the father of Doña Inés, gazed at everything through narrowed, calculating eyes, and nothing that moved caught his eye, rather the richness of the wood of the choir and the chairs in the chamber, of acana and mahogany, terebinth and walnut, box and ebony, and the paneling with embellishment, molding, and inlay of mahogany, and the columns of the choir of blood-red acana, each fluted and round, their richly wrought capitals supported by corbels carved in thistle leaves; sixty feet long, at least, this chapel, the Sevillian said to himself, and fifty-three feet wide, but it contains more riches than a space a hundred times greater could hold, for the tables are of green and pink and white marble and jasper, inlaid, veneered, and outlined in contrasting colors; the altar is of finest jasper trimmed with bronze made golden by fire, and the monstrance is like a flaming ruby adorned with diamonds—and diamonds had to be used in carving such a costly tabernacle; well said he who said that there are sufficient riches here to found a kingdom, certainly there will be more than enough to repay a moneylender, for I see no thing in this sacred place that cannot be melted down or torn from its place to be resold; there is too much here for one little-used room, and the former councilman of this place spoke the truth when these communal lands were expropriated by El Señor: "Note down that I am ninety years old, that I have twenty times been mayor, and that El Señor will build here a nest of locusts that will devour the land; place first the service of God"; and to fulfill the demands of El Señor they uprooted forests, leveled hills, stopped streams, and all, yes, all out of devotion to God, to sing His divine praise with continual choirs, prayers, charity, silence, and study, and also for the fitting interment of our Sovereign's ancestors. But one never knows for whom he labors, and perhaps what today honors God and the dead in this one room can tomorrow, without diminishing the greatness of the Creator, adorn the houses of the living, and this balustrade can be sent to Seville, and that candelabrum perhaps to Genoa, that pilaster to the house of a merchant in Lübeck, the chairs to schools where the children of prosperous and frugal citizens are educated, and the chasubles, dalmatics, capes, albs can easily be transformed into sumptuous attire for our women, for one sells the good cloth in his coffer; these riches are buried here, and no one benefits from them. El Señor must have planned that these marvels would be the treasure of future centuries, but I see them as a profitable annual balance, and in order to obtain them I shall believe that everything I have seen and heard here the last few nights is but a nightmare; things are things and can be touched and measured and exchanged and sold and resold; the objects here are but adornment for useless rites and events my senses cannot credit; no, I did not see the flight of a bat, or the transformation of that bat into a naked woman, or the robbing of sepulchers, or fornication inside them, or the apparition of dwarfs and mutilated old ladies or youths who recline upon rich funereal tombstones, or any of the things my reason cannot comprehend or my interests translate. This age is long in dying, and makes even a hardened merchant like myself see visions and phantoms. Let the old dreams die, Señor; everything you possess here must circulate, move, find a new dwelling place and a new owner. That is reality, and this prodigious edifice will be but the tomb of your ancestors, and of your dreams also, your vampires, your dwarfs, your armless and legless old ladies, your mad youths disguised as statues. Thank you for my title, Señor, although what you reward in me will be your own downfall. Your spectral God is not my real Goddess. I call my deity Reason, alert senses, rejection of mystery, banishment of all that does not fit within the secure treasure chest of common sense where I amass logic and ducats joined together in happy matrimony.

And the fulgurating gaze of the Mad Lady was the gaze of triumph, and as the aged Comendador wedded reason and money, she wedded life and death, past and future, ash and breath, stone and blood: propped in one of the chapel's carved niches, incapable of movement, indifferent to any fear of a fatal fall from the niche to the granite floor, her gaze was of triumph: all the court, all living beings gathered in this deep sepulchral crypt resembled her adored dead, and perhaps with luck no one would ever leave here, everything would remain forever fixed in time, like the figures in that painting above the altar, a strange painting of Christian theme and pagan conception where contemporary naked figures coexisted with those steeped in Sacred History; the perfect exchange of death and life was now being consummated; the reward of life was death; the gift of death was life; the obsessive game of reversal that dominated the insane reason of the Mad Lady had reached its ultimate point of equilibrium. Let nothing upset it, pleaded the Mad Lady, let nothing upset it, and she drifted into a profound dream that also confused the domains of life and death.

The eyes of everyone present turned to scrutinize a dejected El Señor as he occupied the curule chair Guzmán held for him at the base of the altar; all eyes, from those of Inés, hidden behind the grillwork of the choir, to those of the most distant alguacil innocently standing at the foot of the stairway of the thirty-three steps. In all the crush of the assembled throng, no one occupied those steps; it was as if an invisible glass shield sealed access to the stairway. Regarding the crowd before him, El Señor was more aware of certain absences than of the assembled presences, and as he wished to identify those absences, he named them Celestina and Ludovico, Pedro and Simón, asking himself, his fingers clutching the smooth mahogany arms of the chair, whether his dreams of yesterday could eventually bear any relation to the mysteries of today, whether the dreams had announced the mysteries, and whether the enigma, finally, was but ignorance of the logical bond between what youth desired and old age feared, whether the mystery of today was only, how could one know?, the failure of yesterday's dream. Perhaps . . . perhaps it was the student and the bewitched girl, the serf and the monk who invisibly occupied the steps of that never completed stairway, the stairway where every stair was a century and every step a step toward death and extinction, oblivion, inert matter, and then accursed resurrection in a foreign body. Toribio's unfocused gaze, the fear-filled gaze of Brother Julián, the greedy, obsequious gaze of the Sevillian moneylender, the bored gaze of the prelate, Guzmán's impenetrable gaze, told him nothing; they held no answer to the question that El Señor asked himself as he asked them. And he found no response, he retreated into his only sure refuge: his own person.

His real, his royal person. El Señor decided to count only on himself and to rely on the simple oneness of his own person to dominate surprise, crowd, enigma, and disorder. But immediately he asked himself: Is my person sufficient? And the answer was now the first rupture in that simple unity—I, Felipe, El Señor—no, my person is not enough; my person is drained by the power I represent, and that power extends beyond me, for since it antedates me it does not actually belong to me, and as it passes through my hands and through my gaze it seeps away and ceases to belong to me; I, Felipe, am not enough; power is not enough; what is needed are the trappings, the place, the space that contains us and gives a semblance of unity to me and my power: the chapel, this chapel with the painting from Orvieto and the bronze balustrades and the fluted pilasters and carved chairs and high iron grillwork of the nuns' choir and the thirty sepulchers of my ancestors and the thirty-three steps that ascend from this hypogeum to the plain of Castile; thus the illusion of unity was but the complex fabric of a man, his power and his space, and Julián gazing at El Señor seated before the anonymous painting which was said to have come from Orvieto, imagined him imagining himself as an ancient icon, a timeless, spaceless reproduction of Pankreator, but vanquished by the proliferation of spatial and temporal signs in the painting: you, Felipe, El Señor . . . here and now; and as the masked page and the blond youth entered, the enigmas were multiplied rather than resolved, enigmas enslaved the soul of El Señor in the same way the simple couple enslaved the multitude of dumfounded alguaciles and duennas, monks and halberdiers, councilmen and stewards who opened a path for them into the presence of El Señor; and thus he himself, seated upon the curule chair with Guzmán standing by his side, his back to the altar, to the Italian painting, to the offertory table, to the embroidered altar cloths, the ciboria, and the tabernacle itself, became the purveyor of the questions he himself had formulated: Who are they?, why do they look the way they do?, why is the page wearing a mask, hiding his features behind a green and black and yellow feather mask?, why does he have a large green sealed bottle secured in his sash?, who is the youth with the tattered breeches and doublet and tousled blond hair the page is leading by the hand, and what is he clutching in his hand?; the cross, the cross; what is that blood-red cross between the youth's shoulder blades, the cross I now see clearly as a clumsy halberdier twists the boy's arm, makes him moan with pain, forces him to kneel, his back to me as mine is to the altar; my back also bears a cross, the gold-embroidered cross of the cape resting upon my shoulders; and what has dropped from the hands of the youth now forced to prostrate himself, abject and captive, before me?, two rocks, two gray stones, what offering is this?

to whom does he offer it, to me, or to the powers of the altar behind me?; did he intend to stone me in my own temple?, did he intend to stone us both, both Lords, I and the other, I and the Christ without a halo?, is that what he wanted?; and why does my astronomer Toribio rush through the throng to the prostrate boy, the infinitely strange and conquered and defiant youth at my feet, and pick up the two stones, gaze at them with his crossed eyes, weigh them in his hands, seem to recognize them, kiss them, and immediately hold them aloft, exhibit them, exhibit them to Brother Julián the miniaturist, run toward him with the stones?; has my horoscopist friar lost his judgment, or is he merely carrying out to the last detail the function for which I had him brought here: to resolve the enigmas and then position them in the astral chart?; and thus hesitated the royal and unique person of El Señor, made multiple by doubt and the double presence of these strangers, the black-clad page masked in feathers and his young companion; thus there arose a shrill bird-like shrieking from the nuns' cage: it is he, my Sweet Lamb, shrieked Madre Milagros; it is he, my cruel and most beloved confessor, shrieked Sor Angustias; it is he, another Don Juan, shrieked the novitiate Inés; one is of stone and the other living, I have lost my reason; which should I love?, the one that promises the adventure of motionless stone or the one that promises me the misadventure of trembling flesh?, and the twittering shrieks of the nuns aroused the Mad Lady from her dream and she, too, saw the man who was identical to the one she had rescued from the dunes one evening and elevated to the rank of royal heir; and Don Juan himself gazed at his double kneeling before El Señor and then he gazed intently into the mirror he held, still reclining, in one hand, and he said to himself: I am turning into stone and my mirror is but the reflection of my death: we are two, two cadavers; that is the power and the mystery of mirrors, oh, my lucid soul, for when a man dies before a mirror he is in reality two dead men, and one of them will be buried but the other will remain and continue to walk upon the earth: and that one kneeling there, is that I?

In contrast, the masked page did not hesitate. While the splintering of El Señor's soul revealed itself in similar contortions of a face that in doubt and oblivion and premonition and fear and resignation prematurely assumed the features reserved for the moment of death, the page advanced toward him with a firm step. The echo of his footsteps resounded upon the granite floor of the chapel; the steps resounded more because of the hushed silence occasioned by El Señor's evident perturbation than because of the forcefulness of the slight body of the Mad Lady's page-and-drummer. And the Mad Lady, ensconced in her niche, gazed now at her lost drummer and cried out: "You've returned, ingrate, jackanapes; after abandoning me, without my permission, you've returned to cause my ruin, to shatter my equilibrium: damned knave!"

And this aged Queen was so agitated that she fell from the high carved niche where Don Juan had placed her with such delicacy, and lacking arms or legs to brace herself against the fall she tumbled head-first to the granite floor and was knocked unconscious. No one paid the least attention to her, for all their powers of observation were focused on what was taking place before the altar. The page climbed upon the dais and, still masked, approached before the perturbed gaze of El Se-ñor. And also Guzmán's, standing nearby; and Don Juan's, liberated to the imagination of evil and death; and the Comendador's, fearful that these events, more akin to intangible fantasy than to the solidity of his merchant's scales, would turn from its course the stream of precise and precious affairs of commerce; and the nuns', stupefied by the ap-parition of the young man identical to their own lovers. The most alert eyes could scarcely see; not even the most attentive ears could hear. They heard nothing of what the page, after kissing El Señor's hands, whispered into his pallid ear; only a few would see that for an instant the page removed the mask, but everyone, in tune with their Lord's most minute vibration, felt that El Señor shivered like quicksilver when he glimpsed the page's face: gray eyes, upturned nose, firm chin, moist, tattooed mouth imprinted with many-colored serpents that writhed with the movement of full lips; and Don Juan, from his posi-tion upon the slab of the tomb, could see El Señor's ears flush, as if the page had lighted the candles of memory behind them.

And that memory, unknown to everyone except El Señor and the page, stopped the wheels of time, immobilized bodies, suspended breath, blinded gazes, and thus the painter Julián could tear his own gaze from the vast canvas he had painted to focus upon another, still larger, although less detailed canvas: the court of El Señor, fixed, para-lyzed, converted into insensible figures within the space of the royal chapel; and Julián, who gazed, one gaze within this space, could nei-ther hear the words nor see the few trembling gestures El Señor direct-ed to the page and the youth: the protagonists.

The page replaced the feather mask upon his face; he offered a hand to El Señor, who grasped it, arose, and descended from the dais; but even this uncommon movement did not reanimate those who observed incomprehendingly, although luster was restored to eyes that watched El Señor and the page descend from the altar, saw the page offer his other hand to the kneeling youth in tattered clothing, a cross upon his back, his blond locks hiding his face; the page's young companion arose from his position of humiliation, the halberdiers released him, and the trio—the page, the youth, and El Señor—walked toward the neighboring bedchamber separated from the chapel by a black curtain, and passing through the throng that formed a double wall of question-ers, they entered El Señor's chamber.

Guzmán drew back the curtain to allow them to pass. And that was the gesture that revived the movement, sighs, chatter, and exclamations of the court; everyone crowded over, ran across, nudged, or trampled the mutilated body of the Mad Lady, perhaps thinking it was some animal, perhaps El Señor's dog, a forgotten package, a bundle of black rags, a bale of old hay; they thundered over it like a herd of horses, like a drove of oxen; no one saw her die, no one heard the last sigh from that mutilated bleeding old woman, her head split open, her tangled white hair matted with blood, her eyes starting from her head, her torso flattened, a heap of discarded rinds and peels, for everyone buzzed like a swarm of insects before the bedchamber door.

But only those closest—Julián and Toribio, the Comendador and Guzmán—could see what happened; Don Juan only imagined it; Inés only feared it. And this is what those who could see and hear, and lived to tell it, say:

The page approached El Señor; again he whispered something to him, and El Señor gave orders corresponding to the words of the page, for only at the page's instruction did El Señor seem capable of acting; they were to send for a certain Aragonese flautist, and allow the page and his young companion, holding hands, moving extremely slowly, as if underwater, not looking at one another, somnambulists, to walk to El Señor's bed, climb upon it, lie down, and await the indispensable arrival of the flautist; he is on his way, Señor, he was entertaining La Señora in her chamber with his sad, blind trilling; poor solitary and defeated Señora, she seems to be following the road of all our Queens: to be devoured by a Time with a body, a gullet, teeth, claws, scruffy hide, and hunger; they're opening a path for him now, Señor; he's guided by eyes that can see and by his own divining hands, Señor; here comes the flautist, no, no one knows where he came from, or when, or how, or why, only that the page deems him indispensable for the incomprehensible ceremony taking place upon the bed where our Señor has in the past been treated by Guzmán for all his premature ills, and where ill, unmoving, he has been able to watch other ceremonies, divine ceremonies, without being seen; but this ceremony cannot be divine, for the two boys have climbed upon El Señor's own bed and are embracing there as if to console or recognize each other, as if to remember each other; tender, humane gazes, Julián and Toribio may think, but not the prelate who in a high state of agitation cries sodomy, sodomy in the chapel dedicated to the sovereign worship of the Eucharist, sovereign the worship as sovereign should be contrition before a sin becoming more and more prevalent, and St. Luke has said: Nay; but, except you repent, ye shall all likewise perish, and the only way to purge this heinous sin is in the way the youth was purged who was discovered in improper relations with the stableboys: at the stake, by fire, sic contritio est dolor per essentiam; and only vaguely hearing him, for the prelate's admonitions in no way detracted from the force of curiosity outside the seignorial chamber or the force of fatality within it, Julián gazed toward the painting on the altar and asked himself whether Christian contrition must necessarily be repentance of intent, and not repentance for the passion that was cause and effect, as necessary to the sin as to the pardon, and as he met Julián's eyes, the friar who was horoscopist and astronomer, he longed to ask him whether the moment was not approaching to change an act of contrition into an act of charity, an act without the repentance the Bishop judged and proclaimed essential, an act of pardon (Inés, Angustias, Milagros) that did not detest the fault committed, for there is something in Christian *contritio* that as we cleanse ourselves of the sin (Milagros, Angustias, Inés) also washes away our lives, pretending that we have never actually lived them: was it worth the trouble to begin again? Toribio and Julián asked each other with their eyes: Is it worth the pain?, while the page and his companion lay embraced on El Señor's bed; there they are awaiting, Inés, Madre Milagros, Sister Angustias, the arrival of the flautist from Aragon, who now enters the bedchamber, feeling his way, yellow-fingernailed hands extended before him, heavy shoulders, limping walk, his silent rope-soled sandals tied with rags around ulcerated ankles, his flute tied to his belt with a tattered cord: the blind man.

Doubly blind, doubly, Toribio reported to Julián, Julián to the Comendador, the Comendador to an alguacil, the alguacil to a steward; the sound of their voices flowed over the flattened cadaver of the Mad Lady until it reached the agitated honeycomb of nuns hidden behind the distant ornamental ironwork: doubly blind, for now the page blindfolds the blind man with a dirty handkerchief stained with visible remains of dried blood; the blind man remains blindfolded; he is led by the page to the bed and the flautist too climbs upon it, where he sits at one end, legs crossed; he removes his flute from his belt and begins to play a melancholy, monotonous tune with interminably repeated rhythms: music such as we have never heard here, Julián, Toribio, Inés, Madre Milagros, music that smells of smoke and mountain, that tastes of stone and copper, that does not recall in us any recollections, but seems to revive the page's young companion, draws him out of his stupor, causes him to lift his face as if in search of a sun banished from these royal dungeons, lights a flame in his eyes as if truly an errant star were reflected there, Toribio, Julián; and the page is drawing the curtains around El Señor's bed, Inés, Madre Milagros, Sister Angustias, while the light in the eyes of the blond and tattered youth spreads across his entire face and animates his lips; the youth's lips are moving, Guzmán, Toribio, Inés, Madre Milagros, and this is the last thing we who have the privilege of being able to peer through the door to El Señor's chamber can see before the page's hand draws the last curtain and separates the three—the page, youth, and flautist—from eyes avid for these novelties and also from the defeated gaze of a trembling El

Señor seated again upon the curule chair brought to him by Guzmán: all three are hidden by the three curtains that completely close off the bed from head to foot and from top to bottom: more than a bed, it is a fragile tomb, a motionless carriage.

The youth speaks. And El Señor hears what the youth is saying, but his fatigued arm hangs lifelessly by his side, and his hand gropes distractedly for something beside the curule chair, a companion, perhaps a dog that would make him feel less defenseless.

The youth speaks, hidden behind the curtains that envelop El Señor's bed, hidden in the strange company of the page and the flautist. One can hear the flautist's melancholy music accompanying the words of the young pilgrim. Nothing, on the other hand, can be heard from the lips of the page. And these are the pilgrim's words:

II

THE NEW

WORLD

MORNING STAR

Sire: My story begins with the appearance over the sea of the morning star, called Venus, night's last glimmer, but also its perpetuation in the dawn's clear light: Venus, the sailor's guide. One morning in a secluded spot along the coast I came upon an old man, tenacious still, but marked by fatigue. He was building a boat there by the seashore. I asked him where he planned to sail; he did not welcome my questions. I asked whether I might voyage in his company; with his fist he motioned toward a hammer and some nails and planks. I understood the arrangement he was offering, and I labored with him fourteen days and nights. When we had finished, the taciturn old man spoke: looking with pride toward his ark with the stout, weathered sails.

"At last."

We set sail, then, with Venus one summer morning, carrying twenty casks filled with water from the nearby streams. At great risk I had gathered from the villages along the shore—and without permission of their owners—hens and large wheaten loaves, supplies of rope and other tackle, jerked beef, smoked bacon, and a bag of limes. The old man smiled when I returned with these provisions. I recounted the small adventures I had encountered in obtaining them, by night, or at the hour of siesta, slipping and sliding along tile roofs, swimming the wide mouth of a river, and always saving myself by my natural agility.

The old man smiled, I say, and asked my name. I answered by asking his; Pedro, he said, but insisted on knowing mine. I entreated him to give me a name, adding that, with neither mockery nor distrust, I must assure him I didn't know my name.

"Sir Thief"—old Pedro laughed—"or Genteel Pirate, and with good reason: What things do you know?"

"East and west, north and south."

"What names do you remember?"

"Very few. God, and Venus, Mediterranean, Mare Nostrum."

A light breeze bore us swiftly away from the coast. Once out of sight of the shore, I asked instructions of Pedro, who was busying himself with the sails, so I could set the course toward our destination. But the old man had already lost his temporary good spirits, and said in a somber tone: "You tend the sails, I'll take the helm."

And so we sailed on; there was no sense of movement, for the summer sea was as still as glass, and the breeze so soft it raised no swell but swept away the spume and spread the seas with quicksilver. We sailed without incident, for the old man had no doubt about the course he'd set, and at first I obeyed his orders blindly. My will was becalmed; the quiet of the sea inspired similar tranquillity of body and soul. Peaceful sea, soft zephyr. There was little work to be done, so I whiled away hours on end lying on the deck and gazing at the docile passage of the fleecy clouds and the bountiful sun. We left gulls and plants behind, signs of the proximity of land. The old man had steered away from the coast, but I supposed we were never more than two days from land, for, whatever our route, like a flowing needle we'd be stitching a pattern along the widespread cloth of the shore. In itself, the sea is nothing—except the kingdom of the fishes and the tomb of the incautious—its only value that of serving as a briny road to link together the abundant harvests of our provident Mother Earth. I knew well the maps that charted the outlines of our Mediterranean Sea, and although we'd sailed away from the northern coasts, in my mind I pictured myself sailing first toward the south, then to the east, to Mare Nostrum, the sea with no secrets, our cradle, as secure as that land I praise, land our sea contains in its very name, Mediterraneum, sea of marble and olive, sea of wine and sand . . . my sea.

I watched the last gannets gliding above the surface of the water, eating fish from the sea, the sun occasionally glinting from their backs. And when they were no longer there to watch, I missed them. Then my half-closed eyes focused on the sun, and with a flash stronger than those burning rays my dozing reason flamed with surprise and fear. What a fool! Day after day I'd been watching that summer sun, and only now did I realize what it had been telling me: faithfully, persistently, we were following its course. The sun was our guide, a magnet more powerful than any compass; one need only follow its daily path and one can dispense with any navigational needles; we were obedient to its course, our ship was a serf, subservient to the heavenly body.

Obdurately, we were sailing from East to West. The sun rose at our backs to set before our bow. I sprang to my feet, shocked and trembling; I looked at Pedro; he returned a cold, serene, decided, mocking stare.

"You were a long while realizing, boy."

His words broke the strange and unwarranted peace of my spirits, an inferior copy of the benign nature enveloping me; that radiant sun, that clear sky, that good air, that mirrored sea were instantly transformed into the icy certainty of disaster; the calm presaged storm, pain, and certain catastrophe: we were sailing toward the end of the world, the cataract of the ocean, that unknown sea of which only one thing was certain: those who passed the forbidden line of the beyond were claimed by death.

Terror and anger: can such contrasting emotions exist side by side? In me, at that moment, yes. I saw death in the quicksilver sea and I imagined a boiling fury where its waters tumbled precipitously over the very edge of the world. With fury and fear I looked at the old man; I hoped to surprise the gaze of madness in those deep-set eyes hidden beneath the ancient lids. I shouted that he was leading us to disaster, that he had deceived me, and that if his proposition was to put an end to his days in such a terrible manner, mine was to save myself, and not to share his wretched fate. I seized a pole and rushed at Pedro. The old man abandoned the wheel and struck me in the belly with all the frightful force of his callused fist, and in that instant the boat rolled, momentarily freed from control, and I lay groaning on the deck.

"It's your choice, Thief . . . or Pirate," Pedro murmured. "You may choose whether you're to voyage bound hand and foot like a common thief, or standing on your feet, hands free, master, with me, of this sea and the free land we will find on the other shore."

"Free land? Other shore?" I exclaimed. "You're mad, old man! You're going to perish in this mad endeavor, and drag me down to death with you!"

"What is it you reproach me for?" Pedro replied. "The fact that I'm resigned and you're ambitious?"

"Yes. I want to live, old man, and you want to die."

"On my life, I tell you not so. Because I've lived what I've lived, I make this voyage to go on living."

He looked at me enigmatically, and as I didn't understand his reasoning, but persisted in my own—he wished to die, I wished to live—he continued in a guarded tone: "Can't you see it's me, the old man, who has ambitions, and you, the young one, who's resigned? I flee because I must. And you?"

He was asking me whether the events of my short life hadn't disenchanted me with those things that denied life, not life itself.

"Why, then, did you sail with me? Why didn't you stay behind if you don't believe in the new land I seek? Where do you come from, Thief?"

I feared that question: I always fear it, because even as I cannot remember my name, I am more than aware of the reason for that ignorance. I answered the old man: "From everywhere."

"From nowhere, then."

"What I mean is, the only thing I can remember is an endless pilgrimage. Believe me, old man."

"Then I'll call you Pilgrim."

"Yes, I've never stopped, always a wanderer. No corner of the known earth has ever claimed me, made me feel what other men feel that makes them want to put down roots—a name, a hearth, a woman and offspring, honor and property. Do you understand me, old man?"

From the helm Pedro looked at me, pondered, and said no, he couldn't understand such meaningless words, they were too different from what he would have said to explain his own life: "All the things you never had, I had and lost. Lands and harvests: the lands burned, the harvest stolen; descendants: well, my sons were murdered; honor: my women were besmirched by the Liege. And liberty as well, or its illusion, for I came to know how the multitude can be deceived and led into slavery and death in the name of liberty. Do you know anything at all of this, Pilgrim? I think not, and that's why I can't understand your words."

I tried to explain how little I understood myself, for the fleetingness of my recollections was of a different nature, and very few voices came to my aid in explanation. Visions of pale deserts and distant oases, bronzed mountains and indistinct islands, walled cities, temples of death, men's faces, cruel or humiliated, perverse or desiring women, the muted cries of children, galloping horses, fire and flight, dogs howling beneath the moon, old men sleeping beside their camels. Could I reconstruct the memory of a life from such visions? I don't know. I didn't know the precise names of those places and those people any more than I knew my own name or place. Was what I then said to Pedro enough to encompass all those featureless memories?

"I've always lived beside Mare Nostrum. I am a Mediterranean man."

No. It was not enough: at the moment I uttered the words, my cruel memory, unlimited but also without guideposts, dragged me backward in its impetus, backward to a distant and close memory, never making clear what came before and what came after: memory like air, lost sigh of the past and agitated breath of the present, all one. How could I explain this to the old man? Helpless before absolutes I was myself unable to penetrate, I preferred to concede this invalid but immediate argument once I had satisfied, if only temporarily, it's true, my immediate instinct of self-preservation. I felt two principles struggling within my breast. One impelled me to survive at all cost. The other demanded mad adventure in pursuit of the unknown. Between the two, resignation reigned. For that reason, my rebelliousness quelled, the spirit of adventure latent, I said: "Since I, like you, am fleeing, although I have no motive and you say you have more than enough, I accept, old man, this voyage to death. Perhaps in death my poor enigmas will be resolved, perhaps it is my destiny to resolve them at the moment I am dying, and to know only when I am dead. It doesn't matter, it will all have been in vain."

Resignedly, I arose from the deck where I had been thrown by the force of Pedro's blow and the motion of the ship, as Pedro said: "You will see, my boy, that we're not going to our deaths but to a new land."

"Don't be deceived. You have many illusions for a man of your years, and I admire you. At the least, I swear to weep with you when you lose them."

"You'd wager your life against my illusions?" Pedro laughed with a trace of bitterness. "And what will you give me if at the end of the voyage both my illusions and your life survive?"

"Nothing more than I can give you now. My company and my friendship. But I am calm. May you be, too. Believe me, old man, I accept the destiny we will share."

Pedro sighed. "I could believe you better if you believed what I do."

He told me then how one must believe in that other land beyond the ocean. How when the sun sinks in the west every night, it is not devoured by the earth or miraculously reborn in the east at dawn, but has circled around the earth, which must be round like the sun and the moon, for his old eyes had never seen flat bodies in the heavens, only spheres, and our earth would not be the monstrous exception.

He recounted how thousands of times at dusk, his feet planted firmly upon the dry earth of summer or sunken in the winter mud, he had gazed upon the expanse of an enormous open field, free of the accident of mountain or forest, and how whirling where he stood he had seen that the earth and the horizon traced two perfect circles and that the sun, as it nightly bade farewell to the earth, recognized itself in its sister form.

"Poor old man," I said with increasing melancholy, "if what you say is true, then at the end of this voyage we'll have returned to our point of departure and everything will have been in vain. *I* will be right. And you'll be returning to what you remember with horror."

"And you?"

It was difficult for me to say: "To what I have forgotten."

"Then believe as I do," Pedro said energetically, "that God did not create this world to be inhabited only by the men that you and I have known. There must be another, better land, a free and happy land made in God's true image, for I believe the one we have left behind is but an abominable reflection."

And he repeated, his voice trembling: "I don't believe that God created this world to be inhabited only by men that you and I have known, men we have remembered or forgotten . . . it's all the same. And if that is not the case, I will no longer believe in God."

I told him I could respect his faith, but that he needed proof to sustain these questionable convictions. He asked me to bring him a lime from the sack. This I did. We knelt on the deck and he asked me to stand the lime on end. I was convinced of the old man's madness, but again resigned myself to my bad fortune. I tried to do what he asked, but the elliptical faded green fruit again and again rolled over onto its side. I looked at Pedro in silence, not yet daring to point out his error. And as I say, I was resigned. The old man took the lime, held it high between two thick fingers, then smashed it down against the planking of the deck. The base of the lime split open, its juice ran out, but it stood on end.

Pedro handed me the lime: "Your lips are white, Pilgrim. You need to suck one of these little limes every day."

That night neither of us slept. Some wretched suspicion kept us awake until the appearance of our early-morning star. I had nothing to fear but certain death, the fatal moment when we'd be tossed into a foaming cemetery to perish, crushed beneath the monumental opaque waters, black as the deepest rivers of Hell. Nevertheless, as the star appeared, announcing another day of heat and calm, I fancied I'd struggled against sleep to prevent Pedro's worrying that as he slept I would take advantage of his rest to strangle him with a cord, throw him overboard, and undertake the return to the coast from which we'd set sail.

But in truth I'd also feared that as I slept, the old man, for fear of me, would do the same, would kill me with the broken knife he kept beside him at the helm, throw me to the sharks that had for days been following in the wake of the ship, and then continue alone, assured, without misgivings, his willful voyage to disaster.

The disquieting star—sister to dusk and to the dawn—glimmered, seeming to confirm in her round the old man's circular reasoning. And it was he who resolved our fears, he the valiant one who first lay down in a corner of the deck, shaded by the canvas that protected our casks of sweet water.

"Aren't you afraid of me, Pedro?" I shouted from the helm in my white and briny voice.

"The death you foresee for us is a worse risk," the old man said. "If you believe so strongly we're going to perish, why would you kill me now?" And after a brief pause he added: "I want the first person to set foot on the new land to be a young man." And closed his eyes.

I imagined myself master of the ship, free of the old man and his fatal race toward disaster: I imagined returning to the coast we'd left behind twelve days before. And as I pictured myself there, I tried to imagine what I would do once we'd returned to the starting point. Well, Sire: I could imagine only two courses. One would carry me back to an earlier point of departure, and from there to the one before that, and so on, until I'd reached the place and time of my origins. But if I began again from that forgotten origin, what road offered itself to me but the one I'd already traveled? And that road, what could it do but lead me to the shore where I'd found Pedro, and from there, with him on this ship, to the same point we find ourselves, in this very instant, on the sea? I reflected in this way about the sad fate of a man in time, for the great abundance of the past obliged me to forget it and live only this fleeting present: but caught in the memory-less succession of the seconds, I was given no choice: my future would be as obscure as my past.

With my eyes closed I stood thinking about these things. And as I thought, the struggle between survival and risk began to trouble the quiet resignation of my soul. Pedro had closed his eyes. I opened mine.

"Guide me, star, guide me," I fervently pleaded.

I followed the path of the sun, the will of the old man, and my fatal destiny, toward the motionless Sargasso Sea.

WATER CLOCK

And so, Sire, we measured time by water. The saltiness of the sea increased, and we consumed the sweet water in the casks, but everything, except Pedro and me and our ship, was water. We devoured a goodly portion of our provisions, but kept some of the jerked meat, and baited hooks with it, and threw them into the sea. Since sharks abound in all the seas, it wasn't long till one took the bait, as speedy and voracious in falling into the trap of the astute as in attacking the defenseless sailor.

It was with great joy we captured the first squalus, and gaffed it and dragged it over the side; Pedro killed it by beating it on the head with the side of the ax, and with a knife I cut it into thin strips, which we hung from the rigging. We left them there three days to dry, in no hurry now, sure of food and in no way troubled to postpone our banquet. Few things bring two men closer together and force them to forget past quarrels more easily than these fraternal tasks, helping each other to confront a danger, and overcome it. Then we can see how foolish are the disputes of human wills, for nothing can be compared to the menace of nature: nature may lack will, but it abounds in a ferocious instinct for extermination. In this, nature and woman are alike. And here is their greatest danger: their beauty tends to disarm us.

On the thirtieth day of our voyage we ate the savory strips of shark meat, and we laughed heartily upon discovering that our fierce shark had a double reproductive member, that is, that he steered with two virile weapons, each as long as a man's arm from elbow to the tip of his middle finger, and in addition we were cheered by a discussion of whether, when he coupled with the female, the shark exercised both members at one time, or one at a time, in separate couplings. Perhaps that is the reason the female of the shark is known to give birth only once during her lifetime.

I tell you now, Sire, we were completely surrounded by motionless water; I told myself we'd sailed upon the terrible Sargasso Sea, the point where all sailors become fearful and turn back. Not we. I, because I feared the turbulent catastrophe of the future more than the present calmness that delayed that fate. The old man, because neither calm nor torment weakened his confidence in our certain destination, the new world of his dreams. The delightful conversations we had then saved us from the clutches of this indolent ocean. We spoke of the sea, and when Pedro showed me the faithfully—to the extent of man's knowledge—reproduced charts of the ports and harbors ringing our Mediterranean, I could recall, but always without the orientation of any dates, the contours of that remembered sea; but where the charts extended toward the west, marine space faded into an unknown of vague contours.

"That's how it is, son. The mariner's compass can tell us nothing about what lies beyond this point"—his finger touched the island of Iceland—"shown here as Ultima Thule . . ."

". . . where the world ends," I added.

Friends in adversity, father and son, or more accurately, grandfather and grandson, in appearance, we had not because of that ceased to maintain our opposing beliefs.

"Are you still afraid?" the old man asked me.

"No, I'm not afraid. But neither do I believe. And you?"

"I fear your name. Do you swear you're not called Felipe?"

"Yes. Why do you fear that name?"

"Because that name is capable of carrying me to something worse than the end of the world."

"To what, Pedro?"

"To his castle. He lives there, with death."

These are the things the old man said when his spirit grew somber; then I would try to talk again about the sea and boats, and then old Pedro, a man of action and memories as I was one of dreams and forgetfulness, explained the observations leading him to conceive the plan of this lateen-rigged, two-masted vessel with triangular sails superior, he told me, to those on the ancient cogs, for by lying closer to the wind it took better advantage of it. And the absence of a forecastle, as well as the lightness of the wood from which the ship was built, assured greater agility and maneuverability. I saw that now: two men alone, we were able to control this small and docile ship, and we had come this far tacking with scarcely a breeze fore or aft, and were even advancing over the Sargasso, although the water was like oil. Old Pedro had shown himself to be ingenious and full of illusions.

"I must not falter now!"

He told me how, twenty-two years before, he'd tried to embark in search of the new land. "My plan was ruined by three men and a woman; their desires destroyed me, for they wanted only the deceptive promises of our old land. They destroyed me, son, but they saved themselves—although I doubt now whether that imperfect old barge would have carried us very far. So I abandoned my fields and came to the seashore; I exchanged the company of field laborers for that of sailors. It took me a long while to learn what I needed. This ship is almost perfect.''

He said that when a squadron of light ships like this were constructed, and of greater size and with larger crews, they would tame the ocean. "We must guard our secret well, though, lest all come by the route that today belongs only to you and me, my boy, where both solitude and freedom are ours.''

He spoke without lowering his voice; vast was the arched ceiling of this marine cathedral, and if I served as his confessor, those words would never cross my lips for anyone but him to hear.

We were in the fourth day of the second month on the route of the trade winds when our sails swelled and we saw the sure sign of a favorable wind in flying fish. We admired those fish, whose two wings emerge alongside the gills, a handsbreadth long, as wide as your thumb, covered with skin like the wing of a bat. Because we had some fine nets aboard, I was able to capture a few that passed very close by the starboard rail. We ate them. They tasted of smoke.

I can tell you now, Sire, that eating those flying fish was the last pleasure we were to enjoy. The following day, toward midday, the sea lay blue and the wind blew soft; the salt of those calm, even waves was the dew of the burning sun: everything, I say, was harmonious . . . clear, warm beauty. The sea was the sea, the sky the sky, and we were a calm and living part of it all. Then, to the north of our vessel, a tumult burst forth, the azure horizon exploded into tall, brilliant flashes of white; the sea was churned with an anger all the more impressive for being so sudden and so in contrast with the peace and silence the old man and I'd been enjoying an instant before. White waves, though still distant, approached relentlessly, swelling to ever increasing heights. Belly of glass, crowned with phosphorescent plumes, the flotillas of enormous waves devoured each other only to be born redoubled in size.

At last we saw the black tail of the fierce beast threshing the once tranquil waters; we saw it dive and then, a half league from us, shoot like a heavy arrow into the air, opening great jaws of iridescent flesh, turning slowly, diving, again emerging violently from the sea as if it detested both air and water but needed both in equal measure. Sire, first we saw the frightful lime-and-seashell-crusted back, looking like an enormous phantom ship, mysteriously propelled, its driving force the death which clung in that odious dross to the whale's back. Then we saw its bloodshot, aqueous, flaming eye, crisscrossed with coagulated broken veins, appearing and disappearing between the slowly moving, oozing, oily lid; our safe little ship was turned into an uncontrollable raft, whipped by the chaotic, violent, and ever higher waves engendered by the leviathan.

I feared that if we received one blow from that tail we would sink, broken in two. But the ship was proving its good construction. It behaved like a cork, and the old man and I, hanging on to the same mast, my hands grasping his shoulders and his clutching mine, felt our vessel was the plaything of the tumult; but the boat did not fight the waves; rather, it bent to their hostile commands, bobbing over the crests and in this manner keeping us afloat. Pounding foam sprayed over our heads.

I saw the reason for it all. I shouted to the old man to watch the terrible combat an enormous swordfish had launched against the whale, for so close to us was the struggle that we could see every detail of the fish, the jaw filled with ferocious teeth, the hard rough sword struggling to puncture the whale's thick hump, and it was a marvel to watch how the fish played the side of his rapier, not the point, ripping and tearing the leviathan's best defense, the tough striated skin, seeking the opportunity to plunge his sword into the wildly rolling eye of the enemy.

I was grateful that the great fish was employing his sword against the whale and not against our ship, for he could have penetrated our bulwarks a handsbreadth deep, as now, quick as a flash, with an unexpected movement he drove his sword deep into the whale's eye, with the same gusto and to the same depth the male thrusts into the female. I don't know whether we shouted with surprise as we saw how the fish, precise and quivering, knew instinctively how to press his advantage in the battle, for it seemed to move with greater speed than the whale could comprehend, whether Pedro and I cried out in empathetic pain, whether the terrible moan came from the enormous jaws of the suffering, wounded giant, whether a victory cry could have been born of the silvery vibrations of the fish, or whether the ocean itself, wounded along with its most powerful monster, issued a mournful cry from the deep, a great bellow of reddish foam.

But imagine, Sire: the leviathan leaps for the last time, attempting to free itself from the fatal pike driven deep into its eye; then it sinks, perhaps also for the last time, seeking refuge in the deep, and perhaps relief from pain. And as it submerges it drags in its green wake the fish, trembling now, eager to free itself from its prey, victimized in turn by its victim, and carried by it to the silent kingdom where the whale can wait whole centuries for its wound to heal, cured by the sea's medicines, salt and iodine, while the fish, formerly master and now slave to its body's weapon, body and weapon inseparable, will die, its fine brittle skeleton, as silvery as its scales, deposited in crusts of lime and shell on the hide of the great whale. I must rejoice that the arms of man, staff and iron, though propelled by flesh and blood, are not part of our bodies.

There we stood, blindly clinging to the mast, rubbing our soaking shoulders and our hairy necks. When we opened our eyes, we moved apart, made sure the rudder was in good condition, the lines well secured, and that nothing indispensable had been lost. Only then did we look at the sea of blood surrounding us, the red bubbles ascending from the depths capturing the light of the sun, staining it with blood. What awaited us ahead? Drop by drop, our water clock measured the spilled blood of the wounded ocean.

WHIRLPOOL OF THE NIGHT

Life's everyday habits must be immediately reestablished; routine boredom seems like noble perseverance when marvels—by their abundance—acquire the aspect of custom. Thus the old man and I, when we touched the hair at the back of our necks, realized that neither scissors nor blade had come near our unshorn heads for many days; nor had we consulted a mirror in more than two months.

We moved away from the stern and its red wake; who would have dared seek his image in a mirror of blood? For a better tool, I rummaged through a canvas sack for the glass I'd stolen from some sleeping household, and braced myself to look at my face. I saw where salt and sun had left their marks, white where the indication of a question, joy, or fear was wont to wrinkle the skin, but the color of polished wood where the twofold action of sun and spume had touched my face. There was little beard, a fine, golden fuzz, not at all like the gray, tangled and abundant fleece adorning Pedro, but my mane reached my shoulders. A young lion and a bear, companions in the middle of the ocean. I looked at myself, and as I looked asked my reflection: "Where do you come from? Where have you been and what have you learned that there is no trace of malice in you? Can innocence be the fruit of experience? One day, when you remember, tell me."

I showed my aged companion his reflection; we laughed, forgetting the fish and the whale. I sat upon a keg while the old man, with shiny tailor's scissors I'd also stolen on the shore cut my long hair; I put away the glass in my double pocket.

It was growing dusk when we exchanged positions and I performed the barber's rites, trimming Pedro's rough and savage neck; neither of us spoke of what truly occupied our thoughts. For more than two months we'd been sailing in a straight line from East to West, and still no sign of land nearby, no bird or vegetation or floating log or strong-scented breeze of oven or of meat or bread or excrement or stagnant water, as Pedro had hoped—nor precipitous waters and atrocious death, as I had feared. The skies were beginning to grow heavy with clouds.

"Hurry," the old man said. "There's little light left and a storm is threatening."

"That's good," I replied. "I hope the rain will fill our empty casks."

I recall our words, and I connect them with the familiar sound of scissors as I trimmed my friend's neck, because those were the last words and that the last ordinary action we were to say or do. Sire: beneath my feet I felt a growing suction as if a lightning flash were issuing not from the stormy sky but from the tormented waters, a flash passing from my head to my feet; an inverted flash, so it felt to me, striking without the warning the good firmament offers us; that must be so because the sky and land look upon one another openly, while it's different with the kingdom of the sea, which having taken the veil is to the sky and land what the nun is to man and woman.

This was a flash, I say, born of a profound eruption at the very bottom of the sea; liquid fire. The ship creaked frighteningly; the natural night was doubled in another, cyclonic darkness; the storm burst and I gave thanks that the heavens thundered like our boat, that the clouds descended to hover above the mastheads, that real lightning announced real thunderbolts. Each of us ran to a mast; we trimmed the sails, attempting to furl them and lash them down with rope, but the sudden heaving of the boat prevented us; we rolled across the deck and crashed against the bulwarks. I seized a large iron ring embedded in the starboard rail; we had voyaged, sailed, tacked, settled onto the calm Sargasso, been driven by soft trade winds, agitated by the tumult raised by the whale, but what was happening now was totally different from anything we could ever have foreseen. The wheel was uncontrollable, whirling madly at will; Pedro was helpless, his outstretched hands mercilessly drubbed by the wildly windmilling spokes and knobs. The ship wasn't sailing, it was whirling, sucked lower and lower, the Devil's toy, caught in a suction originating in the yawning jaws of the deep.

"Here we are at the edge of the universe," I said to myself, "at the mercy of the cataract; this is what I have dreaded, the hour has come . . ."

For our ship was sinking into a sinister, invisible whirlpool; I knew that, with fear, when I no longer could see the water beneath us, but above us: the phosphorescent crests of the waves were the only light in that black tempest, and if earlier the waves had risen to swamp us, now they threatened to capsize and crush us: the swells receded from us not horizontally but vertically, in a line parallel to our heads, not our outstretched arms; the waves were above us, high over our heads, higher even than masts that no longer pointed toward the clouds. We were descending the watery walls of a bottomless whirlpool, we were a paper boat foundering in a gutter, a fly swimming in honey, we were nothing, there.

And even though I was prepared for this, for I had foreseen and feared nothing else, I observed at that moment, Sire, the vigorous tenacity of life, for I labored then as if hope were possible; my mind racing, I ran toward Pedro, who struggled in vain to control the whirling wheel; the rudder had allied itself with the whirlpool and was our enemy. I pushed Pedro, whipped and befuddled, toward the nearest mast and as best I could lashed him to the pole; the old man moaned all the while, a feeble echo returned to the roar of the storm. There is nothing I could tell you, Sire, that could reproduce the roaring of that tempest; more than a tempest, it was the end of all tempests, the frontier of hurricanes, the sepulcher of storms: a centenary combat of wolves and jackals, lions and crocodiles, eagles and crows could not engender a more piercing, shriller, greater, and more keening outcry than that dark lament of all the wind-whipped seas of the world here reunited, over and around and below us; great, terrible, and without surcease were the boundaries and pantheon of the waters, Sire.

The bound old man moaned: the sparks from his eyes told me he considered himself a prisoner and me the jailer of the ship, and in those flashing glances was perhaps disguised the terror of defeat. We had reached not the new land of his desires but the bottomless well of my fears. I didn't stop to reflect, I acted, telling myself that if salvation was to be had it would be attained only by clinging to the iron rings or the masts, and I myself clung for an instant to the mast, looking into Pedro's resentful eyes, vacillating between anger and sadness, when before us we saw the second mast break like a feeble reed, sucked immediately, a quiet ruin of splinters, into the circling maelstrom.

I lost all hope; the speed with which we whirled toward the belly of the maelstrom tore the ropes loose from the casks, and they began to roll with menacing and chaotic force about the deck, demolishing what remained of the boat's equilibrium. I imagined that within a few brief instants we would founder, deep within the vortex, swept from the deck, for now we could not even see the distant sky and distant crests of the sea we'd left both behind and above us; upturned, standing on end, we looked into our destiny, the blind eye of death in the entrails of the sea.

Then stumbling and falling I ran among the tumbling barrels, thinking feverishly in what manner I might best lash them again or throw them overboard; just in time I reached my iron ring and clung to it at the very moment the most terrible of all the tremors shook the boat.

Everything in it that was not lashed down, casks and rigging, hooks and canvas, chains and harpoons, chests and bags, tumbled over the sides; clinging to my iron ring, I feared I, too, would be swept overboard as I saw them sucked out of the ship by the rapid circular whiplash, the whistling trajectory, our ship traced around the liquid walls of that marine tunnel.

I looked upward; it was like looking toward the highest tower ever built or toward the mountain after the Deluge; we were captive within a cylinder of compacted, fissureless water, a tube uninterrupted to the top of the distant, chiaroscuroed peaks of phosphorescent foam. And beyond was the sky and the storm; but we were part of a space without sky or storm; we were living within the swiftly racing black cave of the whirlpool, in the tomb of the waters. I imagined what lay beneath us, a smooth, narrow, pulsating pit; the infinite well. I called upon my diminished powers of observation and again looked upward; I don't know whether our star Venus was shining once again high above or whether certain forms of luminous waves were being regularly repeated; what is certain is that in the distance there was a point of reference, a providential, fleeting, faint luminosity that permitted me to measure with exactitude the curve of our trajectory within the whirlpool: I counted on my fingers, I counted forty seconds for every revolution—I counted, and my fingers still hurt from that counting—and I found that as I counted between thirty and thirty-six the velocity of the rotation notably diminished, our ship slipped into a calmer segment of the curve, cruelly offering a hope of remission before redoubling its fury to explode, between thirty-seven and forty of my total, with a whiplash force that at every revolution threatened to break forever the nutshell that held us. I looked at the liquid walls of our prison, and what I saw was incredible. Among the objects thrown outside the ship by the force of the whirlpool, some—heavy sacks, and chains, and the anchor— were descending into the vortex with greater velocity than that of the ship itself, while others, with equal speed, were effecting the opposite movement: I saw a yellowish cluster of shriveled limes ascending, I saw pieces of canvas rising and empty kegs and the sail we'd not managed to furl; I saw, an even greater marvel, that the pieces of the splintered mast were also ascending in regular rotation toward the surface of the sea that was our tomb, toward a meeting with the heavens that had forgotten us.

Never had a mind debated so fast and feverishly as in that instant: in every complete revolution of our boat around the circular walls of water I had exactly six seconds to move without fear of being sucked from the boat: swiftly, I reviewed the objects caught in the rigging and still remaining in the boat: strips of shark meat, some lines attached to the embedded iron rings; in vain I sought the ax with which we'd clubbed the shark to death: in the pocket of my water-soaked doublet I felt the shaving mirror, and in the belt of my breeches the black tailor's scissors. And Pedro bound to the mast. And at the helm, the wheel, spinning wildly, weakened now, perhaps, in its precise and precious equipoise as both indicator and guide of the ship.

In the six seconds Providence granted me at each rotation, I ran to the wheel. The vibration had damaged its stability. I returned to my sure hold on the ring. I endured the trembling whiplash as the ship completed its gyration. I returned to the wheel, utilized the scissors as a lever, seized its vibrating base, and struggled like a galley slave to prize loose that wheel on which all my hopes were pinned.

Imagine, Sire, my repeated efforts during that eternal night whose only hour hands were those of my particular sequence: six seconds of feverish activity, thirty-four of obligatory and painful repose, watchful, adding my sweat to the waters that washed over me and at times blinded me, wiping away when I could the thick salt encrusted on my forehead and eyes. I ran toward the mast, waited, I began to free Pedro, waited, continued freeing Pedro, waited, I told him to run with me to the wheel, waited, we ran, I counted, I told him first to seize the base of the wheel, that he count to thirty-six and move only when I moved, now, clutching the wheel—wait, old man, now—I bound him chest and shoulders to the wheel, waited, now I grasped the wheel, wait, old man, now take the line, tie me while I hold myself pinned to the motionless base, now let go, old man, free your arms as I free mine, now we're going to fly, old man, to fly or drown, I don't know which: old man, you told me, didn't you, that the novelty of this ship was its light wood? Invoke that lightness now, Pedro, for your life and mine, pray for us; I don't know what forces of this hostile whirlpool cause certain weights to descend and others to rise, pray that your wheel be of the former, let go, old man, here comes the whiplash of this fearful curve, now . . .

The combined velocity of the whirlpool and the ship threw us overboard, dashed us against the smooth turbulence of the vortex, it was impossible to know whether we were upside down or right side up, we lost all orientation, twins bound to the wheel that had in its turn fallen into the claws of the maelstrom. I closed my eyes, nauseated, choking, blinded by the cataracts of black spume in this ocean tunnel, knowing that my sight was of as little use as my death, perhaps, would be. At first I closed my eyes in order not to lose consciousness, such was the rapidity of the revolutions: no one has ever known such vertigo, Sire, no one; and in that vertigo, light and dark were one, silence and clamor, my being and that of the female who gave me birth, wakefulness and sleep, life and death, all one. Finally I lost all consciousness, calculation, or hope; I was born again, again I died, and only one thought accompanied me amidst all that vertigo:

"You've lived this already . . . before . . . you've lived it . . .

before . . . you knew . . . already,'' the waters murmured in my dead ear.

For the last time, I opened my eyes, the old man and I were still bound to the wheel. I saw the upturned keel of our ship in the heart of the vortex, I heard nothing, for the drumming of the waters obliterated everything. All I saw was that husk of wood fading out of sight forever, consummating its nuptials with the sea.

THE BEYOND

Was there ever a time, Sire, you looked death in the face? Do you know the strange new geography death offers to the passive eyes and stilled hands of the dead? With no proof except that of my own death, I imagine the universe of death is different for every person. Or is the uniqueness of our deaths also wrested from us by the nameless immortal forces of sea and slime, stone and air. Farewell to an age of pride; accept now the certainty that as the senses that served us in life are dead, a new sense with dusty eyelids and waxy fingers is born in each of us in death, awaiting only that moment to lead us toward white beaches and black forests.

I say white and black in order to be understood, but I do not speak of whiteness as we know it in life, the white of bone or sheet, or of the blackness of the crow or of the night. Imagine, if you can, Sire, their simultaneous existence; side by side, at once illuminating and obscuring, the white white because the contrast of black permits it, and the black made black because white lights its blackness. In life these colors are divorced, but when at the hour of death I opened my new eyes of sand, I saw them forever united, one the color of the other, unimaginable alone: black beaches, white jungles. And the sky of death obscured by swift wings: a flock of shrieking, brightly colored birds flew overhead, their number so great they darkened the sun.

I am recounting my first impressions upon dying, as vague and uncertain as my drowsy fatigue, but as precise as the certainty that I would not be astounded by anything I saw, for I was dead, and thus I was seeing for the first time what one sees on the littoral of death. I clung to such simple facts: I had met death in the sea and we had descended into its entrails through a deep tunnel of water; the speeding vortex had led us to the island of the dead, a curious place of vague outlines, a hazy impression of white beach, black jungle, and shrieking birds that cast the veil of their wings across a spectral sun. Phantasmal island, final port of phantasmal voyagers. All of this must be accepted as truth, my will was incapable of offering any opposition; so this was the contract with death, an inability to affirm, to better, or to transform. Final port, a reality without appeal.

Had I come to this bay alone or accompanied? The eyes of the dead voyager search for new and strange directions, Sire, for he has lost the compass of his terrestrial days and cannot tell whether far is near, or near, far. With the ears of death I heard intermittent breathing; with the eyes of death I saw I was approaching a beach, accompanied by moth-er-of-pearl shells washed toward shore by the waves and by a soft dew that bathed both them and me. The dew was cool, the waters of the sea were warm, a green warmness warm as the water of a bath, different from the icy gray seas and cold blue waters I had known in life. I reached the shore of the other world with an armada of seashells that seemed to guide me toward the beach; my face was washed in the warm waves, I felt grainy sand beneath my hands and knees and feet; I was enveloped in crystalline green water, calm and silent as a lake.

I thought I had returned to life; I tried to shout; I tried to shout a single word: "Land!"

But instead of the impossible voice of a dead man I heard a bellow of pain; I looked and saw a floating wineskin adrift in the current of a sleepy river that emptied here into the sea; I saw an enormous monster with the body of a hairless pig, boiled or singed by fire; the monster moaned and stained the limpid waters with red; it was fat and dark and had two teats upon its breast; it was bleeding, carried toward the sea by the slow current. When I saw it, I tried desperately to grab hold of the floating shells around me; I said to myself, this is God-the-Terrible; I said, I'm looking at the very Devil, and I think I fainted from terror.

Perhaps I slipped from swoon to sleep. When I came to myself I seemed to be reclining. My head rested on the sandy beach, my body was caressed by warm waves. I managed to struggle to my feet, blind-ed still by fear and the acceptance of death. I looked toward the sea; the wineskin monster was drifting toward the horizon, inanimate and bleeding. I stepped onto the beach and was bathed in light. It was as beautiful as the sunset: a light slanting horizontally across the beach it bathed in a glossy grayish luster. I told myself that was the light we had in life called pearly.

I stopped looking at the light and turned to see what things it re-vealed. Sire: that beach of the Beyond, the beach I stood upon for the first time, was the most beautiful shore in the world; the beach in a dream, for if death were the most beautiful and desired and now the most complete of dreams, this would be the coast of the Paradise that God reserves for the blessed. A white beach of brilliant sand and thick black forests: I recognized the tree of the desert, the sighing palm. And the clearest of skies, cloudless, pure burning light born of itself, with no winged messengers to interrupt its gaze.

My damp footsteps sank into the sands of Eden. I breathed new odors, like nothing ever smelled before, sweet and juicy and heavy. I thought of the promises of the gods, but here were realities. The immense rolling white perfumed and shining beach of Paradise was a vast sandy treasure chest spilling over with a wealth of precious pearls. As far as my newly recovered and astonished sight could see, large nacreous shells and beautiful pearls covered the expanse of this providential beach. Pearls black as jet, tawny pearls, pearls yellow and scintillating as gold, thick and clustered, bluish pearls, quicksilver pearls, pearls verging upon green, some with diluted tones of paleness, others glowing in incendiary shades, pearls from all the mollusks, margarites, and minute baroques. The refracted light of all the mirrors of the world mixed with the white brilliance of the sands could not match the coruscating splendor of this pearly beach where death had thrown me. I buried my feet in the fabulous riches accumulated here, then quickly squatted to plunge my arms to the elbows in the treasure of this happy shore.

I bathed in pearls, Sire, precious pearls, pearls of all sizes, paragon pearls, graduated pearls, seed pearls; I swam among pearls, and I hungered and thirsted to eat and drink pearls, bushels of pearls, Sire, some the size of a large chestnut, hull and all, and round as all perfection, of a clear and glowing color worthy of the crown of the most powerful monarch, and smaller but no less shimmering baroque seed pearls worthy of being strung in the most divine necklace, then to preserve their pulsating life upon the palpitating breasts of a Queen.

The sea had sewn this beach in pearls, and the sea continued to strew its pearly shells upon the shore where they awaited the dew as one awaits the bridegroom, for they are conceived of the dew and impregnated by the dew, and if the dew is pure the pearls are white, and if the dew is murky, they are dark and shadowy: pearls, daughters of the sea and sky. I had emerged from their cradle and now walked among their coffers, Sire, and I asked myself heatedly whether I was seeing and touching these marvels with the senses I had lost, or through the perceptions of death, and whether when I was resuscitated I would lose them on the spot and see only sands and gull droppings where now I saw great treasures. I raised a large pearl to my mouth; I bit it, almost breaking my teeth. It was very real. Or was it real only in this land of death and dream? It didn't matter: I told myself that whether this were the prize or the price of death, I happily accepted—reward or final end.

I picked up pearls by the fistfuls and only then did I experience the sadness of death and lament the absence of life. I moaned. The only person who would profit from these riches was one who could remember nothing, either of his life or of his death. I longed to be a living man again, Sire, a man of passions and ambitions, of pride and jealousy, for here was the wherewithal to exact the most passionate revenge against the enemies who had harmed us in life, or to confer the greatest favors upon the coldest and most inaccessible of women—or the warmest and most approachable. Neither the fortress of the warrior, nor the palace of the King, nor the portals of the Church, nor the honor of a Lady, I told myself at that moment, could possibly resist the seduction of the man who owned such opulence.

With outstretched arms, fists filled, I offered the pearls to the land of death. My shining gaze was returned by the veiled and inhospitable stares of the true masters of this beach. Only then did I see them, for their enormous carapaces blended with the color of the jungle behind them. I saw gigantic sea turtles, scattered along the verge where the sand ended and the jungle thicket began. And those sad veiled eyes reminded me of my old friend Pedro, and as I remembered him, I felt that the pearls in my hands grew soft and faded and finally died.

"Old man," I murmured, "I was the first to set foot on the new world, as you wished it."

And I threw the pearls back to the pearls. The sea turtles looked at me with suspicious torpor. And at that instant I would have exchanged all the treasures of the beach for the old man's life.

RETURN TO LIFE

I slept a long time on a bed of pearls. When I awakened, I told myself that time hadn't moved: the same light, the same warm waves, the eternal sea turtles watching me from that frontier between the beach and the forest. Everything was exactly the same, but I felt that in my sleep I had deeply penetrated the veil of an imaginary night. If this was Paradise it could not accommodate the contrasts and measures of life—night and day, heat and cold. And nevertheless, I was hungry and thirsty. I decided to investigate the shoreline of this recaptured Eden; no doubt my hunger and thirst were of a new order, not physical, and I was confusing the needs of an errant soul with the demands of a nonexistent body. Who would guide me to the water and the fruit of death?

I seemed to remember, from instinct more than any teaching, that upon our arrival at the other shore, someone waited to lead us to our eternal abode. Someone, or something: beast or angel, dog or Devil. Were the drowsing sea tortoises the guardians of death? As I walked toward them another instinct, stronger than memory, for it is called survival, caused me to put my hand to my waist. I felt the tailor's scissors, secure in the belt of my breeches. The sea turtles' oily eyelids slowly opened and closed: they were the image of passivity, but as I drew closer I could see what preoccupied them.

They were spawning, Sire; two dozen sea tortoises, flattened beneath verdigris shells crusted with ocean debris like that on the back of the whale, were emptying their slimy eggs into nests hollowed from the sand, but at my approach they became alarmed and began to bury their eggs in the sand, waving their short ribbed flippers, uncertain whether to hide their reptilian heads beneath those enormous shells or extend their scaly, blemished necks in challenge. Hunger commanded; I hazarded the risk. With one foot I attempted to raise one of the turtles, but its weight was excessive, it lay as heavily motionless as a rock. Then I saw the nearby river and decided to slake my thirst while I formulated a plan to move one of the sea turtles from its nest.

I walked toward the river. Its mouth was only a narrow notch in the thicket through which the jungle bled its venom. Where the river met the sea a poisonous sand bar had built up, covered with rotting leaves, reeds and slime, and corpses of the wineskin monster I'd seen dying drifting out to sea. The remains lodged on the sand bar were bits of dark, decaying flesh, and the opaque waters of the river's mouth were covered with a thick scum of green slime. I splashed this aside and it was as if I had stirred a hornets' nest; my action seemed to wake a fine cloud of insects from their lethargy; born from the waters or fallen from the sky, they swarmed over my head and hands, seeking out the slight wounds the storm—and the effects of clinging desperately to the ship's wheel during my deliverance—had left on my fingers and elbows, along with deeper gouges on my knees. As I fought the flies, the insects gorged themselves on my blood, quickly glutted; as I swatted them against my skin, I noticed they were as yellow as the bloom of dyer's woad.

I fled before that storm of mosquitoes, quickly bathed my body in the sea, and now I did not hesitate. I walked toward the sea turtles as I searched for a receptacle among the seashells on the beach. With one hand I picked up the deepest shell and in the other I firmly clutched my scissors. I approached the turtle farthest from the others; as I drew near she stretched her neck far outside her shell, at the same time hurriedly covering her eggs with sand. I straddled her carapace, grabbed the scoriaceous neck and drove in the scissors to the hilt—for I knew that these beasts have a sac filled with pure water that permits them to live a long time without thirst, like the camels in the desert. I collected the water in the concave shell and, when this was filled, pulled off parts of my clothing in order to catch even more liquid, which I could suck to satisfy my thirst. By the time I held my shirt to the turtle's neck, only blood ran from the wound, staining it and the sand and the scattered pearls. But I didn't complain, for the blood of the turtle is as good as water. Thus I quenched my thirst, drinking the water from the shell, then squeezing the blood from the moistened doublet onto my lips; and I had already imagined the savor of the flesh of that ageless beast, said to be as ancient as the ocean and, like it, immortal, when I became aware of the terror—a terror more terrible for being totally silent—of the other turtles that were abandoning their fecund nests in the sand and beginning to disperse across the mother-of-pearl shells toward the protective ocean where they would regain their speed and strength.

I feasted then upon a great banquet of turtle eggs, which are similar to those laid by hens except that those of the sea tortoise are covered only by a thin membrane instead of a shell. And as I was eating I watched the spectacle of that powerful squadron of turtles reentering the sea; and so vast was their company that if a large boat had been in their path, they would have slowed its course. They left behind, for my solace, the flesh of one of their companions and the seed of their children. And a beach stained with blood.

Satiated, I lay on my back in the pearly sand and tried to order my thoughts. Hunger and thirst had blinded me; only now, filled and content, could I reason that those had been real feelings, the hunger and thirst of a living body. And those nests of turtle eggs had not deceived me: they were the opposite face of the pearls, for in the pearls I saw another death image. Without the contact of living flesh, pearls grow old and their luster dims: pearls are a moribund promise; the turtle eggs, pearls of nascent life.

Troubled, I rose to my feet; my mortal reasoning was crumbling; it was inconceivable that any living being could be born in the land of death, or that the beasts of death could give birth to life in the ports of the Beyond, whether it be Paradise or Hell: such absurdity was equally foreign both to science and to legend.

"Then there's life," I whispered, "there's life here . . . and death." These words meant changing courses once again, losing my sense of orientation, descending into another maelstrom. There is spilled blood; therefore, there is life. There is life; therefore, I must survive. I must survive; therefore, I must find a companion.

The shining pearly beach stretched toward a distant cape on the horizon. The sea was green as young lemons; the beach a nacreous white; red, the tall palms with clusters of enormous dates much, much larger than those of the desert. Sea turtles and dates: I would not die of hunger. Pearls: I would not die poor. I laughed. Again the noisy flocks of colored birds wheeled overhead, and in the distance at the end of the beach I saw a faint rising spiral of smoke.

Then I ran. I ran, oblivious of any possible menace, indifferent to the dangers of the new and unknown, toward that sign of human life, fearing a deceptive jungle fire, a will-o'-the-wisp, anything except what I most desired, the companionship of my brother . . . Pedro, Pedro. The shells cut my bare feet; I ran to the edge of the sea, fearful that any odor of blood would again attract those dreadful mosquitoes;

it was hot, and I took comfort from splashing in the calm waves; I was finally aware that the sun of this burning landscape was a boiling brazier fiercer than that of any known land: sweat and salt water ran down my body and sand stuck to my skin; long was the distance to that hope-giving smoke.

An hour later—measured by the clock of my belly—I reached the point on the beach, guided by the persevering, wispy column of smoke.

I fell to my knees exhausted; even more than by fatigue, I was overwhelmed by the complete serenity of the landscape, so contradictory to the urgency of my race toward something that might mean life or death to me. The first thing I saw was the upright wheel from our ship planted firmly in the sand. Then I saw a wiry-haired old man, almost nude, tough and tanned, clearing away underbrush at the edge of the jungle, his back turned to the glimmering wealth of pearls.

"Pedro!" I shouted, still on my knees. "Pedro, Pedro, it's me!"

The old man glanced over his shoulder, looked at me without surprise, and said: "Watch the fire. The rocks are good, they spark when you strike them together. And there's plenty of dry wood. It took me many hours to start that fire. Don't let it die out. This is the first fire in the new world."

A PIECE OF LAND

Fire and death were the two things the old man had fled from. Sorrow and captivity: were those the things I had fled? Now that it's all over, and the perfect circle of my pilgrimage is completed, I think of you, Pedro, and if there is any man besides me who knew you, I ask him to remember you with me, how you were, precise, manly, a hard-working man, a man of few words. All I desired after I'd found you again was for you to tell me what had happened, how we were saved. Even though I knew you were a taciturn man, I thought surely you would answer my barrage of questions: Was the wheel lighter than the force of the vortex dragging us toward the bottom of the sea? How did we stay afloat once we'd reached the surface? How had we become separated? Did you stay bound to the wheel when I was torn loose? What force of nature allowed supreme power to be overcome by supreme lightness? Do you know where we are?

Pedro answered only my last question: "This is the new world I so desired."

He didn't pause for me to tell him: You were right, old man, you won the bet, I gambled my life against your illusions and you returned both of them to me, old man. Nor did he tell me those things himself. Now I understand why: what were our past adventures compared to fortune itself: standing upon the new land so desired by him, so denied and feared—yes, it's true—by me. In the labor the old man was undertaking in this land I saw a serene but urgent decision to begin a new life, starting from nothing, to give a name and use, a place and destiny, to everything. Like God the Father, this old man covered with hair as white as a fleecy cloud was presiding over the first day of Creation, and his deep-set eyes, showing the strain of his years, said only one thing: "Hurry, I haven't much time."

I considered then, with warm and enduring emotion, how this man who was more than seventy years old had attempted twenty years before to make the voyage he had now completed. We must hurry. We don't have much time.

Pedro collected the dried branches of the red palm trees that formed the wall of the jungle and asked me to strip them of their long, hard, sharp-pointed stalks to feed the fire, while he, from the stripped stalks, fashioned a variety of sharp instruments, daggers, swords, stakes, to enclose the space cleared from the jungle at the edge of the sand, and sharp spears with which he attempted to split open the enormous green dates fallen at the foot of the palm trees.

"Here," I said, "it should be easier with my scissors."

I picked up one of the heavy fruits; it was like a green ball with a shell so hard it was impossible to open with my bare hands. I drove the scissors into the center of the monstrous date and worked them back and forth until I broke the shell. And of all the marvels I'd seen in my wanderings, there is none greater than having found water in the heart of that fruit, clear, intoxicating water so pure it tasted like wine from Heaven, and savory, too, its white flesh. I handed the marvelous date to Pedro so he might eat and drink; he exclaimed jubilantly we would never have to fear thirst. I told him about the beach of pearls and he smiled, shaking his head.

"It isn't wise to hold pearls in high esteem, for they grow old and their beauty fades."

"But in the other world . . . I mean, in our world . . ."

"We will never go back."

At his reply my blood ran cold, and the pleasure of having discovered the fruit with the limpid water and leathery flesh also cooled. Pedro returned to his labor.

With reeds and mud, shells and branches, using stones as hammers and substituting thorns for nails, the Father of this lost shore of renewed Creation was raising a house, while I, his creature, climbed the palm trees to harvest the savory dates that slaked the thirst of this burning place, and returned to the beach of pearls to collect not its treasures but eggs from the nests of its turtles. While swimming, I discovered seaweed that was good either raw or boiled. The nature of the rough stones found in the dry gullies was such that one had only to strike them together to elicit fire.

And the wheel that had saved us from death became the gate to our stockade. For after exactly six nights had passed, counted by an equal number of pearls I was gathering to mark the passage of time, Pedro had finished his house. Only then did he speak, leading me down to the edge of the sea. From there we turned and looked at the new space claimed from the jungle, cleared to the border of the sand, tight and fenced and roofed.

"Now no Liege can take away the fruit of my labor, burn my home, rape my women, and kill my sons. Now I am free. I have won."

The old man hawked furiously and spat contemptuously into the sea; it was as if he were spitting in the face of the past, as if he hoped the insult of that saliva would be carried by the ocean currents to the shores from which we'd sailed, staining them with his scorn and proclaiming his victory.

I had watched him, night after night, observing the stars in their heavens, and, day after day, wiping his forehead and lifting his face to look at the sun.

"Do you know where we are, Pedro?"

"Very far to the west."

"So I imagined. That was our course."

"But not this far south. We're so far south now, you can scarcely see the northern stars. And the sun sets very late but goes down very fast. The whirlpool must have dragged us far off our course."

I listened to him in silence, considering the unshakable truth of the one thing I think I know, for as I heard those words I felt my destiny was sealed; return was impossible, and once again the warring motivations of adventure and security struggled within me. The old man did not want to return. I had nothing to return to. And this time resignation did not intervene in the conflict between risk and survival, neutralizing them as before; now it denied them by uniting them.

"Old man, when will we venture inland? There must be a fresh stream near here without those flies, for the lands seem well watered, and we can't live forever from the water of the palms. Aren't you eager to know whether we're on an island or an isthmus or on terra firma? Don't you want to know whether this land is inhabited, and if so, by whom?"

"No, you go alone, if you want. I won't leave this place. I have what I've always wanted. My piece of land."

He nodded emphatically, and as I bowed my head—confused because adventure and survival had become one, and resignation, once a saving grace, had become certainty that to stay here meant death— Pedro did something unexpected; he rubbed my head and then hugged me to his breast and said:

"Yes, the wheel did prove to be lighter than the terrible force dragging us toward the center of the vortex. I closed my eyes when we were thrown into it, but then tried to hold them open in spite of the fact I was blinded by the speed and the vertigo, the flood of waters, and the changing light in that whirlpool. I felt as if I were immersed in a sea of metal, my son, where every drop of water was a golden coin sparkling and shimmering before my eyes; at one moment I would see the glittering face of the coin, and the next, the shadowy cross on the reverse. My bones told me we were ascending, like the limes and the shattered mast and the sails. And then, as we burst out of the whirlpool to the level of the whitecaps, my eyes told me the same. I prayed for our salvation, for the vortex had vomited us up only to deliver us unto the will of God.

"All night long we were whipped and battered by the storm and the lines holding us grew slack; more than once I attempted to bind us both, but the ropes securing you yielded to the power of the storm and finally I had to hold you with my own hands. I clutched your arm until there was no feeling left in my own arm and I couldn't tell whether I was holding you or not; I prayed I was, I prayed you would hold on to my arm, that it would be my arm that saved you, son, but as I prayed I was overcome by a deep and lugubrious fatigue; I gave us up for lost; I sank into the tomb of sleep. The gulls awakened me to a peaceful sea. My arms were entangled and I saw a bed of seaweed. I saw land; I moaned the word, but my parched throat prevented me from shouting it, as I wished to shout after twenty years of hope . . . Land! land! the new world! All I could do was turn to you to whisper it. Only then did I realize you weren't with me. I'd been unable to save you. I wept for you. I wanted a young man to be the first to step onto the land of the new world."

Pedro was silent a long moment as I stood, eyes closed, my head resting against his chest, imagining the scene, imagining how Pedro had saved me, imagining what it was to have a father.

Then the old man continued: "I thought you'd been swept away by the great waves of that terrible night. Now you see I could do nothing to save you. You saved yourself. And you knew that, son. For during the stormy night, bound so close together on the wheel that was keeping us afloat, you didn't seem conscious but you murmured these words . . ."

"I've lived this before . . ." My eyes still closed, my head against his breast, I repeated the words with Pedro. "I knew already . . . I'm living this the second time . . . it happened long ago . . . two shipwrecks . . . two survivors . . . two lives . . . only one can be saved . . . one must die . . . so the other may live."

The old man caressed my head again. "Yes, that's what you said. What were you trying to tell me?"

"What did you think, then, Pedro?"

"That you'd given your life for mine, your young manhood for my old age, and it seemed a cruel fate. Didn't you believe, when you were saved, that I had died?"

"Yes. I despised the pearls of that fabulous beach, for I'd gladly have exchanged them for your life."

"Ah, yes, the pearls; you'd have exchanged the pearls for my life. But would you also have given your life for mine?"

I was troubled. "That doesn't matter now, old man. We're here together. We both survived."

But Pedro said then with great sadness: "No, no, remember, what did you mean that night? Try to remember: you knew everything that happened before it had happened. That's why I believe you must know what is going to happen next, what is going to happen again. Tell me: do you remember? In the end, which of us will survive here? You, or I?"

Sire, I never had the opportunity to answer.

THE EXCHANGE

Whoever lives amid sound is frightened by silence. More than darkness, silence is the terror of the night. And more than his confinement, the captive suffers the absence of the sonorous rhythms of freedom. We were surrounded by soft and regular murmurs: the warm waves of the sea, the crackling of the fire on the beach, the rustling of the palm fans.

Why did those sounds that had become customary after more than a week suddenly cease? I listened, my head still against Pedro's breast, and heard the beating of his heart. Then, like an alert bird with eyes on each side of its head, I looked nervously from the jungle to the sea and from the sea to the jungle. I saw nothing at first: nothing to cause or justify the sudden cessation of sound.

My senses quickened. I imagined I had penetrated the forest at our back: there the green was so intense it was black. Again I looked toward the sea: the lemony-green waters, too, were growing dark, taking on the colors of the jungle: the sea, Sire, was a forest of trees.

I withdrew from the embrace of my aged father and, unable to move toward the shore, stood as if enchanted, perceiving finally that the sea was filled with tree trunks, as it had been the other day with the shells of the turtles, and that those floating trunks were advancing toward our beach. I whirled, frightened, as the fire crackling on the beach was echoed in the sound of snapping twigs and branches parted behind us in the jungle.

Stupidly, I managed to pant: "Pedro, did you bring a weapon?"

The old man shook his head, smiling. "We won't need them here in our happy land."

Happy or unfortunate, was it ours alone? Was it really ours? Or did it belong to the beings whose heads I could now see over the edge of the floating tree trunks? I don't say men, Sire, because the first thing I saw were long black manes which I mistook for horses' tails and for a moment I had a strange vision of floating trees manned by dusky centaurs. Only as that armada of trunks drew closer could I distinguish faces the color of the wood itself, and in the interior of the tree trunks I saw heads, round shields, and another forest—this time vertical—of ferocious lances.

Pedro walked tranquilly to the gate of his house and stood there, his hand upon the ship's wheel. I whirled to look toward the woods; the noise in the thicket was increasing; the invisible force from the jungle and the visible army from the sea were marching toward an encounter.

Then thirty or more men leaped from the trunks into the water, blending with its reflected greenness; their bodies were the color of canaries, their lances red, their shields green. And other men like them, similarly armed and naked except for the cloth that concealed their shame, erupted from the jungle.

They looked at us.

We looked at them.

Our astonishment was identical, and we were equally immobilized. I could only think that what seemed to me fantastic about them—the color of their tawny skin and their straight black hair and smooth-skinned, hairless bodies—must, to creatures so different, have seemed incredible in us—my long gold mane, Pedro's curly hair and white beard, his hirsute face and my pallid one. They looked at us. We looked at them. And from that first exchange was born a fleeting, silent question: "Have they discovered us . . . or did we discover them?"

The natives were the first to conquer their astonishment. Several, as if planned beforehand, ran to our small bonfire and with lances and bare feet stamped out the fire, saving only one burning branch. Then one of them, who wore a band of black bird feathers around his waist, spoke to us excitedly and angrily, pointing toward the sky, then toward the extinguished fire, then toward the expanse of the beach of pearls. Finally he raised three fingers of one hand and with the index of the other counted three times the three extended fingers. I looked at Pedro, as if I had such confidence in his wisdom that I believed him capable of understanding their language and the strange signs. An amazing language, in truth, with chirping sounds, for now the multitude of dark men had begun to speak simultaneously, and their voices seemed more like those of birds than men, and I noticed there were no *r*'s in their speech, but many *t*'s and *l*'s.

And since we could answer none of their arguments, the ire of the plumed man increased, and he walked toward Pedro and spoke again, pointing toward the house and the fence of branches bounding the space reclaimed by the old man in this new world. And the group of natives who had surged from the thicket began to pull up the stakes of the fence and throw them back into the forest. Pedro did not move, but blood surged to his face and veins pulsed at his throat and temples. The party of natives pulled down the fence, ripped the branches from the roof, and kicked and tore down everything the old man had built. I searched desperately for an escape, for some response, some way to reason with the savages, and at that instant, born from some miraculously recovered instinct, came an idea born of the exchange—the simple fact that first we'd exchanged looks and then been unable to exchange words, and from the mutual looks had been born an original and duplicated amazement, but only violence had come from the unanswered words.

I shouted to Pedro without thinking, as if someone else were speaking through me, using my voice: "Old man! Offer them your house! Offer them something, quickly!"

Blood glinted in Pedro's eyes, and foam bubbled at the corner of his lips. "Never! Nothing! Not one nail! Everything here is mine!"

"Something, Pedro, something!"

"Nothing! It took me twenty years to best El Señor! Never!"

"Hurry, Pedro, give them your land as a gift!"

"Never!" he screamed like a cornered beast, clinging to the ship's wheel that had saved us once before. "Nothing! This is my piece of land, this is my new home . . . Never!"

The black-plumed chieftain shouted: the natives rushed at Pedro, but the old man struggled against them; he was a hoary lion, striking furiously at the faces and bodies of his assailants; he shouted at me: "Bastard, don't leave me alone! Fight, are you a woman!"

I pulled the scissors from my breeches and raised them to strike; they glinted darkly in the sun and the natives stopped abruptly; they stood back from Pedro as the black-plumed leader shouted something to the men from the sea who were waiting on the beach, lances poised; as one, their weapons flew toward a single target: Pedro's heart.

I was paralyzed with fright, my scissors still in my upraised fist: like the flocks of birds, the flying lances darkened the sky; they pierced the old man's body as one of the natives threw the burning branch onto the remains of the hut, setting fire to the dried branches of the thatching.

The old man did not cry out. His life was ended, standing by the ship's wheel, arms open, eyes and mouth wide, engulfed in the smoke from his burning hut, his body run through by red lances; Pedro was dead, standing at the foot of his little plot of land by the beach. He had obtained what he had so long sought, but he did not keep it long.

I told myself such steadfastness deserved at least this poor glory: the first to step on the new land, the first whose blood was spilled upon it. I shut my eyes as the sound of mockery filled my ears, my own laughter echoing through unshed tears, and I could see upon a black background the cadaver and the blood of the ancient turtle I had killed with the same scissors I still grasped in my hand.

Then I heard no sound at all except the crackling of the fire consuming the pitiful remains of the hut and the body of my friend and grandfather. Slowly the quiet murmur of the waves and palms returned. I opened my eyes; I found myself surrounded by silent natives holding their shields before their breasts. Their black-plumed chieftain advanced toward me. There was nothing in his dark glance except a hope—that could change to a smile or a grimace.

I held out my hand; I opened it. I offered the chieftain the scissors. He smiled. He accepted them. He flashed them in the sun. He did not know what they were. He manipulated them clumsily. He nicked a finger. He threw the scissors upon the sand. Uneasy, he looked at the blood. Uneasy, he looked at me. With great caution he picked up the scissors, as if fearing they had a life of their own. He shouted a few words. Several men ran to one of the tree trunks beached on the sand and took something from it. He ran back to the chieftain and handed him a coarse cloth similar to that of their loincloths. The cloth held something. The chieftain clutched the scissors in one hand. With the other he handed me the small parcel. I hefted its weight in my open hands. The rough, stiff cloth fell open. In my hands lay a brilliant treasure of golden grains. My gift had been reciprocated.

My hands filled with gold, I looked toward Pedro's body.

The warriors retrieved their lances, pulling them from the body of my old friend.

With branches and bare feet, the men from the jungle extinguished the lighted fires. I would swear there was sadness on their faces.

THE PEOPLE OF THE
JUNGLE

I was placed in one of the tree trunks, which were actually long, barge-like canoes, each one hollowed from the trunk of a single tree. And as I was carried away from shore once again, I secretly named this place Tierra de San Pedro, for my poor old friend had died like a martyr, and I could still see the last flames being fed from his body.

A ring of black vultures was already circling over the beach, and I thought how Pedro had finally met the destruction and death he'd been fleeing. I asked myself whether I too was being carried toward my origins, and whether that origin might have been captivity. For if Pedro's end had been the same as his beginning, was I an abnormal exception to a destiny that as it fulfilled itself encountered only the semblance of its genesis? And although I'd learned to love old Pedro I prayed now that I wouldn't inherit his destiny but that his death would free me to find my own, even though it be worse than his. Since the day we'd embarked together we'd shared the same fortunes. Now our destinies would be forever separate.

The fleet of crude canoes did not put out to sea but doubled the cape, and after a short period of silent paddling we sighted the mouth of a great river whose murky waters muddied the sea for several leagues. At a shrill command from the chieftain the armada turned into this broad river flowing between widely separated dark shorelines. The black forests lining either shore were dense and tall, making invisible the source of the sounds hidden in their jungle thickness; intense and mixed, its perfumes were a blending of wild flowers and rotted foliage. The sudden flashes in the milky sky were the eternal birds of this new world, noisy, thick-beaked birds like enormous parakeets, the color of cochineal, green, red, black, and rose. They were masters of the sky; and the masters of the swampy river's edge were the lizards watching us through drowsy-lidded eyes.

And I, Sire, was a captive with a bag of gold in my hands. We paddled upriver. I no longer remembered; I knew; and I gave thanks for the ignorance that permits us to go on living even though we know the only certainty awaiting us is loss of freedom or life. We know the nature of what is to come, we are ignorant only of the time and circumstance; glory be to God who thus alleviates our painful destiny.

We disembarked near an inhabited clearing. As the natives beached the canoes in the mud, we were surrounded by a hundredfold of old men, women, and children. Our return was greeted with the chirping voices I have already told you of, Sire, and their great excitement was engendered not only by my strange presence but also by an obvious feeling of relief. The remnants of a terror slow to disappear still lingered on the faces of the quivering old men, the uneasy young girls, and the women with nursing children pressed to their breasts. The warriors had returned. The dangers had been surmounted. They were returning with a captive: me. I noted there was not a single young male among those who came to meet us, although there were many young boys, some of whom, as old as twelve, were still suckling at their mothers' breasts.

I again became aware of my situation when the black-plumed chieftain showed everyone the scissors and urged me to show my cloth filled with the golden grains. They all nodded enthusiastically and the nearest women smiled at me and the old men touched my shoulder with their trembling hands.

I looked about me and saw that all the houses of this jungle village were of matting laid over four-arched stakes, all of them alike, with no visible signs of superior riches or superior power. The chieftain himself unclasped his belt of black feathers and with great deference walked toward an arbor where he placed the belt in the hands of a wrinkled and shivering ancient seated within a basket woven of palm leaves and filed with balls of cotton. And thus the chieftain was no longer distinguishable from the other canary-colored men, for to me they all looked identical. The ancient, who in spite of the heat seemed to be trembling with cold, murmured something and the young man whom I had taken for the chieftain of this band explained something in reply. Then, as one would a curtain, the young man dropped the dried skins attached to the roof of the arbor, and the ancient disappeared from view.

I was offered a strange bed made of cotton netting hanging between two palm trees, and a bitter root to eat. At that, the everyday life of this village was resumed, and I decided it was greatly to my advantage to participate in it as discreetly as I could; and so for several months I occupied myself in doing the things they all did: tending the fires in the ovens, digging in the earth, gathering red ocher, mixing mortar, cutting reeds and twigs, polishing stones, and also collecting pieces of shell for cutting the fruit that grew wild in various locations in the jungle, fruit never before seen by my eyes, of several colors, flaming red, blush pink, or juicy black, with a rough outer shell, and soft and fragrantly perfumed inside. I also gathered firewood, although I noted it quickly disappeared in spite of the fact that little was used.

I rapidly learned that here everything belonged to everyone: the men hunted deer and captured turtles, the women gathered ant eggs, worms, and several kinds of lizards, and the old men were still dexterous in capturing snakes—whose flesh isn't bad to eat; then these things were routinely divided among the whole community.

This period seemed endless, one day exactly like another; I remember this time very poorly, and see myself very poorly, as if I'd been living in the dark. I clung to one intelligible fact. My scissors had been commended to the care of the ancient secluded in his cotton-filled basket, who was also the possessor of the belt of black feathers he entrusted to a young man only in moments of active danger—as when they had discovered our presence by the smoke on the beach, or when, as on another occasion, the men carried their canoes to the river, paddled upstream and returned with more grains of gold, or descended the river to return with a cargo of pearls from that enchanted beach. Everything was stored in baskets like the one occupied by the ancient, and was carefully covered with deerskins painted with red ocher, all of them stored in the arbor where lived the ancient to whom they then returned the belt of feathers.

Apparently master of the treasures, the ancient was also custodian of my scissors; imagining them in his knotted, blemished hands, I became obsessed finally with the conviction that the gift had been sufficient to assure my peaceful acceptance into this primitive community. As I say, Sire, I clung to one certainty:

The gift had saved me. And also the fact I accepted the gift they made me.

But the more I comforted myself with that thought, the more a terrible doubt came to haunt my tranquillity. At some unforeseen moment, would they demand something more? What could I give them then? With that worry, my will redoubled to blend with these natives in their daily tasks, to be exactly like them in every way, to be an invisible stranger who assisted them in catching snakes and delivering them to the women, and then, like them, eat the communally divided rations. Because I heard it constantly, I learned something of the bird language spoken there. But as it was my intention to be unnoticed, even forgotten, I didn't dare test my knowledge. Thus I learned to understand more than I could speak—although I confess I had a terrible temptation to go to the ancient some night and ask him everything I wanted to know. Scant consolation, Sire, were the weak suppositions I provided myself, measured against a myriad of questions for which there was no answer. Why were we attacked on the beach, and why did the fire seem to infuriate them so? Why such rage against the old man and such obsequiousness toward me in exchange for a pair of scissors? Who was the ancient guardian of the treasures, and what purpose did gold and pearls serve in this miserable land?

This curiosity was not easily reconciled with my intent to assume the color of a stone or a tree, like a lizard. That, at least, was not difficult to do; as they filtered through branches and thick treetops, the rays of the austral sun covered bodies and houses and all the objects of the inhabited area with undulating patterns of light and shadow that blended spectrally into random jungle forms.

Fool that I was, I came to believe that that phantasmal movement of light and shadow did in effect disguise me as it did the lizards, and that I could be two things at once, both curious and invisible. So one evening I approached the arbor occupied by the shivering ancient and dared pull back one of those curtains of skin I have told you of, to look inside. I had only a moment, although that was sufficient to see that certain things were stored there, the greater part of the firewood collected all these months, for example, and some large ears of fruit covered with reddish grains. I noticed also that the old man was completely surrounded with baskets similar to the one that served him perpetually as his bed, and that within them glinted grains of gold. I also saw the ancient's basket was filled with pearls.

At that moment the old man let out a terrifying shriek, exactly like that of those enormous multicolored parakeets, and I dropped the flap and imagined the worst of possible fates. I was especially startled when I realized that the play of light and shadow that had masked me had disappeared and that my hands and body and everything around me stood out clearly in a different kind of light, gray and brilliant as the pearls in which the decrepit ancient seemed to bathe. Everything was metallic light, Sire; the sun had hidden itself, and with it its companion, shadow. I heard thunder in the sky and it began to rain as if the universal deluge were beginning, not the rain we know here, not even in a storm; no, a steady, incessant downpour, as if the heavens had opened. And the commotion and activity provoked by the torrential rainfall was so great that nobody noticed me, and I grew more calm, telling myself the ancient had shrieked because his bones felt the nearness of the rains, not me.

With a great hubbub a few natives dismantled the matting of the huts and carried them away on their backs, while others rescued the canoes from the river front, and another group dedicated themselves to transporting the ancient in his basket along with the baskets filled with gold and pearls and the piles of firewood and the reddish ears of fruit, everything covered now with skins to protect it from the deluge. So equipped, and pounded by the implacable rains, we walked to higher ground, where we were able to watch from a small tree-covered hill the frightening rise of the river that rapidly inundated the space that till then had been ours.

Then the nature of our lives changed. Every afternoon and every night it rained without interruption, filling the sky with terrible thunder and soundless lightning flashes; but during the morning the sun shone brilliantly and then the wood guarded by the ancient would be used with great care; the women would sit beside their modest fires, take those red ears, separate the grain, grind it, and mix it with water to form a white dough they patted between their palms to form a flat biscuit shape which they held over the fire; the smoke smelled of that strange bread made from the red wheat so jealously guarded by the immobile ancient for this epoch of flight and fear. Fear of hunger, Sire, for the jungle fruit had become rotten and inedible; the jungle had been razed by the enormous expanse of river, and there were months when it was difficult to gather food, months when I participated in all their efforts, hunting and scratching beneath stones in the constant rain of the season that turned all the world into a quagmire; months when I even accepted the deer droppings the women sometimes roasted. I understood then why those sparse ears of grain were so precious and why young boys nursed until they were twelve.

I understood, too, why the dry firewood was as prized as gold and pearls, for there was not a dry stick in the whole of the swampy jungle; the golden morning hours barely served to half warm ourselves, and then the afternoon deluge would drown everything once more, bringing with it the torture I had earlier encountered at the sluggish stream by the beach: mosquitoes; clouds of insects that sucked human blood, glutting themselves to the point of bursting; tiny invisible fleas that burrow into your feet and form sacs as big as a chick-pea, swollen with nits you can see when a sharp-edged shell is used to slit open the foot, as formerly it sliced fruit from the stalk. And sleepless nights, Sire, continuous scratching, rolling on the ground from pain and torment, covering your body with mud . . . black, swollen bodies, living fodder for the insects; saving dry wood for food and cutting wet wood to make smoke to frighten away those ferocious enemies that claimed all our attention, for to combat them meant to forget everything else, although the natives tried to survive while employing their time for two purposes: armed with coals, they burned the fields and brush to destroy cover for the mosquitoes, and at the same time the fire trapped the few tiny-horned, dark-skinned deer and facilitated digging in the ground for lizards.

Dry wood and wet wood, glowing bonfires and dank, smoking ones; we wouldn't have survived without the fire and the smoke. Precious firewood, more useful then than all the pearls and gold in the world. Yes, Pedro and I thought that with igneous stone and dry leaves we'd invented the first fire in the new world. Now, surrounded midday to midnight by the burning fires of the jungle, I had at last found the explanation for the natives' attack. But I also asked myself: if saving the sacred fire warranted a mortal battle against those who would squander it, what value did the pearls and gold have, for they defend no one against anything here, or offer any sustenance. Sire, I was soon to know.

WORDS IN THE TEMPLE

At first the sky crackled with dry storms: lights and drums beneath a domed ceiling the color of a dark pearl, lightning that crossed the firmament with the velocity of the flocks of birds, thunder that echoed and reechoed, receding in more distant and muted reverberations to die against the peaks of the remote mountains hooded in clouds.

Then one day the sun again shone as before, and everything seemed fresh and new. The jungle was filled with clusters of wild flowers and sweet-scented groves, and for the first time, far in the distance, I saw the white peak of a volcano. Air clear as crystal, the transparent regions.

The vultures returned before the other birds. Many old people had died in fits of coughing and some young men had died of fever, their trembling greater than the ancient's who stayed always in the pearl-filled basket. I saw several women die after they were bitten by ticks; their feet were cut open with the sharp-edged shells, but blood crept blackly up their legs until they died. Many young boys suddenly disappeared. All the corpses, young or old, disappeared.

The sun was again the great lord of this land. But its return caused no visible signs of joy, as I would have expected. Rather, a nervous silence fell over everyone and I asked myself what new tribulations this season might portend.

One morning I noticed great activity on the hill. The mat huts were again dismantled: the canoes raised high over their heads, the people returned to the shore of the river. Nevertheless, one company of men remained on the hill, caring for the ancient and his treasures. I can tell you that now I understood this clipped, brusque bird language rather well, and thus I understood that they were asking me to remain with them.

They lifted the basket with the ancient onto their backs; they balanced the other baskets on their heads and, taking me with them, plunged into the jungle away from the river and the sea. At first I feared that the leafy forest, its foliage so augmented by the rains of many months, would devour us and that we would lose all sense of orientation. I soon realized, however, that through the banks of sensitive green plants that yielded to the touch of our fingertips, repeated footsteps had left their trace; scarcely a footpath, it was still more tenacious than the pulsating flowering of lichen, orchid, and all the glittering leaves that still held captive in their delicate silvery fuzz the most brilliant drops of the past deluge.

It was a corrupt jungle, Sire, humid and dark, where the tree trunks had never seen or never will see the light of the sun: so tall and thick are the leaves, so deep the roots, so heavily intertwined the ivies, so intoxicating the perfumes of the flowers—so melded into the mud the scattered corpses of men and serpents. So abundant, too, the song of the crickets.

We walked two days, sleeping in those cotton nets they hang between two tree trunks, stopping near strange deep wells of water almost like small lakes lost at the foot of chalky precipices, or in some clearing of the jungle where the bitter orange grows. But soon the tangled thickness reclaimed us, and the more we penetrated its darkness, the more putrid was the odor and the more intense the croaking of the vultures circling high above us.

It smelled of death, Sire, and when finally we stopped, it was because a most extraordinary edifice rose before us. I would never have seen it from afar because the masking expanse of forest seemed to hold it here in the very center of its dark humid body. This broad-based construction with sheer slimy steps and summit open to the air pulsed like the stony heart of the jungle.

For only the summit received the sun; the body of this great temple was sunken in the corrupt black jungle. Oh, my seas, my rivers; I recalled the blue course that gathers the waters of the desert and leads to the mausoleums of the ancient Kings; like those, this was a pyramid, Sire, although it smelled like a charnel house. Then I observed that it was here the vultures satiated themselves, folding their wings at the top of the pyramid and tearing great hunks of flesh decayed by rain, sun, and death. The tumult at the summit, the feast of the vultures, deafened me, and I knew where the corpses that had disappeared from the village during the long summer deluge had been carried. Deafened, I could still see: the jungle liana climbed and wound around the four sides of the temple and moss covered its steps, but this invasion of the jungle still could not hide the temple's many sculptured sills, lavish bands of carved serpents that wound with greater vigor than the clinging roots around the terraced levels of that temple.

The barefoot men of our company effortlessly ascended the steep steps with their baskets on their backs; slipping on the moss, I followed them to one of those carved, niche-like openings. Then I saw they were sumptuous caves of human making, and the ancient was set down in one of them along with the baskets of pearls and gold. The natives left him there and told me to enter.

This grotto in the temple had caught the light, and the gold and pearls shone within the deep cavity beneath the low roof, and in one of the palm baskets, immersed in pearls, still sat the old man, my scissors in his hands—hands like the roots of the jungle. He raised one hand and gestured me to approach, to sit beside him. I squatted on my haunches. And the ancient spoke. Opaque and dead, his voice resonated among the dank walls of this at once lugubrious and resplendent chamber.

"Welcome, my brother. I have awaited you."

THE ANCIENT'S LEGEND

Sire: as I listened to these words in the temple, and the gravity of the ancient's tone as he spoke to me, I understood that he attributed to me the secret knowledge I had of his tongue; and as it is said of certain magicians that with a magic wand they cause water to burst forth from stone, so burst from my lips the language I had learned without speaking during my long months of living with the people of the jungle. What I do not know, however, is whether I am completely faithful to the words of the ancient man in the temple; I do not know how much I forget and how much I imagine, how much I lose and how much I add. I do not know whether it was only much later during my adventures in the new world that I completely understood everything the old man told me; perhaps it is only today that I understand and repeat it in my own style.

I looked at him, immersed in the pearls that perhaps lent him life and in turn received life from his flaccid skin, the man nourishing the pearls, and the pearls the man. I didn't know what to say to him; he told me he had been observing me since the day of my arrival, which had been Three Crocodile day, and in that he had seen a good augury, for on such a day, he said, our mother the earth had risen from the waters.

"I was saved from the sea, my lord," I said simply.

"And you arrived from the East, which is the origin of all life, for the sun is born there."

He said, too, that I had arrived with the shining yellow light of dawn, with the colors of the golden sun.

"And you dared indicate your presence with fire, and on a dry day. You are welcome, my brother. You have returned home."

With a gesture he offered me the temple, perhaps the entire jungle. I could only say: "I arrived with another man, my lord, but that man was not welcomed as I was."

"That is because he was not expected."

Paying no heed to my questioning glance, the ancient continued: "Furthermore, he defied us. He raised a temple for himself alone. He wished to make himself owner of a piece of the earth. But the earth is divine and cannot be possessed by any man. It is she who possesses us." He was quiet an instant, then said: "Your friend wished only to take. He wished to offer nothing."

I looked at the scissors in the hands of the ancient and was again convinced that it was to them I owed my life. And the ancient, gesturing with that rude contrivance I had stolen from a tailor, said something that can be translated like this: the good things belong to everyone, for what is held in common belongs to the gods, and what belongs to the gods is held in common. The words "god" and "the gods" were the first I learned among these natives, for they repeated them constantly, and their "teus" and "teo" are not unlike our "theo."

"He was my friend," I said in defense of old Pedro.

"He was an old man," the ancient replied. "Old men are useless. They eat but they do not work. They are scarcely able to hunt snakes. They should die as soon as possible. An old man is the shadow of death and is unnecessary in this world."

With amazement I looked at this ancient who surely had lived more than a hundred years, at this invalid coddled in a basket filled with pearls and balls of cotton to warm him against a cold born not of the warm humid air of the jungle but of the brittle, icy years of his bones.

I told him that all things decline and die, man and pearl alike, for such is the law of nature.

The ancient shook his head and replied that some lives are like arrows. They are shot into the air, they fly, and they fall. My friend's life was like these. But there are other lives that are like circles. Where they seem to end, they in truth begin again. They are renewable lives. "Such as these is your life and mine and that of our absent brother. Do you know anything of him?"

Imagine, Sire, my confusion as I listened to these incomprehensible statements so familiarly expounded. And imagine, too, as I imagined, how the only thing clear to me was the feeling that my fate depended upon my replies.

I murmured: "No, I know nothing of him."

"He will return someday, as you have returned."

The ancient sighed and told how our absent brother, more than any other, must return, because he, more than any other, had sacrificed himself. And sacrifice is the only manner to assure renewal.

"Let us be attentive"—he spoke very quietly—"to Three Crocodile day, which returned you to this land. That is the day when all things join together and again become only one, as in the beginning."

"We are three, my lord; you, I, and the absent one," I murmured, unsure of what I was saying.

The old man pondered a moment and then said that all abundant things that chaotically proliferate or multiply decline; on the other hand, those things that rise toward oneness live again, and this is the difference between gods and men, for men believe that more is better, but the gods know that less is better.

As he spoke he touched his fingers rapidly, as earlier the young warrior on the beach had done, and he counted on them and gave me to understand that six are fewer than nine, and three are fewer than six.

"Three men clasping hands"—his icy fingers touched mine—"form a circle, readying themselves to be one single man, as in the beginning. Three aspire to oneness. One is perfect, the origin of everything; one cannot be divided, all things that can be divided are mortal, what is indivisible is eternal; three is the first number after one that cannot be divided, two is still imperfect since it can be cut in half; three can devolve into six, nine, twelve, fifteen, eighteen, or return to one; three is the crossing of the roads: unity or dispersion; three is the promise of unity."

The ancient accompanied all these explanations by rapid movements of his hands; stretching an arm outside his basket, he drew parallel lines, erased them, drew some within circles hurriedly traced by his gnarled finger in the dust of this chamber illuminated by treasures whose owners feed upon snakes and ants and turtles.

I added one line in the dust: "What shall we do if we again become one, my lord?"

The ancient stared into the distance, beyond the aperture of our cave, toward the jungle, and said: "We shall become one with our opposite—mother, woman, earth—who is also one being and who awaits only our oneness to receive us in her arms. Then there will be peace and happiness, for she will not rule over us nor we over her. We will be lovers."

I could say nothing, and he said nothing for a long while. Then he looked at me intently and told what I am now going to tell you, Sire:

First was the air and it was inhabited by gods who had no bodies.

And below the air was the sea, and no one knows how or by whom it was created.

And there was no thing in the sea.

And neither was there time in the air or in the sea, so the gods did nothing.

But one of the goddesses of the air called herself goddess of the earth and then since she saw only air and water, she began to ask what her name meant, and when the earth would be created, for that was her dwelling.

She became enamored of her name earth and so great was her impatience that finally she refused to sleep with the other gods until they would give her earth.

And the gods, eager to possess her once again, decided to grant her her whim and they lowered her from the sky to the water and for a long time, until she grew tired, she walked upon the water, and then she lay down upon the sea and fell asleep.

And the gods, desiring her, attempted to waken her, and to do with her what men will, but earth slept and it is not known whether this sleep was like death.

Angry, the gods turned themselves into great serpents and coiled about the arms and legs of the goddess and with their strength they dismembered her and then abandoned her.

And from the body of the goddess were born all things.

From her hair, trees; from her skin, grass and flowers; from her eyes, wells and streams and caverns; from her mouth, rivers; from her nostrils, valleys; and from her shoulders, the mountains.

And from the belly of the goddess was born fire.

And with her eyes the goddess looked at the sky she had abandoned and for the first time she saw the stars and the movement of the planets, for when she dwelt in the sky, she had not seen them or measured their course.

There is no time in the heavens, for in them everything is forever the same.

But the earth needs time in order to be born, to grow, and to die.

And the earth needs time in order to be reborn.

The goddess knew this because day after day she watched the setting and rising and setting of the sun, while the fruits born from the skin of the goddess fell to the ground, and with no hands to pick them they rotted, and no one drank the water of the fountains born from her eyes, and the rivers flowing from her mouth coursed swiftly to the sea, without purpose.

And so the goddess of the earth convoked three gods, one red, one white, and the third black.

And this black god was an ugly, humpbacked dwarf plagued with boils, while the other two were tall, proud young princes.

And the goddess of the earth said to these gods that one of them must sacrifice himself in order that men might be born to pick the fruit, drink the waters, tame the rivers, and make use of the earth.

The two handsome young men hesitated, for each loved himself very much.

The diseased and humpbacked dwarf did not; he neither hesitated nor did he love himself.

He threw himself into the belly of the earth goddess, which was pure fire, and there he perished.

From the flames thus nourished came the first man and the first woman; and the man was called head, or hawk; and the woman was called hair, or grass.

But from the truncated body of the monstrous god who had sacrificed himself came forth only a half man and a half woman, for they had no bodies below their chests, and to walk they hopped like magpies or sparrows, and to beget offspring the man placed his tongue in the mouth of the woman, and so were born two men and two women who were more complete, with bodies as far as their navels, and from them were born four men and four women, whole now as far as their genitals, and these coupled like gods, and their children were born whole as far as their knees, and their grandchildren were completely whole, with feet, and they were the first to be able to walk erect and they populated the world before the watchful gaze of the first lady our mother.

From earth's belly of fire were also born the companions of men, the beasts that escaped from her pyre, and all of them bear on their skins the mark of their birth from the ashes: the spots of the snake, the dark blackish feathers of the eagle, the singed ocelot. And so, too, the wings of the butterfly and the shell of the turtle and the skin of the deer all show to this day their refulgent and shadowed origin.

Only the fishes escaped from between the legs of the goddess lying upon the sea, and for that reason they smell of woman and they are smooth, and quiver, and are the color of pleasure.

And the belly of the goddess contracted for the last time.

And from her smoking entrails rose a column of fire.

And the specter in the flame was the phantom of the humpbacked, boil-plagued god, who ascended to the sky in the form of fire and there shut out the light of the old sun that existed before time and was converted into the first sun of man: the sun of the days and the sun of the years.

Thus was the dwarf rewarded for his sacrifice.

In contrast, the red god and the white god had to bear the price of their pride.

They remained upon the earth, condemned to measure the time of man.

And they wept for their cowardice, for from the sacrifice of the black boil-plagued god were born half-formed men, men who in no way resembled the gods, men born not whole but mutilated, deformed of soul as the body of the god who sacrificed himself to give them life was deformed of body.

As he was telling all this, the ancient traced line after line in the dust of the elaborately embellished cave, before stopping and asking that I count the lines while he continued his account.

He said then that the mother goddess counted as many days as he had drawn lines in the dust, so that all the stars might complete their dance in the sky and so that the yield of all the fruits of the earth might be completed and again begin their cycle of germination.

I counted three hundred and sixty-five lines and the ancient said that this was the exact number of a complete revolution of the sun and thus it proved that there are lives that begin anew as they are ended, for the humpbacked god gave his life for man but was reborn as the sun.

And the ancient said he would tell what the goddess had then said:

I have given the fire of my belly so that men might be born.

I have given my skin and my mouth and my eyes so that men might live.

The humpbacked and boil-plagued black god gave his life so that men might be born of the fire of my belly.

Then he was turned into the sun so that my body might be fruitful and nourish mankind.

What will men give us in exchange for all this?

And as she spoke she realized that men did possess something the gods do not have, for the gods were and are and will forever be, and they owe nothing to anyone.

But man does: he owes his life.

And the debt of his life is called destiny.

And it must be paid.

And in order to direct the destiny of men, the mother earth and the father sun invented and ordained time, which is the course of destiny.

And thus as the sun had its days exactly numbered, man must know the name and the number of his days, which are different from the days of nature, which has no destiny, only purpose; but different, too, from the days of the gods, who possess neither time nor destiny, although it is true that it is they who give them to nature and to man.

With his extended hand, the old man erased five lines in the dust and looked into my questioning eyes.

And he continued to count:

The gods granted twenty days to the destiny of the names of man, calling them the day of the Crocodile, the Wind, the House, the Lizard, the Snake, the Skull, the Deer, the Rabbit, the Water, the Dog, the Monkey, the Grass, the Reed, the Ocelot, the Eagle, the Vulture, the Earthquake, the Knife, the Rain, and the Flower.

But man not only has his day and his name, but his destiny as well is inseparable from the sign of the gods to whom he must offer sacrifices to repay the debt of his life.

And so, in addition to the twenty days of the name of man, were ordained the thirteen days of the gods' being.

And the year of destiny, which is different from the year of the sun's voyage or of the germination of the earth, begins when the first day of the twenty coincides with the first day of the thirteen.

And this happens only when the twenty days have turned thirteen times or when the thirteen days have turned twenty times.

In this way the destinies of the arrow and of circular being are linked, the line of man and the sphere of the gods, and of this conjunction is born total time, which is neither line nor sphere, but the marriage of both.

"Look at these lines, brother, and count them to the point my finger indicates."

As I counted, I asked: "Why twenty and why thirteen?"

"Twenty because this is the natural number of the complete man, who had that many fingers and toes. Thirteen because it is the incomprehensible number of mystery, and thus is fitting for the gods."

I counted two hundred and sixty lines, which, it is true, are twenty times thirteen or thirteen times twenty, and I accepted the fact that for the ancient these were the days of the human year, different from the solar year, and I asked: "And why did you erase those five days from the time of the sun?"

The ancient sighed and recounted the following:

As I sigh, so sighed the goddess, our mother earth, and she wept bitterly throughout the night, imploring men to repay her for the debt of their lives.

But the only thing men could give to repay their lives was life, and the goddess knew that, and she wept, desiring to eat the hearts of men.

The men were afraid and they offered the goddess the other two things they had besides life: fruits as an offering; time as adoration.

The goddess cried out, saying that was not enough, that the fruit was in reality another gift of the earth and the sun to men, and to give something that did not belong to them was not a gift at all.

The goddess cried out, saying it was not enough, that time, too, was a gift of the earth and the sun to men, that men needed it while the earth and the sun did not, and that by giving time to men they had lost their divine eternity, and chained themselves to calendars not fitting to a god.

The goddess cried out, saying it was not enough, that the only gift man could give to the gods was life, and that she would not be stilled until they gave her blood, and she would no longer give fruit if it were not watered with human blood.

Beneath the skin of her mountains and her valleys and her rivers, earth had articulations filled with eyes and mouths: she saw everything, nothing sated her appetites, and men asked themselves whether if in order to go on living they must actually all die to feed the thirst and hunger of the earth and the sun.

Their offerings of the fruits of nature were not enough, for the earth refused to continue to give fruit and with her died the first sun of Fire and the world was covered with ice and we all perished from cold and hunger.

And the prayers of time were not enough, for the earth concerted with the sun so that time disappeared and the second sun of Wind died, when everything was destroyed by tempests and we had to abandon our temples and carry our homes on our backs.

And thus evils succeeded evils; men tried to flee, but where could they flee that was not the earth, always the earth?

"Look, brother, look outside, toward the light, toward the indomitable jungle, and see there the wounds of our sufferings, and recall with me the terrible catastrophes that beset us again and again."

The third sun of Water died; then everything was swept away by the deluge, and it rained fire, and men burned and their cities with them.

Each sun perished because men did not want to sacrifice themselves for the gods, and the price of their refusal was destruction.

Each sun was reborn because men again honored the gods, and sacrificed themselves for them.

And in each catastrophe we lost everything and had to begin again from nothing.

"What sun is today's sun?" I asked.

"The fourth sun, which is the sun of the Earth, which will disappear like the others, in the midst of earthquakes, hunger, destruction, war, and death, unless we keep it alive with the river of our blood."

He said that thus it was foretold, and the destiny of each man was to procure the postponement of the fatal destiny of all men by balancing the death of some against the lives of others.

"But, my lord, I have seen no sacrifice in your land, except the ordinary ones of illness and hunger."

With great sadness the ancient said: "No, we do not kill each other. We live in order to offer our lives to others. Wait and you will understand."

In my fevered mind I tried to put in order the things related by the ancient, and this was my conclusion: If there is more life than death, the gods soon will see that the debt of life is repaid with widespread death; and if there is more death than life, the gods will be without the blood that nourishes them, and they will have to sacrifice themselves so that the life that vitalizes them may begin again. Thus, by dying for the gods, men postpone their total extinction, and the gods postpone their own extinction by dying so that life can begin again. I felt, Sire, poor arrow that I was, that I had penetrated a hermetic circle, both great and round, deep and high, where all the forces of men were directed toward discovering the fragile equilibrium between life and death.

And I said to myself: "Like one drop added to a cup filled to the brim with blood, I have become a part of this life and this death described by the ancient immersed in the gentle pearls and warming cotton."

Perhaps the ancient read my thoughts, for these were his words:

"You have returned, brother. You have come home. Take your place in your house. You will have as many days as the twenty days of destiny to complete your destiny. The gods were generous. As I with my hand, they erased five days from the time of the sun. Those are the masked days. Those are the faceless days, that belong neither to the gods nor to men. Your life depends upon whether you can win those days from the gods who will try to take them from you and win them for themselves. You must try to win the days and store them away against the days of your death. And when you feel death approach, say: 'Stop, don't touch me, I have saved one day. Let me live it. Wait.' And you can do this five times during the life that remains to you."

"And if I win them, will they be happy days for me, my lord?"

"No. They are five sterile and luckless days. But misfortune is still worth more than death. That will be your only argument against death."

As the ancient said these strange things he made many gestures and motions of his hand that helped me penetrate his meaning, although my mind was at times distracted, trying to make order from this chaos of information, and from time to time I fell into pragmatic considerations, as if to compensate for the delirious magic of the ancient. He spoke much of circles, re-creating them with weak movements of his hand. As I listened to him I realized I had never seen a wheel in these lands, unless it had to do with the sun. Nor horses. Nor donkeys. Nor oxen nor cows. I found myself bedazzled by the extraordinary; I felt sudden anguish; I longed for ordinary things. And submerged in the echoes of these fabulous tales, nothing seemed more ordinary than I myself.

"Who am I, my lord?"

For the first time, the ancient smiled. "Who are we, brother? We are two of the three brothers. Our black brother died in the blaze of creation. His dark ugliness was compensated for by his sacrifice. He was reincarnated as a glowing white light. You and I, we who lacked the courage to throw ourselves into the fire, survived. We have paid for our cowardice with the tremendous obligation of maintaining life and memory. You and I. I, the red. You, the white."

"I . . ." I murmured. "I . . ."

"You lived upon the shoulders and nose and flowing hair of the goddess, teaching about life. You planted, you harvested, you wove, you painted, you carved, and you taught. You said that work and love were enough to give in payment for the life the gods gave us. The gods laughed at you and they made fire and water rain down upon the earth. And every time the sun died you fled weeping toward the sea. And every time the sun was reborn, you returned to preach life. I thank you, brother. You have returned from the East where all life is born. The return voyage of our black brother will be more difficult, for although he shines magnificently by day, by night he descends into the depths of the West, he travels the black river of the lower regions, he is besieged by the demons of drunkenness and oblivion, for hell is the kingdom of the animal that swallows up the memory of all things. It will take him longer than it did you to be reunited with me, for by day he gives life and pleads for death, and by night he fears death and pleads for life. You are my white brother, the other founding god. You reject death and praise life.''

"And you, my lord?"

"I am he who remembers. That is my mission. I guard the book of destiny. Between life and death there is no destiny except memory. Memory weaves the destiny of the world. Men perish. Suns succeed suns. Cities fall. Power passes from hand to hand. Princes collapse along with the crumbling stone of their palaces abandoned to the fury of fire, tempest, and invading jungle. One time ends and another begins. Only memory keeps death alive, and those who must die know it. The end of memory is truly the end of the world. Black death, our brother; white life, you; and I . . . red memory."

"And if what you are waiting for comes to pass, and the three of us are together?"

"Life, death, and memory: one single being. Masters of the cruel goddess who has until now governed us, given us nourishment and hunger in turn. You, I, and he: the first male princes since the reign of the female mother goddess—to whom we owe everything, but who also would take everything from us: life, death, and memory."

For a long time he looked at me with his sad eyes as black and decayed as the jungle, as etched and hard as the temple, as brilliant and precious as the gold. He raised the scissors and worked the blades. He said he thanked me for them. I had given him the scissors. They had given me gold. I had given of my labor. He had given me memory. When he asked, finally, the light in his eyes was as implacable and as cruel as the eyes of the mother goddess must have been: "What will you give us now?"

Oh, Sire, as you hear me today, tell me, after listening to all I have recounted and without knowing what is still to tell, you who understand as I the truest truth of that world into which my misfortunes had cast me: tell me—for what I have still to tell will only serve as corroboration—how here all things were an exchange: exchange of life for death and death for life, endless exchanges of looks, objects, existences, memories, with the proposition of placating a predicted fury, of temporizing against the subsequent threat, of sacrificing one thing in order to save another, of feeling indebted to every existing thing, of dedicating both life and death to a perpetual renovating devotion. Everything the ancient had spoken until now seemed pure fantasy and legend until these words made me a participant in that fantasy and a prisoner of that legend: "What will you give us now?"

The old man was asking that I renew our alliance—for him so clear, for me so obscure—with a new offering, something of greater value than his words, as his words had held more value than my life—which I owed to him. What could I offer, wretched being that I was? The ancient spoke of heavens and its gods: my protection lay in common things. There were no wheels here or beasts of burden. Nor had I seen the one thing I still possessed. I put my hand to my breast.

There in the parchment-thin pocket of my wide sailor's doublet I felt the small mirror Pedro and I had used, joking happily, to serve each other as barber on the ship. I took out the mirror. The ancient watched inquisitively. With a gesture of humility and respect I held the mirror to his eyes.

This was my offering; the ancient looked at himself.

I have never seen, and I hope never to see again, a more terrible expression on a human face. His black eyes bulged, the yellow eyeballs seeming to leap from their deep, wasted sockets; all the deaths of all the suns, all the burning bodies, all the destroyed palaces, all the affliction of hunger and tempests of the jungle were instantly distilled in their twin terror. And all the bitterness of recognition. The wrinkles on the ancient's face turned into pulsing worms that devoured his face, leaving only an infernal grimace; the white tufts on his mottled skull stood up in horror; his jaw dropped open as if he were drowning, choking, in loosened strings of phlegm, and thick slobber trickled down the dark wrinkled network of his chin to stain the sparse white stubble. His lips drew back to reveal broken teeth and bleeding gums: he tried to cry out, his knotted hands clutched his hide-like neck: he tried to rise; with the movement, the basket overturned, spilling pearls and cotton balls and scissors; finally the ancient screamed and his voice drowned out the jungle accompaniment of cicadas and parrots; that shriek pierced my heart, and his head struck the dusty floor of this ornate temple chamber.

Over our heads I heard the flapping of the frightened vultures and then the voices and rapid footsteps of the young warriors.

They entered the temple chamber. They looked at me. Then they looked at the fallen ancient who stared at us with open, but lifeless, eyes.

I crouched beside him, my fatal mirror in my hand.

One of the warriors knelt beside the ancient, tenderly caressed his head, and said: "Young chieftain . . . youthful founder . . . first man . . ."

THE TRIBUTES

My mind was a turtle as torpid and sluggish as the one I had killed when first I stepped onto the beach of the new world. In contrast, the thoughts of the warriors raced swift as quicksilver hares; after an instant of sorrow that gave way to extreme astonishment they turned to look at me kneeling there beside the dead ancient, my mirror in my hand. In the brief instant between sorrow and amazement, my lethargic emotions could not completely absorb the meaning of those mysterious words: "Young chieftain . . . youthful founder . . . first man . . ."

I would need time, I told myself, to decipher that enigma: like a gust of wind blowing through my fragmentary memory arose the recollection of other pilgrimages in search of the meaning of the oracle: I tasted sea foam, I breathed the perfume of olive trees—another time, another space, not these environs where enigma was suffocated beneath fearful certainty: the warriors saw in me the murderer of their ancient father, their king of memory, perhaps their god. And in just retribution, they were preparing to kill me.

Why did they not do it? I could not answer that question. I was enveloped in the general agitation, a whirlwind of confused motion and warring lights; the warriors spoke so quickly and excitedly, and I so feared for my life, that it was difficult for me to understand what they were saying; I knew only that I was guilty of a crime, and I attributed the excitement to that knowledge, which surely was shared by the warriors. Blinded and deafened, I envisioned my death, and the only word I understood was the constantly vociferated: "Lizard . . . lizard . . ."

All the warriors were pointing toward the black dripping walls of the treasure chamber, gesticulating toward the numerous swiftly darting lizards that sometimes blended with the stone, sometimes were revealed in the metallic reflections of the gold. They seized me by the arms and legs and head, they lifted me high in the air, and my benumbed brain resigned itself to thoughts of death.

What happened, then, Sire, was something like death. They placed me in the ancient's basket, my knees touching my chin; they poured the pearls over my body and I felt their nacreous grayness revive at contact with a skin aflame with ignorance and fear. They raised me, and also the body of the ancient, and we left the cave and went out upon the precipitous steps of the temple.

From the tumult of that moment, I tried to rescue swift impressions of what was happening. I was held in the arms of the warriors, a captive within the basket. The cadaver of the ancient was being dragged by its feet toward the summit of the pyramid. As the lifeless, inverted body ascended, its eyes stared into mine, as if trying to explain something; and when we reached the highest platform, the corpse was abandoned to the vultures, who fell upon it immediately. The body of the Lord of Memory became mixed with the putrefying flesh of the other dead, already torn by the slashing beaks of the birds of prey.

Then I looked down toward the foot of this wild temple and saw many of the women and old men and young of the jungle people standing silently there; they seemed to bleed, a thick red liquid dripped from their hair and faces, and at their feet, bathed in the same color of blood, were stones and arrows and shields. All looked up toward me; the entire jungle reverberated redly, mingled with the incessant movement of the warriors who now carried the baskets filled with pearls and grains of gold from the chamber and set them about me, distributing them on the slimy steps of the pyramid. They placed the scissors in my hands. I still held the weapon of the crime: my mirror. My cross and orb. The warrior from the beach clasped the belt of black feathers about his waist, the sign of ritual confrontation.

I waited. The devoured cadaver of the ancient at the temple summit. The festival of the vultures. The celerity of the nervous, unseen lizards. The motionless, silent, red-stained natives at the foot of the pyramid. The mound of objects, also red, at the feet of the women and old men and children. I, in the pearl-filled basket amid the other baskets of gold and pearls. I waited.

Then I saw all the butterflies of the jungle; they flew from the thick branches and fluttered over the engrossed vultures at the peak of the pyramid, and I heard a flute, Sire, and little bells, and a drum and many footsteps in the jungle; and the thick branches parted before the slow advance of a majestic bird whose brilliant blue and garnet and crocus-yellow body seemed to float over the jungle thicket as if over a lush verdant sea.

Then the leaves parted wider and I saw a man cloaked in a white mantle edged in purple, and I saw that the bird was his headdress, its plumage forming a luxurious trailing crest; and this man was followed by a motley company of musicians, and men who held scrolls beneath their arms and carried feather fans, and a company of warriors with round leather shields and ocelot and eagle masks and lances that ended in hard stone points and red-painted bows and arrows, and bearers clad only in loincloths who carried on their backs baskets and bundles wrapped in deerskin. And at the end of the procession came other similar men, naked, who bore upon their shoulders a palanquin of woven reeds covered on all four sides by worked and embossed deerskins painted with the yellow heads of plumed serpents and adorned with heavy bands and medallions of purest silver.

Seeing myself thus situated, surrounded and confronted, I prayed that the memory of the ancient who had died because he saw his face in my mirror had flown from his staring eyes and through the mirror would penetrate mine. For now I occupied his place; and I understood nothing or knew nothing, could foresee or imagine nothing. I was the prisoner of a ritual; I was its center, but was unaware of my role in it. I felt older than the ancient, more dead than he, the captive of the basket and the pearls and the mirror I still held in my hand. I tell you, Sire, I prayed for one thing: that the ancient's last glance be captured in the mirror as I was captive in the basket. I wished to affirm my own existence in the midst of so many mysteries and I held the mirror to my face, fearing to see in its reflection the image of my own decrepitude, magically acquired in the swift exchange of glances between the ancient and myself. For if I saw an older face in the mirror, then the ancient had seen a young face and had died of that terror. I looked. And then, only then, as the mercury returned to me my own youthful semblance, I understood that the ancient had not been aware of his own age: he had seen himself for the first time as I saw him . . . and he had never seen a man so old.

Now the warriors descended the steps, carrying the gold- and pearl-filled baskets, and delivered them into the hands of the man with the plumed crest, and he examined the contents of the baskets and then dictated words to the men with the paper scrolls, who traced signs on them with small sharp sticks with different colored points. Then the strange bearers added the baskets of gold and pearls of the people of the jungle to their loads and the young warrior of the black feather belt asked whether all was well, and the man with the crest nodded and said yes, the Lord Who Speaks, or the Lord of the Great Voice—for thus I translated his words—would be content with the tributes of the men of the jungle and would continue to protect them. The man with the crest made a sign to one of the attendants who fanned him constantly, and this man handed the young jungle warrior several of the reddish ears of fruit and many balls of cotton; the warrior prostrated himself and kissed the sandals of the man of the crest, and this, I believed, consummated the transfer of gold and pearls in exchange for bread and cotton, and that had been the purpose of the treasures of the sea and river, and the ancient had been the guardian and executor of the pact, a fact I understood clearly when the warrior of the black feathers thanked the lord of the crest for what he had given in exchange for their proffered treasures: "We thank the lords of the mountain for the gift of the red grain and the white cotton."

Then, sadly, he stood silent while the man of the crest waited with folded arms for him to continue, and I, submerged in my basket, reckoned the exchanges of this ceremony of tributes: the men of the river and the jungle offered gold and pearls in exchange for bread and cloth. What more, then, did the man of the crest expect in payment for grain and cotton?

The warrior of the black plumes again spoke: "In exchange for your protection, we deliver unto you our fathers and women and children gathered here."

My clouded vision returned and I saw that the old men and women and children were painted with the red ocher that had been so laboriously collected. The lord of the crest counted them and dictated words to the scribe and said that this number was good, that it would calm the furies of the day of the Lizard, the day when all the things of the world would bleed unless the goddess of the earth—who on this day suffers bitter cold until she is sprinkled with human blood—was fed. And then the old men and women and children were rounded up by the warriors of the crested lord and he said they would return when the day of the Lizard again coincided with the day of the Last Tempest, when the beautiful goddess of the swamps of creation to whom the gold and pearls of this coast would be dedicated found rest. And he said, too, that they should always guard their treasures well and should always deliver lives on this day, and thus they would always have the fruits of the cotton and the red grain.

"And now," the crested lord concluded, "allow me to salute your chief."

Everyone made way to let him pass and the man of the crest ascended majestically toward the spot where I sat half hidden in my basket. And as he climbed he intoned a chant, accompanied by flutes and bells and drums, and also by the cloud of butterflies and the silence of the jungle, his eyes, constantly focused on the distant sun high above the airy cemetery on the summit of the pyramid.

He stopped before me, and only then did he look at me. I saw his ashen face; he looked at my pale visage. He had expected to encounter the ancient man as usual; he found me, and his features were transformed; the majestic gravity disappeared and in its place appeared first astonishment, and then terror. I merely repeated the words that so intrigued me: "First man . . ."

The crested lord lost all dignity, he turned his back to me and ran down the slimy steps, he slipped and fell, his crest rolled to the base of the temple, he rose, screaming, and scattering everyone before him— the warriors of the people of the jungle and the warriors of the mountain, the men with the fans and the men with the scrolls, bearers and prisoners—he ran to the palanquin decorated with silver and hide and serpents, he knelt beside it, speaking in a low voice, his flaming eyes constantly turning to look toward me, and from an aperture between the skins appeared an arm ringed with heavy, jangling bracelets, a hand the color of cinnamon, with long black-painted nails.

The hand gestured, the crested lord hurriedly arose and in a shrill voice issued many orders: the bearers returned the baskets of gold and pearls to the base of the pyramid, with grotesque movements the warriors freed the jungle people, the men of the feather fans hastily retrieved the ears of grain and the balls of cotton, and all those who had come from the mountain disappeared into the jungle with the swift invisible movements of the lizard.

Sire: now you find me again in the village beside the river. I am confined within my basket, along with my mirror and my scissors. How I wish these objects, the ones with which I arrived, were my only possessions. But no. My trembling body warms and revives the fading pearls. My house is the house of the dead ancient: the bower, a weak structure of reeds. I am enclosed by four deerskins that serve as walls to isolate me from the world, although not from the sounds of the excited natives: shrill conversation, plaintive songs, discussions, and crackling bonfires.

Through the branches this night I can see the black tapestry of the heavens and count its stars, locate them in the heavens, distinguish them one from another. I must accustom myself to this dialogue with the stars. I fear that from now on I shall have no friendship except this cold, brilliant, distant one. As the old man saw himself in the mirror, I shall see myself in the twin star of the dusk and the dawn, Venus, the precious reflection of itself. She will guide my voyage toward absolute immobility. She will be my calendar.

Warriors surround my prison. Again and again I think upon this singular irony. I, the man without memory, occupy the place of the Lord of Memory. I, the stranger arrived from the sea, am the founder. I, naked and dispossessed, am the young chieftain. I, the last of men, am the first.

When I tire of gazing at the stars, I sleep. I do not look at the sky during the daytime, for the sun would set aflame my white eyelashes and pallid lids and blond beard. During the daytime I stare at myself in my mirror and begin to count my wrinkles, my white hairs, my bleeding gums and broken teeth. A prisoner in my basket, I shall wait for old age to devour me, and I shall become as ancient as the old man I killed with my mirror.

Now my mirror will kill me. My fate will be to watch myself grow old and immobile in this fleeting reflection.

THE BURNING TEMPLE

The heart is the kingdom of fear. Oh, moons, suns, days, stars . . . shelter me; water clock, hourglass, book of hours, stone calendar, swelling seas and storms . . . do not abandon me, but bind me to time. Dry smoke, shouting, weeping, wailing, silence: how shall I know finally whether it is the world around me or my own heart in which these mists and sounds originate? Through the way of fear I enter the kingdom of silence. I lose count of the days of Venus, repeating to myself that the days of my destiny in this strange land can be only the number set by the ancient in the temple: the days stolen from the days of the sun, the masked days stolen from the days of my destiny. How shall I know these five sterile days I must steal away from bad fortune for the purpose of delaying the moment of my death? Which signs? Which voices? How much time, my God, has passed since then? How old am I now?

The silence grew deeper. I realized it originated not in my heart but instead enveloped the jungle village.

In vain, Sire, I freed myself from my preoccupations to listen to the sounds of the village; in vain I waited to hear the sounds of life I had once shared with these natives. No footsteps in the dust, no hands rustling grasses, no weeping of children or chanting of ancients or voices of warriors or plaints of women: nothing.

I conjectured: they have fled to another location: I don't know what motivates the peregrinations that lead them from the river to the woods, the woods to the river, the river to a new location, carrying their mats, their baskets of useless treasure, their canoes and their lances, the precious ears from which they make their steaming bread, the balls of cotton from which they weave their beds and clothing. But now they have neither bread nor cloth, and the guilt is mine. Now they have no treasure, except for a few dry branches saved against the time of rain. I am misfortune incarnate; I have given them nothing; I have taken everything from them.

I speculated: they have abandoned me here, they have left me to the ravages of hunger and rain and mosquitoes and the rising river; I shall die, bleeding, drowning, starving. And as I asked myself why they had abandoned me, I could only answer: they fear me. And when I asked, why do they fear me? I replied: I brought bad luck to them, I killed the father of their memory, I left them without recollection, they will be like children now, no, like animals, with no sense of direction to their lives; I am bad fortune; because of me they lost what they were to receive in exchange for the pearls and gold. They have abandoned me along with their useless riches: they have fled to seek for themselves the lands of cotton and red grain.

They had abandoned me. They believed that—situated as I was in the basket beneath the bower of the dead ancient who never moved from this spot and who received water and food only from the hands of his people—I would continue in the way of my predecessor, motionless, and dependent upon them. The fires of survival and adventure sparked again in my breast. I told myself that in this land the two were always united, not, as in the lands I had left behind—how long ago? a thousand years?—separate and conflicting. There, survival is calculation, adventure is risk, resignation is the balance between the two. Here, resignation is death: I had seen it on the red-painted faces of the old men and women and children at the foot of the pyramid: captives offered to the so-called lords of the mountain and their Lord of the Great Voice.

Survival called for risk. I accepted the risk. I struggled within the narrow basket, attempting to free myself from that prison of woven branches; I rocked like a violent pendulum until the basket fell to the ground, spraying pearls and cotton balls across the ground, and I crawled out on all fours. I got to my feet. I still had the mirror and the scissors in my belt; I ventured to part the deerskin curtains.

The last of the fires were dying, almost ash, reduced now to low-hanging smoke. They seemed the only living things. In a tomb of ash and mud and blood lay all the dwellers of this village, children with slashed necks, women eviscerated by stone knives, old men run through by warriors' lances. And the warriors themselves dead upon their shields, also felled by lances. The mat huts and canoes lay in stone-cold ashes. And from the branch of a tree, hanging from the belt of black feathers, the young warrior I had once assumed to be the chief of this wandering tribe.

It was night. I could imagine the legion of vultures already poised in the treetops, hooded by their wings, ready to fall at the first light of dawn upon the feast offered by this immolated village. I thought that as my heart was a victim of fear, the village people had been similar victims of the men of the mountain, of the man with the crest and the men with the fans and all their warriors and bearers, who had thus avenged the rupture of the pact. And as in the darkness I tried to detect the motionless outlines of the warriors and the silhouettes of those voracious vultures, I looked toward the jungle, then toward the hills, and finally toward the splendor of flames on the distant nocturnal horizon.

I did not know how to return to the ocean unless it was in one of the canoes now burned beyond repair. Return to the ocean. It was only at that moment that it occurred to me to question why the men of the mountain demanded the tribute of pearls from the jungle people; why didn't they go directly to the sea and there loot at will the treasures of the beaches?

I didn't know the answer, although I was looking at the evidence. All the inhabitants of this village had died. And their assailants had destroyed everything, even the canoes. Those who had destroyed this village, I told myself, wished to impede even the flight of spirits . . . and mine as well. I didn't know the way through the jungle to the sea. And once on the coast, what would I find except what was before me now: death—buzzards, Pedro's skeleton, the ashes of his poor plot of land on the shores of the new world, and the dying treasure of the beaches?

I saw that the fire in the jungle lay in the direction of the temple. It was in the temple that I had begun to learn the secrets of this land. I felt it was there I must return, and that if it was my fate to die—motionless as an idol—no better place than that pyramid locked in the heart of the jungle. There I would again be what destiny decreed.

The heir of the ancient: I repeated that to myself many times as guided by the nocturnal splendor I moved forward into the jungle, freed of the weight of treasure and mat huts and canoes that had slowed the pace of our caravan when I had for the first time traveled the route to the pyramid. Over and over I repeated that my only inheritance in this immolated, deserted, and intractable land was my relation with the ancient: what he had told me and what he had not been able to tell me, what his dead staring eyes had tried to communicate as his body was dragged toward the summit of the temple.

I slept beside one of those wide deep wells in the plains at the foot of the hills. And in my sleep flashed a new question: why did the men of the mountain kill all the inhabitants of the village by the river, respecting only my life? As if in answer to all my questions, a black spider loomed in my dream, swaying before my eyes; then, terrified, I fell into that well at whose edge I slept, and the well was deep—interminable—and I was still falling, and I would die, crushed against the chalky walls or drowned in the depths of its distant waters; and then high above me glowed the spider, and she was spinning a thread she dropped down to me; it was strong, and with its aid I climbed from the well and with a choking cry I awakened from my nightmare. In my hand I clutched a spider's silken thread.

Trembling, I rose to my feet and guided by the spider's thread raced into the heart of the night. I didn't need to see anything on the wooded hill, not even the flames toward which I ran; branches whipped against my face, I trampled ferns beneath my feet; I advanced blindly, hurrying, indifferent to hissing snakes, hurry, hurry, sweating, panting, toward wherever this thread chose to lead me. Everything was in flames. Fire illuminated the night. The temple was a tall torch of stone and ivy and sculptured serpents and sacrificed lizards. I reached the end of the thread. Through the eyes of madness I saw the waiting spider; when it saw me it scurried toward the foliage that trembled in the light and shadow of the fire. I looked again. Where the spider had been, holding the end of the thread, stood a woman.

I say woman, Sire, in order to be understood by you and your company. I call woman that apparition of dazzling beauty and dazzling horror, and beautiful was her lustrous cotton raiment all embroidered with jewels, and beautiful but terrible the two strands of jewels that as if encrusted there crossed her cheeks, and terrible was the crescent moon that adorned her nose, and both beautiful and horrible the mouth painted in many colors, and only beautiful the soft shining darkness of her limbs. She wore a crown of butterflies on her head, not a reproduction, not metal or stone or any glass were they, not a garland even of dead butterflies: hers was a crown of living black and blue and yellow and green and white butterflies that wove a fluttering wreath above the head of the being I call woman. And she was that, for if I seem to describe something painted or dreamed or some carved statue, her eyes were living and the life of their gaze was directed toward me. And behind the woman, the burning temple.

She raised her arms toward me. The heavy bracelets clinked and jangled: the black fingernails I had seen the other day on this very spot between the deerskin curtains of a palanquin reached out toward me, sought me, beckoned me. How could I refuse that invitation, Sire? How could I resist, how not walk toward her, toward that embrace, how not bury myself in the folds of finespun cotton and adamantine jewels, how not join the end of my spider's thread with hers?

Through my sweat-soaked clothing, my heat-drenched body could sense that she was naked beneath the robe, but I couldn't look upon her body, for my eyes were hypnotized by her mouth: colored snakes that froze and slithered and undulated on the full compelling lips, and I could only imagine the body pressed against mine, which inflamed me as the temple behind us inflamed the night. I tried to imagine the nipples of those black breasts, the jungle of black hair upon the black mound of Venus—my guide, my precious twin, my black star.

Slender, heavy-braceleted arms, black-nailed hands removed my doublet and my breeches, and I was nude, erect, pressed against that terrible and beautiful body; my hands held her waist, her fingers caressed my belly and chest and thighs and buttocks, and fluttered, finally, like butterflies about my sex—stroking, coaxing, cupping, measuring, stiffening; and then with the lightness of butterflies those open, inviting legs shifted and clasped my waist, and I, Sire, sailed away on Venus; I lost all sense of sight and smell, I was mute, deaf . . . king and slave to pure sensation, a deep and thick and throbbing sensation that thrust against the warmest walls of the jungle and the night, for I was coupling with the black jungle; I was one with everything about me, and through the pulsing cave of the woman mounted upon me I touched everything I had feared—thirst and hunger, sorrow and death . . . and then, all want, all need, turned into well-being, into gift, into reward . . . and I was clinging to the back and neck and buttocks of my lover as another night I had clung to the wheel of the ship, knowing that my life was allied to it; now life ebbed from my useless throat and eyes and ears and mouth, flowed from my groin; I was caught in annihilating pleasure, and instead of fleeing this mortal sensation, I clung to it till I felt I was melting into the woman's flesh and she into mine, and we were one, a spider wrapped in its own spinning, an animal captured in traps of its own making: animal pleasure, call it that, Sire: dreamed-of bliss and immediate evil: imprisoned freedom. All my being told me I must never be parted from this union, I had been born to know it, even if knowing it meant death in life. And my most fervent desire was that all my senses die, except sensation; I prayed all the others would leave my body, evaporate into air, spread afar the news I was about to die in the hands of the woman who made love to me at the foot of the burning temple—who was I, as I was she. We were one person, Sire, can you understand me? For only thus can you understand that in that mortal embrace of all earthly delights only one voice spoke, and it was mine, but it issued from her tattooed lips.

And these are the words the Lady of the Butterflies spoke in my voice, said in my name, with her mouth crushing mine, her lips caressing my ear, her teeth nibbling my neck and shoulders and nipples, her fingernails digging into my back:

"Follow the road to the volcano. Ascend. Let yourself be guided. Never look back. Forget from whence you come. Turn your back to the sea that brought you to this shore. You have arrived. Prove who you are. If you are who you are, you will overcome all the obstacles you encounter in your way. Climb. Climb. To the highest point. To the highland. I shall await you there. Do you wish to see me again? Obey me. Have you had pleasure? This night is nothing compared with those I reserve for you. Do not lose your way. Follow the spider's thread. The spider is always by my side. She is a creature without time."

To the possessor of my voice, for it was my voice that issued from her painted lips, I could only ask, without words: "Why did you burn the temple? Why did you order all the people beside the river killed? If I have arrived, where have I arrived? If I am, who am I?"

And with my voice on her lips she answered me: "You will travel twenty-five days and twenty-five nights before we are together again. Twenty are the days of your destiny in this land. Five are the sterile days you will save against death, though they will be similar to death. Count them well. You will not have another opportunity in our land. Count well. Only during the five masked days will you be able to ask one question of the light and one question of the darkness. During the twenty days of your destiny, it will not profit you to ask, for you will never remember what happens on those days—forgetfulness is your destiny. And during the last day you pass in our land, you will have no need to ask. You will know."

Then, Sire, my vision grew clouded as my sight returned, my throat thickened with my returning voice, my nose smarted with returning smell, my ears roared with returning hearing. And as I again became aware of other senses my sense of touch diminished, and with every new flash of light, with every new odor, with every new crashing sound, the Lady of the Butterflies faded away, blended into the jungle as moments before she had blended into my body; she was returning— to the red flame or to verdant growth: whether she entered the smoking temple or the misty jungle, I do not know.

She disappeared.

My groping hands tried to capture the ghosts of her crown of butterflies; they grasped only air.

And feeling life, I felt loneliness, and I went to rest against the blackened stones of the temple and to the temple I swore to have that woman again.

Naked, I climbed the elevated steps where the last fires were dying, and naked, I paused at the summit strewn with incinerated cadavers. The smoking ashes burned my feet. I did not feel them. This was the chamber of the dawn. I offered to Venus my love-drenched body. The white cone of the volcano was illuminated by the light of the morning star.

So passed the days of my destiny in the new world. Of them I remember only five.

THE MOTHER AND THE WELL

I had two guides: the distant volcano and the thread the woman had dropped at the foot of the charred temple. I had two weapons: the scissors and the mirror. Many were my companions when again I plunged into the jungle, as previously I had penetrated the woman's flesh. A brilliant sun. The fluttering butterflies, as uncertain as my soul, hidden in the thick foliage. A host of birds. I recognized the chattering birds that fill these skies, knew now the partridges and hummingbirds that ornament this warm florid jungle whose greatest marvel is a constant mist so fine it does not wet the body: an impalpable dew that surely is the nourishment of the perfumed trees that abound here, some with white flowers and aromatic seed pods, some blush pink streaked like marble, others tiger-spotted, and one with round fruit of rough brown husks. And not least, a splendid unfolding of leaves brilliant as burnished leather disseminating a smoky odor.

The lustrous little short-horned deer are plentiful in this jungle, which led me to think: "This is the first day of my new destiny. I shall call it the day of the Deer."

Scarcely had the thought passed my mind when all the perfumes and colors floated from the flowers and birds, fruit and dew, and formed an enormous rainbow before my eyes. At the slightest touch, the forest of ferns parted to open a path for me. The spider's thread led me to the foot of the rainbow, which was guarded by birds I had not seen before, like small peacocks but without their air of vanity: tame and beautiful birds with green feathers and long tails.

As on the beach of pearls, I could imagine a return to Paradise. But experience caused me to doubt the illusions of this forest and to move forward with caution. Appearances deceive in any land, but here the extraordinary was the rule. And so, surrounded by peace and beauty, I prepared to defend myself against sudden terror. But this brief flicker of my will was quickly defeated by the fatal nature of my journey: I was to follow the route the spider spun for me through the jungle: I would follow, whether it led me to Heaven or to Hell. For more powerful than Heaven, more powerful than Hell, was the promise that awaited me at the end of my road: the Lady of the Butterflies.

As they heard my footsteps the birds with the long green tails were startled and flew away, and in the line of their flight I glimpsed at the end of the rainbow a house washed so white with lime it seemed of polished metal; it swam like a sunlit island in a many-colored mirage of tepid mist. I approached; I touched the walls. They were of baked and painted mud. I repeated: appearances deceive, and in the new world so desired by my poor friend Pedro all that shines is not gold. The spider's thread led into the single door: I followed.

I entered a room as warm as the jungle, clean, and heaped with provisions: ears of grain, odorous herbs, burning braziers, large earthen pots in which thick, aromatic beverages were brewing. I have never seen such cleanliness, and scarcely had my gaze adjusted to the shadow of this room when I heard the sound of a broom and saw a woman slowly sweeping the hard dirt floor. It was an old woman, the most ancient of women, who now looked up to meet my gaze; and if her eyes were as brilliant and black as the coals on the hearth, the toothless smile was as sweet as the honey stored in the green jars of her house.

She did not speak. In one hand she held her broom and with the other made a gesture of welcome, indicating I should make myself comfortable on one of the straw mats placed beside the braziers, and there, silently, smiling and stooped, the tiny old woman served me the savory smoking bread of the land, rolled and filled with deer meat and rosemary and mint and coriander, and little jugs filled with a boiling tasty liquid, thick and dark brown in color. And when I had eaten, she offered me a long thin tube of golden leaves which I began to chew. This food left an acid juice upon my tongue. The little woman laughed soundlessly, smacking her wrinkled, sunken lips which no longer bore any color of life, and she herself took one of those tubes I have described, Sire, and placed it between her lips, leaning over to the coals, and lighted it, inhaling its smoke and then expelling its intoxicating aroma through her mouth. I did as she had done. I coughed. I choked.

The old woman laughed again and indicated that I should take a sip of the dark thick liquid.

We sat there a long while, sucking the roll of herbs and puffing smoke from our mouths until the roll was consumed, and then the old woman threw the end of hers into the brazier and I imitated her, and she said: "You are welcome. We have been awaiting you. You have arrived."

" 'You have arrived.' That's what the ancient Lord of Memory said to me."

"He was mad. He did not speak the truth."

"Who, then, will tell me the truth? Why have you been awaiting me? Who am I?"

The tiny old woman shook her round head; her carefully combed bluish-white hair was pulled tightly back and wound into a knot at the back of her head and held by a delicate tortoise-shell comb.

"You can ask me only one question, my son. You know that. Why do you ask me two? Are these your questions? Choose well. You may ask only one question each day and each night."

"Tell me then, señora, in order that I may know how to count my days, which day is this? Why did today—in this incomprehensible land usually so filled with menace—seem so peaceful?"

I am sure the old woman looked at me with compassion. Her soft and gentle hands smoothed the folds of her simple flower-embroidered white robe as she said: "It is the day of the Deer, the day of serene prosperity and peace in all homes. It is a good day. He who arrives at my house on this day will seem to have found a corner of the garden of the gods. Enjoy it. Rest and sleep. Night will come again."

I was a fool; I had asked what I already knew, what I had already seen, what I already felt. I had wasted my only question on this my first day when there were so many questions that might clarify the mysteries of this land and my presence in it. But lulled by the food and the smoke and the journey, I rested my head upon the ancient woman's lap. Maternally, she stroked my head. I slept.

And in my dream, Sire, I saw the Lady of the Butterflies. She was accompanied by a monstrous animal black as the night, for there was nothing about it that reflected any light; it was like a shadow on four paws, huge and hairy. In vain I looked for its eyes. Only its form was visible. It had no eyes, only a hairy coat and a yawning maw and four twisted paws, for instead of pointing forward, its paws turned backward. The woman with whom I had made love beside the ruined temples was bathed in an aureole of hazy light; the animal that was her companion began to dig in the earth, and as it dug, it growled terrifyingly. When it had completed its task, the diffuse light of my dream became an oblique golden column emanating from the very center of the heavens; it fell into the hole excavated by the beast. That intense golden light was like a flowing river and as it poured into the depths of the cavity, the animal covered it up, throwing dirt upon it with its twisted feet, and the more dirt it scratched into the hole, the more the light faded. The Lady of the Butterflies wept.

Frightened, I asked the old woman who had cradled me: "Mother, kiss me, for I am afraid . . ."

And she kissed my lips, as the woman of the jungle vanished weeping into the night and the animal howled with a mixture of joy and suffering.

I awakened. I reached to touch the lap and hands of the old woman who had cradled me like a baby. My head now rested upon one of the plaited straw mats. I tried to clear my mind. I heard the weeping and howling of my dream. I looked around the room. The braziers were extinguished. The old woman was gone. The jars were broken, the beverages spilled, the brooms broken, and the flowers crushed; the dirt floor had turned to dust and the corners of the hearth were thick with spider webs. My lips felt bruised and tired. I rubbed the back of my hand across them; my hand was smeared with mingled colors. An owl hooted. I picked up the end of the spider's thread and went out of the house. Soft dark mud covered its walls.

It was night, but the spider led me. Closing my eyes, I clung to the thread; the sinister hooting of the owl was nothing compared to the far-off laments and sobs and sounds that seemed to come from the very heart of the mountains; they filled the air as if the entire earth mourned the loss of the light the dark creature in my nightmare had buried in the earth, thus condemning her to the twofold torture of burning entrails and a sightless gaze. As blind as the night, I didn't wish to see and I didn't wish to hear; I prayed that the peace of the day I had spent with the tiny old woman beside her hearth might be prolonged in the silence of a beneficent night.

My prayer was heeded. Total silence fell over the jungle. But now you will see, Sire, of what weak clay we men are made, for having obtained what I most desired, I now detested it. The silence was so absolute it was totally overwhelming, a menace as threatening as the vanished cries and laments. Now I longed for the return of sound, for true horror lies in the heart of silence. One sound, just one sound, would save me now. First, I was captured by silence. Then came real capture at the hands of silent men. I was already undone by my misdirected supplications for silence; I let myself be led by men I did not try to see to places I did not want to know. Lifeless, voluntarily blind, and deaf—so silent were the forest and its men—I once more resigned myself to fate. I knew the shape and form of my destiny when we stopped; I took a step forward and felt only empty space beneath my foot. Arms held me, I heard the bird-like voices. I opened my eyes. I was standing at the edge of one of those wells I have spoken of, so wide and deep that at first view they seemed to be caverns level with the ground; but in their center lie waters so deep they must be the baths of the Evil One himself.

My foot loosened a pebble from the edge of the well; I watched it fall and for many seconds—as long as it took the pebble to reach the sunken mirror of the waters—I listened in vain, and then the cavern was filled with echoes, and the voices of my captors were raised in confused debate, and again and again they repeated the word "cenote, cenote," and then "death," and then "night," and then "sun," and then "life," and I recalled my dream, when I had slept beside one of these wells and fallen into it, and also I remembered I had the right to one nocturnal question and at the top of my lungs I shouted in the language of this land: "Why am I going to die?"

And a voice spoke over my shoulder, so close I would have sworn it was the voice of my shadow, and said: "Because you have killed the sun."

I was not dreaming now, and the naked arms of these natives pushed me toward the well: I lost my footing; I shouted, it isn't true! I fell . . . the animal with the twisted feet killed it! I fell . . . I saw it! I fell into the true night, not the unreal night of dreams, I fell shouting, the animal! the animal: I fell through the black night within the well . . . the animal! It's true! I dreamed it! Then feet-first I struck the water and I heard the distant ringing echo of the voice that had spoken over my shoulder: "Dream now you are going to die so that this night will not be the last, the eternal, the infinite night of our fear . . ."

I sank into the quicksilver breast of the waters.

DAY OF THE WATER,

NIGHT OF THE PHANTOM

I was bathed in light. Night reigned when I had been thrown into the well, and the fear of my executioners was like the night. As I plunged into the water, I had drawn in the last lungful of air and closed my eyes; as soon as I felt myself beneath the surface, my will to survive revived; I swam, but my efforts were to no avail: after a few strokes I came always to the circular wall of smooth, sheer rock, without any handhold. Without hope, I floated, knowing that sooner or later I would grow weak and would sink into the unknown depths of this watery prison. I decided to call this day of my certain death the day of the Water, and I wondered whether this was one of the five days I was to steal from life to hold against death, as the Lord of Memory and the Lady of the Butterflies had so often told me. How would I know? My beautiful and horrible lover had warned me I would remember only those five decisive days, forgetting the other twenty of my destiny in this land. How would I know what I lived but could not remember? And then, as I say, Sire, I was bathed in light.

An undulating brightness, shattered when I had splashed through it, covered the surface of the water; it was again smooth and calm, barely riffled by my quiet floating. First, I sought the deliverance of the thread that in my dream had rescued me from a similar situation. But now the thread was nowhere to be seen. Then I prayed that this well might be like the sea, subject to high and low tides, for then at the ebb tide I might stand on the floor of my prison. Keeping my eyes open wide, I dived into the depths of the well. There I found the reason for the astonishing brightness: the sandy floor of this pool was a burial ground of bones and skulls; and if the sands were brilliant, they were dull compared to the refulgence of the remains of those other men who had died here.

I rose to the surface: I had seen my destiny face to face, bone to bone. I dived again, again I explored the well in the illumination of that deathly light. I saw that in one corner chance had piled up a heap of skulls that formed a small submerged pyramid. I considered: "Perhaps these dead can be of service to my life. Perhaps I can build a platform of washed bones where I can stand and await my death by starvation—or the salvation that came in my dream: the spider's thread."

So I began to work. I swam like a fish to the grisly mound and began to dislodge the crusted skulls that seemed almost a part of the chalky rock, or the rock an extension of the death's-heads. I used my scissors to pry the skulls from the soft stone, rising to the surface when my air was exhausted, filling my lungs, diving again to renew my task.

Thus I passed several hours of the night, resting from time to time, floating calmly on my back on my liquid bed, for more people drown from terror than from water. But in the end my pedestal of bones was still not very tall, and I reached the point where I considered giving up and abandoning myself to the sleep shared by my companions, the skeletons in this sinkhole. There I was beneath the waters, staring into the hollow eye sockets of a skull embedded in the rock. I said to myself that as the ancient Lord of Memory had died of fear upon seeing himself in my mirror, I would take this skull as my mirror; I would kiss it, caress it, press it to my breast, and thus create a compassion I had been denied. I would die embracing my own image, as final and eternal as the night so feared by my tormentors.

As captives pry stones from their dungeon walls, so I pried loose this last skull. But captives have hopes that beyond the loosened stone they will find liberty. I had no such hope. This labor I did for my death.

I loosened the skull, and then, Sire, an icy thread slipped between my fingers, and if it were possible for a man to shout beneath the water, I would have shouted: "The spider's thread!"

And, shouting, I would have thanked my loving and protective lady for saving me. But I immediately realized the thread in my hands was intangible; it was not spun by the spider, but was water . . . more water. And then this filament of cold water turned into a frozen torrent, and the torrent into a true subterranean cataract that scattered the shattered remains of the skulls and burst powerfully from the small hole in the rock that had been plugged only by the last skull. The liberated torrents enveloped me in foam, tumbled me over and over, lifted me from the bottom of the well with their turbulent force, dragging me upward with them toward the night, toward the jungle.

That well was filling with water, Sire, quickly and tumultuously, and I swam upward toward the edge from which I'd been pushed, fighting now to keep from being sucked toward the sunken cemetery by the churning currents of the waters freed by the accident of my labors. Fortune had allowed me to tap the very vein that fed the well, the subterranean river that was father to these deep-flowing waters.

I swam with the upsurging water, lessening now in force. The water did not overflow the top of the well, but leveled a few inches below its rim. My hands touched dry land, my fingers dug in, and I pulled myself up until I could see over the edge of the well. A red sun and a gray sky: these were the first things I saw. A sun the color of blood, blazing in its own fire, bathed in the purple of its rebirth. It, as I, had just emerged. It edged upward in a metallic sky, a sky as flat as the chalky white ground where my nighttime executioners stood staring in amazement, watching me emerge from the well filled by the rushing waters at the very instant the sun was born anew.

I emerged by my own efforts; by my own efforts I scrambled to my feet and met their expressions of amazement, gratitude, and respect. No one came near me now, no one touched me; all stood obediently at a distance. I heard the lament of a flute. The sun quickly shed its terrestrial cloak, rose higher, transformed the gray sky into a bright yellow cupola. Joy exploded. To the music of the flutes were added rattles, bells, and drums; groups of men with red ocher- and clay-painted bodies danced first around me, then preceded me, inviting me to follow them; women and children joined us, offering me small earthen jars of a thick white intoxicating liquid and roasted ears of grain sprinkled with a fiery pepper.

I ate; I followed them, and we came to the foot of a clean, low temple with beautiful ornamental frets. The people who first had wished to sacrifice me and now were honoring me formed two lines, indicating the path I must follow to the foot of the temple. I ascended the short stairway, as astonished now as my former-captors-turned-enthusiastic-hosts. I reached the flat platform of this temple, as low in profile as the bare chalky plain about us, and there, upon a strange stone throne carved in the form of spread wings, I encountered an obese and lavishly robed man wearing a dyed purple mantle, his forehead bound by a jewel-encrusted riband, fanning himself with the feathers of the beautiful tame green bird I had first seen near the home of the provident old mother.

This Fat Prince maintained an appearance of great dignity, but his nervous fanning indicated to me that he shared the reverent amazement of his people. By his side, as nervous as its master, tied to the throne by a silver chain, fretted a marvelous fowl, the largest bird I had ever seen. Its head was bald as an eagle's; from its neck, almost touching the ground, drooped enormous, worn, reddish, inflamed dewlaps; the wings of this great fowl were covered with jewels, with emeralds and jade, and about its neck and tarsi danced beautiful golden chains and copper bracelets and coins of pure gold. The music stirred the bejeweled bird whose ornaments jangled as if in time to the rhythm of the music. This great bird's nest was a large sheet of cotton cloth that covered part of the platform, as well as some objects beside the throne. The Fat Prince of this land rose heavily from his throne, aided by two young men and submissive girls with downcast eyes whose tight white skirts were embroidered like the tunic of the grandmother of the hearth. The obese one bowed before me and, with a gesture, ceded me his throne.

Shaking my head, I refused. The Prince glared at me, offended. The fowl shook its scoriaceous dewlaps. I remembered the fate of Pedro. I took the Prince's place on the throne and he said: "Long-awaited Lord: you have given us back the sun. We thank you."

Instead of asking and wasting a question, I stated: "The sun rises every day."

The Prince sadly shook his head, and in a loud voice repeated my words to the throng at the foot of the temple. When they heard him, they wailed and shouted no, no, not so; the noise of the drums and rattles rose and with satisfaction the Fat Prince looked at his people and then at me.

"It rises for you, our Lord, when you wish it. But for us it dies. We have seen the deaths of many suns; and when the suns die, the deep rivers of our land dry up, nothing grows upon the land, animals die and princes die; the birds die. Cities return to rough stone and disappear beneath the jungle growth. We have died, and fled, and we have returned when you have deigned to return the sun to us. The sun does not die for you, for you are its master. For us it dies every night, and we never know whether it will rise again. You have proved who you are.

We sacrificed you in exchange for the sun, and you returned the sun to us, and with it you returned to earth. We do you honor, Lord, on this day of the Water.''

The Fat Prince raised his fan of feathers and signaled to two young men, who rapidly climbed the temple steps. In their hands they carried two small cloth-covered earthen jars. The Prince dropped his fan and accepted the jars, holding one in each hand. He said to me: "Uncover them.''

I did, and I must tell you, Sire, those jars contained excrement, vile excrement, and with a gesture of repugnance I re-covered the jars as the obese Prince spoke: "Offer this to the bird, who is the bejeweled guaxolotl, and you will be rewarded, for this bird is the prince of the world.''

I arose from the throne and held out the two filthy jars to that fowl he called guaxolotl; the fowl shook its dewlaps and with its own beak lifted the cotton cloth that lay over the shrine and revealed to my eyes a treasure of jewels of gold and polished jade.

"See, my Lord,'' murmured the Fat Prince, "the jeweled bird offers you the gold and jade, the excrement of the gods, in exchange for human excrement. With it he offers power, riches, and glory. Take it all. It is yours.''

What misery. I had before me riches enough to found an empire; but I had possessed the glory of the pearls on the beach where I had been shipwrecked, and I had received the power of gold from the natives beside the river; but I had abandoned both glorious pearls and powerful gold, I had forgotten them amid the rain and mud and mosquitoes, for I had found they could not help me survive in this land. What the obese Prince called the excrement of the gods, would it serve me in any way?

The temptation of this treasure which the fowl guarded was nothing compared to the greatest temptation of my new life: the Lady of the Butterflies, finding her again, making love to her again. And to that end my only treasure was a simple spider's thread of greater worth than all the jade and topaz and emeralds and gold and silver I was offered in appreciation for the return of the sun. To follow the road to the volcano I must travel without any burden. And so I replied to the Fat Prince: "I accept your offering, my Prince. And having accepted, I return it to you in exchange for one question.''

The Prince looked confused, and I continued: "Tell me what I ask of you, for if you know the answer you will know how to defend yourself, and if you do not know, you will be forewarned. I look at your people and I fear that my passage among you may be as disastrous as my time with the people beside the river. Answer this single question, for I know that I may obtain only one answer on this day. Tell me: why were all the people killed who lived beside the river?''

The Fat Prince trembled: "Is my answer worth all the riches, the power, and the glory the jeweled bird-prince offers you?"

I said yes; perturbed, he answered: "They were not killed. They killed themselves. By their own hand they offered themselves in sacrifice."

I bowed my head, as perturbed by this answer as the man who gave it. At my feet, beckoning, lay the spider's thread.

As I left this land, walking across the white plain away from the temple and the well and the people who wished one night to sacrifice me and the next day to honor me, I pondered greatly the answer of the obese Prince. I could still hear the sad lament of their flutes, and their disappointed faces as they watched me leave were still alive in my memory. But above all else, to my feverish imaginings came the spectacle of the people beside the river.

A people immolated by its own hand. So that killing had not been a reprisal on the part of the men of the mountain but a voluntary sacrifice motivated by some other reason: perhaps the death of their Lord of Memory, and with him the death of memory itself? Did they fear their orphaned state, bereft of the knowledge demanded by that place: the sun and rain, the time to collect firewood and the time to burn it, smoke and gold, flight to the hill, the return to the river? They were a fragile, tender people too preoccupied with combating the evil of nature ever to practice human evil.

I loved that people in my memory, Sire, for as one who also lived without memory, I felt I was one of them. And I pardoned them the death of my old friend Pedro, for I understood that his intrusion, as mine, had interrupted the sacred order of things and ages; they did not hate us, they feared our presence would break the perfect cycles of an age that defended them against the evil of nature. The new world was a world of fear, of fleeting happiness and constant anguish: I trembled to think how our measures of duration and of strength, of survival and defeat and triumph, were useless here where everything was born each day only to perish again each night; I trembled to think of an encounter between our energetic concepts of continuity with these that were but a quickly withered flower of a day—uncertain expectation. I pardoned, I say, Pedro's death. I told myself I would also pardon them mine. The intrusion of one white man in these lands was enough . . . no, it was too much.

Night surprised me in the midst of these cavilings, guided always by the spider's thread. I had passed the chalky plain and was traveling a road that penetrated into a forest of tall trees covered with clusters of crescent-shaped green fruit. I also noted that the road, more arduous now, ran uphill. I was leaving rivers and jungle and sea behind. I felt hungry, and I shook one of those trees to satisfy that hunger. I was just preparing to eat when I heard the sound of someone working. I tried to identify the sound and came to the conclusion that a short distance from me someone was cutting wood. I entered deeper into the dark woods with several of the green fruit in my hand, ready to share them with the woodcutter.

In the darkness I could barely make out the stooped figure of a man standing with his back turned to me, violently attacking a tree trunk with an ax. Confidently, I approached. The man turned to face me and I cried out in horror, for the woodcutter's face was nothing but two glowing eyes and a swinging tongue that hung from a slit of a mouth, a smooth lipless wound; and the rib cage of this phantom opened and closed like gates in the wind, and as his ribs parted they revealed a living, beating heart that glowed like the monster's eyes. I was sure I had lost my reason, such was the contrast between my feeling of peaceful friendship and the horror of the vision: then the enormous hanging tongue spoke imperiously: "Dare . . . Take my heart, take it in your hand, dare to do what no one else has ever dared . . ."

Oh, Sire, as you hear me, recall, and sum up my adventures from the time I left your shores and tell me why upon hearing these words I would hesitate: what was seizing that palpitating heart compared to the dangers I had met in the sea, in the center of the vortex, among the warriors on the beach, and in the sacrifice of the well?

I reached out and took that sonorously beating, bloody, dripping heart in my hand. I held it with repulsion, wishing only to return it immediately to its owner—but the phantom moaned with fury, his wounded mouth filled with green spittle, and he howled these words: "Demand what you will: power, riches, glory: they are yours; they belong to he who dares take my heart."

I replied simply: "I want nothing. Here. I return your heart to you."

The creature, who had only eyes, mouth, and tongue, shouted again and his shouts drowned out the sound of his pounding ribs. "Then it is true!" he shouted. "You are the one who rejects all temptation; today you rejected the gifts of the jeweled bird and now you reject mine. What is it you wish?"

I stood silent, the creature's heart in my hand. I looked with cold disdain at this forest tempter. The only thing I possessed was my desire; I would not deliver it in exchange for his heart. For I well knew the law of this land was to reply to an offering with another of greater value: what but my desire could I offer the phantom of the forest in exchange for his heart?

When his ribs, like the shutters of a window, again opened, I returned his heart and I asked the one nocturnal question to which I had a right. "Take your heart. And in exchange, tell me now: why did the inhabitants of the town beside the river kill themselves?"

I feared, Sire, I was wasting another question, and that I would hear the answer I had myself proposed: that they had gone mad when they realized they had lost their memory. I did not fear that answer; it would, at least, reaffirm my reason. But the creature with the glowing eyes raised two hands as smooth as his face (hands without fingernails or lines of fortune or love or life), and pressed those hands against his beating rib cage and said: "They sacrificed themselves for you . . ."

And the phantom began to laugh monstrously. "They sacrificed themselves for you . . ." Howling with laughter, the horrendous forest apparition repeated: "Sacrificed themselves for you . . . sacrificed themselves for you . . ." And with every burst of laughter, his body shrank; the creature hid his face between his hands, and howled: "Fear me, brother, fear me; I am your pursuing shadow; I am the voice you heard last night over your shoulder; I am . . ."

Suddenly the creature stood tall, looked straight into my eyes. I was looking at myself. The phantom of the forest had my face, my body; he was my exact double, my twin, my mirror.

DAY OF THE

SMOKING MIRROR

I say exact, but I am inexact, Sire. For my double was my double in everything except color. My eyes were blue, his were black. My hair was the color of wheat, his the color of a horse's mane. My skin, in spite of the time spent in these lands, was pale and quick to burn, to blister and peel to a pale rose color. My twin's was burnished copper. But he was my twin in every other way: size, build, features, and bearing. Now I can recall the differences. That night I was impressed only by the similarity.

I was not master of my hours there. Much time must have passed between the night of the horrendous nocturnal apparition and my next memory of my voyage. The ancient of the temple and the goddess of the butterflies had warned me; I would recall only five days, those saved from the days of my destiny in this land. Now, before opening my eyes again, I could have dreamed: "One day, ten, five more, how many days had passed since that night the phantom offered me his heart and I offered him my wish in exchange?"

I did not know, and that was an advantage the new world held over me; it knew all my steps across its face, even those I actually would never forget because they were not a part of my memory. But if this was my weakness, perhaps that of the new world was having to assume the memory and responsibility for all my acts. I may have done a great deal, Sire, I may have done very little, but I did something between that night and this dawn. But if I were dreaming this dawn, I was consoled by reason: "Yesterday, only yesterday, you escaped from the well of death, following a night of superhuman labor and wakefulness; you were led to the pyramid of the Fat Prince; you rejected the power and the glory offered by the bejeweled bird; you left behind you the chalky plain; you walked through the forests of tall trees; you encountered the phantom, your dark double. You must have slept deeply, as you have never slept before. There is no body, no matter how young, that can bear so much. Your sleep has been so deep that it seems as if it were the longest of your life; no, more than that; it seems longer even than your life. But the truth is that you slept last night and you awakened today. That is all."

My eyes contradicted my reason. I awakened suddenly, eagerly, breathing rapidly, as one awakens from a nightmare, and I saw a transformed landscape. There was nothing here to recall the warm, florid lands of the coast. It was cold, and my ripped and torn clothing served me badly. It was difficult to breathe; the air was thin and elusive. The luxuriant vegetation of the new world had died, and in its place reigned a no less luxuriant desolation. I was surrounded by a landscape of rock; tumultuous yellow and red stone, at once symmetrical and capricious in its naked shapes of knife and saw, altar and table, cloud and constellation of shattered stone, tall, smooth, sharply outlined cathedrals of sheer rock pierced by twisted thickets and dwarfed gray trees; rock crowned by enormous green-thorned candelabra never before seen by the eye of man, like cathedral organs, tall and dry and armed to defend themselves against any touch, although who would dare touch so forbidding a plant, queen of this petrous desert, whose coarse, prickly habit declared her majestic desire to live isolated in this sterile domain: a hermit plant, a stylite unto herself, O Very Christian Sire who hears me today, both pillar and penitent.

At the foot of this rocky mountain lay a valley of dust so restless and silent that at first I did not notice any life within its reaches, except for the movement of the veils of dry, white whirling dirt, swift and hostile; an icy wind was blowing; and it rent the veils of dust; before me, before my bed of rocks, rose the volcano. I had arrived. I gave thanks. Here my lover was to meet me. I looked around. At my feet was the spider's thread.

Jubilant, I picked it up. Following it, I descended from my harsh eyrie. I no longer thought whether much or a little time had passed between my most recent recollection and this new morning, between my passage through the burning coastlands and my arrival in this cold region. Guided by the spider I descended to the plain, and holding to its thread I moved through the restless dust of the plain, and like the plain I felt crushed by the closeness of the sky and sun which at this height were almost on top of me, and I remembered how distant they had seemed on the coast. I did not understand; terrible was the heat on the beaches I first trod in this new world, and I thought then that nowhere did the blazing sun burn so close to us. Now, I remembered how high and distant it had seemed on the coast and in the jungle; and on this plain of rock and dust, beside the volcano, so nearby, its blaze was lessened. A transparent Host, the sun burned less the nearer I was to it. I realized this, to the astonishment of my body, only at that instant. And as I walked forward I discovered that the dust was also smoke.

In one hand I held the guiding thread. With the other, I tried to fan away the dust and smoke that almost prevented my seeing or breathing. I stretched out my hand before me, Sire, as blind men do, even when someone leads them. And my hand disappeared in that thick haze. My fingers touched other bodies, a swiftly moving line of human bodies hidden by the dust and smoke of this silent dawn at the foot of the volcano. Silence. Footsteps. I drew back a hand throbbing with fear and touched my chest, my face, my sex, for I needed to assure myself of my own existence; and when I knew it was I, that I was there, alive, only then did my sensations begin to float away from reality; and reality insinuated itself, Sire, with such cunning that I believed my sensations were reality. For while I was telling myself I had come into a world of dust, the reality was that the dust was smoke; and while I believed myself to be surrounded by silence, evil and cunning were the murmuring reality on this plain at the foot of the volcano.

Footsteps in the dust. Footsteps amid the smoke. Feet dancing in silence. Feet dancing to a beat not their own, but marked by a different rhythm, one imposed upon them. The spider guided me with its silvery thread. Clutching that thread I lost my fear of the smoke, the dust, and the silent dancing that surrounded me. And free of the fear I realized once again that distance is fear, and proximity, confidence. I began to perceive a persistent music, a monotonous, three-beat rhythm that set the cadence for the silent feet of the dancers; drum and rattle, I said to myself, only a rattle and a drum, but with a persistence and a will for festival, for celebration, for ritual, that converted their rhythm into the very incarnation of this time and this space: the time and the place in which both they, the dancers and the musicians, and I, the pilgrim in these lands, were living, here and now. Nothing beyond the silent dance to the beat of the continual drum and the continual rattle belonged to the reality of this invisible plain that took for a veil the dust and for a coif the smoke. And thus one sees, Sire, how our senses deceive us, thinking we may discover the whole through its parts, never imagining what great universes may be hidden behind the rhythm of a drum and a rattle.

I walked among the silent, hidden dancers of this my new morning in the new world, the third morning of the time that would be granted me here. I felt the nearness of bodies; at times my outstretched hands brushed shoulders and heads, at times feathers and paper streamers and rope touched my chest and legs, but as if they feared my touch, these contacts were fleeting. My bare feet knew only a vast expanse of dust, which is why the sudden contact of my feet with stone was so unexpected: a change of element, like stepping from water into fire, for the dust was liquid and the stone burning hot. And this stone, Sire, rose upward. For a moment I imagined that the spider had led me in an infinite and hidden circle and that I had returned to the rock where I had awakened early this morning. Instinctively I took a step backward to protect my feet from the rough stone and the sheer, hidden reefs of the mountain. But, instead, they found the sharp corners and smooth surface of carved stone.

I climbed. The stone was a stairway of rock. I began to count the steps as I ascended; the sounds of the dance grew fainter and the accompaniment of drum and rattle was fading and the double haze of dust and smoke was dissipating. Thirty-three steps I counted, Sire, not one more, not one less, and as I stepped upon the last, as is natural, I sought the next one, and when I did not find it, when my foot touched air, I was confused. I sought aid by looking upward, for until that moment my gaze had been the captive of the ground. As our senses diminish we depend upon our feet and the earth. As they increase we forget both feet and earth and again we stretch our hands toward heaven. Behind the heights to which I'd climbed, a great white gleaming cone reposed upon a motionless carriage of white clouds. Beneath the clouds, the skirts of the great mountain spread like a black shield of ash and rock protecting the pristine crown of ice, the refulgent field of tiny stars, and the white sea of sand frozen in the heavens.

The haze hovering over the land began to break, and fled, thinner and thinner, across the thirsty face of this desert. From the heights I watched the dissipation of the clouds of dust and I saw a multitude of men and women and children gathered there; I saw that the men were dancing in circles to the rhythm of the drum and the rattle, and that the children stood motionless, waiting, and that the women, kneeling, were variously occupied in pouring liquids and in roasting skinned hares and in patting the dough of the bread of their land and rolling that bread into cylinders that were then sprinkled with red powders and heated upon braziers and in puffing their smoking tubes like the ancient mother of the clean hut where I had taken shelter one night. And there were bundles of rushes there, and beds of hay, and stones like millstones, and piles of rope. I saw the steps, lined with smoking censers, up which I had just ascended, and men with tall crests and golden ear ornaments in the form of lizards sitting on the ledges with enormous conch shells held between their legs. I saw the steep stone stairway that had led me to this summit, the twin of the volcano's peak, as the smoke and the dust, the phantom and I, were also reflections of each other. The insubstantial bodies formed a horizontal alliance, and the volcano rising before my eyes and the pyramid that reproduced its conical and suppliant structure formed a vertical unity. They were the horizontal plain; we, the vertical summit.

I employed the plural for myself before I knew there were others on the high platform of the temple. Alone, on the plain, I had felt I was many. Accompanied, on the pyramid, I felt alone. Again I sought the assurance of the surface where I stood. The sole of my left foot rested upon the hard stone of the temple; my right foot was planted in a white mound of flour or sand—when I saw my foot sunken in that strange matter I thought it one of the two; hastily I withdrew my foot and contemplated the track, the sign of my passage, there imprinted.

And if before I had been blinded by haze, now sound deafened me. Other drums joined the drum, other rattles the rattle, and pipes and bells and flutes similar to those I had heard at the other two temples: the one in the jungle and that at the well; and when I heard that music I resigned myself; destinies meet in these great stone theaters of the new world; here, in the open air, definitive performances were held, here near the life-giving sun; the pyramids were hands of stone raised to touch the sun, aspiring fingers, mute prayers. One sound reigned above all the others, a sound similar to the moan of the dying beast I had seen one day drifting, wounded, out to sea from the putrid river of the first beach I trod. At first I imagined that it rose from the very entrails of the volcano. Only now, when at last I stopped staring at the track of my foot in the white mound, only now did I see upon the steps those men with the lizard ear ornaments blowing into their enormous conch shells.

They extinguished the lighted braziers on all the steps and upon the apex of this temple. Whirling swiftly, I looked all around me. The platform was square, with steps descending on all four sides, and with two narrow troughs down the sides of each stairway. There was a large square block in the center of the platform, a stone three spans—or a little more—in height, and two spans in width. And behind this stone there was a great fire, its flame now extinguished, but its secret ardor of bubbles, oil, and hot ash unsatiated, its flames quick to rise at the touch of one of the many torches on the ground beside many black stone knives shaped much like an iron goad. I walked to where one of them lay amid the thinning smoke and picked it up: it seemed to be made of hardened volcanic ash. And I dropped it in fright when I looked up; several repulsive men were approaching me, their faces painted black and their lips glossy and sticky, as if smeared with honey; they were dressed in long black tunics and their long black hair stank even at that distance. They were singing quietly as they steadily advanced toward me like an unarmed phalanx, and they held the tails of their pleated tunics spread wide as if to hide something behind them; they sang and nervously pointed toward my footprint in the white mound.

"He appeared, he appeared . . ."
"Thus it was spoken . . ."
"Last night we spread the container of ground meal . . ."
"We waited in silence . . ."
"All night . . ."
"We danced in silence . . ."
"All night . . ."
"Thus it was spoken . . ."
"That he would this day return . . ."
"He who is invisible . . ."
"He of the air . . ."
"He of the shadows . . ."
"He who speaks only from the shadows . . ."
"Have mercy upon us and do not harm us . . ."
"We shall honor you upon this day . . ."
"We seek your favor . . ."
"We fear your evil . . ."
"It is You . . ."
"Night . . ."
"Arrived in the day . . ."
"Shadow . . ."
"Appeared with the sun . . ."
"It is You . . ."
"Smoking Mirror . . ."
"It is You . . ."
"So it was spoken . . ."
"The footprint in the ground meal . . ."
"The track of a single foot . . ."
"We will survive . . ."
"He has returned . . ."
"Smoking Mirror . . ."
"Has returned . . ."
"Star of the night . . ."
"Has returned . . ."
"By day . . ."
"Has returned . . ."
"Conquering his twin, the light . . ."
"Has returned . . ."
"Hero of the night, victim of the day . . ."
"Has returned . . ."
"Honor to the fearful god of the shadows . . ."
"Honor to the shadow that dares show himself by day . . ."

"Honor to the conqueror of the sun . . ."

"Smoking Mirror . . ."

Mirror and smoke, mirror of smoke, smoke of mirror: with difficulty I deciphered these words and I clung to their meaning as the voices of the men dressed and bedaubed in black converted them into a litany. And clearly, no combination of words could better describe the plain of dust, the cradle of rocks where that day I had awakened, the pyramid on whose summit I now found myself, with the magnificent whiteness of the tall volcano behind me. Mirror: the sky, the snow, and the rock. Smoke: the land, the music, and the people. That I understood, and as I understood I was consoled. The reason for my uneasiness was of a different origin: the words of the sorcerers had the ring of portent; they marveled at what had happened; my arrival, the testimony of my footprint in the ground meal they had sprinkled there the night before, were proof that I was the one they had waited for.

I was ringed by the malodorous sorcerers, who raised their arms like the wings of the crow; as they approached I could smell and see the blood daubed in their long hair, upon their faces, their clothing and hands. With fear I recalled the animal in the aged mother's hut, pure shadow, a black silhouette inseparable from the night, the executioner of the sun, and I told myself that the spirit of the beast dwelt now in the bodies of these sorcerers. They feared what the beast had done. And so the beast might not kill the sun by night, they would kill the night beneath the sun. I saw my footprint in the ground meal: I was the night that they had waited to capture. In me they would hold the night captive. They surrounded me: they surrounded the mound of spilled meal bearing the mark of my foot, and the chant of those magi, Sire, was directed toward me, it was I they called "Smoking Mirror."

They let their arms fall, and behind them I saw the woman of my desire, my lover, the Lady of the Butterflies. I say it thus, with serenity, to compensate for the disturbance her presence caused in me. To see her again I had confronted all dangers, rejected all temptations, overcome all obstacles. But now, as I looked at her, I was looking at a stranger. She was not looking at me.

It was she. And she was another. She was seated upon a throne of stone, on the skin of an ocelot. No butterflies fluttered about her head. Her head was bare and her long black hair, like the priests', was smeared with blood. She wore a garment of jewels joined together by threads of gold with no cloth to dull the reflecting glitter of agate and topaz, amethyst and emerald; and beneath her sumptuous gown her woman's flesh showed smooth and flowing and naked. At the foot of her throne lay mounds of yellow flowers and pullulating serpents and centipedes, creatures of caverns and dry darkness. At her side lay a broom and long branches of odorous herbs. And at the feet of this terrible lady rested the spider: I recognized her by the spider, and by my lover's painted lips. And from between the opened thighs of the woman projected the head of a red serpent, as if the seed of my love-making in the jungle had gestated.

I looked at her, pleading: "My Lady, do you not know me?"

The woman's cruel eyes did not return my gaze. Two of the sorcerers seized my arms and the others raised high their daggers as they walked to the steps on which were ascending, singing and softly weeping, six women led by young warriors. Sire: you can never have imagined warriors of such elegance and luxury; in all their movements, and in the opulence of their attire, they revealed a care of breeding and of destiny similar to that of the finest charger or the fiercest mastiff. Tall feather crests, copper ear ornaments worked to resemble little dogs; lip rings made from oyster shells; leather necklaces, feathers tied about their shoulders, and, to their feet, the cloven hoofs of the stag. Their faces were covered by ocelot and eagle and alligator masks; the mouths of the women were painted black and they exuded a heavy perfume, they wore no clothing but hummingbird feathers stuck to their flesh, leaving bare their shame, and they wore many bracelets and necklaces on their wrists and neck and ankles. Wailing, they were half carried by the warriors, and some stroked the men's chests and others stared at them with a melancholy gaze and a resigned smile and sad recollection, and all of them were weeping, saddened by their abandonment. Then one of the warriors approached the stone seat where sat the Lady of the tattooed lips. And he said:

"You who cleanse our sins and devour our filth, soiling yourself so that the world may be purified, cleanse our sins; here are the whores who were chosen from among humble families of conquered peoples to satisfy our impure desire; tear that desire from our breasts and allow us to do battle without anxiety, our only desire that of serving the gods and their incarnation upon earth, our Lord of the Great Voice. Into the indecent bodies of these women we have emptied our man's weakness and impurity so we may be strong and pure upon the field of battle. Take them. They have fulfilled their time on earth. They have served. But now they serve no purpose. We renounce the flesh to dedicate ourselves to war. Take them. We offer them to you, you who devour filth, on this day of the Smoking Mirror."

The moment the warrior ceased speaking, the music again sifted across the plain as the dust had in the past, and with joy and great pleasure the musicians began to thump the hollow gourd rattles with their hands and to strike their sticks upon the skin of their drums, and when the sound of the drum was low in tone they whistled loudly, and dancers in richly colored green and yellow mantles holding clusters of roses and feathered fans trimmed in gold, their faces covered by feather head-coverings shaped like the heads of fierce animals, clasped hands and formed large circles, and upon the summit of the pyramid the sorcerers, at a sign from the black-nailed hand of my lover, struck their flint daggers deep into the breasts of the prostitutes, splitting them from nipple to nipple, and then upward through the breastbone, and with blood-caked hands they tore out their hearts, and finally cut off their heads and piled the mutilated bodies by the troughs beside the pyramid steps, where the women's blood flowed to sprinkle the plain of now quiet dust where the tempo of the dance was rising and buffoons ran out feigning drunkenness or madness or pretending to be old women, evoking laughter from the watching women and children. The sorcerers tossed the heads of the warriors' six whores down the temple steps, where they were quickly picked up by old men, who skewered them through the brains and impaled them on lances standing in a row as if in a lance rack.

The black sorcerers placed the smoking hearts of the women in a wooden dish at the feet of the lady who had been my lover. I fell to my knees, Sire, with my arms still held by two of the sorcerers of that group of murderers who were anointing their clothing and faces and hair with the blood of the whores, and I thought of my lost river people, of their simplicity and their lack of greed, of their ordinary life and their extraordinary fate: a people sacrificed by their own hands, and in my name; a people gathered beside the jungle temple to be brought to this high valley of dust and blood, their women given as whores to the warriors of the so-called Lord of the Great Voice, and then offered in sacrifice on the day of the mirror and the smoke. What kind of world was this where beauty and communal ownership of property and love of life coexisted with these ceremonies of crime? In that instant I recalled the frightful apparition in the forest: my double. As he coexisted with me, so the cult of life and the cult of death existed side by side in the new world, for reasons I had still not succeeded in understanding. I was the white god, so the ancient of the memories and the princess of the butterflies had told me: the principle of life, the teacher, the premonitory voice of love, of good and peace. The black god, the enemy, was my brother, the principle of death, of shadow and sacrifice. I thought I had vanquished my phantom twin by refusing him, because of my desire. But my desire was a woman, the woman I saw here now presiding over the pageantry of death.

The warriors knelt before the woman and removed their animal masks: their hair was cut short at the temples, shaved across their foreheads, and their temples painted yellow. They stuck thick thorns through their earlobes and then, one after another, they spoke into the ear of the devouring princess, as penitents speak, Sire, kneeling, and in a low voice. And only after each confession had ended did the woman and the warriors raise their voices, and she asked: ''Who inspired your evil?''

And he replied, "You . . ."

"Of whom were you thinking when you gave yourself to lust?"

"You . . ."

"Where are lust and evil to be found?"

"In the serpent that peers from between your parted thighs."

"Who will cleanse you of your sins?"

"You, you who devour filth, soiling yourself to purify us."

"Who grants me these powers?"

"The smoking mirror."

"How many times may you confess before me?"

"Once in my lifetime."

"When?"

"When I am preparing to die."

"Are you old?"

"I am young."

"Why are you going to die?"

"Because I am going to war."

"Against whom will you do battle?"

"Against the people who still refuse to submit to us."

"Do you prefer death in war to death in old age and infirmity?"

"I prefer it. The aged and the ill die as slaves. I shall go directly to the paradise of soft mists without passing through the icy hell beneath the earth."

"If you survive, do you know that you will never be able to confess or to cleanse yourself again?"

"I know. You hear each man only once. That is why I prefer to die in combat. I shall not survive."

The Lady took sweet-smelling herbs and cleansed the bodies of the warriors, brushing them softly over their backs and chests and legs while the sorcerers opened baskets and cages and removed little colored birds from them, wrung their necks, and placed the small feathered bodies at the woman's feet, and the warriors again put on their animal casques and descended the steps to the plain, where the dancers, the women, and the children had moved aside to make way for a procession led by two dancing satraps with large paper disks bound to their foreheads. Their honey-smeared, black-painted faces glistened in the sun, and they led a group of men whose bodies were stained white. The warriors who had just made their confessions to my lover advanced to meet this procession while the satraps forced the captives—only at that instant did I realize that they were captives—to climb upon some round stones resembling millstones, and they offered them clay pots from which to drink, and each captive raised his pot to the east and to the north, then to the west and to the south, as if offering it to the four corners of the earth, and each, in a plaintive voice, sang the same song:

In vain was I born,
In vain I came to this world.
I suffer, but at least I am here,
I have been born upon earth.

And once the captives were standing upon the stones, the satraps took rope that came from the center of the millstones and tied the rope to the waists of the captives, thus tying them to the stones. Then they gave each captive a lance with feathers stuck to the cutting edge, and a pine war club, and then four warriors walked forward, and they too carried lances, except that their lances had knives on the cutting edge, and two were dressed as ocelots and the other two as eagles, and they raised their round shields and their swords to the sun, and then each warrior began to battle against one captive. But there were captives who swooned and fell to the ground without taking up any weapon, as if they wanted to be killed; and these were scorned by the warriors. And others, seeing themselves tied to the stone, were dispirited, and took up their weapons as if in a trance, and then were vanquished. But others were valiant and the warriors could not subdue them and they sought aid from their companions until among the four they overcame the captive, took away his weapons, and thrusting at him with their knives, bore him to the ground.

The music and dancing burst forth anew; the bleeding captives were freed from the rope and millstone to be dragged by the warriors toward the summit while the plain below was the scene of a colorful dance danced by men wearing sumptuous miter-shaped headdresses from which issued many green feathers, like tall crests, so numerous that the air was green with them.

The warriors, dragging their captives, reached the summit, where the prisoners were taken by the high priests, who tied the prisoners' hands behind them, and also their feet, and many had fainted and thus they were thrown into the great fire onto the heaped coals burning on the high platform; and where each fell he sank into the bed of coals and hot ash, and there in the fire the captive began to writhe and twist; and his body began to crackle like the body of some roasted animal, and great blisters rose over all his body. And at the height of this agony the sorcerers drew him from the fire with a pothook, dragged him to the stone block, and they split open his chest from nipple to nipple, threw the heart at the feet of the Lady, cut off the captive's head and threw both head and body, thus separated, down the steps, where aged men received and quickly dragged away the bodies and pierced the heads through the brain, impaling them upon the lances.

One of the warriors walked to the edge of the platform and the voices and music and dancing ceased so that he might be heard.

"Hidden among the women and children and dancers there are

many lords and spies of the peoples with whom we are waging war, who want secretly to observe our ceremonies this day. Return to your lands and let it be known what happens to our captives. Fear the power of Mexico!''

For the first time, Sire, I heard a man of this high arid plain speak the name of his nation, for as such I took it, allied as it was with the assertion of power, although it could have been the name of their greatest Lord, he of the Great Voice, or of the supreme god to whom all others owed honor. My limited knowledge of this soft tongue forced me to reduce every word to the roots I had so tortuously learned, and whether this was the name of the land, of the lord, or of the god, that name signified several things at one time: umbilicus, death, and moon; umbilicus, I said to myself, is life; and death, death; and moon, the two faces, waning and waxing, of life and death. I had no time to ponder this: in the midst of the silence the warrior who was speaking walked to the filthy high priests who had officiated here, knelt before them, and his companions imitated him and among them they washed their priests' feet, stained with blood and melted pitch and cold ash.

The ritual of the foot washing was slow and elaborate, and in the humility of the warriors before the high priests I read another sign of the structure of this land of the navel of the moon: the fearsome warriors with eagle and ocelot headdresses owed obeisance to the celebrants of death and thus were subjected to a power higher than that of arms. Whom, in turn, must these black priests obey? What power was greater than that of this truncated pyramid of death? Numbed, I looked toward the volcano whose form the temple reproduced, and their summits were identical, ice and fire, snow and stone, ash and fire, blood and smoke; and remembering my ascent from the coast to the volcano, I told myself that this entire land lay in the form of a temple, putrid and vegetal at its base, smoking and petrous on its summit, and that I had climbed the steps of that gigantic pyramid, and that the nation that worshipped the sun and called itself moon was like a series of pyramids, one included within the other, the lesser enclosed by the greater, a pyramid within a pyramid, until the entire land was a temple dedicated to the fragile maintenance of life nourished by the arts of death.

Oh, Sire, you who hear me, the bloody rites I have related must evoke in you a horror as great as mine as I witnessed them, but I wish that you might put yourself in my place on that distant day of the Smoking Mirror, and that in spite of the horror you might share my deep desire to understand what I was seeing, and to grant to the desire for comprehension powers greater than the instinct for condemnation. Unarmed, I myself captive and witness to the fate of other captives, I rejected the temptation to condemn what I did not understand. Very limited was my intelligence of what was happening. And perhaps, I told myself, I must await the end of my pilgrimage, the fifth day of my memory and my questions and their promised answers before I could understand this land. The ceremony of the long day's ritual had not ended, and I still had no understanding of my place in it.

The two priests who held my arms had released me in order to participate in the long and difficult ceremony of the foot washing, for the warriors in their humble task could not clean the melted pitch from the feet of the sorcerers. I decided to test my fortune. I arose, and walked toward the Lady who presided over this festival. The sorcerers looked up at me and intoned hoarse prayers; the kneeling warriors kept their heads bowed. Cautiously, I approached the woman. She, finally, looked at me. She summoned me with her gaze. Everything about her that once had been delight now was terror. There was something in her new presence that prevented me not only from touching her but from even remaining standing before her. Like the warriors before the sorcerers, I fell to my knees, my head bowed, not daring to touch the body that with such pleasure I had made mine in the jungle. I could not, however, resist the urge to question her with my eyes: for the first time that day, I scrutinized the face of my lover. From a distance, and at first glance, it was her face, the face I had known. But closer, Sire, I could note the minute changes on that unforgettable face, the imperceptible traces left on that skin by the passage of time: the faint wrinkles around the eyes, the sudden heaviness of the eyelids, the visible hardness of the lips, the slightest loosening of the flesh on her neck and beneath the still high, firm cheekbones. The passage of time: of what time, Sire? Only three nights earlier I had made love to a girl younger than I; now I was looking at a woman a little older than I, a mature woman, still beautiful, still desirable, but whose features had passed the flush of spring and suggested autumn instead. I thought: it isn't she. The only way to prove whether or not it was she was to resort to my only legitimate weapon: my question for that day.

Impelled by the anxiety of the discovery and my doubt, and without pausing to think, I said: "My Lady, do you not know me?"

She looked at me from an icy distance. "That is the question you ask me today?"

Realizing my error, I shook my head, not daring to touch her hands, which was my desire: the question with which she answered mine was proof that this woman was my lover, the princess of the butterflies, privy to our pact. "No, my Lady, it is not . . ."

"You have the right to ask one question . . ."

"I am surrounded by so many mysteries . . ."

"You may ask only one question each day . . ."

"I know; I have fulfilled our pact during the time I have been apart from you . . ."

Sadly, she looked toward the plain, where activity was renewing: people were eating, women were pouring the liquors of the land into clay pots and preparing the native bread on the stone mortars, and the elders were directing the dances, holding heavy canes adorned with paper flowers soaked with incense. Smoke of the flowers, smoke of the braziers: from afar, beside my Lady, I observed them, and I rejected all temptation to comprehend the present mystery; I must respect the logical order of my questions, climb them like the steps of the pyramid and the land itself; my most profound reason told me I must not skip a single bead in the rosary of cause and effect, or the string of beads would break and scatter, would roll down the steps like the heads of the whores and captives, and I myself would be the prisoner of the day's enigmas without having resolved those of yesterday, and I would understand nothing of what was still to come.

"My Lady," I said finally, "why did the inhabitants of the town in the jungle sacrifice themselves for me?"

She looked at me with a touch of disdain, and strong compassion. "That is what you want to know today?"

"Yes."

Distantly, she gazed at the mixed smokes of the plain, the braziers and the incense, the smokes of human hunger and of the divine hunger of this land. "Because you are the reason for life and we are the reason for death. Because they believed that by sacrificing themselves to you they would not be sacrificed by us. They preferred to die for you rather than be killed by us."

I was deeply disturbed by these words, and my eyes clouded with blood, anger, and sadness; I recalled once again the quiet people of the jungle and I cursed for an instant the order of this new world that made me the cause for the death of innocents. But fear immediately overcame my sad and impotent rage. Sire: I feared that now those declarations spoken by the painted lips of my elusive lover would be inverted, and that in this day's ceremony I would die, sacrificed. This was demanded for the equilibrium of the things of the land of the dead moon.

The ceremony of the foot washing ended and all of them, priests and warriors, saw me kneeling at the feet of the Lady. A new sound rose from the steps, accompanied by an intense aroma, and soon there appeared on the summit richly adorned dancers with long hair and with plumage of rich feathers upon their brows, and they were led by another dancer dressed like a bat, with wings and all else necessary to assure that resemblance; and these dancers whistled by placing a finger in their mouths, and each carried two sacks upon his back; and one of these sacks was filled with incense that they began to sprinkle upon the braziers on the four sides of the platform, as if on the four corners of the world, and they offered the other sacks to the priests, who took them and then approached me: they ordered me to stand.

I looked with terror at the block and the knives and I divined my fate to be that of a whore sacrificed after draining a warrior's pleasure, or that of a captive killed to serve as an example to insubmissive peoples.

There was no time. From their sacks the high priests withdrew objects and clothing and paints, and began to stain my body and face, and to cover my head with white feathers, and to place garlands of flowers about my neck, and long streamers of flowers down my back, and hoops of gold in my ears, and strings of precious stones upon my chest. And they covered me with a rich mantle woven like a net, and covered my lower parts with a piece of richly embroidered linen, and they shod me with brightly painted ankle-high boots of soft deerskin and tied golden bells about my ankles and placed strings of precious stones upon my wrist, up to the elbow, and above the elbow golden arm bands, and again upon my chest the white ornament they call the wind jewel, and upon my shoulders a fringed and tasseled pouch-like ornament of white linen.

Thus transformed, and drenched in an icy sweat, I asked myself whether in this manner they were not preparing me for the maximum sacrifice of the day, but the high priests stood back from me, as if awed, and one of them exclaimed:

"This is, in truth, the Lord of the Night, the capricious and cruel Smoking Mirror, who lost one foot on the day of creation when he dragged our mother, the earth, from the waters, and the earth, our lady and mother, tore off his foot at the joint; this is the other, the shadow, he who always watches over our shoulders and accompanies us everywhere, he who tore the earth from the waters of creation and, exhausted and mutilated, had no time to give light to the earth, and who sees in the light an enemy who mocks his efforts and his sacrifice: the earth was born from the waters and from the shadows, and only because first there was land and then shadow could light exist, and men, and so the Smoking Mirror demands men's deaths to remind them that they emerged from the earth and the shadow, and so castigate their pride. This is, in truth, the Lord of the Night who left one single footprint in the ground meal of the temple on this his day."

As I heard this reasoning, I sought with feverish eyes the hard, cold gaze of my Lady, for through her I knew I possessed a different identity, one I believe destined to labor and peace and life; but as this priest's words accorded me the opposite identity, condemned me, I suddenly realized that the horrible deaths I had witnessed here were in my honor, as the sacrifice of the inhabitants of the jungle had been, and that I would not die now since others would die for me and in my name: the Smoking Mirror. Here my name meant shadow and crime, and in the jungle, light and peace.

How ignorant, Sire, I was and I am of the keys that open the doors of understanding to that world so foreign to our own, for if among us the code of unity prevails and all things aspire to oneness, there what

seemed to be one soon demonstrated the duplicity of its nature: everything there was two, two the people of the jungle, who first killed Pedro and then killed themselves for me; two the ancient of memories:
ancient in my mirror and young in his recollection; two the Lady of the
Butterflies, lover in the jungle and tyrant on the pyramid, devourer of
filth and purifier of the world; two was the sun: beneficence and terror;
two was the darkness: the executioner of the sun, the promise of the
dawn; two was life: life and its death; and two death: death and its life.

As I was two: I, this person who is speaking to you, and a dark double encountered one night in the forest. I was my shadow. My shadow
was my enemy. I must fulfill my own destiny as well as that of my dark
double. Little I imagined, even then, of the fearful burden that this my
double destiny would cast upon my weak shoulders. I barely glimpsed
its horror in the words of my lover, the cruel Lady of this day, when
the sorcerer ceased to speak. And this is what she spoke:

"Every year, on this day, we select one youth. For one year, we
nurture and care for him, and all who look upon him have great reverence for him and pay him great obeisance. For an entire year he
wanders through the land playing his flute, with his flowers and his
smoking reed, free by night and day to wander throughout the land,
accompanied always by eight servants who assuage his thirst and hunger. This youth will be married to a maiden who will surfeit him with
pleasure through the year, for she will be the youngest and most beautiful and most wellborn in this land. And at the end of the year, having
lived like a prince in the land, the young man will return on this day to
this very temple, and as he lies upon the stone, bound hand and foot,
the stone knife will pierce his breast, and from the open wound we will
tear out his heart and offer it to the sun. This is, among us, the most
honorable, the most desirable destiny our land may offer, for the chosen youth will have greater pleasure than any man, first in life and then
in death. And the people will learn that those who have riches and
pleasure in life must come to the end of their lives in poverty and in
pain."

The Lady was silent for a moment, staring at me, her eyes brilliant,
her tattooed lips forming a smiling grimace. Finally she said: "We
have chosen you, stranger, as the image of the Smoking Mirror. Yours
will be the destiny I have just related."

I closed my eyes, Sire, in a vain attempt to exorcise these words,
and in the green star of my mind gratitude for the postponement shone
more strongly than the certainty of my announced death. I would not
die today. But within a year I would return, to die in this very place.
Between the fact of my survival and the fact of my coming death,
which between them were the total destiny the cruel Lady my lover had
proclaimed, was insinuated the unique fact of my other destiny the
same Lady had told me one night in the jungle.

"My Lady," I replied, "I remind you that one night you promised me a different destiny: that I might have five days rescued from death."

"You have saved them."

"You promised that we would meet again at the foot of the volcano."

"We have met."

"You promised that when I found you again, you would multiply my pleasure of that night."

"I have fulfilled my promise. I offer you a pleasure greater than any other: the certainty of one happy year and a precise death. For unhappy are the lives of men who among so many years of misfortune manage to salvage, here and there, only brief hours of happiness; and it is fearful to live without knowing either when or how death will come, for although death is certain, it does not announce its arrival, and thus plunges man into anguish and fear."

"You promised me that on the last day saved from my destiny, I would not have to ask because I would know."

"This is the last day, and now you know: a year of happiness and death at an appointed time await you."

"But, my Lady, since last I saw you I have lived only two of those days . . ."

The woman, Sire, gazed at me with frightening intensity, and for the first time on that day she arose, trembling, burying her long fingernails in the ocelot skin covering her throne, for the first time incredulous, for the first time conquered, Sire, impotent, for the first time doubting herself and her powers. And in that instant the marks of time became more prominent upon her face, as if the years had fallen upon her from above like the pestilent vultures of this land that like my Lady fed upon the world's offal.

I feared she would fall, so unsure was her posture and so violent the trembling of her body. Half risen, clutching the chair of stone, her voice weak and faded, at last she was able to say, the words foaming from her mouth: "Only two days . . . ?"

"Yes," I replied, "I have lived two days and two nights apart from you . . ."

"Two days and two nights . . ."

"Yes . . ."

"That is all you remember?"

"Yes . . ."

With fire in her throat she howled, "That is all you remember, poor miserable fool, nothing more?"

"Nothing, my Lady, nothing . . ."

"Of all the obstacles I placed in your path, of all the tests to which I subjected you, only four times, twice at night and twice by day, they forced you to ask your question and save your day: your life was worth only two complete days?"

"Yes, yes, yes . . ."

If earlier she had looked at me with disdain and compassion, now only pity illuminated her maddened eyes. "Poor fool, poor fool . . . It would have been better had you spent your five days and come here, today, to me, and here with me fulfilled your destiny in our land . . ."

"The destiny you have offered me is death."

"Yes, following a year of happiness. Do you prefer death within two days, with no happiness at all?"

As my only answer, I said: "Yes. I still have this night and two more complete days."

"What will you do with them, poor wretch?"

"I choose to end this day, and tonight to receive the answer to my next question."

"Where will you go?" asked the Lady, newly impassive.

I looked about me. If I descended the steps of the temple toward the great esplanade of the valley, I would meet only the destiny she had promised; I would immediately be amid the people of this high plain who would worship me and honor me, who would give me food and drink, and who would deliver unto me their most beautiful maiden, exactly as the Lady had proclaimed, and after one year I would die on the pyramid. If I took that route, therefore, I would lose the challenges and the answers of my other destiny. If, on the other hand, I descended the steps on the side facing the volcano, if I climbed the volcano itself, if I descended into its ashy crater, the dangers that awaited me there would offer me the security of chance, and in that instant, Sire, for me chance meant liberty and well-being and life, for I already knew that the other road was fatal, I knew its outcome, and knowing the exact date of my death was not, as the Lady had said, a relief, but an unbearable burden that enslaved my soul. If, in spite of everything, I returned to this temple at the end of a year, it would not be, I told myself, without having first exposed myself to all the risks of the two remaining days of my destiny.

"To the volcano, my Lady . . ."

First the high priests chirped with fear, and the warriors brandished their shields, shouting hoarsely, the bat fluttered its wings, the dancers scattered their incense, and with a gaze as icy as the volcano, the Lady answered: "Fool. That is the road to hell. In one day there you may lose what I have assured you for an entire year: your life. If you go to the volcano, you will only hasten your destiny: your death."

"I shall find my own death, my Lady."

"Fool. There is no solitary destiny. Your death will be a common destiny, and you will return to us by way of death."

I looked at her sadly, knowing that I would never see her again, that this time the spider's thread would not lead me to her; now I would travel alone in search of my well-being, not, as before, in search of the redoubled pleasures this woman had promised me one night. How was I to know then that the promised pleasure would be to live one year as a prince in order to die as a slave and thus honor the god of the shadow. I looked sadly at the woman who in offering me this fate believed she offered a reward greater than a new coming together of our bodies.

"Farewell, my Lady."

Wearing the splendid clothing in which they had dressed me here, but with my torn sailor's clothes clinging to my shivering skin, I turned my back upon this company. I descended the steps slowly, looking toward my new goal, the volcano that in the late afternoon light seemed more distant, and as the light diminished, it turned the color of the air, as if it already rejected me, as if it were warning me: "You see, I am moving away from you, cloaked in the transparent air of dusk. You must do the same. Choose another route. Turn yourself into air, so that I not turn you into ice."

Halfway along the road, and before the fire of sunset hid it from my sight, I stopped and turned to look for the last time toward the pyramid. A crown of red sunlight was settling upon the bloody, smoking summit. The temple was a dark beast crouching under the setting sun. Its jaws of carved stone were devouring the blood and dust of the plain.

I turned my back upon the pyramid and walked toward the volcano.

NIGHT OF THE VOLCANO

Long was my road through the plain covered with huge thorny plants, and I gave thanks for the soft boots that protected my feet from constant contact with these needles of the desert. I asked myself, looking at the desolation about me on the route toward the volcano, whether the only nourishment of the people of the arid high plain was the fruit from the jungle and the coast, and whether the reason why the inhabitants of the low areas were subjected and sacrificed was simply the hungers and needs of the inhabitants of the high plains. Something I could not precisely identify told me this was not the case, that there was something more, and that I must reach the site where the Great Lord of this world lived, he who was repeatedly called the Lord of the Great Voice, in order to know the truth about the order my strange presence violated at every step, the order confounded by the novelty of my presence.

As I walked toward the volcano and as night was rapidly descending upon me and the world about me, I kept repeating one certainty, one of the few that consoled me in the midst of so many questions:

"I am an intruder here. I am an intruder in a world unaccustomed to intrusion. A world separate from the world: how long have these people I have known on the coast and high plain lived in solitude, without contact with other peoples? Why not since the beginning of time? A world kept separate by fear; but secure in its reason for being to be able to survive surrounded as it is by portents of disaster. What a fragile balance: death in exchange for possessions, life in exchange for a pair of scissors, the scissors in exchange for gold, gold in exchange for bread, bread in exchange for life, life in exchange for the disappearance of the sun . . . Truly precarious, for all it takes to upset that balance is the intrusion of an unexpected being, an individual as unimportant as I."

For now I tell you, Sire, that the men of the new world only foresee and accept catastrophic change, which in truth is not change but an end to what presently exists, and the catastrophe can be only the work of gods or of nature, but never that of a simple man. That is why, I told myself that night, in order to understand me they must see me as a god or as an element of nature.

I sought, in that dusk, my guide: Venus, the light twin to shadow and the shadow twin to light. Venus, its own twin. I had sailed for the new world, on old Pedro's ship, guided by the morning star. I feared, Sire, that having embarked at the dawn, I would find in the dawn the final port of my destiny in these lands, thus closing a perfect, implacable circle: son of light, having arrived at the hour of light, condemned to light. But I had already seen that my other destiny, my other possibility, was no less fatal: having arrived by night, I was identified with shadow. If I had learned anything in this land, it was that nothing was more feared than the death of the sun. Nothing more feared, then, than the executioner of the sun: son of shadow, having arrived at the hour of shadow, condemned to shadow. I felt myself a prisoner of the perfect circles of a double destiny: day and night, light and shadow. But my soul sought indecision, chance, an opening toward the continuity of life that for me is linear. And who in this world, having achieved the final perfection of closing a circle, would grant me the grace of one night more of life? Having set sail at dawn, having arrived by day, and thus having appeared as the creator of the sun; or having left at dusk, having arrived by night, and so appearing to be the executioner of the sun? Fatal world, new world, where my incomprehensible man-presence was understood only in the light of superhuman forces: the terror of the night would be crushed forever between the two perfect halves of the light; the blessing of the day would be crushed forever between the two perfect halves of the shadow. There was no other final escape for this new world, Sire, and its inhabitants were prepared to honor equally light, if it triumphed, or the shadows, if they conquered. Who would grant me the grace of one hour more of life, the rupture of the miracle, the repetition of uncertainty? Thus I was prisoner of an anguishing contradiction, the most terrible of all: I owed my life to death; I would owe my death to life. The miraculous is exceptional. It must be preserved. Only the perfection of a unique instant may preserve it. That perfection is death.

Pondering these mysteries, I reached the foot of the volcano with the first shadows, and my feet touched cold rock and icy ashes, and in the distance I could see lighted fires on the mountainsides, as if compensating for the coldness of what once had been a boiling basin.

Here and there, I could see where small bonfires were being lighted, and beside them, here and there, a few old men whose fox-like profiles could be distinguished in the dim glow; they were cutting pieces of paper, trimming them and binding them together, and one ancient would take a motionless body, bind its legs, and dress and bind it with the paper, and further along, another old man would pour water over the head of another motionless body, and all about me I could see this ceremony being repeated, those lifeless bodies being shrouded in cloth and paper, and tightly bound, and I noted that around each bonfire were scattered yellow flowers with long green stalks, and youths carrying doors on their backs were approaching some deep holes dug in the ashes; they placed the doors over the holes, and then groups of women wept and strewed dried yellow flowers over those doors, and amid the women's weeping could be heard plaintive voices saying: "Know the door of your house, and use that door to come out and visit us, for we have wept long for you. Come out a little while, come out a little while."

And as I climbed the mountainside, more fires were lighted, and I was aware of moaning voices and increased activity. I accepted what my eyes told me; every bonfire marked the site of a dead person, an ancient tomb revisited or a recently dug sepulcher, and the groups gathered about each body, buried or still unburied, were engaged in various scrupulously observed rites: for one they placed in the winding sheets a little jug filled with water; between the waxen hands of another they secured a strand of limp cotton thread tied to the neck of a small, nervous, reddish-colored dog with bright eyes and a sharp snout; further along, they were burning piles of clothing; beyond that, jewels were being thrown into a fire, and old men were singing softly, sadly: Oh, son, you have known and suffered the travail of this life; and in taking you away our lord has been served, for life in this world knows no permanence and our life is brief, like a man who warms himself in the sun; and the women echoed in chorus, moaning: you went to that darkest of all places where there is neither light nor windows, and you will never again have to return here or leave there; do not be troubled by the childlessness and poverty in which you leave us; be strong, son, do not be bowed down by sadness; we have come here to visit you and to console you with these few words; and the ancients again began to sing, we are now the fathers, the ancients, for our lord has taken away those who were older and more ancient, those who knew better how to speak consoling words for those who mourn . . .

And above these words spoken all about me as I climbed towards the white cone of the volcano, among the mourners indifferent to my task, ululated one high, shrill lament, a flame of words that lay like a protective mantle over the funereal ceremony of that night: "It is not true that we lived, it is not true that we came to endure upon this earth."

I was thankful, Sire, for the darkness, and for their indifference: here the living had voice and eyes only for death, and my painful journey toward the peak in no way disturbed their suffering; they gave no thought to the passing of my shadow amid their sorrow.

I left lamentation and fires behind me; one by one the fires were dying out, abandoning me to a night of mysterious shadow, for although the eternal snows of the volcano must be nearby, a warm lethargy was nevertheless rising from the depths of the ash in whose sandy blackness I was struggling, laboriously lifting one foot after the other, sinking up to my ankles in the extinct fire. How distant, Sire, seemed then the wild volcanos of the islands and bays of Mare Nostrum that in its waters find a mirror to their tremors and a solace for their ruins, while here, in the land of the navel of the moon, the volcanos were extinct, and their mirror was a desolation reflecting that of the moon itself: black desert on land, white dust in the heavens.

I looked up, seeking the moon, desiring its company as I penetrated into the darkness of this night; but there was nothing shining in the sky; a tapestry of black clouds obscured my guide, the evening star; I feared to lose my way, although I was guided by the rising ground. And then, Sire, as if my thoughts possessed powers of convocation, before me, from behind a rock, appeared a man with a great light upon his back.

I stopped, doubting my senses, for that luminous man appeared and disappeared among the volcanic rocks, sowing light and shadow in his passing; and when finally he came toward me, I saw that he was an old man with a great conch shell upon his back, and the light was coming from the shell, illuminating his old man's face, lean and white, so old he seemed to be a skull shining in the night; and behind him I heard shouting and running, and young warriors darted by, hunting an invisible animal in the night, and shooting lighted arrows; and these arrows found their mark in the darkness, and the darkness wounded by the arrows had a form and was bleeding, although its form was but that of the shadows. Sire: I recognized the terrible animal I had seen in the ancient mother's hut, the same shadowy shape, wounded, howling, digging with its back-turned paws in the volcanic ash; the animal would dig, and the old man with the conch shell on his back would laugh, and as the animal tried to bury the light cast by the old man's shell, the old man would run and hide himself again among the rocks, and the animal would howl, enraged, searching for the rays of elusive light, wounded by the fiery arrows of the nocturnal hunters, and then the air was filled with invisible darts descending from the sky, wailing sadly and cursing, and as I looked toward that hail of darts I saw they possessed faces like skulls, not that they were truly skulls, but the mark of sadness and malediction upon their features gave them the appearance of death's-heads, and I knew that these were the skulls of women; damned, sad voices; and the fearsome aggregate of the old man with the shell on his back, and the warriors hunting by night the animal of the shadows, and the skull of the weeping, cursing women was the proclamation of all the actions that seemed to happen simultaneously on this black side of the volcano.

The earth trembled and opened its yawning jaws, and my only sensation was one of falling through a cave of ashes. Perhaps, unaware, I had reached the highest ledge of the volcano, the mouth of the crater, and through it was slipping down into its extinguished entrails; in the distance I heard sounds, the old man's laughter, the barking of the hunted animal, the wailing of those flying women; my mouth was filled with ashes, I tried to stop my fall but my hands grasped ashes, and as upon a different night I had been a prisoner of the ocean whirlpool, now I felt myself a captive of this black-earth vortex; and captured, I was not alone, for in my vertiginous descent into the center of the volcano there passed before my eyes dark forms that seemed to beckon me and lead me toward the most unknown of all lands: I saw a man robed in, and toying with, jewels, a man whose shouts and roars filled me with terror, for that noise was like a howl issuing from the very heart of the mountain; he beckoned to me and still falling I reached out toward him in the blackness, but at the moment I almost touched him he disappeared, and behind him, farther in the distance, appeared a different man holding a banner in one hand and upon his shoulder he carried a staff on which were impaled two hearts, and upon this man's head was a darkness so black it was as if for one precise instant everything else—I, he himself, the sea of ash in which we were drowning—was bathed in light, and all the darkness of the world was gathered in that crown he wore; he, too, beckoned to me, but he immediately faded from view and in his stead I saw a fierce spotted ocelot in the distance devouring the stars born of this deep fertile sky: an upside-down sky, I told myself, the fearful twin, in the entrails of the earth, of the sky we know and worship in the heavens; and through this standing-on-its-head sky, choked in the deepest ashes of the world, again flew those moaning, saddened, cursing skulls, now carrying in their mouths arms and legs torn from the dead; they dropped them, and cried out:

"Where are the doors? I wave these bones before a door, and with their magic, all in the house lie sleeping so the profaner may enter. Is there a door in hell? Only an entrance. Never an exit. Once I was human. I died in childbirth. Where is the door? The profaner stole my hands and my legs. I weep, seated upon rocks by the side of the road. Do not fear me, voyager. The profaner stole my limbs. With them he harmed my children, all children, and he spread plague and pestilence. Do not believe them if they tell you that those are my arms and legs."

And the legs and hands struck me in the face and then plummeted into the great empty space surrounding me, and the invisible women fled through the air, moaning sadly. My head struck against rock, and I lost consciousness.

A damp tongue licking my face awakened me. I was staring into the bright black eyes of a small red dog, like those I had seen on the slopes of the volcano, and by my side flowed a river of icy waters with great pieces of ice piled along its shores, and the dome above my head was of pure ice, with cold tears hanging from it, and beyond the river only white, empty space.

The dog led me to the shore and entered the waters, and as I clung to his back he swam across the icy torrent, leading me as the spider's thread had led me before. But to whom did I owe the animal's assistance? The Lady of the Butterflies had abandoned me, and all that remained of her was the recollection of one night, the sadness of an unfulfilled promise, the warning of the number and order of my days in this unknown land, and an endless mystery: How much time had passed between each of the days I had recalled? How many days had I lived in forgetfulness? What had happened during the time I could not remember? And why, between the memory of the temple of the jungle and the encounter upon the pyramid on the high plain, had time left the traces not of days but of years upon my lover's face? From among these questions, I said, I must choose the one I will ask this night. Ask whom? A voiceless dog, perhaps, or women dead in childbirth, flying like arrows, nothing but face and tears, along the road to the underworld.

And thus, clinging to the swimming dog, I reached the other shore. There the whiteness was accentuated as if formerly white had not been white but simply ice and frozen caverns and the gelid river of this world beneath the volcano; this was whiteness itself: the pure color of the dawn, foreign to anything ever called white; the white of whiteness, a stranger to any other quality. And in this total whiteness, Sire, I could distinguish nothing, so that the pure brilliance was like impenetrable darkness, I felt I was drowning in milk, in snow, in gypsum.

An unbearable wind blew toward me, whipped my soaked clothes, doubling the tall plumes of my crest, lacerating my painted skin like knives, forcing me to creep forward, blinded by pure, unrelieved light. A wind like daggers. Finally its rending force revealed before my eyes two motionless figures hand in hand, pure form, erect, pure whiteness, but still the form of a man and a woman, one figure shorter than the other, one standing with icy legs planted arrogantly apart, the other with its limbs hidden beneath a skirt of snow: a shimmering white pair so identical to the white spaces surrounding them it was impossible to know whether the air, the space, the colorless color of this land were born from the double silhouette, battered by the wind and solidified by the ice, or whether they were the result of the land surrounding them. At the feet of the motionless pair I could discern the whiteness of a heap of bones.

The dog barked, his hackles rising, and turning, he raced back to the river and plunged into its white waters, swimming until he gained the other shore. I stood defenseless before the white pair, and I heard the cavernous laughter of the man as motionless as an ice statue, as resonating as the harsh wind of these deep caverns, and he said: ''You have returned.''

I bit my tongue, Sire, to keep from asking a fruitless question and receiving a fruitless reply; I did not ask, Why have you awaited me? I did not ask anything, and there was no calculation in my silence, rather a sudden exhaustion, as if my soul could accommodate no further astonishment, terror, or doubt before the successive marvels of the new world, but only a passive, warm resignation, like sleep at the end of a fatiguing day. The wind had died down around the icy figure of the man speaking to me. But instead, it whirled violently, to the point of making her almost visible, about the figure of the woman standing beside the man, her hand in his. That motionless frigidity struggled against the whirling wind, until the woman spoke in tones of indomitable hatred:

''You came once before. You stole our red grains and gave them as a gift to men, and because of them men could sow, and harvest, and eat. You delayed the triumph of our kingdom. Without the red bread grains, all men would today be our subjects; the earth would be one vast lifeless whiteness and we, my husband and I, would have emerged from these deep regions to reign over the entire world. What are you seeking now? Why have you returned? This time you will not deceive us. We are warned against your tricks. Furthermore, there is nothing now to steal from us: look at this sterile land; would you steal the wind of death, the bones of death, our frozen whiteness? Do so. You will only give the gift of more death to men, and thus hasten our triumph.''

''No,'' I murmured, grateful for the words of this White Lady, for her breath formed a vapor, warm in spite of its smoking whiteness, around her figure, animating mine. "No, I come only with a question, and I seek an answer of you."

"Speak," said the White Lord of these regions of death.

"Majesties, you see in my attire the signs of an identity that has been imposed upon me, and that I, here before you, confess I fear, for I know that it condemns me to death, blood, sacrifice, shadow, and horror . . ."

"You are dressed in the raiment of Smoking Mirror, who represents all you have said," said the White Lord.

"Nevertheless, you yourselves have spoken of my other identity, that of the giver of life, educator, man of peace. I know it now: I stole the red grain so that men could live. Who am I, Majesties? That is the question to which I am entitled this night."

The White Lady, through the icy drops on her lips and the heavy vapor of her hatred, answered, before the man could speak:

"It does not matter who you have been, but who you will be. You have come here, not understanding the warnings that accompanied you in your descent to our kingdom. You have looked upon the skull faces of the women dead in childbirth, profaners of tombs, who course through the air, moaning sadly, cursing, spreading terrible illness, and harming the children who caused their deaths. You have seen the spotted ocelot of the high rocks devouring the stars and awaiting the rising of the sun. You have seen the old man with the conch shell upon his back, which is the whiteness that shines by night, our light, the light of the darkness. You have heard the moan of the heart of the mountains that is the voice of the sun beneath the earth, condemned to disappear every night and not to know whether he will appear the next morning, and you have seen his rival, the lord who carries darkness upon his head and displays two hearts upon his battle standard—the hearts that were mine and my husband's before we died, before the creation of the world, when there was no need for death. See us now, vanquished each time the sun leaves our caverns; little victorious, however, for scarcely does it reach its zenith in the sky when it begins to decline; it never reaches the status of perfection, eternity in the midday sky, to which it aspires each time it is born—only to lose, and sink inevitably into our kingdoms. You have seen the struggle between the life of men, partial, imperfect, condemned to be born only to die, and the life of the dead, condemned to die only to be reborn. We were at the point of triumph. Every day there were more dead and fewer living: hunger, earthquake, illness, storm, and flood were our allies. Then you arrived, stole the red grains of bread and permitted life to be prolonged. For how long, Thief? Ask yourself that, yes, how long, if men themselves, to the end of maintaining life, assist us in our deadly reconquest through war, the excess of their appetites, and the terror of sacrifice. Do battle, love, and kill to live, O Thief of life, and feel the icy wind

pulsating behind your every action, warning you that even as you believe you are affirming life you are promoting the Kingdom of Death.
My husband and I are patient. Finally all will end in ice. All will come
to us. The sun rises, then hides itself, then rises again: half of life is
already death. We shall gain the other half, because the totality of our
death is life. We are slow; we are patient; our weapon is attrition. And
one day, the sun will rise no more. Then we shall rise to reign over a
land identical to ours.''

I feared, Sire, that the icy cataract of words from this Queen of Hell
would turn me into ice, and my words into coins of snow. I spoke rapidly, savoring the warmth from my mouth, tossing my words like coals
at the feet of the motionless pair: ''Who am I? I have the right to one
answer this night . . .''

I would have wished to see the eyes of the King of Death when after
a perverse silence, as if the two expected that the pause would suffice
to convert me to their condition, he at last spoke: ''You are one in your
memory. You are another in the time you cannot remember.''

And the White Lady added: ''The Plumed Serpent in what you remember. The Smoking Mirror in what you forget.''

As I listened, I hid my face in my hands, and as if she herself had
appeared in this deep region I again heard clearly the words of the
Lady of the Butterflies, spoken on that warm night in the jungle, only
three nights before the night I was now living in the nation of the dead:

''You will travel twenty-five days and twenty-five nights before we
are together again. Twenty are the days of your destiny in this land.
Five are the sterile days you will save against death, though they will
be similar to death. Count them well. You will not have another opportunity in our land. Count well. Only during the five masked days will
you be able to ask one question of the light and one question of the
darkness. During the twenty days of your destiny, it will not profit you
to ask, for you will never remember what happens on those days—forgetfulness is your destiny. And during the last day you pass in our
land, you will have no need to ask. You will know.''

I closed my eyes and quickly I measured that promised time: I had
lived twenty days without memory, and I remembered only three, for
in order to save myself I had felt the need to save only three; and thus I
had abused the Lady of the Butterflies, for I had succeeded in meeting
her again at the pyramid with two full days left to me, two days in
which I had the power to ask, to approach final wisdom, and to remember what might be remembered from the forgetfulness that seemed to
be my burden, here in this land, Sire, and there in the lands I left behind.

I opened my eyes and saw superimposed upon the featureless, icy
mask of the Lady of Death the semblance of my beloved wife of the
jungle and the cruel tyrant of the temple; and when I saw those faces

imposed upon nothingness, but simultaneously alive in their expressions of love and hatred, wedded by passion, I swore they were both speaking to me; one, the voice of warm love in the jungle; the other, the voice of the smoking sacrifice on the pyramid; and the voice of the pyramid was telling me not to be deceived further by the terrible tyrant: false was her first promise to me, the woman of the pyramid was saying, as her more recent promise was false: it is not true, you would not have lived like a prince for a year, drinking in the pleasures of the land, then to die in sacrifice; no, my years are like your minutes, stranger, and your year would have ended there, immediately, as the culmination to the bloody day of sacrifice; fear my words; I would have made you believe that the following night had lasted a year, and the next day I would have said: "I have fulfilled my promise. You have lived your year of happiness. Now you must die. This is your last day. As I told you, today you need not ask: you know."

But while the goddess of the pyramid was speaking, the voice of the woman of the jungle, my lover, also spoke from the depths of the mask superimposed upon the featureless face of the Queen of Death, and that voice was saying, fool, dearest fool, everything I told you on the pyramid was true, the year I offered you would truly have been a complete year, our year, and the woman offered you in marriage would have been I, oh, poor fool, I myself, again your lover for more than three hundred days; that was my true promise, and you refused to take advantage of it; an entire year with me, and then death . . ."

Oh, Sire, these delirious debates coursed through my mind as wildly as the skull women flew through the air, and as I listened to the two voices I could only remember the Cruel Lady's confusion when I told her that two days and two nights remained to me; her amazement, her anger, her confusion, revealed that she herself had been deceived; that a power greater than hers had allowed me to live twenty complete days without memory, but only three in memory. Two days and two nights, wrested from my destiny, remained; these days I would remember; on these days I would live guided by my own will, and on the last day I would know. But what I knew I would not know through the intercession of the Lady of the Butterflies, but because of another power superior to hers. And now I would never know what I would have known had I heard in time the voice of my lover: a year by her side, one whole year with her, one year of love, and then one day of death. I was already in the Kingdom of Death: perhaps with only two days remaining of my own will, and they would be days without love, and then, more swiftly this time, this time not to be denied, the same death my beautiful Lady had had the grace to postpone for a year.

Knowing this, Sire, was to return to my primary condition as orphan: before I had known the friendship of old Pedro, before I had embarked with him that long-ago evening; then I lost him on the beach of the new world, then I lost the people beside the river who had sheltered me, and finally, just today, I lost my lover and her promise; an orphan who had lost all affectionate companionship, all support from the warm closeness of others, father, people, friend, mother, and lover: I was an orphan in the icy, white, cold furrows of death, an orphan reliant upon the aid of an unknown power, the power that had violated the design of mortal love of the princess of the tattooed lips. I asked myself whether this power was not greater than that of these sovereigns of death, and whether I would pass the last two days of my life in their frozen kingdom, then sink forever into a whiteness without memory or time or life. I looked at the Lords of Hell, I thought of myself. And I wept.

But this I must tell you, Sire; as I wept, my tears ran down my cheeks, and from my bowed head they fell upon the heaps of white bones lying at the feet of the monarchs of this icy hell. And as my tears fell upon the bones, they turned into fire, and a wall of flame rose between the Ice Lords and me, and as their snowy raiment burst into flame they moaned and cried out and shrank back as before a living plague or a murdered beast, while the fire curled and licked and spread like red branches through the white cloister until the entire cavern flamed like the corposant of the fatidic ships that sail the seas without crew or rudder.

I obeyed my one certain impulse; I picked up those burning bones and clasped them to my breast; in an instant the clothing in which the bloody sorcerers had dressed me upon the pyramid, crests and mantle, breechclout and sandals, bags and jewels, was reduced to ashes; but see as I saw, oh, Sire, how the fire stopped as it approached my sailor's clothing, my own clothes, those in which I had set sail from your shores, Sire, in search of these adventures, embarked, yes, because of old Pedro's faith in the existence of a world beyond the ocean, but also because of my own triple faith in risk, survival, and the passion of man that now, though not before, linked resignation to the hazards of danger and life upon the earth; see, the flames, as if from a sacred covering, fall back as they touch my worn doublet and torn breeches.

I ran far from the flaming chamber of ice, but the entire cavern was a conflagration of red tongues and yellow lances, and the very river of Hell was a current of fire, and I ran upon it, for as long as I clutched to my chest the bones stolen from the Lords of Death, the fire did not touch me, it was solid ground, even where it flowed like water, and the bones were writhing in my embrace, and were bathed in blood, and were forming into new constellations of shapes, and finally the bones spoke, and I looked at them, incredulous: in my arms I was carrying bones that were no longer bones but covered with flesh that now had human shape and form; and they leaped from my grasp, stood, and ran ahead and behind and beside me; they led me with their hands, and guided me with their voices, they thanked me, and called me giver of life, we thank you, they told me, we thank you, do not look back, seek the Serpent of Clouds in the heavens, look upward, look toward the mouth of the volcano, do not look back, the fire has revealed the eyes of death, save yourself, save us . . .

I felt that powerful arms held me and soft hands caressed me and I knew that my swiftness was not my own but that of the fleeing heap of bones-become-humans who were supporting me and carrying me far away, up toward a sky that was closer every moment. I looked for the constellation that ruled the firmament: the Milky Way of lost sailors that here they call the Serpent of Clouds: the beloved constellation of well-being, the pilgrim's faithful compass, an epistle written upon the night . . . And dizzily searching for the Serpent of Clouds, I thus escaped the fierce eyes of the howling ocelot, the sunken, hollow eyes of the women dead in childbirth, the banners of darkness, and the conch shell of the false light of those regions: their laments and curses whistled past my ears; my eyes were fixed on the nocturnal sky, exhausted, soon to perish, soon to cede its brilliant reign to the solitary star of morning: Venus.

And I saw Venus as I collapsed into the high snow on the volcano through whose crater we had escaped. I sat there, my head buried between my knees and my arms about my legs, not daring to look at the companions of my dream, for surely I had not entered the icy domain of death at all, but lost on the high mountain paths and overwhelmed with fatigue I had reached the summit and had passed the night here, dreaming. I looked at Venus and closed my eyes. A thousand needles prickled behind my hooded eyes. I opened them.

Sire: I was in the midst of a group of twenty young people, ten boys and ten girls, totally naked and indifferent to the cold on the peak and the intemperate dawn: masters of their own bodies, and of their bodies' warmth. They looked at me as they caressed and kissed one another and worshipped their own nakedness, and each woman felt her pleasure in each man, and in each woman each man saw his own perfection. Young, in their prime, strong, and beautiful, these boys and girls lay in pairs around me, and smiled at me; they were as if newly born, breathing with the security that nothing could harm them. Their smiles were my reward: I understood. Their beautiful cinnamon-colored bodies, smooth, full, slim, narrow-waisted, were enough to express the gratitude that shone from them.

Smiling, they whispered among themselves: I could hear their birdlike sounds, and laughter.

One youth spoke: "Young Lord, you have been awaited. With fear by some. With hope by many more, but by no one as eagerly as by us.

It was spoken. You were to come to rescue our bones and return us to life. We thank you."

A long while I observed them in silence, not daring to speak, and even less to propose a question to which, I knew, I now had no right until the following morning.

Finally I said to them: "I do not know whether my journey ends here, or whether I must travel farther."

"Now you will travel with us," said one young girl.

"We will lead you where you must go," said a young man.

"From now on, we will be your guides," said a third.

And then they all stood and offered me their hands: I arose and followed them down the slopes, still dizzy from my experiences of this night, drunk with conflicting sensations. And suddenly, Sire, I stopped, immobilized by a marvel greater than any I had known till now, first astounded and then amused as I realized how slow I had been in reacting to this, the supreme marvel. I burst out laughing, laughing at myself really, as I realized what I had just realized: Sire, in a tone much sweeter than ours, never losing the singing-bird tones, these boys and girls born of the bones wrested from the Lords of Death, the cinnamon color of all the inhabitants of this land, from their very first words—I realized it only now—were speaking in our own tongue, the tongue, Sire, of our Spanish lands.

DAY OF THE LAGOON

Long was our road, as long as the dawn of this my fourth day, guided now not by the spider's thread of the Lady who had abandoned me, but by my new companions, the twenty naked, cinnamon-colored young people who spoke our tongue. I did not dare, Sire, ask them the explanation of this new mystery; the hours of my time in the new world were growing short, and I preferred to ponder for myself the riddles of my pilgrimage, perhaps to resolve them in my spirit, or wait until events revealed their meaning to me rather than waste one of the few questions—only four now—to which I was entitled.

My companions did not speak, and in the early light of dawn our silent ascent was interrupted only by the sound of our feet, league after league, upon the stony earth defended by formations of strange plants grouped like the phalanxes of a vegetal army, the only growth capable of surviving on this high, arid plain, armored plants with leaves like broad sword blades beginning at the level of the ground and spreading upward like a mournful cluster of daggers searching for the light of the sun: intensely green leaves ending in sharp points from which peered the face of their own death; the points of those green daggers of the high plain were dried at the tips into yellowed, frayed, fibrous harbingers of the plant's extinction.

As the sun grew stronger, my companions ripped from the earth rocks as sharp as the points of those desert lances and slashed the base of the plants: from the wounds flowed a thick liquid that each caught in his cupped hands; they told me to do the same; we drank. Then they plucked from the leaves of some tall, thorny shrubs a green fruit covered with fine prickly hair, peeled and ate them, and I plucked one of the same fruits. Thus we assuaged our thirst and hunger; and when we were satisfied, it was as if the senses dulled by the intensity of the night in the volcano had suddenly been awakened from sleep, as if our eyes were seeing anew. I wiped from my lips and chin the juices of that savory fruit my companions called "prickly pear," and from the heights where we had climbed, I saw the marvel this morning held in store for me.

I saw a valley, Sire, sunken in the midst of a vast circle of bare mountains, massive stone, and quiet, extinct volcanoes. And in the center of that valley shone a silver lake. And in the center of the lake, more brilliant than the lake itself, shone a white city of tall towers and golden mists traversed by wide canals, a city of small islands, with buildings of stone and wood along the water's edge.

I gazed in wonderment; I asked myself whether what I saw was not a dream; and as the morning mists lifted, from behind their veils appeared two snow-crowned volcanoes standing like guardians over this city. One resembled a gigantic sleeping man lying with his white head resting upon knees of black stone, and the other took the form of a reclining, sleeping woman covered by a white shroud, and in her my hallucinated eyes saw my lost lover, the princess of the butterflies, turned into icy stone.

We began our descent into the valley toward the city, and I told myself that what I was seeing was but illusion, the well-known mirage of the deserts, and my ears buzzed as if to warn me of the unreality of this new adventure, as unreal, surely, as the preceding night in the white hell in the entrails of the volcano. I did not need to ask, I knew; it was a dream. But were my naked companions also a dream, the masters of my tongue who in my infernal nightmare had been snatched from the feet of the Lords of Death and returned to life as I held them to my burning breast?

These were questions intended only for myself; let them be settled by what was to come; let my few remaining hours answer, they had no need of my questions.

Such was my silent supplication on that dawn, soon interrupted by a sequence of portents that appeared before our eyes in increasingly swift succession, as if announcing our descent from the high desert into this valley enclosed among fortresses of tall, denuded, stony, snowy mountains that stood like a mute chorus to the city lying at our feet: a tapestry of brilliant jewels.

For first there arose in the midst of the sky something I can only describe as a great thorn of fire, a blaze of fire, a second dawn, that dripped and bled as if it had pricked the dome of the sky; this fiery light was broad at its base, narrow at its apex: a pyramid of pure light; in the very center of the sky, it reached to the highest arch of the sky, shooting sparks that scintillated in such profusion it seemed to be raining stars; piercing the sky, this column had its beginnings in the earth, then grew slimmer and slimmer until it reached the sky, a pyramid whose brilliance outshone the sun.

I stopped in fear, Sire, but my young companions gently urged me forward, taking my arms, and in their eyes there was no astonishment, as if they knew, or had experienced, the vision before. And then, although there was no breeze, the lake in whose bosom this magnificent, brilliant city lay was altered; its waters boiled and foamed and rose to great heights, and the waves broke into whirling waterspouts; great was their force and height; and my astonished eyes beheld how those gigantic waves burst against the foundations of the houses by the lake shore, and many of them crumbled and sank, totally inundated.

Then even my companions paused, awaiting the end of this terrible upheaval, and I longed to know the reactions of the inhabitants of the city I had never entered but which from a distance I could see assaulted by such foreboding forces; were they weeping, were they crying out, did they feel fear, or anger? And, finally, what awaited us? For we were advancing toward that city in the midst of portents that by the very fact of their concurrence with our arrival would surely be attributed to us.

A chill ran down my back, and my companions realized it; again they gently urged me forward, as I witnessed a new calamity: a great fire fell from the sun, scattering embers and raining sparks upon the city; this comet extended across the sky, and from it were born three other comets, and all of them raced with violent force toward the east, scattering sparks behind them, until their long tails disappeared into the sky where the sun is born.

And when I turned my eyes from the heavens and looked at the ground, I saw that we were walking along an earth causeway that stretched between the land and the city; the waters had calmed and turned opaquely green, and in some places their turbulence had stirred clouds of mud, and the reeds along the shore were trembling still.

Of the first houses I saw on our approach to the city, many had been battered by the great waves, and others were burning, and lightning was flashing without the warning of thunder, setting the straw roofs on fire, and when finally my companions and I entered the city no one paid us any heed, for these shore dwellers were in a great state of agitation and confusion; people covered their mouths with their hands; some carried jugs of water to put out the fires, but the water only added to the fire, causing the flames to blaze all the higher. But then a warm, fine drizzle began to fall that gradually extinguished the fires, and a warm mist rose, mixed with the smoke from the fires and the dust of the battered houses, and my fearful eyes were incapable of fixing on details; I wanted to absorb everything, to understand everything, but I was blinded by the plethora of sensations: I allowed myself to be guided by my companions, and all I knew was that as we entered the enormous city in the middle of the lake, we became lost in the labyrinths of a market as vast as the city itself, for no matter where my bewildered feet led and no matter how far my confused eyes could see, we were completely surrounded by merchants, and a great chatter and confusion I heard among those selling gold and silver and precious stones and feathers and mantles and embroidered cloths, and those who in this enormous fair were displaying the skins of ocelots and mountain lions and nutrias, and of jackals and deer, and of other predatory animals, badgers and lynx, were importuning Heaven, and the male and female slaves brought there for sale, chained to tall stakes by collars about their necks, were staring at the ground, indifferent to any portents, and merchants were snuffing out with their hands the coals that had fallen upon the fragrant liquidambar tubes like those the old woman had offered me in the white hut at the foot of the rainbow, and upon the cochineal they offered for sale, and beneath the archways they were rapidly covering pottery of all kinds, from great earthen jars to little jugs, all exquisitely adorned in brilliant colors with little figures of ducks and deer and flowers; and there were casks filled with honey and molasses and other sweets, and wood: planks and braces and beams and blocks and benches and boats; and the salt and herb sellers spread hempen cloths over their merchandise; and the dealers in golden grains clasped their merchandise to their breasts, and the golden grains stored in the quills of the geese of this land spilled from the carelessly held containers; and equally frightened were the owners of dark brown-colored grains surely as precious as the gold, for I saw no one more assiduously protecting his property, little bags bursting with this stuff, similar to the beads of a precious rosary; and hurrying through this fair disrupted by the unexpected rain and waves and lightning and fire, in the distance we perceived—and only she stopped our hurried pace—a woman emerging from the haze who also seemed to be clothed in haze, for her rags were dingy white, and her step was hesitant and uncertain, and her weeping profound and lugubrious, and her face invisible behind the curtain of white hair, and her words were one long lament: "Oh, my sons! Oh, my sons! We are lost! Now we must travel far! Oh, my sons! Where can I take you and hide you?"

And just as she had appeared, this lamenting specter disappeared, and it seemed as if we walked through the haze of her body to find ourselves at the edge of a dark canal of stagnant waters scarcely stirred by the passage of shadowy boats that seemed less solid than the water; these vessels were rowed by two-headed monsters who accompanied their slow, silent rowing with moans: "It must have come at last; the end of the world has come; the world has consumed itself and new people will be created; the new inhabitants of the world have come."

How well I remember those phantom voices, Sire, and the monsters rowing calmly along the canal that separated the confused multitude of the marketplace from a great circle of courtyards which we entered across a bridge, whether advancing or fleeing, I do not know, for the disorder of my flight was equal to that of the inhabitants of this confused city whose form and countenance, for such had been my bedazzlement at my entrance into it, I still had not perceived, even less now that I was lost in the labyrinthine courtyards, enclosed within walls of white stones, large and very smooth; and suddenly, Sire, I found myself in the middle of a great plaza, very white and well swept and clean.

I sought the reassuring presence of my young companions and only then did I realize I was alone in the center of that plaza, and that the twenty boys and girls who had led me from the volcano into the heart of the city on the lake had disappeared.

Desolate, I looked all about me in search of them. Then I looked at the walls of this alien fatherland, and one was formed solely of death's-heads, and another of carved stone serpents curled back upon themselves, biting their own tails. There was a tower whose door was in the form of a fearsome, open, fanged mouth. This door was flanked by great blocks of stone depicting women with the faces of devils, with skirts of serpents, and open, lacerated hands.

And in the midst of all this, I alone.

And once again before me, a portentous stone stairway whose steps, I now knew, led to a high temple of blood and sacrifice. And to one side, a palace of rose-colored stone, at whose entrance squatted the statue of a god or prince whose face was raised to the sky; he sat with legs crossed, his arms folded across his chest, and in his lap was a bowl of yellow, flaming, smoking flowers that seemed to beckon to me.

I, poor wretch, entered, breasting the curtain of smoke from twin censers, and I walked along a low, narrow passageway until I emerged into a strange courtyard filled with sound.

I felt I was again in the jungle, but now a jungle of soft rose-colored stone with strutting peacocks, and in shining cages or upon high pedestals, staring intently at me, sat all kinds of birds, from royal eagles to very small, brilliantly colored birds. There were a great number of parrots and ducks, and in a pond stood long-limbed, motionless birds, with rose-colored body, wings, and tail feathers. And secured to stone columns by short chains and heavy collars were ocelots and wolves that did not even deign to glance at me, so engrossed were they in devouring deer, and hens, and small dogs, and in earthen jars and large water jugs were coiled many poisonous vipers and snakes with a rattle-like appendage on their tails, and in feather-filled jugs vipers were laying their eggs and tending their young.

I paused a moment; I would have believed I had entered a deserted palace were it not for the predatory beasts and the birds; then, Sire, I heard the sound of a broom and I smelled the smoke of something burning issuing through the door of one of the chambers opening onto this courtyard.

It was high noon; how much my eyes had seen since the dawn of the fourth day of my memory! I looked at the sun from where I stood in the center of the courtyard, and it blinded me. Absolute silence reigned, as if the walls of this palace might muffle, even kill, the noises from the frightened city I had left behind, but in whose very heart I believed I now found myself. Sun-dazzled, blinded by light that increased with every blinking of my eyes, and panting from the rarefied air of this high city, I entered the chamber where I thought I had detected signs of life: the sound of a broom, and the odor of burned paper.

When I first entered I saw nothing, so strong was the contrast between my dazzled gaze and the intense shadow of this long, empty chamber: narrow, deep stone nave and resounding emptiness. I walked the length of it, entreating my customary vision to return.

I do not know, not even to this day, whether it would have been better to have been blinded by smoke, or sun, or ashes than to see what finally I saw: an almost naked figure, his shame hidden by a loincloth like that worn by the poor of this land, who held, with movements sometimes slow and sometimes brusque and urgent, long pieces of papyrus to a small fire of lighted resins in one corner of the bare chamber, watching them consumed in flames, and then with the broom sweeping up the ashes, and again choosing other long pieces of paper, holding them to the fire, burning them, and sweeping away the residue. Then I noted that the broom fulfilled a double function, that this almost naked man also used it as a crutch. I recognized first his body, quivering with nervous energy one instant, placid the next: one foot was missing.

I walked toward him. He ceased his sweeping. He looked at me.

It was he, again.

It was I, the same semblance that was faithfully reproduced by the mirror I had so carefully guarded in my torn doublet. It was I, but as I had seen myself on the night of the phantom: dark, my eyes black, my hair lank and long and black as a horse's mane. It was my pursuer, the one called Smoking Mirror, the Lord of Sacrifices, the avenger, who on the day of creation lost his foot when it was torn from him by the contortions of a mother earth who was breaking apart into mountains, rivers, valleys, jungles, craters, and precipices.

And these were his words: "Our Lord; you have fatigued yourself, you have exhausted yourself; but you have come to your own land. You have reached your city: Mexico. Here you have come to be seated upon your throne. Oh, it was but a brief time that we kept it for you." Those black eyes, identical except in color to my own, stared at me intently, and now there was in them neither the mockery nor the anger of our former encounter, rather, sorrowful resignation.

"No, I am not dreaming, I am not rousing from a sluggish sleep; it is not in my dreams I see you, I am not dreaming you! I have seen you. My eyes are looking upon your face! You came amid clouds, amid fog. And this was what our kings had told us, our ancestors, those who ruled your city in your absence and in your name, they who are to install you upon your seat, in your place of honor . . . they said you would return. And now it has been accomplished, you arrived after great fatigue, you came with purpose from across the great waters, overcoming all obstacles. This is your land: come and rest; take possession of your royal houses and give comfort to your body."

He raised his head, for all he had said had been said with his head bowed, as if he feared to look at me, and he stared at me inquisitively: "I am not mistaken? You are the awaited Quetzalcoatl, the Plumed Serpent?" As was my custom, Sire, I answered with the simplest truth: "I came from the sea. I came from the east. A storm tossed me upon these shores."

The lame sweeper nodded several times, and hurriedly limped to one corner of the chamber. "I had only one doubt," he said, as he raised a cotton cloth to reveal an enormous bird the color of ashes, a dead crane, and in the crown of the bird's head there was something resembling a mirror, or a spinning bobbin, spiral-shaped and pierced in the center.

"The crane was killed by the boatmen of the lake, and brought to me here in this my black house," added the man with the broom, "and in the mirror in its head I could see the heavens and the constellations, and the stars, and beneath the heavens the sea, and on the sea great mountains advancing across the waters, and from them descended onto the coasts a great number of people who came marching singly and in squadrons, with many weapons, wearing many adornments in the manner of men dressed for war, and these men had very white skin, and red beards, and they showed their teeth as they spoke, and they were like monsters, for half of their bodies were those of men, but the other half was that of a beast with four legs and a fearsome foaming mouth."

He ceased speaking, and again questioned me: "You came alone?" I told him I had.

"I thought not. I thought you came with others.."

He covered the dead bird with the cloth.

He was silent for a long while. And as if they had awaited this silence, through the narrow door of the chamber entered in a great company maidens with cloths folded over their outstretched arms, and they were dressed in elaborately embroidered gowns of white cotton, and warriors with banners whose insignia was an eagle attacking an ocelot, its feet and talons set as if to strike, and albinos who entered as I had, shielding their eyes with their hands to protect them from the sun, and upon seeing me they were grateful for the surrounding shadows, and they approached to touch me and murmured things among themselves, and frolicking dwarfs, leaping and grimacing and thus paying me their respect, and they were accompanied by stately peacocks and small, fleet, short-haired dogs with skins lustrous as a pig's.

Then the maidens robed me in the cloths, and around my neck they placed strings of precious stones and garlands of flowers, and they tied golden bells about my ankles, and upon my arms, above my elbows, they placed golden arm bands, and ear ornaments of highly polished copper in my ears, and once again, upon my head, a crest of green plumes.

And my dark double, naked, supporting himself upon his broom, said to all assembled:

"This is truly the Plumed Serpent, the great priest from the beginnings of time, man's creator, the god of peace and work, the teacher who taught us to plant corn, to till the earth, to weave the feather, and work the stone; this is truly the one called Quetzalcoatl, the white god, the enemy of sacrifice, the enemy of war, the enemy of blood, the friend of life who one day fled to the east with sadness and anger in his heart because his teachings had been repudiated, because the demands of hunger and power and catastrophe and terror had led men to war and to the spilling of blood. He promised to return one day by the same route from the east toward which he had fled, where the great sun rises and the great waters burst upon the shore, to restore the lost reign of peace. We did but guard his throne for his return. Now we give it to him. The signs have manifested themselves. The prophecies have been fulfilled. The throne is his, and I am his slave."

So spoke my dark double, painfully supported by the broom that at times served as his crutch, and my ear, made sensitive by continual contrast between reality and marvel, seemed to perceive in his tones a return to those he had employed on the night of the phantom: imperceptibly, resignation was yielding to a new challenge, and behind the softness of his words was a metallic timbre that made me question his sincerity. Nevertheless, I rejected those doubts; and I did so, Sire, because in truth I did not seek the honors that this man offered me; I had little desire to reign over the great city of the towers and canals; and sadly, in that instant when a throne was offered me, I thought of only two things, everything I desire was centered in them: Pedro, a small piece of land, our own free land, on the coast of pearls would have been sufficient; my young beloved, the Lady of the Butterflies, I longed to find you again, burning and beautiful and terrible, as on the night in the jungle, and make love to you again.

But all my desires and doubts were suspended by the activity of the maidens and the warriors, the albinos and the dwarfs, the small dogs and the vain peacocks; they opened a path for me, indicating the way from this chamber, and when I reached the threshold, I looked back and saw my vanquished double, who was renewing his compelling task of burning papers and sweeping ashes. He did not look at me again.

I went out into the courtyard, and sounds and people before invisible became immediate, present, as if the entire city was reviving from its stupor, the morning's portents annulled, the prophecies of an origin so often invoked in this land fulfilled, feared and desired, yes, as if that past was also future, beneficent at times, but also a stark presentiment of a past as cruel as that they had known formerly; I was led along corridors raised upon jasper pillars that looked down upon great gardens, each with several pools, where there were more birds, hundreds of them, and hundreds of men feeding them, and giving them grass and fish and flies and lizards; they were cleaning the pools, and fishing, and feeding, and grooming the birds, they were collecting their eggs, and treating them and clipping their feathers, and I realized that from these magnificent breeding aviaries came the feathers from which these natives made their rich mantles and shields and tapestries and crests and fans; and we passed through low-ceilinged rooms where there were many cages built of strong wooden bars, and some held mountain lions, and others ocelots, and some lynx, and others wolves; and we came to another courtyard filled with cages built of sturdy poles, and perches, where there was every imaginable species of birds of prey: lanners, kites, vultures, hawks, all species of falcons and many of eagles; and from there we passed into some high-ceilinged rooms where there were men and women and children whose hair and bodies were completely white, and dwarfs and hunchbacks, and crippled and deformed and monstrous people in great numbers, every category of these little men having its own chamber or room; and we passed by something similar to armories whose blazon was a bow and two quivers upon each door, and in these rooms there were bows and arrows, slings, lances, goads, darts, bludgeons and swords, shields and bucklers, casques, greaves and brassards, and poles dipped in pitch with sharp fish bones and rocks embedded in their tips; beyond that house we arrived in a courtyard enclosed on three sides by masonry walls and on the fourth by an enormous stone stairway.

I was led to the stairway by the maidens and warriors, the albinos and dwarfs, and, counting the steps, I climbed—there were thirty-three—and as I reached the summit, low and square like all the others of this land, I could again see, closer now than from the mountains of the dawn but with sufficient distance to perceive its contours, the magnificent city that my double, the dark prince, had just ceded me.

I looked upon the great expanse of the city of the lake, crossed by bridges and canals, and open in vast plazas, tall in thick towers, its dwellings one hundred thousand houses, and frequented by two hundred thousand boats, and I saw only what I already knew: all this splendor was maintained by my poor friends of the jungle and the river towns, it was for this homage that they had repeatedly fulfilled the cycle: pearls and gold in exchange for men, women, and children to the service of this great city and its lords ensconced upon the high lake of the high valley of thin air and transparent visions.

I stepped into the chamber that crowned this construction.

What marvels, oh, Christian Lord who hears me, had I not seen since the whirlpool of the ocean threw me upon the beach of pearls. I wish to omit nothing from my account, either seen or dreamed, even though in that land, I admit it, it was almost always impossible to separate marvel from truth, or truth from marvel. But if I am certain of anything, it is that the chamber into which I now entered was the seat of the ultimate union of fable and reality, for to enter there was to penetrate into the very heart of opulence.

Long and broad was the chamber, and its walls were of pure gold; there was accumulated an unbelievably great quantity of pearls and precious stones—agates, carnelians, emeralds, rubies, topazes—and the very floors were covered with heavy plates of gold and silver, and there were golden disks, and necklaces of idols, fine shields, nose moons of gold, greaves of gold, arm bands of gold, diadems of gold.

Into the chamber came lords and men of the guard, and servants carrying their arms, and maidens with great trays laden with fruits and meat, and some carrying vessels, and there were six ancient lords, and one group of musicians and another of dancers and athletes, and when I sat upon a low bench facing a leather cushion, the maidens offered me victuals—chicken and deer and fragrant herbs—and they served me from their vessels, pouring the sweet-scented beverages into cups of gold, and the six ancients stepped forward to taste each dish as it was served, and as a sign of their respect, they never raised their eyes to my face, and the music commenced—reed pipes, flutes, shell horns, bones and rattles—along with the songs and dances, and a few of the athletes threw themselves on the floor, twirling with their feet a pole as large as a beam, stout, polished, and smooth, tossing it into the air and catching it, and exchanging it among themselves with their feet, a thousand movements in the air so swift and so well executed that I could scarcely believe it could be done; I ate and drank to my fill, marveling at the place and its people; and then came the jesters and buffoons, the dwarfs, with their capering and cavorting, and an old man took the remains from my meal and threw them to the dwarfs and they fell upon them like starving animals.

After we had eaten, all retired from the room with lowered eyes except the maidens, and they disrobed me, bathed me with great care, and again dressed me in a rich mantle.

I held out my hand, Sire, and asked that they leave me my sailor's clothing, my torn doublet and breeches, and what was concealed inside them: my scissors and my mirror. A maiden relaxed for an instant her mask of servitude, as a flash of anger crossed her features: "Young Lord: you must change your clothing four times a day, never wearing the same habiliment twice."

"These are the clothes I was wearing when I was thrown upon these shores," I said simply, but the maiden looked at me, and looked at the clothes, as if I had spoken some kind of witchcraft.

But she herself placed my tattered doublet and breeches at my feet, and along with the other maidens disappeared, leaving me alone in this chamber of treasures.

For a moment, Sire, I thought of the stone chamber of the ancient of memories, where he so zealously guarded his baskets of pearls and ears of grain; in this chamber there was not only treasure to buy a million times over what that old man had guarded, oh, no, Sire. With the treasure of this room one could buy the ransom of all the ports of our Mediterranean Sea, and the lives of all their rulers, great and small, and the love of all their women, of both high and low estate.

Only in that moment of my solitude did I come to the absolute realization that all these treasures were mine, to do with as I would. But since my two sovereign desires—to return with Pedro to the happy beach of the new world and to return with the Lady of the Butterflies to the happy night of my passion—were impossible, I looked once more around this chamber of riches, knowing that it would take more than a month simply to count the gold and silver, the pearls and precious stones, the jewels here collected, and I shouted, as if I wished everyone to hear me, I shouted, so they all would hear me, I seized handfuls of the pearls and necklaces and arm bands and earrings and bracelets and went out of the chamber onto the high terrace from which one could see the total expanse of the splendid lacustrine city, transparent now in the waning, pullulating light of the afternoon; and to the tens of thousands of boats, the open markets, the plazas, the stone towers, the golden haze, the canals of brilliant green, the two snowy peaks that guarded it all, I shouted; to them all, my hands filled with jewels, I shouted:

"Return to your true owners! Restore these treasures to those who wrested them from the jungle, the mines, the beaches, to those who worked and set and polished the stones! Restore the lives of all who died for these treasures! Revive in each pearl a girl given as a whore to a warrior, in every grain of gold revive a man sacrificed because the death of the world was feared, revive the entire world, I will water it with gold, sow it with silver, and bathe it in pearls, let everything be returned to the people, deliver everything I here possess to its true owner—my people of the jungle, my forgotten children, my violated women, my sacrificed men!"

This is what I shouted to the high city from the height of the thirty-three steps on whose summit were guarded the greatest treasures of the world. Believe me, Sire, when I tell you that the distant sounds in the canals and markets, footpaths and towers, seemed suddenly to cease, and only the fading blast of a conch shell filled that enormous vacuum of silence.

I threw the jewels and gold and pearls from the four sides of my high terrace; I watched them roll down the steps up which I had climbed; and from the second side they rolled toward a broad canal; and toward the altars and stone idols below, toward the bloodied walls and black-crusted floors, from the third; and from the fourth, toward the ossuary of death's-heads, the rows of grinning skulls embedded in the stone.

It was to the water, to the stone, and to the bones I threw all treasures that my hands could hold, and not, I told myself, to the forever lost inhabitants of the nomadic villages of the river, the jungle, and the mountain.

Dispiritedly, I returned to my chamber.

At first I did not perceive its brilliance. It was a pool of light, dazzling, a lake of gold and silver, as if here the precious metal had reproduced in miniature the brilliance of that vast enchanted city.

I walked toward the rear of the cloister, seeking a place where I might rest. I needed to think. I seemed to have come to the end of my trials, but I knew very well I still had the remainder of this day, its night, and the following day and night to exhaust my destiny in the land of the navel of the moon. Strange: it was late afternoon and I still had not yet felt the need to ask my question for this day. Others had spoken; others had explained; my prayers had been answered that events respond to my questions. I had feared at dawn that I might waste a question; now, as night fell, I feared I would not find the opportunity to formulate it.

In this brilliant chamber my eyes sought skins, mantles, some semblance of a bed where I might lie. Brilliant chamber: the brilliance had a center and something in that center was hovering in the air, a crown of lights, a constellation of luminous wings . . .

Oh, Sire, how I ran then toward that center of light, how quickly I wished to penetrate the shadow that girded the human figure beneath the crown of butterflies, but I stopped, wild with joy, my heart pounding, unsure of the good fortune that had been bestowed upon me, before that figure gowned in shadow but crowned by the sign of my beloved: the fluttering scepter of the butterflies of light.

"My Lady, is it you?"

The black shadow was silent; then came the reply: "Is that your question for this day?"

It was her voice, revealing knowledge of our pact.

I threw myself upon her bosom, my arms embraced her waist, I sought her face; body and countenance were veiled in black; I grasped her hands, they were sheathed in gloves of black leather. In each hand she held a cup.

She said to me: "Drink. I swore to you we would meet again, and that when we met, your pleasure would be redoubled. You have overcome all temptations and all obstacles. You have reached the summit of power. Drink."

I held to my lips, Sire, the heavy cup of gold she offered me; I drank a thick, fermented, intoxicating liquid that was like swallowing fire from a hearth; no more turbid beverage exists, or one more crystalline: it was like drinking fragrant mud, it was like drinking ground crystal.

I drained the cup, I threw it aside, I sank my head in the lap of my recovered lover, I thought that under the influence of the liquor I was losing my senses, and that my sight was turning to water, my flesh, my hands and knees, my bones; my Lady, my Lady, hear my question of this day, answer it: the White Lady of Death told me in the deep icy hell that I was one in memory and another in forgetfulness, Plumed Serpent in what I remember and Smoking Mirror in what I forget: what does that riddle mean, my Lady?

I don't know how many times in my pitiful drunkenness I repeated this question; and the gloved hands of my dark lover consoled me as a mother consoles her child, as the grandmother of the clean hut had consoled me as I slept in her lap. And only when I ceased to repeat my question, when my trembling ceased, did she speak these terrible words:

"Your question has been wasted. Before the Lords of Death, you answered your own question. I said you would voyage twenty-five days and twenty-five nights before we would meet again. I promised you five days to rescue from death to enable you to come to me. You used only two. Three remained. On the pyramid I offered you the opportunity to renounce those days and once and for all to join me. Forever. In life and in death. You preferred to wager your remaining days.

What a pity. Now you have found me again. But I am not the same. My time is not your time. Mine has a different measure. So much time has passed since we made love in the jungle . . . so much time since we saw each other on the pyramid . . . so much time."

I closed my eyes and clung to her knees. "I still do not understand; you have not answered my question; I know who I was in memory, I recall the days I was able to save from death; what happened to me during the twenty days I have forgotten?"

"Ask that question of the others tonight. Now come to me."

She caressed my head with her gloved hands. She said softly into my ear: "Remember the pyramid. Remember it is I who hear the final confession of every man, the one confession of his life, one time only, at the end of life . . ."

I looked up at the mask of black veils, and I cried out: "But I don't want to die, I want to live with you, I have found you again! I asked two impossible things today as I entered this chamber of treasures, and one of them has become possible: to hold you, to make love to you again, forever! And since I cannot restore life to the man who was like my father, in his name and in the name of the happiness he sought here, I want to make love to you as long as I live . . ."

The Lady of the Butterflies laughed from behind her cascade of black veils. "Are you sure of what you say?"

Yes, I answered, yes, as I parted the veils covering her face, a thousand times yes, as I tore at my lover's clothing, seeking again the cinnamon-colored skin, the black nails, the black jungle of my unrepeatable pleasure . . .

"My unrepeatable pleasure," I repeated loudly, stupidly, as I unveiled the woman's face only to discover it was covered by another mask, of garnet and green and blue feathers, a fan radiating from a center of dead spiders affixed with that resin whose scent I had noted in all the things of this land.

"Your face," I said, "I want your face, I want to kiss you . . ."

"Wait. Before you remove this mask, swear one thing."

"Yes, anything."

"That you will keep it with you always. That, whatever happens, you will never be parted from it. It is my final gift to you. It is the map of the new world your unfortunate old friend so desired. Keep it with you. One day it will lead you back to me . . ."

"A map? I see only a center of spiders upon a field of feathers, how can this guide me . . . ?"

She interrupted: "Have faith in what I say. This is the true map of the new world, not the map navigators draw, or voyagers as they travel into the mountains. Not a map that leads to visible places, but one that will one day lead you back to me, to the invisible . . ."

In the depths of this chamber of treasures, the two of us alone, surrounded by the infinite silence that I myself had imposed upon the city when I threw the jewels from the platform of the pyramid, I removed from the face of my beloved, with great delicacy, with all the tenderness of which I was capable, the mask of feathers and spiders.

Behind the mask appeared the last face of my lover.

I could tell you, Sire, that it was a face devoured by age, a minute network of wrinkles, a deep gaze of opaque passion from the depths of cavernous, livid sockets sunken in jutting, bare bones of forehead and cheek, thinly covered by a skin as yellow as old parchment, and I would speak the truth; I could tell you it was an infinitely ancient face, with the eternal tattoo of the lips erased and wasted by time, conquered by the deep wrinkles that were buried in her lips, that furrowed the corners of her mouth, that disappeared in her toothless gums, and I would speak the truth.

But only half the truth, Sire. For the signs of devastation on the face of my beloved were those of time, yes, but also something worse than time. My beloved, my beloved of the jungle. I looked for the crown of butterflies above the thinned white-haired, wart-covered head of my lover; I watched them fall, dry and dull, lifeless, upon the silver floor of this sumptuous chamber. And I looked at her; such antiquity was the work of illness, of the pox that marked her skin, of the leprosy that corroded her blood, of the tumefaction that burst from the mire of swollen craters, of the filth that oozed from her breasts, of the pestilent swamp of her mouth: my Lady, the devouring goddess of filth, had been devoured by that filth . . .

She peeled off her gloves, I felt her bony, damp, claw-like hands caressing my cheeks, my neck, my chest . . .

"Forever, young pilgrim, did you say forever?"

I sobbed in her lap; I am not sure that I heard clearly all she said.

"I was the young temptress, the lover of my own brother who in my arms lost himself and the kingdom of peace; I was the goddess of games of chance, of all that is uncertain, whom you knew in the jungle; in maturity, I was the priestess who absorbs sins and filth, devours them so they no longer exist; now I am but the witch, the ancient destroyer of young men, the envious one; I must be seated upon the body of a young man; that is my throne . . . you . . ."

Trembling, the ancient woman thrust me from her. "Go, flee, you still have time; you did not understand; I offered you a year in which we might be together, one year of your life as a man, which is not the equivalent of my years as a woman; you did not accept; after a year of making love to me every night you would have died; now we must wait, so long, so long; keep the map, return, look for me, in a hundred years, two hundred, a thousand years, whatever time it takes that you and I be young at the same time, two, together, at the same time, at the same instant . . ."

Judge, Sire, my fever, my madness, my ferocious drunkenness; I was not master of myself; I tore the remaining clothing off the foul and rotted ancient woman, I closed my eyes, I told myself, it doesn't matter, you are drunk, what does it matter? you can have her again, close your eyes, think of the girl in the jungle, think of the woman of the pyramid, she is your only woman, your lover, your wife, your sister, your mother, enjoy the forbidden, make her yours, she is the only woman in the world, do not assess, do not compare, love, love, love . . ."

The ancient one trembled like a little bird, and her small, shrunken, sick body was that of a plucked sparrow; with eyes shut, I put my arms around her.

"Wait," moaned the woman, "wait, you cannot now, oh, pity, now our times no longer coincide, too much time has passed for me since I knew you, but too little time for you, wait, one day my cycle will be complete, I will again be the girl of the jungle, we shall meet again, somewhere, now you cannot . . ."

I had thrown off the mantle in which they had dressed me and, naked, blind, aroused, I pressed myself against her body, my erect penis sought the sex of the ancient one, but instead met stone, flint, impenetrable rock . . .

I drew back, I knelt between the ancient legs, I spread them, and from her hole, Sire, from that burning hole that had been mine, emerged a stone knife, its stone sheath a carved face, and the face was that of my marvelous beloved, the girl of the jungle, the Lady of the Butterflies.

I moaned, my senses reeling, I spun through time, uncertain of the hour, abandoned to the radiance of gold and silver and pearls that like that of the shining butterflies was now reduced to the dullness of ashes; I felt ashes in my mouth, and fire at my back, and suddenly the chamber was filled with a new radiance; I rolled over: torches of fire, great explosions of fire, held on high; it was night, the night was lighted by these men; I looked at their torches, I looked at my dark double, supported on his crutch.

They looked at me.

NIGHT OF REFLECTIONS

My dark double, the lame one called Smoking Mirror, was now wearing a vest on which were painted parts of the human body—skulls, ears, hearts, guts, breasts, hands, feet; around his neck he wore an ornament of yellow parrot feathers; his mantle was the shape of nettle leaves, and was decorated with black dye and tufts of eagle down; the plugs in his earlobes were turquoise mosaic, each supporting a circle of thorns, the nose ornament was of gold set with stones, and upon his head he wore a headdress of green feathers similar to the one I had worn when I took the throne of this accursed city. His gaze was a mirror of passions, the first of the long night of reflections I now had to live: revulsion and anger, scorn and pleasure, secret defeat, inflamed deception, dark victory.

Ashamed of my own nakedness, I picked up my ragged sailor's clothing; I dressed bashfully, clumsily, hastily; I picked up the feather mask, the strange map of the new world the ancient woman had given me, and placed it in my doublet along with my mirror and scissors. The old woman still lay on the floor, shielding her eyes with a pocked arm, her black clothing scattered upon the silver floor, her legs spread, the stone dagger still buried between her thighs.

The heavy smoke of incense invaded the treasure chamber.

The crippled prince raised one arm as he spoke, agitating the feathers of his crest; he addressed himself to the company of priests and warriors who accompanied him, rather than to the ancient woman and myself, although he looked only at us:

"See him; see the Young Lord of love and peace; see the creator of men; see the gentle and charitable teacher; see the enemy of sacrifice and war; see the creator fallen; see his naked and drunken shame; see him intoxicated, lying with his own sister, believing in the stupor of drink that she is his mother, or lying with his mother, believing she is his sister; which is the worse crime?, for which of all his crimes shall we again expel him from the city: usurper, liar, as weak as the men he once created, and contaminated by human clay? Is this the one who will defend us against thunder, fire, earthquake, and shadow? Will his teachings be sufficient to placate the furies of nature that from the heights of the sky and the deepest reaches of the earth threaten us at every instant? See the creator fallen, and tell me whether from the pits of drunkenness and incest, love and peace and labor can be predicated. Go now, messengers and couriers, carry the news: the dream has ended, the god has returned, has sinned, will again flee filled with shame, our law has triumphed, remains, continues, the earth thirsts for blood that it may yield its fruits, the sun hungers for blood that it may reappear at every dawn, the Lord of the Great Voice hungers and thirsts for pearls, maize, gold, birds, the life and death of all things, to answer the challenges of the earth and the sun. You have returned, Young Lord; brief has been your stay upon the throne I yielded to you today; you will flee again; your return will again be what it has always been: a promise. With our words we shall honor that promise. We shall reject it by our acts. One cannot govern with your teachings. But one can govern only by invoking them."

Before I could react to these incomprehensible accusations, the ancient woman moaned with fear, held out her aged arms to the man who spoke, my sumptuously attired double, the man in whom only now I recognized—separating him forever from myself—the Lord of the Great Voice, the oft-mentioned prince of these lands of the dead moon.

The Tlatoani told the woman not to despair, that everything was done well, that she would have the reward of this day and this age, the gift of the moment she was living, the promise offered every time the woman fulfilled this cycle of an always renewed existence.

"Your sister," murmured the lame prince. "Your shame. Your mother."

Oh, Sire, what did these prohibitions matter to me? I did not understand them, I knew them false, I was giddy, my reason whirling, my members tremulous; gorged with nightmares I threw myself at the feet of my recovered lover, I kissed her knees, her thighs, her belly. I tried to kiss her lips; her hand forbade me, sealing my lips; I cared nothing for her cruel mysteries, I would accept whatever she asked of me, one year, and then death, one day, one night, one single moment of love and my life would again have meaning; now, yes, now I would confess before her, my mother, prepared to be heard by her and thus to die for her; I pulled her hand from my lips, I told her she must listen, that my memory was returning, everything I had thought was lost forever, the memory of my life, of our lives, the memory of the world before my voyage to the new world; I saw myself as a child, before speech or memory, a newborn infant wrapped in bloody sheets, fleeing in the arms of a woman, mother, wet nurse, sister, I do not know, through portals and corridors to a stone courtyard where were piled corpses of women, men, and infants like myself, corpses whose clothing indicated their state, peasants, Jews, workmen, mudejares, whores, monks, women and children of the common people, corpses in a castle courtyard, a tumulus of bodies, cadavers heaped on firewood, a few armored guards holding their torches to the enormous pyre, dogs barking at the flames, the flames illuminating their spiked collars bearing a device inscribed in iron, *Nondum, Nondum* . . .

No, Sire, do not tremble, do not cry out like that, let me continue, hear me, she did not want to hear me, she said what you just now said, enough, enough; she pushed me away, as now you rise from your chair, not yet, not yet; wait, Sire, I wanted this time to confess before her, and I remembered death and crime and I did not know why I should confess this, shouting to the Lady of the Butterflies, you preferred me, you gave yourself to me so that I might give you a son, not knowing what I was saying, Sire, or why I was saying it, and the proud man resting on his crutch stared at us through the eyes of a black ocelot, you possessed her only after I had fled, you were always the second, not first, and you despised my sons, you murdered my sons, I said this as if I had actually lived it and was now confessing it, but she finds them again, my mother, my wife, my lover, my sister, she drinks the blood of my sons, she regains youth and life, she again makes love with me, and the ashen butterflies recovered their brilliance and their power of flight, joined together in a sparkling constellation and lighted upon the head of the ancient woman, and at that instant the Lady of the Butterflies disintegrated, fell into dust, and the guards of the Lord of the Great Voice fell upon me, shoved and kicked me to the ground, dragged me far from the remains of my mother and sister, my lover, away from the chamber of treasures onto the great terrace, to the flickering night of the city, bright bonfires, lights trembling in the canals, stilled mirrors in the black lagoon.

We descended the thirty-three steps, we passed through the rooms of the albinos and dwarfs and monsters along the dark gardens where wolves howled, lynx growled, owls hooted, to a great chamber of idols, each with a pot of incense at its stone feet, and like stone were all the visions of my long and brief pilgrimage through this land.

Look, look well, the Lord of the Great Voice, my crippled double, shouted at me, look well, his fist buried in my hair, banging my head against the stone of the idols, look well at your protectors, the powers that assure the rain and the wind and the fertility of the earth, and frighten away devastating earthquakes, droughts and floods, look well, at the eternal opposites, man and woman, light and darkness, movement and quietude, order and disorder, good and evil, the forces that impel the beneficent sun into the heart of the mountains and the forces that revive it from its nocturnal lethargy, at night, the light, shadow in the day, the omen, the double star, twin of itself, the first star at dusk, the first at dawn, world of dualities, world of oppositions, there is life only if two opposites confront each other in battle, there is no peace without war, no life without death, there is no possible unity, nothing is one, everything is two, in constant warfare, and I pretended that everything had become one, everything one, everything all things, I, my somber double shouted at me, you, the prince of unity, of good, of permanent peace, of dissolved dualities, I . . . .

Blood rushed to my eyes.

Smoke blinded me.

I was lying upon the stone of the chapel and when I raised my head I saw only that the Lord of the Great Voice was standing before me, and that we were alone.

And these were his words: "This morning you saw me burning some papers and sweeping away the ashes. Those papers told the story of your legend. In them was the promise of your return. One day you fled toward the east. You went saddened because men had violated your codes of peace, union, and brotherhood. You said you would return one day to restore your kingdom of goodness."

"I do not understand," I said in a hoarse, exhausted voice, "I do not understand, why was that kingdom lost, why did men violate the laws of peace and goodness?"

My double laughed. "You are light and I am shadow. Your sons, men, were born of light. I, from the shadows, was unable to create. Night is nourished from increasing nothingness. You invented men in light and for the light. But even light needs repose, and my kingdom, that of night, shelters man's fatigue. Your sons could be no greater than the sun itself. They, like the sun, would have to sleep, and then I, the demon of dreams, would make them mine, each night, and each night I would cause them to doubt the goodness of their creator, and in the trembling of the night give form to fear, doubt, envy, scorn, and greed, night after night, drop by drop, until I poisoned your sons, divided them, seduced them, made them choose between the temptation of the night and the habit of the day. You made a mistake, my poor brother. You made men free. You allowed them to choose. Who would not choose the delightful prohibitions of night over the insipid laws of day?"

"Even at the price of slavery?"

"They did not know then that upon the disorder of their senses would be raised the sense of my order. Without a single word they became the slaves and I the master, but both—they, to maintain the illusion of their freedom, and I, to maintain the legitimacy of my power—pretended to continue to respect your laws. You fled, saddened; you said you would return. Meanwhile, I would reign as the usurper, as a mere substitute upon your throne, with no legitimacy of my own, every instant fearing your promised return and the end of my power. Look at yourself, drunken, incestuous, unworthy, stupid. You did not resist temptation. The creator is guilty. The creator is as weak as his creatures. Look at yourself. Look . . ."

The Lord of the Great Voice extended to me a staff holding many mirrors. I closed my eyes so as not to see myself. I murmured an argument that suddenly flared in my memory: "The ancient Lord of Memory told me we were three, three were the creators, one of life, another of death, and the third of the memory that sustains life and death . . . And if he was memory, and I life, you must be death, death on earth, not the death I knew beneath the earth . . ."

"The old man lied. We have always been two. Only two. You, the hunchbacked, boil-plagued dwarf who dared leap into the brazier of creation; I, the well-formed and handsome prince who did not have the courage to do so. You returned whole, splendid, golden, rewarded for your sacrifice, with no sign of your former monstrosity but the six toes on each foot and the red cross upon your back: the seal of your passage through the fire, like the spots of the ocelot and the deer. I . . . look at me . . . crippled . . . destroyed by the vengeful contortions of our mother, the earth . . .''

"You and I, alone . . .''

"I alone, from now on. Only I, without your pursuing shadow, my double, the always present accuser, watching me over your shoulder, telling me I err, that I do evil, that my power is cruel and bloody, and also unsure and transitory, that you will return to revive the power of goodness . . . Look at yourself now . . . My legitimacy will be founded upon your failure. Never again will you disturb our order. To-day I burned the papers of your legend. There is nothing more written about you. I shall begin there, I will convert your memory into ashes like those I swept away with my broom.''

I was speaking with my eyes closed. I implored: "Tell me one thing. Answer one question. I have the right to one question tonight.''

My dark double, who saw his dark double in me, waited in silence. I spit blood. I said only: "Tell me: what did I do during the twenty days I have forgotten?''

Sire: the laughter of the one called Smoking Mirror exploded like the wave that had that morning swept over the poorest houses of this city, it burst into echoes against the walls of this sacred room and washed back converted into words, and those words were an irresistible command: "Look, I tell you to look; look in the mirrors on this staff, which is the staff of our lord Xipe Totec, the flayed god, the one who gives his life for the next harvest, the one who escapes from himself as he escapes from his skin; look in the mirrors of his staff, and you will have the answer to your question.''

I opened my eyes. The Lord of the Great Voice held the staff in his left hand, supporting himself upon it. This was now his cane.

A cane of lights: each mirror glittered and every gleam was a terrible scene of death, slashed throats, conflagration, frightful war, and in each I was the protagonist, I was the white, blond, bearded man on horseback, armed with a crossbow, armed with a sword, a cross of gold embroidered upon his breast, I was that man who set fire to temples, destroyed idols, fired cannons against the warriors of this land armed only with lances and arrows, I was the centaur who devastated the same fields, the same plains, the same jungles of my pilgrimage from the coast, my mounted troops trampled whole towns, cities were reduced to dark ashes by my wrathful torches, I ordered the beheading of the festival dancers at the pyramids, I raped the women and branded the men like cattle, I denied the paternity of the sons of whores I left behind me, I charged the poor of this land with heavy burdens and at whiplash set them on their road, I melted into bars the gold, the jewels, the walls and floors of the new world, I spread pox and cholera to the inhabitants of these lands, I, I, it was I who knifed the inhabitants of the town of the jungle, this time they did not immolate themselves in my honor, to honor the god who had returned, the promise of good: this time I killed them, I ordered the hands and feet of rebels to be amputated, I, I, laden with gold and corpses and laments and shadows, I sank into the muddy swamps of a lagoon that receded a little every time a bearer defeated by his burden, a woman branded on the lips, a child born in the desert, fell dead into its waters: the lagoon was a cemetery and I emerged from it, bathed in gold and blood, to reconquer a city without inhabitants, a mausoleum of solitudes . . .

Terrified by these visions, bleating like an animal, pawing like a beast, I pushed away the staff of mirrors; the crippled man lost his balance and fell to the floor beside me.

His face, identical to mine, looked into mine, we were both lying upon the stone floor of the sacred room, staring at each other like animals lying in ambush, our teeth bared in a snarl, saliva dribbling from our jaws, our chests touching the floor, elbows cocked, hands pressing against stone, clawing, we were poised to leap.

"Is that what I did . . . what you have always done . . . !"

I asked it, Sire, but terror and fatigue and shortness of breath drowned out the question and offered it to my double as an affirmation.

Frothing at the mouth, he answered: "That is what you will do . . . The mirrors of this staff see into the future . . ."

I felt, Sire, as if I were going mad: the compass of my mind had lost its directional needle, my identities were spilling over and multiplying beyond all contact with minimal human reason, I was a prisoner of the most tenebrous magic, the magic represented in stone in this pantheon of all the gods and goddesses I could not conquer in this land, who with fearful grimaces mocked my oneness and imposed upon me their monstrous proliferation, destroying the arguments of unity I had meant to carry as an offering to this world, yes, and also the simple unity in which that total unity was to be maintained: my own, the unity of my person. I looked upon the faces of the idols: they did not understand what I was saying.

What proof did I have, except what I had carried from the coasts of Spain in the pocket of my doublet? Against the mirages of this land, against the fatal staff of the flayed god, against the limpid reflection in the head of the crane, against the very name of Smoking Mirror, against the incomprehensible images of the twenty days of my other destiny, the destiny forgotten because it was still to be fulfilled, or perhaps the destiny fulfilled because it was already forgotten, I had opposed my own small mirror, the one Pedro and I used on the ship that brought us here when we performed the office of barber, the mirror I had shown to the distressed ancient of memories in the temple chamber: my mirror, and my scissors.

I removed both from my doublet, stretched out there like a wild beast facing an enemy beast, my double, Smoking Mirror, the Lord of the Great Voice, also stretched out on the floor, serpents, each of us, staring at one another, lying in ambush, awaiting the next movement of the opponent.

"Do you yourself not fear what I have seen in the staff of mirrors?" I asked him.

"I do not fear what resembles me. I feared you in the forest, when you chose your desire over my heart. Today I ceased to fear you when you converted the power I gave you into desire. If you believe that my mirrors lie, look at yourself in your own."

Sire: what that ancient of memories must have felt when I showed him his reflection, I now felt when I saw myself, for my own mirror returned to me the face of the ancient who died of terror when he found he was old: in my own mirror I saw myself burdened with time, upon the threshold of death, stricken and ruined, toothless and desiccated, pale and tremulous, immersed in the basket filled with pearls and cotton; I saw myself, Sire, and I told myself I had never moved from the basket under the bower where the men of the river had placed me one night in their town in the jungle; I told myself that the truth was what I imagined then: sitting in that basket I would wait for death to devour me, to become as ancient as the old man I had killed with my mirror; now the mirror is killing me. I had never moved from that town. Everything else, up to the present moment, I had merely dreamed. It was my destiny to see myself, motionless, grow old in this fleeting image. Moons, suns, days, stars, shelter me, water clock, hourglass, book of hours, stone calendar, tides and tempests, do not abandon me, bind me to time, I lose count of the days of Venus, repeating alone that the days of my destiny in this strange land can be only the number indicated by the ancient in the temple: the days of my destiny stolen from the days of the sun; the masked days stolen from the days of my destiny; I have imagined those five sterile days thieved from evil fortune for the purpose of winning them at the moment of my death; but today I have imagined also the twenty days of the sun stolen from the time of my destiny, the twenty days of my evil fortune, the twenty days of my forgotten death which will inevitably occur in the future. How to measure them? How to know whether one day of my time was a century of this time?

I saw myself, an ancient, in my mirror; I choked back a cry; I longed to rejoin my lover, the old woman, the witch, the atrocious female, the murderess, and be reborn with her into youth; it was not possible; our times would never coincide; she would be young again; I was racing toward old age, toward the image in the mirror, the image of the ancient of the temple; he who granted me the time of my memory and whom I killed with the time of my mirror; blindly, I was approaching the time of space and the space of time; the image of the double lay before me, transfixing me with his eyes of black glass; he had granted me the time of my premonition and I would kill him with my scissors; I raised them, and drove them into his face, ripping the face that was my face, I sliced his gaze with my fragile twin steel blades, again I raised the scissors, I struck the back of the Lord of the Great Voice, my double rolled over with a horrible spasm, and I plunged the scissors into his chest, his belly, and his black blood spread across the broad stones of the chapel, and sprinkled the flowers, insects, brooms, the feet of the stone gods.

I rose to my feet, my hands dripping blood.

Sire: I knew then that I must flee, that the twenty days of carnage of my life beneath the sun of Mexico were counted, that I had only one day to flee from that destiny, to repudiate it with my absence, to return to the sea, return to my true guide, Venus, to cling to her sails and on the sea save myself, or drown, but never to submit to the destiny I had forgotten and which the mirrors of the staff recalled to me.

For the last time I looked at the slashed body of my dark double. Again I looked at my blood-covered hands. The legend had ended. The fable would not repeat itself again. My enemy and I had killed the awaited god of peace, union, and happiness. So died the one called the Plumed Serpent. But also—I thought then—so died the one called Smoking Mirror. And with them died their secret: they were one.

DAY OF FLIGHT

Disoriented, I fled from the sacred chamber and lost myself in the stone labyrinths of the city of the lagoon. I was again the person I had been in the beginning, the castaway in tattered clothing, with three wretched possessions: a mirror, my scissors, and now a mask of feathers and spiders.

I was lost. I did not know whether the palace was the city or the city the palace, where a plaza ended and a market began, where a market ended and a causeway began; I fled clad in the armor of fear—but armed only with my bones, and combating an enormous emptiness: empty, the gardens of the birds and snakes and ferocious beasts; empty, the temples; empty, the markets; empty, the canals, the boats abandoned on the shores of the islands; I fled; the city seemed to flee with me; perhaps it had fled before me, and I was merely following in its flight toward the dawn, my last dawn in this new world where I had arrived a year, ten years, a century, before, accompanied by old Pedro who was searching for a free land, his parcel of happiness, the new world emancipated from the injustices, oppressions, and crimes of the old.

Oh, my dear old friend, you died in good hour, you were spared disappointment; all you would have known here—with different causes, with different clothing, with different ceremonies—were the same cruel powers you thought you had abandoned as you embarked with Venus, and with me, on that long-ago morning.

Hear me, Sire, hear me to the end, do not raise your hand, do not summon your guards, you must hear me: I speak in my love for the girl who succored me, I can speak only as she caresses me, love is my memory, my only memory, I know that now, for the minute we are separated, Sire, she and I, I shall return to the oblivion from which this woman's painted lips rescued me: she is my voice, my guide, in both worlds, without her I forget everything because remembering is painful, only her love can give me the strength to resign myself to the pain of memory: in solitude I shall abandon myself forever to soothing oblivion; I do not wish to remember the old world from which I sailed, or the new one from which I have come . . .

I was fleeing along the causeway that joins the larger island of Mexico to the smaller island of Tlatelolco, when I saw walking toward me a group of naked youths, and in them I recognized the ten boys and ten girls who had led me from the volcano, and who spoke our tongue; they ran toward me, joy in their voices and expressions; and this was the first happy thing I had seen for a long time, contrasting violently with the melancholy silence of the city of the lagoon. They embraced me, they kissed me, but they said nothing explicit beyond the simple expressions of pleasure at meeting me.

I did not want to ask them why they had abandoned me to those terrible solitary encounters with the inhabitants of the palace; I must save my penultimate question for a moment I knew was near, and it must not be asked of them; they—my uncertain judgment and my sure heart told me—would give the final answer.

I let myself be led along the causeway toward the island of Tlatelolco; we entered a large, very clean, and deserted plaza surrounded by walls of red stone. In the plaza were a single low pyramid and several temples; a great silence reigned over all. The dawn was a pearl in the heavens. In the center of the immense plaza stood a wicker basket.

I thought I recognized it; I hurried forward, followed by the twenty young people; there was a man within it; I looked at him; I fell to my knees before him, because of a strange sacred compulsion as well as the desire to look into his face and hear his voice close to mine.

It was the ancient of memories, the same old man, guardian of the most ancient fables, who one day spoke to me in a dank chamber in the pyramid in the jungle and then died of terror when he saw himself in my mirror, who was dragged to the summit of the temple and there, I believed then, devoured by vultures.

And as before, he said to me now, but speaking our Castilian tongue: "Welcome, my brother. We have awaited you."

I touched him with a trembling hand; he smiled; he was not a phantom. Was this old man, in truth, the owner of the secrets of this land, of all lands? But what did he know? He was welcoming me on the day of my flight: the last day of my life in the new world, at the end of the five days of memory that he himself—I was sure of it now—had granted me as an exceptional gift; five days separate from the twenty days he had forbidden to my memory, twenty days, and on this morning I still did not know whether they had been lived in the oblivion of what happened between each of the five remembered days or, as the mirrors of the staff told me, were still to be lived in an uncertain future.

The sun's rays appeared over the walls and low summits of the pyramids of this plaza, and this was my true question—as I rejected the most immediate, closest questions, those I wished at that instant to ask on impulse, who are you, old man?, did you die of terror when I showed you your true face?, were you not fodder for vultures, worms, and snakes in the thick jungle where we abandoned your corpse? Instead, my question was this:

"My lord: Have I already lived the twenty forgotten days, or am I still to live them? For now I know they were, or they will be, days of death, pain, and blood, and I fear alike having lived them yesterday or living them tomorrow."

The ancient with the mottled skull and tufts of white hair smiled a toothless smile. "You are welcome, my brother. We have awaited you. We shall always await you. You have been here before. You do not remember. What does it matter? You have been in many places, and you do not remember. How far my eyes can see. How far beyond this land born from burning seas, which rises from its decaying and abundant coast, ascends through perfumed valleys of fruit, and ends in a desert of stone and fire. I know the many cities you have founded. Beside rivers. Beside seas. In the motionless center of the deserts. Discover who founded those distant and proximate cities and always you will discover yourself, forgotten by yourself. Plumed Serpent you were called in this part of the world. You bore other names in the lands of clay and date palms, of deltas and flood tides, of vineyards and she-wolves. You were born between two rivers. You were suckled on the milk of beasts. You grew to manhood beside the blue and white father of waters. You dreamed beneath a tree. You perished on a hilltop, and were born again. You were always the first teacher, he who planted the seed, he who tilled the land, he who worked the metal, he who predicated love among men. He who spoke. He who wrote. And always you were accompanied by an enemy brother, a double, a shadow, a man who wanted for himself what you wanted for everyone: the fruit of labor, and the voice of men.'' The ancient's long bony finger emerged from the cotton that warmed him, and he pointed toward one of the entrances to the plaza of Tlatelolco.

"You will always fail. You will always return. You will fail again. You will not allow yourself to be vanquished. You know the original order of man's life because you founded it, with men, who were not born to devour one another like beasts but to live in accord with the teachings of the dawn of day, your teachings.''

"I killed him with my own hands; I, too, am a murderer.''

"No, it is merely that you have once again killed your enemy brother. He who struggles against you. He who struggles within you. That dark twin will be reborn in you, and you will continue to struggle against him. And he will be reborn here. Once again we shall suffer beneath his yoke. Once again we shall await your return to kill him.''

"My lord: you are speaking of a fatality without end, circular and eternal. Will it never be resolved with the definitive triumph of one of the two: my double or me?''

"Never. Because what you represent will live only if it is denied, attacked, sequestered in a palace or a prison or a temple. For if your kingdom could be established without opposition it would soon be converted into a kingdom identical to the one you combat. Your goodness, my son, is kept alive only because your double refutes it.''

"And it will never be resolved?''

"Never, my brother, my son, never. Your destiny is to be pursued. To struggle. To be defeated. To be reborn from your defeat. To return. To speak. To remind men of what they have forgotten. To reign for an instant. To be defeated again by the forces of the world. To flee. To return. To remember. An endless labor. The most painful of all labors. Freedom is the name of your task. One word represented by many men.''

"Like me, always defeated, my lord?''

"Look, my brother, my son. Look . . .''

The plaza of Tlatelolco was teeming with life, activity, sounds, music, a thousand small and pleasurable tasks: some were shaping clay with their hands or on a potter's wheel, some were weaving hemp, some dancing and singing; silversmiths, with dexterity and finesse, were casting silver toys: a monkey with moving head and feet that held in its hand a spindle that seemed to spin, or an apple it seemed to eat; patient workers were sorting and adjusting feathers, examining them minutely to see whether they fitted better with the grain, against the grain, or across the grain, on the right side or the reverse, perfectly fashioning a feather animal or tree or rose; children were seated at the feet of aged teachers; women suckled their babes, others were cooking the food of the land, flesh of the doe or buck, rabbit, gopher, all wrapped in the bland little cakes of bread that have the taste of smoke; scribes and poets were speaking loudly or in calm tones of friendship, of the brevity of life, the delight of love, the pleasure of flowers; their voices filled my ears, and all about me that morning, my last morning, I heard their words:

"My flowers will never cease . . ."
"My song will never cease . . ."
"I raise it . . ."
"We, too, raise new songs here . . ."
"Also, new flowers are in our hands . . ."
"With them delight the assemblage of our friends . . ."
"With them dissipate the sadness of our hearts . . ."
"I gather your songs; I string them like emeralds . . ."
"Adorn yourself with them . . ."
"On this earth they are your only riches . . ."
"Will my heart fade away, solitary as the perishing flowers?"
"Will my name one day be nothing?"
"At least, flowers; at least, songs . . ."

The old man watched me looking and listening. And when at last I again looked at him, I was possessed by conflicting sensations of happiness and sadness.

He asked: "Do you understand?"

"Yes."

Then the ancient of memory seized my hand and leaned close to me, and his words were like carved air, written air: "You gave the word to all men, brother. And your enemy will always feel threatened because of fear of the word all men possess. He himself a prisoner. Enclosed in his palace. Imagining there is no voice but his own. Lord of the Great Voice! Hear the voices of all those in this plaza. Know that you are more defeated than all your victims."

He addressed himself to the midday sun. It had risen above the great plaza of life and death, freedom and slavery, unending struggle, and as its light bathed each of these men and women and children who with hands and arms and voices and feet and eyes were keeping something precious present and alive—cheerful labor, friendly wisdom, bodily pleasure, secret hope—a different light, born perhaps of them, bathed me within, illuminated my blood and my bones, rose to my eyes and filled them with luminous tears.

"Have I or shall I live what I now know, my lord?"

"You have and you will live it. Why would you be removed from the conflict of all men, past or future?"

"I shall not forget your words."

"You will not suffer if you believe, as I, that the unity I promised will be born of encounter, of the combat and combination of the two worlds. Of the collapse of the walls that separate us."

"I believed that you lied. In your world I had experienced only signs of a petrified duality."

"We are three, we shall always be three. Life. Death. And the memory that blends them into a single flower of three petals."

"Yesterday?"

"Now."

"Tomorrow?"

"The present that never ceased to be the past and is now the future. Then we shall, as I promised you, reunite with our mother the earth. We shall be one with her and we shall endure all the battles of history, the victory of your defeat, and the defeat of the victorious."

All times were joined in the eyes of the ancient.

I knew it, but I could not read them.

He pressed my hand. "Now go with your friends. They will guide you on your return."

He dropped my hand and sank into his basket of cotton, covering his face with his hands.

For the last time, muffled, the voice of that ancient I had believed forever dead was reborn, muffled by cotton, the basket, the sun, his hands:

"Let no one deceive you, ancient brother, newborn son. Freedom was the shore that man first trod. Paradise was the name of that freedom. Inch by inch, we lost it. Inch by inch, we shall regain it. Let no one deceive you, son, brother. You will never return to this shore. Never again will there be the absolute freedom we knew before the first death. But there will be freedom in spite of death. It can be named. And sung. And loved. And dreamed. And desired. Fight for it. You will be defeated. This is the victory I offer you in freedom's name."

A fearful noise followed these words. The sky filled with clouds. A muddy rain fell upon the plaza. My young companions surrounded me, as if they wished to protect me. They prevented me from seeing what was happening, they forced me to turn around:

"Do not look back . . ."

"Quickly, run . . ."

"The boat awaits you . . ."

I ran with them toward the causeway, while behind us the detonations continued beneath the rain, the shouting at first was stronger than the detonations, then quieter than the dark and persistent rain.

Silence triumphed.

And from the silence arose a new chorus of voices which pursued us as we ran along the causeway:

"The weeping spreads . . ."

"Teardrops fall here in Tlatelolco . . ."

"Where are we going? Oh, friends!"

"Smoke is rising . . ."

"Mist is spreading . . ."

"Water has become bitter; food, rancid . . ."

"Worms pullulate in streets and plazas . . ."

"Brains are splattered on the walls . . ."

"The waters run red . . ."

"Our water is foul, and salty . . ."

"Our birthright is a mesh of holes . . ."

"They place a price upon us . . ."

"A price on youth, on priesthood, on the child and the maiden . . ."

"Weep, my friends . . ."

We stopped beside a heavy boat moored to a stele and built of broad planks bound together with the bodies of serpents.

For the last time I looked at the outlines of the city. Night was falling precipitously, summoned early by the pitch-black clouds, the rain, and whirlwinds of dust that struggled against it, unquelled by the storm: a city bathed in darkness, I did not recognize its new and spectral face: its towers were taller and their infinite windows, all of mirrors, like the staff of the flayed god, glittered in the storm, its walls were cracked and crowned with flickering lights, red, white, blue, green, dust-covered lights that winked and signaled with regularity, unaffected by the fury of the elements, tenacious as the fires I had seen upon my arrival, fires the water had merely fanned.

I heard the tolling of deep bells, an impatient roaring, not merely the solitary sound of the drum and the conch, but of thousands and thousands of hoarse whistles, as if the city were invaded by an army of frogs; great was the croaking, but becoming silent beneath the pestilent gray scum overspreading the landscape, veiling the nearby volcanoes, slowly, heavily, asphyxiatingly veiling the entire valley: a shroud fell over Mexico and Tlatelolco.

It was night. It was also an imitation of night.

NIGHT OF THE RETURN

In spite of everything, conquering this avalanche of shadows, as hidden as a pin in a bog, I saw shining, reborn, distant, but at the level of my gaze, the evening star, illuminating the final night of the vast unknown of this land. Now, at last, I would know.

The serpent boat awaited me. My twenty young friends had stopped with me on the causeway between Mexico and Tlatelolco to contemplate the night of the city. One of them was untying the ropes that moored the boat to a low stone stele. A tense melancholy hovered over our group. It was the moment to say goodbye, but until this moment these youths and I had said nothing, or almost nothing. Nonetheless, I said to myself, smiling, they are the only ones here who speak the tongue of Castile, though with traces of the inhabitants of this land: sweet, singing, stripped of the brutal tones of our own accents; theirs, the trilling of birds; ours, the trampling of boots.

No, I thought immediately, disquieted, they are not the only ones; the ancient of memories, too, spoke to me in Castilian; he replied to my questions in that language . . . My questions. How many I had asked him, how many he had answered; why, if I had the right only to one question each day and another each night, why did he break that agreement in the center of the great plaza of Tlatelolco; why . . . ? The question escaped my lips before I could capture it, before thinking it might be the last I could ask: "Why is that ancient with whom I spoke in the plaza still alive? I swear it: I saw him die of fear one day, and be thrown to the vultures . . ."

The young people looked at one another. A new kind of gaze, stamped by water. I do not know how to explain it, Sire. I had not seen such gazes here before, although, remember, in my passage through this strange land I had seen many eyes of warring passions, terror and tenderness, friendship and hatred, veneration and vengeance, yes, but never such new glances, for the first time new, theirs and mine: who minted the face of the earth?, who made its field burn wordlessly?

One of the youths spoke. I understood him easily as I listened, what sadness and relief I felt: a youth, a boy, who did not speak in the name of the beginning, of legend, power, or tradition, but for himself, here, on this causeway beside the waters of the lagoon of Mexico. "I saw no one in that plaza."

"The old man," I murmured, frightened, "the old man in the basket . . ."

The youth shook his head. "No one. There was no one there but us."

An obscure question blazed in my body: "With whom was I speaking, then? Who answered my questions?"

Now it was a young girl who spoke: "You were talking to yourself. You asked questions. You answered them. We heard you."

If time is a hunter, in that instant I was pierced by its arrow, I fell, wounded, and the oath of my days in this land fell shattered beside me; I managed to stammer: "Then I have dreamed it all . . . Then none of it was true . . . Then I must awaken . . ."

"No, do not awaken," said a youth. "You must finish your voyage, you must return to your land . . ."

"And return here, again and again, to be defeated, always defeated, defeated by crime if I commit a crime when I return, defeated by criminals, if I return to punish them?"

My head was whirling, Señor, words tumbled from my lips, I no longer knew where I was or what day it was . . . I was dreaming. But if I dreamed, where was I dreaming?, how long had I been dreaming? Perhaps in that instant, dreaming that I was standing on the causeway beside a boat, surrounded by my twenty friends, I was sleeping placidly on old Pedro's ship, becalmed in the center of the Sargasso Sea; or perhaps I was dreaming it all, dizzied by the sea, in the center of the vortex that held us captive in the great ocean; or perhaps, truly—as I had then believed—I had emerged from the sea to step upon the beaches of death, and had remained there forever, imagining the phantoms of my life; I did not know, after all, whether perhaps everything was dreamed from the moment I was placed within the basket of the ancient of memory beneath the jungle sky, surrounded by bowers and deerskins, abandoned there with no company but my mirror, destined to dream and one day to awaken and see myself as ancient as the Lord of Memory; I did not know, I did not know in what moment I had ceased to live awake and begun to live asleep; but here we were, on the causeway that joined the islands of a lagoon in a non-existent place called Mexico, the place of the navel of the moon, they and I, I and they, those I had torn from the soil of death, the bones that had come to life when I clasped them to my breast, the most unreal, the most fantastic of all my dreams . . .

Was this, too, a lie?, were they also phantoms?

"We are here," a different girl spoke, simply. "In truth, we exist here."

And they spoke in turn:

"You must go."

"You are the only one who knows of us."

"This is your secret."

"You must not return."

"We shall hide."

"We shall disappear."

"They will not find us."

"They will not sacrifice us."

"We shall emerge when it is necessary."

"Tell no one about us."

"You need not return."

"We shall do what you promised."

"We shall act in your name."

"Do not worry."

"We are twenty."

"We shall live the days you do not remember in your name . . ."

"The days you lost . . ."

"The days you fear . . ."

"Twenty days . . ."

"We are twenty . . ."
"Ten men . . ."
"Ten women . . ."
"One for each of your forgotten and feared days . . ."
"All together . . ."
"Do not return . . ."
"They will not forgive you for it . . ."
"This has been your crime . . ."
"You gave us life . . ."
"They do not know that . . ."
"They do not believe we exist . . ."
"We shall surprise them . . ."
"We shall hide . . ."
"In the mountain . . ."
"In the desert . . ."
"In the jungle . . ."
"On the coast . . ."
"Among the ruins . . ."
"In forgotten villages . . ."
"Among the magueys, cultivating the fiber and the flowing sap . . ."
"Beside the bells . . ."
"Beneath the lash . . ."
"Within the mine . . ."
"In the trapiche, grinding the sugar cane . . ."
"In the dungeons, prisoners again . . ."
"In the milpas, working the corn . . ."
"In all the land . . ."
Did time have words, did it?, did space have hours, did it? What hour, what day was this? I implored them to tell me, that was my last question, Sire:
"What day is this? What hour is this?"
"A day."
"A man."
"A different day."
"A woman."
"Twenty days."
"Ten men."
"Ten women."
"What does it matter?"
"A day."
"The first morning of March."
"Dry earth."
"Black earth."
"The city falls."

"And we."
"A different day."
"The second night of October."
"Wet earth."
"Red earth."
"The city falls."
"And we."
"Twenty days."
"September."
"The rains are dying."
"July."
"Burning mornings, late storms."
"February."
"Whirling dust."
"March."
"The same plaza."
"Sun, the sun."
"October."
"The same plaza."
"Water, the water."
"Twenty days."
"Knife and cannon blast."
"Dogs growl."
"Blood runs."
"We have no weapons."
"Stones are lofted, sticks, and shafts."
"Many men."
"On horseback."
"A man."
"Murdered."
"The same plaza."
"Odor of dust."
"Tattered standards."
"A people."
"Enslaved."
"A land."
"Humiliated."
"And we."
"The city dies."
"The city is reborn."
"They kill us."
"We are reborn."
"Go on your way."
"Do not return."
"We shall be the twenty days of your dark destiny."

"We shall live them for you."

"My question," I implored. "My final question . . ."

"Look at the sky: every star has its time."

"All those times live side by side, in the same sky."

"There is a different time."

"Will you learn to measure it?"

"All times live within a single dead space."

"There history ends."

"History? This one, mine?, the history of many?, which history? I could not ask; I could not answer . . . Once again, these young people born of my embrace spoke as if they could divine my thoughts, as if they were I, multiplied, crossbred, mixed with everything I had seen or touched here. Humankind stood before me on the causeway, beside the lagoon, naked and proud, they spoke in their plural voices.

"The new land gave life to Pedro; in that life your friend culminated his entire existence, his dreams, his sufferings, and his labors. His life was worthwhile. The new world gave him his life, completed."

"Pedro gave his life for you."

"You gave the scissors."

"They gave you gold."

"You gave your labor."

"They gave you memory."

"You gave them a mirror."

"They gave you the gift of their deaths."

"You responded with love: to them, already dead; to a woman, still living."

"She gave you your days."

"The five days of the sun offered you twenty days of shadows."

"The twenty days of the smoking mirror offered you your double."

"Your double offered you his kingdom."

"You exchanged power for the woman."

"The woman gave you wisdom."

"You gave us our lives."

"We give you freedom."

"Can you make a greater offering?"

"You cannot."

"The story has ended."

"To whom will you give your lives?" I asked.

"To the new land that gave life to Pedro."

They embraced me.

They kissed me.

I climbed into the boat.

A youth freed it from its moorings.

The wind and the night drew me far from the causeway. I could no longer see my twenty young friends, or imagine their destinies during the twenty days they would live on my behalf; but they would be days of blood, crime, and pain, that was all I knew, I could understand nothing more of what they told me. I felt impoverished, and alone: I had lost everything, the friendship of old Pedro, the fraternal love of the people of the jungle, the love of the Lady of the Butterflies; I had gained nothing except what I wished to forget: the sacrifice and oppression incarnate in the smoking shadow that dwelt within me, and which, perhaps, I had not truly killed with my scissors. Dizzy, I clung to the single mast of this ship of serpents and saw that I was skimming rapidly across the lagoon of Mexico. But behind me I was leaving not a wake in water but a whirlwind of dust; at the contact of the keel, Sire, the lagoon was turning into earth, the water lay only before me, my stern trailed dust behind it.

I trembled: I was sailing toward a convulsed center where water and dust met, where water was dust, and dust, water; a whirlpool identical to the one I had known in the voyage to these lands, an upside-down spiral of stars, a suction of broken teeth and invisible tongues and a sound of rattles: the mouth of the serpent, I told myself, clinging to the fragile mast of my boat, the great serpent of dust and water of the Mexican lagoon is swallowing me, its coils contracting, everything is returning to the mortal embrace of the great skin spotted by the fire of creation, I closed my eyes, I fell into the pit, I dreamed I was surrounded by liquid walls, cascades of dust, and that, as in the ocean sea, the sky was quickly receding from view, I opened my eyes, Sire, and found that such was not the case, rather, my boat and I, with a movement that cannot be described, were moving in every direction, captive upon a vast subterranean river, or plowing an enormous land beneath the sea.

We were moving in every direction, so that if this was descent it was also ascent; if the boat raced to the right, my rebellious senses indicated it also danced toward the left; in one space and one time my final voyage was leading me, simultaneously, to all places and all moments: in them I found myself, hallucinated, in the center of everything that exists, a center of flaming flowers, yes, but the center was also a desert-like north, a rain of hail, a dominion of owls, a midnight at once black and white; and being in the north, I was at the same time in the south, a blue midday, a flock of parrots, fecund water that rose in warm mists to bathe the moon at its apogee; and being both in the north and the south, I was in the west, a tremulous red dusk, timorous before the nearby darkness, and I was in the east, in the heart of the mountain, on the crest of the dawn, the announcement of the morning star, and being in each of the points of the compass—and still in the center of it all—I was also above the north, watching the fire that spread from the center of the earth to the most distant star of the Pole, but beneath the north, also, in the midst of a cold and cutting storm of ice and knives;

and above the south, in the eye of its deluge, but below it also, in a thick region of repugnant forgetfulness and drunkenness; and being at the occident, I was at the same time above it, witness to the feared extinction of the sun, and beneath, looking for the last time at the forbidding animal with twisted paws that devoured it; and being at the east, I was beneath it, seeing how all hidden things emerged from the earth, how plants began to germinate, rivers to flow, beasts to couple, and men to be born, and above the orient of my simultaneous vision of all things, Venus was gleaming within reach of my hand, near my extended hand, and as at the beginning of my story, I called her morning star, night's last glimmer, but also its perpetuation in the dawn's clear light, the sailor's guide: I repeated that name, the same name, the only name, the name of my destination, go where I go, sailing away from port or in return, embarked victorious or vanquished, Venus, Venus; Vésperes—evening; Vísperas—eve; Víspero—evening star; Héspero—Venus; Hesperia—the Western Land; Hespérides—daughter of the west; España, Spain; España/Hespaña/Vespaña, name of the double star, twin of itself, constant dusk and dawn, silver stele that joins the old and the new worlds and carried me from one to the other borne on her fiery train, star of evening, star of dawn, Plumed Serpent, my name in the new world was the name of the old world; Quetzalcoatl, Venus, Hesperia, Spain, identical stars, dawn and dusk, mysterious union, indecipherable enigma, but cipher for two bodies, two lands, cipher for a terrible encounter.

I tore my mirror from my doublet and turned it toward the star, to capture her, to hold in my mirror all the instants and spaces of my voyage toward the origin of my voyage: at hand, in my hand, the burning star, Venus, Hesperia, Spain, Plumed Serpent, Smoking Mirror: a single name, I clung to the fire of the trapped star, I climbed the mast to be closer to her, fire touched the tip, it burst into flame, St. Elmo's fire, the rough slate-gray sea, heaving tortuously, sky veiled beneath scintillating light, my solitary light in flames, a mirror, a beacon, a coast, my serpent boat burst upon the rocks, I fell from the mast, falling backward, my eyes fast on the fire on the tip of the mast, the fugitive star, restored night, upside-down sky, a single place, no longer all places, a single time, no longer all times, I fell, returned . . .

I was awakened, Sire, by the tattooed lips of a woman dressed as a page.

I was lying face down upon the beach, arms flung wide in a cross.

III

THE NEXT

WORLD

LOVE OF WATER

"Why is everything so still?"

La Señora would spend long hours alone in her bedchamber, her only company that of the creature she had fashioned—inanimate, impervious to all rituals, deaf to all convocations; seated upon fine carpets and cushions and cloths, toying distractedly with the sands of the floor of her rich Arabic bedchamber, she would not look at him, attentive only to the sound of water in the late afternoon outside her window on the high plain and the mountains, divining, listening, imagining the origin of the scant liquid sounds of that flat, dusty, quiet, inhospitable land: she listened intently: she could hear water flowing in the silence of the Castilian afternoon.

"Azucena, Lolilla, where are you?" How long the solitary hours. Where had everyone gone?

For an instant she imagined she had been abandoned, her only companion the creature born of her witchcraft. She imagined herself as the solitary mistress of the palace. Oh, then there would again be shepherds and songs and dances and baths and pleasures . . . hours falling like silver coins. Golden light: stone gilded by the setting sun; the cleft hoofs of goats upon the mountain; the cloven hoofs of bulls upon the plain; invisible water: dripping water in the dungeons, black drops trickling down the walls; water draining from the quarries, water coursing from the grumbling, snowy mountain; narrow, shallow rivers, water of stone; the nearby storm building in the east, distant thunder . . . water . . .

She did not look toward the figure lying upon her bed.

She gazed through the half-open window, sniffing the coming rain, the summer storm, water from the east, the great bath for the dirty land that forbade ablutions, the absorption by water of strength indispensable for war and sanctity and affliction; the increasing drumming of raindrops upon dry earth, on canvas tents of forges and taverns on the work site, on paving stones of the palace. Each drop: pleasure; she had asked nothing more; she had not solicited these love affairs, these diabolical pacts, these black arts: she had sought nothing more than a little indulgence of her senses.

Her head resting upon her closed fist, she dreamed of the East, the Indies, the Crusades; she was living in a castle at the time of the Crusades, discovering unknown pleasures, drop by drop, a rosary of pleasures; everything that is pleasure is foreign, it comes to us from afar, Mihail, Juan, the rosary, the rosary itself came from Syria, beads of the rosary of pleasure, rice, sugar, sesame, melon, lemon, orange, peach, artichoke: a rain of delectable spices, cinnamon, ginger, perfume; a solid sheet of cotton, satin, damask, carpets; a rain shower of new colors, indigo, carmine, lilac.

"Everything that hangs, that one can taste or smell, comes from very far away."

Water, love of water; seas, oceans, rivers, sails and rudders, pitch and distant swallows, oars and anchors, sail, sail far from here to the lands of pleasure, far from the rivers of my English fogs and Spanish shadows, far, far away; here pleasure is evil, phantoms are born of fog and shadow; lands of the sun where pleasure is good, it is to you I long to travel, to the East, to the Indies; who will carry me there? Let us go south, Mihail, to Andalusia, to Cádiz, we shall make love upon the sea, you should never have come here, you should have remained beside the sea . . . love of water . . .

She drank deeply from her water pitcher, then poured what was left upon the sand, as if she wished to create a beach, a shore, a place where she might sail away from the prison of her bedchamber of sands and tiles and cushions; and where she had emptied the pitcher, in the center of the damp stain spreading across the sand, something stirred, as if the sand were germinating, a plant being born from this sterility, a bud, a seed of life, a caterpillar struggling from the cocoon of the damp sands, wet grains of sand, a homunculus, insignificant, diminutive, a living root bursting forth, baptized by the water she had drunk, convoked by water, a moist tuber, the mandrake, torn from the earth of death, born of the tears of a hanged man, of a man burned alive, the mandrake, at last I understand, torn from the burned earth beneath the ashes of Mihail-ben-Sama, Miguel-of-Life, ashes mixed with sand, the root of the mandrake, quickly, two cherries for his eyes: he shall see; a radish for a mouth: he shall speak; wheat, wheat sown upon the tiny head, I have none, bread, the crust of bread, bread crumbs upon his head: his hair shall grow, he shall see, he shall speak; he will tell me his secrets, he knows where the treasures are, little turnip, little man, you were here all the time, hidden in my own bedchamber, where did these sands come from?, oh, they must be the sands of death, ash, and dust collected from beneath all the racks, all the stakes where men have died, mandrake, weeping, mandrake, that they might give you life, drops of their tears, drops of their sperm, mandrake, for the hanged man, the burned man, the impaled man, mandrake, everyone knows, dies with his last erection . . .

How still it is. Where is everyone?

THE DECREE

The voice of the pilgrim was silent.

The music of the blind Aragonese beggar had ceased.

The curtains around El Señor's bed remained drawn, the sails that had brought the shipwrecked sailor to the high plains of Castile, led by a woman dressed as a page, and behind which he had recounted to El Señor his voyage and had divined El Señor's reactions—his trembling, his fear, his anger, his desire to interrupt the narration, to rise from the curule chair and call an end to this unwonted audience, to order all the court to return to their chambers, their cells, their towers—but not his desires: to be left alone with his mortification, then to ask Guzmán for ointments, brews, rings, and magic stones, then to ask Inés to return once again, one more night . . .

Trembling and panting, El Señor half rose to his feet. Though his legs were feeble, his face was a mask severe as stone, and his voice was muted thunder: "Be you hereby warned that it will in no manner be allowed that any person write of the superstitions and the way of life you have heard recounted here, nor allowed that they be repeated by any tongue, for such would be contrary to the service of God Our Lord and our . . ."

And collapsing again onto the curule chair, he joined his hands, cracked his fingers, and added, weighing each word: "We hereby decree . . . that a . . . new . . . world . . . does not . . . exist . . ."

He gazed into the silence around him. With a disdainful flick of his hand, he dismissed the company.

With his own imperious gesture, Guzmán ripped back, one by one, the curtains that veiled the bed's three occupants. "And what, Sire, will you do with the bearers of this news?"

"Guards . . . halberdiers . . . take them into custody . . . place them . . . in the deepest dungeon . . ."

"Torture, surely, Señor; they have not told everything they know . . ."

"Let no one touch them. Guard them zealously. Later I shall speak with them. Not now, Guzmán, I want everyone to leave; you, too; my fatigue is great; be off, all of you, be off!"

RUMORS

Alguaciles and chaplains, monks and stewards, Julián and Toribio, Guzmán and the Comendador, the halberdiers taking charge of the three prisoners, the young pilgrim, the blind flautist, the girl with the tattooed lips dressed as a page, the nuns fluttering behind the iron latticework, the Bishop and his companion, the monk of the order of St. Augustine, the scrubbing girls hidden behind the columns, the huntsmen, Guzmán's men, all hurrying from the chapel, murmuring, lost in amazement, doubt, mockery, deafness, credulity, incomprehension, fear, indifference, hurrying swiftly from the vicinity of El Señor's bedchamber, could you hear anything?, I couldn't, and you?, nor I, what did they say?, nothing, pure fantasy, what did they say?, nothing, pure lies, lands of gold, lands of idols, beaches of pearls, blood, sacrifices, infidels, teach them, truth, the Gospel, barbaric nations, exterminate them, blood and fire, idolaters, by the handfuls, dreams, lies, not one shred of proof, they didn't bring even one grain of gold with them, fucking, they were fucking, two men, two sodomites, no, one was a woman in disguise, and one an old man, a flautist, and one a young man, a sailor, and they were all in one bed together, fucking, Babylon, take your pleasure and you'll die an old man, quarreling and loving make all men equal, madmen, lies, save us, God, from madmen in dangerous straits, but in this palace, eh? fantasies, fairy treasure, God, Our Father, what happened, Mother Milagros?, nothing, daughters, nothing, still another challenge to the Faith, still another, always a challenge, Christianity bleeds from battling against the Infidel, the Body of Christ, the rack of the cross, the redemption of sins, praise, praise, praise be, scurrying like little mice among the sumptuous tombs of the ancestors, trampling unawares over the bulk that is the mutilated body of the Queen called the Mad Lady, avoiding the forbidden stairway that leads to the plain, avoiding the strange painting brought, it is said, from Orvieto, abandoning the icy chapel to its solitary inhabitants, the corpse of the Mad Lady, Don Juan, a statue of himself, resting upon a tomb, and inside another sepulcher, by his own choice, the Idiot Prince, and close to him, hidden, containing her rage, the whorish, farting dwarf, and again through tunnels and courtyards, galleries and kitchens, stables and passageways, bedchambers and dungeons, the rumor: "There is a new world beyond the sea"

"What proof is there? None. It's a tangled tale we've heard, pure fable, dream, imagination, delirium, danger, for that devil's-spawn pilgrim is in league with the other two, his twins, and one of them has planted his ass in La Señora's bedchamber, and the third one is plotting with that crowd of rebels in the work sheds." "Be calm, Don Guzmán, drink up. Thank you for bringing me to these cool and shady mews, and thank you, especially, for notifying me of my elevation to the rank of Comendador. It is a pleasure for me to celebrate it here with you in this place where men's work is done rather than in some site of leisure and luxury, for this place is more fitting to our purposes, that men rise in the world by virtue of their merit—never forgetting our humble origins and hard times, isn't that right, Chief Huntsman?'' "But I, Guzmán, I was born high.'' "That's worse, much worse. If you've come down in the world, it's with even greater energy you must strive to ascend.''

"There's a new world on the other side of the sea''

nonononono, Spain is Spain, not an inch of land exists outside of Spain, it's all here, all here contained within my palace, oh, help me, my Lord, God, and True Man, see me once again prostrate before your altar of mysteries, hear me this time, answer me this time, assure me that everything that exists in the material and the spiritual world is already contained here within my palace, my reason for living, the duplication of everything that exists enclosed here with me forever, I, the last I, with no descendants, here in this reduced space with everything within reach of my hand, everything, everything, not in a limitless, inaccessible, and multiple expanse, the world is trickling through my fingers, the brief life, eternal glory, unchanging world, here there is no room for even one additional idea, one terror, one joy, one challenge, everything is here, everything is enclosed within the walls of my mausoleum, luxury is here, mourning, the war of the soul, and here is art, Brother Julián, science, Brother Toribio, power, Guzmán, honor, my mother, perversion, game, and pleasure, my Señora, love, Inés, and your own plan of eternal well-being and human redemption, Christ Saviour, here, solid, fixed, contained, comprehensible, distilled in their final essences, here good, evil, and the final judgment of everything that exists, do I not thus, for my own reasons, advance your work?, does not everything here advance your work?, until the very end, until with the consummation of all things we too are consumed and my scheme complete, we shall be the only ones, the last ones, we shall have had all, and the final act will take place on this stage so that everything finally is resolved, comprehended, so ambition and war, lust, doubt, offense, and crime disappear, so it be known here, once and for all, which will be condemned and which saved, which is the face of man and which the divine face, one life, my God, one entire life dedicated to lessening the haste, fatigue, and madness of men, enclosing them all here, giving them every opportunity until there are no opportunities left, and thus hastening the last event of the world, your sovereign judgment, the clarification of all mysteries, the certainty that we have achieved your kingdom in Heaven, forever, for the earth shall have ceased to exist, and never again will there be played out upon it the mockery and tragedy of man, there will be only Heaven and Hell, without the accursed intermediary step of life on earth, and this will be so because no one can offer a gift surpassing that of the end of everything, the offering we make of everything that exists, exists for the last time, in order that it all end here with me, with us, and not in the broad and terrifying chance of a new world where everything can begin all over again . . . nononono . . .

"A new world exists"

"Why not, Brother Julián? If all the bodies in the heavens are spheres, the earth will be no exception, and it is possible that it traces a circle from East to West, from the setting to the rising sun, always returning to the original point of departure." "I understand you, Brother Toribio, it is other things that frighten me, not that." "What things?" "If the new world described by that youth and the new universe you describe are real, then they are immense, and fatally diminish the stature of man and of the God who created him." "God does not need to be rewarded, or excused, or aggrandized, Julián, for if there is a God, He is All." "But man, Toribio, man . . ." "Now it is up to us to glorify man and instill pride in him through the art and philosophy and science of man; the new matter and space will not diminish us, Brother, they will not conquer us." "The soul, Toribio . . ." "Pride, Julián, do not fear human pride." "Our soul is escaping from us, dribbling away, hurry, we must stanch the flow . . ."

"Beyond the ocean"

"I'm losing control of things, chance is unraveling all my projects, how was I to foresee what that sailor was going to tell us?, what effect will it have upon the soul of El Señor?, proof, proof, I need proof . . ." "A feather mask?" "Bah, this youth has spoken of fabulous riches, of chambers lined with gold and silver, of rich ornaments, but I have yet to see with my own eyes the tiniest pip of gold, the darkest and most misshapen pearl, nothing, he has brought nothing with him, not the least proof, nothing but a small mirror, a pair of scissors, and a mask such as any Eastern artisan might fabricate . . . Nothing! I do not believe . . ."

"Exists"

"Gold palaces, jade temples, bronze earrings, you say, Lolilla?" "Yes, my mistress, and beaches where pearls grow, and everything the lowest scrubbing girls like ourselves or the most exalted Ladies like Your Highness could dream of." "Oh, Lolilla, Azucena, this afternoon I dreamed how pleasure always comes to me from afar; everything that is pleasurable has come to us from the East, there was nothing here before; what pleasures these new lands must hold! You say a blond youth with a cross upon his back and six toes on each foot has been there? Oh, my splendid scrubbing maids, there are three different—although identical—men; oh, Don Juan, oh, my very own, I know where to seek you, you are not unique, I told you, you can never escape from me, I shall always find you again, oh, my true master, Mus, this is how you reward me, by revealing to me the new land and its pleasures, the new world from whence came my lover, my lovers, and the ardent cinnamon and juicy orange and soft damask, oh, my tiny man, my mandrake, this is how you manifest yourself, thus you first reveal to me the place of treasures, you are faithful to your legend, look at him, Azucena, Lolilla, look what was buried in my sand." "Ay, a snake!" "No, its antidote: the mandrake." "Ay, the sticky turnip, the slobbery root!" "No, the tiny man of secrets; see how the face is coming to life; the cherries are becoming eyes; the bread, hair; the radish, a mouth; he appeared, and I received the news of the new land and its treasures; everything is in accord; the walls of my prison are crumbling; the road to the Indies, the return to the Orient, is opening, oh, what a dream, oh, what mad joy, oh, let my feet touch those distant shores where all men are like you, Juan, for if the three of you are identical, then all the men of the new world must be the same, and my pleasure will know no end . . ."

"A world"

"Arise, Sire, from that unseemly posture, for this is not the moment for penitence and plaint, but for action that will save men's souls; what an urgent task the Redeemer has entrusted to us, He who died to redeem our souls, there is much to do if we are to carry the light of the Gospel to the afflicted nations of which this young pilgrim, if he speaks the truth, has told us." "Who are you, for God's sake? Tell me, Señor Bishop, who is this man accompanying you? I have never seen him before, and I wish to see nothing new here, neither person nor thing, least of all this creature you have brought into my presence, a devil, a demon, the Antichrist: you must recognize him, my sweet Jesus told me, you must recognize him, for your life is bound up in his, and I believe that this is he." "Calm yourself, Señor, calm yourself, this is the Inquisitor of Teruel." "A devil, I tell you, look at his red eyes, see how his flesh clings to his bones, his skin is bone, his face is a skull." "Sire, I owe allegiance to you and to my order, that of St. Augustine; I have been a professor of theology, a defender of the faith, an enemy of heresies, and for these reasons I have succeeded the former Inquisitor of Teruel; I followed with admiration your admirable conduct as you prepared your astute trap for the heresiarchs of your domains, delivering them into your father's hands, may he rest in glory, after endangering your own life by joining with them; I celebrated your zeal in the campaigns against the pertinacious Cathari, the wily Waldenses, and their deformed stepchildren of the North, the Flemish Adamites; great and good accomplishments all, but even greater had you but made use of your natural ally, the ecclesiastical arm of power: error is still not eradicated in Europe, and now you find yourself facing yet another gigantic undertaking: that of evangelizing the savage nations of this new world, if it exists, bringing to them the light of the Faith, and converting them for Christ the King, and having done that, the no less awesome task of extirpating pagan idolatry and protecting the new Faith, our Faith, against the dangers of a reemergence of barbaric and heinous behavior, like that exposed here today." "Yes, yes, I have always so stated, I have always so sworn: war against idolatry, I never doubted that." "One would say, Sire, that you had doubted something." "Nononono." "Arise, Sire, take my hands, look with me at the Sweet Jesus upon the altar of the Eucharist, and with me consider how your obligations are now multiplied." "Nononono." "For if the new world exists you must take it for yourself, your fortune, and your Faith." "Nononono." "And if this world and that world are to be governed, the same rigorous law must pertain to all men, there and here; there must not be, either here or there, even one vassal, no matter how independent of your power, who escapes immediate subjection, who is not subject to your mandates, your censures, your taxes, and your prisons; regard, Señor, with what harmony God's ways are manifested: you may subject all dissidents with one blow, the laws against Moors and Jews extended against idolaters, and the laws against idolaters applied equally to Moors and Jews; sons must pay for the sins of their fathers, for did not the blood of our crucified Lord stain forever the blood of His executioners?, and let the accuser speak in secret, for must he who works in the name of God be held to account for his actions?, nor shall accuser and accused ever confront one another, for would the common thief confront the Supreme Maker?, nor shall the names of witnesses be made public, for who would confuse those who sell their soul to the Devil with those who sell themselves to God?; and thus, investigate everyone, until every man fear to speak or listen to another; let all intellect serve the Faith; and finally, both here and there, impose total silence upon every man, for through the least chink of science or poetry slips heterodoxy, error, the poison of the Jew, the Arab, and the idolater. Sire: do as you will with the riches these new territories hold. But do so in the name of the Faith, for if not, you shall have gained the world but lost your soul, and what profiteth it a man to have gained the world . . ."

"New"

"Oh, Señor Don Guzmán, doubt is excellent when it is a question of securing what we already possess, but it can be fatal if it impedes us in pursuit of what we seek." "Are you out of your mind? Have you swallowed that pack of lies?" "No, but I shall have the prudence, with no illusions, to submit everything I have heard to the harshest test: the same proof that you demand; but you must see things in my manner, Don Guzmán; if the new world does not exist, we shall have lost nothing; but if it does, by chance, exist, we have everything to gain; oh, my dear friend; I cannot ever sleep again in peace for thinking that the riches recounted by that young voyager may exist, and may lie there for centuries, wasted, unless my hand take them and turn them to their true purpose, which is not the adornment of idols, but commerce, the arts, prosperity, change . . . Did you notice how naïvely those natives exchanged their jewels for a mirror or a pair of scissors? Oh, Don Guzmán: these ancient eyes and these feeble ears have never seen or heard of better business . . .''

"Beyond"

"Azucena, Lolilla, I tell you that everything that hangs, that tastes and smells comes from another place, even the rosary of our devotions, which comes from Syria, oh, I shall have it bead by bead, I shall have everything, guided by my homunculus, away from here, far from this accursed cloister of death, I shall be reborn, I shall live, I who have longed for a garden of jasmine and mosques, I who asked only that the shepherds return beneath my window with their flutes and flocks, I who came from misty England in search of the land of the sun and its orange trees and instead found myself on a plain of weeds, my flesh pierced by nettles and thistles, now I shall have the greatest garden in the world at my feet, the free land, the new land, without the burdens and crimes and prohibitions of this accursed plain to which my English aunt and uncle sent me, oh, Don Juan, pleasure will be for everyone or no one, and in the free land woman, to be woman, need not sell her soul to the Devil, oh, I shall beat the Devil at his own game, I shall sell my soul for the second time, he cannot keep his records straight, for so great is his desire to make himself master of souls that he buys them once and twice and a thousand times, I shall deceive the horned and tailed one himself, for if after it is all over I am condemned, what do I lose, my dear scrubbing maids?, and if in deceiving him I win, I win nothing less than a second chance: a second life, in the second land; oh, my most cherished scrubbing lasses, what happiness you have brought me." "Mistress, mistress, remember that the Devil may refuse to come in spite of your potions and spells and fancy words; we have tried everything and nothing happens; where is the Devil? Surely he's not this little bit of a man, this slobbering root that inspires only disgust, not fear, and who would be lucky not to end up as a partner for that clown of a Barbarica." "But I know, Azucena, Lolilla, I know; now I know, now I know where the Devil is . . ."

"The ocean"

be off, be off, far from my chapel, my cocoon, let them take everything, the palace, the servants, the land, everything except this place, my dead, my stairway, my painting, my bedchamber, my nest, my anguish, exterminate idolatry, yes, I promised that, I dictated that to Guzmán, and what is written exists, exists permanently, but how was I to know that there were still more pagans in the world?, the world was closed, its frontiers circumscribed, fenced in, conquered, the heretics and idolaters known, yes, let the idolaters die by my hand and I shall be granted the pardon I bestowed upon the heretics, true pardon, not for my transitory acts on the fields of Flanders, but for my eternal words in this final cloister, who will recall even a single act that has not been recorded?, will the need to exterminate idolaters in the new world be the price for pardoning heretics in the old?, but that Augustinian, that man with the face like a skull, has told me just the opposite, the same law for everyone, extermination for everyone, Jews, Arabs, idolaters, heretics, and if not that, then must it be precisely the opposite?, pardon for everyone, those there and those here?, oh, nonono, I shall save nothing that way if the new world exists, it must be destroyed, for never have I heard of anything that so ferociously mocks my world, a world, that youth said, a world where the natural order must be re-created each day, for its life depends upon the sun and the night and sacrifice, a world that dies with each dusk and which must be re-created with each dawn, nononono, the goal of my world is to be forever fixed, that it may be forever regulated by power, crime, inheritance, my world equal to my palace, the new world the most dissimilar world possible, that world incomprehensible, proliferating, flower of a day, death every night, resurrection every morning, the very thing I saw in the mirror as I ascended the stairway, everything changing, nothing dying completely, nothing expended, everything resurrected, transformed, everything nourished from every other thing, extinction impossible, everything repeated, oh, for all my theorems, all my philosophy, I would be naked, defeated, truly defeated, for everything I offer to the world to force the world to say I cannot repay you, you have won, your obliteration is my defeat, I continue to live but you have succeeded in obliterating your presence, you have killed me, for as you die I die because of you, for as you die I can summon nothing to occupy your place, all that is nothing if now some contemptible boy offers me an entire world, a new world, oh, my God, with what can I repay such an offering?, what could I give in return for such a gift?, with what could I fill the space of the new world?, how many crimes, loves, anxieties, battles, persecutions, dreams, and nightmares would I have to suffer before again being able to reach this trembling needle point of concentration that constitutes my entire existence?, oh, Lord who hears me, tell me, finally, the truth, if I conquer the new world, will I not be the conquered, not it?

"From the other side"

"Since man has observed the order of the heavens, Toribio, when they move, where they move, to what degree, and what that movement produces, could you deny that man, if I may put it this way, that man possesses a genius comparable to that of the Creator of the heavens?"

"No, Julián, I would merely say that in some manner man could fabricate heavens if he could but obtain the divine instruments and materials." "Well, I would be content if I could fabricate a new world using human materials." "Do not doubt it could be done, my brother, for anything is possible; nothing must be rejected; nature, and in particular human nature, encompasses each and every level of existence, from the divine to the diabolic, from the bestial to the mystic; nothing is beyond belief; nothing is beyond possibility; the only possibilities we deny are the possibilities we do not know . . ."

"Of the sea"

"Business dealings for whom, old man? I'll tell you: for El Señor, for his fortune, not ours, and thus this new world, once again, will defer our bettering ourselves, and bind us even more tightly than before to seignorial power . . ." "Oh, Don Guzmán, do you have so little confidence in my astuteness? Look around you; look at the Princes, the monks, at the palace, look at religion itself; what is their common sign? Nonproductivity; for as the monks do not propagate sons, El Señor does not propagate riches; he cannot, it is contrary to his most profound reason for being; if what I know of him from my own account and what you have told me about him is true, then it is also true that his rank, his power, his cult, depend upon loss, not acquisition. El Señor's dynasty confuses honor with loss, glory with loss, rank with loss, power with loss, like the magpie that to no one's benefit steals and hides in her nest everything that glitters. Look closely, Don Guzmán. Reflect seriously upon what we have heard and what I now tell you, and you will find a frightening similarity between the motives that animate El Señor and those that govern life in the new world. Power is a challenge based upon offering something for which there is no possible counter-offering. A challenge, I say, for greatest is the power of the one who ends by having something that is nothing; in the end, loss; in the end, death; in the end, sacrifice: sacrifice, death and loss for others, as long as it is possible, and when it is no longer so, then sacrifice, death and loss for oneself. My solution is very simple; to these negative practices I oppose the very positive proposition of exchanging in order to acquire; to loss, I oppose acquisition. El Señor wished to complete his palace of death? You have seen that he had to come to me for a loan. Does he wish to send an expedition to ascertain the existence or non-existence of a new world? He will have to come to us, the outfitters, the dealers in commodities, the manufacturers of arms. Does he wish to colonize new lands? He will have to come to men like you, Don Guzmán, and to every last ordinary man in this palace, and to the rogues in the cities, and to the impoverished nobles; the new world will belong to us, we will win it with our arms and our brains, and we shall be repaid for our efforts with the gold and pearls that will flow from the hands of the natives into ours, though we will take care to reserve the royal fifth part for El Señor, and to collect payment for his debts in advance, and to make him content, and deceive him. Oh, yes!'' ''Bah, you're a dreamer, too, testy old fool; it was an ill-fated day when I opened the doors of this palace to you. You're dreaming, for whether or not that new world exists, El Señor has decreed that it does not; you heard him.'' ''But a piece of paper will never stay the course of history.'' ''El Señor believes it so; he believes only what is written.'' ''Then we shall win with paper; find me a pen, ink, and parchment, and this very night my letters will go out to the contractors and navigators of Genoa and Oporto, Antwerp and Danzig; the word will spread far and wide . . .''

''Exists''

''The Devil, yes, Azucena, Lolilla, the Devil exists, I know it, but not in the single body of the wise, nibbling, silky-haired Mus, and not in a double body, the mouse's that assumed the flesh of Don Juan and directed his actions. No, look, my duennas: look upon my bed at that body I formed from bits and pieces of the royal cadavers, held with sap from the storax tree and gum acacia; look at it, the eyes from one body, the thighbone from another, the ears from one and hands from another, and that is what the Devil is like; I know him now; he is a soul living amid us; he must be composed as I composed this monstrous body: compose the Devil's soul from portions of the souls of El Señor, his mother, the dwarf, Guzmán, Julián, the astronomer-priest, the Chronicler, the workmen, Don Juan, the Idiot, this pilgrim of whom you speak, the female with the tattooed lips, the blind flautist from Aragon, your own souls, and mine; mix them together and stir them in a great pot over a lighted fire, and even without adding benzoin or aloe, you shall know the soul of the Devil.'' ''His passion, his dream,'' ''Ay, my mistress, who said that?'' ''His fear, his anger, his mortality, his innocence.'' ''Ah, my bones are rattling with fear.'' ''His gluttony, his rebellion, his desire, his misery, his stupidity, his wisdom.'' ''Ay, Lolilla, the voice from beyond the tomb.'' ''Ah, Azucena, the sands are speaking.'' ''His dissatisfaction, his servitude, his grandeur.'' ''Listen, my scrubbing maids, he is speaking; listen, he knows.'' ''His longing to leave a record of his passage through the world; poor creature that he is, the Devil is all these things.'' ''He is speaking, my pretty maids; the radish has become a mouth; my homunculus is speaking.'' ''And as we, too, are all these things, he attempts to seduce us, to make a pact with us, to complete himself through us.'' ''Ay, I'm coming down with the ague.'' ''To play, to love, to weep, to laugh, to do battle, to dream, to wound, to kill, to die, and be reborn with us.'' ''Ay, upon my soul, the little turnip knows how to talk!'' ''For God is none of these things; He is eternal perfection, pure, uncontradicted essence, unopposed oneness.'' ''Ay, the little play toy is talking!'' ''And thus, loving us, He despises us.'' ''Ay, I'm eaten up with fear!'' ''And thus as He summons us to Him, He scorns us.'' ''Ay, upon my oath as a whore, it must be seen to be believed!'' "God asks us to come to Him, but the Devil comes to us; we are like him; he is our most fervent, secret, and compassionate ally.'' "Ay, Azucena!'' "Ay, Lolilla!'' "Ay, St. Thomas!'' "I wouldn't have believed it if I hadn't seen it!''

"A world"

my husband, my King, come out now, don't hide, see, everyone has gone now, there's no one left but me, your Barbarica, your tiny Queen, your squat little piece of real woman, don't deny me that delicious dingalingdong, come out from your hiding place, don't spoil my wedding night, where have you gone? Come, come back to me, let me show you all the things I know that compensate for my defects, you'll see how warm and deep my twat is, you'll see how much I love you . . . and if you don't come to me, you bastard, I hope your knees swell and your eyelids turn red and your skin turns green and you blood turns to poison and your dead fish rots off and if you leave here without me, I hope everyone shouts "bugger" at you everywhere you go!

"New"

tell me, hawk, ferocious hawk, my beautiful falcon, what should I do?, you are my only faithful friend, my only true confessor, not that Friar Julián who sometimes plays the role, you, hawk, tell me, like a mole I have gnawed at the foundations of El Señor's power, with patience I have plotted, I have carried my grudge for a long time, I am no one's man, and I know that from this great disorder a new order will emerge that is favorable to me, whatever the outcome, for if El Señor triumphs, he will remember me as a prudent counselor who forewarned him of the dangers surrounding him, and if his many enemies triumph—the cities, merchants, workmen—they will recognize in me a loyal friend who from within prepared the way for the rebellion, and opened the doors to it, but I did not expect this news, a land beyond the great ocean, a second opportunity for El Señor and his house, *Nondum, Not yet,* yes, now, now, for if El Señor extends his domains he will survive, he will become master of the fabulous riches seen by that youth, he will owe nothing to anyone, and once again, this time perhaps forever, I will be indebted to his accursed dynasty, Don Nobody, but if that new world exists, hawk, if the moneylender is right, then how can I not play a part in the adventure of discovering it, conquering it, and colonizing it? Will I be El Señor's servant forever, with never another opportunity, forever the bored sentry at his idiotic mystic sessions?, shall others win the fame and fortune for which I have so long striven?, the new world, the new world, who will win it, if it exists?, this unenterprising, pusillanimous, sick Señor who, I swear it, whether or not the new world exists, will never set foot upon it because he will never expose his weak body to the fatigue and terrors of scurvy, sargasso, leviathans, vermin, fevers, hand-to-hand combat, the new world, hawk, my elegant hawk, will my arm know how to win it, along with all its treasures?, Guzmán, Don Nobody, the new man, decisive, a man of action, free of diseased blood and morbid anguish, I, an undertaking worthy of my individual energies, I, I, I? The new world, if it exists, hawk, how can I not play a part in it?, oh, hawk, I am beginning to believe not only that it exists but that actually it exists for me, for men like me to demonstrate there in those jungles and seas and rivers and plains and mountains and temples that the universe will belong to action and not contemplation, to strength and not inheritance, to chance and not fatality, to progress and not stasis: to me, and not El Señor, oh, my fine falconet, my friend, my handsome hawk, am I dreaming too?, shall I defeat our puny Felipe both here and there? Yes, I shall act on his behalf, with words, but I shall act for myself in fact, I shall write long chronicles of the discovery to make him believe he is the sovereign of lands he will never know, he will believe everything he sees written, oh, hawk, I begin to burn with desire to cross the great sea, to drive my sword into the blazing shore of the new world, to burn temples, topple idols, conquer idolaters, heroic deeds await us, my fine young hawk, for you will voyage with me, my arm will be your perch, and as you swoop like an arrow to capture your prey, so will I sweep down like a curse upon the treasures of the new lands, and then, hawk, and then . . . what did that pilgrim say?, a beach, a beach of pearls with sufficient riches to captivate the favors of the coldest, most remote, most noble and disdainful lady, and bathe her in pearls, gold, emeralds, to make her mine, heroic feats, La Señora, the new world, the land conquered, the woman conquered, hawk . . .

"Not yet"

Barbarica, Barbarica, stop blubbering, can you not hear me, little dwarf?, can you not see me?, have you eyes only for the tomb where lies our heir?, come to me, little silly, your mistress is calling you, I need your aid, for I have neither arms nor legs, come to me, now I have come back to life I need you more than ever, why do you not hear me?, do you not realize?, I was already dead, little one, dead, I accompanied the corpse of my King and Lord through the highways and monasteries of Spain, dead, I arrived here, at the mausoleum of my son the King, idiots, unruly women made me fall from my niche, they trampled over me like a troop of jennies, they believed that by killing me they killed me, oh, what an error, little Barbarica, what a great error, what a grave error, for how can someone die who is already dead?, and if dead, how not be revived as he is killed?, come, my little Queen-to-be, let us go together, we have much to do, have I not always told you so?, as we die we may lose the five senses of natural life, but we gain the sixth sense of supernatural life, here, pick me up, we will live again, we will begin again, I smell something new, I smell it on all sides, the world is expanding, imbeciles, they look beyond, with vain illusions, with great hopes, they believe they can escape from us, from our law, power and loss, honor and sacrifice, nothingness, we shall conquer, we shall impose the kingdom of nothingness upon the land toward which they gaze with hope, for every forward step they make we shall take two backward, we shall capture the flight of the future in the ice of the past, leave that Idiot Prince in his tomb, abandon him, I promise you better things, Barbarica, I promise myself better things, oh, never again shall I marry a husband who dies before me . . .

"*Nondum*"

"The red stone, the ring of bones, Guzmán. I cannot breathe. How good that you returned, I was choking to death here by myself." "Drink this, Señor, drink this." "Even water turns to pus in my throat." "I beg you, drink, and listen to me." "Loyal Guzmán, what would I do without you? You have attended me, you have warned me, will you now be able to console me for something worse than either madness or lack of breath: the loss of the things that cause me to cling to life, something that is both madness and lack of breath?" "I understand El Señor, but I do not share his judgment, if El Señor will forgive me." "A new world, Guzmán, a world new to me, to my crown. All I sought was the reduction of every existing thing to fit within the space of these walls, and then the quick extinction of my person and my line. I constructed a necropolis; they offer me a universe. The new world will not fit within my tombs." "Señor, I tell you, with the greatest respect, you have triumphed; look at things in this way: in that new world you can duplicate your own and freeze it in time." "What do you mean?" "Something very simple, Sire. Once you told me that for heaven really to be heaven, there could be no heaven on earth." "Yes, I told you, and I told myself: let us construct a hell upon earth so as to assure the need for a heaven that will compensate for the horror of our lives; let us first deserve hell on earth, torture, the stake; first we shall free ourselves from the powers of evil upon earth with the goal of someday deserving the beatitude of heaven in Heaven; Heaven, Guzmán; to forget forever that we ever lived." "And you prayed, Your Grace, to Christ Our Lord, and you said . . ." "Those who attempt to change your image, my God, shall see their work burned, crumbled, destroyed by the combined rage and piety of my armies; never again will new Babylons be raised to deform your sweet likeness, my God." "Señor, then construct your hell in the new world; raise your necropolis upon pagan temples; fix Spain in time outside of Spain; your triumph will be double; never will the times have seen its equal; and no one will be able to surpass your gift: an entire universe consecrated to mortification and death; no one, Señor . . . Raise your cause of stone and sorrow above both worlds, the old and the new." "The new world, Guzmán; you heard that youth; a world that must be remade each day as the sun appears." "Destroy it, Sire, convert it into the mirror of Spain, that whoever sees himself in it see the motionless stone of death, the eternally fixed, the motionless statue of your eternal glory." "Amen, Guzmán, amen." "The new world will fit within your tombs . . ."

"*Plus Ultra*"

this I fear above all, Brother Toribio, that the new world will not in truth be new, but rather a terrible extension of the old world we are living here, did you see El Señor?, did you see how he trembled every time that pilgrim pointed out the similarities between the crimes of that place and our own, the oppressions there and oppressions here?, I tremble, too, Brother, although for reasons different from those that shake our sovereign; El Señor wishes that his life, his world, his experience, be unique and final, a definitive page written for eternity, unrepeatable; he fears anything that opens outward and divests him of his sense of culmination, the final and unquestionable end; the life he lived was to be the last, forever; not only for him, no, but for the species itself; so great is his arrogant will for extinction; on the other hand, I tremble because I fear that in conquering the tyranny of the new world those of the old world will grow in strength and dimension, ally themselves with greed and cruelty, and all this in the name of our sacred Faith; the powers of Mars and Mercury are waxing; they mask themselves with the face of Christ; war, gold, evangelization: we shall lose the opportunity to transfer to the new world that new world you and I, Brother, had so quietly begun to create with our telescopes and paintbrushes, protected here in the sheltering and indifferent shadows of this palace; fear, Brother; we shall be watched; we shall be persecuted, all I have warned you of is certain: we shall be accused, and in the most innocuous of our preoccupations will be discovered error, heresy, traces of the Jew; and as in the new world everything will be destroyed and the diabolical signs of idolatry seen in every action and object, as those artisans of whom the pilgrim spoke will be murdered, their works of stone and feather and metal destroyed, the gold melted down, the statues beheaded—all signs of evil, since evil is what we do not know and what does not know us—thus shall we be burned, you and I, Brother; and we will be unable to defend ourselves; we lack the strength to rebel; your science and my art detest equally disorder and oppression and desire perfect equilibrium between all things necessary and all things possible, a balance between order and freedom; oh, Brother, precarious indeed is the harmony we require, and when we lose it we shall be both victims and executioners of oppression, which will continue as order, before being victims and executioners of rebellion, which always means disorder . . .

"Beyond"

Don Juan, Don Juan, where are you?, it is so dark and lonely in this chapel, the only light shines from the figures in that painting behind the altar, you would almost think the figures are moving, that they wish to speak to us, but that is deception, as the stone in which you have cloaked yourself is deception, I saw you from the choir, from behind the iron latticework I glimpsed you reclining atop one of the sepulchers, and I desired you again, my lover, but now, disguised in stone, how can I distinguish you in the darkness from the other statues, from the Princes and Lords and heirs represented here?, I shall go from tomb to tomb touching the hands of all the dead, kissing the lips of all the statues until I recognize you, Juan, if I rescue you from the stone, if thanks to my lips and my hands I save you from being but one statue more in this pantheon, will you be grateful to me?, will you truly?, that deserves some reward, does it not?, I shall free you from the spell of the stone, and you will free me from the spell of being virgin again, Juan and Inés, Inés and Juan, we shall break one another's spells, one night more with you, Juan, that is all I ask, then I shall seclude myself here forever as a nun in this palace where my father brought me, did you know?, to prove his faith, so no one might doubt the sincerity of our conversion, Juan, you didn't know that, but I do, from childhood I knew nothing else, how they ordered us to wear a round yellow patch over our hearts, how they called us filthy pigs, *marranos*, how they forced all the Jews into one section of the city, and forced us to wear strange clothing, rags that brought scorn upon us, how they made the men let their beards and hair grow, we were sorrowful-looking creatures, one saw hunger in every face, they forced us to eat the flesh of the pig, there were great slaughters, the Jewish quarters of Seville and Barcelona and Valencia and Toledo were completely destroyed, and in the name of devotion they greedily stole our property, we won it back, again and again, my father told me this, we did without clothing, we dared not even keep our Hebrew books of prayers, lest some servant come upon them by accident, what could we do but recant, be converted, in order to survive?, and once converted rebuild our fortunes from nothing in offices scorned by Castilians, for had we not performed them, no one else would, they accused us of seeking easy employment, of refusing to dig or plow, but what my father and his people did, Juan, someone had to do, even though to do it revealed us as Jews and vile people, my father was an old man when I was born, my mother dead in childbirth, I learned these stories late, and I had barely become a woman when my father destined me—as proof of his sincere confession and his faithfulness as a new Christian, and in hope that in time, our names changed and our old ways forgotten, we would be considered pure Christians—to take holy vows and thus, he told me, when the persecution begins again, as inevitably it will, perhaps I will already be dead, or perhaps I shall suffer persecution, but you will be safe, sheltered by your order, office of fire, office of shadows, one must choose between them, oh, Don Juan, I kiss your lips of stone, I give life again to your statue, Don Juan, between the two offices, between persecution and life in the convent, give me one night more, that is all I ask of you before I resign myself to my fate, one night more of love, I touch you, I kiss you, you will be flesh again, be mine again, Don Juan, first El Señor deflowered me, now, the second time, let it be you, Don Juan, and I shall accept my destiny forever, I took Christ as my bridegroom that I might love all men . . .

"*Mudnon*"

"See things as they are, Señor. Do not delude yourself. And in my daring, see the proof of the same fidelity you would demand of a dog, could he speak." "You have a voice, Guzmán." "And my truthful voice tells you that my huntsmen are mingling among the uneasy mob, the noisy grumblers of the work sheds and forges whose discontent is growing; something is about to happen; I do not know exactly what, but I can smell conflict in the air. You must be prepared, the motives for rebellion are mounting: the fruitful land destroyed, insufficient wages, the contrast between your luxury and their poverty, the accidental deaths, the fact that you buried your dead with such ceremony while those who died suffocated under the landslide lay abandoned, their widows wailing, and black crape mockingly adorned the plain; you were prepared to give charity to the poor passing by, but there is nothing for the workmen; they ask themselves who will succeed you, they have no trust in your foreign Lady and they believe that when you die that idiot brought here by your mother will take your place; yes, something is in the air." "What should I do, Guzmán?" "The same thing you did as a young man, Señor; open the doors, let them enter, lock them here inside the palace, and exterminate them." "This time they will be forewarned." "Hope blinds them; nothing is forgotten more quickly than the past; nothing repeats itself like the past." "Again?" "This is destined, Señor." "So you say; but you do not believe in destiny." "I give more than one name to action; the means justify the means." "And the end?" "It is but the means between two actions which in turn becomes means for other actions." "Guzmán; let me tell you something; of all the things that poor shipwrecked lad recounted, nothing impressed me as much as this: that in the new world the death of innocents is justified by the very order of their cosmos. I did not have that justification. How much suffering I could have saved myself! Do you remember what he said? The inhabitants of the new world are equally disposed to honor light if it triumphs, or shadow if it conquers." "Then you must accept their belief as valid, and your undertakings will be justified not only by divine right but by the rights of nature as well." "You have decided, have you not, Guzmán, for yourself, for me? You will go to the new world." "I shall be a simple soldier in the fleets of El Señor and those of the evangelizing God."

"Guzmán, you know the answer; you told me, you brought that old man here, you forced me to contract that debt, you suggested I name him Comendador of the very noble Order of Calatrava; how shall we pay for the expeditions?" "A divine end, human means. Did not the Inquisitor of Teruel give you the solution? Expel the Jews, Señor, take possession of their riches, demand both purity of blood and purity of Faith; both are in peril. We shall carry to the new world the immaculate flag of Christ our Lord; we must not let false converts filter into the evangelization, false Spaniards who have never been willing to work as laborers or herd cattle, or to teach those offices to their sons, but who have sought positions of ease, and ways to earn a lot of money for very little work. And if what you thus amass is not sufficient for your royal purse, consider the cities, Señor; I repeat, that is where the riches accumulate; there are the merchants and sellers and collectors of excises and interests, and the gentlemen's stewards and officers, and tailors, shoemakers, tanners, curriers, tilemakers, spice sellers, peddlers, silk mercers, silversmiths, jewelers, physicians, dyers, doctors, and other similar offices; impose exorbitant taxes upon them and deny them the shelter of statutes, courts, tribunals, and assemblies; while your ancestors were combating the Moors and persecuting the Hebrews, while you did battle against distant heretics and then shut yourself up to construct your necropolis, men of the cities were governing themselves, gaining rights and statutes and courts of justice; they were meeting in assemblies and practicing audacious customs; they speak of the will of all men, they make decisions by a majority of votes, they deny the basis of your unquestionable and unique ordination; impose tributes and outlaw their courts; the Augustinian of Teruel spoke wisely; the same law, for those in the new world and those in the old; enough vacillation, subject the Moor, expel the Jew, humble the free man and the burgher, enough contemplation, the undertaking is too great, too profitable, and too holy; there is a superabundance of accusations, choose one: traitors, sodomites, blasphemers, infanticides, murderers disguised as doctors, poisoners, usurers, heretics, witches, profaners of the Holy Spirit; the method is the same, impose it: act out of fervor for the Faith and the salvation of souls, even though you act against many true Christians, utilize the testimony of enemies, rivals, the merely envious; act without proof of any kind, lock them up in ecclesiastical prisons, torture them, wrest confessions from them, condemn them as heretics and relapsed converts, deprive them of their goods and property, and deliver them to the secular branch of power to be executed: with this one stroke you will fortify your Faith, your political unity, and your depleted coffers." "Guzmán, Guzmán, I lack the strength; you ask me to reconstruct a kingdom and then to construct a new world in its likeness; I wished only to forfeit it all; I wished to end, you wish to begin." "Let me act, then, Señor; sign these papers and I shall act in your name; I shall not importune you except when absolutely necessary, I swear to you; your signature will be sufficient, you can continue to dedicate yourself to your devotions—known to everyone—and your passions—known to none; Inés, I shall bring her to you again, Señor." "Inés? Silence, lackey; Inés, never again; Inés, sold by her father; I have paid for a woman; I desire her, I admit it, but never again, Guzmán, never again; I have never touched the woman I have loved since my youth, because such was my chivalresque ideal; I shall never again touch the woman I love, because I shall not pay for the pleasures of the flesh. I did not touch La Señora; instead I took peasant girls, I took Celestina; I shall not touch a woman who was sold to me in exchange for a loan and a title; no." "Others touch them, Sire." "Silence, Guzmán." "You wish to exorcise the world that lies outside the walls of this palace, but that world has already filtered in here; you know two of the youths who arrived here: the imbecilic heir accompanying your mother and the dreadful shipwrecked sailor accompanying the girl dressed as a page." "Twins . . . the prophecy . . . Romulus and Remus . . . you should have warned me . . . the usurpers . . . those who begin everything anew . . ." "No, not twins, but triplets; a third . . ." "Silence, silence; heed me; obey me." "A third, Señor; you must know the truth; a third, identical to the other two, and more to be feared than they, for he has touched both the touchable and the untouchable; he sleeps with Inés in the servants' quarters, which El Señor has never entered, and he sleeps with La Señora in La Señora's bedchamber, also never entered by El Señor; this third youth has touched El Señor's honor, his wife and his lover, Señor; both are lovers of this audacious burlador, this seducer of women who in addition, on successive nights, has satiated his brutal appetites with Sister Angustias, Madre Milagros, the dwarf Barbarica, the palace scrubbing maids, and have no doubt, would do the same with your own mother, so great is his insatiable lust." "Oh, Guzmán, Guzmán, nonono, you have wounded me deeply, Guzmán, what shall I do with you?" "I am at the feet of El Señor." "I think I no longer have the spirit for either. I constructed this space to renounce the material world and consecrate myself to the spirit; here I exorcised my youth, my love, my crime, my battles, my doubts, in order finally to be alone with my soul, complete, free, suspended, awaiting its ascension into Paradise; but now I believe that events are accelerating, sifting in through a thousand chinks; you opened one of them; you brought me Inés; should I punish you or reward you? Yes, events are accelerating; I believe I must reserve my limited forces and respond to only one of the thousand challenges the world again sets before me; I prayed for an unchanging world, but the world is quivering like a thousand-eyed Argos and all those eyes are staring at me, summoning me, challenging me; I shall respond to one only, and surely that one, the one I must answer with what little strength remains, is not you, or what you do, eternal lackey; poor Guzmán, poor creature; I am sorry for you, so much effort, so much energy, so much devotion, for what?, for what good if you, like Bocanegra, never know your instant of glory, for what good, if now, purely as a whim, as you seek it for the Jews, heretics and burghers, I ordered your execution—the pillory, the rack, the garrote—with no explanation, saying only, 'He had rabies'; poor Guzmán, you have wounded my honor, but I forgive you; do I not wound yours?'' ''Honor, Sire? That concept, so often invoked in this land and so little conforming to the purposes of shrewdness and ambition, needs to be analyzed.'' ''You see, Guzmán, you see, you would like to undo it, take it apart as if it were a clock or a machine; no Guzmán, those of us who possess honor know it cannot be debated or dismantled; one simply has honor, and knows it, with no need for explanations, and those who would like to explain it will never know or possess it; so, Guzmán, everything I have said to you is true; you do not deserve my attention.'' ''You will do better, Sire, to occupy yourself with these papers; sign them.'' ''I shall do it gladly, my loyal, pragmatic Guzmán, because in them I see acts that will make the world more remote, that will abandon me here in this solitary sanctuary of my soul; and if you want me to believe what you have told me, bring me more papers, Guzmán, on paper and with paper domonstrate the reality of what you have told me about Inés and La Señora.'' ''I shall do so, Señor, as soon as possible; in the meanwhile, have you so little curiosity that . . .''

''*artlu sulp*''

''You say the world is round, Toribio; I believe you; does that prove, round as it may be, that the lands described by that sailor are to be found upon it?'' ''No, not at all.'' ''Do you believe what he told us?'' ''Not necessarily; perhaps he merely dreamed it.'' ''And nonetheless, will the whole of Spain go out in search of what may be nothing but a dream?'' ''There is much that is ignominious in this land, but only one greatness: the belief in dreams.'' ''Great madness, Toribio.'' ''Enormous glory, Julián.''

> Great is Felipe, the Lord of Spain,
> Great is our King Sublime.
> He governs the greatest part of the world
> Under his rights divine.

''Did you repeat my arguments, bailiff?'' ''With total fidelity, Your Excellency.'' ''Did El Señor sign the papers I dictated to you?'' ''Here they are, Señor Inquisitor.'' ''The expulsion of the Jews?'' ''Signed and sealed.'' ''The suspension of statutes, courts, chapter meetings, and assemblies?'' ''Signed and seal . . .'' ''The extraordinary taxes

upon the cities and the burghers, their officials?'' "Sign . . ."
"Have them proclaimed immediately, and upon these papers will the
true unity of this kingdom be founded, the unity of power and faith, of
power and riches; for only upon such power will the new world, if it
exists, submit to our will, and at the same time, if it does not, Spain
will subject herself, and that is sufficient.'' "Without suspecting it,
that naïve voyager gave us excellent justification, Your Excellency.''
"Good, good, Guzmán; you have acted with promptness and precision. Take this, take this purse for yourself—and know my generosity . . ." "Señor Inquisitor: with the greatest respect, I beg you to
allow me to refuse it.'' "What is it you wish, then?'' "A promise: that
I be remembered, that I be permitted to head an expedition to the new
lands and prove myself in danger, and thus confirm my loyalty to the
Crown and the Church.'' "So promised, Don Nobody . . ."

> Thus our invincible King,
> Wherever man had trod,
> Has spread around the globe
> The sacred word of God . . .

well, caro amico, here I am an old man enjoying new youth, new
honors, and if we act with discretion, an extensive fortune; I cannot
write you of everything I heard, for the sailor youth's account abounded in evident fantasies and barbaric idolatrous theologies, and the
names he said were impossible to pronounce, Mexicunt, Whazaldat,
Chipitits, which are names of lands and idols over there; but all this is
secondary, and only three things are important: a new world does exist
beyond the ocean; the land is rich, no, opulent; and one can sail there
and return to Europe; I am writing now, as to you in Genoa, to all our
navigator and contractor friends of the North Sea, the Baltic, and the
Mediterranean; we must be audacious and cautious at the same time;
the persecutions our race has suffered at the hands of the Spanish powers force us to be; this is how I see things: in the first euphoria of the
discoveries they will overlook our Jewish origins, for the Spanish will
badly need all the things we have to offer—the maintenance of commerce; an infinite number of ships laden with merchandise, whose port
taxes will support their armadas; the handling of merchandise and administration of royal taxes and tribunals established outside of Spain—
but once religious zeal overcomes practical considerations, have no
doubt, dear Colombo, they will turn against us, they will remember
our origins and doubt the fidelity of our conversion; we shall be persecuted anew; they will wish once again, as always, to take command
of our fortunes under the pretext of the purity of Christianity; let us be
forewarned: let us establish our principal houses in Flanders, in Eng-

land, in Jutland, in the Germanic principalities where pragmatic inclination will always be stronger than religious zeal, so that when the moment comes we have in Spain only a minimum of agents and can transfer to the North the substance of the South; these undertakings and their maintenance over a long period, along with the expenses of war and administration they presuppose, will always be extremely costly; let us act, you and I and all those of our profession, to assure that the riches of the new world are employed to pay our services; and even they may be insufficient, thus forcing the Princes and captains to contract debts with us, as happened during the Holy Crusades that were so favorable to us, making us the creditors of those harebrained knights and even, dear Colombo, permitting us to rid ourselves of undisciplined sons and pass for faithful Christians by the simple expedient of sending our rebellious scions to Palestine; and guard yours carefully, caro amico, though stubborn and audacious, he lacks discretion, and in his eyes shines the fire of a certain madness; mine, a daughter of my later years, is making her vows in the palace from which I write you this July night; your most obedient servant, loyal servitor and faithful friend, I kiss your feet, *Gonzalo de Ulloa, Comendador of Calatrava . . .*

"and never again will Thule be the ultimate boundary of the world"

"Take my breviary, Guzmán; read for my repose, this day is ending." "And so that dying we be faithful and loyal witnesses to the infallible truth that our God spoke to the First Fathers, that sinning they and all their descendants would die . . ." "That sinning, that sinning . . ." "That is what it says . . ." "No, Guzmán, do not accept these words; doubt, doubt, Guzmán; affirm that all evil is done by us, but that it is not born in us; we were born with no sin but the capacity for good and evil, and this our sin is nothing but the freedom that both likens us to and differentiates us from God; for His freedom is absolute, and ours, sad, terrible, profound, and poignantly relative; God's freedom is a fatal attribute, whereas that of man is but a fragile promise; nevertheless, we were conceived without vice or virtue, and before the activity of our personal will there is nothing in us except what God placed there to tempt us, to test us, to condemn us, to diminish us before His presence: the lights and shadows of free will. Hear me, Brother Ludovico, lost companion of my lost youth, hear me and repeat with me, wherever you may be: Adam was created mortal and would have died whether or not he had sinned, God could never have conceived of immortal man, His infinite pride would not have tolerated such a challenge; there were men free of sin, righteous men, before the coming of Christ; God sent Christ to avenge himself upon the rare, but certain, righteousness of men and to impose upon them a sense of pervading guilt; the Redeemer needed to redeem; but newly born children are as free of sin as Adam when he was created; the human race did not perish with the fall and death of Adam, nor did it arise with the torture and resurrection of Christ, for man can always live outside of sin if he so desires, if he so wishes; I love you, beautiful Inés, and I do not know why loving you should be a sin, except that more than a thousand years have lashed my flesh and my conscience, humbling me to the guilt that Christ requires as a condition to His promised redemption; I hear you, Brother Ludovico, I love you, as always, and finally I understand you and repeat your words, words we never spoke because they were flesh of our meeting beside the sea, constructing the aged Pedro's ship so we might sail beyond the end of the world and seek the beginnings of the earth, the earth before sin, the new foundation, the new land, oh, my Ludovico, twin image of my youth, my strength and adventure, woe unto us, for there will be no land but this one where we suffer and where everything is lost; would I follow you today? you, Pedro, who died fleeing from me, cursing me? you, Ludovico? you, poor bewitched Celestina? you, good monk Simón? would I follow in that adventure, the search for a new beginning?; I humble myself, Ludovico, my head touches the cold floor of this chamber, and I tell you I do not know, I do not know, I do not know; with you I believed I could, I believe I wished to, I am what I believed, and when I was with Inés I believed it, too; but God neither wishes nor is; He is all-powerful, He can do anything; see how he has determined things, joined and separated and rejoined our destinies, but for no purpose, for He neither wishes nor is: He does not wish or exist as you and I wish and exist; true, my brother? true, my beautiful, soft, warm Inés? true, Celestina? true, my lost youth, my lost, forgotten, shared dream? true, my unpardonable crime?; we should have embarked that afternoon on the beach on old Pedro's boat, all of us together, you and I; you would pardon me today, you who wished and were while I—tiny God in my somber castle—merely demonstrated I could, could, could . . . Oh, Ludovico, Pedro, Celestina, Simón . . . how have our lives ended? what have hope and forgetfulness and time made of us? it is your, not God's, pardon I should seek, it is to you I should pray, not to the most glorious and pure Virgin and Mother of God, mediatrix of all sinners, do not in the hour of my death abandon me, but with my Guardian Angel and with St. Michael and St. Gabriel and all the other angels of Heaven, and with the blessed St. John the Baptist, and St. Peter and St. Paul, St. James the Greater and St. Andrew and St. John the Evangelist, St. Philip and St. Bernard, St. Francis, St. James the Less, St. Anne and St. Mary Magdalene, my mediators, and with all the other Saints in the court of Heaven, succor me and aid me with your special favor so that my soul through your intercession and by virtue of the passion of Jesus Christ Our Lord may take its place in the glory and beatitude created in the beginning. Amen, Guzmán, amen." "Amen, Señor, and now draw the curtain across your existence, for the world is racing inexorably toward its destiny, and that destiny is no longer yours." "What shall I do with you, Guzmán?" "You have said already: I do not deserve your attention." "Should I reward you, should I punish you?" "It would be reward or punishment for my fidelity." "You have lied to me, Guzmán; you think you know everything, but you lie; I have been in La Señora's bedchamber, I have seen . . ." "Señor . . ." "My honor is intact; my wife's sins are venial: she has created a refuge in the image and likeness of the pleasure she desires; you have accused her of adultery." "I swear to you, Señor . . ." "I have eyes, you said, I have a nose; I know how to see, I know how to smell . . ." "I try to serve El Señor; if I err, it is without ill will, because I am human." "Ludovico, Celestina, my youth, my love— before there was crime—my project is drawing to an end, Guzmán; my mother was right, if I cannot end in extinction, I shall end at the beginning; I shall return to that privileged instant of my life, to that shore, to my four companions, I shall renounce my inheritance, my power, my father, Isabel, it will again be six o'clock on a summer's day near a ship on a beach, we shall set sail, we shall voyage to the new world; we dreamed of it before anyone, we stepped upon its shores before anyone." "You are raving, Sire, you are invoking phantoms, your companions are dead, they are lost, they are nothing, they have been swallowed up by time, the plague, madness." "Poor Guzmán, you know a great deal about hawks and hounds, but nothing of the affairs of the heart. Go now; close the breviary, arise, draw the tapestry, tell the halberdiers to free them and let them enter, I want them here— Ludovico, Celestina . . ."

> Oh, I am the Moor Moraima,
> young, and fair to behold . . .

"Are you singing, mistress?" "Oh, Lolilla, look how happy our mistress is, you're alive again, mistress, and your happiness gives us pleasure." "I am singing, my scrubbing maids, and laughing." "We were terribly afraid for you, Señora, when we saw your husband enter your bedchamber for the first time, without knocking, as if seeking a . . ." "And see what he found, my duennas; just look at that creature lying upon my bed, fabricated from bits and pieces I stole from the sepulchers; see him as El Señor saw him: is this my lover, this mummy, this monster? Yes, Señor, he is my penitence, the proof of my loyalty to your proposals, Sire, the Oriental luxury of a bedchamber and upon the bed, a cadaver, my companion, Sire, the only choice you have left me, the reflection of your funereal will, luxury wherein death resides, the pleasures of the senses subjugated by the domination of a cadaver; see how well I understand you, see how I follow in your path, see how closely bound I am to your most intimate mandates . . . and now, Azucena, Lolilla, let us prepare ourselves for a great voyage, all is ended here; warm my bath water with hot charcoal; the most perfumed soap, Lolilla; clean my most elegant dress, Azucena, scrape well the wax stains left by the candles; bathe me, lather me with soap, take the *torche-cul*, Lolilla, and wash well all my parts so that no odor of man cling there, not one drop of man's love . . . my perfumes, Azucena, and that dress, the one with the lowest décolletage—they say that the eyes are the windows of the soul and décolletage the window of Hell—and my jeweled gloves, and the slippers that fit my feet so sleekly that common people will wonder how I put them on and off, and gold powder for my hair, and remove those precious glass panes from my windows and pack them away so no one will ever again look through them toward a garden that does not exist; the garden is beyond, in the other world, and we are going there.'' ''And this sealed green bottle, mistress; is there something in it?'' ''Don Juan brought that with him from the sea; leave it here on the sands of the chamber.'' ''And the monster, Señora; will he remain on your bed?'' ''Oh, Azucena, Lolilla, my homunculus knows everything, understands everything; he has already told me what we must do with my royal mummy; there will be time; let us make ready; take that cup, Lolilla, the one made from an ostrich egg; fill it and give it to me.'' ''Drink, Señora . . .'' ''Sing, mistress . . .''

A Christian came to my gates,
ah, woe is me,
hoping to deceive . . .

CELESTINA

AND LUDOVICO

I recognized you, said El Señor, when the woman with the tattooed lips, dressed as a page, and the blind Aragonese flautist had entered his bedchamber; Felipe dismissed Guzmán, who, stuttering with rage, and eyes burning, excused himself, saying: ''I would rather a wrathful El Señor castigate me for angering him than a repentant El Señor condemn me for not giving him counsel . . .''

No one looked at him, no one answered him, and when he attempted to station himself outside the door to the chapel the halberdiers prevented him; Guzmán crossed the chapel, walked through corridors, courtyards, kitchens, and mews, and emerged into the night of the tile sheds, taverns, and forges of the work site.

I recognized you, said El Señor, gazing at them with great tenderness. You, Celestina; you, Ludovico; you have returned, it is true, is it not? I was slow to recognize you both; you, Ludovico, do you remember when we talked beside the sea? a dream, a world without God, sufficient grace for every man; you, Celestina, the world of love with nothing forbidden to the body, each body the solar center of the world; I was slow to recognize you, time has wounded you, brother, and favored you, my girl; you cannot see, poor Ludovico, I could not believe you were so old, and you so young, it is you, Celestina, it is truly you? I am, and I am not, she said, the girl you remember is not I, and the girl I was you do not remember, although you met me one day in the forest; is it you, Ludovico? Yes, it is I, Felipe, here we are, we have returned, and you must return with us to that shore by the sea where we destroyed Pedro's ship with our hatchets, you must hear our stories again, hear us again and remember what you told us then, remember what you imagined, then compare it with what actually happened, imagine what actually will happen.

And this is what, in turn, the girl with the tattooed lips and the blind flautist recounted that night.

THE FIRST CHILD

Felipe pleasured himself in that night of love with Celestina and Ludovico: Ludovico in the love of Celestina and Felipe; Celestina, in the love of Felipe and Ludovico. The three, lying together on marten-skin furs, turned one of their sea dreams into reality.

And thus they passed several days. Their pleasure was inexhaustible. They invented words, acts, combinations, desires, recollections, that led them toward the ultimate truth of their bodies; not finding it, they imagined their youth and their love would be eternal. Celestina had been right. The world will be liberated when all bodies are liberated.

Felipe left them by day. He offered no excuses, they were not necessary. The castle was the place where everything they had dreamed was becoming reality. The others, Ludovico said to Celestina—Pedro, Simón, the Eremites, the Moors, the pilgrims, the Hebrews, the heresiarchs, the beggars, the prostitutes—must, like them, be liberating themselves in the diverse forms of their various pleasures. At night, Felipe returned, always with brimming pitchers and trays laden with food.

"We need never leave here," he said to them, "Everything we need is here."

They made love. They slept. But one night Felipe entered the bedchamber and with him a frightful odor penetrated the room.

"Now the smell is of death, not of pleasure," Ludovico said to himself.

He waited until Felipe and Celestina were sleeping, naked, their limbs intertwined. The young student donned his beggar's clothing and left the chamber. A thick cloud of smoke forced him to retreat. He steeled himself to investigate what was happening. Cautiously he walked a long passageway. Death was borne on the wings of the smoke. Choking, he sought refuge. He opened a door and stepped into a bedchamber.

Two women were peering through a high narrow arched window onto the castle courtyard below. They did not see him as he entered. Clutching each other in fear were a beautiful young Lady and a malodorous scrubbing maid in wide skirts. The student approached the window. Seeing him there, the women screamed and embraced each other even more tightly. Brusquely forcing them aside, Ludovico looked out onto the courtyard. The women ran screaming from the room.

He had not seen the women before, but the cadavers, yes. Guards in coats of mail, bloody swords unsheathed, were dragging bodies by the hair or by the feet and throwing them onto a great pyre blazing in the center of the courtyard. He recognized the men, women, and children Felipe had led to the castle.

Ludovico looked about the rich apartment. With a gesture of rage he ripped down a tapestry hanging on one of the chamber walls. Behind the tapestry was a cradle. And in the cradle slept a baby only a few weeks old. A thousand conflicting thoughts raced through the student's feverish brain. All were resolved in one almost instinctive action: he removed the child from the cradle, wrapped him in the same silks that had covered him, and left the room with the infant in his arms.

He believed he was saving an innocent from the terrible slaughter. He returned to Felipe's bedchamber. The youth and the girl were still asleep. Holding the infant aloft to show him to his companions, he almost awakened them. He looked at Celestina's sleeping face and smiled tranquilly; he knew what she was dreaming. He looked at Felipe and his smile froze; he did not know what Felipe dreamed. Beside the seashore each of them except Felipe had told what he desired: Pedro, a world without servitude. Simón, a world without illness. Celestina, a world without sin. Ludovico, a world without God.

Again he looked at Felipe's sleeping face. The prognathic jaw. The laborious breathing. Both characteristics emphasized in sleep. He remembered royal medallions: Felipe was one of them.

He sighed with great sadness and left the chamber, coughing, and protecting the child. In the next room, which was a falcons' mews, he hid the child. Fearfully, he covered him with a hood like those covering the hawks themselves in the hours of sleep.

THE DEATH CART

About midday Felipe left them, and later Ludovico and Celestina heard bells, flute music, and tambourines. The student mashed some food until it was the consistency of gruel, and fed the child he had hidden in the mews, but he told Celestina nothing of what had passed.

At dusk Felipe returned, magnificently arrayed: polished shoes in the Flemish style, rose-colored breeches, brocaded robe lined with ermine, and on his head a cap as beautiful as a jewel; a cross of precious stones lay upon his breast, and orange blossoms on the ermine. He told them he had obtained a signal favor from his father. The student and the girl could remain in the castle. They would become accustomed to palace life. Ludovico could make good use of the great library, and Celestina find delight in the dances and amusements of the court. Their beautiful nights of love would continue forever. Celestina told him, gaily, she didn't recognize him, he was so elegant. Ludovico said nothing. Felipe said: "That is because today was my wedding day . . ."

He left, smiling. Celestina embraced Ludovico, and the student told her all he had learned. They awaited the deepest hour of the night and when they felt sure that the guards were sleeping and the dogs exhausted from being chained all day, they stole from their bedchamber, gathered up the child from the mews, and sought an escape.

Yes, the guards and the dogs were sleeping; but the heavy door of the barbican was closed, and the drawbridge raised above the moat. Then Celestina heard a noise in the courtyard; several men were occupied in piling the charred remains of cadavers onto carts.

Hidden in the shadows of the archways, they waited until the last hour of the night. They took advantage of a moment when the men went to pick up more bodies, and hid in one of the carts, making a place for themselves among burned arms and legs, torsos, and staring into the fiery eyes of corpses with slashed throats. Ashes and blood stained them too; Celestina clutched the infant to her breast, fearfully covering its mouth with her hand, and fighting back the nausea that welled in her throat.

Face down among the cadavers, stained as the cadavers themselves, they shivered in silence as additional charred bodies were thrown on top of them and they heard the creaking wheels of the cart. The huge doors were opened and the drawbridge lowered; Celestina choked back her tears and cradled the infant; the infant cried out; Ludovico shuddered, and Celestina clapped a blood-stained palm over the infant's mouth; the carts rolled on toward the Castilian dawn.

"Did you hear anything?" said one of the drivers.

"No, what?"

"A baby crying."

"What have you been drinking, blockhead?"

"The leftovers from Prince Don Felipe's wedding feast, just like you, you bleary-eyed old sot . . ."

Now, Celestina, now, jump, we're in the woods where they cannot find us, Ludovico whispered, and the drivers saw two figures from the heap of cadavers leap from the cart and run into the thicket.

They stopped, climbed out of the cart, and examined the load of dead bodies they were carrying to dump into a mountain ravine; they knelt, crossed themselves, and said: "Don't tell anyone about this; they'll say we were drunk and give us the beating of our lives."

THE TOLEDO JEWRY

They took refuge in the Jewry of Toledo. At first the Hebrews received them out of pity, seeing them in a great state of fatigue, dressed like beggars and carrying a child in their arms, but later they wished to interrogate the couple, and they went to call upon them. Celestina was bathing the child, and the Jews saw what Ludovico and Celestina had seen with astonishment as the day dawned in the woods after their escape from the cart, stained with blood and ashes: the child had six toes on each foot and a blood-red cross upon his back.

"What does this mean?" the visitors asked each other, and Celestina and Ludovico asked each other the same question.

"Is the child yours?" they asked, and the student replied no, that he and his wife had saved him from death, and for that reason loved him as they would their own.

But after a few months everyone noted that the girl was expecting another child, her own, for her torn garments could not hide the swelling of her belly, and they all said: "So; may the Lord be with you; now you will have a child of your own, may he bless your house."

They lived in a single room behind tall stone arches. There was little light, as the windows were high and very small and covered with oiled paper; the cotton wick floating in a basin of fish oil emitted a strong odor but very little light, although it burned for a long time.

"We stole the child," Ludovico said to Celestina, "but Felipe robbed us of our lives."

The learned doctors of the Synagogue of the Passing came to see the child, and almost without exception they shrugged and said they did not understand the anomalies of the six toes on each foot and the cross upon the child's back. But one stood gravely silent, and one day he sought out Ludovico and spoke with him. Thus he learned that the student was expert in translating Latin, Hebrew, and Arabic, and he took him to the synagogue, and there entrusted him with various tasks.

"Read; translate; we have saved many of the folios which were taken from Rome to the great library of Alexandria, and from there— saved from the great destruction of the civil war waged by Aurelian, and later from the Christian holocaust—were brought to Spain by Hebrew and Arab savants, saved here, too, from the barbaric Goths, and zealously guarded by our people, for all faiths are nourished from a common wisdom. I do not know your faith, nor shall I question you in that respect. We are all sons of the Book, Jews, Moors, and Christians, and only if we accept this truth shall we live in peace one with another. Read; translate; conquer your prejudices, as every man has his own; think how many men have lived before us; we cannot deprecate their intelligence without mutilating our own. Read; translate; find for yourself the things I know and will not tell you, for greater will be your joy if you come to that knowledge by dint of your own efforts, and only thus will you perhaps learn something my long years have not taught me."

This man was an erudite Jew of advanced years, with a long white beard; his head was always covered by a black toque and the tails of his black tunic were gathered together beneath a silver star pinned upon his breast; in the center of this star, inscribed in bas-relief, was the number 1.

THE CABALA

The Cabala descended from Heaven, brought by angels to instruct the first man, guilty of disobedience, in the means by which he could regain his primordial nobility and happiness. First, you will love your Eternal God. He is the Ancient of ancients, the Mystery of mysteries, the Unknown of unknowns. Before creating any form upon this earth, He was alone, formless, resembling nothing. Who could conceive of how He was then, before the creation, since He had no form? Before the Ancient among ancients, the Most Concealed among all concealed things, had prepared the forms of kings and their first diadems, there was neither limit nor end. Therefore, he began to sculpt those forms and trace them in imitation of his own substance. He spread out before him a veil, and upon that veil he drew the kings and gave them their limits and their forms; but they could not survive. For God did not dwell among them; God did not reveal himself even in a form that would permit Him to be present in the midst of creation, and thus perpetuate it. The ancient worlds were destroyed: unformed worlds we call sparks. Because it was the work of God, and God was absent from it, Creation failed. Thus God knew that He himself was responsible for the Fall, and for that reason must also be responsible for redemption, for both would occur within the circle of divine attributes.

And God wept, saying: "I am the Most Ancient of the ancients. There is no one who knew my youth."

THE SECOND CHILD

In the eighth month of Celestina's pregnancy, Ludovico dared ask her: "Who is the father of your child? Do you know?"

Celestina wept and said no, she did not know. They did not know the father or the mother of the child they had stolen from the castle; now they knew only that she was the mother of the child about to be born, but its father was unknown . . .

"Did Jerónimo, your husband, never touch you?"

"Never, I swear it."

"But I did."

"Both you and Felipe."

"Our semen was mixed; poor girl, what will you give birth to . . . ?"

"And three old men in the woods, one after another . . ."

"And the first, then, who was the first?"

"The first man . . . ?"

"Yes . . ."

"El Señor, Felipe's father; Felipe did not dare; his father took my virginity on my wedding night . . ."

"Then you knew . . ."

"Who Felipe was? I always knew."

"Oh, Celestina, you should have spoken; those innocents would not have died . . ."

"Would you have exchanged all the world's pleasure for all its justice?"

"You are right; perhaps not."

"And now, would you exchange knowledge for vengeance?"

"Not yet. I need to know, that later I may act."

"And I, Ludovico?"

"The semen is mixed, I tell you. We shall never know the father of your child."

"I fornicated with the Devil, Ludovico."

Celestina's child was born one dark March night. The midwives came. The air of Toledo was green, and its sky, black silver. The Jews, beneath that dome of blazing phosphorus, sought shelter from the storm with fervent prayers. Lightning flashed like bloodless lances. The child was born feet first. He had six toes on each foot, and a blood-red cross upon his back.

When Ludovico carried the child to be presented at the synagogue, he bowed before his mentor, the erudite ancient. Ludovico glanced up and saw that gleaming on the star upon his protector's breast was inscribed the number 2.

THE ZOHAR

And thus, the Ancient of ancients, intending to rectify the flaw in His creation, which was His absence from the world and the cause of the common Fall of God and man, conceived of redemption as a way to manifest Himself among men and to remain present among them. But as He could not incarnate in human form, or be represented in any icon—not even as an exclamation point or a period—without forfeiting His unknown form in the unknown, manifested Himself in the very origins of the new life. Which was this: life and thought were intermingled. What is thought, is. What is, is thought. And this being so, all human souls, before their descent into the world, will have existed before God, in Heaven, for there, having been thought, they were. But before coming into the world, each soul is composed of a woman and a man joined together in a single being. Upon descending to earth, the two halves are separated and each half animates a different body. According to the works they do and the paths they follow upon the earth, the souls, if they work with love and follow the paths of love, will be reunited in death. But if they have not done so, the souls will pass through as many bodies as are necessary to incarnate love. Thus the damned souls take possession of living bodies, and fearful is the battle within every man: one former soul, incomplete and condemned to wander because of lack of love, takes possession of a portion of each new soul born in search of love. But as it has existed before God, in

Heaven, all that a soul learns on earth it has always known. And this being so, all that has existed in the past will also exist in the future, and all that will be has already been. And this being so, nothing is born or dies completely. Things simply exchange places.

THE SOMNAMBULIST

Celestina soon saw that the resemblance between the two children was not limited to the extreme manifestations of the feet, and the cross, but also that in all other ways, in their bodily proportions and their features, they were identical. She pointed this out to Ludovico; the student could say only that it was a true mystery, and since there was no possible explanation, and as such was its nature, nothing could be done but trust that someday the mystery would reveal itself. He said this grudgingly, for these events, and the reading and translations through which he earned his living in the synagogue, were contrary to the deepest beliefs of his rebellious intelligence: grace is directly accessible to man, without intermediaries; it must be incarnate in matter, direct itself to pragmatic ends, and be explicable by logic.

Ludovico advised Celestina not to venture outside the Jewry, enclosed on four sides by the Puerta del Cambrón, the hills of the Tagus, the old mosque, and St. Eulalia, as it was the couple's invisible protection and to venture out into the Christian sector would endanger their anonymity. But certain afternoons, driven by a waking dream, Celestina left the two children, taking advantage of their napping, or confident that neighbors would respond to their cries, and wandered like a sleepwalker beyond the limits of the Hebrew quarters.

Perhaps only now, twenty years later, did she dare explain the reason for those somnambulistic walks through steep stone alleyways and ancient Arab markets, to the Castle of San Servando, toward the river, to the Alcántara Bridge, to the northernmost ports, and to the southernmost port, Puerta de Hierro, where the fearful, dense, desolate, extensive, profound Castilian plain dies at the feet of the mountains of Toledo.

She looked at people. She sought one face. Many afternoons went by. She recognized no one. No one recognized her. They were all living. Each had been born before or after or at the same time as she. No dead wandered these Toledan streets, no one who could approach her, take her arm, stop her, and say: "I knew you before I died or you were born."

THE SEPHIROT

Everything that exists, everything formed by the Ancient (sanctified be his name!), is born of both male and female. The father is the wisdom from which everything is engendered. The mother is intelligence, as it was written: "To intelligence you shall give the name Mother." From this union is born a son, the major offshoot of wisdom and intelligence. His name is knowledge, or science. These three sum up in themselves everything that has been, is, and will be; at the same time, their union resides within the head of the Ancient of ancients, for He is all and all is He, and thus the Ancient (sanctified be his name!) is represented by the number 3, and has three heads that form but one. God reveals His creation through His attributes, the Sephirot that radiate like rays and extend like the branches of a tree. But all the rays and all the branches emanating from God must return to the number 3, lest they be destroyed in dispersion. Thus the Hebrew alphabet, which is the word of God, has twenty-two letters, and these letters can be combined and arranged in diverse manners, always as long as they are not dispersed and all possible combinations return always to the three mother letters, which are ש, ם, and א. The first is fire. The second water. The third air. From them is born everything that multiplies. And through them everything returns to unity. And from unity again derive the first three Sephirot, which are the Crown, Wisdom, and Intelligence. The first represents knowledge, or science. The second, the one who knows. The third, what is known. The son. The father. The mother. From this trinity are born all other things, manifesting themselves progressively in love, justice, beauty, triumph, glory, generation, and power. Rash would be he who, traveling this route, attempted to go beyond, for wishing to surpass himself he will know only the disintegration of all that preceded him: power, generation, glory, triumph, beauty, justice, love, intelligence, wisdom, and knowledge; and will only commit himself to the desert of the wandering death, seeking a soul to appropriate so he can reincarnate and reinitiate the circle of life, postponing his return to Heaven and reunion with the lost half of his soul. The holy soul, on the other hand, will stop, recognizing that plenitude possesses limits and that these limits assure that plenitude is plentiful, for infinite disintegration is a vacuum, and that soul will renounce ambitious mirages and will turn back upon its steps to return to the threshold of the three, which in turn is the threshold of return to unity. For it is written that every thing shall return to its origin, as from it, it emerged.

CELESTINA

AND THE DEVIL

And so it happened that one night, upon returning to the room they shared, Ludovico found Celestina crouching beside the flames of a brazier, weeping, biting upon a cord, and burning her hands in the flames; she was insensible to the weeping of the two children, and surrounded by little flour-filled cloth dolls.

The student tried to help her and draw her away from the flames, but the girl was possessed of an invincible strength, and she told him to leave her, that her memory was returning, that she had forgotten everything, her dream had been realized: love without prohibitions—a liberated body, she, Ludovico, and Felipe—had been like a drug, she had allowed herself to be lulled by a false illusion, now she was beginning to remember again, she had been violated by El Señor Don Felipe the Fair, taken coldly and brutally by that whoring, incontinent, hurried Prince, on the very night of her wedding with Jerónimo in the grange, and she had said to herself: I shall give myself to the Devil, I have no friend but the Devil, only Satan could be more powerful than this filthy Señor, God has not thought me worthy of His protection, perhaps the Devil will defend me, I shall be his wife, he will give me the power to avenge myself against El Señor and his house, El Señor and all his descendants, and she held her hands to the fire, drew them back, took the cord and bit upon it to relieve her torment, plunged her hands into the fire, invoking him, angel of venom and death, come, take me . . . and amidst the flames, Ludovico, a shadow appeared, visible only in the center of the fire, as if requiring purest light to appear and to be seen, and that form of pure shadow without face or hands or legs, pure darkness revealed by the flames, spoke to me and said:

"Do not weep, woman. There is one who will take pity on you. You have learned what the world offers you if you obey the law of God and as a reward suffer the cruelty of men. Remember that woman was once a goddess. She was goddess because she was keeper of the most profound wisdom. This ancient female sage knew that nothing is as it appears to be, and that behind all appearances there is a secret that both refutes and completes them. Men were unable to dominate the world while women knew these secrets. So they joined together to divest them of their dignity, their priesthood, their privilege: they excised and amended the ancient texts that recognized the androgynous character of the first Divinity, they suppressed mention of the wife of Yahweh, they changed the Scriptures to hide this truth: that the first created being was both masculine and feminine, made in the image and likeness of the Divinity in whom both sexes were joined; in His place they invented a God of vengeance and anger, a bearded goat; they expelled woman from Paradise, to her they assigned guilt for the Fall. Nothing of this is true, it is merely the lie that is indispensable to the foundation of man's power, power without mystery, cruel, divorced from love, separated from real time, which is woman's time, simultaneous time: the power of man is captured within a simple succession of events which in their linear progression lead every thing and every being to death. Hear me, woman: I shall tell you how to conquer death; I shall tell you how to conquer this atrocious masculine order; and I shall tell you secrets, see how much you can do with them, and quickly, your time is brief, I shall demand much of you, you will be exhausted, all you can do is initiate what I ask you, you will not be able to finish it, it is too much for one person, you must realize that in time so you can transmit what you know to another woman in time, before men again wrest from you the forces that today I grant you; remember, let another woman continue what you initiate, for you can only continue what others have initiated in my name. Woman was Goddess. I was Angel.''

''What,'' moaned Celestina, ''what will you teach me, what must I know, I do not understand . . .''

''Your wounded hands are the sign of our communion: fire. The woman who kisses your hands shall inherit what I give to you.''

''When? How shall I know?''

''Look for me in the streets of Toledo. There you shall find me, when fate so decrees.''

''What shall I do in the meantime?''

''Flee to the forest. Spirits and succubi dwell there, the familiars of witches. Seek their counsel. They are the ancient pagan gods, expelled from their altars by cruel Christianity. They will recognize in you the ancient goddesses of the Mediterranean world, condemned to witchcraft by Christian powers and executed in public squares with the same cruelty accorded Christ upon Golgotha. Adore the forbidden goddesses. Disguise them as an innocent game. Fabricate dolls made from rags. Fill them with flour. Flour is the color of the moon. There dwells the hidden goddess of all time.''

''Where? In the forest? In the moon?''

But the invisible vision in the center of the fire had disappeared.

NUMBER 3

Morning, midday, and night. Beginning, middle, and end. Father, mother, and child. Everything that is complete is three times complete. Thrice a saint, truly a saint. Dead three days, truly dead. Three regions make up the heavens: sky, land, and water. Three bodies have the heavens: sun, moon, and earth. Thrice is the rite repeated, and three persons fulfill it. Sacrificial animals must be three years old. The Law ordains three fasts per year and three prayers a day. Three is the number of righteous men. Three flocks come to the well. Guilt extends unto the third generation. Three generations are needed to avenge fathers. Three years without a harvest justify the husbandman's impatience, and the abandonment of his lands. Three days is the guest tolerated. Three times, one circles the funeral pyre. Three are the Furies. Three are the judges of death. Every three years are celebrated the festivals of Bacchus. Three were the first augurs. Three, the first vestals. Three, the books of the Sibyls. Three days pass in the descent into Hell. Three days the soul remains beside the corpse awaiting its resurrection. Thrice are repeated the words that protect voyagers, that induce sleep, that calm the fury of the sea. Thrice Yahweh blessed creation. Heaven offers us three witnesses. Three daughters had Job. Three sons Noah, and from them we have descended. Thrice Balaam blessed Israel. Three friends had Job, and three, Daniel. Three emissaries from Heaven visited Abraham. Thrice Jesus was tempted. Thrice he prayed in Gethsemane. Thrice Simon denied Him. He was crucified at the third hour. There were three crosses on Golgotha. Thrice Jesus revealed himself to His disciples after the Resurrection. Three times Saul desired. Father, Son, and Holy Ghost. Beast, Serpent, and False Prophet. Faith, Hope, and Charity. Three sides has a triangle. One is the root of all. Two is the negation of one. Three is the synthesis of one and two. Three contains both. It balances them. It announces the plurality that follows. Three is the complete number. The diadem of the beginning and the middle. The reunion of the three times. Present, past, and future. Everything ends. Everything begins again.

THE DUEL

Many afternoons Celestina wandered through the streets of Toledo, steep and level, solitary and tumultuous, opening into broad plazas, honeycombs of long narrow lanes, seeking the promise of the Devil. Her search was for one known face.

One late afternoon she passed by a walled garden, and she heard cries in the garden and noises on the other side of the high wall. A cloaked cavalier with a nun in his arms leapt over the wall. The gate opened and two other cavaliers ran into the street, their swords unsheathed. The nun lay in a swoon; the cloaked man was wounded in one leg. He saw Celestina. He entreated her: "Try to revive the novitiate. Take her with you and I shall come for her. Tell me where you live."

Celestina had no time to respond. The armed cavaliers rushed toward the cloaked man and he, tossing his cape over his shoulder, arose and unsheathed his sword. Steel clashed against steel; the cavalier of the cape battled with joyful fervor against his rivals, and in spite of his wounded leg held them at bay. Celestina turned to reviving the nun; she succeeded in getting her to her feet, and, supporting her, led her to a hidden lane not far from the scene of the duel, where the nun again fell to the ground; close by, they could hear the shouted insults, the cry of the vanquished, the hurrahs of the victors. Celestina watched the two men with bloody swords run by, down the wider street, away from the arbor roofed by ivy reaching out from the garden on either side and clasping gnarled fingers above the heads of Celestina and the nun.

"Go, go to him," sighed the nun, "see if they have killed him."

Celestina ran to the site of the duel, where the abductor lay bleeding. A scarlet rosebud bloomed upon the brocade of his breast. Celestina knelt beside the dying man, not knowing exactly what to do: the cavalier of dark beauty looked at her through half-closed eyes, smiled, and managed to say: "Celestina . . . Celestina . . . Is it you, you are young again? Oh, Mother, that I meet you again only as I am again dying . . . I who saw you die before . . . oh, God, oh, Death, have I not always said . . . so distant a challenge . . . !"

And so speaking, he died. Terrified, Celestina ran from the body back to the nun hidden in the shadowy lane. Dead leaves were falling upon her white habit. She asked Celestina the outcome of the duel and the fate of the cavalier, and Celestina said: "He died."

The nun did not weep, but merely sat there beneath the dense ivy bower of that path, with a strange expression in her eyes; finally she said: "He murdered my father for love of me. I loved my father's murderer. My love for the living was greater than my love for the dead. He did not come to deceive me, but my father, buried here in this very convent. He came to mock the sepulcher, to challenge the statue of my father; he invited him to dine this very night at the inn, he refused my pleas to take me with him again, he said he spent only a few days with each woman he loved, one to fall in love with her, another to win her, another to abandon her, one more to find another in her place, and one hour to forget her; I pleaded; he refused; my brothers entered, they challenged him, he laughed; he seized me and fled with me, not for love of me, but to defy my brothers. He scaled the convent wall, we fell, I fainted. He died."

The nun toyed with the dead leaves. "I saw my father's statue tremble, the stone come to life. He would have gone to the rendezvous, I am sure. Now you see, little sad-eyed girl, how nothing has ended as I planned it, but instead in a squalid back-alley duel. Please help me, take me to the door of the convent. My honor is saved. But not my love. Do you know something, child? The worst of it all is that my fancy is still unsatisfied. Don Juan should not have died this way . . . Perhaps in another life. Come, help me, please take me to the convent door.''

TWO SPEAK OF THREE

Ludovico said he believed he understood some part of what he had read and translated, but now he asked the aged doctor with the black robes and with the star upon his breast for an hour of conversation, because for the moment the student could go no further without the vital juices of dialogue, which animates thought and wrests it from the inert page.

''I am listening,'' the aged man said.

''Your texts honor the number 3, but your star is inscribed with the number 2 . . .''

''Which once was one.''

''Do two deny one?''

''Only relatively. Duality diminishes unity. But it denies it absolutely only if the duality is definitive. Two eternally opposite terms could not ever combine their action for a common effect. Pure duality, should it exist, would be an irreversible severance of the continuity of things; it would be the negation of cosmic unity; it would open an eternal abyss between the two parts, and this opposition would merit the epithets of sterile, inactive, static. Evil would have triumphed.''

''Have I read correctly? Can only the third term reanimate inert duality?''

''You have read well. Binaries differentiate. Ternaries activate. Unity confers latent individuality. Duality is severing and unchanging differentiation. A trinity, as it activates the encounter between opposites, is the perfect manifestation of unity. It combines the active with the passive, it unites the feminine principle with the masculine. Three is the being that lives. What would God and the Devil do without a third, except confront one another, immobile, throughout an endless night? Good and evil: man activates them, for God and the Devil are in contention for man.''

''This morning I was translating the Cabalist, ibn-Gabirol, and he says: 'Unity is not the root of totality, for Unity is but one form and totality is both form and matter; three is the unity of totality, that is to say that Unity represents form, and the number 2, matter.' ''

"The sage speaks wisely, for three is the creative number, and without it form and matter would be inert. Nothing develops without the intervention of a third factor; without three, everything would remain forever in static polarity. Youth and old age require a middle age; past and future, the present; sensation and awareness, memory; sum and remainder, substitution. Two equal quantities in themselves are equal only by comparison to a third quantity. The intelligences of form and matter are joined and ordered in the number 3. Beginning from that number, man is armed to confront the world, and life. But he is alone."

"What follows 3?"

"Four is nature, the cycle of constant repetitions: four seasons, four elements. Five is the first circular number: the number of the creature who has five senses, and who enclosed within a circle forms a pentagram, the five points his head, his hands, and his feet: it is the hand of the prophet Mohammed. Six is 2 times 3, perfection of the form and matter incarnate in man: beauty, justice, balance. Seven is man along his way, fate, the progression of life, for as the wise Hindu of the Atharva-Veda says, 'Time moves upon seven wheels.' Eight is liberation, health, the state of well-being resulting from the progression of seven: eight are the ways of Gautama Buddha, the eight rules for emerging from the river of reincarnations and touching the shore of Nirvana. Nevertheless, few are those who achieve such beatitude, and the number 9 signifies redemption and the reintegration of all things upon the threshold of unity: Nirvana is not the final point of human evolution, for he who has reached Nirvana must, in an act of enormous charity and in solidarity with a multitude of suffering creatures, renounce his personality to aid in the work of universal redemption. Such perfection is reached at the number 10: unity truly realized is the collective being, common good. All is for all; nothing is for one; the creature returns to the first Unity of the Ancient of ancients and the Unknown of the unknown: praised be His name!"

"Is there anything beyond that reunion?"

"The number 11, which, as St. Augustine of Hippo wisely said, is the arsenal of sin. Ten closes the great circle of creation and life, redemption and reunion. In eleven there is one small unity, a miserable one opposing divine unity: Lucifer. Eleven is temptation; having everything, we desire more. The multiples of eleven only accentuate this evil and this misfortune; twenty-two, thirty-three, forty-four, fifty-five, increasing dispersion, the always vaster separation between human and divine unity . . . Oh, my young friend: may that number never appear on the star upon my breast."

"Will the number 3 appear instead?"

"This does not depend on me. Will a third child be born?"

THE KNIGHT OF THE
SORROWFUL COUNTENANCE

Celestina expected the nun to kiss her fire-scarred hands, but it did not happen.

The resigned nun disappeared behind the closed doors of the convent and for a moment Celestina stood in the street staring at the corpse of the murdered cavalier, trying to understand his last words, saddened because she understood none of it. What wisdom could she possibly transmit, knowing nothing?

She walked slowly, not knowing whether she was dreaming or waking, far from the scene of the duel, toward the port of Almofada, and as she was passing by an inn she heard a great commotion and a stout, ruddy-complexioned peasant came running out of the inn, raising a great alarm, and when he saw her he took her by the arm and said to her: Here, wench, whoever you may be, please help me, for my master has gone mad and I believe you are the only one who can restore in him a little calm and reason; try to behave like a fine lady, although it matters very little, since he sees nobility where there is only meanness, and perceives fine breeding in those of lowest office.

In the courtyard of the inn four serving boys and the innkeeper were mercilessly tossing in a blanket a thin-shanked old man with a short white beard and eyes of saintly choler; as this unfortunate sailed through the air he shouted and cried out: Knaves, villains, varlets; and the innkeeper shouted even more loudly: Go to the devil, you son of Satan, for you have run through all my wineskins with your rusty old sword till there is nothing left but a sieve, and the knight shouted, no, they were giants, they were magicians and enchanters come to challenge him by night, in the shadows, like cowards, but they had not counted on the always ready sword that had subdued the furies of Brandabarbarán de Boliche, Lord of all Araby, but as that does not apply in this instance, sobbed the peasant, do as your master orders and sit with him to take a meal, for neither master nor meal will be mine after this adventure; I came naked into this world, and naked I find myself now, I neither gain nor lose, and at that moment the knight's bones hit the dust, and as he lay there the serving boys thrashed him with poles, laughing uproariously, and then went about their chores.

"Those cowardly knaves had more arms than the hundred possessed by the titan Briareo," moaned the flogged knight when he could bring himself to speak, amidst sounds of pigs, asses, and hens; with cloths dampened in water his peasant squire soothed his wounds, murmuring, "Whether the pitcher falls upon stone or stone upon pitcher, it's all bad for the pitcher, but you must see. Your Mercy, that there is no evil from which some good does not result, and now you can lift your beard from the mud, your efforts were not in vain, for with them you freed this most illustrious and exalted lady who is here beside me, Señor, and who comes to thank you for the heroic deed you performed last night, which freed her from the captivity of magicians . . .''

The cudgeled knight stared intently at Celestina, then at the peasant, and trembled with rage. "Is this how you mock me, my friend? Do you believe I am so addled my eyes would not clearly see before me this old witch, this bawd?; when she passes by, the very stones shout out, 'Old whore!' and she has rubbed her back raw in every brothel in the land. Though you not believe it, I was once young, and it was at the hands of this same false, stubble-chinned, evil old woman I lost my virtue, for promising to gain me access to the bedchamber of my beloved, she instead in her own chamber drugged me with love philters and took me for herself, I having paid in advance. I know you well, greedy, tongue-clacking, foul-mouthed old witch, may you burn in Hell, shameless, prevaricating sophist, bawd, magpie, trotting around convents to further your vile trade; and you delivered my beloved Dulcinea to another, for more money, what are you doing in these lands? ah, grubby, greedy go-between, you may be a plum, a purple-juiced juror in the tribunal of lust, but you'll not get two prunes from me . . . Be off with her, Sancho, for I am seething with rage, I knew her as a youth, I thought her dead—ha! let Judas believe it!—and may God grant you evil Easters, the bad weed never dies! And you, squire, why do you try to bring me a cat for a hare, and foist off scrubbing girls and whores and bawds in the stead of princesses? Do you think I am blind? Do you think I do not recognize the real reality of things? Windmills are giants. But Celestina is not Dulcinea. Come, Sancho, let us leave Toledo, which Livy wisely labeled *urbs parva*, lesser city . . . for wide is Castile!''

A SICK DREAM

Do you begin to understand, woman? I shall make use of Ludovico. You will tell him what has happened to you. He will scold you affectionately for having wandered beyond the limits of the Jewry: you see?, you were recognized twice. I feared that. You have been in the streets. I, in the libraries. Do we now know the same things? This is what I wrote after reading, and after listening to you. What is thought, is. What is, is thought. I travel from spirit to matter. I return from matter to spirit. There are no frontiers. Nothing is forbidden me. I believe I am several persons mentally. Then I am several persons physically.

I fall in love in a dream. Then I encounter the loved being when I awake. Did you not go to the burial of the cavalier who died in the duel before the convent? I did. Your story wakened my curiosity. I arrived early, before the mourners, even though I assumed they would be few, given the dead man's evil reputation. I looked at him, lying within his coffin. His beard had grown in the two days following his death. I looked at his hands. His fingernails had grown, too. I separated the hands crossed upon his breast. All the lines of fortune and life, intelligence and love, had disappeared from the palms: they were a white wall, two newly whitewashed walls. Upon his breast, other hands—these still blessed with fortune and life, intelligence and love—had placed a paper with these words:

> Let him be warned who doubts God's wrath:
> His hand will not be stayed.
> There is no time that will not come,
> Nor debt that not be paid.

Again I looked at his face. It had changed. It had been transformed. It was not the face of the man you saw die in the street. It was not the face I had seen as I quietly entered the temple, before I had parted his hands and read that paper. He was a different man. Do you understand, Celestina? This horrified me. Once more I looked at the new face of the dead man and told myself: This is the face that one of our children, the one we abducted from the castle, will possess when he becomes a man. How shall I know? I could search through the streets, as you have done, for a man who has the dead man's face. Or I could wait, patiently, for twenty years and then know whether, as he matures, this child will have the dead man's face. Wait. I left the temple of the Christ of the Light, previously the mosque of Bib-al-Mardan, turning my back upon the coffin, murmuring what today I write and read to you:

"One lifetime is not sufficient. Many existences are needed to fulfill one personality."

Two men said they had known you long ago. Both believed you were old; one of them, dead. Imagine what I have read and written and now communicate to you. Each child, one born every minute, reincarnates in each of the persons who die every minute. It is not possible to know in whom we reincarnate because there are no actual witnesses who can recognize that being we reincarnate. But if there were one single witness capable of recognizing me as the person I had been, then what? He stops me in the street . . . before dismounting from a horse, or entering an inn . . . he takes my arm . . . he forces me to participate in a past life that had been mine. He is a survivor; the only one who can know that I am reincarnated.

This child and you. The world and you, Celestina. You have wandered the streets of Toledo searching for the one who could recognize you. You found two men who knew your eternal name and your variable destinies. It does not matter. Go out again. There are others who do not speak—but who see us; those who do not see—but who remember us; those who do not remember—but who imagine us. That is enough to decide our fate, though we never exchange a word. Who are the immortals? This is what I have read, this is what I wrote, let me read it to you:

"Those who lived many times, those who reappear from time to time; those who had more life than their own death, but less time than their own life."

What is the shared wisdom of God and the Devil, Celestina? The Cabala says nothing disappears completely, everything is transformed, what we believe to be dead has but changed place. Places remain; we do not see them change place. But what is time but measurement, invention, imagination? What is, is thought. What is thought, is. Times change space, join together or are superimposed, and then separate. We can travel from one time to another, Celestina, without changing space. But he who voyages from one time to another and does not return in time to the present loses his memory of the past (if it was from the past he arrived) or his memory of the future (if it was there he had his origins). He is captured by the present. The present is his life. And each of us, without exception, returns late to our present: time does not stop to await us while we travel to the past or the future; we always arrive late; a minute or a century, it is the same. We can no longer remember that we were also living before or after the present. Perhaps this was your pact with the Devil: to live in our present without memory of your past or your future, if it was from them you arrived at our today.

I imagine, woman, I only imagine; I read, I write, I listen, I tell you. What did that dead cavalier and the cudgeled knight remember when they saw you? Who you were, where you lived before, where you died before, Celestina? I am thinking for you. If I wished to rid myself of the memory of something hideously sad, this would be my pact with the Devil: "Take my memory and I will give you my soul."

God cannot undo what has been done. The Devil, on the other hand, affirms that he can convert what was into what was not. Thus, through the Devil, God challenges and tempts man. But as we forget a hideous event, do we not also run the risk of forgetting the best of our lives, our parents' love, a woman's beauty, a man's passion, the joy of friendship, everything? This is the Devil's condition, woman: to forget everything or to forget nothing.

Do you know that this morning the elder of our two children, the one we stole from the castle, crawled out the door as if he wished to tell me goodbye. I smiled at him and blew him a kiss. I had scarcely taken two steps before a hand stopped me: a cold, pale, almost wax-like hand. It was a cloaked cavalier.

"Who is that child?" he asked me in a voice deadened by the folds of his cape.

"He is mine," I replied.

"Look at my face," he said to me, uncovering himself.

I looked at him carefully, without noting anything unusual except an excessive paleness similar to that of his hands. He recognized my indifference; he touched his cheek, then extended both hands and showed them to me. "Look. My beard continues to grow. My fingernails continue to grow. Does that not seem extraordinary to you?"

I told him no. Then he turned his hands over to show me his smooth and unlined palms. I concealed my amazement; I know that the cavalier wanted to smile, but pain prevented him; I noticed then the rosette of dried blood upon his breast; I tried to offer my arm to assist him; he stopped me with a disdainful gesture and a few hollow, sonorous words: "Every man born becomes a body for every man who dies. Do you want to know the face the child who crawled out to say goodbye to you a moment ago will possess in twenty years? Go directly to the temple of the Christ of the Light. You will find me there. And you will see the face your son will possess. I was unable to terminate my life."

You say that cavalier died two days ago in a duel? Go, then, Celestina, continue your search, conquer the Devil, seek what you have forgotten in the words of those who speak to you but do not look at you; in the glances of those who look but do not remember you; in the memory of those who do not remember, but imagine you. In that way you will overcome the Devil: you will be the Devil, you will know what he knows, and also what he does not know.

Reality is a sick dream.

WOUNDED LIPS

Celestina saw in the city marketplace a little girl about eleven years old, accompanied by her father. Father and daughter were offering candles, dyes, and honey for sale. This child was very beautiful, with gray eyes and an upturned nose; her skirts were old and patched, and she wore no shoes.

Celestina noticed her because she was like a drop of crystalline water in a sea of blood: nearby, chickens' necks were being wrung, farther away a sheep was being quartered; one man was butchering a pig, another gutting a fish; blood ran between the rough plaza paving stones and down the gutters of the alleyways; urine and offal were thrown from windows, dogs wandered unrestrained, and flies buzzed about the severed animal heads; the water casks emitted a terrible stench, buyers and sellers streamed in and out of dank rooms; and in their fast, penitents shouted their visions from their windows: the Devil, the Devil, the Devil appeared before me; dressed in white, a twelve-year-old bride passed by on the way to St. Sebastian followed by a sparse train of yellowish, pockmarked, hawking and spitting women, and behind her came the munificent, obese, sexagenarian groom, distributing coins among the unruly throng of beggars with ulcerated, never-healing sores upon their arms and chests; children pullulated beneath the archways, fighting among themselves over scraps stolen from the dogs; many children were sleeping in the streets, beneath stairways, on thresholds; a few Dominican priests crossed the plaza, looking like spotted dogs in their habits of white wool and black capes, singing:

> From evil dreams defend our eyes,
> From fantasies and nocturnal fears;
> The phantom enemy is near,
> Free us from all corruption.

And the little girl with gray eyes and upturned nose, shoeless, in patched skirts: Celestina looked at her in the midst of that throng in the old market of Toledo, for there was nothing more beautiful than she. And she looked at her also because two men had recognized her, and one had said to her: You are dead; and they had called her Mother, and old whore. She saw herself in that child. She wanted to see herself there. So she must have looked at that age, before what was to happen had happened, if she had reached the present from the future; after what had happened had happened, if she had come to this morning from the past.

Sadly the child gazed upon sadness: the slaughter of beasts, the child bride, bodies covered with sores, the raving of madmen, a lamb bound by the feet, and a butcher with dagger poised high, preparing to plunge it into the white wool of the tiny animal.

The child ran to plead with the butcher: no, it is just a lamb, I look after them, I protect them from the wolves, I stay awake through the nights with them, do not kill the lamb.

The butcher laughed and shoved the child aside; she fell to the bloody stone. Her father ran to aid her, but Celestina reached her first; she patted her head, and held out her hands to her. The child, eyes filled with tears, kissed them. She looked up, her childish lips now bore the mark of Celestina's wounds; Celestina stared at her hands;

they were hers, the hands of the bashful and happy bride of the wedding in the grange; the signs of her travail had disappeared, a tattoo of wounds gleamed on the child's lips.

"Who are you?"

"I am a shepherdess, señora."

"Where do you live?"

"My father and I live in the woods near the castle of a great Señor whose name is Felipe."

The father drew his child away from Celestina; child, my little girl, what has happened to you? look at your mouth, who injured you, this whore-son butcher? no, this evil, ragged witch, here, everyone, after the vicious creature, look at my daughter's mouth, after her, run, Celestina, knock down tents, stumble over pigs, a house, a stairway, dogs barking, flies buzzing, dank rooms, basins of excrement, madmen shout at you, I have seen the Devil, straw upon the floor, cover yourself, hide, they are going to burn you, witch, flee, wait, night is falling, the marketplace is emptying, the incident is forgotten, you look from the tiny window of your hiding place upon the city spread before you, a steep promontory, encircled by the Tagus, layered in steep grades of stone, a besieged city, accessible only by the north across the desolate plain, defended on the south by the deep ravines of the river, and now, escape, like a mouse scurry through the night, return to the Jewry, awaken Ludovico, what has happened to you?, I must go, I must search, I shall return, wait for me, care for the children, and if I cannot, come to meet me, Ludovico, where, Celestina?, on the beach, on the same beach where we dreamed of embarking for a new world, on the same day, July 14, when Celestina?, twenty years from now.

THE THIRD CHILD

She begged for charity along the roads and in the hamlets, and after walking three days she saw the towers of the castle she thought never to see again, and to the north, the vast forest.

She recognized it. Here she had found refuge when she abandoned Jerónimo: the forest is a fine hiding place for a woman bewitched; and here in the long moonlit nights, surrounded by sounds of the owl and the wolf and the cicada, she was visited by a husband without light or shadow, pure nothingness, who said to her: "I shall reward you, Celestina . . . But your time is brief . . . Do not believe my reward will be eternal . . . Your happiness will be an illusion . . . Transmit to another woman what you know when you know . . . Not yet, not yet . . .''

Here she played with her flour-filled dolls. She took a deep breath. She recognized the odor of damp earth, the whisper of the arching branches of the elms above, and of fallen leaves on the ground, remnants of a forgotten autumn. Here one night she had been taken by three aged merchants. Here she dreamed what her lover spoke into her ear: ''. . . A graceful youth . . . The stigmata of his house: prognathism . . . He will pass by here . . . Detain him . . . You will recognize him . . . He did not want to rape you . . . You know him . . . He is the son of the Señor who so brutally exercised his rights as Lord . . . Take him to the beach . . . The Cabo de los Desastres . . .''

And now one night as she approached a clearing in the woods she saw her.

It was the young girl who had kissed her hands in Toledo. She was tending her sheep and in spite of the full moon and the balmy air had built a small fire to protect herself and her flock. Celestina looked at her with love: the girl was scrubbing her lips with her hand, again and again; she spat, but the wound on her lips would not be erased. It is she, Celestina said to herself, I know, but I do not understand . . . She tried to recall what she knew; everything was a sign, and the directions were so many . . . One lifetime would not be sufficient to follow that network of intersecting roads.

She heard an animal's low whine. The child picked up a burning brand. She held it low; it illuminated a large gray she-wolf. The animal held out a wounded paw, and she knelt beside it and took its paw. The beast licked her hand and lay down beside the fire. Celestina watched, hidden behind a clump of white poplars that seemed to swallow the light of the moon. After a while, the animal gave birth, amidst the brambles and the dust and the bleating of the sheep. It was a boy child. He was born feet first. He had six toes upon each foot, and upon his back the sign of the cross; it was not a painted cross, but part of his flesh: flesh incarnate.

SPECTER OF TIME

That morning Ludovico encountered the ancient of the Synagogue of the Passing kneeling upon a rug and murmuring prayers, huddled in so profound a bow that his head touched his knees. The student waited until the prayer had ended.

"Do you wish to speak?" asked the ancient.

"Yes, but not to annoy you."

"I was waiting for you."

"I have been uneasy."

"I know. You have read much here. Not all of it agrees with what you believe."

"I dreamed aloud one afternoon on the beach. I spoke and I dreamed of a world without God, where every man would create his own grace and offer its benefits to other men so their lives would be transformed. Now I do not know. I do not know because I know that one lifetime is not sufficient to fulfill all the promises of individual grace. I fear, venerable sir, to go to the opposite extreme and believe that spirit is all and matter nothing; the spirit eternal, the matter perishable."

"Nothing dies, nothing perishes completely, neither spirit nor matter."

"But do they develop similarly? Are thoughts transmitted? Are bodies transmitted?"

"Ideas, you know, are never completely realized. At times they recede, they hibernate as some beasts do, and await the opportune moment to reappear: thought bides its time. The idea that seemed dead in one time is reborn in another. The spirit is transported, duplicated, at times substituted; it disappears, one believes it dead, it reappears. In truth, it announces itself in every word we speak. There is no word that is not laden with forgetfulness and memories, colored with illusions and failures; nevertheless, there is no word that is not the bearer of imminent renovation; each word we say simultaneously announces a word we do not know because we have forgotten it and a word we do not know because we desire it. The same happens with bodies, which are matter; and all matter contains the aura of what it was previously and the aura of what it will be when it disappears."

"Then am I living an epoch which is my own, or am I but the specter of another epoch, either past or future?"

"Each of the three."

The ancient of the synagogue arose from his abject position and looked at Ludovico.

He saw the star upon the ancient's breast. Upon it was inscribed, in bas-relief, the number 3.

MEMORY UPON THE LIPS

Come, child, come to my arms, do you remember me?, *señora sí*, I kissed your hands, you wounded my lips, I scrub my mouth but it doesn't come clean, every day the scars bite deeper, like a tattoo, child *señora sí*, a mouth of many colors, let me kiss you, *señora sí*, do you remember me? *señora sí*, my pretty little girl, I would like to be like you forever, to be like you again, once I must have been like you, I no longer remember, what else do you remember?, *señora sí*, a black hairy scorpion, where, child?, between the legs of El Señor, *señora sí*, here in this forest, one night, El Señor on horseback, his shirt open, excited, riding by night, alone, swallowing up the leagues, *señora sí*, lashing the tree branches, like a madman, shouting, drunken, I don't know, lopping off the heads of wheat stalks, you saw him?, *señora sí*, I was hiding, I put out my fire, I hid as you did just now, amid the poplars, trees of light, light of the moon, a she-wolf caught in a trap, El Señor dismounted, laughing, shouting, growling, stripping off his clothes, he freed the she-wolf from the trap, he lowered his trousers, the black scorpion, he seized the she-wolf, the animal defended herself, growled, howled, clawed, he put the scorpion in the she-wolf's bottom, you remember that?, *señora sí*, but my voice, my voice is fading, *señora sí*, he took off his clothes like this?, *señora sí*, so warm, what a beautiful spring, child, your little breasts are budding, little lemons, your fine legs, open them, child, *señora sí*, Toledo, the marketplace, the beheaded sheep, your underarms, how moist, how perfumed, *señora sí*, how bare your little mound, you can count the silken hairs, so few, *señora sí*, open your legs, child, how tight your little cunt, it smells of saffron, my pretty child, my delicious child, *señora sí*, do you like my soft tongue? ah yes, ah yes, I'll kiss you all over, will you let me?, ah yes, ah yes, El Señor, the hairy scorpion, the burning ass of the she-wolf, the red anus of the beast, he took her, he shouted, he laughed, a drunken madman, *señora sí*, your tongue in my mouth, my tongue on yours, forest poplar, bramble, sheep bell, she-wolf, sheep, severed heads of wheat, I absorb it all, all of nature, let nothing escape me, my tongue in your ear, hear my secrets, hear what I know, nothing dies, everything is transformed, places remain, times change, I carried you within me, I was you when I was young like you, I penetrate inside you, the black scorpion, the dark tongue, my time has ended, *señora sí*, your voice is my voice, *señora sí*, I am exhausted, *señora sí*, I give you my life, continue it, *señora sí*, I give to you my voice, I give to you my lips, I give to you my wounds, my memory is upon your lips, men infected me with illness, the Devil with wisdom, daughter of no man, lover of all, I am poisoned, El Señor transmitted his illness to me when he took me on my wedding night, I transmitted it to his son in the castle bedchamber, I was the conduit, through me the father infected the son, they need us, they pursue us, there will be no well-being for man upon earth as long as a single black hole of sulphur and flesh and hair and blood exists, there will be no well-being for woman upon earth while the hairy black scorpion commands, the whip of flesh, the erectile serpent, remember me, child, *señora sí*, grow, try to be like me, I leave you my wounded lips, upon them my memory, upon them my words, you will know and you will tell what I knew and told you, I shall know and I shall tell in time, he told me, act in time, your name is Celestina, you remember the whole of my life, you live it now for me, in twenty years, on an afternoon of a fourteenth of July you will be on the beach of the Cabo de los Desastres, divert paths, deceive wills, alter time, you must be there, we have a rendezvous, *señora sí, señora sí . . .*

SIMON IN TOLEDO

I scarcely recognized her, the monk Simón said to Ludovico one night, as the student served him a plate of lentils and dried codfish, for her voice was hoarse and low, and the rags she wore could not hide the fierce wounds on her face and hands, still bleeding as if a wild beast had wounded her with claw and fang, and her eyes held no light.

She said she had found me by inquiring in every desolate city where houses have been abandoned by their dwellers, where the beasts of the forest, guided by instinct, come and make their dens in halls and bedchambers. I asked her whether she did not fear for the life of the child. She laughed and said: "A child born as this one will never die from a vile plague."

She gave him to me, Ludovico; she told me where you were and asked me to deliver the child to you. She said that without fail she would be at the rendezvous in twenty years. In the houses of the dead everything is open, doors and treasure chests. The servants who have not died have fled. Celestina took a handful of gold and another of jewels from a chest, cackled, and left as if fleeing, as if cloaked, making herself small like the miser who fears the light of the sun will melt her gold.

But first she gave me these coins for you. It was her last generous gesture. She wept as she gave them to me. She had laughed as she took them.

Look carefully at the profile minted on these coins, Ludovico.
The salient jaw.
The heavy, protuberant lip.

The dead gaze.
It is El Señor.

THE ALCAZABA
IN ALEXANDRIA

Ludovico made his farewells to the learned doctor of the Synagogue of the Passing and traveled far, very far, with the three children.

He had read in the texts in Toledo a manuscript wherein Pliny speaks of a people without women, without love, and without money—an eternal society into which no one is ever born. This people lived in a village near the shores of the Dead Sea, fleeing the great cities to the end of perfecting their simple, silent, and austere lives. There Ludovico desired that the three children left in his care grow to manhood.

They sailed from Valencia on a Christian ship that one night left them near the port of Alexandria. They were soon lost in the twisting alleyways of that city, the widow of gods and of men; in his beggar's rags, and despite his great strength, struggling to carry the three children in his arms, he attracted a great deal of attention. Nevertheless, he was well received. He spoke Arabic, he could pay for lodging and meals, and the three boys were singularly quiet and well behaved. They found lodging in a dovecote on a flat rooftop high above the city and from there Ludovico watched the hundred-armed river empty into the waters of the incorporeal sea.

One night, because of the heat, he was sleeping upon the sun-bleached stones of the rooftop, and he dreamed he set out in a small sailboat, and rowed toward the source of the Nile. Only three stars shone in the firmament; there was no other light and a great silence lay over the land of Egypt. As he rowed, he moved closer and closer to the three silent stars until, reflected in the water, they were within reach of his hand. He plunged his hand into the river and fished out a star.

First the star trembled. Then it spoke. It said sun, and the sun appeared. It said wheat, and the shores were covered with undulating heads of grain. It said city, and a white settlement emerged from the sands of the desert. It said children, and three persons, two youths and a girl, appeared and swam beside the boat, guiding it to the shore of the river.

"This is my brother, and this my sister," said one of the youths.

During the first day, the youth who had first spoken sowed the land, harvested its fruit, channeled the waters of the river so they irrigated the desert, formed bricks from the black mud of the shore, constructed a house, and thus provided both sustenance and shelter to his brother and sister.

That night, as an act of gratitude, his sister took him as her husband and they slept together in the house. The other brother lay down in the night air, but brief was his rest. He arose and walked beside the river, wakeful, resentful, barely containing his anger and envy.

At the dawn of the second day, the envious brother entered the house where the couple lay, and killed his sleeping brother. He dragged the corpse to the river and threw it into the waters. The wife-and-sister wept, and walked along the muddy shores, searching for the body of her brother-and-husband. The murdering brother told Ludovico: "You are sleeping on a rooftop. Seal your lips. If you betray me, I shall also kill you in the dream. You will never awaken."

And he walked into the desert, naked and defenseless.

Ludovico went in search of the woman. After a while he found her kneeling beside some rushes that had trapped the body of her dead brother. The woman pressed her lips to those of the dead man and revived him with her breath, passing life from her mouth to his. Then she said: "Lips are life. Mouth is memory. The word created everything."

And the dead man returned to life. But he was a living dead man, not the man he had been before. And as he returned to life he said: "I am yesterday and I know tomorrow. Like me, my children will live their deaths and die their lives. We shall never again be three, alone in the world, conceived by ourselves, with no father to engender us or a mother to give us a name."

And the land was peopled.

Upon the third day of his dream, Ludovico found himself wandering among the multitudes of the city of Alexandria. The many-colored turbans and veiled faces and flowing mantles and unshod feet and thieving hands were indifferent to him, but at the same time he felt threatened by the haste, the harsh voices, the wailing cries. On the stone threshold of a white door he recognized the murderer. He was sitting, legs crossed, before a rickety stool, writing, without pausing, as if condemned to write, as if his well-being depended upon scratching the Arabic characters upon stiff, curled leaves of papyrus, as if by writing he postponed a damnation.

Ludovico approached the scribe. He was not recognized. Flies lighted upon the criminal's face and he brushed them away with one hand, not blinking. Ludovico passed his hand before the scribe's eyes. Again he did not blink. Ludovico read over the blind scribe's shoulder. "One night I killed my brother. Attention. Read and understand. I shall tell you why it happened, how, when, and for what reasons; what I then foresaw, what today I remember, what I shall fear tomorrow. Attention. Stop. Does not my story arouse your curiosity . . . ?"

Ludovico dreamed that the murdered brother and his wife-and-sister that night lay sleeping in the tomb. She awakened and said: "We can leave now. Now you will know the destiny of those who live outside the tomb."

"Yes," replied the murdered man, "but secretly. Let no one see us."

They emerged from their winding sheets as if abandoning their skins. The woman shook out her robe of a thousand colors, and from its folds day was born, and night fell, light was kindled and shadow prolonged, the cloth burst into flame and poured down her body like water; at its touch the living died and the dead were reborn; all the while the couple walked through the same streets of Alexandria toward the numberless mouths of the great river.

Finally he saw them.

The murderer brother lay dead in the abandoned alley, his face stained by spilled ink, his pen clasped tightly in his hand, the scrolls of paper strewn about his body, white, virgin, not a single character upon them.

The couple sailed up the river in a luminous boat, the man naming things in secret, water, sand, wheat, stone, house, the woman asking the waters: "Why did our brother succumb to the temptation to write of his own crime?"

He was awakened by fingers brushing his. Lying beside him was a woman of indeterminate age; veils covered her face and body except for an aperture over her lips. The aperture followed the outline of her lips. The mouth was stamped with many colors; she spoke.

"Flee," she said to Ludovico, "go as quickly as possible to the place I shall tell you. There is your well-being. Here your children will be in danger if the sign they bear is discovered. They will be identified with a sacred prophecy. They will be separated from you and, captive, will await their manhood only to enact once again the struggle of rival brothers . . ."

"What is the prophecy?" asked Ludovico; but the woman wrapped herself in her multicolored veils—the raiment, like her lips—and disappeared into the darkness.

THE CITIZENS OF HEAVEN

With half his remaining gold, Ludovico bought a small boat, provisions, and a compass, and sailed from Egypt toward the coast of the Levant. The three children laughed and crawled on the deck; their eyes and skin glowed with the good health and fortune bestowed by the brilliant Mediterranean sun.

He docked in the port of Haifa; he sold the boat and after a few days on donkeyback arrived at a desert village near the Dead Sea. Without asking anything of anyone, he followed precisely Pliny's instructions for reaching the community. They were received by several men dressed as poorly as Ludovico and the three boys, and all saw a good sign in this arrival, for the desert community was divided into four classes: children, disciples, novices, and the faithful; and the three still very young infants, arriving into the life of the sect so free of the past, could readily ascend in the scale of knowledge and merit. To Ludovico they explained that the reason they joined together there was not the inability to possess goods; rather, it was a will to possess everything in common. Ludovico placed his remaining gold in a common chest.

For ten years Ludovico and the three boys lived the life of this community. They awakened at dawn. They worked the fields watered by wells known to the faithful. Before the midday meal they bathed and turned to the severe tasks of carpentry, ceramics, and weaving. They supped; no one ever spoke during meals. Before going to sleep they could study, meditate, pray, or contemplate. They dressed always like paupers. They forbade all ceremony, for they affirmed that good must be practiced with humility, not celebrated. They abhorred equally the pomp of all churches, those of the East and those of the West, the Hebraic and the Christian, all rites and all sacrifice. And they transmitted their beliefs not in sermons but in ordinary conversation, at the hour of rest, during the day's labor, in a quiet and reasoned voice. No one there noticed the external signs the three boys shared.

"Your body is transitory matter, but your soul is immortal."

"Captive within the body as if within a prison, the soul can aspire to freedom only if it renounces the world, riches, and stone temples, and in contrast serves God with piety, practicing justice toward all men."

"Do harm to no one, neither voluntarily nor at anyone's behest."

"Detest the unjust man and succor the just."

The three boys learned these maxims by memory. Seated at the refectory table according to their age in the time of the community, Ludovico and the three boys finally occupied a high rank, for here age was not judged by external appearances of youth or maturity but by the time spent in the community, and thus the boys were older than some gray-haired men who had arrived more recently. These old men were considered children; Ludovico became a novice; the boys, disciples.

"Equality is the source of justice; it manifests to us true riches."

"Three are the roads to perfection: study, contemplation, and knowledge of nature."

"But also there are dreams."

"Dreams come from God."

"At times, they are the shortcut to the final beatitude the other three roads can procure."

One day in the year when the three boys, in different months, became eleven, Ludovico told the faithful what he had dreamed. He must return to the world to fulfill the dictates of justice. The faithful returned to him the gold coins he had surrendered upon his arrival. Ludovico looked at the coins Celestina had sent from Toledo by the monk Simón. The same prognathic profile, in bas-relief; the pendant lower lip; the dead gaze. But the effigy imprinted there was not the former Señor's but that of his son Felipe.

"The old King?" the captain of the sailing vessel replied as they set sail one afternoon from Haifa.

The captain looked at the coins Ludovico had given him in payment of their passage. He bit one to assure its legality, and added: "He died years ago. His son Don Felipe, may he enjoy glory, has succeeded him."

Ten years of silence and labor, Ludovico said to himself, ten years of bookless study, thinking, contemplating, in silence, remembering everything I have learned, restructuring it in my mind. Felipe predicted it would take longer to achieve pragmatic grace. I shall need less time to change grace through action. He imagined I would be alone, in a miserable little room, bent over charcoal and pitch, philters and mud, growing old before knowing, knowing, an old man, knowing, of no use. But I am not alone. I am I plus my three sons. My small, formidable army. One lifetime is not enough to fulfill a destiny.

He gazed for the last time toward the coasts of Palestine. The desert was sinking into the sea. The desert began in the sea. A people in the desert, without women, without love, and without money. An eternal people, where no one is born. Men came to the community; men left. But no one was seen in birth or in death. And perhaps because of this, he mused, only there could he think clearly and totally of his destiny and that of the three boys bound to his own.

One night in the dog days the captain approached him and after staring for a moment at the motionless, opaque sea, said to him: "I have heard one of your sons praying in the early morning. The things he said are those repeated centuries ago by a sect rebelling against both the law of Israel and the law of Rome: this sect held that all Churches are dens of the Evil One."

"That is so. We have lived ten years among them," Ludovico replied.

"But that is impossible. All the members of the sect were condemned by the Sanhedrin and delivered to the Centurions, who took them out into the desert and abandoned them, bound hand and foot, without bread, and without water. They could not have survived. They were called the Citizens of Heaven."

For an instant, dizzied, Ludovico felt he had never gone there; but also that he had never left.

A long night's sleep dissipated his obscure anxieties.

THE PALACE

OF DIOCLETIAN

This is the city-palace; this is the palace-city; its name is Spalato, space of a palace, city within a palace, a palace converted into a city upon the steep coasts of the Adriatic Sea, the last dwelling of the Emperor Diocletian, plazas that had been courtyards, cathedrals that had been mausoleums, baptistries of Christ formerly temples of Jupiter, churches that had been chapels, streets that had been passageways, gardens that had been orchards, lodgings that had been bedchambers, inns that had been great halls, merchants' stalls that had been anterooms, public dining halls that had been private, wine cellars that had been taverns that had been dungeons, an imperial palace partitioned by time, consumed by usury, blackened by kitchen smoke, cracked by repeated cries, meeting of two worlds, the East and the West, Dalmatia, high cliffs and flat beaches, dirty sands, slippery seaweed and rotted timber, shivering octopuses and sealed bottles, enduring ash and decayed excrement, tunnels, subterranean passages, rusty iron rings, damaged marble, stone worn and polished like antique coins, scratched paintings, waves of conquerors, Byzantine, Croatians, Normans, Venetians, Hungarians, a beehive of dark stone devastated by hordes of Avars who had with greater fury desolated neighboring cities, all of whose refugees came to live in this abandoned palace, this labyrinth of thick walls, soaring on the side of landfall, forest of masts, sky of sails, the palace of Diocletian, its sixteen towers, four gates, waves of fugitives, crossroads, they all came here, from here they scattered across Christian Europe, from the precinct where Diocletian had launched his edict against Christians for having offended the gods of Rome with the sign of the cross, from here they went out, here they came in, through the Porta Aenea, the guardians of the Egyptian secrets of the two brothers and a sister: Osiris, who founded everything upon the word; Set, who was the first murderer; Isis, the sister-and-wife who returned life through her mouth; through the Porta Ferrea the ragged disciples of Simon Magus, forever seeking the lost goddess in temples and brothels, the guardian of secret wisdom, the damned, the expelled, Eve, Helen, the Hetaera of Babylon, she who had been condemned by the Priapic angels of the vengeful God, the demiurge of evil, wise female, feminine sage, lost woman, the piece lacking to complete total knowledge; through the Porta Aurea the bearers of Gnostic and Manichaean heresy, dissatisfied with the work of creation, desirous of a second truth, higher, more perfect, more secret, more total than that consecrated by the Councils of the Church, the incarnate enemies of St. Augustine who saw in the Roman and apostolic Holy See the full realization of the promise initiated with the birth of Christ, while they, disciples of Basilides of Alexandria, of Valentinus, and Nestorius and Marcion, saw a world foundering in pomp, corruption, and surrender to the works of the second God, He who had created evil while the first God created good, and they anticipated the solution of this conflict in a second millennium, a second coming of Christ to earth to purge the world and prepare it for the final judgment; and through the Porta Argentea the zealous guardians of Orphic secrets, recipients of the Pistis Sophia, revealers of the prophecies of the pythonesses, the Sibyls who announce the appearance of a last Emperor, King of peace and abundance, the triumph of true Christianity, which is the religion of selflessness, charity, poverty, and love, the last monarch, annihilator of Gog and Magog:

"His purifying task completed, he will go to Jerusalem, he will deposit his crown and mantle upon Golgotha and will abdicate in favor of God . . ."

"And does history end there?" Ludovico asked of a one-eyed itinerant Greek with hair like black serpents and wearing a black toga as they sat eating fried hake served on lead plates. "Does your story end there?" he asked of this man who disseminated the auguries of the Tiburtine Sibyl beside the busy Porta Argentea, gate in the walls of Spalato.

THE PROPHECY

OF THE THIRD AGE

"No," mumbled the magus. "Three are the ages of man. The first age of the world passed beneath a reign of faith, when the elect, still weak and enslaved, were not yet capable of freeing themselves. Their law was the law of Moses; that age was continued until the One came who said: 'If the Son free you, then shall you be truly free.' The second age was initiated by Christ and continues unto the present hour; it frees us in respect to the past, but in no way affects the future. St. Paul spoke wisely: 'We know in part, and we prophesy in part. But when that which is perfect is come, then that which is in part shall be done away. For now we see through a glass, darkly, but then face to face.' "

The magus cleaned his teeth with a fishbone. "The third age will be initiated in these days we are living. It is imminent. For have we not seen everywhere the fulfillment of the prophecies Matthew put in the mouth of Jesus, that nation shall rise against nation, that there shall be earthquakes and famines and pestilences and all manner of tribulations, and false prophets shall rise, iniquity abound, and the love of many wax cold: the world is growing old and deteriorating. Are we not governed by a false Pope and a King of unchaste countenance? It is time now for the last Emperor to appear and unite all nations into a single flock, for the Sibyl has said: 'Rex novus adveniet totum ruiturus in orbem . . .' "

"And does history end then?" Ludovico insisted.

The magus asked for something to drink. He gulped grossly. He wiped his lips on a black sleeve. "Good does not belong to the age of men. Its triumph is partial. Absolute evil must come so that absolute good may triumph. Absolute good is divine. It is not of the world of men, as is absolute evil. But once the third epoch is begun in peace and abundance—man's precarious blessings—the Antichrist will appear to destroy them in all his fury."

He looked at Ludovico with his cat eyes and continued: "He is absolute evil. Only if he incarnates in the future will history know its apotheosis: the future ends there. Absolute evil will provoke absolute good. The Son of Man will descend upon clouds from Heaven, bearing power and great majesty. And He will send forth His angels with resounding trumpets and gather His elect from the four winds. He will sit upon His throne of glory and to the just He will give possession of the kingdom prepared for them since the creation, saying unto them: For I was hungry, and ye gave me meat; naked, and ye clothed me. And to the damned He will say: Depart from me, and will cast them into the everlasting fire, saying: I was a stranger and ye took me not in, sick and in prison, and ye visited me not. And both the elect and the damned will ask: When did we or did we not all these things?, and the Son of Man will say unto them: Inasmuch as ye have done it even unto one of the least of these my brethren, ye have done it unto me; but inasmuch as ye did it not to one of the least of these, ye did it not to me. Each shall occupy his place in Eternity. And there will be no further human history."

Exalted by his own words, the magus had risen to his feet.

Ludovico looked up to ask: "How will you recognize the Antichrist?"

The magus embraced one of the three boys, who always accompanied Ludovico, listening to his every word; he said only: "Bird of prey; black penis. Where the cadaver is, there will the vultures gather."

"But first, the good King of whom you spoke, how . . . ?"

The magus kissed the cheek of Ludovico's second son. "A cross upon the back. Six toes upon each foot. He will conquer. He will be conquered."

"Where?"

"In the house of the scorpions."

"What place is that?"

"In the only land with the name of Vespers: Spain."

The magus knelt beside the third child, and other disciples, of other persuasions, who had gathered to listen to him, were offended by the Greek's allusions to false prophets; and the mob—upon occasion so credulous, at other times so malicious—began to mock the magus, and they shouted at him, some laughing, others somber, all defiant: "If you are a magus and know so much, perform a miracle, or we cannot believe what you have told here . . ."

Then this terrible one-eyed man with hair like serpents withdrew a scimitar he guarded beneath his black toga and with unexpected strength and ire, as if possessed of a hundred arms, cut the hand from one man, the tongue from another, with two rapid strokes pricked the eyes from one man's sockets, and spat a thick black stinking phlegm upon another's face, and this man's face melted like wax; and to all, the magus cried out: "Were you blind, you would see; maimed, your limbs would be restored; mute, you would speak; sick, you would be healed, but as it is not thus, see how miraculously you have lost eyes, hands, tongue, and health. Men of little faith: who will convince you?"

With clubs and fists, with daggers and hatchets, weeping and vociferating, this crowd fell upon the Greek magus, and tore him limb from limb.

His members were thrown into the sea: the head and the two halves of his trunk, split from his pelvis through his breastbone, like any beast hunted in the forest.

"Never go barefoot, run and play along the beaches and sea walls, but never remove your shoes, never bare your back, always be well covered, listen, speak, mix with everyone, hear them all, learn, survive, compare what we learned in the desert community with what we are living here, we have things to do when you are old enough, something to do together, forget nothing, when you are fourteen we shall leave this city, each will go his separate way, we shall meet again for the final episode, now I want you, with me, to learn, now you are becoming men, I shall gather together everything I know, what little I know, and we shall channel a new course for all this confusion of beliefs, rebellions, and aspirations, we shall join them with my dream on the beach, the promised millennium will take place within history and will be different from Eternity, the world will be renewed within history, without oppression, Pedro, without prohibitions, Celestina, without plagues, Simón, without gods, Ludovico; we shall not return to the original age of gold, nor shall we find it at the end of history, the age of gold is within history, it is called the future, but the future is today, not tomorrow, the future is present, the future is immediate, or it is nothing; the future is here, or there is no such place; the future is now, or there is no such time; we are the future, you three, I . . ."

THE GYPSY

After three days Ludovico and the three boys descended to the beach of Spalato beneath the high walls of the city-palace in search of the remains of the mutilated Greek magus. The boys agreed that as the one-eyed magus had embraced one, kissed a second, and knelt beside the third, he had asked them to perform this act.

The dirty sands were deserted. Ludovico and the boys searched among the spoils of the sea for the parts of the magus's body, but finding nothing they sat down to rest and admire the sunset over the yellow waters of the Adriatic.

Then, as if emerging out of nothing (but the sand deadened her steps), they saw walking toward them clothed in red and saffron robes a gypsy woman of the race so named because they had come from Egypt, one of the many prostitutes and thieves with barbaric earrings dangling in their pierced ears that thronged the streets and houses of Spalato selling their favors, telling fortunes, and at times working as servants, for there is no better guardian of things that can be stolen than a thief himself, and this is the age-old wisdom: children of night, guardians of their mother.

But as the woman approached, Ludovico felt fear; the gypsy's lips were tattooed in the same colors as her billowing dress. It was growing dark; the woman asked them whether they wished her to tell their fortunes, to throw the *naipes*, a word that comes from *naibi*, the most ancient Oriental name for she-devils, sibyls, and pythonesses. Ludovico refused, dismissing her brusquely, for secretly he feared any announcement of a new fate that would alter the destinies of his three sons.

Then the gypsy asked: "Are you searching for the remains of the one-eyed one?"

Ludovico sat silently, waiting, but the boys eagerly responded. The gypsy spoke simply: "It is in the cards."

"Read them," one of the boys said impulsively.

"Yes, read them," the other two chorused.

The gypsy smiled enigmatically: "I have only three cards with me."

The boys reacted with childish disappointment.

"But with three cards one may achieve all the combinations of the tarot; the number 3 signifies the harmonious solution of the conflict of the fall, the incorporation of the spirit with the pair, the formula of each of the created worlds, and synthesis of life: man with his father and mother; with his wife and his child; with his father and his son . . . So spoke the tarot, which contains all enigmas and their solutions."

The woman moved her hands in the air as if shuffling cards; the three boys laughed and mocked her, she doesn't even have three cards!, her cards are pure air!, deceiver, thief, whore!, but the gypsy did not laugh; she looked at one boy and said to him: Run along the shore and pick up that bottle half buried in the sand; and to the second she said: Dive into the water, there is another bottle on the bottom; and to the third: Swim still farther, I see the green crystal gleam of another bottle floating on the waves. The three boys did as she asked. They returned to the beach with three bottles, slimy, green, red-sealed. Only the feet of one boy were wet; the other two, soaked and out of breath, were on all fours on the dirty sand shaking themselves like dogs.

"Get up!" Ludovico shouted with growing terror. "Like men, on two feet!"

The gypsy smiled and said: "These are the remains of the magus; his head and the two halves of his severed torso."

Again the boys laughed, and said they were only three old bottles; they looked at them and shook them: there was something inside, not even wine, not water, a tight sheaf of papers within each bottle. They laughed. They looked at one another. They started to throw them back into the sea. The gypsy screamed and shouted three words, tiko, tiki, tika, it is the word of God, which in all tongues is pronounced the same, theo, teos, deus, teotl, and only these sons of the Devil will disguise it by naming God dog, in reverse, yes, get up, do not tempt me, be men, not dogs, you, boy, your bottle, tiko, which means destiny in the Chinese tongue, you, boy, your bottle, tika, which means fate in the Gypsy tongue, guard them well, never open them or you will have neither fate, chance, nor destiny, they have been sealed for many ages, one comes from the past, destiny; another from the present, chance; the other from the future, fate; this is the gift of the one-eyed magus who gave you an embrace, a kiss, a caress while others mocked him, and once again killed him . . .

"But you said these were the parts of his body," murmured one of the boys.

And the gypsy replied: "The magus was paper. Always he was paper, either a hero or an author of paper. First he was protagonist. When he returned to his hearth from wars and adventures, he wrote. What he lived as a hero is one thing: the centuries sing of it. What he wrote as a poet is a different thing: the letters are silent. He lived the lore that traveled from mouth to mouth. He died what was written upon paper. When he discovered the infidelity of his wife, weary of waiting for him, he lived all his adventures in reverse order. And as he relived them, he wrote about them. He did not stop his ears with wax: he was seduced by the song of the sirens. He did not resist the beauty of the lotus: he ate, and from that time he has lived a dream. Without weapons, he confronted Polyphemus; the Cyclops tore out one of his eyes. He returned to the origin: Ulixes, son of Sisyphus, forever between Scylla and Charybdis, between the monster of imagination—the creature with twelve feet and six heads and serpents' necks and teeth like a shark and barking dogs in the place of its sex—and the monster of nature—the enormous mouth that swallows and vomits out all the waters of the universe; son of Sisyphus, he returned to the origin, condemned to write of his own adventures again and again, to believe that he had finished his book only to begin again, to relate it all from a different point of view, according to unforeseen possibilities, in other time, in other spaces, aspiring from the beginning and to the end of time the impossible: a perfectly simultaneous narration. He was paper. His body was his death. When they killed him and threw him into the sea, he was again paper. He lived again. Guard him well. It is his offering."

She left without another word, and one of the boys swore that she walked into the sea and disappeared, another said no, she walked down the beach followed by a herd of swine, and the third was sure she had entered a cave among the rocks, a cave alternately covered and revealed by the waves, where one heard the frightful roaring of lions and the howling of wolves, but Ludovico stood gazing at the gypsy's footsteps in the sand, and the wind blew and the waves washed over the tracks but the tracks were not erased.

THE THEATER OF MEMORY

They left Spalato before the anticipated time. Three times Ludovico had returned alone to the beach; each time he found there, unerased, the gypsy's footprints. They traveled to Venice, a city where stone and water retain no trace of footsteps. In that place of mirages there is room for no phantom but time, and its traces are imperceptible; the lagoon would disappear without stone to reflect it and the stone without water in which to be reflected. Against this enchantment there is little the transitory bodies of men—solid or spectral, it is the same—can do. All Venice is a phantom: it issues no entry permits to other phantoms. There no one would recognize them as such, and so they would cease to be. No phantom exposes itself to such risk.

They found lodging in the ample solitudes of the island of La Giudecca; Ludovico felt reassured, being near the Hebraic traditions he had studied so thoroughly in Toledo, even though not sharing all their beliefs. The coins Celestina had sent by hand of the monk Simón had been exhausted in the last voyage; Ludovico inquired in the neighborhoods of the ancient Jewry where many refugees from Spain and Portugal had found asylum, as he now did, whether anyone had need of a translator; laughing, everyone recommended he cross the broad Vigano canal, disembark at San Basilio, walk along the estuaries of the shipwrights and sugar merchants, continue past the workshops of the waxworkers, cross the Ponte Foscarini, and ask for the house of a certain Maestro Valerio Camillo, between the River of San Barnaba and the Church of Santa Maria del Carmine, for it was widely known that no one in Venice had accumulated a greater number of ancient manuscripts than the said Dominie, whose windows even were blocked with parchments; at times papers fell into the street, where children made little boats of them and floated them in the canals, and great was the uproar when the meager, stuttering Maestro ran out to rescue the priceless documents, shouting at the top of his voice whether it were the destiny of Quintilian and Pliny the Elder to be soaked in canals and serve as a diversion for brainless little brats.

Ludovico found the described house without difficulty, but its doors and windows prevented the passage of either light or human; the residence of Donno Valerio Camillo was a paper fortress, mountains, walls, pillars and piles of exposed documents, folio piled upon folio, yellowed, teetering, held upright thanks only to the counterpressure of other stacks of paper.

Ludovico circled the building, looking for the house's garden. And, in fact, beside a small sotto portico facing the vast Campo Santa Margherita, extended a narrow iron railing worked in a series of three recurring heads: wolf, lion, and dog; fragrant vines trailed from the walls, and in the dark little garden stood an extremely thin man, the meagerness of his body disguised by the ample folds of a long, draped tunic, but the angularity of his face emphasized by a black hood— similar to those worn by executioners—that hid his head and ears, revealing only an eagle-like profile; he was occupied in training several ferocious mastiffs; he held a long stick on which were impaled pieces of raw meat; he teased the dogs, dangling it above their heads; the barking dogs leaped to snatch the prize, but at every leap the man placed his arm between the raw meat and the beasts' fangs, miraculously barely escaping being wounded; each time, with amazing swiftness, the frail, hooded Donno pulled back the arm grazed by the dogs, and stuttered: "Very well, very well, Biondino, Preziosa, very well, Pocogarbato, my flesh is the more savory, you know how I trust you, do not fail me, for at the hour of my death I shall be in no condition to discipline you."

Then he threw another piece of meat to the mastiffs and watched with delight as they devoured it, fighting among themselves to seize the best portions. When he saw Ludovico standing in the entrance to the garden, he rudely demanded whether he had so little interest in his life that he had to pry into the lives of others. Ludovico asked his pardon and explained that the motive for his visit was not gratuitous curiosity but the need for employment. He showed him a letter signed by the ancient of the Synagogue of the Passing, and after reading it Donno Valerio Camillo said: "Very well, very well, Monsignore Ludovicus. Although it would take many lifetimes to classify and translate the papers I have accumulated throughout my lifetime, we can do some small part, we can begin. Consider yourself employed—with two conditions. The first is that you never laugh at my stuttering. I shall explain the reason this once: my capacity for reading is infinitely superior to my capacity for speaking; I employ so much time reading that at times I completely forget how to speak; in any case, I read so rapidly that in compensation I trip and stumble as I speak. My thoughts are swifter than my words."

"And the second condition?"

The Maestro threw another scrap of meat to the mastiffs. "That if I die during the period of your service, you must be responsible to see that they not bury my body in holy ground, or throw it into the waters of this pestilent city, but instead lay my naked body here in my garden and loose the dogs to devour me. I have trained them to do this. They will be my tomb. There is none better or more honorable: matter to matter. I but follow the wise counsel of Cicero. If in spite of everything I am someday resurrected in my former body, it will not have been without first giving every digestive opportunity to the divine matter of the world."

Daily Ludovico presented himself at the house of Maestro Donno Valerio Camillo and daily the emaciated Venetian handed him ancient folios to be translated into the tongues of the various courts where, mysteriously, he hinted he would send his invention, along with all the authenticating documents of scientific proof.

Soon Ludovico became aware that everything he was translating from Greek and Latin into Tuscan, French, or Spanish possessed a common theme: memory. From Cicero, he translated the *De inven-*

tione: "Prudence is the knowledge of good, of evil, and of that which is neither good nor evil. Its parts are: memory, intelligence, and pre-vision, or pre-sight. Memory is the faculty through which the mind re-calls what was. Intelligence certifies what is. Pre-vision or pre-sight permits the mind to see that something is going to occur before it oc-curs." From Plato, the passages wherein Socrates speaks of memory as of a gift: it is the mother of the Muses, and in every soul there is one part of wax upon which are imprinted the seals of thought and percep-tion. From Philostratus, the *Life of Apollonius of Tyana:* Euxenes asked Apollonius why, being a man of elevated thought, and express-ing himself so clearly and swiftly, he had never written anything, and Apollonius answered him: "Because until now I have not practiced si-lence." From that moment he resolved to remain silent; he never spoke again, although his eyes and his mind absorbed every experience and stored it in his memory. Even after he was a hundred years old he had a better memory than Simonides himself, and he wrote a hymn in eulogy of memory, wherein he stated that all things are erased with time, but that time itself becomes ineradicable and eternal because of memory. And among the pages of St. Thomas Aquinas, he found this quotation underlined in red ink: "Nihil potest homo intelligere sine phantasmate." Man can understand nothing without images. And im-ages are phantoms.

In Pliny he read the amazing feats of memory of antiquity: Cyrus knew the names of all the soldiers in his army; Seneca the Elder could repeat two thousand names in the order they were communicated to him; Mithridates, King of Pontus, spoke the tongues of the twenty na-tions under his dominion; Metrodorus of Scepsis could repeat every conversation he had heard in his lifetime, in the exact original words; and Charmides the Greek knew by memory the content of all the books in his library, the greatest of his age. On the other hand, Themistocles refused to practice the art of memory, saying he preferred the science of forgetfulness to that of memory. And constantly, in all these manu-scripts, appeared references to the poet Simonides, called the inventor of memory.

One day, many months after beginning his work, Ludovico dared ask the always silent Maestro Valerio Camillo the identity of that re-nowned poet Simonides. The Dominie looked at him, eyes flashing be-neath heavy eyebrows. "I always knew you were curious. I told you so that first day."

"Do not judge my curiosity as vain, Maestro Valerio, now it is in your service."

"Search among my papers. If you do not know how to encounter what I myself found, I shall consider you are not as clever as I be-lieved."

After which the agile, stammering, slight Maestro bounded across the room to an iron door he always kept closed, protected by chains and locks; he opened it with difficulty and disappeared behind it.

It took Ludovico almost a year, alternating translation with investigation, to locate a slim, brittle document in Greek wherein the narrator recounted the story of a poet of bad reputation, despised because he was the first to charge for writing, or even reading, his verses. His name was Simonides and he was a native of the island of Ceos. This said Simonides was invited one night to sing a poem in honor of a noble of Thessaly named Scopas. The wealthy Scopas had prepared a great banquet for the occasion. But the waggish Simonides, in addition to a eulogy in honor of his host, included in the poem a dithyramb to the legendary brothers, the Dioscuri, Castor and Pollux, both sons of Leda, the former by a swan and the latter by a god. Half mocking, half in earnest, Scopas told the poet when he had ended his recital that, since only half the panegyric had honored him, he would pay only half the agreed sum, and that he should collect the other half from the mythic twins.

Bested, Simonides sat down to eat, hoping to collect in food what the miserly Scopas had denied him in coin. But at that instant a messenger arrived and told the poet that two youths urgently sought him outside. With increasing bad humor, Simonides left his place at the banquet table and went out into the street, but found no one. As he turned to reenter the dining hall of Scopas he heard a fearful sound of falling masonry and cracking plaster; the roof of the house had collapsed. Everyone inside had been killed; the weight of the columns crushed all the guests at the banquet, and beneath the ruins it was impossible to identify anyone. The relatives of the dead arrived and wept when they were unable to recognize their loved ones lost among all those bodies crushed like insects, disfigured, their heads smashed in, their brains spilled out. Then Simonides pointed out to each kinsman which was his dead: the poet recalled the exact place each guest had occupied during the banquet.

Everyone marveled, for never before had anyone achieved a similar feat; and thus was invented the art of memory. Simonides voyaged to offer his thanks at the shrine of Castor and Pollux in Sparta. Through his mind, again and again, passed in perfect order the mocking, indifferent, scornful, ignorant faces of Scopas and his guests.

Ludovico showed this text to Valerio Camillo, and the Dominie nodded thoughtfully. Finally he said: "I congratulate you. Now you know how memory was invented and who invented it."

"But surely, Maestro, men have always remembered . . ."

"Of course, Monsignore Ludovicus; but the intent of memory was different. Simonides was the first to remember something besides the present and the remote as such, for before him memory was only an inventory of daily tasks, lists of cattle, utensils, slaves, cities, and houses, or a blurred nostalgia for past events and lost places: memory was *factum*, not *ars*. Simonides proposed something more: everything that men have been, everything they have said and done can be remembered, in perfect order and location; from then on, nothing had to be forgotten. Do you realize what that means? Before him, memory was a fortuitous fact: each person spontaneously remembered what he wished to or what he could remember; the poet opened the doors to scientific memory, independent of individual memories; he proposed memory as total knowledge of a total past. And since that memory was exercised in the present, it must also totally embrace the present so that, in the future, actuality is remembered past. To this goal many systems have been elaborated throughout the centuries. Memory sought assistance from places, images, taxonomy. From the memory of the present and the past, it progressed to an ambition to recall the future before it occurred, and this faculty was called pre-vision or pre-sight. Other men, more audacious than those preceding them, were inspired by the Jewish teachings of the Cabala, the Zohar, and the Sephirot to go further and to know the time of all times and the space of all spaces; the simultaneous memory of all hours and all places. I, monsignore, have gone still further. For me the memory of the eternity of times, which I already possess, is not sufficient, or the memory of the simultaneity of places, that I always knew . . ."

Ludovico told himself that Dominie Valerio Camillo was mad: he expected to find burial in the ferocious digestive system of mastiffs, and life in a memory that was not of here or some other place, or the sum of all spaces, or the memory of the past, present, and future, or the sum of all times. He aspired, perhaps, to the absolute, the vacuum. The Venetian's eyes glittered with malice as he observed the Spanish student. Then gently he took him by the arm and led him to the locked door. "You have never asked me what lies behind that door. Your intellectual curiosity has been more powerful than common curiosity, which you would judge disrespectful, personal, unwholesome. You have respected my secret. As a reward I am going to show you my invention."

Valerio Camillo inserted keys into the several locks, removed the chains, and opened the door. Ludovico followed down a dark musty passageway of dank brick where the only gleam came from the eyes of rats and the skin of lizards. They came to a second iron door. Valerio Camillo opened it and then closed it behind Ludovico. They stood in a silent white space of marble, illuminated by the light of the scrupulously clean stone, so marvelously joined that not even a suggestion of a line could be seen between the blocks of marble.

"No rat can enter here," laughed the Donno. And then, with great seriousness, he added, "I am the only one who has ever entered here.

And now you, Monsignore Ludovicus, now you will know the Theater of Memory of Valerio Camillo.''

The Maestro lightly pressed one of the marble blocks and a whole section of the wall opened like a door, swinging on invisible hinges. Stooping, the two men passed through; a low, lugubrious chant resounded in Ludovico's ears; they entered a corridor of wood that grew narrower with every step, until they emerged upon a tiny stage; a stage so small, in fact, that only Ludovico could stand upon it, while the Donno Valerio remained behind him, his dry hands resting upon the translator's shoulders, his eagle's face near Ludovico's ear, stuttering, his breath redolent of fish and garlic. "This is the Theater of Memory. Here roles are reversed. You, the only spectator, will occupy the stage. The performance will take place in the auditorium.''

Enclosed within the wooden structure, the auditorium was formed of seven ascending, fan-shaped gradins sustained upon seven pillars; each gradin was of seven rows, but instead of seats Ludovico saw a succession of ornamental railings, similar to those guarding Valerio Camillo's garden facing the Campo Santa Margherita; the filigree of the figures on the railings was almost ethereal, so that each figure seemed to superimpose itself upon those in front of and behind it; the whole gave the impression of a fantastic hemicycle of transparent silk screens; Ludovico felt incapable of understanding the meaning of this vast inverted scenography where the sets were spectators and the spectator the theater's only actor.

The low chant of the passageway became a choir of a million voices joined, without words, in a single sustained ululation. "My theater rests upon seven pillars,'' the Venetian stammered, "like the house of Solomon. These columns represent the seven Sephirot of the supracelestial world, which are the seven measures of the plots of the celestial and lower worlds and which contain all the possible ideas of all three worlds. Seven divinities preside over each of the seven gradins: look, Monsignore Ludovicus, at the representations on each of the first railings. They are Diana, Mercury, Venus, Apollo, Mars, Jupiter, and Saturn: the six planets and the central sun. And seven themes, each beneath the sign of a star, are represented on the seven rows of each gradin. They are the seven fundamental situations of humanity: the Cavern, the human reflection of the immutable essence of being and idea; Prometheus, who steals fire from the intelligence of the gods; the Banquet, the conviviality of men joined together in society; Mercury's sandals, symbols of human activity and labor; Europa and the Bull, love; and on the highest row, the Gorgons, who contemplate everything from on high; they have three bodies, but a single shared eye. And the only spectator—you—has a single body but possesses three souls, as stated in the Zohar. Three bodies and one eye; one body and three souls. And between these poles, all the possible combinations of

the seven stars and the seven situations. Hermes Trismegistus has written wisely that he who knows how to join himself to this diversity of
the unique will also be divine and will know all past, present, and future, and all the things that Heaven and earth contain."

Dominie Valerio, with increasing excitement, manipulated a series
of cords, pulleys, and buttons behind Ludovico's back; successive sections of the auditorium were bathed in light; the figures seemed to acquire movement, to gain transparency, to combine with and blend into
one another, to integrate into fleeting combinations and constantly
transform their original silhouettes while at the same time never ceasing to be recognizable.

"What, to you, Monsignore Ludovicus, is the definition of an imperfect world?"

"Doubtless, a world in which things are lacking, an incomplete
world . . ."

"My invention is founded upon precisely the opposite premise: the
world is imperfect when we believe there is nothing lacking in it; the
world is perfect when we know that something will always be missing
from it. Will you admit, monsignore, that we can conceive of an ideal
series of events that run parallel to the real series of events?"

"Yes; in Toledo I learned that all matter and all spirit project the
aura of what they were and what they will be . . ."

"And what they might have been, monsignore, will you give no opportunity to what, not having been yesterday, probably will never
be?"

"Each of us has asked himself at some moment of his existence, if
we were given the grace of living our life over again would we live it
the same way the second time?, what errors would we avoid, what
omissions amend?, should I have told that woman, that night, that I
loved her?, why did I not visit my father the day before his death?,
would I again give that coin to the beggar who held out his hand to me
at the entrance to the church?, how would we choose again among all
the persons, occupations, profits, and ideas we must constantly elect?,
for life is but an interminable selection between this and this and that, a
perpetual choice, never freely decided, even when we believe it so, but
determined by conditions others impose upon us: gods, judges, monarchs, slaves, fathers, mothers, children."

"Look; see upon the combined canvases of my theater the passage
of the most absolute of memories: the memory of what could have
been but was not; see it in its greatest and least important detail, in gestures not fulfilled, in words not spoken, in choices sacrificed, in decisions postponed, see Cicero's patient silence as he hears of Catiline's
foolish plot, see how Calpurnia convinces Caesar not to attend the Senate on the Ides of March, see the defeat of the Greek army in Salamis,
see the birth of the baby girl in a stable in Bethlehem in Palestine dur-

ing the reign of Augustus, see the pardon Pilate grants the prophetess, and the death of Barabbas upon the cross, see how Socrates in his prison refuses the temptation of suicide, see how Odysseus dies, consumed by flames, within the wooden horse the clever Trojans set afire upon finding it outside the walls of the city, see the old age of Alexander of Macedonia, the silent vision of Homer; see—but do not speak of—the return of Helen to her home, Job's flight from his, Abel forgotten by his brother, Medea remembered by her husband, Antigone's submission to the law of the tyrant in exchange for peace in the kingdom, the success of Spartacus's rebellion, the sinking of Noah's ark, the return of Lucifer to his seat at the side of God, pardoned by divine decision; but see also the other possibility: an obedient Satan who renounces rebellion and remains in the original Heaven; look, watch as the Genoese Colombo sets out to seek the route to Cipango, the court of the Great Khan, by land, from West to East, on camelback; watch while my canvases whirl and blend and fade into one another, see the young shepherd, Oedipus, satisfied to live forever with his adoptive father, Polybus of Corinth, and see the solitude of Jocasta, the intangible anguish of a life she senses is incomplete, empty; only a sinful dream redeems it; no eyes will be put out, there will be no destiny, there will be no tragedy, and the Greek order will perish because it lacked the tragic transgression which, as it violates that order, restores and eternally revives it: the power of Rome did not subjugate the soul of Greece; Greece could be subjugated only by the absence of tragedy; look, Paris occupied by the Mohammedans, the victory and consecration of Pelagius in his dispute with Augustine, the cave of Plato inundated by the river of Heraclitus; look, the marriage of Dante and Beatrice, a book never written, an aged libertine and merchant of Assisi, and untouched walls never painted by Giotto, a Demosthenes who swallowed a pebble and died choking beside the sea. See the greatest and the least important detail, the beggar born in a Prince's cradle, the Prince in that of the beggar; the child who grew, dead upon birth; and the child who died, full-grown; the ugly woman, beautiful; the cripple, whole; the ignorant, learned; the sainted, perverse; the rich, poor; the warrior, a musician; the politician, a philosopher; one small turn of this great circle upon which my theater is seated is sufficient, the great plot woven by the three equilateral triangles within a circumference ruled by the multiple combinations of the seven stars, the three souls, the seven mutations, and the single eye: the waters of the Red Sea do not part, a young girl in Toledo does not know which she prefers of the seven identical columns of a church or the two identical chick-peas of her supper, Judas cannot be bribed, the boy who cried 'Wolf!' was never believed.''

Panting, for a moment Donno Valerio fell silent and ceased to manipulate his cords and buttons. Then, more calmly, he asked Ludovico: "What will the Kings of this world pay me for this invention that would permit them to recall what could have been and was not?"

"Nothing, Maestro Valerio. For the only thing that interests them is what really is, and what will be."

Valerio Camillo's eyes glistened as never before, the only light in the suddenly darkened theater: "And it is not important to them, either, to know what never will be?"

"Perhaps, since that is a different manner of knowing what will be."

"You do not understand me, monsignore. The images of my theater bring together all the possibilities of the past, but they also represent all the opportunities of the future, for knowing what was not, we shall know what demands to be: what has not been, you have seen, is a latent event awaiting its moment to be, its second chance, the opportunity to live another life. History repeats itself only because we are unaware of the alternate possibility for each historic event: what that event could have been but was not. Knowing, we can insure that history does not repeat itself; that the alternate possibility is the one that occurs for the first time. The universe would achieve true equilibrium. This will be the culmination of my investigations: to combine the elements of my theater in such a manner that two different epochs fully coincide; for example, that what happened or did not happen in your Spanish fatherland in 1492, in 1520, or 1598, coincide exactly with what happens there in 1938, or 1975, or 1999. Then, and I am convinced of it, the space of that co-incidence will germinate, will accommodate the unfulfilled past that once lived and died there: this doubled time will demand that precise space in which to complete itself."

"And then, in accord with your theory, it will be imperfect."

"Perfection, monsignore, is death."

"But at least do you know the space where everything that did not happen awaits the co-incidence of two different times to be fulfilled?"

"I have just told you. Look again, monsignore; I shall turn the lights on again, place the figures in movement, combine spaces, that of your land, Spain, and that of an unknown world where Spain will destroy everything that previously existed in order to reproduce itself: a doubly immobile, doubly sterile, gestation, for in addition to what could have been—see those burning temples, see the eagles fall, see how the original inhabitants of the unknown lands are subjugated—your country, Spain, imposes another impossibility: that of itself, see the gates closing, the Jew expelled, the Moor persecuted, see how it hides itself in a mausoleum and from there governs in the name of death: purity of faith, purity of bloodlines, horror of the body, prohibition of thought, extermination of anything that cannot be understood. Look: centuries and centuries of living death, fear, silence, the cult of appearances, vacuity of substances, gestures of imbecilic honor, see them, the miserable realities, see them, hunger, poverty, injustice, ignorance: a naked empire that imagines itself clothed in golden robes. Look: there will never be in history, monsignore, nations more needful of a second opportunity to be what they were not than these that speak and that will speak your tongue, or peoples who for such lengthy periods store the possibilities of what they could have been had they not sacrificed the very reason for their being: impurity, the mixture of all bloods, all beliefs, all the spiritual impulses of a multitude of cultures. Only in Spain did the three peoples of the Book—Christians, Moors, and Jews—meet and flourish. As she mutilates their union, Spain mutilates herself and mutilates all she finds in her path. Will these lands have the second opportunity the first history will deny them?''

Before Ludovico's eyes, amid the screens and railings and lights and shadows of the gradins of this Theater of Memory of everything that was not but that could sometime have been, passed, in reverse, with the assurance it would be they he watched, animated, incomprehensible images, bearded warriors in iron cuirasses, tattered pennants, autos-da-fé, bewigged lords, dark men with enormous burdens on their backs, he heard speeches, proclamations, grandiloquent orators, and saw places and landscapes never before seen: strange temples devoured by the jungle, convents built like fortresses, rivers broad as seas, deserts poor as an outstretched hand, volcanoes higher than the stars, prairies devoured by the horizon, cities with iron-railed balconies, red-tile roofs, crumbling walls, immense cathedrals, towers of shattered glass, military men, their chests covered with medals and gold galloon, dusty feet pricked by thorns, emaciated children with swollen bellies, abundance by the side of hunger, a golden god seated upon a ragged beggar; mud and silver . . .

Again the lights died down. Ludovico did not dare ask Valerio Camillo how he controlled the illumination of the theater, how he projected or mounted or raised from nowhere these moving images through railings, upon screens, or what was the function of the cords he pulled, the buttons he pressed. He could imagine, yes, that the Dominie was capable of repeating the unspoken words of Medea, Cicero, or Dante through the simple expedient of reading lips: the understandable art of the stutterer.

Valerio Camillo said only: "I shall reveal my secrets to the Prince who will pay the highest price for my invention."

But again Ludovico doubted that any Prince would want to see face to face what was not, but wished to be. Politics was the art of the possible: neither the statue of Gomorrah nor the flight of Icarus.

Every night the translator returned to his miserable room on the long backbone of La Giudecca, resembling, in truth, the skeleton of a flounder, and there found his children engaged in their personal occupations. One would be wielding a wooden sword against the late-evening shadow projected onto the ancient walls of the Church of Santa Eufemia; another, wood shavings tangled in his golden hair, would be sawing, polishing, and varnishing shelves for the books and papers of Ludovico; the third would be sitting tailor-fashion in the doorway, contemplating the bare paving stones of the Campo Cosmo. Then the four would dine on fried sea food, beans, and mozzarella cheese. One night they were awakened by a desperate pounding. One of the boys opened the door. Gasping, his face caked with ashes, his clothing scorched, Dominie Valerio Camillo fell across the threshold. He stretched out his hands toward Ludovico and grasped his wrist with the fierce last strength of a dying man.

"Someone denounced me as a wizard," said the Donno without a trace of a stutter. "Someone slipped a letter into the stone mouth. They tried to take me prisoner. I resisted. I feared for my secrets. They set fire to my house. They prodded me with their blades, to subdue me. They wanted to enter the theater. They tried to break the chains. I fled. Monsignore Ludovicus: protect my invention. What I fool I was! I should have told you my true secrets. The theater lights. A deposit of magnetic carbons on the rooftop of the house. They attract and store the energy of lightning and the supercharged skies above the lagoon. I filter this energy through waterproof conductors, copper filaments and bulbs of the finest Venetian crystal. The buttons. They set some black boxes in motion. There are mercury-coated silk ribbons bearing the images of all the ages, miniatures I have painted, that increase in size as they are projected upon the gradins by a light behind the ribbons. A hypothesis, monsignore, only a hypothesis . . . you must prove it . . . save my invention . . . and remember your promise."

There, upon the brick floor, Donno Valerio died. Ludovico covered the body with a blanket. He asked the boys to hide the body in a boat and bring it the following day to the Dominie's house. Lodovico went to the Campo Santa Margherita that same afternoon. He found a black shell: the house burned, the documents burned. He made his way inside to the locked door. The mastiffs Biondino, Preziosa, and Pocogarbato were huddled there. He called them by name. They recognized him. He unlocked the chains with the Maestro's keys. He penetrated the passageways of the rats and lizards. He reached the marble chamber. He touched the invisible door and it swung open. He entered the narrow space of the stage. Darkness reigned. He pulled a cord. A brilliant light illuminated the figure of the three Gorgons with the single eye beneath the sign of Apollo. He pressed three buttons. On the screens and railings were projected three figures: his three sons. On the gradin of Venus, on the railing of love, the first son was a statue of stone. On the gradin of Saturn, on the railing of the Cave, the second son lay dead, his arms crossed upon his breast. On the gradin of Mars, on the railing of Prometheus, the third, writhing, was bound to a rock, pecked by a falcon that was not devouring his liver but mutilating his arm.

As he turned to leave, Ludovico found himself face to face with his three sons. He whirled toward the auditorium of the theater; the shadows of his sons had disappeared. He looked back at the three boys. Had they seen what he had seen?

"We had to flee with the body of the Maestro," said the first.

"The Magistrati alla Bestemmia came in search of the fugitive," said the second.

"They threatened us; they know your connection with Valerio, Father," said the third.

They left the theater; they retraced their lost steps. Ludovico again chained and locked the door; from a burned-out window he threw the keys into the River of San Barnaba. They recovered the body of Valerio Camillo from the boat and carried it to the garden. Ludovico collected the mastiffs. They removed the clothing from the corpse. They laid it in the garden. More than ever, in death the Dominie, with his sharp profile and waxen flesh, resembled a frail young cardinal. Ludovico loosed the dogs. The bells chimed in the tall campanile of Santa Maria del Carmine.

Valerio Camillo had found his tomb.

THE DREAMERS

AND THE BLIND MAN

"They will search for him throughout the city. They will search for us at our house. It would be best to spend the night here," Ludovico said to the boys. "No one will think to look for us in the most obvious place."

As always, the three boys listened attentively to Ludovico, and lay down beside the padlocked door to sleep. The former student who had one day challenged the Augustinian theologian in the university and had another day escaped across the rooftops of Teruel from the wrath of the Aragonese Inquisition, marveled once again: the boys were almost fifteen years old and they were still absolutely identical. Actually, instead of accentuating their individuality, time had underlined their similarities. He no longer knew which was which: one, abducted one night from the castle of the Señor called the Fair, was the son of unknown parents; a second, true, he was the son of Celestina, but by an unknown father: that same Señor who while Felipe watched had taken her by force on the night of her wedding in the grange?, the three hurried old men who had raped her in the forest?, Prince Felipe?, Ludovico himself?, they who had each pleasured themselves with Celestina in the bedchamber of the bloody castle, occasionally both enjoying her at the same time; and the third—yes, this one was certain, but the most fantastic—was the son of a she-wolf and the dead Señor; that news Celestina had sent upon the lips of Simón; but the girl was half mad and her word was not to be trusted.

He looked at them that night as they lay sleeping. Better they not know. He knew (he remembered; he imagined): when he was twenty, one of the boys, the one abducted from the seignorial castle, would have the face of the cavalier dead in the back-alley duel and mourned in the temple of the Christ of the Light. His name was Don Juan. But although the three are identical today, will they be so in the future? And as they are identical, will all three have the face Don Juan acquired in death? Better they not know; enough. They are all my sons; enough. They are brothers; enough.

Moved by a torrent of love for the three creatures abandoned to his care, he longed to awaken them, to know they were alive and happy and loving.

He sought some pretext for expressing this overwhelming tide of love. Some news that would justify awakening them from their deep sleep—he spoke, he called them, he touched one's head, shook another's shoulder—yes, this news: the time was approaching, it was five years still before the appointed meeting—he lighted a candle, held it to their sleeping faces—but they would return to Spain, the meeting was to be in Spain, and there they would prepare themselves . . .

Only the third boy awakened. The other two continued to sleep. The one who awakened said to Ludovico: "No, Father, leave them alone; they are dreaming of me . . ."

"I have news for them . . ."

"Yes, we already know. We are going to make a voyage. Again."

"Yes, to Spain . . ."

"Not yet."

"We must."

"I know. We shall go together, but we shall be separated."

"I do not understand, my son. What secret is this? You have never done anything behind my back."

"We have always accompanied you. Now you must accompany us."

"We shall go to Spain."

"We shall reach Spain, Father. But it will be a long voyage. We shall take many turnings."

"Explain yourself. What is the secret? You have . . ."

"No, Father. We have made no pacts. I swear it."

"Then . . . ?"

"They are dreaming about me. I shall do what they dream I am doing."

"They have told you that?"

"I know. If they awaken, if they cease to dream of me, Father, I shall die."

"Which one are you, for God's sake, which of the three . . . ?"

"I do not understand. We are three."

"What do you know? Have you read the papers inside those bottles?"

The boy nodded, his head lowered.

"You could not resist the temptation?"

"Not we. You must resist it. We have sealed them again. They are not for you . . ."

"That damned gypsy, that temptress . . ."

The boy again nodded; Ludovico felt they had not fled from Venice in time, that the city had imprisoned them within its own spectral dream, that the destiny Ludovico shared with the three boys was splitting into four different paths. For the first time, he raised his voice: "Hear me; I am your father . . . Without me, the three of you would have died of hunger, or been murdered, or devoured by beasts . . ."

"You are not our father."

"You are brothers."

"That is true. And we venerate you as a father. You gave us your destiny for a time. Now we shall give you ours. Accompany us."

"What enchantment is this? How long will it last?"

"Each one of us will be dreamed thirty-three and a half days by the other two."

"Why that cipher?"

"It is the cipher of dispersion, Father. The sacred number of Christ's years upon the earth. The limit."

"Thirty-three, twenty-two, eleven . . . Distant from unity, the numbers of Satan, the learned doctor of the Synagogue of the Passing told me . . ."

"Then the days of Satan are the days of Christ, for Jesus came to disperse: the power of the earth belonged to One; Jesus distributed it among all men, rebel, humble, slave, poor, sinner, the sick. If all are Caesar, then Caesar is no one, Father . . ."

Ludovico was amazed to hear in the mouth of one of his sons the arguments denying all aspiration toward recovering perfect unity. With sadness he realized he was facing a rebellion that could not be contained; for the first time, he felt old. "Thirty-three and a half days . . . That is little time. We can wait."

"No, Father, you do not understand. Each one will be dreamed those days by the other two and thus he will be dreamed for sixty-seven days. But the one dreamed will actually live an equivalent time; and that makes one hundred and a half days. And because as he ceases to be dreamed by the other two, the one dreamed, not to die, must join one of the dreamers to dream of the third; that now makes two hundred and two days. And as the third ceases to be dreamed he must join the one already dreamed to dream of the one who has only dreamed but has not yet been dreamed; then, three hundred and four days shall have passed."

"That is still not too much; we have more than four years." Ludovico again shrugged his shoulders.

"Wait, Father. We love you. We shall tell you what we have dreamed, once we have dreamed it."

"That is my hope."

"But to tell you what we have dreamed will take as long as dreaming it."

"Nine hundred and twelve days? That is still only half the time I wanted. There are 1,825 days in five years."

"More time, Father, much more, for each one will tell what he dreamed about the other two, plus what the others dreamed about him, plus what he lived in reality as he was dreamed; and then each one must tell the others what he dreamed he was dreaming as he was dreamed; and each must tell what he dreamed as he dreamed what the other dreamed as he was dreamed by him; and then what each one dreamed dreaming he was dreaming the dreamed one; and then what the other two dreamed dreaming that the third one dreamed, dreaming, he was dreaming the dreamed one; and then . . ."

"Enough, son."

"Forgive me. I do not mock you, nor is this a game."

"Then, tell me, how long will all these combinations take?"

"Each one of us will have the right to thirty-three and a half months to exhaust all the combinations."

"That is one thousand and a half days for each of you . . ."

"Yes: two years nine months and fifteen days for each one . . ."

"Which would be eight years and four months for the three of you . . ."

"They will be, Father, will be. For only if we fulfill exactly the days of our dreams can we then fulfill our destinies."

Ludovico smiled bitterly. "At least you know the exact time. For a moment I believed the combinations would be infinite."

The boy smiled in return, but his was beatific. "We must, in turn, tell all the combinations of our dreams to you, for we hold no secret from you."

"That is my hope," Ludovico repeated, but now with a lingering sadness.

"And it is the narration, not the dream, that is infinite."

Ludovico ordered the carpenters on the Squero de San Trovaso to construct for him two lightweight and well-ventilated coffins, for it was not their purpose to lie under the ground but to travel with him and remain undisturbed for long days at a time while each of his sons lived the dream the other two dreamed of him.

From the ship carrying them to land he watched the golden cupolas, the red-tile roofs and ocher-colored walls of Venice fade into the distance. The challenges had been made. One was the infinite destiny the three boys had chosen—violating the warning of the gypsy woman of Spalato, forgetting the instructive example of Sisyphus and his son Ulysses—after reading the manuscripts contained within the three bottles; a second, finite, destiny was that he had chosen for them; it had an hour: afternoon; a day: a fourteenth of July; a year: five years from now; a place: the Cabo de los Desastres; and a purpose: to see Felipe face to face, to settle the accounts of their youth, to fulfill their destinies in history, not in a dream. The times foreseen in the boys' dreams would not work out so that he, Ludovico, could attend his appointment on the Spanish coast. He must, by force, shorten the boys' dreams, steal from them three years and four months, interrupt them in time . . . he must deceive them, prevent one from telling another what he dreamed the dreamed one was dreaming, he must prevent one from being told what the other was dreaming as he was dreamed by him, cut short the dream the third dreamed he was dreaming as he was dreamed . . . cut short their dreams . . . As he told himself these things, Ludovico struggled against the deep and strange love he felt for the three youths placed in his care. He kept his decision to himself: he would have enough integrity, intelligence, and love to reunite his destiny and that of the three boys, make equal sacrifices for all four. But even thinking this, was he not admitting that from now on, none of the four would have the unified destiny a dream dreamed or a will willed?

He calmed his agitation by reflecting: "That is the price of a destiny in history: to be incomplete. Only an infinite destiny like that imagined by the three boys can be complete: that is why it cannot occur in history. One lifetime is not enough. One needs many existences in order to fulfill a personality. I shall do whatever possible to assure that this finite date in history—an afternoon, a fourteenth of July, within five years—does not deprive my sons of their infinite destiny in dream . . ."

And so he laid down a challenge to himself, a self-imposed challenge, an act of voluntary flagellation that would serve as witness to his conscience of the good faith that motivated him. There could be nothing better than to see for the last time the splendid sight of Venice, the glimmering scales of her canals, the sealed light of her windows, her white jaws of marble, her solitary stone squares, her silent bronze doors, the motionless conflagration of her bells, her shipwrights' pitch beaches, the green wings of the lion, the empty book of the Apostle, the blind eyes of the saint: Ludovico was a man forty years old, bald, with olive-colored skin and green protruding eyes, with a sad smile marked by the lines of poverty, love, and study . . . He was seized by enormous bitterness. Felipe had been right. Grace was neither immediate nor gratuitous: one had always to pay history's price: the denunciation of a witch who denied the pragmatic efficacy of grace, Felipe had said then; the foreshortening of dreams that extended beyond calendar years, Ludovico said today.

He did not tear out his eyes. He did not even close them. He simply decided not to see; he would see nothing, never again, he would be voluntarily blind; he, blind, his sons, sleeping, until their destinies flowed together and were again joined—by dissimilar routes, with different purposes—in Felipe's presence; then their pledges could be redeemed: history colored by dream, as well as dream penetrated by history.

He would not see again. They sailed away. In the distance, San Marco, San Giorgio, La Carbonaia, La Giudecca; in the distance, Torcello, Murano, Burano, San Lazzaro degli Armeni. The image his pilgrim's eyes beheld, the most beautiful of all cities, was what would remain. They had not fled in time. No one ever flees Venice in time. Venice imprisons us within her own spectral dream. He would not see again. He would not read again. The dreamer has another life: wakefulness. The blind man has other eyes: memory.

THE BEGUINES OF BRUGES

They say that one winter night, oh, about five years ago, a slow-moving cart drawn by starving horses entered the city of Bruges. Its driver was a very young man of handsome appearance: by his side sat a blind beggar. Patched canvas covered the cart's contents.

A few faces peered out from the narrow windows of the houses, for the night was so silent, and so frozen and hard the ground, that the wheels groaned as if they supported the weight of an army.

Many crossed themselves as they saw that phantasmal apparition advancing beneath the light, persistent snow, through the white streets, across black bridges; others swore that the shadow of the carriage, the beggar and his guide, and their tottering old nags did not reflect in the motionless waters of the canals.

They stopped before the great gate of a community of Beguines.

Aided by the boy, the blind beggar descended and knocked softly at the door, repeating over and over: "Pauperes virgines religiosas viventes . . ."

Snow covered the heads and shoulders of the wretched pilgrims; finally they heard the scraping sound of footsteps approaching the other side of the door, and a woman's voice asked who it was disturbed the peace of this place in that profane hour, saying they could offer pilgrims nothing here, for the community was under a papal interdiction and such grave censure prevented them from celebrating Divine Offices, administering Sacraments, or burying in holy ground . . . I come from Dalmatia, said the blind mendicant; the gypsy of the tattooed lips sent us, added the boy; they heard the sound of other feet, the hissing of awakened geese; the door opened, and more than twenty hooded women in gray wool tunics, veils covering their faces, observed in silence the entrance of the creaking cart onto the grass court of the community.

INSIDE THE WINDMILL

They say that barely three years ago the same cart was dragging along across the fields of La Mancha when a terrible storm broke that seemed to crumble the distant mountain peaks, first dry thunder and then a steady, driving downpour.

The beggar and the boy in the open cart sought refuge in one of the windmills that are the sentinels that take the place of trees on that arid plain.

They turned back the canvas that covered the cart bed and exposed two coffins which they laboriously transported to the entrance of the windmill. Once inside, they deposited the boxes on dry straw and, shaking themselves like dogs, climbed the creaking spiral stairway to the upper floor of the windmill: the wind was madly spinning the sails and the noise inside the windmill was like that of swarms of wooden wasps.

The entrance where they had left the two death boxes was dark. But as they ascended, deafened by the noise of the sails, they were illumined by a strange light.

On the upper floor an old man lay upon a straw pallet. As the beggar and the boy approached, the light in the room began to dim; the shadows rearranged themselves and certain barely visible forms were suggested in the penumbra; then they disappeared, as if swallowed by the darkness, as if they had melted into the rough circular walls of the windmill.

PEDRO ON THE BEACH

"I knew we would find you here. You are Pedro, are you not?"

The old man with the hairy gray body said yes, but that words were unnecessary; if they wanted to help him, to take up nails, hammers, and saws.

"You do not remember me?"

"No," said the old man, "I have never seen you before."

Ludovico smiled. "And I cannot see you now."

Pedro shrugged his shoulders and continued to fit planks upon the skeleton of the boat. He asked the slender youth who accompanied the blind man: "How old are you?"

"Nineteen, señor."

"How I wish," Pedro sighed, "how I wish it would be a young man who first steps upon the beaches of the new world."

SCHWESTER KATREI

No, said the Mistress of the Beghards, we are affected by the interdiction but we were not the cause; it was the Princes of these Low Countries who every day remove themselves further from the power of Rome and endeavor to act with autonomy in collecting indulgences, naming bishops, and allying themselves with merchants, navigators, and other secular powers, thus confusing the aims of Satan and Mercury; we have no idea what will be born of this pact . . .

Ludovico nodded as he listened to these explanations and he told the Mistress that he was familiar with the purposes of the Beguines, which were to renounce riches and come together in a community of poverty and virginity, offering an example of Christian virtue in the midst of the century's corruption, although without segregating themselves from it; but was it not also true that the last Cathari, defeated in the Provençal wars, came to these secular convents seeking refuge and that the sainted women did not refuse them shelter, but here allowed them to regain their strength, to practice their rites, and . . . ?"

The Mistress clapped her hand over Ludovico's mouth; this was a holy place, given to intense devotion to the rules of the imitation of Christ: poverty, humility, the desire for illumination and union with the person of the Divinity: here dwelled the legendary and never sufficiently praised Schwester Katrei, purest of the pure, virgin of virgins, who in her state of mystic union had reached perfect immobility; so great was her identification with God that all movement was superfluous and only from time to time did she open her mouth to exclaim: "Rejoice with me, for I have become God. Praise be God!" Then she would again fall into a motionless trance.

Ludovico asked if he could approach the sainted Sister. The Mistress smiled with compassion. "My poor brother, you cannot see her."

"Is that necessary? I can sense her presence."

He was led to a hut at the rear of the geese- and sycamore-dotted green where dwelt Katrei, the Saint. The snow was beginning to melt beneath a fine, constant rain from the North. The Mistress, with the familiarity of long practice, opened the door of the hut.

Schwester Katrei, naked, sat astride the blind man's young companion; she was shouting that she was mounted upon the Holy Trinity as upon a divine steed; her legs locked about the youth's waist, she shouted, I am illuminated, Mother, I am God; she clawed the boy's back, and God can neither know, nor desire, nor effect anything without me . . . the naked youth's back was covered with bleeding crosses . . . nothing exists without me . . .

The Mistress fell to her knees upon the melting snow and agreed to summon the Cathari who had taken refuge in this region to a meeting in the remote forest of the Duke where they were wont to gather secretly on certain nights of the year.

Ludovico uncovered the cart and the Mistress saw the two coffins lying there.

"No, we cannot bury anyone. That is part of the interdiction."

"They are not dead. They are merely dreaming."

GIANTS AND PRINCESSES

The old man on the pallet in the windmill laughed loud and long; he had an infinite capacity for laughter that was in great contrast to the sadness of his features; tears of laughter ran down the wrinkles in the emaciated cheeks of this man with the short white beard and unkempt moustaches. He laughed for more than an hour and finally, his words interrupted by merriment, managed to speak: "A beggar and a youth . . . A blind man and his guide . . . Whoever would have believed . . . ? Two persons in such condition . . . would be the ones who come to break my spell . . . to free me from this prison . . . where I have lain for so many years . . . ?"

"This windmill is a prison?" Ludovico asked.

"The most terrible of all prisons: the very entrails of the giant Caraculiambro, Lord of the Island of Malindrania. What arts did you call upon to reach here? The giant is zealous . . ."

He requested his arms, which like him lay upon the straw, and the blind man and the youth armed him with his broken lance and dented shield. In vain they searched for the helmet he had requested, until he himself informed them that it resembled a barber's basin.

Between them, they helped him to his feet; the knight's bones clanked like old chains as, supported between the blind man and the youth, he was dragged to the head of the stairway. The moment his foot touched the first step, the circular area of the windmill was again illuminated; they heard plaintive voices, and frightening and guttural sounds, the latter impotently menacing, and the former heart-rendingly pleading: Do not abandon us, you promised to aid us, to free us, turn back, knight, do not leave us, you are escaping only because two corpses have intruded into our domains, you will be damned, you will be accompanied by death, see whether you can free yourself from it after you have freed yourself from us . . .

The old man paused, turned, and said, his eyes filled with tears: "Do not miaow, my unrivaled Miaulina, nor you, peerless Casildea of Vandalia, I am not abandoning you, I swear it, I free myself only to return to the attack and vanquish our captors; do not growl, fearful Alifanfarón de la Trapobana, do not open your gaping jaws, Serpentino de la Fuente Sangrienta, I have not put the final period to our combat, nor will any blue and bedeviled enchanter ever succeed in doing so; the crumbs will not grow stale before they reach my lips . . ."

Huddled beside the circular wall, the youth saw pale and trembling ladies held captive in the enormous, bleeding, and hairy fists of giants, and he said to Ludovico: It is true, what this man says is true; but Ludovico was grateful for his blindness and he smiled, tranquilly unbelieving.

ULTIMA THULE

They set sail one afternoon guided by the evening star. They sailed always toward the west. They caught sharks. They witnessed a mortal combat between a leviathan and a swordfish. They were becalmed on the Sargasso Sea, the limits of the known world, but beyond it they were seized in a deep whirlpool that carried them into the depths of the sea, the marine tomb, the tunnel of the oceans into which endlessly pours the great cataract of the world.

Ludovico stood alone on the beach between the two coffins, his back to the sea; he murmured: "Return. There is nothing behind me."

HERTOGENBOSCH

Schwester Katrei was once again alone and she promised, from that instant, to devote herself to the supreme mortification of her illumined and persecuted faith.

"Go," she told the youth who had robbed her of her virginity, "I shall devote myself to endura, the will for death, motionless, my eyes opened, my mouth closed, fading away little by little. Nothing stands between me and eternal union with God."

The youth kissed the enlightened woman's open eyes and whispered into her ear: "You are wrong, Katrei. The dream is the only intelligent form of suicide."

"Let us go beyond that," Ludovico told the initiates that night in the woods. "If the world is the work of two gods, one good and the other evil, we shall not reach Heaven—as you have believed until now—through purity and total chastity; on the contrary, if our body is the seat of evil we must exhaust that body on earth so we may reach Heaven cleansed of any stain, with no recollection of the body we once possessed, like our father Adam in his primordial innocence; let us remove our clothing, let us not be ashamed of our bodies, as Adam was not ashamed; for if you accept Adam's guilt you must also accept the need for sacraments and priests, the need for a church to mediate between God and his fallen creature; but if you accept that the body is free and deliver yourself unto pleasure, you will be twice worthy on earth, twice free, you shall battle for the innocence of the body by exhausting its impurities and so, from this time forward, you will be called the Adamites, followers of Adam, disrobe . . ."

His young companion revealed to those assembled there his beautiful naked body, and soon all of them were naked and accompanying him in a circle dance around the fire; no one felt the cold that night, but danced among the trees, copulated in the ponds and with the flowers, naked they rode horses and wild pigs, the night was filled with sounds of the horn, they awakened the birds, they dreamed they were floating inside pure globes of crystal, devoured by fish, and devouring strawberries; and they were seen only by the owls and by the eyes of one middle-aged initiate who never removed his peasant cap, as if something was hidden beneath his hat.

When day again dawned over the village of Hertogenbosch, this man, eyes half closed, recounted everything through thin, colorless

lips to a mute retable which had just witnessed the same events seen by
the humble artisan.

DULCINEA

Believe me, I was once young, I was not born as you see me now, old,
and cudgeled, I was young and I was in love, the knight recounted to
the blind man and the youth, and it is not the way of youth to stop and
dream about what he desires, but to rush to seize it quickly, for blessings, if they are not communicated, are not blessings, and let us all
win them, let us all share them, let us all be merry, for thus are fabricated the marvels of the present, and death is distant and pleasure
near at hand; he spoke beneath the sudden sun of La Mancha, the sky
washed clean by the storm and creased by clouds with trailing shadows. I loved Dulcinea, she proved herself virtuous, so I used the
services of the old procuress and possessed the maiden for myself, my
ideas about time began to change, I cursed the cocks because they announced the dawn and the clock because it struck so quickly, the man
said, seated between the two coffins in the cart; we were surprised by
the girl's father, he challenged me, I became violent, he became violent, he ran his own daughter through with his sword, and I him with
mine: it is told that there was never a more bloody day in all Toboso;
father and daughter were buried together beneath a statue that represented the daughter sleeping and the father standing guard over her
with his sword; all this the old man told them as the cart advanced
slowly over earth studded with rocks resembling half-buried bones,
raising clouds of orange, flaming dust. I fled, they placed a price upon
my head, I changed my name, and settled in a place whose name I do
not wish to recall, alone, knowing in my own flesh the truth of what the
old procuress who furnished me Dulcinea's favors had told me: old age
is a hostelry of illness, an inn for thoughts, unremitting anguish, incur-
able wound, stain of the past, pain of the present, morose concern for
the future, neighbor to death, and, standing as tall as possible in the
cart and raising his lance as if to wound the clouds, he said, books
were my only consolation, I read them all, I imagined I could be one of
those flawless knights, rescue those illustrious ladies, vanquish those
perfidious giants and magicians, return to Toboso, break the spell of
my maiden of sleeping stone and restore her to life, as young as the day
she died, Dulcinea, do you remember Don Juan, your young lover?,
see him now, I am returning to you with a basin for a helmet, a broken
sword and a skinny nag, I return to your tomb, the old man said, opening his arms as if to embrace the reverberating expanse of the granite-

strewn plain, I returned convinced that I would rescue her from the enchantment of death and stone, I was once again the young Don Juan, not the aged Don Alonso I had become in order to flee from justice, I begged and pleaded before her tomb; it was not the effigy of the maiden that moved but the statue of the father, noble sword in hand, who spoke to me and said, I wanted to kill you when you were young, but now I see you are old and worthless. I tried to challenge him anew, to invite him to dine, now gladly I would throw myself into the pit of Hell, what were phantoms to me!, but the statue only laughed, and he told me he was condemning me to something worse, that my imaginings and my reading would become reality, that my fragile bones would actually confront monsters and giants, and that again and again I would rush to right wrongs only to be cudgeled, mocked, caged, taken for a madman, and dishonored, the mocker mocked, he laughed, ridicule will kill you, for no one but you shall see those giants and magicians and princesses, you will see the truth, but only you; others will see sheep and windmills, puppet stages, wineskins, sweaty peasant girls and piggish servants where you see reality: armies of cruel despots, giants, frightful hordes of Moors and adorable princesses: that was the statue's curse, said the old man, sinking down beside one of the coffins.

FIRST MAN

Dawn rose upon a beach of pearls and turtles tossed there by the tempest. He thought he had lost Pedro in the storm. He found him at the end of the beach. They constructed a house. They placed limits about a space. They lighted a fire. Floating tree trunks arrived bearing naked men armed with lances. They put out the fire. They killed Pedro. They bore the youth upriver to a village inhabited by an ancient king in a basket filled with pearls. Great rains came. They climbed the mountain. The ancient received the youth in a temple. He called him brother. He told him the story of the creation of the new world. First man. The youth thanked him by offering him a mirror. Young chieftain. The ancient died of terror when he saw himself in the mirror. In the stead of the ancient the men of the jungle placed the youth in the basket of pearls. There he would wait forever, until he died, as ancient as his predecessor.

THE FREE SPIRIT

From province to province they advanced, at a pace that others attributed to the assistance of the Devil; they devastated the lands, destroyed churches, and burned monasteries; at their head was a young, blond heresiarch, his hair bound into three crowning golden bands, his back bared to show the sign of the elect, his feet unshod so as to astound with his twelve toes, his face painted white to glow in the night—to some, the prophet of the human millennium; to others, the Antichrist; for some, a teacher telling of a land without hunger, without oppression, without prohibitions, without false gods or false popes or false kings; entire families joined with him, apostatized monks, women disguised as men, highwaymen, prostitutes, ladies of great breeding who had renounced their wealth to find salvation in poverty but who in truth were only seeking nights of pleasure with him, with the young heresiarch, here called Tanchelm, in other places, Eudes de l'Etoile, names that others gave him, Baldwin, Frederick, Charlemagne, he who had no name, accompanied always by two coffins and a blind beggar who on occasion spoke for him, he stirring up the multitudes of poor who followed after him, only the poor shall achieve the Kingdom of Heaven and the Kingdom of Heaven is here upon earth, seize it, each of you is Christ, Paradise is here, dissolve the monasteries, take the nuns for your women, set the monks to work, in truth I say to you: let the monks and nuns grow the vine and the wheat that sustain us, chop down the door of the rich man, and we will sup with him, persecute the clergy, let every priest hold us in such fear that he will hide his tonsure even if it is covered under cow's dung, march day and night, through all the land, from Louvain to Haarlem, from Bruges to St.-Quentin, from Ghent to Paris, though they slit our throats and throw us into the Seine, Paris is our goal, there where thought is pleasure and pleasure thought, the capital of the third age, the scene of the final battle, the last city, there where the persuasive Devil inculcated in a few wise men a perverse intelligence, Paris, fountain of all wisdom, let us march with our standards, and our candles burning in the light of day, we will flagellate ourselves in the streets, we shall make love in the open, the pain and the delight of the flesh, hurry, we have but thirty-three and a half days to complete our crusade, that is the holy cipher for our processions, the number of the days of Christ upon the earth, but sufficient time to sweep away the corrupt Church of the Antichrist in Rome, there is no authority but ours, our life, our experience, let us recognize nothing except that, follow me, I am but one of you, I am not the leader, do as I do, seduce women, they belong to each of us, weavers, needle sellers, rascals, beggars, Turlupins, the poorest of the poor, the same as I, nothing is mine, everything belongs to us all, there is no sin, there was no Fall, take possession, with me, of the visible empire preparing for the end of the world, preached the young heresiarch to the accompaniment of the blind beggar's flute, be free, the knowing man is in himself heaven and purgatory and hell, the man of free spirit does not know sin, take everything for yourself, nothing is sinful except what you imagine to be so, return with me and my blind father to the state of innocence, let us take off our clothes, take each other by the hand, kneel, swear obedience only to the free spirit, dissolve all other vows, matrimony, chastity, priesthood, God is free, therefore everything was created to be shared, freely, by all, everything the eye can see or desire, stretch out your hand and take, go into the inns, refuse to pay, beat him who would ask you for payment, be charitable, but if charity is denied you, take it by force, women, food, money . . . the hordes of Flanders, Brabant, Holland, Picardy, at their head the beggar kings, a youth with a cross upon his back, and a blind flautist: the end of the world . . .

THE GALLEY SLAVES

Well, master, what must we do? the squire who abandoned me to stay to govern an insalubrious and insipid and inhuman island always used to ask me, and I always replied: "What must we do? Favor and aid the needy and the helpless."

The old man of the sad countenance, lying between the two coffins, clutching in both hands his aching head aggravated by the swaying and creaking of the cart, was silent for a long moment. Then he sighed and said: "Many are the ways that such a holy undertaking may be accomplished, and mine was but one of many. But see what my fate has been, sirs, that I see the truth of things which others hold to be a lie; the enchantment lay upon the others; and greater the enchantment of my enchantment, as I saw that only I, cursed by the statue of Dulcinea's father, saw giants where others, as if enchanted, saw only windmills."

Jolted by the cart, he drew closer to the blind man and the youth; he looked at them with wrathful eyes. "But do you know what my revenge will be?"

He laughed again, and struck his fist against his chest. "I shall declare that my reason has returned. I shall keep my secret. I shall accept that everything I have seen is a lie. I shall try to convince no one."

Cackling, he placed a bony hand upon the youth's shoulder. "I lived the youth of Don Juan. Perhaps Don Juan will dare to live my old age. You, my boy . . . I cannot remember . . . I believe I looked like you in my youth. You, lad, would you agree to continue living my life for me?''

The youth had no time to respond, or the blind man to comment. As the old man raised his eyes he saw on the road ahead a party of a dozen men on foot, strung by their necks like beads along a great iron chain, and all of them handcuffed. Two men on horseback carrying flint-locks accompanied them, and two on foot carrying javelins and swords . . . The old man, reanimated, leaped from the cart, sword in hand, but as the cart did not stop, he fell flat on the ground, where dusty and battered he cried to the youth: ''Aha! here is an example of the purpose of my office: to rout armies and to succor and aid the wretched; will you not accompany me, my boy?, will you not follow adventure with me?, see that injustice, see these galley slaves led against their will, abused and tortured, will you allow a wrong of such magnitude to remain unpunished?, will you not do battle by my side, my boy?''

The youth jumped from the cart, assisted the old man to his feet, and the two serenely awaited the passage of the chain gang.

THE LADY OF THE BUTTERFLIES

But it did not happen that way. Rather, one night, cinnamon-colored hands with long black fingernails parted the deerskin hangings of the bower, and a strangely beautiful woman crowned by glowing butter-flies, her lips painted a thousand colors, entered and said to him: ''Your life is in danger. For days now they have gathered about the bonfires to deliberate. They have decided to offer you as a sacrifice. Take this knife. Come with me. They are sleeping.''

And that night the two of them slit the throats of all the inhabitants of the town in the jungle. Then they made love.

At dawn, she said to him: ''Twenty-five are the days of your destiny in this land. You shall remember twenty, because in those days you will have acted. Five you will forget, for they are the masked days you will set aside from your destiny to save against your death.''

''And at the end of those days, what will happen to me?''

''I shall await you at the summit of the pyramid, beside the volcano.''

''Shall I see you again? Shall I sleep with you again?''

''I promise. For one year you will have everything. You will have me every night.''

''Only a year . . . ? And then?''

The Lady of the Butterflies did not answer.

THE DEFEAT

Felipe, El Señor, Defensor Fides, in the name of the Faith he defended and the sacred power of Rome, had laid siege to the Flemish city where the hordes of the heresiarch and the Brabantine Duke who protected them had taken final refuge.

"All is lost," said the Duke.

He stroked a mole on his cheek and again looked at Ludovico and his young companion. "That is to say, everything is lost for you. I shall make peace with Don Felipe and with Rome. If I lay down my arms I shall have gained something: the right to collect tithes, plus privileges of navigation and letters of commerce for my industrious subjects. And without need of accords, but thanks to the crusade of the heretics, I shall have discredited both the Church, which was so easily challenged and humiliated by your throng, and the mystics who participated in such excesses. The true triumph of this war belongs to the secular and lay cause. The men of the future will remember that it is possible to burn effigies, disband convents, and expel monks, converting the unproductive riches of the clergy into the sap of commerce and industry. They will also remember that mobs guided by mysticism level fields, destroy harvests, harass the burghers, and violate their women. Thus, I shall have triumphed, if I lay down my arms. A thing I shall do. However, they are asking the head of this youth. You, blind man, you may go free. It is a sad thing, but no one sees any danger in you. Go now."

Ludovico hid in the shadows of the Cathedral. There was a terrible odor of vomit and excrement. He heard the Teutonic voices of Felipe's mercenaries. He smelled Felipe's presence; he knew that body, he had loved it, he had possessed it. He spoke to him from the shadows. He did not open his eyes. Not yet. Phantoms do not frighten us because we cannot see them: phantoms are phantoms because they do not see us.

Then he fled. It was night. He kept his ear to the ground. He followed the sounds of the retreat of the Duke and his men. He hitched up the cart. A blind man with two coffins. Dead from hunger, from the war, from the plague, what did it matter? They allowed him to pass beyond the walls. He followed the sounds of the flight of the Duke and his men.

He was guided by the dark drums of execution.

Naked, his hands bound, the young and beautiful heresiarch with the blood-red cross upon his back knelt beside the stump of a tree and laid his head upon it.

The executioner raised high the ax.

SING YOUR TROUBLES

"I only promised to take them to the next town," the blind man protested, "where I am going to bury two of my sons who died of the cholera. I've never seen them before."

They allowed him to continue on his way. They set free the scramble-brained old man in his town-without-a-name, amid the jeers and the anguish of the priest, the barber, the bachelor, and the niece, for everyone knew about the madness of Señor Quijano, but they placed a chain about the neck of the youth, and handcuffed him and strung him to the chain gang.

The captain of the guard said to a subaltern: "Did you see that? That youth has a cross upon his back, and six toes on each foot . . ."

"So, that means nothing to me . . ."

"Don't you remember almost twenty years ago now, when we were serving in the castle guard?"

"Nah, so we served in the guard, so . . ."

"El Señor gave orders to place traps for wolves through all the district, and each Saturday we went out to hunt the beasts; we were to kill immediately any she-wolf we saw, or any child with those same signs of the cross and the feet; don't stop to make sure of anything, he said, kill them quickly, don't you remember?"

"God's blood, how should I remember, it's been so long . . ."

Sing your troubles, they said to him in the dungeons of Tordesillas; they tied a cloth over his face, covering his nostrils and cutting off his breath, and through the cloth they poured streams of water which ran down the back of his nose into his throat; speak, who are you?, you'd better speak up, wretch, for in any case you were condemned to death twenty years ago, no one will ask about you, speak, who are you? . . . I'm drowning, drowning, drowning . . .

THE CIRCULAR DREAM

The black, blood-bedaubed priests took him by the hands and arms, and amid smoking censers, forced him to lie upon the stone at the summit of the pyramid that faced the throne of the woman with the painted lips . . .

He smiled sadly. To reach her he had fled from village to village, through the jungles and valleys of the new world, until he reached the temple beside the volcano; employing all the tricks of the rogue, he had deceived, he had assumed the role of a blond white god who according to the legends of the natives was to return from the East, he had accepted their gifts, he had asked that it all be converted into gold, he had laden himself with heavy pouches, he had made love to the women, he had explored every facet of his cleverness, he had demanded sacrifices in his name, he had presided over the pageantry of death, more, more, always more, the god is insatiable, he exploited their weakness and fear, he ordered the death of the old because they were of no service, of the young because they could serve as nourishment, and of children because they were innocent, he had set people against people, he demanded war as proof of devotion, he knew the burning of villages, he had seen cadavers on the plains, and in his ascent from the coast to the high plain he had promised each nation to free it from the tribute exacted by the next strongest, only to subject it to the taxes of the next nation along his path; he had created a chain of tributes worse than any servitude previously known in these lands. He justified himself by saying he did it in order to survive; one single man against an empire . . . had history ever known an undertaking comparable to his? Alexander's armies, Caesar's legions; he was alone, Ulixes, son of Sisyphus, breaking forever from his father's fatalism: this time the rock, pushed to the summit, would crown it forever. But who would know of this odyssey, who would tell it to generations to come? Was it worth the effort to perform memorable feats with no witnesses to sing of them?

He alone.

The woman of the painted lips whispered into his ear: "You remember nothing more?"

"No."

"You have forgotten the five days?"

"I have lived but twenty."

"And the beautiful year we spent together, you favored and attended, you and I making love?"

"I remember nothing."

He had survived. The black priest raised the flint knife and with a single, swift movement drove it down toward the youth's heart . . .

At the instant the stone knife touched his breast, he awakened.

He breathed a sigh of relief. He was sleeping beside a tree on a pile of dried leaves. He was trembling with cold, and he attempted to stretch his limbs. His hands were tied. He tried to struggle to his feet. He fell back among the damp leaves. A rope bound his feet. Two soldiers walked toward him, cut the rope binding his feet, and led him to a clearing in the forest.

On horseback, the Duke looked at him with sadness, gave the order, and galloped away.

The order was short and decisive: "Take his head to the victorious Señor, Don Felipe, in proof of my good faith."

They forced him to kneel beside the stump of a tree and lower his head until his cheek touched the stump.

The executioner raised the ax high and with a single swift, sure movement drove it toward the youth's neck . . .

In the instant the ax touched his neck, he awakened.

Someone had kicked him in the ribs. He opened his eyes and saw a tall monk wearing the habit of the order of St. Augustine; he had a face like a skull, so tightly did his skin adhere to the bone.

"Are you ready to speak?"

"What would you have me say?"

"Where were you born?"

"I do not know."

"What is the meaning of that cross upon your back?"

"I do not know."

"You know nothing, imbecile, but our former Señor, may he live in glory, surely knew something when he ordered your death twenty years ago when you were scarcely born, after you disappeared one night from the bedchamber of Isabel, Lady of our present Señor; do my words mean nothing to you?"

"Nothing."

"You are very stubborn; in any case, you are going to die, but if you speak you can spare yourself torture. You know nothing?"

"I remember nothing."

"Then sing your troubles."

He scarcely had a moment to glimpse for the last time the brick floor of the cell, the thick stone of the walls, the iron bars covered with drops of water like the dew: they tied a cloth over his face, covering his nostrils and cutting off his breath, and through the cloth they poured streams of water which ran down the back of his nose into his throat . . . I'm drowning, drowning, drowning . . .

THE CABO

DE LOS DESASTRES

Quickly, Pedro, for the first time all three are dreaming at the same time, they must be dreaming one another, for the first time it is not one who acts as the other two dream him, I tell you they are dreaming each other, an infinite, circular dream with no beginning or end, perhaps it is my fault, may God, if He exists, forgive me, they told me that the total cycle of their dreams would be thirty-three and one half months multiplied by three, too much time, I interrupted their dreams three times, I stole time from them, I justified myself by saying that on those three occasions the intensity of their dreams frightened me, their screams, their voices of terror, and loneliness, and death. I do not know whether I did them harm or good by interrupting their dreams at those instants, stealing time from them to gain my own, the ordained day, tomorrow, the ordained date, the fourteenth of July, the ordained year, twenty years after the youths were born, the ordained place, the Cabo de los Desastres, the same beach where we all met twenty years ago, do you remember?, Felipe and Celestina, the monk Simón, and you and I; Celestina will be here tomorrow, I know it, she promised, Simón is now at the site of the palace, he has notified the friar Julián, Felipe, El Señor, will go out to hunt tomorrow, destinies are flowing together, I tear my sons from their dreams in order to immerse them in history, quickly, yes, all right, Ludovico, but I can go no faster, you cannot see, but the storm is terrible, you will not calm it with the music of that flute, it cannot be heard, the squall will drown it out, Ludovico, and I have only two hands to furl the sail, the sky is black, even the lightning flashes are black this night, ay, my poor ship is creaking, you see, it would never have reached the other side of the great ocean, this worthless nutshell could never have withstood even a miserable coastal storm, so many years wasted in building, destroying, building again, perfecting a ship that would carry me far, far away to the new world, to the better world, ay, the mainmast's aflame, St. Elmo's fire, did you lash each one's bottle securely to him, Pedro?, yes, Ludovico, between his belly and his breeches, as you asked me, swear to me, Pedro, you will never tell my secret, that no one will ever know I interrupted their dreams, that everyone will believe that these youths completed the sacred cycle, the thirty-three and one half months, if someday we find ourselves facing El Señor, do not betray me, Pedro, do not make a liar out of me, now, Ludovico, while we can take advantage of that blazing light from the mainmast, now Pedro, throw them into the water, one after another, the three youths, the three dreamers, they will drown, Ludovico, death by water, love for water, you mean, Pedro, if it is their destiny to be saved, they will be saved, if they die, they will continue to dream, and dreaming eternally I do not know whether they will forgive me for having taken their destinies in my hands, perhaps they were destined to end their lives dreaming one another, a fatal circle, and I am awakening them to bind them to my own destiny, the encounter with Felipe, the return twenty years after the illusion and the crime, but I must know, Pedro, can you understand?, they are my work and I am theirs, neither they nor I shall ever be anything but what we have been together, everything they know they learned with me, they are the founding brothers common to all races, all peoples, except with different names, the ones who named, the ones who fell, those who founded everything for a second time upon the ruin of the first creation, making themselves part of it, grace, Pedro, practical grace set free in history, incarnate in the present, in our present, here and now, throw the first one overboard, now the second, now the third, three, always three, a dream in Alexandria, seclusion in Palestine, prophecy in Spalato, a memory in Venice, a crusade in Flanders, a pilgrimage to the new world, an encounter in La Mancha, the roads of liberty, encounters and partings, quickly, Pedro, it is done, Ludovico, and may God forgive you, I do not know who these boys are but I believe you have put them to death as surely as you drown a rabid dog by throwing it into the river in a sack, no, Pedro, creation is eternal, it is repeated time and time again like the dreams of those young men, they are the founders, the brothers who will not this time be able to repeat the crime of brother against brother, as it was written, because I looked after them, I intervened, I saved them for this moment, I took them away from the tempting sister, the enchantress, the woman of the tattooed lips, the gypsy, and now I am returning to them the freedom the dream took from them, I am returning them to history, my history, to see what they can do in it, with it, for it, to see what destiny awaits them, what faces, what names, the brothers, always two, always two, the learned doctor of the synagogue told me two is the static opposition that resolves itself in death, not now, for they were three, history will be changed, three is the number that puts things in movement, animates them, makes fluid what seemed immobile, transforms the cavern into a river, I saved them from the prophecy, one brother did not kill the other, because they were more than two, one brother shall save the others, because they were three, and the ship creaks, the tempest breaks the mast and the fire falls into the sea, the deck shatters, the hull splits apart, jump, Ludovico, the ship is nothing but splinters, tie me to the rudder, Pedro, quickly, my poor ship is foundering, it's sinking, we shall shatter against the rocks, we are drowning, drowning, drowning . . .

MOTHER CELESTINA

࿓

Felipe's father, El Señor, visited them, and asked Celestina's father: "When will the girl be married? Marry her soon, for noblemen are roaming this forest who have lost their lands but not their taste for virgin girls. In any case, remember you must save her maidenhead for me . . ."

He trotted away, laughing, and Celestina remembered with fear the night this same Señor, drunken and shouting, had ridden through the forest looking for trapped she-wolves, and in his erotic fury had fornicated with one of them. This the girl had never told her father; that innocent, thinking thus to defend her against wandering noblemen hungry for a female, decided to dress her as a man from that day forward; she, allowing herself to be disguised, hoped to defend herself against El Señor, although she knew he would as soon rape a lad as a woman or a beast.

With her father, she grew up in the forest. He grew old; at times his fingertips brushed the forever wounded lips of his daughter, and he murmured sadly: "A mouth with pain says no good thing. It was an unlucky day we left the shelter of our forest to go to Toledo."

He avoided speaking with his daughter masquerading as a lad. One day they learned of the death of El Señor. And then the armed men of the heir Don Felipe appeared, their mission to gather all the boys in the forest for the service at arms, and as servants.

"Who will work the land, who will care for the flocks?" were the last words she heard her father speak.

Prince Don Felipe, seeing her dressed as a man, did not guess her true condition, although her features seemed to awaken something disturbing in the heir's memory. She was assigned to the service of the young Señor's mother, where the presence of women was forbidden. As a shepherdess, she had learned to play the flute and she let this be made known to the head steward so she might entertain herself and others, living apart from the servants and the soldiers, before whom she had never disrobed. The Mad Lady respected the musical talents of her new page: she ordered the page to learn to play the drum, for she had forbidden all but funereal sounds now that she lived in continuous mourning. And thus, when the aged Lady began her long pilgrimage with her husband's corpse, she assigned the page to the last position in the procession, playing the drum and dressed all in black, a herald of mourning.

From the castle of Tordesillas the procession advanced to Burgos, and from there to the Carthusian monastery of Miraflores; through great cities, Medina del Campo and Avila, small cities, Hornillos, Tórtolos, Arcos, and middle-sized cities, Torquemada and Madrid. And one day in this city of little merit as the Mad Lady was secluded in the monastery worshipping her husband's remains, the members of her procession dispersed along the servile banks of the Manzanares, and thus the black-clad page with the colored and wounded lips happened to pass by some tanneries along the banks of the river; the smoke from the tanneries recalled to her her childhood in the forest, and as she stood, overcome by nostalgia, a hand seized her arm and a hunched figure spoke into her ear:

"O-ho, there, my girl, whom do you think you're fooling? I can smell a virgin a league away, and there are very few virgins in this town—and may God be praised for it—who have been stitched without me as guide to the needle. When a girl is born I mark her name in my book so I will know which of them escapes my net. You may deceive the rest of the world, but not Mother Celestina, for if I've restored one maidenhead, I've restored a thousand, and a whiff tells me yours has not been touched, and that is bad, my girl, for you should never be miserly with what costs you so little. How have you escaped my register? Are you a stranger in this town? Hear me, my pretty, I may have lost my molars, but the taste for love is still strong on my gums. And if you are a virgin, trust in me, because for every girl that's born, there is a boy, and for every boy, a girl, and there is no one in this world who does not have a mate if he but knows how to find him; a lonely soul neither sings nor weeps, it's a rare sight to see a single partridge in flight, and there is nothing more pitiful, my daughter, than the mouse that knows but one hole, for if that is blocked up he has nowhere to hide from the cat. Who longs for honor without profit? You look like a barren ewe; go change your clothing and show the world what God gave you, for I divine a sublime form beneath that black garb. Yes, you've fallen into good hands . . ."

The girl's wounded lips moved. "Celestina," she said.

"Yes, Celestina," answered the old woman so swathed in black rags that only her face and hands were visible. "I see that my fame has spread afar, and if you find my name evil, ask yourself as I did, was the wind to look after me?, what estate did I inherit?, do I have a house, or a vineyard? But if you think it evil, you will find I have a good name among men; just walk along with me, daughter, and you will see how they greet me, gentlemen, old men, lads, abbots of all rank from bishops to sacristans: you'll see hats tipped in my honor as if I were a duchess. Oh, you accursed, voluminous skirts, tripping over you, I can never go as fast as I want."

"You don't remember me?"

"Daughter, he who scatters his memory in many places finds he has none to spare . . ."

"My lips . . . ?"

"What happened to you, child? Did the Devil kiss you? Come along with me; I'll lend you a veil until I can mend them for you, for there's nothing that cannot be cured with the ointment made from goat's blood and a few hairs from its chin whiskers. I tell you, you fell into good hands when in all of this spoiled meat pie of Madrid you came to this aged lapidary who perfumes ladies' toques, extracts mercury chlorate, knows all there is to know about herbs, and physics babies . . ."

"But I remember you . . ."

"How can that be, daughter? I have lived a lot of years. There is no one who remembers how I used to be, not even I myself. But I tell you what you would like to hear, and what others will tell you one day: methinks you were beautiful; you look different, you've changed. Daughter: the day will come when you won't recognize youself in your own mirror."

"I remember everything. I have lived remembering you, Mother. Along with your kisses and your caresses you left me your memory. I grew up with one body and two memories. And the memory you gave me has been more profound than my own, for I have had to live with yours in silence for twenty years, Mother, unable to speak to anyone about what I remembered. The boys. The three boys. Ludovico. Felipe. The crime in the castle. The nights of love. The dream on the beach. The days in the forest. The pact with the Devil. The rape. El Señor. The wedding in the grange. Jerónimo."

The cloaked and toothless old woman stopped for an instant, looked intently at the girl dressed as a page, and said with great sadness: "He who has little sense or judgment loves almost nothing except what he's missed. The wanderer tired at the end of his long day's travel would be mad to walk back the same path only to return to the place from which he started. I take care of my needs in my own house, and no one outside knows of them. Tumble-down or strong, it's my house, right or wrong. Enough now. Let it never be said of me that I took a single step without hope of gain. Where are you going, daughter, and what is there in it for me?"

"Our procession is going to the palace being constructed on the plain, where the greatest Señor in this land, Prince Don Felipe, has built tombs for his ancestors, and there awaits their remains."

"Remains, you say, palace? Strength, strength, Celestina, be not faint, there were always suppliants aplenty waiting to ease your pain! How many corpses are there?"

"Thirty, they say . . ."

"Ah, I who have exhausted myself going from cemetery to cemetery at midnight seeking the materials necessary to my trade, there's not a Christian or Moor or Jew whose burial I've not attended; I hide and spy on them by day and dig them up by night; just this morning I removed with some eyebrow tweezers seven teeth from a hanged man; do you realize what you are telling me? Go on, get along, I shall prepare my utensils, I shall bid my kindred farewell, I shall leave my affairs in the hands of my faithful Elisia and Areusa, who may be young but are no less sinful, and artful, and skillful whores for it; they will look after my affairs as if they were their own, and I shall follow the faint scent of your virgin's odor—may you soon lose it!—and look for you in the place you have told me of; and tell no one, my girl, for when we have learned something to our gain, we do not noise it about to our harm; very few live to a ripe old age, and those that do never died of starvation!"

THE SEVEN DAYS
OF EL SEÑOR

✤

Many years later, walking through the deserted galleries of the palace, shading his eyes with one hand to protect them from the light filtering through the white leaded windows, El Señor would remember his last encounters with the companions of his youth, Ludovico, the student, blind of his own will, bald, shoulders bowed, dressed in beggar's rags, his face marked by the exertion of memory and questioning, and Celestina, yes, Celestina, no, not young, not that young, so like the other, the bewitched girl they had both made love to twenty years before, but no, not that similar, an illusion, an impression caused by certain features, her figure, gestures that could not withstand close examination: a resemblance born of possession or of memory . . .

Ludovico and Celestina, twenty years later. Somber pleasure illuminated Felipe's pale face; he knew everything; everything was once again a succession of questions; for seven days he had asked what he had already known; they remained in the bedchamber, they ate there, they slept there, at fixed hours alguaciles and stewards, chamberlains and guards attended them; Brother Julián officiated at the early Mass, but at night El Señor asked to be left in total solitude in the chapel; seven days and seven nights: El Señor recalled the narrative told alternately by Ludovico and Celestina: the number 7, fortune, the progression of life, time moves upon seven wheels . . .

FIRST DAY

✤

"The sickness . . ."

"The women of the people, with their sweaty underarms and wide hips, infected your father."

"The accursed malady . . ."

"Your father infected me when he took me on the night of my wedding in the grange."

"Corruption . . ."

"Celestina transmitted your father's malady to you when you and I had her in the castle of the crime."

"Then you were also infected . . ."

"I never touched another woman."

"I never touched my wife."

"Did you know carnal love with any other woman?"

"With a novitiate who then made love with one of these you call your sons . . ."

"My sons are incorruptible."

"But they are sons of corruption: brothers . . ."

"By destiny, not by blood."

"No, Ludovico, at least two of them are my father's sons . . ."

"How do you know that?"

"Celestina's child is my father's son."

"I copulated with three old men in the forest, Felipe; with you, with Ludovico . . . with the Devil."

"The enigma would not be so dark if all three had been born at the same time from the same womb, like the brothers of old."

"And the son of the she-wolf is my father's son . . ."

"But these . . . my will has made them brothers: my sons."

"And if two of them are my father's sons, then the third must be also."

"Who is the mother of the child Ludovico and I stole from the castle?"

"I do not know, Celestina. They are all my father's sons. There is no other possible bond . . ."

"There were two women in the chamber where I found him."

"And if they are my father's sons, all three are my brothers . . ."

"A scrubbing maid . . ."

"Bastards . . ."

"And a young Lady . . ."

"Silence, Ludovico, for the love of Heaven, silence!"

Then, in response to Ludovico and Celestina's story, El Señor told them of his father's death and his mother's voluntary sacrifice, her mutilation, and her decision to live accompanying forever the embalmed cadaver of her husband.

When night fell, he had gone into the chapel he imagined to be deserted, to calm his soul praying before the altar and the painting from Orvieto, when behind him he heard terrible curses; he looked toward the double rows of tombs, and there, poking into each of them, he could see the crooked figure of a woman who seemed brazenly to be admonishing the corpses: "Curses on you! May you be eaten up by canker. May your pores ooze stinking water and evil nits eat your flesh! Who beat me to the robbing of these rich tombs?"

El Señor took her by the arm and asked who she was; the cloaked woman fell to her knees, looked up at El Señor, and begged his forgiveness; she said she was called Mother Celestina, and that in all Spain there was no more honorable woman to be found, that His Maj'sty could ask in the tanneries along the Manzanares, her word was as good as gold in every tavern there; a devout and honorable woman she was who in her pilgrimage had come to this holy place of widespread and well-deserved fame to worship the holy relics of El Señor's ancestors; and although she be the first to do so, she would not be the last, for such a notable mausoleum would attract multitudes desirous of sharing El Señor's pain and paying homage to his affliction.

El Señor yanked back the hood hiding the woman's face; he knew it was she, the girl of the wedding in the grange, the bewitched girl Celestina his father had raped because he, Felipe, did not possess the spirit for it and was saving his virginity for his English cousin, the beautiful Lady of the curls and starched petticoats. Here was a Celestina with no memory of anything, having transmitted everything she had known and experienced to the other woman, the one disguised as a page, who with Ludovico awaited him a few steps away in the bedchamber; Felipe tied up loose ends, Felipe felt rejuvenated, his project against the world was regaining strength, Celestina was an unforeseen ally, she did not remember him but he could reconstruct the youthful face behind that mask marked by greed, promiscuity, gluttony, and wine, the alert and malicious eyes that remembered nothing, in truth, because she lived for the day, her flesh swollen, lax, and wrinkled, the mouth toothless, the nose crisscrossed by broken veins: Celestina . . .

"But you say someone beat you here . . . Who?"

"But look here, Yer M'rcy, there's a leg missing here, and a head there, and here fingernails, and there the scorpion . . ."

"Who?"

They heard weeping and sighing: Celestina took El Señor's hand, placed a finger to her lips, and they walked between the royal sepulchers until they came to the tomb of Felipe's father: there they found Barbarica sniveling and whimpering by the open tomb, and in it, upon the remains of the former whoring Señor, lay the new Idiot Prince brought there by the Mad Lady. The dwarf was startled when she saw El Señor and Mother Celestina; she crossed herself, joined her hands in supplication to Heaven and to earth, do not castigate me, Señor, but see how my husband lies sleeping, nothing brings him to his senses, he lies there just as if he'd been drained; your mother the Queen promised us your throne, but it's a fine job we'll do of occupying it—on that distant day when you're no longer with us, Señor, and may God keep you for many years—if my sovereign husband is stretched out here stupefied forever upon the embalmed remains of your father, El Señor, see . . .

Felipe affectionately stroked Barbarica's head. "Do you truly wish to reign, my little monster, or would you prefer to be with your lover forever?"

"Oh, Señor, both things, if it please Your Mercy."

"You cannot do both. You must choose."

"Oh, most generous Prince, then I wish to remain forever with him . . ."

"Do you know the monastery of Verdín?" El Señor asked Mother Celestina.

"There is no monastery, Señor, where I cannot count a brother among the friars."

"Are you discreet?"

"Have no fear, Most Munificent Prince, I am not one of those women they pillory as witches for selling girls to the abbots . . ."

"Do you know what happens in Verdín?"

"It is a place of bed-fast people, Señor, where all those who tire of life, or of whom life has tired, exhausted old men, disillusioned youths, dishonored families, take to their beds and pledge never to arise until death carries them off feet-first. In short, whoever goes there makes a vow to keep himself between his sheets and never rise again, and it is a marvel to see a father, a mother, children, sometimes even servants, lying there one beside the other, some sighing, some weeping, one pretending to sleep, another saying aloud the Magnificat, some avoiding looking at the others, some staring at each other absently or with enigmatic smiles, the old appealing for a swift passing, the young soon accustomed to living that life, even believing there is no other, that the world outside is pure illusion. No one lasts very long. Death takes pity on those who imitate it."

"There you will take this youth, already sleeping, and the dwarf, with the escort and documents I shall give you . . ."

"But it must be in the same bed!" shrieked Barbarica, who had listened with growing delight to the words passing between El Señor and Celestina.

"Being honorable, I am nonetheless poor," murmured Mother Celestina, "and when lips are sealed, I pray the mouth of the purse be opened . . ."

El Señor tossed a heavy pouch at Mother Celestina's feet, wheeled, and returned to his bedchamber. The maiden-mender and the dwarf fell upon the pouch, squabbling over its possession, but Celestina kicked Barbarica to the floor, as a lustrous black pearl rolled from the dwarf's closed fist.

"So you have hidden treasures, do you, you botch of a woman?"

"It is the Pilgrim Pearl my mistress gave to me."

"It smells of shit."

"It's mine."

"I'll have that pearl, you gimpy she-ass."

"But it's mine, old whore!"

"I'll kick you to sleep, you stinking lump, and once and for all carry the both of you sleeping off to bed, you and your lunatic husband . . . Shackled in irons, and shitting with fear!"

SECOND DAY

❧

My brother, murmured El Señor; your heirs, Ludovico answered, and Felipe nodded: my mother has so proclaimed one of them, but Ludovico shook his head, it cannot be one alone, it must be all three, and in a very low voice made opaque by anguish, El Señor said, "Again dispersion?, the war of brother against brother, the partitioning of my kingdom, the loss of unity represented by my person and my palace: I, this place, the summit?"

He stared toward the high window of the bedchamber, as if the fragmented light of history shone there; he recalled how much pain the pretensions of royal bastards had caused Spain, and how much blood they had spilled to make those pretensions valid; but Ludovico did not relent in his argument: the three in one, the same as in the dream: the first remembers what the second understands and the third desires; the second understands what the first remembers and the third desires; the third desires what the first remembers and the second understands . . .

"Who are they, Ludovico?"

"I myself do not know, Felipe. You have heard the same stories I have."

Celestina assured El Señor that they had told him everything, even things she had not told the youth it had been her fate to find on the beach and bring to the palace.

"The usurpers, Celestina?"

"The heirs, Felipe?"

From the chapel they could hear the chanting of the Mass for the royal dead; El Señor knelt before the black crucifix of the bedchamber and intoned the beginning prayers of the Office of Darkness, Confiteor Deo omnipotenti, beatae Mariae semper Virgini, beato Michaeli Archangelo, beato Joanni Baptistae, sanctis Apostolis Petro et Paulo, omnibus Sanctis, et vobis, fratres: quia peccavi nimis cogitatione, verbo et opere; and striking his breast thrice, repeating, like a spectral echo, the words of the monks in the chapel, Mea culpa, mea culpa, mea maxima culpa.

He was racked by a fit of coughing. Then in a hoarse voice, as if his words were a continuation of the Mass for the Dead, he invoked with credulous conviction the writings of his own testament, with no shade of variation between the tone of his voice as he prayed for the dead and that as he sought the visitation of the unborn: "This I bequeath to you, a future of resurrections that may be glimpsed only in forgotten pauses, in the orifices of time, in the dark, empty minutes during which the past tried to imagine the future."

"The founders, Ludovico?, Felipe?," said Celestina, her voice silvery, as if her words incorporated the antiphony of the canticle being sung in the chapel and the prayer of El Señor, canticle and prayer both of black velvet.

"This I bequeath to you: a blind, pertinacious, and painful return to the imagination of the future in the past as the only future possible to my race and my land . . ."

Beneath all the suns, said Ludovico, in all times, two brothers have been the founders, two brothers have fought each other, one brother has killed the other, and then everything has been founded once again upon the memory of a crime and the nostalgia for death.

"Dies irae, dies illa . . ."

He asked Felipe to return to the origins of all things, two brothers, Abel and Cain, Osiris and Set, Plumed Serpent and Smoking Mirror, rival brothers, the argument over the love of the forbidden woman, the mother, the sister, Eve, Isis, or the Princess of the Butterflies, why have all men at the dawn of their history dreamed, thought, or lived the same thing, spanning all distance, as if all of us, Felipe, all of us before we were born had known one another in a place of common encounters and then, upon earth, been separated only by the accidents of distant spaces, different times, and unknown unknowing? One day we were one. Today we are other.

"Quantus tremor est futurus . . ."

Did Felipe remember how Simonides was saved from the collapse of the house of the wealthy Scopas by Castor and Pollux, the Dioscuri? From the chapel they could hear the phrases repeated by El Señor, kneeling before the crucifix: Lacrimosa dies illa, qua resurget ex favilla, judicandus homo reus. Castor was mortal and died in the battle against the cousins whose women the twins had stolen. And then Pollux, the immortal son of Zeus, rejected an immortality that did not include his brother Castor. He preferred to die with his brother.

"That is the love my three sons hold for one another."

"My three brothers? The usurpers?" asked El Señor, never varying the solemn voice of the funeral chant.

"I tell you I know as much and as little as you yourself."

Celestina, her eyes closed, spoke in the voice of dream: "The twins . . . salvation of sailors and castaways . . . guardians of St. Elmo's fire . . ."

El Señor rose to his feet, Dona eis requiem, Amen, looked toward the map covering one wall of his bedchamber, and said he was thinking, actually, of other signs, other brothers, other rivals, other founders, Romulus and Remus, thrown into the Tiber, suckled by the she-wolf, the founders of Rome. Romulus had raised a wall about the city. Remus had dared leap over it. Romulus killed his brother, and with these words established his power: "So dies he who leaps my walls."

Then he disappeared in the midst of a storm: the exiled founder, the fugitive from himself.

"Consider, I tell you, all the brothers in history . . ."

"But now they are three. One brother will not kill his brother, because if one dies, the other two will not remember, or understand, or desire. Look, and understand, Felipe: for the first time three brothers are establishing a history; three, the number that resolves oppositions, the fraternal cipher of encounter and the mixing of bloods, the dissolution of the sterile polarity of the number 2: understand, and make a place for them in your history . . ."

"They have challenged with their histories my will to end this dynasty now, here, with me. All the things they have recounted they have done to the end of destroying my project of death. They have . . ."

"Et lux perpetua luceat eis."

In exchange for Celestina and Ludovico's accounts, El Señor employed the remainder of the day telling, with sadness, of his never consummated marriage with Isabel, explaining his ideas of chivalric love, and recalling La Señora's misfortune when she fell on the paving stones of the castle and remained there awaiting arms worthy of assisting her: arms that had never taken her as a woman.

And nevertheless, as night fell, Felipe went to the chapel with a light step; he had not felt so young in years; his breast was pounding, his arms pulsing, his mind was clear; but the chapel was filled with shadows, as if inverting the equation between his recovered vigor and the eternity of the stone raised to support the weight of the centuries: El Señor's luminous gaze, and the announcement of death in the lengthening shadows in the holy place. He paused. He looked toward the altar. A young man wrapped in a cape of sumptuous brocade was scrutinizing the painting from Orvieto; by his side, holding a letter in one hand, one of the common laborers from the site was importuning the youth. El Señor, protected by the shadows, moved nearer, and hidden behind a pillar, listened.

"My name is Catilinón, my lord Don Juan, but I am an honest man, and your most faithful servant . . ."

"Who has given you such license?" asked the youth, gazing intently at the painting.

"No one, but that is what I want to ask of you, for such opportunities are as few as hairs on a bald man's head, and though I've had to sweat blood for it, I guess the bread here's as good as that in France; I can take my medicine! I want you to know your well-deserved fame, carried by La Azucena and La Lolilla, has spread to the forges and tile sheds on the job, and when I heard of it I said to myself, Catilinón, that noble Don Juan has need of a servant to look after him, warn him of trouble, and find out things for him, to go ahead of him to clear the way, to follow behind him to cover his flight, to list his love affairs and his feats, to take his place, if necessary, and, with luck, to enjoy a few of his leftovers, for if you give me a heifer, you'll see how swiftly I'll hav'er, and you'll never find this year's bird in last year's bird's nest."

"To me you have the smell of a scoundrel and adventurer. You must remember that the noble lord's adventures are fine deeds, but those of the common man are sins."

"Ah, but my lord Don Juan, alike we go but to our deaths."

"What, a challenge so distant?"

Don Juan again gazed with fascination at the face of the Christ standing alone in one corner of the painting: he saw himself, he saw his face; El Señor looked at the lively gaze of Don Juan, and the dead gaze of the Christ: he recognized the face of the pilgrim from the new world: Don Juan turned toward the scoundrel by his side.

"Be truthful; why have you approached me?"

"There are rumors of insurrection on the work site, and I do not want to be counted among the losers, for any battle the poor engage in is as good as a promise of jail, and when a poor wretch looks for a prize, he gets poked in the eye."

"What is brewing, then?"

"The greatest uproar in all Spain."

"Who are the actors?"

"Men within and men without."

"Without?"

"The discontent of the workmen; the rancor of the humbled; the revenge of the dispossessed; many cloaked Jews; many heretics who arrived disguised as monks in the funeral processions; many exalted merchants and doctors of the towns who are conspiring and arming themselves against tributes, the disbanding of their tribunals, and the new power of the Holy Inquisition . . ."

"And within?"

"Guzmán, who comes and goes both inciting and terrifying us, promising us a government of free men, and menacing us with a reign of madmen and dwarfs; and the old moneylender, the Comendador of Calatrava, who writes letters to his colleagues in other countries; look, I told him I had a cousin in Genoa who is married to a sailor who plies his way back and forth between the two coasts, and Guzmán placed in my hands this letter, so that it might reach Italy, and a contractor there by the name of Colombo. He paid me thirty maravedis—the price of a pound of capon flesh—to do it; I opened it, and read it, and now I hand it over to you; it is proof of a culpable intrigue against El Señor, who might very well give us the price of a whole capon for it."

"And what makes you think, rascal, that I am faithful to El Señor?"

"Nothing, Señor Don Juan, nothing; but by delivering it to you, I prove I am thinking only of you. Good God in Canaan, how salty the sea has become!, everything is in a bad state, and if the longest life is a brief life and only Hell awaits us after death, I prefer to live my life with you, Don Juan, for as you are worse than they, you will defend me equally from a mad dog, a Turk, a heretic, or a phantom, and when we must go to the Devil, you should be able to conquer the Devil himself, so you see why, in spite of everything, I must be faithful to you, for my fear will make a place for zeal, and putting reins to my feelings I will force myself to applaud what my soul might despise. I shall live the lively carnival with you, and reap my harvest while I can, for I have learned that among the poor I shall harvest nothing but sorrows, and with El Señor Don Felipe nothing but jeers, for a fun-poking verse is already circulating that goes like this:

> "Lived a prince of fantastic intentions,
> Of his speech had philippic pretensions,
> From his mother came comic conventions,
> For his tricks, known as prince of inventions,
> Sing ho, sing hey,
> Sing rondelet lolly,
> Sing loud pimps and rogues by profession."

THIRD DAY

"Listen, and you will understand, Felipe. Two slept: the one who understood it all, the pilgrim of the new world, neither desired nor remembered anything."

"You tore them from their dream, Ludovico, their circular and eternal dream; what have you given them in exchange?"

"History. I have returned them to history."

"What is that?"

"That depends upon you."

"Wait . . . the pilgrim . . . the voyager from the new world . . . he dreamed it . . . he was not there . . . Pedro's boat never set sail . . ."

"Pedro drowned in the storm on the Cabo de los Desastres. I saw that in reality. But in the dream he died on the beach of pearls, pierced by a lance."

"Wait . . . then the new world does not exist . . . it was dreamed by a dreamed youth . . . who, you say, understood it all . . . but desired and remembered nothing."

"Except the love of a woman with tattooed lips, and she returned his memory to him."

"No, he could not remember twenty days, having lived five, or five days, having lived twenty . . ."

"My lips returned memory to him, Felipe; once, when he took my virginity on the mountain; again, here in your bedchamber. Only while making love to me does he remember."

"There is no proof . . ."

"I do not know, Felipe . . ."

"I was right . . ."

"The pilgrim was dreamed by the other two . . ."

"My world ends here!"

"But he returned with proof: a map of feathers and spiders."

"Ah, Ludovico, Celestina, what weapons you have provided me."

"The map, Felipe, listen and understand; I did not give it to him, he brought it from his dream . . ."

"I decreed: the new world does not exist, they do not believe me, they prefer to follow after an illusion, all of them will chase after phantoms of gold, they will spill over the great cataract of the sea, I shall be left alone, here . . ."

"I accompanied the young heresiarch of Flanders . . ."

"What is written is true: my decree of non-existence . . ."

"I accompanied the wanderer in La Mancha . . ."

"The spoken word is not true; what that youth told as you were making love with him, Celestina . . ."

"I did not accompany the pilgrim from the new world . . ."

"I am laughing, Ludovico, Guzmán's pitiful ambition!, the Augustinian's pitiful zeal, the moneylender's pitiful calculation, all gone in an expedition against nothing!"

"I stayed behind on the beach with Pedro and the two coffins, waiting . . ."

"I have triumphed! Ah, do not believe that I shall discourage them, on the contrary, I will give them royal seals, fleets, protection, whatever they ask, as long as they set sail and never return . . ."

"The pilgrim was the only one who was dreamed alone, without the company of the other two . . ."

"My palace! Everything concurs: there is no new world, there are no heirs, my family line ends here . . ."

"He was the only one who returned alone by sea, tossed at our feet by the waves . . ."

"I alone!"

"He did not awaken. It was the first time the three dreamed at the same time, Felipe . . ."

"Everything here, unmoving, until the hour of my death!"

"And thus was born my plan to throw them still sleeping into the sea on the day of the appointed meeting, so that they wake together, without the third having been able to tell his dream to the other two, as before . . ."

Then El Señor recounted the details of his last armed crusade against the Adamite heresy in Flanders: how the sacred glory of his triumph had been stained by the blasphemy and desecration of the Teutonic mercenaries in the Cathedral; how he had sworn then to erect a temple, a palace and pantheon of princes, an impregnable fortress of the Holy Trinity. And as a renunciation of battle, how he had thrown the Banner of the Blood from the tower of the citadel into the moat: from that moment forward, nothing but solitude, mortification, and death.

When that night he went for the third time into the chapel, he was surprised to hear contentious voices at the foot of the stairway of the thirty-three steps. The darkness was even deeper, all the easier to hide himself. He saw the gleam of two unsheathed swords. A voice sobbed behind the latticework of the nuns' choir. A trembling servant hidden behind a pillar was muttering impudently. El Señor also trembled, the place he had constructed to protect the Eucharist was again profaned: howling nuns, a dead dog, crossed swords. Like the servant, he trembled. Like the servant, he also hid.

"You have doubly stained my honor, Don Juan," the old Comendador was saying, spurred by anger to a spirit inconsistent with the frailness of his limbs.

"You speak of something you do not possess, old javel," the graceful youth replied, one hand at his waist, one hand disdainfully parrying at sword point the edge of Inés's father's sword.

"You would add insult to injury, liar?"

"May God be a witness! You sold your daughter to El Señor. Is that your honor?"

"You have none, sir, or you would not mention such arguments, for honor lies in silence, especially when it is harmful to the honor of others."

"Honor is appearances, old man, and judging on appearances, you are ruined."

"Honor means respecting the seal of a letter; and you opened mine through the offices of a rogue who has charged us for his faithlessness."

"It is said that honor is the strict fulfillment of duty, and you have failed in all of yours: that you owe El Señor, for having given you rank; that you owe yourself, out of gratitude; and that you owe your daughter, if honor also lies in woman's honor and virtue."

"She gave herself to El Señor and to God, supreme honors on earth and in Heaven; but with neither title nor honor, you seduced her; for that I demand redress."

"Be grateful that even though she was stained, I granted her my favors."

"Monster! Vile knave!"

"Honor is glory that results from virtue, Señor Comendador de Calatrava, and it transcends families, persons, and even the acts of the one who earns it: my honor is greater in seducing than yours in procuring, and a greater feat . . ."

Thoughtful, the Sevillian moneylender lowered his guard and rested his chin on the hilt of his sword. "Let us consider that."

Don Juan laughed, gleefully threw his sword into the air, and caught it again in mid-air. "Yes, let us consider that."

The old man and the youth sat down on the first step of the thirty-three that led from the chapel to the plain.

"You say that honor is appearances," murmured the Comendador.

"For others; not for me, for public reputation could never harm the exalted and profound concept I have of my own honor."

"Then no one can be insulted except by himself?"

"So say the masters of ethics: the whole world cannot injure you if they touch not your soul, for only by his own soul may man be harmed."

"Well, I believe that each of us is the child of his acts, not of his lineage. Plato says there is no King who has not come from low origins, as there is no man of low estate who has not descended from eminence. But the vagaries of time have reversed all ranks, and fortune lowered and raised them. Who then is the nobleman? Seneca answers: He whom nature has shaped for virtue. Such is my case, Señor Don Juan, for my honor rests upon my virtue, my virtue upon my acts, and my acts upon my wealth."

"Thus, to rob you of your wealth is to take your acts, your virtue, and your honor."

"To lose it, sir, would be to lose my soul. And I shall lose it all if you do not return that letter to me."

"Wait; first would you give your life or your honor?"

"I tell you, if each of us is son of his acts, each can be the founder of a dynasty: but there is no lineage—or honor and glory in our lifetime and even after death—without wealth, for our acts procure for us the fame that lives after us. Don Juan: return my letter."

"As God is witness, what a foolish interpretation you give to morality! In these kingdoms it is held as common wisdom that one owes his wealth and his life to the King, but that honor is the patrimony of the soul, and the soul belongs only to God."

"And you, Don Juan, do you prefer honor to death?"

"I don't give a fig for honor; and as far as death is concerned, it is a long day between now and then."

"Don Juan: I believe we can come to an understanding. Return my letter, thus saving my wealth, my acts, my virtue, and my honor, for yours matter not to you."

"But my life matters, javel."

"Do not expose it to danger, then."

"You do not understand, wretched old man. This is my life: the adventure I begin, whether love affair or duel, is the challenge from which I emerge victorious: I live for pleasure, not for God, the King, wealth, virtue, acts, lineage, or honor."

"Then fear me, for I shall have my revenge, even after death."

"If you are saving your vengeance for your death, it is better that you give up hope."

The two men rose to their feet, the moneylender agitated, Don Juan serene.

"Return that letter, Don Juan, or by my honor, I swear . . ."

"What, javel? That by that feeble arm you will kill me?"

"I shall die with honor . . ."

"One is born with honor; but you . . ."

"One also dies with honor . . ."

"What? A challenge so distant?"

"Then take this, swine!"

Holding his sword before him, the old man threw himself upon Don Juan; Don Juan, with one motion, impaled him like a butterfly and raised the frail figure of the Comendador, like a pierced shadow, high in the air . . .

There was a scream from the nuns' choir; Don Juan with a flick of his wrist freed from his blade the body of the old man, which fell noiselessly upon the granite floor of the chapel, and noiselessly Don Juan slipped behind the altar, followed by a terrified Catilinón, the servant exalted by fear and also by the novelty of the incomprehensible codes, arguments, and ceremonies of people of breeding . . . through galleries, courtyards, dungeons, the hiding places of the servants Azucena and Lolilla; as he passed before the altar, the rascally servant knelt and swiftly crossed himself, and there, taking them as his own, repeated the words of his master: "I don't give a fig . . ."

As the nun Inés ran into the chapel and knelt weeping beside the motionless body of her father, El Señor emerged from the shadows and approached the pitiful pair.

Inés raised teary eyes, kissed El Señor's hand which loomed long and pallid beside her, and implored: "Oh, Señor, Señor, see this poor old man dead, a lifetime of labor and cares wasted, dead scarcely after he achieved the honor for which he had so long striven; Señor, if I have pleased you in any way, please me now: promise me that you will erect a statue upon my father's tomb in Seville, a mausoleum of stone that will perpetuate, in death, the honor that was so fleeting in his lifetime . . ."

"That favor will cost me nothing, Inés. Your father's fortune will now pass into my coffers."

Still clinging to El Señor's hand, the nun bowed her head: "I told you one night that of my own will I would return to your bed. That my heart needed to empty itself. Refill itself. Now it is my will."

"But it is not mine."

"How then may I repay you for the honor you accorded my father?"

"Take this ring. Go with it to your superior, Madre Milagros. Tell her it is my order that in twenty-four hours one of the nun's cells be lined with mirrors."

"With mirrors, Señor?"

"Yes. Mirrors are not lacking here. All the materials of the world have been brought to this work site. I preferred stone to mirror, as I preferred mortification to vanity. Now the hour of the mirrors has arrived. Have them cover an entire cell: walls, floors, doors, ceiling, windows. Every inch must be reflection. Then, Inés, you will lead the youth named Juan to that room, and there seduce him."

"Oh, Señor, Don Juan wants nothing from me, or from any woman a second time."

"Then you will seduce him through a third party. I know such a person. Wait until she returns. She is now undertaking a charge for me."

"Oh, Señor, there is something still worse . . . A witch's spell has closed the lips of my purity, making me a virgin again."

El Señor began to laugh as he had never laughed, as if this act not only restored his youth but actually transformed his character; first he laughed softly, then he bellowed; he laughed, laughing, he who had never laughed. And between shouts of laughter, he said to Inés: "Well, you will see that I also have a cure for that ailment. Mother Celestina has restored many virgins; now, for the first time, she will demonstrate her art in the contrary operation: she will unstitch it for you, my beautiful Inés . . ."

FOURTH DAY

"Let me figure this carefully, Ludovico; I want to reason it out; you say that each of the dreams of each of the three youths lasted thirty-three and one half months?"

"Thirty-three and one half months."

"Which makes two years, nine months, and two weeks . . ."

"Which is a thousand and one half days . . ."

"What was your reason, Ludovico . . . ?"

"Life was more brief . . ."

"The dreams of Flanders and the new world could have lasted a thousand and one half days . . ."

". . . than the dream was long."

"Not the dream about La Mancha . . ."

"Two slept: and he who remembered everything, the wanderer of La Mancha, understood and desired nothing."

"I tell you, that boy remembered nothing: he met a mad old man in a windmill, they came across a chain gang of galley slaves, he was captured, he was tortured by water, there was time for nothing more . . ."

"The dream of La Mancha lasted a thousand and one half days."

"That isn't true, Ludovico; the actions do not coincide with the amount of time you mention. I do not understand your arithmetic . . ."

"Arithmythic, Felipe. Between the adventure of the windmill and the adventure of the galley slaves, on the cart, along the highways, we lived a thousand and a half adventures with the Knight of the Sad Countenance. Each day he told a different story. How he was knighted. The stupendous battle with the Biscayan. The meeting with the goatherds. The story the goatherd told about the shepherdess Marcela. The heartless Yanguesans. The arrival at the inn we took for a castle. The night with Maritornes. The adventure of the dead body. The gratifying winning of Mambrino's helmet. The adventure in the Sierra Morena. Beltenebros's penance. The story of the fair Dorotea. The tale of foolish curiosity. The fierce and extraordinary battle with some wineskins. The appearance of the princess Micomicona. The discourse on arms and letters, which took an entire day and a night. The Captive's tale. The story of the young muleteer. The adventure of the troopers. The enchantment of our poor friend. The quarrel with the goatherd. The adventure of the Penitents. The enchantment of Dulcinea. The adventure of the chariot of the Courts of Death. The meeting with the Knight of the Mirrors. The adventure of the lions. What happened in the house of the Knight of the Green Coat. The adventure of the enamored shepherd. The wedding of Camacho the Rich. The Cave of Montesinos. The braying adventure. And that of Maese Pedro's puppet show. The famous adventure of the enchanted bark. The fair huntress. The breaking of Dulcinea's spell. The arrival at the castle of the Duke and Duchess. The adventure of the Dolorous Duenna. The arrival of Clavileño. The island of Barataria, and what happened there to our friend's squire. The love of the enamored Altisidora. Doña Rodríguez. The adventure of the second Dolorous Duenna. The battle against the lackey Tosilos. The encounter with the bandit, Roque Guinart. The voyage to Barcelona and the visit to a miraculous place where through enchantment books reproduce themselves. The Knight of the White Moon. When the knight became a shepherd. The adventure of the hogs. The resurrection of Altisidora. The return of our friend to the village-whose-name-he-did-not-wish-to-remember, for a narrow prison it was for his magnificent dreams of glory, justice, danger, and beauty.''

"You have named fifty stories, but you spoke of a thousand and one half days . . .''

"Fifty accounts are accounts beyond count, Felipe. For from each account came twenty others, inopportunely, tempestuously, unseasonably, and each story contained as many others: the story told by the knight, the story lived by the knight, the story told to the knight, the story the knight read about himself in the press in Barcelona, the oral and anonymous version of the story told as pure verbal imminence before the knight existed, the version written in the papers of an Arabic chronicler, and based upon that, the version of a certain Cide Hamete; the version which to the knight's anger a shameless wretch by the name of Avellaneda had written apocryphally; the version the Squire Panza endlessly recounts to his wife, thus filling her to bursting with both intangible illusions and everyday proverbs; the version the priest tells the barber to kill the long hours in the village; and the version which to revive those same dead hours the barber tells the priest; the story as it is told by that frustrated writer, the bachelor Sansón Carrasco; the story that from his particular point of view Merlin the magician tells about those same events; the story the giants challenged by the knight tell among themselves, and the fantasy fabricated by the princesses whose spells he broke; the story told by Ginés de Parapilla as part of his everlastingly unfinished memoirs; the one that Don Diego de Miranda, seeing it all from the viewpoint of friendship, set down in his diary; the story dreamed by Dulcinea, imagining herself a farm girl, and the story dreamed by the farm girl Aldonza, imagining herself a princess; and, finally, the story staged again and again, for the amusement of their court, by the Dukes in the theater of resurrections . . .''

"What did that maddened knight achieve by repeating to you twenty times each of his fifty adventures and all their versions?''

"Simply the postponement of the day of judgment, which was to recover his sanity, lose his marvelous world, and die of scientific sadness.''

"Then, in any case, he was defeated by destiny . . .''

"No, Felipe; in Barcelona we saw his adventures reproduced on paper, in hundreds and at times thousands of copies, thanks to a strange invention recently brought from Germany, which is a very rabbit of books: if you place a piece of paper in one mouth, from the other emerge ten, a hundred, a thousand, a million pages with the same letters . . .''

"Books reproduce themselves?"

"Yes, there is no longer a single copy, commissioned by you, written only for you, and illuminated by a monk, which you can keep in your library and reserve for your eyes alone."

"A thousand and one half days, you said, but you have accounted only for fifty stories in twenty versions: one half day is missing . . ."

"And will never be completed, Felipe. That half day is the infinite sum of the readers of this book, for as one finishes reading, one minute later another begins to read, and as that one finishes his reading, one minute later another begins it, and so on and so on, as in the ancient example of the hare and the tortoise: neither wins the race; so, too, the book is never without a reader, the book belongs to everyone . . ."

"Then, wretch that I am, reality belongs to everyone, for only what is written is real."

Later El Señor told of his strange experience on the stairway of the thirty-three steps, and how each step devoured a long stretch of time, in such a manner that whoever ascended them lost his life but gained his death, his metamorphosis into matter, and his diabolical resurrection into the body of a beast: it was more worthwhile, then, to perpetuate and re-create the past in a thousand combinations than to extinguish it in the pure linearity of a future without end.

That night El Señor hastened to the chapel. He was well aware of the reasons for his recent exaltation, which harmonized so well with his personal project. The new world was a dream. Two of the bastards, the heirs, his brothers, were eliminated, one locked in a dungeon, the other fast in bed in a monastery; and the third would not be long in falling into the trap baited by El Señor. But what purpose would these triumphs serve (he asked himself) if the very uniqueness of things and their eternal permanence on the written page became the property of every man?

"Power is founded upon the text. The only legitimacy is the reflection of one's possession of the unique text. But now . . ."

He knelt before the altar and looked at the painting from Orvieto. The shadows served up a banquet of form and color. El Señor recognized the faces in the painting.

"Oh, all-merciful God, must I undertake a new battle, this time against the pages being reproduced by the thousands, thus granting power and legitimacy to all those who possess it: nobles and common men, bishops and heretics, merchants and procuresses, children, rebels, and lovers?"

He rose and sought escape from his doubts by walking between the thirty sepulchers—fifteen and fifteen—lining both sides of the chapel: one by one he visited them, brushed their cold tombstones with his fingertips, caressed the veined marble, gazed at the reclining statues that reproduced in stone and bronze and silver the figures which in life had been his ancestors. He read the singular inscriptions on each sepulcher: these funeral texts, at least, would be irreproducible, unique, inseparable from each figure commemorated in this vast vault of rotting bodies.

As he reached the last tomb, that closest to the stairway of thirty-three steps, he trembled, divining at last that the three additional steps, which he had never ordered to be constructed, Providence had reserved for his three brothers. From his conversations with Ludovico and Celestina, only one conviction had been imprinted upon his soul: the three youths were the sons of his father, the fair and whoring Prince of insatiable appetites: his father had been capable of impregnating the very sea, air, and rock.

His head whirled dizzily; his penis dangled between his legs like a black and withered petal; he supported himself upon a tombstone; as a cold sweat stained his clothing, he drew comfort from a single thought: "I ordered thirty steps, one for each of my dead ancestors; the workmen, guided by the hand of Providence, constructed thirty-three; each step thus convokes the death of one of the usurpers who came here; there is no step for me."

He asked himself, panting heavily through thick, foam-speckled lips: Shall I never die, then? And immediately said out loud: "Nor is there a step for my mother. Will she and I live forever?"

"Yes, son, yes," a muffled murmur arose from a black bundle lying in one corner of the chapel and crypt, invisible at a casual glance. Felipe stepped back, surfeited with mystery, hungry for reason; but with the same motive he approached the bundle, knelt beside it, and discovered the mutilated body of his mother, the one called the Mad Lady, as he himself was called by rogues and rascals the fantastic, comic, inventive, pretentious, and deceptive Prince.

Bewilderment silenced El Señor; the severe waxen mask of the old woman's face, barely illuminated by a bitter smile, moved slightly. "Do you believe I am dead? Do you believe I am alive? In either argument, you hit the mark, my son, for he who is born dead cannot die, nor live, he who died in life, and from these opposing explanations is nourished what you can call, if it please you, my present existence. Do not bury me, Felipe, my son: I am not as dead as these, our ancestors; but neither return me to common life, to ambition, to effort, to appearance, to eating and defecating, to clothing, and to dreaming: grant me the place my particular existence deserves, the natural result of my entire life and death, as one day I explained it to a poor fellow I found on the highway coming here, on the dunes of a beach, so long ago it seems to me: do you know, our senses deceive us, they give us no proof of life, neither is their absence proof of death: we are a dynasty, my son, something greater than you or I alone, something more than an entire succession of Princes, individuals perish but legacies are continued, the strength of a man is exhausted but the power of a family line increases, because individuals seize and grasp so as to have something for themselves and thus end by losing everything, while we live on loss, excess, pomp, the sumptuous gift, waste, and thus end by gaining everything; hush, my little son, do not interrupt me, do not answer me, respect your elders, simply listen, every error is repaid, every excess compensated, every crime expiated, history is the secular account of ransom; but if common men pay for their errors by making amends, compensate for excess with a vow of future frugality, and expiate their crime with the pain of repentance, we, quite the reverse, repay error with more errors, compensate for excess with new excesses, expiate crime with worse crimes: everything offered us we return in like nature, a hundredfold, until it culminates in the gift for which there is no possible response: no one can repay us, compensate us, or expiate us, for fear that we will return to them, multiplied and magnified, the very evils they give to us in an attempt to conquer us; do not bury me, little Felipe, or return me to my bedchamber; grant me the place appropriate to me: do it as a reward for my sorrowful love for you; I never wounded you, my son, I never told you all the truth; place me in that niche from which I fell; then order them to wall me in to the level of my eyes, my mutilated body hidden behind common brick; let only my eyes be seen; I shall not speak; I shall ask for nothing; I shall be a walled-in phantom; my eyes will gleam in the growing shadows of your chapel; do not place stone or inscription beneath me; I shall not be dead; we shall not know what date to inscribe for my death, we cannot know what name to put on my tomb-in-life; I shall concentrate my gaze on all the histories of Queens, I shall be the mirror of those who preceded me and the phantom of those who will follow me; from my immured pedestal I shall dream them all, I shall live because of them, I shall live for them, I shall accompany them without their realizing that I, suspended between life and death, inhabit them, I shall be what I was, Blanca, Leonor, and Urraca, I shall be what I am, Juana, and I shall be what I am to be, Isabel, Mariana, and Carlota, eternally beside the tombs of Kings, eternally widowed and disconsolate, eternally near you, my son: from time to time pass before my walled niche, seek my eyes, tell me the sad stories of men and nations; I have more than enough days, I have more than enough deaths . . ."

FIFTH DAY

❧

"The dream of Flanders lasted thirty-three and a half months . . ."

"Which are a thousand and one half days . . ."

"The arrival in Bruges. Schwester Katrei. The nights in the Duke's forest. The crusade of the poor. The free spirit. The free spirit. The final battle against you. The defeat . . ."

"The profaned Cathedral; that is why I constructed this fortress of the Most Holy Sacrament."

"That night, Felipe, I approached you; I asked you to join us: the dream on the beach, you, we . . ."

"You said you were invincible, Ludovico, because nothing could be taken from you . . . You said that if I vanquished you, it would be to vanquish myself . . ."

"Two slept: the one who desired everything, the heresiarch of Flanders, understood and remembered nothing . . ."

"I asked the Duke of Brabant for his head; he delivered it to me . . ."

"Do you have it?"

"In that coffer beneath my bed."

"Show it to me."

"You, girl, you are more agile, drag that chest here to me . . ."

"Open it, Celestina."

"There; it has become wrinkled and black; it has shrunk, but there . . ."

"Look at it, Felipe, this is not the head of the youth."

"True."

"Now you know them; you know that the Duke never delivered to you the head of the young heresiarch who was dreamed, but that of another man . . ."

"Who is he?"

"I cannot see. I do not wish to see."

"Until when, Ludovico?"

"Let me measure my time. Describe the severed head to me."

"It was that of a man of middle age, bald, but the head has shrunk, it now bears a long mane of gray-streaked hair . . ."

"And what more?"

"Half-opened eyes, thin lips, a long nose; it is difficult to describe it to you: the face of a rustic, with no great distinction, a common face . . ."

"Poor man, poor man . . ."

"Did you know him?"

"The Duke deceived you, Felipe; he deceived us all; he delivered to you the head of the most humble of his followers; poor artist, secret painter.''

Then El Señor, to demonstrate his gratitude for this conversation, in his turn told them how he had questioned that painting brought from Orvieto, asking Christ to manifest himself and clearly make known to Felipe, the most faithful of his devoted followers, the truth about his mystic visions: were they prophetic prospects of his destiny in eternal Heaven, or deceitful heralds of a condemnation to repetitive Hell? The painting had not answered. He lashed himself with a penitential whip. The masculine figures with their erect penises had turned toward him. A wound of blood welled from the canvas. Christ had called him a bastard.

For the remainder of the day they did not speak. El Señor summoned to the chapel his most trusted foreman and there instructed him to wall up in her niche the mutilated trunk of the Mad Lady; the foreman said he would need a couple of workmen to help him with the brick and mortar, but El Señor forbade it. All day he listened to the slow progress of the work.

By night El Señor left the chapel and examined the completed job. He thanked the foreman for his efforts and handed him a sack filled with gold pieces. As he felt the weight of his reward, the foreman knelt before El Señor, kissed his hand, and told him that the payment was excessive for such an undemanding task.

"You will have need of it," said El Señor. "I swear to you that you will have much need of it."

The foreman retired, murmuring a thousand thanks, and El Señor walked through the shadows of the chapel toward the altar and its painting.

Now it was he who fell to his knees, stupefied.

The painting from Orvieto, before which he had prayed and cursed so often, the witness to his doubts, blasphemies, solitude, and culpable delays throughout the days and nights of the construction of this palace, monastery, and inviolable necropolis, the scene of his ascent up the stairway to a distant and terrifying future, agent of the words of his testament, spectator to the nuns' fear, the death of Bocanegra, the burial of the thirty cadavers of his ancestors, and the arrival of the mysterious strangers—the page of the tattooed lips and the pilgrim from the new world—that painting, come, it was said, from the fatherland of a few somber, austere, and energetic painters, the painting which in El Señor's imagination had seen, heard, and spoken everything that had happened here, that painting was disappearing before his very eyes; its varnish was cracking and splitting, entire sections were peeling from the canvas like the skin from a grape, like the down from a peach, and the forms painted there, the Christ standing alone in one corner, without a halo, the naked men in the center of the Italian piazza, and all the details contemporary to the place which occupied the foreground, all the many and minute details of the background, all the New Testament scenes, no longer had any discernible or concrete form, they were turning into something entirely different, pure light or pure liquid, and like an arch of light, a river of colors, mingling and blending, were flowing above the head of El Señor, away, away . . .''

With maddened eyes El Señor sought the origin of the force that was stripping his painting and converting it into a stream of chromatic air: with a single brusque movement he turned from the altar and perceived, among the ever increasing shadows of the chapel, the point toward which the forms were fleeing: a monk at the foot of the stairway leading to the plain, a friar holding some object in his hands, something that glittered like the head of a pin or the point of a sword; El Señor lacked the strength to struggle to his feet; he crawled from the altar toward the stairway, following the route of that luminous way which coursed through the heavens of the chapel like an artificial constellation.

When he could see clearly, he stopped.

Brother Julián, a mirror in his hands, stood motionless before the first step of that finite but infinite stairway, completed but incompletable, passable but forbidden, traversable but mortal, and toward the mirror, a triangle, flowed the scrambled, liquid, and dissolved forms of the painting from Orvieto: the triangular mirror swiftly captured and imprisoned them within its own neutral image.

"Julián . . . Julián," El Señor managed to murmur, captive to marvels, as the enormous painting was captive within the tiny mirror.

The priest seemed of stone; absorbed in his task he did not look at him, but said: "Punish me, Señor, if you believe I am stealing something that belongs to you, but pardon me if I but collect what is mine, so that I may give it to others; not mine, not yours: the painting will belong to everyone . . ."

Brother Julián turned his back to El Señor and directed the light of the mirror toward the top of the stairway, the plain of Castile, and the forms momentarily captured there flowed from the triangular mirror.

The mirror emptied; El Señor rose to his feet, choking back a savage growl, the voice of a hunted animal, of a wolf wounded in its own domain by its own descendants, tomorrow's Princes who could not recognize in the poor beast an ancestor incapable of gaining the eternity either of Heaven or of Hell; he tore the mirror from Julián's hands, he threw it to the granite floor and stamped it beneath his feet, but the crystal did not break, nor was the metal band which bound it on three sides altered in shape.

Julián said quietly: "It is to no avail, Señor. The triangle is indestructible because it is perfect. There is no other figure, Sire, which, having three parts, always resolves itself with such exactitude into a single unity. Assign three numbers, whatever numbers you please, to each of the three angles. Add them two by two and write the resultant number on the side linking those two angles. The number of each angle, added to the number that results from the sum of the other two, always comes out the same. What can we, you or I, do against such truth? Behold in this miraculous object the meeting of science and art; the astronomer-priest and I—Toribio and I—fabricated it together.''

"Julián,'' panted El Señor. "In some mysterious manner I always knew you were the creator of that accursed painting . . .''

"You could have accused me at your will, Sire.''

"One day I explained why I did not . . .''

"In order to avoid nonessential disputes, not to give more weapons than necessary to the Inquisition? You have given them everything they need if the decrees that have been published recently and signed with your name are true . . .''

"But you, Julián, you and Toribio, from my most loved and protected order, the Dominicans . . .''

"The Lord's dogs, Señor; as faithful to Him as Bocanegra was to you.''

"You placed that painting there, that black talisman, that mirror with which you have tortured me incessantly . . .''

"Without it, Sire, would you be who you are today and would you know what you know?''

"I always knew what that painting brought me to know even more fully: the angel of my heart will battle eternally against the beast of my blood. So be it; what have you done with that painting, yours and mine?''

"It has been seen by those who needed to see it in this time and place; now it will be seen by those who will need to see it in another time and another place.''

"By whom?''

"Señor; I have read your testaments in the papers Guzmán delivered to me, and which I delivered to my colleague the astrologer. You spoke there of the orifices of time, the dark, empty moments during which the past tried to imagine the future . . .''

"Yes, that I bequeath to them, that is written, a future of resurrections, a blind, pertinacious, and painful return to the imagination of the future in the past as the only future possible to my race and my land . . .''

"I merely fulfill your projects, all of which coincide with those of my order, the Preachers; what have we to preach but what we remember?, and what are we to remember but what we have written or painted? There will be no witness to any identities except what I may have recorded in paintings, portraits, and medallions: thus yesterday's identities will be today's when tomorrow, Sire, be today."

"Such magic has no place in the rules of memory which St. Thomas includes as part of the virtue of prudence. And without prudence, there is no salvation. Would you condemn your soul, Brother Julián, to save your art?"

"Now I can affirm to you, Señor, yes. I would condemn myself, if it save my art, which can save many."

"How pitiful is your pride. Your art, poor Julián, is nothing but empty space behind the altar. Look."

"My art is unsigned, Sire, and thus does not represent an affirmation of stupid individualism but an act of creation: in it matter and spirit are reconciled, and both not only live together but actually live. And before my act, they did not. You see magic in what is new, Señor. I see only what gives life to elusive spirit and inert matter: imagination. And imagination is what changes, not spirit or matter in themselves, rather the manner in which their union is imagined. My painting has already been here, in this chapel. It has been seen. It has seen. It is fitting now that it see and be seen in other places."

"Where, monk?"

"In the new world, in the virgin land where knowledge can be reborn, rid itself of the fixity of the icon and unfold infinitely, in every direction, over all space, toward all time."

"My most naïve friend: the new world does not exist."

"It is too late now to say that, Señor. It exists, because we desire it. It exists, because we imagine it. It exists, because we need it. To say is to desire."

"Go, then, sail in the ship of the mad toward the great precipice of the waters; unfurl, monk, the sails of the navis stultorum . . . Along with your art, fool, tumble over the cataract of the deep, and what will you leave behind you? Look again: empty space."

"Fill it, Sire."

"I? Would it not be better for you yourself to paint another painting above my altar?"

"No. My painting has already spoken. Now let another speak. It is his turn."

"Who, monk, who? You must know, you who know how to hasten disasters . . ."

"Señor: show the severed head of that poor Flemish painter that you keep in a chest in your bedchamber to the empty space my painting occupied . . ."

SIXTH DAY

✻

"Will you never leave here, Felipe?"

"Never, Ludovico. You may doubt everything, except that fact. This is my space, enclosed, determined. Here I shall live until I know what fate Providence has in store for me: eternal Heaven, eternal Hell, or the feared resurrections my mirror announced to me one day as I ascended those stairs leading to the plain."

"Others will leave . . ."

"But no one else will come."

"If you won a world, a new world, would you never visit it?"

"Never, Ludovico, even if it existed. Let others chase after that illusion. My palace contains everything I need to know my fate."

"You climbed that stairway . . . ?"

"Yes."

"You saw only yourself . . . ?"

"Yes . . ."

"You could have seen the world . . ."

"I tell you, the world is contained here within my palace; that is why I constructed it: a replica of stone to forever isolate and protect me against the snares of everything that multiplies, corrodes, and conquers: the canker of ambitions, wars, crusades, necessary crimes and impossible dreams, ours, Ludovico, those of our youth. See to what a bad end we have come. Pedro never knew the world without oppression that he dreamed of; Simón knew nothing but hunger and the plague; Celestina, only the slavery of her body. And you, Ludovico, you shall never know a world without God, filled with human grace."

"We merely initiated those dreams . . ."

"Time has mocked you soundly."

"Perhaps; now others will follow."

"Who, woman?"

"The three youths."

"My poor Celestina; if that is the illusion that sustains you, prepare to pass on your memory, your wisdom, and your wounded lips to another woman, and see yourself in the mirror of the old whore who passed them to you . . . And you, Ludovico, in what do you now place your dream of human grace, direct, Godless, with no need for mediators?"

"In everything I have learned these twenty years. Review everything I have said here and you will know what I know, no more, no less."

"You have spoken to me of divine unity and diabolical dispersion, if I have understood you correctly."

"Exactly. And the human struggle that takes place at all the intermediate grades on that scale. It is your struggle. But you saw only Felipe on the stairway, not the world. You saw the transformations of your individual matter, but not the doors that opened on each side of the steps as you ascended, beckoning you to open them and recognize other possibilities."

"What possibilities, Ludovico? You tell me."

"One lifetime is not sufficient. One needs multiple existences in order to unify a personality. Every identity is nurtured from all other identities. In the present we call ourselves solidarity. In the future we shall call ourselves hope. And behind us in the illusory past, living, latent, everything that had no opportunity to be because it awaited your birth to be given that opportunity. Nothing disappears completely, everything is transformed; what we believe to be dead has but changed place. What is, is thought. What is thought, is. Everything contains the aura of what it was previously, and the aura of what it will be when it disappears. You belong simultaneously to the present, the past, and the future: to today's epic, yesterday's myth, and tomorrow's freedom. We can travel from one time to another. We are immortal: we have more life than our own death, but less time than our own lifetime. You did not open the doors, Felipe. You believe you have the entire world reproduced here within your palace, but you have only yourself; you are nothing, neither unity nor dispersion, not Heaven or Hell or resurrection: nothing, because you have denied the unities which finally joined would integrate your unity, and because you deny them, you have no Heaven, which is the first and last unity; if there is no Heaven there is no Hell; and if there is no Hell there is no dispersion; and lacking the stage of human grace which unfolds between these two poles, you will never know true resurrection, which is to continue to live in others, not in our own skin. Alone, Felipe, you will be only what you have feared: a wolf hunted in your own domains by descendants who fail to recognize you. They will kill you."

"Is there time to do anything different?"

"Your chapel . . ."

"The Theater of Memory . . ."

"Transform it . . ."

"We shall work together, you and I, and Celestina . . ."

"The three youths . . ."

"Search for your Chronicler . . ."

"Bring Julián and Toribio . . ."

"We will add together all our knowledge in order to transform this place into a space that truly contains all spaces, into a time which truly embodies all time: a theater in which we occupy a stage where your altar stands today, and the world will unfold before our eyes, express itself in all its symbols, relations, stratagems, and mutations; the spectators on the stage, the performance in the auditorium; a theater with three revolving concentric circles, one that contains all forms of matter, another that contains all the forms of the spirit, and a third containing all the signs of the stellar universe; as each wheel revolves, all three, concentrically, all the combinations of nature, intellect, and the stars, will be formed, and from each combination will be born a specific form which, although symbolically remaining on our wheels, will actively separate itself from them, ascend your stairway, and go out into the eternal world; then the eternal world will return to us new forms that will descend your stairway and add their number to the triple wheel of our theater: unceasing transformation.''

''What shall we gain, Ludovico?''

''We shall know the truth of the order of things, and our place in them and with them: we shall be both actors and spectators in the very center of the struggle between chaos and intelligence, between dream and reason, between unity and dispersion, between ascent and descent: we shall see how everything that exists moves, integrates, relates, lives, and dies. We shall know everything, because we shall remember and foresee everything in the same instant. And thus, Felipe, we shall regain our authentic human nature, which is divine, and neither God nor Heaven nor Hell nor resurrection will any longer be necessary, because in the single instant which is all times, and in the one space which contains all spaces, we shall have seen and known, forever and from all time, the manner in which everything is related: the totality of manner and form in which we have been, are, and shall be, joined in a single source of wisdom that unifies everything without sacrificing the unity of any part. We shall attend, Felipe, the theater of eternity; we shall carry to its conclusion the secret and feverish dream of the Venetian Valerio Camillo, all things being converted into all men, all men into all things, eternal multiplicity nourishing eternal unity, which in turn simultaneously and eternally nourishes multiplicity. And then, yes, then we shall cry out with jubilation the baptismal words of the emerging era which represents the renascence of all things: what a great miracle is man, a being worthy of reverence and honor! He penetrates the nature of God as if he himself were a god, but he recognizes the race of devils, for he knows it was from them he descended.''

''Do we have time? Would it be sufficient for me to order the beginning of this new construction within the other? Today?''

''A single action is lacking.''

''What is that?''

''I have told you, it depends upon you. You are free.''

''When?''

''Tomorrow.''

''The seventh day?''

For a long time Felipe pondered these arguments in silence. Later he told Celestina and Ludovico how one morning in the month of July he had gone out hunting, expecting to ride through the flowering land of his childhood, and how, instead, a storm had broken that forced him to take shelter in a tent, with a breviary and a dog, far from the hunt arranged by Guzmán. Inexplicably, Bocanegro had fled as if he wished to defend his master from some grave danger. He returned, wounded, with the sands of the coast upon his paws. The hunting dog could not tell the truth the master now knew: Guzmán had wounded the dog when it had tried to defend Felipe from a threat greater than that of a wild boar: the return of the three usurpers . . . No, at the time that was not what worried him; rather, two most unusual events. One was the spirit of rebellion displayed by the band of huntsmen sent to the highest point of the mountain to warn with smoke and fire of the presence of the hart, consequently being deprived of the pleasure of the kill. The second: the inevitability of the final acts of the hunt: formally, El Señor was supposed to signal the sounding of the horns, the quartering of the hart, and the awarding of the prizes and rewards of the day; in actuality, everything had been done independently of his orders, as if truly he had given them.

As always, he went that night to the chapel. Two halberdiers were waiting for him with torches in one hand and bloody swords in the other. Mother Celestina stood uneasily between the two guards, shaking her head.

"Did you carry out my orders?"

"Señor; the foreman of whom you spoke is on the way back to his native village with a pouch of gold tied to his waist, but without hands to carry it or tongue to tell of it."

"Very well."

"And this woman, Señor, returned with your ring, which she says gives her permission to approach you. We found her wandering around the cells, and as she is one of those who damage reputations, who if she enters a house three times engenders suspicion, we brought her here . . ."

El Señor dismissed the halberdiers. From the corner of his eye he glanced at the empty space behind the altar. He asked Mother Celestina: "Are the Idiot and the dwarf in their places?"

"Fast in bed, Yer Maj'sty, beneath the same sheet, until one of them dies on us."

"Did you speak with the nun?"

"Inesilla was awaiting me most impatiently, and caught me as I returned. An angel in disguise! How can that handsome cavalier scorn her, when they seem made for one another? 'Mother,' she said to me, 'serpents are eating away this heart of mine.' Oh, most gentle and fragile feminine sex! I repaired her maidenhead, divining your intentions for that mocker of honor with whose accomplishments the other nuns and the servants Azucena and Lolilla had entertained me; I went to that cavalier Don Juan, as you had arranged with Inesilla, and I said to him, ho, there, woman's whore, little gamecock, downy-cheeked lad, you have deflowered an entire convent, saying—as I believe—that a pleasure unshared is no pleasure at all, Heaven have mercy, even though I am old, do you believe I am unable to receive and give pleasure?, do you believe I have no heart or feelings?, would you not take the sheets as shirttails with me?, would you allow me to die with my virginity intact?, and the cavalier laughed aloud, and said that Troy was stronger, and on the spot undid his breeches, and away . . . but I answered him that Rome wasn't built in a day, and that pleasure is all the greater at night, which is the cloak for sinners, and that I would await him, Yer Mercy, sir, in the cell where I shall now lead you, where he must still be, and where Inesilla has been for hours, heavily cloaked, and disguised in garments like mine."

El Señor and the go-between walked to the palace convent courtyard, then along one of the corridors flanked on both sides by cells. Before one of them Mother Celestina stopped, placed a finger to her lips, quietly opened the Judas window in the door, and signaled El Señor to peer within.

Author of this work, inciter of this act, El Señor stepped back, clapped his hands over his mouth, prey to a delicious fright at what he saw as he peered through the aperture: the barbaric coupling of the cloaked Don Juan and Doña Inés, he in sumptuous brocade mantle, she in the voluminous tatters of the aged Celestina, both mantle and rags raised to the waist, the young cavalier's virile member plunged into the deepest recesses of the novitiate's soft, plump flesh, fornicating, rolling about, she with pleasure, he with fury, her eyes open, his closed, she taking pleasure and he trying to avoid seeing himself in the floor of mirrors, walls of mirrors, windows of mirrors, door and ceiling of mirrors, face down, refusing to look at himself in the floor, face up, seeing himself in the ceiling, again closing the eyes hidden beneath the mantle, forever condemned to seeing himself—or trying to avoid seeing himself—reproduced a thousand times, making love to the same woman, reproduced infinitely in the reflections of reflections, a heaven, earth, air, fire, north and south, east and west of mirrors, she moaning her unceasing pleasure, hidden fire, pleasurable lesion, savory poison, sweet bitterness, dolorous delight, joyful torment, sweet and savage wound, tender death: sweet love; he, neither wishing nor knowing, repeating the words she spoke.

"With a thorn from the limb of a dragon tree I opened anew her virginity," said Mother Celestina, "and I lined the mouth of her pleasure with a double row of fishes' teeth, and placed ground glass deep in her woman's place, then bathed her mound of Venus with drops of bat's blood; I restitched her with a thread as fine as a hair from your head, exactly the same, but strong as the strings of a cittern, so the cavalier would believe he was taking her for the first time, believing she was I, an ancient virgin, and the day will come, El Señor, Yer Mercy, when they will not recognize themselves in those mirrors . . ."

SEVENTH DAY

"Today is the seventh day," said El Señor. "Will you see again, Ludovico? Will you open your eyes?"

"I have already told you, that depends upon you . . ."

"And what is it you expect of me?"

Ludovico reached out to touch Celestina. The girl dressed as a page took the blind man's hand as he began to speak with deliberation. "Twenty years ago chance brought together four men and a woman on the beach of the Cabo de los Desastres. At that time you listened to our dreams. You explained to us why they would be impossible. You did not tell us your dream. We could not therefore tell you why it too would be impossible."

"Do you want me to do that now?"

"Wait, Felipe. You told Pedro that his community of free men would be destroyed, and that in order to survive, its members would be forced to act in the same ways as their oppressors. Freedom would be their goal, but in order to achieve it they would have to employ the methods of tyranny. Therefore, they would never be free."

"Would that not have been the way? And would that oppression not have been worse than mine, since I have no need to justify my acts in the name of liberty, but they, on the other hand, do? I can be exceptionally benevolent, they cannot. Because no one can demand an accounting of me, I can condone failure; they cannot; they would be condemned by others. If the tyranny of a single man is reprehensible, would the tyranny of many men—who would multiply, never diminish, the oppression of the solitary tyrant—be any different? I am able to judge men remembering that within each breast, as in mine, an angel struggles against a beast; they cannot, for the heresy of liberty is the offspring of the Manichaean heresy, which conceives of all things in irreconcilable terms of good and evil. My enlightened discretion as a despot, Ludovico, is preferable to the deformed libertarian zeal of the mob; their oppression is worse than mine."

"And you would not allow even one opportunity for Pedro's dream?"

"Did Pedro's dream offer a single opportunity to me? Besides, the old man is dead; whether drowned in this world or run through by a lance in the other, the effect is the same."

"Pedro's allies are gathered outside your palace. You thought you had rid yourself of his sons by setting your voracious mastiffs on them. But now Pedro has more sons than ever. Your discontented workers. The men of the cities, offended by your capricious decrees. The persecuted races, Moors and Jews, who are as much a part of this Spain as you and I, as Castilian or Aragonese, as Goth, Roman, or Celt. They have been born here, lived and died here; they have left the signs of their labor and their beauty in temples and books. No other land in this old world possesses such a gift: to be the common home of three cultures and three different faiths. Instead of persecuting them and driving them out, search for the way in which they can coexist with Christians, and those three links will form your true fortress."

"This is my fortress, this palace, constructed as the shrine for the two sacraments which are but one: my power and my faith. I do not wish the chaos, the canker, the Babel you propose to me . . ."

"Outside the walls of your necropolis and its strict façade of unity, Felipe, another Spain has been gestating, an ancient, new, and varied Spain, the work of many cultures, multiple aspirations, and different readings of a single book."

"The Book of God can be read only in one manner; any other reading is madness."

"Without your realizing it, many men, inch by inch, have been gaining their human rights as opposed to your divine right. No, enclosed here, you did not realize that, as you were equally unaware of the emptying of your coffers that forced you to go to the Sevillian moneylender . . ."

"Not only words and things must coincide: all reading must be the reading of the Divine Word . . ."

"Be apprised: one city defended the sanctuary it had offered a persecuted man . . ."

". . . for in an ascending scale everything finally flows into one identical being and word: God . . ."

"Be apprised: another city instituted a tribunal against the royal caprice of one of your ancestors . . ."

"God. God. The first, the efficient, the final, and the restorative cause for everything that exists."

"Be apprised: one of the more distant cities began to meet in assemblies of the people in order to debate and vote . . ."

"And thus, the vision of the world is unique . . ."

"Be apprised: yet another city granted freedom to serfs emancipated from their serfdom . . ."

"All words and all things possess a forever established place, a precise function, and an exact correspondence with divine eternity . . ."

"Be apprised: still another city enjoyed a judge who dictated justice in accordance with laws, not caprice, and men's eyes were opened . . ."

"The world of man and the world of God are expressed through a proclamation based upon the word, which can be enriched, combined, and interpreted, yes, but which is in the end immutable, Ludovico . . ."

"Be apprised: one city said secretly of your mandates: obey, but do not fulfill."

"But every enrichment, combination, or interpretation of words leads us always to the same hierarchical and unified perspective, to a single reading of reality. And beyond this canon, all reading is illicit."

"Be apprised: little by little the people of Spain, in secret, have given birth to the institutions of freedom."

"Oh, honor us, God, oh, honorus, God, oh, onerous God . . ."

"Gather into one sheaf all these dispersed events. You will see the plant of liberty germinate. Do not destroy it. Give that opportunity to Pedro's dream."

"What shall I have gained?"

"Spain will thereby be a new world, a world of tolerance, and proof of the virtues of human exchange. And upon this new world we shall found a truly new world beyond the sea, and do there as we do here, coexist with the native cultures."

"You are dreaming, Ludovico; I see no possible coexistence with idolaters and flesh-eaters."

"Our crimes in the name of religion, dynastic power, and belligerent ambition have been no better. If you show yourself to be tolerant here, surely you will be persuasive there. As in that world Quetzalcoatl's morality was perverted by power, that of Jesus has similarly been perverted here. Can we not return together, freed from terror and slavery, to that original goodness, both here and there?"

"You say that all this depends on me?"

"If you will but open your arms to those who in a spirit of rebellion have joined together in the tile sheds, forges, and taverns on this work site, in nearby towns, and among the delegations in the procession that brought your ancestors here."

"You say workmen and burghers, Moors and Jews, surround me and threaten me. I already know that. Is there also rebellion in the religious orders?"

"The thirty processions came from far away, from all extremes, from Portugal and Valencia, from Galicia, Catalonia, and Majorca. The secret adepts of the ancient Waldensian, Cathari, and Adamite heresies joined them disguised as monks and nuns, beggars and pilgrims. You are surrounded, Felipe. Will you receive them in peace?"

"What must I offer them?"

"The shared governing of this kingdom. Their freedom, but also yours. Although you never told us your dream that afternoon by the seashore, you clearly allowed us to see your fears."

"I had none. I knew what I was doing. I demonstrated to my father that I was worthy to succeed him, to increase his power and bring unity to its consummation. Do you want me to sacrifice everything to the dispersion now threatening me?"

"You are not alone. I have three sons. You have three brothers."

"The usurpers, Ludovico?"

"The heirs you never had, Felipe."

"And that I never desired."

"Felipe, my life would not be the same without you: I love you that much. In my sons, your brothers, recognize the bond between your solitary unity and the community of many. They are three, remember: unity that increases without dispersion."

"Be charitable, Ludovico. Let them be patient with me. Let them allow me to disappear in peace. Then they can take everything, and have no need to rebel. Let them allow me to follow my own destiny to its conclusion . . ."

"Nothingness is not a destiny."

"Perhaps the power of nothingness would be: my privilege."

"Will you not share even that?"

"Tell those discontented workers, those rebellious burghers, the Moors and Jews and excommunicated heretics, that out of love they disperse and leave me in peace, enclosed here, without love. That is all I ask."

"Rebellion is one manner of loving. And your destiny is no longer yours: in spite of anything you can do, it is shared now. Do what you will, those three youths have already diverted the course of your destiny merely by coming here; nothing will be as you had previously planned it; nothing will be as you previously desired it . . ."

"Unchanging world . . ."

"Change has begun with the news about the new world. The new world already exists in the imagination or in the desire of all those who heard the third youth speak, or heard of what he told."

"Brief life . . ."

"The second youth has prolonged it, fulfilling his destiny as a holy madman, encountering dynastic continuity in the most humble, scorned, and deformed of women, Barbarica, of all those who dwell within your palace the soul most worthy of love, Felipe, and as he joined himself in matrimony, lighting the spark of rebellion, extending life to the dynasty of all men; the strange ways of a destiny that is no longer yours, Felipe . . ."

"Eternal glory . . ."

"The first youth based it upon immediate pleasure, desire converted into action, passion rooted in the present . . . Felipe, the monk Simón dreamed of a world without illness or death. You countered with the dream of your fears: solitude."

"I said then that if the flesh cannot die, the spirit would die in its name. I would deny men their freedom and men could not barter slavery against death. Thus Simón's dream would be defeated."

"And you added that you would live forever enclosed in your castle, protected by your guards, never daring to go out, fearing to know something worse than your own impossible death: the spark of rebellion in the eyes of your slaves."

"You say that I am surrounded today, and that it is not a spark but a bonfire. But you see: I am not afraid."

"No, you said something different. Try to remember with me. A conversation on the beach twenty years ago. Not that you would fear the simple and irrational menace of the multitude, but rather the rebellion that merely ceased to recognize you. You would kill no one. You would simply decree the non-existence of every person. Why would they not have paid you in the same coin? This would be the world's vengeance: to kill you by forgetting you exist."

"Do I ask anything more? But today's rebels, Ludovico, do recognize me, since they have challenged me . . ."

"Perhaps this is your last opportunity. If you do not recognize them, your horrible dream will be fulfilled. You will be a phantom in your own castle."

"Do I ask anything more? You forget that the other time I ordered them all killed."

"I love you as much as I hate you, and I cannot explain why. You condemned my dream to sterile and solitary pride. You were right. The grace of the knowledge acquired by a single man may perhaps kill God, but it may also kill the one who obtains it. Today I am almost able to say that my hatred toward the egoism of science is capable of casting me once again into the arms of an abominable belief in the Christian God. I have told you my story. I did not follow the path you spoke of that afternoon. Fate joined me mysteriously to the destiny of three children and the wisdom of many men in many places. This I learned: that grace is shared knowledge. No man can keep it for himself. Shared knowledge is true creation, always fragile, maintained by many desires, errors, jubilations, fears, unexpected losses, and sudden discoveries. I cannot separate myself from the three lives I have protected, from my conversations with the learned doctor in the Synagogue of the Passing, from the dream I had on the rooftop in Alexandria, from the ten years that perhaps I lived with the Citizens of Heaven in the deserts of Palestine, from the words of the one-eyed magus in Spalato, from the vision of Valerio Camillo's theater in Venice, from the crusade of the free spirit in Flanders, from our encounter with the old man in the windmill and the tales he told us, from the dream of my third son in the new world, and from the company of both Celestinas, the old and the young. I am all that I know, plus these lives, these stories, and these words. I offer them to you in order that, through all these events, ideas, and destinies joined together here today, I may offer you what few men have had, Felipe: a second opportunity . . ."

"Poor Celestina. She longed so for complete love. Have we ever known it? Did we three have it as we made love those nights in the castle? What excitement, Ludovico! To kill by day and make love by night. My youth ended there; perhaps my life . . ."

"Felipe, listen, a second opportunity. Let them enter: do not kill them this time, do not repeat history, win your freedom, everyone's freedom, by proving that history is not unalterable, purge for all time your first crime by avoiding the second."

"I did not know then. How strange. What a distant memory, Ludovico. I feared not being recognized because I feared not to be loved. I wished to be loved. I loved Isabel. I loved Inés. Yes, I loved the pleasure our companion, the young Celestina, gave me. Ludovico: I have known the old woman, Mother Celestina. She does not remember me. Along with her lips she passed her memory to this woman who accompanies you. Mother Celestina, Ludovico: see the destiny of love, just see . . ."

"A second opportunity, Felipe, do not repeat the crime of your youth . . ."

"But today, do you see, Ludovico?, I fear nothing because I love no one; do you see, Ludovico?, will you finally open your eyes?"

"I shall open them on the day of the millennium."

"What day will that be?"

"Remember the prophecy of the magus of Spalato. The Sybyl announced the coming of the last Emperor, the King of peace and abundance, the triumph of true Christianity, who will vanquish the Antichrist, who will go to Jerusalem, deposit his crown and mantle on Golgotha, and abdicate in favor of God, initiating the third age of history in expectation of the eternal judgment that will put an end to history. It is written that this King will govern over all the peoples of the world, uniting them in one single flock, rex novus adveniet totum ruiturus in orbem. You must be that providential monarch, Felipe, in my name and yours, I beg you, in the name of our lost youth and our regained lives . . ."

"I lack the strength, Ludovico."

"They will help you. That is why I have brought them here. The Sibyl said: a cross upon the back, six toes on each foot. They will set in motion the third age."

"The Antichrist. How shall I know him?"

"This is your opportunity to re-create history, Felipe. Señor: conquer yourself."

El Señor had no strength for further conversation; and that night, while Ludovico and Celestina slept beside the ash-filled hearth in the bedchamber, he again removed the severed head from the coffer, and carried it to the chapel.

He stopped before the space left vacant by the flight of the painting from Orvieto. He took the head by its long gray locks and raised it high, exhibiting it before the altar. The half-closed eyes of the head blinked. El Señor wanted to scream, to throw the head on the granite floor and return to the sanctuary of his bedchamber. But as his hand trembled and the eyes of the head blinked, the empty space began to fill with form and color; El Señor stood transfixed by the miracle; as all the lines, volumes, figures, and perspectives in the painting from Orvieto had poured toward Julián's triangle of light, now new figures, outlines, and colors flowed from the eyes of the severed head toward the space behind the altar, struggling toward composition, seeking their places, unfolding harmoniously, and finally integrating into a triptych with its three panels.

On the first of these, the left wing, El Señor saw the lost promise of an earthly paradise, harmonious clarity, a light joining together all species of creation, animal, vegetable, and mineral; from a pond painfully emerge the first beasts, winged fish, otters, thrushes; a valley enclosed by soft hills leads to a grove of orange trees and a blue lake in whose center rises, the color of the rosy dawn, the fountain of youth: unicorns bathe in its waters, swans, geese, and ducks glide across its surface; immediately behind the fountain, giraffes and elephants stand poised on a plain, and beyond them rise bluish mountains, encircled by spiraling flocks of birds; in the foreground, three figures: a naked youth, seated: the pilgrim of the new world; his face displays innocence, astonishment, and forgetfulness; kneeling beside him is a naked woman with long, copper-colored hair: she has the face of the young Celestina; and standing between them, he, El Señor, his hair longer, but the same thick lips, the same prognathic jaw hidden behind the same beard, the same eyes of serene madness, the same incipient baldness, holding the woman by one hand, offering her to the man. El Señor was delighted with this vision, asking himself how it happened that he would join that man and that woman; he stared at the beneficent tree of life under which the youth sat, palm leaves, a clinging vine, fleshy fruit; still holding high the severed head, he approached the panel depicting Paradise and with horror saw details imperceivable from a distance: a leopard fleeing with a dead rat in its jaws, a scorpion killing a toad, a dark, heavily maned, almost human beast, impossible to identify either as man or animal, devouring a prostrate body, crows nesting in the caves of the mountains and at the base of the fountain of youth, and perched in a dark circle, the timeless bird, the owl, watching over everything . . .

He stepped back, examining the central space of the triptych, and he saw a vast garden of delights, a universe of small human forms interwoven in successive planes to form a sumptuous tapestry of rosy flesh, bodies that resembled flowers, full of grace, the color of mother-of-pearl, entwined in chaste play, a river of flesh flowing from a lower foreground to a second intermediate plane, ending on a third plane that blends into the horizon, the whole bathed in clear blues, delicate roses, olive greens: brilliant and sweet reflections of human felicity; El Señor stared, lost in the vertigo of ideal, unobtainable sensuality; the half-opened eyes of the severed head blinked swiftly and among the figures appear monstrous animals, gigantic fishes, rapacious birds, enormous strawberries, raspberries, cherries, and plums; breast-shaped crystal covers one couple, other bodies are half hidden in the twin shells of a mussel; a solitary man is devouring an enormous strawberry with as much greed as the dark beast its victim, one man has inserted a bouquet of flowers into another's anus and is thrashing his buttocks with a second bouquet, a crow alights upon the sole of an upturned foot whose owner, in an attempt to free himself from the bird of bad omen, is offering it an enormous plum, in the river floats a scarlet fruit from which emerges a crystal cylinder, a man inside the fruit stares at the rat sitting at the other end of the cylinder, each is staring at the other, above them on the fruit floats a bluish globe, a transparent membrane inhabited by a pair of lovers captured forever within a sphere of mirrors, a woman plunged head-first in the river, her parted legs exposed in the air, hides her sex with her hands, but upon that sex nests a crushed raspberry; the bodies, all of them, are prisoners of something, of themselves, of glass, of mirror, of the mussel, the coral, the birds, the shells, or the solitary gaze of the owl.

"Happiness and glass are quickly shattered," the mouth of the severed head spoke in the Flemish tongue; El Señor almost dropped the head; he closed his eyes for an instant, persevered, and looked at the second plane of the central panel of the triptych; again the fountain of youth, and around it a cavalcade of naked men and women mounted on horses, unicorns, wild boars, tapirs, griffons, goats, tigers, bears, an eternal circle of delight and lamentation, orgasmic trembling and exhausted pleasure, white and black women bathing in the stream, birds perched upon their heads: peacocks, storks, and crows. El Señor quickly turned his eyes to the last, the most distant plane of the painting: a frozen mineral lake, in its center a sphere of blue steel topped by horns of pink marble, the fountain of adultery, forbidden couples, black and white, brother and sister, mother and son, father and daughter, woman and woman, man and man, surrounded by an icy world, marble plants, pearl flowers, golden trees, quicksilver streams, all watched over and encircled by four stone castles: El Señor stepped closer, the figures were so tiny, it was so difficult to distinguish the faces, and, near, they were so terrible to see: El Señor covered his face with his hand, and between the cracks of his fingers saw, yes, each face multiplied, repeated everywhere, his own, it was he, he himself, naked, he thrust in a tunnel, fed from the beak of a monstrous bird, it was Isabel, La Señora, his wife, engaged in love-making with a Negro, his mother, the one called the Mad Lady, hidden in the tower of a castle, placing one finger up the anus of a figure hidden inside a different tunnel, Felipe, little Felipe, my darling son, shall I put my finger up your little bottom?, Julián and Toribio, the confessor and the astronomer, peering from inside a vegetal hut, handing an enormous fish to Isabel, the nuns, Milagros, Angustias, Clemencia, Dolores, naked, are caressing one another, cherries capping their heads, and again he, El Señor, kneeling, flowers up his anus, lashed by Ludovico, Celestina inside a crystal cylinder, an apple in her hand, is watched over by the shadows of the Mad Lady and Barbarica the dwarf, Isabel, Isabel, transformed, hairless, unpowdered, all the sadness of the world in her eyes, is staring at a diabolical mouse advancing through a crystal tunnel to eat the face of the Queen, above her in the crystal globe, the prison, Don Juan and Inés coupled in a prison of transparent mirrors, Guzmán, Guzmán is an owl with four arms and four legs, and again Don Juan, the Idiot, and the pilgrim from the new world, naked, with Celestina are plucking fruit in a forest; again, all are mounted upon steeds of passion, all are raked by the same spur, all reined by the same bridle: heaven, earth, sea, fire, wind, heat, cold, and the waxing and waning of the menstrual moon crowning the entire painting: circle, horror, passion, immutable law, warning, warning, fragility, flight, flower of a day: these were the things El Señor saw.

Then the mouth of the severed head spoke again: "That is what you see, corrupt thing that you are . . . I painted something different . . . The sexual act so pure it is a prayer before the eyes of God . . . The act of the flesh with no remorse or fear of God . . . The external man cannot stain the man within . . . Who loves God more? A scorned and subjected people, a people of sinners, of publicans and samaritans who love their fellow beings? See what I painted . . . On the left, the original Paradise, when a malevolent God separated man from woman, who previously had been one, the image of the good God, of the supreme androgynous divinity . . . In the center, Paradise restored by the free spirit of man, without need for

God: there is no Original Sin, all flesh is innocent . . . And now, wretch, look to the right, see the true hell of your own creation . . ."

And so El Señor, motionless as the victims of the Medusa, looked at the last and third panel of the painting, Hell, conflagration, everything aflame, everything bathed in the color of fire, all of them united once again, Inés is a pig seducing an emaciated Don Juan, the other two youths are crucified, the Idiot upon a harp, the pilgrim upon a rebec, both being devoured by serpents, the Mad Lady, naked, is devoured by a salamander, Isabel stands with a die upon her head, Ludovico hides his face as a hooded demon crouches upon his shoulders, a large clothed and crested bird leads a naked Toribio by the hand, Guzmán, yes, Guzmán is pinned to an overturned gaming table, Barbarica is jigging about holding the great rosy phallus of a bagpipe in her hands, the nuns are noseless monsters with gaping mouths and lidless eyes singing notes they read from a staff imprinted on naked buttocks, the monks peer from beneath the psaltery, Toribio lies naked, torturing himself with the iron crank of a machine, he, he himself, El Señor, is an indescribable monster, a human hare wearing a copper caldron as a crown and seated upon a wooden privy stool devouring men one after the other, then expelling them through the seat of the throne of shit, eliminating them into an excremental well, and at the center of everything is the head, the same head he now held by the hair, the severed head, pale, attached to a broken eggshell, the torso and long legs purewhite bone disappearing into enormous blue boats of shoes, face, egg, leg, visage, ovum, bone the color of an atrocious birch tree petrified in spectral whiteness; and beyond, beyond, the conflagration of the world, a flaming edifice, his palace, his life work, the seat of his power, the fortress of his faith, a holocaust, a ruin, a cloaca . . .

Choking back a growl, El Señor forcibly closed the mouth of the severed head; the thin lips and ill-shaven cheeks were hard as stone and resisted closing; he covered the eyes of the head with his hand, closed the lids, the eyelids were flaccid and rough like those of a reptile; he hurled the head against the painting, it burst against the steel sphere in the center of the triptych, the icy fountain of eternal youth; it fell, leaving a star of blood upon the painting; and that line of blood, as it trickled down the painting, wrote upon the pigments in small Gothic characters a name El Señor could barely read:

He ran to close the wings of the triptych, to exorcise forever that monstrous vision of life, passion, the Fall, the happiness and death of everything ever conceived or created; intending only to close the wings of the Flemish painting, he found instead his hands were touching a new painting, and this ultimate image was of the entire world, a perfect sphere, transparent and empty, surrounded by water, the first landscape of the earth illuminated only by moonlight, and there God was but an inferior figure relegated to a position outside the world, as if the world had existed before, long before, God, and the Divinity had only recently arrived, rancorously, weakly, slowly, hurriedly, newly arrived; and toward the top of the painting was written in golden letters, Vides hic terram novam: ac caelum novum: novas insulas.

"Oh, my God, honor us, oh, honor us, God, oh, honorus, God, oh, onerous God!" El Señor cried out. "Is this the end of the world?, is this the beginning of the world?, is this the beginning of the world, or the end of my world?"

THE REBELLION

Most magnificent señores: The affairs of the kingdom become every day more inflammatory, and our enemies are perceiving it. In view of this situation it is our opinion that we must arm ourselves as quickly as possible. First, to castigate tyrants; second, so that we may be secure, where did you find that letter, Catilinón, who gave it to you?, what novelty is this that it is not written by hand but in even and freshly inked letters that smear at the touch of my fingers? I intercepted it, Señor Don Guzmán, it came addressed to the Comendador of Calatrava, who is no more, having been run through by the blade of my master Don Juan; I passed myself off as the servant of the Comendador, for it was with great stealth that hurried messengers who arrived on horseback from Avila commended it to me, and so I said to myself, there's mischief afoot here, and since I cannot enter the King's presence, I deliver it to you, *And above all it is necessary that we all join together to establish order in the badly ordered affairs of these kingdoms, because in the case of such numerous and such important affairs, it is just that they be determined by numerous and most mature counsels,* they are just beginning their deliberations, Catilinón, I must act immediately, spread the word among the workmen, the Moorish captives and Jews liberated by the Idiot, hurry through the forges, tile sheds, workshops, and taverns, the hour has come, El Señor stands petrified before his altar holding a Gorgon's head in his hand, the gates are open, the guards are nowhere to be seen, inside they believe the tempest has passed,

outside, Cato, outside, my rascal, do your work, *We know well, se-*
ñores, that many will revile us with their tongues, and that later many
will defame us with their quills in histories, accusing us of seditious in-
surrection. But between them and us we place God Our Lord as wit-
ness, and as judge, our intentions in this case. For our goal is not to
supplant obedience to the King, our Señor, but to abolish the tyranny
of his consorts, for they hold us as their slaves, not the King them as
his subjects, I am one of you, I, Guzmán, chief huntsman, and you,
overseers, architects and foremen, and which of you will be safe from
the madness and caprice of El Señor?, you have seen what happened
only a few days ago to one of yours, he who left here with his tongue
and hands amputated by order of El Señor so as to be unable to speak
or write of one of the dark mysteries that occur inside there; yesterday
it was he, today it will be someone else, tomorrow you or I; regard the
courage of our estate companions, the burghers of Avila, Toledo, and
Burgos, prepared to take up arms so that these kingdoms be governed
by laws and not by caprice; the gates are open, I swear to that; it is the
moment to act, Jerónimo, Martín, Nuño, injustice is added to injustice, resentment is mounting, yes, twenty years ago El Señor forced
my young bride on the day of our wedding, he besmirched her, because of him she went mad, she was never mine, that is called his
right, his right to rape virgins, I came here to this work, I bided my
time, and my time has come, Martín, Nuño, right, justice, as a warning my brother was ordered to be killed by hunger, thirst, and cold, left
naked and surrounded by troops in the wintertime on a hilltop in Navarre, after seven days my brother died there, by the order of a Lord
inferior to this one who governs us, and if the lesser did so much, what
will the greater not do?, Nuño, in order to be half free and to leave our
homeland, we had to deliver our inheritance to the noble Lord of the
place where we were born, and here you find me, less injured than you,
Jerónimo, Martín, Guzmán, but no less determined, *Do not believe,*
señores, that we are alone in this tumult, for, speaking truthfully,
many generous caballeros who are representative of all three estates
have joined with us, how much did the burial of El Señor's thirty
ancestors cost, brought here by guards and halberdiers amid chants,
canopies, and the prelates of all the orders?, what would have been the
cost of burial of the workman smothered beneath the earth slide and
there mourned by his widow and left to rot?, the oxen are more sure of
food than we, for the beasts have up to two years' provision of hay,
straw, wheat, and rye, whereas there is no provision made for us once
this job is completed and we have eaten up our wages, five ducats every three months, *and thus in Segovia, as well as León, in Valladolid*
and Toledo, in Soria and Salamanca, in Avila and Guadalajara, in
Cuenca and in Burgos, in Medina and Tordesillas, caballeros of the
middle estate are speaking the same words as we, magistrates, jurors,

mayors and recorders, canons, abbots, archdeacons, deans and pre-
centors, learned scholars, captains and marshals, doctors, lawyers,
and university bachelors, physicians and physickers, merchants and
money-changers, notaries and apothecaries, you will be expelled,
Jews, persecuted, Moors, there will be no place for you in this kingdom of purity-of-blood, pure Christians, clean of bloodline, who are
you?, how many are you?, there was a time when the Mozarabic
Christians lived in Mussulman territory and the Mohammedan mudejares in Christian lands, and each tolerated the other and also coexisted
with the Jews, and they called themselves the Three Peoples of the
Book, and San Fernando, King of Castile, proclaimed himself King of
the three religions, and the Moors and Jews brought to Gothic barbarism architecture and music, industry and philosophy, medicine and
poetry, and the Inquisition was held within bounds so as not to surpass
the power of the monarchs, and thus the cities prospered, and institutions of local liberty were taking shape, but now, who will be safe
from the new powers of the Inquisition?, in what innocent act will they
not see suspicion, read guilt, dictate extermination?, how will you defend yourselves against torture, prison, death, and the loss of your
lives, families, and possessions?, to whom will you appeal?, on what
grounds will you appeal?, read, all of you, this decree issued by El Señor: everyone is guilty unless he proves his innocence; will you prove
yours on the rack, Moor?, at the hour of the garrote, Hebrew?, in the
torture of the pillory, serf?, *and also all variety of offices of all and*
each of our cities, shopkeepers, masons, armorers, silversmiths, jew-
elers, jet vendors, cutlers, ironsmiths, foundrymen, bakers, oil sellers,
butchers, spice sellers, salt sellers, waxchandlers, fellmongers, hat
makers, shearers, linen drapers, rope sellers, hosiers, bonnet makers,
harness makers, cobblers, tailors, barbers, chair makers, carpenters,
stonecutters, napkin makers, it is not the hour to seek counsel, it is the
hour to act, yes, Guzmán, to act, here we are in the very precinct of El
Señor, the gates opened, the inhabitants of the palace sleeping or engaged in strange devotions, unaware of everything that is going on,
without opposition we can attack the very heart of oppression, pierce
it, cut off its head with one stroke, pikes, poles, chains, the steel
forged in your forges, Jerónimo, the weapons of the poor, quickly, the
gates are open, *in such a manner, señores, that we are able to speak of*
the general will of this kingdom to undo the injustices that affect us all
and thus, for what it is understood we do, it should be sufficient jus-
tification that we do not ask you, señores, for money to initiate war,
but rather that we ask your good counsel in seeking peace, where is the
rockrose where we used to shelter our flocks, eh?, on this very spot
there was a stream that never ran dry, and nearby a woods that was the
sole refuge for the animals in winter and summer; today only roses of
black crape grow in this devastated garden; and afterward, what?, do

you doubt, Jerónimo?, it is merely that I remember, Martín, I remember, the gates open, so it was with the earlier slaughter, the gates open, be cautious, wait, that is no longer possible, Jerónimo, look at the mob, we are all going, down the stairway leading from the plain to El Señor's chapel, that is the open gate that was never closed, the gate we all respected, imbeciles that we were, it was always open, do you realize the insult?, have they feared us so little?, thirty steps from the plain to the chapel, we have only to descend them to reach the sepulchers, everyone, armed, lances, javelins, pikes, chain, steel, hoes, hatchets, and torches, workers, Arabs, Jews, heretics, beggars, overseers, whores, eremites, Simón, Martín, Nuño, and Jerónimo, all drawn along by the mob and the whinnying of the horses and the bellowing of the bulls which break their fences and trample, terrified, nervous, and sweating, across the plain of Castile, whinnies, bellows, dust, the flight of the crows, everyone down the stairway, *Many youths of these cities, rising up against the latest edicts of El Señor, seek immediate violence and it will take a great effort to persuade them that we must establish a democracy, omnia eo consulta tendebant ut democratia, and they answer that the conquest of liberty cannot be attained by following the paths of the law, de libertate nunc agitur quam qui procurant nullas adeunt leges, omni virtuti pietatique renunciant*, law for those who stain all things?, pity for those who offer none?, Simón, all of you, join us, do not change your clothing, but dressed as monks and nuns join us, beggars, pilgrims, eremites, prostitutes, followers of Peter Waldo, against the excesses of Rome, the crowned serpent, the false pope, the power of the Inquisition, now, march, oh, perfect Cathari, herein dwells the god of evil, let us burn his dwelling place, this is the house of the Devil, Adamites, believers in the innocence of the body of our first father and of all his sons, to the palace, everyone, the gates are open, follow me, Simón, for I have seen the illness and sorrow and poverty of man, follow me, unsheathe your ancient knives, raise high your cudgels, light your torches, *It will be difficult to contain them if we do not act swiftly, and for this reason we ask you, señores, by your leave, that you examine the present letter, then without further delay send your procurers to the Junta of Avila, and be assured that as the situation is inflammatory, the longer you delay in going, so much more you increase the damage to Spain*, but previously, Guzmán, hurry, leave, Señor, leave this chapel, leave your bedchamber, seek refuge in the deepest dungeon until the storm passes, they are already descending the stairway, what are you saying, Guzmán?, one only ascends those steps, no one has descended them, ever, I climbed them to know my own death and resurrection, are they descending in order to know their own life and resurrection?, neither life nor resurrection, Señor, everything is prepared for this moment, as it was twenty years ago the guards are hidden, everything has the appearance of innocence, but everyone is prepared to act, as you acted twenty years ago, Guzmán, I gave you no orders, I still have not finished debating this problem within my own heart, I still am consulting with my own soul, it is too late, Señor, flee, hide, the hordes are descending that stairway, they are armed, I have but followed the example that you yourself provided two decades ago, I am faithful to your lessons, go, Señor, far down to the same dungeons where you will find the pilgrim of the new world and your companions of the past seven days, the blind flautist from Aragon and the girl dressed as a page, quickly, Señor, take this letter, I have always told you, other, worse rebellions lie ahead, crush today's in order to prevent the morrow's, quickly, away, Señor, allow me to act in your name, for as the dog Bocanegra is dead, no one is more faithful than I, Guzmán, *and all the matters we treat in the Junta will be treated in the service of God: First, fidelity to our King, El Señor. Second, the peace of the kingdom. Third, the reparation of the royal patrimony. Fourth, injuries done the native inhabitants. Fifth, neglecting to call into session municipal councils. Sixth, tyrannies invented by some of our own. Seventh, the impositions and intolerable burdens suffered by these kingdoms,* see the sepulchers?, who will give us a burial like that?, see the luxury of the false church, the false pope, and the monarch of the lewd visage, raise the slabs of the tombs, hack at the marble figures, throw those old bones outside their tombs, take up the ciboria, drink the wine, breakfast on the Hosts, there is more bread in this tabernacle than all that our fathers ate in their lifetimes, strike with your hoes against the pillars, turn over the chests, dalmatics, surplices, girdles, dress yourself in them, tumble in one day what it took five fruitless years to build, five years of hard labor to construct a royal cemetery, fuck them!, run through the passageways, courtyards, corridors, kitchens, stables, dungeons, free the prisoners, stuff yourself with victuals, tear down the tapestries, set fire to the stables, to the cells, pray, my sisters, for El Señor, doors barred, padlocked, pray, God save you, Queen and Mother, Queen of Mercy, the prophecy has been fulfilled, the hordes of the Antichrist have arrived, Angustia, Clemencia, Dolores, where has Inesilla gone?, where is she that we do not see her?, who knows, Madre Milagros, she is so turbulent by nature, so curious, bar the door, lock it, Ave María Purísima, conceived without sin, to the bedchambers, they will go there, look for them, El Señor, La Señora, the Idiot, the dwarf, the Mad Lady, hidden, find them, and then, *So that, in order to destroy these seven sins of Spain, we believe that seven remedies must be invented in the Holy Junta, and so it will seem to you, for you are sane men. So that, in treating all these matters, and in finding for them a most complete remedy, our enemies will not be able to say that we with the Junta are rebelling, but rather that we are new Brutuses of Rome, redeemers of the fatherland,* Martín, holding high a torch, ran through the corridors of white leaded windows, opening doors, finding nothing, El Señor, we must take El Señor, that was the order, cut off with one blow the head of the tyrant, La Señora, take La Señora, he opened the door, the bedchamber of white sands and Arabic tiles and caliph's tapestries, La Señora kneeling beside the bed, the cold body on the bed, a dead man, a mummy made of scraps and pieces, motionless, the woman he had seen and desired so many times, he wheeling the handbarrow filled with stone, she walking beneath the sun, the hawk upon her wrist, that vision of soft whiteness, of untouchable beauty, here, within reach of his hand, at last, he threw the burning torch to the floor of sand, conflagration of the desert, desire, take what he wants, do not wait, the hungry body, the incarnate vision, he seized the woman, pulled her from her kneeling position, she did not cry out, she did not speak, blue eyes, brilliant, defiant, moist lips, half opened, twisted, half-naked breasts, infernal, milky white, he embraced her waist, kissed her with fury, she pushed him away, she was pushing him away, finally she recognized him, the beast, she smelled the sweat, the garlic, the shit of the true man's body, she clawed his hairy chest, the tanned arms, the rebellion, what was it?, where was it happening?, what were the reasons?, here, now, take what he had so desired, nothing else mattered, Martín tore off La Señora's clothing, revealing her breasts, he sucked the nipples, threw her to the sand, placed one hand beneath her buttocks, his penis strained against his loincloth, he freed it from between his thighs, like an arrow his sex was erect, pulsing, slavering now, with his other hand he covered the woman's lips, spread open her legs, saw the treasure, the jungle, the bottom of the sea, he was going to enter, he was going to submerge himself in an ocean of silver fish, he was going to enter, the door, swift footsteps on the sand, he was going to enter, Guzmán's blade, the dagger thrust between Martín's shoulder blades, the workman fell heavily on La Señora's wide skirts, she bit one finger, her gaze feverish, Guzmán standing, dagger in hand, Martín mouth down, dead, penis erect, Martín's heavy body, Guzmán hoisted it up by moist armpits, threw it face down on the sand, the sand stained with blood, silence, finally, what do I owe you, Guzmán?, what do I owe you?, silence, Guzmán's closed eyes, the bloody dagger resheathed, nothing, Señora, nothing, I have other things to do, La Señora's loud laughter as Guzmán left the bedchamber, the insulting, godless pride of La Señora, lackey, swine, Don Nobody, how did you dare interrupt my delicious coupling with this male? *We grow tired of obeying without being consulted, and joined together in a Junta born of the general will of the three estates, we shall reestablish the laws of the kingdom diminished by the recent decrees of El Señor our King, we will pay no extraordinary tributes that not be approved by the assemblies of all the people,* and in the kitchens there are geese, young pigeons, eel pies, wine from Luque, from Toro, and Madrigal, here, have some, and you, and you, drink your fill, drink, forget your daily plate of chick-peas, you, beggar, you, whore, you, hermit, let the madmen mumble, the monk Simón and his Shrovetide of mystics, all crammed together in the chapel guarding a triptych they say was painted by one of their own, preventing the altarpiece from being profaned or destroyed, possessors of the temple, the new religion, restored Christianity, the beginning of the third age, purity, the destruction of false images, no, lack of purity, an exhausted body on earth so that the soul arrives in Heaven purified, arguments, flagellations, cries, naked disciples, men and women, ropes of bodies fornicating before the altar, the same as in the Flemish painting, Simón, his arms thrown above his head, shout-ing for order, order, order, Adamites, adepts of the free spirit, the il-luminated, Cathari lying upon the tombs of princes, endura, await death, pass quickly through life without staining the body, perfection, the Insabbatist Waldensians, poverty, destroy luxury, let not a stone remain upon stone, argument, blows and insults between Waldensians and Adamites, destroy the painting, protect it, Arabs scurrying toward the high tower of the astronomer Toribio, do not fear, brother, we shall break nothing, we shall touch nothing, let us pray from on high, we have dragged ourselves like worms for so long, let us sing to Heaven here in the heavens, and the Jews sat down in a courtyard, to wait, *and those converts will no longer be persecuted who with their labor enrich the coffers of Spain, nor mudejares already integrated into Christian communities, nor shall any prosecution continue because of blood,* and Jerónimo, separate from the throngs invading El Señor's palace, searched, descending by the narrow, dank spiral stairways into the deepest dungeons where black water dripped deep beneath the earth, water that never reached the calcined plain where drumming hoofs of horses and bulls resounded, and there in a cell, motionless, he found El Señor seated on a wooden bench, absorbed in his own thoughts, oblivi-ous to everything that was happening, and the old man with the beard fiery as the fires in his forge said to him, do you remember me?, and from his self-absorption El Señor looked at him and shook his head, no; Jerónimo, twenty years ago, the wedding in the grange, I have waited a long time, Señor Felipe, too long, but I am here now with my chains in my hands, chains I forged for you, to kill you in the way I wish, with the product of my labor, to beat you to death, and El Señor looked up, smiled, and said, I do not remember you, I do not know who you are, but I am grateful to you for what you offer me, I await death, I desire death, I have not taken my life because I am a most de-vout Christian, give me what I have most desired, you, a stranger, you, a man with no true reality for me, I shall be grateful to you in eter-nity, and Jerónimo hesitated, looked at El Señor, and said yes, you are right, your torture is life, I shall not give you what you want; he dropped the chains at El Señor's feet, left the black dungeon, strangely elated, strangely sure of his action, the guards took him prisoner outside the dungeon, and Guzmán said, bind him with his own chains, you should have killed me, Jerónimo, and Jerónimo roared, struggled, was subdued, and then, still staring into Guzmán's eyes, he spit in Guzmán's face, Judas, Judas, *nor shall the King have the right to grant posts in perpetuity, nor shall the intimates and courtiers of the crown be freed at his whim, but be prosecuted, as will the King himself, so that the right to resistance shall be established within a new constitutive order in the kingdom, of which the King is but one element,* chapel, passageways, courtyards, stables, kitchens, bedchambers, cells, towers, the halberds of El Señor, the arrows of El Señor, the harquebuses of El Señor, the lances of El Señor, the swords of El Señor, the daggers of El Señor, the axes of El Señor, posted at every exit, beneath every window, beside every opening in this palace of interminable construction, blocked, all the holes through which the mice might escape, the burrows fumigated, explosion of powder in the chapel, arrows in the chests and backs of those running through the courtyards and kitchens, axes in the skulls of those eating in the kitchens, daggers in the hearts of those dozing away their love-making and gluttony in bedchambers, swords in the bellies of those praying in the tower, halberds in the necks of those waiting in the courtyard, not one alive, shouted Guzmán, running from place to place, even those who seem dead, stab them again, run through with your swords anyone that moves and the unmoving as well, two deaths to everyone, three deaths, a thousand, the example will spread, let the members of the Junta of Avila know what awaits them, tear out rebellion by the roots, tear out the eyes of the dead whose eyes remain open, the tongues of those whose mouths remain open, the hands of those with open hands, the heads of them all, ax them, heretics, Moors, beggars, pilgrims, Jews, whores cohabiting with blasphemy and sedition, quickly, the palace is a cup running over with blood, raise it before the altar of the Eucharist: this is my blood, this is my body, *and no decision shall be taken if it does not conform with the will of all and the consent of all,* and from her walled-up niche, through the narrow aperture at the level of her yellow eyes, the Mad Lady watched the slaughter in the chapel, so comfortable, her limbless body propped so easily on that invisible pedestal, nothing but torso and deluded brain, snuggled so closely in that eternal uterus of stone, she had returned to the womb, she watched the death of the enemy, the hordes, those who attempted to deny the very reasons for the life and death of the ancient Queen, dead and living, giving thanks, Felipe, my son, you have again demonstrated that you are worthy of my succession, my blood flows in your blood, Spain is one, great, strong, *We do not doubt, señores, but rather you may marvel, and many in Spain will be scandalized to see a Junta joined, which is a new novelty. But then, señores, you are wise, you know how* to judge the times, considering the bountiful fruit which is expected of this Holy Junta, you must disregard that evil men will think of us as traitors, for from that we shall draw renown as immortals in the centuries to come, Nuño understood only one thing, free the prisoners, he was lost in the honeycomb of subterranean passages of the palace, he approached a cell where a candle sputtered, with the pick he had brought as a weapon he broke the chain and lock and opened the door, here, you are free, the blind Aragonese flautist, the girl dressed as a page, and the youth who had accompanied her to Jerónimo's forge one not so long ago night, he embraced them, you are free, we have taken the palace, the gates were open, El Señor offered no resistance, come with me, come away from here, take me to the chapel, Ludovico asked, there I shall see again, Felipe understood, I can open my eyes again, the three went out, guided by Nuño, the son of askaris on the Moorish border, Ludovico holding the hands of Celestina and the pilgrim from the new world, asking, and the other two, my sons, what do you know of them?, who?, the one they disguised as a prince and called the Idiot, the one they disguised as a seducer of women and called Don Juan, no, I have not seen them, what do they look like?, exactly like this one, Nuño, the three of them exactly alike, no, I haven't seen them, then this is the heir, my son, the free man arrived from the new world, the only one to enter the history of Spain and not be devoured by it, the survivor, my son, they climbed the spiral stairway behind the chapel, stopped an instant behind the altar, the silence in the chapel was more profound than that of the dungeons, I am going to see, son, Celestina, Nuño, I am going to open my eyes again, I lost the mirror that could reflect the entire world, at first I believed that without eyes there would be no memory and consequently there would be no imagination; then I found out that I had seen everything before I closed my eyes, and I could keep it forever; I would have seen no more than any other dead man my age and that would be the measure of my memory and my imagination; I could have slashed my eyes; I did not do it because, in spite of everything, I held the hope of one day again seeing something worthy to be seen, the millennium, the triumph of human grace, God's death, the millennium of man, that day has arrived, I am going to open my eyes, tell me when we reach Felipe's chapel, there I shall open my eyes again, *Because it is a general rule that all good work is received by evil men under guise of something different. This being presupposed, it is beneficial to know that in everything to come, all affairs may succeed in the reverse of our plans, and they may endanger our persons, destroy our homes, and finally, we may lose our lives,* and Lolilla, there's more mischief afoot than we had thought, and tell me the truth, in all this festivity didn't you hope to play a little tune on some heretic's or Moor's or Jew's flute?, well, don't you complain, Catilinón, for you had designs on the fancy purse of the English whore or the blasphemous nun when you should have been content with my old cunt, and I with your mandrake, but don't complain, we've reaped our harvest, my petticoats are filled with jewels, and my doublet with ducats, Lolilla, and now we have the wherewithal to escape from this den of spooks and set up business in Valladolid, Avila, or Segovia, get along now, lady holier-than-thou, hup, you swaggering braggart, this way, bad-mouthed hussy, come on, blustering bastard, let's fun awhile, here, in this cell, look, and they entered the chamber of mirrors where Don Juan was dallying with Doña Inés, rascal, the master shouted to the servant, where were you when I needed you most?, did you not promise to protect me, to scout ahead of my adventures, protect my flights, take my place if it be necessary?, oh, my lord Don Juan, I would gladly take your place in this instant and give you Lolilla in exchange for Inesilla, cackled Catilinón as he helped Don Juan separate himself from the nun, oh, if you must stick your nose in here, tell me why I desire that syphilis-wracked whore, moaned Don Juan, and Lolilla cried out when she saw him, the tip of your taper is all bloody, my lord Don Juan, oh, that holy whore has stripped the skin off it for you, and Don Juan swept his brocaded robe over his injured parts, Doña Inés arose, weeping, Catilinón and Lolilla marveled at seeing themselves reflected in walls of mirror, ceiling of mirror, floor of mirror, what do you have stuffed in your clothing, rascals?, you look as if you're about ready to give birth, sly puss, and you, Sir Cock, have you grown tits?; the servants' faces flushed red as fire, and Don Juan ordered them to remove their clothing and lie down on the floor of mirrors, Inés covered Lolilla in Mother Celestina's rags and Don Juan draped his brocade over Catilinón; Inés and Don Juan dressed themselves in their servants' clothing, stick that fine poker in Lola's pelt, Cato, enjoy yourselves in your prison of mirrors, my crafty bastards, flee with me, Inés, between your legs I recaptured my brother's dream, he awaits us in a brigantine, take the chain and padlock this prison, I smell treachery in the palace, let us flee, I shall look after you, my lover, your presence maddens me, your delicious scepter will heal, your words hallucinate me, we shall live, together, far away from here, your breath poisons me, come, Don Juan, come, Inés, together let us call on Heaven, and if Heaven does not hear us or if its gates close against us, Heaven will be responsible for our passage on earth, not I, *in such a case we shall say that disfavor is favor; danger, security; that robbery is riches; exile, glory; to lose is to win; persecution is the crown; and death is life. Because there is no death as glorious as that of a man who dies in defense of his republic,* funeral drums resound across the plain, more muted than the drumming of oxen's and horses' hoofs again enclosed in fences, the smoke of the taverns and huts dies out, mourning women stare in silence, muffled, old before their time, barefoot children, bleary-eyed, burned by the sun, blond locks on dark heads, bleached by the sun, with round black eyes and torn fingernails, stand clutching the skirts and hands of the women, mangy dogs wander about, storks fly in search of their nests, three lines of El Señor's soldiers, lances raised, black standards, harquebuses at the ready, halberds at rest, stand on three sides of a square of dust, and on the fourth, before the tall midday sun-lighted façade of the uncompleted and uncompletable palace, El Señor sits beneath a black canopy on a throne of carved wood rosettes, he too dressed in black, as prematurely aged as the women in the crowd who have borne thirteen children since they were thirteen years old, the Bishop stands beside him, crimson miter, dalmatic and tunicle, brocade waistband in his chasuble, pastoral staff, beside him the Inquisitor of Teruel, the monk with thin skin drawn taut across the bones, wearing the habit of St. Augustine, on each side of them deacons and subdeacons carrying the cross, acolytes with their tall, richly adorned candlesticks, all dressed in dalmatics and cords of silver cloth, damask and slubbed silk, and behind El Señor, bending to speak into his ear, Guzmán, in ceremonial attire, a short fur cape, velvet cap, black breeches, his hand resting on the hilt of his blade, drums, the first prisoner, Nuño, bound to one of the two stakes driven into the dusty plain, naked except for a loincloth, the guards beat him with rods, a hundred times, his entire body is an open, bleeding wound, then they cover his body with honey, a goat is led to him and begins to lick the honey with its rough tongue, stripping away shreds of skin, Nuño closes his eyes, grits his teeth, flesh and hide, blood and nerve, the goat's rough tongue, the drums roll, the second prisoner, the ringleader, an old man with a beard as fiery as the fires of his forge, the rack, he reaches the stake, they tie him to it so that his feet do not touch the ground, to the large toe of each foot they tie weights of a hundred and forty pounds and wait half an hour, watching him suffer slowly while the Augustinian of Teruel exclaims in his hoarse voice, bulwark of the Church, pillar of truth, guardian of the Faith, treasure of religion, defense against heretics, light against the deceit of the enemy, touchstone of the pure doctrine, accursed scum!, kill the rebels!, I watch you die with pleasure, rebel dogs, we are the ministers of the Holy Inquisition!, and then they coat the naked body with fat and set fire to the stake, and the Inquisitor of Teruel cries, light the flame!, Jerónimo roars like a lion, they have lighted only his sides, so only his ribs are burned, they extinguish the fire, they place upon him a shirt dipped in nitric acid and light it; Jerónimo's beard sizzles, he closes his eyes, his eyelashes and eyebrows are burned away, again they extinguish the fire, they remove the shirt, they seize his clenched fists, force them open, sink needles and nails deep beneath his fingernails, they wash stinking urine over his body, they press his right hand between burning planks, and press, and burn, they squeeze his wrist with iron pincers, they wait, Guzmán has asked to be the executioner, he removes his dagger from its sheath, approaches Jerónimo at the stake, cuts off his penis, stuffs it in the unfortunate man's mouth, he stretches the testicles back until he can stuff them in Jerónimo's anus, he slits open Jerónimo's belly in the form of a cross, rips out the entrails and the heart, cuts the heart in four portions, throws one to each of the four cardinal points, laughs, to Pater Noster, to Ave Maria, to the Credo, and Salve Regina, he gives the final order, cut off his head, impale the head upon a lance at the entrance to the palace, cut the body in four parts and hang them from four poles at the four corners of the palace, such is the will of our King, our Señor, and you, Nuño, son of askaris on the Moorish frontier, know me as you die, I am the son of that impoverished lord of the Ta'if kingdoms who had no money to retain you when you and yours abandoned our lands to weeds and drought, condemned us to poverty, leaving us without hands for labor, believing you would gain a little freedom by becoming the King's subjects and ceasing to be my father's laborers; look at you now, Nuño, I am collecting at the hour of your death the debt of slavery you owe me, and may your body rot here as example and warning to rebels, *We have wished, señores, to write you this letter so that you see what is our goal in calling this Junta, and those who fear to venture their persons, and those who suspect the loss of their properties, will not be cured by following us in this undertaking, or even less in coming to the Junta, because as these are heroic acts, only very exalted hearts may undertake them,* between the two, La Señora and her mandrake, the homunculus with vaguely defined features, cherries for eyes, a radish for a mouth, crumbs for hair, a root for a body, his monstrous appearance hidden as much as possible beneath high boots, heavy breeches, a bejeweled doublet, a loose cap with an eyeshade and long ear flaps, gloves embroidered with precious stones, ruffles on his wrists and a high ruff beneath his chin, between them they lifted the mummy made of royal bits and pieces from the bed in the Arabic chamber, and the little dwarf said, Señora, a great silence reigns now, night has fallen, this is the time to do what I have recommended to you, help me carry your Prometheus, you take his arms and I his feet, he is well joined, his parts well adhered thanks to the storax gum and resinous cáncamo, quietly, Señora, we shall leave together, through the galleries, halls, and small courtyards they went, carrying the mummy, first the feet, carried by the homunculus who was leading, through severe cloisters of strong, square pillars, through forests of arches, beneath the carved ceilings of the storerooms, through a series of eleven doors, until they reached a vast gallery La Señora had never seen, two hundred feet long and thirty feet high, the fronts, sides, and domed ceiling covered by painting, columns embedded in the walls embellished with fascia, jambs, lintels, and railings in a row, in the manner of balconies, the ceiling and the dome with grotesque and elaborate plaster ornamentation, a thousand variations on real and fictional figures, plaster medallions and niches, pedestals, men, women, children, monsters, birds, horses, fruits and flowers, draperies and festoons, and a hundred other bizarre inventions, and at the rear of the room a Gothic throne of roughly worked stone, and behind the throne a semicircular wall with feigned painting of two draperies hanging from their spikes, with flounces and fringe, look, Señora, it seems so real, it deceives many until they come to draw them and touch them; La Señora and her dwarf carried the inert body of royal bits and pieces, fashioned from the worm-eaten nose of the Arian King, an ear from the Queen who stitched flags with the colors of her blood and tears, the very flag that El Señor had one day cast into the putrid moat of the conquered Flemish city, another from the astrologer King who complained that God had not consulted him about the creation of the earth, one black eye from the fratricidal King and a white eye from the rebellious Infanta, the livid tongue of the cruel King who had forced his courtiers to drink the bath water of his concubine, the mummified arms of the rebellious King who had risen in arms against the stepfather who murdered his mother, the blackened torso of the King who violated his own daughter and who died between flaming sheets, the skull of the Suffering and the shriveled sex of the Impotent King, a shinbone from the virgin Queen murdered by the King's halberdier while she prayed, another shinbone from the Mad Lady, a relic of the sacrifice of the present Señor's mother, the twisted lips of the Reprieved, the murderer of his brothers, found dead in his bed after the thirty-three and a half days of the justice of God had passed, the silky hair of the kidnapped Princes whose throats were slit by Hebrews by the light of the moon, the rotted teeth of the King who employed all the days of his reign in celebrating his own funerals, and the feet of the most chaste Queen who never changed her clothing and whose shoes had to be pried off with a spatula when she died, they seated this creature on the throne, the homunculus ran behind the throne, picked up a golden crown encrusted with sapphire, pearl, agate, and rock crystal, a mantle of opaque purple, a scepter and a sphere, and he said to La Señora, you have invoked all the arts of the Devil, you have called upon them all, my mistress, you have attempted everything, except the simplest and most apparent: do it yourself, as this your mummy is seated on the most ancient throne of Spain, crown him yourself, thus, wrap him in the royal mantle, that's it, pry open his afflicted fingers and close them again upon this orb and scepter, La Señora did as he advised, and that very instant the royal mummy blinked, his eyes filled with turbid light, his arm creaked as he raised the scepter, the backs of his knees squeaked, the twisted lips opened, the livid tongue moved, the homunculus shrieked with joy, words tumbled from the crowned mummy's lips, he spoke contradictory words, close, Santiago, after them, I live without living in myself, plus ultra, plus ultra, in my hunger I command, dominate, Castile, dominate, you, the dominant, scorn what you do not know, and since from Spain we come, let us resemble what we were, La Señora fell to her knees and murmured, thank you, thank you, she kissed the hand of the King of Kings, now Spain has an eternal King, a Holy, Caesarian, Catholic Majesty, *We do not doubt, señores, that in our wills both here and there we are one; but the distances of lands forbid communication of persons; from which follows no little harm for the enterprise we have undertaken, to mend the kingdom, for very arduous affairs are long in their conclusion when there are long roads to travel, and let it not be said of us what Don Pedro of Toledo once said, that he hoped death would come to him from Spain, so that it might come to him very late. Only that to the messengers who carry these words you give your entire faith in these words,* El Señor has been magnanimous, too benevolent, said Guzmán, for I have never tired of warning him that the innocent, once pardoned, will not tarry in making themselves his enemy and very quickly will assume the guilt of the accusation, and in my opinion all of you are guilty, faithful allies of the seditious rebels who yesterday fell into our trap, but I am still more faithful to the desires of my Señor, you are free, you, blind man, and you, girl, and you, monk from pestilent cities, the fever of rebellion spreads throughout the kingdom and I am sure that we soon will meet again, you, up to your elbows in intrigue, by the side of the insurgent townsmen of the cities of Castile, I by the side of my King, Guzmán is patient, we will settle our accounts then, and my son?, pleaded Ludovico, he has done nothing, he is innocent, he can be accused of nothing, will he not be freed?, yes, laughed Guzmán, but not now, not with you, I shall free him in my own way, El Señor has granted me that kindness, Celestina kissed the forehead of the pilgrim from the new world, clasped the youth's hands in hers, spoke into his ear, we shall wait, one day we shall triumph, we shall await the new millennium, I give you this appointment, far from here in another city Ludovico has told me of, Paris, the fountain of all wisdom, the fourteenth of July, when this millennium is dying, the fourteenth of July of 1999, I shall look for you, I shall find you, all waters communicate with each other, we shall find one another over the waters, we shall arrive by water, water passes from the Cantabrian to the Seine, from the Tiber to the Dead Sea, from the Nile to the gulfs of the new world, I shall look for you, I shall find you, upon a bridge, I shall pass my memory and my life to another woman, kissing her upon the lips, my lips are my memory, try to remember me, I shall look for you, Guzmán ordered the halberdiers to take Celestina, Ludovico, and Simón from the donjon, lead them to the plain, and abandon them with a week's provisions, he did not understand why El Señor was pardoning them, Guzmán would have subjected them to the rack, the same as the ringleader, Jerónimo, when the two of them remained alone in the cell, Guzmán stared with derision and amusement at the youth, *We wish to make known to Your Mercies that yesterday, Tuesday, which we counted the eleventh, Guzmán came to this town with two hundred musketeers and eight hundred lances, all prepared for war. And certain it is that Don Rodrigo rose no earlier against the Moors of Granada than Don Guzmán against the Christians of Medina. Once at the gates of the town, he told us that he was a captain general and that he had come for artillery. And, as we had not been told that he was captain general, we set ourselves to defend it. So that being unable to reach an agreement by words, we had to determine the matter by arms. Guzmán and his men, as soon as they perceived that we were superior to them in strength of arms, resolved to set fire to our homes and property, because they believed that what we had won by our efforts, we would lose by our greed. Certainly, señores, all the weapons of our enemies, aimed against one point, wounded our flesh, and in addition, the fire destroyed our properties. And above all else, we saw before our eyes that the soldiers were despoiling our women and our sons. But we give thanks to God that, thanks to the good effort of this town of Medina, we sent Guzmán away vanquished,* twenty-four years ago I was brought still a child to your house, Felipe, Isabel said to him that night, a young Princess with starched petticoats and corkscrew curls, do you remember?; I arrived on the eve of a terrible slaughter; we celebrated on the same day our wedding and your crime; today I ask you that our separation coincide with this new slaughter that closes so perfectly the circle of your life, my poor Felipe, I believe that I now know all it is possible to know about you, and I about you, Isabel, everything, my poor dear?, everything, Isabel, all your secrets, and the worst of them, too, the secret that is a greater crime than all of mine, for now you have seen, my crimes are repeatable but yours are not: the dead would have to be revived before you could again commit your unique crime, I shared Celestina with my father, with Ludovico, and perhaps with Beelzebub himself, I shared Inés with Don Juan; on the other hand, Isabel, I could not share you with your first lover, that is why I never touched you, that is why in my love you will always be that most perfect ideal, untouchable, incorruptible, soiled by no one, for only my mind sustains it and nourishes it and only with me will it die: I will share you only with my life and my death; and knowing this, do you believe, Isabel, that your love affair with the one called Mihail-ben-Sama could matter to me—with what relish I sent him to the stake, never invoking his true crime, only a secondary one—or your love-making with the one they called Don Juan, who is now living forever the hell he so feared and the death he so long postponed with a single female in a prison of mirrors; did you always know the truth, Felipe?; always, Isabel; and even so, you loved me, Felipe, in spite of my first love?; I shall always love you, Isabel; only I, among all living beings, shall have known and loved what you could have been; my love, beloved Isabel, has been the votive temple for that precious child who entertained herself in playing with her dolls, waking drowsy duennas, and hiding peach stones in the gardens: you, my child Isabel, you, my eternal lover, you, what you could have been; what I myself could have been; what we could have been together: the withered sheaf of our possibilities, the shattered shell of our realities; Felipe, my poor dear Felipe, I have harmed you greatly, I shall harm you greatly still, I shall leave in your land deep seeds of rancor, I shall live despising Spain until I purge myself completely of Spain, you will know my evil though I journey far from here; and in spite of everything, Felipe, given what we have been, being what we are, knowing our shared miseries and weaknesses, tell me, Felipe, did we learn at last to love one another?; I have always loved you, Isabel, you answer, have you at last learned to love me?; yes, Felipe, a thousand times yes, my child, my sweet muck-working mole, my little saint, my pitiful chained puppy, my wounded bird, my poor scarred man, conquered equally by humility and pride, my tender, impossible lover, sequestered in the stone of the sacred prison you have constructed, my innocent victim of the power you inherited, how am I not to love you to the very enormity of my hatred, he who hates so intensely, at times without realizing, gives all the intensity of his love to the one he thinks to despise; yes, that is why I love you, for the same reasons you love me: I love what could have been; thank you, Isabel, thank you for coming this night for the first time to my bedchamber, without my asking you, of your own will, thank you, look at it, what a poor naked funereal chamber, thank you for coming to me for the first time and—we know, for the last time, is that not so?, no more talk, Felipe, take my hand, take me to your bed, we shall spend this last and first night together, clothed, not touching one another, like a dead brother and sister, like two additional statues lying in the crypt where you have united your ancestors, sleep, sleep, sleep . . . *Do not marvel, señores, at what we have said; marvel at what we have not yet said. Our bodies are fatigued by combat, our houses all burned, our properties all stolen, our children and women with no place of shelter, the temples of God turned into dust; and especially, our hearts so disquieted we fear we shall become mad. We cannot believe that Guzmán and his men sought only artillery; for if this were so, it was not possible that eight hundred lances and five hundred soldiers would cease, as they ceased, to do battle in the plazas and turn to robbing our homes. The damage in sad Medina done by fire, you will want to know, all the gold, silver, brocades, silks, jewels, pearls, tapestries, and riches that were burned, is beyond the power of tongue to tell, there is not a quill that can record it, nor is there heart that can think on it, or mind that can consider it, there are no eyes that can see it*

*without tears; in burning our unfortunate Medina the tyrants did no
less harm than the Greeks in burning powerful Troy. We have such
justice in our demands, señores, that we must never desist in our undertaking. And if it is necessary, we shall send more men into the
country, and aid them with more money and artillery, for it would be
no small affront to Medina if this so just war were not carried to a conclusion. We seek first a compromise: Guzmán provoked the encounter
of arms. What he did in Medina he will repeat, if we permit it, in
Cuenca, Burgos, Avila, and Toledo. To the bearer of the present notice give your entire faith in what he tells you in our behalves and belief,* damp walls of Galicia tapestried with ivy, dead leaves, the ground
icy cold; as the brigantine put out to sea from the port of La Coruña, La
Señora looked at the Spanish coasts for the last time; El Señor lacked
the will to oppose the annulment, he acquiesced in the fact that he had
never touched Isabel, and it did not matter to him now that this truth be
known in all the circles in St. Peter's; some dim-witted cardinal spoke
of canonizing him, believing that chastity was a requisite of sanctity;
El Señor commissioned Julián, the friar, to go to Rome to initiate the
process before the Sacred Roman Rota; no one wanted to accompany
La Señora in her English exile, which for her was only a return to the
land of her father; the maid Azucena wept and explained and made excuses, you are returning to England, my mistress?, and what language
do they speak there?, how could a muddlehead like me get around
there without either understanding or being understood?, I, La Azucena, speak English?, Jehosaphat, not even if it were God's will, and remember, mistress, I know that little men like yours are born beneath
gallows, gibbets, pillories, and racks, are engendered by the tears of
the tortured, ay, poor Jerónimo, cut to pieces like a hunted stag, ay,
poor Nuño, left to bleed to death and rot, his flesh stripped away by a
goat's tongue!, at the feet of both, my Señora, there must be two other
little men like yours, two mandrakes, mistress, waiting for me to go by
the light of the moon, cut off a strand of my hair, tie it to a black dog's
tail, the other end to the mandrake root, and pull, cover my ears, and
amid cries so terrible they cannot be heard, our little men will be
yanked from their dank cradles of mud and tears; I shall put in cherries
for their eyes, and they will see, radishes for their mouths, and they
will speak, wheat on their little heads, and their hair will grow, and a
great carrot between their legs, my mistress, tee-hee-hee, and I shall
have a great dingalingdong to entertain myself with while I grow old,
for I am nothing but an argumentative old whore, and may God keep
me so, although without La Lolilla, my mistress, who do I have to
argue with or play ruff and honors with?, for that scrawny old Lola has
disappeared on us, I don't know where she's got to, and I scare myself
to death thinking that in all the slaughter they may have confused her
with the English whore, begging your pardon, mistress, Your Mercy,

and chopped the bawd in two with an ax, and besides, if the Devil is to carry us off, it will be the same either here or there, but better a known Devil than a Devil still to know, and the scrubbing maid wept and made her goodbyes, and the little dwarf said no, he wouldn't go either, for who would be left to look after the true monarch, the mummy seated on the Gothic throne in the gallery of paintings, columns, and plaster ornaments, who would listen to what he said, applaud the strange movements of his arms, his harsh and trembling gestures, celebrate his witticisms, so clumsy and difficult with that ancient, livid tongue, look after his tidiness, attend to dressing him, change his clothing according to the time, the mode, changing fashions, for that King, the true King, would in truth remain on the throne for centuries and centuries to come, and the little dwarf would be his only page, his buffoon, his confidant, counselor, and executor, and only Julián agreed to accompany Isabel, but he only to an English port, and from there he would continue on to Rome to carry out El Señor's charge, and then, Friar, and then?, Brother Julián leaned on the port railing, watching the deep inlets of the sheer coasts of Galicia fade into the distance, and said to her, Señora, as soon as the kingdom is again at peace, the rebellion of the city communities put down, all the riches confiscated from the insurgents, the Jews expelled and the Moors conquered, everyone will be employed in navigation and discoveries; the new world must exist, because the vanquished desire it so they can flee to it, and the conquerors as well, in order to channel into virgin lands all the energies and discontent that have flowered since the middle of the summer, all done in the name of the unity of Spain, proof of its unique power and evangelizing mission; a thousand ambitions palpitate beneath these reasons, those who can be Nothing here, can be Somebody there; you will see that in leaving their land all the Spanish will become Princes and luminaries, and in the new world the swineherd and smith and laborer will be able to achieve the lineage that being Spanish in Spain he could never achieve; the treasures of the new world will attract both conquerors and vanquished in the Spanish fratricide, and those conquerors, having subdued Spain, will have energy to spare for subduing idolaters; I shall go with them; I have something to do there; together they gazed at the green and golden coast of Galician autumn, La Señora recalled the smoke and flames of pyres consuming cadavers of the two slaughters, one in today's palace, one in yesterday's castle, on reaching Spain, on leaving Spain; then she turned her back to the land and looked at the tossing, slate-gray sea opening in stony waves before the brigantine's advance; England, her country, she had left so late, she told Julián, the friar, she was returning so late, no, it was not too late, it would not be too late, there would still be time, a virgin Queen, humiliated, burdened with vengeance and anguish, thus she would return, thus she would present herself, the home of her uncles, the Boleyns, awaited her, from those forgotten fields of Wiltshire she could plot her revenge, no one knew the Spanish land and its men as well as she, no one would know as well as she how to counsel her own race, reveal the secrets and weaknesses of terrible Spain, Isabel, virgin Queen, returning to her fatherland, filling the seas separating La Coruña from Portsmouth with powerful squadrons of vengeance, English fleets, English pennons, English cannons, and then toward the west, toward the new world, sons of Albion, so the new world would belong not only to Spain, she, Elizabeth again, as she was baptized, would take charge of instigating, pressing, intriguing, harassing, enlightening England so that its men also would set foot on the new lands and there forever confront the sons of Spain, challenging them, as cruel as they, and more, as covetous as they, and more, as criminal as they, and more, but without holy justification, without dreams of becoming gentlemen, without the temptations of the flesh, considering the new world a challenge, not a prize, like the Spanish, exterminators of natives, but without joining their bodies, or living the torments of that divided blood, seekers of treasures they would never find, they would have to wrest the fruits from the hostile land with their sweat and calluses, leisure for the Spaniard, industry for the Englishman, enervation of feelings for the Spaniard, the discipline of strength for the Englishman, illusion of luxury for the former, frugal reality for the latter, oh, yes, orders would be inverted, for the Spaniard—abandoning penitence, scarcity, sadness, and doors closed to ascent in his own land—would find too much leisure, too much opulence, and too great ease for personal grandeur in the new world, and he would sink into a swamp of golden softness, confusing reality with his person, and the Englishman abandoning the same problems in his world, oppression, war, and hunger, would find in the new world no leisure, no opulence, no ease, only the challenge of a new and virgin land that would give him nothing in compensation for his flight but what he conquered with his bare hands, working from nothing; Spain: conquer cities of gold; England: conquer virgin forests, untouched land, solitary rivers, plow furrows where Spain digs mines, build wood cabins where Spain raises palaces of quarried stone, paint white what Spain covers with silver, decide to be, where Spain contents itself with appearing, demand results, where Spain proclaims desires, commit yourself to actions where Spain dreams illusions, sacrifice to work what Spain sacrifices to honor, live the consensus of the hour where Spain lives the expectation of destiny, live forever disabused while Spain passes from illusion to disillusion and from disillusion to new illusion, let England prosper in the hard calculation of efficiency while Spain exhausts herself maintaining dignity, heroic appearances, and the self-gratification of commendation by others, yes, England asked everything that negated her, the dream of pleasure and luxury would not be for her, she sacrificed those dreams gladly so that Spain could swell to bursting, poisoned first from the excess the new world offered her famished austerity, and then from the disenchantments that sense of satiety produced; Spain: on the docks at La Coruña, Julián, I offered a gold ducat to a mendicant; it was my parting gift; and do you know what he said to me: "Look for some other poor man, Señora"; I shall give that same ducat to a beggar in London, and I shall tell him how to multiply it, invest it, reinvest it, lend it on interest and with conditions, attract partners, money-changers, contractors, the Jewish intelligentsia expelled from Spain, fleets of pirates, provocations against Hispanic dignity, all the measures, all of them, Julián: the gold of the new world will pass like water through Spain's hands into England's coffers: I swear it; and for yourself, Isabel, what do you want for yourself, Señora?, this autumn morning, sailing back to my English fatherland, Julián?, Elizabeth wants nothing but the image of a little girl, a Princess with corkscrew curls and starched white cotton petticoats, and she will ask that child, did your dolls arrive safely?, none was broken on the voyage?, where did you bury your peach stones?, oh, the hawk, how it soars, how it spreads its jet-black wings!, have you ever heard of a bedchamber with white sand floors, Arabic tiles, soft tapestries?, will you come with me to the Court of Love where a company of knights dressed in white will compete for your hand against a company of knights dressed in black?, do you hear the little bronze pellets dropping into a basin, marking the hours?, let's play, ring-a-ring o' roses, a pocket full of posies, a-tishoo, a-tishoo, we all fall down, *Yesterday, Thursday, we came to know what we had never wanted to know and heard what we had never wanted to hear: it is fitting to know that Guzmán has burned down the very loyal town of Medina. As God the Lord is our witness, if he burned the houses in that town, he will roast our entrails. But hold, señores, as true that as Medina was lost for Segovia, either no memory shall remain of Segovia, or Segovia will avenge the injury to Medina. We have been informed that you battled against Guzmán, not like merchants, but like captains; not as if unprepared, but defiantly, not like weak men, but like strong lions. And as you are sane men, give thanks to God for the burning, that it afforded you opportunity to achieve such glory. For beyond comparison you must hold greater the fame you earned than the properties you lost. The disasters of war stir us to move the General Junta from Avila to Valladolid, and from there to continue the struggle for the general remedying of the kingdom, occasioned by bad governing and the counsel our Señor the King has received,* conquered in Medina, conquered in Segovia, conqueror in Torresillas and in Torrelobatón, my defeats and victories are all victories, for I provoked and goaded the townsmen to war with tears in their eyes and affronted dignity, bad judges of cold military calculation, but what do such victories and calamities mean to me if I still have not vanquished you?, Guzmán had said to the young pilgrim of the new world brought once again by Guzmán to the site of the first hunt on the spurs of the Cantabrian range, and in view of the coast, you see that I am loyal, youth, you came from here, I bring you again to this very spot, on a clear day from this height one can see the beach and the Cabo de los Desastres, El Señor told me, set him free, one of his brothers sleeps forever, fast in bed in Verdín, and the other purges his pleasure and heresy in a prison of mirrors, the prophecy has been defeated, there are not three now, or two, but only one, let him go free, there is no way he can harm us, and all our efforts must be directed against the rebellious townsmen, who in truth are threatening us, not against a poor wretch who dreamed a new world, he says you were three, that is what the blind flautist and the girl with the tattooed lips led us to believe, but Guzmán is not so easily deceived, I know the truth, there was only one, I never saw the three together, and what the eyes do not behold, the mind does not understand, I saw the same one every time, in different places, in different attires, and with different persons, they are all you, you are all three, I asked El Señor, Sire, let me set him free in my own manner, with as much justice and as much chance as the hart is given in the hunt, and he agreed, and that is why, now, you, the last youth, blond, pursued, you, trembling with cold, in ragged clothing, you, who knew the dangers of the high seas, the beach of pearls, the town beside the river, the virgin jungle, the sacred wells, the smoking pyramids, the snowy volcano, the entrails of the white hell, the city of the lake, the palaces of gold of the new world, that is why you have been running, walking, falling, struggling to your feet, since yesterday, Guzmán said he would give you one day's start, then would follow to hunt you, it has snowed all day, first that fact frightened you, all the footsteps of your route through the mountains, toward the sea, would leave a trail, he had warned you of that, you will have one day's start, but it is snowing, snow erases old trails, one easily finds the fresh track, the wind blows snow from the branches, a good time to run new game, the dogs will be well baited, but by dusk the wind began to blow strong from the knife-edge ridges of the mountain and looking back you saw that it was hidden beneath a cape of white snow and with it the track of your feet; you had won or lost a day's advantage: you can see the signal tied to a lance by the lookouts on the highest point of the mountain, placed so that everyone sees it, even you: it is the call to flush the stag; you stop for a moment in the midst of the storm that as it muffles the sound of horns and trumpets seems to impose an illusory silence over the snowy clearing through which you have fled from the mountain; but suddenly the storm died down, Guzmán loosed one pack of dogs, and then another, and then a third; you count each wave of barking behind you, Guzmán told you, freedom, freedom, you came here to speak of freedom, freedom for the new world beyond the sea, freedom for the new world here, you will see how long your freedom lasts, here or there, you will hear the cry of Spain every time they offer you your freedom: Long live chains!, you hear the steadily approaching horns, Guzmán had instructed the crossbowmen, these are dogs that will not follow a trail if they do not smell blood, kill that boar to excite them, you are a stag, pilgrim, Guzmán had told you, the easy way to kill an animal is from a distance, aiming at its side, the longest part of its body, but more audacious and fatal is to wound it face-on, to drive in your lance to the hilt, turn it, and then allow the hart to be subdued by the dogs, run, youth, run, pilgrim, run, founder, run, first man, run, Plumed Serpent, you do not know the wiles of the wild boars that as they come down from the mountain to graze in wheat fields send two or three little ones ahead, and as they enter the wheat they give them two or three quick thrusts of their tusks, making them squeal, then return to high ground where they can survey the field; they do this three times, until they are assured there is no hunter about, and the fourth time they descend without caution, and are easily hunted; you, no instinct, no wile, you run toward the sea, packs of dogs close behind you, Guzmán mounted, his favorite hawk upon his forearm, wrapped in dark-brown cape, hooded and heavily booted, I told you, hawk, beautiful hawk, fierce hawk, your hour would come, that hour is now, I prepared you for the great hunt, remember Guzmán, brave hawk, you are my weapon, my devotion, my child and my luxury, the mirror of my desires and the face of my hatred, and you see the sea before you through cobwebs of fog, the Cabo de los Desastres, the beach of Celestina's and Pedro's, Simón's and Ludovico's former dreams, the beach of Felipe's deceit, the beach that received you and your two brothers in order to hasten history, destinies, the millennium, in the land of eternal vespers, Spain, Vespers, Hesperia, land of Venus, its own twin, in anguished and interminable search of its other countenance, Spain, you are running, again returning to that beneficent sea, your heart tells you that the sea will save you, in spite of everything, how near the terrible horns, barking, hoof beats, panting, you run like the hart, the fringe of desert between the mountains and the sea narrows, besieging greyhounds block any exit to the right, whippets to the left, the whippets must contain the greyhounds so they will not capture you too soon, you are trapped between two lines of menacing dogs, Guzmán knows his office well, the passage to the sandy beach narrows, you scramble down between icy-crusted dunes, you fall face down upon the beach, your arms flung in a cross, you rise, barking, horns, Guzmán on the height of the sand dunes, laughing, before you the misty sea, behind you, Guzmán and the huntsmen, Guzmán frees the hawk, go, hawk, beautiful hawk, I promised you, I did not deceive you, I swore to you, I will offer you the freshest flesh, that is your prey, soar into the skies with the swiftness of a prayer and swoop down with the speed of a curse, the hawk soars, the dogs run, you have not reached the sea, a greyhound's jaws close about your arm, his fangs sink deep, tear your flesh, a whippet chases away the greyhound, you are free for a moment, you fall, you rise, your feet sink in the slime of the shore, turbulent waves break and die around your knees, the hawk soars, speeding like an arrow, it swoops swift as a curse, fastens onto your arm, digs its steely talons into your flesh, fixes upon your arm with its long tarsi, sinks its beak into the wounds opened by the dog's fangs, you run into the sea, the bird still clinging to you, you struggle, you roll over, you beat at the bird, the falcon is devouring your arm, you try to swim, you cannot with a single arm, you try to drown this ferocious falconet, Guzmán, on horseback, is laughing from the dunes, you plunge the arm in the iron grip of the hawk into the sea, you sink, in the obscured heavens you seek the light of your star, Venus, the sailor's guide, and in the depths of the sea, St. Elmo's fire, flame of inseparable brothers, *Marquis, kinsman: I write to apprise you that Tuesday last, the day of St. George, near the village of Villalar, our army joined battle—in which participated all the viceroys and governors of our kingdoms—against the army of rebels and traitors, in which it pleased Our Lord and His Blessed Mother to give us the victory without any harm to the men of our army, and from the enemy we recaptured the artillery they had taken from us and usurped, and all the ringleaders of the General Junta were taken prisoner and killed. Captain Don Guzmán was outstanding in this action, galloping on horseback, face flushed red, sweat streaming from a brow blackened by the agitation of his soul, hoarse from shouting to our men: Kill the accursed rebels; destroy the impious and dissolute upstarts; pardon no man; you shall enjoy eternal rest among the just if you eradicate from the earth this accursed people; do not forbear in wounding either in the front or in the back these disturbers of tranquillity. Before night fell, one could see the townsmen fleeing for a distance of two and a half leagues; one hundred men were dead on the field, four hundred were wounded, a thousand captured. Not one of our soldiers lost his life. Of the townsmen the most nimble saved themselves, and some who had the foresight to exchange our white crosses for the red crosses fastened to their breasts and backs that distinguished them from us. There reigns in Villalar, the tomb of the townsmen's rebellion, more silence than in a village of only three men. Your most abject servitor and servant, who kisses your hands, kinsman Marquis, your most fervent, faithful and humble adept, etc., etc., etc.,* Guzmán asked a single favor from his King Don Felipe in reward for his actions, and that was to lead an expedition that would cross the great ocean in search of the new world and thereby ascertain its existence or non-existence; El Señor heartily acceded, giving proof of grace and munificence, and urging Guzmán to take with him many of the troublemakers of his kingdoms, men of excessive energy capable of disturbing his calm, so that the prayers and peace of his necropolis would not again be perturbed by heretics, rebels, madmen, and lovers: "For your hand is harsh, Guzmán, you will know how to discipline these upstarts, and how to use them to best advantage in the undertakings of great risk that only those who have nothing to lose will attempt"; Guzmán supervised in Cádiz the construction of a fleet of three-masted caravels with triangular sails rigged on masts distributed along the longitudinal plan of the ships; these caravels were a great novelty, for formerly the varinel had been used on such expeditions, a ship with both oars and sail, and the barque, whose conformation and round sail greatly reduced its maneuverability and speed. As he directed the construction of these new ships, and smiling to himself, Guzmán recalled the labors of the aged Pedro on the beach of the Cabo de los Desastres, for these new ships were as long as the varinel but with decks high as the barque's, combining the advantages of both hulls, eliminating their defects, for the Latin-style triangular sail permitted lying closer to the wind, thereby receiving better advantage of it, and its lighter design resulted in greater agility in speed and maneuverability. El Señor provided for the expenses of the expedition a fund of two million maravedis expropriated from three families of exiled Jews, the Santángel, the Santa Fe, and the Bélez, and as warranty ordered the authorities of towns and villages along the Andalusian coast to provide Guzmán whatever goods he asked for his flotilla, allowing them to collect excise taxes. As additional warranty, El Señor promised that all who signed on board the caravels would be given security, and his promise that no one could harm their persons or their goods because of any crime they had committed. Thus three hundred men signed on, and as he watched them board the caravels with their sparse belongings, Guzmán smiled, guessing that here was the conquered townsman and there the common criminal, in this one he saw an impoverished nobleman, and in that one the pretended convert, in one a laborer of the land, and in another a rancorous smith. If only they had waited a little: Jerónimo, Nuño, Martín, Catilinón . . . He had not again seen that servile rascal given to speaking in proverbs. Had he been killed by mistake in the palace slaughter? Distracted, Guzmán did not notice the strange couple who arm in arm boarded one of the caravels. A hooded man, walking slowly, bent over with pain, one hand protecting his sex and the other resting upon the shoulder of a Mozarab of short stature and effeminate gait dressed in rags, his head shaved and features obscured by grime. It was almost the hour to set sail. Through the narrow windows of Cádiz, from behind the green shutters of their houses, peered pale, suspicious faces. Guzmán knew what they were thinking: they are headed for disaster, they are mad, and we will never see them again. He hoisted the pennants of the caravels. A message arrived from El Señor: wait two more days. Brother Julián, the palace iconographer, will join your expedition. Guzmán's mouth tasted of gall.

CONFESSIONS
OF A CONFESSOR

Up to now, Julián said to the Chronicler, that is what I know. No one knows the things I know, or knows things I do not know. I have been confessor to them all; believe only my version of events; listen to no other possible narrators. Celestina believed she knew everything and told everything, because with her lips she inherited memory and through them she thinks to transmit it. But she did not hear El Señor's daily confession before taking Communion, the details of the vanquished illusions of youth, the meaning of his penances in the chapel, his ascent up the stairway leading to the plain, the defiance of his listing of heresies, his relationship with our Señora, or his late passion for Inés. Furthermore, I heard the confessions of the Mad Lady, those of nuns and scrubbing maids; those of the Idiot and the dwarf before they were joined in matrimony and with my benediction wed; and those of the workmen. I heard Guzmán's confession; and if he believes that, in fleeing in search of the new world, he will leave behind the memory of his guilt, a great frustration awaits him. And I heard, my friend Chronicler, Ludovico's and Celestina's relations in El Señor's bedchamber: only I know the passageway that leads to the wall where hangs the King's ocher map; I pierced holes for my eyes and ears in the eyes of the Neptune that adorns it. Everyone who spoke there, everyone who thought aloud there, everyone who acted there, everyone who listened or was listened to there, gave me their secret voices, as I lent them my penitent ear, for often the confessor suffers more than the one who confesses; he relieves himself of a burden and the confessor assumes it.

Therefore, give no attention or credence to what others tell you, Julián continued, nor hold any faith in the simple and deceitful chronologies that are written about this epoch in an attempt to establish the logic of a perishable and linear history; true history is circular and eternal. You have seen: when she found him on the beach, the young Celestina did not tell all the truth to the pilgrim of the new world, so as not to distract him from his central purpose, which was to narrate before El Señor the dreamed existence of an unknown land beyond the sea; and even less, much less, was La Señora able to tell all the truth to the castaway called Juan when she took him to her bedchamber and there made love with him with such intense fury. How could Guzmán tell anyone except me—as the fires of the secret seal my lips—of his turbulent acts, the debates within his soul, and the designs of his life?, who but I could know, and keep secret, the ignominy of his drugging El Señor and setting the dogs on him?; he conceived of regicide, but he opted to kill our Señor not with a dagger, not with philters of lunacy, but by making potent his impotence, leading him step by step: the shattered mirror restored, pitchers filled after they were emptied, candles that grew taller as they were burned, the howling of the phantasmal dog, the commotion of the nuns in the chapel, Bocanegra's death, the impossible passion with Inés, always greater and greater confrontations with what cannot be.

I kept everything secret, my candid friend, and if now I have told you everything, it is because my need to confess and do penance for the harm I have caused you supersedes all the vows of my priesthood. Including the secrets of the confessional. I am going far away. Someone must know these stories and write them. That is your vocation. Mine carries me to other places. But I do not want this story to be cut short, this hadith-novella, as you say it must be called in order to give to the tale the dignity the Arabic settlers in our peninsula gave to the communication of news. I give you, then, all the news I know—which is all the news—as I told you from the day you returned, exhausted, dressed as a beggar, your arm crippled from the fierce naval battle against the Turk. You saw things clearly, friend; your freedom was not given you in exchange for your meritorious performance in combat; but with only one good arm you were of little service on the galleys. You were abandoned on the Algerian coast and taken captive by the Arabs. They treated you well, but you, a Christian, fell in love with a beautiful Moorish girl, Zoraida, and she with you; you knew spring in autumn. Zoraida's father wished to separate her from you; you were abandoned on the Valencian coast by Algerian pirates and returned to prison in Alicante. That is where I went in search of you once I obtained the roll of those dead, wounded, and repatriated following the famous battle. With my facile hand it was no effort to feign El Señor's signature on your order of liberation, and even less to take advantage of Don Felipe's sleep to seal it with his ring. From the bold terraces of the muscatel, the almond, and the fig, through the vast garden of Valencia, through open land and rice fields I brought you here, disguised as a mendicant, up to the arid Castilian plain to this tower of the astronomer Toribio where the tasks of science and art can ward off, even if only momentarily, the ambush of madness, crime, injustice, and torment that seethes before our eyes. Here you have heard everything: all that happened before your arrival and after it, from Felipe's first crime to the last. I say, deluded creature that I am, that I am telling you the story so you will write it and thus, perhaps, his story will not be repeated. But history does repeat itself; that is the comedy and crime of history. Men learn nothing. Times change, scenes change, names change, but the passions are the same. Nevertheless, the enigma of the story I have told you is that in repeating itself it does not end: see how many facets of this hadith, this novella, in spite of the appearance of conclusion, remain inconclusive, latent, awaiting, perhaps, another time in which to reappear, another space in which to germinate, another opportunity in which to manifest themselves, other names to call themselves.

Celestina made a rendezvous with the pilgrim for a very distant date in Paris, the last day of this millennium. How shall we put a period to this narration if we do not know what will happen then? That is why I have revealed the secrets of the confessional to you, and only to you, because you write for the future, because it does not matter to you what is said today concerning your writing or the laughter your writing provokes: the day will come when no one will laugh at you, but everyone will laugh at the Kings, Princes, and prelates who today monopolize all homage and respect. Ludovico said that one lifetime is not enough: one needs multiple existences to unify a personality. He also said other things that impressed me. He called immortal those who reappear from time to time because they had more life than their own death, but less time than their own life. He said that since a man or woman can be several persons mentally, they can become several persons physically; we are specters of time, and our present contains the aura of what we were before and the aura of what we will become when we disappear. Don't you see, Chronicler, my friend, how this argument coincides with El Señor's repeated malediction in his testament, his bequest of a future of resurrections that can be glimpsed only in forgotten pauses, in the orifices of time, in the dark, empty minutes when the past tried to imagine the future, a blind, pertinacious, and painful return to the imagination of the future in the past as the only future possible to this race and this land, Spain, and all the peoples that descend from Spain?

I, Julián, friar and painter, I tell you that as the conflicting words of El Señor and Ludovico blend together to offer us a new reason born of the encounter of opposites, so in the same way are allied shadows and lights, outline and volume, flat color and perspective on a canvas, and thus must be allied in your book the real and the virtual, what was with what could have been, and what is with what can be. Why would you tell us only what we already know, without revealing what we still do not know? Why would you describe to us only this time and this space without all the invisible times and spaces our time contains?, why, in short, would you content yourself with the painful dribble of the sequential when your pen offers you the fullness of the simultaneous? I choose my word well, Chronicler, and I say: content yourself. Discontented, you will aspire to simultaneity of times, spaces, and events, because men resign themselves to that patient dribble that drains their lives, they have scarcely forgotten their birth when it is time to confront their death; you, on the other hand, have decided to suffer, to fly in pursuit of the impossible on the wings of your unique freedom, that of your pen, though still bound to the earth by the chains of accursed reality that imprisons, reduces, weakens, and levels all things. Let us not complain, my friend; it is possible that without the ugly gravity of the real our dreams would lack weight, would be gratuitous, and thus of little worth and small conviction. Let us be grateful for this battle between imagination and reality that lends weight to fantasy and wing to facts, for the bird will not fly that does not encounter resistance from the air. But the earth would be converted into something less than air were it not constantly thought, dreamed, sung, written, sculpted, and painted. Listen to what my brother Toribio says: Mathematically, everyone's age is zero. The world dissolves when someone ceases to dream, to remember, to write. Time is the invention of personality. The spider, the hawk, the she-wolf, have no time.

To cease to remember. I fear sequential memory because it means duplicating the pain of time. To live it all, friend. To remember it all. But it is one thing to live, remembering everything, and something different to remember, living everything. Which road will you choose in order to complete this novella that I entrust to you today? I see you here, beside me, diviner of time, of the past and the present and the future, and I see how you are looking at me, reproaching me for the loose ends of this narration while I ask you to be grateful to me for the oblivion in which I left so many unfulfilled gestures, so many unspoken words . . . But I see that my wise warning does not satiate your thirst for prophecy: you ask yourself, what will be the future of the past?

For you, I have violated the secrets of the confessional. You will tell me that a secret is the same as death: the secret is a word and an event that have ceased to exist. Then, is all past secret and dead? No, is it not true?, because the remembered past is secret and living. And how can it be saved by memory and cease to be the past? By converting itself into the present. Then it is no longer the past. Then all true past is impenetrable secret and death. Do you wish that, having told you everything of the past I wish to rescue in order to convert it into present, I also tell you what must be secret and dead in order to continue to be the past? And all of it only to give to you what you yourself do not know: a story that will end in the future? Oh, my indiscreet scribe, that is why you ended up in a galley, unceasingly you confound reality with paper, just like the one-eyed magus whose quartered body was thrown into the waters of the Adriatic. Be grateful, I tell you, for loose ends; accept the truth spoken by the Mad Lady: every being has the right to carry a secret to the tomb; every narrator reserves to himself the privilege of not clarifying mysteries, so that they remain mysteries; and who is not pleased, let him demand his money . . .

Who said that? Who? Wait. One minute. He who would know more, let him loosen his purse strings . . . There are so many things I myself do not understand, my friend. For example I, as much as you, depend upon Ludovico and Celestina for an understanding of the story of the three youths . . . For me they were always three usurpers, three youths allied to frustrate El Señor's intent and prolong history beyond the limits of death and immobility indicated by the King; three heirs, three bastards, yes, even three founders, as Ludovico said, but, I swear to you, I never understood that story, those signs, clearly. I repeated to La Señora what Ludovico asked me: a blood-red cross upon the back, six toes on each foot, the kingdom of Rome still lives, Agrippa, his is the continuity of the original kingdoms, phrases, phrases I repeated without understanding, loose ends, accept them, be grateful for them, I tell you . . .

The three bottles? What did the three bottles contain? I do not know that either, I tell you, and he who would know more, let . . . Equality? You ask me for equality, then?, you accept not knowing the things I do not know, and ask only to know what I know, you permit me no secret, nothing I can take to the tomb except what, like you, I do not know?, that is the only agreement you will accept?, oh, my friend, that is the only way you will forgive me for having been the cause of your harm, the galleys, your certainty of death on the eve of the battle, your being crippled in it, your delivery to the Arabs, your prison in Alicante . . . only in that way?

I am going far away, my poor friend. I shall know nothing of what happens here. It is left in your hands, to your eyes and your ears, to continue the story of El Señor Don Felipe. Where I am going, little news will reach me. And certainly, less news, or none, will you have of me. I do not know if a new world exists. I know only what I imagine. I know only what I desire. As a consequence, it exists for me. I am an exasperated Christian. I wish to know, and if it exists, I wish to protect it, and if it does not exist, I wish to adopt it, a minimal community of people who live in harmony with nature, who own no property except those things shared by all: a new world, not because it was found anew, but because it is or it will be like that of the first Golden Age. Remember, my candid and culpable friend, everything I have told you and, with me, ask yourself, what blindness is this?, we call ourselves Christians but we live worse than brutish animals; and if we believe that this Christian doctrine is but a deceit, why do we not abandon it altogether? I am abandoning this palace; I am abandoning my friends, you, my brother Toribio; I am abandoning El Señor. I go with one who needs me more: Guzmán. It is true; do not look at me with such amazement. I know that I go in search of the happy Golden Age; I know that Guzmán goes, with great malice and covetousness, in search of sources of gold, and that his age in the new world will be an iron age, and worse; I know that I seek, tentatively, the restoration of true Christianity, while Guzmán seeks, with certainty, the instauration of fortunate Guzmánism. I am needed more there than here; there will be need of someone who will speak on behalf of the defeated, perpetuate their founding dreams, defend their lives, protect their labors, affirm that they are men with souls and not simple beasts of burden, watch for the continuity of beauty and the pleasure of a thousand small offices, and channel souls, for the glory of God, toward the construction of new temples, the astounding temples of the new world, a new flowering of a new art that will defeat forever the fixity of icons that reflects a truth revealed only once, and forever, and instead reveal a new knowledge that unfolds in every direction for every delectation, a circular encounter between what they know and what I know, a hybrid art, temples raised in the image and likeness of the paradise we all envision in our dreams: color and form will be liberated, expanded, and fructified in celestial domed ceilings of white grape clusters, polychrome vines, silver fruit, dusky angels, tile façades, altars of excessive golden foliage, images, yes, of the paradise shared by them and me, cathedrals for the future, the anonymous seed of rebellion, renovating imagination, constant and unfulfilled aspiration: a vast circle in perpetual movement, sweet friend, my white hands and their swarthy ones joined to do more, much more, than anything I could ever do in the old world, secretly painting culpable paintings to disturb the conscience of a King; hybrid temples of the new world, the solution of all our mute inheritances in one stone embrace: pyramid, church, mosque, and synagogue united in a single place: look at that wall of serpents, look at that transplanted arch, look at those Moorish tiles, look at those floors of sand.

There is no such place? No, my friend, there isn't if you look for it in space. Seek it, rather, in time: in the same future you will investigate in your exemplary—and thereby scandalous—novels. My white hands and their dark hands will juxtapose the simultaneous spaces of the old and the new worlds to create the promise of a different time. I shall assume, my sweet, bitter, lovable, desperate friend, the dreams dreamed and lost by Ludovico and Celestina, Pedro and Simón, on that long-ago afternoon on the beach of the Cabo de los Desastres. Without their knowing it, I shall also assume the dreams of El Señor and Guzmán, of the Comendador and the Inquisitor, for neither they nor we know what we do, only God, whose instruments we are. Guzmán will seek new countries in his desire for gold and riches; El Señor will accept events in order to transfer there the sins, the rigidity, and the will for extinction operating here, but God and I, your servant Julián, shall work together for the most exalted goals. My friend: will the new world truly be the new world where everything can be begun anew, man's entire history, without the burdens of our old errors? Shall we Europeans be worthy of our own Utopia?

Thus, I accept your proposition to teach by example: I shall arrive in the new world cleansed of culpable secrets and odious burdens. Let us be ignorant of the same things, you and I; let us know the same things; and he who wishes to know more, let him loosen his purse strings, and he who is not pleased with what I tell him, let him demand his money. That is what the jester with the broad bedaubed smile used to say when he entertained with his buffoonery in El Señor's castle, with the grimace of the dying day reflected in the twin orbs of eyes beneath a pointed cap pulled low on his brow; how would he not see the glances of carnal cupidity El Señor's father directed toward the beautiful child Isabel, come from England after her parents' death to find refuge and consolation by the side of her Spanish aunt and uncle: starched white petticoats, long corkscrew curls, Elizabeth, yes, that incontinent and whoring Prince desired her as a child, he who had raped every country girl in the district, taken all the honorable maids of his kingdoms by seignorial right, who was pursuing the girls of Flanders while in a latrine in the palace of Brabant his wife was giving birth to his son, our present Señor, he who had satiated his appetites with a she-wolf, scarcely had he seen the budding breasts and the down in the armpits of his English niece—after playing with her and offering her dolls and gifts, then breaking upon the floor the same dolls he had given her as a gift—when he surreptitiously deflowered her.

In whom was the young girl to confide but in the only man in that castle who, like her, played: the jester? But if she said nothing to me, I, who even then entertained her with my brushes and engravings and miniatures, found her weeping one day, and noted the swelling fullness of her belly and breasts, and she, weeping, told me she wept because for two months she had not bled.

I was shocked by the news: what was to be done with the young English girl who was gazed upon with eyes of love by the youthful heir Felipe, and who had committed the indiscretion—worse than the deed—of telling the truth to the most deceitful and disturbed of the courtiers, the jester of bitter features, a buffoon because in all his existence he found no cause for joy? It would be useless to tell the jester that I shared the secret and urge him to guard it. He would have placed a price on his silence, as in the end he did; an intriguer, but stupid, he told El Señor's father he knew the truth.

First our insatiable master ordered that the Princess Isabel be removed for seven months to the ancient castle in Tordesillas, there to receive a disciplined education in the arts of the court, to be accompanied only by a marshal, three duennas, a dozen halberdiers and the famous Jewish physician, the humpbacked Dr. José Luis Cuevas, brought from prison where he was expiating the unconfessed crime of boiling in oil six Christian children by the light of the moon, exactly as an ancestor of his had done with three royal Princes, for which the King of that time had ordered burned alive thirty thousand false converts in the plaza of Logroño. Cuevas was taken to Tordesillas with the promise of being exonerated if he fulfilled well his office in the somber castle, the ancient lodging of many mad royalty. Cuevas attended the birth; he marveled at the monstrous signs on the child and, laughing, said that he looked more like a son of his than of the beautiful young girl; he laughed for the last time: the halberdiers cut off his head in the very chamber of the birth, and they were at the point of doing the same to the newborn child, had not the young Isabel, clutching the child against her breast, defended him as a she-wolf defends her cub.

She said: "If you touch him, first I shall strangle him and then kill myself, and we shall see how you explain my death to your Señor. Your own death is hovering nearby. I know that as soon as we reach the castle, the Señor will order you killed as he ordered the death of this poor Hebrew doctor, so that no one can tell of what happened here. On the other hand, I have promised before God and before man to keep eternal silence if the child leaves here alive with me. Which will have the greater import, your word or mine?"

With this, the halberdiers fled, for well they knew the violent disposition of El Señor's father, and they did not doubt the words of Isabel, who returned to the castle with two of the duennas, while another, with the marshal, carried the child by a different route. Warned by my young mistress of the approximate dates of events, I had circled about the palace of Tordesillas for several days prior to the birth, and cloaked, wearing the hat and clothing of a highwayman, I assaulted the duenna and the marshal, galloped back to the seignorial castle with the bastard in my arms, and delivered him in secret to the child mother, Isabel.

Discretion was my weapon and my desire: the heir, Felipe, loved this girl; he would wed her; the future Queen would owe me the most outstanding favors; I would enjoy peace and protection in which to continue my vocation as friar and painter, and also to extend them to men like you, Chronicler, and to my brother, the astronomer Toribio. But if someone discovered the truth, then what confusion there would be, what disorder, what rancor, what uncertainty for my fortunes; Felipe would repudiate Isabel; Felipe's mother, who had pardoned her husband so many deceptions, would not absolve him of this particular transgression; my fortune would be unsure; I would be defeated, like Oedipus, by incest! Through the alleyways of Valladolid I sought out an ancient blackbird, a renowned procuress expert in renewing maidenheads, and in secret I led her to Isabel's chamber in the castle, where the old curmudgeon, with great art, mended the girl's ill and stole away as she had come, a drone in the shadows.

Isabel wept because of her many misfortunes; I asked her about the infant; that giddy child moaned that, not knowing how to care for him, or nourish him, or anything concerned with him, she had given him into the hands of her friend the jester, who was keeping him in some secret part of the castle. I cursed the girl's imprudence, for she was furnishing more and more weapons to the intriguing buffoon, who, neither late nor lazy, made known to the outrageous and whoring Prince, our Señor, what he knew, and asked him money in exchange for guarding the secret. The Señor called the Fair, you see, was convinced that the duenna and the marshal—following the King's direction—had abandoned the newborn child in a basket in the waters of the Ebro. Therefore, the jester's greedy project was short-lived, for that same afternoon, when all the court was gathered in the castle hall, El Señor, our master, offered the jester a cup of wine to animate him in his buffoonery, and the incautious mime, cavorting and capering, died, choked by the poison.

I set about to look for the lost infant and found him in the most obvious of places: on a straw pallet in the cell occupied by the jester. I gave the child to Isabel's duenna, Azucena. The duenna took him to Isabel and explained to her that when he died the jester had left a newborn child in his pallet. She had decided to care for the child, but her breasts were dry. Could she nurse the babe at the teats of the bitch who recently had whelped in Isabel's bedchamber. Isabel, who was still bleeding from her own childbirth, said yes, and to her uncle, El Señor, she said: "Our son can pass as the son of the jester and Azucena. Do not kill anyone else. Your secret is safe. If you do not touch my son I shall tell nothing to anyone. If you kill him, I shall tell everything. And then kill myself."

But that ferocious and handsome Señor did not wish to kill anyone, he wished to make love to Isabel again, he wished to love without limits, he wished to possess every living woman, every bleeding female, nothing could satiate him; that very morning in the chapel he saw Isabel spit out a serpent at the moment she received the Host, he saw the eyes of love with which his own son Felipe gazed at Isabel, and being unable to make love to her again, and thus desiring her more ardently than ever, he drank until he was drunk, rode out on his dun-colored steed, lopping off heads of wheat with his whip, he encountered a trapped she-wolf, he dismounted, violated the beast, howled like her and with her, satiated all his dark needs, his frustration, and burning fires: animal with animal, the act did not horrify him; it would have been a sin against nature to make love again with Isabel, but not beast with beast, no, that was natural: this is what he told me as he confessed another night, the night when Isabel and Felipe had just been wed and after the cadavers burned on the pyre in the courtyard had been carried away in carts; this he confessed to me, in addition to all his earlier crimes, sure of my silence, feeling the need to pour out his tormented soul before someone.

"Have I impregnated a she-wolf?" he asked me through the grating of the confessional, hoping to find solace for his monstrous imaginings.

"Be calm, Señor, please be calm; such a thing is impossible . . ."

"Accursed breed," he murmured, "madness, incest, crime, the only thing lacking was to make love as beast to beast; what do I bequeath my son? Each generation adds scars to the generation that follows; the scars accumulate until they lead to sterility and extinction; degenerate seeks out degenerate; an imperious force impels them to find one another and unite . . ."

"The seed, Señor, exhausts itself from growing upon the same soil."

"What would be born of my coupling with a beast? Did some dark necessity impel me to renovate the blood with a living but nonhuman thing?"

"In spite of classic wisdom, Señor, nature at times makes strange leaps," I said ingenuously, thinking thus to absolve myself of any knowledge concerning the paternity of Isabel's child, and also to promote the current belief about his origin. "For instance, consider a child," I added, "that is not the son of man and she-wolf but the child of jester and scrubbing maid; he bears monstrous signs of degeneration . . ."

"What signs?" cried El Señor, who had never seen the child.

"A cross upon his back, six toes on each foot . . ."

Now El Señor called the Fair howled, he howled, and his animal cry resounded through the domed ceiling of the church; he left, shouting: "Do you not know the prophecy of Tiberius Caesar?, is this the sign of the usurpers, rebellious slaves, have I engendered slaves and rebels who will usurp my kingdom?, parricidal sons?, a throne raised upon the blood of their father?"

I knew he ordered the child killed, but he disappeared, as also disappeared that same night, to his great sadness, Felipe's companions, Ludovico and Celestina; I knew that El Señor ordered that every Saturday be dedicated to hunting wolves until every wolf was exterminated. Only I understood the reason for these orders. I gave thanks when El Señor died, after playing very strenuously at ball; Prince Felipe occupied his place, and my Señora Isabel ascended to the throne reserved for her.

Isabel displayed great austerity and discretion as the wife of the new Señor, Don Felipe, and I never imagined that the maidenhead restored by the magpie of the alleyways of Valladolid remained intact. My respectful friendship with La Señora was constant. I attempted to entertain her, as I always had, with my enamels and miniatures, and by lending her to read the volumes of courtly love of the *De arte honeste amandi* of Andreas Capellanus, for beneath her dignity I noted an increasing melancholy, as if something were lacking; at times she sighed for her dolls and her peach stones, and I told myself that my Señora's transition from young foreigner to solitary Queen and secret mother of a vanished child had been too swift. The people murmured: When will the foreigner give us a Spanish heir? False pregnancies were announced, followed always by unfortunate miscarriages.

Nothing was more disastrous, however, than the accident that then befell my mistress, her husband being in Flanders at war against the Adamite heretics and the dukes that protected them. The humiliation of the thirty-three and one half days she spent lying upon the paving stones of the castle courtyard transformed my Señora's will; it unleashed forces, passions, hatreds, desires, memories, dreams that doubtless had throbbed for a long time in her soul and had awaited only an astonishing event, both terrible and absurd, like this one, to fully manifest themselves. A mouse, then, and not the virile member of our Señor, gnawed away the restored virginity of my Señora. She called me to her chamber, when finally she returned to it: she asked me to complete the work begun by the Mus; I possessed her, finally breaking the network of fine threads the go-between of Valladolid had woven there. I left her in the spell of a delirious dream, cursing myself for having broken my vow of chastity: a renewable vow, yes, but also less sacred than my resolution to pour all my bodily juices into my art. To perfect that art, I have dedicated myself all these years.

I often went out into the countryside searching for faces, landscapes, buildings, and perspectives that I sketched in charcoal and guarded jealously, later incorporating these details of everyday reality into the figures and spaces of the great painting I was secretly creating in a deep dungeon of the new palace El Señor was constructing to commemorate his victory over the dukes and heretics of the vicious province of Flanders. Thus one morning, as I was wandering through the fields of Montiel, I happened to meet a cart being driven by a blond youth by whose side was seated a green-eyed, sun-burned blind man playing a flute. I asked permission of the blind man to sketch his features. He acceded with an ironic smile. The youth was grateful for the rest; he went to a nearby well, drew a bucket of water, disrobed, and bathed himself. I turned from my preoccupation with the blind man, who could not see me, and gazed at the splendid beauty of the youth, so like the perfect figures rendered by Phidias and Praxiteles. Then, with amazement bordering on horror, I noticed the sign upon his back: a blood-red cross between the shoulder blades; and as I looked at his naked feet, I knew I would count six toes upon each foot.

I controlled my trembling hand. I bit my tongue not to tell the blind man what I knew: the youth was the son of my Señora, the brother of our present Señor, the bastard disappeared on the night when wedding and crime were allied; I told him, rather, that I was a friar and painter of the court, in the service of the most exalted Prince Don Felipe, and then it was he who became perturbed, his expression alternately revealing the desire to flee and the need to know. I asked him what he was hauling in his cart beneath the heavy canvas. He reached out a hand, as if to protect his cargo, and said: "Touch nothing, Friar, or the youth will break your bones on the spot."

"Have no fear. Where are you going?"

"To the coast."

"The coast is long, and touches many seas."

"You are good at prying, Friar. Does your master pay you well to go as talebearer throughout his kingdom?"

"I take advantage of his protection and attend secretly to my vocation, which is not that of informer, but artist."

"And what kind of art would yours be?"

I deliberated for a moment. I wished to gain the confidence of the blind man who was accompanying the lost son of my Señora. I did not, however, tell him what I knew. I tried to tie up loose ends: in some manner this man was involved with the child's disappearance; perhaps he had received him from other hands, but perhaps he himself had stolen him that night from the bloody castle; and who had disappeared at the same time as the child? Felipe's companions: Celestina and Ludovico. I knew the rebellious student; I could not recognize him in the blind man. I took the risk, not knowing whether I would be rewarded with the blind man's good faith or a drubbing from his young companion; I took a stab in the dark.

"An art," I answered him, "similar to your ideas, for I conceive of it as a direct approximation of God to man, a revelation of the grace inherent in every man, man who is born without sin and thus obtains grace immediately without the intercession of the agencies of oppression. Your ideas incarnate in my painting, Ludovico."

The blind man almost opened his eyes; I swear, friend Chronicler, that a ray of strange hope flashed across his obstinately closed eyelids; I pressed his coppery hand in my pale one; the youth dropped the bucket back into the well and approached, naked and drying himself with his own clothing.

"My name is Julián. You can rely on me."

When I returned to the palace, I found my Señora upset from a dream she had just experienced. I asked her to tell it to me, and she did so. Feigning stupor, I replied that I had dreamed the same, dreamed of a young castaway tossed on a beach. Where? My dream, I told her, had a site: the coast of the Cabo de los Desastres. Why? The place of my dream, I said, had a history: the chronicles abound in notices of varinels sunk there with their treasures from the Spice Islands, Cipango, and Cathay, of vessels that had disappeared with all the Cádiz crew and all their captives of the war against the Infidel aboard. But also, as if in compensation, they tell of sailing ships broken upon the rocks because lovers were fleeing in them.

She asked me: "What is the name of this youth of whom we both have dreamed?"

I replied: "It depends upon what land he treads."

La Señora reached out to me: "Friar, take me to that beach, take me to that youth . . ."

"Patience, Señora. We must wait two years nine months and two weeks, which are a thousand and one half days; the time it will take your husband to finish his necropolis of Princes."

"Why, Friar?"

"Because this youth is life's answer to the will-for-death of our Señor, the King."

"How do friars know these things?"

"Because we have dreamed them, Señora."

"You lie. You know more than you are telling me."

"But if I told her everything, La Señora would cease to have confidence in me. I do not betray La Señora's secrets. She must not insist that I betray mine."

"It is true, Friar. You would cease to interest me. Do what you have promised. At the end of a thousand and one half days, bring that youth to me. And if you do so, Brother Julián, you will have pleasure."

I lie, my friend. I did not answer her saying, "That is all a contrite and devout soul could ask"; no, I did not wish to be my Señora's lover; I did not want to waste in her bed the vigor and vigilance I must devote to my painting; and I feared this woman, I was beginning to fear her; how could she have dreamed what had happened between Ludovico and me when the blind man told me he was going to the Cabo de los Desastres, the beach where more than sixteen years before he and Celestina, Felipe, Pedro, and the monk Simón had met, and that this time Pedro's ship would sail in search of the new world beyond the great ocean, and that the youth with the cross upon his back would embark upon it and on a precise day, a thousand and one half days later, on the morning of a fourteenth of July, he would return to the same beach, and that then he could go with me, travel to the palace of Don Felipe, El Señor, and there fulfill his second destiny, that of his origins, as in the new world he would have fulfilled his first destiny, that of his future? I was confused by these explanations; the place and the time, on the other hand, were engraved in my mind; I would then see some way my mistress could recover her lost son. But Ludovico added one condition to our pact: that I find a way to advise Celestina that on the same day she should pass by that beach. Celestina? The blind man knew what Simón had told him when, he said, the blind man had returned to Spain: disguised as a page, she was playing a funeral drum in the procession of the Mad Lady, Don Felipe's mother, who bore throughout Spain the embalmed cadaver of her impenitent husband, refusing to bury him. It was not difficult for me to send a message to the page of the lunatic Queen.

But my Señora, I tell you, frightened me: how did she dream that dream?, was it the potions of belladonna I had administered to calm her delirium?, the recollections of some drawing of mine of real or imagined castaways?, was it the presence in her bedchamber of a furtive Mus I saw moving at times among her bedsheets, hiding, watching us?, was it a white and knotted root like a tiny human figure, almost a little man, I occasionally saw move with stealth among the hangings of the bedchamber?, was it a Satanic pact, something of which I was unaware and that caused me to tremble as I entered my mistress's bedchamber, some horrible secret that damaged and hindered the causes of my art as well as the beliefs of my religion?, and was it not my purpose, candid friend who hears me, to conciliate once again reason and faith through art, to return to human intelligence and divine conviction the unity threatened by separation?, for it was, and is, my belief that religion warring against reason becomes the facile prey of the Devil.

In order to rid myself of this increasing fear of the demonic, and also to rid myself of the increasing sexual appetite of La Señora, I searched for gracile youths that I might lead in secret to her bedchamber; I became, I confess, a vile go-between, as much a procurer as that hymenmending magpie of Valladolid; and in one thing, worse, for these youths led to her bedchamber never left there alive, or if they did, they disappeared forever and no one ever heard of them again; some were found, white and bloodless, in the passageways of the palace and in forgotten dungeons; of others, a very few, I came to know this: one died on the gallows, one on the pillory, another was garroted. I feared more and more for the health of my protectress's mind; I must channel her passions in a manner beneficial to my own desires, and also convincing to hers—whatever they might be. I searched through *aljamas* and Jewries in Toledo and Seville, in Cuenca and Medina. I was searching for someone in particular. I found him. I brought him to the uncompleted palace.

In lands of ancient Castilian Christianity he was called Miguel. In the Jewries he was called Michah. And in the *aljamas* he was known as Mihail-ben-Sama, which in Arabic means Miguel-of-Life. Your husband El Señor, I said, has exhausted his life in the mortal persecution of heretics, Moors, and Jews, and those three bloods and those three religions flow through Miguel's veins; he is a son of Rome, of Israel, and of Araby. Renew the blood, Señora. Enough of this attempt to deceive your subjects; the familiar public announcement of your pregnancy, hoping to attenuate the expectations of an heir, merely forces you to pretense: you must stuff your fathingale with pillows and imitate a condition that is not yours; then follows the equally familiar announcement of a miscarriage. Frustrated hopes are often converted into irritation, if not open rebellion. You must be cautious. Allay their discontent with one theatrical blow: fulfill their hopes by having a son. You may rely on me: the only proof of paternity will be the features of El Señor, your husband, that I introduce upon the seals, miniatures, medallions, and portraits that will be the representation of your son for the multitudes and for posterity. The populace—and history—will know the face of your son only through coins bearing the effigy I have designed that are minted and circulated in these kingdoms. No one will ever have occasion to compare the engraved image with the real face. Combine, Señora, pleasure and duty: provide Spain with an heir.

Conveniently deaf, Chronicler, I did not hear—I swear it, I did not hear—La Señora's answer to my arguments: "But, Julián, I already have a son . . ."

She said it serenely, but there is no worse madness than serene madness; I tell you I did not hear her; I continued; I said: Recover the true unity of Spain: regard this young man, Mihail-ben-Sama, Miguel-of-Life, a Castilian, Moorish, and Hebrew Miguel; I swear to you, Chronicler, do not look at me in that way, that is when I said this to La Señora, I did not say it later, when I took her own son to her, the youth found on the Cabo de los Desastres, when I told you this, I lied, I accept my lie, yes, because I did not know then how this story was going to end, I believed I would never reveal my greatest secret to anyone, I thought today, as I began to speak to you, that the worst secret would be any secret at all, for example, when El Señor told me what he saw in his mirror as he ascended the thirty steps, I said to myself, this will be the secret, the father of El Señor fornicated with a she-wolf, but that she-wolf was none other than an ancient Queen dead for centuries, the one who stitched flags the color of her blood and her tears, a restless soul resurrected in the body of a she-wolf, it was natural that another child should be born of her belly, blood calls to blood, degenerates seek out one another and copulate and procreate: three sons of the Señor called the Fair, three bastards, three usurpers, Felipe's three brothers, is it not enough you know this secret?, is your curiosity not satiated?, I wished to be honest with you, to win your forgiveness, do not now accuse me of something so frightful, I asked La Señora to have a child by Mihail-ben-Sama, you, you were the true culprit, you, a Chronicler made bitter and desperate because your papers are not identical to life, as you would wish, you interrupted my project with your idiotic poem, you removed Mihail from life and placed him within literature, you wove with paper the rope that was to bind you to the galley, indiscreet and candid friend, you sent Mihail to the stake, do you not remember?, you shared a cell with him the night before your exile and his death, how could I have been the iniquitous procurer who delivered a son to the carnal love of his mother?, how was I to know that was what La Señora desired?, she recognized him, yes, she recognized him, the cross, the toes, I believed I was compassionately reuniting a mother and a son, she knew who he was, she knew she was fornicating with her own son, she knew it, and she screamed her pleasure of him, I knew it, and I lamented it with prayers and breast beating: blood calls to blood, the son born of incest has closed the perfect circle of his origin: transgression of moral law; Cain slew Abel, Set, Osiris, Smoking Mirror killed the Plumed Serpent, Romulus, Remus, and Pollux, son of Zeus, rejected immortality at the death of his brother Castor, son of a swan: sons of a witch, sons of a she-wolf, sons of a Queen, these were three, they did not kill one another, their number saved them, but there is no order that is not founded upon crime, if not of blood, then of the flesh: poor Iohannes Agrippa, called Don Juan, it fell to you, in the name of the three brothers, to transgress in order to found anew: not Set, not Cain, not Romulus, not Pollux, your destiny, Don Juan is that of Oedipus: the shadow that walks toward its end by walking toward its origin: the future will respond to the enigmas of the past only because that future is identical to the beginning; tragedy is the restoration of the dawn of being: monarch and prisoner, culprit and innocent, criminal and victim, the shadow of Don Juan is the shadow of Don Felipe: in her son, Don Juan, La Señora knew the flesh of her husband Don Felipe: only thus, Chronicler, only in this way; candid friend of marvels, soul of wax, hear me, I believed I was returning her lost son to her, but instead she recovered her true lover, you are to blame, foolish friend, not I, not I, such was not my intent, I swear it, forgive me, I forgive you, events acquire a life of their own, they escape our hands, I did not propose such a horrible infraction of divine and human laws, you frustrated my project with your literature, now you know the truth, you must now alter all the words and all the intent of this long narration, revise now what I have told you, Chronicler, and try to discover the lie, the deception, the fiction, yes, the fiction, in each phrase, doubt now everything I have told you, what will you do to collate my subjective words with objective truth?, what?, you sent Miguel-of-Life to the stake, and you condemned me to be an accomplice to an incestuous transgression: see the fires of the stake upon every page you fill, Chronicler Don Miguel, see the blood of incest in every word you write: you desired the truth, now save it with the lie . . .

"Señor, this great painting has been sent to you from Orvieto, fatherland of a few somber, austere, and energetic painters. You are the Defender of the Faith. They offer it in homage to you and to the Faith. See its great dimensions. I have measured them. They will fit perfectly within the empty space behind the altar in your chapel.''

SOUL OF WAX

Brother Julián embarked on one of Guzmán's caravels that yesterday set sail from the port of Cádiz; I remained here alone in the astronomer's tower with my pens, paper, and ink. I say alone, because Toribio was working feverishly, as if very little time remained and as if the well-being of the world depended upon his tasks; he paid little attention to my presence. I was grateful for this situation. I could finish the narration begun by Julián. I would be the phantom of King Don Felipe, the wax whereupon were imprinted the footprints of his soul, to the very end. I wanted to be a faithful witness. But from the moment I sat down to write the final section of this hadith, my imagination intruded to divert the worthwhile purposes of my chronicle. First I wrote these words: "Everything is possible." Next, beside them, these: "Everything is in doubt." Thus I knew, by the mere fact of writing them, that I was writing on the threshold of a new era. I longed for the certitude inculcated in me during my fleeting passage through the halls of Salamanca. Words and things coincide: all reading is, in the end, but the reading of the divine word, for, in an ascending scale, everything finally flows into one identical being and word: God, the first, the efficient, the final, and the restorative cause of everything that exists. In this manner the vision of the world is unique: all words and all things possess an established place, a precise function, and an exact correspondence within the Christian universe. All words signify what they contain and contain what they signify. I thought then about the knight Ludovico and his sons had met in the windmill and I began to write the story of a hidalgo from La Mancha who continued to adhere to the codes of certainty. For him, nothing would be in doubt, but everything would be possible: a knight of the faith. That faith, I said to myself, would originate in reading. And that reading would be madness. The knight would persist in the unique reading of the texts and would attempt to transmit that reading to a reality that had become multiple, equivocal, and ambiguous. He would fail time and again, but every time he would again take refuge in reading: born of reading, he would remain faithful to it because for him there was no other licit reading: the sorcerers he knew through reading, and not reality, would continue to interpose themselves between his undertakings and reality.

I paused at this point and decided, audaciously, to introduce a great novelty into my book: this hero of mockery and hoax, born of reading, would be the first hero, furthermore, to know he was read. At the very time he was living his adventures, they would be written, published, and read by others. A double victim of reading, the knight would twice lose his senses: first, as he read; second, upon being read. The hero who knew he was read: Achilles knew no such experience. And this obliges him to create himself within his own imagination. He fails, then, as a reader of the epics he obsessively wishes to transmit to reality. But as object of reading, he begins to conquer reality, to infect it with his insane reading of himself. And this new reading transforms the world, which begins more and more to resemble the world wherein are narrated the knight's adventures. The world disguises itself: the enchanted knight ends by enchanting the world. But the price he must pay is the loss of his own enchantment. He recovers his reason. And this, for him, is the supreme madness; it is suicide; reality delivers him to death. The knight will continue to live only in the book that recounts his story; there will be no other recourse to prove his own existence, it will not be found in the unique reading life gave him, but in the multiple readings life took from him in reality, but granted him forever in the book . . . only in the book. I shall create an open book where the reader will know he is read and the author will know he is written.

Founded upon these principles, reader, I wrote both this chronicle faithful to the last years of his reign, and the life of Don Felipe, El Señor. Thus I fulfilled the fearful charge of the one who had until now narrated this story, Brother Julián, now embarked upon a caravel in the hope of finding beyond the unknown ocean a new world that would truly be a New Spain. I shall suffer and burn the midnight oil. My only hand will tire, but my soul will be illuminated.

CORPUS

Where is everyone?

He dedicated his days to wandering tirelessly through all parts of his palace, attempting, in vain, to hear again the persistent—unnoticed because it was accustomed—sound of picks and bellows, hammers and chisels and cartwheels. But following the torture of Nuño and Jerónimo before the noonday-lighted façade of the palace, a great silence fell over the work site, as if the hand of God had placed over it a large inverted goblet, covering the entire space of the construction, and thus imposing a divine truce.

That day, after the storm and after the death of the workmen, he walked through one of the three doors of the north wall of the palace, which, because it faced the north wind, lacked windows; he gazed for the last time upon the external walls of the palace, the mass of the granite, the tall towers on every corner. Temple of Victory. City of the Dead. Eighth Wonder of the World. He avoided the door leading to the kitchens and also that leading to La Señora's quarters: both evoked bad memories. He chose the door leading to the palace courtyard; he admired for an instant the jamb, the lintel, architrave, and pilasters, the quality of workmanship of the entire door facing, its stone so carefully joined that the seams were invisible, with its columns that finished off, tied together, gave harmony to the door and the low plinth, fascia, and high cornice. He entered, and swore he would never go outside again.

"Where is everyone?"

The nuns were still there; the monks were still there; a minimal staff of kitchen and palace servants remained. The servants, unordered, devoted themselves to quietly preparing El Señor's meals and to attempting to clean his rooms, but as most of the savory dishes were almost always returned untouched to the kitchens, and as El Señor refused to allow them to change the black sheets on his bed, or touch a broom to his chamber, and as he himself never changed the black attire in which he had presided over the final ceremonies of death, the cooks, scullery lads, and chamber servants found very little to do, except what will be seen they did. El Señor ordered the monks to perform a perpetual service for the dead and said to them: "You have but one mission: to pray for the dead and to pray for me."

First he ordered that two friars be continuously before the Most Holy Sacrament of the altar, praying to God for his soul and the souls of his dead, day and night, in perpetual prayer. Then on the day of Corpus Christi, he ordered that thirty thousand Masses be offered for the repose of his soul. The friars were astounded, and one of them dared say to him: "But you still live, Sire . . ."

"Would you bear witness to that?" El Señor replied with a bitter smile, and he added that when the thirty thousand Masses were ended, a new series of equal number should be begun, and so on unto infinity, whether he lived or died.

The outspoken friar said: "You do violence to Heaven."

"I shall temper it with piety," El Señor responded, trembling, and added: "Yes, and may two thousand Masses be said for souls in Purgatory. And at the end of each Mass, say a response for my soul, and with this intent may the appropriate alms be distributed among the poor."

And to Madre Milagros he said: "Have your nuns watch over me. Let them frighten away fear."

"Our Inesilla is lost, Señor. That is what frightens us."

"One nun does not make a convent. Have you not replaced her?"

"Yes, other novitiates have arrived, Sor Prudencia, Sor Esperanza, Sor Caridad, Sor Ausencia . . ."

"I want no intruders. Let them howl like bitches when anyone approaches me, as they howled when they heard the barking and chains and horns of my faithful hound Bocanegra."

During those years, the nuns howled every time an increasingly ancient Mother Celestina came to visit El Señor to assure him that the feared usurper, the Idiot Prince, remained in bed with the dwarf Barbarica at the monastery of Verdín. The stubble-chinned old woman marveled at El Señor's solitude and poverty, shook her head and said things El Señor had decided to allow only her to say: "He who has little sense or judgment loves almost nothing except what he's missed. And you, Don Felipe, you feel great remorse for the years you lost. Would you return to the first age?"

He told himself he would not, and La Celestina told him that word was spreading of the alms distributed here following every Mass; the beggars of the kingdom, in growing numbers, were gathered at the palace gates, they surrounded the palace, they were appropriating the old huts of the workmen and the abandoned taverns and forges, awaiting the daily charity.

Then the old woman would leave and El Señor would sit for long hours in his curule chair beside the fireless hearth and recall the young bride ravished on the day of her wedding with the smith Jerónimo, the girl who accompanied him to the beach and there told her dream of a world free for love and the body, the lover with whom he and Ludovico had shared their nights in the bloody castle. Would they wish to return to the first age?

Occasionally in the late afternoon he ascertained that the couple bound together by sex in the prison of mirrors were still there, moaning, incapable of extricating themselves from one another, like street dogs, the juices of pleasure burned up, the lubricious orifices dried up, desiccated prick and withered cunt yoked together, both wounded—powerless ever to heal—by the ground glass Mother Celestina had introduced into Inés's sex and by the sharp fish's teeth she had set in the lips of Inés's restored virginity. Doña Inés and Don Juan moaned, the nun's face always covered by the coif of her habit, the cavalier cloaked always in his brocaded mantle. El Señor did not wish to see them. It was enough to know they were there, condemned to see themselves one day in what could be seen only when they tired of living with their eyes closed: their own images in a world consisting solely of mirrors.

Everyday, without opening the door of the cell, the servants passed a plate of dried beef beneath the door. They occupied themselves with this chore, and with delivering the leftovers of El Señor's meals to the beggars clustered beneath the tile sheds, who at the hour of the Angelus came to the kitchen door on the north façade to ask for charity. El

Señor never watched Inés and Juan eat. One night a servant dared say to him as he served him dinner in the bedchamber where dust mounted in the corners: "They snarl over the dried beef like beasts, master, and never reveal their faces; they're worse than the hungriest beggars we attend . . ."

El Señor asked the servant to be silent, and ordered that he be lashed for his impudence. It happened that this same night the nuns howled quietly, and a friar entered El Señor's chamber accompanied by an ancient gentleman of learned aspect who said he was Dr. Pedro del Agua; he looked at El Señor with an embalmer's eyes, and even asked in a low voice: "Will it be my fate to embalm both father and son?"

Is there a doctor in Spain who is not a Jew? And is there any Jewish doctor who is not a poisoner? Angrily, El Señor ordered the incautious friar to condemn Dr. del Agua before the Holy Office, and to prosecute him, and torture him, and force a confession from him, and since his name was Marrano, Filthy Pig, del Agua, he should be tortured by water until he burst. And he ordered that from that time nothing should be communicated to him aloud, but only in writing, only in writing, always.

"Only what is written is real. Wind carries away words as easily as it brings them. Only the written remains. I shall believe in my life only if I read it. I shall believe in my death only if I read it."

And thus, after a few day's time, a different friar brought El Señor a document and El Señor read it. It related therein the suffering of the Jews expelled from his kingdom, and this chronicle was signed by an Andrés Bernáldez, priest of Los Palacios; the Jews could not sell their possessions in exchange for gold or silver, as the exportation of these metals was forbidden, thus they have sold houses, properties, and everything they possessed for the pittance pure Christians wished to pay them, they wandered about with them, begging, and finding no one who would buy them; they gave a house for an ass, a vineyard for a little cloth, and then fled Spain in cramped and badly captained ships, and many drowned in storms, and others reached the north of Africa only to become victims of pillage and murder, the Turks killing many of them to steal the gold they had swallowed hoping in this fashion to conceal it, others perished from hunger and epidemics, and there were those who were abandoned naked on islands by their captains; some were sold in Genoa and its villages as men- and maidservants and some were thrown into the sea; staggering, the most fortunate had reached the cities in the north of Europe, Amsterdam and Lübeck and London, and there have been given refuge and accepted in their offices as money-changers, contractors, jewelers, and philosophers . . .

At first El Señor savored the reading of this chronicle, giving thanks that his land was being rid of those who, denying the divinity of Christ, threatened El Señor's personal well-being and solitude. But then he was struck by diarrhea like a hare's or nanny goat's that kept him bed-fast for a week. He persisted, nevertheless, in his decision to heed only what was communicated to him in writing, and to speak only with the ancient Celestina, when she came to visit him, or with his mother, the one called the Mad Lady, when he himself approached the walled-up niche in his chapel.

"What are you doing, Mother?"

Through the opening at the level of the mutilated Queen's yellow eyes, he heard her muted, ancient voice: "I was remembering, my son, when you were a little boy and used to sit at my feet, or upon my knees, during the long winter nights beside the fire in the chimney hearth in our old castle, while I educated you to be a true Prince, re-peating to you the rules every good preceptor inculcates in legitimate heirs. I told you then, son, that it befits no one more than a Prince to have much and good knowledge, but this knowledge must be useful and employed toward heroic and praiseworthy ends. The bee does not settle upon every flower, nor from those from which she sucks does she take more than she has need of to fabricate her honeycombs. The eru-dite Prince need not know everything, but neither may he ignore any of the things leading to the designs of his birth. Thus let it be said of you, my darling son: that you knew everything you should, but that you studied nothing you need not have known. How young I was then, and beautiful, and whole, and you were so small and blond and attentive in your high ermine collar, your pale, delicate hands resting upon my knees, so serious, listening to me: it is not sufficient, my son, that you confess and take Communion every month, but, knowing that in the use of the Holy Sacraments lies your best defense, you must habituate yourself, first, to confessing every two weeks, then every week, and then every day; and do not content yourself with confessing only the sins you have committed since your last Communion, but every day confess first the last ten years of your life, then twenty, then thirty, un-til you are accustomed to confessing your entire life every day. And in order to do this with greater purity, you must not only most forcefully forbid yourself all that is illicit, but even be moderate in the honorable portion of your life, keeping your fasts, even though your physician counsel you differently, suffering your labors with patience, and sur-mounting your passions, for he who is not mortified can never be a Christian Prince. Let your virtue shine forth, oh, my son, my Prince, in the delights of bodily purity, and let it be said of you that you were like the pearl that never leaves its shell except to receive the dew from Heaven: never betray the limits of this virtue, not even in the strict law of most chaste matrimony. This will be a rare marvel in a depraved century! In a perfect body! In a young sovereign! And in a palace filled with adulation, and the delights of the world. For let the fables say what they will of their chaste deities; the poets lie when they say that

Hercules destroyed serpents in his cradle, but here we shall say with all truth, and in all simplicity, that a young King choked within his palace all the serpents of his appetites. Oh, what a great victory! Let the Phoenix make its nest amid heavy perfumes in the high mountains of Araby, that is well and good; but that the Ermine be not stained in the black vapors of Babylon is cause for admiration. The admiration of others, my son: power is appearance, honor is appearance, the Spanish knight and Prince are what they appear to be, for appearance is reality, and reality a fleeting illusion. That a King confined within his bedchamber, penitent, austere, contemplative, may keep himself clean and pure, I can easily understand; but that a King caressed by all delights, feted with music, flattered with entertainments and feasts and a thousand incentives for pleasure, keep himself always so temperate; truly, that has all the signs of a miracle. God placed Adam in Paradise; and here observes St. Augustine: who must guard whom?, Paradise, Adam?, or Adam, Paradise? Answer this question today, my little son, and if you ask me, what are you doing, Mother?, where are you?, I shall tell you I am with you, I, young, and you a child, more than forty years ago, inculcating in you the education of a Prince, asking you to be what your father, my husband, the fair, never was, always looking to your salvation, son, inciting you to chastity, pleading with you never to succumb, never to touch any woman, not even your wife, or to know anything it was not fitting to know, and that you devote yourself to mortification, for I would charge myself with procuring for you an heir who would not lead us to extinction but guide us back to our origins, thus perpetuating our breed. I have fulfilled my part, little Felipe, you have an heir without having stained your body; you would not be like your father who caused me such great suffering, you would be for me what your father never was, chaste, mortified, and prudent; and what you were not, another would be in your name, the heir I rescued from the poking and pinching and sticks of a mob of beggars so that he would do what you would never have to do. Have you deserved, my son, the name of Prince? That I am: I am a young and beautiful Queen, saved by the honor and esteem of her son: you. My name is Juana.''

In the solitude of his dust-filled bedchamber of black sheets, black tapestries, black crucifix, and high narrow window, El Señor pondered his mother's words. Seated there, he was pleasured by a summer's day, the last summer's day he had lived. He knew he would never again see such a day. It would be eternal winter in this solitude. He looked from time to time toward the nuns' choir. Encarnación, Dolores, Esperanza, Caridad, Angustias, Clemencia, Milagros, Ausencia, Soledad: he, Felipe, a recluse among women, seated in eternal penumbra.

On that last summer's day of his life he had ridden through the flowering land of his childhood. He had ridden out to hunt. Guzmán had

prepared everything. His faithful Bocanegra accompanied him. It
rained. He took refuge in his tent and read his breviary. Bocanegra ran
out of the tent. It stopped raining. Everyone gathered around the felled
stag. He was to give the order for the final ceremony: that the horns
sound, the stag be quartered, the hounds be baited, and the prizes and
punishments of the day be allotted. He raised his hand to give the order. But before he gave it, everything happened as if he had already
acted. The culminating moment of the hunt proceeded as if El Señor's
order had been given. As if his most perfect presence were absence itself.

"Where is everyone?"

Who was giving orders in his name? Who was governing in his
stead?, or was it that everything was happening—as it had that night
on the mountain—through inertia, without El Señor's having signed
papers, or ordered or forbidden or rewarded or castigated.

He walked through the courtyards, passed through doors, fatigued
vestibules, wandered through the small cloisters of the convent, the
great square that served as a locutory, with its pilasters of granitic
stone, he passed beneath lunettes of melancholy windows, past walnut
benches with back rests, through the upper level of the convent with its
long walls and cloisters traversed and crisscrossed by a multitude of
arches, beneath the carved ceilings of the storeroom, until he entered a
vast gallery he had never seen before, two hundred feet long and thirty
feet high, the fronts, sides, and domed ceiling covered by painting,
columns embedded in the walls embellished with fascia, jambs, lintels, and railings in a row, in the manner of balconies, the ceiling and
the dome with grotesque and elaborate plaster ornamentation, a thousand variations on real and fictional figures, plaster medallions and
niches, pedestals, men, women, children, monsters, birds, horses,
fruits and flowers, draperies and festoons, and a hundred other bizarre
inventions, and at the rear of the great hall stood a Gothic throne of
carved stone, and seated upon it a man, he tried to recognize him, the
high, starched ruff, damask doublet, tightly laced shoes, one leg shorter than the other, stiff torso, pale, grayish face, drowsy, stupid eyes
with the gaze of an inoffensive saurian, half-open mouth, the lower lip
thick and drooping, heavy prognathic jaw, sparse eyebrows, long wig
of black, oily curls, and crowning the head a bloody white pigeon, the
blood ran down this King's face, yes, this secret monarch who stiffly
raised one arm, and then the other, and governed in his name, now he
knew, now he understood . . . the royal mummy fabricated by La
Señora, the specter of all his ancestors, seated upon this throne and
crowned by a dove, thank you, thank you, Isabel, I am indebted to
you, this phantom governs for me, I can devote myself to the greatest
undertaking: my soul's well-being . . .

Another crown, this one of gold encrusted with sapphire, pearl, agate, and rock crystal, lay on the floor at the feet of the mummy, of this animated corpse that did not stare at him any more intently than he, trembling, stared at it.

Impulsively, he picked up the Gothic crown and fled from the gallery, not hearing the titters of the homunculus hidden behind the throne, and walked hurriedly through mournful passageways, unfinished gardens, secret stairways, tombstones of dark marble, avoiding the chapel and the ceremonies of that Holy Day of Corpus Christi, until he reached the chamber of his wife Isabel, he had seen the mummy there, lying on her bed, he entered: there was nothing there now except the white sand floors, a warm June breeze drifted through the window from which La Señora had ordered the costly windowpanes removed and packed, the shiny tiles of the Arabic bath had been torn out, the bed collapsed. In her absence, Isabel's chamber had begun to resemble El Señor's; hasty abandon, passing glory.

Something glittered, half buried in the sands of the floor.

El Señor walked to it, stooped over, and withdrew a green bottle from its tomb of sand.

He broke the bottle's red seal.

The bottle contained a manuscript.

With difficulty he extracted the manuscript. It was ancient parchment, its stained leaves stuck to one another, and it was written in Latin.

He sat upon the sand, and this is what he read.

MANUSCRIPT OF A STOIC

I

I am writing in the last year of the reign of Tiberius. The Empire inherited from Augustus still maintains its maximum and magnificent extension. From the central navel of its foundation by the sons of the she-wolf, its possessions extend, in great universal arcs, to the north, the Frisian Islands and Batavia, through all Gaul, conquered by Caesar, and to the south and west, from the Pyrenees to the Tagus through the lands where Scipio availed himself of three Lusitanians to murder the rebellious Viriathus and then, everything once having been founded upon revolt, blood, and betrayal, it was necessary to found it all a second time in Numantia, upon the honor of heroic failure: Numantia, where, before surrendering, the Iberians set fire to their homes, killed their women, burned their children, poisoned themselves, thrust daggers into their breasts, cut the hocks of their horses, and those who remained alive after this immolation threw themselves from their towers upon the Romans, lances pointed, trusting that as they crashed to the ground and died they would take with them, impaled, an invader.

All the lands embraced to the east of the Rhone and south of the Danube, from Vienna to Thrace, are Roman; Byzantium, the Bosporus, Anatolia, Cappadocia, Cilicia, and the great crescent that sweeps from Antioch to Carthage are Roman; hers is the Mare Nostrum: Rhodes, Cyprus, Greece, Sicily, Sardinia, Corsica, and the Balearic Islands. The world is one and Rome is the head of that world. Rome is the world, even when its most ambitious citizens temper this truth with glances directed toward what remains to be conquered: Mauritania, Arabia, the Persian Gulf, Mesopotamia, Armenia, Dacia, the Britannic isles . . . Nevertheless, we can say with pride, along with our great founding poet: Romans, masters of the world, a togaed nation.

Like falcons, descend, reader, from this high firmament that permits us to admire the unity and extension of the Empire, to the place where dwells Tiberius, Master of Rome.

Until recently, we narrators could begin our chronicles with this notice: Listen, reader, and you shall have delight. I do not know whether this be my case; I ask forgiveness beforehand as I lead you to Capri, a craggy island of goats anchored in the gulf of Naples, accessible only by one small beach, surrounded by bottomless waters, and defended by sheer cliffs. On its summit: the Imperial Villa, the most inaccessible spot on this small, barren, and impregnable island.

And, nevertheless, this afternoon a poor fisherman who has had the good fortune to catch an enormous mullet does ascend laboriously, though sure-footedly, for from the time he was a child he has competed with the other lads of the island to see who can most rapidly scale the vertical rock formations; he sweats, he pants, his legs are scratched, and with a single hand, in moments of danger, he clings to the sharp yellow rocks; his other arm clutches to his breast the fish with the silver belly and eyes (both in life and in death) half covered by transparent membranes. Night is falling, but the fisherman does not falter in his keen determination to reach the summit where dwells Tiberius Caesar; night is falling but in the enormous eyes of Tiberius Caesar there is no fear, for we all know that he can see in the dark.

At night, he sees by thrusting forward his stout, stiff neck; by day, he shuns the sun, even inside the Imperial Villa wearing a wide-brimmed hat to protect himself from the glare of the sun. Now he has discarded the hat, and as the sky grows dark, he asks his counselor Theodorus to place upon his head a crown of laurel leaves; it is only night, night naturally descending upon us, Theodorus says to Caesar; one never knows, Tiberius replies, the sky grows dark, it may be night, but it may be a storm approaching, crown me with laurel so lightning can never touch me, and make sure, Theodorus, that when I die they bury me more than five feet in the ground, where lightning cannot penetrate and commit my manes to the ignipotent god Vulcan, whom I most fear.

Caesar sits silently in the darkness and listens to the dripping of the water clock that marks time; a time of water; and then, brusquely, he seizes the wrist of his patient counselor who had acquired in the East— and never renounced—the customs of his attire and personal appearance: linen tunic, sandals of palm fiber, and shaved head. Theodorus: this afternoon as I was sleeping my siesta I dreamed again, the phantom returned; who, Caesar?; Agrippa, Theodorus, Agrippa, it was he, I recognized him; that poor youth is dead, Caesar, you know it better than anyone; but not because of me, is that not true, Theodorus, not through any fault of mine?, be frank with me, only in you will I tolerate frankness, you are the son of my rhetoric master, Teselius of Gandara, you can tell me, without fear of retribution, what others, if they spoke, would pay for with their lives . . .

"Caesar; your stepfather, the Emperor Augustus, told you once that it does not matter that others speak evil of us; it is sufficient that we prevent their doing evil; I, Caesar, if I speak evil, I do you good; in what other way would you hear the complaints, rumors, ire, and sorrow of your Empire?"

"I do not care to know what is said; rather, I wish to act against the complainers, the rumor-mongers, the wrathful and sorrowful; make that distinction; and do you never fear, Theodorus, that one day my fury will turn against you, will attribute to you the crimes you inform me of, the opinions you transmit to me?"

The counselor bowed slightly, and Tiberius caught the silvery gleam of his shaved head in the darkness. "Caesar, I run that risk . . . Shall I order the torches to be lighted?"

"I can see at night. Furthermore, I prefer to hear you and not see you. I shall close my eyes. It will be as if I were speaking to myself. I have forgotten how to do that, and that is why I have need of you. But I cannot speak to, or touch, or hear that phantom that visits me every afternoon. It appears at the foot of the triclinium where I have lunched, and later napped, and smiles at me, merely smiles at me . . ."

The counselor looks around the bedchamber. He does not know whether the masks that adorn it are smiling: they are Tiberius's ancestors.

"Since you wish to hear the truth in order that your spirit be calmed, I shall tell you, Caesar, that the first act of your reign was the murder of that poor youth who now appears to you in dreams. Agrippa Postumus, the legitimate grandson of Augustus, his blood heir . . ."

When he speaks, Tiberius always nervously drums his fingers.

"While I am but the son of Augustus's wife, is that not what you mean? But Augustus chose me; dying, he called me to his bedside and told me, you will be Emperor, you, not that idiotic, gross, physically strong but mentally weak, handsome but imbecilic youth, it will be you, it will not be he . . . You will be Caesar, Tiberius."

"The people believe otherwise."

"What do they believe? Tell me, do not be afraid."

"That you took care not to reveal the death of Augustus until you had murdered his true heir, Agrippa Postumus; that the corpse of Augustus was closeted away, hidden, rotting, while you ordered Agrippa to be murdered."

"Augustus Caesar left a letter . . ."

"The people say that Livia, your mother, wrote in the name of Augustus, her husband, to clear the way for you, the stepson, condemning the young Agrippa, the grandson, to exile . . ."

"The youth was murdered by the Tribune of the soldiers."

"The Tribune said that you gave the order."

"But I denied it and ordered the Tribune killed for slandering me . . . for slandering the new Caesar, accepted by the Senate and by the Legions . . . Are these legitimizations not sufficient?"

"In any case, the Agrippa Postumus who died, murdered in his exile on the island of Planasia, and who appears to you every afternoon in your dreams, is merely a specter. Although I believe, Caesar, that no one, not even a phantom, could reach this place; you have chosen your refuge well; the island is a natural fortress."

Then Caesar screams, raises one arm, points a trembling finger, and Theodorus, the son of a rhetoric master, attempts with narrowed eyes to penetrate the darkness that is so familiar to his master; the phantom!, it has returned, this time by night, there!, it entered by that balcony, behind that curtain, light the torch, Theodorus! shouts Tiberius, a coarse, trembling man with enormous eyes and a neck like a bull: as the counselor lights the oakum torch he hears the murmur of a humble and frightened voice: "Caesar . . . the most modest man of this island begs you to accept our hospitality . . ."

The torchlight reveals a mature man, head bowed, a sparse beard, uncombed hair, and dirty fingernails, wearing only a loincloth; his feet are bleeding, his chest and arms gleaming with sweat; the fish he had clamped against his breast, he now holds out in offering to the Emperor.

"Who are you? How did you reach here?"

"I am a fisherman; I offer you the best of my humble hospitality; the fruit of the sea, this beautiful mullet, Caesar, see how large it is, how gray its side, how silver its belly, and how beautiful its fins . . ."

"Then anyone at all could come here . . ."

"Since I was a boy, Caesar, I . . ."

"And you could lead anyone here . . ."

"I do not understand; my fathers taught me that it is proper that the humble offer hospitality to the powerful, and that they, without in any way diminishing their greatness, accept it . . ."

"Innocent; you have shown the way to phantoms."

At Caesar's screams a great number of servants burst into the room; they carry torches, lamps, wax tapers, candles; only after the servants have entered, the guards rush in and take the fisherman prisoner—both the guard and the fisherman are trembling; Caesar, also trembling, is muttering that anyone at all can come here, even a miserable fisherman, even a phantom, the phantom that pursues him every afternoon and now sends messengers by night with poisoned fish; no, Caesar, I swear to you, I caught this fish this very afternoon, it is the largest mullet that has ever been taken from these waters, it seemed to me that I would sin through pride if I kept it for myself and my poor family, it is my homage, Caesar, it is the custom of hospitality; the other fishermen say that Agrippa is not dead, that he has been seen on other islands, on Planasia and on Closa, and that soon he will land here with his army of slaves to reclaim the inheritance of his grandfather, Caesar Augustus, they say he is young and blond, and he appears only at night and never twice in the same place: Agrippa Postumus; I argued with my companions, Caesar, I told them you were the Emperor and that with my fish I would offer to you the hospitality of Capri so that your dreams would be tranquil, and mine also; we wish peace, Caesar, my father died in the civil wars fighting against Cassius and Brutus, I wish only to fish in peace, and honor Caesar . . ."

"Imbecile," says Tiberius, "you have but doubled my nightmares. Guards, smear the mullet in this brute's face, rub its snout and teeth in his face; and now what do you say, imbecile?, will you again dare scale those cliffs behind my palace and make me believe that anyone, even the phantom of Agrippa, can do what you have done?, what do you say?"

"I say, Caesar, that all is well and that I give thanks for having caught a soft-fleshed mullet instead of bringing you a crab . . ."

And Tiberius laughs; he orders a man of his guard to bring a crab from the kitchen, and orders a servant to fetch the relief guard resting at this hour in the barracks, and orders them to scrub the face of the miserable fisherman with the crab until the man weeps, and bleeding and fearing to lose his sight is ejected from the palace.

"And from now on, believe in a usurping phantom," Tiberius yells to the air, to the fisherman, to Theodorus, and to himself; and then he orders a relief guard to take the men of the night watch who had not been able to prevent the passage of a wretched fisherman and who, also, had reached the imperial bedchamber after his own servants had arrived; surely they deceived him, they who comprised that watch were not true soldiers, but slaves freed in their master's wills, *orcivi* liberated by the grace of Orcus, god of death; such grace would be of short duration; let these cowards of the night watch be rewarded, give each man much to drink, and then bind his genitals so he cannot urinate, and so pass the night with his water strangulated and kidneys swollen, and only in the morning when he, Tiberius Caesar, can attend the spectacle, let each and every man of them be thrown into the sea from the heights of the cliff; and have a crew of sailors waiting below on the sea to break with gaffs and oars the bones of those who did not drown, and yes, even these; and let the relief guard look upon my justice.

The counselor Theodorus believes that parricides suffer a worse fate; beat with canes, they are stitched inside a leather bag with a dog, a cock, a monkey, and a serpent, and thrown into the sea.

"Theodorus: I had among my animals a serpent. One day I discovered it, devoured by ants. The augur warned me against the power of the multitudes."

"You do well to show caution, Caesar; you have already seen, you were opposed to attending the contest of the gladiators at Fidanae; the amphitheater collapsed and twenty thousand spectators died; you might have been one of them. Stay away from crowds, Caesar. Remember your ancestor, the second Claudia, whose wax mask hangs there beside the balcony."

"I shall do so. And you try to remember why you have not informed me of that legend now circulating . . ."

"Caesar; you ask so many things of me."

Tiberius claps his hands loudly; fetch my servants, disrobe me; lead me to the bath, bring my little fishes, prepare a feast, and merriment, girls, ephebes, let us forget fishermen and phantoms, let the fishermen return to the sea and phantoms to their ashes; farewell, fisherman, come, little fish . . ."

"Caesar, the rumor is widespread; this apparition is not, of course, the phantom of Agrippa, but the very real person of his slave Clemens, who has taken advantage of a rare physical resemblance, being of the same height and stature as his master, to spread the news that the heir is not dead. This notice is murmured secretly, in the manner of all forbidden stories, in the solitude of the night or under cloak of the similar protection of the multitudes at spectacles, for neither the night nor the mob possesses a discernible face; every fool with a ready ear listens to it; every subversive malcontent; Clemens shows himself only by night and never twice in the same place; who sees him or hears him once will not see him or hear him again, for the man is as swift and intangible as the rumor he disseminates. Publicity, joined to immobility, reveals truth too clearly, Caesar; imposture requires mystery and swift movement from one place to another. All Italy believes that Agrippa lives . . ."

"Agrippa is nothing but ashes; let Italy recognize them . . ."

"The slave Clemens stole them, Caesar."

"Why did you wait so long to tell me this? How do you wish me to be informed, if not by you? Must I wait for some idiot fisherman to climb up here to tell me?"

"Caesar: I have not wished to add fear to fears; of what import is an impersonation condemned to die out, whether by force of ridicule or the force of arms that can mercilessly crush that rabble of slaves? Let the rumor spend itself; no miracle lasts more than nine months; it tires; new marvels will out . . . Furthermore, Agrippa is not the first murdered heir. So too was Caesarion, the son of Julius Caesar and Cleopatra."

Enough; warm water, lustral water; how it soothes me, how it renews me; quickly, my little fish, my tender, docile children. Into the water, I seated and you swimming, swiftly, tenderly, between my legs, little fish, you bronzed and I pale, you slim and I soft, between my legs, little fish, until you find your golden fishhook, my weak flame, my aged, tired penis, my withered testicles, come, little fish; how fruitless, but how delicious, little fish, do not hold back, do not be impatient, it matters not, lick, suck, caress; enough. Theodorus, I am leaving the water, dry me, clothe me, the toga, the laurel, my cothurnus, let everything be prepared at the lunar sigma, my crescent couch, mullets and crabs and warm water to mix with the wine and the amphoras well sealed with plaster; have them bear me there, place me there, have my young nymphs come before me, my perverted youths; eat, drink, read the book of the poetess Elephantis wherein are described more than three hundred postures, one for each night of the year; you, Cynthia, and you, Gaius, and you, Lesbia, place your little tongue into Cynthia's beautiful shaved sex, and you, Cynthia, place between your lips the delicious, dripping penis of our Gaius, and you, Persius, mount Gaius, spread the taut wrinkles of his asshole, loosen with your saliva-moistened fingers the rectum of our ephebe and introduce your long, hard African prick, and you, Gaius, suck the shimmering nipples of our Cynthia, and my children, my little fish, approach, caress with your bronzed hands anything that is unengaged, Lesbia's buttocks, Persius's testicles, Gaius's armpits, and Cynthia's navel; and you, Fabianus, you masturbate, let your hand slide powerfully from the base of your penis to the scarlet head, so, so, let your weighty peaches feel the gentle energy of your hand, let us see the supple, pellucid skin stretched taut and glistening, bursting with blood and semen, I have always asked myself why we do not ejaculate blood, that would be a glorious sight, red blood and white toga, let your veins swell like pig's tripe, so, so, oh, now, shower them, bathe them in silvery milk, all of them, children and men and women, now separate yourselves, all of you, break the chain, drink the semen of our Fabianus, smear it between your breasts, between your legs, scoop it up on your fingers and drink that heavy wine through your anuses, let your bodies be covered with a crust of burning snow from our he-goat, our strong and hairy and handsome stud, so blond he is almost white, covered with red scars in the pit of his buttocks and on the tip of his cock and on his red, red, lips, beautiful red-tipped Fabianus, now, change position, do not come yet, weave a new garland, each of you, seek a different mouth, a different pubis, vagina, penis, testicles, anus, breasts, armpits, feet, navel, feast yourselves, naked, on Venus, struggle face to face, attack without fear and wound to the death, give no quarter, do not fear, there will be no offspring, there will be no fruit, the women are extirpated, the seed of the men is dead, your bodies are pure, washed, shaved, clean, lustral, full . . . enviable Priam Theodorus, who survived all his kin and left no offspring; he was the culmination of his breed, Tiberius wishes also to be the last, he can . . . he must . . .

"You have made much progress toward that end, Caesar: you poisoned your adoptive son, Germanicus; and permitted your daughter-in-law to poison your other son, but then you condemned her to eternal voyaging, bound in chains within a closed litter, her sons imprisoned with her: so far as the world is concerned, they do not exist; you ordered your grandsons murdered: Nero on the island of Pontia, Drusus in the dungeon of your palace; both died of hunger; Drusus tried to eat the stuffing of his mattress; you ordered the youth's remains to be cast to the winds. Caesar: you have no successors, you can be as happy as Priam. Only a phantom threatens you, and that phantom, you know now, is but a slave, he has a name and a body, he can be found, and crucified; you can punish him as you have punished so many. Just punishment, Caesar, worthy of your magnificence and equanimity; the patrician sold as a slave for cutting off his sons' thumbs to render them unfit for war, the legions you decimated because of their cowardice in combat, all the men tortured and imprisoned and deprived of their citizenship . . ."

". . . yes, repeat it all now that I take delight in the pleasure of these bodies, do me this favor, Theodorus, allow me to think of that as I see this, think of sorrow as I see pleasure, my pleasure will be redoubled and I shall be ever grateful to you, look, look, Theodorus, my sex swells merely thinking of it, a miracle, a miracle, do not stint, Persius, Fabianus, my little fish, Lesbia, tell me what I did to Agrippina, the wife of my son Germanicus, when she dared suspect me . . . Cynthia, Gaius, continue . . ."

"You exiled her to the island of Pandateria, Caesar, and as she persisted in telling that you murdered the valiant Germanicus, you ordered a centurion to beat her until she lost one eye, and then, half blinded, the woman ceased to eat, so that she might die of hunger, then you ordered your soldiers to pry open her mouth and force food upon her . . .''

". . . go on, speak, counselor, tell me of unjust punishments, excite me . . .''

"You condemned to death, and burned the books of, a poet who called Brutus and Cassius the last Romans . . .''

". . . I am the last Roman, Theodorus, I alone; Rome is the unity of all history, what the world has always desired, from the beginning of the most desolate tribes and primitive villages, unity, Rome has acquired it, Rome has acquired something more than lands, seas, cities, towns, booty, it has acquired unity: a single law, a single Emperor, there cannot, there must not be anything but dispersion following the Rome that is Tiberius and the Tiberius that is Rome; let a resurrected Agrippa return to the throne, and see the combined power and enormity of Rome trickle through his hands like the sands of the moon; I desire, believe me, I desire as much as I desire to kiss Cynthia's sweet buttocks, for that to happen after I am dead . . .''

"It is happening in your time, Caesar; hear the complaints: you have not filled the vacant posts in the Decurions, nor have you changed the soldiers' tribunes, or the prefects and governors in the provinces: a great uneasiness responds to your negligence . . .''

"Quickly, all of you, each give the one closest to him the black kiss, the excremental kiss, quickly . . .''

"For years you have left Spain and Syria without consular governors, you have allowed Armenia to be enslaved by the Parthians, Moesia by the Dacians, and the Gallic provinces by the Germans. The people say that in all this there is danger and dishonor for the Empire, and they blame you.''

". . . do not speak of obligations, Theodorus, speak of pleasures . . .''

"You ordered a man killed who beat a slave beside your statue, and a man who changed his clothing beside another of your statues . . .''

". . . have you drunk sufficiently?, then urinate, urinate in each other's mouths, quickly . . .''

". . . you ordered a man killed who entered a public urinal wearing a ring that bore your effigy, and still another who entered a brothel wearing a similar ring.''

". . . and now, all the men, on your feet, Fabianus and Persius and Gaius, fornicate, each of you with the one before him, while the women kneel and kiss your testicles, each of you thinking how at the hour of death you will think upon your bodies as ridiculous wrinkled wineskins, and of your acts as indecent buffoonery that condemned you to death; tell, tell, counselor; ally my pleasures . . .''

"You killed a patrician who allowed himself to be honored in his natal village, only because on a different occasion, but on the same date and in the same place, you had been honored; and the time of every village, Caesar, begins upon the day you visit it . . .''

"Minutiae, minutiae, I visit nothing today, I am ensconced in my villa in Capri, content, imagining, imagining the sublime: how to make my death coincide with the death of my Empire. I cannot bear the thought that someone might succeed me, it would be as if our beautiful Cynthia, instead of offering me her buttocks white as animated marble, had begun in this instant to feel the pangs of childbirth, and had lain upon my sigma to give birth, imagine such horror; the same horror I feel when I imagine that anyone could succeed me, lie down in my places, touch Lesbia's breast, pluck a pubic hair from Fabianus, no, no, they must all die first, I die only with my Empire; Theodorus, there must be alerts, executions at the least pretext, let no one remain, I want to die but I want to die the last death, execute, Theodorus, execute, ejaculate, execute and let the corpses be thrown down the mournful steps of the Forum and dragged on gaff hooks to the Tiber . . .''

"It has been done, Caesar . . .''

". . . and as it is our impious custom to strangle virgins, first let the executioners rape them, and then hang them . . .''

"It has been done, Caesar . . .''

". . . let no one commit suicide without my consent . . .''

"Carmulus has just committed suicide, Caesar, that malcontent Carmulus.''

". . . then he escaped me!, you see, counselor, such imprudence, what lack of attention to scruples . . .''

"Agrippina, too, conquered in her exile, she died of hunger, as she desired . . .''

". . . let none other escape me, each of you must be vigilant!''

"No one, Caesar?, not even those who wish to die?''

"Not even they . . .''

"How, then, will you condemn them?''

"By forcing them to live . . .''

"Whom shall we call on, Caesar? Italy is peopled with spies, with informers, with resentful and offended men. It is an enormously cunning mechanism, even those injured by you believe there is no reason their case should be unique and they betray a friend or an enemy, or the relatives of friends and enemies, to other friends and enemies, and thus all Italy is founded upon the revenge of vengeance, and we do not know where it will end; and there are cases of those who have no one in their families whom you have had killed, they feel neglected and swiftly contrive an intrigue that will make them worthy of such an honor; and all the informers listen to them, their only desires are to provide deaths for you; whom shall we call on now . . . ?"

"Listen to the dwarfs, Theodorus, they smell out traitors, they have a great nose for treachery, the gods have granted them that gift in exchange for their misshapen bodies. If a dwarf asks you why it is permitted that this one or that one live, being a traitor to my person, immediately execute the informers, even if they be Fabianus or Cynthia, my lovers; now, tell me from whom I descend, recall my cruel line to me, Theodorus . . ."

"From the Lucians, Caesar, but you changed the surname when those of the family so named were condemned for looting and murder. From the Claudias, Caesar. From the first Claudia, who, to demonstrate that her chastity could not be questioned, threw a rope over her shoulders and dragged from the muddy banks of the Tiber a mired boat laden with sacred objects . . ."

". . . what women, Theodorus, what females!"

"From the second Claudia, condemned as a traitor by the Senate because one day, when the mob in the streets blocked the passage of her litter, she descended and asked publicly that her brother Pulcher be resurrected, and as he had done in life, lose another fleet to the enemy, and thus there would be fewer crowds in Rome and the patricians could pass through the streets without mishap."

". . . yes, yes, what women, they have always despised the mob."

"And the second Claudia would not even dress in mourning to ask clemency as she was judged. Clemency was for slaves and castrati, she said, not for a woman who hoped to encounter all her friends and admirers in Hades, on the other side of the lazy black waters of the River Styx . . ."

". . . yes, yes, Theodorus, that line culminates in me; look, search in your archives and your recollections, search for the most obscure, the least known, the most forgotten testimony of a rebellion against me; an individual rebellion, originating in the crowd, but one that means revolt against us who although we are unique represent a collective ethic incarnate in marble temples and marble laws that I, and only I, can convert into dust and ridicule, not the mob, not the multitudes, not the ants that devoured my serpent: our Roman law, Theodorus, the same for all, sustained in a vast and unified Empire: unique Rome, you can belong to no one but a unique Tiberius; die with me, Rome; and you, son of a rhetorician, search, go forth in your palm sandals, find what I seek and allow me to take pleasure from my children and ephebes and nymphs, what?, have you tired so soon?, quickly, consult Elephantis, a new posture, quickly, my pleasure will not tolerate half measures, and you are here for my pleasure, not your own, quickly, Elephantis to our aid . . ."

II

I, Theodorus, the narrator of these events, have spent the night reflecting upon them, setting them down upon the papers you hold, or someday will hold, in your hands, reader, and in considering myself as I would consider another person: the third person of objective narration; the second person of subjective narration; yes, Tiberius's second person, his observer and servant; and only now, in the seclusion of this cubicle filled with piles of papers I have collected throughout my travels, seated on a rough wooden cot near a window that does not look out upon the sea, my only view the barren ocher rocks of Capri, I can consider myself, in the solitude that is my spare autonomy, first person: I, the narrator.

I have witnessed these events; most monstrous events, for I could understand the Emperor's lewd appetites if, in fact, the children he calls his little fish were normal children, or the women called Lesbia and Cynthia were beautiful females, or handsome youths Fabianus, Persius, and Gaius; but to have to attend these orgies, accepting the beauty imagined by Tiberius and imposed upon his sexual attendants while my eyes see what they see, is something that would perturb the serenity of the most discreet and even-tempered man; the pitiful children are blind, Cynthia and Gaius are dwarfs, Persius a hunchback, Fabianus an albino, and Lesbia a monster who has lost the lower portion of her face, from nose to chin, so that the poor woman's face is partly a great scarred hole, and partly an opening for swallowing ground food, a face dominated by two maddened eyes that attempt to say to me: You who look at me with compassion, tell me how I have come here, what I am doing here, why I repeat these acts I do not understand, why they subject me to this derision and torture . . .

I would like to explain to her that Caesar is very attentive to the birth of deformed beings, he searches for them in circuses, in ports laid waste by sudden plagues, in isolated mountains where incest reigns, and in subterranean quarters in criminal cities, and from there he has brought to his Imperial Villa these poor creatures forced to acquaint themselves with the book of the poetess Elephantis and to represent a beauty whose patrons Caesar has invented, I do not know whether he does this so that the normality of his own body may be comparatively impressive, or whether, compared to his senescence and impotence, the monsters believe, in spite of everything, that they are beautiful because they can still do with their deformed bodies what our Emperor can no longer do with his.

I do not know; nor is it my function to ascertain, choosing among solutions, involving myself emotionally in all this. I fulfill the simple function of witness. Without ever saying so, Tiberius requires a witness of his character; it is that necessity that saves, and will always save, those of us who otherwise would be the first to be thrown to the lions. Once I attended a venatic spectacle with the Emperor; a man fought in the arena against the beasts, and in the end was devoured by them. I was surprised not to see a single spark of fear in the eyes of that gladiator; he was a tranquil man; he expected nothing, he lost nothing.

Perhaps I, too, am a lost man; my death is deferred by Caesar's need for a witness. He must know that I write, that I leave proof of these events, and that the Romans of the future will know of them. Consequently, he knows that I do not assign him endearing traits. Nevertheless, he permits it; furthermore, he desires it. Because, perhaps, I am not merely witness to events, which are only actions, but, more importantly, witness to the character that is the agent of these events. Actions change, and different men may enact them; character does not change, only one man may be its agent. The character Tiberius possesses in these later years has been his character always, although, perhaps, in the springtime of his life no one, not even he, was aware of it; the good man does not become evil, or the evil man good. Power does not alter a man's character; it merely reveals it. If we know this, we shall always understand the character of the powerful. At least, power possesses this virtue; he who retains it can never lie; the light of history is too powerful; it will not serve the powerful to be hypocritical, for the exercise of power will reveal the extent of his hypocrisy. Thus, wise nature balances the fact that she gives much to very few and little to many; the few cannot hide the truth, and this is the penance they serve for having strength; the many can never help but see it, and this is the reward of their weakness.

A man like myself, who understands these things, must, nevertheless, choose between two attitudes as he writes history. Either history is merely the testimony of what we have seen and can thus corroborate, or it is the investigation of the immutable principles that determine these events. For the ancient Greek chroniclers, who lived in an unstable world, subject to invasions, civil wars, and natural catastrophes, the reaction was clear: history can concern itself only with what is permanent; only that which does not change can be known; what changes is not intelligible. Rome has inherited this concept, but has given it a practical purpose: history should be at the service of legitimacy and continuity; future chance must support the act of founding. The law of Rome is an act that defines several and individual chance concerning paternity, possession, marriage, inheritance, and contracts. None of these events would be legitimate without reference to the principle, the act, the general norm—superior to the individual's—that legitimize them. And what is the base of this legitimacy? The nation itself, the Roman nation, its origins, its foundation. And what is the projection of this legitimacy? The entire world, since the Roman nation incarnates universal principles capable of converting pure nature, cosmos, into a social and historical world, into ecumenae. This is the privilege of Rome; this is why she has been able to conquer the world, to impose unity, to be *caput mundis*, but the head of a world conceived as extension of the intangible act of our law, our morality, our civil and military administration, not of a natural world where chance prevails over action, a world which consequently is destined to dispersion. Our success is the best proof of this truth: we are the amphora that gives form to the wine of pure creation.

Before these truths and these disjunctions, I choose to be witness to the fatal chance represented by my master Tiberius, asking myself by virtue of which fates a man can wear the imperial purple who denies all the founding virtues of a society so preoccupied with legitimizing itself and its conquests. I have known the East: why do our preceptors lie when they compare the presumed corruption of the Levantine with their equally presumed belief in the simplicity, strength, and beneficence of Rome? And why, if this is believed, is vice secretly fomented in Rome, the cults of Venus and Bacchus, while pressure is exerted on the poets to exalt the virtues represented by a government that maintains the order so disastrously altered following the murder of Julius Caesar that sad day in March? And by what strange contradiction do all these necessities for true responsibility exempt our master Tiberius?

I know that my questions imply a temptation: that of acting, of intervening in the world of chance and placing my grain of sand upon the hazardous beach of events. If I succumb to it, I may lose my life without gaining glory; my kingdom is not that of necessity but that of whatever fragile liberty I can gain for myself in spite of necessity. To the temptation of action I oppose a conviction: since I neither want nor can influence the events of the world, my mission is to conserve the internal integrity and equilibrium of my mind; that will be the manner in which I recover the purity of the original act; I shall be my own citadel, and to it I shall retire to protect myself against a hostile and corrupt world. I shall be my own citadel and, within it, my own and only citizen.

I confess here that the only temptation to which I shall truly succumb is that of presenting myself to myself—when I write about myself in the third person—in a more worthy, more sympathetic light. The truth is not so beautiful.

But that temptation to act . . . that all too human temptation . . .

III

Caesar: I have been able to find nothing more obscure among my papers, or in the deepest recesses of my memory, Theodorus said to Tiberius that midday, while the naked Emperor, before eating, stood near a great fire as servants showered him with cold water and then rubbed his body with oil; nothing more obscure, nothing more forgotten.

You are Mercury, herald of the gods, Tiberius laughed. No, Caesar, a simple archivist mouse, and a humble traveler of the East; consider my method: first I thought about something no one had ever thought before; that is, I thought the impossible, what I did not know, beginning from your premise: find the most unknown testimony of an individual rebellion that originated in the mob. I reviewed the history of Rome; it is too well documented. Then I reviewed the history of the provinces, one by one, until I came to one of the poorest, the most isolated and insignificant, Judea. Examining its history, I found a recent event (unknown because it was recent, for only the ancient has had time to become memorable) that attracted my attention.

One of your Procurators, Pontius Pilate by name, a subordinate of the Roman governor of Syria and a protégé of your favorite, Sejanus, was deposed and forced to commit suicide last year because of a complaint of excessive cruelty issued by the so-called Samaritans, who centuries ago populated and dominated the northern part of the kingdom of Israel. I asked myself, Caesar, what, however dark a deed, could force the abdication and death of one of Tiberius's Procurators; what strength could a sect or tribe of the desert land of Judea exert to achieve that; and why?; and what are the antecedents?

Suddenly I remembered something I had completely forgotten: five or six years ago in the extreme heat of the month of Nisan I was passing through Jerusalem on the way to Laodicea. I crossed through the heights of the city, through a square called Antonius, or Gabbatha, where there was gathered a great rabble of Jews. I could see, from a distance, two figures standing in the atrium of the praetorium: a man dressed in a toga, washing his hands before the multitude, and beside him, head bowed and crowned with thorns, a figure of mockery, a bearded beggar, lacerated, bleeding, motionless. What is happening? I asked my guide; and he answered: "Caesar's Procurator is administering justice here."

We passed by; I was thirsty; I was tired; I wished to reach Laodicea. I had not remembered that incident until today. But beginning from that, I was able to conjecture upon the answers to my questions. The Procurator is charged both with imparting justice and with maintaining peace; the only threat against the peace of Judea is Hebraic messianism, which preaches the coming of a redeemer of the Jewish people, a descendant of King David who will restore the political sovereignty of Israel. There is a surplus of these redeemers, or messiahs, in Judea, Sire; shake any palm tree in the desert, and from it will fall twenty date clusters and ten redeemers. My inquiry became more circumscribed: was the Procurator Pilate involved in one of these cases? Was I, that afternoon during the dog days, an unconscious witness to an encounter between the Procurator and one of those Jewish prophets?

I unearthed the least-consulted papers in our archives; finally I found a brief bureaucratic report telling of an execution, scarcely five years ago, of a Hebrew magus or prophet or rogue of questionable behavior who fraternized with prostitutes and lived with twelve workmen; he was called the Nazarite, or, as that is translated, the Saint of God. This man, the Nazarite, said he was descended from David and that he was the Messiah of prophecy, the King of the Jews. For some months he wandered about the most remote areas of Judea, preaching this rebellion-of-one that coincides with what you asked me to find, Caesar: a purely individual revolt that originated in the mob, for the Nazarite was the son of a carpenter and was born in a stable. He said, nonetheless, that he was the son of God, born independently of man, and he affirmed that earthly power and riches are of no worth, for all that matters is to save one's soul and win the Kingdom of Heaven, that is, the kingdom of that unique God, the supposed father of the Nazarite.

With these ideas he either irritated or disheartened everyone. He discouraged, Caesar, those who were awaiting a call to arms; instead, the Nazarite preached love for one's fellow, meekness, and other, not in the least martial, virtues, such as offering the other cheek to those who smite us. And he irritated the priests of Jerusalem and the Sadducean aristocracy, our allies, because he expounded before the mob criticisms and reproaches against the Hebrew order and their wise alliance with Rome. He literally walked into the mouth of the wolf: he went to Jerusalem and there incited disorders, outraging the sellers of doves, whipping the money-changers installed in the atrium of the temple, and violating the Sabbath with healings the Jews attributed to Beelzebub, although their only debt was to Aesculapius. He grossly insulted the learned doctors of the law, the Scribes and Pharisees, calling them whited sepulchers and other such pretty names. This permitted the Hebraic aristocracy to denounce him as a dangerous agitator before Pilate, and at first, Caesar, your Procurator seemed doubtful, in spite of the insistence of his wife, who sent him messages telling him to have nothing to do with "The Just" because he made her suffer in dreams; but in the end he capitulated to this argument: the Nazarite says he is King of the Jews; but we, the Hebrew hierarchs, recognize no king but Tiberius; if you free the agitator, Pilate, you will demonstrate that you are no friend of Tiberius Caesar.

Pilate converted necessity into policy; he saw an opportunity in all this to ingratiate himself with the priesthood and the aristocracy, and at the same time to frighten other Jewish insurgents; they, like the Nazarite, threaten both the dominion of Rome and the stability of the Hebrew powers allied with Rome. And, as I have told you, such men abound: one who called himself the Anointed said he had the power to resurrect the dead; another called Jehohanan drowned evildoers in the Jordan as he walked upon the waters. And so on and so forth.

As everyone had agreed, the Nazarite was led to the cross and died there on the fourteenth day of the month of Nisan; but his stubborn disciples say he arose from the dead and ascended into Heaven, and that his kingdom of slaves will be eternal, whereas your kingdom of patricians is but transitory; and in recollection of the sacrifice of their Master, these followers have the custom of making with their hand the sign of the cross upon their face or breast, in the same way we Romans, as a sign of adoration, place our right hand to our lips.

But to return to your Procurator, Caesar. The crucifixion of the Nazarite was the last instance of equilibrium between the power of Rome and that of her Hebrew collaborators. Made arrogant by his political success in ridding himself of the Nazarite, Pilate believed he could use that event to advantage and extend the local power of Rome by confusing it with his own. He had eliminated the prophet; he thought, too, to subject those who had helped crucify him. Naïvely, he did not perceive that the priests and Jewish aristocracy were well aware of the popularity of the Nazarite and that as they forced Pilate's hand they were in truth effecting the lessening of prestige of Roman justice, they were weakening our power and strengthening their own. The truth is that poor Pilate succumbed to this human temptation: not to be content with the balance of power he thought he had achieved and, not being content, desiring to upset it. Why?

To augment his own power, yes, or his representation of a power that was not his; but especially to have life, Caesar, to have the life that is born only, always, of the rupture of an earlier state of equilibrium.

He offended the Jewish powers for whom images are an abomination by having our soldiers parade through Jerusalem carrying standards bearing your image, and by placing in full view in the ancient palace of Herod votive shields bearing your name; have no doubt, Caesar, Pilate imagined his own name there, not yours. Judea is a distant land; why not play the part of an Emperor, feel he was a minor Caesar; had the Nazarite not proclaimed himself King of the Jews, and had not Pilate, without consulting Caesar, acted in Caesar's name, and only to affirm that there was no King but Caesar? Imagine Pilate's confusion, Sire, for as he asked himself these questions he was forced to add others: was the Nazarite the son of God or merely the phantom of God, a specter issued from the reverberating mirages of the desert? Had the representative of Tiberius killed the representative of God; had Tiberius killed God? Pilate, in order to overcome this quandary, had but one road: he persisted in unnecessarily subjugating those who were already subjugated, in provoking their passive resistance, in charging against the treasury of the temple the expenses of an aqueduct for Jerusalem and, finally, in acting with unnecessary cruelty against the Samaritans. He wished, an obscure emissary in an obscure confine of the Empire, to repeat his hour of glory: the moment when he had ordained the death of God. For he thought that if he had merely ordered the crucifixion of an inoffensive agitator, his deed was scarcely memorable. But if he had delivered to death the Son of God, memorable indeed was his glory, and his alone. Your agent, Caesar, could have executed in your name an insignificant medicaster and charlatan, but if he had crucified a God in Pilate's name, then Pilate was greater than Tiberius.

I speculate, Caesar. The truth is that Pilate's confused arrogance endangered our delicate accord with the Hebrews. To the end of salvaging the political reality, Vitellius, Legatus to Syria, had to intervene and depose Pilate. The ancient Procurator came to Rome to seek an audience, and you, wisely, refused; with political reality salvaged, whom would it interest to salvage the mental or administrative reality of a Pontius Pilate? I believe that Pilate went mad; he was seen along the shores of the Tiber, repeatedly washing his hands; finally he committed suicide by drowning himself in those same Tiberine waters, but his drowned corpse was rejected by the river. The people say that the body of Pontius Pilate is borne from river to river, carried to new waters where it is always rejected with repugnance by the flowing current in which no man may ever bathe twice, for as the philosopher says, no water that flows is twice the same. Pilate's body has found no repose.

This is the end of the tale. I hope, Caesar, that this somber and harrowing account has in no way displeased you, and that now I have told it, this unimportant chronicle, this small mystery, will return to the oblivion and obscurity from which it never should have emerged.

I V

As he listened to his counselor's narration, Caesar's servants were singeing his legs with burning nutshells so the hair would grow soft. Afterward, distractedly, Tiberius allowed himself to be dressed; awkwardly, he made that sign of the cross upon his forehead and then, content and laughing, walked to his triclinium and there lay back to lunch.

"I like it, Theodorus, I like it; the sign of the cross; an instrument of torture and death; a sign associated with bodily pain; it pleases me . . . Why not make the sign of the cross the sign of the death, the dispersion, the multiplicity, the multitudinous, that I desire to follow my death? Hear me, counselor, if Rome is unique, if Rome is the apex of history, its unity must never be repeated lest Rome cease to be exceptional. Let all the kingdoms of the future, partial and dispersed, dream of the inimitable unity of Rome; let them struggle among themselves—yes—beneath the sign of that cross, let them fight and bleed for the privilege of occupying Rome, of becoming a second Rome; and from this growing fragmentation let new wars be born resulting in multiplied and absurd frontiers dividing minuscule kingdoms ruled by less and less important Caesars, like your Pilate, struggling to be a third Rome, and so on, and so on, without end . . . without end; oh, thank you, counselor; you have given me the weapons and sign of my desire, the cross of the slaves, the rebellion of a wandering Jew; let the Nazarite and his cross triumph and the power and unity of Rome will be dispersed like ashes and wind and dust . . . No important power will conquer us, not the Germans or the Parthians or the Dacians that today trouble our boundaries, not internal dissension, not license, lust, or decadence of character and discipline, not the loss of civic spirit, not the incapacity of imperial power to dominate the army, not the stagnation of commerce, low productivity, scarcity of gold and silver, not the depletion of the land, deforestation and drought, not plagues and illness, not our increasing disdain for work and subsequent dependence upon conquest, tribute, and slavery, none of these things, but a lugubrious Judaic philosophy of passivity and hope of a kingdom in Heaven . . . Can you imagine a greater triumph of my imagination, can you imagine anything more ridiculous, Theodorus, than the triumph of the most obscure of the Hebraic redeemers and the sign derived from the rack of his torture?''

He laughed; as Tiberius drained the last cup, Theodorus asked: ''Does what you have said imply an order, Caesar?''

''Let's play mora . . .''

Each placed his hands behind his back and then quickly extended them. ''One,'' said the counselor. ''Three,'' said Caesar. Tiberius saw perfectly the number of fingers revealed by Theodorus; Theodorus was painfully mistaken: Tiberius also showed three fingers. Caesar had not looked, he had not guessed; he merely repeated the number he always chose. He always did so; he always won. He had no time to guess or look; he had time only to choose and repeat what he had chosen.

''Yes,'' said Tiberius, ''it is an order.''

''How must I execute it?''

''My augur says that every living man has thirty phantoms behind him; three times ten; that is the precise figure of our dead ancestors. I have added to that with a number of murders.''

''You do well, Caesar; perhaps the function of power is to increase the number of phantoms . . . Will you bequeath your Empire to them?''

''I have no descendants, Theodorus; woe is me; if I had, I would have to divide the Empire among three sons, and make them promise they would divide their three kingdoms among their nine sons, and so on in succession; and in memory of our founding, I would also make them promise to copulate with she-wolves so that the heirs would be born from these beasts, and that as a secret jest, each bears the incarnate cross of the Nazarite upon his back; they would be my heirs, but in a different time, in a time of defeat and dispersion . . . Am I raving, counselor?''

''No, Caesar; you wish to bequeath an empire of phantoms, and we have phantoms to spare. Your desires, if they are true, can be fulfilled.''

''Enough. I have no offspring. I feel drowsy. Let me sleep, Theodorus.''

Tiberius was breathing deeply; I closed the draperies and waited. The soft Capri afternoon enveloped me; I watched the fire dying in the hearth; I listened to the dripping of the water clock that marked the time of Tiberius Caesar, fat, stiff-necked Caesar, sleeping uncomfortably, and breathing with difficulty; I inhaled the wild perfume of the laurel roses that surrounded the Imperial Villa, and said to myself: Take care, Theodorus, those roses smell good but they are poisonous; I stood up and covered my master's face with a silk cloth, for flies were gathering about the remains of his meal, and threads of wine and honey trickled from between the Emperor's thick lips; I was grateful for the adherence to the blessed law of silence.

Then I myself broke that law; I looked at the water clock; it marked the hour. It is told that there are rooms in which no one may enter unless with great need and with prior purification; unless he fulfills the ritual, one will feel afraid . . . and anyone who lies down in these chambers will be thrown forcefully from his bed by impalpable forces, and later found half dead. I walked toward the balcony that faces the wine-dark sea, a sea of nereids and dolphins, the glimmering court of Neptune, the liquid cave of Circe. Again I gazed about the placid imperial chambers; suddenly the dead flames in the hearth sprang to life; I trembled, I hesitated no longer; I drew back the draperies and saw standing there the phantom of Agrippa; the sun was at his back and cast an aureole about his head, but his somber face reflected only the shadow of the chamber. He wore a black tunic, and he stood motionless. Behind him, jumping down from the balcony and scurrying toward the sharp rocks was the fisherman who had shown him the way; the fisherman who had known this route since he was a child, known how to scale the rocks and catch the largest mullets in these seas; his face was marked by the sharp pincers and rough shell of a crab; I saw him no more; he fled. Only pregnant she-goats browsed on the rocky heights.

The phantom of Agrippa entered the chamber as I retreated, never turning my back, attempting to fathom that gaze, so deep, masked, a gaze capable of convoking its own shades; but the phantom was not looking at me, he stared through me absently, as absent as my body seemed before his advance. I could imagine his goal: the triclinium of Tiberius, where my master dozed, where lay his heavy, digesting, impotent, senile body: my master, the master of the world, the murderer, the pervert, and I his servant, his inseparable witness and chronicler, his sycophant; the black and gold phantom of Agrippa Postumus advanced, bent over the sleeping face of Caesar, breathed upon the pale, parchment cheek of Tiberius, and then suddenly, violently, snatched away the silk cloth covering his face and simultaneously withdrew the cushion upon which rested the Emperor's head; and the eyes of my master, who could see in the darkness, opened wide like two lakes of terror; and as my lucid mind witnessed that terror, I questioned: why, if every afternoon at the hour of the nap my master is visited by this phantom, does he now show such fear?, he must be accustomed to it. My courtliness overcame my amazement: I introduced them: "Caesar . . . the phantom of Agrippa."

And Caesar screamed, yes, he could scream, no, no, this is not the phantom, I know the phantom perfectly well, the slave Clemens, this is the slave Clemens, the eyes are different; I can see in the dark, I can distinguish between the two, they are different, the phantom and the slave, Agrippa and Clemens; tell me, slave, how did you become Agrippa?, and the black and gold creature, bent over Caesar, finally spoke, the cushion in his hand: "In the same way that you became Caesar . . ."

He raised his slim, strong, pale arms, he grasped the cushion in both hands and with incredible power thrust it upon Tiberius's face; the renewed flames of the hearth leaped high and duplicated the trembling of the struggling figures; I succumbed to temptation; I ran to the side of the slave, the phantom, whoever this executioner might be, recalling the imploring gaze of the disfigured Lesbia, her humiliation, her horror, and I helped him suffocate my master.

Old and coarse, even so, Tiberius struggled, he shuddered, and finally freed his manes with a fearful death rattle. The terrible visitor removed the saliva and blood-stained cushion; the enormous eyes of Tiberius contemplated the phantom, and he, the phantom or the slave, enjoyed it, he had the right to enjoy this vision. On the other hand, I fled into the courtyard, quietly summoned the guard, and we ran back to the chamber and captured this infernal man who still knelt beside my dead master, as if paralyzed by Tiberius's last gaze: the incalculable abyss of those black and glassy eyes.

V

I, Theodorus, the narrator, am writing all this on the day following the events I describe; I am writing them in triplicate, in accordance with the specific logic of my master's vague testament; and I will place the three writings into three long green bottles, which I will seal carefully with red wax and the imprint of Tiberius's ring.

The slave Clemens, this very morning, was thrown from the heights of the cliffs into the sea, where a crew of sailors awaited his fall to beat him to death with oars and gaffs. I did not attend the spectacle; I am surfeited with blood; enough, enough, I feel nauseated . . .

But this afternoon I descended to the village of Capri and listened to what was being murmured in the taverns and among the nets and fishing boats of the old harbor: the slave Clemens had been thrown into the sea, but the sailors had searched for him in vain to break his bones and club him to death with their oars; in vain, for as he hurtled toward the sea, Clemens, in mid-air, was transfigured into Agrippa Postumus, grandson of Augustus and heir to the Empire; his naked body had been cloaked in a cloud, and the cloud transformed into a white toga, and the toga into wings that deposited the condemned man upon the back of a dolphin that swam with him to a safe port from which the heir will again battle against usurpation at the head of the nameless and numberless legions of the slaves.

I know that all this is fantasy; but who can prevent a legend's being believed by the ignorant?, and what threats are posed by that belief? This I do not know. I have limited myself to following closely the last orders of my master Tiberius; I myself, with a knife, traced last night a bloody cross upon the back of the murdering slave, and in the face of his controlled pain, invoked the words of my master:

Let Agrippa Postumus, multiplied by three, one day be revived from the bellies of she-wolves, so he may contemplate the dispersion of the Empire of Rome; and from the three sons of Agrippa may another nine be born, and from the nine, twenty-seven, and from the twenty-seven, eighty-one, until unity be dispersed into millions of individuals, and as each will be Caesar, none will be he, and this power that now is ours will never again exist. And let these things all come to pass in the ragged reaches of the Empire, beneath the secret sands of Egypt where are buried the trinitarian mysteries of Isis, Set, and Osiris, beneath the arid sun of rebellious and restless Spain, fatherland of the insurgent Viriathus and of the Numantine suicides, on the shore of Lutetia, on an unsubmissive Gaul subjugated by Julius Caesar, a city of inquisitive and suspicious minds, as well as in the deserts of Israel, which knew the teachings of the Nazarite and the vulgar ambition of Pilate. And since the cross of infamy will preside over these lives of the future, as it presided over the death of the Jewish prophet the Nazarite, let the sons of Agrippa—who will bear the sign of the cross upon their backs—be called by the Hebrew name Jehohanan, which means "Grace comes from Jehovah."

This last stricture, I hasten to add for those who may read these papers, was but a small erudite fantasy on my part.

This is not the serious part, what was serious was that in the end, as with the knife I traced a cross upon the back of the rebellious Clemens, I could see his accursed eyes, and in them I saw twice repeated that same bloody cross; that was his gaze. And these were his last words: "My death does not matter. The multitudes will rise again."

I do not know whether I laughed as I cursed him: "May you grow an extra toe on each foot to aid you in arising and in traveling more swiftly . . ."

I do not know whether I laughed; I was not master of my words: in my heart I wished to thank him for not having betrayed me.

VI

The notice of Tiberius's death flies to Rome on the wings of horses no less swift than Pegasus. The funeral flutes will be heard in all Italy and will allow us no sleep; voices will be raised in mournful outcry. This is my pious imagining; my sense of the truth proclaims, on the other hand, that the multitudes will run jubilantly through the streets of Rome, celebrating the death of the tyrant, shouting "To the Tiber with Tiberius," asking that the corpse of my master be dragged there by gaff hooks, raising supplications to Mother Earth that Caesar find no rest save in Hell. Poor, stupid mob. They desire only occasions for rejoicing, for carnivals, circuses, and saturnalias. Why instead of occupying themselves with the dead do they not occupy themselves with the living? Why do they not ask who will succeed Tiberius, and what new misfortunes lie in store for Rome?

But that is not my problem. My stoic spirit dictates to my hedonistic hand the last words of these folios, and I say that in every good action what is praiseworthy is the effort; success is merely a question of chance, and, reciprocally, when it is a question of culpable acts, the intent, even without the result, deserves the punishment of law; the soul is stained with blood though the hand remain pure.

Did I truly assist the slave, or did I struggle unsuccessfully against his efforts to suffocate my master? I have no moral refuge but that of having written what I have reported; if any of these bottles is retrieved by one of my contemporaries, I shall be punished; if my papers are read in a distant future, perhaps I shall be praised. I write today: I run both risks. Whom have we killed here: a phantom of flesh or the flesh of a phantom? Was it all illusion, deception, a comedy of roving, disembodied larvae and mischievous, ghostly lemures? The true history perhaps is not the story of events, or investigation of principles, but simply a farce of specters, an illusion procreating illusions, a mirage believing in its own substance. I, like Pilate, shall wash my hands and wait for time to decide; let the reincarnations herein consigned, herein desired, herein cursed by the last will of Tiberius Caesar, decide.

Having written these things, I seal, as I have said, the three bottles and throw them one by one from the high lookout on Capri into the deep and boundless waters of Mare Nostrum, as black tonight as the velvet shroud that enveloped the remains of my master Caesar, of whom, when I was still a child, my father, master of rhetoric, Teselius of Gandara, said to me: "He is mire mixed with blood."

Yes, the bottles carrying my manuscript will drift to all the limits of the Mediterraneum, to the Hispanic coast and the Palestine coast, but I shall keep for myself the most secret of my secrets: the knowledge that Tiberius's curse had begun to be fulfilled before he had pronounced it, for in truth, on that not so long ago afternoon in the month of Nisan in Jerusalem, when I was traveling on the road to Laodicea, I beheld Pontius Pilate judging three identical men in the Praetorium, three equally ragged and bearded magi or prophets, perhaps three brothers, each crowned with thorns, each wounded by the lash, their lacerated backs marked with the sign of a bloody cross. Which of the three did Pilate condemn as the false Messiah, deliver to the Sanhedrin and death on the cross? What became of the other two? The chronicles say that there were three condemned men on Golgotha. The Nazarite and two thieves. Were, in truth, these thieves the two brothers of the Nazarite?; did Pilate, with the wisdom of Solomon, opt for the death of a single Messiah, depriving the other two prophets of that dignity, condemning them as vile thieves? Did he think thus to balance the relations between the power of Rome and the power of the Jews, giving them something, but not all they requested, giving himself the privilege of killing one God, of refusing the Jews more than one God, of astutely making mock of the Jewish faith in a unique God? Not three: the pantheon— the reunion of all the gods—is the privilege of Rome; so let you, Jews, have one God and two thieves. Rome: one Caesar and many gods. Israel: one God and many Caesars. Pilate and the Nazarite: one Caesar and one God. Poor deceived man: his uniqueness was his mortality; I suspect, on the other hand, that those three identical magi I glimpsed from a distance through the haze of the Levantine dog days will be forever interchangeable . . .

And then I hear titters from the chamber of Tiberius, I hear the moans and cries and sighs of Lesbia and Cynthia, of Gaius, Persius, and Fabianus; I hear the voice of my master Tiberius summoning me to his quarters, come Theodorus, come in, do not be afraid, speak to me of the flesh, Theodorus, ally my pleasures, pain and lust, Theodorus, do not be afraid, come . . .

ASHES

He had a vague impression of his own face. In passing, he caught hasty, fleeting glimpses in the stained mirrors the inhabitants fleeing the palace had left behind, here and there, in a bedchamber, in a tower. He did not see the wrinkles, the gray hair, the marks of time; increasingly, he was surrounded by shadow. The shadows were his old age. He remembered certain courtyards, certain galleries with white leaded windows through which the light of day had formerly filtered. Not now. Inch by inch the shadows were confiscating his palace.

"Where is everyone?"

He commanded and ordered that a hundred poor be dressed in the clothing lying forgotten in the coffers of those who had fled, and that ten thousand ducats be provided to wed poor, orphaned women, preferably of good reputation. The nuns howled quietly when Mother Celestina made her periodic visit on the Sunday before Ash Wednesday. El Señor delighted in verifying the noxious usury time had practiced upon the aged procuress whose upper lip was now streaked with dark fuzz, and whose chin whiskers were thick as a beard. Unconsciously, El Señor repeated the words formerly spoken by the go-between: You've become an old woman; they speak wisely who say that the years take their toll; methinks you were beautiful; you look different; you have changed. And she, for both of them, would reply, laughing, the day will come when you won't recognize yourself in your own mirror, and he was grateful that the increasing shadows of his palace were the only sign of time's passing, but the old vixen was like a dog with a bone, and half whining and half laughing said:

"It's clear that you didn't know me twenty years ago. Ay! Any man who saw me then, and sees me now . . . His heart would break with sorrow. But I know very well that I rose in the world merely to descend, and that I flowered only to wither on the vine; I had pleasure only that I might know sadness; I was born that I might live, lived that I might grow to womanhood, reached womanhood only to grow old, and grew old . . . merely to die. Do you know that, too, Yer Mercy?"

Then she repeated what El Señor wished to know—more than ever after reading the manuscript of Caesar's man, the counselor Theodorus—that the Idiot Prince was sleeping his long sleep with the dwarf in Verdín, that a hawk's murderous beak had seized the pilgrim of the new world by one arm, and that both, bird and youth, had drowned on the coast of the Cabo de los Desastres; the third assurance was in El Señor's own house: the deceiver and the novitiate were forever united, in perverse enactment of love, in the prison of mirrors. And what more? Well, the throng of beggars around the palace was growing larger every day, Señor, and it seems that the kitchens are in service only for them, for Yer Maj'sty never tastes a bite, they say, and the fame of your charity is growing throughout the kingdom.

He was afflicted by many pains, among those of the body, the most troublesome and inordinate was the gout, which caused him the most severe agonies in the separation the corrupt humor was causing in the knuckles and joints of his hands and feet, extremities which were most frightfully sensitive because of their lack of protective flesh, all nerve and bones that in rest tortured him without mercy, as his cries attested; and he was obliged because of the extreme tenderness of his feet to carry with him always a shepherd's crook with which to steady himself. In addition, his gums were constantly inflamed, and his teeth rotting, and for these reasons he commanded and ordered that every sacred relic that existed in his kingdom, and even beyond its confines, be brought to him without consideration of costs or money matters, and one day in December twenty great crates of relics were delivered to him, closed and sealed with many seals and testimonies and wrapped in linen cloth so that rain or snow could not damage them. "As these are relics of very ancient saints and of that time when the sincerity and poverty of Christians shone forth in the Church, many of them are adorned very poorly and roughly, some are in wooden boxes, others in copper of the most elementary workmanship embellished with stones of glass or an occasional pearl of poor quality, all of which is a most faithful testament of the purity, reverence, and truth of those good centuries when there was so much Faith and so little wealth."

So stated the folio delivered with the boxes, and although it was signed by a Rolando Vueierstras, the Apostolic Notary designated to attest and certify to the places from which the relics had been removed and assembled, El Señor thought he recognized a hand he had seen before.

Kneeling before the altar of his chapel and the Flemish triptych so zealously guarded behind its painted panels, El Señor spent entire days kissing an arm of St. Barbara and one of St. Xystus, the Pope, a rib of St. Alban, half of St. Lawrence's pelvic bone, the thighbone of St. Paul the Apostle, and the whole serrated kneecap, complete with hide, of St. Sebastian, Martyr.

With delectation his thick lips caressed the shinbone of Leocadia, Holy Martyr and Virgin, who suffered torment in the dungeons of Toledo, it too still covered with skin and hide, very beautiful, and inviting a thousand kisses.

He carried with him to his bed of black sheets at night an entire jaw-bone of that thirteen-year-old child, stronger than all the giants of the world, that enamored lamb, Inés, Martyr, who when she died said that the blood of her spouse, Jesus Christ, flushed her cheeks with beauty, and now El Señor repeated those words, caressing throughout the night the jawbone of the Martyr: "Sanguis eius ornavit genua mea."

Other nights he carried to his bed an arm of St. Ambrose, but what he most enjoyed was caressing, until he fell asleep embracing it, the head of the valiant St. Hermenegild, King and Martyr, martyred by his father, and to the head he would say: "Such an illustrious martyr would not wish a lesser tyrant and executioner."

Heads abounded on the long list of tariffs paid on the relics brought there, and often El Señor slept with two of them, the very head of the one the Gospel calls St. Simon the Leper, who, they say, was one of the seventy-two disciples, and that of the most holy doctor, St. Jerome, a sane, mature, and grave head; and early one morning, as they carried him his breakfast of dried raisins, the servants were frightened to see beside El Señor's head, resting on the same pillow, protruding like a living thing from between the black sheets, the head of St. Dorothy, Virgin and Martyr.

"And as my arms lack strength," he said to himself, "I shall take strength from the strong, never twisted arm of St. Vincent, Spanish Martyr, native of Huesca, and that of Agatha, Sainted Virgin and Martyr, of noble blood, although according to her doctrine more noble still for being the servant of Jesus Christ."

And he pinned those holy arms to his own sleeves and, with the strength they afforded, wandered interminably through the rows of sepulchers in the chapel.

He ordered that a table be set for dinner in the hall of the seminary, and that the nuns serve a copious collation, as in happier times, and he had placed upon tall chairs all the whole bodies listed among the relics, and with uncertain glances and trembling hands Sisters Angustia and Prudencia, Dolores and Remedios, Milagros and Esperanza, Ausencia and Caridad heaped high with geese and ganders, francolins and pigeons, the lead plates set before the motionless seated bodies of the Holy Martyr Theodoric, presbyter of the time of Clovis, of the glorious Martyr St. Mercury, of the valiant captain of the Holy Legion of Thebes, called Maurice, and that of St. Constant, martyred during the Diocletian persecution. El Señor presided over the table, but he ate only his raisins. And in the place of honor opposite him was seated the tiny, complete body of a sainted and innocent child, a native of Bethlehem, of the same tribe and descendancy as Judah, and he was so tiny he seemed no more than a month old.

"It is true," El Señor said to the child to initiate the conversation, "that the flesh, and even the bone, when they are those of one of such tender years, shrink and contract greatly over a long period of time . . .''

And as the child did not answer him, he directed himself to St. Mercury, whose body, with time and neglect in dust-filled shrines, looked worn and black. "Delight us," he said to him, "by telling us of your suffering during Decius's persecution, and how, after a few years, you were chosen by Our Lord to rid His Church of the evil of the apostate Julian, and to avenge the blasphemies he was uttering against God, and how he died by your hand, the result of a wound you inflicted with a lance . . .''

And as St. Mercury did not answer, and as the dishes were growing cold before his invited guests, El Señor chewed a few raisins and pointed toward the painted domed ceiling of the hall whereon was depicted the Most Holy Trinity seated upon a throne: he explained to his guests that the creatures on high were the angels; that slightly lower they could see the sun, the moon, and the stars, and in the lowest portion, the earth with its animals and plants:

"On that side you see the creation of man; on the other, how he sinned by eating from the forbidden tree, deceived by the envy of the ancient serpent, and how man is cast out of Paradise, and thus is summarized all that is written in the first part of the Acts of St. Thomas, whose chair and whose lecture room these are, and whose doctrine is here propounded. And one sees those two emanations that reside in God, which our theologians call *Ad intra et ad extra.* That of the two divine persons consubstantial *ab aeterno,* and those of all the creatures of the beginning of time.''

In these and other delightful Christian conversations was spent the dinner El Señor offered the martyrs. Then they were all returned to their crystal boxes and their coffers garnished with many gold flowers and ornamental gold braid; El Señor went to lie down with the grave head of St. Jerome, and the servants divided the cold victuals among the beggars.

And as to the miraculous St. Apollonia, patron saint of toothache, there came to the palace in two boxes two hundred and two teeth from her divine jaws, which El Señor esteemed highly as relief for his pain, placing them in golden vessels in the shape of ciboria.

On the first day of Lent, Ash Wednesday, a long document sent by Guzmán was delivered to El Señor. Felipe read it with avid repugnance, while in the chapel the obese and now almost centenarian Bishop, accompanied by deacons, acolytes, and choir, knelt, and removing his miter, sang the hymn "Veni, Creator Spiritus." Guzmán related the news: the dream of the young pilgrim was true, the caravels had reached the very coasts described by the youth; they disembarked on the beach of pearls, they picked up pearls by the handfuls, some even swallowed them. They followed the route of the jungle toward the volcano. The native inhabitants did not know the horse, the wheel, or gunpowder; it was easy to frighten them, for they took the horsemen for supernatural beings, and the harquebuses and cannons for things of magic. They were living, furthermore, in a state of dissension, the weaker peoples subject to the stronger, and all to an emperor called the Tlatoani, whose seat of power was the city of the lagoon. Let El Señor have no worry: the power of arms was at the service of the power of the Faith. As they advanced, the vigorous Spanish forces tore down idols, burned temples, and destroyed the papyri of the abominable religion of the Devil. He had a complaint against Brother Julián, who was constantly intruding in an attempt to save both idols and manuscripts, and who pretended that these savages were as much the children of God as we, and also possessed souls. Guzmán took advantage of the resentment of the various tribes to incite them against the great Tlatoani; the city of the lagoon fell, thanks to the combined action of the Spanish forces and the rebellious tribes. The vast city sank into the swamp; its idols fell, the temples and royal chambers were stripped of gold and silver, the ancient city was leveled and upon it was begun the construction of a Spanish city of severe outlines, similar, Most Christian Señor, to the grid upon which St. Lawrence suffered his martyrdom. I hope thus to respect your intentions, which are to transmit to these domains the supreme virtues of Spain.

Continuing, he recounted that once the imperial city had fallen, its inhabitants saw that they would once again be subjected, and Guzmán did not disenchant them. The natives' wonderment decreased and they rebelled; but Guzmán knew how to respond. He forced the docile to accompany him as an armed retinue against other tribes; he devastated fields; he burned harvests; he burdened the prisoners with chains, branded them like cattle, and divided them as slaves among his troops. Each soldier of this expedition has thus come to have a thousand or more slaves in his possession, and any man who left Spain without a stitch on his back has promptly earned a much higher state in these lands. In great enclosures, as warning to all, he gathered together men, women, and children; the men with fetters about their necks, and the women roped together ten by ten, the children five by five; he dragged them from town to town, through every region, exhibiting them as a warning that whoever wished to escape that fate would be better advised to submit. In each village he branded some, killed others, promised life to many more if they agreed to a life as beasts of burden, he gave license to his soldiers to take any woman who pleased them, and instilled fear in all. Even among the peoples that did not offer resistance he followed this tactic in order to set a good example: he proposed either servitude or death; even of those who agreed to be servants, he killed many; and among those he took with him, chained and bound, he allowed many to die from hunger; actually, he preferred the death of very young children deprived of mother's milk, whom he left along to roads to be seen by all. This rage against children culminated in a town of those called Purépechas, or Tarascans, where the inhabitants, as a gesture to demonstrate their peaceful intentions, delivered several pigs to Guzmán, and he, in return for their gift, gave them a great sack filled with dead children. When he came to the next town, he repeated these exploits. He has left no village between Tzintzuntzan and Aztatlán, between Mechuacán and Shalisco, between the lake of Cuitzeo and the river of Sinaloa, that does not weep for a child, scorn a woman, or hold dear the memory of a man.

Vast are the treasures in the temples, palaces, and mines, surpassing even what that poor dreamer and pilgrim told us. And if my eyes have seen much, my ears have heard more. They tell of a route through the deserts of the north that leads to seven cities of gold. They speak of a people of Amazon-like women warriors who have mutilated their right breasts that they might shoot their arrows with a man's skill. They speak, Señor, of a fountain of eternal youth, hidden in the jungles, where one need bathe only once to recover one's youth. I know that such fantastic stories are but illusions; they nourish, nevertheless, my men's greed and desire for glory, inspiring them to run unparalleled risks; your young pilgrim retrieved nothing from his dream, Sire; in contrast, I send you, along with this letter, the most ample proof of the riches of the new world. It is barely the royal one fifth owed you. The booty has been divided among the enterprising members of this expedition which surpasses in boldness and merit even those of Alexander, Hannibal, and Caesar. No one has refused his share, not even Brother Julián, whom I tolerate only by your mandate. Nevertheless, he does fulfill the charges of the Faith, erecting chapels and churches in all the towns we have conquered. Let no one say, therefore, that only the desire for gold brought us here, but rather, the desire to serve God.

This long document was signed by the Most Magnificent Señor Don Hernando de Guzmán.

El Señor looked up. The senior sacristan, with a golden sieve, was scattering ashes on the floor of the chapel, forming two lines from corner to corner that intersected in the middle of the temple. The choir sang the "Benedictus Domine Deus Israel" while the Bishop, with his shepherd's staff, traced the Latin alphabet in the ashes, and then in the intersecting line, the Greek alphabet, intoning in a voice more burned out than the ashes: "Behold, Israel, that we shall not write here your Hebrew alphabet, in order to demonstrate the ingratitude of your people who, being the first, and the first to whom were made the promises of such sovereign treasures, did not recognize those treasures, preferring to live apart from them, a blind, obscured, and cruel people."

El Señor walked painfully toward the altar, dragging his afflicted feet through the ashes; and there at the foot of the holy table of the Eucharist stood the enormous coffer overflowing with gold, molten gold, gold from ear ornaments, bracelets, idols, floors, ceilings, and collars melted down to remove from them any pagan sign and to invest them with their true value as treasure, money, funds with which to arm armies, combat heretics, erect palaces, placate nobles, endow convents, and regale clerics. El Señor saw the glances of greed which, still in the midst of their prayers of humility, the Bishop, the deacons, the sacristan, and the choir directed toward the coffer.

In a loud voice El Señor said: "Let no one remove this treasure. Let it remain here forever, open, as an offering to God Our Lord. Let no one employ it, divert it, or enjoy any advantage whatsoever from it, except God himself, at whose feet I lay it."

He bent over to pick up ashes from the floor; with his finger he traced a black cross upon his forehead.

He returned to his bedchamber, from which he could watch unseen the ceremonies of this and all other days, of this and all other years.

Many years passed without his hearing the barking of the nuns announcing a visitor. Why did Mother Celestina not return to see him? What had become of Ludovico, the young Celestina, and the monk Simón, abandoned, although free, on the plain? He forgot his mother; surely, she had died, living, or must be living, dead; he respected her will that he abandon her in the walled tomb with neither inscription nor ceremony. In his arthritic hand he wrote: "One governs the world only if he is guided by the hand of God. Respect my solitude. Respect my devotion. What will it profit a man to gain the entire world if he lose his soul? I hunger for God. I hunger for death. Both are one in my desires. Communicate in writing to me the major news. It need not be good. As if unaware, I shall bear it with resignation."

He was right. Occasionally missives reached him, rumors consigned to paper, warnings, proposals, suggestions, decrees that required his signature. He signed many things without even looking at them, others he forgot until he was reminded of the need for his signature. He hesitated; he postponed signing; he hesitated again. Such deliberation earned for him the designation of the Prudent. With horror, he received books printed by heretics who had divorced themselves forever from the tutelage of Rome and were founding new Churches. He guarded as secret the news communicated to him: if it was known by all, he would comport himself as if it were unknown.

Shadows, he said to himself, and not years, are besieging me. My age is measured by the increasing expanse of shadows; inch by inch they are taking possession of my body and my palace.

And so he lived until one night he heard a terrible scream from the chapel. It was the eve of another Ash Wednesday. He grasped his staff. The scream echoed through the domed ceiling of the chapel. He attempted to place it. Slowly he shuffled through the double row of royal sepulchers. As he reached the corner nearest the foot of the stairway, he finally found the origin of the sound: the niche where his mother, the Mad Lady, lived, walled up, and, immured, was dying.

"Son, my son! Where are you?" she cried. "Oh, my son! Have you forgotten me?"

"Where are you, Mother? Who are you now, Mother?"

"Ring the bells," howled the Mad Lady. "Crown me with three thorns of Christ's sovereignty, drive into my hand the nail of the true Cross, and in the other hand let me clasp the sacred cane of St. Dominic of Silos; bind my enormous belly with the girdle of the convent of San Juan de Ortega! I am giving birth, my son, to my last son, I have given birth to six, and all have died, while the bastards of my husband the King live and prosper; I am giving birth to my poor son, the sixth heir of the house of Austria in Spain, born on the sixth day of the month of the Scorpion; with him I shall vanquish the bastards, this one will live, I shall vanquish the accumulated poison of six generations, he is born, bring him to my bed, to my arms, when I was fifteen I was wed to the King, who was forty-four, poisoned by inheritance and his own excesses, a miserable celebration, we were married in a dusty village, Navalcarnero, a miserable celebration, that of Spain, I tell you, a village chosen for our wedding because the place where monarchs are married need never again pay tribute, that is why I was married in a wretched hamlet populated by fleas and goats and cretins and blind men, and I gave birth to dead sons, and now you, this son, bring him to me, this one will live, this one will reign over a ragged and defeated kingdom; the Great Armada, defeated; the gold of the Indies, evaporated; the regiments in Rocroi, defeated; Spain, lost, impotent Spain, your grandeur is that of a pit: the more it is used, the more it disappears, we cannot pay the salaries of the palace servants, we, the Kings of Spain, eat the meat of dogs and chickens, and crumbs smaller than the flies squatting upon them; bring me my son, healthy and lucid, handsome and of good character, my little son, my beautiful little son who will be my answer to the death and misery of Spain; my weak little son, cheeks covered with ringworm, head covered with scales like a fish or a lizard, my son, the bewitched, cover his head with a cap, pus dribbles from his ears, hide his genitals so that no one can see that stubby, livid scorpion's tail, even if they believe he is a woman, no one must see that purulent little stump, the bewitched, crown him, quickly, let his head become accustomed to the weight of the crown, he is five years old, he still cannot walk, his nursemaid must carry him, he is not learning to speak, he communicates only with dogs, dwarfs, and buffoons, his body is rigid, and tense, and impotent, he stutters and slobbers, your greatest pleasure is to crown your head with wounded doves and feel the threads of blood trickling down your yellow face, your bed is icy, your heart inflamed with hatred against me, your moth-

er, who wants only to govern well in your name; you are an idiot prisoner of astute and ambitious men who order me to cut my hair, don the
habit of a nun, cover my face with the veil, and lock me in the castle of
Tordesillas, you are alone, surrounded by intriguers, alone, my son,
bewitched, with your swollen tongue and the stupor in your eyes, imitating the sounds of animals, sitting in corners weeping without reason, gritting your teeth to keep from eating, your blood swarming with
ants, your brain with frogs, your belly with vipers, your hands with
fish, may God bless you: you spend days in a state of insensibility,
prisoner of a lugubrious dream; may the Devil pardon you; you spend
days clawing at yourself, tearing out your thin hair, you are your own
persecutor and executioner; when you see a woman you vomit; a
strawberry of pain is growing in my breast, modesty forbids me to consult a physician, and further, my Christian fervor; is there a physician
who is not a Jew, an Arab, or a convert? I die, happily, before you,
and from the pulpits of Spain my faithful Jesuits sing my praises:
blessed indeed, but not as blessed as the cancer that killed our august
Queen, for the cancer that tortured the Royal Breast encountered there
not only the luminous sphere of her death but the very breath of her
life. What will become of you without your mother, my poor bewitched King? My name is Mariana.''

The voice issuing from the niche faded away, but on that occasion
other voices pursued Don Felipe as slowly and painfully, supporting
himself on his crutch, he walked to the room presided over by the
mummy fashioned of royal bits and pieces by Isabel, his untouched
wife. Through the honeycomb of galleries and courtyards he heard,
echoing through domes of stone and air, rondelets, cruel jests, ditties:
a King without a kingdom is our King, the King is leaping, the Queen
weeping, the Monarchy creaking, nuns speaking, toadies all peeping,
sing ho, sing hey, sing lolly, may God pardon your sire, who, suffering an ill so dire and hoping never to expire, dragged your mother
through the mire, oh, rondelet lolly, sing lolly, lai, lay, why that son of
a bitch scratches his itch with every wench in the kingdom, without
rhyme or reason, sing lolly, sing well, there's still worse to tell, on the
way to perdition, through his benediction, his government's going to
hell, his government's going to hell, sing ho, sing hey, sing rondelet
lolly, sing loud, all ye pimps, sing loud all ye rogues, all randy, at random, yes, sing of the phantom, the phantom, the phantom . . . now
seated upon the Gothic throne Felipe found a rotund and rubicund bewigged King wearing a tricorn atop his head and sprouting two horns
from his forehead; the magnificence of his black-velvet, gold-embroidered coat, his medallions and gold braid, his silver dress sword and
white satin stockings, could not compensate for the calamity of his stupid gaze, his drooping lower lip, the red eagle's beak of a nose crisscrossed by broken veins. And now he was accompanied by a pale ugly

woman with an impudent face that was boldly painted, but to no avail, her rat's hair combed into high peaks of frizzly curls, a saliva-slicked curl plastered over each ear; the bodice of her daring, gauze-thin dress cinched a wrinkled bust, causing her tightly squeezed breasts to bulge over the top of the transparent cloth. A small boy, a faithful replica of his father and mother, a mixture of vulture and rat, sat playing at the feet of his progenitors, and when he saw Felipe on the threshold, he laughed and shrieked, and as if he were rolling a ball rolled a golden and diamond orb toward El Señor.

"What does that old spook want?" shrieked the child, looking, as he posed his question, into the imbecilic, round black eyes of his progenitors.

Felipe fled in terror, wondering whether the specters he saw looked on him as another specter. He fled, returning to his seclusion, his habits, to the passage of years he measured by the stick of the increasing shadow.

At times, seated in his curule chair, aided by the light of a short candle stub that burned his fingers and dripped wax stains on the old, almost illegible, papers in his hands, El Señor reread the manuscript of Counselor Theodorus and pondered, with mortification, any possible relationship between those ancient destinies and his own, that is, the destinies of all those connected with him, for his solitary memory—on behalf of his zealous soul—claimed possession of the beings whose life coincided with his, the destinies of those he loved, but also the destinies of those he despised, those he had combated, those he had ordered killed . . .

His smile was bitter then, and he felt wretchedly mediocre, How insignificant his despotism seemed compared to that of Tiberius Caesar. He would never have time to become a greater tyrant than he; greater were the domains of today's Spain than those of yesterday's Rome, and nevertheless, he could not say, as Caesar had said, I am the head of the world; other powers contested his; heresy was showing its face in the very places he had defeated it, Flanders, the Low Countries, Germany; Mussulman infidels had installed themselves in the very seat of the Second Rome, the Sublime Porte, Constantinople, and from there continued to threaten Christianity and mock the possessive pronoun of Mare Nostrum; the Jews expelled from Spain had carried enlightenment and skills to the kingdoms of the North, and both threatened Spanish hegemony; Isabel's descendants occupied the throne of England, and all their acts seemed directed toward defying him, avenging themselves against him, humiliating him; in any case, power became diluted over such a vast expanse; he did not wish to know, once he had heard them for the first and last times, any of those distant names, Cholula, Tlaxcala, Machu Picchu, Petén, Atacama, not even when they were disguised with holy Hispanic names, Santa María del

Buen Aire, Santiago del Nuevo Extremo, Santo Domingo, Buenaventura: he swore he would never set foot on the new lands; the great crimes were being committed by a swarm of botflies, the little Caesars of the new world, Guzmán, all the Guzmáns. Printing had deprived writing of its uniqueness, it was no longer intended for his eyes alone. Science told him that the earth was round. Art told him that the work of creation was not completed in a single immutable act of revelation, but that it continued to develop, ceaselessly, in new times and new places.

He drew a curtain of rancor over the present that raged so against him, sifting in through the tightly fitted granite blocks of his palace, his monastery, his imperial necropolis. History was a gigantic puzzle; it had left only a few broken pieces in El Señor's transparent hands. He closed his eyes and attempted to determine how the trinitarian heresies that broke the primary unity of Christianity, the secrets recounted here in this very bedchamber by Ludovico, fitted with the key pieces of Tiberius's curse: the Cabala, the Zohar, the Sephirot, the magic number of three, and he imagined that, independent of the will of Tiberius, an invisible plot, a stratagem woven of sand and water, was being delineated throughout the confines of the Mediterraneum; a shared destiny, incarnate always in three persons, three movements, three stages, it could be read on the sheer rock faces of the island of Capri, in the meaningless meeting of the Nile and the hunger-filled alleys of Alexandria, in the spectral community of the Citizens of Heaven in the Palestine desert, in the caves and the palace on the Adriatic coast, in the illusory Venetian Theater of Memory, in this new scar of the Hebrew, Latin, and Arabic world represented by his own palace, monastery, and sepulcher, what secret thought joined the words and acts of Tiberius Caesar, the phantom of Agrippa Postumus, and the rebel slave Clemens; the invisible elect of the desert, the one-eyed magus of the Porta Argentea, and the waves of heretics Felipe had combated in the overcast lands of Flanders?; what ruling idea inspired the construction of these edifices, at once solid and spectral, the palace of Diocletian, the Theater of Memory of Valerio Camillo, the Spanish necropolis of the King Felipe?; what identical prophecies were murmured by the voices of a Roman despot, an Egyptian fratricide, and a Greek magus?; what atrocious and ineradicable mark of the origin of humanity was signaled in those parallel histories separated by centuries and oceans, those of the two brothers and a sister—the benefactor, the murderer, and the incestuous woman—in the sands of the Egyptian river and in the jungles of the new world?; is that what the three youths marked by a cross on their backs and disfigured by hexadigitalism were enacting in this palace: a further act of the representation of the beginning, a painful return to the memory of the first dawn, to the terrible acts of the founding of the city upon earth? Ariadne gave a thread to Perseus in the labyrinth: El Señor dreamed of a woman with tattooed lips, present in Alexandria and Spalato, absent in Capri, Palestine, and Venice, and again present here in Spain and in the Spanish domains beyond the seas—before they were conquered. He awakened, and he asked himself, in that sudden and fleeting lucidity that sometimes accompanies the return to wakefulness: had Ludovico read Theodorus's manuscript, did he know of the curse of Tiberius, or had everything happened independently of will or logic?, was it all a gratuitous series of events separate from any relationship of cause or effect?

Then he knew he would never know.

And nonetheless an insistent spark glimmered in the depths of his questions, his dreams, and his waking. What he knows is as important to the education of a Prince as what he does not know; the bee does not alight on every flower . . .

"You must know these things, my son. It will be you who will one day inherit my position and my privileges, and the accumulated wisdom of our domain as well, for without that wisdom the privileges are but vain pretension."

"You know, Father, that I am reading the ancient writings in our library, and that I am a diligent student of Latin."

"The wisdom to which I refer goes far beyond the knowledge of Latin."

"I will not disappoint you again."

He remembered his father as if he were a stranger, always distant from him, until for the first time he went out into the world, joined the dreamers, the rebels, the children and sinners and lovers, and delivered them to the slaughter in the castle. As a reward, his father gave him Isabel's hand. Shortly thereafter, he died; Felipe inherited the throne, and his mother lay down to await death in the courtyard, later accepted mutilation, and then traveled throughout Spain bearing with her the embalmed cadaver of that Prince, his father, violator of village girls, the whoring Señor who was pursuing the girls of the palace of Brabant while his son was being born in a privy: the spark became a bonfire, only through his mother did he know who his father was, she wanted him for herself alone, if not in life, then in death, for herself alone, let no one come near, no woman, no man, not even a son . . .

"You must know the curse that weighs upon the heirs of Rome . . ."

"I forgive you everything, your women, your appetites, your deceit, everything; but I could never forgive you that . . ."

"I have lived and ruled with that curse upon my head, weighing upon me, robbing nights from my nights and days from my days . . ."

"You shall not transmit that curse to my son . . ."

"Our son, Juana . . ."

"Mine only, for like Rachel I gave birth to him with pain, forgotten, in a Flemish privy . . . while you . . . The First Rome fell, defeated by hordes of slaves. Constantinople, the Second Rome, fell, defeated by the throngs of Mohammed. Spain will be the Third Rome; it will not fall; there will be no other; and Felipe will rule over it.''

"You are mad, Juana; Aragon and Castile can scarcely rule Castile and Aragon . . .''

"My son inherited a plethora of ills from our line; I shall avoid for him that anguish that has eaten away at you, my poor Señor; called the Fair, you are a horror beneath your skin; I shall save my son from the fear of extinction, I charge myself with the responsibility of assuring that our line will never end . . .''

"You are mad, Juana; you speak as if you could revive the dead . . .''

"Even if our phantoms must govern, the line will not be exhausted. You will not bequeath to my son your fear of being the last King, choked and enslaved by the anonymous crowd; he will not be devoured by ants like the serpent in your nightmare. He will know what I wish him to know; he will never know what I do not wish him to know . . .''

If he could, El Señor would have run to his father's tomb; instead, he had to support himself upon his cane; painfully, he made his way from his bedchamber to the chapel blackened by the ceremonies of Ash Wednesday; he was assaulted by a fearful stench, my God, oh, my God, oh, God, the same pestilential smell of the day of victory, the same execrable odor of the Cathedral profaned by the mercenary legions that had won the day for the Faith.

Limping, he approached the altar. He looked at the coffer filled with gold from the new world. It shone like gold. But gold has no odor. And this excrement-filled coffer did; it was overflowing with transmuted excrement, gold into offal, the offering of the new world, oh, God, oh, God, the alchemy of your creation; if your creation is nothing but ruin, then shit is your offering. Oh, God, from what jungle temples, from what idolater's palaces was the gold-become-shit removed?, can it be gold only there, and nothing but excrement here?

"Gold, Felipe, is the excrement of the gods," said a hollow voice from the Flemish triptych behind the altar.

Supporting himself painfully on his shepherd's staff, Felipe hurried breathlessly to his father's sepulcher and rested, feverishly, on the slab of the tomb; Dr. Pedro del Agua had embalmed that body, he would be able to see his father as he had been in life, he had died young and still fair, an elegant and whoring Prince whose body disguised his inner corruption, dead before completing his fortieth year, now Felipe could rip off his doublet, his breeches, he could see the embalmed member that had taken Isabel's virginity, the cloves-and-aloes organ of the man who had possessed and impregnated his wife Isabel, the preserved penis that had done what the son could never do, possess Isabel and give her a son, Isabel, there is nothing there but a scar, a rime frost of ancient vellum, a cobweb between the legs, Dr. del Agua had removed and cut away everything that was corrupt or corruptible, Dr. del Agua castrated my dead father, my father's sex is nothing but a wound, like the sex of a woman . . .

But in that same sepulcher where El Señor's father lay, the Idiot Prince had once been buried atop him, the night of his wedding with the dwarf Barbarica, and there too Barbarica had made love with the double of her lunatic husband, with the deceiver, the whoring, incontinent youth who was his father's true heir, the son of his father and Isabel, Don Juan, and there, beside the embalmed cadaver, lay a green bottle, the second, stopped with plaster and sealed with wax.

El Señor picked it up, slowly returned to his bedchamber, and once again sat in his curule chair.

He extracted the manuscript from the bottle.

And this he read that early dawn in the weak light from his high, narrow window.

THE RESTORATION

Sitting there in the center of the smoking hut, sitting upon her own hands, her face hidden by a white cloth that collects and simulates the imaginary light of this night in the high tropics, the woman is a photographic cell that detects its own movements, indifferent to the internal immobility of fear. She knows that unconscious movement interrupts the imaginary flow of light (the point of light represented in this dark Indian hut by her white mask) and converts it into a buzzing transmitted to the throbbing drum of her brain. There is no relationship between the light and the sound. A white, masked face (hers) comprises the entire hut, with its walls of crumbling adobe and its straw roof, a face that receives the volume, the attack, the duration, and the decadence of real or imaginary sound.

You hear the rhythm of a drum in the same instant that she recounts:

Only once, never to be repeated: the Ancient Woman says she hears the incessant, muted sound of a drum, half martial, half funereal; but she admits she cannot manage to distinguish certain qualities; she asks you whether the heads of the drumsticks are of wood, leather, or sponge; that throbbing and constant sound of mother-of-pearl is a presence, but a distant one. At times, as now, she assures you that the noise forces her to draw into a tense ball that occludes all her orifices. Injection and choked-back scream. A drill in a molar. A surgical incision. An airplane's lift-off. The body becomes, she says, a closed order, exclusive, without reference to the threat that could be a delight. You watch her here, closed, trembling, seated on the ground beside the fire in this hut. She is listening attentively; the leather heads of the drumsticks define (or only recapture) the solemn chant: Deus fidelium animarum adesto supplicationibus nostris et de animae famulae tuae Joannae Reginae.

She repeats the words in a soft and disillusioned tone divested of the original vigor that should be used to justify them. Her hands thud against the loose dust every time she repeats the verb of her desire, return. For a long while she sits silently as you listen to the dry crackling of the branches that feed this fire that must defend us against the cold night of the Sierra Madre. Outside, our men are oiling their bicycles, cutting wood for log bridges and passing by in long lines carrying the rolled-up bridges that tomorrow they will remove from the barrancas. The foliage of the myrtle protects us; and, even more, the mist that since this afternoon has been drifting down from the summit of the Cofre de Perote. The Old Woman sits with crossed legs. You describe her as a poet of antiquity in wide, ragged skirts who recounts her own tale with the hesitation of one who speaks of events that have happened to another. She is not recounting a legend; she has told you that one learns legends by memory; if one changes a single word, it is no longer a legend. Her long silence is neither serene nor neutral; it is not a memory, it is an invention seeking its continuity, its support, in the hour of the jungle that surrounds us.

You say you see her there, closed, trembling, her lips forming the sound of a mourning drum, and you tell yourself that terror is the true state of all creatures, sufficient unto itself, separate from any dynamic relationship whatsoever: terror, a state of substantive union with the earth, terra, and a desire to withdraw forever from the earth. History—this history, another, that of many, that of one alone—cannot penetrate terrified bodies that are both paralyzed upon the earth and cast outside it. Surely, the Old Woman cannot know whether in truth that sound is approaching or whether its proximity is precisely the will to fear. Only when she feels that nature is indifferent to her body, the Old Woman tells you that she hears the always closer moaning, that she feels the touch of other hands upon her body, but she cannot be sure whether both sensations are merely an amplification of the essential rhythms of her brain, as if terror were a powerful electrode applied to the cranium and receptive to the variable energy of its waves.

Only once, never to be repeated: she says she hears that drum again; but in that same instant, as if in the distance, as if searching for a meeting of sound, there is the dissonance of something that could be described as the sound of glass broken in the past, glass that is recomposing; utility and reflection: a pile of broken glass rising from the ground as if the moment of its shattering had been recorded on tape that now, in reverse, reconstructs it; glass: a smoking mirror.

The first squadron passes through the low sky and the Old Woman moves her lips, conscious of the insult. At the same moment someone rings the only bell in this village church. She, who in the midst of the ambush of the action, insists on maintaining the distance of the narration, assuming the need to analyze, more than events, the manner in which events are externalized and interrelated, says that the airplane and the bell, as they join in harmony, proclaim their mutual absence at the instant of their meeting: the fleeting sound of pursuit seems to negate the melodic convention of bronze, but in reality a new sonority—which accounts, the woman assures you, for your fascinated silence—is evoked, beginning from the chance encounter.

You brush the Old Woman's hand. She seems to redouble her concentration. You touch fleetingly what she is always touching. You both know that touch of down and carapace, feathered wing and insect's foot.

"You have made progress," you tell her, calmly. "What is it?"

"A gift. They described it to me. I am trying to reproduce the model. It is very difficult."

She slaps at your curious fingers.

"Stop! Wait till it's finished."

She throws her shawl over her shoulders, feigning sudden cold; a shudder ascends to her ears; translucent porcelain. Then she laughs as if she were imitating herself; she repeats the boisterous laughter of a lost occasion, but now the laugh is not crystalline or audacious as it doubtlessly was once, in the time she is attempting to recover. What you hear now is a parody of another laugh, chained and broken: the difference between the fullness of a wave and the fragility of glass. Then, only for an instant, you imagine that the Old Woman's voice is for you what the sound of the drum is for her.

But suddenly you are distracted. The camp followers are preparing breakfast and into the hut waft the enervating odors of sliced and shredded and crushed chili peppers mixed with fresh tomatoes, chopped onion, and mashed avocado. From the hut entrance, a hand offers two large bowls; you take them and place them beside the woman. She ceases to listen, to speak, or to remember (you realize, or you imagine, that she does all these things concurrently), and squatting, devours the meal as if this were the moment of the invention and offering (and the threat by the hands of forever depriving her) of food. She looks at you with a trace of mockery in the deep-set eyes you can scarcely see beneath the white cloth which has been pushed up, wrinkled above the upper lip to allow her to eat. She says to you, her mouth filled with food, that she eats for the pleasure of eating: a sufficient pleasure. She says that this is not the moment to think or to justify anything. The food serves to connect her, to root her, even more closely with the ground; it is the lead (she says) of a too-light body.

In the distance, the bombardment has begun once again, the indication that day is approaching. But the Old Woman, impervious in serenity as she is in terror, reflects, indifferent to the renewed threat the new dawn promises. Her prolonged pause is like a cinematic dissolve, it is as if she were awaiting the authorization of the first rays of the sun to renew her tale, and as if this nascent light, today, in the Veracruz sierra were in reality the congealed light of a foreseen, promised, surpriseless day.

The fire is going out.

You open your arms wide in a normal stretching gesture that might be confused with praise to the emerging sun that now transforms the cold of night into the fresh heat of a tropical daybreak (announcing, in turn, a long, humid, burning, implacable day). But on the woman's narrow profile, scarcely visible through the white cloth covering her face (illuminated all night from the earth by the weak fire, as now from the east by the ambling sun), there is a question. You ask yourself whether that nascent sun sheds light on itself or upon us. But you cannot help thinking you are merely repeating the question your prisoner asks herself in silence.

As every morning, the Phantoms swoop by swiftly, flying low, strafing indiscriminately; we all protect ourselves, we tuck our heads between our legs and join our hands over our necks. In the distance, the airplanes drop their full loads of fragmentation bombs, circle through the sky, gain altitude, and disappear. The Old Woman, with no motive, begins to laugh, then drags herself across the floor, turning her head from side to side, until she finds what she is looking for. Brusque movement; every morning's sudden fear of death, but as soon as the familiar and momentary threat passes, normality is restored with amazing speed. The Old Woman, like everyone else, had crouched into a fetus shape, flinging from her what she held in her hands. And now, as if nothing had happened, quite naturally, she picks it up, strokes it several times, finds the old container filled with glue, and begins her work. There is almost no light (the fire has gone out; it is not worth the effort to light another; the day is beginning). Following fear, there is silence. From time to time, you look at one another; you wait. Her hands move with agility.

You ask: "What is it?"

"Come closer."

"May I see it?"

"There is little light. Come. Touch it. Do not be afraid."

"Then you have finished?"

You know she smiles, and that her smile is two answers: she finished it some time ago; she will never finish it.

"Yes, come here. What do you think it is?"

"It's in the shape of a bird."

"Yes, but that's incidental. Almost an accident."

"It's like touching a bird. Those are feathers, I'm sure of that."

"And in the center? In the very center?"

"Just a minute . . . no, not feathers, I'd say . . . I'd say they're . . . ants."

"Wrong again. Spiders. The creatures without time."

"But those lines . . . like ribs . . . that seem to divide the cloth . . ."

"You can call it cloth, if you wish . . ."

". . . that seem to divide it into zones . . . of feathers . . . and then separate the feathers from that . . . that field of spiders, you say . . . a field of spiders in the very center, yes . . ."

"Touch it, touch it, run your fingers over it. Follow the ribs to their ends."

"Let me feel it . . . like branches . . . very fine . . . filaments, almost . . . but they end, they end, like darts . . ."

"Arrows. Arrows divide the field. The known field. They partition it. We need light. I wish you could see the colors."

"Dawn is coming."

"There are divisions of green, blue, garnet, and yellow feathers."

"Soon we will be able to see it together."

"The color of each field indicates the kind of bird that can be hunted there. In addition, these are the actual feathers of the birds that inhabit each sector of the jungle. The quetzal, the hummingbird, the macaw, the golden pheasant, the wild duck, and the heron. Each area is irregular, do you feel it?, except for the center. That is regular; it has a perfect circumference. That is the forbidden part of the jungle. There are no feathers there; no one can derive sustenance there; there nothing can be hunted and killed to satisfy the hunger of the body; there dwell the masters of words, signs, and enchantments. Their kingdom is the field of dead spiders that I join with glue to the object you call cloth. And the limits of the cloth are those of the known world. One can go no farther. But one would like to go farther. The tips of the arrows all point outward. Toward the unknown world. They are a limit; they are also invitation. The frontier between the hearth and the marvelous. This is what the Indian woman told me in her tongue as she handed me this offering the first time I came to this land."

You recall the sparse information, given the difficulty of communications, you have been able to obtain. She entered the country on a tourist's visa, and she was a professional anthropologist. At least that's what her papers said. An English father and a Spanish mother, or vice versa, this was not clear. You could not verify her name, or the date of her birth. She was captured while wandering around the camp site, wearing the white cloth mask that covers her face; she said it was for protection against mosquitoes. In the present situation, there was only one possible attitude: suspicion, presumption of guilt. She had said nothing that would prove the innocence of her occupation or that of her appearance in the very place where you are directing the war of resistance. By her voice, her hands, her hunched figure, you deduced that she is old. That is what you call her: Old Woman. She continues to glue the spiders, in silence now. You watch her. Life is renewing all around us. You listen. Water is being drawn by hand, bicycle tires inflated—the whistle of escaping air, bullets introduced into rifle chambers; someone is raking a nearby garden; refugee children nurse at the breasts of women squatting against walls facing the sun. But the beating of the drum envelops and dominates everything else. A naked, bleeding messenger enters the camp and falls to his knees, panting. One hears distant Indian flutes.

"The music of the Nayar," murmured the Old Woman. "I knew a village of Coras where the church had been abandoned. I was there once, and I recall hearing that music of flute and drum. The church was constructed a little more than two centuries ago, after the late Spanish conquest of that rebellious and inaccessible region. The Indians, the ancient fallen princes, were the masons on the construction. The missionaries showed them engravings of the saints, and the Indians reproduced the images in their own fashion. The church was an indigenous paradise, an opaque vessel containing the colors and forms of the lost kingdom. The altars were golden birds chained to the earth. The dome was an enormous smoking mirror. The white faces of the plaster sculptures laughed bestially; the dark faces wept. One could believe that the Coras, only recently defeated, were reaffirming the continuity of their lives by appropriating the symbols of the conquistador and investing them with a form that continued to represent aboriginal heavens and hells. The missionaries tolerated that transformation. After all, the cross governed. And now one sign would represent the same promise, formerly fragmented into a thousand divinities of wind and sun, water and deer, parrot and blazing bramble. When the work was completed, the missionary pointed to the Christ on the altar and said that the church was the place of love because in it reigned the God of love. The Indians believed it. By night they entered the church and beneath the gaze of that tortured Christ who suffered like them, fornicated at the foot of the altar amid soft bird-like laughter and sighs like wounded cubs'. The missionary discovered them and threatened them with all the fury of Hell. And the Indians could not understand why the God of love could not be witness to love. They had been given a promise, which was the same as permission. And suddenly the fulfillment of the promise had become a prohibition. The Indians rebelled, banished the missionary, and filled with mute deception closed the doors of the church of the false God of love. They decided to visit that church, which for them had been converted into the cloister of Hell, only once a year, and disguised as Devils. The walls are cracked and the atrium is overrun with weeds. A devouring desert, a ruined land whose only temples are the magueys. But the firmament overhead is enormous and burning. The Indians paint their bodies black and white and blue, slowly, caressing one another as if they were again dressing in ancient ceremonial garments: the land is the canvas; the origin of paint is vegetal. Afterward, they simulate a collective fornication beneath the dome of the sky. But the acts of that long sensual passion celebrated every Holy Week are identified with the acts of the Christian Passion. The sighs of abandonment in the Garden of Olives, the cup of vinegar, Calvary, the Crucifixion, the company of the two thieves, the wound in the side, the garment wagered at dice, death, the deposition, and the burial of the holy body are interpreted sexually, like a sorrowful sodomy: God, physically, loved men. It is very strange. The church was a symbol and in it they wished to effect a real act. The sun is real, but beneath its rays they enact a merely symbolic act. The ceremony is observed by a masked man on horseback wearing the large sombrero of the horseman. This horseman cloaks his body in a cape of red silk and covers his face with a feather mask. Only on Holy Saturday does he show his face; Christ has arisen, but not the historical Christ who suffered during the reign of Tiberius and was delivered unto Pilate, but the founding god, he who delivered unto men the seeds of corn, who taught them to cultivate and to harvest: a god not belonging to the time of Christ but to the time of a constantly renewed origin. It is very strange. Do you know that place and that ceremony?''

Yes, you know them, but you say nothing to the woman. You suspect the real intent of her question. She repeats it, is still, and then . . . what day is it? she asks. You believe it is useless to answer. Slowly she struggles to her feet. You fear she will fall. You also rise, to take her arm, but your instinct keeps you at a distance, though nevertheless dependent upon her; beside her, but not touching her, you duplicate quite naturally her infirm step, picturing the imminent collapse of that fatigued body; finally, brusquely, she supports herself against the central pole of the hut that holds up the straw roof. You move toward her; she clutches the pole but extends her hands toward you, imploring you with words you cannot hear.

"What? What are you saying? I can't hear you."

You approach her as you would a little girl, or an animal. You try to divine her desire. You cannot escape her odor. Ancient salt. Mineral husks. Herbivorous fish. Rotten oranges. Black and volatile fumes. A second, viscous skin that passes from her hands to your defenseless skin, now that finally you take her like a little girl or an animal, trying to divine her desire, and lead her to the tiny garden behind the hut: the parcel of land barred on three sides by bamboo, the fourth side a thick adobe wall, a pretension of private property the distant bombardment makes ridiculous.

You cannot escape her smell. You cannot stop touching her. The damp rags that envelop her. You feel the vertigo of an elusive memory.

In the forgotten garden everything is weeds, and if once someone tended it, today it bears evidence of different labor: rusted bicycle wheels, saws, a box of nails, some empty gasoline cans. It looks like a garden of metal, a gallery of scrap-metal sculptures. Its only purpose now is to serve as depository for useless objects that may someday, unexpectedly, again become useful. The wire of the wheels can be used for binding wire. The empty cans as floats. The thick, bullet-pocked wall can be used again.

"Don't you see?"

"Yes. A garden. Things."

"No. Something more."

"Nothing is happening here."

"Give me a drink."

You hand her the gourd and look around. The weed-filled garden is indifferent to your gaze, merely describing to you its own nature, compact, green, bounded on three sides by the fence of bamboo tied together with thick maguey rope, the fourth by the wall of crumbling adobe. Weeds emerge from damp ground only to end in split, dried-up, burned tips.

We know this territory inch by inch, from the river Chachalacas to the peak of the Cofre de Perote, and from the Huasteca Tamaulipas to the mouths of the Coatzacoalcos: the besieged half-moon of our last defense against the invader. The rest of the republic is occupied by the North American Army. And facing the Gulf coasts, the Caribbean fleet observes, bombards, and launches raids. Here in Veracruz we were founded by a conquest, and here, almost five centuries later, a different conquest attempts our eternal destruction. We know inch by inch, sierra by sierra, barranca by barranca, tree by tree, this last citadel of our identity.

The Old Woman raises her arm; an age-spotted hand appears from among her rags and a finger points toward the depths of the jungle. Beyond the cimarron trees, sleeping violets, and greedy, spotted tiger-flowers. She points, and then stoops as if to trace a circle in the dust. Her index finger is a knotted scepter. The veils that fall from her head tremble, and she springs like a puma. She digs her fingernails into your chest and you stagger back, off balance; you feel her hands like a tourniquet about your throat and the breath of a weary journey near your mouth: "Why are we staying here? Why do you not take me to a different place?"

She says (and you know) that the question merely passes through lips that are the conduit for the jungle that contemplates you and the jewels the jungle hides. You embrace her in passive combat; in her hand the Old Woman still holds the cloth (you don't know what else to call it: map?, guide for the hunt?, plan of operations?, talisman?): feathers, spiders and filaments. The only drum resounds, always swifter and more muted.

You push the Old Woman aside with a feeling of physical repugnance (the breath; the bestial hands; the filthy clothing; especially that breath of mushrooms and mildew). You tell her firmly, and with rage: "I know the place you mean. It's an abandoned pyramid. We've hidden there several times. And it serves as a depository for weapons. I tell you this because you will never be able to reveal it to anyone."

But as you see her there, thrown to the ground in the garden, staring at the thick wall, you must struggle against the pity the woman evokes. A heavy silence surrounds her, as tangible as actual absence; silence, a deserved repose, like that of death; similar, at least, to the chronic death of dream.

The drum resounds and she lies at the foot of the adobe wall. You do not know what she is waiting for, what she invites you to, what she expects of you, whether she wished to remain there or go to the sumptuous Totonac tomb the jungle has devoured.

The Old Woman writhes on the ground and screams, a scream indistinguishable from the others, those of macaws abandoning the jungle in flocks of terror now that the Phantoms return flying in low formation.

The repeated whistle, impact, explosion, intolerable in their screeching descent, the explosion muffled by the foliage of useless targets: they are devastating jungle . . . nothingness.

You raise your fist to curse them once again: but that is your daily prayer, your sign of the cross; fucking gringo sons of bitches. They fly so low you can read the black insignia on the wings: USAF.

The din strikes against your eardrums with the everyday, irritating sound of a knife scraping against a frying pan. You grasp the maddened dervish beneath the arms and she cries out sharply and tries to hold herself by clawing at the dust at the foot of the bullet-pocked wall; you try to drag her forcibly into the hut where you both should be lying face down for the duration of the bombardment, this time closer and more severe, and furthermore, unforeseen; generally they make their pass only once, in the early morning, dump their load of napalm and lazy dogs and return to their bases. Today they have repeated their daily incursion. What's happening, you wonder; is this a portent of their victory, or of our resistance? That stretch of garden between you and the hut seems fantastically long; the Old Woman is simultaneously an inert bundle and a metal nerve, a bag of rags and a root sunk several meters into the ground; she is an electrical conductor for voices, fears, and desires that perhaps avail themselves of this weakness to install their strength. Other traditions tell that beings of this nature are instantly recognizable, and can penetrate without obstacle all places, sacred and profane: their voice and their movement are those of an imminence that can appear as easily in a temple as in a brothel.

Why do you not dare tear off the white cloth that covers her face? The temple and the brothel. The Old Woman spoke of the Church of Santa Teresa in the Sierra del Nayar. Then she had been there, in that place you fear so greatly. You listened to her describe it and didn't know whether this woman was plotting against your country or against your life; whether she was spying on rebellious forces or spying on you when she came to this hidden camp in the Veracruz jungle. You heard her describe the temple constructed by the Coras under the watchful eyes of the Spanish missionaries and you recalled the time you spent there in a different time, when you believed you had a different vocation: the artist's brush, not the gun. You were sent—you must have been about twenty, no more—with a group of specialists from the Churubusco School to restore the splendor of an old and forgotten painting of enormous dimensions, neglected, damaged by the centuries, humidity, fungus, lack of care, situated behind the altar of that temple of God the Indians had converted into the Devil's brothel. The peeling and blistered surface depicted, in the foreground, a group of naked men in the center of a vast Italian piazza. Their backs were turned to the viewer and their attitude was one of anguish, of desolate waiting, of terror before an imminent end. To the right of this foreground, a Christ wearing the traditional robes of his teaching, blue mantle and white tunic, stared intently at these men. In the background, forming a deep semicircle, fanned out minute scenes of the New Testament. Professionally, your team prepared to limn the damaged oil painting anew, to remedy its wounds, to fix its colors. Someone, many years before, must have lashed the painting with a whip; you would think that blood had run down the canvas, and that the skin of the painting still had not healed.

Your fancy provoked the laughter of your companions; but soon everyone could see that this fantasy revealed a truth: the painting had been painted on top of another; it was difficult to see with the naked eye because both paintings, the original and the one that was superimposed, were very old, and their materials were very similar. You all discussed whether it could be a pentimento; you imagined an aged and remorseful painter who, lacking materials, used the same canvas to cover up a failure and at the same time create another more perfect work. Someone said that perhaps it was a painting in which the outer stratum had tended to separate from the preparatory stratum. Another said that doubtlessly it was an abortive sketch, and the painter had let too much time pass between the preparatory and the final phases.

You X-rayed the canvas, but the results were very confusing. Colors least penetrable by X-ray were predominant in the painting: lead white, vermilion, and lead yellow. The negative barely suggested differentiations among the hidden images: like a succession of ghosts superimposed one upon the other, the figures reflected several times their own specters, the paint was thick, very old, perhaps what you were seeing was merely a faithful rendering of the original, a past restoration, a swarm of artistic repentances, a simple transposition of colors. You asked permission to make one final test: to resort to an infinitesimally small section made with your artist's knife; the painting had already been badly treated, it would be sufficient to lift off a tiny fragment that had cracked by itself, treat it with resin and balsam on a glass slide, and examine it under the microscope to see whether between the layers of color there appeared a subtle film of dirt or yellowed varnish. Your test was successful: the color revealed was not the original color of the painting; an intangible line of time separated the two.

With increasing excitement, but also with great caution, your crew cleaned the painting. You applied solvents to its surface, dividing it into small rectangular zones, scraping away with your knives plaster, fungus, tenacious crusts, and little by little the stripped, false skin of the oil painting peeled away, and little by little, no more than thirty centimeters a day, the oils applied with enormous care, the drops of ammonia, alcohol, turpentine, there appeared before the astonished eyes of your small group of artists the original form of the painting.

It was a strange and vast portrait of a court. It could only be a court of Spain, and not one court, but all courts, centuries reunited in a single gallery of gray stone, beneath an arch of stormy shadows. In the foreground, a kneeling King with an air of intense melancholy, a breviary in his hands, a fine hound lying by his side, a King dressed in mourning, his face marked by repressed sensuality, a fine ascetic profile, thick, drooping lips, noticeable prognathism, self-absorbed but inquiring eyes, thin, silky hair and beard; and forming a circle with the King, two additional figures: a Queen in sumptuous attire, elaborate hoopskirts and belled farthingales, a high ruff, a hawk perched on her wrist—never had you seen in eyes so blue, in skin so fair, an expression of such vulnerable strength and cruel compassion; and a man dressed as a chief huntsman, one hand resting upon the hilt of his blade, a hooded falcon on his shoulder, the other hand forcefully restraining a pack of mastiffs. To the left and rear, a funeral procession trooped onto the canvas; it was led by an old and mutilated woman wrapped in black rags, armless and legless, a yellow-eyed bundle pushed on a little cart by a toothless and chubby-cheeked dwarf draped in clothing too generous for her stature; behind them came a page-and-drummer dressed all in black, with submissive gray eyes and tattooed lips; and behind the drummer, a sumptuous, wheeled coffin and a vast company of mayors, alguaciles, stewards, secretaries, ladies-in-waiting, workmen, beggars, halberdiers, captive Hebrews and Moslems accompanying an endless row of funeral carriages that disappeared into the background of the painting, and also surrounded by bishops, deacons, chaplains, and chapters of all the orders. On the right side of the painting, as if watching the spectacle, crouched a flautist, a beggar with olive skin and protruding green eyes, and behind him a huge monster floated in a sea of fire, a cross between a shark and a hyena, whose gaping mouth devoured human bodies. And in the very center of the painting, behind the circle presided over by the black figure of the kneeling King, in the space formerly occupied by the naked men, a trio of young men, also naked, their arms entwined, their backs to the viewer; on each back was stamped the sign of a cross, a blood-red cross. And beyond this plane, deeper and deeper in the perspective of gray stone and black shadow, a group of half-naked nuns lashed themselves with penitential cilices; and one of them, the most beautiful, held broken glass in her mouth, and her lips were bleeding; processions of hooded monks with tall lighted tapers; in a high tower a red-haired monk observed the impenetrable sky; in a similar tower a one-armed scribe bent over an ancient parchment; an equestrian statue of a Comendador; a plain of tortures: smoking stakes, racks, men twisted with pain, pilloried; scenes of battle and throat slashing; minute details: broken mirrors, mandrakes emerging from the burned earth beneath funeral pyres, half-consumed candles, plague-infested cities, a masked nun with a bird's beak, a distant beach, a half-constructed boat, an ancient sailor with a hammer in his hand, a flight of crows, fading into the boundaries of the canvas a double row of royal sepulchers, jasper tombs, recumbent statues, mere sketches, an infinite succession of deaths, vertiginous attraction toward the infinite; increasing darkness in the background, dazzling chromatic symphony in the foreground: blue, white, golden yellow, vivid red, and orange red.

Of the three youths writhing and twisting in their mutual embrace like Laocoön in his battle with the serpents, only one showed his face. And that face was yours.

The painting had no date, although it was signed: *Julianus, Pictor et Frater, Fecit.*

Like you, everyone was at first astonished to see you depicted in a portrait painted four, five, six centuries earlier . . . There was discussion of coincidences, then everyone joked about it and left the church to eat with the white-clad Indians beneath an enormous sun beating down upon the sick land of the Cora people.

"Silence will never be absolute." This you say to yourself as you listen to her. "Forlornness, yes, possibly; suspected nakedness, that too; darkness, certainly . . ."

This she says as you try to drag her toward the hut; she says it, but she says it with your voice. Black scale falls from her eyelids. The whites of her eyes are shot with green veins. Her eyes gyrate in their sockets like two captive moons: her white veil has fallen away.

"But either the isolation of the place or that of forever embraced figures [she says to you, señor caballero] seems to convoke that reunion of sound [the drum; squeaking carriage wheels; horses; the solemn chant, luminis claritatem; the panting of the woman; the distant bursting of waves upon the coast where you awoke this morning, again in another land as unknown as your name] which in the apparent silence [as if it was taking advantage of the exhaustion of your own defenses] builds layer upon layer of its most tenacious, keenest, most resounding insinuations . . ."

Ants swarm across the livid face of the Old Woman lying on her back in the dust of the garden.

You can say nothing; her wrinkled lips silence yours, and as she kisses you, without wishing it you speak what she says in the name of what she, her body resting upon yours, convokes. Like her, you are inertia transformed into a conduit for energy; you were found along the road; you had a different destiny; she separates her lips from yours and her hands stroke your features, they seem to be drawing, tracing, a second face upon yours. Her fingers are heavy and rough. They seem to hold colors and stones they arrange upon your features, as your former face disappears with every stroke of her fingertips. The fingernails scrape against your teeth as if filing them. Dry palms pass through your hair, as if spreading a blondish, reddish dye, and as they touch your cheeks, those hands create a beard light as plumage. Her fingers work upon your former skin.

"The silence that surrounds us [señor caballero, she calls you, her head resting upon your knees] is the mask of silence: its person."

Her hands claw at the air. You offer her the gourd filled with pulque and she drinks without argument, vitally gross. Again she brushes your lips with her fingers. Pulque dribbles down her quivering chin. You drink what her mouth offers you. You hear her murmuring and feel you are again a child in your mother's lap, far from war, far from death; she tells you that you are young and handsome, a child, sleep, sleep, rest, rest; such clear eyes, such soft cheeks, such moist lips. She strokes your armpits. You raise your arms and cradle your head in your clasped hands; she toys with the moist hair on your chest, the excited nipples of a mischievous child.

"I have managed to deceive you. Every night, when you are not watching me, I have been writing you a letter: My beloved, I think of you constantly from this land filled with the memories of our best years . . . Here everything speaks to me of you; your Lake Como, so dear to you, spreads before my eyes in all its azure serenity, and everything seems the same as it was before; except that you are there, so far away, so far . . . I know how to read at night, señor caballero.''

Laughing, her finger counts your ribs, and creeps into your navel, is moistened by the sweat and dirt accumulated there, faint testimony that for days you have not descended to the river, there is no time, everything one does is indispensable, eating, sleeping, waking, we bathe together in the river, but no one looks at the others, soldiers and camp followers, our bodies are also our uniform, we must win our ultimate battle or we shall have no reason to continue living, the vegetation on the shore hides us, our bodies are the color of the deep grasses swaying on the bed of the tropical river. The belly is a smooth stone in the depths of the placid river. She caresses you, and murmurs. Body hair is moss on the stones that lie in the depths of the turbulent river.

"Air and light. Those of us who still cultivate the deception of the senses require them. Ideas flower, but quickly wither, recollections are lost, sentiments are inconstant. Smell, touch, hearing, sight, and taste are the only sure proofs of our existence and of the reflected reality of the world. You believe that. Do not deny it.''

Scorpius, sweet purple scorpion, raceme of moist mud. She caresses you, clasps you, cups your weight.

"We have left our homes and we must pay the price of such prodigious behavior. Exile is marvelous homage to our origins.''

Her toothless mouth descends upon your belly.

"You believe that time always advances. That all is future. You want a future; you cannot imagine yourself without it. You do not want to provide any opportunity to those of us who require that time disintegrate and then retrace its steps until it come to the privileged moment of love and there, only there, stop forever.''

Her tongue slides along the burning smoothness of your penis; toothless gums imprison you; everything is viscous, dank, open; she touches the live fascine of nerves.

"It is sad that you will not live as long as I; a great pity that you cannot penetrate my dreams and see me as I see myself, eternally prostrated at the foot of tombs, eternally present at the death of Kings, insanely wandering through the galleries of palaces yet to be constructed, mad, yes, and drunk with grief before the loss that only the combination of rank and madness can support. I see myself, dream of myself, touch myself, wandering, from century to century, from castle to castle, from crypt to crypt, mother of all Kings, wife of all Kings, surviving all, finally shut up in a castle in the midst of rain and misty grasslands, weeping another death befallen in sunny lands, the death of another Prince of our degenerate blood; I see myself dry and stooped, tiny and trembling as a sparrow, toothless, whispering into indifferent ears: 'Do not forget the last Prince, and let God grant us a sad but not odious memory . . .' "

You spread your legs for her mouth.

"I said to him: do not dishonor yourself, always be the Emperor, make them bow before you; a monarch is a good shepherd, a president is a mercenary; a republic is a stepmother, a monarchy a mother. You and I will be the mother and father of these people, I said to you as we were climbing from the sea, from Veracruz, toward the plateau, toward Mexico City, seeing frontiers of nopal cactus, naked and swollen-bellied children, dark impassive women wrapped in rebozos; stiff, mute men. We loved them so, didn't we, Maxl? Do you remember, Maxl, when we hid behind the curtains at Miramar and watched how your brother's soldiers beat and shot the rebellious Italians; when we allowed them in Trieste to whip a pregnant woman until punishment turned into a blood bath. They told me that we killed ninety thousand Mexicans. But we were their mother and father. They had no name. Only you and I had a name in this anonymous land. But now, dear Maxl, now that I imagine you alone and besieged, far away, dead, I would like to shout: in the name of those we murdered without moving a finger, in the name of those who died while we danced in Miramar and Chapultepec, for the pity we did not have for you, may you have pity on us! Punish our crimes with your pity. Let your mercy be our torture. Castigate and pierce our bodies with the intolerable humiliation of forgiveness. Do not grant us martyrdom. We do not deserve it. We do not deserve it. Are we victims of Mexico, Maxl, you and I and all our ancestors, all the kings of Flemish and Austrian and Spanish blood who first conquered this Indian land and, finally, in this place exhausted their royal line? No, in the end we are all the children of Mexico, because only by hatred can one measure love for Mexico, and only Mexico's vengeance is measure of its love. Bells are tolling on the hill. Can you hear them, Maxl? Can you not understand that they are attempting to overcome the roar of the Mexican sun, the weeping of guns, the sighs of prayers, and the trembling of that dry land? Give me back the body of my beloved."

Silence pursued. Silence personified. Spurting, bitter milk; death rattles. The Old Woman's mouth holds you, saliva and semen blend, and now she allows the mingled liquids to return from her lips toward their origin, the exhausted testicles breathing with the rhythm of a caged animal: you are bared to the sky.

"There is no possible exchange, my son. A true gift does not admit equal recompense; an authentic offering rises above all comparison and all price. They gave us an empire; could we repay that with simple death, with simple madness? I, poor wretch, returned to seek what I had lost. Again I plunged into these accursed jungles. I let myself be led by the map of the new world, the map of arrows and insects that allows us to abandon the known world and venture where no one has any claim on us, to the heart of the virgin forest, to the pyramid itself.''

You lie beside the adobe wall, panting beneath the sun.

"It was for nought. My place was already taken. Another woman stood on the steps of the pyramid. An Indian woman. She was adorned with necklaces of jade and turquoise, and she clasped a dagger of flint in her hand. I recognized her; it was she who when I disembarked from the *Novara* offered me this gift: this feather mask. Her feet trod the porous stone of the stairway and I could see the wounds of irons and chains on her ankles. I knew she was waiting for someone—perhaps a different man—to lead him a second time. To repeat the eternal journey of defeats and victories, of jungle and sea, plateau and volcano. I pitied her. I returned the map to her. Now I must reconstruct it if I wish to escape from here, to forget, to return to the penumbra that awaits me . . . the castle in the mists . . .''

A messenger enters, panting and bleeding, and falls to his knees.

"Rest now. You will forget everything I have said. All my words were spoken yesterday.''

The Old Woman imitates the breathing of the wounded man who has just reached your camp in the Veracruz sierra, while you rise slowly to your feet, zipping your trousers; you run your fingers through your hair, and with your feet scatter the night's fire: a pyramid of ashes.

"Each of us has the right to carry a secret to the tomb.''

After entrusting your prisoner to the soldiers, you turn off the battery-powered tape recorder that throughout the night has repeated, hypnotically, a single tape, the constant sound of a funeral drum. That tape recorder is the only thing the Old Woman brought with her when she was captured. You expected to hear a message, decipher a code, find something that would implicate her. Only a tape with the sound of a mourning drum. In vain you search for the cloth—you cannot call it, as she does, a map of the jungle—the trance-induced woman fashioned before your eyes in this very hut.

You go out into the garden and you waste precious time poking through the rubbish at the base of the wall. Futile. If only you could remember the exact design of that cloth: surely it was the map of a primitive hunt, the precise composition of the zones of feathers in relation to the center of spiders, the color of the feathers, the directions signaled by the arrows. You have wasted your time. Your arms fall to your sides. You leave the garden and ask about the messenger who arrived at the camp this morning, panting and wounded.

The messenger is lying on a straw mat in the shade. He drinks awkwardly from the gourd you offer him. He tells you that the previous night he had gone to El Tajín as you had ordered to make a recount of the arms hidden inside the pyramid. He had been overtaken there by an electrical storm and had decided to spend the night in the shelter of the jutting eaves of the Totonac temple. Without close examination it is difficult to distinguish between the luxurious vegetation and the elaborate carving of the façade. Shadows of the jungle and shadows of stone integrate into an inseparable architecture. One can easily be deceived. But he swears to you that as he leaned back into one of the openings in the façade, looking for an eave under which he could take shelter, feeling his way with his hands, he touched a face.

He jerked his hand away, but then overcame his fear and played over the wall the flashlight he always carried tied to his belt. First it illuminated only the sumptuary frets of the temple. But finally, inserted in one of the hollows of the pediment that surely had served as airy tombs for royalty, he discovered what he was looking for. And he tells you that he found a strange body there with a profile eroded by time and corruption; an old, perhaps a hundred-year-old, body placed inside a basket filled with cotton and swimming in pearls; a devoured, featureless face with two staring, black, glassy eyes.

He wanted to investigate more closely; he lifted the cape soaked by the storm and devoured by insects, but two events distracted him: behind him, illuminated by lightning flashes, he saw a young Indian girl with a serene gaze and tattooed lips, barefoot, sad, luxuriously attired, her ankles scarred by shackles; as if waiting, she was sitting at the base of the pyramid: in her hands she held a cloth of feathers and arrows, and at her feet lay a circle of dead butterflies; at the same time, he heard an amazing sound, a drum seeming to advance through the jungle, announcing a future or a past execution; he thought he must be dreaming; through the parted undergrowth appeared a funeral procession composed of people of another epoch, white-coiffed nuns, monks in dark-brown hooded robes, lighted tapers, beggars, ladies gowned in brocades, gentlemen in black doublets with high white ruffs, captives with the Star of David on their breasts, other captives with Arabic features, halberdiers, pages, laborers carrying poles across their shoulders, torches and candles. Our messenger was confounded; he extinguished his flashlight and began to run. Above the sound of the drum several shots thundered in unison. The messenger felt a sting on his shoulder and on his arm. He doesn't know how he managed to reach the camp.

Later you give a few orders, you eat the midday mess and inspect the hanging bridges that tonight will permit us to cross the barrancas, attack the flank of an enemy position, and then disappear into the jungle. We attack only by night. By day we prepare ourselves for combat and blend into the jungle and the population. We all dress like the peons of the region: we are chameleons. We eat, we sleep, we make love, we bathe in the river. If they want to exterminate us, they will have to exterminate the jungle, the rivers, the barrancas, even the ruins—the entire earth and sky.

Following the assassination of the Constitutional President and his family, your brother assumed the post of First Minister in the military regime, and he pleaded with you to join him. Freedom, sovereignty, self-determination; vain words that for defending them as if they were something more than mere words cost the President his life . . . You had to face reality. The government that emerged following the coup had solicited the intervention of the North American Army to help maintain order and to assure a transition to peace and prosperity. The division of the world into inviolable spheres of influence was a fact that saved us all from nuclear conflict. These are the things your brother said to you in his office in the National Palace as he pressed a series of buttons that turned on a number of television screens. A dozen apparatus were lined up along a dais; across their smoking mirrors passed scenes that your brother, redundantly, described to you. This was the brutal reality: the country could not feed its more than a hundred million persons; mass extermination was the only realistic policy; collective brainwashing was necessary to assure that human sacrifice would again be accepted as a religious necessity; the Aztec tradition of sumptuary consumption of hearts must be joined to the Christian tradition of the sacrificed God: blood on the cross, blood on the pyramid; look, he said, pointing toward the illuminated screens. Teotihuacán, Tlatelolco, Xochicalco, Uxmal, Chichén Itzá, Monte Albán, Copilco; they are all in use again. With a smile, he pointed out to you that the commentary was different on each program; the public-relations experts had subtly distributed suitable commentators among the twelve channels to lend to the ceremonies a sports, religious, festive, economic, political, aesthetic, or historical emphasis; one announcer, his voice rushed and excited, was giving the scores of the contest between Teotihuacán and Uxmal: so many hearts in favor of this team, so many in favor of the opposing team; another, in an unctuous voice, was comparing the sites of sacrifice with yesteryear's supermarkets; the sacrifice of life would directly contribute to feeding those Mexicans who escaped death; then a smiling, typically middle-class family was flashed upon the screen, the supposed beneficiary of the extermination; a third announcer was extolling the concept of the fiesta, the recovery of forgotten collective bonds; the feeling of communion these ceremonies provided; another spoke in serious tones of the world situation: cruelty and spilling of blood were in no way fatalities inherent only in the Mexican people: all nations were resorting to such practices in order to resolve problems of overpopulation, scarcity of food, and depletion of energy sources:

Mexico was merely employing a solution fitting to its own sensibilities, its cultural tradition, and its national idiosyncrasy: the flint knife was proudly Mexican; and an eminent physician spoke with a solemn air about universal acceptance of euthanasia and the option—neglected because of mass ignorance and an anachronistic cult of machismo—of employing anesthesia, local or general, etc. . . . .

With horror you watched the ceremonies of death on the electronic mirrors in your brother's office. Was it for this that millions of men since the beginning of Mexican time had been born, had dreamed and struggled and died? In your imagination were superimposed other smoky images that supplanted those flashing across the screens of this walnut and brocade office in this palace of tezontle and granite that had been erected on the very site of the temple of Huitzilopochtli, the bloody hummingbird magus, and in the same plaza that had served as the seat of Aztec power: a vast Catholic cathedral erected upon the ruins of the walls of serpents, the houses of the Spanish conquistadors built on the site of the wall of skulls, a municipal palace whose foundations were laid upon the conquered palace of Moctezuma with its courtyards of birds and beasts, its chambers of albinos, hunchbacks, and dwarfs, and its rooms lined with silver and gold: the images of a tenacious struggle against all fatalities, in spite of all their defeats. Your poor people; without moving from where you stood you could re-create here on those blinking screens and outside, beyond the thick curtains of the office, on the enormous plaza of broken stone established over the slime of the dead lagoon, all the struggles against the victories of the powerful, against fatalisms imposed upon Mexico in the name of all historic and geographic and spiritual destinies; television screen and plaza: peoples subjected to the power of Tenochtitlán, torn from their burning coastal lands, their fertile tropical valleys, from poor pasturing plains, from high, cold forests, to nourish the insatiable gaping jaws of Aztec theocracy, its terrible fiestas of a dying sun and the war of the flowers; screen and plaza: an invincible dream, alive in the eyes of slaves, the good founding god, the Plumed Serpent, will return from the East, he will restore the Golden Age of peace, labor, and brotherhood; screen and plaza: from the houses that walk upon the water on the day predicted for the return of Quetzalcoatl descended the masked gods on horseback, carrying fire in their fingernails and ashes between their teeth, to impose a new tyranny in the name of Christ, a God bathed in blood, a people branded like cattle, slaves of the large estates, prisoners chained in the depths of a gold mine that fed the transitory grandeur of Spain, in the end, beggars both conqueror and conquered, the haughty conquistador and the fallen Prince; screen and plaza: a tenacious dream, executioner and victim, Spanish and Indian, white and copper, a new people, a brown race, we shall preserve what our own fathers attempted to destroy, an orphan people of an unknown father and a blemished mother, sons of La Chingada, the queen of all bitches, we shall save the best of two worlds, a truly new world, New Spain, the Christian Saviour redeemed by the sins of history, the Plumed Serpent liberated by the distance of the legend, a people of mixed blood, founders of a new, free community; the father forgiven, the mother purified; screen and plaza: a green, white, and red flag, a victorious people vanquished by their liberators, a republic of rapacious Creoles, greedy leaders, fattened clergy, plumed tricorns, parading cavalry, shining swords, useless laws, proclamations, and speeches; an avalanche of empty words and cardboard medals buries the same ragged, enslaved people eternally bound to peonage, subjected to taxes, given in sacrifice; screen and plaza: foreign flags, the Stars and Stripes, the Napoleonic tricolor, the two-headed Austrian eagle, the crowned Mexican eagle, a land invaded, humiliated, mutilated; screen and plaza: an invincible dream, to give one's life to vanquish death, there is no matériel with which to combat the Yankees in Churubusco and Chapultepec, the French burn all the villages and hang all their inhabitants, a dark, tenacious Indian, fearsome because he possesses all the dreams and nightmares of a people, confronting a blond and dubious prince, fearful because he possesses all the ills and illusions of a dynasty; screen and plaza: the victorious people once again vanquished, their flags fallen, the barefoot soldier returns to the great estates, the wounded soldiers to the sugar-cane mill, the fleeing Indian to be stripped of his property, to extermination; oppressors from within replace those from without; plaza and screen: plumed hats, gold galloon, and the waltz, the ever present dictator seated on a gunpowder throne before a theater backdrop; the learned despot and his court of aged Comtian Positivists, rich landowners, and pomaded generals; plaza and screen: the dream more stringent than the power, the façade falls under machine-gun fire, bayonets rip the curtain and men in wide sombreros with cartridge belts strapped across their chests appear from behind it, the burning eyes of Morelos, the harsh voices of Sonora, the callused hands of Durango, the dusty feet of Chihuahua, the broken fingernails of Yucatan, a shout breaks one mask, a song the next, a laugh shatters a third mask that hid our true face behind the other two, on a bullet-pocked adobe wall appears the authentic face, bare, previous to all histories because it has been dreaming through the centuries, waiting for the time of its history: flesh indistinguishable from bone, inseparable, grimace from smile; tender fortitude, cruel compassion, deadly friendship, immediate life, all my times are one, my past, right now, my future, right now, my present, right now, not indolence, not nostalgia, not illusion, not fatality: I am the people of all histories, and I insist only—with force, tenderness, cruelty, compassion, brotherhood, life and death—that everything happen instantly, today: my history, neither yesterday nor tomorrow: I want today to be my eternal time, today, today, today, today I want love and the fiesta, solitude and communion, Paradise and Hell, life and death, today, not another mask, accept me as I am, my wound inseparable from my scar, my weeping from my laughter, my flower from my knife; screen and plaza: no one has waited so long, no one has dreamed so long, no one has so struggled against the fatality, the passivity, the ignorance others have invoked to condemn him, as this supernatural people who a long time ago should have died of the natural causes of injustice and the lies and scorn oppressors have heaped upon the wounded body of Mexico; screen and plaza: all for this?, you ask yourself, so many millennia of struggle and suffering and rejecting oppression, so many centuries of invincible defeat, a people risen time and time again from its own ashes, only to end like this: the same ritual extermination of their origins, the same colonial suppression of their beginnings, the happy lie at the end . . . again?

Your brother saw your expression and warned you: resistance would be futile, a heroic but empty gesture; a few guerrillas could never defeat the most powerful army on earth; we need order and stability, we must accept the reality of our contemporary world, be satisfied with being a protectorate of Anglo-Saxon democracy, we are interdependent, no one will come to our assistance, the spheres of influence are too perfectly defined, U.S.A., U.S.S.R., China, get rid of your anachronistic ideas, there are only three powers in the world, we are going to realize the dream of universal government, and shelve your moth-eaten nationalism . . .

You seized the paper knife lying on the desk of the First Minister and plunged it into his belly; your brother had no opportunity to cry out, blood spurted from his mouth, choking him; you drove the bronze dagger into his chest, his back, his face; your brother fell against the multicolored buttons and the pictures faded from the screens, the mirrors once again covered with smoke.

You walked calmly from the office, amiably, you bade goodbye to the secretaries: your brother had asked that no one interrupt him for any reason. Slowly you walked the length of the corridors and patios of the National Palace. You stopped for an instant on the stairway and in the central patio before the murals of Diego Rivera. The Military Junta had ordered they be boarded over. They gave as an excuse the imminent need for restoration.

You open your eyes. You see the real world surrounding you and you know that you are that world and that you battle for it. It is not the first time we have fought. Your smile fades. Perhaps it is the last.

"What shall we do with the old woman, sir?"

"I don't know. I don't want to decide."

"Forgive me, sir, but who, if not you?"

"We could stow her away somewhere, Dusty. In some solitary, well-guarded house. How about a madhouse or a convent, Dusty?"

"Is there no superior officer who decides these things?"

"No, sir. There's not enough time."

"You're right. It's also true that we don't have any extra men to look after prisoners . . ."

"Besides, they limit our mobility."

"And as an example, Dusty, as an example. Of course she was a spy, one of the enemy. This isn't her country."

"Very well. Shoot her today. Over there, against the wall behind my hut."

"What's she doing?"

"Writing names in the dust with her finger."

"What names?"

"Names of old bitches: Juana, Isabel, Carlota . . ."

Beneath the sun you walk back toward the Indian hut. You wonder whether as it appears every morning the sun sacrifices its light in honor of our need; or whether that light, in some manner sufficient to itself, spends its transparency in revealing our opacity. But the light gives form and reality to our bodies. You must shake off this nightmare. Because of the light we know who we are. Without it, we would come to invent identity antennae, detectors for the bodies we wished to touch and recognize. You wonder whether it is possible to shoot a ghost. You aren't lying to yourself anymore, you know where you have seen before the eyes of an ancient, mutilated, armless and legless woman wrapped in black rags, the eyes of a Queen of vulnerable strength and cruel compassion. The nightmare calls you again; you were also in that painting . . .

You stop. Beside the entrance to the hut a young native girl with smooth, firm (you are sure) skin, tattooed lips, and scarred ankles is weaving and unraveling, with dexterity and serenity, a strange cloth of feathers. At her side, a soldier is playing a guitar, and singing. You approach the girl. In that instant, the bombardment begins anew.

The lazy dog consists of a mother bomb fabricated of light metal that bursts while still in the air and close to the ground, or when it strikes the ground. Inside the mother bomb there are three hundred metal balls, each the size of a tennis ball, which, as they are liberated from the maternal bosom, scatter independently in every direction, either exploding immediately or lying in ambush in undergrowth or dust, awaiting a child's foot or a woman's hand, blowing off the foot, the hand, or the head of the first woman or child who touches it. The men are all in the mountains.

REQUIEM

Recently he had been assaulted by a terrifying multitude of afflictions.

Five wounds erupted; the nuns of the palace called them wounds so as to suggest that the King's suffering was like that of Christ himself; and Felipe accepted this blasphemy in the name of his hunger for God. One wound on the thumb of his right hand, three on the index finger of the same hand, and another on a toe of his right foot. These five suppurating points tormented him night and day; he could not bear even the contact of the sheets. Finally, the wounds healed, but he was completely incapable of movement. He was transported from place to place in a sedan chair carried, in turn, by four nuns. El Señor observed to Madre Milagros: "Any thing that enters a convent will never leave it; no person, no money, no secret. I could have chosen to be transported by four deaf-mute servants: but thus will you and your Sisters be, Milagros, deaf and mute to everything you see and hear."

He asked them to carry him once more to the dark corner of the chapel where his mother, the one called the Mad Lady, reposed in a wall; he asked her: "Mother, what are you doing?"

Madre Milagros and Sisters Angustias, Caridad, and Ausencia knelt, frightened, and began to pray in a low voice when they discerned through the crack between the bricks the amber eyes of the ancient Queen about whom so much had been conjectured by gossips and tattlers: she had returned to absolute seclusion in the castle of Tordesillas; she had in life buried herself beside the cadaver of her most beloved husband, she had been accidentally killed during the fierce slaughter in the chapel presided over by Guzmán, she had fled to new lands with her farting dwarf and her lunatic Idiot Prince. Now they heard her voice:

"Oh, my son, how wise you were never to abandon the protection of your walls, and never to cross the seas so you might know the lands of your vast Indian empire. No one, no sovereign of our blood, had ever stepped upon the shores of the new world: they were more discreet than I. But consider, my dear son, my dilemma: my handsome husband, blond as the sun, was only second in succession; we were living in the shadow of the Emperor, Maxl's brother, in the court in Vienna; amid the frivolity of balls and court etiquette we were living on crumbs from the imperial table, always second, never first, mere delegates, representatives in Milan and Trieste of the true power in an unredeemed and rebellious Italy subjected to the power of Austria. How could we help but hear the song of the siren? An empire, our own empire, in Mexico, our land, discovered, conquered, and colonized by our royal line, but not one royal foot had sunk into the sands of Veracruz. Maxl, Maxl, the poison of incestuous generations was more concentrated in you, my beloved, the hereditary traits, the prognathic jaw, the brittle bones, the thick, parted lips: even so, your blue eyes and your blond beard gave you the aspect of a god; but you could engender no sons. I told you that night in Miramar, if we cannot have children, we shall have an empire. The good Mexicans offered us a throne; we would be good parents to that people; but the Emperor, your brother, refuses us aid: he envies you; accept the aid of Bonaparte; his troops will protect us from the handful of rebels who oppose us. We disembarked from the *Novara* into the burning tropics, a sky filled with vultures, a jungle of parrots, an aroma of vanilla, orchid, and orange, we climbed to the dry plain, so like this of Castile, my son, to the site of our ancestor's power, the conquered city, Mexico, the rebellious country, Mexico: an ancient legend, Maxl, a white, blond-haired and bearded god, the Plumed Serpent, the god of good and peace; but they did not want us, my son, they deceived us, my son, they fought to the death against us, they faded into the jungle, the mountains, the plain, they were peons by day and soldiers by night, they attacked, they fled, they lay in ambush, an invisible army of barefoot Indians; we reacted with the fury of our blood: hostages, villages burned, rebels shot, women hanged; nothing subdued them, the French Army abandoned us, first you wanted to flee with them, but I told you that one of our dynasty would never undertake cowardly flight, I would go to Paris, to Rome, I would force Napoleon to live up to his promises, I would force the Pope to protect us; they scorned me, they humiliated me, I became demented, they tried to poison me, they allowed me to spend one night in the Vatican, the first woman ever to sleep in St. Peter's, then I went to our villa at Lake Como, I received your letters, Maxl, you, alone, abandoned, your letters: If God allows you to recover your health, and if you can read these lines, you will know in what measure I have been buffeted by adversity, one blow after another, since you went away. Misfortune dogs my footsteps and destroys all my hopes. Death seems to me a happy solution. We are surrounded. Imperial messengers have been hanged by the Republicans within sight of us, in trees across the river. The Austrian hussars have been unable to come to our aid. Our munitions and provisions are exhausted. The good Sisters bring us a little bread made from the flour of the Hosts. We eat the meat of mules and horses. We live in our last refuge, the Convent of the Cross. From its towers one can look out over the panorama of the city of Querétaro. I do not know how long we can resist. I shall comport myself to the end like a sovereign defeated but not dishonored. Farewell, my beloved. I answered him: My beloved, I think of you constantly from this land filled with the memories of our best years . . . Here everything speaks to me of you; your Lake Como, so dear to you, spreads before my eyes in all its azure serenity, and everything seems the same as it was before; except that you are there, so far away, so far . . . My letter, my son, arrived too late; the bullet-pierced body, convulsed at the base of the firing wall, refused to die. A soldier approached and fired the coup de grâce into his breast. The black tunic burst into flame. A majordomo ran and snuffed out the flame with his livery. The body was taken to a convent to be embalmed so it could be returned to the family. The carpenter, from Juárez's army, had never seen him in his lifetime. He did not measure correctly. They brought him down from the Hill of the Bells on a caisson of the Republican Army, inside the too-small box, his legs dangling outside the coffin. Naked, the body was laid out on a table. But they had to wait a long time before taking up the scalpel and opening the body cavity. There was no disinfectant naphthaline in the convent. They found a flask of zinc chloride. This liquid was injected into his arteries and veins. The process took three days. Four bullets had penetrated his torso, three through the left breast, and one through the right nipple. A fifth bullet had burned his eyebrows and brow. Beneath the sun one eye had burst from its socket, as if throughout his life he had stared at it without blinking. They searched through the churches for eyes the color of his: blue. Saint by saint; virgin by virgin—only black eyes. Blue had fled from the gaze of that country. They clothed him in a campaign tunic of blue cloth. A row of golden buttons from waist to neck. Long breeches, tie, kid gloves. There was so little left. Barely a rushing of wind. They inserted eyes of black glass in the hollow sockets: no one could have recognized him. Exhausted gases escaped from the opened belly, bubbled in his ears, covered his lips with green spume. The body lay convulsed. A soldier fired the coup de grâce into his breast and then leaned against the adobe wall to smoke. After two weeks, the body turned black. The zinc injections had destroyed the roots of the hair. It was impossible to recognize beneath the glass of the coffin— that bald head, that beardless chin, those false eyes, that flesh first swollen and then sunken—the imperial profile known on gold medallions. The features were erased. My beloved had the face of the beaches of the new world. Again his body crossed the great ocean, on the same ship that had brought us there, the *Novara*. No one could recognize him. I never saw him again. Look at me, my son; I am that ancient mad doll dressed in a lace dressing gown and coiffed in silk, shut up in a Belgian castle, escaping at times to search beneath the trees of the misty meadows a nut, a little fresh water; they wish to poison me. My name is Carlota.''

That day El Señor abandoned the niche of his mother, the Mad Lady, with great sadness; he did not need to threaten the nuns to silence; it was sufficient to look upon their four bloodless faces, transparent with fear. In the sedan chair they carried him back to the bedchamber and lifted him onto his bed. During that time he was experiencing the first onslaught of a dropsy that swelled his belly, his thighs and legs; and this rheum was accompanied by an implacable thirst, a tormenting passion, for dropsy is fed most unrestrainedly by that which is most delicious to it: water. While he was in that condition, he received a folio signed by the grandees of the kingdom, wherein they explained the lamentable state of the royal coffers owing to droughts, scarcity of laborers, attacks by buccaneers upon galleons carrying back treasures from the new world, and the financial astuteness of the families of Jews settled in the north of Europe.

With his afflicted hand El Señor tortuously wrote orders for monks of the kingdom to go from door to door begging alms for their King. And to prove his Christian humility, he asked that on Holy Thursday he be carried to the chapel for the ceremony of the washing of feet, and that for that purpose be brought seven of the poor from among the multitude of beggars perpetually surrounding the palace awaiting scraps from the palace meals. He insisted, in spite of the pain of movement, on performing this rite of humility. On the morning of Holy Thursday he approached the poor on his knees, supported by Sister Clemencia and Sister Dolores, and with a damp cloth in his wounded hand and a basin of water Sister Esperanza held for him, he proceeded to wash the feet marred with scabs and wounds and buried thorns. After he washed each pair of feet, bowing down, still kneeling, he kissed them; then the hand of one of those poor fell upon his shoulder; El Señor checked his anger, looked up, and met the gaze of Ludovico, the resigned, green, protruding eyes of the former theology student.

First Felipe wept upon Ludovico's knees, embracing them, while the beggar's hand rested upon El Señor's shoulder and the frightened nuns watched and the Bishop continued the Divine Services before an altar draped with black crape, like the effigies and sepulchers in the chapel. Then El Señor made a gesture that meant all is well, do not be alarmed, let us talk. Ludovico leaned over until his head touched Felipe's.

"My friend, my old friend," murmured El Señor. "Where have you come from?"

Ludovico looked at El Señor with affectionate sorrow. "From New Spain, Felipe."

"Then you triumphed. Your dream was realized."

"No, Felipe, you triumphed: the dream was a nightmare . . . The same order you desired for Spain was transported to New Spain; the same rigid, vertical hierarchies; the same style of government: for the powerful, all the rights and no obligations; for the weak, no rights and all obligations; the new world has been populated with Spaniards enervated by unexpected luxury, the climate, the mixing of bloods, and the temptations of unpunished injustice . . ."

"Then neither you nor I triumphed, my brother, but Guzmán."

Ludovico smiled enigmatically, he took Felipe's face in his hands and stared directly into his sunken, hollow eyes.

"But I sent Julián, Ludovico," said El Señor. "I sent him to temper—to whatever degree possible—Guzmán's acts, the acts of all the Guzmáns."

"I do not know." Ludovico shook his head. "I simply do not know."

"Did he construct his churches, paint his pictures, speak in behalf of the oppressed?" asked Felipe in an increasingly anguished voice.

"Yes." Now Ludovico nodded. "Yes, he did the things you speak of: he did them in the name of a unique creation capable, according to him, of transposing to art and to life the total vision of the universe born of the new science . . ."

"What creation?, what does he call it?"

"It is called Baroque, and it is an instantaneous flowering: its bloom so full that its youth is its maturity, and its magnificence its cancer. An art, Felipe, which, like nature itself, abhors a vacuum: it fills all voids offered by reality. Its prolongation is its negation. Birth and death are the only acts of this art: as it appears, it is fixed, and since it totally embraces the reality it selects, totally fills it, it is incapable of extension or development. We still do not know whether from this combined death and birth further dead things or further living things can be born."

"Ludovico, you must understand, I believe nothing I am told, only what I read . . ."

"Then read these verses."

From his threadbare clothing Ludovico removed a folio which he offered to El Señor, who unfolded it and read in a low voice:

> Pyramidal, earthbound, melancholy,
> Born a shadow, he advanced toward Heaven,
> The haughty apex of vain obelisks,
> And thought to scale the stars . . .

Then:

> And the King, who affected vigilance,
> Even with opened eyes maintained no vigil.
> He, by his own hounds harassed—
> Monarch in a different time well honored—
> A timid deer become,
> With ear receptive
> To the quiet calm,
> The slightest movement.

The atoms move and
An inner ear, acute,
Hears the faint sound
Which alters, even sleeping . . .

"Who wrote this about me? Who dared write these . . . ?"

"The nun Inés, Felipe."

Trembling, El Señor tried to draw away from Ludovico; instead, his head merely settled more firmly against the beggar's breast; the nuns watched, stupefied, and redoubled their breast-beating.

"Inés is confined in a prison of mirrors in this palace, Ludovico, bound by the chain of love to your son, the usurper called Juan."

"Hear me, Felipe, lean close to my lips. The hordes that invaded your palace broke with pickaxes all the chains and locks from the prisons; they never paused to see who inhabited the cells, but ran from cell to cell shouting , 'You are free!' "

"I did not order the slaughter, Ludovico, I swear it. Guzmán acted in my name . . ."

"It does not matter. Hear me: those imprisoned lovers are a scrubbing maid and a rogue, Azucena and Catilinón; in the commotion of the day they replaced Inés and Juan . . ."

"I do not believe you; why would such lowly subjects endure that prison, never revealing who they were?"

"Perhaps they preferred imprisoned pleasure to joyless freedom. I do not know. Yes, I do know: for the pleasure of feeling they were of exalted rank and to receive treatment reserved for those of breeding, they accepted the identity of their disguises . . . at the cost of death."

"And Inés? And Juan? What of them?"

"They fled with me. Disguised, we embarked in the caravels of Guzmán. Yes, along with the painter-priest, we would temper the excesses of your favorite: against his sword, our art, our philosophy, our eroticism, our poetry. It was not possible. But have no fear. The nun Inés has been silenced by the authorities: she will never write another line. She has sacrificed her library and her precious mathematical and musical instruments to devote herself, as her confessor and her Bishop ordered, to perfecting the vocations of her soul."

"That is good, yes, that is good. And Don Juan?"

"Again, have no fear. He met his destiny. He abandoned Inés. He impregnated Indian women. He impregnated those of Spanish blood. He left his descendants throughout New Spain. But on a certain All Souls' Day, which the Mexican natives celebrate at tombside amid a profusion of yellow flowers, he decided to return to Spain. He had learned of the disappearance of his brothers, of your sterile enclosure in this place, of the heirless throne you would leave behind you. He returned to claim his rights as bastard. On his way, he stopped in Seville. Do you remember that you promised Inés to erect a stone statue on her father's grave?''

''Yes, and I honored my word. It cost me nothing: when her father died, the nun's property became mine.''

''What have you done with it?''

''I do not know, I do not govern, I do not know . . . wars against heretics, expeditions, persecutions, territorial skirmishes, my unfinished palace, I do not know, Ludovico.''

''Don Juan visited the Comendador's grave. He stared at the statue with irony, and it came to life, vowing to kill Don Juan. A challenge so distant? said Juan, and he invited the statue to dine. The Comendador asked that the dinner be celebrated in the sepulcher itself; Don Juan acceded. The host served Juan wine of gall and vinegar; the deceiver cried out that flame was splitting his breast, he struck at the air with his dagger, he felt that in life he was being consumed by flames; he clung to the statue of Inés's father, and with him Don Juan sank forever into the sepulcher, death-in-life and life-in-death hand in hand.''

''How do you know all this? Did you see it happen?''

''His servant told me, an Italian rogue named Leporello.''

''And you trusted the word of such a man?''

''No, but like you, what is written. Here: read this catalogue of his love affairs, read of the life and death of Don Juan, handed me by his servant at the exit to a theater.''

''Then that was the end of the youth you had cared for, Ludovico?''

''Perhaps he was destined to that end, ever since the face of the cavalier mourned in Toledo was transfigured into that of my son. But I am not sad. He met his destiny. And his destiny is a myth.''

''What is that?''

''An eternal present, Felipe.''

''You have seen all these things you tell me, and read them? You can see again? You are no longer blind?''

''Not now, Felipe. I opened my eyes that I might read the only thing that was saved from our terrible time.''

''The millennium . . . you said you would open your eyes at the time of the millennium . . .''

''I was more modest, my friend. I opened them to read three books: that of the Convent Trotter, that of the Knight of the Sorrowful Countenance, and that of the deceiver Don Juan. Believe me, Felipe: only there in those three books did I truly find the destiny of our history. Have you found yours, Felipe?''

''I still have it, it is here. I shall never leave my palace.''

''Farewell, Felipe. We shall not meet again.''

''Wait; tell me about yourself; what did you do in the new world, how, when, did you return . . . ?''

"You must use your imagination. I have served the eternal present of myth. Farewell."

Ludovico extricated himself from El Señor's embrace; the King continued to wash, and kiss, the feet of the beggars. When he was finished, he looked toward the place where the friend of his youth had stood. He was not there. El Señor searched the chapel with his eyes: in the distance, Ludovico was ascending the stairway that led to the plain. El Señor bit the foot of one of the beggars; the beggar cried out; the priests looked at one another with alarm. Ludovico was ascending the thirty-three steps that were the way to death, reduction to matter, and subsequent resurrection; in supplication Felipe stretched out his arms. Then he asked the nuns to carry him before the altar and support his outstretched arms; let his hands never touch those treasures of the new world; let his feet never touch the steps of the accursed stairway; the transitory world, enemy of the soul's salvation, sifted into his solitude through them; temptation, the temptation to touch gold, the temptation to flee up the stairway.

"A phantom distills its poison in my blood and its madness in my mind, I wish only to be a friend of God."

In spite of his fatigue, a feverish El Señor asked the nuns to carry him in the sedan chair to the cell of mirrors.

They arrived. They entered. El Señor asked Madre Milagros to uncover the two cloaked figures that lay copulating upon the floor of mirrors.

The blessed woman crossed herself and parted the ancient tatters. She revealed two skeletons in the posture of coitus.

Following the fatigue of a fever of seven days' duration there erupted on El Señor's thigh, a little above the right knee, an abscess of malign appearance which little by little grew larger and more inflamed, causing him enormous pain. And on his chest appeared four additional abscesses. As the abscess on his thigh did not heal, though it maturated, the doctors decided that it was necessary to lance it open, a process which was to be feared because the place was so dangerous and so sensitive, and all feared he might die of the pain.

Don Felipe listened serenely to these arguments and asked that before the doctors intervened, the nuns carry him on his litter to a place he would indicate. He directed them to the hall of the Gothic throne so that he might see, perhaps for the last time (for grave and silent were his premonitions), the monstrous monarch fabricated by La Señora from bits and pieces of royal cadavers, who, he was convinced, governed in his name while he lay swooning within his solitude, illness, and shadow of two twin bodies: his palace and his own.

Madre Milagros and Sisters Angustias, Asunción, and Piedad carried the litter; they entered the vast gallery with its carved ceilings and domes, its Gothic throne, and behind it the semicircular wall with the feigned painting of two flounced and fringed draperies hanging from their spikes.

"Look, what beautiful draperies," said Sor Piedad, who had eyes only for such fripperies. "May I go and pull them and see what is behind them?"

"There is nothing behind them, little innocent," said Madre Milagros. "Can you not see it is a thing painted to deceive the eye?"

But El Señor's horrified eyes saw only the figure seated upon the throne: a tiny man, although somewhat larger than the last time he had seen him, wearing a black cap, a uniform of coarse blue flannel with a yellow and scarlet band fastened about the great soft belly, a toy sword, black boots, the eyes of a sad lamb, a trimmed moustache: his right arm was raised in a salute and he shrieked in a high-pitched voice: "Death to intelligence! Death to intelligence!"

Where was the mummy?

"Quickly, take me from here," El Señor cried to the nuns.

"You, supposed King, do not run," shrieked the tiny man. "You stole my crown, my precious crown of gold, sapphire, pearls, agate, and rock crystal; return it to me, thief!"

The four nuns, with El Señor on his litter, fled that chamber, as El Señor's spirit clamored within him: My God, what have you done to Spain?, were all the prayers, the battles for the Faith, the illumination of souls, the penitence and sleepless nights insufficient?, has a homunculus, a mandrake, the son of gallows and stakes, been seated upon the throne of Spain?

Exhausted, he agreed that on the Day of the Transfiguration they might lance his abscess. There arrived to attend him a licensed surgeon from Cuenca, Antonio Saura, who was aided by a physician from Madrid and a Hieronymite priest named Santiago de Baena, for El Señor did not wish to be treated by secular hands only, as one never knew whether in truth they were the hands of a convert, a filthy pig of a Jew, but rather let divine eyes witness what the hands wrought.

When they opened the abscess, the physicians removed a great quantity of corrupted matter, for the whole thigh had become a pocket of pus so deep it almost touched the bone. As it was so large, nature, not content with the passage provided by art and knife, opened two additional mouths through which El Señor expelled such a quantity of pus that it seemed a miracle a person so frail did not die of it, although the priest Baena tried to pacify their spirits, saying: "It is laudable pus."

Don Felipe's skin was pale and transparent, his fine hair, his beard and moustache, silken snow, and this fearsome whiteness was the more startling in contrast to the black attire he had never changed from the time he had resolved to shut himself up in his palace.

After they had lanced the abscess, he ordered all those gathered there, doctors, surgeons, priests, nuns, and servants, to give thanks to God. Kneeling, they thanked God for mercy granted. With this El Señor was consoled and felt a great calm, believing he was imitating martyred saints whose pain had been alleviated as they were transported to the Passion of the One who had died to redeem them. He said he was hungry, and he was speedily brought some chicken broth. When he had drunk it he felt very cold, and from his bed he stretched out his hand and sought his faithful mastiff Bocanegra. He imagined that the hound still lay by his side, and smiling and shivering, said to him: "You see, Bocanegra? After eating, the finely bred Spaniard and his dog experience a chill."

Nevertheless, he remained in a state of torment from which he never emerged, for every time they treated him they syringed and pressed upon the wound to remove the corruption. Between morning and evening, on occasions of most terrible pain, El Señor filled two porringers with pus.

Thin and wasted with corruption, he at times slept overlong, but at others suffered from a most grievous inability to sleep at all. At times great diligence was necessary to awaken him during the day, depending upon the extent to which the evil vapors of his rotted leg had risen to his brain, and then Madre Milagros, who was often at his bedside serving whatever the occasion demanded, would say, a little gruffly: "Do not touch the relics!"

And then El Señor, startled by this voice, would open his eyes and see the relics placed beside his bed, a bone of St. Ambrose, the leg of St. Paul the Apostle, and the head of St. Jerome; three thorns from the Crown of Christ, one of the nails from His Cross, a fragment of the Cross itself, and a shred of the tunic of the Most Holy Virgin Mary; and, supported against the bed, the miraculous staff of St. Dominic of Silos. In these relics he sought the well-being the physicians were unable to afford him; and upon awakening—thanks to the cries of the aged Madre Milagros—and seeing the relics, he was wont to comment: "For these relics alone I would call this house a thousand times blessed. I have never had nor do I desire treasure more divine."

But as with morbid melancholy these words recalled to him the treasures arrived from the new world, he soon sank again into gloomy lethargy.

He happened to overhear some conversations between his physicians. "I do not dare open the abscesses on his chest," Saura said to Baena. "They are too near the heart."

The Hieronymite assented. One afternoon, this same Brother Santiago came to El Señor with a letter: a filthy sheet of paper that had been handed to him, he said, at the gates of the palace by a beggar indistinguishable from any of those who in increasing numbers gathered about the palace. But this beggar, Baena smiled, said he had been the most faithful of all El Señor's favorites, and that El Señor owed him more than he owed the King. Such effrontery impressed the small friar with the intense iron-colored eyes and high receding forehead. "Here then, Sire, is the letter."

Most Holy, Caesarian, and Catholic Majesty: I believed that having labored in my youth I would profit in my later years and find rest, and thus for forty years I busied myself, never sleeping, eating badly, my weapons at the ready, exposing myself to danger, spending my fortune and my youth, all in the service of God, in leading sheep to His pasture, all in lands very remote from our hemisphere, and unknown, and not recorded in our writings, and in advancing and spreading far and near the name of my King, winning for him and bringing beneath his yoke and royal scepter many great seigniories of many barbaric nations and peoples, won by my own person and at my own expense, without being aided in anything, and often obstructed by many envious men who since have burst like leeches from sucking my blood. I devoted myself fully to this undertaking of conquest and only because of it were clergy, Inquisitors, officials, and other minor clerks able to establish themselves in the new world, they who now accuse me of appropriating treasures for myself, of packing and sacking them and even secreting them on my own person, so that the correct sum, the royal one fifth owed to Your Most Holy, Caesarian, and Catholic Majesty never reached its destiny; and, further, they accuse me of excessive cruelties against the natives, as if there were other recourse when dealing with the tenacious idolatry of these savages; of living in concubinage with idolatrous Indian women, as if a man were able to choose between what there was and what did not exist; of lack of loyalty, bad governing, intrigue, and tyranny: why then, Señor, did I risk my life in my own behalf, on behalf of my King and my God, only to gain nothing for myself, only to deliver it all to the Church and Crown? I merely defended the rights you had granted me by royal decree. Today I have nothing, while in contrast the Church and Crown have everything. I find myself old and poor, in debt, I am seventy-three years old and that is not the age to be on the road, rather it is the age to pluck the fruit of my labors. Most Holy, Caesarian, and Catholic Majesty: I merely seek justice. I ask no more than the tiniest part of the world I conquered. Thanks to me, Your Majesty is master of a new world won without either danger to or exertion of Your Royal Person. Again I plead that Your Majesty be pleased to set in order, etc. etc. etc. . . . .

El Señor skipped over the requests to read the ridiculous signature: the Most Magnificent Señor Don Hernando de Guzmán. He laughed. He laughed until he cried. The chief huntsman, the intriguer, the secretary who had far exceeded the will of his Señor. El Señor laughed for the last time. He looked severely at Friar de Baena. "Tell that Don Nobody that I do not know him."

This was his last pleasure. As he suffered so greatly from the wound and aperture, and the mouths through which nature herself discharged her poisons, he became so racked with pain, so sensitive, that it was impossible for him to shift his weight or turn over in the bed. He was forced, night and day, to lie on his back, never turning to one or the other side.

Thus the royal bed was converted into a pestilential dung heap emitting the most evil odors: El Señor lay in his own excrement.

For thirty-three days, the duration of this illness, they could not change his clothing, nor would he tolerate it; they could not move him or raise him even slightly in order to clear away the result of his natural wants and the pus that streamed from abscesses and wounds.

"I am buried in life. And life has a foul stink."

It being necessary one time to raise his leg slightly for the purpose of wiping away the matter collected there and cleaning beneath his knees, he felt such excessive pain that he said he absolutely could not tolerate it, and when the physicians replied they must treat him, El Señor said with great feeling: "I protest, for I shall die in torment."

With these words they were so fully convinced of his pain that they abandoned the treatment. Many other times as they treated him, overcome by agonizing pain, he ordered them to cease and desist. Other times he broke into divine praise, commending to God his efforts. As he was limited to one position, unable to turn over, great sores appeared upon his back and buttocks; not even these parts were to escape pain.

Because of pain in his head, perpetual thirst, horrendous odors, he was unable to retain food. One day after partaking of a simple broth of fowl and sugar, he vomited forty times. And when he did not vomit he was shaken by diarrhea like that of a goat, which flooded his black sheets with greenish feces. Protesting, servants were called who, covering their noses and mouths with damp cloths, crawled beneath the bed and with knives worked a hole through the wooden planks and thin straw mattress so the mixture of excrement, urine, sweat, and pus could be drained. These lackeys fled from the room, their faces and bodies bathed in filth, and it was Madre Milagros, in an act of delicious contrition, who knelt to place a basin beneath the opened hole.

"I am nothing but skin and bones," said Felipe, "but no one will bear them with more honor than I, since it is a question of dying."

The basin filled eleven times every day, and when to all the pus and corruption was added the color of blood, El Señor asked for Extreme Unction, wishing to confess and take Communion for the last time, but the priests feared he would vomit the Host and they told El Señor that this would be a horrible sacrilege.

Then El Señor asked: "If I were well, would I not finally defecate the Host? Is it a worse offense that it be expelled through my mouth?"

But to himself he wondered whether his sinner's body was unfitting even to receive the Saviour's body. "Does the Devil dwell in me?"

Once again he sank into the heavy, putrid, melancholy humors that flooded through his body toward his brain; at times these humors were dank and half digested, at others less terrible, more lively. From his head they occasionally spread to the region of his heart, causing him sad assaults that greatly disquieted him. Finally he said: "The only healthy portions of my body are my eyes, my tongue, and my soul."

The last night, nevertheless, he was awakened by an unfamiliar tickling. Madre Milagros and three nuns were sleeping on the floor of his bedchamber. Candle stubs flickered low, sputtering, slowly consuming themselves. Trembling shadows stretched across the fetid chamber. The nuns slept with their heads covered beneath cloths redolent of oil of bergamot. Again El Señor felt the tickling in his nose. Weakly he felt for a handkerchief to wipe away the mucus which like all his bodily fluids drained steadily from him. But with horror he realized this was not drainage but rather something seemingly advancing under its own power; it contracted, paused, and again advanced toward the opening of Felipe's nostril.

He placed a waxen hand to his nose and extracted a white worm; he choked back a scream, he blew his nose on the handkerchief; a colony of tiny white eggs exploded into the cloth of fine linen, the spawn of the white worm that writhed on the palm of his hand.

He screamed. The nuns arose, the halberdiers guarding the entrance to the bedchamber, the physicians drowsing in the chapel, the monks praying before the altar, all appeared at the door. With a candle in her hand Madre Milagros approached him, and in a faltering voice El Señor said: "Come; it is the hour."

He ordered that among them they carry him to the chapel, his pain no longer mattered, or the stench, nothing, he wished to be placed in his coffin, for since he was not worthy to receive the Body of Jesus Christ, he was at least worthy of attending his own death, so long desired, of attending his own funeral, he who in this place of corpses had granted repose to all Spanish royalty, had constructed this palace of death; he believed that he was confessing, as they carried him from the bedchamber to the chapel, suffering enormous pain, he shouted, Lord, I am not worthy, I confess, Pedro, I acknowledge my sins, Ludovico, mea culpa, Celestina, I am unworthy, Simón, forgive me, Isabel, forgive me, forgive me, forgive me; they laid him in the lead coffin which for days had awaited him before the altar, and once there he grew calm, he felt sheltered by the white silk that lined the coffin, protected by the cloth of black gold that covered the exterior, and by the cross of crimson satin and the golden nails.

Buried in his coffin, he asked that they open the panels of the Flemish triptych and that one priest read him the Apocalypse of St. John, that the nuns sing the Requiem, and that another priest note down his last will and testament:

Domine, exaudi orationen meam, Et clamor meus ad te veniat,

So he carried me away a spirit into the wilderness, and I saw a woman sit upon a scarlet-colored beast, full of names of blasphemy, having seven heads and ten horns,

I command and order,

Chorus Angelorum te suscipiat et cum Lazaro quondam paupere aeternam habes requiem,

And the woman was arrayed in purple and scarlet colors, and decked with gold and precious stones and pearls,

I would be crowned with the Gothic crown of gold, agates, sapphire, and rock crystal, the first crown of Spain, and I would wear it to my grave,

Ego sum resurrectio et vita,

Having a golden cup in her hand full of abominations and filthiness of her fornication with the Kings of the earth,

Where is Celestina? What became of her? Why did I forget to ask Ludovico?

Qui credit in me, etiam si mortuus fuerit, vivet,

The great Babylon, the mother of harlots;

Simón? What became of Simón? Why did Ludovico not tell me of Simón's fate?

Et omnis qui vivit et credit in me, non morietur in aeternum,

The waters which thou sawest, where the whore sitteth are peoples, and multitudes, and nations, and tongues,

I command and order: Find the third bottle, there were three, I found only two, I read only two, seek the third bottle, I must read the last manuscript, I must know the last secrets,

In tuo adventu suscipiant te Martyres,

And I saw the woman drunken with the blood of martyrs,

I would be shaved and depilated, and I would have my teeth extracted, ground, and burned so they cannot serve witches for their evil spells,

De profundis clamavi ad te, Domine,

And the woman which thou sawest is that great city which reigneth over the Kings of the earth.

The relics shall not be dispersed or pawned, but rather they shall be preserved and together be handed down in succession,

Libera me, Domine, de morte aeterna, in die illa tremenda,

And upon her forehead was a name written: MYSTERY.

I would that all papers opened or sealed, all that be found and that treat our affairs and things past, be burned,

Dies illa, dies irae, calamitatis et miseriae,

And I saw an angel standing in the sun; and he cried with a great voice, saying to all the fowls that fly in the midst of Heaven: Come, and gather yourselves together unto the supper of the great God, that ye may eat the flesh of Kings,

Requiem aeternam dona eis, Domine,

Hear me, all of you, centuries will pass, wars will pass, hungers will pass, death will pass, but this necropolis will remain, dedicated to the eternal cult of my soul, and on the last day of the last year of the last age there will be someone praying beside my sepulcher,

Et lux perpetua luceat eis,

I would have two perpetual anniversaries, the day of my birth and the day of death, and vespers, nocturns, Mass, and responses, all sung, and I command and order that because of my devotion, and in reverence for the Most Holy Sacrament, there be two priests continually before it by night and by day, praying to God for my soul and the souls of my dead, unto the end of the centuries,

Dies illa, dies irae, calamitatis et miseriae,

And there fell a noisome and grievous sore upon the men which had the mark of the beast,

I command and order: upon my death, I would that thirty thousand Masses be said: violence shall be done unto Heaven,

Requiem aeternam dona eis, Domine,

Thus were blended together lugubrious chants and the mournful glow of the guttering candles, the reading of St. John and the smoke of incense, the mandates of El Señor and the concentrated light in that impenetrable Flemish triptych on the altar, the garden of delights, the millenary kingdom, the eternal Hell wherein El Señor saw all the faces of his life, his father and mother, his bastard brothers, his wife, the companions of his youth, that distant afternoon on the beach, the open sea before their eyes, the true fountain of youth, the sea, but he turned his back, he returned to the brown and arid high plain and there constructed a royal palace, monastery, and cemetery upon the quadrangle of a grill, similar to that which knew the torture of St. Lawrence, a harmony of austere lines, mortified simplicity, rejection of all sensual, infidel, and pagan ornament, a convergence of the tumult of the universe into a single center dedicated to the glory of God and the honor of Power: from his coffin, principal and witness to his own funeral exequies, he gazed at the Flemish painting as he had first gazed at it, a painting brought, it is said, from Orvieto, asking of it, demanding of it, whether these acts of his death agony were of sufficient merit to open the doors of Paradise to he who suffered them.

But first he needed to know once again, now dying, whether the sum total of the events, dreams, passions, omissions, visions, and revisions of his life had been directed by the hand of God or the hand of the Devil: in truth, neither the Divinity nor the Devil had ever clearly manifested himself; was the man who, like him, now asked himself the eternal question not worthy of compassion?; why does God prefer mortal man's blind faith to the tangible certainty of His existence were He to manifest it?; would the man never enter Paradise who, like him now, again posed the eternal question to God: why if you are Good do you tolerate Evil, allow the virtuous to suffer, and exalt the perverted? That is the reason, the King Don Felipe told himself, his gaping mouth attempting to capture the thin air of a chapel smoky with candles, incense, chants, and prophecies, he had so often allowed fate, indifference, or simple court etiquette to act freely on his behalf, without his intervention; if God so acted, what could He demand of one of his poor creatures?; that was the reason he had so often acceded to the proposals of others: Guzmán, the Inquisitor of Teruel, the Comendador of Calatrava, his own father, called the Fair; that is the reason, too, he had so often acted with such profound awareness of the indissoluble unity of good and evil, of the angel and the beast: the Chronicler, Brother Julián, Ludovico's and Celestina's freedom, that of Toribio in his tower. I acted or I failed to act, he murmured while the sensual images of the Flemish painting faded, or were erased, from his sight, because God and the Devil refused to manifest themselves clearly; if it be God's work, be it praised; if it be the Devil's, I am not to blame: I did not act, I failed to act; I did not condemn, I forgave—or if I condemned, it was for the secondary and not the principal reason. If I sinned, why, oh, my God, did you not intervene to prevent it?

He screamed for a consecrated Host, but no one heard him, no one came to give nourishment to his soul: everyone was singing or praying or kneeling around his coffin as if he were already dead.

He would have to confess himself.

Therefore, he interrogated himself about the occasions when he had acted, the times he had truly exerted responsibility: he deceived the messianic hordes in his youth, he delivered them to slaughter in the castle, he denied his sex to Isabel, he bestowed it upon Inés, he defeated the Flemish heretics, he ordered this necropolis to be constructed with all haste: as these were acts of which he had been conscious, for which he had been responsible, was virtue to be found in them? And what was the virtue of a King? From his coffin he gazed up into the gray domes of the Citadel of the Faith: it was also a Basilica of Power, and the virtue of a King lay in his honor, and his honor in his passion, and his passion in his virtue, and his virtue, thus, in his honor; honor was called the sun of a monarchy, and the further the kingdom's subjects moved from it, the greater cold and the greater dispersion they would know; El Señor had attempted to concentrate everything in one place—this palace, monastery, and tomb, and in one person—his, the final, heraldic place and person, definitive in their will for a conclusion, as definite as was the act of revelation in their will to create; the immutable icon of the honor of Power and the virtue of Faith, with no descendants, no bastards, no usurpers, no rebels, no dreamers, no lovers . . .

In his innermost ear, putrescent now with writhing worms, he heard the horrible laughter of Guzmán and of the Sevillian usurer elevated to the rank of Comendador, of the citizens who had fought against him in Medina and Avila, Torrelobatón and Segovia, and found their tomb in Villalar: honor is invoked by a King's tyranny; the government of common men works against honor, and then later ignores it; virtue is born of an individual's excellence and is determined by his interests; whatever that individual desires is good. And to those small and ambitious men who defied the central concept of honor, and opposed it with these new words, liberal, progress, democracy, El Señor in his death agony said: then live dispersed, far from the sun of honor; appreciate riches more than life, cling to existence to enjoy fortune, be ruled by general laws, as the rebellious burghers have demanded, obey what should be done and avoid the forbidden; and on the day of your disenchantment, sirs, again turn your eyes toward my sepulcher and understand the rules of the honor that was mine: give all importance to fortune, but none to life, avoid what the law does not forbid, and do what it does not demand: such, sirs, is the virtue of honor. His gaze was obscured by nests of minute white eggs; oh, my God, oh, my Devil, how can freedom and passions exist side by side?, is the honor of a monarch not a better restraint to passions than the ambition of a merchant?

He did not know the answer. He could not answer. The question remained forever suspended mid humors of incense and candle fat and pus, excrement, and sweat from his wounds. The physicians approached. They placed cantharides upon his feet and freshly killed doves upon his head. Dr. Saura said: "To prevent vertigo."

Then scullions came from the kitchen carrying boiling caldrons and from them Friar de Baena removed the steaming entrails of bull, hen, dog, cat, horse, and falcon and placed them upon El Señor's stomach. "To raise his temperature and make him sweat."

El Señor tried to counter: "It is futile. I have but one age. I was born in a privy; I died in another. I was born an old man."

But he could no longer speak. He felt changed. He felt as if he were a different person. He murmured to himself: "A phantom, day by day, I decay."

Then the two surgeons approached the coffin with fine, sharp knives in their hands. First they cut open the stinking black garments and revealed the hairless, chalky-white body. El Señor shouted: he could not hear his own voice and he knew no one would hear it again, not ever. The physicians, the nuns, and priests; it was they who were deaf; not he, not he.

They opened the four abscesses on his chest. Three, they said, were filled with pus. The fourth was a cave of lice.

With his knife, Saura opened the body cavity. The two doctors explored it, they extracted the viscera and, as they tossed them one by one into the same caldron that had held the beasts' entrails, commented:

"The heart the size of a nut."

"Three great stones in the kidney."

"The liver, filled with water."

"The intestines, gangrenous."

"A single black testicle."

THE THIRTY-THREE STEPS

Then there was a long absence.

"Where is everyone?"

Then there was a great silence.

"Close your mouth, Your Mercy, for the flies of Spain are very insolent."

He felt great fatigue, and simultaneously great relief. Relief was death. Fatigue, the long centuries he still must live, though dead; not only his time, but all the time remaining, necessary for drinking to the dregs his unfulfilled destiny. The centuries still to be lived by Queens announced by his mother, by Kings who would occupy the Gothic throne.

"Time and I are worth two."

As day dawned he could distinguish from the depths of his coffin two figures peering in to look at his corpse. One he recognized immediately: the astronomer, Brother Toribio, with his one unfocused eye and his aureole of flaming hair. He looked at the King's corpse and said: "Poor fool. He died still believing the earth was flat."

But the other . . . the other . . .

He tried to recognize him, and recognizing him, remember him. Condemned to the galleys, wounded in the great naval battle against the Turks, prisoner in Algiers, dead, surely, and forgotten in the dungeons to which his indiscreet pen had led him; what lie had Brother Julián once told him?: "The Chronicler, Sire? Forget him. He's been taken to the prison and tower of Simancas, where so many leaders of the rebellious burghers had died, and, like them, decapitated . . ." And now here he was, alive, peering into the coffin to look upon his dead body. He had but one hand. That hand clutched a long green bottle with a broken seal.

"Poor Señor. He died without knowing the contents of the third manuscript contained in this bottle left by the Pilgrim in the cell from which Guzmán led him to a cruel hunt. Poor Señor. Like the whore of Babylon, upon his forehead I read the word: MYSTERY."

"You are too compassionate, Miguel," the astrologer said to the writer. "To assure that everyone will read what you write, you are capable of foolishly risking your head. Be content with the two books you have written in the solitude of my tower, sheltered by me and by El Señor's apathy: the chronicle of the Knight of the Sad Countenance, which everyone will read, and the chronicle of the last years of our sovereign, which will interest no one."

"And the manuscript contained in this bottle, Friar, who will read it? I did not write it. One of the youths brought it with him from the sea."

"Publish it, if you wish. Let everyone read it except the Señor lying here. Look at his embalmed body, shrouded in bindings like a mummy . . ."

The Uranic friar gestured, his arms wide: "And then look at this marvelous triptych of the millenary kingdom painted by a humble Flemish artist, a follower of the Free Spirit, to suggest in secret all the truths of the human world, as rebellion against the Church, which claims to be the kingdom of God in all souls, and against the monarchy, which claims to be the kingdom of God upon earth. Do you think El Señor ever understood the meaning of this defiance which in spite of everything was installed here in his own chapel and seen by him every day? But El Señor is dead."

"Must we not thank him for that?"

"Yes, for his lack of curiosity, for never coming to my tower and surprising us in our endeavors. He is dead, I tell you. My science, your literature, and this art have survived him. All is not lost. Let others weep for him, not you, not I, not the soul of the painter of Hertogenbosch."

They disappeared.

From his coffin, Felipe spent the day scrutinizing that Flemish painting, still unable to penetrate the mysteries Brother Toribio attributed to it. To what age did that painting belong? Well, he believed he understood everything in the manuscript of Theodorus, Tiberius Caesar's counselor, which was about the past, but he understood nothing in the manuscript of a strange war in the jungles and mountains of the new world, which was the future. And this triptych . . . He was unable to place it either in the past or in the future. Perhaps it belonged to an eternal present.

When night fell, he slept.

He awakened with a start in darkness. Had they already placed him in the tomb? Was he covered by a slab of marble? And were those faint sounds shovelfuls of earth? No, it had been his will to be buried here in this rotting-house beside his ancestors. Had the heretics triumphed, madmen, pagans, infidels?, had they, to avenge themselves, thrown him with others into a common grave beside the corpse of Bocanegra? No, he could smell the dead wax of the chapel, the consumed incense, the metallic wind of refuse heaps that blew down the thirty-three steps . . .

Footsteps in the night. Night heavy. Nightmare.

A shadow fell upon his dead face.

A figure.

A phantom: he knew because he was looking at it, but the figure was not looking at him. A phantom does not look at us. For it, we do not exist. That is what frightens us.

He felt a fearful attraction toward that being standing so close beside the coffin, not looking at him, as if El Señor no longer existed either in life or in death. Felipe placed his wounded and bound hands upon the white silk of the coffin, he pushed, and sat up within the coffin, he could move, he did not feel the pain of the past years, he swung one leg outside the coffin, then the other, he emerged from the leaden box, he stood, graceful, light of foot, joyful; he looked toward the triptych on the altar: it had become an enormous mirror of three panels, and in them Felipe saw himself in triplicate: one, the youth of the day of the wedding and the crime in the castle; another, the man of middle years who had conquered the heretics of Flanders and ordered the construction of this necropolis; the third, the pale, ill old man who in life had rotted within this rotting-house.

"Choose," said the voice of the phantom.

He turned to look, but the specter turned its back. Again he looked toward the triptych. He decided to be the young man, to relive his life, to seize the second opportunity that death offered him; the other two mirrors darkened, only the first still shone; the bindings that shrouded him unrolled of their own accord and fell to the granite floor. Felipe saw himself dressed as he had been on the day of his wedding to Isabel, magnificent, magnificent, lustrous shoes of Flemish style, rose-colored breeches, a brocaded, ermine-lined doublet, and upon his head a cap as beautiful as a jewel, and upon his breast a cross of precious stones, and, scattered on the ermine fur, orange-blossom petals. He saw in the mirror of the painting his own features at sixteen, genteel, almost feminine but marked by the stigmata of his house: prognathic jaw, thick, always parted lips, heavy eyelids. But above everything else he was aware of his young body, the body of the imaginary voyage on Pedro's boat in search of the new world, accompanied by Simón, Ludovico, and Celestina: his skin tanned, his hair bleached by ocean gold, his muscles strong, his flesh firm.

He heard the phantom's footsteps receding from the altar and the coffin, along the sepulcher-flanked nave. He followed, eager to be seen by the phantom, by anyone, now that he was again young, now that death offered him a second opportunity. But as he passed his coffin he paused, immobilized by a sight that raised his hackles; the ancient, shrouded King, he himself, still lay there, dead, wrapped in white bindings and crowned by the Gothic crown of gold incrusted with pearl, sapphire, agate, and rock crystal. He did not know what he did then, or why he did it; he did not know whether he felt love, hatred, or indifference for those remains; he merely experienced a passion, a necessary passion, neither homage nor profanation: a transport that determined his action. He removed his cap. He removed the crown from the body. He placed the cap on the body. He placed the crown upon his own head.

The phantom, still not looking at him, his back turned, paused at the foot of the stairway.

Then finally he turned and looked at the young Felipe. The Prince's eyes narrowed, he tried to guess, remember, or, perhaps, foresee the phantom's features, a youth like himself, a strange mixture of racial heritages, blond and tightly curled hair, black eyes, swarthy skin, a long, beautiful nose, sensual lips. Naked. He held out his hand, inviting Felipe to follow him. "You do not remember me? I am called Miguel in Christian lands, Michah in the Jewries, Mihail-ben-Sama in Arabic *aljamas:* Miguel-of-Life. You ordered me burned alive one day beneath your palace kitchens. You did not condemn me for the principal reason, but rather, the second."

He invited Felipe to follow him: to ascend, step by step, that unfinished stairway. Felipe fell to his knees; he prostrated himself; he spread his arms wide in a cross before his victim; no, no, that stairway leads to death, I ascended it one day with my mirror in my hand, and in it saw what I never want to see again, my old age, my death agony, my death, decomposition, my return to brute matter, my metamorphoses, the transmigration of my soul, my resurrection in the form of a wolf, hunted in my own domains by my own descendants, Michah, Mihail, Miguel de la Vida, forgive my crime, honor your name, Miguel-of-Life, do not take mine from me again . . ."

The one called Miguel smiled. "That time, like Narcissus, you looked only at yourself in your mirror. This time, Felipe, you will see the mirror of the world. Come."

The young Prince looked behind him: the sepulchers, his own lead coffin, the nuns' choir, the altar, the triptych, the entrance to his bare bedchamber of secret pleasures and harsh penitences where without moving from his bed he could attend divine ceremonies. He thought of his father. He thought that if he turned his back to the stairway and flew toward that subterranean world he, like falcons hungry for their prey, would confuse the cloistered darkness of the chapel with the infinite space of night, he would strike against pilasters, stone arches, iron grillwork, and would be crippled, and die again.

He grasped the phantom's burning hand.

He raised one foot and placed it on the first step of the stairway.

"This time do not look at yourself; look at your world; and choose a second time."

Slowly Felipe climbed, holding the feverish hand of Mihail-ben-Sama.

This time he closed his eyes to avoid seeing, as he had before, himself; rather, the world; and on each step the world offered the temptation to choose anew, choices dating from the dawn of time, but always in the same, if transfigured, place: this land, land of Vespers, Spain, Terra Nostra.

And as he ascended each step he heard the double voice of Mihail-ben-Sama, one voice which was two voices, each voice precise, clear, vague, urgent, two, but one; one, but two.

Androgynous creator of a being invented in his image and likeness	Father creator of an incomplete man: where is woman?
The first being fecundates himself, multiplying himself like the earth, unstained	Man violates woman, and both offend Nature, which expels them from the sick garden
Harmony of the world of the sons prolongs the original harmony of the world of the fathers	Brother kills brother in order to possess a subjugated woman and an inhospitable earth
A diversity of peoples, tongues, and beliefs is the result of a mixing of bloods that strengthens the unity of the human genre	The domination of vanquished woman and earth sets peoples against peoples: insufficiency is exalted as superiority, necessity as reason
Everything is shared by all	Yours and mine

Ours

I must die: I shall return transformed	I must die: I shall never return to this earth
I must live: I desire death	I must die: I desire glory
I am a river	I am a shadow
Everything changes	Nothing must change
Everything remains	Everything must continue
I understand what moves	I understand only what does not move
I love what I do not understand	I despise what I do not comprehend
I recognize myself in what is different	I exterminate what is different
Let my blood be mixed with that of all other men	Let my blood be purified with leeches and cauterization
May my body be reborn enriched by mixed bloods	Let my body die impoverished by the purity of blood
I love the labor of my renewed hands: I re-create Paradise	Unworthy of my ascetic hands is the labor of slaves
I construct gardens	I erect pantheons
Fountains and sweet-scented stock	Stone and shroud
My body fuses	My body separates
Love or solitude	Honor or dishonor
Awareness of my earthly senses	Ignorance of anything that separates me from eternal salvation

Freedom of body and mind open to all fecundation	Oppression of body and mind subjected to penitence
Community	Power
Tolerance	Repression
Many	One
Christians, Moors, and Jews	Fine breeding, pure blood
The Spanish	I, the King
New world	Old world
The Alhambra	The Escorial
Doubt	Faith
Diversity	Unity
Life	Death

"Did you choose, Felipe? Were you able to choose again?"

The double voice of the burning phantom awakened El Señor from his fleeting dream. That voice faded away. He opened his eyes. He had climbed the thirty-three steps of his chapel. Sun punished his eyes. A valiant and vigorous valley lay before him. Harsh crust of stone. Vast flowering of rock. He looked toward the end of a mountain gorge where arose a compact cone of live rock. And on the summit of this rock, as if born of it, a gigantic cross of stone cast its shadow across El Señor's face; this cross rested upon a double pediment, the first of which was backed by the figures of the four Evangelists; on the corners of the second, smaller pediment stood images of the four cardinal virtues; and to reach these pediments one had to ascend an enormous stairway carved from live rock, for a crypt had been excavated from the heart of the rock, guarded over by a railing of three bodies crowned by a battlement of angels, insignia, and pinnacles accompanying the figure of St. James the Apostle.

Disoriented in space, wounded by a sun he had not seen since in this same place he had witnessed the torture of Nuño and Jerónimo, vanquished by time, Felipe whirled away; he felt trapped, he looked for an exit: a beast trapped by fear, he did not notice the presence of a short old man with a three days' growth of beard, wearing a uniform of rough gray cloth and a battered cap bearing a copper plate.

"May I offer my services, Señor?" asked this obsequious little man.

"Where am I . . . please . . . where . . . ?" Felipe managed to murmur.

"Why, at the Valle de los Caídos, the Valley of the Fallen."

"What? What fallen?"

"God's blood, man, those who fell for Spain, the monument of the Holy Cross . . ."

"What day is this?"

"As for the day, well, who's the man who knows what day it is. As for the year, I know that it is the year 1999. Has the Señor never visited the Valley of the Fallen? Allow me, my card. I am a licensed guide and I can . . ."

Felipe stared at the enormous stone cross: "No, I have never visited it. You see, I went away more than four hundred years ago."

The little man, until this moment obliging, if indifferent, looked for the first time at Felipe's face, his attire, his general appearance. He stammered: "By my faith . . . you see, so many tourists pass this way . . . all alike . . . I always say the same things . . . I know the words by rote . . ."

And eyes rolling, he threw his cap to the ground and ran from Felipe yelling and waving his arms, his grating voice echoing through the mass of carved rock: "Come one, come all. Hark what I say! There is a man there who claims to have been gone for four hundred years! Come, come, come hear what I have to tell!"

That night, seeking protection for his terror and hunger among the stunted growth of scrub oak and juniper, blackberry and hawthorn clinging to the craggy mountainside, and listening to the always closer sound of the horns and the sputtering torches of the night hunt, the occasional sound of a gun and the unceasing barking of the mastiffs, Felipe approached a small bonfire burning in the hollow of a rock, carefully protected from the north winds.

An instinctive sense of relief and gratitude impelled him to throw himself at the feet of the man watching a battered old coffeepot, and slicing a rough loaf of bread.

The mountaineer patted Felipe's snout, and he raised great liquid, mournful eyes to gaze into those of the man who offered him a slab of bread and a slice of ham. The eyes were black, but the hair was blond and tightly curled, the skin swarthy, the nose long and beautiful, and the lips sensual.

Snout and fang, Felipe tore at the ham and bread. Nearer and nearer came the fearful sounds of the hunt, but by the side of this young mountain man, his friend, he was no longer afraid. He even understood the words when the man, his booted feet stamping out the remains of the fire, spoke, slowly, and with a tinge of uncertainty in his words, but with the clear intent of being understood by the wolf: "Yes. The truth is this. If I speak of a place, it is because it no longer exists. If I speak of a time, it is because it has already passed. If I speak of a person, it is because I desire him."

THE LAST CITY

It must have snowed for several hours. The river has risen. The current inundates the stone Zouave on the Pont de l'Alma. Dark waters whirl about the prow of the Ile Saint-Louis. The Luxembourg is shrouded in white. The Montsouris garden recognizes itself in a desolate dawning light. A terrible white beauty blinds the Parc Monceau. Frost outlines the china-ink trees of the Montparnasse cemetery. Snow blankets the Père Lachaise cemetery like a late sacrifice. Snowy tombs of Francisco de Miranda and Charles Baudelaire, Honoré de Balzac and Porfirio Díaz. Silvery webs in gardens and pantheons.

Gilded webs on the smooth ceiling of the apartment in the Hôtel du Pont-Royal. The red suite. Flaming velvet. Outside, the snow is a melted standard and the river the lion rampant of the banner. Inside, white stucco. Vines. Cornucopias. Cherubs. Plaster sculpture. Red velvet and white plaster. Mirrors. Stained. Spotted with age. They multiply the space of the narrow apartment.

Long ago the elevator cage ceased to function. Tarnished bronze. Beveled crystal. Outside. On the other side of the double door. You have not opened it. Not in a long time. You avoid the mirrors. They are enormous, full-length, with opaque gold frames and peeling quicksilver. Others are small, hand mirrors. One is black marble, streaked with blood. Another, very small and square, covered with fingerprints. Another, round, its frame crowned with a two-headed eagle. Another, triangular. Many more. You avoid them. The Argentinian Oliveira warned you: none of them reflects the space of the place you inhabit. A string of narrow rooms: living room, bedroom, dressing room, bath, each opening onto the next. No mirror reflects your face. You touch them; you do not look at them; you do not look at yourself. You touch everything with your only hand. Buendía, the Colombian, warned you when you arrived in France: Paris seems much larger than it really is because of the infinite number of mirrors that duplicate its true space: Paris is Paris, plus its mirrors.

Late in life an aged Pierre Menard proposed that all beasts, men, and nations be apportioned a supply of mirrors that would reproduce infinitely their and other figures and their and other territories, for the purpose of appeasing for all time the imperative illusions of a destructive ambition for possession, although dominion only assures us the loss of what we have conquered as well as what is already ours. Only to a blind man could such a fantasy occur. And of course he was, in addition, a philologist.

Oliveira, Buendía, Cuba Venegas, Humberto the mute, the cousins Esteban and Sofía, Santiago Zavalita, the man from Lima who lived every minute wondering at what precise moment Peru had fucked everything up, and who had come to Paris a refugee like all the others, wondering, like all the others—with the exception of the Cuban rumba-rhythm queen—at what moment Spanish America had fucked everything up. You haven't seen them lately. If they are still alive, even today they are surely declaring, along with you, fucked-up Peru, fucked-up Chile, fucked-up Argentina, fucked-up Mexico, the whole fucked-up world. Today: the last day of the dying century. Today: the first night of the next one hundred years. Although deciding whether the year 2000 is the last year of the preceding or the first year of the coming century lends itself to infinite discussion. We are living within a shattered specter. Only Cuba Venegas, that flabby, garish old rumba queen with the swelling heart-shaped buttocks, maintained her strange Antillean optimism to the end, singing melancholy boleros in her sung-out voice in the lowest dives in Pigalle. She said, unaware of the paraphrase: "All good Latin Americans come to Paris to die."

Perhaps she was right. Perhaps Paris was the exact moral, sexual, and intellectual point of balance between the two worlds that tear us apart: the Germanic and the Mediterranean, the North and the South, the Anglo-Saxon and the Latin.

On the anniversaries of their respective deaths, Cuba Venegas carried flowers to the tombs of Eva Perón in Père Lachaise and of Ché Guevara in Montparnasse.

How long ago seemed those nights on the top floor of the old house in the rue de Savoie when everyone used to get together to drink the bitter maté prepared by Oliveira; the blond Lithuanian Valkyrie would put tangos on the record player, and serve pisco and tequila and rum, and everyone played the game of Superfuck, a card game in which the winner was the one who collected the most cards representing ignominy and defeats and horrors. Crimes, Tyrants, Imperialisms, and Injustices were the four suits of this deck, replacing clubs, hearts, spades, and diamonds.

"W'ich is bes'?" inquired Cuba Venegas. "T'ree or four of de beeg business, or de rrrrrun of de ahmbassador?"

"It depends," said Santiago, of Lima, Peru. "I have five of a kind: United Fruit, Standard Oil, Pasco Corporation, Anaconda Copper, and I.T.T.''

" 'Oh, frohm Cooba wis de music!' " cried the rumba queen. "Henry Lean U'will-son, Choel Poyn-sett, Espru-ill Bra-don, Chon Pueri-phooey, an' Nattani-yell Debbis. W'at de fock you t'ink of dat, baybee?''

" 'My bitter heart, conceal your sorrow . . .' '' you murmured, and turning to address the mute, Humberto: "I'll give you an Ubico and two Trujillos for three Marmolejos.''

"Do you know how"—Oliveira commented in his unmistakable Porteño cadence as he dealt the cards—"Marmolejo came to power in Bolivia? He joined the line filing through to greet the President on the day of the celebration of national independence, and when he came to the President in the line, emptied his pistol into his belly. Then he removed the Presidential sash, fastened it across his chest, and walked out onto the palace balcony to receive the acclamation of the crowd. What do you have, Humberto?''

The mute held out his five martial cards: Winfield Scott's squadron, Achille Bazaine's army, Castillo Armas's mercenaries, the "worms" of the Bay of Pigs, and Somoza's National Guard.

"Full house!" shouted Buendía. "Masferrer's Tigres, Duvalier's Tonton Macoutes, and the Brazilian DOPs, plus an Odría and a Pinochet.''

"That's shit, you're wiped out, you and your momma and your papa," Oliveira crowed triumphantly, spreading his four Prisons on the card table: the cisterns of the Fort of San Juan de Ulúa, Dawson Island, the cold plain of Trelew, and the Sexto in Lima . . . O.K., top that . . .''

"Just sweeten the pot and deal the cards again," the Valkyrie proposed as she filled their glasses.

"Just when Santa Anna was winning the battle of San Jacinto against the Texas fifth columnists, he lost because he stopped to eat a taco and take his siesta.''

"You, Zavalita, what do you have?''

"Three of a kind, mass exterminations in the public plazas: Maximiliano Hernández Martínez in Izalco, Pedro de Alvarado at the festival of Toxcatl, and Díaz Ordáz in Tlatelolco.''

"The last two are the same things, that's only a pair, you bastard.''

" 'Your destiny's deceiving, I'm grieving, and leaving, to follow you forever . . .' " intoned Zavalita, tossing his cards face down on the table.

"What were you saying about Santa Anna?''

"When they blew off his leg he buried it after having it borne beneath a canopy to the cathedral in Mexico City. And when the Yankees captured him he sold them half the nation. Then later he sold another little piece to buy European uniforms for his guards and to construct equestrian statues of himself from Carrara marble."

Humberto's lips formed a silent "Son-of-a-bitching Diego."

"And the cousins?" asked Buendía.

"Esteban and Sofía? Shhhh," said the Valkyrie, "they're in the bedroom."

"A bust!" you exclaimed dispiritedly. "One Juan Vicente Gómez, an Indian branded by Nuño de Guzmán in Jalisco, a slave in the mines of Potosí, a slave ship in Puerto Príncipe, and a General Bulnes campaign of extermination against the Mapuche Indians."

"Ché, Buendía"—again the Porteño—"tell about J. V. Gómez's two deaths."

"Well, Juan Vicente Gómez announced his death so that his enemies would come out into the streets of Caracas to celebrate. He hid behind the drapes in a palace window and observed the celebrations through little raccoon eyes, meanwhile issuing orders to his police: throw him in jail, torture that one, shoot that one over there . . . When he actually did die, they had to exhibit his body in the Presidential chair, dressed in gala sash and uniform, for all the people to file by, touch, and verify: 'It's true, this time he's really dead.' What a crock!"

"I trade you dis Gómes for two of de Péres Jiménes an' de t'rone of gold in Bati'ta's bat'room in Kukine," crooned the rumba queen. 'De emeral' green of de sea sparkles deep in your beeoutiful eyes . . .' "

" 'Your lips wear the blush of the blood that seeps from the coral . . .' "

" 'Your voice is a poem of love, a divine and inspiring chorale . . .' "

" 'The sun-drunken palms brush your cheeks, and echo my sighs . . .' "

"At Christmas Bastista ordered enormous gift boxes wrapped in bright paper and ribbons to be sent to the mothers of the young men who fought in the Sierra Maestra and in the urban underground. They opened them to find their sons' mutilated bodies."

"C.I.A. Poker!" shouted Oliveira, sweeping in all the chips from the center of the table.

"Farewell, Utopia . . ."

"Farewell, City of the Sun . . ."

"Farewell, Vasco de Quiroga . . ."

"Juárez should never have died, ay, have died . . ."

"Nor Martí, chico . . ."

"Nor Zapata, mano . . ."

"Nor Ché, ché . . ."

"Farewell, Lázaro Cárdenas . . ."

"Farewell, Camilo Torres . . ."
"Farewell, Salvador Allende . . ."
" 'I'll become once again the wandering troubadour . . .' "
" 'Who wanders in search of his love . . .' "
" 'Forgotten, discarded, downtrodden . . .' "
"De good ol' days, *chico*, de good ol' days." Cuba Venegas began to sob.

Slowly you wander through the succession of rooms, all linked by French doors. You touch everything. No, you do not touch the red velvet of the furniture, the curtains, and walls. You touch all the objects you have gathered together here and carefully arranged on wardrobes, consoles, commodes, cabinets, antique writing desks with wire-mesh doors, rickety eighteenth-century secretaries, night tables, glass shelves, marble tables. The black pearl. A dog's heavy spiked collar with a device emblazoned on the iron, *Nondum, Not yet*. Tall green empty bottles, eternally moldy, some imperfectly sealed with cork, some stoppered with red seals after having been opened with evident haste—when? by whom?—still others sealed with an imperial seal. You open, often, the long case of Cordovan leather that houses in beds of white silk the ancient coins you love to caress, effacing even more the blurred effigies of forgotten Kings and Queens. With your only hand you withdraw papers guarded in a Boulle cabinet, thin, transparent, faded chronicles. You compare their calligraphy, the quality of the inks, their resistance to the passage of time. Documents written in Latin, Hebrew, Arabic, Spanish: codices written with Aztec ideograms. Characters like spiders, like flies, like rivers, like stone . . . cloud glyphs.

You soon tire of reading. You never know whether to feel sad or happy that these papers, these mute voices of men of other times, survive the deaths of the men of your time. Why preserve these writings? No one will read them now because there will be no one to read, or write, or make love, or dream, or wound, or desire. Everything that is written will survive untouched, because there will be no hands to destroy it. Is this sure desolation preferable to the uncertain risk of writing only to see one's work proscribed, destroyed, burned on great pyres while uniformed masses shout, death to Homer, death to Dante, death to Shakespeare, death to Cervantes, death to Kafka, death to Neruda? Your eyes are tired. But there is no way you can get eyeglasses. Your body is fatigued. If only you could see yourself in a mirror and know that you were seeing yourself, not other men, other women, other children, motionless or animated, repeating forever the same scenes in the theater of mirrors. You have lost count. You no longer know your age. You feel very old. But what you can see of yourself when you disrobe—your chest, your belly, your sex, your legs, your only hand and arm—is young. You cannot remember now what the arm and hand you lost in battle looked like.

Once again you begin your wanderings through the apartment. You touch everything. The greasy gauntlet, its amputated fingers dried out and stiff. The rings of red stone, and bone. The ciborium filled with teeth. The ancient boxes ornamented with rope of gold and filled with skulls, thighbones, and mummified hands. One day, laughing darkly, you fitted two of those relics to your stump: an arm and a hand not yours. Afterward, you were nauseated. You know it all so well. You can touch and describe all the objects with your eyes closed. There are days when you entertain yourself doing just that, testing your memory, fearful as you are that you will lose it completely. Even if the roof of the hotel collapsed you could enumerate, describe, and place all the objects in this apartment in the Pont-Royal. A ustorious mirror. Two stones of unequal size. A pair of tailor's scissors, varnished black. A basket filled with pearls, cotton, and dried grains of corn. You entertain yourself thinking that one day, perhaps, you can nourish yourself from the bread of the new world and then lie down to await death, bedfast and apathetic like the Spaniards in Verdín and the Cathari dedicated to endura. But up till now they still bring you your one daily meal. Invisible knuckles rap at your door. You wait several minutes to make sure that the silent servant has retired. You open the door. You pick up the tray. You eat with great deliberation. Your movements have become old, arthritic, minimal, repetitive, futile.

Then after the meal you return to your preoccupation: reviewing the objects. Of course there is a coffer bursting with the treasures of ancient America, tufts of quetzal feathers, bronze ear ornaments, gold diadems, jade necklaces. And a dove killed with a single knife slash: you look at the wound upon the white breast, the bloodstains on the feathers. A hammer, a chisel, a hyssop, an ancient bellows, rusty chains, a jasper monstrance, an ancient marine compass.

But you receive the greatest pleasure from the maps. A faded navigational chart, an authentic medieval portolano: the outlines of the Mediterranean, the limits, the Pillars of Hercules, Cape Finisterre, Ultima Thule, the ancient names of places lovingly retained on this chart: Gebel-Tarik, Gades, Corduba, Carthago Nova, Toletum, Magerit, in Spain; Lutetia, Massilia, Burdigala, Lugdunum, in France; Genua, Mediolanum, Neapolis, in Italy; the flat earth, the unknown ocean, the universal cataract. You compare this map of Mare Nostrum with the map of the virgin jungle, the mask of green, garnet, blue, and yellow feathers with a black field of dead spiders in the center, the nervature dividing the zones of feathers, the darts that protrude from the cloth.

But the most mysterious of your maps is that of the waters, the Phoenician chart so ancient you scarcely dare touch it, so brittle it seems to wish to be immediately converted into dust and to disappear along with the mysteries it describes: the secret communication of all waters, sub-aquatic tunnels, the passageways beneath the earth where flow all the liquid channels of the world, nourishing one another, seeking a common level, rushing headlong from high mountains, bursting from deep wells, whether their origin be swamp or volcano, whether they spring from the desert or the valley, born of ice or fire: the liquid corridors from the Seine to the Cantabria, from the Nile to the Orinoco, from the Cabo de los Desastres to the Usumacinta, from the Liffey to Lake Ontario, from a deep sacrificial pool in Yucatan to the Dead Sea in Palestine: *atl*, the root of water, Atlas, Atlantis, Atlantic, Quetzalcoatl, the Plumed Serpent that returns along the routes of the great waters, the esoteric highways from the Tiber to the Jordan, from the Euphrates to the Schelde, from the Amazon to the Niger. Esoteric: esoterikos: *I cause to enter.* Maps of initiation; charts of the initiated. There is a banal inscription written in the left-hand margin of this map, in Spanish: "The nature of waters is always to communicate with one another and to reach a common level. And this is their mystery." An amphora filled with sand.

You have not opened your windows since summer. You drew the heavy drapes. You live with your lights turned on, night and day. You could no longer tolerate the smoke, the stench of burned flesh and fingernails and hair. The suffocating perfume from the chestnut and the plane trees. The smoke from the towers of Saint-Sulpice. You used to be able to see the towers from your window on the seventh floor of the hotel. You could not tolerate the rows of flagellants and penitents marching every day through the rue Montalembert toward the Boulevard Saint-Germain, or the clamor of proliferating life, new arrivals, thronging along the rue du Bac toward the Quai Voltaire and the Seine: the river boiled, the transparent Louvre exhibited itself shamelessly, spaces seemed to expand, the Gioconda was not alone, the wild ass's skin shrank in the feverish hand of Raphaël de Valentin, Violetta Gautier lay dying in her bed of camellias, singing softly:

> Sola, abbandonata
> In questo popoloso deserto
> Ch'appellano Parigi . . .

A line of barefoot men, obscured by the smoke, entered the frightful stench and rigorously programmed death of the Church of Saint-Sulpice. Javert pursued Valjean through labyrinthine black waters.

You locked yourself in your apartment. You had sufficient money. The coffer overflowing with ancient Aztec, Maya, Totonac, Zapotec jewels. They told you you could use them while in exile to organize the resistance and aid those who had been banished. Guardian of the coffer, yes, but it was also your subsistence. You, too, are an exile. You read the last newspaper and flushed it down the toilet, torn into little pieces. You watched shocking headlines and judicious commentaries swirl away in a whirlpool of uselessly chlorinated water. The facts were true. But they were too true, too immediate, or too remote, compared to the real truth. That has always, you suppose, been the contemptible fascination of the news: it is its immediacy today that makes it obsolete tomorrow. Fact: the microbic world acquired immunity faster than science could neutralize each new outburst of bacterial independence: chlorine, antibiotics, all vaccines, were useless. But why, instead of taking the minimal steps for safety, did the human world feel itself so attracted, one might almost say mesmerized, by the victory of the microbic world? The ordinary justification, the commonplace, was that once all sanitary programs were abandoned, it was left to nature herself to resolve the problem of overpopulation: the five billion inhabitants of an exhausted planet that was, nonetheless, incapable of ridding itself of its acquired habits: greater opulence for a few, greater hunger for the great majority. Mountains of paper, glass, rubber, plastic, spoiled meat, wilted flowers, inflammable matter neutralized by non-inflammable matter, cigarette butts, junked automobiles, the minimum and the maximum, condoms and sanitary napkins, printing presses, tin cans and bathtubs: Los Angeles, Tokyo, London, Hamburg, Teheran, New York, Zurich: museums of garbage. Epidemics furnished the desired effect. The plagues of the Middle Ages had not distinguished between man or woman, young or old, rich or poor. The modern plague was programmed: in new sterilized cities safe beneath plastic bells, a few millionaires, many bureaucrats, a handful of technicians and scientists, and the few women needed to satisfy the elect, were saved. Other cities stimulated death by offering solutions in harmony with what had formerly been called, without the least trace of irony, the national character. Mexico resorted to human sacrifice, religiously consecrated, politically justified, and offered as a sports event on television spectaculars; the spectator had a choice: certain programs were dedicated to reenactments of the War of the Flowers. In Rio de Janeiro, a military edict imposed perpetual carnival, with no time limits, until the population died of pure joy: dance, alcohol, masquerades, sex. In Buenos Aires a suburban machismo was fomented, a tightly woven intrigue of jealousy, insult, and personal drama, instigated by tangos and gauchoesque poems: the knives of vengeance gleamed, millions committed suicide. Moscow was both more subtle and more direct: millions of copies of Trotsky's works were distributed, and then any person found reading them was ordered to be shot. No one knows what happened in China. The inhabitants of Benares and Addis Ababa, La Paz, Jakarta, Kinshasa, and Kabul simply perished of hunger.

At first, Paris accepted the recommendations of the world council on depopulation. Insofar as it was possible, the obligatory deaths would be natural: hunger and epidemic, though it would be left to each nation to find its own specific and idiosyncratic solutions. But Paris, the fountain of all wisdom, where a persuasive Devil inculcated into some few wise men a perverse intelligence, opted for a different course. Just this spring you watched the debates on television. All possible theories were expounded and criticized with Cartesian subtlety. After everyone had spoken, an aged Rumanian playwright, a member of the Académie, with the aspect of a gnome, or perhaps more exactly, and using the lingua franca of the century, of a leprechaun of the verdant bosques of Ireland: this elf, with tufts of white hair ringing his bald head, and an extraordinary gaze of candor and astuteness, proposed that they merely give equal opportunity to both life and death.

"On the one hand, increase the birth rate, and on the other, the extermination. No generality can prosper without its exception. How can everyone die if no one is born?"

"Thank you, M. Ionesco," said the announcer.

Your only meal is always the same. The faded menu announces it to be a *grillade mixte* comprised of testicles, black sausage, and kidneys. When you have eaten, you open the door again. You deposit the empty tray on the hall carpet. Several hours later, silent footsteps approach. You hear noises, and then the footsteps retreat. The elevator does not function. No letters or telegrams arrive. The telephone never rings. On the television screen, always the same program, the same message you read in the last headline of the last newspaper you bought before closing yourself in here. Again you open the box holding the coins. You look at the profiles blurred by the touch of human hands. Juana the Mad, Felipe the Fair, Felipe II, called the Prudent, Elizabeth Tudor, Carlos II, called the Bewitched, Mariana of Austria, Carlos IV, Maximilian and Carlota of Mexico, Francisco Franco: yesterday's phantoms.

You are not sure whether you sleep by day or night, wander the apartment, touching objects, avoiding objects, by day or night. Time does not exist. Nothing works. The electric lights grow more faint each day. The thirty-first of December, 1999. Tonight they will go out completely. You will wait for them to come on again, in vain. You have conquered the mirrors. They will reflect only darkness. You will not open the drapes. You know by memory the location of every object. You will not need the candle stubs hidden in a drawer beside your bed. And you have only one match left. You allow your slippers to slide from your feet. You dress in a black Tunisian caftan trimmed with gold cord. You hold the manuscripts you found in the bottles. You repeat the texts in a low voice. You know them by memory. But you perform the acts of normal reading, you turn every page after murmuring its words. You see nothing. Outside it is snowing. A procession is passing beneath your windows. You imagine it: tattered pendants, hairshirts and scythes. They must be the last. You smile. Perhaps you are the last. What will they do with you? And suddenly, as you ask yourself that question, you are unexpectedly able to tie together the loose ends of your situation and that of your readings in the darkness, you become aware of the evident, you combine the images you saw for the last time from your window before drawing the drapes, holding the old writing in your hand, those most ancient histories of Rome and Alexandria, the Dalmatian and Cantabrian coasts, Palestine and Spain, Venice, the Theater of Memory of Donno Valerio Camillo, the three youths marked with a cross on their backs, the curse of Tiberius Caesar, the solitude of the King Don Felipe in his Castilian necropolis: an opportunity is offered to all the things that could not manifest themselves in their time, an opportunity to make our time coincide fully with another, unfulfilled time; several lifetimes are needed to integrate a personality: did the press and television not repeat that to the point of nausea? Every minute a man dies in Saint-Sulpice, every minute a child is born on the quays of the Seine, only men die, only children are born, women neither die nor are born, women are merely the vehicle for childbirth, they were made pregnant by the same men who were then led immediately to their exterminations, each child was born with a cross on its back and six toes on each foot: no one explained this strange genetic mutation, you understood, you believed you understood, the triumph was of neither life nor death, life and death were not the opposing forces, gradually, in the time of the epidemics, or later, in the time of indiscriminate extermination, all the present inhabitants, all those—with the exception of the centenarians—born in this century had died; the others, those who impregnated, those who were impregnated, those born, those who continued to die, are beings from another time, the struggle has not been between life and death but between the past and the present: Paris is inhabited by mere phantoms, but how, how, how?

Feverishly you part the heavy drapes and open the window. Wounded feet drag through the snow. You hear a flute. From the street, eyes stare toward your window. Green, protruding eyes stare at you from the street below, summon you. You know the origin and the destination of the footsteps in the street. Each day they have been fewer. The procession used to go toward Saint-Germain. This one is headed toward Saint-Sulpice. They are the last. Then you were mistaken. Death has triumphed; many were born, but many more died. In the end, more died than were born. Perhaps there remain only these final victims who now march through the snow toward Saint-Sulpice. What will the executioners do when their task is finished? Will they kill themselves? Who are the executioners of the executioners? That flautist staring toward your window, that monk with the dark, expressionless gaze, the colorless face? That girl who . . . ? Three persons gaze toward your window. The last. The girl with gray eyes, upturned nose, and tattooed lips. The girl whose multicolored skirts move gently, scattering shadow and light. You stare at the three. They stare at you. You know they are the last.

You summon reason to save you from extremes—the commonness of the event and the impenetrability of the mystery. You are in Paris. In Mexico you did not fully understand your Descartes; in effect, he said that reason that was sufficient unto itself, accounting only for itself, is bad reason, insufficient reason. And now you temper Descartes with Pascal: so necessarily mad is man that it would be madness not to be mad: such is the turn of the screw of reason. And thinking of Pascal, you think of your aged Erasmus and his praise of a madness that relativizes the pretended absolutes of the former world and the present world: Erasmus wrested from the Middle Ages the certainty of immutable truths and imposed dogmas; for modernity he reduces the absolute of reason and the empire of the self to ironic proportions. Erasmian madness is the checkmate of man by man himself, of reason by reason itself, not by sin or the Devil. But it is also the critical consciousness of a reason and an ego that do not wish to be deceived by anyone, not even by themselves.

You ponder with sadness the fact that Erasmism could have been the touchstone of your own Spanish American culture. But Erasmism sifted through Spain defeated itself. It suppressed the ironic distance between man and the world in order to deliver itself unto the voluptuosity of a fierce individualism divorced from society, but dependent upon the external gesture, the admirable attitude, the appearance sufficient to justify—before oneself and before others—the illusion of an emancipated uniqueness. A spiritual rebellion that ends by nourishing the very things it meant to combat: honor, hierarchy, the posture of the man of breeding, the solipsism of the mystic, and the hope of a learned despot.

Looking at the street for the first time in many months, seeing the three persons who from the street are trying to see you, you wonder whether modern science can offer hypotheses other than those of immediate news, hermetic mystery, or humanist madness. You wonder: if the world has been depopulated by epidemic, hunger, and programmed extermination, with what has nature filled what it abhors, the vacuum? Antimatter is an inversion or correspondence of all energy. It exists in a latent state. It is actualized only when energy disappears. Then it takes its place, liberated by the extinction of former matter.

The overcast sky of this night of St. Sylvester in Paris prevents your seeing any refulgence. Quasars, the universe's wandering energy sources, are born of and converted into potential matter by the collision of galaxies and antigalaxies; antimatter awaiting the extinction of something it can replace. If this is true, a whole world identical to ours—insofar as it is capable of integrally replacing, to the maximum and minimum detail, our world—awaits our deaths to occupy our places. Antimatter is the double or specter of all matter: that is, the double or specter of everything that *is*.

You smile. Science fiction always based its plots upon one premise: other, inhabited worlds exist, superior in force and wisdom to our own. They keep close watch over us. They threaten in silence. Someday we will be invaded by Martians. Wells/Welles: Herbert George and George Orson. But you believe you are witnessing a different phenomenon: the invaders have not arrived from another place, but from another time. The antimatter that has filled the vacuum of your present gestated, awaiting its moment, in the past. Martians and Venusians have not invaded us, rather heretics and monks from the fifteenth century, conquistadors and painters from the sixteenth century, poets and entrepreneurs from the seventeenth century, philosophers and revolutionaries from the eighteenth century, courtesans and social climbers from the nineteenth century: we have been occupied by the past.

Then are you living an epoch that is yours, or are you a specter from another time? Surely that flautist, that monk, and that girl staring at you from the snowy street ask themselves the same question: Have we been transported to a different time, or has a different time invaded our own?

Would you dare think the unthinkable as you stand and hold back the drape with your only hand? Are you looking at a transposition of the historic past into a future that will have no history?

And obsessively, because you are who you are and are from where you are, you tell yourself that if this is true, the transposition must surely be that of the least realized, the most abortive, the most latent and desiring of all histories: that of Spain and Spanish America. Then you mock yourself with a grimace of secret scorn. Would an Indonesian not say the same, a Burmese, a Mauritanian, a Palestinian, an Irishman, a Persian? Idiot: you have been thinking like a white-wigged Encyclopedist. How can one be a Persian? How, in truth, is it possible to be a Mexican, a Chilean, an Argentinian, or a Peruvian?

And you. What will they do with you? This is the first day—you suddenly realize—they have not brought your single meal. They are going to let you die from hunger. Perhaps they do not know you are there in your suite in the Hôtel du Pont-Royal. It isn't important. The logic of extermination is imposed independently of your existence. Undoubtedly, they have killed your servant. Would it serve any purpose to speed matters up, to go down to the street, join the three beings staring toward your window? It's all the same. Whoever the true executioners may be, these, others, you will die, ignored, no one will bring you food. You must sleep and recognize your death in dream.

You wonder whether you are the only one to perish this way, like the ancient Cathari; you smile. And in that very instant you cease to believe that you are you: this is happening to someone else. Not to just anyone else. To Another. The Other.

You are overwhelmed by vertigo. In that instant, like St. Paul to the Corinthians, you would shout: "I speak as a fool. I *am* more."

You return to yourself. You return to your wretched body, your blood, your guts, your feelings, your amputated arm: with your sound arm you cling to yourself as your only life preserver. You are you. You are in Paris, the night of the thirty-first of December of 1999. You passed a day before the monument to Jacques Monod, near Rodin's statue of Balzac in the Boulevard Raspail. Chance, captured by invariability, becomes necessity. But chance alone, and only chance, is the source of all novelty, of all creation. Pure chance, absolute but blind freedom, is the very foundation of the prodigious edifice of evolution. Without the intervention of this creative chance, every thing and every being would be petrified, preserved like peaches in a can.

Withdrawing your only hand, you allow the curtain to fall closed. You will never again see those three survivors. The silence of the city beneath the snow tells you everything. Everyone is dead. The order of the factors does not alter the product. The men arrived from the past have died, the women of the present impregnated by them, and the children destined for the future, the newborn infants on the quays of the Seine: all Caesars, all Christs, then none a Caesar, none a Christ. Reason? Madness? Irony? Chance? Antimatter? The rules of the game have been fulfilled: every day as many died as were born. The flautist, the monk, and the girl, being the survivors, are necessarily the executioners. Now they will ascend to kill you, and then they will kill themselves.

You go to your bedroom. Lie down, dream, die. Then you hear the sound of knuckles rapping on your door.

They have come for you.

You did not have to descend to seek them.

You did not have to die dreaming.

You open the door.

The girl with the porcelain skin, the long chestnut hair, the full multicolored skirts and gypsy necklaces is looking at you with deep, gray eyes. " 'I have sung women in three cities, but it is all one.' " Women? Cities? " 'They mostly had gray eyes; I will sing of the sun.' " She stares at you, seemingly forever. Then the tattooed lips move, as many-colored as the necklaces and skirts: "*Salve.* I have awaited you."

Bedazzled heart.

"Yes."

You disguise your amazement.

"We had a rendezvous, do you remember? Last fourteenth of July, on the bridge."

"No, I don't remember."

"Pollo Phoibus."

" 'I will sing of the sun,' " you say, not knowing what you say.

"The words written upon your breastplate gleamed, faded, and others appeared in their place . . ."

" 'Nothing disabuses me; the world has me bewitched,' " you say as if another spoke for you.

"You fell from the Pont des Arts into the boiling waters of the Seine."

" 'Time is the relationship between the existent and the non-existent.' "

"For a moment I saw your only hand above the water."

" 'And what if suddenly we all turned into someone else?' "

"I threw the sealed green bottle into the river, praying you would cling to it and be saved."

" 'Transformed utterly: A terrible beauty is born.' "

"May I come in, then?"

You shake your head. You emerge from your trance. "Forgive me . . . Excuse . . . my lack of courtesy . . . When one is alone one forgets . . . one forgets . . . the rules of conduct. Forgive me; come in, please. You are welcome."

The girl enters the darkness of the apartment.

She takes your hand. Hers is icy. She leads you gently through the living room. In the darkness you cannot see what she is doing. You hear only the swish of her skirts and the chink of the beads of her necklace upon her breasts.

"Bocanegra's collar . . . Fray Toribio's ustorious mirror. All the mirrors . . . Fray Julián's triangular mirror that Felipe was unable to destroy when the painter removed the painting from Orvieto . . . The round mirror Felipe held as he ascended the thirty-three steps in his chapel . . . The black blood-streaked mirror in which La Señora and Juan looked at themselves one night . . . The small hand mirror you stole in Galicia before embarking with Pedro to discover new lands . . . the same mirror in which the ancient of the basket of pearls saw himself . . . the same mirror in which you looked upon me, crowned with butterflies . . ."

You curb the anguish in your voice. "We're in the dark. How do you know?"

"Only in darkness can I see myself in these mirrors," she replies, her voice as serene as yours is altered. "Didn't you yourself, as you opened the door, see me in this same darkness? Didn't you see my eyes and my lips?"

She moves close to you. She smells of clove, of pepper, and aloes.

She speaks into your ear: "Aren't you tired, Pilgrim? You have traveled far since you fell from the bridge that afternoon and were lost in the waters that tossed you onto the shore of the Cabo . . ."

You seize her shoulder, you hold her away from you. "That isn't true, I've been shut up here, I haven't left this place, I haven't opened my windows since summer, you are telling me things I've read in the chronicles and manuscripts and folios I have here in this cabinet, you've read the same things as I, the same novel, I've not moved from here . . ."

"Why not believe the opposite?" she asks after kissing your cheek. "Why not believe that we two have lived the same things, and that the papers written by Brother Julián and the Chronicler give testimony to our lives?"

"When? When?"

She places her hand beneath the cloth of your caftan, she caresses your chest. "During the six and a half months that passed between your fall into the river and our meeting here, tonight . . ."

Lifeless, you surrender, your head touches hers. "There wasn't time . . . All that happened centuries ago . . . These are very ancient chronicles . . . It is impossible . . ."

Then she kisses you, full upon the lips; moistly, deeply, long: the kiss itself is another measure of time, a minute that is a century, an instant that is an epoch, interminable kiss, fleeting kiss, the tattooed lips, the long narrow tongue, the palate bursting with sweet pleasure, you remember, you remember, every moment of the prolongation of that kiss is a new memory, Ludovico, Ludovico, we all dreamed of a second opportunity to relive our lives, a second opportunity, to choose again, to avoid the mistakes, to repair the omissions, to offer the hand we did not extend the first time, to sacrifice to pleasure the day we had before dedicated to ambition, to give a second chance to all that could not be, to all that waited, latent, for the seed to die so the plant could germinate, the coincidence of two separate times in one exhausted space, several lifetimes are needed to integrate a personality and fulfill a destiny, the immortals had more life than their own deaths, but less time than their own lives . . .

You are delirious; you feel you have been transported to the Theater of Memory in the house between the Canal of San Barnaba and the Campo Santa Margherita; you draw away from the kiss of the girl with tattooed lips; you are filled with memories, Celestina has transmitted to you the memory that was passed to her by the Devil disguised as God, by God disguised as the Devil, you draw away with repugnance, you remember, you did not read it, you lived it, you lived it during the last one hundred and ninety-five days of the last year of the last century, during the past five thousand hours: there will be no more life: history has had its second chance, Spain's past was revived in order to choose again, a few places changed, a few names, three persons were fused into two, and two into one, but that was all: differences of shading, unimportant distinctions, history repeated itself, history was the same, its axis the necropolis, its root madness, its result crime, its salvation, as Brother Julián had written, a few beautiful buildings and a few elusive words. History was the same: tragedy then and farce now, farce first and then tragedy, you no longer know, it no longer matters, everything has ended, it was all a lie, the same crimes were repeated, the same errors, the same madness, the same omissions as on any other of the true days of that linear, implacable, exhaustible chronology: 1492, 1521, 1598 . . .

The violence of a warrior. The acclivity of a saint. The nausea of an ill man. You feel all this in your body. Celestina caresses you, calms you, embraces you, leads you to your bedroom, tells you, yes, what you remember is true, what you do not remember also, the curse of Caesar and the salvation of Christ are inextricably blended, the elect were not one, as God and the King desired, or two, as all rival brothers feared, or three, as Ludovico and the ancient dreamed in the beautiful Synagogue of the Passing in Toledo; each and all were the elect, all the children born here, all bearers of the same signs, the cross and the six toes, all usurpers, all bastards, all anointed, all saviors, all led, scarcely born, to the extermination chambers in Saint-Sulpice, all children of the total past of man, all fertilized by a transposition of ancient semen from the deserts of Palestine, the streets of Alexandria, the devastated hearth of the astute son of Sisyphus, the beaches of Spalato, the stone squares of Venice, the funereal palace on the Castilian plain, the jungles and pyramids and volcanoes of the new world; first the children died, and then the women, the men, only at the end, with no opportunity for fecundation, and last of all, the executioners, with no one to kill, except themselves . . .

"Night and fog. The final solution. What tragic jest is this, Celestina? Did everyone have to die before the executioners could finally die? I . . ."

"Here. Take the mask of the jungle."

"But the dogma, Celestina, I heard it every day during the processions, anathema, anathematized be those who believe in a resurrection different from that of the body we possessed in life."

"Your body, my love . . ."

"I don't understand . . ."

"The dogma was proclaimed so that heresy would flower, ever more deeply rooted; all things are transformed, all bodies are their metamorphoses, all souls are their transmigrations . . . Take the mask, quickly . . ."

"They accept nothing from women, that's what the *patron* of the Café Le Bouquet said to his wife; the penitents accept nothing from women; woman is blemished, she is bloody, she is the vessel of the Devil . . ."

"Only persecuted and in secret am I able to perform my role; forgive me, I am of little worth; consecrated, I am as cruel as my persecutors; condemned, I maintain the flame of forgotten wisdom. I had to survive. The mask, quickly, we have very little time . . ."

In the darkness you touch Celestina's face. It is covered by another mask of feathers, dead spiders, darts . . .

"You're wearing it . . ."

"I am wearing mine, you must wear yours, quickly . . ."

"Yours . . . Mine is here, beneath my pillow. But yours, where . . . ?"

"Do you remember a shop window, an antique shop, on the rue Jacob? I broke in. I stole it. How did it get there? I do not know. Put on your mask, and I mine. Identical. Quickly. There is no time. There is no time. What time is it?"

Out of the corner of your eye you glance at the alarm clock on the night table; its phosphorescent hands and numbers indicate three minutes before midnight.

You wish to dispel the mists of vertiginous necromancy that overwhelm you, effacing all sense of internal or external equilibrium; the woman smells of clove, of pepper, and aloes. "Almost midnight. We need twelve grapes. I'm sorry not to be able to offer you champagne. There's no room service. What shall we sing? *Las Golondrinas? Auld Lang Syne?*"

You laughed: New Year's Eve in Paris, without champagne. What a laugh, what truth, what salvation!

"Don't you think that's funny? Where's your sense of humor?"

"Quickly, there is no time."

"Then what has passed?"

Celestina is silent for an instant. Then she says: "Ludovico and Simón died at five minutes before midnight. They were the last. The student killed the monk. Then he killed himself. I want you to understand: we were not the executioners. We escaped them because we never looked at them. They believed we were phantoms; they looked at us, not we at them. We survived so we could come to you. You are right: the executioners never knew about you. I protected you. I brought you food every day. It has been months since anyone lived in this hotel. Ludovico and Simón died when they fulfilled their mission: to leave me here with you. There will be no more bodies in the naves of Saint-Sulpice. Quickly, we must don the masks."

You obey her.

The chamber begins to glow with warm luminosity, the color of new grass, a light like ground emeralds: the mask has slits at the level of the eyes; you look at Celestina, masked. She approaches, she removes your caftan, revealing your nakedness, the caftan falls to the floor. Naked, with the terrible stump of your mutilated arm. Celestina removes her necklaces and underskirts, her smock and sandals. Clothing and adornments slide to the floor: you are both naked, facing one another, so long since you have made love to a woman, she looks at you, you look at her, you come together, you embrace her with tenderness; she embraces you with passion.

The masks fall. The light born of your masked gazes remains. You lead Celestina to the bed. You kiss one another, slowly, caress one another, she kisses your whole body, you kiss her whole body, you tell yourself you are re-creating one another with your touch, she with her two hands, you with your one, you kiss one another's lips, eyes, ears, her breath moistens the hair of your pubis, yours the young perfume of her armpits, your hand caresses one nipple, your lips moisten the other, she moans, she scratches your shoulder, she strokes your buttocks, sticks her finger in your asshole, her fingernails stroke the fascine of pleasure between your asshole and your balls, she lifts the weight of your heavy milk-pouch, you are over her, your legs spread apart, your tongue washes her navel, descends along her belly till your face is buried in the bronze locks of her mound, you nose through the curls, open a way with your tongue, through the hidden, elusive, quivering folds to the moist and palpitating clitoris, her lips, her tongue, her palate, her controlled little teeth devour your prick, she licks your testicles, places her tongue in your asshole, you spread your legs even wider, you seek the acid savor of her asshole, you leave it gleaming and moist as a copper coin abandoned in a rainy alleyway, you move apart from her, with your only hand you lift her legs, you place them on your shoulders and, very slowly, you enter, first the pulsing purple head, little by little, the rest of your prick, to the throat, to the frontier of pleasure, to the blackest and most submissive boundaries of the trembling cave, you do not want to come yet, think of something else, you want to wait, both together, something else, you lived once along the rue de Bièvre, the ancient beaver canal that flowed into the Seine, now a narrow little alley of quiet hawkers' cries, the odor of couscous, the high laments of Arabic music, aged beggars, mischievous children, hopscotches drawn on the pavement, Dante lived there once, he wrote there, he began to write, Paris, the fountain of all wisdom and the source of the divine writings, where the persuasive Devil inculcated a perverse intelligence in some few wise men, the Inferno, you repeat the verses in silence, don't come yet, nondum, not yet, midway along the journey of our lives, a dark wood, we lose our way, wilderness, harsh and cruel, the recollection of terror, that isn't what you want to remember, more recent, not yet, a canto, nondum, the canto, the twenty-fifth canto, that's it, ed eran due in uno, ed uno in due, the girl cries out, you say the verse aloud, due in uno, uno in due, she screams, closes her eyes, you look upon her face convulsed by the orgasm, her trembling thighs, her tempest-ridden sex, now, yes, now you come, with her, you flood her black, rosy, pearly, recessed cunt with silver and venom and smoke and amber, ed eran due in uno, ed uno in due, the pleasure is prolonged, the juices, the semen, the ocean, she is still shivering, you howl like a beast, you cannot withdraw, you do not want to withdraw, you sink into the woman's flesh, the woman blends into the man's flesh, two in one, one in two, your arm, your arm is beginning to grow, your hand, your hand is growing, fingernails, open palm, take, receive, again, let the lost half of your fortune, your love, your intelligence, your life and death reappear: you raise the arm you had lost, it isn't your arm, the arm you scarcely remember, the arm you lost in a manhunt, Lepanto, Veracruz, the Cabo de los Desastres, my God, your arm is the girl's arm, your body is the girl's body, her body is yours; crazed, in that instant you look for the other body in the bed, you have not dreamed this, you have just made love to a woman in your bed in your room in the Hôtel du Pont-Royal, the girl is no longer here, yes, she is here, no, she is not, there is but one body, you look at it, you see yourself, your two hands touch full breasts, your erect nipples, your strange new hips, young and firm, your slender waist, your swelling buttocks, your hands, search, search with the terror of having lost the emblem of your manhood, you brush the mat of hair, seek . . . no, you touch your still-hard penis, moist and slippery, your exhausted, still-trembling testicles, you search further, below your balls, between your legs, you find it, your hole, your vagina, you insert your finger, it is deep, it is the same, the one you have just possessed, it is the one you will possess again, you speak, I love you, I love myself, your voice and the girl's speak at the same time, they are a single voice, let me make love to you again, I want to make love again, you introduce your own long, new, pliant penis, sinuous as a serpent, into your own, open, pleasured, palpitating moist vagina; you make love to yourself, I make love to myself, I fertilize you, you fertilize me, I fertilize myself, my male and female selves, we shall have a son, then a daughter, they will make love, they will fertilize one another, they will have sons and daughters, and those sons and daughters will have sons and daughters, and the grandsons and granddaughters, great-grandsons and great-granddaughters, bone of my bones, flesh of my flesh, and the two shall be one flesh, and in joy thou shalt bring forth children, and blessed is the ground for thy sake, thorns and fruit shall it bring forth to thee, and in the smile of thy face shalt thou eat bread, till thou return unto the ground, for out of it wast thou taken: for dust thou art, and unto dust shalt thou return—without sin, and with pleasure.

Twelve o'clock did not toll in the church towers of Paris; but the snow ceased, and the following day a cold sun shone.

ESCH IS LUTHER
To Carlos Fuentes
by Milan Kundera

When, during January 1969, in Prague, in Wenceslas Square, a Czech student took his own life by fire to protest the Russian occupation of his country, I had the feeling that this horror did not belong to Czech history. There was no precedent for this act; it came from a terrible elsewhere.

Not the world war, not the concentration camps, not the Stalinist terror, but the burning corpse of Jan Palach filled me with a sense of the apocalypse.

A scholarly definition occurred to me: an act is moral if it can serve as an example for everyone; but how can one imitate a boy who immolated himself? Did not that act project us beyond Europe and the moral experience of Europe?

For weeks after his death, the streets of Czech cities were filled with excited demonstrators. One slogan inspired them: "Jan Palach is the Jan Hus of today."

In fact, Jan Palach, an adolescent, bore no resemblance to Jan Hus, one of the great intellectuals of the fifteenth century. Hus did not want to die. Rather, this was the only course open to him if he wanted to remain faithful to himself and his beliefs. The example of Hus, burned as a heretic, is difficult but not impossible to follow. To imitate the other Jan is inconceivable.

Nevertheless, there is incontestably something in common between these two deaths: fire. The Czech people, petrified in the terrible moment of January 1969, saw the history of their country as if in fast motion: like the passage between two flames, the one that burned the body of Jan Hus and the one that burned the body of Palach. With the first, their country appeared on the scene of Europe; with the second, it disappeared from it.

2

The Second World War—the Hitlerite delirium—must have provoked an apocalyptic feeling in certain Germans. Thomas Mann transformed that moment into a watchtower from which he could take in all of German history in a glance.

Doctor Faustus (1947) is not only a novel about a composer called Adrian Leverkühn, but equally a reflection of four centuries of German music. Adrian is not only a composer, but the composer who terminates the history of music (indeed, his greatest composition is called *Apocalypse*). Moreover, he is not only the final composer (author of the Apocalypse); he is also Faust.

Just as a Czech, overwhelmed by the death of Palach, couldn't but think of the death of Jan Hus, a German, confronted by this apocalyptic moment, eyes fixed on the diabolism of his country, thought of the contract the devil made with that mythic character who incarnated the German spirit. The entire history of his country surged before his eyes as the adventure of one sole character; of one sole Faust.

3

The year when the flame passed from the body of Jan Hus to the body of Jan Palach, a few hundred meters from Wenceslas Square, in my studio in Prague I was writing *Life Is Elsewhere*. Suddenly, through the character of Jaromil (an authentic poet, and a police informer), I thought I saw the entire history of poetry, to the degree that—in certain pages of the novel—the face of my hero disappeared behind those of Rimbaud and of Mayakovsky, and his death is confused with those of Lermontov and of Shelley.

I experienced the Stalinism of the 1950s as a time when "the poet reigned alongside the executioner" (*Life Is Elsewhere*). And when poetry identifies itself with terror, then one is taking part in *the apocalypse of poetry*. Lit by this apocalyptic explosion, the past (of a nation, a civilization, an art, a region) appears suddenly telescoped: Jaromil is confused with Rimbaud; Jan Palach with Hus.

Several years after Palach's death, I came to France, and everyone asked me what I thought of communism, of Marxism, of the revolution. Nothing interested me less than this sort of question. I had before my eyes that flame which traversed five centuries, and I thought of Thomas Mann. I thought of the art of the novel, which, alone of all the arts, is capable of becoming that privileged place where humanity's distant past can converse with its present. To arrange this rendezvous seemed to me one of the three or four great tasks, one of the three or four great possibilities available to the future of the novel.

And today I think of Carlos Fuentes: in his *Terra Nostra* (1975), this new possibility of the novel has been realized in a far more radical fashion than anyone could have imagined.

4

Serenus Zietblom, the narrator of *Doctor Faustus,* set himself the task of writing his *souvenirs* of his friend Adrian Leverkühn at the end of the Second World War. From time to time, he interrupts his narrative to comment on contemporary events. It is precisely these passages which rang flat and falsely to my ears when, recently, I reread Mann's novel. We know, alas, that the last war, presented by Mann as the final apocalypse, which also held the promise of the resurrection of the West, was nothing more than an episode. It was one phase of a much longer process and was followed by no resurrection.

I deduced that, from the watchtower of the novel, one can see the past but not the future and that it is very difficult to find the right spot to set up a watchtower.

If Fuentes has known how to find that spot—that incontestable locus of the apocalypse—it is thanks to great artistic ruse (or wisdom): he did not search in real history but in myth. The watchtower from which he views history is called the year 1999, the end of the millennium. His description of the apocalypse will thus not be contradicted by the reality of the real year 1999, because Fuentes is talking about a mythic date, not a real one.

It is not the political predictions of the author which are at the root of *Terra Nostra* but something more profound. "Historic time is stretched so taut that it is hard to see how it will not snap," Cioran writes. This "tension of historic time" (of that time which today hurtles on, accumulating events, approaching a paroxysm), and the personal experience Fuentes has of this tension, is, it seems to me, the hidden source, the subterranean force, of the unbelievable, apocalyptic dream which is *Terra Nostra.*

5

Carlos Fuentes has several times compared the contemporary Latin American novel to that of Central Europe.

Latin America and Central Europe are in effect two border areas of the West: two parts of the world where the West (Westernness) has become problematic; two parts of the world where the survival of the West is not a theoretical question but forms part of the most concrete reality.

Beginning in 1914, Central Europe lives obsessed with the end of things: Karl Kraus writes *The Last Days of Mankind;* Robert Musil composes *The Man without Qualities,* where a society constructs its future at a time when it has none; Hermann Broch, in *The Sleepwalkers,* studies the gradual decline of Western values; Jaroslav Hašek describes a world where liberty survives only under the mask of idiocy; Franz Kafka imagines a world where history is already forgotten and where life takes place in a present bereft of memory.

The causes of this "obsession of the end" are not hard to understand. The collapse of an empire, traditionally understood as a model of Europe ("little Europe"), appeared as foreshadowing a more general collapse, which, of course, took place quickly enough: Hitler, Stalin, and, finally, the real start of the end of Central Europe, most of which was included for an unforeseeably long time in Russia's civilization. Too bad if, at the same time, the discordant noise of progress assaults our ears: "Every advance brings the end closer and such happy catchwords as 'farther' and 'forward' make us hear the lascivious voice of death encouraging us to hurry" (*The Book of Laughter and Forgetting*).

In a different but no less radical (because it is so ancient) way, the West is at issue in Latin America. The West took the continent by conquest, and its legitimacy has never been sure. Even if Latin America's culture is Western, it belongs to the Third World as well and shares all its anti-Western reflexes. Latin America, as Fuentes says, is a façade and one always wonders what is hidden behind it.

Western historical time interrupted Indian time in Latin America. Gabriel García Márquez's village of Macondo in *One Hundred Years of Solitude* keeps its pathetic solitude—the solitude of a world outside history.

But the world deserted by history can avenge itself and one day could banish history to its own exile. History, abandoned, alone, will be forgotten in a world which would have got rid of the Western mirage of "historic time." Fuentes sees history in that solitude; he sees it as if it were already finished; he dreams of it as one dreams of the dead.

Be that as it may, in Central Europe and in Latin America, the novel puts history in question in a way not seen until now.

6

The novel speaks of a world without a future, but the world prefers to debate the future of the novel.

In a long interview on American TV, Fuentes said: "Outside of scientific knowledge, logic, and politics, there is the knowledge of the imagination. There are many things which neither historiography nor logic nor science can discern. There are things which only a Dostoevsky sees."

Still, in the last few decades, one has the impression that the romanesque procedures of literature have exhausted themselves and that "a Dostoevsky" has nothing to see or to say.

This impression sometimes engenders a radical reaction. One sees only one way of avoiding the shame of eclecticism: the total renunciation of the conventions of the novel. One begins to distinguish on one side the traditional novel (whose time is past) and on the other the modern novel (which is not conceived as a new phase of literature's evolution but as confrontation, rupture, and negation).

This renunciation also concerns that which was the basis of the romanesque—the character (an imaginary being not identical to the author), about whom everything has now been said. All of a sudden, the notion of the character is itself exhausted, used up. In the 1920s, Proust and Joyce explored the whole universe of the human soul; they touched its limit. Following this logic, it is easy to think that Kafka, during the same period, in depriving K. of his visible face, of his past, even of his name, effected a kind of definitive decapitation of the romanesque character as such.

Still, it seems to me that the development of the novel is not over yet and that what appears to be an end is nothing but a change of direction. The camera of romanesque knowledge turns slowly toward other horizons. I don't think Kafka decapitated the character: he was only interested in other aspects of man and he had another idea of what was essential for human life.

K. does not enchant us by the universe of his soul; if his soul is a universe, then it is besieged, dried out, absorbed by another universe—the world that surrounds it and toward which its possibilities of action are tragically limited. By virtue of this new human condition (as Kafka conceived of it), the physical face, the character's past, his name, etc., lose all interest.

But one must never forget: what is basic (with Kafka as with all great novelists) is *discovery* (of the unknown aspects of human life and of the new possibilities of the novel). *Renunciation* (of old conventions) is nothing more than a consequence—inevitable, perhaps, but secondary.

Paradox: renunciation is immediately visible; it is thus an easily perceived sign of modernity. In contrast, what is new, what constitutes a discovery, is much harder to discern.

The reader's eye is accustomed to conventions: the renunciation of convention is thus picked out instantly. In contrast, the discovery of the new holds itself outside all conventions. The conventional spirit cannot register it. For a conventional person, *Doctor Faustus* is just a conventional novel.

That is why minor works which noisily assert their rejection of conventions without bringing us anything new are often preferred to works which, without proclaiming their renunciation, discover and reveal.

Among these, *The Sleepwalkers* of Hermann Broch is the book I admire ceaselessly. It contains the germ of all the possibilities of the post-Proustian novel.

Broch's greatest performance in *The Sleepwalkers* is probably the character of Esch (this portrait says more about the man of our century and about the irrational forces that guide his conduct than any other book). Esch appears in the novel at the age of thirty; we do not know and never will what he was up to until then. His past remains absent, just like K.'s in *The Trial*.

And if the past is absent, so is "psychology," at least in the sense that writers before Broch (and his generation) understood it: the search for psychological causality, the quest for hidden motivations in the depths of biography. Despite this "renunciation" (that is, the renouncing of those novelistic procedures dubbed psychological), Esch is completely "alive" for us. Broch explains his character's attitudes by minute descriptions (which are, however, *phenomenological*, not psychological).

During one of his descriptions, Broch develops the comparison between the criminal and the rebel. He writes: "Esch was a rebel. He was a rebel the way Luther was."

Instead of informing us about Esch's childhood and youth, Broch tells us Esch was like Luther. His character's individual past is unimportant. Esch's attitude can be traced beyond his life. Esch's past is Luther.

The novelty of Broch's conception of character is discrete (although it is consistent: Passenow, another character in *The Sleepwalkers,* is linked to St. Augustine, to Seneca, to Zeno, and to Pythagoras). It is nonetheless clear: a character is no longer conceived as an inimitable uniqueness but rather as a locus of continuity, as a window which gives out on man's distant past.

That which we call psychological analysis in the art of the novel has not been the exclusive property of a Richardson or a Stendhal. It was one of the secular tasks of the novel in an era fascinated by the discovery of the individual, of his irreplaceable non-interchangeable nature.

The principle *Esch is like Luther* is not Broch's property. It is the general orientation of the novel in a century in which "the tension of historic time" seems close to its paroxysm and in which man looks backward to summarize the history of his civilization.

8

The principle *Esch is like Luther* is transformed in the aesthetic of *Terra Nostra* as the principle *Esch is Luther*.

If the principle *Esch is like Luther* is not Broch's exclusive property, the principle *Esch is Luther* belongs only to Fuentes. It cannot be imitated except at the risk of turning into pastiche.

Toward the end of *Terra Nostra*, Fuentes shows us the key to his method: "A life is not sufficient. Several existences are needed to make up a person." And he follows with a Cabalistic allusion: "Each child born at each instant reincarnates each person who dies at each instant." And: "It is not possible for us to know who we are reincarnating, because there exists no witness capable of recognizing in me the person I was."

The ancient mythology of reincarnation is materialized in a romanesque technique. *Terra Nostra* is an immense dream in which history is performed by endlessly reincarnated characters who say to us: it is always us, we are the same who go on playing the game of history. Historical continuity resides not only in the causal linkage of events but also in the identities of the actors.

"Several existences are needed to make a sole person." That's why Philip I is confused with his grandson Philip II (who, in the novel, becomes his son); why Celestina traverses the centuries, and the wife of Philip II goes to England to become Queen Elizabeth. Characters from books—Don Juan and Don Quixote—join real characters, and at certain times the silhouettes get confused: Don Quixote becomes Don Juan and Don Juan becomes Don Quixote.

If Esch is Luther, the history which leads from Luther to Esch is simply a private story of Luther–Esch. The structural consequences are overwhelming. The novel has always been built on the notion of temporal space which couldn't go beyond the dimensions of one life. To imagine a romanesque story lasting a thousand years or even a hundred would have seemed nonsensical.

And if Ludovico discovers in Mexico a new undiscovered continent, if he then finds himself in Palestine in Roman times, and if he appears during the last summer of our century, in Paris, with Celestina—she who was the mistress of Philip I and Philip II—the time of the novel becomes limitless. The private story of all these characters (reincarnated, immortal) is nothing more than the story of history itself.

If Esch is Luther, the novel enters the realm of the "fantastic." The fantastic of *Terra Nostra* is not far from madness, but that folly (baroque folly) does not oppose the novel as an aesthetic category. On the contrary, *Terra Nostra* is the spreading out of the novel, the exploration of its possibilities, the voyage to the edge of what only a novelist ("a Dostoevsky," as Fuentes says) can see and say.

In Moravia, where I was born, there has always been a bizarre custom. One June day, the boys of the village dress in traditional garb and get on horseback. One of them, his face covered, a rose in his mouth, may not speak: he's the king. The others accompany him, sabers in their hands, through the surrounding villages. I have always been struck by the beauty of that column, but the verses the horsemen shout are a monotonous litany, and I have always been stupefied by the unintelligibility of the spectacle. "For in the past a group of people had something important to say, and they come alive again today in their descendants life deaf-and-dumb orators holding forth by means of beautiful and incomprehensible gestures." That was the initial inspiration of *The Joke*.

For Cervantes, history was the barely visible background of adventure.

For Balzac, it became a "natural" dimension without which man is unthinkable.

Today, at last, history appears like a monster, ready to assault each of us and to destroy the world. Or else (another aspect of its monstrousness), it represents the immeasurable, incomprehensible *mass* of the past—a past which is unbearable as forgetfulness (because man will lose himself), but also as memory (because its mass will crush us).

Let us read the last pages of *Terra Nostra*. Philip II lies in his coffin in the Escorial. As often happens in poetry marked by the baroque tradition (a tradition which is as strong in my country as in Carlos's— another parallel between Central Europe and Latin America!), the corpse is aware of being dead. Philip of *Terra Nostra* lives his death. One day, he rises and leaves his coffin. He encounters a tour guide who panics and runs away. But Philip is also afraid of the guide and flees to the mountains. There he finds some peasants around a small fire. We are in the distant future. An old mountain man strokes his head and Philip is suddenly full of "a sense of comfort and gratitude."

The encounter between Philip and the guide and the villagers is not only "beautiful like the encounter between an umbrella and a sewing machine." It makes us hear the uninterrupted dialogue between our present and humanity's immemorial past—that dialogue which only the novel of our late epoch (of the West's late epoch) knows how to hear and say.

Translated by David Rieff